Travel Discount Coupon

This coupon entitles y...
when you book yo...

TRAVEL NETWORK®
RESERVATION SERVICE

Hotels ♦ Airlines ♦ Car Rentals ♦ Cruises
All Your Travel Needs

Here's what you get: *

♦ A discount of $50 USD on a booking of $1,000** or more for two or more people!

♦ A discount of $25 USD on a booking of $500** or more for one person!

♦ Free membership for three years, and 1,000 free miles on enrollment in the unique Miles-to-Go™ frequent-traveler program. Earn one mile for every dollar spent through the program. Earn free hotel stays starting at 5,000 miles. Earn free roundtrip airline tickets starting at 25,000 miles.

♦ Personal help in planning your own, customized trip.

♦ Fast, confirmed reservations at any property recommended in this guide, subject to availability.***

♦ Special discounts on bookings in the U.S. and around the world.

♦ Low-cost visa and passport service.

♦ Reduced-rate cruise packages.

Visit our website at http://www.travnet.com/Frommer or call us globally at 201-567-8500, ext. 55. In the U.S., call toll-free at 1-888-940-5000, or fax 201-567-1838. In Canada, call toll-free at 1-800-883-9959, or fax 416-922-6053. In Asia, call 60-3-7191044, or fax 60-3-7185415.

* To qualify for these travel discounts, at least a portion of your trip must include destinations covered in this guide. No more than one coupon discount may be used in any 12-month period, for destinations covered in this guide. Cannot be combined with any other discount or program.
**These are U.S. dollars spent on commissionable bookings.
***A $10 USD fee, plus fax and/or phone charges, will be added to the cost of bookings at each hotel not linked to the reservation service. Customers must approve these fees in advance.

Valid until December 31, 1997. Terms and conditions of the Miles-to-Go™ program are available on request by calling 201-567-8500, ext 55.

MEF123

Frommer's

22nd Edition

FRUGAL TRAVELER'S GUIDES

Mexico
FROM $35 A DAY

by Marita Adair

Assisted by Herb Felsted and
Carla Martindell Felsted

Macmillan • USA

ABOUT THE AUTHOR

Marita Adair's lifelong passion for Mexico's culture, people, and history began at age 11 on her first trip across the border to Nogales. An award-winning travel writer, she logs about 10,000 miles a year traveling in Mexico—by all means of conveyance. Her freelance photographs and articles about Mexico have appeared in numerous newspapers and magazines.

MACMILLAN TRAVEL

A Simon & Schuster Macmillan Company
1633 Broadway
New York, NY 10019

Find us online at **http://www.mgr.com/travel** or
on America Online at Keyword: **Frommer's**

ISBN 0-02-861143-8
ISSN 0899-2835

Editor: Ian Wilker
Assistant Editor: Jim Moore
Production Editor: Lynn Northrup
Design by Michele Laseau
Page Creation by Toi Davis, Tom Missler, Natalie Hollifield, CJ East, Heather Pope, Stephanie Hammett and Jerry Cole
Digital Cartography by Ortelius Design
Map copyright © by Simon & Schuster, Inc.

SPECIAL SALES

Bulk purchases (10+ copies) of Frommer's and selected Macmillan travel guides are available to corporations, organizations, mail-order catalogs, institutions, and charities at special discounts, and can be customized to suit individual needs. For more information write to: Special Sales, Macmillan General Reference, 1633 Broadway, New York, NY 10019.

Manufactured in the United States of America

Contents

List of Maps

AN INVITATION TO THE READER

In researching this book, I discovered many wonderful places—resorts, inns, restaurants, shops, and more. I'm sure you'll find others. Please tell me about them, so I can share the information with your fellow travelers in upcoming editions. If you were disappointed with a recommendation, I'd love to know that, too. Please write to:

Marita Adair
Frommer's Mexico from $35 a Day
Macmillan Travel
1633 Broadway
New York, NY 10019

AN ADDITIONAL NOTE

Please be advised that travel information is subject to change at any time—and this is especially true of prices. We therefore suggest that you write or call ahead for confirmation when making your travel plans. The authors, editors, and publisher cannot be held responsible for the experiences of readers while traveling. Your safety is important to us, however, so we encourage you to stay alert and be aware of your surroundings. Keep a close eye on cameras, purses, and wallets, all favorite targets of thieves and pickpockets.

A FEW WORDS ABOUT PRICES

In December 1994, the Mexican government devalued its currency, the peso. Over the ensuing months, the peso's value against the dollar plummeted from 3.35 pesos against U.S. $1 to nearly 7 pesos against U.S. $1. The peso's value continues to fluctuate—at press time it was around 7.5 pesos to the dollar. Therefore, to allow for inflation, prices in this book (which are always given in U.S. dollars) have been converted to U.S. dollars at a rate of 7 pesos to the dollar, with 15 percent added for inflation. Inflation for 1996/1997 is forecast at around 36%. Many moderate-priced and expensive hotels, which often have U.S. toll-free reservation numbers and have many expenses in U.S. dollars, do not lower rates in keeping with the sinking peso.

Mexico has a Value-Added Tax of 15% (Impuesto de Valor Agregado, or IVA, pronounced "ee-bah") on almost everything, including restaurant meals, bus tickets, and souvenirs. (Exceptions are Cancun, Cozumel, and Los Cabos, where the IVA is 10%.) Hotel taxes are 17% everywhere except Cancun, Cozumel, and Los Cabos, where they are 12%. The IVA will not necessarily be included in the prices quoted by hotels and restaurants. In addition, prices charged by hotels and restaurants have been deregulated. Mexico's new pricing freedom may cause some price variations from those quoted in this book; always ask to see a printed price sheet and always ask if the tax is included.

WHAT THE SYMBOLS MEAN

✪ Frommer's Favorites

Hotels, restaurants, and attractions you should not miss.

Ⓢ Super-Special Values

Hotels and restaurants that offer great value for your money.

The Best of Mexico on a Budget

The faint tinkle of organ grinder music drifted up to my room at the Hotel Gillow from somewhere on a street below in Mexico City's Centro Histórico. The familiar carnival-like tune filled me with one of those "ah ha, this is Mexico" moments, prompting me to reminisce about why I love this huge, colorful, and culturally rich capital so much, and why I continue to be fascinated by this country after decades of travel here.

Traveling in Mexico is akin to walking through history. Within a few footsteps of my hotel were khaki-suited organ grinders—themselves cultural icons surviving from a bygone era—churning out tunes on their old wooden German machines. Just a couple of blocks away were 300 years of Aztec artifacts, housed in the Museo Templo Mayor; the strikingly beautiful stone baroque facade of the Palacio del Iturbide; the truly palacial Museo Nacional de Arte; the Museo Serfin, with its rare collection of indigenous costumes; the ornate Teatro Bellas Artes; and Diego Rivera's murals in the Palacio Nacional—and really, that's just a few of the name attractions.

At around $17 a night at the time, the Gillow was a terrific buy, with a good restaurant, quiet, carpeted rooms, good beds, nice bathrooms, and remote control TV with U.S. channels—the kind of deal you can find all over Mexico but in very few other places in the world. However, a good deal at the Gillow and my admiration of Mexico City's Centro Histórico were but two of the many satisfying rediscoveries I made this year—others were the positive side of Mexico's recent run of bad luck, and that inflation failed to soar prices as I had expected. Bargains were—and still are—everywhere: perfectly comfortable and safe $10-to-$25-a-night hotel rooms, and *comida corridas* (Mexico's multicourse, fixed-priced lunches) for $1.75 to $3. (Mexico's exception to this widespread value appears to be the resorts of the Baja Peninsula, particularly Cabo San Lucas. There, the U.S. dollar has become, unofficially, the standard currency; prices charged in U.S. dollars do not, of course, fluctuate in correspondence with the peso's value.)

Because of *La Crisis* (as Mexicans call the aftermath of the 1994 peso devaluation), Hurricane Roxanne's rampage across the Yucatán Peninsula, and the earthquake that rocked the Pacific coast near Manzanillo, I began the year gloomily anticipating finding numerous boarded-up restaurants, hotels, and other businesses during my annual research travels. But my worst fears failed to take shape.

Mexico

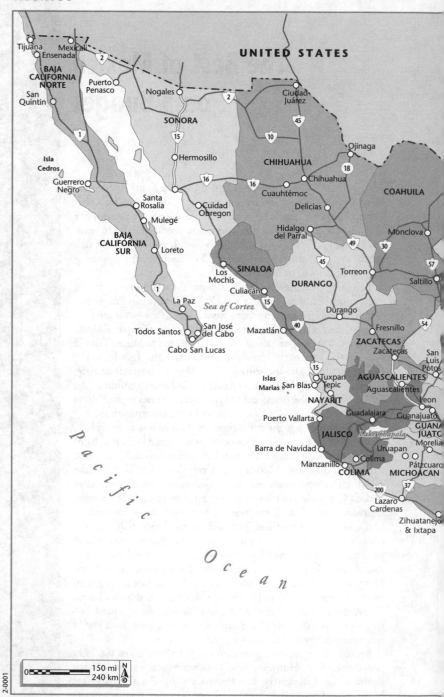

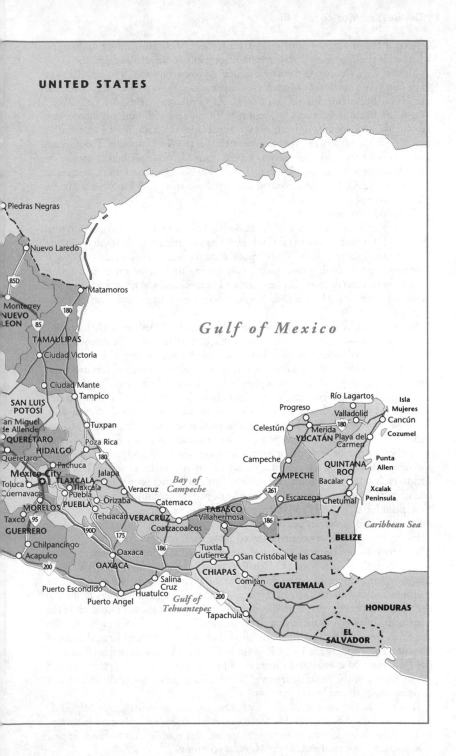

UNITED STATES

Piedras Negras

Nuevo Laredo

85D

Matamoros

Monterrey
NUEVO
LEON
85
180

TAMAULIPAS

Ciudad Victoria

Ciudad Mante

Tampico

SAN LUIS
POTOSÍ

an Miguel
de Allende

QUERÉTARO

Tuxpan

Poza Rica

HIDALGO

Queretaro

Pachuca

180

Mexico City

Jalapa

Toluca

TLAXCALA

Tlaxcala

Cuernavaca

Puebla

Orizaba

MORELOS

PUEBLA

Veracruz

Tehuacán

VERACRUZ

Taxco

95

Coatzacoalcos

GUERRERO

190D

175

Chilpancingo

Oaxaca

186

Acapulco

200

OAXACA

Puerto Escondido

Huatulco

Salina
Cruz

Puerto Angel

Gulf of
Tehuantepec

Tapachula

Gulf of Mexico

Río Lagartos

Isla
Mujeres

Progreso

Valladolid

Celestún

Merida

180

Cancún

YUCATÁN

Playa del
Carmen

Cozumel

Campeche

QUINTANA
ROO

Punta
Allen

CAMPECHE

Bacalar

*Bay of
Campeche*

261

Escarcega

Chetumal

Xcalak
Peninsula

Catemaco

TABASCO

Villahermosa

186

Caribbean Sea

Tuxtla
Gutierrez

San Cristóbal de las Casas

BELIZE

CHIAPAS

Comitan

200

GUATEMALA

HONDURAS

EL
SALVADOR

3

Instead, I found a frenzy of new construction and Mexicans rustling up business wherever it could be found, while responding rapidly to the national disasters.

Mexico City was crowded with foreigners there on business. The new Crowne Plaza opened on Reforma Boulevard, and another chain is opening a luxury hotel near the Hotel Presidente Inter-Continental. As Guillermo Arias, my taxi-driver/tour-guide friend in Mexico City, told me, "Foreigners with business interests are keeping the best hotels as full as they ever were before the crisis, maybe more so." A new state-of-the-art archaeology museum opened at the nearby ruins of Teotihuacán, and the gardens of the Bellas Artes have been restored. Passenger buses now run directly from the Mexico City airport to Toluca, Puebla, Querétaro, and Cuernavaca. Of all the Mexico City restaurants included in our two 1996 Frommer's Mexico guides, only one had closed.

The good news gets even better.

In the Pacific coastal village of Barra de Navidad, where the earthquake rattled the Hotel Tropical and several other buildings to the ground, resident Trayce Blackstone explained that "While the earthquake was scary and destructive, it may have been a blessing too, since we are getting new paved streets and almost everything that was damaged has been replaced or repainted and given a facelift." The luxurious Grand Bay Hotel on Isla Navidad, across from Barra, was readying for its opening.

Just a few weeks after Roxanne pounded the Yucatán, I sped along Highway 307 south of Cancún—it had been nearly impassable immediately after the storm, flooded and clotted with downed trees. The hurricane's winds blew out almost every window in its path, yet hotels stood proudly sporting new paint, mattresses, furniture, and roofs—and shiny replacement glass glistened everywhere. "The day after the hurricane a man came through selling fresh palm fronds," John Swartz of La Rana Cansada in Playa del Carmen chuckled, "and of course we all bought them." Woven palm roofs (*palapas*) are a functional and handsome architectural staple in much of Mexico. Teams of *palaperos* (professional palapa weavers) worked at such a furious pace that everywhere I went for hundreds of miles, handsome new palapas appeared completed. I saw numerous young men peddling along the narrow highway with palm fronds tied to each side of their bicycles, bound to some construction project for which a sale of palm leaves was assured. Hurricane-downed palms thus became a source of fresh palm leaves. . . . All in all, there were innumerable examples of Mexican ingenuity, creating opportunity out of devastation.

Incredibly, almost everywhere I checked along the Caribbean coast, hoteliers were adding rooms—not because of the storm, but in readiness for a progressive future, for which this coast is poised. The Cabañas Paamul is gearing up for a major expansion on their pretty little bay; Lago Bacalar's Rancho Encantado has added four gorgeous *casetas* with Maya-themed murals on the walls and more tours to the Río Bec ruin route; developers are staking out the undeveloped beaches just north of the Majahual/Xcalak Peninsula; in Xcalak proper, small hotels are appearing on the Río Bec ruin route; and lavish private beachfront homes are going up like mad south of Cancún. The owner of the Hotel Albatros in Playa del Carmen razed his funky old hotel and erected a smashingly handsome pueblo-style one in its place. He and others explained the building frenzy: "We're taking advantage of the low cost of building materials and labor right now."

It was much the same in Mexico City, Oaxaca, Puerto Vallarta, San Miguel de Allende, and Cabo San Lucas. For those whose businesses earn payment in dollars, and those without debt with exorbitant interest, this was the year to invest in new construction—not at all bad for the Mexican economy.

"New" archaeological sites are open near Puebla and Tlaxcala and, in Campeche and Yucatán, along the Río Bec ruin route. A car/passenger ferry will run the route across Chetumal Bay from Chetumal to the Xcalak/Majahual Peninsula in Quintana Roo state. New, deluxe buses and routes are being added countrywide.

Still, despite such prosperity, *La Crisis* is troubling for most Mexicans. Until only a few years ago, the middle class bought little on time and seldom used credit cards. But as Mexico's inflation spiraled upward, loans for homes and cars and use of credit cards increased. When the devaluation hit, and there was no ceiling on interest, ordinary people found themselves paying 80% to 150% interest on debts. These are the people we've seen profiled in our newspapers. The less affluent populace earned even fewer pesos after the devaluation, and the rising cost of transportation and food (which still seem relatively inexpensive to us because our dollar buys more) made purchasing basic commodities very difficult. Many of these people began small businesses: In Pátzcuaro, Berta Servin Barriga marshaled the women of a whole farming community to form a crafts cooperative; their colorfully embroidered cloth depictions of farm scenes sell at the co-op. Tricycle taxi drivers proliferated on the Yucatán Peninsula; in downtown Mexico City, between the Alameda and the Zócalo, there are more street vendors and street stalls selling food, toys, clothes, tools, and kitchen gadgets.

The U.S. newspapers have picked up many stories of crisis-panicked Mexicans who've turned to thievery. I don't want to diminish safety concerns or the terrible experience of being victimized, but I must say that the average tourist meets far more kind, hardworking people than thieves and blackguards. To me these working people with the smiling faces are Mexico's unpaid goodwill ambassadors, the ones who generate warm memories when we're nestled once again in our homes far away. Of course, they don't make headlines. After a trip to a South American country this year, where rampant crime forced me to guard my possessions every minute, I returned home grateful for the relative safety of my own hometown; but more than that, I viewed Mexico with fresh, appreciative eyes.

In fact, my enthusiasm for Mexico was so keen this year that I spent Thanksgiving on top of Temple II at Calakmul, munching a chicken sandwich with ruins specialist Serge Rìou, musing over the mysteries of this site only 75 miles north of Guatemala. It was such a clear and beautiful day that from our lofty perch we could see El Mirador, another Guatemalan site 30 miles south, jutting up through an ocean of jungle. For Christmas, I headed off to Oaxaca to immerse myself in the amazing *Noche de los Rabanos* (Night of the Radishes). Every year on December 23, dozens of ingenious Oaxaqueños carve elaborate religious and festival scenes out of enormous radishes and display them on the zócalo for thousands of viewers to see. Every room in the city was booked for the event and for Christmas. On Christmas Eve the Cruz family, owners of the Casa Arnel in Oaxaca, embraced me and several dozen guests and friends with a warm welcome and memorable midnight dinner on the patio. It's a traditional gift the family gives its guests at Christmas every year, along with nightly *posadas,* a Mexican custom commemorating the Holy Family's search for an inn.

This year, as always, it was difficult to leave Mexico and plunge into months of remembering and writing about the places I've been. But in just a few days I sallied south again for a more slow-paced respite, drinking in more of Mexico City; after that, it was on to the soothing, slow-paced streets of 16th-century Pátzcuaro . . . and then who knew where else.

It was such a pleasure to meet so many of you as I rambled through Mexico. I hope to cross paths with more of you and share travel tales about our journeys in the land of our southern neighbor. See you there.

—Marita Adair, May 16, 1996

1 The $35-a-Day Premise

I love budget travel because it puts me close to the sights and sounds of Mexico, to its culture and people. Traveling on a budget in Mexico is anything but a hardship. You can stay at charming inns (see "The Best Budget Hotels" below), eat well (see "The Best Comida Corridas") and in fine surroundings (see "The Best All Around Restaurants" below), and enjoy low-cost or free entertainment almost everywhere, as well as low-cost transportation (see "Eighty Tips for Saving Money in Mexico" below). Even otherwise expensive resort cities such as Puerto Vallarta or Cancún offer rich, culture-filled experiences for cost-conscious travelers, and this book will tell you where to find them.

Because of the devaluation of the peso and inflation running as high as 25% to 50%, there may be some surprises when it comes to deciding how much money travel in Mexico will cost. Before the devaluation, it was possible to travel comfortably on our budget. Even now, two years after the devaluation, Mexico is still a travel bargain.

The premise of the book is that two people can travel for $35 a day each, combining their money for a room at $20 to $25 per person per night and $10 to $15 per person daily for meals. But anyone traveling solo could sleep and eat in comfort for the beginning cost of one person in a pair—$20 to $25 for a room and $10 to $15 for meals. And as you page through the book you'll see that it's often possible to get by on much less than that even in heavily touristed areas, but especially inland, away from the resorts. And though this book's title covers only the cost of a daily room and meals, I'm dedicated to showing you many ways to avoid overspending and to cut the cost of travel on everything from transportation to sightseeing, while throwing in shopping gems along the way.

I had a great travel year updating this issue, and next year promises to be just as bargain filled.

2 Best Bets on a Budget

THE BEST CULTURAL EXPERIENCES

There are moments in Mexico that visitors vainly wish they could shelve away intact, to be brought out and savored again and again at home. But even though such experiences are fleeting, they leave an indelible mark in memory and breathe all that's best about Mexico whenever they come to mind.

- **The Callejoneada** (Zacatecas): Nothing compares to the exhilaration of following a band of horns and drums, a burro laden with barrels of fiery mezcal (from which you imbibe frequently using a cup hung around your neck), and a group of merry people swinging hands and dancing through the narrow streets (*callejons*) of Zacatecas until the wee hours—legally disturbing the peace. See chapter 9.
- **The Estudiantinas** (Guanajuato): When University students (*estudientes*) dressed in medieval garb sing their way through the streets of Guanajuato accompanied by crowds and a burro laden with tequila (from which you take liberal cups of the liquor), it's unforgettable. Crowds follow along nipping, dancing, and singing along until exhaustion sets in. Often, especially during the Cervantino Festival, the estudiantinas appear spontaneously in restaurants. Their mixed voices are so wonderful you wish for a recording. See chapter 9.

- **Hanging Out in the Plazas:** Plaza-sitting is how Mexicans and visitors alike take time out. In Mexico, the town plaza is the center of life, and a prime location for watching the heartbeat of a place. Four come to mind as premier plazas:

  The **Veracruz's Plaza de Armas** (see chapter 8) features nearly nonstop music provided by marimbas, strolling trios, and harpists singing spontaneous poems to diners—all for the price of a tip. You'll usually want to leave a large one. **Oaxaca's Zocalo** (see chapter 14) surrounded on three sides by outdoor restaurants and centered around a wrought-iron bandstand, is vibrant with balloon, craft, and flower vendors, children playing, old and young sitting on iron benches chatting. Concerts are given almost nightly in the bandstand. **Mexico City's Alameda** (see chapter 11) has perhaps the most grimly dramatic history of all—heretics were burned at the stake here during the colonial period. Today it's a people's park in the heart of the Centro Histórico where lovers sit, cotton candy vendors spin out their pink delight, and the sound of organ grinders drifts over the changing crowd. At Christmas, Santas change places with the Three Kings for picture-taking against elaborate seasonal backrops. And **San Miguel de Allende's Jardín** (see chapter 9) is the local focal point for meeting, sitting, painting, and sketching. During festivals, it swirls with dancers, parades, and unbelievably elaborate fireworks that shower everything with sparks of fire. Almost any night the portals around it hold mariachi bands tuning up as they wait to be hired.
- **Mariachi Serenades:** On the Plaza Garibaldi in Mexico City (see chapter 11), under the portals of El Parian in Tlaquepaque near Guadalajara (see chapter 10), and in San Miguel de Allende (see chapter 9), numerous groups of the elegantly clad musicians play their lustrous brass and stringed instruments and belt their songs unforgettably. Anytime you hear mariachis in Mexico this dreamy yet intensely alive feeling settles over you—you'll kick back and say, "Now *this* is Mexico."
- **Fireworks:** Pyrotechnic displays are seen so frequently in Mexico that it's easy to take them for granted. Their makers are so creative they beat any laser show ever made—I'm convinced fireworks are a kind of national genious. They appear somewhere almost nightly in Acapulco (see chapter 6), and at almost every festival countrywide.
- **Regional Folk Dancing:** Be it the Ballet Folklorico in Mexico City or Guadalajara (see chapters 10 and 11), or the almost nightly park performances in Mérida (see chapter 15), or hotel Fiesta nights countrywide, these celebrations of culture never become tiresome, no matter how many you've seen.
- **Festivals:** You don't really know Mexico until you have a few festivals under your belt, preferably some in small towns. At these, the pageantry of dancers wearing elaborate and carefully carved masks, and costumes that may shimmer with satin and sequins or be humbly homemade, plays out sometimes for hours but often for days.

THE BEST ARCHAEOLOGICAL SITES

- **Teotihuacán:** So close to Mexico City, yet centuries away. You feel the majesty of the past in a stroll down the pyramid-lined Avenue of the Dead from the Pyramid of the Sun to the Pyramid of the Moon. Imagine what a fabulous place this must have been when the walls were stuccoed and painted in brilliant colors. Unlike Palenque, where important personages were honored with their likenesses carved in stone, we don't yet know what the builders of Teotihuacán looked like. See chapter 12.

- **Monte Alban:** A grand ceremonial city built on a mountaintop overlooking the city of Oaxaca, Monte Alban leaves visitors with more questions than it answers: Why were they obsessed with deformed humans and who were they exactly? See chapter 14.
- **Palenque:** In a dense jungle setting, the long-ago makers of these powerful Chiapan ruins carved histories in stone that allow them to speak through the centuries to us. Just imagine the ceremony that must have taken place the day King Pacal was buried below ground in a secret pyramidal tomb; it remained untouched from A.D. 683 to its discovery in 1952. See chapter 14.
- **Uxmal:** No matter how many times you see Uxmal, the splendor of its stone carvings is awesome. A stone rattlesnake undulates across the facade of the Nunnery complex there, and 103 masks of Chaac, the rain god, project from the Governor's Palace. See chapter 15.
- **Chichén-Itzá:** Stand beside the giant serpent head at the foot of El Castillo pyramid and marvel at the mastermind who conspired to position the building precisely so that shadow and light would form a serpent's body slithering all the way to the giant head each March 21 and September 21. See chapter 15.

THE BEST FESTIVALS AND CELEBRATIONS

Some of the country's most memorable celebrations, such as Holy Week, are solemn religious events that often employ elaborate and colorful pageantry. Others, however, are the kind of nonstop revelry endemic to a country that knows how to put on a whale of a fiesta.

- **Gueleguetza:** On the Mondays following the last two weekends in July **Oaxaca's** Fiesta Guelaguetza, or Feast of Monday of the Hill, is an extravaganza of regional dancing featuring groups from all over the state. See chapter 14.
- **Days of the Dead:** In **Oaxaca,** The Días de los Muertos (Days of the Dead), November 1 and 2, blend Indian and Hispanic customs. Markets brim with marigolds and other brilliant flowers, and piles of special breads, all of which are offerings for altars seen all over town and built to honor the dead. Night cemetery tours are ways tourists can observe this unique tradition. See chapter 14. In **Pátzcuaro,** the country's most widely attended cemetery event takes place with nightly candlelit vigils on the island of Janitzio on Lake Pátzcuaro. By day, vendors from all over the state sell a fabulous array of crafts in the Plaza Grande. See chapter 13.
- **Holy Week:** This solemn weeklong commemoration involves the village of **Pátzcuaro** and others surrounding it with nightly candlelit processions through the streets, and daily masses and other religious events. Nearby **Uruapan's** central plaza fills with crafts as artisans from all over the state arrive for this week-long, once-a-year market (see chapter 13 for both). In **Oaxaca,** from the Thursday before Palm Sunday through Easter Sunday, religious processions fill the streets while various parts of the community sponsor fairs, concerts, fireworks, and other entertainment. See chapter 14. The Silver City of **Taxco** hosts one of the most compelling Holy Week commemorations in the country, beginning the Friday a week before Easter with nightly processions and several during the day. Thursday evening, villagers from the surrounding area carrying saints are followed by hooded members of a society of self-flagellating penitents. Others are chained at the ankles, and still more carry huge wooden crosses and bundles of penetrating thorny branches. On the Saturday morning before Easter, the Plaza Borda fills for the procession of three falls, reenacting the three times Christ stumbled and fell while carrying his cross. See chapter 12.

- **Christmas:** Unique in the country, December 23 in **Oaxaca** is the Night of the Radishes, when the Oaxaqueños build fantastic sculptures out of radishes (the most prized vegetable cultivated during the colonial period), as well as flowers and dried corn husks. They are on display on the zócalo. On December 24 each Oaxacan church organizes a procession with music, floats, and crowds bearing candles that parade to the zócalo before returning to parish churches. See chapter 14.
- **New Years:** In Oaxaca, New Year's Eve is celebrated with the Petition of the Cross, where villagers from all over come to a forlorn chapel on the hill beyond Tlacolula (about 22 miles southeast of Oaxaca, near the ruins of Mitla) to light candles and express their wishes for the coming new year. Mock bargaining, with sticks and stones to represent livestock and produce, is part of the traditional way of expressing hopes for the new year. Tiny symbolic farms and fields are built in the hope for real prosperity. See chapter 14.

THE BEST BEACH VACATIONS

Almost as valuable as knowing the best beaches is knowing which beaches are not so inviting—such as San Blas, north of Puerto Vallarta, and most of the coast of Veracruz. In both places the hard-packed sand is as appealing as a concrete parking lot.

- **Mazatlán:** The waterfront is lined with wide golden yellow beaches where water sports are a big draw—parasailing, banana boats, etc. The best stretch is known as Playa Sábalo, but beaches line the ocean especially northward beyond the marina, all the way to Los Cerritos. On Isla de las Piedras (Stone Island) on the ocean side of the small village there, a pale-sand beach, bordered by coconut groves, stretches for miles. On Sunday afternoons the palapa restaurants there have music and dancing, attracting families and young people; on other days the beach is almost empty. See chapter 5.
- **Puerto Vallarta:** The spectacularly wide Bandera Bay is lined with fine beaches, and many economical places to stay. Boat excursions take you to other nearby beaches to spend the day and dine on fresh fish beneath a woven palm umbrella. See chapter 5.
- **Barra de Navidad:** The golden sands of Barra de Navidad Bay spread from this village to its neighbor Melaque. Inexpensive hotels are right on the beach or very near to it. See chapter 5.
- **Manzanillo:** Beaches spread out all along Bahia Manzanillo and Bahia Santiago, the two big bays on which Manzanillo is built. But one of the best beaches—and certainly the most accessible—is Playa Las Brisas, fronted by small hotels and condominiums. See chapter 5.
- **Zihuatanejo/Ixtapa:** This resort duo packs a lot of good beaches into a relatively small area. Best and most beautiful of those close to Zihuatanejo is Playa La Ropa, but the wide beautiful beach at Playa Las Gatas, with its beachside eateries and snorkeling possibilities, is a great place to spend time too. On the next bay over from Zihuatanejo, all the luxury hotels in Ixtapa front Playa Palmar, a fine wide strip of beach. Just offshore Isla Ixtapa boasts a good beach and snorkeling area and lots of palapa restaurants serving incredible fresh fish. See chapter 6.
- **Puerto Angel:** The town beaches are beautiful on the small bay here, and townsfolk keep the trash picked up that coastal currents deposit. Nearby are a number of almost uninhabited beaches that can be reached by taxi or bus; discovering them is one of the treats of a leisurely Puerto Angel vacation. See chapter 6.
- **Puerto Escondido:** Some people love this spot for the enormous breakers that roll into Playa Zicatela—it's a world-class surfing beach. Others love sharing the beauty

on the town beach with fishermen who pull their colorful *pangas* under the shade of palms leaning so far over they almost touch the ground. See chapter 6.

- **Isla Mujeres:** There's only one small best beach here—Playa Norte—but it's a dandy. From this island you can dive in the cave of the sleeping sharks, snorkel right off shore, and take a fascinating boat excursion to the Isla Contoy National Park, where there's great birdlife and a fabulous uninhabited beach. See chapter 17.
- **Playa del Carmen:** The town beach, fronted by small hotels and little restaurants, is a beautiful wide one. Topless sunbathing, although illegal, seems to be permitted here. From here you're just a ferry ride away to the island of Cozumel, not far from the ruins of Tulum and Cobá, and near the snorkeling lagoons of Xcaret and Xel-Ha. See chapter 17.
- **The Yucatán's Quintana Roo Coast:** The best beaches in the country are in Cancún and south of it, almost all the way to Chetumal. All along the coast are some extraordinarily inexpensive places to stay right on the powdery, nearly white-sand beaches. Among the most beautiful is the palm-lined beach at Xpuja. See chapter 17.

THE BEST ACTIVE VACATIONS

- **Biking:** Several outlets in Puerto Vallarta now feature mountain bike trips into the mountains surrounding this picturesque village. See chapters 2 and 5.
- **Scuba Diving:** The coral reefs off the island of Cozumel are Mexico's premier diving destination, but diving off Isla Mujeres is excellent too. On the Yucatán mainland, diving the deep, dark *cenotes* (sinkholes or natural wells) is an interesting twist on underwater adventuring. See chapter 17. There's also a fascinating sea world at Cabo Pulmo off Los Cabos in the Sea of Cortez, around the islands off Loreto, and at Ixtapa/Zihuatanejo, Puerto Vallarta, and Manzanillo. See chapters 3, 5, and 6.
- **Sportfishing:** Billfishing for graceful marlin and sailfish is among the popular sports in Los Cabos, La Paz, Mazatlan, Manzanillo, Cozumel, Playa del Carmen, and Zihuatanejo, but you may hook any number of other edible fish while searching for them. Serious fisherfolks will find bonefish near Punta Allen south of Tulum, where the Cuzan Guest House caters to them. Most of the major fishing towns have annual contests. See chapters 3, 5, 6, and 17.
- **Surfing:** Surfers congregate on Puerto Escondido's Zicatela Beach where large curling waves challenge the best in the sport. Playa Costa Azul, on the outskirts of San Jose del Cabo, is another surfing beach popular for its broad waves. At Las Islitas Beach near San Blas (north of Puerto Vallarta) surfing champions match wits with the mile-long waves which are best in September and October. See chapters 3, 5, and 6.
- **Hiking and Mountaineering:** Tough challenges can be found on the slopes of volcanoes in central Mexico—Paricutín, Orizaba, Popocatépetl, and Ixtaccíhihuatl. In the Copper Canyon, hiking the deep canyons and lofty ridges requires a good guide and plenty of stamina. See chapters 4 and 12.
- **River Rafting:** The Usumacinta River, which divides Mexico from Guatemala, offers an extraordinary opportunity to steep yourself in jungle scenery and to visit the almost inaccessible Maya ruins of Yaxchilán. See chapter 14.
- **Boating the Maya Canals:** Ancient narrow canals made by the Maya go inland from the Caribbean through the jungle to a place near the ruins of Muyil. Travelers can experience this adventure from the Punta Allen Peninsula. See chapter 17.

THE BEST PLACES TO GET AWAY FROM IT ALL

A few places in Mexico come to mind as total escapes for a moment, a day, a week, or more of sublime tranquility. Some of these could double as romantic escapes if you're not expecting posh digs.

- **Batopilas** (Copper Canyon): After seven hours of passing nary a soul on a twisty, narrow, dirt mountain road you enter a near-ghost town remaining from 18th- and 19-century silver-mining booms and preserved as though someone sealed it for safekeeping last century. The feel of yesteryear is indelibly imprinted in the stucco walls and cobbled streets. This outpost has no telephones or newspapers. Electricity, a recent installation, makes the one or two televisions operable. See chapter 4.
- **Casa de la Tortuga and El Burro Boracho** (Ixtapa): Six miles north of Ixtapa, this Pacific Coast hideaway started out as a simple-but-wonderful place to have a delicious lobster or shrimp lunch, a swim in the ocean, and a stroll on the beach without bumping into a soul. With rooms for a few guests, now it's a complete getaway that's hard to beat for simplicity and tranquility, without phones or other worldly interruptions. See chapter 6.
- **Isla Mujeres:** If there's one island in Mexico that speaks relaxation, this is it. Though the island has plenty of hotels and restaurants, there are no crowds, just people bringing laziness to new heights, stretched out and dozing beneath shady palms or languidly strolling about, "dressed up" in flip flops, tee shirts, and shorts. See chapter 17.
- **The Costa Turquesa:** Away from the busy resort of Cancún, a string of heavenly quiet getaways offer tranquility on beautiful beaches. These especially include Pamul, Xcalacoco, and Xpuja. See chapter 17.
- **The Punta Allen Peninsula:** South of the Tulum ruins another string of beachside budget inns offers some of the most peaceful getaways in the country, where life among the birds and palms has never been anything but leisurely. See chapter 17.

THE BEST MUSEUMS

- **Museo de Occidente de Gobierno de Estado** (Colima): Also known as the Museo de Antropología, this small museum has an exquisite selection of pre-Hispanic pieces, primarily from Western Mexico—including hundreds of the clay dancing dogs of Colima. See chapter 5.
- **Museo de Antropología de Jalapa** (Veracruz): Second only to the Museo de Antropología in Mexico City, this outstanding museum houses pre-Hispanic remains of cultures from Mexico's East Coast—Huastec, Totonac, and Olmec—plus a small, but fine ethnography section of everyday life among peasant folk of the region. See chapter 8.
- **Museo Pedro Coronel** (Zacatecas): Outstanding for its collection of paintings from contemporary world masters. See chapter 9.
- **Museo Rafael Coronel** (Zacatecas): Houses a fantastic collection of rare marionnettes and thousands of Mexican dance masks. See chapter 9.
- **Museo del Pueblo de Guanajuato** (Guanajuato): A priceless collection of more than 1,000 colonial-era civil and religious pieces gathered by the muralist José Chávez Morado. See chapter 9.
- **Museo de Antropología** (Mexico City): Counted among the world's most outstanding museums, it contains the riches of 3,000 years of Mexico's past on the first floor. On the second floor are fabulous examples of Mexico's rich and still-thriving indigenous cultures. See chapter 11.

- **Museo Teotihuacán** (Mexico City): The new museum at the ruins of Teo-tihuacán, outside of Mexico City, like the Maya Museum in Chetumal, is a modern gleaming, state-of-the-art arena for displaying old and recent finds at the site. Punch a button, and interactive exhibits light up to speak the area history. It too has a glass floor that visitors walk on to see a miniature layout of the archaeological zone below. See chapter 11.
- **Museo Franz Mayer** (Mexico City): A rare collection of furniture and utilitarian decorative objects dating from the 16th to the 19th centuries, collected by a German immigrant to Mexico who bequeathed the collection. See chapter 11.
- **Museo del Templo Mayor** (Mexico City): With 6,000 objects displayed, no other museum shows the variety and splendor of the Aztec Empire the way this one does. See chapter 11.
- **Museo Amparo** (Puebla): This museum offers audio-cassette tours and exhibits showing the function of pre-Hispanic art in society, as well as displays of a unique collection of pottery and clay figures from Mexico's pre- to post-Classic periods. See chapter 12.
- **Museo de Artes Populares** (Puebla): In a two-story convent this huge collection of the state's regional costumes, pottery, and everyday utensils is displayed as if in use. Plus there are cavernous rooms showing works in clay, leather, straw, and papier-mâché from villages statewide. See chapter 12.
- **Centro Cultural Mexequense** (Toluca): On the grounds of a former hacienda, this cultural center houses four cultural entities and a library: The huge **Popular Arts Museum,** showcasing work of the state's fine craftsmakers; the **Charro Museum,** with fine examples of costume adornments; the **Museum of Modern Art,** with works from Mexico's finest artists; and the **Museum of Anthropology,** with examples from the state's 10 most important archaeological sites. See chapter 12.
- **Museo de la Cultura Maya** (Chetumal): This new museum showcasing Maya archaeology, architecture, history, and mythology is one of the best in the country. It features interactive exhibits and a glass floor that allows visitors to walk above replicas of Maya sites. See chapter 17.

THE BEST SHOPPING

Hardly a tourist returns from Mexico without at least one craft tucked in a bag. Some people bring an empty bag for purchases, and some haul their loot by the trunk- or truckful. Sure bets for superior shopping are found in more than a half dozen cities and villages.

- **Dolores Hidalgo:** A few miles north of San Miguel de Allende, this village is fast becoming the best-known pottery producing village in Mexico. Almost every block has factories or store outlets devoted to the colorful Talavera-style pottery. See chapter 9.
- **San Miguel de Allende:** Street after street of shops carrying textiles, brass, tin, iron, pottery, glass, and much more are housed here in colonial-era mansions. See chapter 9.
- **Tonala and Tlaquepaque:** Two villages near Guadalajara, they are renowned for pottery, papier-mâché, and hand-blown glass. More than 400 artisans have workshops in Tonala. See chapter 10.
- **Mexico City:** Shopping highlights include the Fonart stores, the Museo de Artes y Industrias Populares, the Avalos Brothers glass factory, and the Bazar Sábado, Lagunilla Market, and La Ciudadela Market. See chapter 11.

- **Puebla:** A pottery center before the conquest of Mexico, it's Talavera-style tile adorns building facades and church domes throughout the area. Factories produce highly collectable tile and colorful tableware with unique motifs. See chapter 12.
- **Toluca:** The Friday Toluca Market is one of the grandest in the country—exhausting in its enormity and fascinating in its contents. The huge Casart, the state-owned crafts shop, is one of the best in Mexico; it features locally made baskets, pottery, glass, Persian-style carpets from Temoaya, and more. See chapter 12.
- **Taxco:** Mexico's "Silver Capital" features more than 200 stores selling the metal worked into fine jewelry and decorative objects. See chapter 12.
- **Pátzcuaro:** Deep in the Sierra Madres, this village and the smaller ones surrounding it feature beautiful cotton textiles, wood carving, a captivating variety of pottery, lacquerware, and straw weaving. One nearby village is Santa Clara del Cobre, Mexico's "Copper Capital," where shops glimmer with copper. See chapter 13.
- **Oaxaca:** A colonial city with good shops and crafts markets, it's also ringed by crafts villages specializing in pottery, wool Zapotec rugs and other textiles, and colorful, imaginative wood carving. See chapter 14.
- **San Cristóbal de las Casas:** Deep in the heart of the Maya highlands, San Cristóbal's shops, open plazas, and markets feature the distinctive waist-loomed wool and cotton textiles of the region, leather shoes, and handsomely crude pottery, genre dolls, and Guatemalan textiles. See chapter 14.

THE HOTTEST NIGHTLIFE

In Mexico nightlife runs the gamut from quiet supper clubs with a dance floor (although there aren't many of these), to beachside dance floors with live bands, to rousing or tranquil extended "happy hours" in seaside bars, to some of the flashiest discos known to humankind. Yes, *discos*. These flamboyant 1970s-style clubs may be passé in the rest of the world, but in Mexico "dees-cohs" are more than alive and well, they have a thriving life of their own. Most nightspots start around 9:30 or 10pm and close up somewhere between 2am and sunrise.

- **Baja California:** Cabo San Lucas is the nightlife capital of Baja, though after-dark fun is centered around the party ambience and camaraderie found in the casual bars and restaurants rather than a flashy disco scene—but you'll find those too. See chapter 3.
- **Mazatlán:** Though this clean beachside city doesn't have the breadth of nightlife of other resorts, it does have Valentinos, one of the most well-known and popular discos in the country. Dramatically perched on a rocky outcropping overlooking the sea, this all-white, Moorish-looking building has a high-tech light show complete with green laser beams. See chapter 5.
- **Puerto Vallarta:** Here you can find mariachi hotspots that rollick until the wee hours or work yourself into a dancing frenzy at an almost all-night disco. See chapter 5.
- **Acapulco:** For hot nightlife this city is tops in the country, with lots of the latest discos, several of which have a wall of windows overlooking the bay. But establishments featuring pulsating Caribbean and salsa sounds can be just as crowded as the most "in" disco. See chapter 6.
- **Cancún:** From live music in hotel lobby bars to the most sophisticated discos around, there are a lot of options in Cancún for staying out until the sun comes up. See chapter 16.

THE BEST BUDGET INNS

Some inns stand out for their combination of hospitality and simple-but-colorful surroundings. These are places guests return again and again.

- **Posada Terranova** (San José del Cabo; ☎ 114/2-0534): The best budget inn in town, the rooms are invitingly bright and clean, and the patio restaurant serves good American- and Mexican-style meals. See chapter 3.
- **Los Cuatro Vientos** (Puerto Vallarta; ☎ 322/2-0161): A quiet, cozy inn set on a hillside overlooking Banderas Bay, it features colorfully decorated rooms built around a small pool and central patio, daily continental breakfast, and the absolute best venue for sunset in Puerto Vallarta. See chapter 5.
- **Hotel Flor de María** (Puerto Escondido; ☎ 958/2-0536): Charming in every way from the hospitable owners Lino and María Francato, to the rooms, which are individually decorated with Lino's fine artistic touches, and the restaurant, which is the best in town. See chapter 6.
- **Mesón de Alférez** (Jalapa; ☎ 28/18-6351): The owners of the lovely Posada del Cafeto created another hotel in the 1808 home of the Spanish Viceroy's representative. Rooms, named after historic Jalapa streets, are furnished in a colonial style with colorful accents warming the colonial-era stone. See chapter 8.
- **Posada del Cafeto** (Jalapa; ☎ 28/17-0023): Travelers are delighted to discover this comfortable town house-turned-hotel with its colorful rooms and Mexican tile accents. Coffee is available for guests mornings and evenings. See chapter 8.
- **Hotel Gillow** (Mexico City; ☎ 5/518-1440): The secret is you get a lot for your money—modern hotel, perfect location between the Zócalo and Alameda, comfortable beds, remote control television with U.S. channels, excellent lighting, good restaurant, and a staff that is likely to remember you from one visit to the next. See chapter 11.
- **Hotel Rancho Taxco Victoria** (Taxco; ☎ and fax 762/2-0010): With a fabulous hillside setting overlooking all of Taxco and its pristine 1940s decor, this hotel gets special marks as an inexpensive inn that exudes all the charm of old-fashioned Mexico. See chapter 12.
- **Hotel Mansión Iturbe Bed and Breakfast** (Pátzcuaro; ☎ 434/2-0368): Few budget hotels offer more free perks for guests—welcome drink, hot water for instant coffee in the lobby early each morning, full breakfast in Doña Paca, the hotel's great little restaurant, free daily paper, two hours of free bicycle rental, and the fourth night free. It's all in a 17th-century town house on Pátzcuaro's Plaza Grande. See chapter 13.
- **Hotel Posada de la Basílica** (Pátzcuaro; ☎ 434/2-1108): A mansion-turned-hotel, this appealing colonial-style inn has comfortable rooms with fireplaces built around a lovely patio with a view of the village. See chapter 13.
- **Las Golondrinas** (Oaxaca; ☎ 951/6-8726): I receive more favorable letters about this hotel than any other in the country. Small and simple, but colorful, with homey touches of folk art and pathways lined with abundant foliage, this hotel thrives on repeat visitors who pass the word to their friends. See chapter 14.
- **Casa Mexilio Guest House** (Mérida; ☎ 99/28-2505, or 800/538-6802 in the U.S.): Host Roger Lynn has created the atmosphere of a private home rather than that of a hotel in this 19th-century town house, and he offers some of the most unusual guided tours of the area. See chapter 15.
- **Hotel Mucuy** (Mérida): Among the most hospitable budget hotels in the country, owners Alfredo and Ofelia Comin strive to make guests feel at home, with

cheery, clean rooms, comfortable outdoor tables and chairs, a communal refrigerator in the lobby, and laundry and clothesline facilities. See chapter 15.

- **Cabañas Paamul** (Cancún-Tulum Highway; ☎ **99/25-9422** in Mérida): Seven coral-colored bungalows face a beautiful small cove and wide beautiful cream-colored beach, and the cerulean blue Caribbean. Reef diving and snorkeling are within five minutes' walking, but the next closest civilization is at Puerto Aventuras, 2¹/₂ miles distant. See chapter 17.

THE MOST AUTHENTIC CULINARY EXPERIENCES

- **Casa Puntarenas** (Zihuatanejo): A modest spot with a tin roof and nine wooden tables, Puntarenas is one of the best places in town to try one of Mexico's finest food treats—fried whole fish served with toasted bolillos, sliced tomatoes, onions, and avocado. See chapter 6.
- **Fonda del Refugio** (Mexico City): Elegantly casual, you'll find specialties here from all over the country, such as manchamanteles (tablecloth stainer) on Tuesday, and albondigas en chile chipotle (meatballs in chipotle sauce) on Saturday. See chapter 11.
- **Fonda Don Chon, Mexico City:** Ever had a hankering for armadillo *en chimole*, a heap of toasted grasshoppers, chrysanthemums stuffed with tuna, or perhaps a pile of ant eggs sauted in butter and wine sauce, or maybe in a sauce of fruity guanabana? Don Chon gets back to the basics of authentic Mexican cuisine at his restaurant, billed as the "Cathedral of Pre-Hispanic Cooking." More traditional fare is served too, but even if you don't eat here, it's worth a trip just to read the menu and examine the walls of articles and accolades written about this famous place. See chapter 11.
- **Los Almendros** (Mérida, Cancún, Ticul, and Mexico City): This family-owned restaurant chain features Yucatecan specialties. Their famous Poc-chuc, a marinated and grilled pork dish, was created at the original restaurant in Ticul some years ago. See chapters 11, 15, and 16.
- **Fonda de Santa Clara** (Puebla): Serving regional food, the menu here includes such local dishes as pollo mole poblano, mixiotes, and tinga. There are seasonal specialties as well, like fried grasshoppers in October and November, maguey worms in April and May, chiles enogada in July through September, and huitlacoche in June. See chapter 12.
- **Las Pichanchas** (Tuxtla Gutiérrez): Chiapan variations on sausages, tamales, and beef are featured in this festively decorated restaurant named after the holy pot used to make nixtamal masa dough. See chapter 14.
- **El Fogón de Jovel** (San Cristóbal de las Casas): Chiapan food is served at this handsome old townhouse, with dining under the portals and rooms built around a central courtyard. The waiters wear local indigenous costumes. The scrumptious food highlights the specialties of Chiapas. See chapter 14.

THE BEST COMIDA CORRIDAS

To do as the Mexicans do, begin your day with a light breakfast, then have your main meal at lunch. Many Mexican restaurants around the country offer a fixed-price lunch of three or four courses that can be delicious, filling, and astonishingly cheap. It's called the comida corrida. Here are some places where you'll find great deals.

- **Doney's** (Mazatlán): This tried-and-true favorite, in a converted colonial home immediately south of the plaza in old town, is regarded by many locals as the best moderately priced restaurant downtown. See chapter 5.

- **Cafeteria/Nevería Chantilly** (Manzanillo): Always busy, this chrome-and-Formica restaurant, opposite the main plaza, does a full-house business at lunch, with a comida that might begin with fresh fruit cocktail, followed by soup, rice, the main course, dessert, and coffee. See chapter 5.
- **Café El Retiro** (Guanajuato): For decades this has been the most dependable restaurant in town. Service is fast, informal, and friendly, and the portions of home-style food are generous and well flavored. See chapter 9.
- **Truco 7** (Guanajuato): With one of the most cozy settings in the country, Truco 7 is crowded almost any time, but at lunch it's worth the short wait for the generous three- or four-course comida corrida. See chapter 9.
- **El Cortijo** (Puebla): Everyone knows this is the place for a good comida corrida, so it's crowded at lunch. But once seated, the *cubierto* (or comida corrida) starts with a fruit cocktail; followed by a choice of two soups; a mid-course of perhaps paella or spaghetti; then the main course, which might include a choice of pork leg, mole, fish, or chicken. Then of course it's siesta time. See chapter 12.
- **Las Viandas de San José** (Morelia): In a handsome mansion centered on an open patio, enjoy the comida corrida, which starts with vegetable crudités, followed by soup dipped from a tureen by the hostess, several choices of main course served with rice or potatoes, and then dessert. See chapter 13.
- **La Sorpresa** (Mitla, Oaxaca): On the back patio of an old hacienda that houses the Museum of Zapotec Art, this little restaurant puts out a value-packed, multi-course midday meal featuring regional food that's not only filling but excellently prepared. See chapter 14.
- **El Méson** (Oaxaca): Wow, do you ever get taste and value for your peso here. The excellently priced comida corrida is filling and costs almost nothing. For only a few pesos more you can enjoy the all-you-can-eat breakfast and lunch buffets. See chapter 14.
- **Mi Tierra** (San Cristóbal de las Casas): Upon arrival in San Cristóbal I'll head to this restaurant just for the filling and wonderfully prepared comida corrida. It comes with soup; choice of three entrees such as pork in adobo sauce, barbecue ribs, perhaps chicken curry, or poblano chile; fruit-flavored purified water; and dessert—all in a cozy setting with classical music playing in the background. See chapter 14.
- **Restaurant Tuluc** (San Cristóbal de las Casas): Another of Mexico's dependable restaurants offering a comida corrida that you'll remember and return to for the several choices of everything in a warm setting that you'll enjoy lingering in for coffee and dessert. See chapter 14.
- **Restaurant Curva** (Cancún City): Open only six hours a day, the six tables are always full for the value-priced four course lunch. There's usually a choice of main courses, such as beef tips, pozole, pollo adobado, or pollo frito. See chapter 16.
- **Carmelita's** (Isla Mujeres): Small, with only three tables, but good, this is the place for a filling, inexpensive meal of perhaps a Maya tamal, paella, cochinta pibil, or pozole on Sundays. See chapter 17.

3 Eighty Tips for Saving Money in Mexico

AIR TRAVEL

1. "Low season" in Mexico runs from Easter Sunday through approximately December 20, and airlines often offer discounted airfares. Many of these fares are un-advertised, especially during the slowest months mentioned above (mid-summer),

and again in January, when the Christmas travelers have dispersed and hotel and airline occupancies are low.

2. Airfare to Mexico City is less expensive if you travel to the city on a Friday, Saturday, or Sunday and return on a Saturday or Sunday.

3. Charter flights from cold-weather cities in the United States—most run only in winter—often offer a considerable savings over scheduled airlines because they go directly to the destination (avoiding the necessity of overnighting en route), and they usually include low airfare and hotel. However, these same charters often offer round-trip airfare only, allowing more independent travelers to choose a less expensive hotel, and the option of staying longer and returning on a later charter flight.

4. Regional airlines affiliated with Mexicana and Aeroméxico cost much more to book from the United States than if booked in Mexico and paid in pesos. Of course if a connection is critical you'll want to book from the United States, but if you can wait, or want to take a chance that seats will be available, you can save at least one-third or sometimes even one-half of the fare.

ACCOMMODATIONS

5. Low season yields even greater discounts in hotel rates than airfares—prices are 20% to 50% lower than during high season. There's often a lull after New Year's in such sought-after places as Cancún, Cozumel, and Puerto Vallarta. During January, prices can fall to somewhere between high- and low-season norms.

6. In most places July and August are very slow, but there are some exceptions. Mexicans and Europeans take vacations in those months, and some hotels in a few destinations thus raise their prices; these include some hotels in Isla Mujeres, Playa del Carmen, Veracruz, and Barra de Navidad.

7. Rooms with air-conditioning are almost always more expensive than those with only fans. Rooms with a view of the street may be more expensive (not to mention noisier) than those with windows opening onto an airshaft. Sea views cost more than garden or street views at the same resort. A room with a balcony or patio, however, will cost the same as one without.

8. Hotels a block or two from the beach cost 50% to 75% less than those right on the sand.

9. Fewer and fewer hotels in Mexico have rooms without private baths. The few bathless rooms listed in this book will be somewhat cheaper, but not necessarily by very much, than those with baths.

10. It is generally cheaper for two people to share a room with one bed than for them to share a room with two beds.

11. If you ask a desk clerk to price a room, the quote he or she gives you may not be for the cheapest room available. Ask to see a cheaper room by saying *"quiero ver un cuarto más barato, por favor"*—it can't hurt.

12. Package vacations that include the cost of air transportation and hotel will usually save you money—except right after a currency devaluation, as 1995 proved. Package prices may have been negotiated at pre-devaluation rates.

13. To check out package deals, look for hotels listed in this book with toll-free reservation numbers in the United States; they may be a part of a package offered by a scheduled or charter airline or wholesale package dealer. (Most hotels in this book are not included in package vacations.) To evaluate the value of a package, call the airline to determine the cost of round-trip airfare and if possible call the hotel for their per-day rack (public), promotional, and discount rates. This will give you

some idea of the actual cost as compared to the package cost. Take into consideration that round-trip transportation from the airport to your hotel is often included in package rates and can save you $20 to $30 in such places as Cancún, Puerto Vallarta, and Acapulco.

14. In Cozumel, you can save money by purchasing diving packages, which include the price of the hotel and usually two dives. If the dive operates from the hotel, you will also save on transportation costs. Many divers, however, save more money by staying in a cheaper hotel and booking dives directly with a diving concession. This method may be particularly practical in the fall, when stormy seas often preclude diving, and you therefore won't have to pay for unused dives.

15. In Mexico City, many of the top hotels cut weekend rates substantially, since most of their business is midweek. The discounts are usually unadvertised.

16. In Acapulco, midweek rates in some hotels are lower than on the weekends, when an influx of people from Mexico City often fills hotels. Especially affected are hotels in the moderate- to low-price range. Many super-luxury hotels slash midweek rates too; a hotel charging $180 to $200 on the weekend may charge only $80 midweek.

17. By law, hotel rates should be posted within view of the reception desk, but often they are not. If a hotel's quoted rate seems too high, ask to see their official rate sheet and ask about discounts and promotional rates. Walk away if the price seems too high.

    Additionally, budget quality hotels may charge you 10% to 15% more if you want a receipt. Since it isn't wise to pay a desk clerk for a room without getting a receipt for your payment—for example, readers have reported paying an evening clerk on check-in, only to discover upon checkout that the day clerk has no record of the transaction—I carry a pad of receipts, so they won't have to use their official ones. As an alternative, I've asked them to write, sign, and date an informal receipt in my notebook.

18. If you're traveling in the off-season (and not during a Mexican holiday), it is not necessary to make reservations. Arrive at your destination early in the day and target your choice of hotel. This will save you the price of a long-distance call to reserve a room and the uncertainty of knowing if your reservation deposit has been received. Mexican hotels often do not respond to reservation requests made by mail, even though they will honor such requests.

19. When calling from outside Mexico for a reservation, you'll almost always be asked from where you are calling. If you say you're from the United States or some other country, the price may go up. Instead, say you're calling from a nearby Mexican city and you're more likely to get good rates.

20. If you have reserved a room, ask the going rate for a room on arrival. If it is less than the rate you reserved, register as a new client and take a room at the lower cost. If you've paid a deposit, ask that it be applied to your new account. You may have to debate the point, but it will be worth it. Only if you've used the hotel's U.S. toll-free reservation number can the hotel logically justify a higher rate for your reservations.

21. If you arrive in a city without a hotel reservation, call a hotel from the public telephone/fax office in most bus stations and airports. For only the cost of a local call, you'll be assured of a room when you arrive. In addition, you will not incur hefty taxi fares. If you don't speak Spanish and if the person at the telephone office isn't busy, ask him or her to make the call for you.

22. At the airports in both Mexico City and Acapulco and at bus stations in Acapulco, hotel associations staff 24-hour hotel reservation services. They make your reservation and you prepay one night, for which you're given a paid voucher to present

to the hotel. Use this book to approach the associations with suggestions for hotels. If your preferred hotel isn't a member of an association, they'll probably allow you to use the phone to call for a reservation. Hotels often allow these reservation outlets to use promotional or discount rates—ask about these rates first.

23. Bed-and-breakfast hotels are slowly beginning to appear in Mexico. They offer good values, especially the Hotel Cuatro Vientos in Puerto Vallarta, the Pensión Casa Carmen in San Miguel de Allende, and Hotel Mansión Iturbe in Pátzcuaro.

24. In San Miguel de Allende and Taxco, you can arrange a long stay at small apartments or in family homes for $100 to $200 a month. There's no central reservation service, so take a room in a hotel for a few days and check bulletin boards around town for this type of deal.

25. Most hotels allow children under age 12 to stay for free in their parents' room. Many hotels will accommodate kids with a roll-away bed. When making your reservation, always verify that the hotel has this service and take down the name of the person with whom you spoke.

26. Although Mexican campsites are not of the same quality as those in the United States, most beach destinations have designated camping areas. I mention several in this book.

27. In Mexico, hotels on the main square are often slightly higher priced than hotels a block or two away.

28. Finally, some destinations *do* have cheaper places to stay than those I've written up for this book. But I purposely have not listed rock-bottom hotels in this guide because of frequent reports of thefts at such places—especially of cameras and money from backpackers. Although nothing can guarantee complete security, I have chosen hotels that feel safe.

DINING AND DRINKING

29. Generally the least expensive, most filling items on Mexican menus are local specialties such as enchiladas, tacos, chilaquiles, carne tampiqueña, and milanesa.

30. Other inexpensive meals (which come in a bowl) include sopa tlalpeño—a hearty vegetable soup—and pozole soup, in its different regional varieties.

31. Free coffee refills are rare in Mexico, so you pay by the cup at 75¢ to $1.25 a shot. To make your own coffee or tea, pack a travel-size coffee pot (or an immersion coil), a heat-resistant plastic cup, instant coffee or a tea bag, and powdered milk. (Having a coil or a hot pot is also very handy if you are ill and can stomach only chamomile tea or bouillon.)

32. Trail mix, granola bars, and fruit from the market are great to bring along for snacks. You can also prepare instant soup (not easily found in Mexico) with your own hot-water maker in your room and save $1 to $4 on the cost of a bowl of soup in a restaurant.

33. Mexico's abundant fresh-fruit markets and bakeries are ideal for concocting inexpensive breakfasts.

34. The *comida corrida,* Mexico's traditional noontime fixed-price menu, often includes an entire meal, from soup to dessert. It can be a good value if portions are large and if a beverage and dessert are included. If the comida corrida is over $4, you're probably better off ordering from the à la carte menu.

35. In most restaurants, the fresh large bolillo rolls and butter the waiter brings are included in the cost of the meal. Some restaurants, such as the Chalet Suizo and the Hostería Santo Domingo in Mexico City, however, charge extra for rolls and butter. Other restaurants, such as the Café El Popular in Mexico City, put a

tempting basket of sweet rolls on the table and charge you for what you consume. You see the added charge on the bill.

36. Although eating in American-style restaurants such as Denny's, Vips, and Lyni's surely isn't classic Mexican dining, these places offer value and dependable food. They are especially good deals in Mexico City and Guadalajara, where there are fewer economical restaurants.

37. Since Mexico has a value-added tax (IVA) of 10% in Cancún, Cozumel, and Los Cabos, and 15% in the rest of the country, determine the amount of your tip from the cost of your meal *before* the tax has been included. For meals costing under $3, leave loose change; for meals costing $4 to $5, leave 6% to 10%, depending on the quality of service. For meals above $5, include a 10% to 15% tip.

38. Avoid buying a beverage with each meal by drinking water—yes, water. Most restaurants serving tourists (and many serving primarily Mexicans) use purified water from large commercial jars. To get free water and not bottled water (for which you pay), ask if they have *agua purificada natural de la garrafon* (noncarbonated, purified water from the big bottle dispenser) *sin hielo* (without ice). The garrafon (big bottle of purified water) is often within view in the dining room, and you can point to it if you don't speak Spanish. If the waiter puts a small bottle of commercially produced purified water on the table, it'll cost $1.50 to $3 extra.

39. At 75¢ to $2 each, soft drink or beer costs can add up as you travel, especially in hot-weather destinations. To quench thirst more economically, carry a small water jug and replenish it with bottled water purchased at a grocery store for around 75¢ to $1 per gallon.

40. Mexico produces excellent wine, beer, and rum which are considerably less expensive than imported spirits.

41. If your craving for beer, soft drinks, and liquor is acute, save money by buying them at a grocery store and have drinks in your room, patio, or balcony rather than at a restaurant or bar. A soft drink, for example, can cost as little as 25¢ at a corner grocery and as much as 75¢ to $2 at a restaurant.

42. Mexicans recycle soft drink bottles, and you'll be charged more if you take bottles with you from a grocery store or *abarote* (neighborhood store). Usually, clerks will ask if your drink is to go (*para llevar*) or to drink there. Often, though, they pour the whole bottled drink into a fresh plastic bag, stick a straw in it, and send you off clasping the loose neck of your portable container at no extra charge.

43. Happy hours, when drinks are two for the price of one, proliferate, especially in resort areas. Often there are also happy hours at lobby bars in major cities.

44. Sports bars offer TV or video sports entertainment without a cover charge.

SIGHTSEEING, OUTDOOR ACTIVITIES, & NIGHTLIFE

45. In Puerto Vallarta you can save money on horse rentals by going directly to the owner of the horses rather than making arrangements through a travel agent.

46. Bring your own snorkeling gear to beach destinations and save $5 to $10 on the cost of daily rental.

47. Use the walking tours and suggested strolls in this book to see towns instead of taking commercial tours.

48. For a leisurely and inexpensive orientation to a spread-out destination such as Cancún, Acapulco, or Manzanillo, take a city bus along the main thoroughfares for 25¢ to 50¢.

49. In Acapulco, hotel tour desks and reception areas and travel agencies often dole out coupons for free admission to discos—a savings of $10 to $16.

50. If you're female, look for ladies' nights, when women pay no cover charge at discos.
51. In Mexico City, trolley-bus tours of the Centro Histórico for around $3 are a good orientation to downtown, after which you can return for a more in-depth tour on foot.
52. Free weekend concerts are often presented in central parks and plazas all over Mexico. For example, concerts are held on Tuesday, Thursday, and Sunday evenings in Guadalajara's Plaza de Armas. In Querétaro, on Saturday night there's free entertainment on the Plaza Independencia. Mérida has free entertainment in city parks almost nightly. In Cuernavaca, orchestras perform on Sunday afternoons in the gazebo on the Plaza de Armas. Oaxaca entertains the public in its main square at least six nights a week. Mérida hosts entertainment almost nightly in its parks and plazas. In Veracruz, marimba and harp musicians play for diners around the Plaza de Armas.
53. Almost all museums and archaeological sites are free to the public on Sunday and Mexican holidays—a savings of $1.50 to $7.
54. Most archaeological sites charge visitors $3.50 to $8.50 for using their personal video cameras. If you are visiting many sites, you'll save a lot of money by not using your video camera or by saving it for the most important sites. A few sites charge visitors for using still cameras, so consider whether the lighting conditions and site are worth this expense.

MONEY MATTERS

55. One or two of the several currency exchange booths at the Mexico City airport offer exchange rates far better than those at banks and at other exchange booths in the same row. At the Cancún airport you can lose substantial amounts of money by using the first exchange booth you see—compare exchanging $100 at seven pesos to the dollar (700 pesos) and at 6.5 pesos (650 pesos) to the dollar. There's a 50 peso ($7.15) difference. As a general rule, take a few minutes to scout the exchange houses for the best rate and then change only enough to tide you over until you can go to a bank, which usually offers better deals.
56. Try not to carry U.S. $100 bills, which may not be exchangeable; there's a surfeit of counterfeit bills circulating in that denomination, and banks, exchange houses, and others are wary of accepting them.
57. Carry at least $50 in U.S. one-dollar bills to avoid overtipping in pesos. For example, a 10-peso tip ($1.43 at seven pesos to the dollar) may be too much, but five pesos (about 71¢) might not be enough. Using one-dollar bills helps conserve small-denomination peso bills and coins, which are in short supply.
58. Carry enough cash to cover a weekend or holiday, since travelers checks and credit cards may be difficult to use at those times.
59. Do not rely on your credit card in out-of-the-way places or in many budget hotels and restaurants. Such places often do not accept credit cards, and you will waste time looking for a bank and could pay dearly for a cash advance.
60. Some establishments charge an additional 3% for use of a credit card, but they usually tell you first.
61. If credit cards are accepted and incur no additional fees, use them whenever possible. The exchange rate may be in your favor when the peso-to-dollar rate is determined later during billing. Such savings can be considerable.
62. Always count your change, especially at taxi ticket booths, where shortchanging is common. One reader wrote me about having saved money equivalent to the cost of this book by following this tip at the Mexico City airport.

63. Most hotel and restaurant prices you'll see posted in Mexico include the 10% to 15% IVA tax. Look at the bottom of menus for information about whether the tax is included in meals; ask *before* you rent a room or order a meal.
64. A 10% to 15% tip is sometimes, though not often, included in bills, most often in the Yucatán. Restaurants which serve many visitors from Europe (where the tip is customarily included in the cost of food) may tack it onto the bill when it is presented to you.

TRANSPORTATION

65. Inner-city bus service in Puerto Vallarta, Cancún, Acapulco, Manzanillo, Mazatlán, Guadalajara, Pátzcuaro, Oaxaca, and much of Mexico City is so good and inexpensive (15¢ to 50¢ per ride) that there's little need for a taxi.
66. Most airports and bus stations in large cities have *colectivo* (shared) or fixed-rate taxis to town. The colectivo is always the least expensive way to go. Usually the fixed-rate taxis at bus stations, especially in Mexico City and Guadalajara, are much cheaper than those hailed on the street.
67. At airports with relatively few incoming flights, such as Tuxtla Gutiérrez, San Luis Potosí, León, and Villahermosa, buy your colectivo van ticket as quickly as possible; as the most inexpensive transportation available, colectivos fill and leave quickly. If you miss them, you'll have to rely on very expensive taxis as transportation.
68. In Acapulco, Manzanillo, and Oaxaca, returning to the airport in a colectivo van costs a third the price of a taxi. In most other cities, there is no colectivo transportation to return to the airport, so you must hail a taxi.
69. If a fixed-rate taxi driver at a bus station or airport tries to tell you that the ticket you paid for isn't enough for the zone or hotel you're going to, tell him to take it up with the ticket seller—don't fork over more money.
70. Except for Mexico City, taxis in Mexico aren't metered. In other cities, you must agree on a price before you get in. Taxi prices to the most common destinations are usually posted inside the front door of most hotels. Use these prices as guides to taxi costs, since taxi drivers are notorious for bargaining high.
71. A Volkswagen Beetle (which are made in Puebla, Mexico) with manual transmission and without air-conditioning, is the least expensive car you can rent in Mexico. Save money by reserving a rental car before you leave the United States. Avis's prepay rental deal is a substantial cost saver. Weekly rentals and those with mileage included are the best deals, but watch out for high deductibles.
72. During high season and Mexican holidays, rates for car rentals are inflated. Rentals also cost more during weekends at resorts and weekdays in business-oriented cities.

● SHOPPING

73. Bargaining is expected in markets. Start at half the price first quoted to you and agree finally on something in between. You'll get a cheaper per-item price if you buy more than one of the same item. If the vendor senses that you're prepared to walk away, the price will often come down. Even in stores with fixed prices, discounts are often available if you are buying many things, but you'll have to ask for them.
74. In resort areas, especially Acapulco and Puerto Vallarta, resort clothing is often a bargain, especially when there's a sale. Be careful about Mexican-made zippers; sometimes they aren't up to the task.

LAST, BUT NOT LEAST

75. Pack plenty of insect repellent and suntan lotion. When available, these commodities cost at least triple what they do in the States. Lotions with an SPF rating are almost impossible to find.

76. Although prices have risen recently, prescription drugs are often less expensive in Mexico than in the States and can be purchased without a prescription. Drugstores, however, won't sell drugs that are controlled in the States—tranquilizers for instance. High-priced antibiotics cost about the same in Mexico as they do in the United States. Aspirin and over-the-counter sinus medications are difficult, if not impossible, to find in Mexico.

77. Save money on long-distance calls by calling collect. If that's not possible, then the least expensive option is to use a *larga distancia* office, found in most towns. Generally there's a service charge of about $2.50 to $3.50 in addition to the cost of the call. Using the phone in your hotel room can be the most expensive way to call; a hefty service charge is often added to the price of the call—even if you are calling a toll-free number. Many budget hotels, however, charge the same rates as those at a larga distancia office; ask before you call.

78. Save money on laundry by doing it yourself. Bring a self-sealing plastic bag of powdered detergent; as an extra, it keeps your suitcase smelling fresh. Budget hotels often also offer very inexpensive laundry service. For a small tip, you can usually have everything ironed as well. Be wary of getting delicate items laundered at hotels.

79. If the copy of *War and Peace* you brought along didn't last the trip, you can exchange it for a different book at one of the many hotels listed in the book that have an honor book exchange. Novels from the United States for sale at Sanborn's and other outlets in Mexico often cost at least twice the U.S. cover price.

80. The *guarda equipaje* (baggage storage) at the Mexico City airport costs a minimum of $2.75 for an hour or 24 hours of storage. Bus stations charge 75¢ and up, but they won't keep baggage as long. Hotels, however, will store guests' luggage free in a locked closet especially for this purpose. There's usually no limit on the length of time luggage can be stored.

2 Planning a Trip to Mexico

Before any trip, you need to do a bit of advance planning. When should I go? What's the best way to get there? How much will this trip cost me? And can I catch a festival during my visit? I'll answer these and other questions for you in this chapter.

1 Mexico's Regions in Brief

BAJA CALIFORNIA   A peninsula longer than Italy, Baja stretches 876 miles from its border with California, and northernmost city of Tijuana, to **Cabo San Lucas** at its southern tip where the Sea of Cortéz meets the Pacific Ocean. Formed by volcanoes that left multicolored mountains and mysterious caves later painted by Indians, today this craggy desertscape is framed on both sides by deep blue waters. Culturally and geographically set apart from mainland Mexico, development has been slow. Baja California Sur (Southern Baja) achieved statehood only in 1974. Even now only a few roads penetrate Baja California, but for centuries a few intrepid souls have staked their lives on its promise. Slowly the peninsula has evolved into a vacation haven noted for its fishing, diving, leaping dolphins, sea lions, colonies of migrating whales, and posh resorts. Though much of Baja is expensive, with planning, there are still many possibilities for enjoyable vacationing on a budget, especially in **Loreto, Santa Rosalia,** and **La Paz.**

THE COPPER CANYON   The Copper Canyon is so remote, so rugged, and so gorgeous in its multicolored mountain grandeur that few other areas in Mexico create more curiosity, or more dreamy praise. Soaring from sea level to over 9,000 feet and covering 390 miles between **Los Mochis** on the Pacific Coast to **Chihuahua** in northern Mexico, the railroad, which took several entrepreneurs from 1863 to 1928 to complete, skirts the edge of more than 20 canyons in a network said to be four times larger than the Grand Canyon. You can take the train straight through on a 15-hour ride, but staying overnight en route is the only way to really see the canyons. Rustic-but-comfortable lodges house visitors who can opt for a leisurely armchair-type trip or one filled with character-building adventure from hiking and backpacking to strenuous horseback trips through the mountains. The intriguing terrain is the home to Tarahumara Indians who live in caves and small farming settlements. Seeing this region requires both planning and flexibility.

THE PACIFIC COAST   Few regions in Mexico vary in terrain as dramatically as this coast. The northern portion, going south from Arizona, opens to a beautiful sienna- and milky brown-colored desertscape that, with its western edge rimmed by the Sea of Cortéz, has been likened to Arizona with water. It encompasses Puerto Penasco, an offbeat holiday beach town, and Guayamas (not so touristically interesting, but noted for giant-size shrimp). Toward **Los Mochis** the desert becomes cultivated with sugarcane, and by **Mazatlán** the setting is more tropical with cultivated fruit plantations. At **Puerto Vallarta,** forested mountains meet the sea on the beautiful and wide Banderas Bay; it has a lush tropical feel. To the south of Puerto Vallarta for 50 miles or so agriculture has largely replaced trees, but then gorgeous tropical forests rise again north of **Chamula** and continue to **Manzanillo,** interspersed with horizon-to-horizon banana, mango, and coconut palm plantations. This area encompasses laid-back **Barra de Navidad** and its sister town **Melaque,** both on large bays rimmed by cream-colored beaches. The highway inland from Manzanillo to the city of **Colima** covers more mountains, with some fairly beautiful scenery in mountain passes. At **Zihuatanejo/Ixtapa** you'll find more deep-green forests around the town; to the south, fruit plantations stretch almost all the way to **Acapulco,** affording brief glimpses of the ocean. Tree-covered mountains still remain around Acapulco, though hillside development has marred them some, but in some places the natural vegetation has been replaced with tropical gardens around plush hillside villas. Traveling inland from Acapulco to **Taxco,** the thinly covered mountainous landscape can be refreshing after the rainy season, but blisteringly hot and desertlike at other times. Taxco, a delightful hillside colonial-era city famed for its hundreds of silver shops, is surrounded by thinly forested mountains. Farther south along the coast from Acapulco, the short, scrubby forests, interspersed with agricultural plots, give way to a boulder-laden scrub forest terrain around the nine gorgeous bays of **Huatulco.** Twisty mountain roads go inland to **Durango, Guadalajara,** and beautiful **Lake Chapala,** and from there to the mountain resort town of **Mazamitla** and on into the gorgeous mountainous state of Michoacán.

Of all these destinations the least budget friendly is Acapulco, where economical lodgings are a step down compared to what you get for the same price almost anywhere along this coast. Puerto Vallarta and Mazatlán combine the most to do with the best economical lodgings, especially in their downtown areas, while Barra de Navidad and Puerto Angel offer the most relaxation for the least money.

THE CENTRAL REGION   This region encompasses the area from the Texas border as far south as **Mexico City,** and includes the heaviest concentration of population and beautiful colonial cities, many of which were founded during Mexico's early silver mining centuries. The rugged mountain terrain proved a tough obstacle when bringing silver out of the mines, so many of the towns were established both to refine the metal and to provide safety for its transport on the way to the capital and to coastal ports. From the almost barren, cactus-filled desert of the Texas border all the way to **San Luis Potosí,** in north-central Mexico, the hint of the Sierra Madre Oriental to the east and the Sierra Madre Occidental to the west is visible in unending barriers of hazy mountains in the distance. These two ranges along with the Sierra Madre del Sur on the southern Pacific Coast begin to merge in the middle as the country narrows into the tail of its cornucopia shape. It's flat from **Saltillo** to the pristinely preserved colonial city of **Zacatecas.** Veering to the west you enter mountains slightly going to **Guanajuato,** and twist through them east of **Querétaro** heading along the Fray Junipero Serra Mission Route, or farther southeast to the silver mining region around **Pachuca.** South of Saltillo dozens of hopeful roadside vendors sell strands of rattlesnake skins and ground snakeskin powder.

At major crossroads where vehicles slow down, vendors proffer armloads of leather and fleece-lined vests, hubcaps, cheese, strawberries and cream, or perhaps caged parrots.

From Mexico City northward the region is made up of seven high mountain valleys, all with natural drainage except Mexico City. Except for immediately around the capital, the valleys are known for their agricultural produce, namely cattle, goats, cheese, and grain. Around Querétaro, Guanajuato, and **Dolores Hidalgo** vineyards in vast tracts produce grapes to feed the country's wine industry. Except for **Monterrey,** the budget traveler can expect excellent value for the travel dollar, even in the country's capital.

THE MID-EAST REGION   The northern part of this region—eastward from **Monterrey** to **Ciudad Victoria**—passes fertile flatlands with distant mountains to the west. Between **Ciudad Mante** and the mountain town of **Tamazunchale** is some of Mexico's most incredible mountain scenery. Tropical forests threaten to overgrow the roadway, and humble huts have immense hedges of giant varigated crotin, cactus, and red hibiscus. Mango, orange, and lime trees shade these minimal abodes in an almost edenic scene. This region is traversed by Highway 85; between Ciudad Mante and Tamazunchale it's a twisty two-lane paved road with white-knuckle hairpin curves. You're torn between devouring the fabulous vistas and attending to the road, which is the kind where oncoming trucks speed around curves traveling in your lane. When the road rises to the top of the mountain ridges (as it does many times) you see ripples of seemingly uninhabited forests and mountains completely to the horizon. It's as though no other Mexico exists beyond the purple hue of these mountains. Occasionally, Huastec Indians trudge up from the valleys to the highway, some of them wearing regional clothing and a few women wearing their hair twisted around bulky yarn in elaborate traditional hairdos. Roadside stands sell honey, cone-shaped brown sugar (*piloncillo*), and huge squash cooked in brown sugar. After such a drive, the scenery beyond Tamazunchale is almost anticlimactic until you reach the colonial mountain city of **Pachuca,** capital of the state of Hidalgo. Around Pachuca, numerous mountain villages grew up around silver mines during the colonial era.

Throughout this region you have the pleasure of seeing Mexico as it was 40 or more years ago—except for bustling Pachuca, the area is becomingly rural and rustic with no vestiges of the hectic, commercial, resort-heavy Mexico of the present day. Enjoy this region at a slow pace and bring a flexible spirit.

THE GULF COAST   Little traveled by tourists, this whole coast has marvelous pockets of scenery and culture and encompasses the long, skinny state of Veracruz. Highway 180 leads down from **Matamoros** at the Texas border, providing a few glimpses of the Gulf, which in some places is the same cerulean blue as the Caribbean. Roads are not always in the best shape, since torrential rains can leave vast stretches of potholes. But the mostly two-lane road is paved and flat almost until you reach **Lake Catemaco.** There it undulates gently among almost flat grassy fields humped strangely with unexplored mounds left by the Olmecs more than 3,000 years ago. Four highlights make this region worth seeing: the ruins of **El Tajín** near the mountain village of **Papantla; Jalapa** and the magnificent Museo de Antropología there; lively, colorful **Veracruz,** the colonial port city with a terrific Latin beat; and the region around the placid Lake Catemaco, known for its beautiful setting and splendid collection of birds and other wildlife, and for a surprising number of *curanderos* (healers who use chants, herbs, and magic), who advertise with signs outside their homes. You'll see sugarcane fields almost the whole length of the coast, and coffee is grown around Jalapa as well. Near **Santiago Tuxtla** and

Lake Catemaco produce from abundant fruit plantations spills over into roadside stands with pyramidal mounds of fruit in colorful displays. Cattle raising, however, has made this area one of the wealthiest in the nation. This is another region to choose if you're longing for Mexico of yesteryear, for another cultural face of Mexico, and for some of the most economic hotels and restaurants in the country. It's easily traveled by bus.

TARASCAN COUNTRY   This region, in the state of Michoacán, encompasses two completely different colonial-era towns—**Pátzcuaro,** with its rural colonial architecture, and stately **Morelia,** where rich colonial citizens built handsome mansions. Isolated by mountains from the rest of the country, Michoacán's forests provide raw material for an enormous furniture industry, and the state is the country's leading producer of avocados. The area's Indians—the Tarascan, or Purépecha, people—appear to be disappearing as the indigenous groups shed their regional costumes, but the language and culture are still readily visible. An enormous number of craft communities produce pottery, textiles, and colorful furniture, and all are easily reached by local bus. Monarch butterflies winter in the eastern part of the state in a forest of omeyel fir trees. This is one of the most economical regions to visit and one not overrun with other tourists.

SOUTHERNMOST MEXICO: OAXACA, CHIAPAS & TABASCO STATES   This ruggedly mountainous region steeps travelers in the living color and texture of Zapotec, Mixtec, and Maya cultures. Although most people don't drive from one area to the other (they usually fly), a new toll highway from near Puebla to **Oaxaca** makes Oaxaca more accessible by car. The climate is hotter and more arid in Oaxaca than in **San Cristóbal de las Casas,** where high altitudes and lush, vegetation-covered mountains provide the cool mountain air. As you approach San Cristóbal from any direction, you see small plots of corn tended by colorfully clad Maya, many of whom are seen along highways with loads of firewood on their backs. Of the three, Tabasco is the least interesting. Oaxaca and Chiapas are rich in crafts from wood carvers to potters and weavers, and both offer fine accommodations and dining for budget travelers.

THE YUCATÁN PENINSULA   Traveling this remote peninsula provides an opportunity to witness several contrasting faces of Mexico—its ties to an ancient past, its giant leaps into an upscale, fast-moving future, and its timeless natural beauty. Within its confines, one can see pre-Hispanic ruins such as **Chichén-Itzá, Uxmal,** and **Tulum** and the living descendants of the cultures who built them, as well as the ultimate in resort Mexico—**Cancún.**

Edged by the rough deep-aquamarine Gulf of Mexico on the west and north and the clear cerulean-blue Caribbean Sea on the east, the peninsula covers almost 84,000 square miles, with nearly 1,000 miles of shoreline. Covered with dense jungle, the porous limestone peninsula is mostly flat, with thin soil supporting a low, scrubby jungle that contains almost no surface rivers. Rainwater is filtered by the limestone into underground rivers. *Cenotes,* or collapsed caves, are natural wells dotting the region. The only sense of height comes from the curvaceous terrain rising from the western shores of Campeche inland to the border with Yucatán state. This rise, called the Puuc hills, is the Maya "Alps," a staggering 980 feet high. Locally the hills are known as the Sierra de Ticul or Sierra Alta. The highways undulate a little as you go inland, and south of Ticul there's a rise in the highway that provides a marvelous view of the "valley" and misty Puuc hills lining the horizon. Ancient Maya near the Puuc hills developed a decorative style that incorporated geometric patterns and masks of Chaac (the Maya rain god), thus giving the style its name—Puuc.

The interior is dotted with lovely rock-walled villages inhabited by the kind, living Maya of today along with crumbling henequén haciendas surrounded by fields of maguey. Henequén, a yuccalike plant with tough fiber ideal for binder twine was the king crop in the Yucatán in the 19th century. Though the industry has declined in the past century, the spiny plant is still used today to produce rope, packing material, shoes, and purses. Besides henequén, other crops grown on the mostly agricultural peninsula are corn, coconuts, oranges, mangoes, and bananas.

The Yucatán's interior stands in strange contrast to the hubbub of the touristed 20th-century Caribbean Coast. From Cancún south to Chetumal the jungle coastline is interrupted by development of all kinds from posh to budget, but also hosts an enormous array of wildlife including hundreds of species of birds. Beaches from Cancún south to Chetumal are almost uniform in their powdery, drifting beauty. The western side of peninsula fronts the Gulf Coast and is the complete opposite of the Caribbean Coast. The beaches, while good enough, don't compare to those on the Caribbean. But nowhere else can you see flocks of flamingos as you can at national parks near **Celestún** and **Río Lagartos.**

This peninsula is excellent for a driving trip, since roads are generally flat, well kept, and not heavily trafficked. Outside the resorts, the Maya continue life as they did before the invasion of tourists began in 1974. Besides the friendly Maya faces you can meet in any village where you stop, you see men on bicycles with a hunting rifle and cork-capped water gourd on the shoulder turning from the highway down bumpy, narrow dirt tracks into the thick jungle.

Even in Cancún you can plot an economical vacation, but your bucks will go much farther on the islands of **Isla Mujeres** and **Cozumel** and farther still down the coast south of Cancún.

2 Visitor Information, Entry Requirements & Money

SOURCES OF INFORMATION

The **Mexico Hotline** (☎ 800/44-MEXICO in the U.S.) is a good source for very general informational brochures on the country and for answers to the most commonly asked questions. If you have a fax, Mexico's Ministry of Tourism also offers **FaxMeMexico** (☎ 503/385-9282). Call, provide them with a fax number, and select from a variety of topics—from accommodations (the service lists 400 hotels) to shopping, dining, sports, sightseeing, festivals, and nightlife. They'll then fax you the materials you're interested in.

More information (15,000 pages worth, they say) about Mexico is available on Mexico's World Wide Web home page, **http://mexico-travel.com.**

The **U.S. Department of State** (☎ 202/647-5225 for travel information, ☎ 202/647-9225 for bulletin board information), offers a **Consular Information Sheet** on Mexico, with a compilation of safety, medical, driving, and general travel information gleaned from reports by official U.S. State Department offices in Mexico. You can also request the Consular Information Sheet (☎ 202/647-2000) by fax. The **Center for Disease Control hotline** (☎ 404/332-4559), is another source for medical information affecting travelers to Mexico and elsewhere.

MEXICAN GOVERNMENT TOURIST OFFICES Mexico has tourist offices throughout the world, including the following:

United States: 70 E. Lake St., Suite 1413, Chicago, IL 60601 (☎ 312/565-2778); 5075 Westheimer, Suite 975-West, Houston, TX 77056 (☎ 713/629-1611); 10100 Santa Monica Blvd., Suite 224, Los Angeles, CA 90067 (☎ 310/203-8191); 2333

Ponce de Leon Blvd., Suite 710, Coral Gables, FL 33134 (☎ **305/443-9160**); 405 Park Ave., Suite 1401, New York, NY 10022 (☎ **212/838-2947**); and the Mexican Embassy Tourism Delegate, 1911 Pennsylvania Ave. NW, Washington, DC 20006 (☎ **202/728-1750**).

Canada: One Place Ville-Marie, Suite 1526, Montréal, PQ H3B 2B5 (☎ **514/ 871-1052**); 2 Bloor St. W., Suite 1801, Toronto, ON M4W 3E2 (☎ **416/ 925-1876**). 99 W. Hastings #1610, Vancouver, British Columbia V6C 2W2 (☎ **604/669-3498**).

Europe: Weisenhüttenplatz 26, D 6000 Frankfurt-am-Main 1, Germany (☎ **49/ 69-25-3413**); 60–61 Trafalgar Sq., London WC2 N5DS, United Kingdom (☎ **171/734-1058**); Calle de Velázquez 126, 28006 Madrid, Spain (☎ **341/ 261-1827**); 4 rue Notre-Dame-des-Victoires, 75002 Paris, France (☎ **331/ 4020-0734**); and via Barberini 3, 00187 Rome, Italy (☎ **396/482-7160**).

Asia: 2.15.1 Nagato-Cho, Chiyoda-Ku, Tokyo 100, Japan (☎ **813/580-2962**).

STATE TOURISM DEVELOPMENT OFFICES   Two Mexican states have tourism and trade development offices in the United States: **Casa Guerrero State Promotion Office,** 5075 Westheimer, Suite 980-West, Houston, TX 77056 (☎ **713/552-0930;** fax 713/552-0207); **Casa Nuevo León State Promotion Office,** 100 W. Houston St., Suite 1400, San Antonio, TX 78205 (☎ **210/ 225-0732;** fax 210/225-0736).

OTHER SOURCES   The following newsletters may be of interest to readers: *Mexico Meanderings,* P.O. Box 33057, Austin, TX 78764, aimed at readers who travel to off-the-beaten-track destinations by car, bus, or train (six to eight pages, photographs, published six times annually, subscription $18); *Travel Mexico,* Apdo. Postal 6-1007, 06600 Mexico, D.F., from the publishers of the *Traveler's Guide to Mexico,* the book frequently found in hotel rooms in Mexico, covers a variety of topics from archaeology news to hotel packages, new resorts and hotels, and the economy (six times annually, subscription $18).

For other newsletters, see "For Seniors" under "Tips for Special Travelers," below.

ENTRY REQUIREMENTS

DOCUMENTS   All travelers to Mexico are required to present **proof of citizenship,** such as an original birth certificate with a raised seal, a valid passport, or naturalization papers. Those using a birth certificate should also have a current photo identification such as a driver's license. And those whose last name on the birth certificate is different from their current name (women using a married name, for example) should also bring a photo identification card *and* legal proof of the name change such as the *original* marriage license or certificate (I'm not kidding). This proof of citizenship may also be requested when you want to re-enter either the United States or Mexico. Note that photocopies are *not* acceptable.

You must also carry a **Mexican Tourist Permit,** which is issued free of charge by Mexican border officials after proof of citizenship is accepted. The Tourist Permit is more important than a passport in Mexico, so guard it carefully. If you lose it, you may not be permitted to leave the country until you can replace it—a bureaucratic hassle that takes several days to a week at least. (If you do lose your Tourist Permit, get a police report from local authorities indicating that your documents were stolen; having one *might* lessen the hassle of exiting the country without all your identification.)

A Tourist Permit can be issued for up to 180 days, and although your stay south of the border may be shorter than that, you should ask for the maximum time, just in case. Sometimes officials don't ask—they just stamp a time limit, so be sure to say "six months" (or at least twice as long as you intend to stay). If you should decide to extend your stay, you'll eliminate hassle by not needing to renew your papers.

This is especially important for people who take a car into Mexico. Additional documentation is required for driving a personal vehicle in Mexico (see "By Car" under "Getting There," below).

Note that children under age 18 traveling without parents or with only one parent must have a notarized letter from the absent parent or parents authorizing the travel.

Lost Documents   To replace a **lost passport,** contact your embassy or nearest consular agent (see "Fast Facts: Mexico," below). You must establish a record of your citizenship and also fill out a form requesting another Mexican Tourist Permit. Without the **Tourist Permit** you can't leave the country, and without an affidavit affirming your passport request and citizenship, you may have hassles at customs when you get home. So it's important to clear everything up *before* trying to leave. Mexican customs may, however, accept the police report of the loss of the Tourist Permit and allow you to leave.

CUSTOMS ALLOWANCES   When you enter Mexico, customs officials will be tolerant as long as you have no illegal drugs or firearms. You're allowed to bring in two cartons of cigarettes, or 50 cigars, plus a kilogram (2.2 lb.) of smoking tobacco; the liquor allowance is two bottles of anything, wine or hard liquor; you are also allowed 12 rolls of film.

When you're re-entering the United States, federal law allows you to bring in duty free up to $400 in purchases every 30 days. The first $1,000 over the $400 allowance is taxed at 10%. You may bring in a carton (200) of cigarettes or 50 cigars or 2kg (4.4 lb.) of smoking tobacco, plus 1 liter of an alcoholic beverage (wine, beer, or spirits).

Canadian citizens are allowed $20 in purchases after a 24-hour absence from the country or $100 after a stay of 48 hours or more.

Going Through Customs   Mexican customs inspection has been streamlined. At most points of entry tourists are requested to punch a button in front of what looks like a traffic signal, which alternates on touch between red and green signals. Green light and you go through without inspection; red light and your luggage or car may be inspected briefly or thoroughly. I've been seeing more red lights these days; seems the government is stepping up their inspections.

MONEY

CASH/CURRENCY   In 1993, the Mexican government dropped three zeroes from its currency. The new currency is called the *Nuevo Peso,* or New Peso. The purpose was to simplify accounting; all those zeroes were becoming too difficult to manage. Old Peso notes were valid through 1996. Paper currency comes in denominations of 10, 20, 50, and 100 New Pesos. Coins come in denominations of 1, 2, 5, and 10 pesos and 20 and 50 *centavos* (100 centavos make one New Peso). The coins are somewhat confusing because different denominations have a similar appearance. You may still see some prices written with *N* or *NP* beside them, which refer to New Pesos. Currently the U.S. dollar equals around NP$7.50; at that rate an item costing NP$5, for example, would be equivalent to U.S. 67¢.

These changes are likely to cause confusion among U.S. and Canadian travelers to Mexico in several ways. Before the New Peso was instituted, merchants and others skipped the small change, now they don't. Small change (a peso or less than a peso) is often unavailable so cashiers often offer gum or candy to make up the difference. Centavos will appear on restaurant bills and credit cards, but are paid differently depending on if you pay in cash or by credit card. On restaurant bills that you pay in cash, for example, the centavos will be rounded up or down to the nearest five centavos. Credit-card bills, however, will show the exact amount (not rounded), and will have *N* written before the amount to denote that the bill is in New Pesos. Be sure to double check any credit-card vouchers to be sure the *N* or *NP* appears on the total line.

Getting change continues to be a problem in Mexico. Small-denomination bills and coins are hard to come by, so start collecting them early in your trip and continue as you travel. Shopkeepers everywhere seem to always be out of change and small bills; that's doubly true in a market.

Note: The dollar sign ($) is used to indicate pesos in Mexico. To avoid confusion, I will use the dollar sign in this book *only* to denote U.S. currency.

Only dollar prices are listed in this book; they are a more reliable indication than peso prices. Many establishments dealing with tourists quote prices in dollars. To avoid confusion, they use the abbreviations "Dlls." for dollars and "m.n." (*moneda nacional*—national currency) for pesos.

Every effort has been made to provide the most accurate and up-to-date information in this guide, but price changes are inevitable.

EXCHANGING MONEY The December 1994 devaluation of the peso has had varied meanings for tourists. First, the rate of exchange fluctuates daily, so be careful not to exchange too much of your currency at once. Don't forget, however, to allow enough to carry you over a weekend or Mexican holiday, when banks are closed. Cash can sometimes be difficult to exchange because counterfeit U.S. dollars have been circulating recently in Mexico; merchants and banks are wary, and many, especially in small towns, refuse to accept dollars in cash. In general, avoid carrying the U.S. $100 bill, the one most commonly counterfeited. Since small bills and coins in pesos are hard to come by in Mexico, the U.S. $1 bill is very useful for tipping.

Bottom line on exchanging money of all kinds: It pays to ask first and shop around. Banks in Mexico often give a less favorable rate of exchange than the official daily rate, and hotels usually exchange less favorably than do banks. Exchange houses are generally more convenient than banks since they have more locations and longer hours, and the rate of exchange may be the same as a bank or slightly lower. Personal checks may be cashed but not without weeks of delay—a bank will wait for your check to clear before giving you your money. Canadian dollars seem to be most easily exchanged for pesos at branches of Banamex and Bancomer. *Before leaving a bank or exchange house window, always count your change in front of the teller before the next client steps up.*

Banks are open Monday through Friday from 9am to 1:30pm; a few banks in large cities offer extended afternoon hours. Most banks won't exchange money until 10am, when they receive the day's official rate. Large airports have currency-exchange counters that often stay open whenever flights are arriving or departing. Don't go for the first one you see in an airport—there's usually more than one, and you'll often find a better exchange rate farther along the concourse.

TRAVELER'S CHECKS Traveler's checks are readily accepted nearly everywhere, but they can be difficult to cash on a weekend or holiday or in an out-of-the-way place. Their best value is in replacement in case of theft. I usually arrive in Mexico with half of my money in cash (in $1, $20, and $50 bills) and half in traveler's checks ($20 and $50 denominations). Mexican banks sometimes pay more for traveler's checks than for dollars in cash, but in some places *casas de cambio* (exchange houses) pay more for cash than for traveler's checks. Additionally, some but not all banks charge a service fee to exchange either traveler's checks or dollars.

CREDIT CARDS & ATMS   You'll be able to charge some hotel and restaurant bills, almost all airline tickets, and many store purchases on your credit cards. You can get cash advances of several hundred dollars on your card, but there may be a wait of 20 minutes to two hours. You can't charge gasoline purchases in Mexico.

VISA ("Bancomer" in Mexico), MasterCard ("Carnet" in Mexico), and, less widely, American Express are the most accepted cards. The Bancomer bank, with branches throughout the country, has inaugurated a system of **automatic-teller machines (ATMs)** linked to VISA International's network. If you are a VISA customer, you may be able to get peso cash from one of the Bancomer ATMs.

ATM machines are also associated with other banks and may work with your own bank ATM. There's usually a $200 limit per transaction. Two cautions about using automatic teller machines are in order: First, though ATMs are located next to banks, or in a bank lobby, use the same precautions you would at home—don't use one at night, or on a lonely street, etc.; second, don't depend on them totally for your extra cash—you might not always have access to one, and you'll be out of luck if the machine eats your card.

BRIBES & SCAMS

You will probably find yourself in situations in Mexico where bribes—called *propinas* (tips) or *mordidas* (bites)—are expected, or where con artists are working their trade. Here's how to deal with them.

BRIBES   Extortion, of course, exists everywhere in the world, but in Mexico as in other developing countries, the tolls are smaller and collected more often.

Border officials appear to be slipping back into the petty-extortion habit they largely shed during the administration of President Salinas de Gortari. Just so you're prepared, here are a few hints based on my experiences.

First rule: Even if you speak Spanish, don't say a word of it to Mexican officials. This allows you to appear to be innocent, even dumb, all the while understanding every word. Some border officials will do what they're supposed to do (stamp your passport or birth certificate and perhaps lightly inspect your luggage) and then wave you on through. If you don't offer a tip of a few dollars to the man who inspects your car (if you're driving), he may ask for it, as in "Give me a tip (*propina*)." I usually ignore this request, but you'll have to decide for yourself based on your circumstances at the time, especially if the official decides a complete search of your belongings is suddenly in order. If you're charged for the stamping or inspection, (for example, the inspector says "One dollar"), followed by an outstretched hand, ask for a receipt (*recibo;* "ray-SEE-bow"). If he says there's no receipt, don't pay the bribe. By then he's probably already nonchalantly waved you ahead anyway, the quicker to hit up the next unsuspecting victim. You can also simply ignore the request or pretend not to understand it, and walk on.

Officials don't ask for bribes from everybody. Travelers dressed in a formal suit and tie, wearing pitch-black sunglasses and a scowl, are rarely asked to pay a bribe. Those who are dressed for vacation fun or seem good-natured and accommodating are targets. Whatever you do, avoid impoliteness, and absolutely *never* insult a Latin American official! When an official's sense of machismo is roused, he can and will throw the book at you, and you may be in trouble. Stand your ground, but do it politely.

How do I know when paying a bribe would be better than fighting it? Here are a couple of scenarios: A driving rain is drenching the world outside and the scowling border guard orders everyone out of the vehicle to unpack belongings for inspection—in the rain. Cut your losses and offer a bribe. You're stopped for a traffic infraction that you did or didn't commit, and the policeman keeps inspecting your car documents, your driver's license, or your Tourist Permit, finding things "wrong." If you're in a hurry, offer a bribe. If you're not, offer to follow him to the station. He'll probably not want to do that and will find some way to save face—your credentials are all right after all—and move on. You must allow him to save face.

How much should I offer? Usually $3 to $5 or the equivalent in pesos will do the trick. There's supposedly a number **to report irregularities** with customs officials (toll free ☎ **91-800-00148** in Mexico). Your call will go to the office of the Comptroller and Adminstrative Development Secretariat (SECODAM). It's worth a try. But be sure you have some basic information, such as the name of the person who wanted a bribe or was rude, and the place, time, and day of the event.

SCAMS   As you travel in Mexico, you may encounter several types of scams. The **distraction scam** is found frequently on the Mexico City subway, or on crowded buses, but it can happen on a busy city street, market, or festival, anywhere. Someone in front of you on the subway or street drops to the ground searching for something. You're mildly distracted as you manage to get around the person in the way, probably with people crowding you from behind. By the time you're beyond the distraction, a hand has already found its way to your wallet—even when it's stowed in a front-facing fanny pack or your front pants pocket. As a variation, an impeccably dressed man or woman tells you that you've got a foreign substance, like white powder or a wet paintlike substance, on the back of your nice jacket. He (usually it's a male, but sometimes it's a "married couple") spends a long time helping you remove the stain with his nicely pressed handkerchief. Your thanks are so profuse for this kind assistance to you, the foreigner, that you don't realize until later that your wallet is missing. A variation of this one, starring the impeccably dressed local again, occurs in hotel lobbies: He or she strikes up a conversation with you, and while your head is turned your purse, bag, or packages disappear. Or the lobby is filled with well-dressed people and you turn your attention away from your belongings for a second, and the next thing you know a well-dressed someone with straight-faced aplomb has disappeared with your purse or valise on his or her arm. If you catch the villain, he or she will feign mortification switching quickly to indignant anger while proclaiming that the object looked just like his or hers. Another variation is the unaccompanied, frightened or perhaps lost child, who takes your hand for safety on the subway. Who would deny a child a hand—right? Meanwhile the child, or an accomplice, manages to plunder your pockets. Needless to say, these people are really slick and outwardly unsuspicious looking.

More and more in Mexico City I'm confronted with the **"I've just been robbed and lost everything" scam.** A distraught person appearing to be in wide-eyed shock and on the verge of tears approaches you and says, "Someone just stole my purse!" (Or vehicle, or wallet, etc., etc.) "Can you give me money to take a bus home." Then it turns out he or she lives in Tijuana or some other distant city, and the pesos required for the trip are substantial. Often the perpetrator of this one has hungry, poorly dressed children in tow, and maybe a hopeless-faced or teary-eyed wife as well. Or well-dressed, innocent-looking teenagers accompany the truthful-sounding con artist, and you think, "These people are middle class and educated—how can this be a scam?" And of course, they'll need food money, because the trip takes several days.

Then, naturally they've got to pay for transportation to the bus station. It really tugs at your heart strings. I usually say I've just run out of money myself, and they quickly move on to the next target.

Because hotel desk clerks are usually so helpful, I hesitate to mention the **lost objects scam** for fear of tainting them all. But here's how it works. You "lose" your wallet after cashing money at the desk, or you leave something valuable such as a purse or camera in the lobby. You report it. The clerk has it, but instead of telling you he does, he says he will see what he can do; meanwhile, he suggests you offer a high reward. This scam has all kinds of variations. In one story a reader wrote about, a desk clerk in Los Mochis was in cahoots with a bystander in the lobby who lifted the reader's wallet in the elevator.

Another scam readers have mentioned might be called the **infraction scam.** Officials, or men presenting themselves as officials, demand money for some supposed infraction. Never get into a car with them. I avoided one begun by a bona fide policeman-on-the-take in Chetumal when my traveling companion feigned illness and began writhing, moaning, and pretending to have the dry heaves. It was more than the policeman could handle.

Legal and necessary car searches by military personnel looking for drugs are mentioned elsewhere in this book. Every now and then, however, there are police-controlled illegal roadblocks where motorists are forced to pay before continuing on their way.

Along these lines, if you are stopped by the police, I also suggest you avoid handing your driver's license to a policeman. Hold it so that it can be read but don't give it up.

Then there's the **taxi ticket scam.** This usually happens at taxi ticket booths in airports and bus stations. You're vulnerable because you may be a new arrival to the country and not yet have your peso legs, your Spanish may not be up to par, or you're preoccupied with getting where you're going. You give the ticket seller a 50-peso bill, and the seller returns change for 20 pesos. I'll say this elsewhere: *Count your change before leaving the booth!* Better yet, when you hand the seller the bill, say out loud the amount of the ticket and the amount of the bill and say *cambio* (KAHM-bee-oh) which means change.

The **shoeshine scam** is an old trick, used most often in Mexico City. Here's how it works. A tourist agrees to a shine for, say, 15 pesos. When the work is complete, the vendor says "That'll be 50 pesos" or $15 dollars, and insists that the shocked tourist misunderstood. A big brouhaha ensues involving bystanders who side with the shoeshine vendor. The object is to get the bewildered tourist to succumb to the howling crowd and embarrassing scene and fork over the money. A variation of the scam has the vendor saying the price quoted is per shoe. To avoid this scam, ask around about the price of a shine, and when the vendor quotes his price, write it down and show it to him *before* the shine.

Similar to the shoeshine scam because of the pronunciation of numbers is the *dos* (two) and *doce* (twelve) scam. Usually taxi drivers work this one. You ask how much and he holds up two fingers or says "dos." You think the ride costs two pesos. At drop off he says "That'll be two U.S. dollars," looking at you as though you're especially stupid to think he'd ever accept two pesos. Or he says "dos" ("dohs") pesos, but when you get to your destination he says "doce" ("DOH-say") pesos. Or he says "doce," which you understand to refer to pesos, and then he wants 12 *dollars* before you depart. The same confusion can cause an uproar over *tres* ("trays"), which means three and *trece* ("TRAY-say"), meaning thirteen; *quince* ("KEEN-say"), which means fifteen, and *quinientos* ("KEEN-ee-ehn-tohs"), the word for 500; or *cuatro* ("KWAH-troh"), which means four and *catorce* ("kah-TOHR-say"), which means 14.

Tourists are suckered daily into the **iguana scam,** especially in Puerto Vallarta and nearby Yelapa beach. Someone, often a child, strolls by carrying a huge iguana and says "Wanna take my peekchur?" Photo-happy tourists seize the opportunity. Just as the camera is angled properly, the holder of the iguana says (more like mumbles) "One dollar." That means a dollar per shot! Sometimes they wait until the shutter clicks to mention money.

Although you should be aware of such hazards and how to deal with them, I log thousands of miles and many months in Mexico each year without serious incident, and I feel safer there than at home in the United States. So I must reiterate that you are more likely to meet kind and helpful Mexicans than you are to encounter those who've mastered thievery and deceit. And as you can see by these scams, Mexicans with bad intentions prefer to use stealth and wit more than an outright holdup to take your possessions. (See also "Emergencies" and "Safety" under "Fast Facts: Mexico" later in this chapter.)

3 When to Go

HOLIDAYS

On national holidays, banks, stores, and businesses are closed; hotels fill up quickly; and transportation is crowded. Mexico celebrates the following national holidays: **January 1,** New Year's Day; **February 5,** Constitution Day; **March 21,** Birthday of Benito Juárez; **March–April** (movable), Holy Week (Good Friday through Easter Sunday); **May 1,** Labor Day; **May 5,** Battle of Puebla, 1862 (Cinco de Mayo); **September 1,** President's Message to Congress; **September 16,** Independence-penance Day; **October 12,** Day of the Race (Columbus Day in the U.S.); **November 1–2,** All Saints' and All Souls' days (Day of the Dead); **November 20,** Anniversary of the Mexican Revolution; **December 11–12,** Feast Day of the Virgin of Guadalupe (Mexico's patron saint); **December 24–25,** Christmas Eve and Christmas Day.

MEXICO CALENDAR OF EVENTS

January
- **Three Kings Day.** Commemorates the Three Kings' bringing of gifts to the Christ Child. On this day the Three Kings "bring" gifts to children. January 6.
- **Feast of San Antonio Abad,** Mexico City. Blessing of the Animals at the Santiago Tlatelolco Church on the Plaza of Three Cultures, at San Juan Bautista Church in Coyoacán, and at the Church of San Fernando, two blocks north of the Juárez/Reforma intersection. January 17.

February
- **Candlemas.** On January 6, Rosca de Reyes, a round cake with a hole in the middle, is baked with a tiny doll inside representing the Christ Child. Whoever gets the slice with the doll must give a party on February 2.
- ✪ **Carnaval.** This celebration resembles New Orleans's Mardi Gras, with a festive atmosphere and parades. In Chamula, however, the event harks back to pre-Hispanic times with ritualistic running on flaming branches. On the Tuesday before Ash Wednesday in Tepoztlán and Huejotzingo, masked and brilliantly clad dancers fill the streets. In some towns there will be no special celebration, in others a few parades.

Where: Especially celebrated in Tepoztlán, Morelos; Huejotzingo, Puebla; Chamula, Chiapas; Veracruz, Veracruz; Cozumel, Quintana Roo; and Mazatlán, Sinaloa. **When:** Date is variable but always the three days preceding Ash Wednesday and the beginning of Lent. **How:** Transportation and hotels will be clogged, so it's best to make reservations six months in advance and arrive a couple of days ahead of the beginning of celebrations.

- **Ash Wednesday.** The start of Lent and time of abstinence. It's a day of reverence nationwide, but some towns honor it with folk dancing and fairs. Movable date.

March

- **Benito Juárez's Birthday.** Small hometown celebrations countrywide, especially in Juárez's birthplace—Guelatao, Oaxaca.

◐ **Holy Week.** Celebrates the last week in the life of Christ from Good Friday through Easter Sunday with somber religious processions almost nightly, spoofing of Judas, and reenactments of specific biblical events, plus food and craft fairs. Among the Tarahumara in the Copper Canyon, celebrations have pre-Hispanic overtones. Businesses close, and Mexicans travel far and wide during this week.

Where: Special in Pátzcuaro, Taxco, Malinalco, and among the Tarahumara villages in the Copper Canyon. **When:** March or April. **How:** Reserve early with a deposit. Airline seats on flights into and out of the country will be reserved months in advance. Buses to these towns or to almost anywhere in Mexico will be full, so try arriving on the Wednesday or Thursday before Good Friday. Easter Sunday is quiet.

May

- **Labor Day.** Workers' parades countrywide and everything closes. May 1.
- **Holy Cross Day,** Día de la Santa Cruz. Workers place a cross on top of unfinished buildings and celebrate with food, bands, folk dancing, and fireworks around the worksite. Celebrations are particularly colorful in Valle de Bravo, in the state of Mexico, and Paracho, Michoacán. May 3.
- **Cinco de Mayo.** A national holiday that celebrates the defeat of the French at the Battle of Puebla. May 5.
- **Feast of San Isidro.** The patron saint of farmers is honored with a blessing of seeds and work animals. May 15.

June

- **Navy Day.** Celebrated by all port cities. June 1.

◐ **Corpus Christi.** Honors the Body of Christ—the Eucharist—with religious processions, masses, and food. Celebrated nationwide. Festivities include numerous demonstrations of the Roman *voladores* (flying pole dancers) beside the church and at the ruins of El Tajín. In Mexico City children, dressed as Indians, and their parents gather before the National Cathedral on the Zócalo, carrying decorated baskets of fruit for the priest's blessing. *Mulitas* (mules), handmade from dried corn husks and painted, often with a corn-husk rider, and sometimes accompanied by pairs of corn-husk dolls, are traditionally sold there on that day.

Where: Particularly special in Papantla, Veracruz. **When:** Variable date, 66 days after Easter. **How:** By bus from Tampico, Tuxpan, or Poza Rica. Make reservations well in advance.

- **Saint Peter's Day,** Día de San Pedro. Celebrated wherever St. Peter is the patron saint and honors anyone named Pedro or Peter. It's especially festive at San Pedro Tlaquepaque, near Guadalajara, with numerous mariachi bands, folk dancers, and parades with floats. June 29.

July
- **Virgin of Carmen.** A nationally celebrated religious festival centered in churches nationwide. July 16.
- **Saint James Day,** Día de Santiago. Observed countrywide wherever St. James is the patron saint and for anyone named Jaime or James or any village with Santiago in its name. Rodeos, fireworks, dancing, and food. July 25.

August
- **Fall of Tenochtitlán,** Mexico City. The last battle of the conquest took place at Tlatelolco, ruins that are now a part of the Plaza of Three Cultures. Wreath-laying ceremonies there and at the Cuauhtémoc monument on Reforma commemorate the event when thousands lost their lives and the last Aztec king, Cuauhtémoc, surrendered to Hernán Cortés. August 13.
- ✪ **Assumption of the Virgin Mary.** Celebrated throughout the country with special masses and in some places with processions. Streets are carpeted in flower petals and colored sawdust. At midnight on the 15th a statue of the Virgin is carried through the streets; the 16th is a running of the bulls. On August 15 in Santa Clara del Cobre, near Pátzcuaro, Our Lady of Santa Clara de Asis and the Virgen de la Sagrado Patrona are honored with a parade of floats, dancers on the main square, and an exposition of regional crafts, especially copper.

  Where: Special in Huamantla, Tlaxcala, and Santa Clara del Cobre, Michoacán. **When:** August 14–16. **How:** Buses to Huamantla from Puebla or Mexico City will be full, and there are few hotels in Huamantla. Plan to stay in Puebla and commute to the festivities.

September
- **Independence Day.** Celebrates Mexico's independence from Spain. A day of parades, picnics, and family reunions throughout the country. At 11pm on September 15 the president of Mexico gives the famous independence *grito* (shout) from the National Palace in Mexico City. At least half a million people are crowded into the Zócalo, and the rest of the country watches the event on television. The enormous military parade on September 16 starts at the Zócalo and ends at the Independence Monument on Reforma. Tall buildings downtown are draped in the national colors of red, green, and white, and the Zócalo is ablaze with lights; it's popular to drive downtown at night to see the lights—truly spectacular. It's also elaborately celebrated in Querétaro and San Miguel de Allende, where Independence conspirators lived and met. September 16 (parade day).

October
- **Cervantino Festival.** Begun in the 1970s as a cultural event bringing performing artists from all over the world to the Guanajuato, a picturesque village northeast of Mexico City. Now the artists travel all over the republic after appearing in Guanajuato. Check local calendars for appearances. Early to mid October.
- **Feast of San Francisco de Asis.** Anyone named Frances, Francis, or Francisco and towns whose patron saint is Francisco celebrate with barbecue parties, regional dancing, and religious observances. October 4.
- **Día de la Raza,** Day of the Race, or Columbus Day (the day Columbus landed in America). Commemorates the fusion of the Spanish and Mexican peoples. October 12.

November
- ✪ **Day of the Dead.** What's commonly called the Day of the Dead is actually two days, All Saints' Day, honoring saints and deceased children, and All Souls' Day,

honoring deceased adults. Relatives gather at cemeteries countrywide, carrying candles and food, often spending the night beside graves of loved ones. Weeks before, bakers begin producing bread formed in the shape of mummies or round loaves decorated with bread "bones." Decorated sugar skulls emblazoned with glittery names are sold everywhere. Many days ahead, homes and churches erect special altars laden with Day of the Dead bread, fruit, flowers, candles, and favorite foods and photographs of saints and of the deceased. On the two nights of the Day of the Dead, children dress in costumes and masks, often carrying mock coffins through the streets and pumpkin lanterns into which they expect money will be dropped.

Where: The most famous celebration is on Janitzio, an island on Lake Pátzcuaro, Michoacán, west of Mexico City, but it has become almost too well known. Mixquic, a mountain village south of Mexico City, hosts an elaborate street fair, and around 11pm on both nights, solemn processions lead to the cemetery in the center of town where villagers are already settled in with candles, flowers, and food. Cemeteries around Oaxaca City are well known for their solemn vigils and some for their carnaval-like atmosphere. **When:** November 1–2.

- **Revolution Day.** Commemorates the start of the Mexican Revolution in 1910 with parades, speeches, rodeos, and patriotic events. November 20.

December

✪ **Feast of the Virgin of Guadalupe.** Throughout the country the Patroness of Mexico is honored with religious processions, street fairs, dancing, fireworks, and masses. The Virgin of Guadalupe appeared to a young man, Juan Diego, in December 1531 on a hill near Mexico City. He convinced the bishop that the apparition had appeared by revealing his cloak, upon which the Virgin was emblazoned. It's customary for children to dress up as Juan Diego, wearing mustaches and red bandanas. The most famous and elaborate celebration takes place at the Basílica of Guadalupe, north of Mexico City, where the Virgin appeared. But every village celebrates this day, often with processions of children carrying banners of the Virgin and with *charreadas* (rodeos), bicycle races, dancing, and fireworks. December 12.

Where: Basílica of Guadalupe. **When:** The week preceding December 12.
How: Public transportation will be packed, so your best bet is a taxi, which will let you off several blocks from the basílica.

- **Christmas Posadas.** On each of the 12 nights before Christmas it's customary to re-enact the Holy Family's search for an inn, with door-to-door candlelit processions in cities and villages nationwide. You may see them especially in Querétaro and Taxco.

- **Christmas.** Mexicans extend this celebration and leave their jobs often beginning two weeks before Christmas all the way through New Year's. Many businesses close, and resorts and hotels fill up. On December 23 there are significant celebrations. Querétaro has a huge parade. In Oaxaca it's the "Night of the Radishes," with displays of huge carved radishes, as well as elaborate figures made of corn husks and dried flowers. In the evening of December 24 in Oaxaca processions culminate on the central plaza. On the same night Santiago Tuxtla, Veracruz celebrates with dancing the *huapango* and with *jarocho* bands in the beautiful town square. In Quiroga, Michoacán, villagers present Nativity plays (*Pastorelas*) at churches around the city on the evenings of December 24 and 25.

- **New Year's Eve.** As in the United States, New Year's Eve in Mexico is the time to gather for private parties and to explode fireworks and sound noisemakers. Places with special festivities include Santa Clara del Cobre, with its candlelit procession of Christs, and Tlacolula near Oaxaca, with commemorative mock battles for good luck in the new year.

4 Outdoor Sports, Adventure Travel & Wilderness Trips

Mexico's resort areas and two largest cities, Mexico City and Guadalajara, have numerous **golf** courses and ample opportunity for other such leisure sports (**tennis, racquetball, squash, water skiing, jet skiing and powerboating,** and the like).

If adventure sports, wilderness trips, and eco-tours are more your bag, you'll find Mexico strangely behind the times—which can be a good or bad thing, depending on your perspective. The natural wonders are there in overwhelming abundance—from the head-high surf of the Pacific to the crags of the Sierra Madre, from cloud forest in Chiapas and Tamaulipas states to tropical jungle in the Yucatán. There are numerous wildlife spectaculars: the winter monarch butterfly migration in Michoacán; the gray-whale migration off the Baja Peninsula in February and March; the brilliantly colored birds, like the keel-billed toucan, that live no farther north than Mexico.

The problem is that outdoor adventure sports and activities haven't caught fire the way they have in the States or even in nearby Costa Rica, which draws huge numbers of adventure travelers. There aren't very many expert Mexican adventure-tour leaders, and Mexican companies specializing in natural history are few. As a result, most of the national parks and nature reserves are understaffed and/or not staffed by knowledgeable people. Most companies offering this kind of travel are U.S. operated, with trips led by specialists. If you're an experienced backcountry traveler, there are many lonely places awaiting you in Mexico. If, on the other hand, you're trying your hand at something new, the Mexican outback is not the place to be testing your independence, and you should definitely work with one of the outfitters or tour operators listed below.

Surfing off Baja, mountain biking into the Sierra Madre back of Puerto Vallarta, deep-water sportfishing off Mazatlán and Baja or fly-fishing for bonefish off the Yucatán, horseback riding and pack tours in the Copper Canyon, snorkeling and scuba diving off Puerto Vallarta or at Cozumel's famed Palancar Reef, kayaking the Sea of Cortez, and serious mountaineering on the likes of Pico de Orizaba or Popocatepetl are all trips run by various adventure-tour operators in Mexico. The following companies offer a variety of off-the-beaten-path travel experiences:

- **The American Wilderness Experience,** P.O. Box 1486, Boulder, CO 80306 (☎ **303/444-2622** or 800/444-0099), leads catered camping, kayaking, biking, and hiking trips in Baja California and the Copper Canyon.
- **ATC Tours and Travel,** Calle 5 de Febrero no. 15, 29200 San Cristóbal de las Casas, Chiapas (☎ **967/8-2550;** fax 967/8-3145), a Mexico-based tour operator with an excellent reputation, offers specialist-led trips primarily in southern Mexico. In addition to trips to the ruins of Palenque and Yaxchilán (extending into Belize and Guatemala by river, plane, and bus if desired), they also offer horseback tours and day-trips to the ruins of Toniná around San Cristóbal de las Casas, Chiapas; birding in the rain forests of Chiapas and Guatemala (including in the El Triunfo Reserve of Chiapas where you can see the rare quetzal bird and orchids); hikes out to the shops and homes of native textile artists of the Chiapas highlands; and walks from the Lagos de Montebello in the Montes Azules Biosphere Reserve, with camping and canoeing.

- **Baja Expeditions,** 2625 Garnet Ave., San Diego, CA 92109 (☎ **619/581-3311,** or 800/843-6967 in the U.S.; e-mail 72234.1520@compuserve.com., offers natural history cruises, whale-watching, sea kayaking, and scuba-diving trips out of La Paz, Baja California. One trip retraces John Steinbeck's journey as he wrote it in "Log from the Sea of Cortez."

- **Columbus Travel,** 900 Rich Creek Lane, Bulverde, TX 78163-2872 (☎ **210/885-2000,** or 800/843-1060 in the U.S. and Canada), has a variety of easy to challenging adventures, primarily in the Copper Canyon and Michoacán. They can design trips for special-interest groups of agriculturists, geologists, rockhounds, and birdwatchers. The company also arranges trips to see the monarch butterflies in Michoacán.

- **Mexico Sportsman,** 202 Milam Building, San Antonio, TX 78205 (☎ **210/212-4567;** fax 210/212-4568), is sportfishing central for anyone interested in advance arrangements for fishing in Cancún, Cozumel, Puerto Vallarta, Ixtapa/Zihuatanejo, Cabo San Lucas, and Mazatlán. The company offers complete information from the cost (nothing hidden) to the length of a fishing trip, kind of boat, line and tackle used, and whether bait, drinks, and lunch are included. Prices are as good as you'll get on-site in Mexico.

- **Mountain Travel • Sobek,** 6420 Fairmount Ave., El Cerrito, CA 94530 (☎ **510/527-8100** or 800/227-2384), the granddaddy of adventure outfitters, leads groups into the Copper Canyon and kayaking in the Sea of Cortez.

- **Naturequest,** 934 Acapulco St., Laguna Beach, CA 92651 (☎ **714/499-9561** or 800/369-3033), specializes in the natural history, culture, and wildlife of the Copper Canyon and the remote lagoons and waterways off Baja California. A 10-day hiking trip ventures into rugged areas of the Copper Canyon but they offer a less strenuous trip to Creel and Batopilas in the same area. Baja trips get close up with nature with special permits for venturing by two-person kayak into sanctuaries for whales and birds, slipping among mangroves, and on into shallow bays, estuaries, and lagoons.

- **One World Workforce,** Route 4, Box 963A, Flagstaff, AZ 86001 (☎ **520/779-3639**) in its "Hands On Conservation Trips" offers working volunteers a chance to help with sea turtle conservation at Bahia de Los Angeles, Baja (April 28 through June 16), and a similar turtle project (July 30 through November 30), at the Majahuas Ecological Reserve 60 miles south of Puerto Vallarta. Overnight visits (two days and one night) from Puerto Vallarta to the Majahuas reserve can also be arranged.

- **PanAngling Travel Service,** 180 North Michigan Ave., Chicago, IL 60601 (☎ **312/263-5246**) focuses on fishing off the Yucatán Peninsula and the Baja Peninsula near East Cape and Cabo San Lucas. Yucatán fishing includes bonefish and tarpon fishing, and stays at some remote and unique lodges.

- **The Cloud Forest Adventure,** c/o Fred S. Webster, Jr., 4926 Strass Dr., Austin, TX 78731 (☎ **512/451-1669**), offers once- or twice-a-year, weeklong trips (usually in June) to America's northernmost tropical cloud forest and the Rancho El Cielo in the remote mountain El Cielo Biosphere Reserve 50 miles south of Ciudad Victoria, Tamaulipas State, in northern Mexico. The trips are sponsored by the Gorgas Science Foundation of Texas Southmost College. The area is rich in birds, orchids, and bromeliads and is home to endangered black bear, jaguar, and ocelot. Two nature movies explaining the region are available from the foundation—*At A Bend In a Mexican River,* about birds and nature along the Río Sabinas, and *El Cielo, Forest in the Clouds,* exploring the adjacent mountain range and what visitors may see.

- **Trek America,** P. O. Box 189 Rockaway, NJ 07866 (☎ **201/983-1144,** or 800/ 221-0596 in the U.S.; fax 201/983-8551) organizes lengthy, active trips that combine trekking and hiking (with van transportation) with camping in the Yucatán, Chiapas, Oaxaca, the Copper Canyon, and Mexico's Pacific Coast, and touching on Mexico City, and Guadalajara.
- **Ultimate Bicycle Tours,** 1123 Los Palos Drive #1, Salinas, CA 93901 (☎ **800/ 337-TOUR**), offers bicycling tours around Puerto Vallarta that also include options for sea kayaking, fishing, horseback riding, hiking, and surfing.
- **Victor Emanuel Tours,** P.O. Box 33008, Austin, TX 78764 (☎ **512/328-5221,** or 800/328-VENT), is an established leader in birding and natural-history tours.
- **Zapotec Tours,** 2334 W. Lawrence Ave., Suite 219, Chicago, IL 60625 (☎ **312/ 973-2444** or, outside Illinois, 800/44-Oaxaca in the U.S.), offers a variety of tours to Oaxaca City and the Oaxaca coast (including Puerto Escondido and Huatulco), and two specialty trips—for Day of the Dead in Oaxaca, and the "chocolate route" in the states of Tabasco and Oaxaca. Coastal trips emphasize nature. In Oaxaca City tours focus on the immediate area with visits to weavers, potters, and markets. They are also the U.S. contact for several hotels in Oaxaca City and for the Oaxaca state route of AeroMorelos airlines (serving the Oaxaca coast and Oaxaca City). Call them for information, but all reservations must be made through a travel agent.

5 Health, Safety & Insurance

STAYING HEALTHY

Of course, the very best way to avoid illness or to mitigate its effects is to make sure you're in top health when you travel and that you don't overdo it.

Important note: Antibiotics and other drugs that you'd need a prescription to buy in the States are sold over-the-counter in Mexican pharmacies, but Mexican pharmacies don't have the common over-the-counter sinus or allergy remedies we're accustomed to finding easily. If you're prone to this trouble, bring your own supply of pills.

COMMON AILMENTS It's a rare person indeed who doesn't experience some degree of gastric upheaval when traveling; see the box on Moctezuma's Revenge for tips on preventing and dealing with **travelers' diarrhea.**

Altitude Sickness is another problem travelers experience; Mexico City is at an elevation of more than 7,000 feet, as are a number of other central Mexican cities. At high elevations it takes about 10 days to acquire the extra red blood corpuscles you need to adjust to the scarcity of oxygen. At very high elevations, such as Ixta-Popo Park outside Mexico City (13,000 ft.), you may not sleep well at night.

Altitude sickness results from the relative lack of oxygen and the decrease in barometric pressure that characterizes high elevations (over 5,000 ft./1,500m). Symptoms include shortness of breath, fatigue, headache, and even nausea.

Take it easy for the first few days after you arrive at a high elevation. Drink extra fluids but avoid alcohol. If you have heart or lung problems, talk to your doctor before going above 8,000 feet.

Mosquitoes and gnats are prevalent along the coast and in the Yucatán lowlands. Insect repellent (*rapellante contra insectos*) is a must, and it's not always available in Mexico. If you're sensitive to bites, pick up some antihistamine cream from a drugstore at home. Rubbed on a fresh mosquito bite, the cream keeps the swelling down and reduces the itch.

Ay Caramba! Moctezuma's Revenge

Turista, or Moctezuma's Revenge, are the names given to the persistent diarrhea, often accompanied by fever, nausea, and vomiting, that attacks so many travelers to Mexico. Doctors, who call it travelers' diarrhea, say it's not caused by just one "bug," or factor, but by a combination of consuming different food and water, upsetting your schedule, being overtired, and experiencing the stresses of travel. Being tired and careless about food and drink is a sure ticket to turista. A good high-potency (or "therapeutic") vitamin supplement, and even extra vitamin C, is a help; yogurt is good for healthy digestion and is becoming much more available in Mexico than in the past.

Preventing Turista: The U.S. Public Health Service recommends the following measures for prevention of travelers' diarrhea:

- *Drink only purified water.* This means tea, coffee, and other beverages made with boiled water; canned or bottled carbonated beverages and water; beer and wine; or water you yourself have brought to a rolling boil or otherwise purified. Avoid ice, which may be made with untreated water. However, most restaurants with a large tourist clientele use only purified water and ice.
- *Choose food carefully.* In general, avoid salads, uncooked vegetables, and unpasteurized milk or milk products (including cheese). Choose food that is freshly cooked and still hot. Peel fruit yourself. Don't eat undercooked meat, fish, or shellfish.

The Public Health Service does not recommend you take any medicines as preventatives. All the applicable medicines can have nasty side effects if taken for several weeks. In addition, something so simple as clean hands can go a long way toward preventing turista. I carry packages of antiseptic towelettes for those times when wash facilities aren't available and to avoid using a communal bar of soap.

How to Get Well: If you get sick, there are lots of medicines available in Mexico that can harm more than help. Ask your doctor before you leave home what medicine he or she recommends for travelers' diarrhea.

The Public Health Service guidelines are the following: If there are three or more loose stools in an eight-hour period, especially with other symptoms (such as nausea, vomiting, abdominal cramps, and fever), see a doctor.

The first thing to do is go to bed and don't move until the condition runs its course. Traveling makes it last longer. Drink lots of liquids: Tea without milk or sugar or the Mexican *té de manzanilla* (chamomile tea) is best. Eat only *pan tostada* (dry toast). Keep to this diet for at least 24 hours, and you'll be well over the worst of it. If you fool yourself into thinking a plate of enchiladas can't hurt or beer or liquor will kill the germs, you'll have a total relapse.

The Public Health Service advises that you be especially careful to replace fluids and electrolytes (potassium, sodium, and the like) during a bout of diarrhea. Do this by drinking Pedialyte, a rehydration solution available at most Mexican pharmacies, or glasses of fruit juice (high in potassium) with honey and a pinch of salt added, or you can also try a glass of boiled pure water with a quarter teaspoon of sodium bicarbonate (baking soda) added.

Though they proliferate in the deserts, most readers won't ever see a scorpion (*alacrán*). If you're stung, go to a doctor.

MORE SERIOUS DISEASES   You shouldn't be overly concerned about tropical diseases if you stay on the normal tourist routes and don't eat street food. However, both dengue fever and cholera have appeared in Mexico in recent years. Talk to your doctor, or a medical specialist in tropical diseases, about any precautions you should take. You can also get medical bulletins from the U.S. State Department and the Center for Disease Control (see "Sources of Information," above). You can protect yourself by taking some simple precautions. Watch what you eat and drink; don't swim in stagnant water (ponds, slow-moving rivers, and Yucatecan *cenotes,* or wells); avoid mosquito bites by covering up, using powerful repellent, sleeping under mosquito netting, and staying away from places that seem to have a lot of mosquitoes. The most dangerous areas seem to be on Mexico's west coast, away from the big resorts (which are relatively safe).

EMERGENCY EVACUATION   For extreme medical emergencies there's a service from the United States that will fly people to American hospitals: **Air-Evac,** a 24-hour air ambulance (☎ **800/854-2569** in the U.S. or call collect: 510/786-1592). You can also contact the service in Guadalajara (☎ **3/616-9616** or 91-800/90345).

SAFETY

Boisterous drunks aside, I've never had trouble of any kind in Mexico and seldom feel suspicious of anyone or any situation. You will probably feel physically safer in most Mexican cities and villages than in any comparable place at home.

Crime, however, is more of a problem in Mexico than it used to be. Be smart, be careful, take all the normal precautions you'd take to deter pickpockets and muggers traveling to any large American city, for example.

Keep a photocopy of your credit cards, driver's license, and passport or birth certificate in a separate place from where you're keeping the originals. (In case you lose, or are relieved of, the originals, these copies will make replacement easier.) Use hotel security boxes or in-room safes for your passport and other valuables.

Keep your things with you on the less responsible village buses and some second-class buses on country routes.

And, of course, *never* carry a package back to the States for an acquaintance or a stranger.

See "Sources of Information" at the beginning of this chapter for how to contact the U.S. State Department for their latest advisories. At press time their crime cautions included warnings about bold highway holdups in the Yucatecan state of Campeche (including robbery of buses on Highway 186 heading east from Escarcega, and between Escarcega and Candalaria); about criminals representing themselves as police or official authorities in the northwestern state of Sinaloa; and particularly about robberies and murders on Highway 15 and the adjacent toll highway, from the U.S. border and on down the Pacific Coast. They urge travelers to contact them for security information before traveling to Chiapas.

Lastly I urge you not to let these cautionary statements deter you from traveling in Mexico. Were I to write a similar section about travel in the U.S., it would take several pages. Mexico is a wonderful country, and your good experiences with its people and culture will far outweigh any negative incidents. I eagerly return there year after year.

INSURANCE

HEALTH/ACCIDENT/LOSS   Even the most careful of us can experience the Murphy's Law of travel—you discover you've lost your wallet, your passport, your airline ticket, or your Tourist Permit. Always keep a photocopy of these documents in your luggage—it makes replacing them easier. To be reimbursed for insured items once you return, you'll need to report the loss to the Mexican police and get a written report. If you don't speak Spanish, take along someone who does. If you lose official documents, you'll need to contact both Mexican and U.S. officials in Mexico before you leave the country.

Health Care Abroad, Wallach and Co. Inc., 107 W. Federal St. (P.O. Box 480), Middleburg, VA 22117 (☎ **540/687-3166** or 800/237-6615), and **World Access,** 6600 W. Broad St., Richmond, VA 23230 (☎ **804/285-3300** or 800/628-4908), offer medical and accident insurance as well as coverage for luggage loss and trip cancellation. Always read the fine print on the policy to be sure that you're getting the coverage you want.

6   Tips for Travelers with Special Needs

FOR SENIORS   Mexico is a popular country for retirees—for decades, North Americans have been living indefinitely in Mexico by returning to the border and recrossing with a new tourist card every six months. Recently, but not uniformly at every border crossing, Mexico has begun to crack down on this practice by refusing readmittance to someone they remember just crossed over. So if you've been in Mexico for six months and haven't decided on permanent residency yet, and want to return immediately for another stay on a Tourist Permit, you'll have to exercise caution about where and when you recross.

Some of the most popular places for long-term stays are Guadalajara, Lake Chapala, Ajijic, and Puerto Vallarta—all in the state of Jalisco; San Miguel de Allende and Guanajuato in the state of Guanajuato; Cuernavaca, Morelos; Alamos, Sinaloa; and to a lesser extent Manzanillo, Colima, and Morelia in Michoacán. Crowds don't necessarily mean there are no other good places: Oaxaca, Querétaro, Puebla, Guanajuato, Tepoztlán, and Valle de Bravo have much to offer, even though Americans have yet to collect there in large numbers.

The following newsletters are written for prospective retirees: *AIM,* Apdo. Postal 31–70, 45050 Guadalajara, Jal., Mexico, is a well-written, candid, and very informative newsletter on retirement in Mexico. Recent issues evaluated retirement in Aguascalientes, Puebla, San Cristóbal de las Casas, Puerto Angel, Puerto Escondido and Huatulco, Oaxaca, Taxco, Tepic, Manzanillo, Melaque, and Barra de Navidad. Subscriptions cost $16 to the United States and $19 to Canada. Back issues are three for $5.

Finally, **Sanborn Tours,** 1007 Main St., Bastrop, TX 78602 (☎ **800/531-5440**), offers a "Retire in Mexico" Guadalajara orientation tour.

FOR SINGLES   Mexico may be an old favorite for romantic honeymoons, but it's also a great place to travel on your own without really being or feeling alone. Although offering an identical room rate regardless of single or double occupancy is slowly becoming a trend in Mexico, most of the hotels mentioned in this book still offer singles at lower rates.

Mexicans are very friendly, and it's easy to meet other foreigners. If certain cities such as Acapulco, Manzanillo, Cabo San Lucas, and Huatulco have so many twosomes as to leave single travelers feeling as though an appendage is missing, places like

Isla Mujeres, Playa del Carmen, Puerto Vallarta, Mazatlán, San Blas, Cancún, Zihuatanejo, Ixtapa, Puerto Angel, Puerto Escondido, and Celestún are great places to go on your own.

If you don't like the idea of traveling alone, then try **Travel Companion Exchange,** P.O. Box 833, Amityville, NY 11701 (☎ **516/454-0880;** fax 516/454-0170), which brings prospective travelers together. Members complete a profile, then place an anonymous listing of their travel interests in the newsletter. Prospective traveling companions then make contact through the Exchange. Membership costs $99 for six months or $159 for a year.

For Women   As a frequent female visitor to Mexico, mostly traveling alone, I can tell you firsthand that I feel safer traveling in Mexico than in the United States. Mexicans are very warm and welcoming people, and I'm not afraid to be friendly wherever I go. But I use the same common-sense precautions I use traveling anywhere else in the world—I'm alert to what's going on around me.

Mexicans in general, and men in particular, are nosy about single travelers, especially women. They want to know with whom you're traveling, whether you're married or have a boyfriend, and how many children you have. My advice to anyone asked these details by taxi drivers or other people with whom you don't want to become friendly is to make up a set of answers (regardless of the truth): "I'm married, traveling with friends, and I have three children."

If you're a divorcee, revealing such may send out the wrong message about availability. Drunks are a particular nuisance to the lone female traveler. Don't try to be polite—just leave or duck into a public place.

Generally lone women will feel comfortable going to a hotel lobby bar, yet are asking for trouble by going into a pulquería or cantina. In restaurants, as a general rule, single women are offered the worst table and service. You'll have to be vocal about your preference and insist on service. Don't tip if service is bad.

For Men   I'm not sure why, but non-Spanish-speaking foreign men seem to be special targets for scams and pickpockets. So if you fit this description, whether traveling alone or in a pair, exercise special vigilance.

FOR FAMILIES   Mexicans travel extensively in their country with their families, so your child will feel very welcome. Hotels will often arrange for a baby-sitter. Several hotels in the middling-to-luxury range have small playgrounds and pools for children and hire caretakers on weekends to oversee them. Few budget hotels offer these amenities.

Before leaving, you should check with your doctor to get advice on medications to take along. Bring along a supply just to be sure. Disposable diapers cost about the same in Mexico but are of poorer quality. Gerber's baby foods are sold in many stores. Dry cereals, powdered formulas, baby bottles, and purified water are all easily available in midsize and large cities.

Cribs, however, may present a problem. Except for the largest and most luxurious hotels, few Mexican hotels provide cribs. However, rollaway beds to accommodate children staying in the room with parents are often available. Likewise, childseats or highchairs at restaurants are rare.

Many of the hotels I mention, even in noncoastal regions, have swimming pools, which can be a treat at the end of a day of traveling with a child who has had it with sightseeing.

FOR PEOPLE WITH DISABILITIES   Travelers who are unable to walk or who are in wheelchairs or on crutches discover quickly that Mexico is one giant obstacle course. Beginning at the airport on arrival, you may encounter steep stairs before finding a well-hidden elevator or escalator—if one exists. Airlines will often arrange wheelchair assistance for passengers to the baggage area. Porters are generally available to help with luggage at airports and large bus stations, once you've cleared baggage claim.

In addition, escalators (there aren't many in the country) are often not operating. Few handicapped-equipped rest rooms exist, or when one is available, access to it may be via a narrow passage that won't accommodate a wheelchair or someone on crutches. Many deluxe hotels (the most expensive) now have rooms with baths for the handicapped and handicapped access to the hotel. Those traveling on a budget should stick with one-story hotels or those with elevators. Even so, there will probably still be obstacles somewhere. Stairs without handrails abound in Mexico. Intracity bus drivers generally don't bother with the courtesy step on boarding or disembarking. On city buses, the height between the street and the bus step can require considerable force to board. Generally speaking, no matter where you are, someone will lend a hand, although you may have to ask for it.

Few airports offer the luxury of boarding an airplane from the waiting room. You either descend stairs to a bus that ferries you to the waiting plane that's boarded by climbing stairs, or you walk across the airport tarmac to your plane and ascend the stairs. Deplaning offers the same in reverse.

7 Getting There

BY PLANE

The airline situation in Mexico is changing rapidly, with many new regional carriers offering scheduled service to areas previously not served. In addition to regularly scheduled service, charter service direct from U.S. cities to resorts is making Mexico more accessible from the United States.

THE MAJOR INTERNATIONAL AIRLINES   The main airlines operating direct or nonstop flights from the United States to points in Mexico include **Aero California** (☎ 800/237-6225), **Aeroméxico** (☎ 800/237-6639), **Air France** (☎ 800/237-2747), **Alaska Airlines** (☎ 800/426-0333), **American** (☎ 800/433-7300), **Continental** (☎ 800/231-0856), **Lacsa** (☎ 800/225-2272), **Mexicana** (☎ 800/531-7921), **Northwest** (☎ 800/225-2525), **United** (☎ 800/241-6522), and **USAir** (☎ 800/428-4322).

Southwest Airlines (☎ 800/435-9792) serves the U.S. border. The main departure points in the United States for international airlines are Chicago, Dallas/Fort Worth, Denver, Houston, Los Angeles, Miami, New Orleans, New York, Orlando, Philadelphia, Raleigh/Durham, San Antonio, San Francisco, Seattle, Toronto, Tucson, and Washington, D.C.

Excursion and package plans proliferate, especially in the off-season. A good travel agent will be able to give you all the latest schedules, details, and prices, but you may have to investigate the details of the plans to see if they are real deals. You'll also have to sleuth regional airlines for yourself (see "By Plane" under "Getting Around," below), since most travel agents don't have that information.

CHARTERS   Charter service is growing, especially during winter months and usually is sold as a package combination of air and hotel. Charter airlines, however, may sell air packages only, without hotel. Check your local paper for seasonal charters.

Well known **tour companies** operating charters include **Club America Vacations, Apple Vacations,** and **Friendly Holidays.** You can make arrangements with these companies through your travel agent.

BY TRAIN

For getting to the Mexican border from the United States by train, call **Amtrak** (☎ **800/872-7245**) for fares, information, and reservations.

BY BUS

Greyhound-Trailways (or its affiliates) offers service from around the United States to the Mexican border, where passengers disembark, cross the border, and buy a ticket for travel into the interior of Mexico. At many border crossings there are scheduled buses from the U.S. bus station to the Mexican bus station.

BY CAR

Driving is certainly not the cheapest way to get to Mexico, but it is the best way to see the country. Even so, you may think twice about taking your own car south of the border once you've pondered Mexico's many bureaucratic requirements for doing so.

In 1994, Mexico's Ministry of Tourism published its own *Official Guide: Traveling to Mexico by Car.* Unfortunately its information can be inconsistent, unclear, or inaccurate. Of possible use, however, is the list it includes of the times at which you'll find government officials on duty at border crossings to review your car documents and issue Temporary Car Importation Permits. To get a copy, inquire at a branch of the regional Mexican Government Tourism Office.

It's wise to check and double-check all the requirements before setting out for a driving tour of Mexico. Read through the rest of this section, and then address any additional questions you have or confirm the current rules by calling your nearest Mexican consulate, Mexican Government Tourist Office, AAA, or Sanborn's (☎ **800/222-0185** in the U.S.). To check on road conditions, or to get help with any travel emergency while in the country, there's a 24-hour number (toll free ☎ **91-800/9-0329** in Mexico) that you can call. Another 24-hour help number (☎ **5/250-0123** or 5/250-0151) is in Mexico City. Both numbers are supposed to be staffed by English-speaking operators.

In addition, check with the U.S. State Department (see "Sources of Information" at the beginning of this chapter) for their warnings about areas where driving the highways can be dangerous. Their current warnings regarding crime and highway travel are in "Safety," above.

CAR DOCUMENTS   To drive a personal car into Mexico, you'll need a Temporary Car Importation Permit, granted upon completion of a long and strictly required list of documents (see below). The permit can be obtained either through Banco del Ejército (*Banjercito*) officals, who have a desk, booth, or office at the Mexican customs (*Aduana*) building after you cross the border into Mexico. You can obtain the permit before you travel through Sanborn's Insurance and the American Automobile Association (AAA), each of which maintains border offices in Texas, New Mexico, Arizona, and California. These companies may charge a fee for this service, but it will be worth it to avoid the uncertain prospect of traveling all the way to the border without proper documents for crossing. However, even if you go through Sanborn's or AAA, your credentials *may* be reviewed again by Mexican officials at the border—you must have them all with you since they are still subject to questions of validity.

The following requirements for border crossing were accurate at press time:

- *A valid driver's license,* issued outside of Mexico.
- *Current, original car registration and a copy of the original car title.* If the registration or title is in more than one name and not all the named people are

traveling with you, then a notarized letter from the absent person(s) authorizing use of the vehicle for the trip is required; have it ready just in case. The car registration and your credit card (see below) must be in the same name.

- *An original notarized letter from the lien or lease holder*, if your registration shows a lien or lease, giving you permission to take the vehicle into Mexico.
- *A valid international major credit card.* Using only your credit card, you are required to pay a $12 car-importation fee. The credit card must be in the same name as the car registration.

  Note: Those without credit cards will forego the $12 importation fee and instead will be required to post a cash bond based on the value of the car. The rules and procedures are complicated (and expensive), so contact AAA or Sanborn's for details.
- A signed declaration promising to return to your country of origin with the vehicle. This form is provided by AAA or Sanborn's before you go or by Banjercito officials at the border. There's no charge. The form does not stipulate that you return through the same border entry you came through on your way south.

You must carry your Temporary Car Importation Permit, Tourist Permit, and, if you purchased it, your proof of Mexican car insurance in the car at all times.

Important reminder: Someone else may drive the car, but the person (or relative of the person) whose name appears on the Car Importation Permit must *always* be in the car at the same time. (If stopped by police, a nonregistered family member driver, driving without the registered driver, must be prepared to prove familial relationship to the registered driver.) Violation of this rule makes the car subject to impoundment and the driver to imprisonment and/or a fine.

Only under certain circumstances will the driver of the car be allowed to leave the country without the car. If it's undrivable, you can leave it at a mechanic's shop if you get a letter to that effect from the mechanic and present it to the nearest Secretaria de Hacienda y Credito Público (a treasury department official) for further documentation, which you then present to a Banjercito official upon leaving the country. Then you must return personally to retrieve the car. If the driver of the car has to leave the country without the car due to an emergency, the car must be put under customs seal at the airport, and the driver's Tourist Permit must be stamped to that effect. There may be storage fees. If the car is wrecked or stolen, your Mexican insurance adjuster will provide the necessary paperwork for presentation to Hacienda officals.

If you receive your documentation at the border (rather than through Sanborn's or AAA), Mexican border officials will make two copies of everything and charge you for the copies.

The Temporary Car Importation Permit papers will be issued for six months, and the Tourist Permit is usually issued for 180 days, but they might stamp it for half that, so check. It's a good idea also to overestimate the time you'll spend in Mexico, so that if something unforeseen happens and you have to—or want to—stay longer, you'll have avoided the long hassle of getting your papers renewed.

Important note: Whatever you do, don't overstay either permit. Doing so invites heavy fines and/or confiscation of your vehicle, which will not be returned. Remember also that six months does not necessarily work out to be 180 days—be sure that you return before whichever expiration date comes first.

Other documentation is required for an individual's permit to enter Mexico—see "Entry Requirements," above.

MEXICAN AUTO INSURANCE   Although auto insurance is not legally required in Mexico, driving without it is foolish. U.S. insurance is invalid in Mexico; to be insured there, you must purchase Mexican insurance. Any party involved in an accident who has no insurance is automatically sent to jail, and his or her car is impounded until all claims are settled. This is true even if you just drive across the border to spend the day, and it may be true even if you're injured.

I always buy my car insurance through **Sanborn's Mexico Insurance,** P.O. Box 310, Dept. FR, 2009 S. 10th, McAllen, TX 78505-0310 (☎ **210/686-0711;** fax 210/686-0732 in Texas or 800/222-0158 in the U.S.). The company has offices at all the border crossings in the United States. Their policies cost the same as the competition's do, but you get legal coverage (attorney and bail bonds if needed) and a detailed mile-by-mile guide to your proposed route—to me, this last part is the kicker. With the ongoing changes in Mexico's highway system it's inevitable that your log will occasionally be a bit outdated, but for the most part having it is like having a knowledgeable friend in the car telling you how to get in and out of town, where to buy gas (and which stations to avoid), what the highway conditions are, and what scams you need to watch out for. It's especially helpful in remote places. Most of Sanborn's border offices are open Monday through Friday, and a few are staffed on Saturday and Sunday. You can purchase your auto liability and collision coverage by phone in advance and have it waiting at a 24-hour location if you are crossing when the office is closed. The annual insurance includes a type of evacuation assistance in case of emergency, and emergency evacuation insurance for shorter policies is available for a small daily fee. They also offer a medical policy.

AAA auto club also sells insurance.

All agencies selling Mexican insurance will show you a full table of current rates and recommend the coverage they think is adequate. The policies are written along lines similar to those north of the border, with the following exception: The contents of your vehicle aren't covered. It's no longer necessary to overestimate the amount of time you plan to be in Mexico because it's now possible to get your policy term lengthened by fax from the insurer. However, if you are staying longer than 48 days, it's more economical to buy a nonrefundable annual policy. For example, Sanborn's Insurance quotes a car (registered to an individual, not a business) with a value of $10,000 can be insured for $137.82 for two weeks or $73.91 for one week. An annual policy for a car valued between $10,000 and $15,000 would be a reduced rate of $519, which you get by joining Sanborn's Amigo Club for $40. (The Amigo Club membership offers hotel discounts, emergency air ambulance, and a newsletter.) Be sure the policy you buy will pay for repairs in either the United States or Mexico and will pay out in dollars, not pesos.

PREPARING YOUR CAR   Check the condition of your car thoroughly before you cross the border. Parts made in Mexico may be inferior, but service generally is quite good and relatively inexpensive. Carry a spare radiator hose and belts for the engine fan and air conditioner. Be sure your car is in tune to handle Mexican gasoline. Also, can your tires last a few thousand miles on Mexican roads?

Don't forget a flashlight and a tire gauge—Mexican filling stations generally have air to fill tires but no gauge to check the pressure. When I drive into Mexico, I always bring along a combination gauge/air compressor sold at U.S. automotive stores that plugs into the car cigarette lighter, making it a simple procedure to check the tires every morning and pump them up at the same time.

Not that many Mexican cars comply, but Mexican law requires that every car have **seat belts** and a **fire extinguisher.** Be prepared!

CROSSING THE BORDER WITH YOUR CAR   After you cross the border into Mexico from the United States and you've stopped to get your Tourist Card and Car Permit, somewhere between 12 and 16 miles down the road you'll come to a

Mexican customs post. In the past all motorists had to stop and present travel documents and possibly have their cars inspected. Now there is a new system under which some motorists are stopped at random for inspection. All car papers are examined, however, so you must stop. If the light is green, go on through; if it's red, stop for inspection. In the Baja Peninsula the procedures may differ slightly—first you get your Tourist Permit, then farther down the road you may not be stopped for the car inspection.

RETURNING TO THE U.S. WITH YOUR CAR   The car papers you obtained when you entered Mexico *must* be returned when you cross back with your car or at some point within the time limit of 180 days. (You can cross as many times as you wish within the 180 days.) If the documents aren't returned, heavy fines are imposed ($250 for each 15 days late), and your car may be impounded and confiscated, or you may be jailed if you return to Mexico. You can only return the car documents to a Banjercito official on duty at the Mexican customs (*Aduana*) building *before* you cross back into the United States. Some border cities have Banjercito officials on duty 24 hours a day, but others do not; some also do not have Sunday hours. On the U.S. side customs agents may or may not inspect your car from stem to stern.

BY SHIP

Numerous cruise lines serve Mexico. Possible trips might cruise from California down to the Baja Peninsula (including specialized whale-watching trips) and ports of call on the Pacific coast or from Miami to the Caribbean (which often includes stops in Cancún, Playa del Carmen, and Cozumel).

From a budget point of view, these are expensive if you pay the full price. However, if you don't mind taking off at the last minute, several cruise-tour specialists arrange substantial discounts on unsold cabins. One such company is **The Cruise Line, Inc.,** 4770 Biscayne Blvd., Penthouse 1–3, Miami FL 33137 (☎ **305/ 576-0036** or 800/777-0707 or 800/327-3021).

PACKAGE TOURS

Package tours offer some of the best values to the coastal resorts, especially during high season—from December until after Easter. Off-season packages can be real bargains. However, to know for sure if the package will save you money, you must price the package yourself by calling the airline for round-trip flight costs and the hotel for rates. Add in the cost of transfers to and from the airport (which packages usually include) and see if it's a deal.

Packages are usually per person, and single travelers pay a supplement. In the high season a package may be the only way of getting to certain places in Mexico because wholesalers have all the airline seats. The cheapest package rates will be those in hotels in the lower range, always without as many amenities as higher-priced hotels. You can still use the public areas and beaches of more costly hotels without being a guest.

Travel agents have information on specific packages.

8 Getting Around

An important note: If your travel schedule depends on an important connection, say a plane trip between points, or a ferry or bus connection, use the telephone numbers in this book or other information resources mentioned here and find out if the connection you are depending on is still available. Although I've done my best to provide accurate information, transportation schedules can and do change.

BY PLANE

To fly from point to point within Mexico, you'll rely on Mexican airlines. Mexico has two privately owned large national carriers: **Mexicana** (☎ **800/531-7921** in the U.S.) and **Aeroméxico** (☎ **800/237-6639** in the U.S.), in addition to several up-and-coming regional carriers. Mexicana and Aeroméxico both offer extensive connections to the United States as well as within Mexico.

Several of the new regional carriers are operated by or can be booked through Mexicana or Aeroméxico. Regional carriers are **Lone Star Airlines** (☎ **14/20-9154** in Chihuahua, or 800/877-3932 in the U.S.) which flies from El Paso and Dallas/Fort Worth to Chihuahua, **Aero Cancún** (see Mexicana), **Aero Caribe** (see Mexicana), **Aerolitoral** (see Aeroméxico), **Aero Monterrey** (see Mexicana), **Aero Morelos** (☎ **73/17-5588** in Cuernavaca; fax 73/17-2320). For points inside the state of Oaxaca only—Oaxaca City, Puerto Escondido, and Puerto Angel—contact Zapotec Tours (☎ **312/973-2444,** or outside Illinois, 800/44-Oaxaca in the U.S.), and **Aerovias Oaxaqueñas** (☎ **951/6-3824** in Oaxaca). The regional carriers are expensive, but they go to places that are difficult to reach. In each applicable section of this book, I've mentioned regional carriers with all pertinent telephone numbers. (For tips on saving money on regional carriers, see "Eighty Tips for Saving Money in Mexico" in chapter 1.)

Because major airlines can book some regional carriers, read your ticket carefully to see if your connecting flight is on one of these smaller carriers—they may leave from a different airport or check in at a different counter.

AIRPORT TAXES   Mexico charges an airport tax on all departures. Passengers leaving the country on an international departure pay $12 in cash—dollars or the peso equivalent. (That tax is usually included in your ticket.) Each domestic departure you make within Mexico costs around $6, unless you're on a connecting flight and have already paid at the start of the flight; you shouldn't be charged again if you have to change planes for a connecting flight.

RECONFIRMING FLIGHTS   Although airlines in Mexico say it's not necessary to reconfirm a flight, I always do. Aeroméxico seems particularly prone to cancelling confirmed reservations. Also, be aware that airlines routinely overbook. To avoid getting bumped, check in for an international flight the required hour and a half in advance of travel.

BY TRAIN

The Mexican government would like to privatize the railroads and has systematically downgraded passenger service from the high it reached a few years ago. You can't count on diner or club cars or Pullman (sleeping) cars, even on overnight journeys. No matter what is promised, *always* be prepared with food, water, and toilet paper.

There are two major train hubs: Mexico City and Guadalajara. Several trains leave from the border areas in Texas and California. If you plan to get on and off before your final destination, tell the agent your exact schedule when you purchase your ticket. First-class trains are often filled, especially on holidays or with tour groups.

In general, Mexico's bus system is a much better and faster mode of transportation, but some people love train travel so that they're willing to overlook the inconveniences of the Mexican system.

There is one place in Mexico where train travel is not only a splendid way to see the area, but also the only practical way: the Copper Canyon. The famous old Chihuahua al Pacífico railroad carves through the enormous canyon and rugged Sierra Madre, linking Los Mochis on the Sea of Cortez with the northern city of Chihuahua. See chapter 4 for all the details.

SERVICE CLASSES   **Segunda** (second class) service is usually hot, overcrowded, dingy, and unpleasant. **Primera** (first class) can be the same unless you make sure to ask for **primera especial** (a first-class reserved seat) a day or so before you travel if possible. The top-of-the-line accommodations on trains are **Pullman compartments** (*alcolba* or *camarín*) for overnight travel. These convert to private sitting rooms during the day. Cramming extra people in either size compartment is very uncomfortable and is not recommended. Some first-class trains have a Pullman and diner; others have only a diner, and most have comfortable reclining chairs.

Service and cleanliness may vary dramatically. The cars, for example, may be clean at the origin of the run, but little may be done en route to keep them that way. Trash may accumulate, toilet paper may vanish, the water cooler may run dry or have no paper cups, and the air temperature may vary between freezing and sweltering. Conductors range from solicitous to totally indifferent.

A BOOKING AGENT   I suggest that you contact **Mexico by Train** (not to be confused with Mexico by Rail), P.O. Box 2782, Laredo, TX 78044 (☎ 800/ 321-1699; fax 210/725-3659). Given 15 days notice, they will prepurchase your train tickets to anywhere in Mexico and mail them to you. For holiday travel, make plans at least 30 days ahead of your proposed trip.

If you leave from Nuevo Laredo, a company representative will meet you at La Posada Hotel, check for your proper citizenship identification, secure Mexican Tourist Permits, transfer you across the border and through customs, and put you aboard a first-class bus to Monterrey to connect with the southbound *Regiomontaño* train that leaves from Monterrey going to Mexico City (see "By Train," above, and specific chapters for train information). For its services, it charges a percentage above the cost of the train ticket. The additional cost of this service may be worth it when you consider the tightness of your travel schedule, the hassle of going to the train station yourself, and the uncertainty of being able to reserve a seat at the last minute.

TRAVEL TIME   From Nuevo Laredo, it's a 25-hour, 735-mile ride to Mexico City. Other border towns are farther from the capital. The trip from Ciudad Juárez, across from El Paso, takes more than 35 hours to Mexico City. From Nogales, the trip takes 26 or 36 hours, depending on which train you take. From Mexicali, the fast train takes 30 hours to Guadalajara and 45 hours to Mexico City. Pacific coast trains and those from Mexico City to the Yucatán are notorious for running as much as 24 hours behind schedule.

BY BUS

Except for the Baja and Yucatán peninsulas, where bus service is not as well developed as in other parts of the country, Mexican buses are frequent, readily accessible, and can get you to almost anywhere you want to go. Buses are an excellent way to get around, and they're often the only way to get from large cities to other nearby cities and small villages. Ticket agents can be quite brusque or indifferent, especially if there's a line; in general, however, people are willing to help, so never hesitate to ask questions if you're confused about anything. *Important Note:* There's little English spoken at bus stations, so come prepared with your destination written down, then double-check the departure several times just to make sure you get to the right departing lane on time.

Dozens of Mexican companies operate large, air-conditioned, Greyhound-type buses between most cities. Travel class is generally labeled first, second, and deluxe, referred to by a variety of names—*plus, de lujo, ejecutivo, primera plus,* and so on. The deluxe buses often have fewer seats than regular buses, show video movies en route, are air-conditioned, and have few stops; some have complimentary refreshments.

Many run express from origin to the final destination. They are well worth the few dollars more you'll pay than you would for first-class buses. First-class buses may get there as fast as a deluxe bus, but without the comfort; they may also have many stops. Second-class buses have many stops and cost only slightly less than first-class or deluxe buses. In rural areas, buses are often of the school-bus variety, with lots of local color.

Whenever possible, it's best to buy your reserved-seat ticket, often via a computerized system, a day in advance on many long-distance routes and especially before holidays. Schedules are fairly dependable, so be at the terminal on time for departure.

Many Mexican cities have replaced the bewildering array of tiny private company offices scattered all over town with new central bus stations, much like sophisticated airport terminals.

Keep in mind that routes and times change, and as there is no central directory of schedules for the whole country, current information must be obtained from local bus stations.

For long trips, *always* carry food, water, toilet paper, and a sweater (in case the air-conditioning is too strong).

A Safety Precaution: The U.S. State Department notes that bandits target long-distance buses traveling at night, but there have also been daylight robberies as well. I've always avoided overnight buses, primarily because they usually must negotiate mountain roads in the dark, which I prefer not to risk. Because of the increase in bus hijackings, I also suggest only using buses that travel via a toll road, where hijackings seldom occur. (See "Sources of Information," above, for contact info, and "Safety" in "Fast Facts: Mexico," below, for specific areas of caution.)

See the Appendix for a list of helpful bus terms in Spanish.

BY CAR

Most Mexican roads are not up to U.S. standards of smoothness, hardness, width of curve, grade of hill, or safety marking. Never drive at night if you can avoid it—the roads aren't good enough; the trucks, carts, pedestrians, and bicycles usually have no lights; and you can hit potholes, animals, rocks, dead ends, or bridges out with no warning. Enough said!

You will also have to get used to the "spirited" style of Mexican driving, which sometimes seems to ask superhuman vision and reflexes from drivers. Be prepared for new procedures, as when a truck driver flips on his left-turn signal when there's not a crossroad for miles. He's probably telling you the road's clear ahead for you to pass—after all, he's in a better position to see than you are. It's difficult to know, however, whether he really means that he intends to pull over on the left-hand shoulder. Another strange custom decides who crosses a one-lane bridge first when two cars approach from opposite directions—the first car to flash its headlights has right of way. Still another custom that's very important to respect is how to make a left turn. Never turn left by stopping in the middle of a highway with your left signal on. Instead, pull off the highway onto the right shoulder, wait for traffic to clear, then proceed across the road. Other driving exasperations include following trucks without mufflers and pollution-control devices for miles. Under these conditions, drop back and be patient, take a side road, or stop for a break when you feel tense or tired.

GASOLINE   There's one government-owned brand of gas and one gasoline station name throughout the country—**Pemex** (Petroleras Mexicanas). Each station has a franchise owner who buys everything from Pemex. There are two types of gas in Mexico: *nova,* an 82-octane leaded gas, and *magna sin,* an 87-octane unleaded gas. Magna sin is sold from brilliantly colored pumps and costs around $1.15 a gallon;

nova costs slightly less. In Mexico, fuel and oil are sold by the liter, which is slightly more than a quart (40 liters equals about 10½ gallons). Nova is readily available. Magna sin is now available in most areas of Mexico, along major highways, and in the larger cities. Plan ahead; fill up every chance you get, and keep your tank topped off. *Important Note:* No credit cards are accepted for gas purchases.

Here's what to do when you have to fuel up. First rule is to keep your eyes on the pump meters as your tank is being filled. Check that the pump is turned back to zero, go to your fuel filler cap and unlock it yourself, and watch the pump and the attendant as the gas goes in. Though many service-station attendants are honest, many are not. It's better to ask for a specific peso amount rather than say "full." This is because the attendants tend to overfill, splashing gas on the car and anything within range.

As there are always lines at the gas pumps, attendants often finish fueling one vehicle, turn the pump back quickly (or don't turn it back at all), and start on another vehicle. You've got to be looking at the pump when the fueling is finished because it may show the amount you owe for only a few seconds. This "quick draw" from car to car is another good reason to ask for a certain peso amount of gas. If you've asked for a certain amount, the attendant can't charge you more for it. (Just for convenience's sake, I'll note that, at the current exchange rate, the $10 fill-up you'd ask for at home would be approximately 70 ["say-*ten*-tah"] pesos in Mexico. See the Appendix for pronunciation of other useful round numbers.)

Once the fueling is complete, let the attendant check the oil or radiator or put air in the tires. Do only one thing at a time, be with him as he does it, and don't let him rush you. Get into these habits, or it'll cost you.

If you get oil, make sure the can that is tipped into your engine is a full one. If in doubt, have the attendant check the dipstick again after the oil has supposedly been put in. Check your change and, again, don't let them rush you. Check that your locking gas cap is back in place.

DRIVING RULES   If you park illegally or commit some other infraction and are not around to discuss it, police are authorized to remove your license plates (*placas*). You must then trundle over to the police station and pay a fine to get them back. Mexican car-rental agencies have begun to weld the license tag to the tag frame; you may want to devise a method of your own to make the tags more difficult to remove. Theoretically, this may encourage a policeman to move on to another set of tags, one easier to confiscate. On the other hand, he could get his hackles up and decide to have your car towed. To weld or not to weld is up to you.

Be attentive to road signs. A drawing of a row of little bumps means there are speed bumps (*topes*) across the road to force you to reduce speed while driving through towns or villages. Slow down when coming to a village whether you see the sign or not—sometimes they install the bumps but not the sign!

Mexican roads are never as well marked as you'd like—when you see a highway route sign, take note and make sure you're on the right road. Don't count on plenty of notice of where to turn, even on major interchanges; more often than not, the directional sign appears without prior notice exactly at the spot where you need to make a decision. Common road signs include these:

Camino en Reparación	Road Repairs
Conserva Su Derecha	Keep Right
Ciudado con el Ganado, el Tren	Watch Out for Cattle, Trains
Curva Peligrosa	Dangerous Curve
Derrumbes	Falling Rocks

Deslave	Caved-in Roadbed
Despacio	Slow
Desviación	Detour
Disminuya Su Velocidad	Slow Down
Entronque	Highway Junction
Escuela	School (Zone)
Grava Suelta	Loose Gravel
Hombres Trabajando	Men Working
No Hay Paso	Road Closed
Peligro	Danger
Puente Angosto	Narrow Bridge
Raya Continua	Continuous (Solid) White Line
Tramo en Reparación	Road Under Construction
Un Solo Carril a 100 m.	One-Lane Road 100 Meters Ahead
Zone Escolar	School Zone

TOLL ROADS Mexico charges among the highest tolls in the world to use its network of new toll roads. As a result they are comparatively little used. Generally speaking, using the toll roads will cut your travel time between destinations. The old roads, on which no tolls are charged, are generally in good condition but overall mean longer trips—they tend to be mountainous and clotted with slow-moving trucks.

MAPS Guia Roji, AAA, and International Travel Map Productions have good maps to Mexico. In Mexico, maps are sold at large drugstores like Sanborn's, at bookstores, and in hotel gift shops.

BREAKDOWNS Your best guide to repair shops is the Yellow Pages. For specific makes and shops that repair them, look under "Automoviles y Camiones: Talleres de Reparación y Servicio"; auto-parts stores are listed under "Refacciones y Accesorios para Automoviles." On the road, often the sign of a mechanic simply says TALLER MECÁNICO.

I've found that the Ford and Volkswagen dealerships in Mexico give prompt, courteous attention to my car problems, and prices for repairs are, in general, much lower than those in the United States or Canada. I suspect other big-name dealerships give similar satisfactory service. Often they will begin work on your car right away and make repairs in just a few hours, sometimes minutes. Hondas are now manufactured in Mexico, so those parts will become more available.

If your car breaks down on the road, help might already be on the way. Radio-equipped green repair trucks manned by uniformed English-speaking officers patrol the major highways during daylight hours to aid motorists in trouble. These **"Green Angels"** will perform minor repairs and adjustments for free, but you pay for parts and materials.

MINOR ACCIDENTS When possible, many Mexicans drive away from minor accidents to avoid hassles with police. If the police arrive while the involved persons are still at the scene, everyone may be locked in jail until blame is assessed. In any case you have to settle up immediately, which may take days of red tape. Foreigners who don't speak fluent Spanish are at a distinct disadvantage when trying to explain their side of the event. Three steps may help the foreigner who doesn't wish to do as the Mexicans do: If you're in your own car, notify your Mexican insurance company, whose job it is to intervene on your behalf. If you're in a rental car, notify the rental company immediately and ask how to contact the nearest adjuster. (You did buy insurance with the rental—right?) Finally, if all else fails, ask to contact the nearest Green Angel, who may be able to explain to officials that you are covered by insurance.

See also "Mexican Auto Insurance" in "By Car" under "Getting There," above.

PARKING   When you park your car on the street, lock it up and leave nothing within view inside (day or night). I use guarded parking lots, especially at night, to avoid vandalism and break-ins. This way you also avoid parking violations. When pay lots are not available, small boys usually offer to watch your car for you—tip them well on your return.

CAR RENTALS   With some trepidation I wander into the subject of car-rental rules, which change often in Mexico. The best prices are obtained by reserving your car a week in advance in the United States. Mexico City and most other large Mexican cities have rental offices representing the various big firms and some local ones. You'll find rental desks at airports, all major hotels, and many travel agencies. The large firms like Avis, Hertz, National, and Budget have rental offices on main streets as well. Renting a car during a major holiday may prove difficult if all the cars are booked or not returned on time. To avoid being stranded without a vehicle, if possible plan your arrival before the anticipated rush of travelers.

I don't recommend renting a car in Mexico City for one-day excursions from the city. It can be a real hassle, and parking is also a problem.

Cars are easy to rent if you have a charge or credit card (American Express, VISA, MasterCard, and the like), are 25 or over, and have a valid driver's license and passport with you. Without a credit card you must leave a cash deposit, usually a big one. Rent-here/leave-there arrangements are usually simple to make but very costly.

COSTS   Don't underestimate the cost of renting a car. And unfortunately, the devaluation of the peso has not resulted in lower car-rental costs in Mexico. When I checked recently for rental on May 15 (after Easter when rates go down) the basic cost of a one-day rental of a Volkswagen Beetle, with unlimited mileage (but before 15% tax and $15 daily insurance) was $44 in Cancún, $45 in Mexico City, $38 in Puerto Vallarta, $45 in Oaxaca, and $25 in Mérida. Renting by the week gives you a lower daily rate. Avis was offering a basic seven-day weekly rate for a VW Beetle (without tax or insurance) of $180 in Cancún and Puerto Vallarta, $150 in Mérida, and $216 in Mexico City.

So you can see that it makes a difference where you rent, for how long, and when. If you have a choice of renting in Mérida and driving to Cancún, you might save more money than if you rent in Cancún. Mileage-added rates can run the bill up considerably. Car-rental companies usually write up a credit card charge in U.S. dollars. *Important Tip:* Take advantage of Avis's prepay offer. You *prepay* the daily rental by credit card before you go and receive a considerable discount. Under this plan, you pay tax and insurance in Mexico. As an example, working through Avis here in the States, I recently prepaid a week's use of a VW Beetle in Cancún for $167 (before tax and insurance), which averages $23.86 daily. If I had chosen to pay in Cancún *after* using the car, the weekly rate would have been $267, or $38.14 daily (before tax and insurance).

RENTAL CONFIRMATION   Make your reservation directly with the car-rental company. Write down your confirmation number and request that a copy of the confirmation be mailed to you (rent at least a week in advance so the confirmation has time to reach you). Present that confirmation slip when you appear to collect your car. If you're dealing with a U.S. company, the confirmation must be honored, even if the company has to upgrade you to another class of car—don't allow them to send you to another agency. The rental confirmation will also display the agreed-on price, which protects you from being charged more in case there is a price change before you arrive. Insist on the rate printed on the confirmation slip.

DEDUCTIBLES   Be careful—deductibles vary greatly; some are as high as $2,500, which comes out of your pocket immediately in case of car damage. Hertz's deductible is $1,000 on a VW Beetle; Avis's deductible is $500 for the same car. You will be asked to sign two separate credit card vouchers, one for the insurance, which is torn up on your return if there's no damage to the car, and one for the rental. Don't fail to get information about deductibles.

INSURANCE   Many credit-card companies offer their cardholders free rental-car insurance. *Don't use it in Mexico*, for several reasons. Even though insurance policies that specifically cover rental cars are supposedly optional in Mexico, there may be major consequences if you don't have one. First, if you buy insurance, you pay only the deductible, which limits your liability. Second, if you have an accident or your car is vandalized or stolen and you don't have insurance, you'll have to pay for everything before you can leave the rental-car office. This includes the full value of the car if it is unrepairable—a determination made only by the rental-car company. While your credit card may eventually pay your costs, you will have to lay out the money in the meantime. Third, if an accident occurs, everyone may wind up in jail until guilt is determined, and if you are the guilty party, you may not be released from jail until restitution is paid in full to the rental-car owners and to injured persons— made doubly difficult if you have no rental-car insurance. Fourth, if you elect to use your credit-card insurance anyway, the rental company may ask you to leave them with a cash bond, or a credit-card voucher with a high amount filled in.

Insurance is offered in two parts. **Collision and damage** insurance covers your car and others if the accident is your fault, and **personal accident** insurance covers you and anyone in your car. I always take both.

DAMAGE   Always inspect your car carefully, and mark all problem areas using this checklist:

- Hubcaps
- Windshield (for nicks and cracks)
- Tire tread
- Body (for dents, nicks, etc.)
- Fenders (for dents, etc.)
- Muffler (is it smashed?)
- Trim (loose or damaged?)
- Head and taillights
- Fire extinguisher (it should be under the driver's seat, as required by law)
- Spare tire and tools (in the trunk)
- Seat belts (required by law)
- Gas cap
- Outside mirror
- Floor mats

Note every damaged or missing area, no matter how minute, on your rental agreement or you will be charged for all missing or damaged parts, including missing car tags, should the police confiscate your tags for a parking infraction (which is very costly). I can't stress enough how important it is to check your car carefully. A tiny nick in a windshield can grow the length of the glass while in your care, and you'll be charged for the whole windshield if you didn't note the nick at the time of rental. Car companies have attempted to rent me cars with bald tires and tires with bulges;

a car with a license plate that would expire before I returned the car; and cars with missing trim, floor mats, or fire extinguishers. They've also attempted to charge me for dings that were on the auto when I rented it, which they were unable to do because the dings were marked on the agreement.

FINE PRINT   Read the fine print on the back of your rental agreement and note that insurance is invalid if you have an accident while driving on an unpaved road.

TROUBLE NUMBER   One last detail to see to before starting out with a rental car: Be sure you know the rental company's trouble number. Get the direct number to the agency where you rented the car and write down its office hours. The large firms have toll-free numbers, but they may not be well staffed on weekends.

PROBLEMS, PERILS, DEALS   At present, I find the best prices are through Avis, and that's the company I use; generally I am a satisfied customer, though I sometimes have to dig in my heels and insist on proper service. I have had even more difficult problems with other agencies. I have encountered certain kinds of situations within the past four years that could occur with any company. These problems have included an attempt to push me off to a no-name company rather than upgrade me to a more expensive car when a VW Beetle wasn't available; poorly staffed offices with no extra cars, parts, or mechanics in case of a breakdown. Since potential problems are varied, I'd rather deal with a company based in the States so at least I have recourse if I am not satisfied.

SIGNING THE RENTAL AGREEMENT   Once you've agreed on everything, the rental clerk will tally the bill before you leave and you will sign an open credit-card voucher that will be filled in when you return the car, and a credit-card voucher for the amount of the deductible, which will be used only if there is damage. Read the agreement and double-check all the addition. The time to catch mistakes is before you leave, not when you return.

PICKING UP/RETURNING THE CAR   When you rent the car, you agree to pick it up at a certain time and return it at a certain time. If you're late in picking it up or if you cancel the reservation, there are usually penalties—ask what they are when you make the reservation. If you return the car more than an hour late, an expensive hourly rate kicks in. Also, you must return the car with the same amount of gas in the tank as it had when you drove out. If you don't, the charge added to your bill for the difference is much more than for gas bought at a public station.

BY RV

Touring Mexico by recreational vehicle (RV) is a popular way of seeing the country. Many hotels have hookups. RV parks, although not as plentiful as those in the United States, are available throughout the country.

BY FERRY

Ferries connect Baja California at La Paz and Santa Rosalía with the mainland at Topolobampo and Mazatlán. In the Yucatán, ferries also take passengers between Puerto Juárez and Isla Mujeres, Playa Linda and Isla Mujeres, and Playa del Carmen and Cozumel.

BY HITCHHIKING

You see Mexicans hitching rides (for example, at crossroads after getting off a bus), but as a general rule hitchhiking isn't done. It's especially unwise for foreigners, who may be thought to carry large amounts of cash.

9 Recommended Books

An endless number of books have been written on the history, culture, and archaeology of Mexico and Central America. I have listed those I especially enjoyed.

HISTORY   Dennis Tedlock produced an elegant translation of the *Popul Vuh*, a collection of ancient Maya mythological tales (Simon & Schuster, 1985). *A Short History of Mexico* (Doubleday, 1962) by J. Patrick McHenry is a concise historical account. A remarkably readable and thorough college textbook is *The Course of Mexican History* (Oxford University Press, 1987) by Michael C. Meyer and William L. Sherman. Bernal Díaz's *The Conquest of New Spain* (Shoe String, 1988) is the famous story of the Mexican Conquest written by Cortés's lieutenant. *The Crown of Mexico* (Holt, Rinehart & Winston, 1971) by Joan Haslip, a biography of Maximilian and Carlota, reads like a novel. Eric Wolf's *Sons of the Shaking Earth* (University of Chicago Press) is the best single-volume introduction to Mexican history and culture that I know. *Ancient Mexico; An Overview* (University of New Mexico Press, 1985) by Jaime Litvak, is a short, very readable history of pre-Hispanic Mexico.

The Wind That Swept Mexico (University of Texas Press, 1971) by Anita Brenner, is a classic illustrated account of the Mexican Revolution. Early this century Charles Flandrau wrote the classic *Viva Mexico: A Traveller's Account of Life in Mexico* (Eland Books, 1985), a blunt and humorous description of Mexico. Jonathan Kandell's *La Capital, Biography of Mexico City* (Random House, 1988) is assiduously researched, yet wonderfully readable.

Life in Mexico: Letters of Fanny Calderón de la Barca (Doubleday, 1966), edited and annotated by Howard T. Fisher and Marion Hall Fisher, is as lively and entertaining today as when it first appeared in 1843, but the editor's illustrated and annotated update makes it even more contemporary. Scottish-born Fanny was married to the Spanish ambassador to Mexico, and the letters are the accounts of her experiences. *My Heart Lies South* by Elizabeth Borton de Treviño (1953) is a humorous, tender, and insightful autobiographical account of the life of an American woman married to a Mexican in Monterrey; it begins in the 1930s.

Several modern writers have attempted to view Mexican culture through the lens of history. Harry A. Franck's *Trailing Cortés Through Mexico* (Frederick A. Stokes, 1935) and Mathew J. Bruccoli's *Reconquest of Mexico* (Vanguard Press, 1974) pursue the conquest route of Cortés, interweaving history with customs of rural and city life of this century.

CONTEMPORARY MEXICAN LIFE   *Five Families* (Basic Books, 1979) and *Children of Sanchez* (Random House, 1979), both by Oscar Lewis, are sociological studies written in the late 1950s about typical Mexican families. Irene Nicholson's *Mexican and Central American Mythology* (Peter Bedrick Books, 1983) is a concise illustrated book that simplifies the subject.

A good but controversial all-around introduction to contemporary Mexico and its people is *Distant Neighbors: A Portrait of the Mexicans* (Random House, 1984) by Alan Riding. In a more personal vein is Patrick Oster's *The Mexicans: A Personal Portrait of the Mexican People* (HarperCollins 1989), a reporter's insightful account of ordinary Mexican people. A book with valuable insights into the Mexican character is *The Labyrinth of Solitude* (Grove Press, 1985) by Octavio Paz. The best single source of information on Mexican music, dance, and mythology is Frances Toor's *A Treasury of Mexican Folkways* (Crown, 1967).

Anyone going to San Cristóbal de las Casas, Chiapas, should first read *Living Maya* (Harry N. Abrams, 1987) by Walter F. Morris, with excellent photographs by

Jeffrey J. Foxx, all about the Maya living today in the state of Chiapas. Peter Canby's *The Heart of the Sky: Travels Among the Maya* (Kodansha International, 1994) takes readers on a rare but rugged journey as he searches to understand the real issues facing the Maya of Mexico and Guatemala today. For some fascinating background on northern Mexico and the Copper Canyon, read *Unknown Mexico* (Dover Press, 1987) by Carl Lumholtz, an intrepid writer and photographer around the turn of the century.

PRE-HISPANIC MEXICO   Anyone heading for Yucatán should first read the wonderfully entertaining accounts of travel in that region by the 19th-century traveler, New York lawyer, and amateur archaeologist John L. Stephens. His book *Incidents of Travel in Central America, Chiapas and Yucatán*, and also the account of his second trip, *Incidents of Travel in Yucatán*, have been reprinted by Dover complete with Frederick Catherwood's original illustrations. Dover has also released Diego de Landa's *Yucatán Before and After the Conquest* (Dover, 1978), written in the 1560s. Friar Diego's account is a detailed description of Maya daily life, much of which has remained the same from his time until today. Another must is *The Maya* (Thames and Hudson, 1987) by Michael Coe, which is helpful in relating to the different Maya periods. *A Forest of Kings: The Untold Story of the Ancient Maya* (William Morrow, 1990) by Linda Schele and David Freidel, uses the written history of Maya hieroglyphs to tell the dynastic history of selected Maya sites. You'll never view the sky the same after reading *Maya Cosmos: Three Thousand Years on the Shaman's Path* (William Morrow, 1993) by David Freidel, Linda Schele, and Joy Parker whose personal insights and scholarly work take us along a very readable path into the amazing sky-centered world of the Maya. *The Blood of Kings: Dynasty and Ritual in Maya Art* (George Braziller, 1986) by Linda Schele and Mary Ellen Miller, is a pioneer work and unlocks the bloody history of the Maya. The most comprehensive guide to Maya ruins is Joyce Kelly's *An Archeological Guide to Mexico's Yucatán Peninsula* (University of Oklahoma, 1993).

Michael Coe's *Mexico: From the Olmecs to the Aztecs* (Thames and Hudson, 1994), takes us through the latest discoveries and theories regarding Mexico's ancient Indian cultures (but excludes the Maya, which are covered in his other book *The Maya,* mentioned above). For the latest on the mysterious Olmec culture don't miss *The Olmec World: Ritual and Rulership* (The Art Museum, Princeton University and Harry N. Abrahms, 1996), the splendid catalog of a major exhibition of privately owned Olmec art in the United States. Major Olmec scholars in the United States provided essays on current theories about Mexico's little-studied "mother culture."

Several fictionalized accounts of Aztec life have been written. These include Gary Jenning's *Aztec* (Avon, 1981), a superbly researched and colorfully written account of Aztec life before and after the Conquest. Equally revealing is *The Luck of Huemac,* by Daniel Peters (Random House, 1981), a compelling novel about four generations of an Aztec family between the years 1428 and 1520.

ART & ARCHITECTURE   A book that tells the story of the Indians' "painted books" is *The Mexican Codices and Their Extraordinary History* (Ediciones Lara, 1985) by María Sten. *Mexico Splendors of Thirty Centuries* (Metropolitan Museum of Art, 1990), the catalog of the 1991 traveling exhibition, is a wonderful resource on Mexico's art from 1500 B.C. through the 1950s. Another superb catalog, *Images of Mexico: The Contribution of Mexico to 20th Century Art* (Dallas Museum of Art, 1987) is a fabulously illustrated and detailed account of Mexican art gathered from collections around the world. Elizabeth Wilder Weismann's *Art and Time in Mexico: From the Conquest to the Revolution* (HarperCollins, 1985), illustrated with

351 photographs, covers Mexican religious, public, and private architecture with excellent photos and text. *Casa Mexicana* (Stewart, Tabori & Chang, 1989) by Tim Street-Porter, takes readers through the interiors of some of Mexico's finest homes-turned-museums or public buildings and private homes using color photographs. *Mexican Interiors* (Architectural Book Publishing Co., 1962) by Verna Cook Shipway and Warren Shipway, uses black-and-white photographs to highlight architectural details from homes all over Mexico.

FOLK ART Chloè Sayer's *Costumes of Mexico* (University of Texas Press, 1985) is a beautifully illustrated and written work. *Mexican Masks* (University of Texas Press, 1980) by Donald Cordry, based on the author's collection and travels, remains the definitive work on Mexican masks. Cordry's *Mexican Indian Costumes* (University of Texas Press, 1968) is another classic on the subject. Carlos Espejel wrote both *Mexican Folk Ceramics* and *Mexican Folk Crafts* (Editorial Blume, 1975 and 1978), two comprehensive books that explore crafts state by state. *Folk Treasures of Mexico* (Harry N. Abrams, 1990) by Marion Oettinger, curator of Folk and Latin American Art at the San Antonio Museum of Art, is the fascinating illustrated story behind the 3,000-piece Mexican folk-art collection amassed by Nelson Rockefeller over a 50-year period, and also includes much information about individual folk artists. The fantastically colorful sculpted animals and figures of Oaxaca's wood-carvers is the subject of *Oaxacan Woodcarving* (Chronicle Books, 1993), by Shepard Barbash and photographed by Vicki Ragan is both a finely illustrated exposition of colorful work from wood-carvers in Oaxaca, and an insightful glimpse of the rural communitities where the artists live.

NATURE *A Naturalist's Mexico* (Texas A&M University Press, 1992), by Roland H. Wauer, is a fabulous guide to birding in Mexico. *A Hiker's Guide to Mexico's Natural History* (Mountaineers, 1995), by Jim Conrad, covers Mexican flora and fauna and tells how to find the easy-to-reach and out-of-the-way spots he describes. Most comprehensive of all the birding guide books is *A Guide to the Birds of Mexico and North Central America* (Oxford University Press, 1995), by Steve N. Ottowell and Sophie Webb, an encyclopedic volume with hundreds of color illustrations. *Peterson Field Guides: Mexican Birds* (Houghton Mifflin), by Roger Tory Peterson and Edward L. Chalif, is an excellent guide to the country's birds. *Birds of the Yucatán* (Amigos de Sian Ka'an) has color illustrations and descriptions of 100 birds found primarily in the Yucatán peninsula. *A Guide to Mexican Mammals and Reptiles* (Minutiae Mexicana), by Norman Pelham Wright and Dr. Bernardo Villa Ramírez, is a small but useful guide to some of the country's wildlife.

10 FAST FACTS: Mexico

Abbreviations Dept.=apartments; Apdo.=post office box; Av.=Avenida; Calz.=Calzada (boulevard). "C" on faucets stands for *caliente* (hot), and "F" stands for *fría* (cold). pB (*planta baja*) means ground floor.

Business Hours In general, Mexican businesses in larger cities are open between 9am and 7pm; in smaller towns many close between 2 and 4pm. Most are closed on Sunday. Bank hours are Monday through Friday from 9 or 9:30am to 1pm. A few banks in large cities have extended hours.

Camera/Film Buying a camera can be inconvenient in Mexico, but there are cheap, imported models available. Film costs about the same as in the United States.

Take full advantage of your 12-roll film allowance by bringing 36-exposure rolls. Also bring extra batteries: AA batteries are generally available, but AAA and small disk batteries for cameras and watches are rare. A few places in resort areas advertise color film developing, but it might be cheaper to wait until you get home.

Important note about camera use: Tourists wishing to use a video or still camera at any archaeological site in Mexico and at many museums operated by the Instituto de Historia y Antropología (INAH) may be required to pay $3.50–$5.50 per video camera and/or still camera in their possession at each site or museum visited. (In some museums camera use is not permitted.) If you want to use either kind of camera or both, the fee must be paid for each piece of equipment. When you pay the fee, your camera will be tagged, and you are permitted to use the equipment. Watchmen are often posted to see that untagged cameras are not used. Such fees are noted in the listings for specific sites and museums.

It's courteous to ask permission before photographing anyone. In some areas, such as around San Cristóbal de las Casas, Chiapas, there are other restrictions on photographing people and villages. Such restrictions are noted in specific cities, towns, and sites.

Cigarettes Cigarettes are much cheaper in Mexico than in the United States, even U.S. brands, if you buy them at a grocery or drugstore and not a hotel tobacco shop.

Doctors/Dentists Every embassy and consulate is prepared to recommend local doctors and dentists with good training and modern equipment; some of the doctors and dentists even speak English. See the list of embassies and consulates under "Embassies/Consulates," below, and remember that at the larger ones, a duty officer is on call at all times. Hotels with a large foreign clientele are often prepared to recommend English-speaking doctors. Almost all first-class hotels in Mexico have a doctor on call.

Drug Laws Briefly, don't use or possess illegal drugs in Mexico. Mexicans have no tolerance for drug users, and jail is their solution, with very little hope of getting out until the sentence (usually a long one) is completed or heavy fines or bribes are paid. (*Important Note:* It isn't uncommon to be befriended by a fellow user, only to be turned in by that "friend"—he's collected a bounty for turning you in. It's a no-win situation!) Bring prescription drugs in their original containers. If possible, pack a copy of the original prescription with the generic name of the drug.

I don't need to go into detail about the penalties for illegal drug possession upon return to the United States. Customs officials are also on the lookout for diet drugs sold in Mexico, possession of which could also land you in a U.S. jail because they are illegal here. If you buy antibiotics over the counter (which you can do in Mexico)—say, for a sinus infection—and still have some left, you probably won't be hassled by U.S. customs.

Drugstores Drugstores (*farmacías*) will sell you just about anything you want, with a prescription or without one. However, over-the-counter medicines such as aspirin, decongestants, or antihistamines are rarely sold. Most drugstores are open Monday through Saturday from 8am to 8pm. If you need to buy medicines after normal hours, ask for the *farmacía de turno*—pharmacies take turns staying open during off-hours. Find any drugstore, and in its window may be a card showing the schedule of which drugstore will be open at what time.

Electricity The electrical system in Mexico is 110 volts, 60 cycles, as in the United States and Canada. However, in reality it may cycle more slowly and overheat your appliances. To compensate, select a medium or low speed for hairdryers, and curling irons, though they may still overheat. Older hotels still have electrical outlets for flat two-prong plugs; you'll need an adapter for using any modern electrical apparatus that has an enlarged end on one prong or that has three prongs to insert. Many first-class and deluxe hotels have the three-holed outlets (*trifacicos* in Spanish). Those that don't may loan adapters, but to be sure, it's always better to carry your own.

Embassies/Consulates They provide valuable lists of doctors and lawyers, as well as regulations concerning marriages in Mexico. Contrary to popular belief, your embassy cannot get you out of a Mexican jail, provide postal or banking services, or fly you home when you run out of money. Consular officers can provide you with advice on most matters and problems, however. Most countries have a representative embassy in Mexico City, and many have consular offices or representatives in the provinces.

The Embassy of **Australia** in Mexico City is at Jaime Balmes 11, plaza polanco, Torre B (☎ **5/395-9988** or 566-3053); it's open Monday through Friday from 8am to 1pm.

The Embassy of **Canada** in Mexico City is at Schiller 529, in polanco (☎ **5/724-7900**); it's open Monday through Friday from 9am to 1pm and 2 to 5pm (at other times the name of a duty officer is posted on the embassy door). In Acapulco, the Canadian consulate is in the Hotel Club del Sol, Costera Miguel Alemán, at the corner of Reyes Católicos (☎ **74/85-6621**); it's open Monday through Friday from 8am to 3pm.

The Embassy of **New Zealand** in Mexico City is at Homero 229, 8th floor (☎ **5/250-5999** or 250-5777); it's open Monday through Thursday from 9am to 2pm and 3 to 5pm and Friday from 9am to 2pm.

The Embassy of the **United Kingdom** in Mexico City is at Lerma 71, at Río Sena (☎ **5/207-2569** or 207-2593); it's open Monday through Friday from 9am to 2pm. There are honorary consuls in the following cities: Acapulco, Hotel Las Brisas, Carretera Escénica (☎ **74/84-6605** or 84-1580); Ciudad Juárez, Calle Fresno 185 (☎ **16/7-5791**); Guadalajara, paulino Navarro 1165 (☎ **3/611-1678**); Mérida, Calle 58 no. 450 (☎ **99/28-6152** or 28-3962); Monterrey, privada de Tamazunchale 104 (☎ **83/78-2565**); Oaxaca, Ev. Hidalgo 817 (☎ **951/6-5600**); Tampico, 2 de Enero 102-A-Sur (☎ **12/12-9784** or 12-9817); Tijuana, Blv. Salinas 1500 (☎ **66/81-7323**); and Veracruz, Emparan 200 pB (☎ **29/31-0955**).

The Embassy of the **United States** in Mexico City is next to the Hotel María Isabel Sheraton at paseo de la Reforma 305, at the corner of Río Danubio (☎ **5/211-0042**). There are U.S. Consulates General in Ciudad Juárez, López Mateos 924-N (☎ **16/13-4048**); Guadalajara, progreso 175 (☎ **3/625-2998**); Monterrey, Av. Constitución 411 poniente (☎ **83/45-2120**); and Tijuana, Tapachula 96 (☎ **66/81-7400**). There are U.S. Consulates in Hermosillo, Av Monterrey 141 (☎ **621/7-2375;** Matamoros, Av. primera 2002 (☎ **88/12-4402**); Mérida, paseo Montejo 453 (☎ **99/25-6366**); and Nuevo Laredo, Calle Allende 3330 (☎ **871/4-0512**). In addition, Consular Agencies are in Acapulco (☎ **74/85-6600** or 5-7207); Cabo San Lucas (☎ **114/3-3566**); Cancún (☎ **98/84-2411** or 84-6399); Mazatlán (☎ **69/13-4444**, ext. 285); Oaxaca (☎ **951/4-3054**); puerto Vallarta (☎ **322/2-0069**); San Luis Potosí (☎ **481/2-1528**); San Miguel de Allende (☎ **465/2-2357** or 2-0068); Tampico (☎ **12/13-2217**); and Veracruz (☎ **29/31-5821**).

Emergencies The 24-hour Tourist Help Line in Mexico City is **5/250-0151.**

Legal Aid International Legal Defense Counsel, 111 S. 15th St., 24th Floor, Packard Building, Philadelphia, PA 19102 (☎ **215/977-9982**), is a law firm specializing in legal difficulties of Americans abroad. See also "Embassies/ Consulates" and "Emergencies," above.

Mail   Mail service south of the border tends to be slow and undependable—though it is improving. If you're on a two-week vacation, it's not a bad idea to buy and mail your postcards in the arrivals lounge at the airport to give them maximum time to get home before you do.

For the most reliable and convenient mail service, have your letters sent to you c/o the American Express offices in major cities, which will receive and forward mail for you if you are one of its clients (a travel-club card or an American Express traveler's check is proof). They charge a fee if you wish to have your mail forwarded.

If you don't use American Express, have your mail sent to you care of Lista de Correos (General Delivery), followed by the Mexican city, state, and country. In Mexican post offices there may actually be a "lista" posted near the Lista de Correos window bearing the names of all those for whom mail has been received. If there's no list, ask and show them your passport so they can riffle through and look for your letters. If the city has more than one office, you'll have to go to the central post office—not a branch—to get your mail. By the way, in many post offices they return mail to the sender if it has been there for more than 10 days. Make sure people don't send you letters too early.

In major Mexican cities there are also branches of such U.S. express mail companies as UPS, Federal Express, and DHL, as well as private mail boxes such as Mail Boxes Etc.

Newspapers/Magazines   Two English-language newspapers *The News* and *The Times* are published in Mexico City and carry world news and commentaries, plus a calendar of the day's events including concerts, art shows, and plays. Newspaper kiosks in larger Mexican cities will carry a selection of English-language magazines.

Pets   Taking a pet into Mexico entails a lot of red tape. Consult the Mexican Government Tourist Office nearest you (see "Information, Entry Requirements & Money," above, in this chapter).

Police   Police in general in Mexico are to be suspected rather than trusted; however, you'll find many who are quite honest and helpful with directions, even going so far as to lead you where you want to go.

Rest Rooms   The best bet in Mexico is to use rest rooms in restaurants and hotel public areas. Always carry your own toilet paper and hand soap, neither of which is in great supply in Mexican rest rooms. Public facilities, usually near the central market, vary in cleanliness and usually have an attendant who charges a few pesos for toilet use and a few squares of toilet paper. Pemex gas stations have improved the maintenance of their rest rooms along major highways. No matter where you are, even if the toilet flushes with paper, there'll be a waste basket for paper disposal. Many people come from homes without plumbing and are not accustomed to toilets that will take paper, so they'll throw used paper on the floor rather than put it in the toilet; thus, you'll see the basket no matter what quality of place you are in. On the other hand, the water pressure in many establishments is so low that paper won't go down. Thus the disposal basket again—which can be a disgusting sight. But better that than on the floor. There's often a sign telling you whether to flush paper.

Taxes   There's a 15% IVA tax on goods and services in most of Mexico, and it's supposed to be included in the posted price. This tax is 10% in Cancún, Cozumel, and Los Cabos.

Telephone/Fax Telephone area codes are gradually being changed all over the country. The change may affect the area code and first digit or only the area code. Some cities are even adding exchanges and changing whole numbers. Often a personal or business telephone number will be changed without notification to the subscriber. Telephone courtesy messages announcing a phone number change are nonexistent in Mexico. You can try operator assistance for difficult-to-reach numbers, but often the phone company doesn't inform its operators of recent changes. People who have fax machines often turn them off when their offices are closed. Many fax numbers are also regular telephone numbers; you have to ask whoever answers your call for the fax tone (*por favor darme el tono por fax*). Telephone etiquette in Mexico does not prompt the answerer to offer to take a message or to have someone return your call; you'll have to make these suggestions yourself. In addition, etiquette doesn't necessarily demand that a business answer its phone by saying its name; often you'll have to ask if you have the right place.

Time Central standard time prevails throughout most of Mexico. The west-coast states of Sonora, Sinaloa, and parts of Nayarit are on mountain standard time. The state of Baja California Norte is on Pacific time, but Baja California Sur is on mountain time. Though adoption of **Daylight Saving Time** was announced at least twice before, and didn't happen, beginning in October 1996, it will occur—by presidential decree.

Water Most hotels have decanters or bottles of purified water in the rooms, and the better hotels have either purified water from regular taps or special taps marked *agua purificada*. In the resort areas, especially the Yucatán, hoteliers are beginning to charge for in-room bottled water. If the water in your room is an expensive imported variety such as Evian, for sure there's an extra charge for using it. Virtually any hotel, restaurant, or bar will bring you purified water if you specifically request it, but you'll usually be charged for it. Bottled purified water is sold widely at drugstores and grocery stores.

3

Baja California Sur

Georgia O'Keeffe probably would have loved Baja's painted-desert colors and sculpted terrain beside the sea, but others might find it barren. Baja is a place that, depending on your mood, can be boring or breathtakingly beautiful. Its austere but dramatic landscape resembles the American West placed beside a brilliant blue sea. Or it brings to mind a moonscape dotted with palm trees and turquoise bays. Scattered along its coastline and tucked among its mountains are tropical hamlets and little towns planted like oases at the end of a long road.

A peninsula longer than Italy, Baja California stretches 876 miles from Tijuana at its northern edge to Los Cabos at its southern tip. Its desert terrain rises from both coasts—the Pacific Ocean to the west and the Sea of Cortez to the east—to form a spine of craggy mountains that can change from burnt sienna to vermilion, orange, purple, apricot, or rose, depending on the time of day. Whole forests of majestic cardon cactus, spiky Joshua trees, and spindly ocotillo bushes populate this raw, untamed landscape where volcanoes once roared. Baja's wide-open spaces seem to echo with geological time: It's easy to imagine the toothy Sierras heaving up while seas rolled across the flatlands at their feet.

Baja has always been a land of striking opposites and paradox. It has some of the most beautiful beaches in Mexico, many isolated and blissfully unpopulated; others lined with semipermanent trailers and RVs that have settled in with their satellite dishes on the sand. Though it's the southern playground of America's west coast, Baja can seem like one of the least crowded corners of Mexico. The terrain and climate can be as inviting as a Caribbean isle or as unforgiving as a norther.

Baja is a land of secrets, a place that takes patience to penetrate. Its mountains are riddled with caves painted with bold prehistoric pictures and petroglyphs, but reaching them is an adventure requiring horses, mules, or Jeeps. A wealth of marine life plays beneath the waves: Besides the flying marlin and other game fish that have lured wealthy anglers to this peninsula since the 1950s, there are cavorting dolphins, colonies of sea lions, giant manta rays, and lagoons full of whales that migrate to Baja's bays in the winter to breed. This land's hidden beauty brings out the explorer in visitors.

The superb sportfishing that is still Baja's main draw has been imperiled by overzealous commercial fishing, especially from long-liner vessels that cruise the Sea of Cortez, dragging thousands of fishing lines. Marlin, tuna, dorado, shark, and swordfish are their targets, but dolphins, manta rays, and any other sea creatures caught along the way are destined to die as well. Environmentalists and sportfishing operators are keeping a close eye on boats they encounter at sea and continue to protest the use of long-liners.

Fortunately for travelers, Baja is much more than an angler's paradise. Sailing, kayaking, windsurfing, hiking, whale watching, spelunking to explore ancient cave paintings, and camping on isolated, wild beaches draw more and more visitors to Baja each year. Golf has become a major attraction in Los Cabos, where at least four championship courses are open for play.

Many of Baja's best-loved activities are difficult to organize independently. Most can be arranged through local travel agencies, but this adds to the price of playing in Baja. Also keep in mind that many organized trips require a minimum of four to six people; consider traveling with a small group of friends.

Shopping, especially in Cabo San Lucas and La Paz, has become much more varied and interesting in the past few years, as have the dining and lodging options.

EXPLORING BAJA CALIFORNIA SUR

If you're driving on Mexico Highway 1 (the Transpeninsular Highway) from Tijuana at the U.S. border in Baja California Norte to Cabo San Lucas at the southern tip of the Baja (1,125 miles), count on 25 hours of driving time (excluding stops) and at least two overnight stops. The distances are vast, and there are numerous side trips to explore isolated coves and beaches, to observe whales in the bays, and to inspect caves painted with ancient pictures—all of which lengthen the journey.

With the exception of such detours, you'll stay on Highway 1 until you're south of La Paz, where Highway 1 goes to San José del Cabo, and Highway 19 branches off to Cabo San Lucas. The two-lane highway is reasonably well maintained (watch for occasional potholes and rocks) but has no shoulders, so drive carefully and fill your tank at every opportunity—the stretches between gas stations can be long. Livestock is not fenced, so you should never drive after dark.

There are express buses that start in Tijuana and go all the way to the capital, La Paz, with minimal intermediate stops. In La Paz you change for one of the many buses south to Los Cabos (San José del Cabo and Cabo San Lucas) or points in between. Bus service is frequent enough that you can use it to see Baja's main towns. The buses have improved dramatically in the past few years, with deluxe service including air-conditioning, reclining seats, restrooms on board, and even movies on TV.

Ferryboats operate between La Paz (Pichilingue dock) and Los Mochis (Topolobampo dock); between La Paz and Mazatlán; and between Santa Rosalía and Guaymas. One ferry system, owned by the private company SEMATUR, uses several large, multideck ships that carry from 100 to nearly 700 passengers, as well as cars and freight. Several companies offer special-interest tours in Baja, from kayaking, scuba diving, and whale watching to exploring Baja's prehistoric cave paintings by donkey. See "La Paz," below, for details on these companies.

Baja brings out the creativity of budget-minded travelers, for as a rule its price structure is rather upscale. Baja first became popular as a private fishing club for wealthy Americans. Some of this country-club ambience still exists, especially in Los Cabos, and has tended to inflate prices. Budget hotels and restaurants exist but are fewer and farther between than in many other parts of Mexico.

Travelers driving foreign-registered vehicles in Baja have little trouble with customs until they try to take their cars on the ferries to the mainland. In such cases drivers must meet all the requirements listed in "Crossing the Border with Your Car" (see "Getting There" in chapter 2). Tourism officials say it is best to complete the vehicle permit paperwork at the border when you first enter Baja.

BAJA'S UNPREDICTABLE WEATHER   Baja is a land of extremes: It can be skillet-hot in summer and cold and windy in winter—so windy that fishing and other nautical expeditions may be grounded for a few days. Though winter can be warm enough for water sports, bring a wetsuit along if you're a serious diver or snorkeler, as well as a change of warm clothes for unexpectedly chilly weather. Rather than setting your heart on one activity, such as fishing or whale watching, have some alternatives in mind.

During the rainy season, August through October, rains on the peninsula may be heavy enough to cause flash flooding. Motorists may be stranded in bumper-to-bumper traffic for hours. Always travel with drinking water and food.

THE PESO IN BAJA   Baja seems impervious to peso devaluations, since most restaurants and many hotels (even budget hotels) quote prices in dollars. Prices are set more on what the traffic will bear than on what the peso is doing against the dollar, or on the actual cost of doing business. It's true, however, that compared to mainland Mexico, there's little agriculture in Baja, and most foodstuffs (and other daily required objects), must be shipped in, adding to the cost. Unlike elsewhere in Mexico, where most posted prices include tax, in Baja, most posted prices don't include the 10% federal tax (it's added to your bill), and many places add an additional 10% to 15% for service. (Whether tax is or isn't included is usually in fine print at the bottom of a price sheet.) Almost always the price will be better in pesos, so ask for the peso price and pay in pesos when possible.

1 Los Cabos

Los Cabos means "The Capes" and refers to **two resort towns** that perch on the southern tip of Baja 22 miles apart: **San José del Cabo** and **Cabo San Lucas.** Because each has its own distinctive character and attractions, I have treated them separately. It is possible to stay in one and make a day-trip to the other.

The twisting, winding stretch of highway between the two towns, with its drop-dead clifftop vistas, is commonly called the **Corridor.** The highway has been widened to four lanes and is still being refined. The construction of several large-scale resort developments along the Corridor is drastically changing the wild terrain. Some of the area's most dramatic beaches and coves lie along this road, and the view is outstanding in January and February, when gray whales often spout close to shore. You'll need a car to explore this area thoroughly; consider renting one for a day.

Note: The **one airport** that serves both towns is $7^1/2$ miles northwest of San José del Cabo and 22 miles northeast of Cabo San Lucas.

SAN JOSÉ DEL CABO
122 miles SE of La Paz, 22 miles NE of Cabo San Lucas, 1,100 miles SE of Tijuana

San José del Cabo retains the air of a provincial Mexican village, with one- and two-story pastel buildings crowding the narrow streets and a shady plaza, church, and bandstand at its heart. This town of 24,000 seems older and more typically Mexican than Cabo San Lucas, and even though it does have a modest nightlife, San José is the more sedate of the two Cabos.

ESSENTIALS
GETTING THERE & DEPARTING   By Plane   Aero California (☎ 3-0848 at the airport), has nonstop or direct flights from Los Angeles, Tijuana, and

San José del Cabo

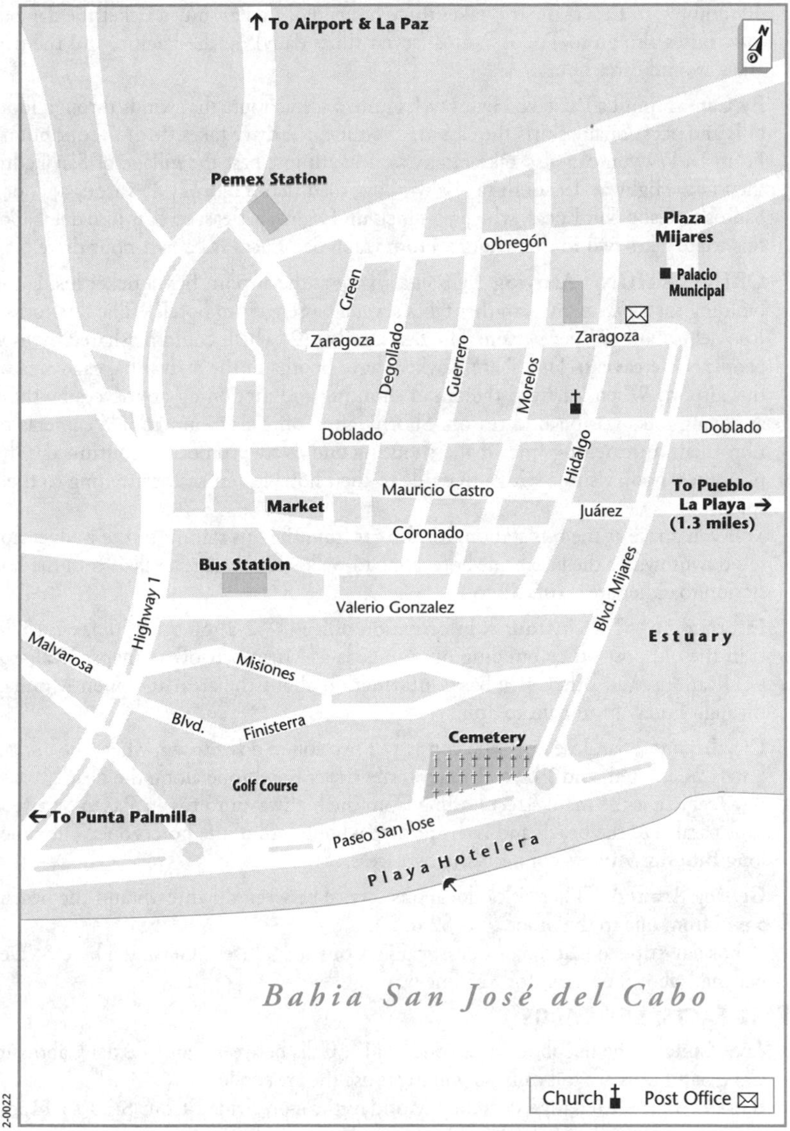

To Airport & La Paz
Pemex Station
Plaza Mijares
Palacio Municipal
Obregón
Green
Zaragoza
Degollado
Guerrero
Morelos
Zaragoza
Doblado
Doblado
Hidalgo
Mauricio Castro
To Pueblo La Playa (1.3 miles)
Market
Juárez
Coronado
Bus Station
Blvd. Mijares
Highway 1
Valerio Gonzalez
Estuary
Malvarosa
Misiones
Blvd.
Finisterra
Cemetery
Golf Course
To Punta Palmilla
Paseo San Jose
Playa Hotelera
Bahia San José del Cabo
Church
Post Office
2-0022

Phoenix; **Alaska Airlines** (☎ **2-1015,** 2-1016, or 2-0959 at the airport), flies from Los Angeles, San Diego, Seattle, and San Francisco; **Continental** (☎ **2-3880**), flies from Houston; **Mexicana** (☎ **2-0606** or 2-1530) has direct or connecting flights from Denver, Guadalajara, Los Angeles, Mexico City, Puerto Vallarta, and Mazatlán.

By Bus The bus station (Terminal de Autobuses) on Valerio González a block east of Highway 1 (☎ **2-1100**), is open daily from 5:30am to 7pm—though buses can arrive and depart later. The company **Aguila** operates first- and second-class buses between Cabo San Lucas and La Paz almost hourly from 7am to 7pm (for points farther north you usually change buses in La Paz). The trip to Cabo San Lucas takes

40 minutes; to La Paz the trip takes three hours. For La Paz, buy a ticket the day before. Buses also go to Todos Santos (seven times daily) on the Pacific, and the trip takes around three hours.

By Car   From La Paz take Highway 1 south, a scenic route that winds through foothills and occasionally skirts the eastern coastline; the drive takes three to four hours. From La Paz you can also take Highway 1 south just past the village of San Pedro then take Highway 19 south (a less winding road than Highway 1) through Todos Santos to Cabo San Lucas, where you pick up Highway 1 east to San José del Cabo; this route takes two to three hours. From Cabo San Lucas it's a half-hour drive.

ORIENTATION   Arriving   Upon arriving at the airport, buy a ticket inside the building for a *colectivo* (a van that takes several passengers to hotels). The fare to San José del Cabo is $7 per person. The taxi fare is $12, which could be shared by four people. **One caveat:** Timeshare hawkers have booths in the arrival/baggage area of this airport. When I arrived the din of shouting and motioning at arrivees by these annoying folks was beyond reason. Shortly after, officials mounted TV cameras to film them, threatening fines if the shouting and overt promotion continued. The promoters hook visitors with a free ride to their hotel in return for listening to their spiel.

If you arrive at the bus station, it's too far from the bus station to the budget hotels downtown or the beachside hotel zone to walk with luggage. A taxi from the bus station to either area costs $2 to $4.

Information   The city **tourist information office** (☎ 2-2960 ext. 150; fax 2-1570) is in the old post office building on Zaragoza at Mijares. It offers maps, local free publications, and other very basic information about the area. It's open Monday through Friday from 8am to 3pm.

City Layout   San José del Cabo consists of two zones: **downtown,** where the budget hotels are located, and **Playa Hotelera,** the ritzier hotel zone along the beach.

Zaragoza is the main street leading from the highway into town; **Paseo San José** runs parallel to the beach and is the principal boulevard of the hotel zone. The mile-long **Bulevar Mijares** connects the two areas.

Getting Around   There is no local bus service between downtown and the beach; a **taxi** from one to the other costs $2 to $4.

For day-trips to Cabo San Lucas, catch a **bus** for $2 (see "Getting There & Departing," above) or a cab for $25 one way.

FAST FACTS: LOS CABOS

Area Code   The telephone area code is 114. Calls between San José del Cabo and Cabo San Lucas are toll calls, so you must use the area code.

Banks   Banks exchange currency Monday through Friday from 8:30 to 11am. There are two banks on Zaragoza between Morelos and Degollado.

Beach Safety   Of all the beaches in San Jose del Cabo (even those fronting the Zona Hotelera), only Playa la Puebla, a public beach, is safe for swimming.

Mosquito Repellent   Gnats, mosquitos, and flies often appear without warning. Be prepared with a remedy to slap on in an instant.

Municipal Market   It's on Mauricio Castro and Green, two long blocks south of the main street, Zaragoza. It's short on handcrafts but long on produce and local color.

Post Office   The Correos, on Mijares at Valerio Gonzalez on the south side of town, is open Monday through Friday from 8am to noon and 2 to 6pm and Saturday from 8 to 11am.

Telephone Long-distance calls can be made from the offices on Zaragoza near Morelos and Doblado opposite the hospital; the offices are open daily 8am–9pm.

FUN ON & OFF THE BEACH

San José del Cabo is a fine place to unwind, play golf, shop, and absorb authentic Mexican flavor. Although the area is ideal for water sports, the currents and undertow make swimming risky at Playa Hotelera, the town beach. Only Playa la Puebla is safe for swimming. At the moment San José has no marina, and ecological concerns have halted the construction of one between the town beach and Pueblo La Playa. Beach aficionados who want to explore the beautiful coves and beaches along the 22-mile coast between the two Cabos will have to bear the cost of a rental car ($45 per day and up). Frequent bus service between San José del Cabo and Cabo San Lucas makes it possible to take in the pleasures of both towns (see "Getting There & Departing," above).

FESTIVALS The festival of the patron saint of San José del Cabo is celebrated on **March 19** with a fair, music, dancing, feasting, horse races, and cockfights. **June 19** is the festival of the patron saint of San Bartolo, a village 62 miles north. **July 25** is the festival of the patron saint of Santiago, a village 34 miles north.

BEACHES The nearest beach safe for swimming is **Pueblo la Playa** (also called "La Playita"), located about 2 miles east of town: From Bulevar Mijares, turn east at the small sign PUEBLO LA PLAYA and follow the dusty dirt road through cane fields and palms to a small village and beautiful beach where a number of *pangas* (skiffs) belonging to local fishermen are pulled ashore. The Hotel La Playita's adjacent restaurant (see "Where to Stay" below) offers the only formal sustenance on the beach. There are no shade palapas. A taxi to Puebla la Playa beach from San José costs about $3.

Estero San José, a nature reserve with at least 270 species of birds, is located between Pueblo La Playa and the Presidente Inter-Continental Forum Hotel. The estuary is protected as an ecological reserve. A building at the edge of the water is gradually being turned into a cultural center, though it was closed when I checked. Just beside it is a pathway to enter the estuary on foot.

A fine swimming beach with beautiful rock formations, **Playa Palmilla,** 5 miles west of San José, is located near the Spanish-colonial–style Hotel Palmilla—an elegant place to splurge on lunch or dinner. To reach Playa Palmilla, take a taxi to the road that leads to the Hotel Palmilla grounds for about $7, then take the fork to the left (without entering the hotel grounds) and follow signs to Pepe's restaurant on the beach. To return, catch a cab from the Hotel Palmilla, though it's a long walk into the hotel grounds where the cabs are stationed.

For a list of other beaches worth exploring if you have a rental car, see "What to See & Do" in Cabo San Lucas.

WATER SPORTS Fishing The least expensive way to enjoy deep-sea fishing is to pair up with another angler and charter a *panga,* a 22-foot skiff used by local fishermen from Playa la Puebla. Several panga fleets offer sportfishing trips, usually from 6am to noon, for $25 per hour. (There's a three-hour minimum.) The cost can be divided between two or three people—weigh the savings against how much elbow room you think you'll need to catch a big one. For information contact **the fisherman's cooperative in Pueblo la Playa, or Victor's Aquatics** (☎ **2-1092,** or 800/521-2281; fax 2-1093) at the Hotel Posada Real. Victor has a full fishing fleet with both pangas ($165 for six hours) and cruisers ($360–$440). Outfitters supply the boat and tackle, and the client buys the bait, drinks, and snacks.

Snorkeling/Diving   Trips start around $66 per person and can be arranged through **Tourcabos** (☎ 2-1982), the dive shop at the **Hotel Palmilla** (☎ 2-0582).

Surfing   Playa Costa Azul at km 29 on Highway 1 at Playa Azul on the southern edge of San José is the most popular surfing beach in the area. Surfers stay in run-down shacks or camp on the beach; spectators can watch from the beach or highway lookout point at the top of the hill south of Costa Azul.

Whale Watching   From January through March, whales congregate offshore. Victor's Aquatica in the Hotel Posada Real, and fishermen at Pueblo la Playa will take small groups out to see the whales; a 4-hour trip runs about $40 per person.

LAND SPORTS   Golf   Los Cabos is rapidly becoming a major golf destination, with several new courses open and others under construction. The most economical greens fees are at the nine-hole **Club Campo de Golf San José** (☎ 2-0905), on Paseo Finisterra across from the Howard Johnson Hotel. The course is open from 7am to 4pm (to 4:30pm in summer). Club guests can use the swimming pool. The greens fee is $15 for nine holes. Carts cost $30.

New courses have opened along the Corridor between the two towns, including the 27-hole course designed by Jack Nicklaus at the **Palmilla Golf Club** (Palmilla resort, ☎ 2-1701 or 2-1708); the 18-hole Nicklaus course at **Cabo del Sol** (at the Cabo del Sol resort development in the Corridor); and an 18-hole course at **Cabo Real** (by the Melia Cabo Real Hotel in the Corridor, ☎ 114/2-9000, ext. 9205). Campo de Carlos, a planned golf resort community in the Corridor close to Cabo San Lucas, is slated to have two 18-hole courses.

Horseback Riding   Horses can be rented near the **Presidente Inter-Continental, Fiesta Inn,** and **Palmilla** hotels at $15 to $20 per hour. Most people ride on the beach.

Tennis   Tennis is available at the two courts of the **Club Campo de Golf Los Cabos** (☎ 2-0905) for $10 an hour during the day, $20 an hour at night. Club guests can use the swimming pool.

SHOPPING

The town's handful of tourist shops are clustered around **Bulevar Mijares** and **Zaragoza,** the main street. The **municipal market** on Mauricio Castro and Green sells edible and utilitarian wares.

WHERE TO STAY

Because San José has only a handful of budget hotels, it's best to call ahead for reservations. If this isn't possible, try to arrive early, when other guests are checking out.

Hotel Colli. Hidalgo 10, 23400 San José del Cabo, B.C.S. No phone. 12 rms (all with bath). FAN. $20 single; $25 double.

Minimally decorated with boxy, contemporary furniture, these small, clean rooms occupy the second and third floors of an apartmentlike building. Those facing the street have private balconies. The rooms are typically taken by long-term guests, but you may find an available room. The hotel is one block south of Zaragoza (and the main plaza) on Hidalgo.

Posada Señor La Mañana. Obregón 1, 23400 San José del Cabo, B.C.S. ☎ and fax **114/ 2-0462.** 19 rms (all with bath). FAN. $165–$237 single or double per week; $28–$40 single or double daily.

Remodeled in 1995, this comfortable two-story guesthouse, set in a lush grove of fruit trees, offers cheery rooms with tile floors and new furniture. There's a small swimming pool, and guests have cooking privilges in a large fully equipped kitchen beside two spacious breezy palapas. Ask about discounts. It's next to the Casa de la Cultura, behind the main square.

Posada Terranova. Degollado, 23400 San José del Cabo, B.C.S. ☎ **114/2-0534.** Fax 114/ 2-0902. 20 rms (all with bath). A/C TV. $35 single; $40 double.

At the nicest budget hotel in town, each of the bright white rooms has two double beds, handsome Mexican tile floors and counters, nice bathrooms, and powerful air-conditioning. The ground-floor restaurant (open daily from 7am to 10pm) has an inviting front patio restaurant and an enclosed dining room and serves reasonably priced Mexican and American dishes. The posada is on Degollado, between Zaragoza and Doblado.

Worth a Splurge

La Playita Resort. Pueblo la Playa, Apdo. Postal 175, 23400 San José del Cabo, B.C.S. ☎ **114/2-4166.** 22 rms, 2 suites (all with bath). A/C TV. High season, $66 single or double. Low season, $55 single or double. Free parking.

Opened in 1995, this is the only hotel on San José's only beach that's safe for swimming. Just steps from the water and lineup of fishing pangas, the two stories of sunlit rooms frame a patio with a small swimming pool. Each room is spacious, with pastel furnishings and nicely tiled floors and baths. Two large suites on the second floor have small refrigerators. Next door, the hotel's La Playita Restaurant is open from 9am to 7pm. To find the hotel from Bulevar Mijares, follow the sign pointing to Puebla la Playa on a dirt road for about 2 miles to the beach. The hotel is on the left facing the water and at the edge of the tiny village of Puebla la Playa.

Tropicana Inn. Mijares 130, San José del Cabo, B.C.S. 23400. ☎ **114/2-1580.** Fax 114/ 2-1590. 40 rms (all with bath). A/C TV TEL. Dec 21–April 30, $65 single or double; May 1– Dec 20, $55 single or double. Free limited parking in back.

Opened in July 1991, this handsome colonial–style hotel is a true oasis in sunny San José. Set just behind (and adjacent to) the Tropicana Bar & Grill, it frames a beautiful plant-filled courtyard with a graceful arcade bordering the rooms and inviting swimming pool. Each nicely furnished, medium-size room in the L-shaped building (which has a two- and a three-story wing) comes with Saltillo tile floors, two double beds, a window looking out on the courtyard, a gaily tiled bath with a shower, coffee pot, and complimentary in-room coffee. Each morning, freshly brewed coffee, delicious sweet rolls, and fresh fruit are set out by the office for the hotel guests. There's room service until 11pm from the adjacent Tropicana Bar & Grill (owned by the hotel). The inn is located behind the restaurant, a block south of the town square.

WHERE TO EAT

Meals for Less than $5

Asadero Los Candiles. Calle Degollado at Calle Zaragoza. No phone. Tacos $1.75–$2.50; baked potatoes $2.50–$3. Daily 5–10pm. TACOS/MEXICAN.

A few wooden tables sit above the street on the porch of this restaurant, though locals seem to prefer the bar stools facing an open grill, where the aroma of grilled meat whets their appetites. You can eat cheaply here by ordering a taco macho (a combination of marinated beef, cheese, and chilis) and a baked potato topped with cheese and sour cream. Vegetarians will enjoy the veggie brochettes. Beer is served in a chilled mug.

Las Hornillas. Calle Manuel Doblado 610. ☎ **114/2-2324.** Half-chickens $4; 3 tacos with beans $3.50; chicken fajitas $6. Daily noon–10pm. CHICKEN/MEXICAN.

A true neighborhood eatery, Las Hornillas is the best place in town for chicken roasted on a spit over a wood fire, served with tortillas, beans, and rice. Plants and bird cages hang about the dining room, and there is a sink set to one side so you can wash up after your messy chicken feast. The fajitas can easily feed two moderately hungry adults. It's located about two blocks before Highway 1.

Meals for Less than $10

El Café Fiesta. Blv. Mijares 14 at Zaragoza. ☎ **114/2-2908.** Breakfast $3–$6; main courses $3–$8. Daily 7am–10pm. MOSTLY VEGETARIAN.

On a shady edge of the Plaza Mijares tables and chairs are set out under the trees and inside the largish dining room. Patrons enjoy a variety of hot and cold coffees, fruit-flavored margaritas, submarine sandwiches, platters of food with fresh whole wheat pita bread and tortillas, plenty of fresh fruits and salads, and chicken and beef fajitas for those who prefer meat.

Pescadería el Mercado del Mar. Blv. Mauricio Castro (also called Highway 1) at Coronado. ☎ **114/2-3266.** Seafood cocktails $2–$4.75; main courses $4–$10. Daily noon–10pm. SEA-FOOD.

Opened in 1993, this tiny popular seafood café offers dining under a palapa roof. A large wood-burning smoker sits at the far end of the room, and occasionally the aroma of smoking fish permeates the restaurant. Start with the *toritos,* small grilled chilies caribe stuffed with smoked marlin, then move on to shrimp teriyaki, or fish in mango sauce. If you catch fish while you're in Los Cabos, consider having it smoked here for a flavorful souvenir. The restaurant is set amid a row of businesses on the east side of Highway 1 at the north end of town near where Coronado meets Highway 1.

Worth a Splurge

Damiana. San José town plaza. ☎ **114/2-0499.** Reservations recommended during the Christmas and Easter holidays. Appetizers $5–$12; main courses $12–$25. Daily 11am–11pm. SEAFOOD/MEXICAN.

This casually elegant restaurant on the east side of the town plaza is decorated with burnt orange walls and cloth clad tables and chairs in bright pink, lavender, and or-ange. Mariachis add to the romantic ambience by playing nightly from 8 to 9pm (mid-December to March) in the tropical courtyard, where candles flicker under the trees and bougainvillea. For an appetizer, try the mushrooms diablo—a moderately zesty temptation. For a main course the seafood pasta or grilled lobster tail are fla-vorful choices. You can also enjoy brunch almost until dinner. There is an interior dining room, but the courtyard is the most romantic dining spot in Los Cabos.

Tropicana Bar & Grill. Mijares 130. ☎ **114/2-1580.** Breakfasts $4–$6; sandwiches $6–$7.50; main courses $8–$17 . Daily 8am–midnight. SEAFOOD/MEAT.

The Tropicana remains a popular mainstay for tourists and locals alike. Its bar has a steady clientele day and night and often features special sporting events on satel-lite TV. The dining area, where candlelight flickers in the evening, is in a pretty garden with a tiled kitchen at one end. All meats and cheeses are imported, and din-ners include thick steaks and shrimp fajitas. Paella is the Sunday special. The restau-rant is one block south of the Plaza Mijares.

Zipper's. Playa Costa Azul just south of San José. No phone. Burgers and sandwiches $7–$9; main courses $7–$15. Daily 8am–10pm. BURGERS/MEXICAN/SEAFOOD.

Mike Posey and Tony Magdeleno own this popular, breezy hangout. Fronting the best surfing waters at the far south end of the beach heading toward Cabo San Lucas, Zipper's has become somewhat of a surfer hangout. The burgers, which are given that back-home flavor with imported beef and catsup, are the restaurant's biggest draw. Steaks, lobster, beer-batter shrimp, deli sandwiches, and Mexican combination plates round out the menu, which is printed with dollar prices.

SAN JOSÉ AFTER DARK

San José's nightlife revolves mainly around the restaurants and large hotels. Bulevar Mijares is the town's restaurant row, along which you can amble until you find the restaurant or watering hole with the most appealing music.

Bones Bar and Disco. Hotel Presidente Inter-Continental Forum, Paseo San José. ☎ 114/2-0211.

Flashing lights, fog machines, and other environmental stimulants keep the dancers moving to a pounding beat at this disco by the Hotel Presidente Inter-Continental Forum. If you're not into dancing, the bar has pool tables and video games. It's open nightly from 8pm to 2am, or until whenever the crowd winds down.

Iguana Bar & Grill. Mijares 24. ☎ 114/2-0266.

This lively open-air bar and restaurant is sheltered by a broad thatched roof and has a patio under the stars. Live music and dancing on Friday and Saturday get cranking around 9:30pm and can last until 1am. If you're hungry, the house specialty is barbecued ribs. The place is open daily from 11am to 1am. Drinks run from $2 to $4.50.

Tropicana Bar & Grill. Mijares 30. ☎ 114/5-2684.

This is definitely the most popular place in town. Patrons become ensconced in leather barrel chairs in the large bar, where, during the day, they tune in to American sports events on the big-screen TV. Come evening, guitarists play from 6 to 11pm. After 9pm on some nights a band plays for those inclined to dance. The Tropicana is open daily from 7am to 1am. Drinks go for $3 and up.

CABO SAN LUCAS

110 miles S of La Paz, 22 miles W of San José del Cabo, 1,120 miles SE of Tijuana

Cabo San Lucas, with a population of 25,000, is the faster growing of the two Cabos and outshines San José in nightlife and restaurant diversity. In the past few years, the number of swanky new hotels and condos has nearly doubled around the harbor and amid the steep hills that frame the picturesque blue bay where private American yachts have been dropping anchor since the 1950s. That era marked the beginning of the town's fame as a mecca for hunters of marlin and other big-game fish, and many of its popular watering holes still retain the air of a yacht club mixed with the good-natured silliness of a fraternity party. San Lucas is definitely the party capital of Los Cabos, and its attitude is far flashier than that of San José. It's also the priciest resort in Baja—the peso devaluation has had little effect, since most prices are posted in dollars.

ESSENTIALS

GETTING THERE & DEPARTING **By Plane** For arrival and departure information see "Getting There & Departing," above, in San José del Cabo. Local airline numbers are as follows: **Aero California,** (☎ 3-3700, 3-0848 at the airport); **Alaska Airlines** (☎ 2-1015 or 2-1016, or 2-0959 at the airport); and **Mexicana** (☎ 2-1530, or 2-0606 at the airport).

By Bus The bus terminal (☎ 3-0400) is on Héroes at Morelos; it is open daily from 6am to 9:30pm.

Autotransportes   Aguila buses go to San José del Cabo about every hour between 6:30am and 8:30pm on the Vía Corta (short route). First-class buses to La Paz leave every 90 minutes between 6am and 6pm. Some La Paz–bound buses stop in Todos Santos. On this line you change buses at La Paz if you're going on to Tijuana. The trip from San José del Cabo takes 40 minutes; from La Paz, the Vía Corta (shorter route) buses take 2¹/₂ hours, and the other buses take four hours.

By Car   From La Paz, take Highway 1 south past the village of San Pedro, then Highway 19 south through Todos Santos to Cabo San Lucas, a 2-hour drive. (Todos Santos has several restored historic buildings and makes a pleasant stop for a meal— try the Café Santa Fe, which draws diners from Los Cabos with its fresh fish and Italian cuisine.)

ORIENTATION   Arriving   Upon arriving at the airport, ignore the dozens of timeshare sellers who offer free rides to town (in exchange for listening to their sales pitch). Instead, buy a ticket for a colectivo van from the authorized transportation booth inside the building. Several people going to the same place share the cost. When I checked, the collective price in dollars for a ride to town was almost twice as high as the quoted price in pesos—around U.S. $6. The taxi fare is $20, which could be shared by four people. The highway between the airport and Cabo San Lucas was widened to four lanes in 1993.

It is not too far to walk with light luggage from the bus station to most of the budget hotels. A taxi from the station to most hotels should be under $5.

Information   The Hotel and Motel Association functions as the **information office** in Cabo. It's on Madero between Hidalgo and Guerrero (☎ **3-4180;** fax 3-2211). The English-language *Los Cabos Guide, Cabo Life,* and *Gringo Gazette* distributed free at most hotels and shops, have up-to-date information on new restaurants and clubs. *Note:* Beware of the hundreds of "visitor information" booths along the street—they're actually time-share hawkers.

City Layout   The small town spreads out north and west of the harbor of **Cabo San Lucas Bay,** edged by foothills and desert mountains to the west and south. The main street leading into town from the airport and San José del Cabo is **Lázaro Cárdenas;** as it nears the harbor, **Bulevar Marina** branches off from it and becomes the main artery that curves around the waterfront. Both Cárdenas and Bulevar Marina are paved, as are several other streets; otherwise, tourists and vehicles lumber over streets that are dusty and rutted.

Getting Around   A **taxi** from downtown to the farthest hotels, such as the Solmar near Land's End or the Melia on Medano Beach, should run between $4 and $8.

For day-trips to San José del Cabo, catch a bus for $2 (see "Getting There & Departing," above) or a cab for $25 one way.

You'll see **car-rental** specials advertised in town, but before signing on, be sure you understand the total price after insurance and taxes have been added.

FAST FACTS: CABO SAN LUCAS

Area Code   The telephone area code was changed in 1993 from 684 to 114. Calls between Cabo San Lucas and San José del Cabo are toll calls, so you must use the area code.

Beach Safety   *Before swimming anywhere it's important to ask if the water is safe.* Undertows and large waves can suck unsuspecting bathers out to sea. Medano Beach, close to the marina and town, is the only beach that is safe for swimming. The Hotel Melia Cabo San Lucas, on Medano Beach, has a roped off swimming area to protect swimmers from zooming water jets and boats. Colored flags signaling

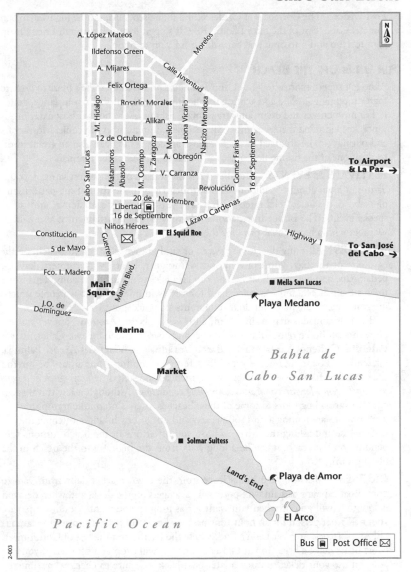

A. López Mateos
Ildefonso Green
A. Mijares
Felix Ortega
Rosario Morales
Alikan
12 de Octubre
Morelos
Calle Juventud
M. Hidalgo
Leona Vicario
Narcizo Mendoza
Gomez Farias
16 de Septiembre
Cabo San Lucas
Matamoros
Abasolo
M. Ocampo
I. Zaragoza
A. Obregón
V. Carranza
Revolución
20 de Noviembre
Libertad
16 de Septiembre
Niños Héroes
Constitución
5 de Mayo
Fco. I. Madero
J.O. de Dominguez
Guerrero
Marina Blvd.
Main Square
Marina
Market
Lázaro Cardenas
■ El Squid Roe
■ Melia San Lucas
Playa Medano
Highway 1
To Airport & La Paz →
To San José del Cabo →
Bahía de Cabo San Lucas
■ Solmar Suitess
Land's End
Playa de Amor
El Arco
Pacific Ocean
Bus ▣ Post Office ⊠

2-003

swimming safety aren't used in Cabo and neither are lifeguards. *You swim at your own risk.*

Currency Exchange   Banks exchange currency Monday through Friday from 9 to 11am. Currency exchange booths, which are found all along Cabo's main tourist areas, aren't competitive, but they're convenient.

Groceries   The biggest and best supermarket is Supermercado Plaza, (☎ **3-0939**), in Plaza Aramburo, on Cárdenas at Zaragoza. It also has a good bakery. It's open daily from 7am to 10pm.

Pharmacy   The largest drugstore in town, with a wide selection of toiletries as well as medicines, is Farmacía Aramburo, in Plaza Aramburo, on Cárdenas at Zaragoza; open daily from 7am to 9pm.

Post Office   The Correos is at Cárdenas and Francisco Villa, on the highway to San José del Cabo, east of the bar El Squid Roe. It's open Monday through Friday from 9am to 1pm and 3 to 6pm and Saturday from 9am to noon.

FUN ON & OFF THE BEACH

Although superb sportfishing put Cabo San Lucas on the map, there's more to do here than dropping your line and waiting for the Big One. But if that's your fancy, go for it. For most cruises and excursions, try to make fishing reservations at least a day in advance; keep in mind that some trips require a minimum number of people. Most sports and outings can be arranged through a travel agency; fishing can also be arranged directly at one of the fishing fleet offices at the far south end of the marina.

FESTIVALS & EVENTS   **October 12** is the festival of the patron saint of Todos Santos, a town about 65 miles north. **October 18** is the festival of the patron saint of Cabo San Lucas, celebrated with a fair, feasting, music, dancing, and other special events. The Bisbee International Marlin Fishing Tournament is also held in October with a huge dollar prize for the winner.

BEACHES   All along the curving sweep of sand known as **Medano Beach,** on the east side of the bay, you can rent snorkeling gear, boats, waverunners, kayaks, pedalboats, and windsurf boards. You can also take windsurfing lessons. This is the town's main beach and is a great place for safe swimming as well as people watching from one of the many outdoor restaurants along its shore.

Beach aficionados may want to rent a car (see "Getting Around," above) and explore the half-dozen out-of-the-way beaches and coves between the two Cabos: **Playas Palmilla, Chileno, Santa María, Barco Varado,** and **Vista del Arcos.** Palmilla, Chileno, and Santa María are generally safe for swimming—but always be careful; the others are for the view only or for experienced snorkelers. *Always check at a hotel or travel agency for directions and swimming conditions.* Although a few travel agencies run snorkeling tours to some of these beaches, there's no public transportation: Your options are renting a car ($60 per day and up) or bus-hiking—catching the bus to San José and asking the driver to drop you off at one of the beach turnoffs (depending on the beach, it can be a long walk from the highway to the beach in the blazing sun).

CRUISES   **Glass-bottom boats** leave from the town marina daily from 9am to 4pm. Boat captains bargain with potential passengers on the dock, and when demand is low they will go out when you want for as long as you want. Count on paying about $15 per person for an hour tour past sea lions and pelicans to see the famous "El Arco" (Rock Arch) at Land's End, where the Pacific and the Sea of Cortez meet. Most boats make a brief stop at Playa de Amor or will drop you off there if you ask; you can use your ticket to catch a later boat back. (Be sure to check what time the last boat departs.)

Whale-watching cruises are not to be missed when gray whales migrate to the Los Cabos area between January and March. The sportfishing boats, glass-bottom boats, and cruise catamarans all offer whale-watching trips ranging from $30 to $50 for a half-day trip. You can also spot the whales from shore; good whale-watching spots include the beach by the Solmar Suites hotel on the Pacific and the beaches and cliffs along the Corridor.

A **sunset cruise** on the 42-foot catamaran *Pez Gato* (☎ **114/3-3797** or 114/3-2458) departs from the Hacienda Hotel dock at 5pm. The 2-hour cruise costs $30, which includes margaritas, beer, and sodas. Similar boats leave from the marina and the Plaza las Glorias hotel. Check with travel agencies or hotel tour desks.

SNORKELING/DIVING   Several companies offer snorkeling; a two-hour cruise to sites around El Arco costs $25, and a four-hour trip to Santa Maria costs $45, including gear rental. Among the beaches visited on different trips are Playa de Amor, Santa María, Chileno, and Barco Varado. Snorkeling gear rents for $6 to $10. For scuba diving, contact **Amigos del Mar** (☎ 114/3-0505; fax 114/3-0887, or 800/344-3349 in the U.S. or fax 213/545-1622) at the Marina. Diving specialist Ricardo Sevilla is the man with the Cabo diving answers. Dives are made along the wall of a canyon in San Lucas Bay, where you can see a "sandfalls" that even Jacques Cousteau couldn't figure out—no one knows its source or cause. There are also scuba trips to Santa María Beach and places farther away, including the Gordo Banks and Cabo Pulmo. Dives start at $45 for a one-tank dive and $66 for two tanks; trips to the coral outcropping at Cabo Pulmo start at $110. Two hours from Cabo San Lucas, Cabo Pulmo is rated for beginners and up. Gordo Banks, for advanced divers, is an underwater mountain about 5 miles offshore with a black coral bottom and schools of gamefish and manta rays. Resort courses cost $100 per person, and open water certification costs around $400. The months from April through November are the best times to dive, but diving is busiest from October to mid January, so it's important to make reservations in advance if you're planning to dive then.

SPORTFISHING   Go to the town marina on the south side of the harbor. There, you'll find several fleet operators with offices near the docks. The best deals are offered by the *panga* fleets, where five hours of fishing for two or three persons costs $150 to $200. To choose one, take a stroll around the marina and talk with the captains—you may be able to agree on an economical deal. Try **ABY Charters** (main office at the Giggling Marlin restaurant, ☎ 114/3-0831), **Rafael's Fleet** (☎ 114/3-0018), or **Baja Mar Fleet** (☎ 114/3-2259), all of which are located at the sportfishing dock at the far south end of the marina. The going rate for a day on a fully equipped cruiser with captain and guide (many of the larger hotels, like the Solmar, have their own fleets) starts at around $300. These have bathrooms aboard. Divide the price between four persons, and you'll fish in far greater comfort. (See also "Outdoor Sports, Adventure Travel & Wilderness Trips" in chapter 2 for companies that can arrange fishing in advance.)

The fishing really lives up to its reputation: Bringing in a marlin weighing more than 100 pounds is routine. Angling is good all year, though the catch varies with the season: Sailfish and wahoo are best from June through November; yellowfin tuna, from May through December; yellowtail, from January through April; black and blue marlin, July through December; and striped marlin are prevalent year-round.

The "catch and release" program is encouraged in Los Cabos. Anglers reel in their fish, which are tagged and released unharmed into the sea. The angler gets a certificate and the knowledge there will still be billfish in the sea when he or she returns.

SURFING   Good surfing can be found from March to November all along the beaches west of town, and there's a famous right break at Chileno Beach, near the Cabo San Lucas Hotel east of town.

OTHER SPORTS   Bicycles, boogie boards, snorkels, surfboards, and golf clubs are available for rent at **Cabo Sports Center** in the Plaza Nautica on Boulevard Marina (☎ 114/3-4272); the center is open Monday through Saturday from 9am to 9pm, Sunday from 9am to 5pm. For information about playing **golf** in Los Cabos, see "Fun On & Off the Beach" in San José del Cabo, above.

You can rent **horses** at the Hacienda Hotel (☎ 114/3-0123) or the **Melia San Lucas** (☎ 114/3-0420) for around $20 per hour. They have guided beach rides and sunset tours to El Faro Viejo (the Old Lighthouse) for $30 to $45 per person and to the Pacific for sunset riding on the beach.

HISTORIC CABO SAN LUCAS   Sports and carousing are Cabo's main attractions, but there are a few cultural and historical points of interest. The stone **Iglesia de San Lucas** (Church of San Lucas) on Calle Cabo San Lucas close to the main plaza was established in 1730 by Spanish missionary Nicolás Tamaral; a large bell in a stone archway commemorates the completion of the church in 1746. Tamaral was eventually killed by the Pericúe Indians, who reportedly resisted his demands that they practice monogamy. Buildings on the streets facing the main plaza are gradually being renovated to house restaurants and shops, and the picturesque neighborhood promises to have the strongest Mexican ambience of any place in town.

ATV TRIPS   Expeditions on ATVs (all-terrain vehicles) to visit Cabo Falso, an 1890 lighthouse, and La Candelaría, an Indian pueblo in the mountains, are available through travel agencies. The three-hour tour to Cabo Falso includes a stop at the beach; a look at some sea-turtle nests (without disturbing them) and the remains of a 1912 shipwreck; a ride over 500-foot sand dunes; and a visit to the lighthouse. Tours cost around $50 per person or $60 for two riding on one ATV. The vehicles are also available for rent at $30 for three hours.

La Candelaría is an isolated Indian village in the mountains 25 miles north of Cabo San Lucas. Described in *National Geographic,* the old pueblo is known for the white and black witchcraft still practiced here. Lush with palms, mango trees, and bamboo, the settlement is watered by an underground river that emerges at the pueblo. The return trip of the tour travels down a steep canyon, along a beach (giving you time to swim), and past giant sea-turtle nesting grounds. Departing at 9am, the La Candelaría tour costs around $88 per person or $110 for two on the same ATV. A 220-pound weight limit per vehicle applies to both tours.

DAY TRIPS TO LA PAZ   Day trips to La Paz booked through a travel agency cost around $80, including lunch and a tour of the countryside along the way. Usually there's a stop in La Paz at the weaving shop of Fortunato Silva, who spins his own cotton and weaves it into wonderfully textured rugs and textiles.

SHOPPING

Your first stop should be the open-air market on Plaza Papagayo on Bulevar Marina opposite the entrance to Pueblo Bonito and behind it facing the Plaza Aranmburo. Like several makeshift open markets around town you'll find what the beach vendors are selling including T-shirts, blankets, onyx objects, touristy junk, and some nice crafts and jewelry. Be sure to bargain. Most shops are on or within a block or two of Bulevar Marina and the plaza.

Casas Mexicanas. Calle Cabo San Lucas across from the plaza. ☎ **114/3-1933.**

This tiny shop in front of Mi Casa restaurant has a small selection of interior design items. Open daily from 4 to 10pm.

Cuca's Blanket Factory. Cárdenas at Matamoros. ☎ **114/3-1913.**

This open-air stand sells the standard Mexican cotton and woolen blankets with an added attraction—you can design your own and have it ready the next day. Open daily from 9am to 9pm.

Galeria Gattamelata. Hacienda Hotel Road. ☎ **114/3-1166.**

In the Medano Beach area, this handsome gallery specializes in antiques and colonial-style furniture. Open daily from 9am to 9pm.

Glass Factory. West of Hwy. 1. No phone.

Combine shopping, touring, and a look at local culture with a trip to the glassblowing factory on the outskirts of town. Glassblowers from Guadalajara and Baja work around enormous gas furnaces and blazing fires. The glassblowers will help you blow your own masterpiece, while a showroom at the front displays more professional work. The tour is free, but visitors are expected to purchase something. Small shot glasses with green glass cacti on the front are about $2 each. The factory is open Monday through Saturday from 8am to 3pm. To get there by car, turn west off Highway 1 north of Cabo San Lucas opposite the post office on Calle Farías or Mendoza, then drive about five dirt blocks inland. A taxi to the factory (your best choice) costs about $4.

Mamma Eli's. Calle Cabo San Lucas west of the plaza at Madero. ☎ **114/3-1616.**

One of the nicest shops in Los Cabos, Mamma Eli's has three levels packed with a high-quality selection of folk art, crafts, clothing, and furniture. Open Tuesday through Sunday from 9am to 1:30pm and 4 to 7pm.

Necri. Blv. Marina. ☎ **114/3-0283.**

One of the oldest shops in town, Necri is packed with tastefully selected handpainted tableware, pewter trays, and folk art. Open Monday through Saturday from 9am to 8pm.

Plaza Bonita. Blv. Marina at Lázaro Cárdenas.

This large terra-cotta colored plaza on the edge of the marina has been around since 1990 and is finally filling with successful businesses. **Libros** (☎ 114/3-1770), at the front of the mall, is a great bookstore with lots of English-language novels and magazines and a good selection of books on Baja. A branch of **Dos Lunas** (☎ 114/3-1969) sells colorful sportswear. **Cartes** (☎ 114/2-1770) is filled with irresistible handpainted ceramic vases and dishes, pewter frames, carved furniture, and handwoven textiles. Most shops in the plaza are open daily from 10am to 9pm.

El Rancho. Guerrero s/n between Madero and 5 de Mayo. ☎ **114/3-0593.**

Three enterprising young Americans opened this unique store selling primarily pottery and furniture they found on nearby Baja ranches. The farm folk of Baja make pottery and furniture for their own use, but they never sold to outsiders until now. The shop, rustically decorated the way ranch houses are in Baja, features beautifully formed lidded casseroles, pitchers, and jars often with an animal head handle or etched on the side. Furniture includes shelves, twig hat hooks, and beautiful branch chairs with rush seats. Each piece is unique. It's open Monday through Friday from 9am to 2pm and 4 to 9pm and Saturday from 9am to 4pm.

Rostros de Mexico. Cárdenas at Matamoros. No phone.

Walls of wooden masks and carved religious statues are the draw at this gallery whose name means "Faces of Mexico." Open Monday through Saturday from 10am to 2pm and 4:30 to 9pm, Sunday from 10am to 2pm.

Temptations. Cárdenas between Matamoros and Blv. Marina. ☎ **114/3-1015.**

Cool cotton clothing for women is the main attraction here, with brands like Maria de Guadalajara. Prices are about double what you'd pay on the mainland for the same thing, but the selection is good. It's open Monday through Saturday from 8am to 8pm.

WHERE TO STAY

Budget accommodations are scarce in Cabo San Lucas. The handful of inexpensive hostelries often have no vacancies, so it's wise to call ahead for reservations or arrive early when other travelers are checking out.

All hotel prices listed here are for high season, in effect from November to April; summer rates are about 20% less.

Hotel Dos Mares. Emiliano Zapata, 23410 Cabo San Lucas, B.C.S. ☎ and fax **114/3-0330.** 40 rms (all with bath). A/C or FAN. $22 single or double with fan or A/C.

This three-story hotel, built around a pool, had been repainted when I checked, but it still seemed unkempt. Air-conditioning is gradually being added, and some rooms have small refrigerators. Ask to see the room first—some lack windows, bathroom doors, or toilet seats. The hotel is opposite the marina and Plaza Las Glorias Hotel, and next to Siesta Suites, on Zapata between Hidalgo and Guerrero, about a block inland from Bulevar Marina. Parking is scarce; try the lot at the marina.

Hotel Marina. Blv. Marina at Guerrero, 23410 Cabo San Lucas, B.C.S. ☎ **114/3-0030.** Fax 114/3-1499. 24 rms, 7 suites (all with bath). A/C. $35 single or double; $55 suite.

This two-story hotel on the harbor has 24 very basic rooms and seven generous suites, some of which overlook the nice, large pool and others that overlook the street. Each regular room is clean, but minimally furnished with tile floor, one or two double beds, and small tile bathroom. The street-side suites are quite large but dark and can be a bit noisy; each comes with two double beds, wood furniture, a balcony, a large tile bath, and a small freezer. The hotel's outdoor café is open daily from 8am to 11pm. Parking is congested. Try the lot at the marina, two blocks south.

Las Margaritas Inn. Cárdenas at Zaragoza (Apdo. Postal 354), 23410 Cabo San Lucas, B.C.S.☎ **114/3-0450.** Fax 114/3-1696. 16 apartments (all with bath). A/C. $38 one bed; $46 two beds; $55 two-bedroom suite. Free parking; unprotected.

Located in Plaza Aramburo, in the heart of town across from the marina, this three-story property features 14 one- and two-bedroom apartments attractively decorated in white and pastels with contemporary furniture and furnished kitchens. Each bedroom has a double bed, and the living rooms have sleeper sofas. Two rooms don't have air-conditioning. All rooms on the second and third stories open off the balconies overlooking the busy parking lot; when traffic is slow, you can catch a view of the marina across the street. Plaza Aramburo is one of the busiest places in town and has the least expensive grocery store and pharmacy. Noise is a problem here. It's between Guerrero and Hidalgo.

Worth a Splurge

Hotel Mar De Cortez. Cárdenas at Guerrero, 23410 Cabo San Lucas, B.C.S. ☎ **114/3-0032.** (Reservations: 17561 Vierra Canyon Rd., Suite 99, Salinas, CA 93907; ☎ and fax **408/ 663-1904,** or 800/347-8821.) 66 rooms, 16 suites (all with bath). A/C. $35 single; $55 double. Free parking; guarded.

In a great location, on Cárdenas three blocks from the marina in the center of town, this attractive two-story hotel arranged its Spanish-style white stucco building around a rambling, landscaped courtyard with a huge pool and shaded by huge palms and banana trees. The front of the hotel has been completely rebuilt to house shops. Each of the smaller rooms of the older section has dark-wood furniture and one double or two single beds, a desk, and a tiny front porch facing the courtyard. Those in the newer section have two double beds; suites have one king bed and a sleeper couch or two doubles and a sleeper couch. A semi-outdoor bar with a fireplace under its thatched roof for the sometimes-cool winter nights provides a pleasant gathering place for guests who share the general feeling of camaraderie here. There's also a restaurant with a TV and a freezer for storing your fish. The place books up quickly, apparently because many patrons are regulars who return every year.

Siesta Suites. Zapata at Hidalgo (Apdo. Postal 310), 23410 Cabo San Lucas, B.C.S. ☎ and fax **114/3-2773.** 15 suites (all with bath and kitchenette). A/C or FAN. $45 single or double with fan; $55 single or double with A/C.

Reservations are a must at this immaculate small inn, which opened in early 1994. The rooms have white tile floors and white walls, kitchenettes with seating areas, refrigerators, and sinks. The mattresses are new and firm, and the bathrooms are large and sparkling clean. The proprietors are accommodating, offering free movies, a barbeque pit and outdoor patio table on the second floor, comfortable lobby with TV, and water for sale. They can also arrange fishing trips. Weekly and monthly rates are available. The hotel is 1 1/2 blocks from the marina, where parking is available.

WHERE TO EAT

It's easy to pay a lot for very mediocre food in Cabo, so try to get a couple of unbiased recommendations before settling in for a meal. If people are only drinking and not dining, take that as one cue, since many seemingly popular places are great for the party atmosphere but lousy on the food. Prices, as a rule, decrease the farther you walk inland from the waterfront. Besides the restaurants mentioned below dozens of good, clean taco stands and taco restaurants are all over the downtown area. These are truly the least expensive good eats in town. Streets to explore for other good restaurants include Hidalgo, Cárdenas, and the Marina at the Plaza Bonita. And just to make you feel at home, U.S. franchise chains proliferate downtown and include Kentucky Fried Chicken, Subway, Pizza Hut, Mrs. Field's (beside the Giggling Marlin), TCBY, Baskin Robbins, Dairy Queen, and Domino's Pizza. One caveat: The tip is often added onto the bill.

Cafe Europa. Blv. Marina s/n. ☎ **114/3-3699.** Main courses $4–$8, coffee $1.75–$2.50. Daily 8am–midnight. COFFEE/PASTRY/LIGHT MEALS.

Gabriel Moreno and Kent Mignon opened this small, cute place that's had several other locations. This one, one-half block north of the Hotel Plaza Las Glorias, attracts a clientele hankering for a place to sit and sip or have a light meal while watching all the passing activity on Bulevar Marina. The appealing menu offers quiche, fruit smoothies, muffins, cinnamon rolls, bagels and cream cheese, carrot cake, coffees many ways, nachos, burritos, fritatas, sandwiches, and lasagna.

The Fish Company. Av. Guerrero at Zapata. ☎ **114/3-1405.** Breakfast $2.50–$3.50; main courses $4.50–$12. Daily 8:30am–10pm. MEXICAN/SEAFOOD.

Owner Miguel Olvera has a good share of fans among local diners tired of high prices and small portions. His small restaurant has only a dozen or so cloth-covered tables, but they're nearly always full. Main courses usually come with rice or baked potato, beans, and tortillas. Fishermen can have their catch prepared to eat here with all the same accompaniments for $5 per person. If you're tired of fish, the *carne asada* is great. The restaurant is one-half block inland from Boulevard Marina and the Plaza Las Glorias Hotel.

✪ **Mama's Royale Cafe.** Hidalgo at Zapata. ☎ **114/3-4390.** Breakfast special $2.50; breakfast à la carte $2.50–$4; lunch $5–$7. Daily 7am–2pm. BREAKFAST/LUNCH/INTERNATIONAL.

What a great place to start the day. The shady patio decked with cloth-covered tables and the bright, inviting interior dining room are both great places to settle in. And what food. Spencer Moore presides over this eatery with well-prepared breakfast selections that include grilled polish sausage, french toast stuffed with pecans and cream cheese and topped with pineapple, eggs benedict, great hash browns, fruit crêpes, and of course traditional breakfasts, plus free coffee refills. The lunch menu includes Mexican specialties such as enchiladas and quesadillas, fresh fish and shrimp, sandwiches and burgers.

Ⓢ Pollo de Oro Rostizado. Av. Cárdenas, by Squid Roe. ☎ **114/3-0310.** Breakfast $3–$3.50; chicken $1.75–$5; ribs $2–$4; comida corrida $3–$3.50. Daily 7am–11pm. ROAST CHICKEN AND RIBS.

In the midst of glitzy prime real estate, this simple red-and-white wood-frame eatery has been dishing out delicious roast chicken and rib plate meals and preparing box lunches for fisherfolk for at least a decade. Platters of whatever you choose (a whole, half, or quarter chicken for example) are tasty and filling and come with flavorful rice, salad, and fresh corn tortillas. The green sauce, set at each table, is great dabbed on chicken. The daily comida corrida features chicken in mole sauce, chile rellenos, and steak ranchero. It's beside Squid Roe and opposite Plaza Bonita.

Ⓢ Tacos Chidos. Zapata s/n. ☎ **114/3-0551.** Breakfast $2.50–$3.50; fish taco $1 each; fruit smoothie $1.50–$1.75; main courses $2–$4.75; comida corrida $2.75. Mon–Sat 7am–10pm. MEXICAN.

At this tiny, friendly family-run place with an open kitchen behind the wooden counter, you can sit on a stool and watch the preparation of some of the most delicious cheap eats in Los Cabos. Everything's fresh and homemade, including the corn tortillas and several different salsas. Fish tacos made with fresh dorado are superb. The fresh fruit smoothies are the best in town. It's between Hidalgo and Guerrero, about a block in from Bulevar Marina.

Worth a Splurge

✪ Cabo Steak House. Marina Sol Condominium, Camino Hotel Hacienda. ☎ **114/3-3231.** Appetizer $5–$6; main courses $15–$16.50. Daily 4pm–11pm. STEAK.

I know, I know, the Sea of Cortez is lapping at your feet, so why would you want steak? Because maybe you're all fished out and dying for a terrific steak. The steaks here are worth the outlay. Most of the meat comes from Mexico's northern cattle-producing state of Sonora, and it's fork tender. The menu is short but good, and all main courses (steak, ribs, and veal) come with baked potato and perfectly cooked vegetables. The outdoor patio overlooking the condo's large inner grounds and running the length of the interior dining area is the best place for an evening meal. *Note:* The prices on the menu don't include the 10% tax.

✪ Mi Casa. Calle Cabo San Lucas at Madero. ☎ **114/3-1933.** Appetizers $2.75–$6; main courses $11–$20. High season Mon–Sat 1–10pm. Low season Mon–Sat 5–10pm. MEXICAN.

The building's vivid cobalt-blue facade is your first clue that this place celebrates Mexico, and the menu confirms your impression. This is one of Cabo's finest gourmet Mexican restaurants. Traditional specialties such as manchamanteles, cochinita pibil, and chiles enogados are everyday menu staples. Fresh fish is prepared with delicious seasonings and recipes from throughout Mexico. Especially pleasant at night, the tables, scattered around a large patio, are set with colorful cloths, traditional pottery, and glassware. The restaurant is across from the main plaza.

CABO SAN LUCAS AFTER DARK

Cabo San Lucas is the nightlife capital of Baja, though after-dark fun is centered around the party ambience and camaraderie found in the casual bars and restaurants on Boulevar Marina or facing the marina, rather than around a flashy disco scene. You can easily find a happy hour with live music and a place to dance or a Mexican fiesta with mariachis.

MEXICAN FIESTAS AND THEME NIGHTS   Some of the larger hotels have weekly "Fiesta Nights," "Italian Nights," and other buffet-plus-entertainment theme nights that can be fun as well as a good buy. Check travel agencies and the following hotels: the **Solmar** (☎ 114/3-0022), the **Finisterra** (☎ 114/3-0000), the **Hacienda** (☎ 114/3-0123), and the **Melia San Lucas** (☎ 114/3-0420). Prices range from $12 (drinks, tax, and tips are extra) to $30 (which covers everything, including an open bar with national drinks).

Sunset Watching
Whale Watcher's Bar. In the Hotel Finisterra. ☎ **114/3-0000** or 114/3-0100.

At twilight, settle into this watering hole on the slender point that leads to Land's End where the two seas meet and watch the sun sink into the Pacific.

The high terrace offers a splendid view of sea and beach, as well as frolicking whales from January to March. Mariachis play on Friday, Saturday, and Sunday from 5 to 8pm. The bar is open daily from noon to 11pm. "Whale margaritas" cost $4; beer, $3. There are two-for-one drinks during happy hour from 4 to 6pm.

Happy Hours and Hang Outs
If you shop around, you can usually find an *hora alegre* somewhere in town between noon and 7pm. On my last visit, the most popular places to drink, carouse, and hang out until all hours were the Giggling Marlin, El Squid Roe, Rio Grill, and the Cabo Wabo Cantina.

Giggling Marlin. On Cárdenas at Zaragoza across from the marina. ☎ **114/3-0606.**

Live music alternating with tapes blasts the merry patrons here, who occasionally jump up to dance on the tables and bar. A contraption of winches, ropes, and pulleys above a mattress provides entertainment as couples literally string each other up by the heels—just like a captured marlin. The food is only fair here; stick with nachos and drinks. There is live music Wednesday through Sunday from 9pm to midnight during high season. The Giggling Marlin is open daily from 8am to midnight; the bar stays open to 1am. Beer runs $1.75 to $2.50; schooner margaritas cost $4–$6. Drinks are half price during happy hour from 2 to 6pm.

Latitude 22+. Blv. Lázaro Cárdenas. ☎ **114/3-1516.** Drinks $2–$5. 24 hours. AMERICAN.

This raffish restaurant/bar never closes. License plates, signs, sports caps, and a 959-pound blue marlin are the backdrop for U.S. sports events that play on six TVs scattered among pool tables, dart boards, and assorted games. Besides the assorted entertainment, food from hamburgers to chicken fried steak is offered, or have breakfast any time. Latitude 22+ is located one block north of the town's only traffic light.

Rio Grill Restaurant and Bar. Blv. Marina 31-A at Guerrero. ☎ **114/3-1335.**

The curving bar in the middle of the room has a cozy neighborhood feeling, with tourists and locals taking advantage of the two-for-one happy-hour margaritas. Soft music plays during dinner. On Thursday through Sunday live rhythm-and-blues and reggae bands play from 9:30pm to 12:30am. On Thursdays at 8:30pm enthusiastic patrons partake in "Karaoke Kraziness." Río Grill is open daily from 7am to midnight. Margaritas are $3 or three-for-one during happy hour, 5 to 9pm.

El Squid Roe. Blv. Marina, opposite Plaza Bonita. ☎ **114/3-0655.**

El Squid Roe is one of the late Carlos Anderson's inspirations, and it still attracts crowds with its two stories of nostalgic decor and eclectic food that's far better than you'd expect from such a fun party place. As fashionable as blue jeans, this is a place to see and be seen. There's a patio out back for dancing. It's open daily from noon to 3am. Beer costs $1.75–$2; margaritas cost $3–$4.

Dancing

Cabo Wabo Cantina. Guerrero at Cárdenas. ☎ **114/3-1188.** Cover $15 for live shows (includes two drinks); otherwise free.

Owned by the band Van Halen and its Mexican and American partners, this "cantina" packs in youthful crowds, especially when rumors fly that a surprise appearance by a vacationing musician is imminent. Live rock bands from the United States, Mexico, Europe, and Australia perform frequently on the well-equipped stage. When live music is absent, a disco-type sound system blasts out mostly rock and roll; conversations are drowned out by the music. Overstuffed furniture frames the dance floor. For snacks, the "Taco-Wabo," just outside the club's entrance, stays up late, too. The cantina is open nightly from 8pm to 4am. Drinks run $3 to $5.

A ROAD TRIP TO TODOS SANTOS

Artists, entrepreneurs, and foreign residents are turning the small town of Todos Santos into one of the most charming spots in Baja. Long the agricultural center of southern Baja, Todos Santos lies 65 miles (an hour's drive) north of Cabo San Lucas on Mexico Highway 19. The ride up the Pacific Coast passes a fabulous blooming desertscape, gorgeous wild beaches, isolated campgrounds, wild burros and mules, and a few solitary homes. Several farms in the area specialize in organic produce that is shipped to gourmet restaurants in Los Cabos and southern California. The town of 3,500 residents is undergoing a real-estate boom, with entrepreneurs investing in older mansions around the town plaza for use as private homes, shops, and restaurants. During the Festival Fundidor, October 10 through 14, celebrating the founding of the town in 1723, streets around the main plaza are filled with food, games and wandering troubadors. Many of the better crafts stores (there aren't a lot of these), and the Café Santa Fe are closed from the end of Septemher through the end of the festival. Todos Santos is a good stopover for those traveling between Cabo and La Paz, and the town is well worth a day's visit, which can be arranged through tour companies in Los Cabos.

Where to Stay & Eat

Hotel California. Calle Juárez between Morelos and Marquez de Leon. ☎ **114/5-0002.** Fax 114/5-2333. 16 rms (all with bath). FAN. $35 single; $42 double.

This hotel is benefiting from the town's popularity, and reservations are a good idea in high season. Grouped around a courtyard, the plain, but very clean rooms face either the street or a courtyard and small pool; most have been refurbished with fresh paint, tiled bathrooms, and new curtains. The hotel restaurant serves breakfast, and other restaurants are nearby. Parking is available on the street.

Café Santa Fe. Calle Centenario 4. ☎ **114/5-0340.** Appetizers $12–$13; main courses $12–$15. Wed–Mon noon–9pm. Closed Sept. 29–Oct. 18. ITALIAN.

Much of the attention Todos Santos is receiving these days can be directly attributed to this superb café. Owners Ezio and Paula Colombo have completely refurbished a large stucco house across from the plaza, creating several dining rooms and a lovely courtyard located beside a garden of hibiscus, bougainvillea, papaya trees, and herbs.

The Italian cuisine emphasizes local produce and seafood; try the homemade ravioli stuffed with spinach and ricotta in a gorgonzola sauce or the ravioli with lobster and shrimp. In high season the wait for a table at lunch can last for hours; once seated, patrons tend to take their time, lingering over espresso and tiramisu.

2 La Paz

110 miles N of Cabo San Lucas, 122 miles NW of San José del Cabo, 980 miles SE of Tijuana

La Paz means "Peace," and few things are more peaceful than relaxing in an open-air café along La Paz's palm-fringed seaside boulevard as the sun sets across the saucer-shaped bay. This laid-back yet thriving port city of 180,000 is also the capital of the state of Baja California Sur. As a port city it lacks the feeling of a tourist town, though there's plenty to do nearby. Many visitors use La Paz as a launching point for whale watching and birding expeditions or sea kayaking, diving, or fishing trips. At Espiritu Santo and Los Islotes it's possible to swim with sea lions. Beaches line the malecón (the main waterfront drive), and others are within a 20-mile radius. Although this casual capital is enjoyable anytime, its carefree charm bursts into full bloom each February—La Paz has the biggest Carnaval celebration in Baja.

ESSENTIALS

GETTING THERE & DEPARTING   By Plane   Aero California (☎ 112/5-1023) has flights to La Paz from Los Angeles, Loreto, Tijuana, and Mexico City. **Aeroméxico** (☎ 112/2-0091, 2-0093, or 2-1636), flies in from Ciudad Obregón, Culiacán, Los Mochis, Guaymas, Hermosillo, Mexico City, Guadalajara, Tijuana, Tucson, and Los Angeles.

By Bus   The Central Camionera (main bus station) is at Jalisco and Héroes de la Independencia, about 25 blocks southwest of the center of town; it's open daily from 6am to 10pm. The bus lines first-class **Tres Estrellas de Oro** (☎ 112/2-6476), second-class **Aguila** (☎ 112/2-7094 or 5-7330), and second-class **Transportes de La Paz** serve La Paz with buses from the south (Los Cabos) and north (as far as Tijuana). From Los Cabos it's $2^1/2$ to $3^1/2$ hours to La Paz (if you take the short route—the Vía Corta); from Loreto to La Paz it's five hours. Buses leave every two or three hours for Los Cabos (south) and points north (Loreto and beyond). It's best to buy your ticket in person the day before, though Tres Estrellas de Oro says reservations can be made over the phone.

To get to the station, catch the "Ruta INSS" city bus near the corner of Revolución and Degollado by the market. It's often crowded, so be prepared to stand. The fare is about 50¢. Taxi fare from downtown to the station runs $2 to $3.50.

To get to Pichilingue, the ferry pier, and close to outlying beaches, the **Aguila** line has a station, sometimes called the "beach bus station," on the Malecón at Independencia (☎ 112/2-7898). The station is open daily from 7am to 6pm, but buses to the ferry have shorter hours.

By Car   From San José del Cabo, Highway 1 north is the longer, more scenic route; you can travel a flatter and faster route by taking Highway 1 east to Cabo San Lucas, then Highway 19 north through Todos Santos. A little before San Pedro, Highway 19 rejoins Highway 1 north into La Paz; the trip takes two to three hours. From Loreto to the north, Highway 1 south is the only choice; the trip takes four to five hours.

By Ferry   Two **SEMATUR car ferries** serve La Paz from Topolobampo (the port for Los Mochis) Monday through Saturday at 10pm (a 10-hour trip) and from

Mazatlán Sunday through Friday at 3pm. In La Paz tickets are sold at the SEMATUR office at 5 de Mayo no. 502.

The SEMATUR car ferry departs for Topolobampo Monday and Wednesday through Saturday at 8pm (a 10-hour trip) and for Mazatlán on Sunday through Friday at 3pm (an 18-hour crossing). The dock is at Pichilingue, 11 miles north of La Paz. Passengers pay one fee for themselves and another for their vehicles. The one-way fare per passenger to Topolobampo is $15 in Salón class—about 440 bus-type seats in one or more large rooms on the lower deck. To Mazatlán, one-way fares are $22 for Salón class (which can become very crowded); $43 for Turista class (a tiny room with four bunks, chair, sink, window, and individual baths/showers down the hall); and $65 for Cabina class (a small room with one bunk, chair, table, window, and private bath). *Note:* All these classes are not available all the time, and ferry schedules change.

SEMATUR ferries are usually equipped with a cafeteria and bar. Nevertheless, it's wise to bring some of your own food and bottled water. Also, reserve as early as possible and confirm your reservation 24 hours before departure; you can pick up tickets at the port terminal ticket office as late as the morning of the day you are leaving. Ferry tickets are sold at the office at 5 de Mayo no. 502 at Guillermo Pieta, La Paz, B.C.S. 23000 (☎ **112/5-3833** or 5-4666). Though the office is open daily from 7am to 1pm and 4 to 6pm, you can only purchase tickets between 7 and 10am. Tickets can also be purchased at the SEMATUR office at the Pichilingue ferry dock (☎ **112/ 2-9485;** fax 112/5-6588); it's open daily from 7am to 1pm and 4 to 6pm. Several tour agencies in town book reservations on the ferry, but it is best to buy your ticket in person at the ferry office.

Important note: Those planning to take their cars on the ferry to the Mexican mainland will be required to meet all the requirements listed in "Crossing the Border with Your Car" (see "Getting There" in chapter 2), and all travelers going to the mainland need tourist cards. Tourism officials in La Paz say it's best to get your car permit and tourist card when you first cross the border at Tijuana, since the system is set up more efficiently there.

Buses to Pichilingue depart from the "beach bus terminal" (☎ **112/2-7898**) on the Malecón at Independencia 10 times from 7am to 2:30pm. Bus fare is $1. A taxi from downtown La Paz to the dock will cost around $10.

ORIENTATION   Arriving by Plane   The airport (☎ **112/2-9386**) is 11 miles northwest of town along the highway to Ciudad Constitución and Tijuana. Airport colectivos (minivans) to downtown cost around $10 (they run only from the airport to town, not vice versa). The taxi fare to or from the airport is about $16.

Arriving by Bus   Buses arrive at the **Central Camionera,** about 25 blocks southwest of downtown. A cab from here to hotels into the center of town will run $3 to $3.50.

Arriving by Ferry   Buses line up in front of the ferry dock at Pichilingue to meet every arriving ferry. They charge about $1 for the ride into town, stopping at the "beach bus station" on the Malecón at Independencia—within walking distance of many downtown hotels if you're not encumbered with luggage. A taxi from the ferry into downtown La Paz (11 miles) costs around $10.

Information   The most accessible **tourist information office** is on Obregón across from the intersection with Calle 16 de Septiembre (☎ **112/2-1199,** 112/2-7975, or 112/2-5939). It's open Monday through Friday from 8am to 8pm. The extremely helpful staff speaks English and can supply information on La Paz, Los Cabos, and the rest of the region.

Another source of tourist information is **tourist services in the lobby of the Hotel Los Arcos** (☎ 112/1-5577 or 5-4794), open daily from 9am to 2pm and from 4 to 7pm. Jack and Jackie Velez have been operating this service for years as part of their sportfishing business and are extremely knowledgeable about the area. The English-speaking staff can help with everything from airline schedules to whale-watching trips, not to mention water sports, tours, and cruises.

City Layout   Although La Paz sprawls well inland from the **Malecón** (the seaside boulevard, **Paseo Alvaro Obregón**), you'll probably spend most of your time in the older, more congenial downtown section within a few blocks of the waterfront. The main plaza, **Plaza República,** is bounded by Madero, Independencia, Revolución, and 5 de Mayo. The plaza is a centered on an iron kiosk where public concerts are held frequently in the evenings.

Getting Around   Because most of what you'll need in town is located on the Malecón between the tourist information office and the Hotel Los Arcos or a few blocks inland from the waterfront, it's easy to get around La Paz on foot. There are public **buses** that go to some of the beaches north of town (see "Fun On & Off the Beach," below), but to explore the many beaches within 50 miles of La Paz, the best bet is to rent a car. There are several auto-rental agencies on the Malecón.

FAST FACTS: LA PAZ

Area Code   The telephone area code is 112. Phone numbers were changing all over town when I was there. Call information if you have difficulty reaching a number.

Banks   Banks generally exchange currency Monday to Friday 9am to noon.

Long Distance Telephone   The Libreria Contempo (☎ 2-7875) on Arreola at Obregón, next to Las Perlas Hotel, has a lineup of private telephone booths for making long distance calls. It's open Monday through Friday from 10am to 3:30pm and 5 to 9:30pm, Saturday from 10am to 9:30pm and Sunday from 10am to 5pm.

Marinas   La Paz has three marinas: Marina de La Paz, at the west end of the Malecón at Legaspi (☎ 5-2112 or 5-1646); Marina Palmira, south of town at km 2.5 on the Pichilingue Highway (☎ 5-3959); and Marina Fidepaz, at km 4.5 Carretera Norte.

Municipal Market   Three blocks inland at Degollado and Revolución de 1910, the public market sells mainly produce, meats, and utilitarian wares and is open Monday through Saturday from 6am to 6pm and Sunday from 6am to 1pm.

Parking   In high season street parking may be hard to find in the downtown area, but there are several guarded lots, and side streets are less crowded over all. Overnight parking costs $3 to $5.

Post Office   The Correos is three blocks inland at Constitución and Revolución de 1910 and is open Monday through Friday from 8am to 6pm and Saturday from 8am to 1pm.

FUN ON & OFF THE BEACH

La Paz combines the unselfconscious bustle of a small capital port city with beautiful, isolated beaches not far from town. Everything from whale watching and sea kayaking to beach tours, sunset cruises, and visits to the sea lion colony can usually be arranged through travel agencies in major hotels or along the Malecón. These can also be arranged through agencies in the United States that specialize in Baja's natural history. (See chapter 2, "Outdoor Sports, Adventure Travel & Wilderness Trips.")

FESTIVALS & EVENTS   February features the biggest and best **Carnaval/Mardi Gras** in Baja. In March there's the **Festival of the Whale.** May 3 features a **festival**

celebrating the city's founding by Cortés in 1535. The annual **marlin-fishing tournament** is in August, with other fishing tournaments scheduled in September and November. And on **November 1–2,** the Day of the Dead altars are on display at the Anthropology Museum.

BEACHES   Within a 10- to 45-minute drive from La Paz lie some of the loveliest beaches in Baja, many rivaling those of the Caribbean with their clear, turquoise water. The beach-lined Malecón (the waterfront drive), is the most convenient beach in town. More exclusive and nicer is the beach immediately north of town at La Concha Beach Resort; outsiders may use the hotel restaurant/bar and rent equipment for snorkeling, diving, skiing, and sailing. It's 6 miles north of town on the Pichilingue highway at 5.5km. A taxi ride to La Concha costs $6. The other beaches are all farther north of town, but midweek you may have these far distant beaches to yourself.

At least 10 public buses from the "beach bus station" at Independencia on the Malecón depart from 8am to 2:30pm for beaches to the north. The buses stop at the small **Playa Coromuel** (3.1 miles), **Playa Camancito** (5 miles), **Playa Tesorso** (8.9 miles), and **Pichilingue** (10.5 miles; from the ferry stop, walk north on the highway to the beach). Ask when the last bus will make the return trip. The one-way fare is $1. Both Pichilingue and Coromuel beaches have a palapa-shaded bar or restaurant, which may not be open midweek. Other beaches have no shade, and no rentals of chairs or umbrellas, so you're destined to sit in the blazing sun on whatever you brought, and most likely consuming food you packed.

The most beautiful of these outlying beaches is **Playa Tecolote,** found approximately 18 miles from La Paz on a paved road that ends there. The water is a heavenly cerulean blue. There are several restaurants, but service is limited midweek. To get to **Playa Tecolote,** take a bus as far as Pichilingue and from there a taxi the remaining 8 miles. Making arrangements for the taxi to return may be difficult. The road is paved as far as **Playa Tecolote** and **Playa Balandra** (18 miles), and turnoffs to these and other beaches are well marked.

For more information about beaches and maps, check at the tourist information office on the Malecón.

WHALE WATCHING   Between January and March (and sometimes as early as December), 3,000 to 5,000 gray whales migrate from the Bering Straits to the Pacific Coast of Baja. The main whale-watching spots are Laguna San Ignacio (on the Pacific near San Ignacio), Magdalena Bay (on the Pacific near Puerto López Mateos—about a two-hour drive from La Paz), and Scammon's Lagoon (near Guerrero Negro).

Though it is located across the peninsula on the Sea of Cortez, La Paz has the only major international airport in the area and thus has become the center of Baja's whale-watching excursions. Most tours originating in La Paz go to Magdalena Bay, where the whales give birth to their calves in calm waters. Several companies arrange whale-watching tours originating either in La Paz or other Baja towns or in the United States. Twelve-hour tours from La Paz start at around $100 per person, including breakfast, lunch, transportation, and an English-speaking guide. Make reservations

Impressions

Below the Mexican border [of Baja California] the water changes color; it takes on a deep ultramarine blue—a washtub bluing blue, intense and seeming to penetrate deep into the water; the fishermen call it "tuna water."

—John Steinbeck, Log from the Sea of Cortez, 1941

at Viajes Coromuel at the Hotel Los Arcos travel desk (☎ **112/2-2744,** ext. 608 or 2-8006), or Viajes Buendía Osório (☎ **112/2-6544** or 112/5-0467). Most tours from the United States offer birding, sea kayaking, and other close-to-nature experiences during the same trip. (See "Outdoor Sports, Adventure Travel & Wilderness Trips" in chapter 2 for details).

You can go whale watching without joining a tour by taking an Aguila bus from La Paz to Puerto López Mateos or San Carlos at Magdalena Bay (a three hour ride) and hiring a boat there. It's a difficult trip to do in one day, but there are a few very modest hotels in San Carlos. Check at the La Paz tourist office for information.

IN & ON THE WATER   Scuba-Diving Trips   Best from June through September, arrangements can be made through Fernando Aguilar's Baja Diving and Services at Independencia 107-A (☎ **112/2-1826;** fax 112/2-8644). Diving sites include the sea-lion colony at Los Islotes; distant Cerralvo Island; the sunken ship *Salvatierra*; a 60-foot wall dive; several sea mounts (underwater mountains) and reefs; and a trip to see hammerhead sharks and manta rays. Rates start at $65 to $75 per person for an all-day outing and two-tank dive. Baja Expeditions, Sonora 586 (☎ **112/5-3828;** fax 112/5-3829) in La Paz (see chapter 2 for information in the U.S. and Canada) runs live-aboard and single-day dive trips to the above-mentioned locations and other areas in the Sea of Cortez.

Sea Kayaking   Extremely popular in the many bays and coves near La Paz, many enthusiasts bring their own equipment. Kayaking trips can be arranged in advance with several companies from the U.S. (See "Outdoor Sports, Adventure Travel & Wilderness Trips" in chapter 2 for company descriptions.) Locally **Mar y Aventuras** (☎ **112/2-2744,** ext. 608 or 112/5-4794), also arranges kayaking trips.

Cruises   The most fascinating one is to Isla Espíritu Santo and Los Islotes to visit the largest **sea-lion** colony in Baja, stunning rock formations, and remote beaches, with stops for snorkeling, swimming, and lunch. If conditions permit, you may even be able to snorkel beside the sea lions. Both boat and bus tours are available to Puerto Balandra, where pristine coves of crystal-blue water and ivory sand are framed by bold rock formations rising up like humpback whales. Viajes Coromuel at the Hotel Los Arcos (☎ **112/2-8006**); Viajes Palmira (☎ **112/2-4030**) on the Malecón across from Hotel Los Arcos; and other travel agencies can arrange these all-day trips, weather permitting, for $40 per person. Sometimes a minimum of four to six people is required.

Sportfishing   La Paz is justly famous for its sportfishing and attracts anglers from all over the world; its waters are home to more than 850 species of fish. Here's a list of the most sought after fish and when you can find them: black marlin, August through November; crevalle, January through October; dorado, June through December; roosterfish, snapper, and grouper, April through October; marlin, May through July; needlefish, May through September; sailfish, June through November; sierra, October through June; wahoo and yellowfin tuna, April through December; and yellowtail December through May. The most economical approach is to rent a *panga* (skiff) with guide and equipment for $125 for three hours, but you don't go very far out. Super pangas, which have a shade cover and comfortable seats, start around $160 for two persons. Larger cruisers with bathrooms start at $240.

Sportfishing trips can be arranged through hotels and tour agencies. One of the best-known operations is Jack Velez's **Dorado Velez Fleet;** call him for reservations at the Hotel Los Arcos Fishing Desk (☎ **112/2-2744,** ext. 608) or write to him at Apdo. Postal 402, La Paz, B.C.S. 23000. Other operations include the **Mosquito Fleet** (☎ **112/2-1674**) and **Baja Fishing** (☎ **112/2-1313**). Ask what the price includes, since you may need to bring your own food and drinks. (See also "Outdoor Sports, Adventure Travel & Wilderness Trips" in chapter 2 for booking La Paz fishing from the U.S.)

HISTORIC LA PAZ When Cortés landed here on May 3, 1535 he named it Bahía Santa Cruz, which didn't stick. In April 1683, Eusebio Kino, a Spanish Jesuit priest, arrived and dubbed the place Nuestro Señora de la Paz (Our Lady of Peace). It wasn't until November 1, 1720, however, that a permanent mission was set up here by Jaime Bravo, another Jesuit priest. He used the same name as his immediate predecessor calling it the **Mision de Nuestro Señora de la Paz.** The mission church stands on La Paz's main square on Revolución between 5 de Mayo and Independencia, and today the city is called simply La Paz.

The **Anthropology Museum,** on Altamirano between Constitución and 5 de Mayo (☎ **112/2-0162**), features large, though faded, color photos of Baja's prehistoric cave paintings. There are also exhibits on various topics, including the geological history of the peninsula, fossils, missions, colonial history, and daily life. All information is in Spanish. Admission is free (donations are encouraged); it's open Monday through Friday from 8am to 6pm and Saturday from 9am to 2pm.

El Teatro de la Ciudad (Av. Navarro 700; ☎ **112/5-0004**), is the city's cultural center, with performances by visiting and local artists.

The **Casa de Gobierno,** across the plaza from the mission church on Madero between 5 de Mayo and Independencia, houses the **Biblioteca de las Californias** (Library of the Californias). The small collection of historical documents and books is the most comprehensive in Baja and is open to the public Monday through Friday from 8am to 8pm. Free international films are sometimes shown in the evenings.

City tours of all the major sights are offered by most tour agencies. Tours last about three hours, include time for shopping, and cost $25 per person.

A DAY-TRIP A day-trip by car or guided tour to **Los Cabos** at the southern tip of Baja California, where the Pacific Ocean meets the Sea of Cortez, will take you past dramatic scenery and many photogenic isolated beaches. A guided tour that includes lunch and a glass-bottom-boat tour to El Arco in Cabo San Lucas costs $45 to $60 per person and can be booked through most travel agencies. Most tours last from 7am to 6pm, and some include breakfast.

SHOPPING

La Paz has little in the way of folk art or other treasures from mainland Mexico. The dense cluster of streets behind the Hotel Perla between 16 de Septiembre and Degollado is chock-full of small shops, some tacky though others quite upscale. Serdan from Degollado south offers dozens of sellers of dried spices, piñatas, and candy. The municipal market at Revolución and Degollado, however, has little of interest to visitors.

Antigua California. Paseo Obregón near Martinez. ☎ **112/5-5230.**

This shop manages to stay in business as others come and go and carries a good selection of folk art from throughout Mexico. It's open daily from 10am to 2pm and 4 to 8pm.

Artesanías Cuauhtémoc (The Weaver). Abasolo 3315 between Jalisco and Nayarit. ☎ **112/2-4575.**

If you like beautiful handwoven tablecloths, placemats, rugs, and other textiles, it's worth the long walk or taxi ride to Artesanías Cuauhtémoc, also called "The Weaver."

Fortunato Silva, an elderly gentleman, weaves wonderfully textured cotton textiles from yarn he spins and dyes himself. He charges far less than what you'd pay for equivalent artistry in the United States. It's open Monday through Saturday from 9am to 2pm and 4 to 6pm and Sunday from 10am to 1pm.

WHERE TO STAY
DOUBLES FOR LESS THAN $15

Hotel Posada San Miguel. 16 de Septiembre and Domínguez, La Paz, B.C.S. 23000. ☎ 112/2-1802. 15 rms (all with bath). FAN. $7.50 single; $10 double.

Tidy and Spartan, this two-story (no elevator) hotel is on a busy street in the downtown commercial district, three blocks inland from the waterfront. The rooms are arranged around an attractive, small courtyard full of plants and flowers. Rooms are almost hospital clean, with painted concrete floors, colorful light cotton bedspreads, and metal doors and windows that look out on an exterior walkway. Reserve in advance if possible—the hotel is often booked. There are several guarded parking lots near the hotel; overnight parking costs $3 to $5.

Pensión California. Degollado 209, La Paz, B.C.S. 23000. ☎ 112/2-2896. 26 rms (all with bath). FAN. $6.75 single; $9 double.

In the middle of town, three blocks inland from the Malecón at Madero, this rather grim pension is housed in an old red-and-white colonial home. The clean, but run-down, cell-like rooms are painted bright blue and white and furnished with ceiling fans, fluorescent lighting, lumpy pillows with meager pillowcases, and well-used mattresses on concrete bases. The showers have no curtains. Rooms are arranged around a large, unkempt courtyard spilling over with plants, trees, Mexican paintings, and bric-a-brac.

DOUBLES FOR LESS THAN $25

Hotel Gardenias. Serdán 520 at Guerrero, (Apdo. Postal 197), 23000 La Paz, B.C.S. ☎ 112/2-3088. Fax 112/5-0436. 56 rms (all with bath). A/C TV TEL. $16.50 single; $20 double. Free parking; guarded.

Though on a side street a bit far from the mainstream of La Paz, there's something charming about this old-timey hotel that could make it worthy of repeat visits. It's ideal for those with cars or anyone seeking inexpensive relaxation (though it's noisy during Mexican holidays). The decor is a blend of neo-Spanish colonial and 1950s motel. The bright pink-and-white Gardenias is popular with Mexican families. Set back on grounds, the two-story building surrounds a large courtyard and pool. The huge rooms have worn carpet, dated furniture, and chenile bedspreads, but they're very clean. The hotel coffee shop is open daily from 7:30am to 3pm. The Hotel Gardenias is about a 30-minute walk from the center of downtown, three blocks inland from the Malecón.

Hotel Lorimar. Bravo 110, La Paz, B.C.S. 23000. ☎ 112/5-3822. Fax 112/5-6387. 20 rms (all with bath). A/C. $18 single; $22 double. Prices may be 30 to 40 percent higher in high season. Closed September and the first half of October.

This modest hotel on a shady street is a cheery, peaceful hideaway offering friendly, personal service. The rooms in the two- and three-story buildings are immaculately clean; those facing the back patio are the best choice. The hotel is well known among La Paz regulars; make reservations early during holidays and peak seasons. The upstairs restaurant has a great view from the porch. The Lorimar is located between Madero and Mutualismo. There are usually parking spaces available on Bravo.

Hotel Miramar. 5 de Mayo at Domínguez, La Paz B.C.S. 23000. ☎ **112/2-8885.** Fax 112/ 2-0672. 26 rms (all with bath). A/C TV TEL. $20 single or double; $25 triple.

One block west of the main plaza, the Miramar sits on a quiet side street with far less traffic noise than on the Malecón. The good-sized rooms have minirefrigerators, small desks, one or two double beds, tile floors, and TV with a VCR. Some rooms don't have windows or only have small windows facing the hallways. Others on the third floor have a bit of an ocean view. A security guard keeps an eye on cars parked on the street in front of the hotel at night.

DOUBLES FOR LESS THAN $35

Hotel Aquario's. Ramírez 1665, La Paz, B.C.S. 23000. ☎ **112/2-9266.** Fax 112/5-5713. 60 rms (all with bath). A/C TV TEL. $27 single; $30 double. Free parking.

This popular, well-maintained three-story motel frames a protected parking lot and pool. Each of the comfortable, neat rooms comes with a small balcony, one or two double beds, a table and two chairs, and a bathroom with a tub as well as a shower. The on-premises restaurant/bar is open daily from 7am to 11pm. Laundry service is available. You'll find the hotel six blocks inland from the Malecón; take Degollado and then make a left on Ramírez.

Hotel Mediterrane. Allende 36-B, La Paz, B.C.S. 23000. ☎ and fax **112/5-1195.** 5 rms (all with bath). A/C or FAN. $30–$40 single or double.

This small two-story inn on a side street off the Malecón has bright rooms with pale wood furnishings, upholstered chairs, and cool tile floors. The hotel sits behind Bistro Paradiso/Trattoria La Patza, where meals are served from 7am to 11pm daily. Street parking is available.

El Mesón. Felix Ortega 2330, La Paz, B.C.S. 23000. ☎ **112/5-7454.** Fax 112/5-7464. 8 rms (all with bath). A/C TV TEL. $30 single or double (including continental breakfast). Free parking; guarded.

The sedate decor and courteous clerks make this a regular choice for discerning travelers more interested in a comfortable room than a tourist-oriented location. The handsome rooms have an Asian flair, with large tiled baths, sliding shower doors, double or king-size beds, and verandas. The classy Mexican restaurant known for its polite service and generous portions is open daily from 7am to 11pm. A pianist croons romantic ballads Thursday through Sunday from 7 to 11pm at the piano bar. El Mesón is situated in a quiet residential neighborhood 13 blocks east of the Malecón at the intersection of Ortega and Calle Bravo.

DOUBLES FOR LESS THAN $50

Hotel Perla. Paseo Obregón, 1570 (Apdo. Postal 207), La Paz B.C.S. 23000. ☎ **112/2-0777.** Fax 112/5-5363. 101 rms (all with bath). A/C TV TEL. $45–$50 single or double (but there's almost always a 20% discount); Free parking; guarded.

Well situated in the center of the Malecón between Callejón La Paz and Arreola, this attractive four-story hotel overlooks the bay. The rooms have white textured walls and chunky, blond-wood furniture, including king-size beds in 10 rooms. Amenities include purified tap water, a pool and sun deck on the second floor, travel agency, La Cabaña disco, laundry service, and room service. A local favorite is the hotel's airy streetside restaurant, La Terraza, a great spot for margaritas and sunsets over the water. Try to get one of the 28 rooms with a sea view.

WHERE TO EAT

La Paz has a growing assortment of good, reasonably priced restaurants. You get more for your money here than in San José or Cabo San Lucas.

Restaurants along the seaside **Malecón** tend to be more expensive than those a few blocks inland. Taco stands abound and appear during mealtimes on the downtown streets.

Coffee lovers might wish to visit **La Casa del Buen Café** on Serdán near Bravo. Coffee beans imported from Guatemala, Cuba, and southern Mexico are sold by the kilo (great as souvenir gifts); brewed coffee costs 25¢ to 50¢. The shop is open Monday through Friday from 10am to 2pm and 4 to 8pm and Saturday from 9am to 2pm.

MEALS FOR LESS THAN $5

Fuente de Sodas Daisy. 16 de Septiembre and Paseo Obregón. No phone. Breakfast $2–$3.50; tortas $1.50; fresh juices 85¢–$1.50. Daily 8am–10pm. MEXICAN/AMERICAN.

You can't miss the bright purple sidewalk tables just around the corner from the Malecón. The stools at this tiny lunch counter are also a vivid purple, and their occupants are young and hip. The licuados and juices are blessedly refreshing, and the cuban tortas, quesadillas, tacos, and hamburgers hit the spot as a snack or a meal. The few tables under the sidewalk tree are usually occupied, but you may find a seat for a late-afternoon coffee-and-postcard break.

El Quinto Sol. Domínguez 12. ☎ **112/2-1692.** Breakfast $1.50–$2.50; soup $1.75; main courses $2.50–$4.50. Mon–Sat 7am–9:30pm. HEALTH FOOD.

A longtime favorite among local vegetarians, El Quinto Sol is part café, part health-food store with a great selection of herbs and grains. It's easy to fill up for little money on a large serving of brown rice and steamed vegetables; veggie burgers and fries; or a huge bowl of fruit, yogurt, and granola. They make unusual but nutritious drinks not found in other health food restaurants, including one made from chaya leaves (supposedly filled with vitamins). The restaurant is one block east of the Plaza República at the corner of Independencia and Domínguez.

✪ **Tacos Hermanos González.** Mutualismo and Esquerro. No phone. Tacos $1.15 each. Daily 10am–7pm. FISH TACOS.

Pedestrians literally stop traffic at this busy intersection as they line up for the best tacos in town. Bowls of salsas, cilantro, cabbage, mayonnaise, and other condiments line the edges of the taco carts, where the González brothers wrap chunks of deep-fried fish into warm corn tortillas. You can hardly resist the aroma. Pick up a taco to go or stand on the corner with a cluster of impromptu diners—you'll probably want seconds.

MEALS FOR LESS THAN $10

✪ **Bismark II.** Degollado and Altamirano. ☎ **112/2-4854.** Breakfast $2.50–$3.50; main courses $3.50–$17. Daily 8am–11pm. SEAFOOD/MEXICAN.

Seafood doesn't get any better than at Bismark, whether you have fish tacos, chile rellenos stuffed with lobster salad, marlin "meatballs" and paella, breaded oysters, or a sundae glass filled with ceviche or shrimp. Extremely fresh dorado, halibut, snapper, or whatever is in season can be prepared in many ways. Chips and a creamy dip are served while you wait. The decor of pine walls and dark wood chairs reminds me more of a country café than what you'd expect for a seafood restaurant. But it's cool, and service is excellent, though it gets very crowded at lunch so get there early. Walk seven blocks inland on Degollado to Altamirano and plan on lingering over a late lunch. The owners will call a cab for you if you wish.

Carlo 'n Charlie La Paz-Lapa. Obrégon at 16 de Septiembre. ☎ **112/2-9290.** Appetizers $3.50–$6; main courses $3.75–$13. Daily noon–midnight. INTERNATIONAL.

La Paz's branch of the infamous Carlos 'n Charlie's has an ambience that's more formal than usual with cloth-covered tables and wonderful air-conditioning. There's live music in the back patio on Thursday, Friday, and Saturday nights with a bar only. The food is predictably well prepared, and portions are generous. For a taste of local seafood, try the whole fried red snapper.

○ **Rosticería California.** Serdán 1740. ☎ **112/2-5118.** Main courses $3–$7. Daily 8am–8pm, Sun 8am–6pm. MEXICAN CHICKEN.

Tasty chicken is the main dish here: it comes roasted, fried, and sometimes cooked in soup. Whole- and half-chicken orders are served with salad, french fries, tortillas, and salsa. Ignore the tacky leatherette booths in the front, there's better seating on the patio in back. The Rosticería is five blocks inland from the Malecón on Degollado; turn right on Serdán, and you'll find it not far from the public market.

Trattoria La Pazta. Allende 36. ☎ **112/5-1195.** Main courses $5–$7.50. Wed–Mon 4–10pm. (Closed September and first half of October.) ITALIAN.

The trendiest restaurant in town, La Pazta gleams with black lacquered tables and white tile; the aroma of garlic and espresso floats in the air. The menu features local fresh seafood such as pasta with squid in wine and cream sauce and crispy fried calamari. Lasagna is baked in a wood-fired oven. There's an extensive wine list, though service is a bit lacking, and everything on the menu may not be available. The restaurant is in front of the Hotel Mediterrane, one block inland from the Malecón.

LA PAZ AFTER DARK

A night in La Paz should begin in a café along the Malecón as the sun sinks into the sea, often painting a luminous Maxfield Parrish sort of scene with gold-tinged, almost iridescently glowing colors streaking across the broad bay behind the palm trees. Always have your camera ready at sunset.

A favorite ringside seat at dusk is a table at **La Terraza,** next to the Hotel Perla. La Terraza makes good schooner-size margaritas. **Pelicanos Bar,** in the second story of the Hotel Los Arcos, has a good view of the waterfront and a clubby, cozy feel. **La Paz-Lapa** has live music on the weekends. The liveliest of all is **La Cabaña nightclub** in the Hotel Perla, featuring one or two bands Tuesday through Sunday playing Latin rhythms. It opens at 9:30pm, and there's a $7 minimum consumption requirement. An inexpensive alternative is to stroll along the Malecón and people watch, stopping for a drink or snack or to hear some wandering mariachis.

The poolside bar overlooking the beach at **La Concha Beach Resort,** Km 5.5, Pichilingue Hwy. (☎ 112/2-6544), is the setting for Mexican fiestas at 7pm on Friday nights and barbecues at 6:30pm Saturday nights during holidays and busy tourist seasons. The cover is $15, and round-trip taxi fare from downtown is $16.

The Copper Canyon 4

The Copper Canyon (Cañon del Cobre), said to be four times larger than the Grand Canyon, is actually made up of some 20 canyons. Along its rim runs the famed *Chihuahua al Pacífico* (Chihuahua to the Pacific) railway. Acclaimed as an engineering miracle, it is 390 miles long and has 39 bridges (the highest is over 1,000 feet above the Chinipas River, the longest is $1/3$ of a mile in length) and 86 tunnels (one over a mile long). It loops down to sea level and up to 9,000 feet through some of Mexico's most majestic pastel-colored, rugged mountain and pine-forest country.

EXPLORING THE COPPER CANYON

With the exception of those in Creel, most of the hotels in the canyon are overly expensive—even considering that rates in most cases include three meals. (The late 1994 devaluation only seemed to drive prices higher). But you can see the Copper Canyon on a budget. With perseverance, it's possible to plan a trip yourself, balancing train stops with hotels, obtaining your train tickets, and making your reservations—especially if you use Creel as a base. Using a travel agent or one of the tour operators mentioned below can ease the uncertainty of travel, but if you prefer not to you can contact the hotels directly and buy your ticket when you arrive in Los Mochis or Chihuahua (See "Buying a Ticket," below). Or you can travel off-season without hotel reservations and take potluck. **Creel** ("Stop 5," below), with the most budget-priced hotels and some of the best side trips, is the most economical choice as a base for canyon travel. **Batopilas,** while too far away from "civilization" to be considered a "base," has both economical and luxury lodgings and offers the priceless cultural experience of the canyonlands. If you purchase your own train ticket, avoid peak canyon travel times (see below) and try to buy your ticket a day or two in advance, since at times the train is booked to capacity.

The *Chihuahua al Pacífico* train runs between **Chihuahua** and **Los Mochis** through the Copper Canyon country. Generally speaking, either Los Mochis or El Fuerte, on the line's west end, is the preferable starting place for this trip—the most scenic part of the 12- to 15-hour journey is between El Fuerte and Creel, and the chances of seeing it in good daylight are best if the trip begins in Los Mochis or El Fuerte. If the train from Chihuahua to Los Mochis runs on schedule (and it has all the times I've taken it), you'll also get daylight during the best part of the trip, but if you don't want to take a chance, start in Los Mochis or El Fuerte. Chihuahua, however, is a more interesting city than Los Mochis.

A trip on the train with stops to stay at lodges en route is an adventure, fraught with the possibility of uncertainty—sold-out trains, delays, full hotels, being out in the middle of nowhere on an excursion when your Jeep breaks down, and so on— even when you've planned every last detail. Accommodations are comfortable but rustic; most don't have electricity (lanterns provide light), and only in Creel and El Fuerte are there telephones (though Cerocahui may have one soon). Rooms have wood-burning stoves for heat in winter, and most, except where noted, have private bathrooms.

Be sure to start the journey with the money you'll need, since changing money outside of Creel is almost impossible, and credit cards are fairly useless. Peak travel times in the canyon are from the end of February through April, and October through early November. Off-season months are June, July, and August (which can be dry, dusty, and extremely hot in the canyon bottoms, but pleasant enough above), January (very cold with snow in the highlands), mid-November, and December. You can pass through the Copper Canyon in one 15-hour day, spending a night in Chihuahua and another in Los Mochis, but you'd miss the essence of the canyon. I'd recommend at least one or two overnight stops along the way.

The four-night, five-day trips often planned by tour companies seem too brief to me. These allow for flying into either Chihuahua or Los Mochis, with one night in each city as you begin and end a trip, and two nights in the canyon, usually at El Divisadero. This is homogenized canyon travel—everyone has exactly the same limited travel experience. I suggest you begin and end your trip in Chihuahua (taking the train twice), skip Los Mochis, spending two nights en route (at El Divisadero, Creel, and/or Bahuichivo), and a night or two in El Fuerte, where you board the train back to Chihuahua. This allows for overnighting at the five stops enroute, or some variation of that. Such a trip would take around 10 days, after which you'll have a real vacation to remember.

If you spend a night en route, you'll have roughly 24 hours at each destination— usually enough time for one or two excursions. While every stop is interesting, Creel and Cerocahui offer the most possibilities. Creel, a rustic lumber town, offers the only economical lodgings in the canyon and great hiking and overnight camping—and van tours, too.

Drivers from all canyon hotels await trains, and if you don't have a reservation you can ask a driver about room availability. However, the hotels are quite small, and groups often fill them up, so it's almost imperative to make reservations in advance, especially in peak season.

A Safety Note: Bandits have held up the *Chihuahua al Pacífico* train several times in recent years. But there have been no robberies since armed guards began riding the trains. The guards aren't friendly, but then public relations isn't their mission. It's also no secret that hidden farmlands in the Copper Canyon are the domain of marijuana farmers and that some prominent names in the state are rumored to be linked to it. This has never affected one of my trips, though. If you are hiking the backwoods, and come across a field of marijuana, leave very quickly—no one growing an illegal crop wants to be discovered.

1 Los Mochis

126 miles SW of Alamos, 50 miles SW of El Fuerte, 193 miles SE of Guaymas, 260 miles NW of Mazatlán

Los Mochis, in Sinaloa State, is a low-lying city of 350,000 founded in 1903 by an American, Benjamin Johnson of Pennsylvania. It is a wealthy city in a fertile agricultural area, and aside from the enormous sugar mill at the northwestern end of town, there's not much of note. The city's architecture is distinctly American. The town's importance to the tourist is as a boarding point for the Chihuahua al Pacífico train, and for ferry connections to Baja California or road travel south down the Pacific Coast to Mazatlán and beyond, or north to Alamos and Guaymas.

ESSENTIALS

GETTING THERE & DEPARTING **By Plane** **Aeroméxico** (☎ 68/15-2570 for reservations) and its subsidiary **Aerolitoral** have direct service from Chihuahua, Hermosillo, and Mazatlán. **AeroCalifornia** (☎ 68/18-1616) flies to and from Los Angeles, La Paz, Guadalajara, Mexico City, Culiacán, and Tijuana.

By Train The **Chihuahua al Pacífico** (Copper Canyon train) runs between Los Mochis and Chihuahua once daily. It leaves Los Mochis at 6am (mountain/Los Mochis time); taxis charge $6.50 from downtown to the station. From Chihuahua it leaves at 7am and arrives in Los Mochis around 7pm (first class fare either way is $26.50). Complete Copper Canyon train information is in Section 2 of this chapter.

By Bus Los Mochis is marginally served by buses. Most passing through are de paso. The first-class station is at Degollado 200 (near Juárez), ☎ 68/12-1757. From here, **Elite** sends buses to and from Tijuana, Monterrey, Nogales, and Cd. Juárez. **Autotransportes Transpacíficos** (same station and phone) services Nogales, Tijuana, Mazatlán, Guadalajara, Querétaro, and Mexico City. There are several choices for second-class service. **Transportes Norte de Sonora,** Avenida Morelos 335 Pte., at Zaragoza (☎ 68/12-0411 or 68/12-0026), and **Transportes del Pacífico,** Avenida Morelos 337 Pte. (☎ 68/12-0347 or 68/12-0341), next door, make the same runs, but almost all are de paso. For buses that originate here and pass through Navojoa (crossroads to Alamos), go to the ticket booth in the back of the station. Eleven buses go to Navojoa, the first at 5am and the last at 5pm. There are two places to catch the bus to El Fuerte (a 1 1/2 to 2 hour trip). The first is at the Mercado Independencia, where the bus stops at the corner of Independencia and Degollado. The other is at the corner of Cuauhtémoc at Prieto, close to the Hotel America. Ask hotel desk clerks or the tourism office for a schedule. El Fuerte buses, which run frequently throughout the day, are the school-bus variety, and the purser stows luggage in the back of the bus. Were it not for the numerous stops en route, the trip would take an hour. A taxi to or from El Fuerte takes about an hour and costs around $50.

By Car Coastal Highway 15 is well maintained in both directions leading into Los Mochis. (For more information on travel conditions on Highway 15 from the U.S. border, see "Safety" in Fast Facts in chapter 2.)

By Ferry The SEMATUR ferry from La Paz, Baja California, to nearby Topolobampo leaves La Paz Monday through Saturday at 11am and arrives in Los Mochis at 7pm—an eight-hour trip.

From Topolobampo the SEMATUR ferry to La Paz, Baja California, leaves Monday through Saturday at 10pm and arrives in La Paz at 8am. Service ranges from a seat (Monday through Saturday, $10) to Cabina Especial, which is a private room with a bed and bathroom, (Wednesday and Thursday only, $40). For tickets and information, contact **SEMATUR** at the ferry pier in Topolobampo (☎ **68/62-0141;** fax 68/62-0035) or better yet, in Los Mochis call Viajes Paotam (☎ **68/15-1914** or 68/15-8262). Reservations are highly recommended. The ferry has restaurant and medical facilities, video movies, and a disco. A taxi from your Los Mochis hotel to the ferry dock (13 miles) costs about $10.

ORIENTATION   Arriving   The airport is 13 miles north of town. Transportation is controlled from the airport, but to return you'll have to hire a taxi. A taxi from the airport into town is $5 per person. All bus stations are downtown within walking distance of the hotels. If you arrive by ferry in Topolobampo, you'll have to bargain with waiting taxis for the fare to Los Mochis. The train station is about 3 miles from town, and taxis charge around $6.50 to take you to the central city.

Information   The **City Tourist Office** is in a back corner of the State Government building at Cuauhtémoc and Allende (☎ **68/12-6640**) and has a helpful staff and usually someone who speaks English. The office is open Monday through Friday from 8am to 3pm.

City Layout   Los Mochis contains no central plaza. To acquaint yourself with this city, use the Hotel Santa Anita, Avenida Leyva at Avenida Obregón, as an orientation point. The bus stations, hotels, and restaurants are within a few blocks of here.

Plaza Fiesta Las Palmas, at the corner of Obregón and Rosales, is the shopping mall and the main spot where people of all ages gather, an interesting slice of Mexican life. **Ley,** a large store, sells everything from groceries to clothes to TVs. Hotels, restaurants, and the Plaza Fiesta Las Palmas are all within walking distance of downtown.

FAST FACTS: LOS MOCHIS

American Express   The local representative is Viajes Araceli, Av. Alvaro Obregón 471-A Pte. (☎ **68/15-5780;** fax 68/15-8787).

Area Code   The telephone area code is 68.

Time   The entire railroad operates on central time, even though Los Mochis is in the mountain time zone.

EXPLORING LOS MOCHIS

For most travelers, Los Mochis is a stopover en route to somewhere else. There isn't much of importance here, but the town is pleasant, and you can enjoy some of the best seafood in Mexico.

A city tour, hunting and fishing trips, and boat rides around Topolobampo Bay can be arranged through the **Viajes Flamingo** travel agency, on the ground floor of the Hotel Santa Anita (☎ **68/12-1613** or 68/12-1929); it's open Monday through Saturday from 8:30am to 1pm and 3 to 6:30pm. The boat ride is really just a spin in the bay and not noteworthy, although the bay is pretty.

Topolobampo also has a nice beach, though the town isn't much. To get to Topolobampo, catch the bus at the corner of Obregón and Degollado, across from the Hotel Catalina.

WHERE TO STAY

Doubles for Less than $25

Hotel Fenix. Angel Flores 365, Los Mochis, Sin. 81200. ☎ **68/12-2623.** 40 rms (all with bath). A/C TV TEL. $14 single; $19 double.

This is a good downtown choice, but make reservations or arrive before noon, as it fills up early. It's clean and carpeted and offers laundry and dry-cleaning service. A small cafeteria, serving Monday through Saturday from 7am to noon and 5 to 10pm, opens onto the hotel lobby. From the Hotel Santa Anita, walk left to Hidalgo, turn left one block to Flores, right to the hotel. It's between Hidalgo and Independencia.

Hotel Lorena. Obregón 186 Pte., Los Mochis, Sin. 81200. ☎ **68/12-0239** or 68/12-0958. 50 rms (all with bath). A/C TV TEL. $14.75 single; $21.50 double.

All the rooms in Hotel Lorena open onto wide hallways lined with comfortable rocking chairs, with groups of tables and chairs at either end of the hall. All rooms have windows, but only a few have views. Owner Yoni Felix speaks English. A ground-floor restaurant is open daily from 7am to 11pm.

To get here from the Hotel Santa Anita, turn right to Obregón, then left two blocks to Guillermo Prieto. The hotel is across Prieto on the corner.

Doubles for Less than $45

Hotel Corintios. Obregón 580 Pte., Los Mochis, Sin. 81200. ☎ **68/12-2300** or 12-2277. 39 rms (all with bath). A/C TV TEL. $37 single; $42.75 double. All rates include continental breakfast. Free parking.

Nestled behind a rather campy Greek-columned entrance is this pleasant two-story hotel built around a small rear-entry parking area. Rooms are light, carpeted, and sizable, with two comfortable double beds. The marble bathrooms have tub-showers, large thirsty towels, and purified water from the tap. A complimentary continental breakfast is served in the small restaurant, open from 7am to 10pm. For those catching the train to Chihuahua, fruit, juice, and coffee are available before you get in your cab at 5:15am.

Worth a Splurge

Hotel Santa Anita. Leyva at the corner of Hidalgo (Apdo. Postal 159), Los Mochis, Sin. 81200. ☎ **68/18-7046.** Fax 68/18-7046. 133 rms (all with bath). A/C TV TEL. $65 single; $75 double. Free parking.

Among the nicer hotels in Los Mochis, the rooms are nicely furnished, although some are small. All are carpeted and have comfortable beds, color TVs with U.S. channels, and tap water purified for drinking. The hotel's excellent and popular restaurant is off the lobby. There are two bars, one with live music at least one day a week.

Another special feature: Every morning at 5:20 a private hotel bus takes guests to the *Chihuahua al Pacífico* train, which departs daily at 6am. That saves the $6.50 taxi ride. The hotel also provides pickup at the train station for a small fee for their guests. The lobby travel agency, Viajes Flamingo (☎ **68/12-1613** or 68/12-1929), is about the best in town; you can buy your train tickets here and find out about all the other touristic activities in the area.

WHERE TO EAT

✪ **El Farallon.** Obregón s/n. ☎ **68/12-1428.** Main courses $4.25–$7.50. Daily 8am–11pm. SEAFOOD.

Locals and tourists say this is the best seafood restaurant in downtown, with tender filets of fresh snapper, dorado, and halibut served in a nautical setting. Go ahead and splurge on giant shrimp in garlic and oil. You won't be disappointed. And in the morning, you can order a conventional breakfast, but most folks wouldn't dream of passing up the seafood. To get here from the Santa Anita, turn right on Leyva and right again for one block on Obregón. It's on your left at the corner of Obregón and Flores.

El Taquito. Leyva at Barrera. ☎ **68/12-8119.** Breakfast $2–$3; main courses $3–$5.75. Daily 24 hours. MEXICAN.

Any time of the day or night, El Taquito has its share of locals enjoying some of the best food in town or lingering over a multiple cups of coffee. The café looks like an American fast-food place with orange Formica tables and booths. The tortilla soup comes in a large bowl, and both breakfast and main-course portions are quite generous. From the Hotel Santa Anita, turn left on Leyva, cross Hidalgo, and go one block. It's on your right.

2 The Copper Canyon Train

The Chihuahua al Pacífico Railway's name conceptualizes the idea of linking arid, desertlike Chihuahua with the natural port of Topolobampo, a few miles west of Los Mochis. American Albert Kinsey Owen, who invested in the project of building the railroad, envisioned it as the shortest route for goods from Kansas City to the Pacific.

The longest train stop where passengers can see the canyons is the 15-minute pause at El Divisadero—barely enough time to dash to the canyon's edge for a look, or to grab a delicious taco at one of the stands, or to hurredly buy something from one of the dozens of colorful Tarahumara who sell their violins, baskets, and carved dolls there; time isn't sufficient to do all three.

Train Departure Times

From Los Mochis		From Chihuahua	
Los Mochis	6am (mountain time)	Chihuahua	7am
El Fuerte	7:25am	Creel	12:25pm
Bahuichivo/Cerocahui	12:15pm	El Divisadero	1:45pm
El Divisadero	1:30pm	Bahuichivo/Cerocahui	3:30pm
Creel	3:15pm	El Fuerte	6:15pm
Chihuahua (arrives)	8:50pm	Los Mochis (arrives)	7:50pm

Note: The railroad runs on central time, although Los Mochis is on mountain time. This means that if the train is scheduled to depart Los Mochis at 7am railway time, it pulls out at 6am local time. Be aware of that when reading a printed schedule.

BUYING A TICKET　In Los Mochis, the Ferrocarril Chihuahua al Pacífico station (☎ 68/15-7775) is about 3 miles from the center of town on Avenue Onofre Serrano, a half mile past Bulevar Gaxiola. This is the station for El Nuevo Chihuahua—Pacífico, which runs between Los Mochis and Chihuahua from both directions simultaneously daily. The ticket window is supposed to be open daily from 5am to 1pm, but it's best to go to the station early in the morning in case the window closes early. A one-way ticket in either direction in Primera Especial costs $24, or double that if you want a round-trip ticket. *Note:* There's a 10% extra charge for any stops you make en route.

There are four ways to obtain tickets. The first is from a local travel agency in Los Mochis or Creel. The second is at the train station a day ahead or the same day of your travel (same-day ticket purchase isn't advised since there may be no seats, and if you're traveling with a group it's best to get tickets in advance). A third way is through **Mexico by Train** (see "Getting Around" in chapter 2). A fourth way, is through a U.S. travel agency specializing in the Copper Canyon and selling air/train/hotel packages (not tickets alone). The least preferable option is to use a travel agent in Chihuahua because several agencies may sell the same seat more than once, requiring travelers to decide how to share a seat. In Los Mochis I've had good luck using Viajes Flamingo at the Hotel Santa Anita.

If you plan to stop off en route, you must tell the ticket agent at the time you purchase your ticket and know in advance how long you will be staying at the various stopoffs. Once purchased, the ticket is good for those dates only and cannot be changed. A reserved seat is a necessity, but your reserved seat number may be good only until your first stopoff; thereafter, when you reboard you'll have to take what's available. On a recent trip, conductors had my name on a list at each stop and had an assigned seat for me—but that's not to say you can count on that efficiency every time. You can buy a ticket for shorter distances along the way, enabling you to spend as much time as you like in any location, but if you're traveling during a peak season, it may mean you'll have to take your chances finding a seat when you reboard the train—or stand in any available space between cars, as many locals do.

Travel Agents   A tour company specializing in the Copper Canyon area can save headaches. A true specialist in Copper Canyon adventure tours is **The California Native**, 6701 West 87th Place, Los Angeles, CA 90045 (☎ **800/926-1140**). I also highly recommend the services of **Columbus Travel**, Route 12, Box 382B, New Braunfels, TX 78132-9701 (☎ **210/885-2000**, or 800/843-1060 in the U.S.; fax 210/885-2010), which arranges group tours as well as individualized and special-interest trips in the Copper Canyon. You can also join groups organized by **Sanborn's Tours**, 1007 Main St., Bastrop, TX 78602 (☎ **800/531-5440**), or **Armadillo Tours International**, 901 Mopac Expy. S., Building 2, Suite 120, Austin, TX 78746 (☎ **800/284-5678**), though you don't have to travel with a group to use any of these agencies.

WHAT TO PACK   Although Los Mochis is warm all year-round, Chihuahua can be blistering in summer, windy just about any time, and freezing or even snowy in winter. Both cities are wealthy, and Chihuahua in particular can be somewhat on the dressy side.

The canyon is blue-jeans and hiking-boot country, but pay special attention to the climate. From November through March it may snow; even in the tropical bottom of the canyon, you may need a sweater. In the upper elevations, be prepared for freezing temperatures at night, even in spring and fall. Long johns and gloves are a must in winter. Sturdy shoes or hiking boots are essential anytime if you plan even a little walking and hiking.

CONDITIONS OF TRAVEL   The first-class Chihuahua al Pacífico has adjustable cloth-covered seats, air-conditioning in summer (usually), and heating (maybe) in winter. There's no dining car, but soft drinks and sandwich plates are available from the porter. And at some of the momentary stops along the line food vendors come to the train vestibule doors, selling an assortment of pies, tacos, empanadas, fruit, and soft drinks. Toilet paper and water may not be replenished; bring your own along with any favorite snacks and water.

The train stops many times; beginning in Los Mochis, the following are stops with hotels:

STOP 1: EL FUERTE

Though not yet in the Copper Canyon proper, the train stops here first. El Fuerte, with cobblestone streets and handsome old colonial mansions, is a former silver-mining town about an hour and a half out of Los Mochis. Were it not for its proximity to the railroad, El Fuerte might have become a ghost town, as Alamos did. But instead it is now one of the prettiest towns along the train route, well worth visiting for a night and a day. The town has a plaza and bandstand, and historic houses around the square. I prefer to skip Los Mochis and start my train journey here.

The **bus stop** (not really a station) is about 1 1/2 blocks from where the bus from Los Mochis lets you off on the cobblestoned street. Ask directions to the plaza and hotel. The train station is several miles from town. Taxis meet each train and cost $4.25 per taxi into town; get others to share the price in advance so you look like a group together—otherwise the taxi charges per person.

EXPLORING EL FUERTE

Canyon country hasn't begun yet, and the main reason for stopping here would be to explore the town, visit nearby villages, go birdwatching, fish for black bass and trout, or hunt for duck and dove. The hotel can arrange guides and all equipment.

WHERE TO STAY & EAT

Besides the restaurants at the hotels mentioned here, there are inexpensive restaurants on or near the central plaza.

El Fuerte Lodge. Montes Claros 37, El Fuerte, Sin. 81820. ☎ **689/3-0226.** 21 rms (all with bath). A/C. $55 single or double.

Owner Robert Brand and his wife have taken one of the oldest homes in El Fuerte and turned it into a charming inn loaded with antiques and character. All 21 rooms have double or king beds, tiled baths (with plenty of water pressure for great hot showers), and colonial furnishings that make you feel like you're staying in a museum. An excellent bilingual guide leads trips to nearby villages and knows all about the flora and fauna in the area. The hotel's restaurant menu includes plenty of dishes for those unaccustomed to Mexican food and is said to be the best in town. The gift shop/gallery has a wonderful display of paintings of the area and a great selection of Casas Grandes pottery. The hotel provides motor transport from the Los Mochis airport for $50 one-way, getting you out into the country as soon as you land. Taxis from the El Fuerte bus or train stop cost $4.25.

STOP 2: BAHUICHIVO & CEROCAHUI

This is the first stop in canyon country. Bahuichivo consists mainly of the station and a few humble abodes. Your destination is the village of **Cerocahui** (elev. 5,550 ft.), in a valley about 6 miles from the train stop. Because of the rough, teeth-jarring road, the ride (often on a school bus) lasts an hour before you see the village, which is home to 600 inhabitants. The Hotel Paraíso del Oso is about a mile before the village. Another hotel, the Misión, is in Cerocahui village.

EXPLORING CEROCAHUI

Built around a mission church, Cerocahui consists of little more than rambling unpaved streets and a hundred or so homes. Mountains surround the town, but you have to take an excursion for real canyon vistas. In Cerocahui tourists are besieged by children vying to be their escorts to the **waterfalls.** Both hotels can arrange **horseback riding** to the falls and other lookout points ($6–$8 per hour) and trips by truck to **Cerro Gallego** ($20 per person), a lookout high in the mountains around the town and worth the trip. It's possible to see the waterfall on arrival and schedule the Gallego trip for the next morning, have lunch, and make the train. The Urique trip (see below) would require another day or two.

The Paraíso del Oso offers a trip to the mining town of **Urique** at the bottom of the Urique Canyon (one of the several canyons that make up the Copper Canyon). You can go down and back in a day or schedule an overnight. The Urique day-trip costs $40 per person, minimum three people.

WHERE TO STAY & EAT

✪ **Paraíso Del Oso.** A mile outside Cerocahui. No phone (reservations: contact Columbus Travel, 900 Ridge Creek Lane, Bulverde, TX 78163-2872 ; ☎ **210/885-2000,** or 800/843-1060). 15 rms (all with bath). $85 single; $115 double. Rates include all meals.

Opened in 1990 and slightly more rustic than the Hotel Misíon, the lodge's stream-side setting is what you come to the canyon country for. And it's at the foot of a toothy mountain with a natural rock profile of an *oso* (bear)—thus its name. The food is worth writing home about, and the night sky features an incredible number of stars (unless the moon is full). Each room has two double beds and pine-log furniture. There's no electricity, though there are solar-powered lights in the dining room. The emphasis here is on the cultural and natural history of the area, which can be experienced on foot or by guided horseback trips (the horses live here too). There is a cash bar, a small-but-good library (with both novels and Mexican history), and topographical maps of the area.

STOPS 3 & 4: POSADA BARRANCAS & EL DIVISADERO

Stops 3 and 4 are only 2 miles apart. Stop 3 (coming from Los Mochis) is in front of the Hotel Posada Barrancas and opposite the Mansion Tarahumara. Stop 4 is El Divisadero proper (elev. 9,000 ft.), consisting of the Hotel Cabañas Divisadero-Barrancas, taco stands at train time (delicious), and the most spectacular overlook of the canyon that you'll be able to see if you make no overnight stops en route. The train stops for only 15 minutes, just long enough for a mad dash to the lookout to see the view and to make some hurried purchases from the Tarahumara Indians who appear at train time to display their beautiful baskets, homemade violins, and wood and cloth dolls.

Hotels can arrange various excursions, including visits to cave-dwelling Tarahumara, hiking, and horseback riding.

WHERE TO STAY & EAT

Hotel Cabañas Divisadero-Barrancas. El Divisadero. No phone (reservations: arrangements can be made at Av. Mirador 4516 [Apdo. Postal 31238, Col. Residencial Campestre], Chihuahua, Chih. 31300; ☎ **14/16-5136;** fax 14/15-6575). 50 rms (all with bath). $100 single; $142 double. All rates include three meals.

The first hotel constructed in the canyon, at the first train stop in the canyon, caters to groups and remains popular because of its location on the edge of the canyon overlook—with the most spectacular view of any hotel in the canyon. The restaurant has a large picture window, perfect for sitting and gazing for hours. Each room is beautifully rustic with foot-loomed, brightly colored bedspreads and matching curtains, two double beds, a fireplace, and 24-hour electricity.

Hotel Posada Barrancas Rancho. El Divisadero. No phone (reservations: contact the Hotel Santa Anita, Apdo. Postal 159, Los Mochis, Sin. 81200; ☎ **681/8-7046;** fax 681/2-0046). 36 rms (all with bath). $85 single; $130 double. All rates include meals.

The train stops right in front of this inn, and hotel employees arrive to help with luggage. Rooms are comfortable, each with two double beds and a very warming iron wood-burning stove. Like those in other lodges, meals are a communal affair in the cozy living/restaurant area, and the food is quite good. You can hike to the Tarahumara caves and to the rim of the canyon, where a more expensive sister hotel, the Mirador, has a beautiful log-walled enclosed restaurant/bar with a magnificent view. Ask also about horseback riding.

Mansión Tarahumara. El Divisadero. No phone (reservations: contact the Mansion Tarahumara, Calle Juárez 1602-A Col. Centro, Chihuahua, Chih. 31000; ☎ **14/15-4721,**

or ☎ and fax 14/16-5444). 45 rms (all with bath). $70 single; $100 double. All rates include meals.

Built like an enormous stone castle, the Mansión Tarahumara is perched on a hillside opposite the train stop at Posada Barrancas. A van meets the train and carries guests and luggage across the tracks to the hotel. This is among my favorite of the canyon lodges because of the setting, the rooms, and the management's interest in guest comfort. Rock-walled bungalows are behind the castle, and each has a big fireplace and a wall heater and is nicely furnished with two double beds and windows facing the view.

The castle contains the restaurant, with a lovely view from its big windows and a large area ideal for dancing or live entertainment, which the hotel sometimes sponsors. Most nights a guitarist stops in for a sing-along after dinner. Besides the usual cave tours or horseback riding, the hotel can also arrange guided hiking to the bottom of the canyon or to Batopilas (see Batopilas description in "Stop 5: Creel," below).

STOP 5: CREEL

This rustic logging town (elev. 8,400 ft., pop. 6,000), with paved streets, offers the only economical lodgings in the canyon, as well as some of the best side trips, especially hiking and overnight camping.

ESSENTIALS

GETTING THERE & DEPARTING   By Train   When you're ready to get off the train, keep a lookout for the station because the trains stop here for only a few minutes. When you're ready to reboard, be sure to be at the station before the arrival time of the train. You'll need to be ready to jump on when you see it coming.

By Bus   **Estrella Blanca,** with facilities next to the Hotel Korachi, serves Creel and Chihuahua every two hours from 6am to 5:30pm. Direct buses make the trip in four hours; de paso buses take five. (See also buses to Batopilas in "Exploring Creel & Environs," below.)

By Car   From Chihuahua, follow the signs to La Junta (but you don't go there), until you see signs to Hermosillo (you don't go there either) but follow them until you see signs to Creel (left). These you do follow into Creel; the trip takes about five hours on a paved road. There is now a well-maintained road, paved part of the way, between Creel and El Divisadero; the drive takes an hour or less.

ORIENTATION   The train station, around the corner from the Mission Store and the main plaza, is in the heart of the village and within walking distance of all lodgings except the Copper Canyon Sierra Lodge. Look for your hotel's van waiting at the station (unless you're staying at the Casa de Huespedes Margarita, to which a flock of kids will manhandle your gear for two blocks). There's one main street, López Mateos, and almost everything is on it and within walking distance.

Fast Facts   The telephone **area code** is 145. There's **electricity** 24 hours daily in all Creel hotels. The best sources of **information** are the Mission Store and the hotels. Several businesses and many of the hotels offer long-distance **telephone** service; look for signs proclaiming LARGA DISTANCIA or ask at your hotel.

EXPLORING CREEL & ENVIRONS

You'll occasionally see the Tarahumara as you walk around town, but mostly you'll see rugged logging types and tourists from around the world.

Sierra Madre *Indígenos:* The Tarahumara

Within the Copper Canyon region live the reclusive Tarahumara Indians, in tiny settlements of small log huts in summer and in caves in winter. They have remained aloof from modern civilization, retreating to the rugged canyons and subsisting on corn, tortillas, beans, and herding a few goats and cattle. The men wear sandals, white loincloths, and colorful headbands. Women, who often go barefoot, wear colorful cotton skirts and ruffled blouses. Although they weave fine thick wool blankets, they don't wear wool, even in harsh canyon winters. Social and ritual gatherings are centered around tesguino, a fermented corn drink, and because of the frequency of these gatherings, many Tarahumara men are alcoholics. Their Semana Santa (Easter Week) and other religious festivals are unique. The Tarahumara tend to suffer from malnutrition and respiratory diseases, but their plight has been addressed by Jesuit priests such as Father Verplancken, who established a fine clinic and hospital in Creel. In past years a group of volunteer U.S. medical professionals known as The Flying Doctors provided health care to remote rancherias. Many Tarahumara children attend boarding school in Creel or Cerocahui, returning home on weekends.

There are several stores around Creel that sell Tarahumara arts and crafts. The best is **Artesanías Misión** (Mission Crafts), which has quality merchandise at reasonable prices, with all profits going to the Mission Hospital run by Father Verplancken, a Jesuit priest, and benefiting the Tarahumara. Here you'll find Tarahumara crafts: dolls, pottery, woven purses and belts, drums, violins (a craft inherited from the Spanish), bamboo flutes, bead necklaces, bows and arrows, cassettes of Tarahumara music, wood carvings, baskets, and heavy wool rugs, as well as an excellent supply of books and maps relating to the Tarahumara and the region. It's open Monday through Saturday from 9:30am to 1pm and 3 to 6pm and Sunday from 9:30am to 1pm. It's beside the railroad tracks, on the main plaza.

NEARBY EXCURSIONS

Close by are several canyons, waterfalls, a lake, hot springs, Tarahumara ranchería and cave dwellings, and an old Jesuit mission. Six miles north of town is an "ecotourism" complex called San Ignacio de Arareko (for information, call **145/6-0120** or 145/6-0078). A lake, hiking and biking trails, horses, cabins and a craftshop are featured, all under the control of the indigenous peoples of the *ejido* (communal area). It's a pleasant change from the almost total control of Copper Canyon tourism by the mestizo population. **Batopilas,** an overnight jaunt, is a fascinating 18th-century silver-mining village at the bottom of the canyon. You can ask for information about these and other things to do from your hotel.

Whether you go by foot, horseback, bus, or guided tour, if you're planning to do any strenuous hiking, rock climbing, or adventuring, it's strongly recommended you take along someone who knows the area—you're in the wilderness out here, and you can't count on anyone coming along to rescue you should an accident occur.

A nice walk you can do on your own is to head out of town on Avenida López Mateos, past the Motel Parador de la Montaña; go past the lumber mill and keep going, taking the left fork in the road when you pass the cemetery. Continuing along this road, you come to a valley where the Tarahumara live; you'll see their footpaths, domestic animals, and cave dwellings. If you continue on this same road, you pass the **Valley of the Mushroom Rocks,** about 2¹/₂ miles from town, and finally reach the tiny village of **San Ignacio,** where there is a 400-year-old mission. From here, you can continue on to **Lake Arareco,** about 4¹/₂ miles from Creel.

If you are driving, the partially paved road between Creel and El Divisadero now makes that village a possible day-trip from Creel (see "Stops 3 & 4," above, for details on El Divisadero). The trip takes around an hour one way. The unpaved part is generally in good condition; however, if you are traveling during or just after rains, it may not be in the best shape. Ask about it before starting out.

ORGANIZED TOURS   Hotels offer organized tours. The Motel Parador de la Montaña has 10 different tours, ranging from 2 to 10 hours and priced at $9.25 to $35.50 per person (four people minimum); it costs $50 per person (four people minimum) for the Batopilas trip. The Hotel Nuevo and Casa de Huespedes Margarita offer the most economical tours in town, priced around $12 for a day-long canyon and hot-springs tour. All tour availability depends on if a group can be gathered, and your best chance of that is at Margarita's Plaza Mexicana or the Parador de la Montaña, both catering to groups. The Copper Canyon Sierra Lodge arranges packages throughout Tarahumara land—but you have to arrange them from the United States.

BATOPILAS   You can make an overnight side trip on your own from Creel to the silver-mining village of Batopilas, founded in 1708. It's a seven- to nine-hour trip from Creel by bus (school-bus type), and about six hours by Suburban, along a narrow dirt road winding down through some of the most beautiful and spectacular scenery in the Copper Canyon. The mountains rise up on one side of the road and drop precipitously on the other side to a stream that alternately trickles and roars. In Batopilas, which lies beside a river at the bottom of a deep canyon, the weather is tropical, but can be a bit chilly in the evenings. There are a beautiful little church and several walks and a hike to Misión Satevó that you can do from there. The town itself is like something from an 18th-century time warp: The dry goods store has the original shelving and cash register; cobblestone streets twist past whitewashed homes; miners and ranchers come on horseback; and Tarahumara are frequent visitors. A considerable number of pigs, dogs, and flocks of goats wander at will—this is Chihuahua's goat-raising capital.

Getting to Batopilas   In Creel, take a bus from the Restaurant Herradero, on López Mateos s/n, three doors past the turn-off to Margarita's Plaza Mexicana. A bus (cost $6.50) goes to Batopilas on Tuesday, Thursday, and Saturday, leaving Creel at 7am and arriving midafternoon. A Suburban (cost $11.50) leaves on Monday, Wednesday, and Friday at 10:30am, also arriving about midafternoon. Both bus and van return the following day. There are no bathrooms, restaurants, or other semblance of civilization along the way, but the bus may stop to allow passengers to stretch and find a bush. Tickets are sold at the restaurant.

Where to Stay & Eat in Batopilas   Batopilas has several little restaurants and hotels/guesthouses, beginning at around $1.75 per person per night. There are no telephones, though, so you can't make firm reservations. The likelihood of vacancies at the basic-but-comfortable, 10-room **Hotel Mary** (formerly called the Parador Batopilas) can be obtained at the Parador de la Montaña in Creel. All rooms share the hotel's two baths and cost $16.50 double per night. There's also the rustic **Hotel Batopilas** and **Hotel Las Palmeras** with five or six rooms each, and if all else fails, you can probably find a family willing to let you stay in an extra room. One night isn't enough for a stay here, since you arrive midafternoon and must leave at 7am or 10:30am the next morning.

A much more expensive lodging choice is the **Copper Canyon Riverside Lodge,** owned by the Copper Canyon Sierra Lodge 14 miles outside Creel. Created from a handsome old Batopilas mansion, rooms are normally booked as part of an eight-day package that includes three nights at their lodge in Creel, three nights in Batopilas, two nights (coming and going) in Chihuahua, transfers, and meals at their hotels. However, if a room is available, drop-ins will be accommodated.For information check with **Copper Canyon Lodges,** 2741 Paldan Dr., Auburn Hills, MI 48326 (☎ **810/340-7230,** or 800/776-3942 in the U.S.; fax 810/340-7212).

Restaurants are informal here, so bring along some favorite snacks and bottled water to tide you over, although most provisions like that are available at the general store. Upon arrival ask for directions to Doña Mica's (everyone knows her). She serves meals on her plant-surrounded front porch, but it's best to let her know in advance when to expect you. On short notice, however, she can probably rustle up some scrambled eggs on her ancient wood-fired stove.

WHERE TO STAY

For a small town, Creel has quite a number of places to stay because of its popularity with international tourists and loggers on business. Be sure to have a reservation during high season.

Doubles for Less than $25

Casa de Huespedes Margarita. López Mateos 11, Creel, Chih. 33200. ☎ and fax **145/ 6-0045.** 23 rms. (17 with bath). $3.50 sleeping bag space (10 spaces); $5 share in four-bed dormitory; $21.50 single or double private room; $24.75 double private cabaña. All rates include breakfast and dinner.

With its youth hostel–type atmosphere, this signless white house between the two churches on the main plaza is the most popular spot in town with international backpacking, student, and minimal-budget travelers. It's also one of the cleanest hotels in the country. Rooms have pine details and tile floors and are decorated with frilly curtains and spreads; there is plenty of hot water and gas heat in each. Meals are taken family style around a big dining table. Nonguests can eat here, too—just let them know in advance; breakfast, lunch, and dinner are $5 each. Margarita is adding more private rooms to the hotel and has built another more deluxe hotel as well (see below). She's one of the best sources of information in the area and does all she can to help budget travelers enjoy their stays.

Doubles for Less than $50

Margarita's Plaza Mexicana. Calle Chapultepec s/n, Creel, Chih. 33200. ☎ and fax **145/ 6-0245.** 26 rms (all with bath). $26.25 single; $33 double (including two meals).

Margarita is one of the most popular and enterprising hoteliers in Creel. She's transformed an old town house into a charming inn filled with Tarahumara folk art. The rooms (including a honeymoon suite) are gaily furnished with wood chairs and dressers from Michoacán and decorated with paintings of Tarahumara scenes. Gas wall heaters take the chill off winter nights. A mural of Semana Santa celebrations covers one wall in the large dining room where guests take breakfast and dinner. Vegetables and salads are prepared with purified water. The hotel is near the Parador Montaña, three blocks west of the plaza.

Pensión Creel. Av. López Mateos 61, Creel, Chih. 33200. ☎ **145/6-0071** or 145/6-0021. Fax 145/6-0200. 11 rms (all with bath). $30.75 single; 39.50 double (including breakfast).

The Pensión Creel's cabins are painted Mennonite blue and are furnished with double beds. One has a fireplace; two others have kitchens. Bathrooms sport tub/ shower combinations, and each room has a coffee pot. There's a new dining room where meals other than breakfast are served by arrangement. The lobby, next to the dining area, has a phone for guest use and a small gift shop. The owners also own the Santa María purified water plant and a laundry, so you can fill up water jugs and get your laundry done, too. They sell topographic maps of the canyon as well. Three-night backpacking trips to the bottom of the canyon, among other tours, are offered for 4 to 10 people. The pensión is two blocks west of the plaza on López Mateos, then 1/2 block south on Chapultepec. Just ask anyone.

Hotel Nuevo. Francisco Villa 121, Creel, Chih. 33200. ☎ **145/6-0022,** or 14/17-5539 in Chihuahua for reservations. Fax 145/6-0043. 40 rms (all with bath). $23–$47.50 single or double.

There are two hotel sections at the Nuevo, the older one across the tracks from the train station next to the restaurant and variety store, and newer log cabañas in back; these are carpeted, have TVs, and are the higher priced rooms. All have a heater or fireplace. There is a nice hotel restaurant open from 8:30am to 8pm, plus a small general store that sells local crafts as well as basic supplies. Ask at the store about rooms.

La Posada de Creel. Domicilio Conocido (Apdo. Postal 7), Creel, Chih. 33200. ☎ and fax **145/6-0142.** (Reservations: P.O. Box 3, Cleburne, TX 76033; ☎ **817/558-9979;** fax 817/641-9979.) 10 private rms (all with bath), 11 sleeping rms (with shared bath). Private room $35 single or double; sleeping room $10 per person.

The old Motel Chavez has been remodeled and transformed into a pleasant hostelry. The bright white and green building houses private rooms with double beds and private baths and sleeping rooms with bunk beds for four persons. There are several showers on both floors of the two-story building and space to congregate in the plaza. The hotel sits right along the train tracks two blocks from the station on an unnamed street.

Worth a Splurge

Motel Parador de la Montaña. Av. López Mateos s/n, Creel, Chih. 33200. ☎ **145/6-0075.** Fax 145/6-0085. (For reservations in Chihuahua, contact Calle Allende 114, Chihuahua, Chih. 31300; ☎ 14/10-4580; fax 14/15-3468). 49 rms (all with bath). $60 single or double.

The largest hotel in town (and at night the most popular gathering place), is the Parador de la Montaña, located four blocks west of the plaza. The rooms are comfortable, each with two double beds, a high wood-beamed ceiling, central heating, a tiled bath, and very thin walls. Guests congregate in the restaurant, the bar, and the lobby with its roaring fireplace. The bar is the town's evening action spot. The motel caters to groups and offers at least 10 overland tours, priced from $10 to $50. They hope to offer helicopter tours in the near future. The hotel can give you information about the Hotel Mary in Batopilas.

WHERE TO EAT

El Caballo Bayo. López Mateos 25. ☎ **145/6-0136.** Sandwiches $2.50–$3; steak dinners $8.25. Daily 2pm–10pm. AMERICAN.

Travelers who've grown weary of Mexican food and are yearning for a taste of home are happy at this bright, clean restaurant with peaked wood ceilings and cheery tablecloths. The menu is diverse, with burgers and fries, club sandwiches, T-bone steaks from Chihuahua, and shrimp from Los Mochis. The restaurant is across the street from the Motel Parador Montaña.

Restaurant Estela. López Mateos 65. No phone. Breakfast $2; main courses $3; comida corrida $2.25. Daily 7am–9pm. MEXICAN.

Simple but wholesome food with down-home flavor is the keyword of this small family restaurant. Five plastic topped tables provide the base from which to eat a tempting bowl of chicken soup, or the memorable *guisado* (stew), or any other dish on the menu. The gracious owner (and cook) oversees a clean, tight ship. From the plaza, Estela's is 1¹/₂ blocks past the Motel Parador.

Restaurant Las Rejas. In the Motel Parador de la Montaña, Av. López Mateos. ☎ **145/6-0075.** Breakfast, sandwiches, and hamburgers $1.50–$2.50; main courses $2.50–$5.75. Daily 7:30–11:30am and 12–10:30pm. INTERNATIONAL.

This is the largest and most popular restaurant in town for an all out dinner of soup, salad, steak, dessert, and coffee or just a simple grilled half-chicken dinner. There's full service from the cozy little bar attached, which is open all day and evening until around midnight. With its hanging lanterns, high wood-beamed ceiling, huge fireplace, and friendly atmosphere, Las Rejas is well worth a stop, though the food is less than exceptional. This is the gathering place for out of towners. It's two blocks west of the plaza.

Restaurant Veronica. Av. López Mateos 34. No phone. Soup 75¢–$2; antojitos 25¢–75¢; comida corrida $2.50. Daily 7:30am–11pm. MEXICAN.

The painted ceiling and walls provide a perfect backdrop for five tables. The menu del día includes a large bowl of vegetable soup, assorted antojitos, seafood, sandwiches, and a daily comida corrida. The burritos de pollo are large and filling and greasy. The restaurant is two blocks west of the plaza.

3 Chihuahua

213 miles S of El Paso, 275 NW of Torreón

Chihuahua (elev. 4,700 ft.; pop. 1,000,000), a city of wide boulevards and handsome buildings, is the capital of Chihuahua, the largest and richest state in Mexico. The money comes from mining, timber, cattle raising, many *maquiladoras* (U.S. assembly plants), and tourism—it's one of two major departure points for the Copper Canyon train. Population is booming in Chihuahua largely because of the manufacturing plants, and the city has lost much of its frontier feeling. Wide boulevards and handsome historic buildings dot the downtown area that also has its share of modern buildings, fine hotels, shops, restaurants, and luxury neighborhoods.

Aside from its industry, Chihuahua boasts a modern university and a museum in the house where Pancho Villa lived, but few, if any, of the tiny Chihuahua dogs.

ESSENTIALS

GETTING THERE & DEPARTING By Plane Southwest Airlines, ☎ **800/531-5601,** serves El Paso from various U.S. cities. **Lone Star Airlines** (☎ **14/20-9154,** or 800/877-3932 in the U.S.) started daily flights (using nifty 30-passenger Dornier twin-prop aircraft) from El Paso and Dallas/Fort Worth to Chihuahua in 1994. **Aeroméxico** (☎ **15-6303**) and its subsidiary **Aerolitoral** fly direct from El Paso, Guadalajara, Hermosillo, Ciudad Juárez, Mexico City, Monterrey, Torreón, Tijuana, Culiacán, La Paz, and Los Mochis, with connecting flights from Los Angeles and San Antonio. **Transportes Aeropuerto** (☎ **14/20-3366**) controls taxi service from the airport ($5.75 per person). Taxis from town charge $10 for up to four people.

By Train The **Chihuahua al Pacífico** (☎ **14/15-7756**; fax 14/10-9059) leaves Chihuahua daily for its route through the Copper Canyon to Los Mochis. (The complete train schedule and the train route are in Section 2 of this chapter.) The station in Chihuahua is two blocks behind the prison on 20 de Noviembre, near the intersection with Ocampo. The train is scheduled to leave promptly at 7am daily. Arriving passengers from the west will pay $2.50 per person for the taxi ride to town.

Important Transportation Information To get to the train station from the Plaza Principal and Avenida Juárez, take a bus named "Cerro de la Cruz." It lets you off two blocks from the station. Public transportation is handy to use if you are going to the station to buy tickets. However, for getting to the station for the early-morning train departure, it's best to arrange transportation through one of the travel agencies recommended under "Canyon Arrangements" in "Fast Facts." They pick up clients taking the train each morning; taxis that early can be scarce.

By Bus The Central Camionera (also called the Terminal de Autobuses) is on the outskirts of the city on Avenida Juan Pablo II, 5 miles northeast of town, en route to the airport. Buses leave hourly heading for major points inland and north and south on the coast. You can get information on most lines at ☎ 14/29-0242 or 14/29-0244. **Omnibus de México** has deluxe service to Ciudad Juárez at 8am and 6pm, Mexico City at 3:15pm, and Monterrey at 9:30pm. **Transportes Chihuahuenses** the big local line, offers deluxe service to Ciudad Juárez at 8am and 2pm.

To travel to Creel, look for the Estrella Blanca line. Buses leave every two hours from 6am to 6pm. Direct buses make the trip in four hours; de paso buses take five.

Transportes del Norte (☎ 14/29-0242) and **Autobuses Estrella Blanca** (☎ 14/29-0242) also run buses hourly from the border through Chihuahua to points south. **Omnibus de México** has Real Ejecutivo (deluxe) service from Juárez, Mexico City, and Monterrey. **Futura & Turistar** (☎ 14/29-0242) also have deluxe service to Monterrey and Durango.

By Car Highway 45 leads south from Ciudad Juárez, Highway 16 south from Ojinaga, and Highway 49 north from Torreón. For the drive to Creel, see "Getting There & Departing" in "Stop 5: Creel" above.

ORIENTATION Arriving From the **airport,** it's a half-hour trip downtown on the express van for $5.75 per person. **Transportes Aeropuerto** (☎ 14/20-3366) runs colectivo service to and from downtown for the same price. Taxis charge $10 for the trip from town. The Central Camionera (bus station) in Chihuahua is 5 miles northeast of the town center and west of the airport. Taxis from the **bus station** to town costs around $5.75 per person.

Information The **Tourist Information Center** (☎ 14/10-1077 or 14/29-3300, ext. 4515 or 1061) on Libertad at Carranza in the Government Palace, is just left of the altar and murals dedicated to Father Hidalgo. It's open Monday through Friday from 9am to 7pm, and Saturday and Sunday from 10am to 2pm.

City Layout The town center is laid out around the Plaza Principal, bounded by Avenidas Libertad and Victoria (which run northeast–southwest) and Avenida Independencia and Calle 4 (which run northwest–southeast). The cathedral is at the southwest end of the plaza, and the city offices are on the northeast end. Standing on Independencia with the cathedral on your left, odd-numbered streets (and blocks) will be to your right, and even-numbered streets (and blocks) to your left.

Getting Around Local **buses** run along main arteries beginning at the central plaza. **Taxis** can be taken from the town center to most major sights. For early-morning transportation to the train station, it's best to make pickup arrangements with one of the travel agencies, since taxis are scarce at that hour.

Chihuahua

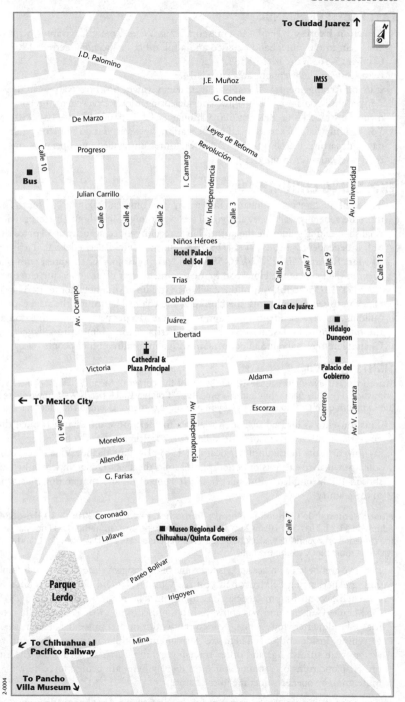

To Ciudad Juarez ↑

J.D. Palomino

J.E. Muñoz

G. Conde

IMSS

De Marzo

Leyes de Reforma

Revolución

Progreso

Calle 10

Bus

I. Camargo

Av. Independencia

Av. Universidad

Julian Carrillo

Calle 6

Calle 4

Calle 2

Calle 3

Niños Héroes

Hotel Palacio
del Sol

Calle 5

Calle 7

Calle 9

Calle 13

Trias

Doblado

Casa de Juárez

Juárez

Hidalgo
Dungeon

Av. Ocampo

Libertad

✝
Cathedral &
Plaza Principal

Palacio del
Gobierno

Victoria

Aldama

← To Mexico City

Escorza

Guerrero

Av. V. Carranza

Calle 10

Av. Independencia

Morelos

Allende

G. Farias

Coronado

Calle 7

Lallave

■ Museo Regional de
Chihuahua/Quinta Gomeros

Paseo Bolívar

Parque
Lerdo

Irigoyen

↙ To Chihuahua al
Pacifico Railway

Mina

FAST FACTS: CHIHUAHUA

American Express The local representative is Viajes Rojo y Casavantes, with one agent in the Hotel San Francisco and a full office at Vicente Guerrero 1207 (☎ **14/15-4636;** fax 14/15-5384).

Area Code The telephone area code is 14.

Canyon Arrangements If you wait to make overnight hotel reservations in the canyon until you are in Chihuahua, consider using a local travel agent. I recommend Turismo Al Mar, Reforma 400, Chihuahua, Chih. 31000 (☎ **14/16-5950**). You can buy train tickets yourself at the station, however, but do so before your day of departure. (See also Section 2, above, for recommended tour operators and train reservationists in the U.S.)

EXPLORING CHIHUAHUA

To see all the sights of Chihuahua in one day, I recommend taking a city tour. The tours are generally well done, and you'll see everything. Three-hour city tours, with English-speaking guides are the norm. Three recommended agencies are **Torres del Sol,** Independencia 116-2 (☎ **14/15-7380**) in the Hotel Palacio del Sol, **Turismo Al Mar,** Reforma 400 (☎ **14/16-5950,** and **Viajes Rojo y Casavantes,** with one agent in the lobby of the Hotel San Francisco and a larger office at Vicente Guerrero 1207 (☎ **14/15-4636**). Any of these will pick you up at your hotel for tours. They'll take you to see the museums, the churches, the colonial aqueduct, the state capital building, the state penitentiary, and more. Cost is $15 per person plus admission to the museums. The fascinating seven-hour trip to the Mennonite village near Cuauhtémoc costs about $33 per person, with a minimum of four people.

SIGHTS IN TOWN

Museo de la Revolución. Calle 10 no. 3014, at the corner of Mendez. ☎ **14/16-2958.** Admission $1. Daily 9am–1pm and 3–7pm. Bus: "Colonia Dale" heads west down Juárez, turning south onto Ocampo, and will let you off on the corner of Ocampo and Mendez.

This museum is located in Pancho Villa's former house on what was once the outskirts of the city. Luz Corral de Villa, Villa's legitimate wife (he had others, they say), lived in the house until her death in 1981. Exhibits include Villa's weapons, some personal effects, lots of period photos, and the 1922 Dodge in which he was shot in 1923, complete with bullet holes. It's one of the most interesting museums in the country.

Museo Regional de Chihuahua (Quinta Gameros). Paseo Bolívar 401. ☎ **14/16-6684.** Admission $1.25. Tues–Sun 10am–2pm and 4–7pm. Heading away from the Plaza Principal with the cathedral on your right, walk eight blocks on Independencia to Bolívar, turn right, and then walk one more block; it's on the right.

If you've ever been to France and visited some of the kingly palaces there, you'll think you're experiencing déjà vu when you see Quinta Gameros, an exact replica of a French Second Empire neoclassical mansion. The mansion was built in 1910 for Manuel Gameros and was converted to a museum in 1961. Pancho Villa used it as a headquarters for a while. Notice the wealth of decorative detail from floor to ceiling, inside and out. There are permanent exhibits of turn-of-the-century art nouveau furnishings and other traveling exhibits. Artifacts from the ancient pre-Hispanic ruins of Paquimé, once on display here, are being moved to a new museum to be opened sometime in the future.

Museo Casa de Juárez. At the corner of Juárez and Calle 5a. No phone. Admission 20¢. Tues–Sun 9am–3pm and 4–7pm. From the Plaza Principal (Cathedral on your left), walk two blocks on Independencia, then turn right on Juárez for one long block; it's on the left almost at Calle 5.

This was the Mexican National Palace in 1864 when Benito Juárez was leading the fight for independence from the French occupation. Detailed exhibits tell the history of that stormy epoch and how the armed struggle proceeded from place to place; also, you'll see the various plans and constitutions that were drawn up, with photographs, documents in Spanish, and exhibits of period furnishings.

Palacio del Gobierno. Av. Aldama between Guerrero and Carranza. ☎ **14/10-6324.** Admission free. Daily 8am–10pm. From the Plaza Principal, walk east on Independencia one block, then turn left on Aldama for two long blocks; cross Guerrero, and you'll find the entrance on the left.

The Palacio del Gobierno is a magnificently ornate structure dating in part from 1890 (the original structure, the Jesuit College, was built in 1718). A colorful, expressive mural encompasses the entire first floor of the large central courtyard, telling the history of the area around Chihuahua from the time of the first European visitation up through the Revolution. In the far-right corner, note the scene depicting Benito Juárez flanked by Abraham Lincoln and Simón Bolívar, liberator of South America.

Also in the far-left back courtyard is a plaque and altar commemorating the execution of Miguel Hidalgo, the father of Mexican independence, at 7am on July 30, 1811; the plaque marks the very spot where the hero was executed in the old building, and the mural portrays the scene.

Hidalgo's Dungeon. In the Palacio Federal, Av. Juárez at Guerrero. No phone. Admission 20¢. Tues–Sun 10am–6pm. From the Plaza Principal, walk on the pedestrian-way Calle Libertad for three long blocks, cross Guerrero, and turn left on it to the corner of Juárez. Turn right $1/2$ block; the entrance to the museum is on the right, below the post office.

Father Miguel Hidalgo y Costilla was a priest in Dolores, Guanajuato, when he started the War of Independence on September 15, 1810. Six months later he was captured by the Spanish, brought to Chihuahua, and kept in a dungeon for 98 days, before being shot with his lieutenants, Allende, Aldama, and Jimenez. The four were beheaded, and their heads hung in iron cages for $9^1/2$ years on the four corners of the Alhóndiga granary in Guanajuato, as examples of what happens to revolutionaries. It was here in this cell that Hidalgo was kept on bread and water before his execution. The night before his death, he wrote a few words on the wall with a piece of charcoal to thank his guard and the warden for the good treatment they gave him. A bronze plaque commemorates his final message.

WHERE TO STAY
DOUBLES FOR LESS THAN $20

Hotel Reforma. Calle Victoria 809, Chihuahua, Chih. 31300. ☎ **14/10-6848.** 49 rms (all with bath). $5.75 single; $6.50 double.

This old mansion was evidently a fancy place when it was built in 1913. Today it's a humble shadow of its former self but possibly enjoyable if you can get one of the brighter rooms facing the street, with French doors opening onto little balconies. Rooms facing the back have small windows opening outside. Many rooms face the large, covered inner courtyard, which serves as the lobby, and these rooms are dark. Ice, made from purified water, is available in the lobby. There's a simple-though-good restaurant, Cafetería Reforma, which is open daily from 8am to 11pm. To get here from the Plaza, go past the cathedral $2^1/2$ blocks on Calle Victoria; it's on your right just past Ocampo.

Hotel Bal-Flo. Calle 5 no. 702. Chihuahua, Chih. 31300. ☎ and fax **14/16-0335.** 91 rms (all with bath). A/C TV TEL. $14 single; $16.50 double. Free parking.

All rooms at the Bal-Flo are heated and carpeted. Some units have windows on the street; others open onto an air shaft. Mattresses are just okay. The proprietor, Sr. Baltazar Flores, speaks English and is quite helpful. The cafeteria, open daily from 7am to 11pm, serves good, inexpensive food. To find the hotel, with the cathedral front on your left, walk four long blocks on Independencia, then turn right for two blocks on Niños Héroes; it's left around the corner on Calle 5.

DOUBLES FOR LESS THAN $25

Hotel Santa Regina. Calle 3 no. 102, Chihuahua, Chih. 31000. ☎ **14/15-3889.** Fax 14/10-1411. 102 rms (all with bath). A/C TV TEL. $19.75 single; $21.50 double. Free parking.

The three-story Santa Regina has carpeted rooms that are heated in winter and TVs that receive U.S. channels. More than half the rooms have windows facing outside; others have windows on the hall. To get here from the Plaza Principal, walk two blocks on Independencia to Doblado and turn right for one block to Calle 3. Turn right again; the hotel is between Doblado and Juárez.

WHERE TO EAT

For some very inexpensive meals, head for several small restaurants on Calle Victoria behind the cathedral. The **Cafetería Reforma,** in the Hotel Reforma, serves a comida corrida from 1pm until it runs out and is open daily from 8am to 11pm. The **Restaurant San Juan,** a few doors down, offers one of the least expensive comida corrida in town from 1 to 3pm and is open daily from 8am to 10pm.

MEALS FOR LESS THAN $2.50

Liveer Restaurante de Auto Servicio. Calle Libertad 318. ☎ **14/15-4902.** Main courses $1–$2.50; plate lunch $1.25–$2.25. Daily 11am–9pm. MEXICAN.

This is a walk-down-the-line–style cafeteria. Bright and clean, it serves a variety of main dishes, side dishes, salads, desserts, and drinks at reasonable prices. You can also get hot snacks "to go" from the window out front.

To get here from the Plaza Principal, walk 1 1/2 blocks on the pedestrian-way Libertad; it's on the right opposite the Salinas y Rocha store.

Pepe's Tacos al Pastor. Juan Aldama 504. No phone. Tacos (order of 4) $1.25; Tortas $1. Daily 9am–11pm. MEXICAN.

Order your tacos or torta as you enter, then doctor it (them) from the condiments lining the counter. Take your trophy back to one of the small metal tables in back, sit down with your favorite beverage, and let the essence of Mexico slide into your system. With your back to the cathedral, walk right one block, then left on Aldama 2 1/2 blocks. It's on your right.

MEALS FOR LESS THAN $5

Degá. In the Hotel San Francisco, Calle Victoria 409. ☎ **45/16-7550.** Breakfast $2.25–$4.75 (buffet $5); main course $5–$8.50; Sun buffet $6.50; plato mexicano $4.25. Daily 7am–11pm. MEXICAN/INTERNATIONAL.

The restaurant/cafeteria/bar at this popular downtown hotel draws both downtown workers and travelers. The breakfast buffet features superb omelets made to order. The plato mexicano is laden with a tamale, chile relleno, beans, chips, and guacamole. Fish, charcoal-grilled chicken, barbecue, and salads are all reasonably priced. American breakfasts and burgers are included in the extensive menu. From the cathedral walk to Victoria and turn right; it's one block down on your right, before Av. Ocampo.

✪ **La Parilla.** Calle Victoria 420. ☎ **14/15-5856.** Steaks $5–$8; fajitas $6.50; tacos $2.75–$5. Daily 12–11pm. STEAKS.

With its ranch-style café decor of dark-wood tables and plastic-covered chairs, La Parilla features Chihuahua-bred beef cuts—sirloin, filet mignon, and club. Some meat platters come with consommé, salad, and potato; the menu turístico includes salad or soup, steak, and mashed potatoes. There are 11 kinds of tacos and lots of side orders, like northern-style pinto beans cooked in beer, melted cheese, tortilla soup, and grilled onions.

From the cathedral walk to Victoria and turn right; it's 1¹/₂ blocks down on your left, just before Av. Ocampo and just past, and across the street from, the Hotel San Francisco.

CHIHUAHUA AFTER DARK

Most downtown action takes place in hotel lobby bars. At the Hotel San Francisco, Victoria 409, behind the cathedral, there's live music in the lobby bar on Monday through Saturday, with happy hour from 5 to 8pm. The Hotel Palacio del Sol, at Independencia 500, has different live entertainment nightly in the lobby bar. The Hostería 1900, at Independencia 506 has live entertainment on weekends from 9:30pm to 2am and is popular with a young crowd, as is Chihuahua Charlie's Bar and Grill at Av. Juárez 3329.

EXCURSIONS FROM CHIHUAHUA
THE MENNONITE VILLAGE OF CUAUHTÉMOC

Two hours west of Chihuahua, this village makes an unusual side trip. Originally from northern Germany, the Mennonites became an official reformist religious sect under Menno Simons in the early 16th century. With a strict Bible-based philosophy governing their daily lives, prohibiting them from engaging in war and many aspects of popular culture, they immigrated to other lands rather than violate their beliefs.

The group of 5,000 that in 1920 migrated to Cuauhtémoc from Canada petitioned the Mexican government for permission to settle here and maintain their own community traditions; Cuauhtémoc was little more than desert then, and Mexico was trying to develop its lands. The Mennonites have transformed this desert into a productive and prosperous farming community. Very few still maintain their 16th-century customs, religion, dress, and language (a dialect of Old German); the traditional horses and buggies have largely been replaced by cars and pickup trucks, an occasional satellite dish can be spotted, and in recent years, one of their daughters was crowned Miss Chihuahua. They are especially famous for their delicious cheese, fine woodwork, and embroidery, as well as their agricultural products.

An all-day Mennonite tour to Cuauhtémoc includes a visit to the Mennonite village and agricultural lands and a cheese factory, plus lunch in a Mennonite home, meeting the people and learning about their culture and history. The tour companies mentioned in "Fast Facts" can arrange the tour.

THE RUINS OF PAQUIMÉ

This is another interesting side trip. The Paquimé ruins (A.D. 900–1340) are near the town of Casas Grandes, about five hours north of Chihuahua on Highway 10. Here you'll find the pueblolike, mud-walled remains of northern Mexico's most important pre-Hispanic city, and a visitor's center, which opened in 1994. Few tour agencies arrange a trip from Chihuahua unless there is a group of six or more. You can stay over in the nearby town of Nuevo Casas Grandes, about 5 miles northeast of the ruins.

5 Puerto Vallarta & the Central Pacific Coast

Mazatlán, Puerto Vallarta, and Manzanillo—the modern resort cities of Mexico's Central Pacific Coast—have come of age. They are linked to major cities by air and are guarded from the sea by towering walls of high-rise luxury hotels. Although the resorts advertise somewhat homogeneous beach holidays, each city possesses its own distinctive Mexican *ambiente;* you'll experience this local character more directly traveling on $35 or so a day than you would staying in resorts where you feel like you never left home.

The budget-conscious tourist does not need to hang a hammock alongside the luxury hotels. There are still perfectly comfortable, inexpensive hotels and restaurants in the older downtown sections of most cities along the Pacific coast, and the villages near each of the cities are generally less expensive.

This chapter describes the central section of Mexico's Pacific coast and its sparkling resort cities, which, from north to south, are Mazatlán, in the state of Sinaloa; Puerto Vallarta, in the state of Jalisco; and Manzanillo, in the state of Colima. The route south from the U.S. border along Mexico's 2,000-mile-long Pacific coast, with its hazy desert pinnacles, makes for scenic meandering. The northern reaches of the coast edge the Sonoran Desert, but once you get south of Culiacán, the lush tropical climate is perfect for beach resorts.

EXPLORING THE CENTRAL PACIFIC COAST

Mexico's central Pacific coast caters to so many kinds of vacationers it's impossible to suggest one resort city over another. Mazatlán, with a loyal following of repeat visitors, is also a mecca for sportfishing, and like Manzanillo, it's less expensive overall than Puerto Vallarta. Puerto Vallarta is very picturesque and sophisticated, with excellent restaurants, shopping, and nightlife. Manzanillo is all about good food, good sunsets, and relaxation. Along this section of coast, villages such as San Blas, Bucerías, Barra de Navidad, and Melaque are still laid-back, almost undiscovered, and relatively inexpensive. Inland, Colima (the capital of the state of Colima) offers a beautiful and slow-paced colonial-style alternative to a beachside vacation. Excursions to these smaller villages offer an altogether different kind of experience. Several are so close together that you can easily try them all out before heading home.

The best time to go is off-season, especially September to mid-December, when prices are their lowest and the hotels are less crowded; some are almost empty. However, don't overlook the high season; many hotels offer surprising discounts or are half empty, even in peak season.

ALONG HIGHWAY 15 FROM NOGALES TO MAZATLÁN

From the U.S. border, along Highway 15 from Nogales to Mazatlán, there are several interesting stops that merit a brief visit or overnight. **Kino Bay,** 70 miles west of Hermosillo on the Sea of Cortez, is a popular oceanside village with numerous inns in its two villages—Kino Viejo and Kino Nuevo.

Hermosillo, Sonora (pop. 500,000), capital of the state of Sonora, is an agricultural center. There are several hotels in the town center. Outside of town on Highway 15 traveling south toward Ciudad Obregón is the **Ecological Center of Sonora,** a nicely done 2,471-acre, mostly open-air museum set aside to protect plants and animals native to the desert. About 112 miles south of Hermosillo is **Guaymas, Sonora** (pop. 130,000), a rather lackluster port city noted for its fishing. Modest hotels line the main street (Highway 200) leading to the main plaza. **Ciudad Obregón, Sonora** (pop. 270,000), 75 miles south of Guaymas, is a modern city by Mexican standards (it was founded in 1928). The city is devoted to agriculture, including cotton, rice, and sesame.

About 42 miles farther south is **Navojoa, Sonora** (pop. 125,000), a wheat-growing center with many flour mills. Just 35 miles west of Navojoa is **Alamos, Sonora** (pop. 25,000), once a great silver-mining village and today one of Mexico's most wonderfully preserved colonial-era towns. It was laid out by order of the king of Spain in the 1600s to cater to the rich silver mines in the area but was deserted by 1900. Many of its centuries-old mansions, which line the streets, have been restored, and several are hotels. It's definitely worth the trouble to visit and to kick back in Alamos's almost somnolent pace. The **Museo Costumbrista de Sonora** in Alamos exhibits artifacts from the city's history. In June, **Mexican jumping beans** start to crackle in the hills, and locals gather them for sale as a curio in local stores.

About halfway between Alamos and Culiacán is **Los Mochis,** a popular boarding point for the **Copper Canyon Train,** also called *Chihuahua al Pacífico*. Los Mochis, the canyons, and Chihuahua (at the other end of the line) are covered in chapter 5. **Culiacán** (pop. 560,000), 130 miles south of Los Mochis, is a town with both modern and colonial elements in a rich agricultural area abounding in cotton, peanuts, tomatoes, and poppies. The city's trade in illegal drugs is well known. From Culiacán, it's an easy three-hour drive to Mazatlán, the most northerly of Mexico's large Pacific resort cities. Pretty country, with rolling uplands gradually yielding to fertile tropic savannahs, separates the two cities.

1 Mazatlán

674 miles NW of Mexico City, 314 miles NW of Guadalajara, 976 miles SE of Mexicali

Mazatlán was once best known as a resort for sportfishermen who came to catch sailfish and marlin. You can still hire a boat for big-game fishing or guns and a guide for a hunting expedition to the countryside at some of the most reasonable prices in Mexico. But nowadays, Mazatlán is better known as a world-class beach resort, and with good reason—17 miles of inviting sandy beaches extend northward from the original old city. Hotels, restaurants, shops, and clubs now cozy up those beaches as this city of 500,000 grows to accommodate its yearly influx of a million visitors.

Compared to many Mexican cities, Mazatlán is a mere child, barely 200 years old. The city has no ancient ruins and very few great legends. It does, however, possess an interesting 20-block historic area called Old Mazatlán, which dates back to the 19th century (see "Architecture," below).

ESSENTIALS

GETTING THERE & DEPARTING   By Plane   There are some direct or non-stop flights to Mazatlán, most from the west coast of the United States. See chapter 3, "Planning a Trip to Mexico," for a list of international carriers serving Mexico. (**Alaska Airlines'** local telephone number is **69/85-2730** at the airport or toll free **95-800/426-0333** in Mexico.) From elsewhere in Mexico, **Aero California** (at the airport ☎ **13-2042**, 16-2190, or 16-2191) flies in from Tijuana, Guadalajara, and Mexico City. **Aeroméxico** (☎ **13-1111** or 13-1621) has flights to Mazatlán from Mexico City, Los Mochis, Durango, Tijuana, and León. **Mexicana** (☎ **82-7722**) offers service from Mexico City, Guadalajara, and Los Cabos. The regional carrier **Noroeste** (at the airport ☎ **14-1455**) flies from Ciudad Obregón, Culiacán, Hermosillo, Durango, Chihuahua, and Mexicali. Check with a travel agent for the latest **charter flights.**

By Bus   First-class and deluxe **Tres Estrellas de Oro** and **Elite** buses (☎ **81-5308**) depart almost hourly for Guadalajara and Mexico City; Tres Estrellas also has service to Guaymas, Mexicali, and Los Mochis. **Transportes Norte de Sonora** (☎ **81-3684** or 81-3846) has daily service to San Blas, Nogales, and Agua Prieta. **Transportes del Norte** (☎ **81-2335**) serves Durango and Monterrey. **Transportes del Pacífico** (☎ **82-0577**) goes to Mexico City, Tijuana, Nogales, Los Mochis, Tepic, and Escuinapa.

The second-class bus station is located directly behind the first-class station across the lot where the buses park. The best way to figure out which line serves your desired destination is to check the names posted on the buses; drivers also call out their destinations as they're getting ready to depart. From this station **Autotransportes Concordia** has 12 buses daily to Concordia and one bus to Copala; **Autotransportes Escuinapa** has several daily buses to Escuinapa; from there you can transfer to Teacapán. Taking a public bus to Copala and Concordia is less expensive than the tour price. Traveling for the day to Concordia is no problem; just make sure you verify the time of the last bus back. Copala presents a different dilemma; there is only one daily bus to and from there, and the town offers few places to stay overnight, so check the schedule carefully before departing. Bus fare to Concordia is $2 and $3.50 to Copala. There are frequent buses to Escuinapa, and from there you can catch a local bus to Teacapán.

By Car   Take International Highway 15 from Nogales, Arizona, to Culiacán. In Culiacán you may want to change to the four-lane tollway that makes Mazatlán only a 10-hour drive from the United States. But get ready for a shock to your budget—the tollway costs about $70. Because of the high cost, the road is little traveled, and motorists on it find themselves somewhat isolated. The paucity of traffic has made it appealing to robbers, and there have been a few reports of motorists being robbed along the tollway. Ask about conditions before traveling or check with the U. S. State Department (see chapter 3 for State Department information). Gas up in Culiacán, too, in case the gas stations on the tollway are closed.

By Ferry   Passenger ferries operated by **SEMATUR** run between Mazatlán and La Paz, Baja California. The ferry leaves Friday through Wednesday at 3pm and arrives

Mazatlán Area

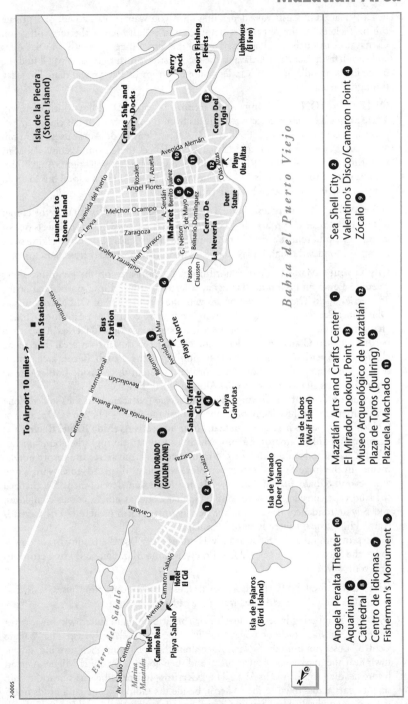

Isla de la Piedra (Stone Island)

Ferry Dock

Sport Fishing Fleets

Lighthouse (El Faro)

Cruise Ship and Ferry Docks

Cerro Del Vigia ⑬

Launches to Stone Island

Avenida del Puerto

G. Leyva

Avenida Alemán ⑩ ⑪

Rosales

T. Azueta

Angel Flores

⑫

Olas Altas

Playa Olas Altas

Melchor Ocampo

A. Serdán

Market Benito Juárez ⑧ ⑨
⑦

Zaragoza

5 de Mayo

Deer Statue

Gutiérrez Nájera

Juan Carrasco

G. Nelson

Belisario Domínguez

Cerro De La Nevería

Paseo Claussen

⑥

Bahía del Puerto Viejo

Train Station

To Airport 10 miles →

Insurgentes

Bus Station

⑤

Playa Norte

Avenida del Mar

Reforma

Internacional

Revolución

Sabalo Traffic Circle ④

Playa Gaviotas

Avenida Rafael Buelna

Carretera

Garzas

③

ZONA DORADO (GOLDEN ZONE)

R.T. Loaiza

② ①

Gaviotas

Isla de Venado (Deer Island)

Isla de Lobos (Wolf Island)

Isla de Pajaros (Bird Island)

Hotel El Cid

Avenida Camaron Sabalo

Playa Sabalo

Esero del Sabalo

Av. Sabalo Cerritos

Marina Mazatlan

Hotel Camino Real

2-0005

Angela Peralta Theater ⑩
Aquarium ⑤
Cathedral ⑧
Centro de Idiomas ⑦
Fisherman's Monument ⑥

Mazatlán Arts and Crafts Center ①
El Mirador Lookout Point ⑬
Museo Arqueológico de Mazatlán ⑫
Plaza de Toros (bullring) ③
Plazuela Machado ⑪

Sea Shell City ②
Valentino's Disco/Camaron Point ④
Zócalo ⑨

in La Paz at 9am. Costs vary depending on if you want a seat, a bed, or a private cabin. Tickets for the ferry must be purchased in advance at the ferry office on Carnaval or through travel agents. To find the ferry office, go south on Olas Altas and turn left on Alemán; Carnaval is the second street; turn right, and you'll find the office in the middle of the block. Ferries return from La Paz to Mazatlán Thursday through Tuesday.

ORIENTATION **Arriving** The **airport** is about 10 miles south of town. **Transportes Terrestres** colectivo minivans from the airport to hotels charge $7 per person; a taxi from the airport will cost $12. The **Central de Autobuses** (main bus terminal) is at Río Tamazula and Chachalacas. To get there from Avenida del Mar, walk three blocks inland on Río Tamazula; the station is on your right. A taxi from the bus station to most hotels will cost around $3. You can catch a local bus for 50¢, but you may have to change buses en route.

Information The **City and State Tourism Office** is on Olas Altas at the corner of Escobedo, near Old Mazatlán (☎ **69/81-5837;** fax 69/81-5835). This is one of the most helpful tourist offices in the country with a friendly English-speaking staff. It's open Monday through Friday from 8am to 3pm and Saturday from 9am to 1pm.

City Layout Mazatlán extends north from the port area on the peninsula along **Avenida Leyva** and **Avenida Barragan,** where the cruise ships, sportfishing boats, and ferries dock. The downtown begins with the historic area of **Old Mazatlán** and **Olas Altas Beach** to the south. The waterfront drive continues north for 17 miles, changing names often. Traveling north, it begins as **Avenida Olas Altas** then becomes **Paseo Claussen** parallel to the commercial downtown area. The name changes to **Avenida del Mar** at the beginning of the **North Beach** area, where several moderately priced hotels are located. The curving seaside boulevard, or **Malecón,** runs all the way from Olas Altas to North Beach.

About 4 miles north of downtown lies the Sábalo traffic circle in the Golden Zone near Punta Camarónóa rocky outcropping over the water. The **Zona Dorada,** or Golden Zone, begins here as **Avenida del Mar** intersects **Avenida Rafael Buelna** and becomes **Avenida Camarón Sábalo,** which leads north through the abundant hotels and fast-food restaurants of the tourist zone. From here, the resort hotels, including the huge El Cid Resort complex, continue to spread northward along and beyond **Sábalo Beach.** The new **Marina Mazatlán** development has changed the landscape considerably north of the Golden Zone, as hotels, condo complexes, and private residences rise around the new marina. North of here is **Los Cerritos** (Little Hills), the northern limit of Mazatlán.

Keep in mind that Mazatlán is fully 17 miles long. Use the landmarks of downtown, the Sábalo traffic circle, El Cid Resort, Marina Mazatlán, and Los Cerritos to find your way.

GETTING AROUND The downtown transportation center for buses, taxis, and pulmonías is on the central plaza facing the cathedral.

By Bus Lumbering buses, some with air-conditioning and tinted windows, cover most of the city and make getting around this long resort relatively easy. The **"Sábalo Centro"** buses run from the Golden Zone along the waterfront, then turn into downtown near the market and central plaza, and then go on to Avenida Miguel Alemán before heading south at Olas Altas. The **"Cerritos–Juárez"** line starts near the train station, cuts across town to the Malecón beside the Golden Zone, and heads north to Cerritos and back. The **"Sábalo Cocos"** line runs through the Golden Zone, heads inland to the bus station and on to downtown by a back route (instead of the waterfront), also stopping at the market. The **"Playa Sur"** line goes to the area where the sportfishing and tour boats depart. The buses run daily from 6am to 11pm and charge around 25¢.

By Pulmonía   These Jeep-type open-air vehicles carry up to three passengers. Pulmonías (literally "pneumonias") have surreylike tops and open sides to let in the breezes. As a rule they're cheaper than taxis, but you should still settle on a price before boarding.

By Taxi   In 1994 Mazatlán began a new taxi service called **Eco Taxi.** The green-and-white cabs have set fares, which are posted.

FAST FACTS: MAZATLÁN

American Express   The office is on Camarón Sábalo in the Centro Comercial Balboa shopping center, Loc. 4 and 16 (☎ **69/13-0600**), between the traffic circle and El Cid Resort; it's open Monday through Friday from 9am to 5pm and Saturday from 9am to noon.

Area Code   The telephone area code is 69.

Banks   Foreign currency is exchanged at most banks Monday through Friday from 9 to 11am.

Climate   As the northernmost major beach resort on the mainland, Mazatlán can be cooler in summer than the resorts farther south. The wettest month is September.

Legal Aid   The District Attorney's Office (Ministerio Publico Especializado de Turismo) is in the Golden Zone, across from the large Hotel Los Sabalos, at Rodolfo T. Loaiza 100 (☎ **69/84-3222**). They help tourists with legal problems and complaints.

Market   The Mercado covers the downtown block bordered by Serdán, Juárez, Ocampo, and Valle.

Post Office   The Correo is downtown on the east side of the main plaza, on Juárez just off Angel Flores.

Spanish Classes   Classes in Spanish, with a maximum of six students, begin every Monday at the **Centro de Idiomas,** three blocks west of the cathedral near 21 de Marzo and Canizales. In addition to small-group and individual instruction, the language center offers a homestay program and a person-to-person program that matches students with local people of similar interests and vocations. On Friday at 7pm the center holds free Spanish and English conversation groups open to both visitors and locals. The school also offers special tours for those enrolled in its programs, including a once-a-month walking tour of Old Mazatlán. For more information, call or write Dixie Davis, Belisario Domínguez 1908, Mazatlán, Sin. (☎ **69/82-2053;** fax 69/85-5606).

Telephones   Most telephone numbers for the Golden Zone, from the Camino Real hotel south to the Playa Mazatlán Hotel, begin with a 1, except those at the Los Sabalos Hotel and at the retail complex housing the El Sheik restaurant and Valentino's disco. Numbers in downtown and along Avenida de Mar begin with an 8.

FUN ON & OFF THE BEACH

To orient yourself, hike up and enjoy the panoramic view from the famous **Faro** (lighthouse), on the point at the south end of town. It's the second-highest lighthouse in the world (only Gibraltar is higher), towering 447 feet over the harbor. The hike begins at the end of Paseo Centenario near the sportfishing docks. There's a refreshment stand at the foot of the hill, but you may want to take along some water for

---

A Week-Long Party: Mazatlán's *Carnaval*

The week before Lent (usually in February) is Mazatlán's famous **Carnaval,** or Mardi Gras. People come from all over the country and abroad for this flamboyant celebration. Parades, special shows, the coronation of the Carnaval Queen, and many other extravaganzas take place all over town (for event information, check at major hotels or the Tourism Office and look for posters). Every night during Carnaval week, all along the Olas Altas oceanfront drive in the southern part of town, music fills the street with roving mariachi groups, the local traditional *bandas sinaloenses* (lots of brass instruments), and electrified bands set up under tarpaulin shades. Everyone dances, laughs, and mills about. The crowd increases each day, until on the last night (Shrove Tuesday), the Malecón is packed with musicians, dancers, and people out for a good time. The following day, Ash Wednesday, the party is over. People receive crosses of ashes on their foreheads at church, and Lent begins.

If you plan to be in Mazatlán for Carnaval, spring break, or Semana Santa (Holy Week), be sure to make reservations several months in advance. Hotels fill up, and prices usually rise, too.

---

the 45-minute climb. The view is nearly as spectacular from the top of **Cerro de la Vigía** (Lookout Hill), accessible by car from Av. Olas Altas.

FESTIVALS IN NEARBY VILLAGES   On the weekend of the first Sunday in October, **Rosario,** a small town 45 minutes south on Highway 15 known for the gold altar screen of its colonial church, holds a **festival honoring Our Lady of the Rosary.** Games, music, dances, processions, and festive foods mark the event. From May 1 to 10 Rosario holds its **Spring Festival.**

In mid-October, the village of **Escuinapa** holds a **Mango Festival.**

BEACHES   At the western edge of downtown is the rocky, pebbly **Playa Olas Altas,** a lovely stretch of pounding surf not suitable for swimming. Around a rocky promontory to the north of Olas Altas is **Playa Norte** with several miles of good sand beach.

At the Sábalo traffic circle, Punta Camarón juts into the water, and on either side of the point is **Playa Las Gaviotas.** Farther north, **Playa Sábalo** is perhaps the very best beach in Mazatlán. The next point jutting into the water is Punta Sábalo, beyond which is a bridge over the channel that flows in and out of a lagoon. North of the bridge the landscape has been redesigned for the Marina Mazatlán development. Beyond the marina lie even more beaches stretching all the way to Los Cerritos. Remember that all beaches in Mexico are public property, so feel free to wander where you like.

Another beach that makes an enjoyable outing is on the ocean side of **Isla de la Piedra** (Stone Island) on the southeast of town. From the center of town, board a "Circunvalación" or "Playa Sur" bus from the north side of the zócalo for the ride to the boat landing, called Embarcadero Isla de la Piedra. Small motorboats make the five-minute trip to the island every 15 minutes or so from 7am to 7pm and charge $1.25 round-trip. When you alight on the island, walk through the sleepy little village to the ocean side, where the pale-sand beaches, bordered by coconut groves, stretch for miles. On Sunday afternoon, the palapa restaurants on the shore have music and dancing, attracting families and young people; on other days the beach is almost empty. Carmelita's has delicious fish called *lisamacho,* served grilled and slightly blackened (over an open fire) with fresh, hot corn tortillas and salsa for about $10 a kilo (2.2 lb.).

Camping here is possible but not recommended because there are no facilities.

CRUISES & BOAT RENTALS   The **Fiesta Yacht Cruise** runs a large double-decker boat every morning at 11am, leaving from the south beach near the lighthouse. The three-hour cruise takes in the harbor and bay; bilingual guides explain the marine life while a marimba band plays. Tickets cost $12 per person (youngsters five to eight pay half price). Purchase tickets through a major hotel or travel agency.

Amphibious boats heading for Isla de Venados (Deer Island), one of three big islands off the coast, leave from the beaches of the **El Cid Resort** (☎ 69/13-5611) throughout the day for $6.50 round-trip. When you buy your ticket, you can rent snorkeling gear for an additional $5.

DEEP-SEA FISHING   It's slightly cheaper to enjoy deep-sea fishing in Mazatlán than in other parts of Mexico. Rates are $170 per day for a 24-foot *panga* for up to three persons; $265 per day for a 38-foot cruiser for up to four persons; and $292 per day for a 36-foot cruiser for up to 10 passengers; rates do not include fishing licenses and gratuities. Try the **Star Fleet** (☎ 69/82-2665; fax 69/82-5155), the **Aries Fleet** (☎ 69/16-3468, or 800/633-3085 in the U.S. and Canada), or **Mike Mexemins' Faro Fleet** (☎ 69/81-2824 or 69/82-4977). Locals suggest making fishing reservations for October through January at least a month in advance; at the very least, do it the minute you arrive in town.

WATER SPORTS   Among the best places to rent water-sports equipment—from snorkeling gear to Hobie Cats—are the Aqua Sport Center at the **El Cid Resort** (☎ 69/13-3333) and the Ocean Sport Center at the **Camino Real Hotel** (☎ 69/ 13-1111).

TENNIS, GOLF & OTHER OUTDOOR SPORTS   Mazatlán has more than 100 **tennis** courts. Try the courts at the **El Cid Resort,** Camarón Sábalo (☎ 69/ 13-3333), though hotel guests have priority; the **Racquet Club Gaviotas, Ibis,** and **Río Bravo** in the Golden Zone (☎ 69/13-5939); and **Club Deportivo Reforma** on Rafael Buelna (☎ 69/83-1200). Many larger hotels in Mazatlán also have courts.

As for **golf,** try the 18-hole course at the **El Cid Resort** (☎ 69/13-3333), mainly used by hotel guests; or the nine-hole course at the **Club Campestre Mazatlán** (open to the public), on Highway 15 on the outskirts of downtown (☎ 69/84-7494).

In addition to its worldwide reputation for year-round sportfishing (especially for sailfish and marlin), Mazatlán is known for good **hunting,** principally duck and dove. For information about transportation, guides, equipment, and licenses, call the **Aviles Brothers** (☎ 69/81-3728) or the **Tourism Office** (☎ 69/81-5837 or 81-5838).

You can rent horses for **horseback riding** on Isla Piedra for $10 per hour.

SPECTATOR SPORTS   There's a bullring on Rafael Buelna, about a mile from the Golden Zone (take the "Sábalo-Cocos" bus). From December through early April, **bullfights** are held every Sunday and on holidays at 4pm; locals recommend arriving by 2pm. Tickets range from $7 for general admission (ask for the shady side—*la sombra*) to $25 for the front of the shaded section; tickets can be purchased in advance at most travel agencies and tour desks.

Mexican **rodeos,** or *charreadas,* are held at the Lienzo Charro (ring) of the **Association of Charros of Mazatlán** (☎ 69/83-3154). Tickets are available through most major hotels and travel agencies.

At Playa Olas Altas, daring **cliff divers** take to the rock ledges of El Mirador and plunge into the shallow, pounding surf below. The divers perform sporadically during the day as tour buses arrive near their perch and sometimes dive with torches at 7pm. After the dive they collect donations from spectators. The public buses don't travel along this section of the waterfront; your closest stop is the Shrimp Bucket restaurant. From here walk north along the water about two blocks; El Mirador is on your left.

MUSEUMS

Museo Arqeológico de Mazatlán. Sixto Osuna 76, a block in from Paseo Olas Altas. ☎ **69/85-3502.** Admission $1. Tues–Sun 10am–1pm and 4–7pm.

This small but attractive museum exhibits both pre-Columbian artifacts and occasional contemporary artists. To get here from Olas Altas, walk inland on Sixto Osuna 1½ blocks; the museum is on your right. Art exhibits are also sometimes held in the Casa de la Cultura across the street from the museum.

Acuario Mazatlán Aquarium. Av. de los Deportes 111, half a block off Av. del Mar. ☎ **69/81-7815** or 69/81-7817. Admission $2 adults, $1 children 3–14. Daily 9:30am–6:30pm; sea lion-, bird-, and fish-feeding shows almost hourly 10:30am–5pm.

Children and adults alike interested in the sea will love this aquarium, one of the largest and best in Mexico. To find the aquarium from Avenida del Mar heading toward the Golden Zone, turn right on Avenida de los Deportes; it's one block down on your left.

Museo de Conchas (Sea Shell Museum). Rodolfo Loaiza 407, in the Golden Zone. ☎ **69/13-1301.** Free admission. Daily 9am–7pm.

Shell collectors and kids will enjoy this vast, fascinating collection of shells and shell art, much of which is for sale. To reach the museum from the Hotel Playa Mazatlán, turn left on Loaiza and walk two long blocks; it's on your right.

ARCHITECTURE   Two blocks south of the plaza stands the lovely and historic **Angela Peralta Theater** (☎ 69/82-4447), which in 1989 celebrated its first full season since the initiation of its renovation four years earlier. The theater was named for one of the world's great divas, who, along with the director and 30 members of the opera, died in Mazatlán in the 1863 cholera epidemic. Some city tours make a stop at the theater; if you're visiting on your own, ask the guard if you can go in. The theater is open daily from 8:30am to 7pm; the fee for touring the building is 75¢. For information on scheduled performances call or check at the box office at the theater.

The 20-block historic area near the theater, including the small square **Plazuela Machado** (bordered by Fras, Constitución, Carnaval, and Sixto Osuna), is packed with beautiful old buildings and rows of colorful town houses trimmed with wrought iron and carved stone; many buildings have recently been restored as part of a city project. Small galleries are beginning to appear in these houses as the neighborhood becomes the center of Mazatlán's artistic community. Check out the **town houses** on Libertad between Domínguez and Carnaval and the two lavish **mansions** on Ocampo at Domínguez and at Carnaval. For a rest stop, try the Café Pacífico (decorated with historic pictures of Mazatlán) on Plazuela Machado.

The **Plaza Principal,** also called Plaza Revolución, is the heart of the city, filled with vendors, shoeshine stands, and people of all ages out for a stroll. At its center is a Victorian-style wrought-iron bandstand with a diner-type restaurant underneath. Be sure to take a look at the **cathedral** with its unusual yellow-tiled twin steeples and partially tiled facade. It's on the corner of Calle 21 de Marzo and Nelson.

ORGANIZED TOURS   In addition to twice-daily **city tours** (for $12), there are excursions to many colorful and interesting villages nearby, such as Concordia or Copala (see below). Some towns date back to the Spanish conquest during the 16th century; others are modest farming or fishing villages. Information and reservations are available at any travel agency or major hotel.

Mazatlán Jungle Tour   Some might say that David Perez's "Jungle Tour" is misnamed, but it's still worth doing. It consists of a $1^1/_2$-hour boat ride past a Mexican navy base, Mazatlán's shrimp fleet and packing plants, and into the mangrove swamps to Stone Island. There's a three-hour stop at a pristine beach where the sand dollars may be the world's largest. Horseback rides on the beach are $6 for a half-hour ride. After the beach stop, feast on *pescado zarandeado* (fish cooked over coconut husks, green mangrove, and charcoal). Tours last from 9am to 3:30pm and cost $30 per person. Days vary, so call **69/14-2400** (☎ and fax) for dates and reservations.

SHOPPING   Most stores are open Monday through Saturday from 9 or 10am to 6 or 8pm. Very few close for lunch, and some stores are open on Sunday afternoon.

The **Golden Zone** is the place to shop. For a huge selection of handicrafts from all over Mexico, visit the **Mazatlán Arts and Crafts Center,** at Calle Gaviotas and Loaiza (☎ **69/13-5423**). Streets throughout the Golden Zone have a good selection of clothing, fabrics, silver jewelry, leather, art, and other Mexican crafts.

The **Centro Mercado** in Old Mazatlán is another kind of shopping experience. Here you'll find women selling freshly gathered shrimp under colorful umbrellas; open-air food stalls; and indoor shops stacked with pottery, clothing, and crafts (mostly of lesser quality). Small galleries and shops are beginning to appear in Old Mazatlán; one of the nicest is **NidArt Galleria,** on Av. Libertad (☎ **69/81-0002**).

La Gran Plaza is a large shopping mall just three blocks inland from the waterfront on Avenida de los Deportes. The plaza has a large supermarket, department stores, and specialty shops and is a good place for buying basic supplies.

WHERE TO STAY

The hotels in downtown Mazatlán are generally older and cheaper than those along the beachfront heading north. As a rule, room rates rise the farther north you go from downtown. The three major areas to stay are Olas Altas and downtown, the North Beach, and the Golden Zone (Zona Dorada). Mazatlán hotels fill up quickly during Carnaval and Easter week; some of the choicest rooms are reserved a year in advance, and room rates generally rise 30% to 40%.

DOWNTOWN SEAFRONT/PLAYA OLAS ALTAS

The old section of Mazatlán is spread around a picturesque beach a short walk from downtown. It was here that the movie stars of the past came to play in the sun and surf; the hotels where they stayed are still here, seeming to whisper of their former glory. All are right on the waterfront, and their seaside rooms have private balconies with beautiful views of the cove and the sunset. There are a few nice seafront restaurants along here, too, which are open from early until late, making it easy to dine near your hotel.

Hotel Belmar. Olas Altas 166,82000 Mazatlán, Sin. ☎ **69/86-1111.** Fax 69/81-3428. 150 rms (all with bath). A/C TV TEL. $12 single without ocean view; $14 single with ocean view; $14 double without ocean view; $17 double with ocean view. Free parking; guarded.

The Belmar was built in the early 1900s and must have been a grand hotel in its prime. Although this is a popular place with foreigners who come year after year, it's hard not to wish for a major renovation for this grand dame, which has fallen into disrepair. Its swimming pool and location are attractive features. Three stories of rooms face the ocean, swimming pool, and parking lots; all rooms have two double beds, tiled baths with showers, and worn furnishings. Those on the top floor have cable TV with U.S. channels. In the winter, the hotel fills up with Americans and Canadians who stay for weeks and months. Reservations are a must at Carnaval time. To reach the hotel from El Shrimp Bucket restaurant, walk left (south) on Olas Altas two blocks.

✪ **Hotel La Siesta.** Av. Olas Altas 11, 82000 Mazatlán, Sin. ☎ **69/81-2640.** Fax 69/3-7476. 57 rms (all with bath). A/C TEL. $17 single; $19 double; $22 triple.

A fresh coat of tan paint makes the Siesta blend into its surroundings among the old mansions of Mazatlán. Inside, three levels of green-and-white railings surround a central courtyard. The rooms facing the ocean have balconies opening to sea breezes, pounding waves, and the roar of traffic. Those at the back of the hotel are more quiet but less charming. All have two beds, white walls with arched ceilings, a small table and chair, good lighting, and dependably hot water in the shower. There's a jug of purified water on each level. TVs cost extra. The courtyard houses the popular El Shrimp Bucket restaurant, where live marimbas and recorded music play until 10pm. This is the nicest hotel in old Mazatlán and fills up quickly. Reservations are strongly advised. To get here from the deer statue on Olas Altas, go right one block.

Downtown

This downtown area, spreading from the main plaza to Playa Norte and Olas Altas, includes the commercial hub of the town with bustling streets, countless shops, chronic parking problems, and small Mexican restaurants. Beware of traffic noise; at some hotels an interior room may be preferable.

Hotel Central. Domínguez Sur 2, 82000 Mazatlán, Sin. ☎ **69/82-1888** or 69/82-1866. 67 rms (all with bath). FAN TV TEL. $12 single; $13 double.

Although the exterior looks a bit grim, the Central offers pleasant, clean rooms with good beds; most have one single and one double bed, and 40 have TVs. There's less street noise here than at the hotels closer to the plaza. The small café upstairs is open Monday through Saturday from 8am to 8pm. To get here from El Shrimp Bucket restaurant (if you're facing the restaurant), walk one block left on Olas Altas, turn right on Angel Flores, and walk four blocks, then turn right on Domínguez; it's on your right halfway down the block.

Hotel Santa Barbara. Juárez and 16 de Septiembre, 82000 Mazatlán, Sin. ☎ **69/82-2120.** 31 rms (all with bath). A/C or FAN. $9 single or double without A/C; $14 single or double with A/C.

The neighborhood around the Santa Barbara is no longer a tourist hangout, and many of the restaurants and shops have closed. Still, it's an inexpensive and quiet area near both the beach and downtown. The Santa Barbara offers a small lobby with a TV and plastic chairs; the rooms are simple, clean cubicles. All are pleasantly decorated with chenille bedspreads or matching spreads and drapes, wood furniture, and peach walls; five double rooms are air-conditioned. To get here from the waterfront, walk one long block up Juárez; the hotel is on the left.

Playa Norte

The waterfront between downtown and the Golden Zone is Mazatlán's original tourist strip. Moderately priced hotels and motels line the street across from the beach, where taco and souvenir vendors set up shop on weekends. Señor Frog's, Mazatlán's most famous tourist restaurant, is in this neighborhood, as is the bus station (though those with heavy luggage might still want to take a cab to reach their hotels). In summer as well as May and September, many hotels along this beach cut their prices.

Hotel Del Sol. Av. del Mar (Apdo. Postal 400), 82000 Mazatlán, Sin. ☎ **69/85-1103.** Fax 69/85-2603. 21 rms (all with bath). A/C TFL. $15 single or double; $25 with kitchenette. Free parking.

This modern brown motel with shuttered windows is on the waterfront near the Pizza Hut and the street leading to the aquarium. It looks small from the street but extends far back. Most rooms are modern and small; some have kitchenettes. Facilities include a small pool, a separate children's pool, and a travel agency.

Olas Altas Inn. Av. del Mar 719, 82000 Mazatlán, Sin. ☎ **69/81-3192.** Fax 69/85-3720. 50 rms (all with bath). A/C TV TEL. $40 single or double. Free parking; enclosed.

New in 1994, the Olas Altas appears remarkably different from its neighbors with its thoroughly modern mauve-and-gray color scheme. Rooms have two double or one king-size bed; cable TV; and pink, blue, and gray decor. The small pool and restaurant are located by the main street; room service is available.

THE GOLDEN ZONE (ZONA DORADA)

The Golden Zone is an elegant arc of golden sand bordered by a palm-lined boulevard. Flashy hotels and a sprinkling of elaborate beach houses with high walls and watchdogs edge the sea. The sunset view here is unique because of the three islands just offshore, which seem to melt gradually into the fading colors of evening. In summer as well as May and September, many hotels along this beach cut their prices.

Apartments Fiesta. Ibis 502 at Río de la Plata, 82110 Mazatlán, Sin. ☎ **69/13-5355.** 7 apts (all with bath). A/C or FAN. $200–$400 for a month; $70–$100 for a week; $20 single or double for a night.

A real find for long-term stays, the bright-blue-and-orange Fiesta has one- and two-bedroom apartments, all with kitchens, clustered around a small courtyard. Each apartment is decorated differently with a variety of wooden tables, chairs, and beds. The proprietors, Yolanda and Francisco Olivera, are very accommodating hosts. They don't take reservations far in advance and prefer that you call a week before you plan to visit. The complex is two blocks inland from Camarón Sábalo, an easy walk from the beach.

✪ Hotel Suites Don Pelayo. Av. del Mar 1111 (Apdo. Postal 1088), 82000 Mazatlán, Sin. ☎ **69/83-1888.** Fax 69/84-0799. 96 rms, 72 junior suites (all with bath). A/C TV TEL. $32 single or double; $35 suite for two. Free parking; enclosed.

After a total refurbishing in 1994 and 1995, the Don Pelayo is the top choice on North Beach. The waterfront rooms have small balconies; all rooms have a king-size bed or two double beds, satellite TV, and central air-conditioning (without individual controls). The lighting and furnishings are gradually being improved. Suites have minibars and kitchenettes. Facilities include a restaurant, bar, two pools, and tennis courts. The hotel is very popular with families.

El Quijote Inn. Av. Camarón Sábalo (Apdo. 934-966), 82000 Mazatlán, Sin. ☎ **69/14-1134.** Fax 69/14-3344. 67 rms and suites (all with bath). A/C TV TEL. $55 single or double for a studio without ocean view; $98 for up to four persons for a studio with ocean view; $124 for a one-bedroom suite for up to four persons; $187 for a two-bedroom suite for up to six persons. Free parking; guarded.

The brown, pink, and orange color scheme may be outdated, but the suites at the El Quijote are some of the best values in town. Most have a Murphy bed that folds into the wall and is far more comfortable than the couches provided at similar establishments. All rooms, except the studios, have full kitchens with a bar and barstools along with a dining table; those with ocean views have arched windows and balconies. There are a fair-size pool and a hot tub beside the beach, but the hotel does not have a restaurant.

WHERE TO EAT

Mazatlán is a great town for tasty seafood prepared in a variety of ways and boasts one of the largest shrimp fleets in the world. Yet seafood here is not cheap, and often Mexican plates are the best bargain.

An alternative to eating in a restaurant is to stop at one of the many **loncherías** scattered throughout the downtown area. At these, a *torta* or *lonche* (a sandwich on a small French roll) stuffed with a variety of meats, cheeses, tomatoes, onions, and chiles generally costs $1 to $1.50.

DOWNTOWN, OLAS ALTAS & NORTH BEACH

Meals for Less than $5

✪ **Pastelería Panamá.** Juárez and Canizales. ☎ **69/85-1853.** Breakfast $1.80–$3.60; sandwiches $2–$4; coffee 75¢. Daily 7am–10pm. FAST FOOD.

Busy, busy, busy describes all five locations of this successful chain. Everyone in Mazatlán must visit one location at least once a day for a leisurely coffee, a quick sandwich, or a sweet roll or piece of chocolate cake. To reach the place from the cathedral, walk straight (with the plaza behind you) one block on Juárez to Canizales; the restaurant is across the street on your right. The branch in the Golden Zone on Camarón Sábalo is the largest in the chain and is constantly busy. Going north on Loaiza, the Pastelería Panamá in the Golden Zone is on the right at Las Garzas, almost equidistant between the Sábalo traffic circle and the Mazatlán Arts and Crafts Center.

Tortas Hawaii. Nelson at Valle. No phone. Sandwiches and chicken $2–$5. Daily 9am–10pm. SANDWICHES/CHICKEN.

At this version of a Mexican fast-food restaurant, you place your order at the counter for a large, round torta (Mexican sandwich) stuffed with a variety of meats and melted cheeses. The tortas are quick, inexpensive, and tasty—some locals swear they're the best sandwiches in the city. At the front of the restaurant there's a chicken stand selling half or whole chickens roasted with rice, beans, and tortillas. To get to the restaurant, walk (with the cathedral on your right) two blocks down Nelson; it's on your right at the corner of Valle. There's another branch on Camarón Sábalo at the end of Loaiza in the Golden Zone.

Meals for Less than $10

Bahía Mariscos. Mariano Escobedo 203. ☎ **69/81-2645.** Main courses $5.50–$14. Daily 11am–5pm. SEAFOOD.

A charming old mansion in Olas Altas has been transformed into this delightful restaurant specializing in bountiful seafood lunches. The campechana bahía is a delicious medley of shrimp, octopus, oysters, and calamari, and the fried whole fish is the best you'll find in the city. To get here from El Shrimp Bucket (at M. Escobedo and Olas Altas), walk south one block and turn left on Escobedo; the restaurant is on your left.

✪ **Copa de Leche.** Olas Altas 33 Sur. ☎ **69/82-5753.** Breakfast $1.50–$4.50; main courses $4–$10; soup $2–$4.50. Daily 7am–11pm. MEXICAN.

This shaded sidewalk café on the waterfront at Playa Olas Altas has the feeling of Mazatlán in the 1930s. The food is consistently as good as the ocean view. The menu includes *alambre* barbecue (beef cooked with onion, peppers, mushrooms, ham, and bacon); wonderful seafood soup loaded with squid, shrimp, and chunks of fish; and great shrimp with chipotle sauce. Inside the café, the bar is an old wooden boat, and the dining tables are covered with linen cloths. To get here from El Shrimp Bucket (at M. Escobedo and Olas Altas), turn south and walk half a block down Olas Altas; the café is on your left.

✪ **Doney's.** Mariano Escobedo 610. ☎ **69/81-2651.** Soup or salad $1.50–$8; main courses $4.50–$12; Mexican plate $2.50–$6. Daily 8am–10pm (comida corrida served noon–4pm). MEXICAN.

This tried-and-true favorite, in a converted colonial home immediately south of the plaza, is regarded by many locals as the best moderately priced restaurant downtown. The mood is serene under the brick domes covering the interior courtyard. Inside, stained glass, handsome woodwork, and old sepia photographs add a turn-of-the-century flavor, especially when piano music fills the air. The large bilingual menu includes what some claim is the best apple pie in town. From the plaza with the city hall on your left, walk one block down Angel Flores, then turn left on Cinco de Mayo; the restaurant is at the end of the block at Escobedo.

Worth a Splurge

Señor Frog's. North Beach Malecón, Av. del Mar. ☎ **69/85-1110** or 69/82-1925. Main courses $7–$15. Daily noon–1:30am. MEXICAN.

A sign over the door says just another bar & grill, but the line waiting to get in indicates just the opposite. The decor is delightfully silly; the food and loud music are great; and the atmosphere is friendly and lively. Revelers have been known to dance on the tables late into the night. The food is among the best in town. Try the great ribs, Caesar salad, or mango crêpes. The restaurant is on the waterfront drive at Playa Norte next to the Frankie Oh! disco.

El Shrimp Bucket. Av. Olas Altas 11 at Escobedo in the Hotel La Siesta. ☎ **69/81-6350** or 69/82-8019. Reservations recommended during major holidays. Mexican plates $3.50–$8; seafood and steak $7–$15. Daily 6am–11pm. MEXICAN/SEAFOOD.

A total remodeling in 1994 has rejuvenated the somewhat weary El Shrimp Bucket, making it once again one of the most popular restaurants in town. You can sample great shrimp in the air-conditioned dining room or under umbrellas in the center courtyard. The marimbas start tinkling around 7pm, and for wining, dining, and dancing, this is a great place for a splurge. El Shrimp Bucket is on Olas Altas at the corner of Escobedo.

NORTH BEACH & THE GOLDEN ZONE

La Costa Marinera. Privada Camarón. ☎ **69/14-1928.** Main courses $4–$10. Daily 11am–11pm. MEXICAN/SEAFOOD.

Set just above the sand in a quiet section of Playa Sábalo, Costa Marinera is festooned with seashells and other nautical bric-a-brac. Shrimp is prepared at least half a dozen ways, all delicious, especially the "adobo"—made with roasted red peppers and almonds. Some dishes are brought sizzling to the table on ceramic grills. Large groups fill the many separate dining rooms, especially at lunch. To find the restaurant look for the Oceano Palace Hotel on Camarón Sábalo heading north and turn left just afterwards—if you reach the Pueblo Bonito you've gone too far—and look for the palm-frond roof on the right at the end of the unmarked street.

Jungle Juice. Las Garzas and Laguna. ☎ **69/13-3315.** Breakfast $2–$4; main courses $4.50–$12. Restaurant, daily 7am–1am. Bar, daily 4pm–1am. MEXICAN.

A front patio surrounded by lattice and an upstairs bar hung with piñatas give this semi-open-air restaurant a festive touch. Smoothies and many kinds of juices are its specialties, as are vegetarian plates and meat dishes grilled over mesquite on the patio. This casual spot also serves good breakfasts and makes a nice stop after shopping in the Golden Zone. Look for daily specials on the blackboard. To get here from Pastelería Panamá on Sábalo, turn right on Las Garzas; it's a block down on your right. (Heading north on Loaiza, Las Garzas and the Pastelería Panamá are on the right after the Sábalo traffic circle but before the Mazatlán Arts and Crafts Center.)

Locos Locos. Plaza Bonita, Camarón Sábalo. No phone. Breakfast $1.50–$3; soup $1.75; shrimp $9; seafood platter for two $16. Daily 7am–11pm. MEXICAN/SEAFOOD.

If you want to eat by the water, this is a good economical place to do it. The small Plaza Bonita is nearly empty except for three small, popular cafés set just above the sand and water. Of the three, Locos Locos is the best choice for seafood. If you're there with a friend, order the seafood platter for two, which comes with a pile of shrimp, lobster, grilled fish, and octopus, plus potato, vegetables, and lime pie. Try any fish or shrimp dish. The plaza is between the Fiesta Inn and the Caravelle Beach Club; Locos Locos is the last restaurant on your right as you face the beach.

Pura Vida. Calle Laguna. ☎ **69/16-5815.** Breakfast $1–$3; sandwiches and salads $2.50–$4. Mon–Sat 8am–10pm. VEGETARIAN/HEALTH FOOD.

Nearly hidden behind thick plants, Pura Vida has several small seating sections with green wooden picnic tables and a central lunch counter. Fabulous veggie and white chicken sandwiches are served on whole wheat rolls, and though there are plenty of meat substitute dishes like soy burgers, you're better off sticking with the vegetable selections. There are plenty of juice and smoothie combos to choose from as well. To get here from Pastelería Panamá on Sábalo, turn right on Las Garzas, then left one block down onto Laguna. The café is on your right. (Going north on Loaiza, the Pastelería Panamá and Las Garzas are on the right almost equidistant between the Sábalo traffic circle and the Mazatlán Arts and Crafts Center.)

MAZATLÁN AFTER DARK

There's a free **fireworks show** every Sunday, beginning at 8pm, on the beach fronting the Hotel Playa Mazatlán, R. T. Loaiza 202, in the Golden Zone (☎ **69/13-4444** or 69/13-5320). The display is visible from the beach or from the hotel's Terraza Playa restaurant.

This hotel also presents an excellent **Fiesta Mexicana,** complete with buffet, open bar, folkloric dancing, and live music. Fiestas are presented on Tuesday, Thursday, and Saturday year-round beginning at 7pm; try to arrive by 6pm to get a good table. Tickets are $25.

DISCOS & BARS

Café Pacífico. Frías and Constitución. ☎ **69/81-3972.** No cover.

If you're staying downtown or would prefer a quiet atmosphere, this bodegalike bar in a restored historic building on Plazuela Machado is a pleasant place to spend some time. The doors are inset with stained glass, and the thick roof beams and walls are decorated with braided garlic, dried peppers, and old photographs. Another room contains a pool table. Beer is $1.50; margaritas cost $2. It's open daily from 11am to midnight. There's a second, newer café that is open the same hours on Loaiza in the Golden Zone by the artisans market.

Joe's Oyster Bar. Loaiza 100, on the beachfront at Los Sábalos Hotel. ☎ **69/83-5333.** No cover.

Beer, burgers, fresh oysters, and loud music are the house specialties at this casual open-air disco. Beer costs $2, and margaritas go for $3. It's open daily from 11am to 2am.

Valentino's. Punta Camarón, near the Camarón Sábalo traffic circle. ☎ **69/83-6212.** Cover $5.

Dramatically perched on a rocky outcropping overlooking the sea, this all-white, Moorish-looking building houses one of the area's most popular discos. There's a good high-tech light show complete with green laser beams. For a break from the pulsating dance floor there are pool tables in another room and some quiet (relatively) areas for talking. Drinks run $1.50 to $5. It's open daily from 9pm to 4am.

ROAD TRIPS FROM MAZATLÁN
TEACAPÁN: ABUNDANT WILDLIFE & A RUSTIC VILLAGE

Teacapán is the quintessential Mexican fishing village. It's just two hours south of Mazatlán (82 miles) at the tip of an isolated peninsula which extends 18 miles down a coastline of pristine beaches. Mangrove lagoons and canals border its other side. Palm and mango groves, cattle ranches, and an occasional cluster of houses dot the peninsula, which ends at the Boca de Teacapán, a natural marina separating the states of Sinaloa and Nayarit. Shrimping boats line the beach at the edge of this marina, backed by the worn houses and dirt streets of town.

Birdwatchers hire local fishermen to take them out around the lagoons, where they can see herons, flamingos, Canadian ducks, and countless other species of birds. Inland, the sparsely populated land is a haven for deer, ocelot, and wild boars. There's talk of making the entire peninsula into an ecological preserve, and thus far, residents have resisted attempts by developers to turn the area into a large-scale resort. For now, visitors are treated to the ultimate peaceful refuge.

Note to drivers: To reach Teacapán, drive south from Mazatlán on the highway to Escuinapa. There are no signs marking the right turn for the road to Teacapán; ask for directions in Escuinapa.

Where to Stay & Eat
Rancho los Angeles. Km 25 Carretera Escuinapa-Teacapán. No phone. Reservations: contact Palmas 1-B, Colonia Los Pinos, Mazatlán, Sin. 82000; ☎ and fax **69/81-7867.** 14 rms, 1 bungalow (all with bath). A/C or FAN. $33 single or double on the waterfront; $27.50 single or double in the bungalow; $22 single or double by the main street.

Dr. Ernesto Rivera Gúzman and his sons have created this small resort at the edge of the sea in the midst of coconut groves. The best rooms are in the hacienda-style building with terraces and a clean blue pool beside a long beach. The single rustic bungalow is a few feet from the main building; other rooms are in a motel-like structure beside the main road to town. Boat tours and horseback riding are available. The hotel's small restaurant serves meals on the patio by the pool.

COPALA: AN OLD SILVER TOWN

Popular tours from Mazatlán stop here for lunch only, but Copala is well worth an overnight stay. The town was founded in 1565; from the late 1880s to the early 1900s, it was the center of the region's silver mining boom. When the mines closed, the town became nearly deserted. Today, it's a national historic landmark, with 600 full-time residents and a part-time community of retired Canadians and U.S. citizens devoted to Copala's picturesque solitude. In fact, some residents were less than pleased when the area received electricity in 1979.

Every building in town is painted white, and most have red-tile roofs splashed with fuschia-colored bougainvillea. Cobblestone streets wind from the entrance to town up slight hills at the main plaza and the Cathedral of San José, built in 1610. The town bustles around noon, when the tour buses arrive, and visitors stroll the streets surrounded by small boys selling geodes extracted from the local hills. By 3pm, most of the outsiders have left, and you can wander the streets in peace and visit the century-old cemetery, the ruins of old haciendas, and the neighborhoods of white villas. The town's burros, roosters, and dogs provide the main background noise, and few cars clatter up the streets.

Note: Copala is an easy two-hour drive from Mazatlán, but it is only served by one bus a day (see "By Bus" under "Arriving and Departing," above, at the beginning of the Mazatlán section). You may be able to talk one of the tour bus drivers into giving you a lift back to Mazatlán for a small fee.

Where to Stay & Eat
Daniel's. At the entrance to town. ☎ **69/86-5736.** 10 rms (all with bath). FAN. $25 single or double (including breakfast).

Daniel's restaurant is Copala's best-known landmark, revered for the sublime banana-cream coconut pie served with nearly every meal. Owner Daniel Garrison restored his uncle's turn-of-the-century home into the restaurant, set against a backdrop of the Sierra Madre foothills. The restaurant fills with guests at lunch time, and later in the day becomes the favored hangout of local expatriates. To the side of the restaurant is a small hotel housing large guest rooms with bathrooms, comfortable beds, and windows looking out to the countryside. Daniel's also offers Copala tours from Mazatlán; call the number listed above or check at the Hotel San Diego in Mazatlán for information. Daniel's is less than a 10-minute walk to town.

2 Puerto Vallarta

620 miles W of Mexico City, 260 miles W of Guadalajara, 175 miles N of Manzanillo, 300 miles S of Mazatlán, 112 miles S of Tepic.

The gorgeous village of Puerto Vallarta boasts tropical mountains right beside the sea, coves and beaches, white buildings with red-tile roofs, and streets of brick and cobblestone. The construction of luxury hotels and shopping centers—mostly on the outskirts of the original town—has developed the town into a city of 250,000 people without destroying its charm. With miles of high-rise hotels flanking the picturesque village center, Puerto Vallarta does a better job than any other coastal city of balancing Mexico's sophisticated resort environment with captivating colonial-era charm. In fact, I always recommend this city as the spot for a Mexican coastal vacation to people who want a taste of inland Mexico combined with the best of Mexico's hotel and restaurant services, shopping, and sports.

Once an agricultural village on the Bay of Banderas, Puerto Vallarta ceased to be a secret when a film of Tennessee Williams's *Night of the Iguana*, starring Richard Burton, Ava Gardner, and Deborah Kerr, was made here. Elizabeth Taylor came along for the filming, and the romance between Burton and Taylor became headline news, throwing Puerto Vallerta into the world's limelight. After Taylor's love affair, the tiny seaside village grew into a booming resort with a good highway and airport. Restaurants, shops, and hotels here are some of the country's best.

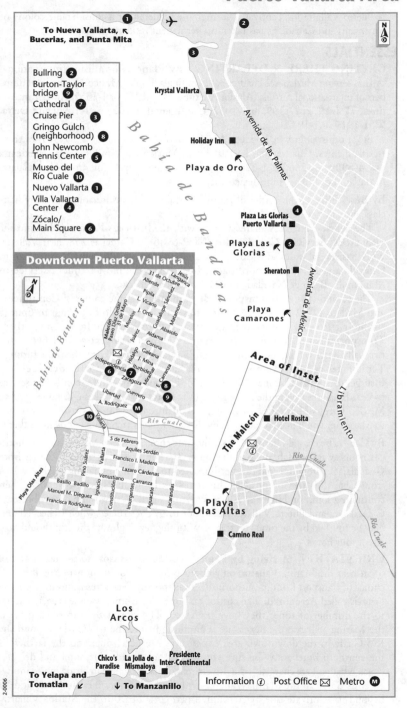

Puerto Vallarta Area

To Nueva Vallarta,
Bucerias, and Punta Mita

Bullring **2**
Burton-Taylor
bridge **9**
Cathedral **7**
Cruise Pier **3**
Gringo Gulch
(neighborhood) **8**
John Newcomb
Tennis Center **5**
Museo del
Río Cuale **10**
Nuevo Vallarta **1**
Villa Vallarta
Center **4**
Zócalo/
Main Square **6**

Krystal Vallarta

Avenida de las Palmas

Holiday Inn

Playa de Oro

Bahia de Banderas

Plaza Las Glorias
Puerto Vallarta **4**

Playa Las
Glorias **5**

Sheraton

Avenida de México

Playa
Camarones

Downtown Puerto Vallarta

Bahia de Banderas

31 de Octubre
Allende
Jesús Langarica
Pipila
L. Vicario
L. Ortis
Guadalupe Sánchez
Matamoros

Malecón
Paseo Díaz Ordáz
31 de Mayo
Morelos
Juárez
Aldama
Corona
Galeana
Abasolo

Independencia
Hidalgo
J. Mina
Iturbide
Miramar
Zaragoza
E. Carranza

Libertad
Guerrero

A. Rodríguez **M**

Vallarta

Río Cuale

5 de Febrero
Aquiles Serdán
Francisco I. Madero
Lazaro Cárdenas

Pino Suárez
Basilio Badillo
Manuel M. Dieguez
Francisca Rodríguez
Ignacio
Constitución
Venustiano
Insurgentes
Carranza
Aguacate
Jacarandas

Playa Olas Altas

Area of Inset

The Malecón

Hotel Rosita

Río Cuale

Libramiento

Playa
Olas Altas

Camino Real

Río Cuale

Los
Arcos

Chico's
Paradise
La Jolla de
Mismaloya
Presidente
Inter-Continental

To Yelapa and
Tomatlan
↓ To Manzanillo

Information ⓘ   Post Office ✉   Metro **M**

2-0006

135

Puerto Vallarta has captivated so many foreigners that a considerable colony of Americans and Canadians has taken up permanent residence here.

ESSENTIALS

GETTING THERE & DEPARTING **By Plane** For a list of international carriers serving Mexico, see chapter 3, "Planning a Trip to Mexico." Some local numbers of international carriers: **Alaska Airlines,** ☎ 1-1350 or 1-1352; **American Airlines,** ☎ 1-1972, 1-1799, or 1-1032; **Continental, 1-1025** or 1-1096; and **Delta,** ☎ 1-1919 or 1-1032.

From other points in Mexico, **Aeroméxico** (☎ 4-2777 or 1-1055) flies from Aguascalientes, Guadalajara, La Paz, León, Mexico City, and Tijuana. **Mexicana** (☎ 4-8900, 1-1266, or 1-0243) has direct or nonstop flights from Guadalajara, Mazatlán, Los Cabos, and Mexico City.

By Bus **Elite,** at the corner of Basillio Badillo and Constitución, has many first-class buses to Guadalajara.

The deluxe-class **ETN** shares a space with the first-class **Primera Plus** and the second-class **Servicios Coordinados** (☎ 2-6986) at Cardenas 258, near Vallarta. ETN has several buses to Mexico City and Guadalajara. Primera Plus buses go to Guadalajara. Servicios Coordinados buses have the most frequent service to Manzanillo, Barra de Navidad, and Melaque/San Patricio.

The second-class **Autotransportes del Cihuatlan,** at the corner of Constitución and Madero (☎ 2-3436), has hourly buses to Manzanillo from 5am to 6pm (a six-hour trip) and almost as frequent service to Melaque (a 4¹/₂-hour trip). **Transportes Norte de Sonora,** at Carranza 322, near Insurgentes (☎ 2-6666), has two daily buses via the short route to San Blas (a three-hour trip); the route through Tepic takes at least five hours to reach San Blas. **Transportes del Pacífico,** Insurgentes 282 at Carranza (☎ 2-1015), has both first- and second-class service to Guadalajara traveling the short route (Vía Corta), which takes 6¹/₂ hours, and to Mexico City, which takes 14 hours. If you intend to head north, for instance to Mazatlán, you'll need to go to Tepic first and then catch a direct bus from there.

By Car The coastal Highway 200 is the only choice between Mazatlán to the north (six hours away) or Manzanillo to the south (3¹/₂ hours). The eight-hour journey from Guadalajara through Tepic can be shortened to six hours by taking Highway 15A from Chapalilla to Compostela (this bypasses Tepic and saves two hours), then continuing south on Highway 200 to Puerto Vallarta. A new toll highway between Guadalajara and Puerto Vallarta was about to be constructed when I checked and may be finished by the time you travel. With the new highway, the trip should take about four hours.

ORIENTATION **Arriving by Plane** The airport is close to the north end of town near the Marina Vallarta, only about 6 miles from downtown. You'll have a choice of transport from the airport: the **Transportes Terrestres** minivan (*colectivo*) or taxis called **Aeromovil.** The cost of taxi or collectivo minivans accrue according to the number of zones they have traversed. The closest zone to the airport is the Marina Vallarta; the next zone is anything before the Río Cuale; beyond the Río Cuale in the downtown area constitutes the next zone; and the farthest is the southern hotel zone. Be sure you know the area of your hotel and double-check what you are charged—the drivers make mistakes. A shared ride in the minivan costs $3.50 to the Marina Vallarta or downtown before the Río Cuale and $6 beyond it. A private ride by Aeromovil taxi costs $8.50 to the Marina Vallarta, $10 to downtown before the river, $16.75 beyond the river, and $20 to the southern hotel zone.

Important note: Colectivos run only when they fill up after flights arrive, so avoid tarrying in the arrivals hall or you'll miss the colectivos. Between such times, only Aeromovil taxis operate. Another option is to walk about a block to the highway and hail a passing taxi; this option is cheaper than Aeromovil but more expensive than the colectivo. City buses also pass on the highway on their way to town and are useful if you have only a small bag. Coming in from the airport north of town, you'll pass (on your right) the **Terminal Maritima** (Cruiseline Pier), the **Marina Vallarta** development, and many luxury hotels; the Malecón, downtown in the village proper, is lined with restaurants, and shops, and a few hotels. However, most downtown hotels are off the Malecón.

Arriving by Bus   If you arrive by bus, you'll be south of the river on Madero, Insurgentes, or Constitución and close to all the hotels I have recommended below. Most of the bus "stations" are small offices or waiting rooms for the various lines. The city has planned a central bus station away from this downtown area for years, but so far, there's no movement on this idea.

Information   The **State Tourism Office,** at Juárez and Independencia (☎ **322/ 2-0242,** 322/3-0844, or 322/3-0744; fax 322/2-0243), is in a corner of the white Presidencia Municipal building on the corner of the main square. This is also the office of the tourist police. It's open Monday through Friday from 9am to 9pm and Saturday from 9am to 1pm.

City Layout   The seaside promenade, or **Malecón** (also known as **Paseo Díaz Ordaz**), follows the rim of the bay from north to south in the village, and the town stretches back into the hills a half a dozen blocks. The area north of the **Río Cuale** is the oldest part of town—the original Puerto Vallarta. The area south of the river, once only beach, has become as built-up as the old town in the last decade, although it's less sophisticated and more rustic. Today the best budget lodgings, as well as the bus "stations," are here.

Once you're in the center of town, you'll find nearly everything within walking distance. Puerto Vallarta has grown to the north and south of the original village along the beach. **Marina Vallarta,** a resort-city-within-a-city, is at the northern edge of the hotel zone not far from the airport—you pass it on the right as you come into town from the airport. It boasts luxury hotels and condominium projects, a huge marina with 300 yacht slips, a golf course, restaurants and bars, an office park, and a shopping plaza. Between it and downtown are many more luxury hotels, such as the Krystal and Fiesta Americana. **Nuevo Vallarta,** another planned resort, is just north of Marina Vallarta across the Ameca River in the state of Nayarit (about 8 miles north of downtown). It also has hotels, condominiums, a yacht marina, and a convention center. For now, though, Nueva Vallarta is too difficult to reach by public transportation, and all the hotels here are out of budget range. **Bucerías,** a village of cobblestone streets, villas behind walls, and small hotels is on the far side of Banderas Bay 19 miles beyond the Puerto Vallarta airport. **Punta de Mita,** at the northern end of the bay, has always been a daytime beach hangout with palapa-style restaurants. A new resort is under construction there now, and access to Punta Mita isn't available now.

Going in the opposite direction, south of the original village about 6 miles on **Mismaloya Beach** (where *Night of the Iguana* was filmed) lies the Jolla de Mismaloya Resort & Spa, and just beyond it is **Boca de Tomatlán,** which marks the farthest development to the south. Between it and downtown are more luxury hotels on the beach and mountainside.

Avenida de las Palmas (formerly called Carretera Aeropuerto, or Airport Highway) is the new name of the multilane thoroughfare leading from town to the northern hotel zone. It's been completely repaved and landscaped, transforming the area from unsightly to chic.

GETTING AROUND **By Bus & Colectivo** **City buses** run from the airport through the expensive hotel zone along 31 de Mayo (the waterfront street), across the Río Cuale, and inland on Vallarta, looping back through the downtown hotel and restaurant districts on Insurgentes and several other downtown streets. These buses will serve just about all your transportation needs frequently and cheaply; it's about 35¢ a ride. Buses run generally from 6am to 11pm. The no. 02 **minivan** bus (colectivo) goes south every 10 to 15 minutes to Mismaloya Beach from Plaza Lázaro Cárdenas, a few blocks south of the river at Cárdenas and Suárez. Check with the driver to make sure this is your bus because another no. 02 goes farther to Boca de Tomatlán (a fishing village) and may not stop at Mismaloya. To get to the northern hotel strip from old Puerto Vallarta, take the "Ixtapa" or "Aeropuerto" bus. These same buses may also post the names of hotels they pass such as Krystal, Fiesta Americana, Sheraton, and others. City buses now also pass into and through the Marina Vallarta area, where they were once prohibited.

By Boat The town pier (*muelle*), also called Terminal Maritima, where you depart for fishing excursions and catch pleasure boats to Yelapa, Las Animas, and Quimixto, is north of town near the airport and a convenient, inexpensive bus ride from town. Just take any bus marked "Ixtapa" and tell the driver to let you off at the Terminal Maritima (ter-MEEN-ahl mah-REE-tee-mah).

By Taxi Most trips from downtown to the northern hotel strip and Marina Vallarta cost between $4 and $5; to or from Mismaloya Beach to the south costs $15. With such good bus service, however, there's little reason to use them.

FAST FACTS: PUERTO VALLARTA

American Express The local office is located in the village at Morelos 660, at the corner of Abasolo (☎ **322/3-2995** or 91-800/0-0555 toll free in Mexico). It's open Monday through Friday from 9am to 6pm and Saturday from 9am to 1pm.

Area Code The telephone area code is 322.

Climate It's hot all year. Humidity rises dramatically during the summer rainy season between May and October. Rains come almost every afternoon in June and July and often continue through evening.

Currency Exchange Bancomer has a branch on Juárez at the corner of Mina. It's open from 9am to 1:30pm; foreign currency can be exchanged only from 9:30am to noon.

Pharmacy The CMQ Farmacia, Badillo 365 (☎ **322/2-1330**) is open 24 hours. It's south of the river between Insurgentes and Aguacate.

Post Office The post office (Correo) is on Mina between Juárez and Morelos. It's open Monday through Friday from 9am to 7:30pm, Saturday from 9am to 1pm, and Sunday from 9am to noon.

U.S. Consular Agency The office is at Miramar and Libertad, on the second floor of Parian del Puente 12A, just north of the river bridge near the market (☎ **322/2-0069,** 24 hours a day for emergencies). It's open Monday through Friday from 9am to 1pm.

FUN ON & OFF THE BEACH

Travel agencies can provide information on what to see and do in Puerto Vallarta and can arrange tours, fishing, and other activities.

Note: Beware of "tourist information" booths, especially along Ordaz and the Malecón—they are usually time-share hawkers offering "free" or cheap Jeep rentals, cruises, breakfasts, and so forth as bait. If you're suckered in, you may or may not get what is offered, and the experience will cost at least half a day of your vacation.

FESTIVALS Santa Cecilia, the patron saint of mariachis, is honored for a solid 24 hours on **November 22.** Beginning at midnight on the 22nd until midnight of the 23rd, different mariachi groups take turns playing in the cathedral. That evening there is a parade of mariachis and a fireworks display in the central plaza. The week leading up to **December 12**—the "birthday" of Mexico's patron saint, the Virgin of Guadalupe—there are processions of *las peregrinas* (religious pilgrims) and much merrymaking.

BEACHES Its beaches are Puerto Vallarta's main attraction. They start well north of town, out by the airport, with **Playa de Oro** and extend all around the broad Bay of Banderas. The easiest to reach is **Playa Olas Altas,** also known as **Playa Muertos** or **Playa del Sol,** just off Calle Olas Altas, south of the Río Cuale. The water is polluted here so the beach is good for sunning but not for swimming. **Playa Mismaloya** is in a beautiful sheltered cover about 6 miles south of town along Highway 200. The water is clear and beautiful. Entrance to the public beach is just to the left of the Mismaloya hotel. Colorful palapa restaurants dot the small beach and will rent you a beach chair for sunning, or you can stake out a table under a palapa for the day. Using a restaurant's table and palapa is a reciprocal arrangement—they let you be comfortable, and you buy your drinks, snacks, lunch there. Before choosing your spot, be sure you'll want to eat and drink there by briefly inspecting the set-up they have. The *Night of the Iguana* was filmed at Mismaloya. You can still see and hike up to the stone buildings that were constructed for the movie, on the point framing the south side of the cove. The Jolla de Mismaloya Resort is to the right of the public beach and restaurants there are available to outsiders as well. This and all beaches in Mexico are public.

Animas and **Yelapa** beaches are very good but are reached only by boat. These are larger than Mismaloya and are similarly set up with restaurants fronting a wide beach. If you aren't keen on taking an expensive boat trip see how to do it less expensively in "Boat Trips," below.

BOAT TRIPS Puerto Vallarta offers a number of different boat trips, including **sunset cruises** and excursions to **Yelapa** (a tiny town on a lovely cove), **Las Animas Beach,** and **Quimixto Falls.** Most of these make a stop at **Los Arcos** for snorkeling; some include lunch; and most provide music and an open bar on board. Most leave around 9:30am, stop for 45 minutes at Los Arcos, and arrive at the beach destination around noon for a 2^{1}/2-hour stay before returning around 3pm. These beaches have many colorful restaurants where you can take a table under a shady umbrella on the beach while you sun, eat, and buy drinks. It's customary to make your food and drink purchases at the restaurant whose table you occupy, so on arrival visitors are besieged by restaurant representatives to take a seat at many of them. Pick one that suits you and enjoy your time there. At Quimixto, where the shoreline is rocky and there's no beach, visitors can take the half-hour hike to the falls or rent a horse for a ride to the falls. Prices range from $20 for a sunset cruise or a trip to one of the beaches with open bar to $35 for an all-day outing with open bar and meals. Travel agencies have tickets and information.

If you prefer to spend a longer time at Yelapa or Las Animas without taking time for snorkeling and cruise entertainment, then try the **water taxi** south of the Río Cuale by the Hotel Marsol on Francisco Rodriguez. For around $15 roundtrip, boatmen advertise direct trips to Las Animas, Yelapa, or Quimixto. Supposedly, this water taxi takes off at 10:30 and 11am and returns at 3:30pm. In reality, however, the operators of this service would rather sell the lengthy tour and don't seem too enthusiastic about the direct trips, which take 40 minutes each way; a direct trip from these folks costs only slightly less than an excursion with all the trimmings. There's also another water taxi next to the Hotel Rosita (north of the river at Díaz Ordaz and 31 de Octubre), which advertises direct trips daily at 11am for $7.

WATER SPORTS   Puerto Vallarta offers good diving and snorkeling; there's a **national underwater park** at Los Arcos, an island rock formation. Underwater enthusiasts from beginner to expert can arrange scuba diving at **Chico's Dive Shop,** Díaz Ordaz 770–5 by Carlos Obrien's (☎ 322/2-1895). Chico's also has branches at the Marriott, Vidafel, Vila del Palmar, Camino Real, and Continental Plaza hotels. **Vallarta Divers,** in the Marina del Rey Condominium at Marina Vallarta (☎ 322/1-0492), also offers scuba outings, as well as resort courses and PADI and NAUI certification courses. Dives cost around $40–$60 with equipment; the price varies depending on how far you go. Snorkeling trips cost around $35.

Waterskiing, parasailing, and other water sports are available at many beaches along the Bay of Banderas.

FISHING   A fishing trip can be arranged through travel agencies or through the **Cooperativo de Pescadores** (Fishing Cooperative) on the Malecón, north of the Río Cuale next door to the Rosita Hotel and across from McDonald's (☎ 322/2-1202). Fishing charters cost $200 to $300 a day for four to eight people. Price varies with the size of the boat. Although the posted price at the fishing cooperative is the same as through travel agencies, you may be able to negotiate a lower price at the cooperative. It's open Monday through Saturday from 7am to 2pm, but make arrangements a day ahead.

Note: Most fishing trips include equipment and bait but not drinks or snacks, so arrange to bring along refreshments.

GOLF   Puerto Vallarta has two golf courses. The one nearest town is the 18-hole private course at the Marina Vallarta (☎ 322/1-0171), for members only. Most of the luxury hotels have memberships, which their guests can use. North of town about 10 miles is the 18-hole Los Flamingos Club de Golf (☎ 329/8-0606) fronting the highway a few miles beyond the turnoff for the Nuevo Vallarta development. It's open from 7am to 5pm daily, with a bar (no restaurant) and full pro shop. The greens fee is $30, plus $15 for club rental and $25 for a motorized cart or $5 for a pull cart.

BULLFIGHTS   Bullfights are held from December through April on Wednesday afternoon at the bullring "La Paloma," across the highway from the town pier. Tickets can be arranged through travel agencies and cost around $25.

ESCORTED TOURS   Hotel travel desks and travel agencies can arrange a **Tropical Tour** ($20) or a **jungle tour** ($20). The "Tropical Tour" is really an expanded city tour and includes the workers' village of Pitallal, the posh neighborhood of Conchas Chinas, the cathedral, the market, the Taylor-Burton houses, and lunch at Chino's Paradise.

Horseback-riding trips can be arranged through travel agents or directly by going to the horse owners who gather at the end of Basilio Badillo, south of the Río Cuale by the Restaurant Corral. Rides cost around $6–$8 an hour. Horsemen arrive about 9am, and rides take off around 9:30am and return around 1:30pm. Ask for Fernando Peña, one of the horsemen who can also take riders from his house on the outskirts of town and into the mountains. Arrange this with him a day ahead.

Mountain Bike Tours, Badillo 381 (☎ 322/2-0080), offers **mountain-bike trips** to outlying areas. Trips cost around $30 for four hours and include bike, helmet, gloves, water, and an English-speaking guide. Trips start at around 8am. Make arrangements a day ahead.

Sierra Madre, D. Ordaz 732-B, at Vicario (☎ **322/3-0661**), may be a sophisticated cover for time-share sales of the Westin Reginas in Mexico, huge photos of which cover the back wall. The trendy storefront features a safari theme, as well as ecologically oriented books, T-shirts, postcards—and trips. Supposedly, funds generated by trips go toward several government and privately sponsored ecological reserves and studies. Among the trips they offer are treks to the mountain foothills 1¼ hours away, an "Artistic Mexico" trip featuring nearby villages and artisans, mountain-bike tours, whale watching, and horseback riding, all conducted by ecologically oriented leaders who point out local flora and fauna. Prices range from $15 to $45 depending on the trip. It's open daily from 9am to 10pm.

You can also tour the **Taylor/Burton villas** (Casa Kimberley; ☎ **322/2-1336**), the two houses owned by Elizabeth Taylor and Richard Burton, located at 445 Calle Zaragoza. Tours cost $5, and proceeds go toward cleft-palate operations for area youngsters.

A **house-and-garden tour** of four private homes in town is offered every Thursday and Saturday during high season by the **International Friendship Club** (☎ **322/2-6060**) for a donation of $20 per person. The tour bus departs from the main plaza by the tourism office (which has information about this event) at 11am. Proceeds are donated to local charities.

A STROLL THROUGH TOWN   Puerto Vallarta's tightly knit cobblestone streets are a delight to explore (with good walking shoes!); they are full of tiny shops, rows of windows edged with curling wrought iron, and vistas of red-tile roofs and the sea. Start with a walk up and down the Malecón, the seafront boulevard.

Among the sights you shouldn't miss is the **municipal building,** on the main square (next to the tourism office), which has a large Manuel Lepe mural inside in its stairwell. Nearby, up Independencia sits the **cathedral,** topped with its curious crown; on its steps women sell colorful herbs and spices to cure common ailments. Here Richard Burton and Elizabeth Taylor were married the first time—she in a Mexican wedding dress, he in a Mexican *charro* outfit.

Three blocks south of the church, head uphill on **Libertad,** lined with small shops and pretty upper windows; it brings you to the **public market** on the river. After exploring the market, cross the bridge to the **island in the river;** sometimes a painter is at work on its banks. Walk down the center of the island toward the sea, and you'll come to the tiny **Museo del Cuale,** which exhibits pre-Columbian ceramics and works by local artists; it's open Monday through Saturday from 10am to 4pm. Admission is free.

Retrace your steps back to the market and Libertad and climb up steep Miramar to **Zaragoza.** At the top is a magnificent view over rooftops to the sea. Up Zaragoza to the right two blocks is the famous pink arched bridge that once connected Richard Burton's and Elizabeth Taylor's houses. This area, known as **Gringo Gulch,** is where many Americans have houses.

SHOPPING   Excellent-quality merchandise is brought to Puerto Vallarta from all over Mexico. Prices are higher than those in the places where the goods originated, and if you're planning to visit other parts of Mexico, you might want to wait and make your purchases at the source. In Tonala and Tlaquepaque (suburbs of Guadalajara), six hours away by bus, prices are considerably lower.

Puerto Vallarta's **municipal market** is just north of the Río Cuale where Libertad and A. Rodríguez meet. The *mercado* sells clothes, jewelry, serapes, shawls, leather accessories and suitcases, papier-mâché parrots, stuffed frogs and armadillos, and of course T-shirts. Be sure to do some comparison shopping before buying. The market is open daily from 8am to 8pm.

The **Río Cuale** under the bridge is lined with a variety of shops.

Calle Libertad, next to the market, is the place to buy *huaraches*—comfortable, practical sandals made of leather strips and rubber-tire soles. Buy a pair that fits a little tightly—they stretch out quickly and can become too floppy.

CRAFTS & FOLK ART   South of the Río Cuale   The **Olinala Gallery,** Cárdenas 274 (☎ **322/2-4995**), has two floors of fine indigenous Mexican crafts and folk art, including an impressive collection of authentic masks and Huichol beaded art. It's open Monday through Saturday from 10am to 2pm and 5 to 9pm. Though it occupies a small space, **Talavera Etc.,** Vallarta 266 (☎ **322/2-4100;** fax 322/2-2413), has a wide selection of Talavera dinnerware, tiles, sinks, and so forth, plus handmade jewelry and many silver reproductions of classic Mexican jewelry. Owner Jackie Kilpatrick will pack and ship your purchases or pack them so you can take them with you as checked luggage. The shop is located between Cárdenas and Carranza and is open Monday through Saturday from 10am to 2pm and 5 to 8pm.

La Rosa de Cristal Vidrio Soplado Artesanías, Insurgentes 272, between Cárdenas and Madero (☎ **322/2-5698**), has the best prices and greatest selection in Puerto Vallarta of Mexican blown-glass objects in all colors. It all comes from their factory in Tlaquepaque near Guadalajara; seconds are in the back. The shop is open Monday through Saturday from 10am to 8pm.

North of the Río Cuale   The **Sergio Bustamante Gallery,** Juárez 275 near Zaragoza (☎ **322/2-1129**), is open Monday through Saturday from 10am to 9pm. Bustamante's fantastic creatures emerging from eggs and other surreal and colorful images are his trademarks. His gold and silver jewelry is for sale in abundance. Two more Bustamante stores are at Ordaz 546 and Ordaz 700.

Gallery Indígena, Juárez 270, between Guerrero and Zaragoza (☎ and fax **322/2-3007**), is a large shop featuring silver, Oaxaca pottery and wood carvings, lacquer chests, dance masks, pre-Hispanic pottery reproductions, and Huichol Indian art. Owner Ignacio Jacobo is usually on hand. Ask about shipping items to the United States and delivery to Puerto Vallarta hotels. It's open Monday through Saturday from 10am to 3pm and 5 to 9pm.

La Reja, Juárez 501 (☎ **322/2-2272**), next to Querebines, has a great selection of Mexican ceramics and some lovely Guatemalan fabrics; it's open Monday through Saturday from 9am to 2pm and 4 to 8pm. **Querubines,** Juárez 501A (☎ **322/2-3475**), offers Guatemalan and Mexican wares, including embroidered and handwoven clothing, bolts of foot-loomed fabric, wool rugs, jewelry, straw bags, and Panama hats. It's open Monday through Saturday from 9am to 9pm and Sunday 10am to 6pm. It's at the corner of Galeana.

Arte Mágico Huichol, Corona 178 (☎ **322/2-3077**), has several rooms of Huichol Indian art. It carries very fine large and small yarn paintings by recognized Huichol artists, as well as intricately beaded masks, bowls, and ceremonial objects. The gallery is open Monday through Saturday from 10am to 9pm. **Nacho's,** Libertad 160A (☎ **322/2-3007**), sells beautifully made silver jewelry from Taxco and lacquerware from Olinala. Nacho's is open Monday through Saturday from 10am to 2pm and 5 to 8pm.

El Baúl, Juárez 512, inside Las Margaritas between Corona and Galeana (☎ **322/3-2580**), has fine decorative objects, colorful furniture, pottery, glass, and pewter; it's open Monday through Saturday from 10am to 2pm and 4:30 to 8pm. **Nevaj,** Morelos at Libertad (☎ **322/2-6959**), has quality folk art from Central and South

America and Mexico; it's open Monday through Saturday from 10am to 2pm and 5 to 9pm.

Instituto de la Jalisciense, Juárez 284 (☎ **322/2-1301**), is the state-operated store, featuring crafts from Jalisco as well as a few other states. It's at Zaragoza catercorner from the zócalo; hours are Monday through Saturday from 10am to 2pm and 4 to 8pm. **El Charro,** Juárez 400 (☎ **322/3-1611**), sells everything for the cowboy or cowgirl—from saddles to belts, lariats, serapes, sombreros, and *china poblana* outfits (a sort of national costume of Mexican women). Located near the zócalo at Iturbide, the store is open daily from 10am to 8pm.

CONTEMPORARY ART   The following galleries carry contemporary Mexican and/or foreign artists: **Galería Uno,** Morelos 561 at Zaragoza (☎ **322/2-0908**), is the leading art gallery, open Monday through Saturday from 10am to 8pm; **Galeria Pacífico,** Río Cuale opposite Le Bistro Jazz Café (☎ **322/2-2748**), is open Monday through Saturday from 10am to 9pm.

WHERE TO STAY

Most of the bargain hotels are south of the Río Cuale. You may find even better prices than those quoted below if you travel between May and December 15—the slowest months of the off-season. Prices go up from 25% to 50% from mid-December through Easter week, when all the best rooms are generally booked. It's best to have reservations in high season, but if you want to chance it arrive early in the day to start your search.

SOUTH OF THE RÍO CUALE

An ideal base, this area is in the heart of the downtown dining district, near numerous shops, and it's close to the beach. The nightlife, shopping, and dining on the other side of the river are also close by.

Along Madero and not far from the city's bus stations lie several hotels, among them the **Analiz** and the **Azteca,** with the lowest rates in town. Avoid the Villa del Mar on Badillo, which has balconies dangerously near electrical wiring for the city—*at least one guest was electrocuted when he touched the balcony rail.* One drawback of hotels in this area is that many have rooms with windows facing an indoor hallway. When the windows are open, your neighbors can look in; when they're closed, you may feel as if you're in a closet. Another drawback is that some appear to rent rooms by the hour at night. Ask to see the room before deciding.

🆂 **Hotel Azteca.** Madero 473, 48300 Puerto Vallarta, Jal. ☎ **322/2-2750.** 46 rms (all with bath). FAN. $7.50 single; $10 double; discounts for stays of a week or more.

This four-story (no elevator) hotel is one of the best buys in town. Many wintering northerners return to this hotel year after year. Though the rooms are very plain and basically furnished with a bed and crude table and chairs, the Villa Señor family keeps the place clean, well maintained, and safe. No visitors are allowed after 10:30pm. Rooms face the interior walkway and courtyard and are brighter than most that have this architectural arrangement. The hotel is 5¹/₂ blocks west of the beach between Jacarandas and Naranjo.

Hotel Belmar. Insurgentes 161 and Serdán, 48300 Puerto Vallarta, Jal. ☎ and fax **322/ 2-0572.** 29 rms (all with bath). FAN. High season, $15 single; $22 double. Low season, $10 single; $17 double.

All rooms in this very clean and comfortable hotel have Mexican tile floors, balconies, and one or two double beds. The push-out windows are good for security as they are very high up, but they don't have screens. Almost all rooms have TVs, or you can rent one. There's a $5 deposit for towels. The hotel is at the corner of Madero and Insurgentes.

⑤ Hotel Yasmin. Badillo 168, 48380 Puerto Vallarta, Jal. ☎ **322/2-0087.** 27 rms (all with bath). FAN. $15 single; $17 double.

The Yasmin is a great budget choice located only about a block from the beach. The hotel is a neat, hidden retreat with three stories of rooms (no elevator) built around a shady garden courtyard. The freshly painted rooms are clean and come with tile floors, firm beds with nice plaid bedspreads, small baths, and full-length mirrors. The popular Café de Olla is just off the reception/patio area. Noise created by restaurant patrons and the delightful strolling musicians catering to them lasts until about 11pm. The hotel is five blocks south of the river on Vallarta between Olas Altas and Pino Suárez.

⑤ Posada Río Cuale. Serdán 242 (Apdo. Postal 146), 48380 Puerto Vallarta, Jal. ☎ **322/ 2-0450** or 2-0914. Fax 322/20914. 21 rms (all with bath). A/C. High season, $32 single; $46 double. Low season, $21 single; $29 double.

This delightful two-story hotel is an excellent choice one block from the beach. Its large rooms have arched brick windows and wooden shutters; the quietest are away from Calle Vallarta. At night the pool becomes a lighted fountain, and the courtyard around it is part of the popular Restaurant Gourmet, which has mariachi music on Friday, Saturday, and Sunday from 7 to 11pm during high season. Park in front on the street. The hotel is one block south of the Vallarta Bridge at the corner of Aquiles Serdán.

Worth a Splurge

✪ Hotel Molino de Agua. Vallarta 130 (Apdo. Postal 54), 48380 Puerto Vallarta, Jal. ☎ **322/ 2-1907** or 2-1957, or 800/826-9408 in the U.S., 800/423-5512 in California. Fax 322/2-6056. 12 rms, 4 suites, 25 cabins (all with bath). A/C. High season, $80–$90. Low season, $75–$80. Free parking; protected.

This complex of cabins and small buildings reached by winding walkways is nestled into lush tropical gardens beside the river and sea; it's half a block south of the river on Vallarta at Serdán. Although the hotel is on a main street and centrally located, it's a completely tranquil oasis with big trees and open space. Some units are individual bungalows with private patios, and there's a small three-story building near the beach. Its amenities include a whirlpool beside the pool and an excellent restaurant/ bar, the Aquarena, as well as its offshoot, the Lion's Court, in the garden. The hotel is on the right immediately after you cross the Vallarta Bridge going south.

NORTH OF THE RÍO CUALE

This is the center of the original town, where the market, principal plazas, church, and town hall all lie. It's an excellent base for nearby dining, shopping, and nightlife on both sides of the river.

✪ Los Cuatro Vientos. Matamoros 520, 48350 Puerto Vallarta, Jal. ☎ **322/2-0161.** Fax 322/2-2831. 13 rms (all with bath). FAN. $40 single or double (including continental breakfast). Low-season discounts.

Though new owners Dan and Rosemarie Larsen of Kansas took over in 1995, this quiet, secluded inn is running as smoothly as before. Set on a hillside overlooking Banderas Bay, Los Cuatro Vientos features rooms built around a small central patio and pool. A flight of stairs takes you to the second-floor patio, pool, and the cozy Chez Elena restaurant, which is open in the evenings. The cheerful, spotless, and differently colored rooms have small tiled baths, brick ceilings, red-tile floors, and glass-louvered windows facing outdoors. Each is decorated with simple Mexican furnishings and accented with local crafts. The whole rooftop, with a panoramic view of the city, is great for sunning, and it's the best place in the city for drinks at sunset. Continental breakfast is served on the terrace for guests only from 8 to 10:30am.

The hotel offers special packages for students attending Spanish language classes at the Puerto Vallarta branch of the University of Guadalajara. Also ask about the week-long Women's Getaway offered several times a year. The program includes cultural discussions, exercise classes, hikes, some meals, and optional massages, facials, manicures, and pedicures. To find the hotel from the central plaza, walk two blocks east on Iturbide; turn left at Matamoros and walk up Matamoros (the hill gets very steep) for three blocks; it's on the right just before the corner of Corona.

Hotel Encino. Juárez 122, 48300 Puerto Vallarta, Jal. ☎ **322/2-0280** or 2-0051. Fax 322/2-2573. 75 rms (all with bath). A/C TEL. High season, $18 single; $27 double. Low season, $15 single; $20 double.

The hotel's spotless rooms are cheerfully decorated with turquoise-blue furniture set against white walls and tile floors. Most rooms have their own private balconies with sliding glass doors and views of the ocean, river, or mountains and town. From the rooftop pool and the restaurant/bar Vista Cuale there are lovely vistas of mountains and sea. The four-story hotel has an elevator. If you walk four blocks south of the central plaza on Juárez, you'll find it at A. Rodriguez, just before the bridge crosses the river.

۞ Hotel Rosita. Ordaz 90 (Apdo. Postal 32), 48300 Puerto Vallarta, Jal. ☎ and fax **322/2-1033.** 103 rms, 9 suites. FAN. High season, $33 single; $37 double. Low season, $17.25 single; $25 double. Ask about discounts Sept., Nov., May, June.

Vacationers have been flocking to the Rosita for decades both for its ideal location on the beach and for its prices. Rooms, with dated but coordinated furnishings, are well kept. Some are carpeted, and some have tile floors. Those with air-conditioning are on the street side. A palm-shaded pool and restaurant open for all meals are by the beach. It's nine blocks north of the main plaza at the corner of Díaz Ordaz and 31 de Octubre, opposite McDonald's.

Worth a Splurge

۞ Hacienda Buenaventura. Paseo de la Palma (Apdo. Postal 95-B), 48310 Puerto Vallarta, Jal. ☎ **322/4-6667,** or 800/307-1847 in the U.S. Fax 322/4-6400. 155 rms (all with bath). A/C TEL. High season, $50 single; $60 double. Low season, $35 single; $45 double. Ask about low season discounts.

Located right on the expensive hotel strip, this congenial hotel offers colonial atmosphere inside and out without the area's high prices. Hacienda-style rooms, which have soft colors on stucco walls and alcove-type windows, are built around tropical gardens containing a functioning aqueduct. The far end of the gigantic pool encircles a large palapa-roofed swim-up bar, and the other end fronts the restaurant, La Cascada. Although the Hacienda has no beachfront of its own, guests are provided passes to the facilities next door at the luxury Hotel Krystal. Some rooms have TVs. The hotel's sibling, Hotel Buenaventura, in the village on the beach, is only slightly higher in price.

WHERE TO EAT

South of the river is still the best area for finding inexpensive-to-moderate restaurants, as well as some of PV's top eateries. Some restaurants now close during low season. Many places have a breakfast special or comida corrida priced much lower than their regular meals. You can find inexpensive fruit, vegetables, and picnic fixings at the **municipal market** beside the Río Cuale where Libertad and Francisco Rodríguez meet. The **Supermercado Gutierrez Ruiz,** Serdán and Constitución, has an especially large bakery and cold cut and cheese selection, as does **Gigante** on the northern hotel strip fronting Avenida de las Palmas.

SOUTH OF THE RÍO CUALE

Archie's Wok. Francisco Rodríguez 130. ☎ **322/2-0411.** Appetizers $2.50–$4; main courses $4–$10. Mon–Sat 2–11pm. ASIAN/ECLECTIC.

Archie's Wok stirs up delightfully eclectic Asian fare, including Filipino egg rolls, Thai coconut fish, and chicken Singapore. For dessert, there are homemade fudge brownies and lime pie. To find Archie's from the Vallarta bridge, cross the bridge and walk four blocks south on Vallarta, turn right on Carranza for two blocks and left on Olas Altas for four blocks, turn right on F. Rodriguez; it's ahead on the left going toward the water. It's actually a pleasant walk since the streets are short.

Café de Olla. Badillo 168. ☎ **322/3-1626.** Main courses $2.50–$6.50. High season, Tues–Sun 10am–11pm. Low season, Tues–Sun noon–11pm. MEXICAN.

This small and inviting place gets high marks from locals and tourists. It's almost always full in the evening. You'll find large portions of New York steak, fish and shrimp, American-style barbecue ribs and chicken, Oaxaca-style tamales, and a great plato mexicana. It's six blocks south of the Vallarta bridge near the corner of Olas Altas.

Ⓢ **Dianita.** Madero 243. No phone. Breakfast $1.50–$2.50; tortas and hamburgers $1–$1.50; comida corrida $3. Daily 8am–6pm; comida corrida 12:30–6pm. MEXICAN.

Five sets of covered plastic tables and chairs scattered in front of an open kitchen decorate this tiny, economical eatery. The comida corrida draws in tourists and locals, who know to arrive early while there are still four or five selections left. Dianita is between Vallarta and Constitución.

✪ **El Dorado.** Pulpito 102. ☎ **322/2-1511.** Breakfast $2.50–$6; main courses $3–$8; salad or sandwiches $3–$6. Daily 8am–9pm. MEXICAN.

Mention Puerto Vallarta and someone will ask, "Did you go to El Dorado?" What makes this open-air palapa-roofed restaurant special is a combination of good food, beachfront location, and excellent margaritas. Lots of Americans living in PV come often for sunset margaritas and in the morning for a hearty breakfast by the ocean. Try the *huevos motuleños*—Yucatan-style eggs—on tortillas with black beans, cheese, and tangy salsa. In the late afternoon watch the surfers and parasailors while sipping a cool drink. Seafood is another specialty, and iced tea is always available.

To get here, walk nine blocks south of the river on Vallarta, then turn right onto Pulpito to its end at the beach.

✪ **Memo's la Casa de Hotcakes (The Pancake House).** Badillo 289. ☎ **322/2-6272.** Breakfast $2.50–$5. Low season, daily 8am–2pm. AMERICAN/MEXICAN/BREAKFAST.

Owner Memo Barroso hosts the village's best and most popular breakfast eatery where patrons receive true value and good food. The patio restaurant is invitingly open, with lots of tile and blue and white stucco. The menu is definitely not limited to plain pancakes. Mouth-watering pancakes and waffles are imaginatively mixed with apples, caramel, raisins, granola, chocolate, nuts, and even peanut butter. You can also enjoy great eggs Benedict, eggs Florentine, cheese blintzes, breakfast burritos, and huge omelets. Egg dishes come with delicious hash browns. A large section of the menu is called "light and fruity" and features a wide assortment of fruit, yogurt, and granola, plus whole-wheat pancakes and waffles and egg dishes using only the egg whites. The coffee keeps coming, but you only pay for it once.

From October to May, Memo offers a very popular **cooking school** on weekday evenings at his restaurant, featuring local seafood and Mexican specialties. Memo's is on "restaurant row," six blocks south of the Vallarta bridge between I. Vallarta and Constitución.

Ⓢ **Restaurant Gilmar.** Madero 418. ☎ **322/2-3923.** Breakfast $1.50–$2.50; main courses $2.50–$6; comida corrida $2.50; pozole $1.75. Daily 7:30am–11pm (comida corrida served 1–6pm). MEXICAN/SEAFOOD.

The personal attention of owner Gilbert Martínez makes this modest but colorful Mexican diner a pleasant stop with good food. The house specialty is *carne asada a la tampiqueña*, which comes with beef, salad, beans, rice, a quesadilla, an enchilada, and guacamole. Try the spicy shrimp "diabla" style. Free coffee refills come with breakfast, and there's a full liquor bar. You can get here by walking two blocks south of the river on Vallarta and then turning left onto Madero for 3¹/₂ blocks.

Worth a Splurge

✪ **Restaurant Argentino los Pibes.** Badillo 261. ☎ **322/2-1557.** Grilled meat $10–$15; pasta $5–$6. Daily 6pm–midnight. ARGENTINIAN GRILLED MEAT.

The food is so authentic and delicious here you may later dream of your meal, and you certainly won't forget it. Argentinian Cristina Juhas, along with her *pibes* (kids)— daughter Vanina and son Nicolas the chef—opened this restaurant in 1994. You select your meat cut from a tray of fresh meat (portions are huge), and while it's being prepared, you can try one of the wonderful empanadas filled with meat, corn, or ham and cheese or savor an order of alubias, which are marinated beans eaten with bread. The homemade sausage is delicious, and you won't find better chimchuri sauce anywhere. Besides beef, there's baby pig, lamb, and chicken fixed several Italian ways. Try the crêpes Los Pibes (cooked with apples and orange liqueur) for dessert. This slice of Argentina is 5¹/₂ blocks south of the Vallarta bridge between Vallarta and Constitución.

JUNGLE RESTAURANTS

On the mountainous outskirts south of Puerto Vallarta several **"jungle restaurants"** aimed at crowds of tourists offer open-air dining in a cool tropical setting by the sea or beside a mountain river. The idea is to come for lunch and spend the afternoon eating, drinking, and swimming in the river. Most of these restaurants have some sort of live entertainment, be it mariachis or roving troubadours playing Mexican ballads.

Chico's Paradise. Km 20 on Hwy. 200, south of town. ☎ **322/2-0747.** Main courses $8–$60. Daily 11am–6pm. MEXICAN/SEAFOOD.

Lunch at this lively tropical place, perched on the edge of a river gorge under a big thatched roof, can easily be a day's outing. Arrive early (by noon) to get a good table, then enjoy the river view and the mariachis. Among the tasty dishes are barbecued ribs, fish *sarandeado* (grilled in a special way), seafood *cazuelas* (casseroles), black-bean soup, and seafood platters for two. After dining, hike down to the river to swim and sunbathe or explore the crafts and souvenir shops on the premises. Bring along your swimsuit, tennis shoes, and beach towel.

The restaurant is about 13 miles south of town on the main highway. Round-trip cab fare is around $30 (get a group of four to share). You can also take the no. 02 minivan (50¢) to Boca de Tomatlán, a fishing village, and then get a taxi from there; it's a relatively short distance to Chico's.

If you want to taste Chico's but don't want to leave town, go to **Chico's II,** Río Cuale 34 (no phone), a pleasant open-air restaurant underneath the Vallarta bridge at the beach end in old Puerto Vallarta. The menu is almost the same as at the original Chico's. This branch is open daily from 8am to 11pm. **Chico's III** is on the Río Cuale by the Insurgentes bridge.

NORTH OF THE RÍO CUALE

✪ **Café San Cristóbal.** Corona 172. ☎ **322/3-2551.** Coffee $1–$1.50; pastries 65¢–$1.25; sandwiches $3. Daily 8am–10pm. COFFEE/PASTRIES/SANDWICHES.

If you're longing for a good cup of coffee, a light meal, or a gathering place to meet locals and other foreigners, this comfortable café fits all the requirements. It's a great spot for coffee, pastries, sandwiches, and conversation. The brew, which features Mexican coffees from the states of Veracruz, Nayarit, and Chiapas, comes most any way imaginable—over ice, hot, or with milk. You can also get latte, cappuccino, or espresso, and there's Mexican chocolate as well. There are fresh cheese and pâté, quiche, bread, cheese and fruit plates, lemonade, and licuados. The cream cheese, cucumber, tomato, and bean sprout sandwich on fresh homemade bread is delicious. This café is three blocks north of the main plaza between Morelos and Juárez.

✪ **Papaya 3.** Abasolo 169. ☎ **322/2-0303.** Breakfast $2–$3.75; soups, salads, and sandwiches $2.80–$3.50; main courses $3.80–$5.75. Mon–Sat 8am–10pm, Sun 9am–5pm. VEGETARIAN.

Opened in 1991, this fine, small restaurant serves innovative and delicious meals. Juice and fruit drinks include tropical shakes like the "Cancún," with a blend of guayaba, coconut, melon milk, or *rompope*. Yogurt shakes come with fruit. The Shanghai salad is a large plate of steamed vegetables. Pastas are topped with imaginative sauces, and many main courses feature chicken or fish. Papaya 3 is north of the river between Morelos and Juárez.

⑤ **La Placita.** Mina 452. ☎ **322/2-1194.** Breakfast $1.50; comida corrida $2.50. Daily 8am–noon breakfast; 1–5pm lunch. MEXICAN HOME COOKING.

Local residents clued me in to this great peso saver in the heart of the village. Family operated, it's crisp and clean with lavender walls and cloth-covered tables. The comida corrida comes with soup; your choice of three main courses such as pork in adobo sauce, barbecue ribs, or perhaps chicken in poblano chile; fruit-flavored purified water; and dessert. It's two blocks north of the main plaza between Juárez and Hidalgo.

Rito's Baci. Domínguez 181. ☎ **322/2-6448.** Pasta $4–$6.50; salads and sandwiches $2–$4.50; pizza $8.25–$12. Daily 1pm–midnight. ITALIAN.

Rito Calzado's grandfather emigrated from Italy, so the tradition of Italian food comes naturally to this small, welcoming restaurant. Two popular pastas are the lasagne and spaghetti with oil and garlic. Pizza lovers favor the Margherite, which has tomatoes, oregano, and garlic, and the Horacio, which has tomatoes, oregano, and basil. Sandwiches come hot or cold. If you're really hungry, the Italian sausage sandwich is a two-handed operation. Rito's offers free home or hotel delivery. It's six blocks north of the main plaza between Morelos and Juárez.

✪ **Tutifruti.** Morelos 552. ☎ **322/2-1068.** Breakfast $2.75–$3.25; cinnamon coffee 50¢; fresh juices or licuados $1.35–$1.75; sandwiches $1.75–$3.50. Mon–Sat 8am–10pm. VEGETARIAN/AMERICAN.

This small, clean corner eatery is a good spot for a quick snack on stools that pull up to three narrow counters. The menu includes hot or cold sandwiches and hamburgers with all the trimmings, as well as fruit plates and yogurt. Eat at the counter or take your meal out. To get here from the main plaza, walk four blocks north on Morelos; it's on the right corner at Corona.

Worth a Splurge

Le Bistro Jazz Café. Río Cuale. ☎ **322/2-0283.** Breakfast $3–$7.50; main courses $6–$9; wine and mixed drinks $2.50–$7. Mon–Sat 9am–11pm. INTERNATIONAL.

Of all Puerto Vallarta's restaurants, this one is the best at combining good food, a serene and sophisticated environment, attentive service, and entertainment—though it sometimes achieves its elite appeal by being somewhat snobby. Nevertheless, the black-and-white dining area spreads out on decks overlooking the river. The cozy bar with couches and sitting areas is also outdoors. At breakfast, the appealing menu includes omelets, crêpes, and eggs Benedict. Lunch, light and casual, features sandwiches as well as chicken and steak. The evening menu has both Mexican and international offerings, mostly fish, seafood, and steaks. Many varieties of coffee are available all day. A great collection of recorded jazz plays in the background all day. The bistro is below the Insurgentes bridge on the left if you're arriving from the main plaza.

PUERTO VALLARTA AFTER DARK

Wander down the Malecón after dark, and you'll hear music pouring out from a dozen inviting restaurant/bars with their windows open to the sea.

RESTAURANT/BARS

Ándale. Olas Altas, 425 at A. Rodriguez. ☎ **322/2-1054.**

South of the river, Ándale can be one of the wildest watering holes in town for all ages. The restaurant upstairs is a bit quieter, with tables overlooking the street. Margaritas cost $1.75, and beer is $2. It's open daily from 10am to 4am or later.

Carlos O'Brian's. Paseo Díaz Ordaz 786 (the Malecón), at Pipila. ☎ **322/2-1444** or 322/2-0356.

Eager patrons form a long line out front in the evening as they wait to join the party inside. Late at night, the scene resembles a rowdy college party. Revelers have been known to dance on the tables and chairs. During the day, this place serves just good food. Drinks run $2 to $5. It's open daily from 11am to 2am. Happy hour is from 6 to 8pm.

Mariachi Loco. Cárdenas at Vallarta. ☎ **322/3-2205.** Cover $2.

Musicians start warming up in the early evening, but around 10pm, it really gets going with rancho music. At 11pm the mariachi show begins, with 10 vibrant mariachis. Afterward, the mariachis stroll and play as guests join in impromptu singing. After midnight the mariachis play for pay, which is around $8.50 for each song. There are a set-price meal and an à la carte menu, plus lots of drinks. It's open daily from 3pm to 2am. Food is served from 3pm to 10pm, and music is continuous from 10pm to 2am.

Mogambo. Paseo Díaz Ordaz 644 (the Malecón). ☎ **322/2-3476.** No cover.

Live jazz lures in passersby to sit beneath the crocodiles and other stuffed creatures on the walls of this African-theme bar/restaurant, which looks across the street to the ocean. Drinks are $2.50 and up; specialty coffee is $3.50. It's open daily from noon to 1am, with live jazz nightly from 8pm to 1am.

Restaurant/Bar Zapata. Upstairs at Paseo Díaz Ordaz 522 (the Malecón). ☎ **322/2-4748.** No cover.

Photographs and memorabilia from the Mexican Revolution surround you as you listen to live South American music at this restaurant/bar. You can sit at the bar on one of the revolving horse-saddle stools and enjoy national (as opposed to imported) drinks, which cost $2.50 and up. It's open Monday through Saturday from noon to midnight, and Sunday from 6pm to 2am, with music until midnight. Happy hour runs from noon to midnight.

SPORTS BARS & DISCOS

The discos in Puerto Vallarta are loud and expensive but a lot of fun. Admission is $4 to $16, and you'll generally pay $3 for a margarita, $2 for a beer, more for a whiskey and mixed drinks. Keep an eye out for the free disco passes frequently available in hotels, restaurants, and other tourist spots. Most discos are open from 10pm to 4am.

The Malecón now has competition for the after-dark crowd. The new hip area is the south side of old Puerto Vallarta, containing parts of Vallarta, Cárdenas, Carranza, and Badillo. Some of the newer places heavily frequented by tourists are **La Esquina** (the Corner), Vallarta and Cárdenas, for televised sports, drinks, and fun; **King's Head,** a semi-English-style pub with TV on Vallarta at Carranza, open from 10am to 1am; and **Diva Disco,** on Vallarta, where Friday night is ladies' night.

Christine. In the Krystal Vallarta Hotel, Av. de las Palmas, north of downtown off the airport road. ☎ **322/2-1459.** Cover $10.

With its Victorian "streetlamps" and ceiling spangled with tiny lights, the interior of this place is a cross between an octagonal jewelbox and a turn-of-the-century gazebo. When the opening light show starts, however, the stage fogs up, lights swing down and start flashing, and suddenly you're enveloped in booming classical music like you've never heard before. After the show, video screens and disco sounds take over. Drinks go for $2.50 to $7. The disco is open nightly from 10pm to 4am; the opening light show begins at 11pm. *Note:* No shorts (for men), tennis shoes, or thongs.

Friday Lopez. In the Hotel Fiesta Americana Puerto Vallarta, north of downtown off Av. de las Palmas. ☎ **322/4-2010.** Cover $5; women free on Wed.

Live bands and the colonial-style setting keep everyone hopping in this festive nightspot. Classic rock and roll is the music of choice. Drinks run $2.50 to $6. This place is open nightly from 10pm to 4am.

MEXICAN FIESTAS & HOTEL EVENTS

La Iguana. Cárdenas 311, between Constitución and Insurgentes. ☎ **322/2-0105.** Admission $25 per person.

La Iguana offers an evening of entertainment that includes an open bar and an all-you-can-eat buffet. The owner-chef-showman-host, Gustavo Fong Salazar, originated the concept of Mexican folk shows for tourists, which have since become popular all over the country. The eclectic show features Mexican folkloric dancing, mariachis, rope-twirling, piñatas, fireworks, and an orchestra for dancing. The show takes place on Thursday and Sunday from 7 to 11pm.

Krystal Vallarta Hotel. Av. de las Garzas, north of downtown off the airport road. ☎ **322/2-1459.** Admission $30.

Mexican fiestas are held just about every night at major hotels around town and generally include a Mexican buffet, open bar, and live music and entertainment. Shows are usually held outdoors but move indoors when necessary. One of the best is hosted by the Krystal Vallarta on Tuesday and Saturday at 7pm.

SIDE-TRIPS FROM PUERTO VALLARTA
PLAYA YELAPA: A PICTURESQUE SANDY COVE

To visit a cove out of a tropical fantasy, you only have to take a two-hour trip by boat down the coast. Go to the town marina and catch the 9am boat, the *Serape*, to Yelapa for $15 to $20 round-trip; the return is around 4pm. The fare includes two drinks on board, but you need to bring your own lunch or buy it in Yelapa. Several other boats and cruises go to Yelapa and include lunch and open bar for $40 to $50. Travel agencies can provide tickets and information, but get reservations two or three days in advance in high season.

Once you're in Yelapa, you can lie in the sun, swim, and eat fresh grilled crayfish or seafood at a restaurant right on the beach. You can also have your picture taken with an iguana (for $1 a shot!), let local "guides" take you on a tour of the town or up the river to see the waterfall, and hike up to visit Rita Tillet's crafts shop on the edge of the mountain.

Note: If you use a local guide, agree on a price before you start out!

For inexpensive accommodations, ask around to see if residents are renting rooms.

BUCERÍAS: A QUIET COASTAL VILLAGE

Only 11 miles north from the Puerto Vallarta airport, Bucerías (Boo-sah-REE-ahs) is a small coastal fishing village of 8,000 people in Nayarit State on Banderas Bay. It's beginning to catch on as an inexpensive alternative to Puerto Vallarta.

Before you reach the town center in Bucerías, turn left when you see all the cook stands. You'll see cobblestone streets leading from the highway to the beach and hints of the villas and town homes behind high walls. Bucerías has already been discovered by second-home owners and by about 1,000 transplanted Americans as a peaceful getaway; casual tourists are beginning to discover its relaxed pace as well.

To get here from Puerto Vallarta, take a minivan or city bus to the stop opposite the entrance to the airport; then catch a minivan marked BUCERÍAS (they run from 6am to midnight and cost $1.15 one way). The last stop is Bucerías's town square, where it departs for the return to Puerto Vallarta.

Exploring Bucerías

Come here for a day-trip from Puerto Vallarta just to enjoy the uncrowded beach and good seafood at the restaurants on the beach. If you are inclined to stay a few days, you can relax inexpensively and explore more of Bucerías while staking out an appealing place for a return trip. Sunday is street-market day, but it doesn't get going until around noon, in keeping with Bucerías's casual pace.

Where to Eat

In addition to the seafood restaurants near the town square and the beach, there are inexpensive outdoor kitchens on the street fronting the highway that serve delicious grilled chicken marinated in orange juice.

Adriano's. Av. Pacifico 2. ☎ **329/80008.** Breakfast $2.25–$3.75; seafood $5–$8; beer 85¢. Daily 8am–11pm. SEAFOOD.

Just off Bucerías's main square at the far left end of the beach, Adriano's is an inviting place to eat while spending the day on the beach. (They have a shower and bathroom just for their beach clientele.) The extensive menu includes french toast and shrimp omelettes at breakfast, seafood, and nachos. Though large, this restaurant isn't on the bus tour route, so you won't be abandoned in favor of a busload of tourists.

SAN BLAS: FOR BIRDWATCHERS & SURFERS

San Blas is a rather ugly Pacific coast fishing village of 10,000 people in Nayarit State, but it's one of the country's premier birding spots. Birding enthusiasts come often and stay long. Surfers do too, since some of Mexico's best surfing waters are at Las Islitas Beach.

Upon your arrival, the dirt streets and ragtag central square will make you wonder "Is this it?" The uninviting wide beaches with hard-packed, thick-grained, grayish-colored sand are shaded by too few palm trees. At night, especially during the rainy season, the whole town is infested with "no-see-ums" that require an armor of insect repellent. Were it not for its reputation as a birders' mecca and surfers' delight, the town would likely languish as an undesirable outpost. Still, most of the year it attracts an assortment of tourists, some of whom are looking for an inexpensive retreat on this increasingly expensive coast, and others who come just to see the birds or to surf. The few hotels are often full, especially on major Mexican holidays.

Essentials

Transportes Norte de Sonora buses from Puerto Vallarta take the short route, but be sure to specify which route you want since the long route through Tepic takes five hours. As an alternative, you can take a **Pacífico bus** to Las Varas and change buses to San Blas; there may, however, be a wait—try to get to Las Varas before noon.

Only 150 miles from Puerto Vallarta, San Blas is an easy 3½-hour trip, now that the new non-toll highway bypasses Tepic. This new two-lane paved highway, which starts at Las Varas off Highway 200 (a sign announces Las Varas), goes through the villages of Santa Cruz and Aticama before connecting with the two-lane highway into San Blas. Signs are few, so if you're driving, keep asking directions.

As you enter the village, you'll be on **Avenida Juárez,** the principal street, which leads to the main plaza on the right. At its far end sits the old church, with a new church next to it. Across the street from the church is the bus station, and on the other side of the churches is the *mercado* (market). After you pass the square, the first one-way street to your left is **Batallón,** an important street that passes a bakery, a medical clinic, several hotels, and Los Cocos Trailer Park and ends up at **Borrego Beach,** with its many outdoor fish restaurants. Nearly everything is within walking distance, and there are public buses that go to the farther beaches—Matanchen and Los Cocos—on their way to Santa Cruz, the next village to the south.

The **Tourist Office,** next door to McDonald's restaurant on Avenida Juárez, is open Monday through Friday from 9am to 3pm.

As for the **climate,** October is the wettest month of the rainy season, which runs from May through October and witnesses the worst of the "no-see-um" attacks. Summer is hot and steamy.

Exploring San Blas

After you've walked around the town and taken the river cruise, there's not a lot to do besides relax, swim, read, walk the beach, and eat fish—unless you're a serious birdwatcher or surfer. During the winter, however, you can also look for **whales** off the coast of San Blas.

Port of San Blas   Like Acapulco, San Blas was once a very important port for New Spain's trade with the Philippines. Pirates would attempt to intercept the rich Spanish galleons headed for San Blas; as a result the town was fortified. Ruins of the fortifications, complete with cannons, the old church, and houses all overgrown with jungle, are still visible atop the hill **La Contadura.** The fort settlement was destroyed during the struggle for independence in 1811 and has been in ruins ever since. Also, it was from San Blas that Fr. Junípero Serra set out to establish missions in California in the 18th century.

The view from La Contadura is definitely worth the trouble to get there. The entire surrounding area stretches out before you, a panorama of coconut plantations, coastline, town, and lighthouse at Playa del Rey. To reach the ruins from San Blas, head east on Avenida Juárez about half a mile, as if going out of town. Just before the bridge, take the stone path that winds up the hill to your right.

Beaches & Water Sports   One of the closest beaches is **Borrego Beach,** south from the town plaza on Batallón until it ends. This is a gray sand beach edged with palapa restaurants selling fish. For a more secluded place to swim, pay a fisherman to take you across Estuary El Pozo at the southwest edge of town to the "island," actually **El Rey Beach.** Walk to the other side of the island, and you might have it all to yourself, or try the beach on the other side of the lighthouse on this island. Bring your own shade, as there are no trees. The fisherman "ferry" charges about $1 one way and operates from 6am to 6pm. Canoes and small boats can also be rented at the harbor on the west side of town, following Avenida Juárez.

About 3 miles south of San Blas is **Matanchen Bay.** If you're driving, head out Avenida Juárez toward Tepic, cross the bridge, and turn right at the sign to Matanchen. A bus also stops there on its way south to the village of Santa Cruz; it departs from the bus station on the main square at 9 and 11am and 3 and 5pm. Check on the return stops at Matanchen Bay, which are generally an hour later. There's a little settlement here where you can have a snack or a meal or rent a boat and guide for the jungle-river cruise.

Half a mile past the settlement is a dirt road to **Las Islitas Beach,** a magnificent swath of sand stretching for miles with a few beach-shack eateries. This is a famous surfing beach with mile-long waves, and real and would-be surfing champions come from Mexico and the United States to test their mettle here, especially during September and October, when storms create the biggest waves. If you don't have a surfboard, you can usually rent one from one of the local surfers. The bodysurfing at Islitas and Matanchen is good, too. A taxi to Islitas will cost about $5 from downtown San Blas.

Farther south from Matanchen is beautiful **Playa Los Cocos,** lined with coconut palms. It's also on the bus route to Santa Cruz, but double check on stops and schedules before boarding in San Blas.

Jungle Cruise to Tovara Springs   Almost the moment you hit San Blas, you'll be approached by a "guide" who offers "a boat ride into the jungle." This can be exciting but expensive, depending on how many people share the cost, which is about $35 for a boatload of one to four people for the three- to four-hour trip from the bridge at the edge of town on Juárez. It's less ($25–$30) for the shorter, two-hour, trip from the Embarcadero near Matanchen Bay, out of town. Either way it's worth it if you take the early-morning cruise through shady mangrove mazes and tunnels and past tropical birds and cane fields to the beautiful natural springs, La Tovara, where you can swim. There's a restaurant here, too, but stick to soft drinks or beer. This is one of Mexico's unique tropical experiences, and to make the most of it, find a guide who will leave at 6:30 or 7am. The first boat on the river encounters the most birds, and the Tovara River is like glass early in the morning, unruffled by breezes. Around 9am the boatloads of tour groups start arriving, and the serenity evaporates like the morning mist.

Note: The guide may also offer to take you to "The Plantation," which refers to pineapple and banana plantations on a hill outside of town. The additional cost of this trip is not worth it for most people.

Birdwatching　As many as 300 species of birds have been sighted here, one of the highest counts in the Western Hemisphere. Birders and hikers should go to the Hotel Las Brisas Resort in San Blas (see "Where to Stay," below) to buy a copy of the booklet *Where to Find Birds in San Blas, Nayarit* by Rosalind Novick and Lan Sing Wu. With maps and directions, it details all the best birding spots and walks, including hikes to some lovely waterfalls where you can swim. Ask about birding guides at the Hotel Garza Canela. A day's tour will cost around $100, which can be divided among the participants. Birding is best from mid-October to April.

Where to Stay

Hotel Garza Canela. Calle Paredes 106 Sur, 63740 San Blas, Nay. ☎ **328/5-0112** or 328/ 5-0480. Fax 328/5-0308. 42 units, 5 minisuites (all with bath). A/C FAN TV. $55 single; $65 double; $100 suite (including breakfast). Free parking.

A block inland from the waterfront and nestled among pretty gardens of palms, hibiscus, and other tropical plants are the cottagelike fourplexes and other buildings of this oasislike resort. The name changed in 1995 from Las Brisas Resort to Garza Canela, but the owners are the same. You'll find a tranquil ambience, two pools (one for toddlers), and one of the best restaurant/bars in town—just a few of the details that make this the nicest place to stay in San Blas. Rooms are modern, bright, airy, and immaculate, with well-screened windows and fans and air-conditioning. Several rooms have a kitchen and come with king-size beds; otherwise, most have two double beds, and a few have an extra single bed. Each room has an in-room safety-deposit box. The manager, María Josefina Vazquez, is one of the most knowledgeable and helpful people I've met on the Pacific coast.

To get here, walk south from the square on Batallón about six blocks, turn right on Campeche across from the Marino Inn, then turn left on the next street, Paredes Sur.

Motel Posada del Rey. Calle Campeche 10, 63740 San Blas, Nay. ☎ **328/5-0123.** 12 rms (all with bath). FAN. $18 single; $22 double.

Rooms at the Posada del Rey are arranged around a tiny courtyard entirely taken up by a little pool; six rooms have air-conditioning. An open-air bar on the third floor provides a lovely view of the ocean and palms. The motel is one block inland from the waterfront at El Pozo Estuary, five blocks south of the town plaza. Turn right at the Marino Inn, and you'll find the hotel straight ahead two blocks on the right.

Where to Eat

For an inexpensive meal, in high season or on weekends, try fresh grilled fish from one of the little shacks on the beach. The prices are the same at all these places. From town, take Avenida Batallón south from the plaza—follow your nose when you smell the fish being grilled.

Ⓢ **McDonald's.** Juárez 36 Pte. No phone. Appetizers $2–$5; main courses $3–$7. Nov–June daily 7am–10pm; July–Oct Wed–Mon 7am–10pm. MEXICAN.

Forget the golden arches, this family run restaurant has been operating here for at least four decades. It's the best place in town for a good, reasonably priced meal from soup through the ample seafood platter. You can chose from a variety of beef and chicken centered meals, as well as Mexican specialties. It's a half a block west of the town square.

✪ **Restaurant El Delfín.** In the Hotel Garza Canela, Calle Paredes 106 Sur. ☎ **328/5-0112.** Main courses $4–$11. Daily 8am–9pm. INTERNATIONAL.

This hotel restaurant serves the best food in San Blas in a beautiful air-conditioned dining room with marble floors and a pink-and-green decor. Soft light, soft music, and comfortable captain's chairs add to the serene ambience. The chef masterfully draws from a wide repertoire of sauces. Try the exquisite shrimp and mushroom in epazote sauce, or filet of beef in tarragon and Parmesan cheese sauce. There are pasta dishes with seafood as well. The homemade soups and desserts also deserve encores.

3 Manzanillo

160 miles SE of Puerto Vallarta, 167 SW of Guadalajara, 40 miles SE of Barra de Navidad

Outsiders think of Manzanillo, Colima State, as a resort community, but this city of 90,000 is today Mexico's foremost Pacific port. Sea traffic, as well as fishing and iron-ore mining, generate more income than the tourist business. Manzanillo remains one of the Pacific coast's hidden retreats; it lacks major air links and is more than 150 miles from both Puerto Vallarta and Guadalajara. Tourists don't come in droves, as they do to those cities.

Manzanillo first began to attract foreigners seeking relief from north-of-the-border winters in the 1970s; condominiums were built on hillsides and the beaches. Today, lots of their little private enclaves on some of the most prime bay property are strung out for more than 20 miles from town center toward the airport. There are few hotels relative to private dwellings and to other Mexican resort cities, and the hotels are just as scattered as the condominiums.

Manzanillo still isn't much to look at; its town center faces the port and railroad tracks, and outlying roadways are veiled in a swirl of dust. Recently the city has begun a long-overdue program to beautify itself, widening and resurfacing its streets and planting palms and flowers in the center medians. The deficiencies in the appearance of the town and its main boulevards are compensated for by the beauty of the bays, the excellent climate, the few good beaches, and the town's relaxing pace. Manzanillo has a delightfully laid-back ambience as well as some very good restaurants, and it's the ideal point from which to launch further explorations north to the coastal villages of Barra de Navidad and Melaque and inland to Colima, the state capital.

ESSENTIALS

GETTING THERE & DEPARTING   By Plane   The airport is 45 minutes northwest of town at Playa de Oro. The colectivo airport service, **Transportes Terrestres** (☎ 333/4-1555), picks up passengers at hotels. Call a day ahead for reservations. One way, the cost is $7 to $11; by taxi it costs $20. **Aeroméxico** (at the airport ☎ 333/3-2424) and **Mexicana** (at the airport ☎ 333/3-2323) offer flights to and from Mexico City and Guadalajara. There are connecting flights several times a week from Monterrey, and a few from cold weather cities in the U.S. and Canada. **American West** (☎ 800/235-9292 in the U. S.) flies from Phoenix and **Aero California** (☎ 333/4-1414) has flights from Los Angeles.

By Bus   Manzanillo's Central Camionera (bus station) is about 12 long blocks east of town. If you follow Hidalgo east, the Camionera will be on your right. **Auto-transportes Colima** (also known as Los Altos; no phone) goes to Colima every 30 minutes. On a Directo the trip takes 1¹/₂ hours with two stops. An Ordinario leaves every 15 minutes and takes two hours, stopping frequently. Both types of bus drop off passengers within two blocks of Colima's main square rather than Colima's outlying Central Camionera. To Barra de Navidad (1¹/₂ hours north) and to Puerto

Vallarta (five hours north) the company with the most frequent service is **Auto Camiones de Pacífico** and **Cihuatlan** (☎ 2-0515). It offers deluxe service (de paso), which they call "Primera Plus" (not to be confused with a line by the same name) six times a day and ten daily second-class buses. **La Línea** (☎ 2-0123) has Plus (first-class) service to Colima (1¹/₂ hours) and Guadalajara (4¹/₂ hours) seven times daily. **Servicios Coordinados** (☎ 2-0210) has frequent first-class buses to Guadalajara. **Primera Plus** (☎ 2-0210) has deluxe buses with video movies and air-conditioning hourly to Guadalajara and Puerto Vallarta.

By Car Coastal Highway 200 leads from Acapulco and Puerto Vallarta. From Guadalajara, take Highway 54 through Colima (outside Colima you can switch to a toll road, which is faster but less scenic, into Manzanillo).

Motorists' advisory: Motorists planning to follow Highway 200 south from Manzanillo toward Lázaro Cárdenas and Ixtapa should be aware of recent reports of random car and motorist hijackings on that route, especially around Playa Azul. Before heading in that direction, ask locals and the tourism office about the current state of affairs.

ORIENTATION Arriving Manzanillo's **Central Camionera** (bus station) is about 12 long blocks east of town. Here you can buy a sandwich, send a fax, make a long-distance call, or store luggage (look for the *guarda equipaje*). Taxis to town line up out front and cost around $6 to the town center.

Information The **tourism office** (☎ 333/3-2277 or 333/3-2264) in Manzanillo is on the Costera Miguel de la Madrid 4960, 8.5 km. It's open Monday through Friday from 9am to 3:30pm.

City Layout The town is at the end of a 7-mile-long beach, **Playa Azul,** whose northern terminus is the **Santiago Peninsula.** Santiago is 7 miles from downtown; it's the site of many beautiful homes and the best hotel in the area, Las Hadas. There are two lagoons; one, **Laguna de Cuyutlán,** is almost behind the city, and the other, **Laguna de San Pedrito,** lurks behind the beach. Both are good sites for birdwatching. There are also two bays. **Manzanillo Bay** encompasses the harbor, town, and beaches; it's separated by the Santiago Peninsula from the second bay— **Santiago.**

Downtown activity centers around the **plaza,** officially known as the Jardín Alvaro Obregón, which is separated from the waterfront by railroad and shipyards. The plaza has a brilliant poinciana tree with red blossoms, a fountain, kiosk, and a view of the bay. Large ships dock at the pier nearby. **Avenida México,** the street leading out from the plaza's central gazebo, is the town's principal commercial thoroughfare. Walking along here you will find a few shops, small eateries, and juice stands.

GETTING AROUND By Bus The local buses (*camionetas*) make a circuit from downtown in front of the train station. They go out along the lagoon opposite Playa Azul and then along the Bay of Manzanillo to the Santiago Peninsula and the Bay of Santiago to the north. The main buses are "Las Brisas," which goes to the Las Brisas crossroads then to the Las Brisas Peninsula and back to town; "Miramar," "Santiago," and "Salahua" buses go to outlying settlements along the bays and to most restaurants mentioned below.

Buses marked "Las Hadas" go to the peninsula and make a circuit by the Las Hadas resort and the Sierra Manzanillo and Plaza las Glorias hotels. This is an inexpensive way to see the coast as far as Santiago and to take a tour of the Santiago Peninsula.

By Taxi Taxis in Manzanillo supposedly have fixed rates for trips within town, as well as to more distant points, but they aren't posted; ask your hotel staff what

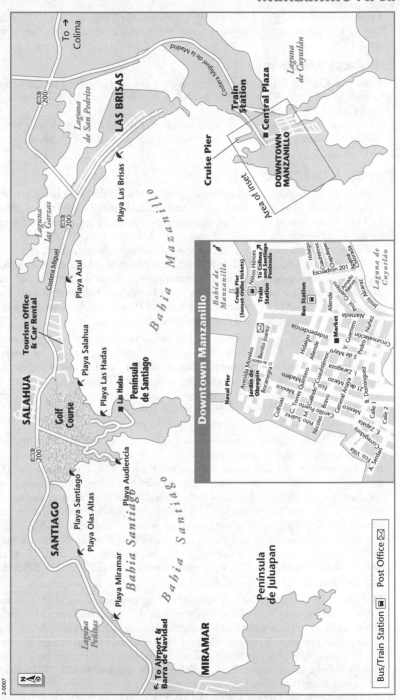

To → Colima

Costera Miguel de la Madrid

LAS BRISAS

Laguna de San Pedrito

Laguna Las Garzas

Train Station

Central Plaza

Cruise Pier

DOWNTOWN MANZANILLO

Laguna de Cuyutlán

Playa Las Brisas

Area of inset

Costera Miguel

Playa Azul

Bahía Mazanillo

SALAHUA

Tourism Office & Car Rental

Playa Salahua

Playa Las Hadas

■ Las Hadas

Península de Santiago

Golf Course

Playa Audiencia

SANTIAGO

Playa Santiago

Playa Olas Altas

Bahía Santiago

Bahía Santiago

Playa Miramar

Laguna Peñitas

← To Airport & Barra de Navidad

MIRAMAR

Península de Juluapan

Downtown Manzanillo

Bahía de Manzanillo

Cruise Pier (Sunset cruise tickets)

Niños Héroes

Train Station

To Colima and Santiago Peninsula ↗

Hidalgo

Cuauhtémoc

Escuadron 201

Bus Station

Allende

Jesús Alcaraz

Prol. Guerrero

Alameda

Nuñez

Amado Nervo

Aquila Adorada

Laguna de Cuyutlán

Naval Pier

Avenida Morelos

Jardín de Obregón

21 de Marzo

Benito Juárez

Bocanegra

Independencia

Hidalgo

Allende

Pedro

V. Guerrero

5 de Mayo

Circunvalación

■ **Market**

L. Zaragoza

Colimas

G. Torres Quintero

Nicolás Bravo

M. Calindo Puerto

FCO. Cuauhtémoc

21 de Marzo

México

General Anaya

Madero

B. Domínguez

México

Pino Suárez

Camillo

A. Serdán

Fco. Villa

Corregidora

E. Zapata

Calle 1

Calle 2

Bus/Train Station ■   Post Office ⊠

157

2-0007

a ride should cost to get a feel for what's right, and then bargain. A taxi from the Central Camionera to the Salahua area costs around $7; a taxi to town center costs about $5.

FAST FACTS: MANZANILLO

American Express   The local representative is Bahías Gemelas Travel Agency, Costera M. Madrid, 10 km (☎ **333/3-1000** or 333/3-1053; fax 333/3-0649).

Area Code   The telephone area code is 333.

Bank   Banamex downtown is just off the plaza on Avenida México; it's open Monday through Friday from 9:30am to 1:30pm but changes foreign currency only until 12:30pm.

FUN ON & OFF THE BEACH

Activities in Manzanillo depend on where you stay. Most of the resort hotels here are completely self-contained, and they have restaurants and sports on the premises. This isn't necessarily true of my hotel recommendations, however, since several of them do not have pools and are not on the beach.

Beaches La Audiencia Beach, on the way to Santiago, offers the best swimming, but **San Pedrito,** shallow for a long way out, is the most popular because it's much closer to the downtown area. **Playa Miramar,** on the Bahía de Santiago past the Santiago Peninsula, is another of the town's popular beaches, well worth the ride out here on the local bus from town. The major part of **Playa Azul** drops off a little too steeply for safe swimming and is not recommended for waders.

BIRDWATCHING   There are many lagoons along the coast. As you go from Manzanillo up past Las Brisas to Santiago, you'll pass **Laguna de Las Garzas** (Lagoon of the Herons), also known as **Laguna de San Pedrito,** where you can see many white pelicans and huge herons fishing in the water. They nest here in December and January. Back of town, on the road leading to Colima (the capital), is the **Laguna de Cuyutlán** (follow the signs to Cuyutlán), where birds can usually be found in abundance; species vary between summer and winter.

DIVING   Susan Dearing pioneered diving in Manzanillo and has come up with some unusually intriguing underwater scenery. Many locations are so close to shore there's no need for a boat. Close-in dives include the jetty with coral growing on the rocks at 45 feet, and a nearby sunken frigate downed in 1959 at 28 feet. Divers can see abundant sea life, including coral reefs, sea horses, giant puffer fish, and moray eels. Dives requiring a boat cost $65 each with a three-person minimum. Offshore dives cost $50 per person. Dearing is certified in scuba (YMCA and CMAS) and lifesaving and CPR by the Red Cross, and she offers diver certification in very intensive courses of various durations. For reservations contact her at the Hotel La Posada (☎ and fax **333/3-1899**), at the spa at the Hotel Sierra (☎ **333/3-2000,** ext. 250), or by cellular phone (90-335-80327).

FISHING   Manzanillo is also famous for its fishing, particularly sailfish. Marlin and sailfish are abundant year-round. Winter is best for dolphinfish and dorado (mahimahi); in summer wahoo and roosterfish are in greater supply. The international sailfish competition is held around the November 20 holiday, and the national sailfish competition is in November before Thanksgiving. Fishing can be arranged through travel agencies or directly at the **fishermen's cooperative** (☎ **333/2-1031**) downtown where the fishing boats are moored.

I can recommend **Gerardo Montes** (☎ **333/2-0817** or 333/2-5085), whose boats, the *Albatros I* and *II* are generally docked by the Naval Station. Fishing costs $35 per hour in a 28-foot boat and $45 per hour in a 38-foot boat with a five-hour minimum. The cost can be shared by up to seven people in the larger boat and up to four in the smaller boat.

SUNSET CRUISES   Many charter boats are available along the waterfront. For a sunset cruise, buy tickets from travel agents, at Las Hadas, or downtown at La Perlita Dock (across from the train station) fronting the harbor. Tickets go on sale at La Perlita daily from 10am to 2pm and 4 to 7pm and cost around $15 for the La Perlita cruise. Cruises from Las Hadas cost $20. The trip is a peaceful one; there's no music or entertainment, but both cruises include two drinks. During high season, it's a good idea to buy the ticket a day ahead, since hotels and travel agencies in town also book this cruise. But during low season you can take a chance and just show up at 5pm. Cruises last $1^{1}/_2$ to 2 hours.

TOURS   Because Manzanillo is so spread out, you might consider a city tour. I highly recommend the services of Luís Jorge Alvarez at **Viajes Lujo,** Av. México 143-2, Manzanillo, Col. 28200 (☎ **333/2-2919;** fax 333/2-4075). Office hours are Monday through Friday from 9am to 2pm and 4 to 7pm and Saturday from 9am to noon, but tours can take place at any time. A half-day city tour costs around $20. Other tours include one to Colima ($40) and to Barra de Navidad ($40), which includes a stop at a banana and coconut plantation. Luís uses air-conditioned vehicles and speaks English.

SHOPPING   Only a few shops carry Mexican crafts and clothing, and almost all are downtown on the streets near the central plaza. You can also try exploring the new American-style malls on the road to Santiago.

LAS HADAS   Anyone who has ever heard of Manzanillo has heard of Las Hadas; say "Las Hadas," and a lot of people think that is Manzanillo. You may remember it from the movie *10*, which featured Bo Derek and Las Hadas. Las Hadas, the self-contained Eden that put Manzanillo on the map, is the brainchild of the Bolivian entrepreneur Antenor Patino. The area features lavish Moorish-style architecture that started a trend in Mexico. Though it's architecturally stunning and frames its own private bay, it's not quite the unique tourist draw it once was, now that Mexico has many luxury hotels. There are four restaurants, four bars, two pools, a marina, a golf course, and lots of stylish shops. Tours of the property have been suspended, but if you'd like to see it, go before sunset and tell the guard you're going to the Benedetti's Pizza restaurant, on the waterfront adjacent to the hotel complex. It's a good place to eat, relax, and view the yachts at anchor.

Las Hadas is on the Santiago Peninsula. From the Costera, turn left at the golf course and follow the signs to Las Hadas. You can also take a city bus marked "Las Hadas" from in front of the train station.

WHERE TO STAY

The strip of coastline on which Manzanillo is located can be divided into three areas: **downtown,** with its shops, markets, and continual activity; **Las Brisas,** the hotel-lined beach area immediately to the north of the city; and **Santiago,** the name of a town and peninsula, which is virtually a suburb situated even farther north at the end of Playa Azul. Transportation by either bus or taxi makes all three areas fairly convenient to each other. Reservations are recommended for hotels during the Christmas and New Year's holidays.

DOWNTOWN

Hotel Colonial. Av. México 100 and Gonzales Bocanegra, 28200 Manzanillo, Col. ☎ **333/ 2-1080** or 333/2-1134. 40 rms (all with bath). A/C (25 rms) FAN (15 rms). $13–$15 single; $15–$17 double.

An old favorite, this three-story colonial-style hotel changes little from year to year. It still offers the same beautiful blue-and-yellow tile, colonial-style carved doors and windows in the lobby and restaurant. Rooms are decorated with the same minimal furniture, red-tile floors, and basic comforts. In the central courtyard there is a restaurant/bar. The highest rates are for rooms with air-conditioning. With your back to the plaza, walk one block inland on Juárez to the corner of Galindo; the hotel is on the right corner.

LAS BRISAS

Buses run out to Las Brisas from downtown. Look for "Brisas Direc" on the signboard. It's a 6-mile trundle around Manzanillo Bay, ultimately curving southward. Most hotels, bungalows, and condominiums are on the single main road.

⑤ Hotel Star. Lázaro Cárdenas 1313, 28200 Manzanillo, Col. ☎ **333/3-2560** or 333/3-1980. 39 rms, 2 suites. A/C FAN. $16–$21 single or double; $24 suite single or double.

In a row of modest hotels, the Hotel Star stands out for its tidy appearance and careful management. It features a two-story sunny complex facing a courtyard and a pool by the beach. The color scheme combines red-tile floors with orange bedspreads and curtains. Rooms are comfortable but sparsely decorated with rattan furniture. The higher prices are for rooms with air-conditioning and TV. Both suites have air-conditioning and TVs, and one has a kitchen.

SANTIAGO

Three miles north of Las Brisas is the wide Santiago Peninsula. The settlement of Salahua is on the highway at one end where you enter the peninsula to reach the hotels Las Hadas, Plaza las Glorias, and Sierra Manzanillo, as well as the Mantarraya Golf Course. Buses from town marked "Las Hadas" go every 20 minutes into the interior of the peninsula and pass by these hotels. Past the Salahua turnoff and at the end of the settlement of Santiago, an obscure road on the left is marked "Zona de Playas" and leads to the hotels on the other side of the peninsula, including Hotels Marlyn and Playa de Santiago. To get to the latter hotels, take a bus to the main Santiago bus stop. Get off there and transfer to a taxi (available at all hours).

Hotel Marlyn. Peninsula de Santiago (Apdo. Postal 288), 28200 Manzanillo, Col. ☎ **333/3-0107.** 38 rms, 4 bungalows (all with bath). A/C or FAN. High season, $20 single; $25 double. Low season, $15 single; $20 double.

White and airy, this hotel faces Audiencia Bay on the Santiago Peninsula. It has a little pool and a beachfront café. Some rooms have a sea view. Rates are lower for rooms with only fans.

Hotel Playa de Santiago. Santiago Peninsula (Apdo. Postal 147), 28860 Manzanillo, Col. ☎ **333/3-0055** or 333/3-0270. Fax 333/3-0344. 105 rms. FAN TEL. $35 single or double. Free parking.

This is one of those 1960s–era hotels aimed at the jet set who've since migrated around the peninsula to Plaza Las Glorias and Las Hadas. You get the essence of glamour at a fraction of the price, and the hotel is on a small beach. Rooms in the main hotel building are small and clean with nearly up-to-date furnishings, tile floors, tiny closets, and balconies facing the ocean. Most have two double beds. The restaurant/bar is positioned for its views, and there are a pool and tennis court.

WHERE TO EAT

For picnic fixings, there's a big supermarket, the **Centro Comercial Conasuper,** on the road leading into town, half a block from the plaza at Morelos. The huge store sells food, produce, household goods, clothes, hardware, and more. It's open daily from 8am to 8pm.

Benedetti's Pizza. Las Brisas. ☎ **333/4-0141.** Pizza $5–$12; main courses $3–$6. Daily 10am–6pm. PIZZA.

Since there are several branches in town (some called Giovanni's Pizza), you'll probably find a Benedetti's not too far from where you are staying. The variety isn't extensive, but these pies taste quite good; add some chimichurri sauce for a new flavor. In addition to pizza, you can select pasta, sandwiches, burgers, fajitas, salad, Mexican soups, cheesecake, and apple pie. This branch is on the Costera de la Madrid, on the left just after the Las Brisas turn; it's next to Goodyear Tire.

Ⓢ Cafetería/Nevería Chantilly. Juárez and Madero (across from the plaza). ☎ **333/2-0194.** Breakfast $2–$3; main courses $1.50–$4.50; comida corrida $3.50. Sun–Fri 7am–10pm (comida corrida served 1–4pm). MEXICAN.

Join locals at this informal corner café facing the plaza. The large menu includes club sandwiches, hamburgers, carne asada a la tampiqueña, enchiladas, fish, shrimp, and vegetable salads. The full comida corrida, a real value, might begin with fresh fruit cocktail, followed by soup, rice, the main course, dessert, and coffee.

Juanito's. Costera Madrid, km 14. ☎ **333/3-1388.** Breakfast $2–$4; hamburgers $2–$3.25; main courses $3–$6. Daily 8am–11pm. HAMBURGERS/MEXICAN/AMERICAN.

It's long way to come for a meal, but Juanito's is worth it. This immaculate family run restaurant offers a simple recipe for success—serve the most popular culinary mainstays of the United States and Mexico. John "Juanito" Corey and his wife, Esperanza, are always on duty serving hamburgers and fries, hot dogs, club sandwiches, fried chicken, barbecued chicken and ribs, tacos, tostadas, enchiladas, milk shakes, lemonade, pie, and ice cream. They have added a few items besides fast food, such as beef or fish filet and chicken in white sauce. The hamburgers taste just like those back home, although they're smaller, and the portion of fries is not as large as in the States. Juanito's is 8¹/₂ miles from downtown Manzanillo on the highway going to Barra de Navidad, before the Club Maeva resort. To get here from town center, take the "Miramar" or "Fco. Villa" bus. Juanito's also offers long-distance and fax service to the public.

Ⓢ Restaurant Emperador. Balvino Davalos 69. ☎ **333/2-2374.** Breakfast $1.50–$2.75; main courses $1.25–$3; comida corrida $2.50. Daily 7am–10pm. MEXICAN.

Space is scarce in this eight-table eatery, but there's no lack of clients because patrons receive a lot for the money. A hearty comida corrida might consist of a choice of two soups, followed by rice or green enchiladas, a choice of carne de cerdo, fish filet or chiles relleno (all with beans), plus small salad, dessert, and coffee or tea. It's quick, and the service is friendly. It's in the front of the Hotel Emperador, a block west of the plaza almost at the corner of Carrillo Puerto.

Restaurant Roca del Mar. 21 de Marzo 204. ☎ **333/2-0302** or 333/2-0424. Breakfast $1.50–$2.50; main courses $1.50–$6. Daily 7:30am–10:30pm. MEXICAN.

Cool, friendly, and open to the breeze, this popular restaurant is one of the best meeting places downtown. The large menu includes salads of chicken, fruit, seafood, and fresh vegetables, plus sandwiches, Mexican food, and seafood. It faces the main plaza, between Morelos and Juárez on the same side of the street as Helados Bing and the Bar Social.

Worth a Splurge

✪ Willy's. Las Brisas crossroads. ☎ **333/3-1794.** Reservations required. Main courses $7–$13. Daily 7pm–midnight. SEAFOOD/INTERNATIONAL.

You're in for a treat at Willy's, one of Manzanillo's most popular restaurants. It's breezy, casual, and small, with perhaps 13 tables inside and 10 more on the narrow balcony over the bay. Among the grilled specialties are shrimp filet imperial wrapped in bacon; red snapper tarragon; dorado basil; robalo with mango and ginger; homemade pâté; and coconut flan. The food has flair and wins over locals and tourists alike. Double back left at the Las Brisas crossroads, and you'll find Willy's on the right down a short side street that leads to the ocean. From the train station, take a "Las Brisas" bus and ask the driver to let you off at Willy's; then walk half a block toward the ocean.

MANZANILLO AFTER DARK

Nightlife in Manzanillo consists mainly of finding a splendid sunset and dining spot, followed by a good night's sleep. However, for the more active tourist, **Carlos 'n Charlies** (see "Where to Eat," above) is always a good choice for both food and fun. **Le Cartouche Disco,** at Las Hadas resort, opens at 10pm and has a cover charge of around $16. **El Bar de Felix,** between Salahua and Las Brisas by the Avis rental-car office, is open Tuesday through Sunday from 9pm to 2am; there's no cover charge. Next door and open the same days, **VOC Disco** opens from 10pm to 4am and charges a $12 cover. The 11pm light show splatters light beams over the waterfall, rock walls, and large central dance floor. **Jalapeños Restaurant** (by the Ford agency on the Costera) entertains patrons with live Mexican music from 9:30 to 11pm on Friday and Saturday nights. Most of these establishments have a dress code that prohibits patrons wearing *huaraches* (sandals) or shorts, but the prohibition generally applies to males rather than females.

SIDE TRIPS FROM MANZANILLO
COLIMA: A COLONIAL CITY WITH FINE MUSEUMS

Founded in 1523 by conquistador Gonzalo de Sandoval, the youngest member of Cortés's band, the attractive capital of the state of Colima is today a balmy metropolis featuring a colonial-era town center and a number of interesting museums.

From Manzanillo, you can reach Colima in an hour by taking a picturesque road that skirts the 12,870-foot Volcano de Colima, which last erupted in 1991. Also visible on this trip is the 14,000-foot Nevado de Colima, which actually lies in the state of Jalisco. Colima can also be reached by frequent bus service from the central bus station in Manzanillo. See "By Bus" under "Getting There & Departing," above, for exact information on reaching Colima from Manzanillo.

Hotels and restaurants are on or near the main square. For a fine lunch I highly recommend **Los Naranjos,** Barrera 34 (☎ 2-0029), near Madero.

Note: Policemen are abundant in this city and seem overly eager to hand out citations for speeding and other minor infractions such as driving the wrong way on a street—so beware!

Exploring Colima

Important note: Colima's museums are closed on Sunday.

Museo de Occidente de Gobierno de Estado (Museum of Western Cultures). Galvan at Ejército Nacional. No phone. Free admission. Daily 9am–7:30pm.

Also known as the Museum of Anthropology, this is one of my favorite museums in the country. It has many pre-Hispanic pieces, including the famous clay dancing dogs of Colima. There are fine examples of clay, shell, and bone jewelry; exquisite human and animal figures; and diagrams of tombs showing unusual funeral customs.

Museo de la Cultura Popular María Teresa Pomar (Museum of Popular Culture). University of Colima, 27 de Septiembre and Manuel Gallardo Zamora. ☎ 2-5140. Free admission. Mon–Sat 9am–2pm and 4–7pm. From the Museum of Western Cultures, go left out the front door and walk five blocks to the wide Avenida Galvan, at Ejército; cross the street, and the museum will be on your right. (The front wall says Instituto Universitario de Bellas Artes.)

One of the city's most interesting museums, this attraction contains regional costumes and musical instruments from all over Mexico. There are also photographs showing the day-to-day use of costumes and masks and folk art from Oaxaca, Guerrero, and elsewhere. The section devoted to Mexican sweet bread (*pan dulce*) is set up like an authentic bakery, with each bread labeled. At the entrance is a shop selling Mexican folk art.

Museo de Historia de Colima. Portal Morelos 1. ☎ **2-9228.** Free admission. Tues–Sat 10am–2pm and 4–8pm.

Opened in 1988, this is the city's newest showcase, dedicated to state history. Its beautiful colonial building on the plaza opposite the Hotel Ceballos is the former Hotel Casino, the birthplace of former Mexican president Miguel de la Madrid Hurtado. The collection includes pre-Hispanic pottery, baskets, furniture, and dance masks. More than 5,000 pre-Hispanic pieces are packed away awaiting the renovation of the upper floor. After seeing the pottery here and at the Museo Occidente (see above), you'll begin to understand why the Aztec name for Colima meant "place where pottery is made." Colima is also known for its variety of pre-Hispanic tombs, and one of the best displays here shows drawings of many kinds of tombs. You may be asked to leave your purse or bag with the guard as you enter.

Sala de Exposiciones. Portal Morelos 1. No phone. Free admission. Tues–Sat 10am–2pm and 4–8pm, Sun 10am–2pm.

Next to the Museo de Historia de Colima (see above) opposite the main plaza, this museum is sponsored by the University of Colima. It's a changing showcase for fine artists from all over the world.

Defy Gravity in Comala

From the old Colima bus station, three blocks south of the central plaza at Nicolás Bravo and Medellin, buses run to Comala every 15 minutes. The trip takes 20 minutes and costs 50¢ cents ($7 by taxi).

This picturesque little village is near a mysterious **magnetic zone** out on the highway. Get one of the taxi drivers on Comala's square to run you out to this area a few miles from town. When he gets there, he'll kill the engine. Then the magnetic pull takes control, and the car gathers speed uphill without engine power. The phenomenon was discovered by accident a few years ago when a motorist had car trouble but couldn't get the vehicle to stop.

Comala is liveliest on Sunday, when roving bands of **mariachis** gather to serenade diners under the arcades around the central plaza. As many as five different groups sing at once. The food, drink, and atmosphere of this village make for a perfect day. Arrive before 3pm for a good seat in one of the three participating restaurants that supply the wholesome revelry, which gets going at around 3:30pm.

On the outskirts of town is an **artisans' school** that's open Monday through Friday. Visitors are welcome to come in and browse.

BARRA DE NAVIDAD & MELAQUE: A QUIET, RELAXING BEACH GETAWAY

Only 1¹/₂ hours north of Manzanillo (65 miles), this pair of modest beach villages (only 3 miles apart from each other) has been attracting vacationers for decades. It appeals to those looking less for expensive, modern, and sophisticated destinations and more for quaint, quiet, and inexpensive hideaways. From Manzanillo, the highway twists through some of the Pacific coast's most beautiful mountains covered in oak and coconut palm and acres of banana plantations. *Travel update:* A recent earthquake rattled Barra to the core, causing damage to many buildings, though all repairs have been made. As one local said: "It was a blessing in disguise because now we are getting new streets and many civic improvements. The town looks better than before."

Buses from Manzanillo run the route up the coast frequently on their way to Puerto Vallarta and Guadalajara. Most stop in the central villages of both Barra de Navidad and Melaque. From here Puerto Vallarta is a five hour bus ride. By car, take coastal Highway 200 north; it takes three to four hours from Manzanillo.

In the 17th century, Barra de Navidad was a harbor for the Spanish fleet, and it was from here that galleons set off in 1564 to find China. Located on a gorgeous crescent-shaped bay with curious rock outcroppings, Barra de Navidad and neighboring Melaque (both are on the same wide bay) boast a perfect beach and a peaceful ambience. So far only Barra has been "discovered," primarily by a small number of people who come from December through Easter and on Mexican holidays. Other times it's a quiet getaway, with lots of empty hotel rooms and an easy pace.

Before the devaluation Barra's pace was about to quicken with the completion of the first phase of the long-awaited **Isla Navidad Resort** project. But completion of the project and opening of the large resort hotel across the water from Barra's main pier are on hold. However, the resort's 18-hole golf course is complete. Hillside homes and condominiums are part of the planned project.

The **tourism office** for both Barra de Navidad and Melaque is in Barra at the end of Legazpi (heading out of town) in the DIF building complex (☎ and fax **335/ 5-5100**). The office is open Monday through Friday from 9am to 7pm and Saturday from 9am to 1pm.

In Barra, the main beachfront street, **Legazpi,** is lined with hotels and restaurants. From the bus station, beachfront hotels are two blocks straight ahead across the central plaza. Two blocks behind the bus station and to the right is the lagoon side, with its main street, **Morelos/Veracruz,** and more hotels and restaurants. Few streets are marked, but 10 minutes of wandering will acquaint you with the village's entire layout.

A special request: If you have any good used clothing or toys, you can deposit them with Philomena Garcia at Los Pelicanos Restaurant in Melaque (see "A Side Trip to Melaque," below). She'll distribute them among needy children in the area.

Exploring Barra De Navidad

Swimming and enjoying the lovely beach and bay view take up most tourists' time. Renting a small boat can be done in two ways. Go toward the Malecón on Calle Veracruz until you reach the tiny boatmen's cooperative with fixed prices posted on the wall. You can also walk a short bit farther to the thatched gazebo at the end of the Malecón itself. Prices are the same. A round-trip to the village of **Colimilla,** just across the lagoon and popular for its many pleasant restaurants, costs $7 for up to eight people, and you stay as long as you like; a 30-minute **tour around the lagoon** costs $12; out on the sea, it costs $25. **Sportfishing** is $15 per hour for up to six people. **Waterskiing** costs $15 per hour.

Unusual **area tours, house and apartment rentals,** and **sports equipment rental** can be arranged through **The Crazy Cactus,** Jalisco 8 (☎ **335/5-6099**), a gift shop and upstairs **restaurant** operated by Trayce Blackstone and Mari Blanca Perez. Besides gifts for sale, you'll find bicycles, boogie boards, snorkeling equipment, and life jackets to rent. Among the unique tours is one along the coast to lagoons and mangroves and another to nearby small towns for market days and shopping. **El Medico,** Av. Veracruz 230 (☎ **335/5-5008** and fax 335/5-5807), rents yachts, camping and fishing equipment; they also organize fishing tournaments and sell fishing lures and yacht parts. **Beer Bob's Books,** Av. Mazatlán 61, between Sinaloa and Guanajuato, is a book lover's institution in Barra and sort of a community service Bob does for fun. His policy of "leave a book if you take one" means vacationers can select from thousands of neatly shelved trade paperbacks. When beer was cheap, he kept a cooler stocked and browsers could sip and read. When the price of beer went up, Bob put the cooler away, but he's still called Beer Bob.

Where to Stay

During low season (May through November) it doesn't hurt to ask for a discount, even on rates already lowered.

✪ **Hotel Barra de Navidad.** Legazpi 250, 48987 Barra de Navidad, Jal. ☎ **335/5-5122.** Fax 335/5-5303. 60 rms (all with bath). FAN. High season, $41 single or double. Low season, $13–$15 single; $27 single, $35 double.

At the northern end of Legazpi, this popular, comfortable hotel on the beach has a friendly management and fine balconies overlooking the beach and bay. Rooms with a street view cost the least in each category. A second-floor terrace restaurant overlooks the bay and swimming pool. Hotel patrons rave about the food; the restaurant is open for all meals.

Hotel Bogavante. Legazpi s/n, 48987 Barra de Navidad, Jal. ☎ **335/5-5384.** Fax 335/5-5808. 20 rms (all with bath). FAN. High season, $20 single; $25 double. Low season, discounts.

Although it was once shabby, this newly renovated hotel sports fresh paint and new tile throughout, making it a good value right on the beach. First-floor rooms come with a single and double bed, and second-floor rooms hold from four to eight people. Third-floor rooms all have kitchens and living areas. About half the rooms have ocean views. The hotel is near the north end of Legazpi.

✪ **Hotel Delfín.** Morelos 23, 48987 Barra de Navidad, Jal. ☎ **335/5-5068.** Fax 335/5-6020. 25 rms, 3 apts (all with bath). FAN. High season, $25 single; $32 double. Low season, discounts. Free parking in the front.

One of Barra's better-maintained hotels, the three-story Delfín is on the landward side of the lagoon. It offers nice, well-cared-for rooms, each of which has a red-tile floor and either a double or two single beds (no elevator). Outside each room are tables and chairs on the covered walkways. The tiny courtyard with a small pool and lounge chairs is shaded by an enormous tree. A small but excellent breakfast buffet is served from 8:30 to 10:30am in the lovely second-level breakfast terrace (see "Where to Eat," below).

Where to Eat

✪ **Hotel Delfín.** Morelos 23. ☎ **335/5-5068.** Breakfast buffet $3.75–$4.50. Daily 8:30am– 10:30 am. BREAKFAST.

The second-story terrace of this small hotel is the most pleasant place to begin the day in Barra. In high season, the self-serve buffet offers an assortment of fresh fruit, juices, granola, yogurt, milk, pastries, eggs, and the delicious banana pancakes for which the restaurant is rightfully well known. In low season you select your order from a list, and it's delivered to your table. During both seasons, each table receives a large pot of coffee. Fresh-grilled German sausage, snacks, and beer are served afternoons during high-season.

Panchos. López de Legazpi 53. No phone. Breakfast $2–$3; main courses, $4–$10. High season, daily 9am–10pm. Low season, daily 8am–7pm. SEAFOOD.

Rancho's is on the beach, toward the far end of Legazpi. The most popular place in town, it's where locals hang out for food and conversation. Pull up a chair on the sand floor and join them. The spicy deviled shrimp was invented here, and the ground marlin ceviche, in a sauce of tomatoes and mildly hot peppers, is fabulous.

Café y Restaurant Ambar. Av. Veracruz 101-A. No phone. Breakfast $2–$4; crêpes $2–$7. Daily 8am–11pm (happy hour 1pm–midnight). Closed Sept. CREPES/VEGETARIAN/MEXICAN.

At the corner of Veracruz and Jalisco opposite the Restaurant y Ceñaduría Patty (see below), you'll find this cozy thatched-roof upstairs restaurant open to the breezes. The crêpes are named after towns in France; the delicious crepa Paris, for example, is filled with chicken, potatoes, spinach, and green sauce. Mexican specialties include tortas and quesadillas. For something lighter, try a seafood or fruit salad. This highly recommended restaurant lies one block inland from the Hotel Tropical on Legazpi.

✪ **Veleros.** Veracruz 64. ☎ 335/5-5838. Main courses $4–$8. Low season, daily noon–11pm. High season, daily 8am–11pm. SEAFOOD/BEEF.

Watch the small boats glide across the glassy lagoon in this clean and casual restaurant at the water's edge. Decorated with striped-cloth-covered tables, it is a tranquil spot for a lengthy meal. Depend on impeccable service and consistently good food. Seafood specialties include shrimp brochette and fish filet, but there are also steak and chicken.

Barra de Navidad After Dark

There's always a group gathered for sunset at one of the restaurants on Legazpi—the "in" place varies from year to year. During high season there is always happy hour from 2 to 6pm at the **Hotel Sands** poolside/lagoonside bar.

At the **Disco El Galleón,** in the Hotel Sands on Calle Morelos, cushioned benches and cement tables encircle the round dance floor. It's all open air, but garden walls restrict air flow, and there are few fans so you can really work up a sweat dancing the night away. It serves drinks only, no snacks. Admission is $4, and it's open on Friday and Saturday from 9pm to 2am.

EXPLORING MELAQUE (SAN PATRICIO)

For a change of scenery, you may want to wander over to Melaque (also known as San Patricio), 3 miles from Barra on the same bay. You can walk on the beach from Barra or take one of the frequent local buses from the bus station near the main square in Barra for 50¢. The bus is marked "Melaque." To return to Barra, take the bus marked "Cihuatlán."

Melaque's pace is even more laid-back than Barra's, and though it's a larger village, it seems smaller. It has fewer restaurants and less to do. It has more hotels, or bungalows, as they are usually called here, but none with the charm of Barra. If Barra hotels are full on a holiday weekend, then Melaque would be a second choice for accommodations. The paved road ends where the town begins. A few yachts bob in the harbor, and the palm-lined beach is gorgeous.

If you come by bus from Barra, you can exit the bus anywhere in town or stay on until the last stop, which is the bus station in the middle of town, a block from the beach. Restaurants and hotels line the beach, and it's impossible to get lost, but some orientation will help. Coming into town from the main road, you'll be on the town's main street, **Avenida López Mateos.** You'll pass the main square and come down to the waterfront, where there's a trailer park. The street going left (southeast) along the bay is **Avenida Gómez Farías;** the one going right (northwest) is **Avenida Miguel Ochoa López.**

Where to Eat

Besides the restaurant below, there are also many rustic palapa restaurants in town on the beach and more farther along the bay at the end of the beach. You can settle in on the beach and use one of the restaurants as your base for drinking and dining.

Los Pelicanos. North end of Melaque beach. Breakfast $2.25–$3; main courses $5–$9; lobster for two persons $30. High season, daily 9am–10pm. Low season, daily 9am–7pm. INTERNATIONAL.

Friendly ex-Pennsylvanian Phil Garcia, along with her spouse, Trine, prepares meals like you might find at home. During high season there might be pork roast and mashed potatoes along with her usual seafood specialties. Year-round you can find burritos, nachos, and hamburgers. The tender fried squid is delectable with one of Phil's savory sauces. Order lobster 24 hours in advance. Many Barra guests come here to stake a place on the beach and use the restaurant as a day-long headquarters for sipping and nipping. It's a peaceful place just to watch the pelicans bobbing just in front of this restaurant. The restaurant is at the far end of the bay before the Hotel Legazpi.

6 Acapulco & the Southern Pacific Coast

This southern part of Mexico's Pacific coast encompasses its oldest resort, Acapulco, and its best pair, modern Ixtapa and its neighbor, Zihuatanejo, a centuries-old oceanfront fishing village. Southeast of Acapulco lie the small laid-back coastal villages of Puerto Escondido and Puerto Angel, both of which front beautiful bays.

Only a four-hour drive north of Acapulco, the resort city of Ixtapa opened in the mid-1970s beside the seaside village of Zihuatanejo. Here you can experience the best of Mexico—sophisticated high-rise hotels in Ixtapa alongside the colorful village of Zihuatanejo—and you'll pay less overall for a vacation than you would in Acapulco.

Acapulco, on the other hand, has historical glamour. The largest and most colorful resort of them all, Acapulco caught the world's attention in the late 1930s when Hollywood stars began arriving. Behind them came a groundswell of tourists, and the city became internationally known as the place to see and be seen. It has retained this exciting edge even into the mid-1990s.

This chapter encompasses two states, Guerrero and Oaxaca, both of which contain stunning coastlines and lush mountainous terrain. Outside the urban centers, roads are few, and both states are still poor despite decades of tourism.

EXPLORING THE SOUTHERN PACIFIC COAST

Most people traveling to this part of Mexico have sun, surf, and sand firmly entrenched in their imaginations, and tend to camp themselves in a single destination and relax. Each of these beach towns—from Ixtapa and Zihuatanejo in the north to Acapulco and on through the Oaxacan resort of Puerto Escondido—stands alone as a holiday resort worth enjoying for a few days, or for a week or more. If you've got a little more time and some wanderlust, several of the coastal resorts covered in this chapter could be combined into a single peripatetic trip.

Each has a distinct personality—your choices range from a city that offers every luxury to sleepy towns offering only basic-but-charming seaside relaxation.

Acapulco City offers the best airline connections, the broadest range of all-night entertainment, some very sophisticated dining, and a wide range of accommodations, from hillside villas and luxury resort hotels to modest inns on the beach and in old Acapulco. Beaches are wide, clean, and numerous, but the ocean is polluted—though cleaner than in the past. It's a good launching pad for side trips to colonial Taxco (Mexico's "Silver Capital"), only $2^1/_2$ hours away using the toll road, and to Ixtapa/Zihuatanejo. The latter offers all that Acapulco has but on a smaller, newer, less hectic scale, plus excellent beaches and clean ocean waters. Since the two are only a four- to five-hour drive apart, many people fly into Acapulco (where air service is better), spend a few days there, and go on to Ixtapa/Zihuatanejo by bus or rental car.

Puerto Escondido is a six-hour drive southeast of Acapulco on coastal Highway 200. Most people don't drive or take a bus from Acapulco to Puerto Escondido, though that's easy enough to do. Usually Puerto Escondido, noted for its surfing waves, laid-back beachside village, inexpensive inns, and nearby nature excursions, is a traveler's sole destination (after a stop to change transport in Mexico City or Oaxaca). But many travelers combine it with a trip to or from the inland city of Oaxaca. The two are six hours apart by serpentine highway, or less than an hour by air.

The small village of Puerto Angel, only 50 miles southeast of Puerto Escondido or 30 miles northwest of the Bays of Huatulco, could be a day-trip from either of those destinations, or a quiet place to vacation for several days providing you aren't big on nightlife and grand hotels of which there are none in Puerto Angel. A couple of hotels serve very good food, and there are beachside restaurants serving fresh fish; but otherwise dining is limited. However, visiting nearly unoccupied beaches near Puerto Angel can be a prime activity.

1 Zihuatanejo & Ixtapa

360 miles SW of Mexico City, 353 miles SE of Manzanillo, 158 miles NW of Acapulco

Zihuatanejo, a picturesque, authentically Mexican oceanside village, complements Ixtapa, a tranquil, sophisticated oceanfront resort created in 1976. With the explosion of population from 4,000 in 1976 to 85,000 today, the pleasing pair is also developing some of the vibrancy of Puerto Vallarta, including excellent restaurants, shopping, and nightlife. In comparison to both Puerto Vallarta and Acapulco, food and lodging are still reasonably priced—if you know where to look. Ixtapa is my favorite of all Mexico's planned resorts, primarily because it has retained its tranquillity while offering the visitor a taste of both village life and modern Mexico.

ESSENTIALS

GETTING THERE & DEPARTING   By Plane   See chapter 2, "Planning a Trip to Mexico," for information on flying to Zihuatanejo/Ixtapa from the United States and Canada. Here are the local numbers of some international carriers: **Aeroméxico** (☎ **755/4-2018,** 755/4-2022, or 755/4-2019), has flights from all its U.S. cities and connecting flights through Mexico City. **Continental** (☎ **755/4-2579** at the airport), serves Ixtapa through Houston. **Mexicana** (☎ **755/3-2208,** 755/3-2209, or 755/4-2227 at the airport), has flights from all its U.S. gateways as well as Mexico City and Guadalajara. **Northwest** has weekly flights from Minneapolis–St. Paul in the high season.

Ask your travel agent about **charter flights,** which are becoming the most efficient and least expensive way to get here.

Taxis are the only option for returning to the airport from town and charge around $5.50 to $10 one way.

By Bus There are two bus terminals in Zihuatanejo: the **Central de Autobuses Camionero,** from which most lines operate, and the **Estrella de Oro station,** on Paseo del Palmar, near the market and within walking distance of downtown hotels.

At the **Central de Autobuses,** several companies offer service to Acapulco and other cities, including first-class **Estrella Blanca** (☎ 755/4-3478), and second-class **Flecha Roja** (☎ 755/4-3477 or 755/4-3483). Estrella Blanca's buses are air-conditioned—most of the time—and depart for Acapulco hourly from 6am to 10pm; the cost is $8.50 one way. Keep in mind, however, that the Estrella Blanca station in Acapulco is far from the hotels I've recommended in that city and means a costly taxi ride on arrival. Flecha Roja buses to Acapulco run every hour or so; these stop in Zihuatanejo and take on passengers as space permits. They cost as much as first-class buses, but there are at least 10 stops en route, and the trip takes six hours instead of the promised four. **Frontera** has buses to Puerto Escondido and Huatulco daily at 6:30 and 9pm, but check on travel time—it could be a 12- to 14-hour trip.

To go north to Manzanillo or Puerto Vallarta, you must buy a ticket for Lázaro Cárdenas (Estrella Blanca has service every 30 minutes) and change buses there.

Estrella de Oro (☎ 755/4-2175), runs five first-class and three deluxe daily buses to Acapulco between 7am and 10pm. You can purchase advance reservation tickets with seat assignments in Ixtapa at **Turismo Caleta** in the La Puerta shopping center next to the tourism office (☎ 755/3-0044; fax 755/3-2024). In Acapulco the Estrella de Oro station is near many budget hotels.

The trip from Mexico City to Zihuatanejo takes five hours (bypassing Acapulco); from Acapulco, four to five hours. From Mexico City, Tres Estrellas de Oro buses to Zihuatanejo depart from the Terminal Central de Autobuses del Sur (South Bus Station) near the Tasqueña Metro line.

From Zihuatanejo, it's three or four hours to Lázaro Cárdenas, another six or seven to Manzanillo, and an additional six to Puerto Vallarta, which doesn't include time spent waiting for buses.

By Car From Mexico City, the shortest route is to take Highway 15 to Toluca, then Highway 130/134 the rest of the way, though on the latter highway gas stations are few and far between. The other route is Highway 95D (four lanes) to Iguala, then Highway 51 west to Highway 134.

From Acapulco or Manzanillo, the only choice is the coastal highway, Highway 200. The ocean views along the winding, mountain-edged drive from Manzanillo can be spectacular.

Motorists' advisory: Motorists planning to follow Highway 200 northwest up the coast from Ixtapa or Zihuatanejo toward Lázaro Cárdenas and Manzanillo should be aware of reports of car and motorist hijackings on that route, especially around Playa Azul. Before heading in that direction, ask locals and the tourism office about the status of the route when you are there and don't drive at night. According to tourism officials, police patrols of the highway have been increased, and the number of crime incidents has decreased dramatically.

ORIENTATION Arriving by Plane The Ixtapa-Zihuatanejo airport is 15 minutes (about 7 miles) south of Zihuatanejo. **Transportes Terrestres** minivans, (or colectivos), transport travelers to hotels in Zihuatanejo for $3.75, to Ixtapa for $5, and to Club Med for $5.75; colectivo tickets are sold just outside the baggage-claim area. A taxi will cost $14 to Zihuatanejo, $17 to Ixtapa, and $20 to Club Med.

Arriving by Bus In Zihuatanejo, the **Estrella de Oro bus station,** on (Paseo del Palmar, at Morelos), is a few blocks beyond the market and is within walking distance of some of the suggested downtown hotels I have suggested. The clean,

Zihuatanejo & Ixtapa Area

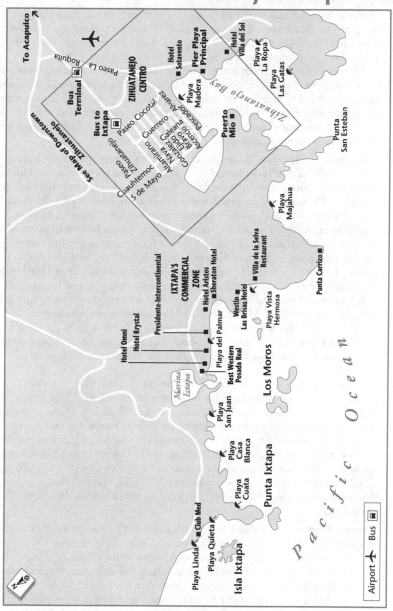

To Acapulco

Paseo La Boquita

Bus Terminal

Bus to Ixtapa

ZIHUATANEJO CENTRO

See Map of Downtown Zihuatanejo

Paseo Cocotal

Paseo Zihuatanejo

Gonzalez

Nava

Alzuhimano

Ejido

Bravo

Galeana

Ascencio Alvarez

pescador

Guerrero

Cuauhtemoc

5 de Mayo

Clauhtemoc

Hotel Sotavento

Pier Playa Principal

Hotel Villa del Sol

Playa La Ropa

Playa Las Gatas

Playa Madera

Zihuatanejo Bay

Puerto Mío

Punta San Esteban

Playa Majahua

Villa de la Selva Restaurant

Punta Carrizo

Presidente-Intercontinental

IXTAPA'S COMMERCIAL ZONE

Hotel Aristos

Sheraton Hotel

Westin

Las Brisas Hotel

Playa Vista Hermosa

Hotel Omni

Hotel Krystal

Playa del Palmar

Best Western Posada Real

Los Moros

Marina Ixtapa

Playa San Juan

Playa Casa Blanca

Punta Ixtapa

Playa Cuata

Playa Linda

Club Med

Playa Quieta

Isla Ixtapa

Pacific Ocean

N

Airport ✈ Bus ▣

warehouselike **Central de Autobuses,** the main terminal where all other buses converge, is a mile or so farther out, opposite the Pemex station and IMSS Hospital on Paseo Zihuatanejo at Paseo la Boquita. A taxi from either bus station to most Zihuatanejo hotels costs $2; continuing to Ixtapa costs around $5 or so.

Information   The **State Tourism Office** (☎ and fax **755/3-1967**) in La Puerta shopping center in Ixtapa, across from the Presidente-Inter-Continental Hotel is open

Monday through Friday from 9am to 2pm and 4 to 7pm and on Saturday from 9am to 2pm. The **Zihuatanejo Tourism Office** is on the main square by the basketball court, at Alvarez (☎ and fax **755/4-2001,** ext. 120), and is open Monday through Friday from 9am to 3pm and 6 to 8pm.

Time-share booths in both towns formerly masqueraded as information booths, but the State of Guerrero clamped down on their deceptive practices. Booths must be clearly marked by their business names and cannot carry signs claiming to be tourist information centers. Time-share employees must wear uniforms and may not leave their stands to accost passersby. If you encounter any problems or false claims from the time-share operators, contact the tourist office.

City Layout   The fishing village and resort of **Zihuatanejo** spreads out around the beautiful Bay of Zihuatanejo, framed by downtown to the north and a beautiful long beach and the Sierra foothills to the east. Beaches line the perimeter and boats bob at anchor. The heart of Zihuatanejo is the waterfront walkway **Paseo del Pescador** (also called the **Malecón**), bordering the Municipal Beach. Rather than a plaza as in most Mexican villages, Zihuatanejo's centerpiece is the **town basketball court,** which fronts the beach. I use it as a point of reference for directions. The main thoroughfare for cars, however, is **Juan Álvarez,** a block behind the Malecón. Sections of several of the main streets are designated as zona peatonal (pedestrian zone blocked off to cars). The area is zigzagged and seems to block parts of streets haphazardly.

A cement-and-sand **walkway** runs from the Malecón in downtown Zihuatanejo along the water to Playa Madera, making it much easier to walk between the two points. The walkway is lit at night. Access to Playa la Ropa is via the main road, **Camino a Playa la Ropa,** about a half-hour walk from downtown. A road is under construction between Playa La Ropa and Playa Las Gatas; until it's finished the only access is by boat.

A good highway connects "Zihuat" to **Ixtapa,** 4 miles to the northwest. The 18-hole Ixtapa Golf Club marks the beginning of the inland side of Ixtapa. Tall hotels line Ixtapa's wide beach, **Playa Palmar,** against a backdrop of lush palm groves and mountains. It's accessed by the main street, **Bulevar Ixtapa.** On the opposite side of the main boulevard lies a huge area of small shopping plazas (many of the shops are air-conditioned) and restaurants. At the far end of Bulevar Ixtapa, **Marina Ixtapa** has opened with excellent restaurants, private yacht slips, and an 18-hole golf course. Condominiums and private homes surround the marina and golf course, and more developments are rising in the hillsides past the marina en route to Playa Quieta and Playa Linda.

Getting Around   A **shuttle bus** goes back and forth between Zihuatanejo and Ixtapa every 10 or 15 minutes from 5am to 11pm daily, charging about 50¢ one way. In Zihuatanejo it stops near the corner of Morelos/Paseo Zihuatanejo and Juárez, about three blocks north of the market. In Ixtapa it makes numerous stops along Bulevar Ixtapa. A taxi from one town to the other costs about $4 one way; from midnight to 5am rates increase by 50% (agree on a price before getting into a cab).

Special Note: The highway leading from Zihuatanejo to Ixtapa widens and narrows in odd ways—keep your eyes on the white line, or you'll end up in a parking lot or on a side street paralleling the highway. Going out of town toward Acapulco, the outside lane ends without warning, sending unwary drivers into a graveled area before the lane picks up again farther on. Surprise speed-control bumps (*topes*) dot the thoroughfare and appear on other streets as well—keep your eyes peeled. Most of the topes on the highway from Zihuatanejo to Acapulco have been removed, thus speeding up the trip.

Street signs are becoming more common in Zihuatanejo, and good signs lead you in and out of both towns. However, both locations have an area called the Zona Hotelera (Hotel Zone), so if you're trying to reach Ixtapa's hotel zone, you may be confused by signs in Zihuatanejo pointing to that village's own hotel zone.

FAST FACTS: ZIHUATANEJO & IXTAPA

American Express   The main office is in the Westin Hotel (☎ **755/3-0853**; fax 755/3-1206).

Area Code   The telephone area code changed in 1995 from 753 to 755.

Banks   Ixtapa has only one bank, Bancomer, in the La Puerta Centro shopping center. Zihuatanejo has four banks, but the most centrally located is Banamex, Cuauhtémoc 4. Banks change money from 10am to noon on weekdays.

Climate Summer is hot and humid, though tempered by the sea breezes and brief showers; September is the wettest month.

Gasoline There's a busy Pemex station in Zihuatanejo, by the Central Camionera on the highway leading to Acapulco and the airport, and another near the airport entrance.

Laundry The Lavandería Super Clean, on Gonzales at Cuauhtémoc (☎ **755/ 4-2347**), is open Monday through Saturday from 8am to 8pm. Drop off your clothes or call for pick up and delivery.

FUN ON & OFF THE BEACH

The **Museo Arqueología de la Costa Grande,** near Guerrero, at the east end of Paseo del Pescador, tracks the history of the Costa Grande (comprising the area from Acapulco to Ixtapa/Zihuatanejo) from its significance in pre-Hispanic times, when it was an area known as Cihuatlán, through the colonial era. Most of the museum's pottery and stone artifacts show evidence of extensive trade with other far-off cultures and far-off regions, including the Toltec and Teotihuacán cultures near Mexico City; as well as the Olmec culture on both the Pacific and Gulf coasts; and from areas known today as the states of Nayarit, Michoacán, and San Luis Potosí. Some items are from a site found several years ago near the airport. Among the tribute items indigenous groups from this area paid the Aztecs were cotton *tilmas* (capes) and *cacao* (chocolate). The museum is nicely done and worth the half-hour or less it takes to stroll through and read; information is given in Spanish. Admission is $1, and it's open Tuesday through Sunday from 10am to 5pm.

ZIHUATANEJO BEACHES At Zihuatanejo's town beach, **Playa Municipal,** the local fishermen pull up their colorful boats onto the sand. Small shops and restaurants line the waterfront, making this a great spot for people watching and for absorbing the flavor of daily village life. This beach is protected from the main surge of the Pacific.

Besides the peaceful Playa Municipal, Zihuatanejo has three other beaches (*playas*): Madera, La Ropa, and Las Gatas. **Playa Madera Beach,** just east of the Playa Municipal Beach, is open to the surf but generally tranquil. Many attractive budget lodgings overlook this area from the hillside.

South of Playa Madera is Zihuatanejo's largest and most beautiful beach, **Playa La Ropa,** a long sweep of sand with a great view of the sunset. Some lovely, small hotels and restaurants nestle into the hills, and palm groves edge the shoreline. Although it's also open to the Pacific surge, the waves are usually gentle. A taxi from town costs $2.

Playa Las Gatas, a pretty, secluded beach can be seen across the bay from Playa Ropa and Zihuatanejo. The small coral reef just offshore makes it a good spot for snorkeling and diving. The open-air seafood restaurants on this beach also make it an appealing lunch spot for a splurge. Small launches with shade run to Las Gatas from the Zihuatanejo town pier, a 10-minute trip; the captains will take you across whenever you ask between 8am and 4pm, and the round-trip fare is $2.75. Usually the last boat back leaves Las Gatas at 4:30pm; be sure to double-check! Snorkeling and water-sports gear can be rented at the beach.

IXTAPA BEACHES Ixtapa's main beach, **Playa Palmar,** is a lovely white-sand arc edging the hotel zone, with dramatic rock formations silhouetted in the sea. The surf here can be rough; use caution and never swim where a red flag is posted.

Several of the nicest beaches in the area are essentially closed to the public as lavish resort developments rise and claim them. **Playa Quieta,** on the mainland across from Isla Ixtapa, is largely claimed by the all-inclusive Club Med and Qualton Club.

The remaining piece of beach used to be the launching point for the boats to the Isla Ixtapa, but it is gradually being taken over by a private development. Now, the Isla Ixtapa-bound boats leave from the jetty on **Playa Linda,** about 8 miles north of Ixtapa. Water taxis here ferry passengers to Isla Ixtapa for about $3 round-trip. Playa Linda is the primary out-of-town beach, with water-sports equipment and horse rental available.

Playa las Cuatas, a pretty beach and cove a few miles north of Ixtapa, and **Playa Majahua,** an isolated beach just west of Zihuatanejo, are both being transformed into large resort complexes. You may be able to reach them by boat, but you won't be able to get there by land as the building continues. Lovely **Playa Vista Hermosa** is framed by striking rock formations and bordered by the Westin Brisas Hotel high on the hill.

WATER SPORTS & BOAT TRIPS Probably the most popular boat trip is to **Isla Ixtapa** for snorkeling and lunch at El Marlin restaurant. Though you can book this outing as a tour through local travel agencies, you can also go on your own from Zihuatanejo by following the directions to Playa Linda above and taking a boat from there. Boats leave at 11:30am for Isla Ixtapa and return around 4pm. Along the way, you'll pass dramatic rock formations and the Los Moros de Los Péricos islands, known for the great variety of birds that nest on the rocky points jutting out into the blue Pacific. On Isla Ixtapa you'll find good snorkeling and a nature trail through an unfenced area with a few birds and animals. Snorkeling, diving, and other water-sports gear is available for rent on the island. Be sure to catch the last water taxi back at 4pm—and be sure to double check that time.

Separate day-trips to **Los Moros de Los Péricos islands** for **birdwatching** can usually be arranged through local travel agencies, though it would probably be less expensive to rent a boat with a guide at Playa Linda. The islands are offshore from Ixtapa's main beach.

Sunset cruises on the trimaran *TriStar,* arranged through **Yates del Sol** (☎ 755/4-3589), depart from the town pier at Puerto Mío. The sunset cruise costs $40 and includes an open bar. An all-day trip to Isla Ixtapa on this yacht begins at 10:30am, costs $60, and includes an open bar and lunch. Schedules, along with special trips, vary, so call for current information.

Fishing trips can be arranged with the boat cooperative at the Zihuatanejo town pier (☎ 755/4-2056) and cost $100 to $250, depending on the size of the boat, how long the trip lasts, and other factors (though most trips last six hours). The cost is higher for a trip arranged through a local travel agency; the least expensive trips are on small launches called *pangas;* most have shade. Both small-game and deep-sea fishing are offered, and the fishing here rivals that found in Mazatlán or Baja. Trips that combine fishing with a visit to near-deserted ocean beaches that extend for miles along the coast from Zihuatanejo can also be arranged. Sportfishing packages including air transportation and hotels can be arranged through **Mexico Sportsman,** 202 Milam Building, San Antonio, TX 78205 (☎ 210/212-4567; fax 210/212-4568). San Lushinsky at **Ixtapa Sportfishing Charters,** 33 Olde Mill Run, Stroudsburg, PA 18360 (☎ 717/424-8323; fax 717/424-1016) is another fishing outfitter.

Boating and fishing expeditions from the new **Marina Ixtapa,** a bit north of the Ixtapa hotel zone, can also be arranged.

Sailboats, windsurfers, and other water-sports equipment rentals are usually available at various stands on Playa la Ropa, Playa las Gatas, Isla Ixtapa, and at the main beach, Playa Palmar, in Ixtapa. **Parasailing** is also available at La Ropa and Palmar. **Kayaks** are available for rent at the **Zihuatanejo Scuba Center** (see below), hotels in Ixtapa, and some water-sports operations on Playa La Ropa. The rate is about $5 per hour.

Scuba-diving trips are arranged through the **Zihuatanejo Scuba Center,** on Cuauhtémoc 3 (☎ and fax 755/4-2147). Fees start at around $65 for two dives, including all equipment and lunch. Marine biologist and dive instructor Juan Barnard speaks excellent English and is very knowledgeable about the area, which has nearly 30 different dive sites, including walls and caves. Diving is done year-round, though the water is clearest May through December, when there is 100-foot visibility or better. The nearest decompression chamber is in Acapulco, though local divers are hopeful that the one in Zihuatanejo will be repaired soon. Advance reservations for dives are advised during Christmas and Easter.

Surfing is good at Petacalco Beach north of Ixtapa.

GOLF, TENNIS & TOURS   In Ixtapa, the **Campo de Golf Ixtapa** (☎ 755/ 3-1062; fax 755/3-1030) has an 18-hole course designed by Robert Trent Jones, Jr. Bring your own clubs or rent them here. The greens fee is $50; caddies cost $15; and electric carts cost $30. Call for reservations (☎ **755/3-1062** or 755/3-1163). The **Club de Golf Marina Ixtapa** (☎ **755/3-1410;** fax 755/3-0825), designed by Robert von Hagge, has 18 challenging holes. Greens fees are $45; $55 with cart. Call for reservations (☎ **755/3-1410;** fax 755/3-0825).

To polish your **tennis** serve in Ixtapa, try the **Campo de Golf Ixtapa** (☎ 755/ 3-1062 or 755/3-1163) and the **Club de Golf Marina Ixtapa** (☎ **755/3-1410;** fax 755/3-0825); both have courts that are lit at night, and both rent equipment. Fees are $7 per hour, $10 per hour at night.

For **horseback riding, Rancho Playa Linda** (☎ 755/4-3085) offers guided trail rides from the Playa Linda beach (about 8 miles north of Ixtapa). Guided rides begin at 8:30, 9:45, and 11am, and 3:30 and 5pm. Groups of three or more riders can arrange their own tour, which is especially nice a little later in the evening for sunset (though you'll need mosquito repellent in the evening). Riders can choose to go along the beach to the mouth of the river and back through coconut plantations, or stay along the beach for the whole ride (which usually lasts 1 to 1¹/₂ hours). The fee is $20. Travel agencies in either town can arrange your trip, but will charge a bit more for transportation. Reservations are suggested in the high season.

A **countryside tour** of fishing villages, coconut and mango plantations, and the Barra de Potos Lagoon, which is 14 miles south of Zihuatanejo and known for its tropical birds, is available through local travel agencies for $25 to $30. The tour typically lasts 5¹/₂ hours and includes lunch and time for swimming.

For **off-the-beaten track tours,** contact Alex León Pineda, the knowledgeable owner of **F4 Tours** in the Los Patios Center in Ixtapa (☎ 755/3-1442; fax 755/ 3-2014). His countryside tour goes to coconut and banana plantations, small villages where brickmakers work in the traditional fashion and residents live in palm thatch huts, and to the beach at La Saladita, where fishermen and the tour clients prepare a lunch of fresh lobster, dorado, or snapper.

SHOPPING
ZIHUATANEJO

Like other resorts in Mexico, Zihuatanejo has its quota of T-shirt and souvenir shops. But it's becoming a better place to buy Mexican crafts, folk art, and jewelry. The **artisan's market** on Calle 5 de Mayo is a good place to start a shopping spree before moving on to specialty shops. The **municipal market** on Avenida Benito Juárez (about five blocks inland from the waterfront) is also good, especially the stands specializing in huaraches, hammocks, and baskets. The market area sprawls over several blocks and is well worth an early morning visit. Spreading inland from the waterfront three or four blocks are numerous small shops worth exploring. Besides the places listed below, check out **Alberto's** at Cuauhtémoc 15 and **Ruby's** at Cuauhtémoc 7 for jewelry.

Shops are generally open Monday through Saturday from 10am to 2pm and 4 to 8pm; many of the better shops close on Sunday, but some smaller souvenir stands stay open, though hours vary.

Boutique D'Xochitl. Ejido at Cuauhtémoc. ☎ **755/4-2131.**

This is my favorite place to pick up light crinkle cotton clothing that's perfect for tropical climes. Hours are Monday through Saturday from 9am to 9pm, Sunday from 2 to 9pm.

Casa Marina. Paseo del Pescador 9. ☎ **755/4-2373.**

This small complex extends from the waterfront to Álvarez near 5 de Mayo and houses four shops, each specializing in handcrafted wares from Mexico and Guatemala. Items include handsome rugs, textiles, masks, papier-mâché, colorful wood carvings, and silver jewelry. Café Marina, the small coffee shop in the complex, has shelves and shelves of used paperback books in several languages for sale. It's open daily from 9am to 9pm during the high season and from 10am to 2pm and 4 to 8pm during the rest of the year.

Coco Cabaña Collectibles. Guerrero and Álvarez. ☎ **755/4-2518.**

Located next to Coconuts Restaurant, this gorgeous shop is crammed with carefully selected crafts and folk art from all over the country, including fine Oaxaca wood carvings. Owner Pat Cummings once ran a gallery in New York, and the inventory reveals her discriminating eye. If you purchase something, she'll cash your dollars at the going rate. It's opposite the Hotel Citali and is open Monday through Saturday from 10am to 2pm and 6 to 10pm. It's closed September and October.

Galería Maya. Bravo 31. ☎ **755/4-3606.**

This small folk art store is packed with Guatemalan jackets, *santos*, silver, painted wooden fish from Guerrero, tin mirror frames, masks, lacquered gourds, rain sticks, and embroidered T-shirts. It's open Monday through Saturday from 10am to 2pm and 6 to 9pm.

Mueblart. Álvarez 13-B. ☎ **755/3-2530.**

You'll wish you owned a nearby beach house after browsing through this handsome collection of handcrafted furniture; or you can simply ship your purchases back home if you'd like. Smaller items include wooden and gourd masks and wicker baskets in bright colors. The store is across the street from the Hotel Avila. It's open Monday through Saturday from 11am to 2:30pm and 5 to 9pm.

IXTAPA

Shopping gets better in Ixtapa every year as several fine folk art shops become established. There are several plazas with air-conditioned shops carrying fashionable resort wear and contemporary art, as well as T-shirts and jewelry. Brand-name sportswear is sold at shops that include **Ferroni, Bye-Bye, Aca Joe,** and **Navale.** All these shops are within the same area on Bulevar Ixtapa, across from the beachside hotels, and most are open from 9am to 2pm and 4 to 9pm, including Sundays.

La Fuente. Los Patios Center on Bulevar Ixtapa. ☎ **755/3-0812.**

This terrific shop carries gorgeous talavera pottery, wicker tables in the form of jaguars, handblown glassware, masks, tin mirrors and frames, and wood and papier mâché miniatures. It's open daily from 9am to 2pm and 4 to 9pm.

Mic-Mac. La Puerta Center on Bulevar Ixtapa. ☎ **755/3-1733.**

The owners of La Fuente created a second shop featuring embroidered and appliquéd clothing from Guatemala and Mexico, textile wall hangings, and ceramic and brass home accessories. Mic-Mac is open daily from 9am to 2pm and 4 to 9pm.

WHERE TO STAY

The term "bungalow" is used loosely in Zihuatanejo, as it is elsewhere in Mexico. A bungalow may be an individual unit with a kitchen and bedroom, or a bedroom only. It also may be hotel-like in a two-story building with multiple units, some of which have kitchens. It may be cozy and nice or rather rustic, and there may or may not be a patio or balcony. Beware of vanishing belongings, however, if your room has a balcony.

Because the most economical hotels are in Zihuatanejo rather than in Ixtapa, all the places I recommend—with one or two exceptions—are in this village or near its beaches, Madera and La Ropa. Zihuatanejo contains some of the best low-budget accommodations on the Pacific coast.

Playa Madera and Playa La Ropa, separated from each other only by a craggy shoreline, are both accessible by road. Prices here tend to be higher than those in town, but some people find that the beautiful and tranquil setting is worth the little extra. The town is just 5 to 20 minutes away, depending on whether you walk or take a taxi.

Note: If you arrive without reservations during the busiest times of the year—the Christmas holidays and Easter week—take the first room available. Then, with more time, search for what suits you best.

IN TOWN
Doubles for Less than $25
Casa Aurora. Nicolás Bravo 27, 40880 Zihuatanejo, Gro. ☎ **755/4-3046.** 12 rooms (all with bath). FAN. High season, $9 single; $18 double. Low season, $7 single; $15 double.

Located a few minutes from the beach, this hotel offers small rooms with well-worn furniture, good window screens (unusual in local hotels), and a comfortable second-story porch. All rooms have hot water, two or three lumpy single beds, and louvered windows. The best rooms are no. 12 (a double) and no. 13 (a triple), with windows facing the street. The management also rents apartments on Playa Ropa. From the museum walk inland on Guerrero two blocks to Nicolás Bravo and turn left; the hotel is on your right.

Casa Bravo. Nicolás Bravo 11, 40880 Zihuatanejo, Gro. ☎ **755/4-2548.** 9 rms (all with bath). FAN. $14 single; $18 double.

A good value for its budget price, this two-story hotel offers clean, plain rooms with mismatched furniture and bare bulbs above the beds. Three second-story rooms at the front of the building have balconies, though they let in a bit of street noise. Guests can lounge in a hammock in the open-ceilinged lobby. You'll find this hotel by walking inland on Guerrero to Bravo and turning right; the hotel is on your left.

Hotel Susy. Juan Alvarez 3 (at Guerrero), 40880 Zihuatanejo, Gro. ☎ **755/4-2339.** 20 rms (all with bath). FAN. High season, $25 single or double. Low season, $20 single or double.

Consistently clean, with lots of plants along a shaded walkway set back from the street, this two-story hotel offers small rooms with louvered glass windows with screens. Upper-floor rooms have balconies overlooking the street. Facing away from the water at the basketball court on the Malecón, turn right and walk two blocks; the hotel is on your left at the corner of Guerrero.

✪ **Posada Citlali.** Vicente Guerrero 3, 40880 Zihuatanejo, Gro. ☎ **755/4-2043.** 17 rms (all with bath). FAN. $20 single or double.

The small rooms in this pleasant three-story hotel are arranged around a shaded plant-filled courtyard decked out with comfortable rockers and *equipale* (leather-covered) chairs. Bottled water is in help-yourself containers on the patio. Furnishings in each room include an orange chenille bedspread and a large wall mirror with a shelf beneath it. The stairway to the top two floors is narrow and steep. The hotel is near the corner of Álvarez and Guerrero.

Posada Michel. Calle Ejido 14, 40880 Zihuatanejo, Gro. ☎ **755/4-7423.** 17 rooms (all with bath). A/C or FAN. $9 single; $18 double.

Though far from spacious, this small hotel offers immaculately clean rooms for a great price. Pink is the predominant color throughout, from the front doorway down the narrow hallways and on to the rooms. Bathrooms, however, have bright green tile and come without shower curtains or toilet seats. To get here from the waterfront, walk two blocks inland on Guerrero and turn right on Ejido; the hotel is on your right.

Doubles for Less than $55

Hotel Imelda. González 11, 40880 Zihuatanejo, Gro. ☎ **755/4-7662.** Fax 755/4-3199. 45 rms (all with bath). A/C or FAN TV. High season, $20–$30 single; $25–$40 double. Low season discounts. Free parking; enclosed.

Despite its proximity to the market area, this hotel is well maintained and remarkably quiet. Each room has a tile floor and tile bath (no shower curtain), a large closet, louvered windows without screens, and two or three double beds. There's a long lap pool and a cheerful restaurant, Rancho Grande, which offers an inexpensive *comida corrida*. Higher prices are for rooms with air conditioning. To get here from the museum, walk inland four blocks and turn left on González; the Imelda is on your right between Cuauhtémoc and Vicente Guerrero.

PLAYA MADERA

Madera Beach is a 15-minute walk along the street, a 10-minute walk along the beach pathway, or a $2 taxi ride from town. Most of the accommodations are on Calle Eva S. de López Mateos, the road overlooking the beach. If you walk 15 minutes east of town beside the canal, crossing a footbridge and following the road running uphill, you will intersect Mateos. An easier route is along the footpath from the end of Paseo Pescador, by the museum, to Playa Madera. Most hotels are set against the hill and have steep stairways.

Doubles for Less than $35

Arca de Noa. Calle Eva S. de López Mateos, Playa Madera, 40880 Zihuatanejo, Gro. ☎ **755/4-2272.** 10 rms (all with bath). FAN. $12 single; $23 double.

An excellent value, the Arca de Noa is a two-story green house set back from a front patio landscaped with flowers and a shaded sitting area. The neat, pleasant rooms have large windows with glass louvers, white walls, and bright-colored bedspreads. Guests can use the kitchen and dining room. Four rooms have sea views. Facing Mateos, take the road to the right; the hotel is midway up the block on your right.

✪ Bungalows Ley. Calle Eva S. de López Mateos s/n, Playa Madera (Apdo. Postal 466), 40880 Zihuatanejo, Gro. ☎ **755/4-4563** or 4-4087. 6 rms (all with bath). A/C or FAN. $30 double with fan; $40 double with A/C; $56 for two-bedroom suite with kitchen and fan for up to four persons, $90 with A/C; $111 for up to six persons.

No two suites are the same at this small complex, one of the nicest on Playa Madera. If you're traveling with a group, you may want to splurge on the most expensive suite (called Club Madero), which comes with a rooftop terrace with tiled hot tub, outdoor bar and grill, and a spectacular view. All the rooms are immaculately clean; the simplest are studios with one bed and a kitchen in the same room. Most rooms have terraces or balconies just above the beach. Clients praise the management. To find the complex, follow Mateos to the right up a slight hill; it's on your left.

Doubles for Less than $55

✪ Bungalows Pacíficos. Calle Eva S. de López Mateos, Playa Madera (Apdo. Postal 12), 40880 Zihuatanejo, Gro. ☎ and fax **755/4-2112.** 6 rms (all with bath). FAN. High season, $50 single or double. Low season, $40 single or double.

The three-story building is arranged in tiers down the steep hillside, and the beach is just a five-minute walk away. Tranquil and comfortable, each room has a bedroom and a narrow alcove with two additional beds facing the doors that open to terraces and sea views. All the rooms have fully equipped (though humble) kitchens with a small dining table and large jugs of purified water. The rooms open onto large terraces that serve as a living area with a table and chairs, a hammock, flowering plants, and magnificent views. The owner, Anita Hahyner, will gladly answer all your questions in four languages, including English, and seems to know everyone in town. Birdwatchers will be delighted here; over 74 species of birds have been spotted and catalogued by guests from their terraces. Facing Mateos, take the road to the right until you reach its terminus overlooking town; the hotel is on the left.

IXTAPA

Although the hotel listed below is priced beyond our budget range, it remains the best bargain in Ixtapa, which caters primarily to the charter- and package-tour business. If you want to stay at a hotel on Ixtapa's beautiful beach, your best bet is to buy a hotel-and-airfare package in advance.

Worth a Splurge

Best Western Posada Real. Bulevar Ixtapa, 40880 Ixtapa, Gro. ☎ **755/3-1625** or 755/3-1745, or 800/528-1234 in the U.S. Fax 755/3-1805. 110 rms. A/C TV TEL. $75 single or double; $120 triple. Free parking.

Each of the plain, motel-type rooms here has two comfortable double beds or one king-size bed, a wall-desk/counter and minicouch, and air-conditioning. Small windows in some rooms offer sea views, but none of the rooms has a balcony. Request a room on the lower floors; there are no elevators in this four-story hotel. Among the facilities are two pools, two outdoor restaurants, a gift shop, and a travel desk. The Lighthouse Restaurant and Euforia Disco (both open only in high season) are set apart on the front part of the property, just off Bulevar Ixtapa, and Carlos 'n Charlie's (see "The Club & Music Scene," below) is next door. Booking directly with the hotel or buying a package may be cheaper than reserving through the Best Western chain. Parking is in an open lot off Bulevar Ixtapa. To get here from the Krystal, walk about five minutes toward the marina; the hotel is not visible from the street but sits down a marked drive to your left.

WHERE TO EAT

Zihuatanejo's **central market,** located on Avenida Benito Juárez (about five blocks inland from the waterfront), offers cheap, tasty food. The food is best at breakfast and lunch because the market activity winds down in the afternoon. Be sure to choose what's hot and freshly cooked. The market area is one of the best on this coast for shopping and people watching.

IN ZIHUATANEJO
Meals for Less than $5

Café La Marina. Paseo del Pescador 9. ☎ 755/4-2373. Pizzas $3.75; sandwiches $1.50–$3; Wednesday-night spaghetti $3.50. Mon–Sat 11am–9pm. PIZZA/SANDWICHES.

This popular beachfront hangout has only a handful of tables on its front porch, and its service is lackadaisical. Yet it dishes out pizza, with toppings that range from pineapple to ham and seafood. Large tortas (sandwiches) come with bean sprouts and avocado. The Wednesday-night spaghetti with pesto or bolognese sauce is said to be the best in town. While you wait, browse through the many shelves stacked with English paperbacks for sale. Facing away from the water at the basketball court, turn left and walk down Paseo del Pescador; the café is on your right by the Casa Marina shops.

Casa Puntarenas. Calle Noria, Colonia Lázaro Cárdenas. No phone. Soup $1.35; main courses $2.25–$5. 6:30–9pm. MEXICAN/SEAFOOD.

A modest spot with a tin roof and nine wooden tables, Puntarenas is one of the best spots in town for fried whole fish served with toasted *bolillos*, sliced tomatoes, onions, and avocado. The chilis rellenos are mild and stuffed with plenty of cheese; the meat dishes are less flavorful. To get to Puntarenas from the pier, turn left on Álvarez and cross the footbridge on your left. Turn right after you cross the bridge; the restaurant is on your left.

Nueva Zelanda. Cuauhtémoc 23 at Ejido. ☎ 755/4-2340. Tortas $2–$3.50; enchiladas $2–$4; fruit-and-milk licuados $1.50; cappuccinos $1.65. Daily 8am–10pm. MEXICAN.

One of the most popular places in town, this clean open-air snack shop welcomes diners with rich cappuccinos sprinkled with cinnamon and pancakes with real maple syrup. But the mainstays of the menu are tortas and enchiladas. For only 5¢ more, you can order a cappuccino to go (say "para llevar") and get twice as much coffee.

You'll find Nueva Zelanda by walking three blocks inland from the waterfront on Cuauhtémoc; the restaurant is on your right. There's a second location (☎ 755/3-0838) in Ixtapa in the back section of the Los Patios shopping center.

Ruben's. Calle Adelita s/n. ☎ 755/4-4617. Burgers $2.25–$3.25; vegetables $1.50; ice cream $1. Daily 6pm–11pm. BURGERS/VEGETABLES.

The choices are easy here—you can order either a big sloppy burger made from top sirloin beef grilled over mesquite or a foil-wrapped packet of baked potatoes, chayote, zucchini, or sweet corn. Homemade ice cream plus beer and soda fill out the menu, which is posted on the wall by the kitchen. Guests snag a waitress and rattle off their orders, grab their own drinks from the cooler, and tally their own tabs. Rolls of paper towels hang over the tables on the open porch and shaded terrace. Ruben's is a popular fixture in the Playa Madera neighborhood—though the customers come from all over town. To get here from Mateos, turn right on Adelita; Ruben's is on your right.

La Sirena Gorda. Paseo del Pescador. ☎ **755/4-2687.** Breakfast $2–$3; main courses $3–$5. Thurs–Tues 7am–10pm. MEXICAN.

For the best inexpensive breakfast in town, head to La Sirena Gorda for a variety of eggs and omelets, or hotcakes with bacon, as well as fruit with granola and yogurt. For lunch or dinner try the house specialty, seafood tacos with fish prepared to taste like machaca or carnitas or covered with mole. There's always a short list of daily specials, such as blackened red snapper, steak, or fish kebabs. Patrons enjoy the casual sidewalk-café atmosphere. To get here from the basketball court, face the water and walk to the right; La Sirena Gorda is on your right just before the town pier.

Meals for Less than $10

Casa Elvira. Paseo del Pescador. ☎ **755/4-2061.** Main courses $3.50–$11. Daily noon–10:30pm. MEXICAN/SEAFOOD.

Casa Elvira almost always has a crowd, drawn in by its neat, clean atmosphere and by the wide selection of inexpensive low-cost lunches and dinners on its bilingual menu. House specialties are snapper (or whatever fish is in season) and lobster; the restaurant also serves meat dishes and chicken mole. The most expensive seafood platter includes lobster, red snapper, and jumbo butterfly shrimp. Facing the water and the basketball court, turn right; Casa Elvira is on the west end of the waterfront near the town pier.

Garrobos. Álvarez 52. ☎ **755/4-2977.** Main courses $3–$11. Tues–Sun 2–10pm. MEXICAN/SEAFOOD.

This very popular, roomy restaurant offers large meat and seafood dishes attractively presented with rice and two vegetables. It also serves the Spanish dish paella and the local specialty, *tiritas de pescado*, little strips of marinated fish (as with ceviche, the fish is "cooked" by the lemon or lime juice). In the evening trios often serenade diners. To reach Garrobos, turn left on Alvarez with your back to the basketball court; the restaurant is on your right beneath the Hotel Raúl Tres Marías Centro.

Worth a Splurge

✪ **Restaurant Paul's.** 5 de Mayo s/n. ☎ **755/4-2188.** Main courses $7–$12. Daily 6–10pm. INTERNATIONAL/SEAFOOD.

It's hard to find a seat after 7pm at this small open-air restaurant, where the Swiss chef has attained a fanatical following. It must be the only place in town that serves fresh artichokes as an appetizer, and the ubiquitous fish filet is covered with a smooth, delicately flavored shrimp and dill sauce. The pasta comes topped with a pile of shrimp and fish in a light cream sauce, and the pork chops and beef medallions are thick and juicy. To get to Paul's from the main pier, turn right on Álvarez and walk one block, then turn left onto 5 de Mayo; Paul's is on your right before the church.

Bakeries

El Buen Gusto. Guerrero 4. ☎ **755/4-3231.** All items 25¢–$2.25. Mon–Sat 7:30am–10pm. BAKED GOODS.

Small but packed with goodies, this pastry shop offers what's usually found in a Mexican bakery—then goes beyond expectations by offering banana bread, French bread, doughnuts, and cakes. To get here from the museum, walk half a block up Guerrero; the bakery is on your left.

Panadería Francesa. Gonzalez 15, between Cuauhtémoc and Guerrero. ☎ **755/4-4520.** Bread and pastries 25¢–$1.80. Daily 7am–9pm. BAKED GOODS.

Here you can buy sweet pastries to accompany your take-out cappuccino to go from nearby Nueva Zelanda (see above). You can also grab a long baguette or loaf of whole-wheat bread for picnic supplies. To get here from Nueva Zelanda, turn left on Gonzalez; the shop is on your right.

IN IXTAPA
Meals for Less than $10
✪ **Golden Cookie Shop.** Los Patios Center. ☎ **755/3-0310.** Breakfast $3–$4; sandwiches $3–$5; main courses $3–$6. Mon–Sat 8am–3pm and 6–10pm. PASTRIES/INTERNATIONAL.

Although the name is misleading—there are more than cookies here—Golden Cookie's freshly baked cookies and pastries are worthy of a detour, and the coffee menu is the most extensive in town. The large sandwiches, made with fresh soft bread, come with a choice of sliced deli meats. Chicken curry is among the other specialty items. To get to the shop, walk to the rear of the shopping center as you face Mac's Prime Rib; walk up the stairs, turn left, and you'll see the restaurant on your right.

✪ **Mamma Norma.** La Puerta Center, Bulevar Ixtapa. ☎ **755/3-0274.** Breakfast $2.75–$3; main courses $4.50–$80; pizza $5.75–$7. Daily 8am–11pm (deliveries made 3–11pm). ITALIAN/AMERICAN.

At one of the most popular restaurants in Ixtapa, you can choose from 17 kinds of pizza (they deliver too), 8 different pasta dishes (including a spicy puttanesca), and regional Mexican dishes including cochinita pibil. You'll also find a generous antipasto, burgers, sandwiches, and ice cream. To get to Mamma Norma from the tourist office, walk to the back of the La Puerta Center and look for the sidewalk tables covered with red cloths.

Toko Tukan Natural. Los Patios Center. ☎ **755/3-0717.** Breakfast $2.75–$3; tacos and sandwiches $3–$4. Daily 8am–11pm. FRUIT/SANDWICHES/VEGETARIAN.

With outdoor tables shaded by umbrellas, this casual restaurant is popular for breakfast and brunch. The fruit plates are amply loaded. Other offerings include fresh fruit and vegetable drinks, as well as salads, including a noteworthy seafood salad. There's also a good selection of tacos and sandwiches, all of which come with meat. At breakfast, hotcakes come plain or with bananas, nuts, raisins, or apples. The restaurant faces the boulevard beside Aca Joe.

Worth a Splurge
✪ **Beccofino.** Marina Ixtapa. ☎ **755/3-1770.** Breakfast $2.75–$3.75; pastas $6–$11; main courses $8–$14. Daily 9:30am–midnight. NORTHERN ITALIAN.

This restaurant is a standout in Mexico. Experienced owner Angelo Rolly Pavia lays before his guests the flavorful northern Italian specialties he grew up knowing and loving. Once seated at the breezy marina location, diners peruse a menu that includes dishes with rice and with short, long, and wide pastas. Ravioli, a house specialty, comes stuffed with the seafood in season. The garlic bread is terrific, and there's an extensive wine list.

ZIHUATANEJO & IXTAPA AFTER DARK
With an exception or two, Zihuatanejo nightlife dies down around 11pm or midnight. For a good selection of clubs, discos, hotel fiestas, special events, and fun watering holes with live music and dancing, head for Ixtapa. But keep in mind that the shuttle bus stops at 11pm, and a taxi ride back to Zihuatanejo after midnight costs 50% more than the regular price. During off-season (after Easter or before

Christmas) hours vary: Some places are open only on weekends, while others are closed completely.

THE CLUB & MUSIC SCENE

Many discos and dance clubs stay open until the last customers leave, so closing hours vary. Most discos have a ladies' night at least once a week when admission and drinks are free for women. Call to check the days.

The Bay Club and Samba Café. Camino a Playa La Ropa, Zihuatanejo. ☎ **755/4-4844.** No cover.

It's fun to dance under the stars on the beautifully lit patio surrounded by tropical plants. The restaurant/bar is perched on a hillside, with a splendid view of the town lights and bay. Live music ranges from jazz and tropical to soft rock. The mesquite-grilled dinners are expensive, but come after dinner to enjoy the music with an appetizer or dessert. Drinks cost between $1.75 and $3.50, and snacks range from $3 to $7. A full dinner goes for $9 and up. The club is open daily during high season from 9:30pm to midnight; happy hour is 5 to 7pm. It's closed in the off-season.

Carlos 'n Charlie's. Bulevar Ixtapa (just north of the Best Western Posada Real), Ixtapa. ☎ **755/3-0085.** Cover (including drink tokens) after 9pm for dancing, $2.50.

Decorated with all sorts of nostalgia, bric-a-brac, silly sayings, and photos from the Mexican Revolution, this restaurant/nightclub offers party ambience and good food. The eclectic menu humorously includes iguana in season (Alka-Seltzer and aspirin are on the house). Out back by the beach is an open-air section (part of it shaded) with a raised wooden platform called the "pier" for "pier-dancing" at night, thus mixing the sound of the surf with recorded rock and roll. The restaurant is open daily from noon to midnight; pier dancing is nightly from 9pm to 3am.

Christine. In the Hotel Krystal, Bulevar Ixtapa, Ixtapa. ☎ **755/3-0456.** Cover $4.50.

This flashy streetside disco is famous for its midnight light show, which features classical music played on a mega sound system. A semicircle of tables in tiers overlooks the dance floor. No tennis shoes, sandals, shorts, or jeans are allowed, and reservations are advised during high season. Drinks cost $1.50 to $5. It's open daily during high season from 10:30pm to the wee hours; the light show is at midnight. (Off-season hours vary.)

Euforia Disco. Bulevar Ixtapa, Ixtapa. ☎ **755/3-1190.** Cover $4.50.

You can't miss the Euforia Disco, next to the Lighthouse Restaurant and in front of the Best Western Posada Real at the turnoff to Carlos 'n Charlie's. Levels of tables rise on one side of the circular dance floor, behind which is a volcano that actually erupts. Go early in time to see the sound-and-light show. No shorts are allowed. Drinks cost between $1.75 and $4. Ask about seasonal discounts on the admission. It's open daily during high season and on holidays from 10pm to the wee hours and is closed in the off-season.

Señor Frog's. Bulevar Ixtapa in the La Puerta Center, Ixtapa. ☎ **755/3-0272.** Cover (including drink tokens) after 9pm for dancing.

A companion restaurant to Carlos 'n Charlie's, Señor Frog's has several dining sections and a warehouselike bar with raised dance floors. Rock and roll blares from large speakers, and even those stopping by for dinner sometimes dance by their tables between courses. The restaurant is open daily from 6pm to midnight; the bar is open until 3am.

HOTEL FIESTAS & THEME NIGHTS

Many hotels hold Mexican fiestas and other special events that usually include dinner, drinks, live music, and entertainment for a fixed price ($30 to $40). The **Sheraton Ixtapa** (☎ 755/3-1858) is famous for its Wednesday-night fiesta; good Mexican fiestas are also held by the **Krystal Hotel** (☎ 755/3-0333) and **Dorado Pacífico** (☎ 755/3-2025) in Ixtapa and the **Villa del Sol** (☎ 755/4-2239) on Playa La Ropa in Zihuatanejo. The Sheraton Ixtapa is the only one that offers these in the off-season. The **Westin Brisas Ixtapa** (☎ 755/3-2121) and the **Sheraton Ixtapa** also put on theme nights featuring the cuisine and music of different countries. Call to make reservations (travel agencies also sell the tickets) and be sure you understand what the fixed price covers (drinks, tax, and tip are not always included).

A SIDE TRIP TO SLEEPY TRONCONES

The tiny fishing settlement of Troncones, 20 miles northwest of Ixtapa, has become a favorite escape for visitors to Ixtapa and Zihuatanejo. The main thing to do is stroll the long, empty beaches, swim in the sea (if the surf is not high), and feast on seafood at one of the fishermen's-shack restaurants or at El Burro Borracho (see below). But there are other things to do here: Horse rentals can be arranged; hotel owners can provide information on hiking in the jungle or to nearby caves; you can take part in the small village's fiestas.

There are no direct telephone lines yet to Troncones, which is inhabited by all of 250 people. The phones listed below are cellular, and the fax lines are in Ixtapa or Zihuatanejo. Unfortunately, no public buses serve this area; to get here, you'll have to join a tour or hire a taxi in Ixtapa/Zihuatanejo. For about $20, a driver will take you and return at the hour you request to bring you back to town.

If you have your own car, follow the highway northwest through Ixtapa, past the Marina Ixtapa, and continue past the Ciudad Altamirano turnoff. Mark your odometer at this turnoff—14 kilometers ahead is the sign pointing left to El Burro Borracho. When you reach it, turn and continue 3.5 kilometers until you reach the ocean. Turn left. El Burro Borracho is the last restaurant on the right. From that location you can get directions to the rest of the inns.

WHERE TO STAY

All the lodgings mentioned below may offer discounts on rentals of as much as 50% in low season.

El Burro Borracho. Los Troncones, Guerrero, 6 miles north of Ixtapa on Highway 200. ☎ **755/7-0777.** Fax 755/3-2417. 3 bungalows (all with bath). 5 RV spaces. High season $45 single; $55 double. Low season $25 single or double; RV space $10–$15. Rates include continental breakfast.

Anita Lapointe, the owner of El Burro Borracho, offers three rustic stone bungalows all with private bathroom, kingsize bed, and a hammock on the porch. In addition, guests can use the fully equipped kitchen, library, and satellite TV. Boogie boards and kayaks are available for rent. Five full-hookup RV spaces and a place to camp are available as well. Local artisans from Troncones provide El Burro Borracho with hand-embroidered dresses and blouses, lace, and other locally made art. The beachfront restaurant is the one recommended for the area.

Casa Canela. Los Troncones, Guerrero, 6 miles north of Ixtapa on Highway 200. ☎ **755/ 7-0777.** Fax 755/4-3296. 2-bedroom house (3 baths). High season $90 per day for the house; $535 per week. Rates include continental breakfast.

Opposite El Burro Borracho, Anita Lapointe also offers this complete house, with two bedrooms, three bathrooms, a kitchen, porch, garden, and satellite TV. The house will sleep up to six people. It isn't on the beach, but the beach is just across the road.

✪ **Casa de la Tortuga B&B.** Los Troncones, Guerrero, 6 miles north of Ixtapa on Highway 200. ☎ **755/7-0732.** Fax 755/3-2417. (Reservations: write Apdo. Postal 37, 40880 Zihuatanejo, Gro.) 6 rooms. High season $50–$100 single or double. Rates include full breakfast.

Dewey and Karolyn MacMillan, a young American couple, recently renovated their isolated paradise on the beach at Troncones; they've used Mexican tiles and created a garden setting. Casa Tortuga is a six-bedroom home with four bathrooms, a dining room, kitchen, laundry, pool, TV and VCR, and a book and video library. Individual rooms are available, or you could rent the whole place for your vacation; it will sleep up to 12 people. A palapa-covered bar is just steps from the beach and ocean.

Casa Ki. Los Troncones, Guerrero, 6 miles north of Ixtapa on Highway 200. No phone. Fax 755/3-2417. 3 bungalows (all with bath). $45 single; $55 double. Rates include continental breakfast.

Ed and Ellen Weston offer these three separate bungalows in a garden setting right on the beach. Each one is furnished with a king-size bed, private bathroom, and porch with a hammock to while away some relaxing hours.

La Puesta del Sol. Los Troncones, Guerrero, 6 miles north of Ixtapa on Highway 200. No phone. Fax 755/3-2417. 2 rms (both with bath). $55–$65 single; $60–$70 double. Rates include continental breakfast.

Next to El Burro Borracho is this small inn, run by Malury Wells. Its two large separate units are on the beach. One has a kitchenette; it commands the higher rates. In either room, you have a choice of a king-size or single bed. Guests use the El Burro Borracho restaurant.

WHERE TO EAT

Several palapa-topped restaurants are near Troncones and are worth a try—just make a casual inspection for cleanliness. Or you can try this place:

El Burro Borracho. Troncones Beach. ☎ **755/3-0089.** Fax 755/3-2417. Main courses $2–$9. Daily 8am–9pm. AMERICAN/SEAFOOD.

Mike Bensal's casual beachfront restaurant is not your ordinary greasy-spoon beach shack. Here are a few winners from the menu, which features a lot of seafood and grilled dishes: shrimp tacos, filet mignon with mashed potatoes and mushroom gravy, the "ultimate" hamburger, barbecue pork ribs, and grilled chicken breast with tamarindo chipotle sauce. You can kick back with a margarita, iced cappuccino, a glass of wine, or cold beer. If you're here on a day-trip from Ixtapa/Zihuatanejo, you can spend the day here if you like, using the beach and this restaurant as headquarters, and have your taxi return here to pick you up.

2 Acapulco

262 miles SW of Mexico City, 170 miles SW of Taxco, 612 miles SE of Guadalajara; 158 miles SE of Ixtapa/Zihuatanejo, 470 miles NW of Huatulco

To the world, Acapulco has a perennially romantic reputation and a jet-set image. Acapulco first grabbed the world's attention in the 1950s when it was the stomping ground of Hollywood celebrities. And though by now it could be considered old-hat among Mexico's resorts, it is still growing and attracting celebrities. A plethora of new villas and condominiums has appeared seemingly overnight on the mountain slopes. The latest development is the enormous Acapulco Diamante project running along the coast from Puerto Marqués almost to the airport. It includes the new Sheraton, Camino Real, and Vidafel resort hotels, and even more hotels are on the drawing board.

Acapulco's nightlife never dims; the vibrant variety of this city's discos and clubs is hard to top in Mexico. And to anyone who knows it, the view of Acapulco Bay, flanked by mountains and beaches, is breathtaking day or night.

Acapulco, however, is a real city of about 1 million now, rather than simply a resort. It has its share of grit along with glitz. There are slums as well as villas, and some of the hotels could use a facelift. The city continues to work hard to maintain the glamour that originally put it on the map. A program called "ACA-Limpia" ("Clean Acapulco") has cleaned up the bay, where whales have been sighted recently for the first time in years, and has spruced up the Costera. And the itinerant vendors that once hawked their wares to tourists on the beaches and sidewalks have been moved to newly created market areas, such as the Diana traffic circle on the Costera.

ESSENTIALS

GETTING THERE & DEPARTING   By Plane   See chapter 3, "Planning a Trip to Mexico," for information on flying from the United States or Canada to Acapulco. Local numbers for major airlines that have nonstop or direct service to Acapulco are: **Aeroméxico,** ☎ **74/85-1600** for reservations or 74/66-9104 at the airport; **American,** ☎ **74/84-1244** or 74/84-1179 for reservations or 74/84-0372 at the airport; **Continental,** ☎ **74/66-9063** or 74/66-9064 at the airport; **Mexicana,** ☎ **74/84-6943** or 74/84-6890 or 74/84-1815 at the airport; and **Taesa,** ☎ **74/66-9067** for reservations, or 74/86-4576 or 74/81-1214 at the airport.

Within Mexico, Aeroméxico flies from Guadalajara, Mexico City, Toluca, and Tijuana; Mexicana flies from Mexico City; and Taesa flies from Laredo, Mexico City, and Guadalajara. Regional carriers include **AeroLibertad,** flying from Ixtapa/Zihuatanejo and Oaxaca, and **AeroMorelos,** flying from Cuernavaca and Puebla. Check with a travel agent about charter flights.

Transportes Terrestres (☎ **74/83-6500**) has colectivo service to and from the airport. Call the day before your departure for a reservation. The one-way trip costs around $7 per person. The service picks you up 1 1/2 hours (for flights within Mexico) to two hours (international flights) before your departure time. **Taxis** cost about $15 to $20.

By Bus to/from Mexico City   Buses to Acapulco leave from the **Terminal Central de Autobuses del Sur** (Tasqueña Metro line) for the four- to six-hour trip. Travel time depends on the number of stops and whether travel is by the toll road (faster) or the old road (slower). **Estrella de Oro** and **Estrella Blanca** have hourly service from Mexico City to Acapulco, but try to reserve your seat a few days in advance. There's little difference in quality between express and deluxe service, but get a directo if you want to arrive without a lot of stops in between.

From Acapulco, **Estrella de Oro** (☎ **74/85-8705** or 74/85-5282) has frequent direct buses to Mexico City. **Oro Plus** has service to Mexico City daily at 7:45, 10, and 11am; 10:15pm; and 1am. All Oro passengers must check luggage that is over 1 foot long. The baggage-check counter is to the right of ticket sales. **Turistar Plus** buses to Mexico City cost roughly double those of Estrella Blanca.

To/from Ixtapa & Zihuatanejo: Estrella Blanca (☎ **74/83-0802**) has several direct buses daily, and **Turistar** has Plus service daily at 6:30am and 5pm. From Acapulco, **Estrella de Oro** runs several daily buses to Ixtapa/Zihuatanejo.

Acapulco Bay Area

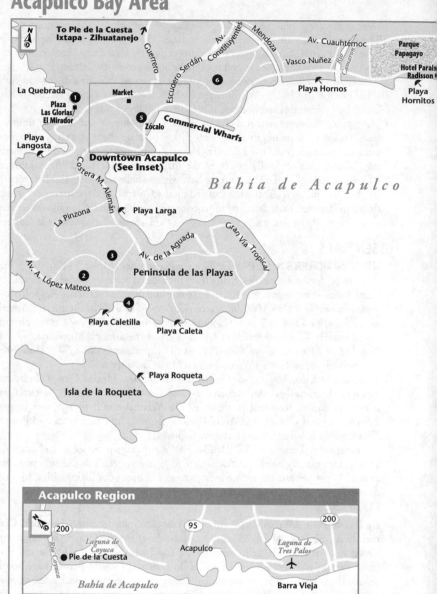

To Pie de la Cuesta Ixtapa - Zihuatanejo

Guerrero

Av. Constituyentes

Mendoza

Av. Cuauhtémoc

Parque Papagayo

Escudero Serdán

Hotel Parais Radisson

Vasco Nuñez

Rio Camarón

6

La Quebrada

Market

1

Plaza Las Glorias/ El Mirador

Playa Hornos

Playa Hornitos

5

Zócalo

Commercial Wharfs

Playa Langosta

Downtown Acapulco (See Inset)

Bahía de Acapulco

Costera M. Alemán

La Pinzona

Playa Larga

Av. de la Aguada

Gran Via Tropical

3

2

Av. A. López Mateos

Peninsula de las Playas

4

Playa Caletilla

Playa Caleta

Playa Roqueta

Isla de la Roqueta

Acapulco Region

200

95

200

Laguna de Coyuca

Acapulco

Laguna de Tres Palos

Rio Coyuca

Pie de la Cuesta

Bahía de Acapulco

Barra Vieja

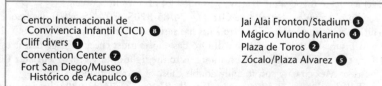

Centro Internacional de
  Convivencia Infantil (CICI) **8**
Cliff divers **1**
Convention Center **7**
Fort San Diego/Museo
  Histórico de Acapulco **6**

Jai Alai Fronton/Stadium **3**
Mágico Mundo Marino **4**
Plaza de Toros **2**
Zócalo/Plaza Alvarez **5**

188

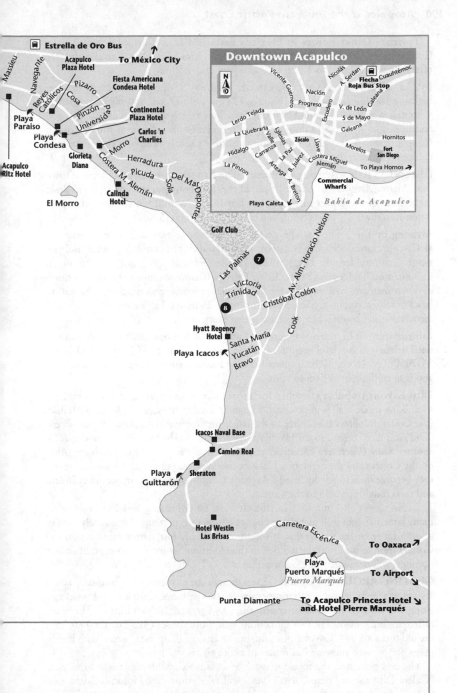

To/from Other Points in Mexico: Estrella Blanca has service to Taxco, Chilpancingo, Mexico City, Puerto Escondido, and Huatulco. **Estrella de Oro** offers three daily buses to Taxco (at 7 and 9am and 4:30pm).

By Car From Mexico City, you can take Highway 95 south or the curvy toll-free highway (six hours). You can also take Highway 95 D, the toll highway (3¹/₂ to 4 hours), which costs around $80 one way. The free road from Taxco is in good condition, so it's worth taking to save around $40 in tolls from there through Chilpancingo to Acapulco. From points north or south along the coast, the only choice is Highway 200.

ORIENTATION   Arriving by Plane The **airport** is 14 miles southeast of town near Puerto Marqués, over the hills east of the bay. **Transportes Terrestre** has desks at the front of the airport where you can buy tickets for minivan colectivo transportation into town ($7 per person); you can also go by taxi ($20).

Arriving by Bus The **Estrella de Oro** bus station is a distance from downtown at Cuauhtémoc 1490 and Massieu, within walking distance of some budget-range accommodations. Local buses pass the terminal going both directions on Cuauhtémoc. The relatively new (1990) **Estrella Blanca** terminal at Ejido 47 is north of downtown and farthest from the hotels I have recommended below. The station has a hotel-reservation service, **Sendetur,** open 24 hours. Just before you exit you'll see a taxi ticket booth where rates are set for every hotel.

Information The **State of Guerrero Tourism Office** operates the **Procuraduria del Turista** on street level in front of the Convention Center (☎ **74/84-4583** or 74/84-7050, ext. 165 or 175). It offers maps and information about the city and state and is open daily from 9am to 9pm.

City Layout Acapulco stretches for more than 4 miles around the huge bay, so walking to see it all is impractical. The main boulevard, **Costera Miguel Alemán** (the Costera), follows the outline of the bay from downtown on the west side, where "Old Acapulco" began, to the Hyatt Regency Hotel on the east side. It continues by another name **(Carretera Escénica)** all the way to the airport. Most hotels are either on the Costera and the beach or a block or two away; as you go east from downtown they become increasingly luxurious. **Avenida Cuauhtémoc** is the major artery inland and runs roughly parallel to the Costera.

Street names and numbers in this city can be confusing and hard to find—many streets are not well marked or change names unexpectedly. Fortunately, you're seldom far from the Costera, so it's hard to get really lost. Street numbers on the Costera seem to have nothing to do with their location, so don't conclude that similar numbers will necessarily be close together.

GETTING AROUND   By Bus Even though the city has such a confusing street system, it's amazingly easy and inexpensive to use city buses. Two kinds of buses run along the Costera: pastel color-coded buses and regular "school buses." The main difference is the price. The new air-conditioned tourist buses **(Aca Tur Bus)** are 75¢; the old buses are 40¢. Covered bus stops are located all along the Costera, with handy maps on the walls showing bus routes to major sights and hotels.

The best place near the zócalo to catch a bus is beside Sanborn's, two blocks east. "Caleta Directo" or "Base-Caleta" buses will take you to the Hornos, Caleta, and Caletilla beaches along the Costera. Some buses return along the same route; others go around the peninsula and return to the Costera. To get to the restaurants and nightspots in the upscale hotel district on the north and east sides of the bay, catch a "Base–Cine Río–Caleta" bus beside Sanborn's. It runs inland along Cuauhtémoc to the Estrella de Oro bus terminal, then heads back to the Costera and beach at the Ritz Hotel and continues east along the Costera to Icacos Beach near the Hyatt Regency Hotel. "Zócalo Directo" and "Caleta Directo" buses follow the same route in the opposite direction.

For expeditions to more distant destinations, there are buses to Puerto Marqués to the east (the bus is marked "Puerto Marqués–Base") and Pie de la Cuesta to the west (the bus is marked "Zócalo–Pie de la Cuesta"). Be sure to verify the time and place of the last bus back if you hop one of these!

For a cheap way to get to the discos and restaurants east of town near the Las Brisas Hotel, take a "Base" bus as far as the Hyatt Regency. Then take a "Las Brisas" bus the rest of the way. Las Brisas buses are infrequent, however, and you could wind up waiting a long time. City buses stop at 10pm.

By Taxi   Taxis charge $2 to $8 for a ride within the city and more if you go farther out. For approximate prices, ask at your hotel or scan one of the taxi tariff lists found in the lobbies of most major hotels. Always establish the price with the driver before starting out. Report any trouble or overcharges to the Procuraduria del Turista—the tourist assistance Office on the Costera next to the Convention Center (☎ 74/84-4416).

FAST FACTS: ACAPULCO

American Express   The main office is at Costera Alemán 709, east of the Diana traffic circle (☎ 74/84-1095 for travel services, 74/84-5200 for financial services, 74/84-5550 for customer service, 74/84-6060 for tours); another branch is at the Hyatt Regency on Costera Alemán near the naval base (☎ 74/84-2888).

Area Code   The telephone area code is 74.

Climate   June through October is the rainy season; June, September, and October are the wettest months, whereas July and August are relatively dry.

Consular Agents   The United States has an agent at the Hotel Club del Sol on Costera Alemán at R. Católicos (☎ 74/85-6600), across from the Hotel Acapulco Plaza; it's open Monday through Friday from 10am to 2pm. The agent of Canada is also at the Hotel Club del Sol (☎ 74/85-6621), open Monday through Friday from 9am to 1pm. The agent of the United Kingdom is at the Las Brisas Hotel on Carretera Escénica near the airport (☎ 74/84-6605); it's open Monday through Friday from 9am to 6pm.

Currency Exchange   Banks along the Costera are open Monday through Friday from 9am to 1 or 1:30pm (though hours for exchanging money may be shorter) and generally have the best rates. Casas de cambio (currency-exchange booths) along the street may have better exchange rates than hotels.

Parking   It is illegal to park on the Costera at any time.

Post Office   The central post office (correo) is on the Costera near the zócalo and Sanborn's. Other branches are located in the Estrella de Oro bus station on Cuauhtémoc, inland from the Acapulco Ritz Hotel, and on the Costera near Caleta Beach.

Safety   Pay careful attention to warning flags posted on Acapulco beaches! Riptides claim a few lives every year. Red or black flags mean stay out of the water; yellow flags signify caution; and white or green flags mean it's safe to swim. Don't swim on any beach that fronts an open sea, but don't let down your guard on the bays either. It's difficult to imagine how powerful an undertow can be.

As always, tourists are vulnerable to thieves. This is especially true when you're shopping in a market; lying on the beach; wearing jewelry; or carrying a camera, purse, or bulging wallet. Tourists out for a morning walk on the beach should be especially alert. Pay attention to joggers coming from both directions—one knocks you down, then they rob you. To remove temptation from would-be thieves, purchase a waterproof plastic tube on a string to wear around your neck at the beach—it's big enough for a few bills and your room key. Street vendors and hotel variety shops sell them.

Telephone Numbers   As mentioned above, the area code for Acapulco is 74, a recent change from the old code, which was 748. Be aware that now all Acapulco numbers begin with "8," but many people have not made the transition and still give their numbers without the "8" or still print the area code as 748.

Tourist Police   If you see policemen in uniforms of white and light blue, they're from a special corps of English-speaking police who assist tourists.

FUN ON & OFF THE BEACH

Great beaches and water sports abound in Acapulco. It's also pleasant to take a walk early in the day (before it gets too hot) around the **zócalo,** called Plaza Álvarez. Visit the **cathedral**—the bulbous blue onion domes make it look more like a Russian Orthodox church, and it was actually designed as a movie theater! From the church, turn east along the side street going off at a right angle (Calle Carranza, which doesn't have a marker), where there's an arcade with newsstands and shops.

A fabulous view of Acapulco awaits you from the top of the hill behind the cathedral. Take a taxi up the hill from the main plaza, following the signs leading to **La Mirador.**

City tours, day-trips to Taxco, cruises, and other excursions and activities are offered through local travel agencies.

BEACHES   Here's the rundown, from west to east around the bay. **Playa la Angosta** is a small, sheltered, and often-deserted cove just around the bend from **La Quebrada** (where the cliff divers perform).

South of downtown on the Peninsula de las Playas lie **Caleta Beach** and **Caletilla Beach.** They are separated by a small outcropping of land containing the new aquarium and water park, Mágico Mundo Marino. Here you'll find thatch-roofed restaurants, water-sports equipment for rent, and the brightly painted boats that ferry passengers to Roqueta Island. You can rent beach chairs and umbrellas for $6 per day. Mexican families favor these beaches because they're close to several inexpensive hotels. In the late afternoon, fishermen pull their colorful boats up on the sand and sell their catch and sometimes oysters on the half shell.

The pleasure boats dock at **Playa Larga,** also south of the zócalo. Charter fishing trips sail from here. In the old days, these downtown beaches—Larga, Caleta, and Caletilla—were what Acapulco was all about. Nowadays the beaches and the resort development stretch the entire 4-mile length of the bay's shore.

Going east from the zócalo, the major beaches are **Hornos** (near Papagayo Park), **Hornitos, Condesa,** and **Icacos,** followed by the naval base (La Base) and **Punta del Guitarrón.** After Punta del Guitarrón, the road climbs to the legendary hotel Las Brisas, where many of the 300 casitas (bungalow-type rooms) have their own swimming pools (there are 250 pools in all). Past Las Brisas, the road continues to **Puerto Marqués** and **Punta Diamante,** about 12 miles from the zócalo. The fabulous Acapulco Princess and Pierre Marqués hotels dominate the landscape.

The bay of Puerto Marqués is an attractive area for **swimming.** The water is calm, the bay sheltered, and waterskiing available. Past the bay lies **Revolcadero Beach** and a fascinating jungle lagoon.

Warning: Each year in Acapulco at least one or two unwary swimmers drown because of deadly riptides and undertow (see "Safety" in "Fast Facts," above). Swim only in Acapulco Bay or Puerto Marqués Bay—but be careful of the undertow no matter where you go!

Other beaches are difficult to reach without a car. **La Pie de la Cuesta** is 8 miles west of town (buses leave town every 5 or 10 minutes). You can't swim here, but it's a great spot for watching big waves and the sunset, especially over coco locos (refreshments made with a fresh coconut with the top whacked off) at one of the rustic beachfront restaurants hung with hammocks. If boys try to collect money from you for sitting under the thatched palapas on the public beach, you don't have to pay them.

If you are driving, continue west along the peninsula, passing Coyuca Lagoon on your right, until you have almost reached the small air base at the tip. Along the way, you'll be invited to drive into different sections of beach by various private entrepreneurs, mostly small boys.

BAY CRUISES & ROQUETA ISLAND   The deck of a boat is a wonderful place from which to view the whole bay, and Acapulco has a variety of them to choose from—yachts, huge catamarans and trimarans, single- and double-decker—you name it. Cruises are offered morning, afternoon, and evening. Some offer buffets, open bars, and live music; others have snacks, drinks, and taped music. (The music, by the way, may be loud enough to preclude talking.) Prices range from around $20 to $60. The operators of these cruises come and go, and their phone numbers change so frequently from year to year that it's pointless to list them here; to find out what cruises are currently operated, contact any Acapulco travel agency or hotel tour desk. They usually have a scrapbook with pictures and brochures so you can get a good idea about what a cruise entails before booking it.

A Trip to Roqueta Island   Boats from Caletilla Beach to Roqueta Island—a delightful place to snorkel, sunbathe, hike to a lighthouse, or eat lunch—leave every half hour from 10am until the last one returns at 5pm. The cost is $5 round-trip or $7 on a glass-bottom boat (use the same ticket to return on any launch). You may disagree, but I don't think the glass-bottom boat ride is worth the bucks; you circle the bay looking down at a few fish, then a diver swims down to a statue of a madonna. Purchase tickets directly from any boat that's loading or from the **information booth** on Caletilla Beach (☎ **74/82-2389**). The booth also rents inner tubes, small boats, canoes, paddleboats, and beach chairs; it can also arrange waterskiing and scuba diving.

WATER SPORTS & BOAT RENTALS   An hour of **waterskiing** can cost as little as $30 or as much as $60. Caletilla Beach, Puerto Marqués Bay, and Coyuca Lagoon have waterskiing facilities.

Scuba diving costs $40 for 1 1/2 hours of instruction if you book directly with the instructor on Caleta Beach. It costs $45 to $55 if you make arrangements through a hotel or travel agency. Dive trips start around $50 per person for one dive.

Boat rentals are the least expensive on Caletilla Beach, where an information booth rents inner tubes, small boats, canoes, paddleboats, and beach chairs; it can also arrange waterskiing and scuba diving (see "Bay Cruises & Roqueta Island," above).

For **deep-sea fishing** trips, go to the pale-pink building of the boat cooperative opposite the zócalo. Charter fishing trips from here run from $100 to $150 for seven hours, arranged through the **boat cooperative** (☎ **74/82-1099**). Booked through a travel agent or hotel, fishing trips start around $150 to $200 for four people. The fishing license, food, and drink are extra.

Death-Defying Divers

High divers perform at La Quebrada each day at 12:45, 7:30, 8:30, 9:30, and 10:30pm for $4 admission. From a spotlit ledge on the cliffs in view of the lobby bar and restaurant terraces of the Hotel Plaza Las Glorias/El Mirador, each solitary diver plunges into the roaring surf 130 feet below after praying at a small shrine nearby. To the applause of the crowd that has gathered, he then climbs up the rocks and accepts congratulations and gifts of money from onlookers. The best show is at 10:30pm, when they dive with torches.

You can watch from the hotel's terraces for the price of an obligatory drink: $9.50. However, you might try arriving at the lobby bar 30 minutes before a performance and ordering less expensive drinks; they don't always collect the cover charge from people who are already there. You could also get around the cover by having dinner at the hotel's La Perla restaurant. The buffet is $35. Reservations (☎ 74/83-1155) are recommended during the high season.

Parasailing, though not without risks (like landing on a palm tree or a building), can be a fantastic thrill. The pleasure of floating high over the bay hanging from a parachute towed by a motorboat is yours for $45. Most of the parachute rides operate on Condesa Beach.

WATER PARKS

Mágico Mundo Marino. Caleta and Caletilla Beaches. ☎ **74/83-1215** or 74/83-1193. Admission $5 adults, $3 children. Daily 9am–7pm (restaurant, daily 10am–5pm).

It's easy to spend an hour or more at this water park and aquarium. Wander among tanks of sea lions, turtles, and dolphins, as well as aquariums of tropical fish and exhibits of shells. Other attractions include popular movies (many from the United States), a pool with a water slide, an ocean swimming area, jet-ski rentals, two bars, and an attractive terrace restaurant overlooking the water.

Centro Internacional de Convivencia Infantil (CICI). Costera Alemán, at Colón. ☎ **74/84-1970.** Admission $7 adults, $3 children (under 2, free). Daily 10am–6pm.

This sea life and water park east of the Convention Center offers a variety of swimming pools with waves, water slides, and water toboggans. Dolphin shows at noon and 2:30 and 5pm are in English and Spanish. Bird shows are at 11:15am and 1:15 and 3:45pm. Amenities include a cafeteria and restrooms.

GOLF, TENNIS & BULLFIGHTS A round of 18 holes of **golf** at the **Acapulco Princess Hotel** (☎ **74/84-3100**) costs $107 for nonguests and $70 for guests. At the **Club de Golf Acapulco,** off the Costera next to the Convention Center (☎ **74/84-0781** or 74/84-0782), you can play nine holes for $35 or 18 holes for $46.

Tennis at one of the tennis clubs open to the public costs around $11 per hour. Try the **Club de Golf Acapulco** (☎ **74/84-4824** or 74/84-0782), open daily from 7am to 7pm. Singles cost $11 per hour; doubles, $16.

Traditionally termed the Fiesta Brava, the **bullfights** are held during Acapulco's winter season at a ring up the hill from Caletilla Beach. Tickets purchased through travel agencies cost around $40 and usually include transportation to and from your hotel. The festivities begin each Sunday in winter at 5:30pm.

FUERTE DE SAN DIEGO The original Fort San Diego was built in 1616 to protect the town from pirate attacks. At that time, the port was wealthy from its trade with the Philippine Islands, which, like Mexico, were part of Spain's enormous empire. The fort you see was rebuilt after extensive damage by an earthquake in 1776. Today the structure houses the **Museo Histórico de Acapulco** (Acapulco Historical Museum), filled with exhibits that tell the fascinating story of Acapulco, beginning with its role as a port for conquest of the Americas and going through the conversion of the natives to Catholicism and the city's trade with the Orient. The first room has changing shows. Recently, it displayed artifacts from the Aztec Templo Mayor excavation in Mexico City. Other rooms chronicle Acapulco's pre-Hispanic past and the coming of the conquistadores, complete with Spanish armor. There are also displays about the Spanish imperial conquest of the South Seas, for which Acapulco was a base, and a 6-foot-tall model of a Manila *galeón*, the famous ships that sailed back laden with treasures from China. (See "The Spice Bazaar: Acapulco's Colonial Past.") Artifacts from the China trade, including fine chests, vases, textiles, and furniture, are also on exhibit.

To reach the fort, follow Costera Alemán past old Acapulco and the zócalo; the fort is on a hill on the right. You can also reach the fort by a road through a military zone; coming from the main plaza, look for the road on the left (landward) side of the Costera. If you're in good shape, you can climb a cascade of stairs opposite the cargo docks. There is no phone.

Note: Although the fort is open Tuesday through Sunday from 10:30am to 4:40pm, the best time to visit is in the morning, since the "air-conditioning" is minimal. Also, the $3 admission is waved on Sundays.

SHOPPING   Acapulco is not the best place to buy Mexican crafts, but there are a few interesting shops. The best places are at the **Mercado Parazal** (often called the **Mercado de Artesanías**) on Calle Velásquez de León near 5 de Mayo in the downtown zócalo area (when you see Sanborn's, turn right and walk behind it for several blocks). Stall after covered stall of curios from all over the country are here, including silver, embroidered cotton clothing, rugs, pottery, and papier-mâché. Artists paint ceramics with village folk scenes while waiting for patrons. It's a pleasant place to spend a morning or afternoon.

Shopkeepers are vigilant and not too pushy, but they'll test your bargaining mettle. The starting price will be astronomical, and getting the price down may take more time than you have. But as always, acting uninterested often brings down prices in a hurry. Before buying silver here, examine it carefully and be sure it has ".925" stamped on the back (this signifies that the silver is 92.5% pure). The market is open daily from 9am to 8pm.

The **Costera Alemán** is crowded with boutiques selling resort wear. These stores have an abundance of attractive summer clothing at prices lower than those you generally find in the United States. If they have a sale, that's the time to stock up on some incredible bargains. Pay close attention to the quality of zippers; sometimes Mexican zippers are not up to the task. One of the nicest air-conditioned shopping centers on the Costera is **Plaza Bahía,** Costera Alemán 125 (☎ 74/86-2452), which has two stories of shops and small fast-food restaurants, including a tempting pastry shop—Café Paris. The center is located just west of the Fiesta Americana Acapulco Plaza Hotel. In front of the hotel there is a fine silver shop called **Fini.**

WHERE TO STAY

The good downtown hotels are bargains. Crime is a reality in any city, so take normal precautions and use common sense. If you need a room upon arrival, both the Estrella de Oro and Estrella Blanca bus stations have **hotel-reservation services,** operated by the Hotel and Motel Association. The staff here will either call a hotel of your choice or try to find one to suit your requirements. If they make the reservation, you pay them for one night in advance (they'll give you a voucher for the hotel). The drawback is that they can make reservations only at hotels that belong to the association. However, they may allow you to use the telephone to call a nonmember hotel yourself.

If you plan to make reservations before leaving home, be aware that the hotel may quote you a higher price than if you walked in off the street and asked for a room. This practice seems to be waning in favor of more honesty, but be aware that it could happen. If you arrive in person and plan to spend more than a couple of nights, it's sometimes possible to negotiate a lower rate—especially in low season.

Important note about prices: Almost all hotels raise their rates during Christmas and Easter weeks, some even double them.

EAST OF DOWNTOWN NEAR HORNOS BEACH

East of the zócalo along the Costera, most lodgings are beyond budget range, but several area hotels offer budget rates off-season (May through November).

Doubles for Less than $25

Hotel del Valle. Espinoza 150,39300 Acapulco, Gro. ☎ **74/85-8336** or 74/85-8388. 18 rms (all with bath). A/C or FAN. High season, $20 single or double with fan; $23 single or double with A/C. Lower rates available in low season.

This little hotel has a small pool in front, and the beach is only a block away. There is a variety of rooms. Those with air-conditioning have telephones, and those with fans have two twin beds. Six rooms have tiny kitchens and rent for $8 more. To find the hotel, use the Hotel Plaza Las Glorias on the Costera as a landmark. Walk opposite it half a block inland, and you'll see the hotel on the right facing Papagayo Park.

DOWNTOWN—ON LA QUEBRADA

Up the hillside west of the zócalo, near the cliff divers' area known as La Quebrada, lie several busy streets dotted with some of the best budget hotels in town. The disadvantage of this area is that every evening until around 11pm, tour buses roar up and down the hill for the high divers' act.

Doubles for Less than $15

Hotel Angelita. Quebrada 37, 39300 Acapulco, Gro. ☎ **74/83-5734.** 10 rms (all with bath). FAN. $8 single; $12 double.

This three-story white stucco hotel on Quebrada a few blocks west of the zócalo advertises *limpieza absoluta* (absolute cleanliness), and that's what you'll find in this bright place. Simply furnished white rooms have blue-tile baths, and the airy central hallway is lined with plants. The two largest rooms have balconies.

DOWNTOWN—THE ZÓCALO/LA PAZ AREA

There are several budget hotels on La Paz, which runs southwest from the zócalo for several blocks.

Doubles for Less than $15

✪ **Hotel Asturias.** Quebrada 45, 39300 Acapulco, Gro. ☎ **74/83-6548.** 15 rms (all with bath). FAN. $9 single; $14 double.

This little charming budget hotel gets high marks for cleanliness and friendly management. There's also a nice pool that is just big enough to cool off in. Rooms are clean and airy, with tile floors and small tile baths (no toilet seats). Louvered glass windows in each room face the open common walkways of the hotel's interior, letting in light and air—as well as mosquitoes. Each room has two double beds, and some also have a single. To find the hotel from the zócalo, walk up Quebrada three blocks; the hotel is on the left opposite the Secretaría de Finanzas. You will notice it by its blue columns flanking a wide stucco arch over the front porch. Prices are twice those quoted here during Christmas and Easter week.

Hotel Isabel. La Paz 16 Centro, 39300 Acapulco, Gro. ☎ **74/83-9816.** 36 rms (all with bath). FAN. Single $6; double $10.

A short walk from the zócalo, the Isabel offers four stories of plain, clean rooms with marble-tiled floors and tile baths with pull-string showers. Windows are built-in louvered; they have no glass or screens and are not closable. Rooms in the front have small balconies overlooking bustling La Paz. Those in the back have windows on the interior. It stands out a bit from other buildings since it's the only four-story building in the area and has a dark-blue base with white on top.

Hotel María Antonieta. Azueta 17, 39300 Acapulco, Gro. ☎ **74/82-5024.** 30 rms (all with bath). A/C or FAN. $7–$10 single; $10–$20 double.

This well-kept two-story hotel offers rooms off an airy central corridor festooned with plants. Each clean white room comes with two double beds, white spreads and curtains, and louvered glass windows, but only 15 have hot water. Upstairs rooms have larger windows and are brighter. Higher-priced rooms have air-conditioning. The hotel, located at the corner of La Paz, three blocks southwest of the zócalo, has a communal kitchen and dining area.

Doubles for Less than $30

Ⓢ **Hotel California.** La Paz 12, 39300 Acapulco, Gro. ☎ **74/82-2893.** 24 rms (all with bath). A/C or FAN. High season, $10 single; $20 double. Year-round, $22 rm with A/C.

The rooms at the Hotel California are arranged around a paved open patio. All have fans (two are air-conditioned) and are decorated with nice white drapes and Formica furniture. The hotel is a block southwest of the zócalo; two blocks east on the Costera are convenient bus stops.

Hotel Misión. Felipe Valle 112, 39300 Acapulco, Gro. ☎ **74/82-3643.** 27 rms (all with bath). FAN. $14 single; $27 double.

Enter this hotel's plant-filled brick courtyard, shaded by an enormous mango tree, and you'll step back to an earlier Acapulco. This tranquil 19th-century hotel lies two blocks inland from the Costera and the zócalo. The original L-shaped building is at least 100 years old. The rooms have colonial touches such as colorful tile and wrought iron and come simply furnished with one or two beds and minimal hot water. Breakfast is served on the patio. On Thursdays, beginning at 2pm, the specialty is an elaborate pozole spread cooked out on the patio; bowls of the regional favorite cost around $3. Soft drinks and beer are usually available all day.

ON PLAYA LA ANGOSTA

If you stand on the zócalo and face the water, to your right the Costera leads to hotels on the hilly peninsula that curves back into the bay. Their location gives these hotels great views of the city and bay; luxury hotels were built here in the 1950s. On the back side of the peninsula is Playa la Angosta. To get there, take any bus along the Costera, which runs along the base of the peninsula, and get off at the Hotel Avenida. Walk a block to Playa la Angosta; the hotels are side by side on the left facing the bay.

Doubles for Less than $35

Ⓢ **Hotel Villa Romana.** Av. López Mateos 185, Fracc. Las Playas, 39300 Acapulco, Gro. ☎ **74/82-3995.** 9 rms (all with bath). A/C. High season, $27 single; $30 double. Low season, $20 single; $25 double.

With terraces facing the sparkling Playa la Angosta, this is one of the most comfortable inns in the area, ideal for a long stay. Some rooms are tiled and others carpeted, and all have small kitchens with refrigerators. There is a small plant-filled terrace on the second floor with tables and chairs and a fourth-floor pool with a splendid view of the bay.

NEAR PLAYAS CALETA & CALETILLA

The layout of streets on the peninsula that separates the two beaches is confusing, and the disorganized street names and numbers are enough to drive one to tears. A street will be named Avenida López Mateos, but so will the street meeting it at a 90° angle. Some streets have two names, while others have none; many buildings have two street numbers.

The following hotels are easy to find. Simply take a "Caleta" bus to Mágico Mundo Marino, a popular local tourist attraction, and you'll be within walking distance (one to four blocks) of any of the hotels.

Doubles for Less than $45

Hotel Lindavista. Playa Caleta s/n (Apdo. Postal 3), 39300 Acapulco, Gro. ☎ **74/82-5414.** Fax 74/82-2783. 43 rms. A/C or FAN. $42 single or double with fan; $50 single or double with A/C. Rates include breakfast. Ask for a discount. Free parking.

The old-fashioned Lindavista snuggles into the hillside above Caleta Beach. Older American and Mexican couples are drawn to the well-kept rooms, beautiful views, and slow pace of the area here. Most of the rooms have air-conditioning, and those that don't have fans. There are a small pool and a terrace restaurant/bar. Cozy as the Lindavista is, the quoted prices are way too high—negotiate a discount or ask about multinight packages. Coming from Caleta Beach, you'll find the hotel up the hill to the left of the Hotel Caleta.

WHERE TO EAT

THE COSTERA FROM PAPAGAYO PARK TO ICACOS BEACH

Meals for Less than $5

100% Natural. Costera Alemán at Yucatán. ☎ **74/84-4462.** Breakfast $2–$3.50; main courses $3–$6; fruit and vegetable drinks $1.75–$2.50; sandwiches $2.50–$4. Daily 7am–11pm. MEXICAN/VEGETARIAN.

You'll see branches of 100% Natural in just about every area of Acapulco, some with green awnings and others with yellow. Actually those with green signs are rival chains of those with yellow signs, but their menus are quite similar. They both feature soups, salads, sandwiches, fruit, yogurt, shakes, and pasta dishes that please vegetarians and carnivores alike. Although each restaurant is part of a franchise, they're individually owned, so the hours vary; some stay open 24 hours. This branch is on the east end of the Costera between the Romano Days Inn and the Magic Disco.

Antojitos Mayab. Alemán 151. No phone. Main courses $2–$5; comida corrida $3. Daily noon–midnight (comida corrida served noon–5pm). YUCATÁN.

A cool, clean little eatery, this place has carved its own niche among Acapulco's quick-food places, offering a few specialties from the Yucatán area. Nowhere else in town will you find tacos filled with cochinta pibil or escabiche, in addition to the usual fillings of chicken or shrimp. Antojitos include turkey *panuchos* (a small flat corn cake topped with turkey, onions, beans, and cheese), empanadas, and tostadas. Yucatecan tamales are served after 5pm. You'll find this restaurant opposite the new blue La Gran Plaza shopping center, next to McDonald's and half a block from the Ritz Hotel.

Meals for Less than $10

Italianissimo. Diana Circle, Costera Alemán. ☎ **74/84-0052.** Main courses $5–$11. Daily noon–midnight. ITALIAN.

The restaurant makes dishes with pizzazz, and all the pastas are homemade. The Italian-style decor is complemented by cool gray marble floors, plus it's air-conditioned. Try the scampi Stroganoff with vodka sauce. For appetizers, try the Caesar salad or mussels in white-wine sauce. The new location, beside/behind the Aca-Joe clothing store at the Diana traffic circle, is easy to miss if you don't know it's there.

Restaurant Cocula. Costera Alemán 10. ☎ **74/84-5079.** Breakfast $3–$5; main courses $3–$8. Daily 7am–1am; happy hour 6pm until closing. MEXICAN.

You can dine on the patio out front or on one of the two levels of terraces. Appetizers include guacamole, black-bean soup, and watercress salad. Grilled meats are the specialty, and you can choose from among red snapper, shrimp, broiled chicken, quail, spiced pork sausage, ribs, shish kebab, and mixed grill. The restaurant is on the inland side of the east end of the Costera, across from Acapulco 2000.

Restaurant Fersato's. Costera Alemán 44. ☎ **74/84-3949.** Breakfast $2.50–$4; main courses $3–$8. Daily 7am–midnight; happy hour 7–10pm. MEXICAN.

The big dining room at Fersato's, beneath the tile roof and stone arches, is decorated with colorfully clad tables. There's an extensive menu of authentic Mexican food, plus seafood, chicken, and steak. Try the mole, the black beans, or the mixiotes with chicken or lamb wrapped in maguey leaves. The restaurant is on the inland side of the Costera across from the State of Guerrero Cultural Center, CICI, and the Acapulco Dolphins Hotel.

La Tortuga. Lomas del Mar 5. ☎ **74/84-6985.** Main courses $3.50–$7. Daily 10am–1am. MEXICAN.

This small, congenial outdoor restaurant with cloth-covered tables occupies two greenery-filled terraces shaded by enormous mango trees. The extensive menu offers a good sampling of food from several Mexican regions, such as Oaxaca tamales, chicken mixiotes, and tortilla soup. Specialties include shrimp-filled crêpes and the Tortuga combination, which has grilled meat, tostadas, enchiladas, stuffed peppers, guacamole, beans, and chips. You can also select from one of the 13 kinds of tortas.

To find this place, walk half a block inland from the Costera at the corner of Lomas del Mar and across from the Hotel Torre de Acapulco, which is next door to the better-known El Presidente.

DOWNTOWN/ZÓCALO AREA

To explore this area, start right at the zócalo and stroll west along Juárez. After about three blocks you'll come to Azueta, lined with small seafood cafés and streetside stands selling fresh oysters and clams on the half shell.

Meals for Less than $5

La Granja del Pingue. Juárez 10. ☎ **74/83-5339.** Breakfast $2; main courses $2–$4; lunch special $3. Daily 7am–10pm. INTERNATIONAL.

This restaurant offers an eclectic menu that includes burgers and fries, Tex-Mex chili, and a lunch special usually in the American home-cooking genre. It also claims to have the best coffee in town, with free refills. The dining area, an attractive shaded patio hung with piñatas, is prime gathering ground for foreigners in town and a great place to exchange paperbacks. This place is two blocks west of the zócalo.

San Carlos. Juárez 5. ☎ **74/82-6459.** Breakfast special $2–$5; main courses $2–$4; comida corrida $2.50. Daily 7:30am–11pm (comida corrida served 1–6pm). MEXICAN.

Western-style food such as charcoal-broiled chicken and fish is served at chuck-wagon prices on the front patio of this place or in its open, fan-cooled dining room. Colorful tablecloths brighten this cheery café a few steps west of the zócalo. On Sunday and Monday one of the many specialties is chicken mole; on Thursday and Saturday they feature pozole. There are at least 11 main-course choices for the comida corrida.

Meals for Less Than $10

✪ **El Amigo Miguel.** Juárez 31, at Azueta. ☎ **74/83-6981.** Main courses $3–$8. Daily 10:30am–9:30pm. MEXICAN/SEAFOOD.

Red tablecloths and fish on the wall decorate this simple restaurant three blocks west of the zócalo. Fresh seafood is king here. The large open-air dining room is usually brimming with seafood lovers. Try the stuffed crab, snapper, or baby shark. To accommodate the crowds, El Amigo II is open directly across the street.

✪ **Mariscos Pipo.** Almirante Breton 3. ☎ **74/83-8801** or 74/82-2237. Main courses $4–$12. Daily 11am–8pm. SEAFOOD.

Diners can look at photographs of Old Acapulco on the walls while sitting in the airy dining room of this place, decorated with hanging nets, fish, glass buoys, and shell lanterns. The English-language menu lists a wide array of seafood, including ceviche, lobster, octopus, crayfish, and baby-shark quesadillas. This local favorite is five blocks west of the zócalo on Breton, just off the Costera, behind the large curved building with "edifício stibadores" in sky-high green letters.

Sanborn's. Costera Alemán and Escudero. ☎ **74/82-6167.** Breakfast $3.50–$5; main courses $3.50–$8. Daily 7:30am–11pm. AMERICAN/MEXICAN.

The best of the American-style restaurants, Sanborn's offers a cool dining area. Reminiscent of upscale dining rooms of the 1950s, it features American colonial decor, brass light fixtures, and well-padded booths. It's especially good for breakfast, though it also has good enchiladas, club sandwiches, burgers, *sincronizadas* (ham and cheese melted between corn tortillas), pastas, and fancier fare such as fish and steaks. Beer, wine, and cocktails are served. For an inexpensive snack, buy pastries to go at the store's bakery. Upstairs are clean bathrooms.

You'll find this branch two blocks east of the zócalo on the Costera. The other Sanborn's is in a high-rise building on the Costera at Condesa Beach near the El Presidente Hotel (☎ 74/84-4465).

CALETA/CALETILLA BEACH AREA

The area around Caleta and Caletilla beaches used to be rather down-at-the-heels, but not long ago, the municipal authorities pumped lots of money into public facilities here. Now the beaches have nice shady palapas, clean sand, and fine palm trees. Three buildings have been built to house *vestidores* and *regarderas* (changing rooms, showers, and lockers) and restaurants.

Little dining places line the outer periphery of the buildings. To find a good meal, wander along the rows of restaurants, looking for busy spots where people are eating (*not* just sipping drinks). Study menus, which will either be displayed or handed to you on request. Although the restaurants may tend to look all the same, you'll be surprised at the differences in price. *Filet de pescado* (fish filet) might be $4 at one place and twice as much at another; beer can cost anywhere from $1 to $2. Some places offer inexpensive fixed-price meals for around $2 to $3.

Worth a Splurge

✪ **Madeiras.** Carretera Escénica 33. ☎ **74/84-4378.** Reservations required. Fixed-price dinner $28. Daily 7–11pm (two seatings: 7–8:30pm and 9–11pm). MEXICAN/CONTINENTAL.

Enjoy an elegant meal and a fabulous view of glittering Acapulco Bay at night at Madeiras, east of town on the scenic highway before the Las Brisas Hotel. The several small dining areas have ceiling fans and are open to the evening breezes. If you arrive before your table is ready, have a drink in the comfortable lounge. Selections might include roast quail stuffed with tropical fruits; or fish cooked in orange sauce. There are such old favorites as filet mignon, beef Stroganoff, and frogs' legs in garlic and white wine. Wines are reasonably priced if you stick to the Mexican labels.

ACAPULCO AFTER DARK
SPECIAL ATTRACTIONS

The **"Gran Noche Mexicana"** given by the **Acapulco Ballet Folklórico** is held in the plaza of the Convention Center every Tuesday, Thursday, and Saturday night at 8pm. With dinner and open bar the show costs $45; general admission (including three drinks) is $20. Call for reservations (☎ **74/84-7050**) or consult a local travel agency.

Another excellent **Mexican fiesta/folkloric dance show,** which includes *voladores* (flying pole dancers) from Papantla, is held at Marbella Plaza near the Continental Plaza Hotel on the Costera on Monday, Wednesday, and Friday at 7pm. The $35 fee covers the show, buffet, open bar, taxes, and gratuities. Make reservations through a travel agency.

Many major hotels also host Mexican fiestas and other theme nights that include dinner and entertainment. Consult a travel agency for information.

NIGHTCLUBS & DISCOS

Acapulco is more famous for its nightclubs than for its beaches. The problem is that the clubs open and close with shocking regularity, making it very difficult to give specific recommendations that will remain accurate. Some general tips will help. Every club seems to have a cover charge around $20 in high season, $10 in low season, and drinks can cost anywhere from $2.50 to $7.

Now that Acapulco has so many discos, many periodically waive their cover charge or offer some other promotion to attract customers. Another trend is to have a big cover charge with an open bar. Call the disco or look for promotional material around hotel reception areas, at travel desks or concierge booths, and in local publications.

No Mexican resort would be complete without a **Carlos 'n Charlie's** (Costera Alemán 999; ☎ **74/84-1285** or 74/84-0039). You'll find the usual posters, silly sayings, bric-a-brac, sassy waiters, and menu humor ("splash" for seafood, "moo" for beef). The food is good and the place always packed. The place is on the Costera east of the Diana traffic circle and across from the Hotel Las Torres Gemelas (which is next door to the more visible Presidente Hotel and near the Fiesta Americana Condesa Hotel).

In addition, the high-rise hotels have their own bars and sometimes have discos. Informal lobby or poolside cocktail bars often offer live entertainment.

Note: When the managers of local discos say no shorts, they mean no shorts for men; they welcome women in them.

Acapulco also has its own spectacular cultural and convention center, the **Centro Acapulco,** on the eastern reaches of the bay between Condesa and Icacos beaches. Designed with extravagant Mexican taste, the centro has rolling lawns, and the entrance is via a grand promenade framing a central row of pools and high-spouting fountains. Within the modern center are several forms of entertainment, including a mariachi bar, piano bar, disco, movie theater, live theater, café, nightclub, several restaurants, and outdoor performance areas.

Baby-O. Costera Alemán. ☎ **74/84-7474.** Cover $15–$20.

Baby-O's can be very selective about who they let in when it's crowded. Your chances of getting in here increase greatly if you're young, pretty, and female. Your next best shot is to be older, affluent looking, and male. Across from the Romano Days Inn, this intimate disco has a small dance floor surrounded by several tiers of tables and sculpted, cavelike walls. It even has a hot tub and breakfast area. Drinks run $4 to $5.

Extravaganzza. Carretera Escénica. ☎ **74/84-7154** or 74/84-7164. Cover $15–$20.

If you have something trendy to wear, you might venture into this snazzy neo-deco chrome-and-neon extravaganza, perched on the side of the mountain between Los Rancheros Restaurant and La Vista Shopping Center. You can't miss the neon lights. The plush, dimly lit interior dazzles patrons with a sunken dance floor and panoramic view of Acapulco Bay. The door attendants wear tuxedos, so don't expect to get in wearing shorts, jeans, T-shirts, sneakers, or sandals. It opens nightly at 10:30pm; fireworks blast off at 3am. Call to find out if reservations are needed. National (as opposed to imported) drinks run $5 to $6.

Fantasy. Carretera Escénica. ☎ **74/84-6727** or 74/84-6764. Cover $15–$20.

This club has a fantastic bay view and sometimes waives the cover charge as a promotion. Periodically during the evening it puts on a good show with green lasers, which it also shoots out across the bay. The dress code does not permit shorts, jeans, T-shirts, or sandals. Reservations are recommended. Located in the La Vista Shopping Center, it's open nightly 10:30pm to 4am. Drinks go for $6.

The News. Costera Alemán. ☎ **74/84-5902.** Cover (including open bar) $15–$20.

The booths and love seats ringing the vast dance floor can seat 1,200, so this disco can double as a concert hall. But though high-tech in style, it's laid-back and user-friendly. It doesn't even have a dress code! Across the street from the Hyatt Regency, it opens at 10:30pm nightly.

INLAND TO TAXCO

Taxco, Mexico's "Silver Capital" is only a 2^1/$_2$- to 3-hour drive from Acapulco using the new toll road. The colonial charm of the picturesque hillside village and its museums and hundreds of shops selling silver make it an ideal day trip. Many people find the city so charming that they regret not planning to stay a couple of nights at least. Travel agents in Acapulco can arrange the trip either for the day or overnight. See chapter 12, "Side Trips from Mexico City," for a complete description of this fascinating village.

3 Puerto Escondido

230 miles SE of Acapulco, 150 miles NW of Salina Cruz, 50 miles NW of Puerto Angel

Puerto Escondido (PWER-toh ehs-cohn-DEE-doh) translates to "Hidden Port." Although this town of 50,000 has been "discovered," touristic development here hasn't yet transformed it. Anyone who wandered into Acapulco half a century ago might have found a similar scene and a similar ambience. So catch Puerto Escondido before it's gone forever. The lush palm-lined beach off the town center is one of the most beautiful in the country, with colorful boats pulled up on the sand—it makes for the kind of scene long since gone from more developed resorts.

When looking out on the Bahía Principal and its beach, you'll see to your left the eastern end of the bay, consisting of a small beach, Playa Marinero, followed by rocks jutting into the sea. Beyond this is Playa Zicatela, which attracts surfers like a magnet. By way of contrast, the western side of the bay, to your right, is about a mile long with low green hills (and a lighthouse) descending to meet a long stretch of fine sand. The coastline is slowly being developed. Where there was once nothing, Zicatela Beach now has restaurants, bungalows, surf shops, and hotels, although the construction there is well back from the shoreline. Westward, the beaches are not quite as accessible by land, but hotels are overcoming this by constructing beach clubs reached by steep private roads and jeep shuttles.

Laziness is a state of mind here—sipping a cool bottle of something refreshing, feeling the sea breeze, watching the pelicans soar and wheel and then come down to race across the surface of the water. Duck into a fan-cooled restaurant by day or return in the cool evening and find informal groups discussing the day's events.

GETTING THERE & DEPARTING   By Plane   AeroMorelos has several daily flights between Oaxaca and Puerto Escondido flying a 40-passenger turboprop. **Aerovega** also serves the route to and from Oaxaca with one, and sometimes two, daily morning flights using a five-passenger AeroCommander. Tickets for both these lines are handled by Turismo Rodimar (see below). **Mexicana** (☎ **958/2-0098**) flies from Mexico City to Puerto Escondido five days per week.

If space on flights to Puerto Escondido is booked solid, you have the option of flying Aeroméxico into the Huatulco airport six days per week. This is an especially viable option if your destination is Puerto Angel, which lies between Puerto Escondido and Huatulco but is closer to the Huatulco airport. There is frequent bus service between the three destinations.

Aerotransportes Terrestres sells colectivo transportation tickets to the airport through **Turismo Rodimar** near the east end of the pedestrians-only zone (☎ **958/ 2-0734** or tel/fax 958/2-0737). The price is $2.25 one way and includes pickup at your hotel.

By Bus   Buses are frequent between Acapulco, Oaxaca, and south along the coast to and from Huatulco and Pochutla, the transit hub for Puerto Angel. Puerto Escondido's several bus stations are all within a three-block area. For **Gacela** and **Estrella Blanca,** the station is just north of the coastal highway where Perez Gasga crosses it. First-class buses go from here to Pochutla and Huatulco hourly, and almost hourly to Acapulco and Zihuatanejo. Five daily direct buses with assigned seats go to Acapulco, one to Zihuatanejo, and two to Mexico City. The most comfortable bus to Mexico City (12 hours) is the deluxe Futuro de Lujo bus leaving at 7 and 10pm.

A block north at Hidalgo and Primera Poniente is **Transportes Oaxaca Istmo.** The office is in a small restaurant. Several buses daily leave for Pochutla (1 hour),

Salina Cruz (5 hours), or Oaxaca (10 hours via Salina Cruz). **Autotransportes Turisticas** has twice daily first-class service to Oaxaca, via Pochutla (7 hours). The terminal for **Lineas Unidas, Estrella del Valle,** and **Oaxaca Pacífico** is two blocks farther down on Hidalgo, just past 3rd Oriente. All buses go to Oaxaca via Pochutla; four are ordinario, and three are directo buses, leaving at 8:15am, and 10:15 and 10:45pm.

Cristóbal Colón buses, Primera Norte 207, serve Salina Cruz, Tuxtla Gutiérrez, and San Cristóbal de las Casas. It also has two first-class buses to Oaxaca, via Salina Cruz, at 4 and 9pm. Here you can enjoy an air-conditioned waiting room.

By Car From Oaxaca, Highway 175 via Pochutla is the least bumpy road. The 150-mile trip takes five to six hours. Highway 200 from Acapulco is also a good road. Don't attempt to come from Oaxaca via Zimatlán—about 100 miles of it is unpaved and in poor condition.

From Salina Cruz to Puerto Escondido is a four-hour drive, past the Bahías de Huatulco and the turnoff for Puerto Angel. The road is paved but can be rutty in the rainy season.

ORIENTATION **Arriving** The airport is about $2^{1}/_{2}$ miles from the center of town near Playa Bacocho. Prices for the Aerotransportes Terrestres minibus to hotels are posted: $3.25 per person. Arriving by bus, you will be deposited at one of the terminals described above. Minibuses from Pochutla or Huatulco will let you off anywhere en route, including the spot where Perez Gasga leads down to the pedestrians-only zone.

Information The **State Tourist Office, SEDETUR** (☎ **958/2-0175**), is about a half mile from the airport, at the corner of Carretera Costera and Bulevar Benito Juárez. It's open Monday through Friday from 9am to 2pm and 5 to 8pm and Saturday from 10am to 1pm. A kiosk at the airport is open for incoming flights, and another, near the west end of the paved tourist zone, is open Monday through Saturday from 9am to 2pm and 5 to 8pm.

City Layout Puerto Escondido is oriented roughly east-west, with the long Zicatela Beach turning sharply southeast. Residential areas lying behind (east of) Zicatela Beach tend to have unpaved streets, while the older town (with paved streets) lies north of the Carretera Costera (Highway 200). The town streets were recently numbered, with Avenida Oaxaca the dividing line between east (oriente) and west (poniente), and Avenida Hidalgo the divider between north (norte) and south (sur). Formerly they were named after historic dates and famous people. But the streets are not marked, so finding your way involves a bit of guesswork and asking directions.

South of this is the tourist zone, through which Avenida Perez Gasga makes a loop. Part of this loop is a paved pedestrian-only zone (or PZ) along which are found many hotels, shops, restaurants, travel agencies, and other services. Actually, in the morning, taxis, delivery trucks, and private vehicles are allowed. But at noon it becomes a closed zone, and chains are fastened at each end. However, motorbikes and bicycles get in, so don't become complacent.

Avenida Perez Gasga angles down from the Highway at the east end, and on the west, where the PZ terminates, it climbs in a wide northward curve to cross the highway, after which it becomes Avenida Oaxaca.

The **beaches,** Playa Principal in the center of town and Marinero and Zicatela, southeast of the town center, are interconnected, and it's easy to walk from one to the other, crossing behind the separating rocks. Puerto Angelito, Carrizalillo, and Bacocho beaches are west of town and can be reached by road or boat. Surfers find

---

Eco-Tours & Other Unusual Explorations

The Turismo Rodimar Travel Agency, on the landward side just inside the PZ (☎ **958/2-0734** or 958/2-0737; open daily 7:30am to 10pm), is an excellent source of information and can arrange all types of tours and travel. Manager Gaudencio Díaz speaks English. He can arrange individualized tours or formal ones such as **Michael Malone's Hidden Voyages Ecotours.** Malone, a Canadian ornithologist, takes you on a dawn or sunset trip to **Manialtepec Lagoon,** a bird-filled mangrove lagoon. The cost is $25 to $30 and includes a stop on a secluded beach for a swim. Another all-day tour to **Chacahua Lagoon National Park** is $30. These are true eco-tours—small groups touching the environment lightly.

An interesting and slightly out-of-the-ordinary endeavor is **Jorge Perez' Aventura Submarina,** located "on the strip" (Zicatela Beach, Calle del Morro s/n, in the Acuario building near the Cafecito; ☎ **958/2-1026**). Jorge, who speaks fluent English and is a certified scuba-dive instructor, guides individuals or small groups of qualified divers along the Coco trench, just offshore. He also arranges surface activities such as deep-sea fishing, surfing, trips to lesser known yet nearby swimming beaches, and dirt bike tours into the mountains. If you want to write ahead, contact him at Apdo. Postal 159, Puerto Escondido, Oax. 71980.

Anna Marquez, also well known in the area as a nature tour leader, can be found at the Hotel Flor de María (☎ **958/2-0536**).

Fishermen keep their colorful *pangas* (small boats) on the beach beside the PZ. A **fisherman's tour** around the coastline in his boat will cost about $35, but a ride to Zicatela or Puerto Angelito beaches will cost only $3. Most hotels offer or will gladly arrange tours to meet your needs.

Zicatela Beach's big curling waves are the best for board surfing. Playa Bacocho hosts most of the expensive hotels.

Getting Around   Almost everything is within walking distance of the pedestrian zone. Taxis cost no more than $1.50 to $4.50 to beaches or anywhere in town. Mountain bikes ($9/day or $2.25/hour) and Honda motor bikes ($33.50/day or $7.75/hour) can be rented at Mango Club, Av. Perez Gasga 605-E, on your right just as you enter the PZ on the east. For intrepid walkers, it is now possible to walk beside the sea from the Playa Principal to the tiny beach of Puerto Angelito. However, I recommend the hike only for the hardy because it's rather arduous, and the sun beats down unrelentingly. Carry water and wear a hat!

FAST FACTS: PUERTO ESCONDIDO

Area Code   The telephone area code is 958.

Currency Exchange   Near the middle of the PZ is a money-exchange office, Puerto Bahias, open Monday through Saturday from 9am to 2pm and 5 to 8pm.

Safety   Crime in Puerto Escondido is on the rise, and beach muggings are not unknown. Don't leave your belongings unattended on the beach and deposit other valuables in the hotel safe. Positively do not take a midnight stroll down the deserted beach and be careful even during the day. And respect the power of waves and undertow. Drownings occur all too frequently.

Seasons   Seasons vary from business to business. Most, however, consider high season to be mid-December through January, then again before, during, and after Easter week. A third high season occurs in July and August, during school and business vacations.

Telephone   There are numerous businesses offering long-distance telephone service, and several offer credit card convenience. One is several doors west of the Hotel Las Palmas (near the center of the PZ) and is open daily from 9am to 10pm. Another is at the west end of the PZ (beach side) and is open daily from 7:30am to 10pm.

SWIMMING, SURFING & OTHER THINGS TO DO

BEACHES   Playa Principal and Playa Marinero, both adjacent to the town center and on a deep bay, are the best swimming beaches. Zicatela beach adjoins Playa Marinero and extends southeasterly for several miles. The surfing part of Zicatela, with large curling waves, is about 1 mile from the town center.

Barter with one of the fishermen on the main beach for a ride to **Puerto Angelito** and other small coves just west of town, where the swimming is safe and the pace decidedly calmer than in town. Both places have clear blue water excellent for snorkeling and can provide equipment; palapas and hammock rentals are available for $1 per day. Enjoy fresh fish, tamales, and other Mexican dishes cooked right at the beach by local entrepreneurs. **Playa Bacocho** is on a shallow cove farther to the northwest and is best reached by taxi or boat.

Warning: Swimming at a beach that fronts on open sea is risky. The waves (and undertow) are unpredictable—you're floating peacefully in shoulder-deep water when suddenly the water sinks to knee level and before you can blink it's crashing over your head. Don't follow the surfers' example; they have surfboards to cling to, and they know waves and tides. Despite big warning signs, there are several drownings every year. Swim at the beach in town or at other sheltered beaches in bays and coves.

SURFING   Zicatela Beach, 1 1/2 miles southeast of Puerto Escondido's town center, is a world-class surf spot. A **surfing competition** in August, and **Fiesta Puerto Escondido,** held for at least 10 days each November, feature Puerto Escondido's well-known surfing waves. The tourism office can supply exact dates and details.

SEEING NESTING RIDLEY TURTLES   The beaches around Puerto Escondido and Puerto Angel are nesting grounds for the endangered Ridley turtle. Tourists can sometimes see the turtles laying eggs or observe the hatchlings trekking to the sea.

Escobilla beach near Puerto Escondido and another near Barra de la Cruz beach near Puerto Angel seem to be favored among other nesting grounds for Ridley turtles. Furthermore, in 1991 the Mexican government established the **Centro Mexicano la Tortuga,** known locally as the Turtle Museum, for the study and life-enhancement of the turtle. Present are examples of all species of marine turtles living in Mexico, plus six species of fresh water turtles and two species of land turtles. The center is located on Mazunte Beach, near the town of the same name. Hours are 9am to 5pm daily, and entry is $2.25. Buses go to Mazunte from Puerto Angel (50¢) about every half hour, and a taxi will take you there for $3.50 to $4.50. You can fit this in with a trip to Zipolite Beach, the next one closer to Puerto Angel.

SHOPPING   The PZ sports a row of tourist shops selling straw hats, postcards, and Puerto Escondido T-shirts plus a few stores featuring Guatemalan and Oaxacan clothing as well as art and souvenirs from various parts of the country. Interspersed among the hotels, restaurants, and shops are pharmacies and minimarkets selling basic necessities.

WHERE TO STAY

Even the more expensive hotels have their share of mosquitoes, so bring insect repellent.

DOUBLES FOR LESS THAN $15

✪ **Castillo de Los Reyes.** Av. Perez Gasga s/n, 71980 Puerto Escondido, Oax. ☎ **958/2-0442.** 16 rms (all with bath). FAN. High season, $11.50 single; $13 double. Low season, $10 single; $11.50 double.

Don Fernando, the proprietor at Castillo de los Reyes, has a gift for making his guests feel at home. Guests converse around tables on a shady patio near the office. Your white-walled room may have a special touch—perhaps a gourd mask or carved coconut hanging over the bed. There's hot water, and the rooms are shaded from the sun by aging palms. It's on your left as you go up the hill on Perez Gasga after leaving the pedestrian zone (you can also enter Perez Gasga off Highway 200).

DOUBLES FOR LESS THAN $20

Hotel San Juan. Felipe Merklin 503, 71980 Puerto Escondido, Oax. ☎ **958/2-0336** or 2-0518. Fax 958/2-0612. 26 rms (all with bath). FAN. High season, $14.50 single; $18 double. Low season, $11.25 single; $14.50 double. Free parking; limited.

The San Juan is a good budget choice in the area, located at the top of the hill, just off Avenida Perez Gasga and near the Hotel Crucero. It's easy to get to as you come into town on the bus or by car, but the return trip on foot up the hill after a hot day at the beach is rough. A new restaurant (open only during the high season) has been added to the pretty patio on the right as you enter. The sparkling clean and bright but spare rooms have painted concrete floors. Each has either two double beds and one twin bed or a double and a twin bed, small closets, and windows with screens. Second- and third-floor rooms have fantastic views from the balcony walkway. *Note:* The hotel will not quote rates or make reservations by phone.

Hotel Nayar. Av. Gasga 407, 71980 Puerto Escondido, Oax. ☎ **958/2-0113** or 2-0319. Fax. 958/2-0547. 41 rms (all with bath). FAN TV. High season, $15 single; $19 double. Low season, $11 single; $15 double. Free parking.

Enter the Nayar via a cobbled drive shaded by enormous palms. There's parking for several cars along the entryway. On the left is a nice-size pool. This is an old-fashioned, rambling two-story hotel with clean but dated rooms, each with either one or two double beds or two twin beds. All have balconies, but only upper-story rooms have views. Fifteen rooms have air-conditioning ($5.50 extra). It's past the PZ, up the hill where Avenida Perez Gasga turns north.

DOUBLES FOR LESS THAN $30

✪ **Hotel Las Palmas.** Av. Perez Gasga s/n, 71980 Puerto Escondido, Oax. ☎ **958/2-0230** or 958/2-0303. 38 rms (all with bath). FAN. High season, $20 single; $25 double. Low season, $15 single; $20 double.

This traditional favorite has an overgrown courtyard surrounded by a three-story U-shaped building in the center of the tourist zone facing the ocean and the beach. Each nicely furnished room has a double and a twin bed covered with tasteful foot-loomed bedspreads and matching drapes. The windows and glass doors offer two choices: You either shut all the curtains for privacy (no natural light) or leave them open and have natural light but no privacy. The louvered windows are screenless. The best rooms are on the second and third floors, facing the sea. While the food isn't particularly outstanding, the hotel's beachfront restaurant location is a comfortable place to dawdle away the hours watching the beach scene. Beside the restaurant is a comfy shaded bar with lounge chairs where guests become engrossed in thick novels.

Hotel Loren. Av. Gasga 507, 71980 Puerto Escondido, Oax. ☎ **958/2-0057.** Fax 958/2-0591. 23 rms (all with bath). FAN. High season, $25 single or double. Low season, $20 single or double. Free parking; enclosed.

This four-story hotel faces an open interior patio with an inviting pool. The best views are from small private balconies on the upper levels (no elevators). Rooms are immaculate but sparsely furnished, each with two double beds, a chair, and a table. The hotel is tucked in a shady bend of Avenida Perez Gasga past the west end of the pedestrian zone (it can also be reached off Highway 200), around the corner from both the Hotel Nayar and the Hotel Paraíso Escondido.

Hotel Rocamar. Av. Perez Gasga 601, 71980 Puerto Escondido, Oax. ☎ **958/2-0339.** 18 rms (all with bath). A/C or FAN. High season, $23 single or double with fan. Low season with fan, $20 single or double; with A/C $25 single; $29 double.

Although the Rocamar is across the street from the beach, you'll be at the west end of the pedestrian zone, only seconds away from the surf on the city's Playa Principal and surrounded by restaurants. Each of the tidy rooms has screens on the windows, a shower, and a fan (15 rooms) or air-conditioning (3 rooms).

DOUBLES FOR LESS THAN $40

✪ **Hotel Flor de María.** Playa Marinero, 71980 Puerto Escondido, Oax. ☎ and fax **958/ 2-0536.** 24 rms (all with bath). FAN. $30 single; $35 double.

This is a real find. Canadians María and Lino Francato built their cheery three-story hotel facing the ocean, which you can see from the rooftop and common walkways linking rooms in the upper stories. Built around a garden courtyard, each room is colorfully decorated with Lino's beautiful trompe l'oeil still-lifes and landscapes— he's even painted some of the headboards. All room have windows facing the outdoors, double beds with orthopedic matresses, and small safes. On the roof you'll find great views, a small pool, shaded hammock terrace, and an open-air bar (open 5–9pm) with evening happy hour specials and a TV that receives American channels. This is a great place to be for sunset. The first-floor restaurant is highly recommended (see "Where to Eat," below). The hotel is a half block from Marinero Beach on an unnamed street at the eastern end of the beach.

WORTH A SPLURGE

✪ **Hotel Santa Fe.** Calle del Morro (Apdo. Postal 96), 71980 Puerto Escondido, Oax. ☎ **958/ 2-0170.** Fax 958/2-0260. 51 rms, 8 bungalows (all with bath). A/C TEL. High season, $65 single; $75 double; $85 bungalow. Low season, $49 single; $56.25 double. Free parking.

This very good hotel is about half a mile southeast of the town center off Highway 200. It is located just where Marinero and Zicatela beaches join and overlooks a rock outcropping that's a prime sunset-watching spot. The hacienda-style buildings have tiled stairs and archways laden with blooming bougainvillea. The ample rooms have large tile baths, colonial furnishings, handwoven fabrics, Guerrero pottery lamps, and both air-conditioning and ceiling fans. There's a small pool in the central patio. Some rooms don't have telephones, but who are you going to call anyway? Bungalows are next to the hotel, and each comes equipped with a living room, a kitchen, and a bedroom with two double beds. Rates quoted in pesos are much higher than those quoted in dollars. Park in front of the hotel entrance.

WHERE TO EAT
MEALS FOR LESS THAN $5

Bananas. Av. Perez Gasga s/n. ☎ **958/2-0005.** Breakfast $1.75–$2.25; sandwiches $1.75– $3; breakfast buffet $2.75. Daily 7:30am–12:30am. MEXICAN.

You'll see this bamboo-and-thatch-roofed two-story restaurant/bar at the eastern entrance to the PZ. Breakfast includes fresh yogurt, crêpes, and fresh-fruit drinks. A range of light appetizers includes quesadillas with potato or squash flowers, tacos, and stuffed tortillas. Happy hour is every night from 6 to 8pm, with live music in high season.

✪ **Carmen's La Patisserie.** Playa Marinero. No phone. Pastries 50¢–$1.25; sandwiches $1.50–$2. Daily 7am–7pm. FRENCH PASTRY/SANDWICHES/COFFEE.

Dan and Carmen are the proprietors of this tiny-but-excellent café/bakery that has a steady and loyal clientele. Carmen's baked goods are positively unforgettable. By 8am on one weekday there was only one mango creme roll left, and other items were disappearing fast. The coffee, perhaps the best in town, has a flavor and fullness that keeps you asking for refills. Taped international music provides a soothing background, and a paperback exchange creates another reason to linger. Fruit, granola, and sandwiches (croissant or whole wheat) round out the menu. Dan and Carmen also provide space for an English-speaking AA group here.

La Patisserie is near, and across the street from, the Hotel Flor de María. A second shop, El Cafecito (open 6am) is on Zicatela Beach, near Bruno's Surf Shop. Surfers and observers gather here to critique each other.

✪ **María's Restaurant.** In the Hotel Flor de María, Playa Marinero. ☎ **958/2-0536.** Breakfast $2.25; main courses $3.50–$5.50. Daily 8–11am, noon–3pm and 6–10pm. INTERNATIONAL.

Probably the best restaurant in Puerto Escondido, meals are served in the first floor open-air dining room of this beachside hotel. There's a regular daily menu as well as one featuring daily specials that include María Francato's homemade pasta dishes. What's available on either menu is based on what's fresh that day. María's is at the east end of Playa Marinero, about half a block up a short unnamed street from the beach.

Taquería Fiord. Av. Perez Gasga. No phone. Tacos, quesadillas, and sandwiches $1–$3.50. High season, daily 7am–midnight; low season, daily 3–11pm. MEXICAN.

Take a seat on a backless chair at one of the uncovered wooden tables here and try the food. Chances are you'll forget what the place looks like once you've tried an inexpensive taco de pollo on a whole-wheat tortilla with its generous portion of chicken, sliced onion, fresh cilantro, lime, and salsa. The restaurant is at the east end of the PZ, on the landward side.

MEALS FOR LESS THAN $10

✪ **Art & Harry's Bar and Grill.** Av. Morro s/n. No phone. Seafood $2.25–$6.75; steaks $8–$11. Daily 10am–10pm. SEAFOOD/STEAKS.

Located about three-fourths of a mile southeast of the Hotel Santa Fe on the road fronting Zicatela Beach, is the robust watering hole where the sun seems to go down in a more spectacular fashion if you are eating one of their monster shrimp cocktails, or savoring fork-tender pieces of budget- and diet-busting grilled beef. A few hours spent here in the late afternoon and early evening watching the surfers and tourists, the sun as it sinks, and the resident cat (no dogs allowed) will give you a sense of Puerto Escondido.

Nautilus. Av. Perez Gasga. No phone. Breakfast $1.75–$2.75; main courses $3.50–$9; comida corrida $5. Daily 8am–midnight. INTERNATIONAL/SEAFOOD.

Here at the west end of the pedestrian zone, you may hear exhilarating mariachi music, Billie Holiday, or Patsy Cline coming from the tape player. From the second-story dining room there's a fabulous bay view for watching fishermen and brown pelicans. Breakfast selections include German and continental dishes. Usually there are several tourist specials featuring soup through dessert in various price ranges. For splurge specialties, try *huachinango* or vegetarian dishes Hindu style with fruit, wine, and curry. Pastas are more moderately priced, as well as chicken and a small selection of vegetarian dishes.

Restaurant Santa Fe. In the Hotel Santa Fe, Calle del Morro s/n. ☎ **958/2-0170.** Breakfast $2–$4; main courses $4–$12. Daily 7am–10:30pm. INTERNATIONAL.

The atmosphere here is cool and breezy, with great views of the sunset and the waves on Zicatela Beach. The seafood dishes are a little expensive, but the vegetarian and pasta dishes are reasonably priced and creative, adapting traditional Mexican and Italian dishes. One of my favorites is the house specialty, chiles rellenos: mild green peppers stuffed with cheese, raisins, and nuts; baked in a mild red-chile sauce; and served with brown rice, beans, and salad. My other favorite is the tostada special—big crispy tortillas heaped high with beans, lettuce, cheese, avocado, and salsa. The restaurant is across the street from the beach about half a mile southeast of the town center.

Spaghetti House. Playa Principal. ☎ **958/2-0005.** Main courses $5–$7.25; pasta $3.25–$5; pizza $4.25–$11.25. Daily noon–11pm. ITALIAN.

This restaurant faces the beach and is open to great sea breezes and the sound of pounding rolling surf. Pasta runs the gamut from basic spaghetti napoletana to cannelloni and seafood fettuccine. Seven salads and seven varieties of pizza, plus an extensive bar list, ought to please most anyone. It is a couple of doors toward the beach at the eastern entry to the PZ.

PUERTO ESCONDIDO AFTER DARK

Sunset-watching is a ritual you won't tire of since there are many good lookout points. Watch the surfers at Zicatela from the Los Tres Osos restaurant or mingle with them at Art and Harry's Bar and Grill, both about a quarter of the way down the beach near the end of current development. For another great sunset view, go to the Hotel Santa Fe at the junction of Zicatela and Marinero beaches or the rooftop bar of Hotel Flor de María. Dedicated sun worshipers might want to spring for a cab (about $1.75) or walk half an hour or so west to the Hotel Posada Real, overlooking Playa Bacocho. The hotel's clifftop lawn is a perfect sunset-watching perch. Or you might climb down the cliff side (or take the hotel's shuttle bus) to the pool-and-restaurant complex on the beach below. The food isn't great, but the restaurant is an amazing sight, with an artificial tropical lagoon in the middle and leopard-skin swings at the bar.

There are several choices for after-dark entertainment in Puerto Escondido. **El Tubo** is an open-air beachside disco just west of Restaurant Alicia on the PZ. **Son y la Rumba** features live Latin music and dancing, across and up the hill from Las Palmas. **Cocos,** near the east end of the PZ, and **Tío Mac,** also near the east end, feature live music during high season and have happy hours from 6 to 8pm. Both the **Posada Real and Villa Sol,** on Bacocho Beach, have Beach Clubs where one can dance the night away. Most nightspots are open until 3am or until the customers leave.

4 Puerto Angel: Laid-Back Sun & Sand

Fifty miles southeast of Puerto Escondido and 30 miles northwest of the Bays of Huatulco is the tiny fishing port of Puerto Angel (PWER-toe on-HEL). Once known only to a handful of vacationers who came here regularly (mostly from Mexico City and Oaxaca), today Puerto Angel, with its unpaved streets and budget hotels, is very popular with the international backpacking set and those looking for an inexpensive and restful vacation. A small, beautiful bay and several inlets provide peaceful swimming and good snorkeling, and the village's out-of-the-way position assures a sleepy, tranquil atmosphere. The population of Puerto Angel is listed as 15,000, but the figure is misleading because it includes the surrounding farming area. On any given day you'll see very few people in the village, and many of these are tourists. Fishermen leave very early in the morning and return with their catch by late forenoon. Taxis make up most of the traffic, although the bus from Pochutla passes every half hour or so.

ESSENTIALS

GETTING THERE & DEPARTING   There are no direct **buses** from Puerto Escondido or Huatulco to Puerto Angel; however, numerous buses leave Puerto Escondido and Huatulco for **Pochutla,** 7 miles north of Puerto Angel, where you can transfer for the short ride to the village. If you arrive at Pochutla from either Huatulco or Puerto Escondido, you may be dropped at one of several bus stations that line the main street; if so, walk one or two blocks toward the large sign reading "POSADA DON JOSÉ." The buses to Puerto Angel are in the lot just before the sign. Ask for the "amarillos" buses (to Puerto Angel). That's what the locals call them—they're yellow—although the name of the line is Estrella del Valle. Estrella del Valle buses originating in Huatulco (about every hour, $1.50) drop off passengers at their station in Pochutla. Buses depart from Pochutla for Puerto Angel every 20 or 30 minutes and cost 50¢. Pochutla has many taxis, and they will be glad to take you to Puerto Angel or Zipolite Beach for $3.50 to $4.50, or to the Huatulco airport ($18) or Puerto Escondido ($23).

The bus will let you off in Puerto Angel near the small market in the central part of town. The town center is only about four blocks long, oriented more or less east–west. There are few signs in the village giving directions, and off the main street much of Puerto Angel is a narrow sand-and-dirt path. The navy base is toward the far (west) end of town, just before the creek-crossing toward Playa Panteón (Cemetery Beach).

If you're traveling **by car,** take coastal Highway 175 to Puerto Angel.

ORIENTATION   Puerto Angel now has several **public telephones.** Primary of these is a TelMex office, just past the turnoff to La Buena Vista and across from the Casa de Huespedes Anahi. It's open daily from 7am to 10pm. Their numbers are ☎ **958/4-3055** and 958/4-3063, and they will accept messages to be picked up (Spanish only). Another public long-distance phone is available at the small restaurant next to Gambusino's Travel Agency and near the entrance to the Hotel Soraya. The office is open daily from 7pm to 10pm.

If you want to stash your luggage while you look for lodgings, Gambusino's Travel Agency offers **luggage storage** for $1.25 during their office hours (Monday through Saturday from 10:30am to 2pm and 4 to 6pm). It's about half a block up the street opposite the pier.

The closest **bank** is Bancomer in Pochutla, which will change money Monday through Friday from 9 to 10:30am; however, it's not uncommon for it to run out of cash. It may be hard to change foreign currency with locals in Puerto Angel. Your best bet is simply to come with enough pesos for your stay.

The **post office** (correo), open Monday through Friday from 9am to 3:30pm, is on the curve as you enter town.

BEACHES, WATER SPORTS & BOAT TRIPS

The golden sands of Puerto Angel and the peaceful village life are the attractions here, so in the "where to soak" category let's begin with **Playa Principal** in the central village. You can't miss it, as the beach lies between the pier from which the bulk of the local fishing fleet works and the Mexican navy base. On one end near the pier, fishermen pull their colorful boats on the beach and unload their catch in the late morning while trucks wait to haul it off to processing plants in Veracruz. The rest of the beach is for enjoyment, and except on Mexican holidays, it's relatively deserted. It's important to note that Pacific coast currents deposit trash on Puerto Angel beaches. The townsfolk do a fairly good job of keeping it picked up, but those currents are constant.

Playa Panteón is the main **swimming** and **snorkeling** beach. It's about a 15-minute walk from the town center, straight through town on the main street that skirts the beach. Just before you reach Playa Panteón you pass the panteón (cemetery), on the right, for which the beach is named.

The 3.7 miles of paved road to the village of **Playa Zipolite** (See-poh-lee-teh) is walkable but only for the hardy in the midday sun. Taxis charge around $4.50 for single passenger (taxis are expensive here), or you can catch a taxi colectivo on the main street in the town center and share the cost. If you walk, the heat can sap the last bit of your energy, so at least wear a hat and, better still, carry drinking water.

Zipolite is a beach without protection from the open sea. Consequently, swimming can be very dangerous—*people die swimming here.* The dangerous currents attract rather than deter surfers, however; along the beach you'll find many surfers ensconced in hammocks under numerous palapas. Beyond a large rock outcropping at the far end of the beach is an area where nude bathing has been tolerated for several years. *One caveat:* Police could roust au naturel bathers at any time, as they are technically breaking the law. Even more serious is the possibility of drug busts. Mexican jails are not as pleasant as those in the United States. In Mexico you are under Mexican law. DON'T RISK IT!

Hotels in Playa Zipolite are basic and rustic—most are made with crude walls and palapa roofs. Prices run from $10 to $35 a night with the highest prices being charged on Mexican holidays. Thefts from hotel rooms are not uncommon, and hotel operators sometimes band together to run off tourists who keep hanging around even though it's well known that they've run out of money.

Besides these beaches, there are others reachable primarily by boat. One of the pleasures of a lengthy stay in Puerto Angel is discovering these hidden beaches, taking a lunch and drinks and spending the day. Local boatmen can give details and quote rates for this service, or ask at your hotel.

In Playa Panteón some of the palapa restaurants and a few of the hotels rent **snorkeling** and **scuba** gear and can arrange **boat trips,** but all tends to be quite expensive. And above all, be cautious about the gear—particularly scuba gear. Often the chaps who rent from the beach have rusted and worn equipment and are hardly interested in either your capability or safety. One reliable boatman, **Mateo López,** at the Posada Cañon Devata (see "Where to Stay," below), will take you fishing or snorkeling. He emphasizes that aside from being a lifelong fisherman, he is also fully insured.

WHERE TO STAY

Two areas in Puerto Angel have accommodations: **Playa Principal** in the tiny town and **Playa Panteón,** the pretty beach area beyond the village center. The bus will let you out at either place—but in Playa Panteón you'll be stuck with your luggage while you look for lodging. A taxi to Playa Panteón from town is around $1.75.

Between Playa Panteón and town are numerous bungalow and guesthouse setups with budget accommodations.

During the high season—December, January, around Easter, and July and August—rates can go up, and you should reserve well in advance.

DOUBLES FOR LESS THAN $15

Capy's. Apdo. Postal 44, 70902 Puerto Angel, Oax. ☎ **958/4-3002**. 14 rms (all with bath). FAN. Year-round, $6–$8 single; $10–$12 double.

You'll see Capy's sign hanging over the street; it's on the right, before the cemetery and Playa Panteón. Go up a flight of stairs to the second-story restaurant, and someone can show you one of the very clean rooms. It's a good budget choice, with simple furnishings and well-screened windows. Room 6 has a great patio out front with a splendid bay view.

The pleasant, covered open-air restaurant is open daily from 7am to 10pm. Breakfast is served between 7am and noon; lunch and dinner are served from 1 to 10pm.

DOUBLES FOR LESS THAN $20

⑤ Hotel La Cabaña de Puerto Angel. Apdo. Postal 22, 70902 Pochutla, Oax. ☎ **958/4-0026**. 23 rms (all with bath). FAN. All year, $16.50 single or double.

Covered in vines and plants, with lots of shade, this hacienda-style hotel is efficient and accommodating, with a friendly, helpful staff; owner Diego Oropeza is truly gracious. The clean, sunny rooms have louvered windows and screens, ceiling fans, and double beds. The rooftop patio is a nice place to sunbathe peacefully, and a hot pot of free coffee awaits guests every morning at 7am in the lobby. The hotel is on Playa Panteón on the landward side of the road, just steps from the beach and several restaurants.

Posada Rincón Sabroso. Playa Principal, 70902 Puerto Angel, Oax. No phone. 8 rms (all with bath). FAN. $9 single; $15 double. Low-season discounts available.

A sign on the street marks the entrance, and a flight of stairs takes you up to the Posada. Rooms have nice tile floors, plaster walls, and screened windows. Hammocks hang between posts on the tile patio walkway, which is also furnished with tables and chairs outside each room. Recent sprucing up, plus its attractive prices, make this one of the best budget choices for in-town stays. The Posada is on the right as you enter town, opposite the main pier and by the Hotel Soraya.

DOUBLES FOR LESS THAN $30

✪ La Buena Vista. Apdo. Postal 48, 70902 Puerto Angel, Oax. ☎ and fax **958/4-3104**. 18 rms (all with bath). FAN. $24 single; $29 double.

To find La Buena Vista, follow the road through town and shortly you'll see a sign on the right pointing to the hotel. It's on a hillside, so to get to the lobby/patio you follow the sign, taking a left at Casa de Huespedes Alex, after which you climb a formidable flight of stairs. This will take you to the lobby, where you'll discover why this hotel's name means "good view," with the bay and village in the distance. The rooms, each with a natural tile floor, one or two double beds, and well-screened windows, are tastefully furnished with Mexican accents. On the upper floor is a wonderful, little, reasonably priced restaurant with bay views. It's open for breakfast from 7:30 to 11am and for dinner from 6 to 10pm.

✪ Posada Cañon Devata. Calle Cañon del Vata (Apdo. Postal 10), 70902 Puerto Angel, Oax. ☎ and fax **958/4-3048**. 10 rms, 4 bungalows (13 with bath). $14–$25 single; $17–$29 double; $38 bungalow or El Cielo room for two. Closed May–June.

The most inviting place in Puerto Angel is a three-minute walk almost straight up from Playa Panteón. Americans Suzanne and Mateo López run this ecologically sound, homey, cool, green, and wooded oasis in a narrow canyon. Hotel water is recycled for the benefit of the resident plants and critters. Rooms are agreeably rustic-chic, with fans, beds covered in Guatemalan tie-dyed cloth, and Mateo's paintings hanging from the walls (the paintings can be bought). The patio restaurant serves delicious food featuring home-baked bread and the posada's own organically grown vegetables. Don't miss climbing to the appropriately named El Cielo to see the bay bathed in the light of the setting sun and to enjoy the happy hour from 5pm until dark. Mateo also offers fishing and snorkeling trips (see "Beaches, Water Sports & Boat Trips," above). Note: Reservations are by fax only.

To find it, walk just past the Hotel Cabaña del Puerto Angel to where the road more or less ends; turn right and go down the sandy path to an area with a few parked cars. Walk across the tiny bridge on your right and follow the stairs on the left until you reach the restaurant, where someone is around to rent rooms and serve food.

WHERE TO EAT

In addition to the restaurants below and those mentioned under hotels above, there are four or five palapa-topped restaurants on the main beach in town as well as on Playa Panteón. Hawkers from these various establishments implore you to try their restaurants, but they're all similar in price, menu, and service. Breakfasts generally cost $2.25 to $4.50, and meat or seafood plates run $3.50 to $11. Watch for overbilling in these restaurants.

✪ **Restaurant Cañon Devata.** At Posada Cañon Devata, Calle Cañon Devata. ☎ **958/ 4-3048.** Breakfast $1.75–$4.50; sandwiches $3.50; dinner $6–$7. Daily 7:30am–4pm and 7–8:30pm. Closed May–June. VEGETARIAN.

It's always a few degrees cooler under the thatched palapa in the middle of the canyon area. Fresh flowers centered on the thick wooden tables set the mood. Guests partake of some of the healthiest cooking around, mainly vegetarian dishes with occasional fish specialties. The restaurant is in the hotel by the same name, on the right, past the Hotel Cabaña de Puerto Angel.

✪ **Villa Florencia.** Bulevar Virgilio Uribe. ☎ **958/4-3044.** Breakfast $1.50–$2.25; pasta dishes $3.50–$5; pizzas $4–$6. Daily 7am–10pm. ITALIAN.

One of the best restaurants in town is Lulu and Walter Pelliconi's delightful slice of Italy. Their generous servings are prepared in a spotlessly clean kitchen that contains a purifier for all water used on the premises. Pasta products are imported from Italy, and the chefs use only extra virgin olive oil. The restaurant is located near the pier and the bus drop-off in the central village.

Overland Along the Central Route: South from Laredo to San Luis Potosí

Although neither easy nor cheap, touring the country by car is still the best way to a rich experience of the real Mexico. This chapter deals with the first leg of most people's overland journey into Mexico; it follows the southward "central route" from Nuevo Laredo at the Texas border through **Monterrey,** a sprawling city that is a gateway to mainland Mexico; **Real de Catorce,** a fascinating ghost town; and **San Luis Potosí,** a prosperous, sophisticated colonial city. A lot of the information that begins this chapter is intended to help drivers find their way—if you'll be traveling by bus, train, or plane, look to the sections covering Monterrey and San Luis Potosí for complete transportation information.

Most people who drive into Mexico from the eastern or midwestern United States use the Laredo, Texas–Nuevo Laredo, Tamaulipas, border crossing. (There are certainly other important border crossings. For information on entering the country at Nogales, see "Along Highway 15 from Nogales to Mazatlán" in chapter 5, "Puerto Vallarta & the Central Pacific Coast"; for crossing into Mexico at McAllen or Brownsville, Texas, see "Exploring the Gulf Coast" in chapter 8, "Overland Along the Gulf Coast."

It's a 10- to 12-hour drive from Nuevo Laredo to San Luis Potosí. It can be done in a day if you leave the border by 7 or 8am in order to arrive in San Luis before dark. However, I recommend a stay along the way, at either Monterrey, Matehuala, or Real de Catorce.

But first things first—to get from Laredo to San Luis Potosí and the Silver Cities, or Mexico City, Guadalajara, the Pacific Coast resorts, or the Gulf Coast (and perhaps on to the Yucatán), you'll first have to get to the city of Monterrey.

FROM THE BORDER TO MONTERREY

Many people drive to the border, leave their cars in a protected lot on the U.S. side, cross over, and take the train or bus into Mexico. For information on secure places to park for extended periods in Laredo, call the Laredo Convention and Visitors Bureau (☎ 210/722-9895).

CROSSING AT LAREDO, TEXAS   After driving into Mexico at Laredo, don't stop at the customs building that is immediately on the right after crossing. There's another location about 2 miles farther into the city, and that's where you obtain your Car Importation

Permit and Tourist Permits, and where your car's contents may or may not be inspected. To get the Car Permit, do this: After crossing, turn right at the first corner (avoiding the customs building and parking lot on the right immediately after you cross) and then bear left along that road; on your right you'll see railroad tracks running parallel to the road. When you see the end of the train station on the right, look to your left for another building marked "Inspecion de Vehiculos"; it's a block or so farther (past the cement pillars). That's where you present all your documents for crossing. (For requirements for crossing the border with your car, see "Getting There, By Car" in chapter 2, "Planning a Trip to Mexico.") When you're all set, you can begin traveling south on Highway 85.

CROSSING AT COLUMBIA, TEXAS   The new Mexican Highway 22 is finished, with a new border crossing at Columbia, Texas, 32 miles northwest of Laredo, and customs officials are on duty on both sides. One of its primary purposes was to give truckers a faster alternative route to Mexican Highway 85, but they seldom use it. So the Columbia crossing is also a good alternative if the Nuevo Laredo crossing is congested, as it often is on holidays and during strikes and protests on the Mexican side. Highway 22 links with Highway 85 south of Laredo; drivers heading to Monterrey and beyond then choose either to continue on the free road or take the toll road.

THE HIGHWAY TO MONTERREY   Depending on the road you take, Monterrey is either a 2^1/$_2$- or 3-hour trip from the border.

Drivers may find the extra cost of the toll road (Highway 85D) well worth it—you'll face a slightly shorter (118 miles instead of 143) and much less stressful trip from the border to Monterrey. The four-lane toll road has very little traffic, and cars make the trip to Monterrey in only 2^1/$_2$ hours. The toll road ends about 30 minutes before Monterrey, leaving motorists to fend for themselves in Monterrey's crazy maze of traffic.

However, you may find the road-use toll expensive—it's $10 from either Columbia or Laredo to Monterrey. Here's one way to decide: If traffic is heavy before you reach the point where you'll have to choose (you'll see signs for the *cuota,* or "toll"), then take the toll road; if traffic is light, then the free road should not be too congested.

The trip from Laredo to Monterrey on Highway 85 and then from Saltillo to San Luis Potosí is a long and boring ride through desert studded with cacti and Joshua trees. But the new toll roads shorten the drive and reduce tedium, and after summer rains the desert can blossom beautifully.

ROUTES FROM MONTERREY INTO THE INTERIOR

From Monterrey, roads branch out toward whatever your main destination may be. Listed below are the chief routes to the major tourist destinations of the Mexican interior. (For more details on these routes see "En Route To . . . " at the end of the Monterrey section.)

TO THE SILVER CITIES   Highways 54 and 57 head south from Monterrey and the nearby city of Saltillo. Highway 57 leads to San Luis Potosí, Guanajuato, and San Miguel de Allende; Highway 54 is the most direct route to Zacatecas and Aguascalientes.

TO MEXICO CITY   The capital is a 20-hour journey by bus or car along the excellent Highway 57.

TO GUADALAJARA   From Saltillo, Highway 54 leads straight through Zacatecas to Guadalajara.

TO THE PACIFIC COAST   Highway 40 goes southwest from Saltillo through Durango to Mazatlán on the Pacific coast.

TO THE GULF COAST & THE YUCATÁN   Highway 85 from Monterrey offers quick access to Mexico's east-coast gateway city of Ciudad Victoria.

1 Monterrey

146 miles S of Laredo, Texas; 53 miles NE of Saltillo

Monterrey, capital of the state of Nuevo León, is Mexico's third-largest city (with 3.5 million residents in the metro area) and the nation's main industrial center. Its setting is spectacular: Hemmed in by towering, craggy mountains, one of which (Cerro de la Silla, or "Saddle Mountain") has become a symbol of the city. This modern city "holds court" in the Gran Plaza with fountains, monuments, and modern and historic buildings in the heart of the city center.

Longtime citizens of this city are proud of its recent achievements and can spout off a long list of reasons to visit their city. But in reality, it's primarily a city based on commerce, rather than the tourist trade. The biggest reason to make a stopover in Monterrey would be to see an exhibit at the Museo de Arte Mexicano Contemporaneo de Monterrey (MARCO).

With the industrial sprawl has come serious noise and air pollution, the latter often in the form of a pink pall that hangs in the valley 24 hours a day. Traffic stays in a snarl, and road signs are dismayingly ill placed. But Monterrey, named in 1596 for the Count of Monterrey, Viceroy of New Spain, retains some colonial touches among its shiny new buildings and factories: the town hall, the Government Palace (state capitol of Nuevo León), mansions and hotels, churches and monasteries, and the parks and squares that the colonial planners always laid out in new towns. Hardly the stereotypical laid-back, charming colonial Mexican town filled with flowers all year and mariachis each evening, Monterrey is a raw, muscular city, crowded and expensive, that produces a great deal of Mexico's wealth.

ESSENTIALS

GETTING THERE & DEPARTING   By Plane   Monterrey has multiple daily air connections with Mexico City, plus nonstop flights to Cancún, Chicago, Chihuahua, Dallas/Fort Worth, Guadalajara, Houston, Los Angeles, Mazatlán, San Antonio, San Luis Potosí, Tampico, and Tijuana. **Domestic flights** are operated by Aeroméxico, Mexicana, AeroLitoral, SARO, and AVIACSA. **International flights** are shared by Aeroméxico, American, Continental, and Mexicana.

By Bus   Greyhound buses and their affiliates in the U.S. border towns can usually provide information on bus schedules leaving from the Mexican side to the Mexican interior. In Laredo, Texas, call **210/723-1321.**

From Monterrey you can travel to almost anywhere in Mexico. Frequent buses run between Monterrey and Nuevo Laredo (a 3- to 4-hour trip) and Monterrey to Saltillo (1¹/₂- to 2-hour trip). Count on a 10- to 12-hour trip to Mexico City. Buses to other areas are frequent—San Luis Potosí, Zacatecas, Durango, Guadalajara, etc. Deluxe buses are being added at a rapid rate; try to use that class of service whenever there's a convenient choice especially on long trips. Deluxe buses stop less frequently and are more comfortable. See "Getting Around, By Bus" in chapter 2, "Planning a Trip to Mexico," for more information.

By Car   See "From the Border to Monterrey," above, for instructions on getting from Laredo, Texas, to Monterrey. There's another border crossing at Eagle Pass,

Texas; from there you can take Mexican Highway 57 south through Sabinas and then go east shortly after Monclova to Monterrey. However, it's much faster to take U.S. Highway 83 from Eagle Pass to Laredo (about 120 miles) and cross the border there.

See "En Route To . . . " at the end of this section for more details about routes from the Monterrey area to points throughout Mexico.

ORIENTATION   Arriving by Plane   To get from the airport into Monterrey, a distance of about 19 miles, take one of the minibuses run by Aeropuerto Transport-aciones or a more expensive taxi.

Arriving by Bus   The bustling bus station on Avenida Colón, about 4 miles outside the city center, is an $8 taxi ride away. Buses marked "Centro" and/or "Central" make the trip from the center of town to the bus station and back.

For taxis, you'll strike a better deal by skipping those in front of the station and walking to the street just in front; bargaining saves bucks.

Information   The state of Nuevo León maintains an **Infotur** tourist-information office at the corner of Zaragoza and Matamoros, just off the Gran Plaza (down at street level; ☎ **83/45-0870** or 83/45-0902), open Monday through Friday from 9am to 1pm and 3 to 7pm and Saturday and Sunday from 10am to 5pm. Look for the publication *Guía Monterrey* ("Monterrey Guide") for the latest happenings.

City Layout   The touristic heart of the city is centered on both the modern **Gran Plaza,** which extends north to south from Juan Ignacio Ramón to Avenida de la Constitución and east to west between Ignacio Zaragoza and Juan Zuazua, and the adjoining **Zona Rosa,** a pedestrians-only shopping-and-restaurant area between Zaragoza and Morelos. **Avenida Colón** is the main market street.

The intersection of Juárez and Aramberri divides Monterrey's street addresses. All numbers north or south of **Aramberri** are *norte* (north) or *sur* (south), respectively. All numbers east or west of **Juárez** are *oriente* (east) or *poniente* (west), respectively; the numbers start at this intersection (you might call it the "zero point") and go up.

Getting Around   Most of the downtown area is easily walkable. For most other attractions mentioned above, the "Ruta 1" buses are the ones to use—but verify it before getting on. Monterrey's **monorail** is operational but is of limited value to the tourist at this time. Check with the tourism office for expanded routings. Traffic is frantic and clogged in Monterrey, so if you're driving, it might be better to park the car and leave it until you're ready to depart.

FAST FACTS: MONTERREY

American Express   The American Express office is located at Padre Mier Poniente 1424 (☎ **8/318-3380**).

Area Code   The telephone area code is 8.

Consulates   The U.S. Consulate is at Constitución 411 Poniente (☎ **8/45-0692**).

EXPLORING MONTERREY

Monterrey is a thriving business center but not a major tourist destination, even though there are lots of Americans in town on business. Still, if you have time, check out a few of the attractions.

THE MAJOR ATTRACTION

Museo de Arte Contemporáneo de Monterrey (MARCO). Gran Plaza at Zuazua and Ocampo (☎ **8/42-4901** or 8/42-8455). $4 adults, free for children 5 and younger; free for all on Wednesday. Tues, Thurs–Sat 11am–7pm; Wed, Sun 11am–9pm.

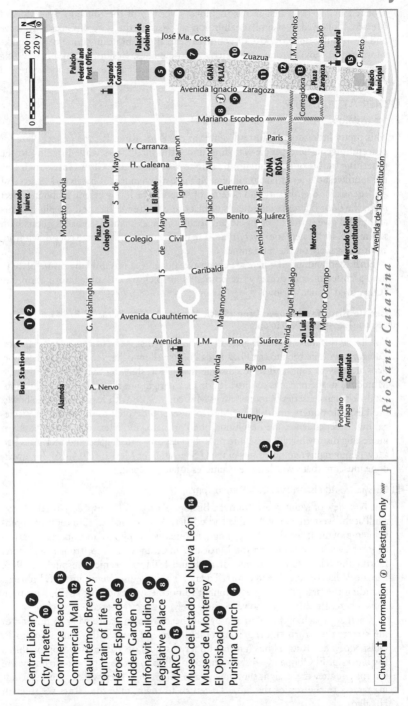

Central Library **7**
City Theater **10**
Commerce Beacon **13**
Commercial Mall **12**
Cuauhtémoc Brewery **2**
Fountain of Life **11**
Héroes Esplanade **5**
Hidden Garden **6**
Infonavit Building **9**
Legislative Palace **8**
MARCO **15**
Museo del Estado de Nueva León **14**
Museo de Monterrey **1**
El Opisbado **3**
Purísima Church **4**

Church ✝ ▪ Information ⓘ Pedestrian Only ⁄⁄⁄⁄

Opened in 1991, its first shows included a version of the touring "Splendors of Mexico," followed by a similar exhibition showcasing the state of Oaxaca. Massive and beautifully done, MARCO is one of several city buildings intended to make Monterrey a moving force in Mexico's artistic circles. Besides important traveling shows, it also displays a permanent collection. A cafeteria and excellent bookstore and crafts shop are on the first floor.

OTHER ATTRACTIONS

Plaza Hidalgo.

This pretty little square is just off center of the Zona Rosa. It's the perfect plaza for peaceful pigeon- and people-watching under the shady trees while listening to the refreshing burble of the fountain. Be sure to visit the stately **Gran Hotel Ancira** on the southwest corner of Jardín Hidalgo. It's one of a handful of hotels in Mexico that are legends for their beauty and decades of service. The lobby ceiling is about 60 feet high; the floor is alternating squares of black and white marble; and the plush chairs and tables give it the air of an elegant living room. A pianist serenades guests with soft music. In the center of everything, a magnificent grand staircase coils down from an ornate gallery on the mezzanine.

Both food and lodging here are expensive, but this is certainly the prime place to have a coffee or cool drink, write postcards, or pick up city tour information (see "Organized Tours," below).

Museo de Historía de Nuevo León (State Museum). Gran Plaza. ☎ **8/344-4165.** Free admission. Tues—Sun 10am to 6pm.

You'll find this museum in the graceful old building that is catercorner to the plaza and Zaragoza, with its back to the Plaza Hidalgo. Its yellow-ocher facade and arched porticos are easy to spot, and there's a stone inscription showing that it was the Palacio Municipal in the previous century. Inside on the right are rooms honoring illustrious locals. Upstairs, a series of rooms shows Mexico's origins with fossils and stone bowls, pre-Hispanic pottery from all over Mexico, a section devoted to the country's Viceregal Era, Independence, the Revolution, the Porfiriato, and Mexico's reform years. An interesting display highlights Monterrey's chief exports—steel, glass, and beer. And last, a few photographs remind visitors of the U.S. invasion of Mexico (1914–16). It's a well-done museum that's worth the few minutes it takes to look it over.

El Obispado. Admission 50¢. Daily 9am to 5pm.

The best view of Monterrey is from the Bishop's Palace—El Obispado—perched atop a hill at the western end of Avenida Padre Mier. Built in the late 18th century to provide employment for the poor during a famine, it has played an important part in Monterrey's history. During the Mexican-American War, U.S. troops slept here. During the yellow fever epidemics of 1898 and 1901, it became a hospital. In 1913, Pancho Villa converted it to a fort. Today it's a museum. Many historical objects, including the first printing press brought to northern Mexico (in 1813), have been moved here. Its chief asset, however, is its view of the city—excellent.

When approaching El Obispado by car, head west on Padre Mier to the end of the street; then turn right, go one block, turn left, and follow the signs to El Obispado. The "Ruta 4" bus (green with a red stripe) on Padre Mier stops within a few blocks of El Obispado—a short but steep climb to the top (get off the bus where it turns left after the straight shot down Padre Mier, then keep walking up the winding streets to the top of the hill). To return to town, take the "Ruta 69" bus on Hidalgo.

Cuauhtémoc Brewery. Av. Universidad Norte 2202. ☎ **8/75-2200.**

Since Monterrey is synonymous with beer, go on a free tour held Tuesday through Friday at 11am, noon, and 3pm. An added bonus on Tuesday through Sunday from 9am to 5pm is the beer garden where visitors can sit and sip free Carta Blanca. Take a taxi to the brewery or any "Ruta 1" bus from Avenida Juárez.

Museo de Monterrey. Av. Universidad.

While at the beer garden (see "Cuauhtémoc Brewery," above), cross the street to the big building that houses the Museo de Monterrey. Its splendid collection includes works of Orozco, Rivera, Siqueiros, and Tamayo.

Sports Museum of Monterrey. Av. Universidad. Tues–Fri 9am–5pm and Sat–Sun 10am–6pm.

At the end of the parking lot for the above-mentioned Museo de Monterrey, this museum features an accumulation of memorabilia of all the sports dear to the Mexican heart. Also included here is a **Sports Hall of Fame.**

Kristaluxus Factory. José María Vigil 400, Colonia del Norte at Ruíz Cortinez. ☎ **83/51-9869** or 83/51-9393. Mon–Fri 9am–1pm and 2:30–6:30pm, Sat 9am–1pm.

Monterrey is famous for its lead crystal, and there is a factory with a showroom specializing in the manufacture and sale of this beautiful product. Prices are only slightly lower than those in the stores handling the crystal in town, but the selection is much greater. All sales are final. Tours through the factory are held Monday through Friday at 10:30am, but call ahead to make arrangements.

There is no satisfactory bus service to Kristaluxus, so plan to take a taxi or the city tour, as it's quite a distance from anywhere else.

ORGANIZED TOURS

GUIDED TAXI TOURS   Walk along Hidalgo near Plaza Hidalgo and every taxi driver and licensed tourist guide you encounter will offer to take you on a tour of Monterrey's sights—for a price. These guides carry identification and an official rate sheet, which you will see as soon as you attempt to bargain for a lower price. It's good to compare prices with several drivers and the official rates before making a commitment. Test the guide's English, then set down exactly what the tour will cover. A good city tour should take you to the Palacio del Gobierno, Palacio Federal, Purísima Church, El Obispado, University City, and perhaps the markets, all in about three hours. The "official" rate is $40 (regardless of the value of the peso) for the carload. A four-hour tour in the guide's car to Horsetail Falls for one to five people is $45.

BUS TOURS   The major downtown hotels (Ancira and so forth) provide information and sell tickets for city tours. The tours have a minimum group number, and the places visited vary daily.

A NEARBY ATTRACTION

COLA DE CABALLO (HORSETAIL FALLS)   This 80-foot waterfall is located on a private hacienda named Vista Hermosa. Turn right off Highway 85 to the village of El Cercado and travel about 4 miles up a rough but passable road. The road winds around for about 3 miles from the main road (making the falls accessible only by car or taxi) and leads to a parking area where horses and burros can be hired for the final half mile to the falls. If you walk, it's hard to resist the blandishments of the children who accompany you on burros, making reduced offers all the way until, when you're nearly there, they start bargaining about the return trip. I walked both ways and found it no particular strain. There's a small fee to enter.

SHOPPING

The city's four main markets offer good shopping possibilities for Mexican crafts. The **Mercado San Luis** is the first one on your right if you're walking from downtown on Ocampo. The rafters are jammed with funeral wreaths and huge, colorful piñatas in whimsical shapes of elephants, burros, pigs, and so on. At eye level you'll notice piles of hats and pottery and some of the largest casserole dishes you've ever seen, plus multitudes of baskets.

Across the street, behind **Más Que Todo** (another market), the **Mercado Colón** has more curios than its neighbor markets in baskets, pottery, hammocks, ceramic horses' and cows' heads, copperware, guitars, live ducks, parakeets, parrots, and rabbits.

Cross the street pathway from the Colón to the **Mercado Constitución** and its load of baskets, pottery, miniature piñatas, puppets, lacquered gourds, and handmade toys, including toy airplanes.

An eight-block walk from the city center brings you to the **Mercado Juárez,** an even bigger feast for the senses. Here you'll find a huge section of fresh flowers, more funeral wreaths, baskets big enough to be transformed into clothes hampers, blown-glass animals, sequin portraits of Christ and Mary, stuffed frog bands, huaraches, kitchen utensils (including tortilla presses and hand juicers), wick lanterns, and medicinal soaps and herbs.

For a truly superb collection of Mexican arts and crafts, stop at **Carapan,** Hidalgo Ote. 305 (☎ **8/45-4422**), not far from Plaza Hidalgo. Antiques and modern items, silver and tin, glass and pottery, textiles and toys—the collection is eclectic and obviously done with an expert's eye. Sr. Porfirio Sosa, the owner, has created a work of art (his shop) from works of art—the best of Mexican crafts—but prices are fairly high. It's open Tuesday through Saturday from 9am to 1pm and 3 to 7pm.

WHERE TO STAY

Since this is one of the three largest cities in Mexico, it's relatively high-priced compared to a provincial town, and good budget choices are few. The prime area for accommodations is in and around the Zona Rosa (the modern district near the Gran Plaza), and Plaza Hidalgo, a small park between the Hotel Ancira and the Gran Plaza. The hotel listed below is in the desirable area.

El Paso Autel. Zaragoza 130 Nte., 64000 Monterrey, N.L. ☎ **8/340-0690.** Fax 8/344-4647. 65 rms (all with bath). A/C TV TEL. $27 single or double. Free interior parking.

Within a short walk of the Gran Plaza, this four-story motel (with elevator) is close to restaurants and museums. The carpeted rooms, though dated with furniture from the 1940s to the 1970s, are light, airy, well maintained, and heated in winter. Beds have firm mattresses. The swimming pool is a welcome sight at the end of a day on the road. The restaurant off the lobby serves good plain food. To get here from the northwest corner of the Gran Plaza, walk five blocks north on Zaragoza. It's on the left, on the corner of Martínez.

WHERE TO EAT

Monterrey's best budget-priced downtown eateries look like American chain restaurants, with plastic-laminate counters and booths and illustrated menus. But the food is Mexican and very tasty, so it's easy to ignore the atmosphere.

La Puntada. Av. Hidalgo Ote. 123. ☎ **8/340-6985.** Breakfast $1.50–$2.50; main courses $1.50–$3. Mon–Sat 8am–10pm. MEXICAN.

A light, bright Mexican lunch place, La Puntada features chrome-and-plastic tables and chairs, a lunch counter, lots of windows, and a loyal local clientele. Though modern, it's also somehow very Mexican. The menu includes breakfast plates, sandwiches, tacos, and other Mexican treats. The most expensive item on the entire menu is T-bone steak. With hotcakes just slightly more than a dollar, this is probably the best breakfast bargain downtown. To get here from the Gran Plaza, walk three blocks west on Morelos to Galeana. Go left one block, then turn right at the next street (Hidalgo); the restaurant is ahead at the corner of Hidalgo and Juárez.

Sanborn's. Escobedo 920. ☎ **8/343-1834.** Breakfast $2.50–$4; main courses $3–$6. Daily 7:30am–11pm. MEXICAN.

Despite its gringo-sounding name, Sanborn's is a Mexican chain of variety stores with restaurants that you'll learn to rely on in your Mexican travels. The stores are bright; modern; spacious; air-conditioned; and stocked with jewelry, gifts, clothing, luggage, stationery, candies and nuts, books (many in English), records, newspapers, and magazines—you name it. The restaurants, usually with a section of booths or tables and also a lunch counter, serve a blend of international and Mexican food that's tasty though not extraordinary. Sanborn's is in the Zona Rosa. From the Gran Plaza, walk one block down Morelos to Escobedo and turn left; it's about half a block down on the right and behind the Hotel Colonial.

EN ROUTE TO . . .

CIUDAD VICTORIA & THE GULF COAST Ciudad Victoria (covered in chapter 9) is 180 miles away and takes about four hours to reach by bus or car. Fill up the tank in Monterrey, as unleaded gas may be scarce until Ciudad Victoria. From Monterrey, go southeast on Highway 85, a two-lane road that's mostly straight and fast, with plenty of greenery and the majestic Sierra Madre range towering up on the right (west). There's little else to be seen, however, except an occasional passing car, bus, or cyclist, plus lazy cattle grazing by the road. Between Linares and Ciudad Victoria is sugarcane country.

The first town of size is 50 miles southeast, **Montemorelos,** Nuevo León, described as Mexico's "Naranjiera" (Orange) Capital. It doesn't have too much to offer, except the mid-July fiesta, the pecan fair in mid-September, and the sight of the orange and lemon trees in bloom from February to March.

Some 30 miles south of Montemorelos is **Linares,** Nuevo León, a clean, pleasant town of 62,000 that's the center of a farming area and some small industry (bricks, furniture). Ciudad Victoria is approximately 100 miles south of Linares.

SALTILLO Taking Highway 40 toward Saltillo, you'll find **Chipinque Mesa** about 13 miles from Monterrey. Turn left at Colonia del Valle, pay a small toll, and drive up the pine-covered slopes of the **Sierra Madre.** The road culminates in a breathtaking view of Monterrey from a 4,200-foot plateau.

You can also travel 15 miles along Highway 40 to the village of **Santa Catarina.** Turn left here, go 2 miles more, and you'll find yourself at **Huasteca Canyon,** a massive rock formation framing dangerously deep ravines.

About 27 miles from Monterrey on Highway 40 are the **García Caves** (Grutas de García), with the usual stalactites and stalagmites, huge chambers, and a subterranean lake.

Saltillo is the mile-high capital of the state of Coahuila, famous for the manufacture of multicolored striped serapes. But for the most part it has ceased to be of touristic interest. Should you desire to detour here anyway, good hotels are located in the

Real de Catorce: Ghost Town in the Mountains

There is one fascinating stop along the long, dull road from Saltillo to San Luis Potosí; at Matehuala 140 miles south of Saltillo you'll reach the turn-off to the ghost town of **Real de Catorce,** one of Mexico's most unusual places—like an 18th-century town preserved in a time capsule and hidden in the mountains west of Matehuala. Photographers, historians, lovers of the unusual in Mexico, and people who don't mind uncertainty in their travels will count this among the high points of a trip south of the border. *Important Note:* Fill up with gas in Matehuala—there's no gas in Catorce.

On the northern edge of Matehuala there's a sign on Highway 57 that is the Spanish equivalent of "Turn Here for Ghost Town." Although it's only 38 miles from the turnoff from Highway 57 to Real de Catorce, it takes 1 to 1½ hours to drive on a well-maintained but teeth-jarring cobblestone road that winds up to 9,000 feet in the mountains, passing an onyx quarry and several tiny, crumbling adobe-walled mining villages. You'll know you've arrived at Catorce when you reach the tunnel, which is 2 miles long and the only entrance into the town. Since it's one way, young men at both ends regulate traffic with walkie-talkies; there's a small fee for this service. Usually there is little traffic, but in the past, deaths from fumes occurred during the busy October 2 festival season when a stalled car stopped traffic in the tunnel. After passing through the tunnel, take the narrow high street to the right, up into the town.

After the discovery of silver in 1773, Real de Catorce became one of Mexico's top three silver-producing towns by the early 1800s, with a population of over 40,000. Streets lined with mansions owned by wealthy mine owners sprouted side by side along with an opera house and a mint. The Mexican Revolution brought the downfall of the town; the mines were flooded, and townspeople fled to safety elsewhere and never returned, although many descendants retain ownership and in recent years a few mines have reopened. Catorce is finally experiencing a renaissance of sorts, and many structures are in the process of being restored. The latest population census attributes almost 11,000 people to this town, but locals guess that only around 2,000 people live in the immediate area.

What travelers find on arrival is a neat mountaintop town of mostly closed-up crumbling rock-walled and stucco buildings, some of them mansions, with cactus and brush growing on the rooflines; a church that attracts 25,000 penitents every October 2; a mint that is sometimes open for tours; a stone cockfighting arena; a

center of downtown on Calle Victoria and streets near it. The few good shops are on Calle Victoria as well.

SAN LUIS POTOSÍ   Since the loop around Saltillo was constructed, there's little reason to stop there. Most people barrel on down Highway 57 for the first night at San Luis Potosí, which is possible by starting early in the day at the border. Between Saltillo and San Luis Potosí is a barren desert of scrubby grass, cactus, and Joshua trees on a road that's nearly straight and is one of the most boring in the country. There's usually unleaded gas in the main towns along this route, but fill up at every chance anyway.

Matehuala (alt. 5,085 ft.; pop. 55,000) is the second-largest city in the state of San Luis Potosí, although you wouldn't know it as it's so small in appearance. But it's fascinating cemetery; a small museum; and a few stores selling food, mining equipment, and Huichol Indian clothing and folk art. Miners and prospectors come to town on horseback and hitch their steeds outside the stores. Sanborn's Auto Insurance/Travel in McAllen, Texas, sells a book about the town, *The Incredible City,* by Lucy H. Wallace. Another book often found in Matehuala is *El Real de Catorce* (in Spanish) by Octaviano Cabrera Ipiña.

In winter, bring your heavy clothes, for you're almost 2 miles high, and the hotels have no heat. Hiking boots are useful, since exploring the area on foot is one of the pleasures here. It's also possible to find horses to rent, done very informally, of course, since no one does that exclusively for a living.

Although the town is off the beaten track, the small hotels sometimes fill up by nightfall. The **Vista** tries hard, and though each room has a bathroom, rooms are still humble. Find it after driving through town toward the cemetery. It has a restaurant, but no written menu. **El Real,** in a three-story restored town house has pleasingly rustic rooms, with private bathrooms, and a cozy restaurant with wildly varying food preparation and service. Several people traveling together are often allowed to share a room meant for two to four people; sometimes these are rowdy people. Since the hotel's overnight guard often stays at Real II, there's no control when noisy guests get out of hand. The facade of an old mansion remains at the **Hotel El Real II** (all with bath), but the interior was gutted to make the stylish rooms here with a plant-filled courtyard. The inattentive management is the same as at the El Real. Doubles in these hotels run around $25 to $35 a night. One phone (☎ and fax **488/2-3733**) serves the whole town, and you can try to make a reservation by fax. Best times to try are around 9am and 5pm weekdays. The phone may be continuously busy since people line up to use it, so keep trying. On weekends Mexico Citians make a mad dash for Catorce, so to beat a possible crowd, arrange to arrive by 3pm on a Thursday or Friday. Sunday through Thursday or Friday morning there should be rooms available. Any day though, if you arrive by 3pm and there are no vacancies, you'll still have time to look around briefly and return to the highway before dark. If you can't arrive by 3pm, spend the night at Matehuala, then get an early start the next day.

In general remember that this is a rustic village, and the employee pool is small and inexperienced. Besides the above-mentioned hotel restaurants, there are a couple of good-but-simple restaurants in town.

a tidy town with a good central market and several adequate hotels in town and on the highway. If you're heading to Real de Catorce, Matehuala is the location of the turn-off. **El Mesquite Restaurant,** on the highway before you enter Matehuala, offers cabrito that's wonderfully flavored, not greasy and not goaty tasting.

Once you arrive in San Luis, the scenery improves.

The Silver Cities   To get to the Silver Cities from Monterrey, follow the route described above through to San Luis Potosí. Highway 57 goes all the way to Mexico City, but most people use this route to branch off to the Silver Cities (chapter 10), beginning with San Luis Potosí and southwest of there on Highway 110 to Dolores Hidalgo and Guanajuato and on Highway 111 to San Miguel de Allende.

2 San Luis Potosí

261 miles NW of Mexico City, 216 miles NE of Guadalajara

San Luis Potosí, set more than a mile high in central Mexico's high-plains region, is among the most picturesque and prosperous mining cities of Mexico, and once you visit this bustling city of half a million, you'll see why. It has rich colonial architecture accented by the city's long, momentous history. Capital of the state of the same name, San Luis Potosí was named for Louis, saintly king of France, and "Potosí," the Quechua word for "richness," borrowed from the incredibly rich Potosí mines of Bolivia, which San Luis's mines were thought to rival. San Luis was formally founded in 1583 by Spaniard Fray Magdalena and Captain Caldera on the site of the Chichimec town of Tanga-Manga; the indigenous people had been living on this spot for three centuries before the Spaniards arrived.

The Spaniards came in search of silver and found it, mostly at a small town called San Pedro, 25 miles from San Luis Potosí. But San Luis's mineral springs made it a better place to settle than San Pedro, so this became the mining center. As a state capital, San Luis Potosí exudes prosperity and sophistication, much the way Morelia does. You'll note shady plazas, brick-paved streets, and stunning colonial architecture.

Along with the prospectors came the friars in search of converts: The Franciscans were the first, followed by the Jesuits and the Carmelites. San Luis owes much of its architectural heritage to the vigor—and lavish expenditure—of these groups.

Later, during the Mexican Revolution, the "Plan of San Luis" was proclaimed here. The city has in fact twice been the capital of Mexico—in 1863 and 1867—when Benito Juárez led the fight against European intervention, governing the country from the Palacio de Gobierno (on Plaza de Armas). From this palace he pronounced the death sentence on Maximilian and his two generals.

Today San Luis Potosí lives on industry rather than silver. Everything from automobiles to mezcal is produced in the factories ringing the city, but fortunately the colonial center has been preserved intact.

GETTING THERE & DEPARTING **By Plane Mexicana** (☎ 48/17-8920 or 48/17-9020) flies to/from the capital daily, as well as Chicago, San Antonio, Monterrey, and Morelia.

Aerolitoral (☎ 48/22-2229) flies between Monterrey and Guadalajara. For return transportation to the airport, call **AeroTaxi** (☎ 48/11-0165 or 48/11-0167). One way, the fare will be around $12.

By Bus There are two bus stations here; the large Central Camionera, on the outskirts of town, has the most departures. The old station in town has buses running the 3¹/₂-hour route between San Luis Potosí and San Miguel de Allende.

City buses marked "Central" go to the bus station from the Alameda park opposite the train station for around 25¢. The bus station is divided between first- and second-class buses. First-class buses are at the end beyond the restaurant. The **Flecha Amarilla** group has hourly buses to León and Querétaro, 16 buses a day to Mexico City and Morelia, 8 to Guanajuato, 4 to Pátzcuaro. **Estrella Blanca** has direct service to Zacatecas six times a day. **ETN** offers frequent premier service to Querétaro, Mexico City, and Guadalajara. **Del Norte** buses go to Queretaro and Guadalajara. **Primera Plus** buses go frequently to Morelia, Queretaro, León, and Mexico City. The **Tamaulipas Primera** line goes to Matehuala. **Elite** buses go to Guadalajara, and **Oriente** buses go to León, Guadalajara, Lagos de Moreno, and Querétaro. **Futura** buses run often to Saltillo, Querétaro, and Mexico City. It's an eight-hour bus ride from Monterrey or Saltillo and only three hours from Zacatecas or Aguascalientes.

San Luis Potosí

To Monterrey and Saltillo

Uresti

Azteca

Old Train Station

To Ciudad Valles and Tampico →

Plaza España

New Train Station

Av. 20 de Noviembre

Xochitl

Othón

Alameda Park

Universidad

Templo de San José

Negrete

Lanzagorta

Parrodi

Constitución

Insurgentes

Arriaga

Juan Sarabia

Moctezuma

Escobedo

Plaza San Juan de Dios

Plazuela del Carmen

Villerias

5

4

6

Los Bravo

Morelos

Mercado Hidalgo

Plaza Arriaga

Hidalgo

Zaragoza

Juárez

Reforma

Calle Bocanegra

Jardin Hidalgo

Iturbide

Guerrero

Galeana

Allende

5 de Mayo

3

Mier y Teran

J. de Los Reyes

Carmona

Plaza Fundadores

Aldama

J. de León

Plaza de San Francisco

Vallejo

Calle Abasolo

Calle Comonfort

Carranza

Madero

Universidad

2

1

Independencia

Arista

Obregón

i

Bolívar

Reforma

F. Nieto

Zapata

Ocampo

Pedro Moreno

N

FONART store **2**

Instituto Potosino de Bellas Artes **6**

Museo Casa de Othón **4**

Museo de la Revoluciones **3**

Museo Nacional de la Máscara **5**

Museo Regional Potosino **1**

227

By Car   It takes between six and seven hours to drive the 335 miles from Monterrey to San Luis Potosí; see "En Route To . . . ," above, for the details. From Mexico City, take Highway 57; from Guadalajara, take Highway 80. There's dramatic scenery on the second half of the trip between Aguascalientes and San Luis Potosí—hair-raising hills and scenic "pueblitos."

ORIENTATION   Arriving   The **airport** is about 7 miles from downtown. A taxi to the city center is expensive, but the cost can be shared. A colectivo van is more economical, though don't tarry in the terminal since they leave quickly.

The city's **Central Camionera** (bus station), on Guadalupe Torres at Diagonal Sur, is about 2 miles from the center of town on Highway 57 next to the Motel Potosí. To find city buses to town (50¢) go out the front entrance of the station, turn left, and walk two blocks to the corner of Dolores Jimenez y Muro. There you'll find buses to "Alameda Centro" (the Alameda is a huge park). Get off at the second Alameda stop, which will put you across from the train station. Cabs from the bus station to town cost $3.50 to $4, depending on your bargaining ability.

Information   The **State Tourism Office** is at Carranza 325 (☎ **48/12-9939** or 48/12-9943; fax 48/12-6769). This is one of the better tourism offices in Mexico, with a helpful staff, excellent maps, and descriptive literature. It's open Monday through Saturday from 9am to 8pm. To find it, from the Jardín Hidalgo walk three blocks west on Carranza. The office is on the south (left) side of the street.

City Layout   The **Jardín Hidalgo** is the historic city center, bounded on all sides by colonial-era buildings and narrow one-way streets—Carranza/Los Bravo, Madero/Othón, Allende/5 de Mayo, and Hidalgo/Zaragoza. It's a delightfully walkable city; most of the museums, restaurants, and hotels are downtown and close to the jardín. Many of the city's historic structures now house museums and restaurants.

FAST FACTS: SAN LUIS POTOSÍ

American Express   The local representative is Grandes Viajes, Av. Carranza 1077 (☎ **48/17-6004;** fax 48/11-1166).

Area Code   The telephone area code is 48.

Banks   Banamex, one block off the main plaza (Jardín Hidalgo) to the left of the cathedral, will change traveler's checks or money Monday through Friday from 9am to 1pm.

Climate   It's warm and pleasant year-round here—the average annual temperature is 67°F. Rain is rare, with an average annual rainfall of 14 inches; the rainy season is from April through November, and the coolest weather is between November and March.

EXPLORING SAN LUIS POTOSÍ
A STROLL AROUND THE HISTORIC CENTER

The center of town is the **Jardín Hidalgo,** a large plaza dating from the mid-1700s and shaded by magnolia and flamboyan trees; before that it was a bullring. After the plaza was laid out, the **Palacio de Gobierno** was begun. What you see today of this building has been much repaired, restored, and added to through the centuries—the back and the south facade were redone as recently as 1973. The front of the building retains much of the original 18th-century decoration, at least on the lower floors.

The **bandstand** in the center of the plaza was built in 1947 (although in colonial style), using the pink stone famous to the region. You'll see the stone throughout San Luis. The band usually plays here on Thursday and Sunday evenings, free, beginning around 7:30 or 8pm.

Across the plaza from the Government Palace is the **cathedral.** The original building had only a single bell tower, so the one on the left was built in 1910 to match, although today the newer tower looks to be the older. The **Palacio Municipal,** on the north side of the cathedral, was built in 1850 by the Count of Monterrey and was loaded with great wealth—paintings and sculpture—little of which has survived the plaza's stormy history. When the count died in 1890, the palace was taken over by the bishop, and later in 1921 by the city government. Since that year it has been San Luis's city hall, peaceful for many years until it was firebombed on January 1, 1986, because of political differences. It has all been restored and functions again with business as usual.

The area south of the Jardín Hidalgo is a grid of narrow streets lined with graceful, and for the most part unmodernized, old mansions. These low, elaborate ancient homes are built in the Spanish style, each containing a lush central garden courtyard. It's well worth a stroll down here to peek through the delicate iron traceries that cover the windows, and if you're lucky you can catch glimpses of cool, aristocratic rooms lined with gilt and velvet, looking as they have for almost a century.

Heading north out of the Jardín Hidalgo, stroll along Calle Hidalgo. This street is reserved for pedestrians, and it's a treat to walk from the jardín almost all the way to the city's Central Market.

Southeast of the Jardín Hidalgo is one of the city's most famous squares, **Plazuela del Carmen,** named for the Templo del Carmen church. From the jardín, walk east along Madero-Othón to Escobedo and the plazuela. The entire area you see was once part of the lush grounds of the Carmelite monastery, built in the 17th century. The church survives from that time and is perhaps the Potosinos' favorite place of worship, but the convent has been destroyed. The beautiful **Teatro de la Paz** now stands on the site, having been built there in 1889.

Attached to the Teatro de la Paz and entered to the right of the theater's main entrance, the **Sala German Gedovius** (☎ **48/12-2698**) has four galleries for exhibitions of international and local art. It's open Tuesday through Sunday from 10am to 2pm and 4 to 6pm.

The square is a fine place to take a rest by the fountain before heading on a few blocks east to get to the shady and cool **Alameda,** the city's largest downtown park. All around the sides of the park are vendors selling handcrafts, fruits, and all manner of snacks. Just across Negrete is the magnificent **Templo de San José,** with lots of ornate gold decorations; huge religious paintings; and *El Señor de los Trabajos,* a miracle-working statue with many retablos testifying to the wonders it has performed.

PLAZAS

San Luis Potosí has many more plazas than the two most famous ones mentioned above. **Plaza de San Francisco** (also called **Plaza de Guerrero**) is south of the Palacio de Gobierno along Aldama, between Guerrero and Galeana. This shady square—lush with ivy, iris, vine-covered trees, and royal palms—takes its name from the huge monastery of the Franciscan order at the south side of the plaza. The Church of San Francisco, on the west side, is dated 1799 and is really worth visiting. Note the

---

Impressions

There are city parks and squares in other countries, but in none do they play the same intimate and important part in the national domestic life that they do in Mexico.

—Charles Flandrau, Viva Mexico, 1908

beautiful stained-glass scenes all around the dome; the carved, pink-stone altar; and the radiant statue of the Virgin surrounded by angels and golden rays. There are also several other lovely statues and paintings, and a spectacular crystal chandelier shaped like a sailing ship hangs from the center of the dome.

Another square with a church to visit is **Plaza de los Fundadores,** at the intersection of Obregón and Aldama (northwest of the Jardín Hidalgo). Take a peek through the baroque doorway of the Loreto Chapel, dating from the 16th century, and the neighboring headquarters of the Compañia de Jesús—the Jesuit order. In the chapel is a magnificent golden sunburst over the altar, a reminder of past glories.

It's a ways from downtown, but if you have transportation you might be interested in a visit to **Parque Tangamanga** (☎ **48/17-6217**), one of the largest parks in Mexico, located on Diagonal Sur at the intersection of Tata Nacho. It covers acres and acres, with three lakes; a Hollywood Bowl–type outdoor theater; a planetarium and observatory; a library; a museum; a children's playground; every kind of sports field you can think of; and many picnic sites set up with barbecue pits, tables, and benches, with slatted shelters for shade. The park is open daily from 6am to 6pm (free admission).

Museums

❂ **Museo Regional de Arte Popular.** Ex-Hacienda de Teneria in Parque Tangamanga. ☎ **48/17-2926.** Free admission. Tues–Sun 9am–4pm. Bus: Ruta 32 from behind the Del Carmen church.

Near the center of this large and well-kept urban park is the new home of this small gem of a museum housed in a 19th-century hacienda. Previously it was located on the Plaza de San Francisco where FONART, the government crafts store, is now. The exhibits of Potosino crafts are stunning: ceramics, inlaid wood, papier-mâché "sculptures," basketry, musical instruments, masks, lacy altars made of wax, and local designs in weaving and rebozos. After the bus lets you off at the park entrance, it's a long walk to the museum, and roads are poorly marked; I suggest a taxi.

❂ **Casa de la Cultura.** Av. V. Carranza 1815. ☎ **48/13-2247.** Free admission. Tues–Fri 10am–2pm and 4–6pm, Sat 10am–2pm and 6–8pm. Transportation: Take a cab or any of the city buses running west on Carranza.

Somewhat removed from the city center, this museum is housed in a splendid neoclassical building constructed at the turn of this century, surrounded by large landscaped gardens. There are works of art, historical pieces, handcrafts, and a collection of archaeological items. Adjoining is the Center of Historical and Geographical Studies. All kinds of national and international cultural events are held here.

❂ **Museo Nacional de la Máscara (National Mask Museum).** Villerias 2. ☎ **48/12-3025.** Free admission. Tues–Fri 10am–2pm and 4–6pm, Sat–Sun 10am–2pm; tours in Spanish are available. From the Jardín Hidalgo (Plaza de Armas), walk east along Madero-Othón to Escobedo and the Plazuela del Carmen. The museum is south, just off the plaza.

Just across from the Teatro de la Paz, the National Mask Museum is the only museum of its kind on the national level in Mexico. It's loaded with regional dance masks from all over the country and is a must-see. In addition to its permanent and temporary exhibits, it offers lectures and workshops on mask making, theater, painting, movies, and history, plus hosts a national mask contest at Carnaval (Mardi Gras) time.

Museo Casa de Othón. Calle Manuel José Othón 225. ☎ **48/12-7412.** Free admission. Tues–Sun 10am–2pm and 4–6pm. Walk two blocks east of the Jardín Hidalgo on Othón; the museum is on the left.

This is the birthplace and home of the poet Othón, who lived from 1858 to 1906. Here are the traditional furnishings of the poet's time, his original poetry manuscripts, and beautiful, tender letters he wrote to his wife. Literary readings and lectures are occasionally held here.

SHOPPING

The best one-stop shopping here is at the ✪ **FONART** store (☎ **48/12-7521**) on the Plaza de San Francisco. The building was originally part of the Convent of San Francisco, founded in 1590. Today it houses the offices of the Casa de la Cultura, and, on the ground floor, a branch of FONART, the government-operated crafts store. This one is especially well-stocked with some of the country's best crafts. It's open Monday through Saturday from 10am to 2pm and 4 to 7pm.

It's several blocks along the pedestrian Calle Hidalgo from the Jardín Hidalgo to the city's **Mercado Hidalgo,** a mammoth building devoted mostly to food but also carrying some baskets, rebozos, and straw furniture. While here, be sure to try some *queso de tuna,* a specialty of the region. Although called a "cheese," it's a sweet paste—something like dried figs or dates with a molasses or burnt-sugar taste—made from the fruit of the prickly-pear cactus. It's delicious and comes in pieces of various sizes, ranging from a taste to a kilo.

But the walk along **Hidalgo** is in itself an introduction to the city's commercial life. Hardware stores, craftspeople's shops, shoe stores, groceries, and taverns all crowd the street. Past the Mercado Hidalgo is another big market, the **Mercado República.**

WHERE TO STAY

Hotel María Cristina. Juan Sarabia 110, San Luis Potosí, S.L.P. 78000. ☎ **48/12-9408.** Fax 48/12-8823. 75 rms (all with bath). TV TEL FAN. $25 single; $27 double. Free parking; guarded.

This is one of San Luis Potosí's better downtown hotel choices. Furnishings are non-descript but perfectly comfortable, and the carpeted rooms are large. The rooftop pool is a plus after a long drive, and the rooftop restaurant serves a substantial comida corrida. The parking garage is adjacent. You can get here from the Jardín Hidalgo by walking three blocks east on Othón and turning left onto Juan Sarabia; the hotel is on the right, reached by a flight of stairs up to the lobby.

Hotel Plaza. Jardín Hidalgo 22, San Luis Potosí, S.L.P. 78000. ☎ **48/12-4631.** 32 rms (30 with bath). $11–$13 single; $13–$14 double. Discounts are sometimes available. Free parking (guarded parking for six cars).

If you prefer older buildings with the wistful air of better days, try the small Hotel Plaza, conveniently located on the south side of the Jardín Hidalgo. Rooms are clean, quiet, and old-fashioned with worn bathrooms, old carpets, wallpaper from long ago, chenille bedspreads, and meager furnishings. Higher prices are for rooms that face the plaza. Other rooms face one of two inner courtyards (one covered, the other open) well back from the street. A few rooms have TVs, and there's a TV in the second floor sitting area.

Hotel Principal. Juan Sarabia 145, San Luis Potosí, S.L.P. 78000 ☎ **48/12-0784.** 18 rms (all with bath). $9 single; $12 double.

Although this two-story hotel is directly across from the more expensive María Cristina, that is where the similarity ends. But a pretty entryway tiled in green, white, and gold greets the visitor in this family hotel. The rooms are a bit worn but clean, pleasant, and freshly painted. Some have tiled floors, and others are carpeted. Rooms on the street side will be noisy. To find it from the Jardín Hidalgo, walk three blocks east on Othón and turn left on Juan Sarabia; the hotel is on the left.

WHERE TO EAT

Café Florida. Juan Sarabia 230. ☎ **48/12-5669.** Breakfast $1.25–$3; main courses $1.75–$5. Daily 7am–midnight. MEXICAN.

A short walk north of the hotels María Cristina and Principal, and across from the Jardín de San Juan de Díos, this clean and cheerful restaurant offers good value and service in an attractive, color-coordinated setting with stained-glass accents. Besides regional dishes, you can order beer, malts, and desserts—something for everyone, even a separate smoking section. To find it from the Jardín Hidalgo, walk three blocks east on Othón and turn left onto Juan Sarabia; the restaurant is on the right 1¹/₂ blocks farther.

✪ **Posada del Vierrey.** Jardín Hidalgo 3. ☎ **48/12-7055.** Breakfast $2–$3; main courses $3.50–$6; comida corrida $3.50. Daily 7am–midnight. MEXICAN.

One of the city's most popular restaurants faces the Jardín Hidalgo and is actually three interconnected mansions. It has great atmosphere—a delightful covered courtyard with a bubbling fountain and singing birds—and is the best place to sample local specialties like *enchiladas potosinos* (known elsewhere as empanadas, these come filled with cheese).

Overland Along the Gulf Coast

8

One of the least-traveled parts of Mexico, the Gulf Coast is also one of the country's most interesting—and economical—places to visit. Your money will go farther here than almost anywhere else in the country. Friendly and gracious, the Gulf Coast is like the Mexico of many years ago, and its prices are like those of bygone times as well—an immensely appealing discovery in this country filled with costly and contrived resorts.

The region is studded with archaeological ruins left by indigenous groups. The **Huastec** occupied the area running from the north of the Cazones River to Soto la Marina, which includes portions of Veracruz, Tamaulipas, and San Luis Potosí; the **Totonac** lived from south of the Cazones River to the Papaloapan River, in mid- to upper-Veracruz; and the **Olmec,** a civilization dating back 3,000 years, lived from Río Papaloapan to La Venta in southern Veracruz and northern Tabasco. Pyramidal sites dot the coast, some of which, like **El Tajín** and **Zempoala,** make for excellent off-the-beaten-track travel. First-rate museums along the way are devoted to explaining these cultures and their impact on Mexico. At least 15% of the people speak Indian languages: Otomi is spoken around Puebla spilling into Veracruz; Huasteco, a Maya-linked language, is spoken in Tamaulipas and San Luis Potosí; and Nauahtl and Totonaco are used in both Puebla and Veracruz.

EXPLORING THE GULF COAST

This chapter follows the highways south from the Texas border along the Gulf Coast, but you don't have to drive all the way down the Gulf Coast to see such highlights as Veracruz and the Zempoala ruins, the ruins of El Tajín, Jalapa, or Lake Catemaco. Many people fly from Mexico City to Veracruz and base their exploration of the Gulf Coast from that exuberant city. Veracruz can be easily reached from Mexico City by bus or car as well.

If you're traveling by car or bus from the Texas border, you can travel from either Brownsville/Matamoros down coastal Highway 180 or from McAllen/Reynosa down Highway 97 to Highway 180, through Ciudad Victoria all the way to Lake Catemaco. You won't see much of coastal waters until Tampico, unless you detour off the highway to one of the coastal villages. All along this route maintenance crews burn roadside weeds, and the resulting smoke and flames can be dangerous for driving—be very careful.

If you're traveling by ground transportation from the border, plan to spend your first night in Ciudad Victoria or Tampico. From either of these cities, you'll be within five hours of the other towns in this chapter.

Monterrey and Ciudad Victoria both have airports, and bus travel from either is easy. In Veracruz state, Veracruz has the most flights from the United States, but if you want to fly from Mexico City to Minatitlán (south of Catemaco), it's very easy to work your way north from there by bus.

Veracruz is a natural base for side trips to Jalapa, the capital of Veracruz, and to the ruins of Zempoala, but allow three days. Getting to and seeing Papantla and El Tajín requires around three days. Don't plan to spend less than two nights in Catemaco and two in the Tuxtlas.

1 Ciudad Victoria

420 miles N of Mexico City, 173 miles SE of Monterrey

The capital of the state of Tamaulipas, Ciudad Victoria was founded in 1750 and in 1825 became the namesake of Mexican revolutionary Guadalupe Victoria, the country's first president. *Tamaulipas* means "between mountains," which the city is—distantly. Today, far from being a one-burro town, Cuidad Victoria is home to 208,000 residents, modern architecture, clean wide streets, and two town squares.

ESSENTIALS

GETTING THERE & DEPARTING   By Plane   AeroCalifornia (☎ 131/2-4050) has one flight from San Luis Potosí.

By Bus   For bus information from the Texas border, call the **Greyhound affiliate** in Brownsville/Matamoros (☎ 210/546-7171). Mexican buslines operating in and out of Ciudad Victoria with deluxe service include **Elite** (☎ 131/6-7225), which serves the Mexico City and Guadalajara routes, and **Omnibus de Oriente** (☎ 131/6-0138) to the same two cities plus Reynosa. Buses of the **Tres Estrellas de Oro** line (☎ 131/6-7225) are de paso on their frequent trips to Mexico City, Querétaro, San Luis Potosí, León, Morelia, Matamoros, and Reynosa. **Transportes del Norte** (☎ 131/6-7336) has four daily buses to Mexico City, eight to Tampico and Monterrey, three to Reynosa, seven to Nuevo Laredo, one to Ciudad Valles, and six to San Luis Potosí. **Omnibus de México** (☎ 131/6-7945) offers express service to Guadalajara, Mexico City, and Reynosa, as well as local service to Reynosa, Matamoros, Mexico City, and Querétaro.

By Car   Highway 101 from Matamoros (across the border from Brownsville, Texas) is probably the best road, and the drive takes 4¹/₂ hours. Highway 97 from Reynosa (across the border from McAllen, Texas) is less well maintained and subject to occasional potholes. From Monterrey to Ciudad Victoria, it's a pleasant 4-hour drive, and from Ciudad Valles, it's about the same; both are on Highway 85, a good, paved two-lane highway.

ORIENTATION   Arriving   The **airport** is 12 miles from downtown; shared minivans meet flights and cost $6–$8 per person, while a taxi will charge around $16. The **bus station** is 15 blocks northeast of the town center. Taxis to the bus station from the center cost around $5; the city bus is 75¢.

Information   The **State Tourism Office,** eight blocks south of Plaza Juárez at 16 Rosales #272, near 5 de Mayo (☎ 131/2-1057; fax 131/2-0481), is open Monday through Friday from 9am to 7pm.

City Layout   There's a confusing street-naming custom in Ciudad Victoria. Locals call streets going north and south by their number rather than by their names, but street signs have only the name. Ask for both when getting directions.

Touristic interest centers on the two downtown plazas—Plaza Hidalgo and Plaza Juárez. **Plaza Hidalgo** is bounded by Morelos and Hidalgo going east and west and Colón and J. Tijerina going north and south. The Hotel Sierra Gorda (see "Where to Stay," below) is here. At the **Plaza Juárez,** eight blocks directly west of Plaza Hidalgo, you'll find the **Centro Cultural,** the **State Government Palace,** the state-run *artesanías* shop, a theater, restaurants, and galleries. The plaza is bounded by Juárez and Morelos going east and west and Manuel González/Calle 15 and 5 de Mayo/Calle 16 going north and south. The **Presidencia Municipal** (city hall) is another block west on the corner of Hidalgo and Madero/Calle 17.

Getting Around   Plenty of taxis circle the main plazas, but most sites are within walking distance of either of the central plazas.

Fast Facts   The telephone area code is 131.

EXPLORING CIUDAD VICTORIA

Check local newspapers for what's going on at the **Centro Cultural,** on the **Plaza Juárez,** the performance site of most traveling entertainment. It's almost worth a trip to Plaza Juárez and the **Government Palace** to see the beautiful stone statue of the Huasteca fertility goddess Izcuinan Tlazolteotl, unearthed by a farmer near Altamira, Tamaulipas in 1988. Tall, slender, and exquisitely graceful, with carvings front and back, it's a post-Classic piece dating from between A.D. 900 and 1200.

On weekend evenings the state band plays in the **Plaza Hidalgo.**

The small but worthwhile **Museo Histórico de la Universidad Autónoma de Tamaulipas,** Calle 9 and Matamoros (☎ 131/2-6125), is operated by the University and dedicated to the state's history from pre-Hispanic to the present time. In addition to old photographs, there's a large display of pre-Hispanic artifacts of the Huasteca Indians—a good introduction to this indigenous group about which you'll hear a lot as you journey along the coast. The museum is open weekdays from 9am to 7pm.

SHOPPING   Ciudad Victoria's municipal **market,** two blocks east of Plaza Hidalgo between Morelos and Hidalgo, is one of the cleanest in the country, with a good selection of craft shops around its perimeter.

The government-operated **Tienda Artesanías Voluntario Tamaulipas** is opposite the Palacio del Gobierno on Plaza Juárez, Calle 16/Hidalgo. Besides a few crafts from other parts of the country, there's regionally made Tula pottery and woven furniture and palm baskets from Bustamante. It's open Monday through Saturday from 9:30am to 1pm and 4:30 to 8pm.

WHERE TO STAY

Hotel Sierra Gorda. Plaza Hidalgo (Apdo. Postal 107), Ciudad Victoria, Tam. 87000. ☎ **131/2-2010.** Fax 131/2-9799. 86 rms (all with bath). AC or FAN TV TEL. $21–$37 single; $40 double. Parking $1.

The five-story Sierra Gorda continues to be Victoria's prime downtown hotel. Rooms have carpeted walls, which cut down on noise, and tap water is purified; there are ice machines on each floor. Five less expensive rooms with ceiling fans and black-and-white TVs are usually occupied. All others are air-conditioned and have color TVs. Ask for the "promotional" rates. The hotel restaurant serves good, reasonably priced food.

Into the Mists of the El Cielo Cloud Forest

About 50 miles south of Ciudad Victoria near the town of Gómez Farías, the unique 357,134-acre **El Cielo Biosphere Reserve** was finally set aside in 1985 as an ecologically protected area. Only two other known areas in the world (in China and Germany) have the unusual characteristics of the reserve. Visibly different ecosystems stretch upward from an elevation of 656 to 6,235 feet (more than a mile). On the eastern side there's tropical selva and mountainous woods (the cloud-forest area); on the western side is oak/pine forest, scrubby brush, and cactus. The gulf side of El Cielo gathers cloud moisture (about 103 inches a year) that filters through the limestone rocks down to rivers, providing waters for irrigation that converts infertile fields into a breadbasket for hundreds of miles all the way to the coast. The desertlike landward side of the reserve receives only about 12 inches of moisture a year.

The reserve is divided into sectors by use and is rich in orchids and bromeliads. In addition, there are at least 255 species of birds (175 are migratory), almost 200 varieties of butterflies, 40 kinds of bats, 60 different snakes, and 21 types of frogs. The reserve also shelters the endangered black bear, as well as jaguar and ocelot. The fragile, unspoiled section nearest the top is off-limits to everyone but authorized scientists.

One part of the reserve was opened to tourism in 1991 with the building of 12 rustic state-operated cabins near the small settlement of San José. Some cabins are similar to bunkhouses, and others are individual units, all with indoor baths for night use and outhouses for day use. Marked paths around the cabin area identify some of the trees, but for the most part visitors are on their own for hiking,

Motel Paradise Inn. Carretera Victoria-Matamoros (Hwy. 101), 1km at Libramiento, Ciudad Victoria, Tam. 87000. ☎ **131/6-8181.** Fax 131/6-8371. 30 rms (all with bath). A/C TV TEL. $33 single; $36 double. Free parking; guarded.

If you are driving south to another destination and only want to overnight without the hassle of going downtown, stay at this modern motel, conveniently located on the north side of town. It is very similar to a U.S. motel—clean and carpeted, with good beds, a nice pool, and a pleasant bar/restaurant off the lobby.

WHERE TO EAT

Restaurant Palenque. Colón 223. No phone. Noon buffet $3.50. Main courses $2–$5. Daily noon–midnight. REGIONAL.

Restaurant Palenque is a light and airy place with off-street parking. Patrons seat themselves on *equipales* (chairs with leather seats and backs) and are kept comfortable by fans set in the high ceilings. There is also a bar. The buffet draws in locals. Walk north of the Plaza on Colón for 2$^{1}/_{2}$ blocks, and you'll see the restaurant between Guerrero and Bravo.

Restaurant San Remo. Hidalgo 315. ☎ **131/2-8243.** Cocktails $2.50–$5. Main courses $3–$6. Daily 9am–8pm. SEAFOOD.

For a break from the standard beef-laden menu of northern Mexico, try this long and narrow hole-in-the-wall—you'll be pleasantly surprised. The seafood is good, and there's an offering or two of meat. To find the San Remo from the Centro Cultural and Plaza Juárez, walk a half block east on Hidalgo.

birdwatching, and so forth. A restaurant is available for guests and scholars, but it wouldn't hurt to bring some snack provisions and other essentials.

Though it's only about 25 miles from Gómez Farías, the cabins are accessible only by four-wheel-drive vehicles that take a jolting 2-hour trip. The crude, rocky, narrow roads throughout the reserve are left over from logging days and will remain unimproved. (There are no nearby rentals for rugged vehicles, so you must drive in your own.)

August and September, as well as the period from March through June, are the best months for seeing flowers. Half the rain falls between July and September. Bring a water canteen for hiking, warm clothing for winter months, and lots of socks and two or three changes of shoes since nothing dries quickly. There's no late-night electricity, so a flashlight is a necessity. Be prepared for rain year-round. Beware of rattlesnakes and fer de lance snakes and the painful *mala mujer* (bad woman) plant with fine hairs that penetrate the skin and cause infection.

To enter El Cielo or to reserve a cabin, contact biologist Hector Zamora Treviño, **Dirección de Turismo,** Gobierno del Estado del Tamaulipas, Apdo. Postal 568, Ciudad Victoria, Tam. 87000 (☎ **131/2-3242** or 131/2-9938), or inquire at the **State Tourist Office** in Ciudad Victoria (see "Information," above, for address). Birdwatching trips are also sponsored to another part of the reserve by the **Gorgas Science Foundation,** Southmost College, Brownsville, Texas, which has similar cabin facilities. You can request a 50-minute video about El Cielo from the foundation.

2 Ciudad Valles

140 miles S of Ciudad Victoria, 85 miles SW of Tampico

Ciudad Valles (VAH-yes), a city of 130,000 in the state of San Luis Potosí, is a good place to take a break in your journey to other places. Permeated with a slow-paced, small town ambience, it doesn't seem as large as the population indicates. On your way here, you'll pass many stands selling honey and *piloncillo* (cone-shaped unrefined brown sugar), and you'll see people grinding the raw sugar and cooking it in huge vats. Squash, deep-cooked in brown sugar, hangs temptingly from the rafters of these roadside stands. Stop for a soft drink and look around.

ESSENTIALS

GETTING THERE & DEPARTING   By Bus Ciudad Valles has frequent service from both Monterrey and Tampico, mostly on de paso buses, and less frequent service from Ciudad Victoria. Most first-class buses will be full at the Tampico station, but the second-class station just opposite has frequent buses and a better opportunity for a seat.

By Car Highway 110 from Tampico is well maintained and mostly flat. Highway 85 from Ciudad Victoria is well maintained with a few curves.

Fast Facts The **telephone area code** is 138. Hotels can provide most **information.**

EXPLORING CIUDAD VALLES

Relax and do what the local people do in the evening. Go to the **market,** piled high with fresh herbs and spices, or during the day walk around the **zócalo** and enjoy the fountain and the view over the Río Valles.

Before heading out the next morning, return to the market, where Huasteca Indian women wearing beautiful yarn-and-ribbon headdresses sell huge, fresh, steaming Huasteca tamales. Or look for a restaurant in the market area with a SE VENDE ZACAHUIL sign out front; it sells a version of the huge pig-leg tamal wrapped in a banana leaf.

The **Huasteca Anthropology Museum,** south of the market area at Juan Sarabía and Calle Rotarios, is definitely worth a visit. The huge collection of Huasteca artifacts is somewhat dusty, but the mass and variety of material are wonderful. It's open Monday through Friday from 9am to 1pm and 3 to 6pm.

If you enjoy rum, you will enjoy a tour through the **Destilería Huasteca** (☎ 138/ 2-0357). These folks make Ron Potosí, and it is interesting to see how a truly superior rum is made. Admission is free; call ahead to see if you may drop by. The entrance to the distillery is on your right about a mile south of town on Highway 85.

WHERE TO STAY & EAT

Hotel Valles. Blv. 36 Nte. (Hwy. 85), Ciudad Valles, S.L.P. 79050. ☎ **138/2-0050.** Fax 138/ 2-0050 (ask for the tone). 100 rms (all with bath). A/C TV TEL. $35–$39 single; $39–$46 double. Free parking; secure. Arriving from Ciudad Victoria, you'll find it on the left side before reaching the town center.

The best hotel in town, the Valles is an elaborate hacienda-style motor hotel landscaped with abundant palm trees and gardens and a splendid 100-foot pool. Rooms are large and comfortably furnished; higher prices are for rooms in the newer section. The hotel's restaurant/bar, La Palapa, is open daily from 6:30am to 11pm. The fixed-price daily lunch is a better deal than ordering à la carte, since a main course costs about the same as the set price lunch. El Estate, the steak-and-seafood restaurant on the grounds in back of the hotel, is more expensive.

FROM CIUDAD VALLES TO PAPANTLA & EL TAJÍN

There is no short route to Papantla, so bite the bullet and take Highway 110, a well-maintained blacktop, eastward toward the Gulf Coast and Tampico and Tuxpan. By the time you travel here, a toll road may also be open inland to Papantla. If you choose to stop or stay a night en route, choose Tampico or Tuxpan but not Pozo Rica, an ugly petroleum-centered city.

TAMPICO   Tampico began as a simple Huasteca village on the south bank of the Río Pánuco. The Spanish founded a small village nearby in 1554. As other settlements arose and commerce increased over the centuries, quarrels ensued over distribution of goods and customs duties. Finally the Tampico of today was chartered in 1823 as Santa Anna Tampico. As a major Gulf shipping port and principal oil center, it was more prominent during Mexico's rowdier days between about 1850 and 1940. It has mellowed since, but it has little to offer the casual tourist.

Several modest to upscale hotels are located within a few blocks of the main plaza, on Madero and Mirón between Colon and Serdan, but their elevated prices suggest that they cater more to the business traveler. The few restaurants near the hotels are rather utilitarian. The number and character of bars announces that this is a seaport.

More conveniently located for the motorist are several mid-range hotels northwest on Highway 80/180 (Calle Hidalgo), where there's also a better selection of restaurants.

TUXPAN Nearly 115 miles south of Tampico and about 40 miles north of Poza Rica is the town of Tuxpan, a clean and pleasant city. Situated on the banks of the Río Pantepec 6 miles upstream from the Gulf, it's a good rest stop but otherwise has few attractions, save for beach aficionados or fishermen. The wide beach here, lined with restaurants, has packed sand, and the water is shallow and choppy.

If you land here overnight, there are several passable and inexpensive hotels on Juárez, a block off the river. Each has its own restaurant.

POZA RICA If you are continuing south to Poza Rica, before heading inland to Papantla and El Tajín, the new toll-road may be finished. Poza Rica is an ugly oil industry town, best to avoid or get through as fast as you can. It is, however, a bus transportation hub, so you may wind up changing buses here.

3 Papantla & the Ruins of El Tajín

140 miles NW of Veracruz, 47 miles SE of Tuxpan

The best reasons to visit Papantla, a city of 159,000, include its proximity to the impressive ruins of **El Tajín** (el ta-HEEN)**,** the frequent shows of the *voladores* (flying pole dancers), and its festivities around **Corpus Christi Day.** El Tajín is one of Mexico's most important, but still mysterious, archaeological sites. Vast excavation in recent years has revealed more unusual buildings and more of its history.

Papantla is the former vanilla capital of the world. The hybrid symbol of the community, displayed at both entrances to the city, is a very large concrete vanilla bean with inscribed hieroglyphs. Vanilla extract can be purchased here for about half of what it costs in the States. The long, slender, almost-black vanilla beans are also for sale, but more than likely you'll see them fashioned into figures, flowers, or a dozen different designs.

ESSENTIALS

GETTING THERE & DEPARTING   By Bus Wherever you're coming from, it's often easier to take one of the frequent buses to Poza Rica and change there for a bus to Papantla. There are two bus stations in Papantla. The first-class **ADO station** (☎ 784/2-0218) is downhill north of the plaza, at the corner of Venustiana Carranza and Benito Juárez. From here, four deluxe buses leave daily for Poza Rica, two to Tuxpan, seven to Jalapa, and two to Veracruz. Frequent de paso buses also go to Poza Rica, Jalapa, Veracruz, Minatitlán, and Villahermosa.

From the **second-class station** at 20 de Noviembre no. 200, buses (mostly the school-bus type) depart for Poza Rica every 10 to 15 minutes (watch out for pickpockets!) and to Tecolutla every 40 minutes. There are also eight departures daily to Jalapa and 12 to Veracruz.

By Car See "From Ciudad Valles to Papantla & El Tajín," above, for directions from the north. If you're driving up from the south, Papantla is a 4- to 5-hour mountainous drive (if there is no fog) from Jalapa, via Misantla, Martínez de la Torre, and finally Highway 180 on the coast. From Veracruz Papantla is about five hours away along Highway 180.

ORIENTATION   Arriving If you arrive by a Transportes Papantla bus you'll be six blocks from the center of town, which is at the top of the hill. To get to town center, walk out the front door of the bus station, turn left, and go up Juárez six blocks to the central park, cathedral, and Hotel El Tajín. You'll be at the bottom of the hill if you arrive at the ADO station.

City Layout Coming into town, you'll most likely arrive at the bottom of the hill. Fix your eyes on the cathedral and blue facade of the Hotel El Tajín at the top of the hill. That's the center of town, with a shady **zócalo** (main square), hotels, markets, plaza, and restaurants.

Getting Around   City buses go to the ruins of El Tajín (see below), and taxis are available around the central plaza. Almost everything worth seeing is within easy walking distance of the central plaza.

Fast Facts   The **telephone area code** is 784. The **climate** is sultry, rainy, and hot in summer, cold and rainy in winter; hotels are unheated.

EXPLORING PAPANTLA & EL TAJÍN

In Papantla, you might want to visit the lovely, shady, ceramic tile zócalo, where couples and families sit while gray squirrels with rust-red underbellies beg for food. The cathedral wall facing the square is covered with an artist's impression of El Tajín done in concrete. On top of a hill overlooking the city is an enormous statue of a *volador* (flying pole dancer).

FESTIVALS   The **Feast of Corpus Christi,** the ninth Sunday after Easter, is surrounded by a very special week in Papantla. Well-known Mexican entertainers perform. Also the native voladores (see "The Ruins of El Tajín," below) make special appearances. Lodging is scarce during this week, so be sure to book ahead.

THE RUINS OF EL TAJÍN   The major attraction is the nearby ruins of El Tajín, which are definitely worth seeing. Of the 150 buildings identified at the site, 20 have been excavated and conserved, transforming them from essentially grass-covered mounds into a semblance of their original form. At least 17 ball courts have been found, though only 5 are visible. Mural fragments led archaeologists to discover a Teotihuacán-influenced mural at the top of Building 11, which has been restored.

The ruins at Tajín are divided into the old section (Tajín Viejo) and the new section (Tajín Chico). The most impressive structure, which is in the old section, is the **Pyramid of the Niches.** The pyramid, made of stone and adobe, has 365 recesses on all four sides of the building. The pyramid was once covered in red-painted stucco, with the niches painted black. It is one of the most unusual pre-Columbian structures in Mesoamerica, though there is a similar one near Cuetzalan, Puebla. Near the Pyramid of the Niches is a restored **ball court** with beautiful carved reliefs on the vertical playing sides depicting religious scenes and sacrifices.

The **Temple of the Columns** is in the new section. A stairway divides the columns, three on either side and each decorated with reliefs of priests and warriors and hieroglyphic dates. Many mounds are still unexcavated, but with the reconstruction that has been done so far, it's increasingly easier to see the ruins as a city. The view from atop one of the pyramids, overlooking the rich, green forests dotted with mounds and excavated buildings, is very impressive.

The *voladores* are an additional attraction; they are local Totonac Indians who perform their flying upside-down pole dance. When you hear the sounds of a drum and flute, the voladores are ready. Five of them, dressed in satin pants, vests, and cone-shaped hats with ribbons and small round mirrors, climb the tall pole (donated by Pemex) to the top, where there is a square revolving platform. One dancer stands on the platform beating a drum and playing a flute while the four others perch on the four sides of the platform and attach themselves by their waists to a rope. When the time is right, the four lean over backward and fall off, suspended by the rope, revolving 13 times before they reach the ground. The number 13 corresponds to the number of months in the Aztec calendar.

A small but impressive **museum** greets you as you approach the esplanade. Inside are selected pieces from the site, including two burials, some exquisite pots, and two restored wall paintings. Perhaps most interesting are two large models of the area, giving you the effect of seeing the site from the air; this is helpful, as the entire archaeological zone covers about 4 square miles.

Across from the museum is a small snack/gift shop, as well as a small restaurant. In a semicircle facing the volador pole are several more gift shops. Admission to the site and museum is $2; it is free to all on Sunday. The fee for a personal video camera is $4. Use of a tripod requires a permit from INAH (the Instituto Nacional de Antropologia y Historia) in Mexico City. If you watch a performance of the voladores, one of them will collect an additional $2 from each spectator. The site is open daily from 9am to 5pm; the voladores fly around Friday through Sunday at 11am and 4pm, although any time a tour bus arrives they tend to suit up.

To get to El Tajín from Papantla, look for buses marked "Chote/Tajín," which run to El Tajín from beside the Juárez market (opposite the front of the church, at the corner of Reforma and 20 de Noviembre) every hour beginning at 7am—but don't count on always finding these buses. As an alternative, buses marked "Chote" pass more frequently and will leave you at the Chote crossroads; from there, wait for a bus for the short distance to El Tajín or take a taxi from there for around $5. From Veracruz, take Highway 180 to Papantla; from there, take Route 127, which is a back road to Poza Rica, going through Tajín.

ORGANIZED TOURS   The hotels in "Where to Stay," below, will arrange a guided all-day tour of a vanilla plantation, a typical Totonac house, and the El Tajín archaeological site for $25 per person.

SHOPPING   Two principal markets are in Papantla, both near the central plaza. **Mercado Juárez** is opposite the front door of the church. **Mercado Hidalgo** is a block or two down Reforma on the left, away from the plaza. The latter has a better selection of locally made baskets and regional clothing. Besides vanilla, **Xanath,** a popular local liqueur, makes a good gift and costs around $13; **Vreez,** another type, costs $11. Embroidered blouses and dresses are sold in the market.

WHERE TO STAY

Hotel Premier. Enríquez 103, Papantla, Ver. 93400. ☎ **784/2-1645** or 784/2-0080. 20 rms (all with bath). A/C TV TEL. $25 single; $30 double. Free, secure parking a half block away.

The Premier's second-floor lobby is reached through a mirror-lined hallway. Opened in 1990, this hotel is a fine alternative to Papantla's otherwise meager selection of hotels. Rooms are nicely furnished and have tile floors, baths with showers, and some have small balconies overlooking the zócalo. Others toward the back are windowlesss and quiet and are reached through a tunnel-like hallway.

El Tajín Hotel. Nuñez 104, Papantla, Ver. 93400. ☎ **784/2-0121,** 784/2-1623, or 784/2-0644 or 784/2-1623. Fax 784/2-1062. 60 rms (all with bath). A/C or FAN TV TEL. $13–$18 single; $13–$23 double. Free, secure parking a half block away.

Walk along the cathedral wall up the hill to the thriving El Tajín Hotel, the building with the bright-blue facade near the top. The rooms here are small and tidy; some have king-size beds. The Restaurant Tajín in the hotel is clean and inexpensive (but the coffee is terrible).

WHERE TO EAT

Mercado Juárez has numerous cookshops that in the morning bring in some outstandingly delicious *zacahuil* (the huge tamal cooked in a banana leaf). Look around until you see a cook with a line of patrons—that's where you'll get the best zacahuil. Outside the market, rolling cart vendors sell steamy hot atole.

Besides zacahuil, be sure to try delicious molotes, small football-shaped creations of fried masa that are served as appetizers.

⑤ **Cenaduría M.Y.R.**, 16 de Septiembre no. 117. No phone. Molotes 75¢; tostadas 80¢–$1.50; main courses $2–$3. Daily 6–11pm. REGIONAL.

Cenadurías are dinner places, so don't come for lunch. A Formica and folding chair sort of place, the M.Y.R. is short on atmosphere but makes up for it in taste. This is the best place to try *molotes.* And you may want to top off any meal with fresh bananas and cream. This cenaduría is across from the church on the uphill side.

✪ **Plaza Pardo.** Enriquez 105. ☎ **784/2-0059.** Breakfast $2–$3.25; sandwiches $1.50–$3; main courses $2–$5. Daily 7:30am–10:30pm. MEXICAN/AMERICAN.

This cheerful place, located across from the main plaza, has the look of an old-fashioned ice-cream parlor. Try the coconut (*coco*) or pecan (*nuez*) ice cream; the strawberry malts (*malteadas de fresa*) are so fresh and frothy you'll be certain you're having something healthy! You can also get a full meal morning to night.

4 Jalapa

188 miles NE of Mexico City, 65 miles NW of Veracruz, 111 miles NE of Puebla

Capital of the state of Veracruz, Jalapa (pronounced "ha-LAP-a" and spelled "Xalapa" by its residents), is an interesting town to explore for a day or more. Although modern, the city is riddled with old, narrow streets that wind up and down. In addition to being the jalapeño-pepper capital of Mexico, Jalapa is the hometown of António López de Santa Anna, whose various terms as president of Mexico spanned 22 years; one of his haciendas is now a museum southeast of town.

Earlier in the city's history, Cortés and his troops passed through nearby Xico on their way from the Gulf Coast to the Aztec capital of Tenochtitlán for the first time. Chroniclers of the Conquest described the hazards of the trip and particularly noted the *chipi chipi,* a fine but pelting rain that is a frequent part of Jalapa life. Coffee plantations surround the city for miles around, so take time out for a cup of the excellent local brew.

ESSENTIALS

GETTING THERE & DEPARTING   By Plane   Veracruz, two hours south of Jalapa, has the closest major airport, although some charter flights use the small Jalapa airport.

By Bus   The trip to or from Papantla takes about six hours over the long route through Perote (with an incredible number of rest stops but also an incredible number of alpine views); if you're in a hurry, be sure to ask for one of the 10 daily buses going the short route (4 hours) via Cardel or take a bus going directly to or from Poza Rica, where you can change to a bus to or from Papantla.

Both **ADO** and **AU** buses have much the same routes, with frequent service to and from Mexico City and Veracruz. Three ADO buses from Zempoala leave at very odd hours.

By Car   From Mexico City, Puebla, Tlaxcala, or Papantla, there is danger of dense fog between Perote and Jalapa. Reckless drivers pass even when they can't see ahead on the narrow two-lane highway. On a clear day this drive will remind you of Switzerland, with spotted cows grazing on verdant hillside pastures.

From Veracruz, take Highway 180 to Cardel and then turn left (west) onto Highway 140 past the coffee plantations.

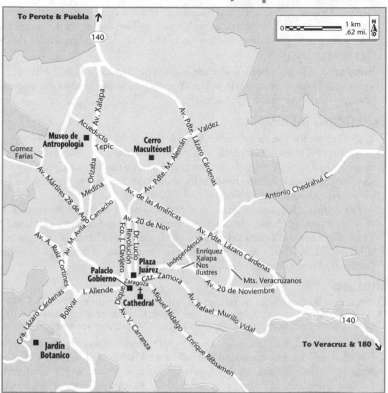

To Perote & Puebla ↑

140

0 1 km / .62 mi. N

Av. Xalapa
Acueducto
Tepic
Museo de Antropología
Gomez Farias
Ortizaba
Medina
Av. Mártires 28 de Ago
Av. M. Ávila Camacho
Cerro Macultéoetl
Av. Pdte. Lázaro Cárdenas
Av. Pdte. M. Alemán
Av. Pdte. Valdez
Antonio Chedrahuí C.
Av. de las Américas
Av. 20 de Nov
Dr. Lucio Revolución
Fco. J. Clavijero
Av. A. Ruiz Cortines
Av. 20 de Nov
Independencia
Av. Pdte. Lázaro Cárdenas
Enríquez
Xalapa
Nos
Ilustres
Palacio Gobierno
Plaza Juárez
Gtz. Zamora
Zaragoza
Mts. Veracruzanos
Av. 20 de Noviembre
I. Allende
Diligue
† **Cathedral**
Miguel Hidalgo
Av. -V. Carranza
Av. Rafael Murillo Vidal
Enrique Rébsamen
Gra. Lázaro Cárdenas
Bolívar
■ **Jardín Botánico**
140
To Veracruz & 180 ↘

ORIENTATION   Arriving   The bus station, **Caxa,** is about a mile and a half east of the town center just off Calle 20 de Noviembre. It resembles a sophisticated airport, with arrivals upstairs and departures downstairs and an overhanging roof for protection from the elements. Inside it's sleek, with shops, telephone and fax service, car rental, guarded luggage, and a fast-food cafeteria in the center. A **tourist booth** is open daily from 7am to 10:30pm. Taxis are downstairs; prices here are controlled, so there is no haggling. Buy your ticket at the kiosk. Tickets to the center of town cost around $1.75.

Information   The **State Tourism Office** is some 12 blocks (about a mile) north-west of the town center on Av. Camacho 191 at Bravo (☎ **784/14-4622**). Little English is spoken, but they have maps and literature. Hours are Monday through Friday from 9am to 3pm and 6 to 9pm and Saturday from 9am to 1pm.

City Layout   Jalapa is a hilly town with streets seemingly without much order, which is very confusing to the visitor. The center of town is the beautiful **Plaza Juárez,** where on a clear day the Pico de Orizaba is visible to the southwest. Facing and across the street (north) from the plaza is the **Palacio Municipal** (city hall), while just east is the **Palacio del Gobierno** (state offices). Across (north) from this is the **cathedral.** A tunnel runs under the park and connects **Avenidas Zaragoza** and **Ávila Camacho,** two of the main arteries, which cross the city, randomly changing name and direction in the process.

Getting Around   The hotels and restaurants I have recommended (see "Where to Stay" and "Where to Eat," below, are within easy walking distance of the central Plaza Juárez. Taxis in Jalapa are inexpensive—around $1.75 to $2 to most places in the city. City buses are 20¢.

Fast Facts   The **telephone area code** is 28. The **climate** is humid and warm in summer and humid and chilly in winter. Year-round, be prepared for the *chipi chipi* (chee-pee chee-pee) rain that comes and goes.

EXPLORING JALAPA

Take a look at the murals by José Chávez Morado in the **Palacio de Gobierno** and glance into the massive **cathedral,** with its disconcerting floor that inclines upward toward the altar. Walk through the streets and admire the bougainvillea, fruit trees, and flowers. Jalapa is halfway between the mountains and the tropics, so it has both coffee plantations and sultry breezes.

The Agora, a hangout for artists, students, and other cosmopolitan types, is just off Plaza Juárez. For books, records, films, conversation, and concerts look here first. Then, check out the **Teatro del Estado,** at Manuel Ávila Camacho and Ignacio de la Llave. This is Jalapa's official cultural center and home of the Jalapa Symphony Orchestra. There's always something going on.

MUSEUMS

✪ **Museo de Antropología de Jalapa.** Av. Jalapa at Av. Aqueducto. ☎ **28/15-0920** or 28/15-4952. Admission $2.50. Museum, Tues–Sun 9:30am–5pm; shop, Tues–Sun 10am–4:30pm. Bus: "Museo" from Plaza Juárez or on Avenida Jalapa or Avenida Americas.

Many people come to Jalapa just to visit this suburban museum operated by the University of Veracruz. It's second only to the world-renowned anthropological museum in Mexico City and worth a the visit if you're anywhere nearby. Designed by Edward Durrell Stone's firm (who designed the Kennedy Center in Washington, D.C.), it's divided into sections devoted to the Indian groups on the Gulf Coast—Huastec, Totonac, and Olmec—and to specific sites relating to each group. Good maps illustrate the regions and sites. An ethnographic section shows the daily modern life of these groups (except the Olmec).

A signature giant Olmec head is the first thing you see on entering, and you will see four more before you finish. Although the gigantic Olmec pieces are the most visible and the Olmec culture is the oldest (it began around 1500 B.C.), each subsequent culture left powerful artifacts—it's unlikely you'll see pieces as magnificent as these in other museums. The museum is highly recommended, especially if you plan to visit any of the actual sites in your travels.

There is a shop/bookstore to the right of the lobby. Near the shop is the auditorium where music recitals at noon on Sunday ("Domingos Culturales") are often held.

Museo de Ciencia y Tecnología. Av. Murillo Vidal s/n. ☎ **28/12-0666.** Admission $5. Tues–Sun 10am–5pm (last ticket sold 3pm). Bus: "Vidal" or "Torre" from the Plaza.

This museum is unique for Mexico. Although it deals only peripherally with Mexico and its history, it provides an outlook on the world of physical and natural science not often seen. There are exhibits of old cars (like an MG-TD) and steam engines (old No. 8 is here), and even a few old airplanes (like the Stinson Reliant). Hands-on demonstration exhibits explain electromagnetics, optics, acoustics, mechanics, and the workings of the human body. The 16 model sailing ships and several model oil tankers are especially interesting. A major exhibit on space allows you to peer into mock-ups of U.S. and Soviet modules and then watch the giant-screen theater presentation of NASA's *El Sueño del Realidad* (*The Dream Is Alive*) or *Sobre Las Alas*, a historical overview of aviation. All in all, this is an exciting way to spend a few hours or an afternoon.

✪ **Hacienda Lencero.** Km 9 on Hwy. 140 toward Veracruz. No phone. Admission $3.25; free Spanish-speaking guides on request. Tues–Sun 10am–5pm. Drive or take a taxi ($12 round trip) about 9 miles south of town on Highway 140 toward Veracruz, past the country club; watch for the signs on the right. You can also catch a bus marked "Banderilla-P. Crystal-Lencero" on Avenida Lázaro Cárdenas. The bus will stop either in the village of Lencero or at a nearby spot along the highway. From either stop it's a walkable distance to the hacienda.

Known today as the Hacienda Lencero, or sometimes the Museo de Muebles (Furniture Museum), this fabulous country estate 9 miles southeast of the town center was the home of António López de Santa Anna from 1842–1856, president of Mexico 11 times. Here he retreated from the world, but on occasion he opened his doors to receive countless notable visitors. Purchased by the state of Veracruz in 1981, the hacienda is one of the best museums of its kind in the country.

Rooms in the sprawling mansion are filled with furniture from Mexico, Europe, and Asia, depicting a type of elegance found in Mexico during the 19th century. Among them is Santa Anna's bed with the national emblem of an eagle holding a snake in its beak. The carefully tended grounds are awash with flowers and shaded by centuries-old trees. Next to the grand house, the spacious servants' quarters, with a gracious, wide covered patio facing a lake fed by a natural spring, has been converted into a **restaurant** serving light snacks, pastries, and soft drinks.

SHOPPING

At the **Casa de Artesanías,** Paseo de la Laguna (☎ 28/17-0804), the quantity and quality of crafts vary from time to time, but you can usually pick up packaged Veracruz coffee, cans of jalapeño peppers, baskets from Papantla, and pottery from San Miguel Aguasuelos—all local products. The store is open Monday through Friday from 9am to 1pm and 4 to 7pm and on Saturday from 9am to 3pm. It's on Calle Dique, off Zaragoza, six blocks south of Plaza Juárez and near a lakeside park.

A good place to pick something for yourself or for a gift that is typical of the region is **Café Colón,** downtown at Primo Verdad 15. The staff roasts, grinds, and packages coffee here, and it's available for purchase ground or *en grano* (whole bean) by the kilo or partial kilo. Walk two blocks east from the Parque Juárez on Zaragoza, then north half a block on Primo Verdad. Café Colón is on the right.

WHERE TO STAY

✪ **Mesón de Alférez.** Sabastiano Camacho 2, Jalapa, Ver. 91000. ☎ 28/18-6351. Fax 28/14-9665. 9 rms, 11 suites (all with bath). TV TEL. $18 single; $23 double; $36 suite. Free parking nearby; secure.

The owners of the lovely Posada del Cafeto (see below) also own this wonderful hotel in the 1808 home of the former Spanish viceroy's representative. Rooms, named after historic Jalapa streets, are furnished in colonial style; bright accents of color warm the colonial-era stone. Some rooms feature a cozy loft bedroom overlooking a living room. The dining room, Hostería La Candela, is located in what had been the private chapel. The dining room is open from 7:30am to 10pm, and meals are accompanied by pleasant music and attentive service. To find the Mesón from the Plaza, go one block east on Zaragoza to the corner of Sabastiano Camacho; it's close to the Hotel Monroy. The entrance is actually on Zaragoza.

✪ **Posada del Cafeto.** Canovas 12, Jalapa, Ver. 91000. ☎ 28/17-0023. Fax 28/12-0403. 28 rms (all with bath). TEL. $14 single; $17 double. Free parking nearby; secure.

What a treat it is to discover this colorful and comfortable town house-turned-hotel, opened in 1987. It was named for the coffee industry in the region, so there's coffee available morning and evening, and guests can help themselves. The owners gave the rooms colorful Mexican style, with bright bedspreads, royal-blue metal doors and window frames, white walls with painted flower designs, and Mexican tile accents. Windows let in plenty of light (and also some cold in winter). Each room is slightly different—some are small, but all come with two single beds, two doubles, or one of each. A small restaurant, open daily 7am to 10am and 5 to 10pm, serves coffee, pastries, fruit, and yogurt. From the Plaza Juárez, walk four blocks east on Zaragoza, then one block south where it bends. Canovas is the first street on your right, and the Posada is farther down on the right.

WHERE TO EAT

Walk almost any block in the downtown area, and you'll find restaurants of all kinds. **Callejón del Diamante** is a narrow pedestrians-only street 1 1/2 blocks from Plaza Juárez with half a dozen restaurants—La Fonda and La Sopa El Mayab among them. Prices are reasonable, and most are open Monday through Saturday from 8am to 10pm. To find them, turn your back to the cathedral and walk left on Enríquez across Lucio one block; the callejón will be on the left.

Restaurant la Casona del Beaterio. Zaragoza 20. ☎ **28/18-2119.** Breakfast $2–$5; main courses $2–$7; comida corrida $3.50. Daily 8:30am–10:30pm. MEXICAN.

This delightful place near the zócalo supplies good food and service in a charming atmosphere. Tables and chairs are plain, but there are high-beamed ceilings, plants, and photos of old Jalapa on the walls. The menu lists a variety of chicken dishes, such as *pechuga maguey* (chicken breast in rich liquor). You can find La Casona on Zaragoza, two blocks east from Parque Juárez on the south side of the street; it's at the end of a row of restaurants.

Salon Don Quijote. Lucio 4 (in the Hotel Mexico). ☎ **28/17-3365.** Breakfast $2.50–$3.50; main courses $3–$6; comida corrida $3; paella (Sun only) $6. Daily 7am–10pm (comida corrida served 1–5:30pm). MEXICAN.

For years this restaurant, far back in the parking lot of the Hotel Mexico, has been serving the best comida corrida downtown. It begins with fruit, then soup, vegetables, meat, rice, dessert, and coffee. You can't go wrong here. It's half a block east of Plaza Juárez, facing the left side of the cathedral, and has lovely stained-glass windows.

5 Veracruz & the Ruins of Zempoala

145 miles E of Mexico City, 68 miles SE of Jalapa

Veracruz (Vay-rah-CROOS), today a delightfully raucous port town, is intriguing for its combination of European and African influences. It also features a clean and impressive shoreline. Despite its reputation as a good-time town—especially during Carnaval, just before Lent—there's a refreshingly relaxed atmosphere in this city of 328,000 residents, more like the Mexico of many years ago.

No trip to Veracruz is complete without indulging in two local customs: drinking coffee at La Parroquia and listening to marimba music beneath the portals of the Plaza de Armas.

Veracruz has been Mexico's principal port almost since Hernán Cortés landed here on Good Friday in 1519. Within three months, however, he moved his forces 45 miles north to a place called Quiauixtlan, a small Indian settlement known today as Villa Rica. Six years later, in 1525, Cortés's forces re-settled near the mouth of the

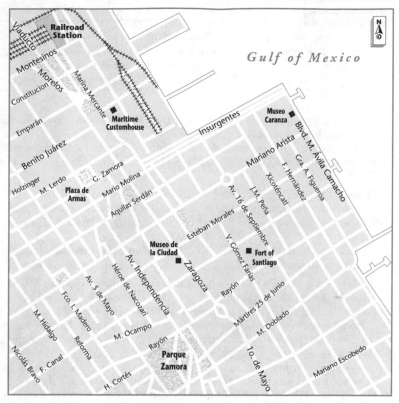

Río Huitzilapan at what is now Antigua (about 14 miles north of modern Veracruz). This move was somewhat more permanent—the ruins of several massive stone houses such as the House of Cortés (La Casa de Cortés) still stand there. Then, in 1599, the settlement was moved south to the original landing site, and Villa Rica de la Vera Cruz ("the Rich Town of the True Cross")—Cortés's name for the town—became permanent.

The Spaniards once shipped most of their gold and silver out of the port, and looting pirates periodically corralled the townfolk in the parish church or abandoned them on an island in the bay while they methodically ransacked the town. The citizens in turn built a high wall around the old town (around the Plaza de Armas) and constructed a massive fort, San Juan de Ulúa, on what was then an island in the harbor (now connected to the mainland by a curving pier). Despite these formidable precautions, the pirates pillaged the port in 1654 and again in 1712. Later the French invaded in 1832 and 1861, and the Americans attacked in 1847 and 1914.

ESSENTIALS

GETTING THERE & DEPARTING   By Plane   Mexicana (☎ **29/32-2242;** at the airport 29/21-4020) flies to Veracruz from Mexico City five times daily and from Mérida twice daily. **AeroLitoral** (☎ **29/35-0701**), an Aeroméxico affiliate, flies from Ciudad Juárez, McAllen and San Antonio (Texas), Minatitlán, Monterrey, Tampico, and Villahermosa. **Aeroméxico** (☎ **29/35-0142;** at the airport 29/34-3428, or toll free 29/91-800/3-6202), flies from Mexico City. **Aerocaribe/Aerocozumel** (☎ 29/

Impressions

*A chronic complaint along the coast of Veracruz is the blast of Boreas called the
"Norther." It swoops down upon the sea like a bird of prey, sending ships ashore,
and laying low many a forest monarch and many a residence on land.*
—Fredrick A. Ober, *Travels in Mexico and Life Among the Mexicans,* 1884

37-0260; at the airport 29/34-5888) arrives from various locations in the Yucatán,
Guatemala, Belize, and Cuba.

The airport is $2^1/2$ miles from the town center. Minibuses of **Transportación
Terrestre Aeropuerto** (☎ 29/37-8719) go out for every departing flight and cost
$10.50.

By Bus   There are frequent buses from Jalapa, Orizaba, Córdoba, and Mexico City
to Veracruz. From Veracruz's **ADO** station (☎ 29/37-5744), buses leave frequently
for Orizaba, Córdoba, and San Andrés Tuxtla; buses to Jalapa leave every 30
minutes.

From the **Central Camionera** (☎ 29/37-6790), frequent buses head from
Veracruz to Mexico City—a 7-hour trip. Six buses daily go directly to Catemaco.

By Car   Veracruz is less than two hours away from Jalapa via Highway 140 to the
coastal Highway 180 and the toll road into Veracruz, or cut off before the coast at
Puente Nacional and go south to Veracruz on toll-free Highway 146.

From Mexico City, Córdoba, or Orizaba, take Highway 150 to the coast and then
drive north on Highway 180 to Veracruz; it's less than a 2-hour drive from the latter two cities.

If you're driving from Oaxaca to Veracruz city or any of the other northerly spots
in Veracruz state, it's probably best to take Highway 131 north to Tehuacán, then
veer north in Tehuacán and drive to Highway 150D. Take 150D east through
Orizaba and on to Veracruz.

ORIENTATION   Arriving   If you arrive **by plane,** don't tarry long in the airport
before getting to the colectivo minivans that await each flight and cost $3: They fill
up and leave rapidly and don't return until the next expected flight. The **bus station**
is many blocks south of the Plaza on Díaz Mirón (between Orizaba and Molina).
Since the bus station is a good distance from downtown, try to make your onward
reservations when you arrive in Veracruz.

The **Central Camionera** (main bus station) is 20 or so blocks south of the town
center on Diaz Mirón between Orizaba and Molina. Taxis cost around $1.75 to the
Plaza de Armas. "Díaz Mirón" buses go to and from the town center. Catch the out-
bound on Avenida 5 de Mayo (two blocks west of the Plaza de Armas).

Information   The **tourism office** (☎ 29/32-1999), with its enthusiastic staff, is
right downtown on the Plaza de Armas. The office is on the ground floor of the
Palacio Municipal (Town Hall), on the east side of the square; it's open daily from
9am to 9pm, although sparsely staffed from 1 to 4pm.

City Layout   Parallel to the shoreline, **Paseo del Malecón (Insurgentes)/Bulevar
Camacho** runs north and south; it goes into the town center and out to the beaches
and resorts south of town. (Technically, the Malecón is named Insurgentes, but that
name is seldom used.) City life gravitates around the **Plaza de Armas,** one block west
of Malecón. It's bounded by Lerdo and Zamora going east and west and by
Independencia and Morelos going north and south. Most museums, restaurants, and
hotels are either here or within a short walk.

Getting Around   City buses are inexpensive (around 25¢ to 40¢) and easy to use. I have mentioned those that get you to and from the most important places in town. **Taxis** cost around $2 to get almost anywhere in the downtown area, including the bus station.

FAST FACTS: VERACRUZ

American Express   Viajes Olymar represents American Express. They have offices in Plaza Mocambo, Local A-18 (☎ **29/21-9923**), as well as on Bulevar Camacho 2221, Col. Zaragoza (☎ **29/31-4636;** fax 29/31-3169).

Area Code   The telephone area code is 29.

Climate   You'll find it hot and sultry in summer and mild in spring, fall, and winter, with windy, sand-blowing *nortes* (northers) from November to March.

Consulate   The U.S. Consulate is located on Víctimas del 25 de Junio, no. 384, almost at the corner of Gómez Farías (☎ **29/31-0142**). It's open Monday through Friday from 9am to 1pm.

High Season   The peak tourist season falls in June, July, and August and then December through March.

Post Office   The correo (post office), located on Avenida de la República, near the Maritime Customs House, is open Monday through Friday from 8am to 8pm.

EXPLORING VERACRUZ

More than anything else, you'll remember the liveliness of Veracruz after you visit here. There is a certain carefree spirit about this bustling seaport. From 1 or 2pm until the early morning, you'll hear **mariachi** and **marimba** bands playing in and around the **Plaza de Armas/zócalo,** and on Tuesday, Thursday, and Saturday from 8 to 10pm, the city band plays in front of the **Palacio Municipal,** where local couples often dance a unique form of the waltz known as **danzón.** Up and down the **Malecón** and in the square, people gather to socialize, listen to the music, or sell trinkets. It's a lively town, especially on Sunday, which seems to be the big socializing day, and Parque Zamora hosts evening dancing.

Sightseeing trolleys—open-air, rubber-wheeled trolleys, replicas of those that ran on rails in Veracruz until the early 1980s—leave from Insurgentes (corner of 16 de Septiembre, on the Malecón opposite the Emporio Hotel) every hour daily (unless the weather is bad) from 10am to 11:30pm, making an hour-long tour through town. The cost is $1.75 round-trip.

The **Ballet Tradicional de México** (☎ **29/31-0574** or 29/32-6693 for reservations) performs at the Teatro J. Clavijero. Tickets cost $3 to $5. Check with the tourism office (see "Information," above).

For the three days before Ash Wednesday, **Carnaval** takes place in Veracruz, and it's one of the best in Mexico. Visitors from Mexico City pack the streets and hotels; those without rooms live out of their cars. Indians, who've walked a day's journey from their villages, spread their crafts on the sidewalks. Even the townspeople, normally attentive to their own affairs, join the crowds in the music-filled streets.

There are fabulous floats (in Spanish, *carros alegóricos*, "allegorical cars") made with true Mexican flair—bright colors, papier-mâché figures (even the Muppets showed up on one float), large flowers, and live entertainment. Groups from the neighboring villages don their peacock- and pheasant-feathered headdresses in preparation for the dances they will perform during the festivities. There are costumed Draculas and drag queens and women in sparkling dresses parading down the streets. Most of the other activities center in Plaza de Armas and begin around noon, lasting well into the night.

If you plan to be in Veracruz for the three days of Carnaval, reserve hotel space months in advance, as everything's jammed full at this time. On the Sunday before Ash Wednesday, the longest and most lavish of the Carnaval parades takes place on the Malecón. Parades on Monday and Tuesday are scaled-down versions of the Sunday parade (ask at the tourist office about the parade routes on Monday and Tuesday), and by Wednesday, it's all over.

MUSEUMS & AN AQUARIUM

San Juan de Ulua. ☎ **29/38-5151.** Admission $4.50. Tues–Sun 9am–5pm. Bus: "San Juan de Ulua" from the *parada* (stop) across from Calle Juárez on Avenida de la República. Drive across the bridge that heads north out of the Plaza de Armas between Avenida de la República and Avenida Morelos, then turn right past the box storage and piers.

Built as a limestone-rock fortress against pirate invasion, the structure became infamous instead as a prison noted for extreme cruelty and for the famous people who were incarcerated there, among them Benito Juárez. He later led the Reform Movement from the fort and became one of the country's most revered presidents. English-speaking guides charge for tours, or you can go on your own.

Baluarte Santiago. At the corner of Rayón and Gómez Farías. ☎ **29/31-1059.** Admission $2.50. Tues–Sun 10am–4:30pm. From the Plaza de Armas, walk five blocks south on Independencia, then turn left (east) onto Rayón and walk for two more blocks.

This bulwark was built in 1636 as part of the city's fortifications against the pirates, but this bastion is all that's left of the old city walls and the original nine forts. It's remarkable to see the type of construction that was used in those days—it's solid, to say the least. A collection of pre-Hispanic gold jewelry, recovered several years ago by a fisherman along the coast some miles north of Veracruz, is on permanent display.

City Museum. Zaragoza 397. ☎ **29/31-8410.** Admission $1. Tues–Sun 9am–3pm. From the Palacio Municipal, walk 4 1/2 blocks south on Zaragoza; the museum is on the right.

Recently restored, this 120-year-old building was converted into the City Museum years ago. Twelve rooms on two levels off the beautiful interior courtyard house archaeological relics from pre-Columbian Gulf Coast sites. The collection is small compared to those of the museums in Jalapa and Villahermosa, but the displays are attractive. Olmec, Totonac, and Huastec Indian cultures are represented here. Several rooms display regional costumes and crafts.

El Acuario. Plaza Acuario Veracruz, Blv. M. Ávila Camacho at Playón de Hornos. ☎ **29/37-4422.** Admission $5 adults; $1.75 children ages 2–12. Daily 10am–7pm. The Plaza Acuario Veracruzana is at the eastern edge of downtown where Bulevar Ávila Camacho meets Xiconténcatl. Walking along the Malecón, you'll find it about 15 blocks from the corner of Insurgentes (Malecón) and Camacho. Buses marked "Mocambo-Boca del Río" stop here.

Opened in the fall of 1992, the aquarium has become a major attraction in the state. Located in a shopping center (where there are numerous restaurants), the aquarium is one of the largest of its kind in Latin America, with nine freshwater and 15 saltwater tanks featuring the marine life of the area and all of Mexico. The circular *gran pecera* (large tank) gives the illusion of being surrounded by the ocean and its inhabitants—including sharks.

Venustiano Carranza Museum. Malecón between Xiconténcatl and Hernandez. No phone. Free admission. Tues–Sun 9am–4pm. The Faro (lighthouse) is a block west of the Pemex Tower on the Malecón, next to the Hotel Emporio.

Located on the second floor of the headquarters of the 3rd Naval Military Zone and the site of the port's second lighthouse, this small museum is dedicated to Venustiano Carranza, who became president of Mexico in 1917. A leading figure in Mexico during the Revolutionary period, Carranza served as First Chief of the Constitutionalistic Army. He was assassinated in 1920 by killers vaguely linked to Álvaro Obregón, who sought to overthrow him. The museum consists of four rooms: Carranza's office/bedroom; two rooms of photographs showing Carranza at various stages of his life (including a facsimile of his autopsy report); and a room with a copy of the Constitution, a portrait of Carranza, and a diagram of the trajectory of the bullets that killed him.

MORE ATTRACTIONS

GUIDED BOAT TRIPS   Guided boat tours of the harbor (most in Spanish only) pass many of the sights listed above, as well as many of the international tankers and ships docked in the port. Launches leave sporadically (depending on the weather and demand) from the dock in front of the Hotel Emporio. The cost is $2 for adults and 75¢ for children ages two to eight, plus a tip for the guide. If the group is small, the price may go up to $4 per adult.

BEACHES   Veracruz has beaches, but none of them is very good because the grayish sand is hard-packed, and the Gulf water tends to be shallow. There are points all along the waterfront downtown where people swim, but the nearest legitimate beach is at the **Villa del Mar,** an open-air terrace and palm-lined promenade with changing rooms and showers at the southern end of town. To get there, take the "Playa V. del Mar" bus, which travels south on Zaragoza. The trip takes 15 minutes.

About 5 miles south of Veracruz along the Gulf Coast is the beach of **Mocambo,** where boats, snorkeling equipment, and waterskis can be rented. There are **public pools** at both Villa del Mar (entrance $1.50) and Mocambo (entrance $2) beaches.

A little farther past Mocambo at the mouth of the Jamapa River is **Boca del Río.** Both places can easily be reached by taking the buses that leave every 30 minutes (on the hour and half hour) from the corner of Serdán and Zaragoza near the municipal fish market. The bus stop is marked with the sign COSTA VERDE or BOCA DEL RÍO; the trip takes 30 minutes.

SHOPPING

The Veracruz **market** (near the corner of Madero and Gonzales Pages) is one of the most interesting in Mexico—it's possible to find just about anything from caged parrots to live iguanas with tethered feet and tied tails. You can shop for curios in little shops along the **Malecón** opposite the Hotel Oriente and around the corner toward the pier. Here, the wares include more typical beachside junk—full shark's jaws, tacky shell art, ships in a jar, and the like.

A VISIT TO THE NEARBY VILLAGE OF ANTIGUA & RUINS OF ZEMPOALA

On Highway 180, about 14 miles north of Veracruz, is the village of **Antigua,** on the Río Antigua. It's not well known today, but for 75 years, beginning in 1525, it was a seat of Spanish power. The village, situated on the banks of the river, is small and primitive. Beside the old church on the main plaza are the ruins of several massive stone structures, one of which is known as **la Casa de Cortés,** although he never occupied it. In ruins now with trees growing up from the interior and thick vines rooted to the rock walls, it's still interesting to see. An ancient cypress tree is said to have been used to tie up Cortés's ships. The village is well known for its seafood restaurants and is especially festive on weekends.

About 25 miles north of Veracruz, past Antigua on the way to Jalapa, are the ruins at **Zempoala** (or Cempoala), surrounded by lush foliage and rich agricultural land. Though nowhere near the size of El Tajín, this pre-Hispanic Totonac site is still noteworthy. Both El Tajín and Zempoala flourished during the Classic Period

(A.D. 300 to 900); although Tajín was later abandoned in the 13th century, Zempoala continued to thrive and was the capital of the Totonacs during the Spanish Conquest. Zempoala, which means "place of the 20 waters," was named for the many rivers that once converged at the site, but which are not visible today. When the conquerors saw Zempoala for the first time, the whitewashed stuccoed walls glimmered like silver in the tropical sun—which naturally drew the Spaniards closer. Though disappointed in not finding a city covered in silver, the Spaniards still made friends, and this city of Totonac Indians became Cortés's first ally. The Spaniards spent considerable time here, learning about the Totonacs' hatred of the Aztecs and about the Aztec Emperor Moctezuma, before heading overland to the Aztec capital of Tenochtitlán.

Most buildings at Zempoala date from the 14th and 15th centuries—quite late for pre-Columbian structures. It was, however, inhabited before the time of Jesus Christ. The **Great Temple** resembles the Temple of the Sun in Tenochtitlán, probably as a result of Aztec influence during the 15th century. The **Temple of the Little Faces** has stuccoed faces set into the walls, along with hieroglyphs painted on the lower sections. The **Temple of Quetzalcoatl,** the feathered serpent god, is square, and the **Temple of Ehecatl,** god of the wind, is, as usual, round.

Admission to the archaeological site is $2; it's open daily from 9am to 6pm. A permit for use of a video camera costs $4. You can get to the archaeological site on buses of the TRV (Transportes Regionales Veracruzianas), which run hourly from Veracruz; the trip takes 1 1/2 hours and is truly a beautiful journey through tropical forests. If you're going by car, driving time is 40 minutes north on Highway 180 through Cardel; the ruins of Zempoala are just north of Cardel.

WHERE TO STAY

Veracruz has a good assortment of hotels, but be careful of noise in this town—car and truck noise combines with marimba and mariachi music, for this is a festive town whose residents stay up until the early morning hours. High season is June, July, August, and the period from December through March.

Note: Veracruz is a favorite weekending spot for tourists from the capital city, and they fill every means of transportation on Friday. The flood of people traveling back up into the mountains is reversed on Sunday. Importers and exporters fill hotel rooms on weekdays. Arrive as early in the week and as early in the day as possible.

Doubles for Less than $25

⑤ Hotel Concha Dorada. Miguel Lerdo 77, Veracruz, Ver. 91700. ☎ **29/31-2996.** Fax 29/31-3121. 50 rms (all with bath). FAN TV TEL. $16.50–$20 single; $18–$23 double.

The six-story Concha Dorada is on the Plaza de Armas at the corner of Morelos, almost next door to the Hotel Colonial and Hotel Prendes. The hotel's prices are based on its prime location. The clean, smallish rooms are somewhat dark and musty and have tidy armoires suspended on the walls, tile floors, and lights over the bed. Twelve rooms are air-conditioned, and these command the highest prices, along with a few doubles that have televisions. The small inner rooms, while a bit claustrophobic, are bound to be quieter than those facing the plaza or street.

Hotel Prendes. Independencia 1064, Veracruz, Ver. 91700. ☎ **29/31-0241.** Fax 29/31-0491. 34 rms (all with bath). A/C TV TEL. $20 single or double. Free parking.

The Prendes faces the action on the Plaza de Armas, but the entrance is on Independencia. An elevator takes you to the three floors of nicely furnished, spacious guest rooms, all of which have good beds. Exterior rooms have balconies and wood-louvered French doors; interior rooms are much quieter but have no windows.

Ⓢ Hotel Villa Rica. Camacho 165, Veracruz, Ver. 91700. ☎ **29/32-4854.** 32 rms (all with bath). FAN. $10 single; $12 double. Parking nearby $2.

Right at the northern (beginning) end of Bulevar Manuel Ávila Camacho, the four-story Villa Rica attracts Mexican families and young people on vacation who want to stay near the beach but not that far from downtown. The rooms are adequate, with fans and stenciled wall decoration. To get here from the market, walk 10 blocks east toward the Gulf; the hotel is on the corner of Figueroa and Doblado.

DOUBLES FOR LESS THAN $35

Ⓢ Hotel Baluarte. Canal 265, Veracruz, Ver. 91700. ☎ **29/32-6042.** Fax 29/32-5486. 81 rms (all with bath). A/C TV TEL. $20 single; $25–$30 double. Free parking.

This is an excellent choice for comfort and value. Five stories tall, the hotel is modern and attractive and in a quiet location. The rooms are clean and comfortable. Guests can use the hotel's own parking lot across the street, and a small air-conditioned restaurant off the lobby is good for breakfast or a light meal. To get here from the Plaza de Armas, walk five blocks south on Independencia, then turn left (east) on Canal toward the Gulf for five blocks to 16 de Septiembre; the hotel is on the left, catercorner from the Baluarte Santiago. It is also five blocks west of the Malecón.

Ⓢ Hotel Colonial. Plaza de la Constitución, Veracruz, Ver. 91700. ☎ **29/32-0193.** Fax 29/32-2465. 182 rms (all with bath). A/C TV TEL. $22–$25 single; $27–$32 double. Parking $2.50 daily.

The pleasant and ideally located Colonial has two sections; the older section has centrally controlled air-conditioning, and the higher-priced newer section has individually controlled air-conditioning. Rooms are very comfortable, and all the expensive hotel services are here, including private covered parking and an indoor pool on the second floor. The Colonial faces the Plaza de Armas; there's an entrance on the plaza and another through the garage.

WORTH A SPLURGE

Hotel Mocambo. Boca del Río (Apdo. Postal 263), Veracruz, Ver. 91700. ☎ **29/22-0205.** Fax 29/22-0212. 125 rms, 4 suites (all with bath). A/C TV TEL. $70 single or double. Free parking.

The Mocambo, built in 1932, is 9 miles southeast of the town center on one of Veracruz's best stretches of beach. One of the city's first and best hotels, it has hosted presidents, movie stars, and governors. Never out of fashion, it has become a comfortable, stylish hotel with the right amount of old-fashioned touches. The palatial hotel contains 129 rooms, wide halls, terraces, a sauna, a Jacuzzi and four pools (two indoor), a tennis court, Ping-Pong tables, and a restaurant; it's definitely a splurge hotel. Most rooms have ocean views, but the cost of rooms varies depending on quality of view and the size of the room. At least 32 rooms have balconies, and 30 rooms are carpeted. Inquire about the cheaper (standard) rooms, since that might not be the first price you are quoted, and children under age 10 stay free in the same room with their parents. Even if you don't decide to stay here, you might want to come out for a look, a meal, or a swim. The beach is public—you needn't stay at the hotel. If you're not driving, take the bus marked "Mocambo" from Zaragoza and Serdán by La Prosperidad restaurant; buses stopping at the hotel's front gate go into town.

WHERE TO EAT

The restaurants under the portals that surround Plaza de Armas are the best places for eating, drinking, and merrymaking. Although they're more expensive than places a few blocks away, their prices are not outrageous.

On Landero y Coss between Arista and Serdán is the **municipal fish market,** its street level chockablock with little *ostionerías* (oyster bars) and shrimp stands. Take a stool, ask the price, and order. Look upstairs for more good places.

The **Paris** is a *panadería* and *pastelería* (bakery and pastry shop) that sells a very wide selection of Mexican rolls and pastries for 5¢ to 50¢. You can't miss the assortment and the smell at Av. 5 de Mayo at the corner of Molina.

MEALS FOR LESS THAN $5

ⓢ Café Andrade. Calle Hernandez y Hernandez. No phone. Desserts $1–$2.50; sandwiches $1.50–$2.50. 10am–8pm. COFFEE/SNACKS.

If you want to take a break from touring, this is a great place for coffee and a light snack. The local brew is served up six ways hot and three ways cold. You can also buy it in bean form or ground by the kilo ($3 to $5). Light snacks include sandwiches, croissants, pies, and wonderful cookies from the village of Xico. There are other locations in the Plaza Mocambo and on Calle Molina downtown. This branch is 2¹/₂ blocks east of the Baluate Museo Santiago.

Café El Portal. Independencia at Zamora. ☎ **29/31-2759.** Appetizers $2–$5; main courses $2.25–$8; comida corrida $4.25–$5.75. Daily 6am–midnight. MEXICAN.

Catercorner from the Plaza de Armas, and occupying the former home of the ever-popular Café La Parroquia, the Café El Portal is developing a character and clientele all its own. From the cavernous dining room huge windows on two sides look onto the Plaza de Armas and Independencia where a parade of strolling troubadours, harpists, roving marimba players, and shoeshine men ply their trades. Elsewhere old photos of Veracruz decorate walls. You can enjoy coffee, an excellent comida corrida, plus traditional Mexican cuisine such as crêpes huitlacoche, tinga (a specialty of Puebla state), and grilled chicken.

ⓢ Comedor Familiar "Laurita." Mercado de Pescadores, local 26 (upstairs). No phone. Seafood cocktails $2–$3.75. Main courses $2–$6. Daily 7am–7pm. SEAFOOD.

Laurita's is a pretty basic establishment located at the side of the second-floor market, but if you lust for fresh seafood, you can find instant gratification here. Their shrimp cocktail is terrific, and the *campechano* (shrimp and oyster cocktail) and *vuelva a la vida* (large seafood cocktail) are meals in themselves. The entrance is on Serdán (up the stairs) at the corner of Cos.

✪ Gran Café de La Parroquía. Av. Insurgentes s/n. No phone. Breakfast $2–$4; coffee $1–$1.50; main courses $2.50–$8. Daily 7am–1am. MEXICAN/COFFEE.

A trip to Veracruz without having coffee at La Parroquía is like going to New Orleans without eating beignets. In 1994, the original La Parroquía moved from its longtime location opposite the Plaza de Armas to its current spot; almost next-door is a second branch facing the harbor two blocks before the Hotel Emporio. Bright and always busy, with music (usually marimba) at almost any hour, this restaurant has customers who ritualistically occupy the same tables at the same time every day. Novice Parroquía patrons can catch onto the ritual quickly. Two waiters scurry about with big aluminum kettles, one with thick black coffee and the other with hot milk. Order the rich café lechera, and you'll get a few fingers of coffee in the bottom of your glass. Then pick up your spoon and bang on the glass to call the waiter with the milk—La Parroquía is filled with the constant chime of banging spoons. If there's too much coffee in your glass, pour the excess into the waiter's coffee kettle, then he'll pour the milk. Though the café is known for coffee and pastries, its main courses are also quite good.

La Paella. Zamora 138. ☎ **29/32-0322.** Breakfast $1.25–$3; main courses $3–$8; comida corrida $3 Mon–Fri, $4.25 Sun. Daily 8:30am 10pm (comida corrida served 1–4pm). SPANISH.

Devotees of Spanish food will undoubtedly like La Paella, where the four-course comida corrida is popular but portions are small. Three of the courses include such internationally known Spanish specialties as crema bretona, paella valenciana, and tortilla española (potato omelet). The walls are festooned with bullfight posters. La Paella is right at the southeast corner of Plaza de Armas, near the tourism office and next door to KFC—look for its very colonial-tiled facade.

FROM VERACRUZ TO LAKE CATEMACO & LOS TUXTLAS

Highway 180 southeast from Veracruz is a good and uneventful road with numerous glimpses of the Gulf and deserted beaches as you drive along the bar separating the Gulf from the Alvarado Lagoon. The fishing village of **Alvarado,** founded in 1518 and celebrated locally for successfully warding off an attack by the U.S. fleet in 1846, is an excellent spot for a fresh seafood lunch at one of the many small restaurants lining the lagoon shore.

Some 30 miles farther along, the 5,000-foot extinct volcano **San Martín** begins to show through the haze on the horizon, and soon the road starts climbing into the lush, green foothills. You are now entering Olmec country.

6 Lake Catemaco & Los Tuxtlas

355 miles SE of Mexico City, 99 miles SE of Veracruz

The beautiful and interesting region around Lake Catemaco includes two Tuxtlas—San Andrés Tuxtla and Santiago Tuxtla. The area offers natural beauty and the remains of the Olmec culture.

About 6¹/₂ miles long and almost 5 miles wide, **Lake Catemaco,** dotted with islands, was formed by the long-ago eruption of volcanoes. Ringed by lush forested mountains and two volcanoes, it is one of the most beautiful lakes in Mexico. At least 556 species of birds live or migrate here. Between Catemaco and **San Andrés Tuxtla** is tobacco country; broad green fields are awash in the tall leggy plant between July and October. The region is dotted with enormous barns for drying the aromatic leaves and with smaller facilities where the leaves are sorted and sold. Just over the mountain from San Andrés is **Santiago Tuxtla,** a handsome colonial town with one of the most beautiful palm-studded plazas in Mexico. On one side of the plaza is the Museo Regional containing Olmec artifacts, and the on-site Museum of Tres Zapotes is 12 miles away. The entire region lies only a few miles from undeveloped beaches on the Gulf of Mexico and within reach of the 500-acre Balzapotes Scientific Station to the northeast near the coast.

ESSENTIALS

GETTING THERE & DEPARTING   By Bus   From Veracruz, there are approximately 18 daily departures, but most of these go only as far as the cigar-making town of San Andrés Tuxtla, 7 miles short of Catemaco. You can take one of the five daily first-class buses, which go directly to Catemaco from Veracruz. You can also go to San Andrés Tuxtla and catch a local bus or hire a taxi for the last short leg. First-class service out of Lake Catemaco is limited, so check departure times when you arrive in town. Reserve tickets as far in advance as possible.

Second-class service from Catemaco is more frequent on **Autotransportes Los Tuxtlas.** Buses make the run to Veracruz throughout the day. They go to San Andrés and Santiago Tuxtla every 10 minutes from midnight to 6pm and every hour in the evening. The terminal is located on Calle Cuauhtémoc (though this won't help you much, as the streets aren't marked), a short walk from the main plaza; ask for directions.

By Car   Coming into Catemaco—whether you're driving south from Veracruz or west from Villahermosa—you'll take the free Highway 180 to Catemaco.

When leaving the Catemaco area, Highway 180 will also be your route out of town—whether you're continuing on to Tabasco, Chiapas, or Oaxaca states, or to the Yucatán Peninsula, you can take Highway 180 along the Gulf Coast through Acayucan and Minatitlán to Villahermosa. A new toll road reduces driving time between Acayucan and Minatitlán, and a good four-lane divided highway continues part of the way toward Villahermosa. This is the route to the Yucatán.

An alternate route to Tuxtla Gutiérrez is via Highway 185, which goes south from Acayucan. This route traverses the Isthmus of Tehuantepec through terrain that is, for the most part, rolling and green. Near Juchitan, on the Pacific coast, Highway 190/200 goes west to Oaxaca and east to Tuxtla Gutiérrez.

ORIENTATION   Arriving   The first-class **ADO bus station** in Catemaco is located behind the church, on the corner of Aldama and Bravo. The lake is a block or so behind the station. The cathedral and main plaza are left up the hill, and the Hotel Koniapan and the southern end of town facing the lake are to the right.

Fast Facts   The **telephone area code** is 294. As for the **climate,** Lake Catemaco is a balmy oasis in a region where the rule is muggy heat. Free from extremes of heat and cold, it's more like year-round eternal spring. It's hottest from March through May. A jacket is handy December through February. Always be prepared for rain—there are only 150 days of sun on average. The **high season** in this area is July, August, Christmas, and Easter week.

EXPLORING THE LAKE CATEMACO AREA

The lake region is located between the only mountains on the steaming coastal plain that reaches from Tampico to the Yucatán. Two volcanic peaks—**San Martín** and **Santa Marta**—reach to nearly 5,600 feet. North of Catemaco is **Monte Cerro Blanco,** where it is rumored that wizards (*brujos*) meet each March. Brujos put out signs in Catemaco the way doctors do in other towns.

Many artifacts have been found in the area, once the site of a pre-Hispanic village. Townsfolk who were children when Catemaco's streets were prepared for paving remember playing with pre-Hispanic artifacts unearthed by bulldozers. **Isla Agaltepec,** one of four large islands in the lake, was an Olmec ceremonial site.

FESTIVALS   The El Carmen Church on the zócalo is visited by thousands of pilgrims each year around July 16, the **Feast of El Carmen.** Look for testimonial drawings around the portals. The interior walls are stenciled with a pattern of golden-yellow and white flowers, while the ceiling is laced with gilded arches. There's also a blessing of the fleet during the festival, and decorated boats sail up and down the shore giving free rides.

ECO-TOURS   The forests in the area of Los Tuxtlas represent the northernmost tropical rain forest on the continent. Some of the more than 500 varieties of migratory and local bird life are apparent even on a brief walk along the lake. Mammals and reptiles are represented by around 100 species each, along with almost 50 species of amphibians. More than 1,000 types of bromeliads have been identified in the region, and they are still being counted. Many area hunters supplement their diets by taking squirrels, armadillos, iguanas, and wild pigs. A serious education and preservation effort has been mounted on the part of both public and private interests in the area. For information on educational and scientific expeditions and summer camps, contact Operadora Turística de Los Tuxtlas at the Hotel Playa Azul (☎ 294/ 3-0761).

BOAT TRIPS   If you're sports-minded, boats are available for **waterskiing** or **fishing.**

You can also take a **tour** of the lake by boat, passing the black-sand lake beaches, the river, a shrine honoring the local miraculous Virgin, numerous flocks of white herons, a mineral spring called Arroyo Agrio (literally "Sour Brook") for its acid content, and another spring called Coyamé—you may have seen its water bottled and on your dinner table.

The most interesting part of the tour is the two **monkey islands.** In an experiment to readapt monkeys to the wild, the University of Veracruz brought several families of macaco monkeys from Thailand to two small islands on the lake. One group has learned to swim between the two islands, while the other group has not. Because the university sends out food each day, the monkeys line up in hopeful expectation when they see approaching boats; have your cameras ready, for as soon as they discover there's no food, they disperse.

In April and May, hundreds of **herons** nest on a tiny island called **Isla de las Garzas** (Heron Island), and the tour boats pass by for a look. Another stop may be **Nanciyaga,** a rather touristy private nature reserve ($2 entrance). Guides lead you across the jungle stream and wind through the woods to a mud-facial house (optional; $2 donation suggested).

The cost of the 1^1/$_2$-hour lake tour is about $5 per person for a boatload of up to six people; a private boat for up to six people ranges from $18 to $25. Two **boat cooperatives** operate from the Malecón. Look for posted prices.

BEACHES   The cheapest way to get to two volcanic-sand beaches—**Playa Azul** and **Playa Hermosa**—is by bus. Take the "Monte Pio" bus (one leaves every 1^1/$_2$ hours) from the second-class bus terminal or look for the "La Margarita" bus from the town square (though the latter runs only about three times a day). You can also walk or hitch the 1^1/$_4$ miles. Be forewarned that these "beaches" are more aptly described as narrow spits of dirt. For real beaches, you have to go to the ocean (reached by the "Monte Pio" bus in about 1^1/$_4$ hours). The "La Margarita" bus goes out to the Cuetzalapan River on the opposite side of the lake, known for its cold, transparently clear waters; flowers; bird life; and interesting rock formations.

WHERE TO STAY

Cabañas Don Armando. Carretera Sontecomapan km. 2.5, Catemaco, Ver. 95870. No phone. 9 rms, 1 suite (all with bath). FAN. High season, $20 single or double. Low season, $15 single or double. Free parking.

Somewhat removed from town but only a 3-minute downhill walk from the shore, this delightful retreat has a stunning view of the lake and its environs. Beds are firm and the rooms spotless. The suite is a second-floor minipenthouse that sleeps up to five people; the other rooms are all on the ground floor. Fans and the breeze keep you cool. With the small restaurant/bar and an attractive pool, there's no need to go into town.

Hotel Catemaco. Carranza 8, Catemaco, Ver. 95870. ☎ and fax **294/3-0203.** 19 rms (all with bath). A/C TV TEL. $20 single; $30 double. Free parking.

The clean Hotel Catemaco, located directly on the plaza, has a good-sized pool out back. The rooms, which have long-distance service, feature Formica furniture, tile floors, two double beds with overbed lights, and air-conditioning, which accounts for the rather high prices. The hotel may not fill up at these rates, so try offering a lower price.

Hotel Los Arcos. Madero 7, Catemaco, Ver. 95870. ☎ **294/3-0003.** Fax 294/3-0250. 35 rms (all with bath). FAN TV TEL. $17 single; $20 double. Free parking.

The three-story Los Arcos has nice, well-kept rooms with red-tile floors, louvered glass windows, and ceiling fans; there's also good cross-ventilation. All rooms come with TVs, but only one has air-conditioning. To reach the rooms you pass through motel-style walkways that also serve as balconies with either street or lake views. To get here from the ADO bus station, turn left out the front door, go around the church, and then walk one block past the church.

Posada (Motel) Koniapan. Malecón and Revolución, Catemaco, Ver. 95870. ☎ **294/3-0063.** Fax 294/3-0939. 21 rms (all with bath). A/C or FAN TEL. $14–$17 single or double. Free parking.

This motel is a favorite place to stay in Catemaco; it's located across the street from the lakeshore. Rooms are bright and clean and come with screened windows, small tile baths, neocolonial furniture, and two double beds. Upstairs rooms have private balconies and views of the lake. There's a clean pool in the front yard; the open-air restaurant next to it is sometimes open. Room prices may be a bit higher in July and August. To get here from the ADO bus station, turn right out the front door and go straight for two blocks; the hotel is on the right facing the lake.

WHERE TO EAT

Althoughthe lake is famed for its whitefish (*mojarra*), fare in Catemaco is not always of the highest quality. In addition to whitefish, smoked pork is a specialty and is quite good. *Pelliscadas* are salted tortillas fried in lard and topped with various sauces or cheese, and local clams are made into ceviche.

When the **street market** is in operation around the Hotel Los Arcos, little cookshops are set up. The market is the cheapest, most colorful place to sample the lake's mojarra or dozens of other kinds of food. Prices, which are not set, depend on how the fishing season's going, how much money has been made that day, and how prosperous you seem to be. (Ask the price before you order!)

Hotel Catemaco. Carranza 8. ☎ **29/3-0203.** Breakfast $2–$3; main courses $3–$7. Daily 8:30am–11pm. MEXICAN.

Perhaps the best all-around restaurant, Hotel Catemaco offers indoor and outdoor dining for breakfast, lunch, and dinner. A view of the town's busy plaza adds to the most refined, pleasant decor in town. The specialty is steak, and to help you know which cut to order, there's a lighted diagram of a cow with cuts marked in Spanish and English.

La Luna. Malecón. ☎ **29/3-0050.** Breakfast $1.50–$3; main courses $3–$5. Daily 8am–9pm. MEXICAN.

Facing the lake across the street and a few doors west of La Ola, La Luna offers tasty meals. A good-sized mojarra can be cooked one of eight deliciously different ways, and the *carne ahumado* (smoked pork) will make you want to return for more. The food compensates for the less-than-stellar view of the lake.

SIDE TRIPS FROM CATEMACO
SAN ANDRÉS TUXTLA: PART COLONIAL, PART CARIBBEAN

Seven miles northwest of Catemaco, San Andrés Tuxtla (pop. 125,000) is the administrative center of the region. Along the way there, you'll pass fields of tobacco between July and October, alternating with corn in the off-months. At Sihuapan, about halfway between Catemaco and San Andrés, you'll see signs to **El Salto Eyipantla,** a 150-foot waterfall with 244 steps leading down to it. There's no charge to enter the area, but many "volunteer" guides vie for tips. There's a good restaurant at the top of the stairs.

San Andrés, a lovely, prosperous town with an interesting mix of colonial, Caribbean, and 1960s architecture, is centered around a pretty square with a frilly white-iron kiosk and church. If you arrive by bus, you'll be by the market packed with locally grown fruits. The town center is up the hill.

This is such a clean, inviting town that you may want to do what the locals do—pull up a chair at the Hotel del Parque (catercorner from the main plaza), order café con leche, and watch the town saunter by.

While here, you might like to go by the **Tabacos de San Andrés** factory, a large and poorly lit barnlike building where some 20 workers ferment, process, cut, roll, and pack La Prueba and Ejecutivo brand cigars. Visitors are welcome Monday through Friday from 9am to 1pm and 3 to 7pm. It is a fascinating procedure even for a nonsmoker. The factory is on the road toward Catemaco, on the right just past the turn-off into San Andrés.

Where to Stay & Eat

Hotel del Parque. Madero 5, San Andrés Tuxtla, Ver. ☎ **294/2-0198.** Fax 294/2-3050. 39 rms. A/C TV TEL. $17 single; $22 double. Parking $1.75.

If you want to be right in the heart of things, there's no better place than the Hotel del Parque. Catercorner across the main plaza, this 1960s-style hotel offers comfortable rooms and a pleasant management.

The restaurant (open daily 8am to 11:30pm), which is both indoors and outdoors under the portals facing the street, is the social center of downtown San Andrés. The menu lists a wide assortment of inexpensive Mexican dishes, including regional specialties of enfrijoladas with chicken, fried bananas with black beans, and dishes from the Yucatán and Oaxaca. Coffee comes four ways, all inexpensive, and there's an extensive cocktail list.

SANTIAGO TUXTLA: A COLONIAL TOWN WITH A LOVELY PLAZA

Some 13 miles from Lake Catemaco and 8 miles from San Andrés Tuxtla, thriving Santiago Tuxtla (pop. 50,000) is reached by a winding drive over hill and dale. Along the way, you'll pass herds of grazing cattle and green rolling hills planted with sugarcane, corn, oranges, bananas, and mangoes, much of it for sale at neatly arranged roadside stands.

The **Museo Tuxteco** (formerly the Regional Museum of Anthropology), facing the beautiful main square, is the reason most tourists seek out this picturesque town. In addition to a small but important selection of mostly Olmec artifacts, there are articles from the Huasteca and Totonac cultures. The museum is open Tuesday through Saturday from 9am to 7pm, Sunday from 9am to 3pm. Admission is $3.25. On Sunday it is free.

On the plaza opposite the museum is a 45-ton **Olmec head** with a scowling face. The **market,** next to the museum, has several good small cookshops, and there's a hotel, Los Castellanos, with a decent restaurant/bar across the park.

9 The Colonial Silver Cities

A visitor to Mexico who has not made the rounds of the Silver Cities hasn't seen the country's heart. The outstanding architectural beauty of these cities places them among Mexico's finest colonial showpieces. More evocative of Spain than Mexico, **Guanajuato** is almost a fairy-tale town. The museums and architecture of **Zacatecas** will linger on in your memory. **San Miguel de Allende,** a city of fine restored mansions and cobblestone streets, offers some of the country's best restaurants and shops, as well as good, inexpensive hotels. **Querétaro** preserves its charm around its Plaza de la Independencia.

This heartland of Mexico lies between the mountain ranges of the Sierra Madre, spread across a high plateau sculpted by rains and rivers over the eons. Now a maze of highlands and valleys called the Valley of Mexico, this was once Anahuac, the center of ancient Mexican civilization.

When the conquistadores subdued Tenochtitlán (where Mexico City would later arise) in the early 1500s, they sent their armies and colonists into the other parts of the Valley of Mexico in search of mineral wealth. They found lead, tin, zinc, iron, antimony, and gold in abundance, but what made the early Spanish governors (and the cities of the northern valley) rich was silver. So rich were the mines here that the Silver Cities of the northern Valley of Mexico became incredibly wealthy and stayed that way for centuries.

There are other old Mexican Silver Cities besides those included in this chapter: Taxco (see chapter 12) is known today as the "Silver Capital of Mexico" and Real de Catorce (see chapter 7), now an extraordinary "ghost town," was one of Mexico's top three silver-producing towns in the early 19th century.

EXPLORING THE COLONIAL HEARTLAND

This chapter presents the Silver Cities as you would find them traveling overland, from the border cities of El Paso or Laredo. But no matter how you're traveling in Mexico, the Silver Cities are easily accessible, despite their locations in mountain valleys.

Coming overland from El Paso or Laredo, Zacatecas is the first real colonial city you'll encounter. From Zacatecas, Highway 45 runs south through Aguascalientes and León to Guanajuato; both San Miguel de Allende and Querétaro are within reasonably short drives.

If your trip to the Silver Cities begins in Mexico City, the capital is linked to Querétaro by a fast, limited-access toll highway, and from Querétaro you can be in San Miguel de Allende and Guanajuato or any other of the Silver Cities in a few hours via good two-lane paved roads.

If you wish to travel by bus, getting to portions of the Silver Cities is easier than ever now: Flecha Roja/Estrella de Oro buses depart directly from the Mexico City airport bound for Querétaro, and from Querétaro it's a short bus ride to San Miguel. Or if your trip begins in Guanajuato or San Miguel de Allende, the Leon/Guanajuato airport runs buses direct to Guanajuato and San Miguel—this makes for an extremely easy trip. Other bus service in the region is fast, frequent, comfortable, and inexpensive.

As for how to allot your time, much depends on your particular interests. As a bare minimum, I recommend two to three days *each* in San Miguel de Allende, Zacatecas, and Guanajuato. Querétaro is an easy day-trip from San Miguel de Allende. Though most museums in Mexico close on Mondays, this is not a hard-and-fast rule in Zacatecas, so if museums are important to your visit, Monday may be a good day to spend in Zacatecas, which has some of the most unusual museums in the country.

1 Zacatecas

392 miles NW of Mexico City, 117 miles NW of San Luis Potosí, 197 miles NE of Guadalajara, 186 miles SE of Durango

A city made rich by silver mines, Zacatecas has magnificently preserved colonial architecture, picturesque brick streets ascending the hillsides, a slew of good museums, and a real dearth of tourists. The fame of the city's fine museums beckons most visitors, who arrive only to be captivated by the city's unique architectural beauty. It's safe to say that this is Mexico's most beautiful and best-preserved colonial city. You can see the town's beauty on a walk through the streets lined with marvelous buildings and from the hilltops that dominate the town, most notably from the Cerro de la Bufa.

The capital of the state of the same name, Zacatecas was already an old town when the Spaniards arrived in 1546. The name comes from the Nahuatl words *zacatl* (pasture) and *tecatl* (people)—Zacatecas, then, means "people of the pasture."

ESSENTIALS

GETTING THERE & DEPARTING   By Plane   **See "Getting There, By Plane," in chapter 3, "Planning a Trip to Mexico," for a list of carriers serving Zacatecas from the United States. From points within Mexico, **Mexicana (☎ **492/2-7429**; at the airport 492/5-0352) flies nonstop to Zacatecas from Morelia, Mexico City, and Tijuana (the flight from Tijuana is booked months in advance for the Christmas holidays). Nonstop service is also available on **Taesa** (☎ **492/4-0050** or 492/2-2555) from Ciudad Juárez, Guadalajara, Mexico City, Morelia, and Tijuana. Transportation from the airport to town is about $18 by taxi, about $6 by minibus.

By Bus   Almost a dozen bus companies provide service in and out of Zacatecas. **Camiones de los Altos** has 11 buses leaving the Central Camionera for Guadalajara daily. There are hourly buses to Fresnillo. **Transportes Chihuahuenses** and **Transportes del Norte** also operate to and from Zacatecas and various cities to the north and west. For those who are just passing through Zacatecas and who want to take the suggested side trip to Guadalupe, **Transportes de Guadalupe** goes there every 15 minutes from the Central Camionera (where you'll be if you arrive by bus) for around 50¢.

By Car Highway 54 comes from Saltillo and Monterrey (a five- to six-hour drive), Highway 40/49 from Torreón, Highway 45 from Durango, and Highway 54 from Guadalajara. Highway 45D is a toll road in various spots all the way from Querétaro through Irapuato, León as far as Aguascalientes. It's fast but expensive.

ORIENTATION **Arriving** The airport is located about 18 miles north of Zacatecas. **Aero Transportes** (☎ 492/2-5946) provides minibus transportation to and from the airport; allow 30 minutes for the ride. The **Central Camionera** (bus station) is on a hilltop a bit out of town; a taxi to town costs $4. Red Ruta 8 buses go to and from the station frequently and can be found in front of the station.

Information Downtown on Hidalgo, across from the cathedral, is a one-room **Infotur office;** it's open Monday through Saturday from 9am to 2pm and 4 to 7pm.

City Layout The touristic heart of Zacatecas is centered on the **Plaza de Armas,** facing Hidalgo, flanked by government buildings and the cathedral, and opposite the tourism office. The late-night *callejoneadas* wind up here with their last burst of singing, dancing, drinking, and band playing.

Getting Around Zacatecas has excellent inner-city **bus** service. To reach the Central Camionera (bus station), take a Ruta 8 bus at the Plaza de la Independencia. Ruta 7 goes to the Motel del Bosque and teleférico. Frequent buses go to and from Guadalupe from the local bus station a block past the Hotel Gallery.

FAST FACTS: ZACATECAS

American Express American Express is handled by Viajes Mazzoco, a travel agent at Enlace 115 (☎ **492/2-5559** or 492/2-5159; fax 492/2-5559).

Area Code The telephone area code is 492.

Climate It's cool enough year-round to require a sweater or other warm wrap. Hotels aren't heated.

Elevation The city is situated at a lofty 8,200 feet. It's very hilly here, and you'll be doing a lot of climbing, which tends to make people winded.

Food Store The Casa Jaquez, Av. Hidalgo 202 at Callejón de la Bordadora, is a convenient supermarket and wine shop that's open Monday through Saturday from 9am to 10pm and Sunday from 9am to 4pm.

Population 108,000.

Post Office The post office (correos) is at Allende III, ¹/₂ block from Av. Hidalgo.

EXPLORING ZACATECAS

Zacatecas is so picturesque that many travelers regret not having planned at least three nights here—or more if they have come on days when the museums are closed. In addition to its marvelous architecture and museums, Zacatecas is famous among craftspeople for its stone and wood carvings, leatherwork, silvermaking, and thread-pulled designs (drawnwork) on textiles. Zacatecan handcrafts can be found directly across from the cathedral in the Mercado González Ortega. There are a few other stores on Hidalgo and Tacuba that sell crafts and antiques. Huichol Indians sometimes sell their crafts around the Plaza Independencia.

FESTIVALS

During Semana Santa, or the **Holy Week** before Easter each year, Zacatecas hosts an international cultural festival the town hopes will soon rival the similar Cervantino festival in Guanajuato. Painters, poets, dancers, musicians, actors, and other artists from around the world converge on the town.

The annual **Fería de Zacatecas,** which celebrates the day the city was founded, begins the Friday before September 8 and lasts for two weeks. Cockfights, bullfights,

Zacatecas

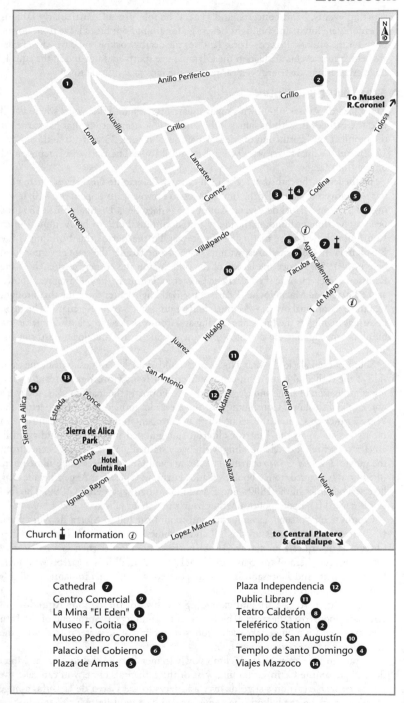

Church ✝ Information ⓘ

Sierra de Alica Park

Hotel Quinta Real

To Museo R.Coronel ↗

to Central Platero & Guadalupe ↘

Cathedral **7**
Centro Comercial **9**
La Mina "El Eden" **1**
Museo F. Goitia **13**
Museo Pedro Coronel **3**
Palacio del Gobierno **6**
Plaza de Armas **5**

Plaza Independencia **12**
Public Library **11**
Teatro Calderón **8**
Teleférico Station **2**
Templo de San Augustín **10**
Templo de Santo Domingo **4**
Viajes Mazzoco **14**

sporting events, band concerts, and general hoopla prevail. Particularly famous toreadores are hired, and bullfight tickets go for around $4; buses leave from downtown for the gigantic Plaza de Toros (and for the nearby cockpit) on days when fights are held. Sports events are held in the Olympic-size sports stadium and in the equally huge gymnasium; there are even car races at the racetrack outside town.

A STROLL AROUND TOWN

The **Plaza de Armas,** the town's main square on Avenida Hidalgo, is where you'll find the **cathedral,** with its fantastically ornate pink stone facade that has earned it the moniker the "Parthenon of Mexico Baroque." It took 23 years to build (1729–1752), and the final tower wasn't completed until 1904. The Eucharist is represented on the front facade.

To the left of the cathedral is the 18th-century **Palacio de Gobierno,** where vice-regal-era governors lived. By the time of Mexico's revolt against Spain in 1810, it was owned by Don Miguel de Rivera (Count of Santiago de la Laguna). Since 1834 it's been a government building; inside is a modern mural (1970) by António Pintor Rodríguez showing the history of Zacatecas. To the left of this building is the **Residencia de Gobernadores,** with its ornate stone facade; the state governor lived here until 1950. Notice the facade of the building on the corner, to the left of the Radisson Hotel opposite the Palacio de Gobierno. Formerly the building was known as the **Palacio de Mala Noche** (Palace of the Bad Night) after the mine that brought wealth to its original owner—Manuel de Rétegui, a benevolent Spaniard. The Plaza de Armas highlights the fine stone carving and ironwork, a hallmark of Zacatecas, on buildings throughout the downtown. Stone carving is still a major industry in the area.

South of the Palacio de Mala Noche on Avenida Hidalgo, opposite from the right side of the cathedral is the 19th-century **Mercado Jesús González Ortega,** a striking combination of stone and elegant ironwork. Formerly the main market, today it's home to stylish shops. Continuing past the mercado, immediately on the left is the **Plaza Francisco Goitia,** the venue for frequent open-air artistic performances. On the right you'll pass the **Teatro Calderón** (inaugurated first in 1836 and again in 1891 after a fire), a stately building with lovely stained-glass windows. Scenes from the movie *The Old Gringo* starring Jane Fonda and Gregory Peck were filmed here (the film was adapted from a book by Carlos Fuentes). Opera star Angela Peralta sang here several times in the 1800s, and Plácido Domingo sang here in 1990. The theater is named for a poet/political writer from the state of Jalisco.

Continue on Hidalgo, cross Juárez, and mount the hill to **Sierra de Alica Park** (the street changes names up the hill and becomes Avenida Gral. Jesús González Ortega). The **equestrian statue** (1898) portrays none other than Gen. González Ortega himself, hero of the Battle of Calpulalpan. Behind it is a gazebo with marvelous acoustics and a pleasant, shady park good for a picnic or a romantic stroll. It's also well lit in the evening.

Beginning at Alica Park and extending southward, the famous **Aqueduct of Zacatecas** looms over the street. The wealth of this mining city at the end of the 18th century allowed it to undertake such impressive public works. Water passed along the aqueduct to a large cistern downtown.

To take in the city all at once, climb slowly (remember the altitude) to the Motel del Bosque on the Cerro Grillo hill, west of the cathedral. Here, you can take the **teleférico** (cable car) on a sky ride over Zacatecas to the **Cerro de la Bufa,** a huge knob of a rock on the hilltop (the name, created by a local Basque citizen who was reminded of that part of the animal's anatomy, means "pig's bladder"). When the sun

Impressions

To think of Mexican colonial architecture—whether churches, or houses, or hospitals, or haciendas—as a scattering of remarkable buildings is to be astonished at the wrong thing. This was not an architecture of imperial display, marking the high points of the system, but the intimate expression of the life of New Spain.
—Elizabeth Wilder Weismann, *Art and Time in Mexico*, 1985

is low in the sky, turning the sandstone town into a golden wonder, and the lights begin to twinkle, Zacatecas seems magical. Watch the time, though, as the teleférico (☎ **492/2-5694** or 492/2-6013) operates only from 12:30 to 7:30pm, and if it's windy it's not open at all. The cost for a ride is $2 one way or $3 round trip; you can hike up either hill and walk down the other if you wish. Before making that long climb, look to see if the cars are running; they may be in repair or out of service because of winds. A glance will tell you.

Up on Cerro de la Bufa, beside the Museo de la Toma Zacatecas (see below) is the beautiful church **La Capilla de la Virgen del Patrocinio,** patron of Zacatecas. At the very top of the hill is an observatory used for meteorological purposes. Around the far side of the hill is the Mausoleo de los Hombres Ilustres de Zacatecas, where many of the city's important revolutionary fighters still keep watch over their town below.

CHURCHES

Many of Zacatecas's churches are notable. **San Agustín** underwent construction in 1613, but its dedication had to wait until 1782. It has been a Catholic church, then a Protestant church (sadly stripped of its elaborate architectural ornamentation), a casino, a hotel, and tenement housing. Today it's an enormous, beautiful shell used for art exhibitions, conferences, and storage and display of pieces of its past glory. The state's **natural history museum** is also housed here. Note the mosaics of carved-stone chunks crammed into the archways and other niches. These pieces formerly decorated the church's ramparts, but now no one knows quite where. Other parts of the interior contain stonework that reveals how beautiful the exterior must have been. The church is five blocks south of the cathedral; walk past the Hotel Posada de la Moneda and turn right on the next street. The church is open Monday through Saturday from 10am to 2pm and 4 to 7pm and on Sunday from 10am to 5pm. There's no admission.

To the right of the Museo Pedro Coronel is the **temple of Santo Domingo,** completed in 1749, with its characteristic pink-stone facade. It was built by the Jesuits; after their expulsion, the Dominicans assumed responsibility and have taken care of it until today. Inside are stunning gilded altarpieces. During a surge of modernization, the baroque main altarpiece (*retable*), was replaced with the neo-classical masterpiece you see today. It too is stunning, but many still mourn the loss of the original.

Four miles from Zacatecas proper is the **Convent of Guadalupe,** the most famous church in the region. See "A Side Trip to Nearby Guadalupe," below, for details.

MUSEUMS

✪ **Museo F. Goitia.** Enrique Estrada 102, Col. Sierra de Alica. ☎ **492/2-0211.** Admission $3.50. Tues–Sat 10am–1:30pm and 5–7:30pm; Sun 10am–4pm. Walk seven short blocks south of the cathedral on Hidalgo, cross Juárez, and continue up the hill. Turn right on Manuel Ponce (look for the aqueduct) and walk two more short blocks. Look for the imposing white "palace" behind the park.

Located behind the park, this former governor's palace was built in 1945. The graceful marble stairway was supposedly constructed so that one may walk down its steps in perfect rhythm while humming the "Triumphal March" from *Aïda*. Formerly occupied by three governors, it was converted into a high school before becoming this very fine museum. Second-floor exhibits showcase the work of Francisco Goitia (1882–1960).

Born in Zacatecas, Goitia's reclusive, hermit-like lifestyle set him apart from some of his contemporaries who basked in political limelight and trappings of success. After studying in Europe he chose Mexicans and the Mexican landscape as his themes, and he lived humbly, like the people he painted. Because he lived to paint and cared little for money, he was often without funds, which seemed to bother his friends more than Goitia; from time to time, though, he accepted the painting positions they offered him. Acclaimed as one of the greatest paintings in Mexico, his *Tata Jesus Cristo* depicts the contrasting figures of two people in mourning illuminated by a single candlelight. A copy of *Tata Jesu Cristo* is in this museum. (The original is in the Museo de Arte Moderno in Mexico City.)

Works of other Zacatecan artists, including Pedro Coronel, Rafael Coronel, Julio Relas, and José Kuri Breña, are also shown here.

✪ **Museo Pedro Coronel.** Plaza de Santo Domingo. ☎ **492/2-8021.** Admission $3.50. Fri–Wed 10am–2pm and 4–7pm. (Closed Thurs). Facing the cathedral, walk left to the next street, De Veyna, and turn left and walk one block to Plaza de Santo Domingo and the museum (next to the Santo Domingo Church).

Pedro Coronel (1923–1985), born in Zacatecas, was considered the most gifted of Rufino Tamayo's students, and his use of color rivals his master's. He attended the National School of Painting and Sculpture, but his search for artistic development took him to Paris. He later painted murals in Geneva, Switzerland, and Mexico.

During his years abroad, and after, Coronel began collecting works of art from around the world. A small selection of his works, along with his fabulous collection of art from Africa, India, China, Tibet, Thailand, Egypt (including a sarcophagus), and ancient Greece and Rome, is displayed in this cavernous colonial-era building. Also displayed are works of such artists as Dalí, Picasso, Miró, Kandinsky, Braque, Roualt, Calder, Motherwell, Segal, Chagall, Coronel, and others. Especially notable is the large collection of native pre-Hispanic art and masks downstairs, matched by a similar display of African masks directly above it. Coronel's sculptures are placed around the first-floor portals. To the left as you enter is the Biblioteca Elias Amador, a long room laden with volumes devoted to the history of Zacatecas.

Museo de la Toma de Zacatecas. Cerro de la Bufa. ☎ **492/2-8066.** Free admission. Tues–Sun 10am–5pm. Bus: Ruta 7 from the Plaza de la Independencia to the Motel del Bosque and teleférico. Take the teleférico to El Cerro de la Bufa (see above) and the museum or walk by following the directions to the mine entrance (see below) and weaving a few more short streets to the hilltop; taxis from the center of town are $3.50.

The Museum of the Taking of Zacatecas, founded in 1984, displays pictures and exhibits explaining the battle between the Federales and the Revolucionarios in the hills surrounding Zacatecas in June 1914. When Pancho Villa arrived from the north to seal the fate of the Federales in this battle, it marked the turning point in the victory of the Revolution.

La Mina "El Eden." Cerro Grillo. ☎ **492/2-3002.** Admission $3.50 (includes train and tour). Daily noon–7pm. One entrance is near the teleférico exit and the Motel del Bosque. For the train and tour, take the other entrance a few blocks up Avenida Juárez (which becomes Avenida Torreón). From the cathedral walk down Hidalgo to Juárez (four blocks), turn right on Juárez (which becomes Torreón), and walk about three blocks, passing the long, narrow Alameda (park) and the red Seguro Social building. Turn right at the next street, Dovali Jaime, which leads straight to the mine entrance.

Opened in 1586, this mine was carved by hand by the indigenous population, which was forced into slavery by the Spanish. The Indians (mainly Caxcanes) began working in the mine at the age of 10 or 12 and lived to about 36 years of age. Accidents, tuberculosis, or silicosis caused their early deaths. The mine was extremely rich, yielding gold, copper, zinc, iron, and lead in addition to silver, but it was closed after only 60 years when an attempt to use explosives resulted in an inundation of water in the lower levels. Be sure to take the 40-minute mine tour, beginning with a short ride on the small train 1,720 feet into the mine. A Spanish-speaking guide takes tourists to interesting points in the mine, which is dramatically lit. Visitors can view the special miners' altar by crossing a shaky (but short) suspension bridge over a deep, dark, water-filled crevasse. The tour is worthwhile even if you don't speak Spanish.

✪ **Rafael Coronel Museum.** Calle Chevano, between Juan de Tolosa and Vergel Nuevo. ☎ **492/2-5661.** Admission $3.50. Thurs–Tues 10am–2pm and 4–7pm. Bus: Ruta 5, 8, or 10. Facing the cathedral, walk left up Hidalgo to the Founder's Fountain (about two blocks), then take the left fork (Calle Abasolo) two more short blocks; at the large yellow-ocher building and traffic triangle, take the right fork. You'll spot the large, old temple ahead.

First stroll through the gorgeous tranquil gardens and ruins of the former Convento de San Francisco, filled with trailing blossoms and verdant foliage and framed by ancient arches and the blue sky. A small wing contains Coronel's drawings on paper.

Once you step inside the mask museum, you'll be dazzled by the sheer number of fantastic masks—4,500 of them—from all over Mexico; they're so exotic they look as if they could be from all over the world. There are entire walls filled with bizarre demons with curling 3-foot-long horns and noses; red devils; animals and unidentifiable creatures spitting snakes, pigs, or rats; conquistadores—anything the mind can conjure up. The masks, both antique and contemporary, are festooned with all manner of materials from human hair and animal fur, fabric, plant fibers, and bones to metal screening, steel wool, sequins, plastic, and glitter.

An amazing marionette museum is a great place to bring children. There are entire dioramas showing a bullfight, battling armies, and even a vision of hell. These marionettes are some of the hundreds created during the last century by the famous Rosete-Aranda family of Huamantla, Tlaxcala, where there is also a puppet museum. This superb collection was donated by the artist Rafael Coronel, younger brother of Pedro Coronel, whose work is found in the Museo Pedro Coronel and the Museo Goitia (both in Zacatecas).

Also in the museum, to the left after you enter, is the Ruth Rivera room, where some of Diego Rivera's drawings are on display. Ruth Rivera is the daughter of Diego Rivera and the wife of Rafael Coronel. The museum also has a delightful ground-floor café for coffee and pastries and a small gift shop.

A SIDE TRIP TO NEARBY GUADALUPE

The most famous religious edifice in the region, aside from the cathedral, is the Convento de Guadalupe, in Guadalupe, about 4 miles east of Zacatecas on Highways 45/49. Transportes de Guadalupe buses go to Guadalupe from the Central Camionera in Zacatecas, or there's a Ruta 13 bus to Guadalupe at López Mateos and Salazar just up from the Hotel Gallery. The bus stops a block from the convent. It leaves about every 15 minutes or so and costs 50¢ for the 20-minute ride. A taxi to Guadalupe will run about $8. If you're driving, look for a red-brick church and steeple and turn right just past it onto Calle Independencia.

Convento de Guadalupe. Calle Independencia, Guadalupe. Museum $2.50. Tues–Sun 10am–4:30pm.

Dating from 1707, the convent now houses the ✪ **Museo de Arte Virreinal de Guadalupe** (☎ 492/3-2089 or 492/3-2386). As you enter through a small park/courtyard with stone mosaics, look up at the different domes and doorways of the convent. The museum building is to your right. Inside the convent proper, every wall seems to be covered by paintings; one series of huge paintings describes the life of St. Francis of Assisi on the ground floor and the life of Christ on the floor above.

Remember while touring these holy grounds that they were reserved for men of the cloth; the public was not meant to see the grounds, the paintings, or the sumptuous "cells" where the Franciscan monks spent their spare time. You may catch a glimpse of the brown-robed monks through a slatted wooden door; today part of the building is still in use as a college of instruction in the Franciscan order. The third Franciscan monastery established in the New World, the convent educated missionaries and sent them northward into what is now northern Mexico and the southwestern United States as part of the cultural conquest by the Spaniards. The Dominican order, also important in the Conquest, appears in the artwork of the convent as well, but the brown-robed Franciscans are the more familiar figures. The three knots of their sashes signify their vows of obedience, penitence, and poverty—the occasional fourth knot signifies the additional vow of silence.

The chapel to the left of the main building (as you face the convent from the front court/park) is called the **Capilla de Napoles.** It must have taken a king's ransom in gold to decorate it, with gold ranging in quality from 6 karat on the lower walls up to 22 karat in the dome above. Guides are available for a tour or to open the chapel, which is visible from either the organ loft or the ground floor—be sure to tip the guide for opening the doors and turning on the lights.

Museo Regional de la Historia. Jardín Juárez, Guadalupe. ☎ **492/3-2386** or 492/3-2089. Free admission. Tues–Sun 10am–4:30pm.

This museum contains fine examples of carriages and antique cars collected from all over Mexico, many of which formerly belonged to ex-presidents and famous historical figures. Representative forms of transportation from pre-Hispanic times to the present are particularly interesting. The museum is located in Guadalupe to the right side of the convent.

✪ **Centro Platero de Zacatecas.** Ex-Hacienda de Bernardez, Guadalupe. ☎ **492/2-1007.** Free admission. Mon–Fri 10am–6pm, Sat 10am–2pm.

Since Zacatecas ranks first in Mexico in the production of silver and fourth in gold, it seems only fitting that the art of metalworking is being reborn here. Young silversmiths are learning the trade in an old hacienda that once belonged to the counts of Laguna, located in the Fraccionamiento Lomas near the golf course. The students are trained not only in the art of jewelry making, but also in business so that they'll be capable of opening their own stores. An association of mining engineers and other local groups support the school and students. Most of the unusual jewelry designs are taken from the balconies and other architectural ironwork in Zacatecas; after you've seen them, you'll view Zacatecas's buildings with new eyes. The jewelry is sold at the school, and there's an equally large selection at the **Centro Commercial "El Mercado,"** next to the cathedral in central Zacatecas.

Visiting this school is convenient if you're also visiting the Convento de Guadalupe, since the two are more or less in the same vicinity (but not close). The school is about a mile north of the highway, zigzagging past newly constructed upscale homes on streets that don't yet have name signs. You'll be glad you took a cab, which costs about $4 from Guadalupe.

ORGANIZED TOURS

Cantera Tours (☎ 492/2-9065; fax 492/2-9121) has an office located a block south of the cathedral at the far end of the Centro Comercial "El Mercado" on Avenida Hidalgo. They primarily host groups and have never seemed particularly welcoming to individual tourists or small groups of four, but they're the only game in town, and a city tour can be arranged for a price of course. Such a tour covers Zacatecas and the surrounding region (the Convento de Guadalupe, Cerro de la Bufa, the teleférico, and so on). Another five-hour guided tour covers the nearby town of Jerez and the ruins of Chicomostoc (the Zona Arqueológica La Quemada) and is the only way to get directly to Chicomostoc unless you have a car. Prices for these two tours are $17 and $20 per person and require a minimum of two and five people, respectively. The office is open Monday through Saturday from 9am to 2pm and 4 to 7pm.

For a group of ten people or more, Cantera Tours also sponsors the **Callejoneada Zacatecana,** a traditional walk through the city's *callejones* (the little curving alleys, byways, and plazas) accompanied by music and dancing, on Saturdays beginning around 9pm (8pm in cold weather). Be sure to ask if there will be one while you're in town. Or, if you want a free tour, just join a group as it marches through the streets—they're hard to miss with the drums and horns and a flower-bedecked burro laden with barrels of mescal.

WHERE TO STAY

DOUBLES FOR LESS THAN $20

⑤ Hotel Colón. López Velarde 508, 98000 Zacatecas, Zac. ☎ **492/2-0464** or 492/2-8925. Fax 492/2-0464. 37 rms (all with bath). TV TEL. $11 single; $13 double. Parking available on the street.

Just a little farther up the hill from the Motel Zacatecas Courts (see below), this hotel is basic but well maintained and clean. The beds are good, and the floors are made of terrazzo. It can be noisy, as the hotel sits between two busy streets—López Mateos and Ramón López Velarde. It's a three-story hotel; you enter on the middle level, and there's a floor above and one below. Basement rooms are dark. To reach this hotel, face the cathedral and then walk/wind to the right around to Calle Tacuba. Bearing continuously left, the street first becomes Guerrero, then Ramón López Velarde as you go down the hill; it's a total of about five or six blocks to the hotel.

DOUBLES FOR LESS THAN $30

Motel Zacatecas Courts. López Velarde 602, 98000 Zacatecas, Zac. ☎ **492/2-0328.** Fax 492/2-1225. 92 rms (all with bath). TV TEL. $17 single; $20 double. Free enclosed parking.

This clean but somewhat worn modern-style hotel has carpeting, hot water 24 hours a day, and laundry and dry-cleaning services. Adjacent to the hotel are a travel agency and pharmacy. The clean, cheerful restaurant has economical meals and is open daily from 7am to 10:30pm. Facing the cathedral, walk/wind around it to the right until you reach Calle Tacuba. Bearing continuously left, this street first becomes Guerrero then Ramón López Velarde as you go down the hill; it's a total of about six or seven blocks to the hotel.

Posada de los Condes. Juárez 107, 98000 Zacatecas, Zac. ☎ **492/2-1412** or 492/2-1093. Fax 492/4-0072. 58 rms (all with bath). TV. $18 single; $22 double. Free parking in front.

This is a good choice on the busiest corner in town—the intersection of Avenidas Juárez and Hidalgo. The building's facade is about 300 years old, though the inside was remodeled in 1968. Rooms facing the street have French doors opening onto small iron-railed balconies; other, quieter rooms have no windows but do have ceiling ventilation. Be sure to specify which you prefer. Rooms that receive no direct sun are chilly in winter. The rooms are in good shape; each is clean and carpeted and has good mattresses, a TV (with two U.S. channels), and hot water from 7am to midnight. To find the hotel from the cathedral, walk three blocks south on Hidalgo and bear left on Juárez; the hotel is on the right side of the street.

WORTH A SPLURGE

☉ Continental Plaza. Av. Hidalgo 703, Col. Centro, 98000 Zacatecas, Zac. ☎ **492/2-6183** or 800/882-6684 in the U.S. Fax 492/2-6245. 115 rms (all with bath). A/C TV TEL. $75 single or double. Free parking.

In the heart of historic, beautiful Zacatecas opposite the cathedral, this hotel (formerly the Paraiso Radisson) opened its doors in 1989 behind the facade of a former colonial-era building that most recently housed the Hotel Reina Cristina. The lobby holds a popular bar and good restaurant. The spacious, heated rooms on six floors are fashionably decorated. Rooms facing the plaza have a ringside seat on Zacatecas; from here you can see the mountains; the central plaza; the cathedral; and those exuberant and loud callejoneadas that end here anywhere between 11pm and 1 or 2am. Other rooms, facing the interior courtyard, are quieter. All rooms come equipped with TVs broadcasting four U.S. channels; some have king-size beds, and others have two double beds.

WHERE TO EAT

Between the Plaza de la Independencia and López Mateos runs **Calle Ventura Salazar,** which is lined with taco shops, snack shops, and hole-in-the-wall eateries just fine for a quick bite at ridiculously low prices. The food market is on the north side of the Plaza de la Independencia, bounded on the left by the Callejon del Traffico, a narrow walkway to the left of the market entrance.

MEALS FOR LESS THAN $10

☉ Café Nevería Acrópolis. Av. Hidalgo and Plazuela Candelario Huzar. ☎ **492/2-1284.** Breakfast $3.50–$4; antojitos $1.80–$5.50; cakes $1.50–$2.50; sandwiches $1.50–$2.50; coffees $1–$3. Daily 8:30am–10pm. MEXICAN/SNACKS.

During the day this is a soda fountain, sweetshop, and ice-cream parlor; it turns into a hip coffeehouse in the evening. Along the wall are photos and signatures of famous people, including Gregory Peck and Jane Fonda, who stayed in Zacatecas for the filming of *The Old Gringo*. This café is a great place for a late-afternoon sightseeing break with tea or coffee and a slab of heavily iced cake, although service be slow. The café is just across the little street to the right of the cathedral.

☉ La Cantera Musical Fonda y Bar. Tacuba 2. Centro Comercial "El Mercado." ☎ **492/2-8828.** Breakfast $1.50–$5; lunch $2.50–$9; dinner $3–$8. Daily 8am–11pm. MEXICAN/REGIONAL.

Locals consider La Cantera one of the best Zacatecan-style restaurants in town. Against a background of Mexican music, Mexican art, handcrafted tiles, and an arched brick ceiling, colorfully dressed women press and fry masa into tortillas. The flavorful *pozole rojo* is loaded with chunks of pork and hominy; other dishes are equally filling. The restaurant is below the Mercado González Ortega by the cathedral in the central city.

Restaurant Mesón La Mina. Av. Juárez 15. ☎ **492/2-2773.** Breakfast $2–$3.50; antojitos $2–$4; main courses $2.50–$8; comida corrida $3.50. Daily 8am–11pm (comida corrida served 1–5pm). MEXICAN.

One of the plain-but-popular eateries in Zacatecas, this restaurant lies just a few doors up from the Hotel Condesa. Locals, especially men with plenty of spare time, congregate here for TV, conversation, newspaper, and coffee. The front of the restaurant is café-like with chrome and Formica. In the back of the restaurant, cheery cloth-covered tables, carved-wood chairs, an old darkwood bar, and red-tile floors provide a pleasant colonial ambience. The extensive menu includes soup, tacos, chilaquiles, beef filets, chicken, and pork chops with fries. There's also a full bar. A popular breakfast on chilly Zacatecas mornings is *leche para café* (hot, steamed milk accompanied by a jar of instant coffee) and a basket of pan dulce.

WORTH A SPLURGE

✪ **La Cuija.** Tacuba T-5, Centro Comercial "El Mercado." ☎ **492/2-8275.** Main courses $4–$10. Daily 2pm–midnight. MEXICAN.

When you see La Cuija etched in the entry-door glass and the stylishly dressed tables beyond, you'll know you should splurge at this place. Appetizers are referred to as "something to open the mouth," and the quesadillas de flor de calabaza are especially good reasons to open up. The succulent *lomo zacatecano*—broiled pork with a delicate red-chile sauce—is a favorite dish. The pastas are fresh-tasting and an interesting change from Mexican fare. In the evenings, there's often live music. It's located at street level, on the back side of El Mercado.

✪ **Hotel Quinta Real.** Av. Rayón 434. ☎ **492/2-9104.** Breakfast $4–$6; main courses $6–$11. Daily 7am–11pm. REGIONAL/INTERNATIONAL.

White linen tablecloths, chairs covered with pastel tapestry, high-beamed ceilings, and plants everywhere create an elegant but comfortable ambience at this restaurant. The wraparound dining room faces the center of the former bullring from which this hotel was created. Diners can gaze out at the twinkling lights in the courtyard's potted trees and the illuminated aqueduct that arches gracefully high above. An inventive menu features all sorts of dishes, including red snapper au poblana with poblano peppers on top and chicken breast covered with coconut paste. For dessert, try *cajeta* (goat's milk candy) crêpes, crêpes Suzette, or chocolate mousse. Even if you don't eat here, drop by for a drink or canapés just to enjoy the unusual setting. To get here, walk seven short blocks south of the cathedral on Hidalgo, cross Juárez, and continue to Manuel Ponce; the hotel is under the aqueduct on the left.

ZACATECAS AFTER DARK

El Malacate. Mina El Eden. ☎ **492/2-3002.** Cover $12.

Have you ever been to a disco located in a silver mine 1,050 feet underground? Call in advance to reserve a table since it's a very popular place. The entrance is at the end of Calle Dovale Jaime, which is the street just past the Seguro Social building on Avenida Torreón. The club is open Thursday through Sunday from 9:30pm to 2am.

ALONG HIGHWAY 45 FROM ZACATECAS TO GUANAJUATO

CHICOMOSTOC: 12TH-CENTURY RUINS About 34 miles south of Zacatecas (about 1¼ miles off Highway 54 en route to Guadalajara), is the **Zona Arqueológica La Quemada,** an archaeological site developed by the 12th-century Nahuatlacas tribe. The pyramids here vaguely resemble those at Mitla and Monte Albán much farther south. The largest pyramid, called the **Temple,** has been restored and offers visitors their first glimpse into this fascinating aspect of Mexico's past. The rest of the site is not very well preserved, but the 11 pillars of granite give you an idea of the size of the grandiose palace that once stood here. Stone-paved avenues and terraces crowded with foundations of houses mark the **Ciudadela,** which is topped by an observatory from which the Nahuatlacas studied the movements of stars and planets and maybe even tracked the course of early extraterrestrial visitors. You can visit the ruins Tuesday through Sunday from 10am to 5pm. Admission is $2.50, free on Sunday.

If you don't have a car, getting to Chicomostoc may present a challenge, since the public bus lets you out only on the highway, leaving you with a walk of a little over a mile to reach the ruins. If you're vigorous, you can make the walk with no trouble. Alternatively, you can take a guided tour through Cantera Tours (see "Organized Tours" in Zacatecas, above).

AGUASCALIENTES On your way to Guanajuato, you'll pass through Aguascalientes (pop. 514,000), which is only 84 miles south of Zacatecas. *Aguascalientes* means "hot waters," and the city is famous for its hot springs. It was founded by the Spanish in 1575 as a place of protection and rest along the silver highway between Mexico City, Guanajuato, and Zacatecas, as well as a center of food cultivation for the mining region. Today Aguascalientes is known for its copper mining, embroidery, and knitwear. In the streets beside and behind the cathedral and the Plaza Principal, you'll note several stores selling the products of these industries.

With growth, the city has lost some of its colonial charm, although the people here are still friendly and relaxed. The main plaza, around which are several moderately priced hotels and restaurants, dates from the colonial era, and it's a pleasant place to stroll. The main tourist attraction in Aguascalientes is the **José Guadalupe Posada Museum** on the Plaza Encino. Posada was a 19th-century engraver and writer, and his skeleton caricatures of politicians and political events are famous countrywide; the museum has a large collection.

The biggest fair in Mexico, the **Fería de San Marcos,** is held here annually from April 19 to May 10. Festivities include industrial expositions, fireworks, cultural events, rodeos, and bullfights with renowned bullfighters from all over the world. At Aguascalientes, you can choose between the toll or free road to León, which is approximately 85 miles southeast of Aguascalientes. Heavy traffic can make the narrow, two-lane free road frustratingly slow.

LEÓN Mexico's leather and shoe capital has thousands of shoestores lining its streets. Unfortunately, uncontrolled growth has resulted in an ugly city, made more so by the contrast between this city and clean Aguascalientes, beautiful Zacatecas, or historic Guanajuato. There's an international airport in León. From León, there are both a fast, inexpensive toll road and a free road to Guanajuato. The drive takes 15 to 45 minutes depending on which route you take.

2 Guanajuato

221 miles NW of Mexico City, 35 miles SE of León, 58 miles W of San Miguel de Allende, 130 miles SW of San Luis Potosí, 102 miles N of Morelia, 175 miles SE of Zacatecas

Steeped in history, Guanajuato is one of Mexico's hidden colonial-era gems. Except during the October Cervantino Festival, relatively few foreign tourists find their way to Guanajuato, but it's a popular weekend trip for people from Mexico City. Clean and beautifully preserved, Guanajuato should be high on your list of the finest places to visit in Mexico.

It was founded in 1559 around the Río Guanajuato, and its narrow, winding streets reflect the past meanderings of the river. Floods plagued the town, and finally the river was diverted, leaving an excellent bed for what has now become a subterranean highway with cantilevered houses jutting over the roadway. Guanajuato was

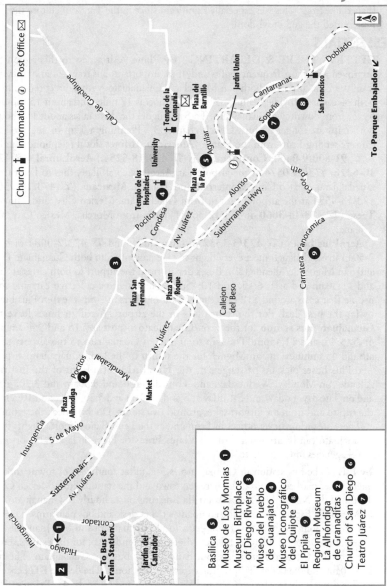

Church † Information ⓘ Post Office ⊠

Museo de Los Momias **1**
Basílica **5**
Museum Birthplace of Diego Rivera **3**
Museo del Pueblo de Guanajuato **4**
Museo Iconográfico del Quijote **8**
El Pípila **9**
Regional Museum La Alhóndiga de Granaditas **2**
Church of San Diego **6**
Teatro Juárez **7**

one of the most important colonial cities (along with Querétaro, Zacatecas, San Miguel, and San Luis Potosí) from the 16th through the 18th centuries. Its mines produced a third of all the silver in the world; and like the gold-rush towns in the United States, it bloomed with elaborate churches and mansions, many in the Moorish style. Today Guanajuato seems like an old Spanish city that has been dumped lock, stock, and barrel into a Mexican river valley.

The name "Guanajuato" is a Spanish adaptation of the Tarascan word *guanaxuato*, meaning "hill of frogs." To the Tarascans, the rocks above town appeared to be shaped like frogs. This was especially significant since in the Tarascan culture the frog represented the god of wisdom.

ESSENTIALS

GETTING THERE & DEPARTING   By Plane   Air access to this region has improved with more frequent flights and, most important, bus transportation directly from the León airport to both San Miguel and Guanajuato, with a direct return from both places as well. The León/Guanajuato airport is 17 miles and about 15 minutes by car from downtown Guanajuato. To San Miguel the drive takes about 1¹/₂ hours; both trips are longer by bus. Check chapter 3, "Planning a Trip to Mexico" for carriers serving León from the States. (**American Airlines'** local telephone number is ☎ **91-800/9-0460; Continental's** is ☎ **473/18-5254.**) **AeroLitoral** (☎ **473/ 16-6226; 473/14-0574** at the airport), an Aeroméxico affiliate, flies to León from Guadalajara, Mexico City, Monterrey, and Tijuana. **Mexicana** (☎ **473/14-9500;** 473/13-4550 at the airport) flies in from Guadalajara, Mexico City, and Tijuana. **Taesa** (☎ **473/14-3660** or 473/12-3621) arrives from Morelia, Mexico City, and Tijuana.

AeroPlus buses (☎ **473/3-1332** in Guanajuato and ☎ **473/2-0084** or 473/ 2-5043 in San Miguel) meet every flight to take passengers to both Guanajuato ($4), and San Miguel de Allende ($7). Buses depart from the airport to both cities at 2:15 and 11:30am and at 1, 6:45, and 10:45pm. There's also a colectivo carrying four people that costs around $18 each, or $72 for one person—but the AeroPlus bus is by far the best deal. For the return bus to the airport, AeroPlus buses leave the **Guanajuato bus station** for the León/Guanajuato airport at 7:15 and 9:45am and 4:45, 5:45, and 11:45pm. The trip to and from Guanajuato to the airport takes around 45 minutes. In San Miguel, for the return to the León/Guanajuato airport, AeroPlus buses pick up passengers at the **Hotel Aldea** (in front of the Instituto Allende) on Monday, Wednesday, and Thursday at 6 and 8:30am and 3:30, 4:30, and on Tuesday, Friday, and Saturday at 5 and 8:30am and 3:30, 4:30, and 10:30pm; the trip to and from the airport takes around two hours. Double-check these times.

There are airline ticket offices in León and at the León/Bajío airport. Flights from Guanajuato can be arranged through **Viajes Frausto,** Plaza de la Paz 10, or other travel agencies in Guanajuato.

By Bus   The bus station in Guanajuato is 3¹/₂ miles southwest of town, and frequent buses marked "Central" go between town and the station. From Mexico City's Terminal del Norte, the **Flecha Amarilla** line runs buses hourly to Guanajuato. Go to Area 6 ("6 Espera") to find the company's ticket desk and bus platforms. The trip can take as long as six hours if you get a local bus that stops in San Juan del Río, Querétaro, Dolores Hidalgo, and San Miguel de Allende. Ask for the express. From Mexico City **Estrella Blanca** has four daily express buses to Guanajuato. The first is at 10am and the last at 6:15pm; the trip takes five hours. The deluxe **ETN** coaches go five times daily to Mexico City and also to León and Guadalajara. **Primera Plus** has seven direct buses to and from Mexico City.

From Guanajuato, **Flecha Amarilla** makes six trips "Vía Presa" (the short route) to San Miguel de Allende; the last is at 2:30pm. The trip takes 1¹/₂ hours. Flecha Amarilla has service every 20 minutes to Dolores (a two-hour trip). From Dolores, there's frequent service to San Miguel de Allende—a good thing to know if you've missed the limited service on other lines to San Miguel. Flecha Amarilla also goes to Querétaro, San Luis Potosí, and Mexico City, as well as to Aguascalientes and Guadalajara. Times and itineraries change frequently, so your best bet is to invest 25¢ for a bus ride to the Central and make your choice.

By Car If you're descending upon Guanajuato from the north, see "Along Highway 45 from Zacatecas to Guanajuato," above. From Mexico City there are two routes. The faster route, although it may look longer, is Highway 57 north and northwest to Highway 45D at Querétaro, west through Salamanca to Irapuato, where you follow Highway 45 north to Silao, and then take Highway 110 east. That route is a four-lane road almost all the way. The other route continues north on Highway 57 past Querétaro, then west on Highway 110 through Dolores Hidalgo and continues on "the scenic route" to Guanajuato. From San Luis Potosí, the quickest way to Guanajuato is through Dolores Hidalgo.

ORIENTATION   Arriving by Bus   The modern station, about $3^{1}/_{2}$ miles southwest of town on the road to Celaya, opened in February 1990 and has all the latest conveniences—shops, baggage storage, telephone center with fax and long distance, and a cafeteria-style fast-food restaurant. If you aren't carting much luggage, take one of the buses marked "Centro" into town. Otherwise, taxis are readily available.

Arriving by Car   Try not to lose your sanity while finding a place to park. Such a winding, hilly town as Guanajuato defies good verbal or written directions. Just be alert for one-way streets, and after winding around through the subterranean highway a bit, you'll get enough bearings to park. If in doubt, follow the signs marked Teatro Juárez or Jardín Unión, which will get you to the center of town, where you can park and collect your wits. In fact, consider parking your car until you leave town, since the frustration of parking and driving in the city could spoil your visit.

Information   The **tourist information office** is at the Plaza de la Paz 14, across from the basílica (☎ **473/2-0086** or 473/2-1574; fax 473/2-4251). It's open Monday through Friday from 8:30am to 7:30pm and Saturday, Sunday, and holidays from 10am to 2pm. The English speaking staff will provide city and area information and a detailed free map of the city with a map of the entire state of Guanajuato on the back.

City Layout   Guanajuato is a town of narrow streets twisting up the mountains and interspersed by pleasant parks, plazas, and churches. The hilly terrain and tangle of streets are difficult to represent on a map—using our map or any other, you'll soon learn they aren't to scale, nor is every narrow street or connecting stairstep walkway shown.

Among all Guanajuato's plazas and parks, the **Plaza de la Unión** (or Jardín de la Unión) is the true heart of the city—the place where students, locals, and visitors gather more than any other. On one side are both the Teatro Juárez and Templo de San Diego, and it's within walking distance of almost all the city sights. As another point of orientation, the statue of *El Pípila,* high on a mountainside overlooking the town, is in line with the Teatro Juárez and Plaza de la Unión.

If you're driving, an excellent point of reference is the **Scenic Highway** (Carretera Panorámica), from which you can see the city from above. It starts north of town off the road to Irapuato, passes El Pípila, continues south to the dam (Presa de la Olla), and finally loops around north again to the Valenciana Mine and Church.

Getting Around   Walking is the only way really to get to know this labyrinthine town. For longer stretches, just hop on the main **bus,** marked "Presa-Estación," which operates from one end of town at the railroad station to the other end at Presa de la Olla. Buses use the subterranean highway when going south, and there are subterranean bus stops along the way; for example, there's one near the Teatro Juárez, off the Jardín de la Unión. **Taxis** are abundant and generally reasonably priced, but as usual you should establish the price before setting out.

FAST FACTS: GUANAJUATO

Area Code   The telephone area code is 473.

Climate   This high-altitude city has mild temperatures in summer, but in winter it can dip to freezing. Bring warm clothing and remember that most hotels have no heat.

Elevation   6,724 feet.

Language School   Every year the positive experiences at the **Instituto Falcón** prompt numerous readers to write letters of commendation—more than I receive about any other place in the country. The Instituto Falcón (Callejón de la Mora 158, Guanajuato 36000, Gto.; ☎ **473/2-3694**) is directed by Jorge Barroso, who provides skilled and dedicated tutors for those wishing hourly or intensive studies at all levels. He can also arrange for boarding with local families.

Population   75,000.

Post Office   The post office (correo) is located on the corner of Navarro and Carcamanes, near the Templo de la Compañía.

Seasons   Guanajuato has several high seasons during which hotel and, in some cases, restaurant prices go up, and unreserved rooms are hard to find. The high seasons are Christmas, Easter week, all of the Cervantino Festival, and July and August when Mexicans and Europeans vacation.

EXPLORING GUANAJUATO
FESTIVALS

Every year, from about October 7 to 22, the state of Guanajuato sponsors the **Festival Cervantino (International Cervantes Festival),** two weeks of performing arts from all over the world. In recent years, the festival has featured marionettes from Czechoslovakia, the Elliot Feld Dance Company from New York, the Cuban National Ballet, and a host of Mexican artists. The shows are held in open plazas and theaters all over town. These same groups also tour Mexico after the festival, so there's a chance of seeing them elsewhere. Book rooms well in advance during the festival; if Guanajuato is full, consider staying in nearby San Miguel de Allende.

For ticket information and a schedule contact Festival Cervantino, Mineral de Cata s/n (Ex Cava), Guanajuato, Gto. 36060 (☎ **473/2-0959**). Once you know the schedule, you can order tickets through Ticketmaster in Mexico City (☎ **5/325-9000**). Keep your confirmation number; you'll need it to pick up your tickets in Guanajuato.

THE TOP ATTRACTIONS

✪ **Iglesia de San Cayetano (Templo de la Valenciana).** Valenciana. Free admission. Daily 9am–6pm.

The magnificent church, built in 1765 by the first Count of Valencia, is one of the most beautiful colonial churches in churrigueresque style—a true masterpiece and one of the finest churches in Mexico. It's absolutely filled with luxurious floor-to-ceiling carvings of white cedar covered with 18-karat gold. This baroque art form, unique to Mexico, merged the Spanish artistic style with the abundant gold of Mexico. You'll also find some beautiful paintings here. If you're lucky, you may be able to catch a concert of baroque music performed on the large organ.

✪ **Teatro Juárez.** Jardín de la Unión. ☎ **473/2-0183.** Admission $1.75, 50¢ additional with still camera, $2 additional with video camera. Tues–Sat 9am–1:45pm and 5–7:45pm, Sun 9am–1:45pm.

Built in 1903 during the opulent era of the Porfiriato, this theater is now the venue for many productions, especially during the Cervantino festival. Outside are bronze sculptures of lions and lanterns, and inside the five-story U-shaped theater is embellished with carved ornamentation in a flurry of red, gold, and blue.

⭐ **Museum Birthplace of Diego Rivera.** Calle Positos 47. ☎ **473/2-1197.** Admission $1.75. Tues–Sat 10am–1:30pm and 4–6:30pm, Sun 10am–2:30pm.

This is the house where the artist Diego Rivera was born on December 8, 1886. It has been refurbished and made into a museum. The first floor of this three-story house is furnished as it might have been in the era of Rivera's birth. Upstairs there's a fine collection of Rivera's early works. He began painting when he was 10 years old and eventually moved to Paris, where he became a Marxist during World War I. The house contains sketches of some of his earlier murals that made his reputation, but most of the works on display are paintings from 1902 to 1956. On the third floor is a small auditorium where lectures and conferences are held. The house is north of the Plaza de la Paz, 1¹/₂ blocks beyond the Museo del Pueblo.

⭐ **Museo del Pueblo de Guanajuato.** Calle Positos 7. ☎ **473/2-2990.** Admission $1.75. Tues–Sat 10am–2pm and 4–7pm, Sun 10am–2:30pm, open all day during the Cervantino Festival.

North of the Plaza de la Paz and before the Rivera museum (see above) lies this 17th-century mansion that once belonged to the Marqués San Juan Rayas. It holds a priceless collection of more than 1,000 colonial-era civil and religious pieces gathered by local distinguished muralist José Chávez Morado. Chávez murals can be seen in this museum as well as in the Regional Museum La Alhóndiga down the street. In addition to the Chávez collection, contemporary displays upstairs show Mexican artists. Every other year, the museum hosts the Biennial of Diego Rivera, a truly fine exhibit of Mexico's up-and-coming artists.

⭐ **Regional Museum la Alhóndiga de Granaditas.** Mendizabal 6. ☎ **473/2-1112.** Admission $2.50 (50¢ extra with still camera), free for students with ID cards, free for all on Sun. Tues–Sat 10am–2pm and 4–6pm, Sun 10am–2:30pm.

Continuing a long block farther on the same street as the Rivera museum (see above), you'll see the huge Alhóndiga on the left (the entrance is on Positos). The Alhóndiga de Granaditas was built between 1798 and 1809 as the town granary. It was so splendid that it was called El Palacio del Maiz (the Corn Palace). The Spanish took refuge here as El Pípila and company burned down the doors to the Alhóndiga, but they still had not lost the war. A year later, the heads of the revolutionaries Hidalgo, Allende, Aldama, and Jiménez were brought here and hung in iron cages on the four outside corners of the building, where they remained from 1811 to 1821 to remind the populace of what happens to those who rebel. The name plaques below the cornice on the four corners of the building commemorate the four heroes of this stormy period. From 1864 to 1949 the building served as a prison.

The Alhóndinga is now one of the best museums in Mexico. There are two levels with rooms off the courtyard. You'll see numerous pre-Columbian relics, including pots, decorative seals and stamps, terra-cotta figurines, and stone implements. The lower level (on which you enter) has rooms filled with regional crafts and the pre-Hispanic art collection of José Chávez Morado—the artist responsible for the splendid murals on both stairwells (and whose collection is in the important Museo del Pueblo de Guanajuato). Mexico's most complete collection of pre-Hispanic stamps was donated to the museum by American archaeologist Frederick Field. The museum contains Chupícuaro ceramics dating from A.D. 350 to 450 from the southeast part of the state; they were saved when the Solis Dam was constructed in 1949 and are a type of ceramics rarely seen in Mexico. A long corridor contains bronze masks of the revolutionary heroes as well as an eternal flame in their honor.

Upstairs is a Bellas Artes section with exhibits (both temporary and permanent) of national and international artists. There are also several rooms showing the history of the state of Guanajuato, particularly its revolutionary history, and an exhibit on the region's dozen mines, the first of which was begun in 1557 on the orders of Charles V. There are some interesting lithographs showing the city in the 18th and 19th centuries, in addition to 20th-century photographs.

✪ **El Pípila.** Free admission. Daily 24 hours. Go via automobile or bus (marked "Pípila") or on foot along a rugged winding pathway (wear comfortable shoes). Walk up Calle Sopeña from the Jardín de la Unión and turn to the right up Callejón del Calvario. A sign on the wall reads AL PÍPILA ("To El Pípila").

Nicknamed El Pípila, this dramatic mountaintop monument is dedicated to the brave young miner who on Hidalgo's orders set fire to the Alhóndiga de Granaditas, the strategically situated grain warehouse in which the Royalists were hiding during the War of Independence. On September 16, 1810, Hidalgo, a radical priest who had appealed for Mexico's independence from Spain, led an army that captured Guanajuato. In this bloody battle, 600 inhabitants and 2,000 Indians were killed, but the revolution was on its way. Guanajuato became the rebel capital; however, its history was short—10 months later Hidalgo was captured and shot in Chihuahua, and his head was sent to Guanajuato to be exhibited.

Today, El Pípila's statue raises a torch high over the city in everlasting vigilance, and the inscription at his feet proclaims AUN HAY OTRAS ALHÓNDIGAS POR INCENDIAR—"There are still other alhóndigas to burn."

The monument sits high above the town, with a great view overlooking the whole city—it's the best spot in town for photos. You can climb inside the statue for another dramatic view of the city below. There's a little park where kids play ball and families picnic.

✪ **Museo de los Momias (Mummy Museum).** Calzada del Panteón. ☎ **473/2-0639.** Admission $2.50, $1 extra with still camera or $2.50 with movie camera. Daily 9am–6pm. At the northwestern end of town is the Calzada del Panteón, which leads up to the municipal cemetery. It's a steep climb on foot, but the bus labeled "Presa-Estación" runs along the Plaza de la Paz/Sopeña, and this will take you to the foot of the cobbled hill. For this trip, Guanajuato's cab drivers invariably tend to charge what the traffic will bear.

First-time visitors find this museum either grotesque or incredibly fascinating: Mumified remains of Guanajuato's residents, some of which are garbed in clothing from centuries past, are on display in tall showcases and glass caskets. Dryness, plus the earth's gases and minerals, have caused decomposition to halt in certain sections of the Panteón. Because of space limitations, people are buried for only five years; then, if the relatives can't continue to pay for the graves, the bodies are exhumed to make room for more. Those on display were exhumed between 1865 and 1985. The mummies stand or recline grinning, choking, or staring. It's impossible to resist the temptation to go up and look at them (everybody does), and this is the only graveyard I've seen with souvenir stands next to the main gate, selling sugar effigies of the mummies.

Museo Iconográfico del Quijote. Manuel Doblado 1. ☎ **473/2-6721.** Free admission. Tues–Sat 10am–6:30pm, Sun 10am–2:30pm.

This museum, a long block southeast of the *jardín* and past the Hostería del Frayle, holds a fascinating collection of art based upon Don Quijote. Once you get past the captivating life-size wood carving of the Don and Sancho, you enter (almost physically) into the lives of Cervantes and Don Quixote by way of the wall and ceiling murals that enclose you in the next room and the works of art all around. In the remaining galleries, there are exhibits of artists who found inspiration from the classic tale of Don Quijote such as Salvador Dalí, Picasso, Raul Angiano, José Guadalupe Posada, Daumier, José Moreno Carbonero, and Pedro Coronel.

OTHER ATTRACTIONS

The **Church of San Diego,** on the Jardín de la Unión, stands almost as it did in 1633, when it was built under the direction of Franciscan missionaries. After a 1760 flood that nearly destroyed it, reconstruction was completed in 1786; half the funds were given by the Count of Valenciana. The pink cantera stone facade is a fine example of Mexican baroque (churrigueresque).

The **Plazuela del Baratillo,** just off the Jardín de la Unión, has a beautiful fountain (a gift from Emperor Maximilian) at its center, and you'll always find people sitting around it peacefully, some in the shade and others in the sun; late in the afternoon the *plazuela* is almost exactly divided between *sol* (sun) and *sombra* (shade). The **Plazuela San Fernando** is larger and has a stone platform where very often there will be local Mexican dances with the younger generation decked out in bright costumes.

The magnificent **university** was founded in 1732, but its entrance was rebuilt in 1945 in a stately manner so the building now dominates the whole town. The university is just behind **Plaza de la Paz,** and it's open every day. Visitors are welcome.

The **Church of the Compañía de Jesús,** next to the university, was built in 1747 by the Jesuit order as the biggest of their churches at that time. It is distinctly churrigueresque on the outside, but the interior, which was restored in the 19th century, is not. This church was built as part of the Jesuit university, founded in 1732 on orders of Philip V on the site of the present university; it's the last of 23 universities built by the Jesuit order in Mexico.

NEARBY ATTRACTIONS

For a suburban outing, hop any bus that says "Presa" (try the bus stop in the Subterranean near Jardín de la Unión) to the **Parque de la Acacias** and the **Presa de la Olla,** the artificial lake. There are several parks and lots of trees—it's a good place for a lazy afternoon.

While in the neighborhood, you might note the **Government Palace** on Paseo de la Presa with its pink-stone front and green-tile interior. The neighborhood around here is residential and will give you another glimpse of Guanajuato away from the bustle of the plazas.

The most famous silver mine is **La Valenciana,** said to have produced a fifth of the silver circulating in the world from 1558 to 1810. It can be reached by taking Route 30, the Dolores Hidalgo road, 3 miles northeast of town (the bus is "Vallenciana SAHOP"). The mine was closed about 40 years ago but then reopened, and a caretaker is there to show you the eight-sided vertical shaft (1,650 feet deep) and the once-grandiose courtyard. You can take a look down the long mine shaft (but you can't go down) from which silver is still being extracted today, along with about 50 other minerals and metals. Silver products from this mine are sold in the adjoining silver shop. While you're in the area, you may also want to see the **Iglesia de San Cayetano/La Valenciana** described in "Top Attractions," above, and FONART mentioned in "Shopping," below. All through this mountainous area, more than a dozen mines produced silver. Some are now abandoned, and some, like Valenciana, are still functioning.

Also around here there were more than 150 splendid mansions on the haciendas of wealthy colonial mine owners. Most are now either in ruins or restored and privately owned, but you can visit the ✪ **Museo Ex-Hacienda San Gabriel de Barrera,** which I certainly recommend. Located about 2 miles from town on the ancient road to Marfil, the museum is housed in one of the most luxurious of the 18th-century grand haciendas, with a magnificent main house, a gold-adorned chapel, and acres of lovely gardens. You can wander through Italian gardens, English gardens, Chinese gardens, and cactus gardens, all decorated with beautiful statues and fountains from the various countries represented. The hacienda, which had remained in the family for two centuries, was sold to the Mexican government in 1979 and is now a museum furnished with Mexican and European furniture and open to the public. You can visit it any day from 9am to 6:30pm; admission is $2, plus $1 for a still camera or $2.75 for a video camera.

The recommended Hotel San Gabriel de Barrera is also here—see "Worth a Splurge" under "Where to Stay," below, for information on this and for directions on how to arrive here from town.

ORGANIZED TOURS

If you understand Spanish, try **Transportes Turísticos de Guanajuato** (☎ 473/ 2-2838 or 473/2-2134) with offices below (on the right of) the Basílica Nuestra Señora de Guanajuato, which offers 3¹/₂ hour tours of the city. They cost $5 per person with a minimum of six participants; for two-person tours, the cost is $15 per person. Tours in English cost more, and readers have complained about the cost of them and the poor quality of English spoken by the guides.

SHOPPING

The **Mercado Hidalgo,** housed in a building (1909) that resembles a Victorian railroad station, has a cavernous lower level and an upper balcony that encircles the whole building. It's stacked with lots of stalls that sell every conceivable kind of pottery and ceramic ware, even items imported from Japan. From this balcony, you can look down onto one of the neatest layouts in Mexico with symmetrical rows of stalls and little eateries providing splashes of orange, green, red, brown, and black—the tones of the fruits and vegetables. The market is open every day from morning to evening.

The **Gorky González Workshop,** Calle Pastita, by the stadium, is a good place to pick up Talavera-style pottery. Hours are irregular, but you may be able to browse through the small showroom Monday through Friday from 9am to 2pm and 4 to 6pm.

Across the street from the Iglesia de San Cayetano, at Valenciana, is the **Casa del Conde de la Valenciana,** which now houses a fine **restaurant** by the same name, decorative art galleries, and the government-sponsored **FONART** store (☎ 473/ 2-2550). Though small, the latter has a selection of the finest crafts from all over Mexico. It's open daily from 10am to 6pm. The Alcocer family, descendants of the count, still own and manage these properties. To get here take the "Valenciana SAHOP" bus by the Alhóndiga.

A half a block from the Plaza de la Unión is **Artesanías Vazquez,** Cantarranas 8 (☎ 473/2-5231), an outlet of the family ceramic factory in Dolores Hidalgo. It's small but loaded with the colorful Talavera-style pottery for which Dolores is famous; there are plates, ginger jars, frames, cups and saucers, serving bowls, and the like.

WHERE TO STAY

During the International Cervantes Festival held in mid-October, rooms are virtually impossible to find unless you have a reservation, and even then it's good to claim your room early in the day. Some visitors have to stay as far away as Querétaro, León, or San Miguel de Allende and come to Guanajuato for the day.

DOUBLES FOR LESS THAN $25

⑤ Casa Kloster. Alonso 32, 36000 Guanajuato, Gto. ☎ **473/2-0088.** 18 rms (1 with bath). $7 per person.

A European-style pension, this two-story hotel is located on a quiet side street one block northwest of the Jardín de la Unión and Juárez, across from Teléfonos de México. Run by a warm, friendly family, the Kloster has a large central courtyard bursting with birds and flowers; the plain but very clean rooms surround the courtyard. Most rooms have two beds, but several hold three or four. The common baths (two upstairs and one downstairs) are also spotlessly clean. One room for six people has a private bath. No meals are served, but don't be surprised if you're invited to share morning coffee in the family kitchen.

Hotel Alhóndiga. Insurgencia 49, 36000 Guanajuato, Gto. ☎ **473/2-0525.** 31 rms (all with bath). TV. $15 single; $20 double. Free parking for seven cars.

Located just off the Plaza Alhóndiga and half a block downhill from the Museo Alhóndiga, this hotel is within walking distance of all the downtown sights. A four-story hotel (no elevator), it has small, basic rooms, tile baths, and good beds covered with garish bedspreads. Front rooms are the nicest but also the noisiest, as this is a major corner (if there is such a thing in Guanajuato). The hotel has a restaurant.

Hotel El Minero. Alhóndiga 12-A, 36000 Guanajuato, Gto. ☎ **473/2-5251.** Fax 473/2-4729. 20 rms (all with bath). TV. $14 single; $16 double.

Only two blocks beyond the Museo Alhóndiga, this four-story (no elevator) hotel, is a good, clean economical choice. The carpeted rooms have small tile baths with showers, and most have a double and a single bed. The hotel restaurant is next door.

DOUBLES FOR LESS THAN $35

Hostería Del Frayle. Sopeña 3, 36000 Guanajuato, Gto. ☎ **473/2-1179.** Fax 473/2-1179, ext. 38. 37 rms (all with bath). TV TEL. $28 single; $34 double.

Half a block southeast of the Plaza de la Unión, this hotel is a perfect place to sample quarters as they might have been in colonial times. During Guanajuato's golden era ore was processed here before it went to the mint. Today, the building has been charmingly converted into a hotel. Each room has tall wooden doors, old hardwood floors, and comfortable, cozy furnishings with a hint of yesteryear. It's drafty and nippy in winter though, so bring your long johns; be prepared to climb lots of stairs. Housekeeping can be a bit lax, so check your room first. Management is friendly, and there's a bar to the left of the lobby.

✪ Hotel Embajadoras. Parque Embajadoras, 36000 Guanajuato, Gto. ☎ **473/2-0081** or 473/2-4464. Fax 473/2-4760. 27 rms (all with bath). TV TEL. $28 single; $34 double. Free parking.

This is the best choice out of downtown on the tree-lined street heading toward Paseo Madero. Spread out on shaded grounds, it's attractive, comfortable, and quiet. Rooms, all of which have red-tile floors, are small, clean, and plainly furnished. Covered walkways with chairs link the rooms. There's a patio at the rear with tables, chairs, and a hammock. A good, reasonably priced restaurant/bar takes care of meals. To reach the hotel, take a taxi or the "Paseo de la Presa" bus.

WORTH A SPLURGE

✪ Casa de Espíritus Alegres B&B. La Ex-Hacienda la Trinidad no. 1, 36250 Marfil, Gto. ☎ and fax **473/3-1013.** 5 rms, 2 suites (all with bath). $60 single; $70 double; $85 casita (all include breakfast).

Folk art and atmosphere abound in this "house of good spirits," owned and operated by two artists who have incorporated 20th-century comfort into parts of a 16th-century hacienda. Some of the rooms have their own fireplaces, and all are uniquely and colorfully decorated, fulfilling the promise of "a skeleton in every closet." A garden suite is decorated with antiques from India and has its own patio and fireplace. The *casita* has its own kitchen and living room. A tent pavilion with white marble floors is the place for happy hour. Breakfasts, overlooking the patio, feature Californian and Mexican cuisine, with generous helpings of fresh fruit. Guests have full use of the living room, decked out in folk art and books as well as paperback novels for loan. The owners also have a small folk art shop downstairs. The facility is sometimes used for workshops and can be rented by groups. Frequent "Marfil" buses run from the highway just outside the grounds into downtown Guanajuato some 2 miles distant. Get specific directions when you make your reservations.

WHERE TO EAT

If you find yourself hungry in the **Mercado Hidalgo** area, stop and try one of the many inexpensive eateries inside or outside to the left of the huge Mercado edifice. Observe the sign that says (in Spanish): "Avoid disappointment, ask to see the price list!"

Good pizza is served at branches of Pizza Piazza. One is at Cantarranas near the Jardín Unión (☎ **473/2-4259**).

MEALS FOR LESS THAN $5

✪ **Truco 7.** Truco 7. ☎ **473/2-8374.** Breakfast $1.25–$2.50; comida corrida $3; main courses $2.50–$4. Daily 8am–11:30pm (comida corrida served 1:30–4pm). MEXICAN.

With its economical prices and warm, colorful atmosphere, this place has quickly established its popularity with both locals and foreigners. The three dining rooms are small and a bit crowded yet nicely decorated with leather equipal tables and chairs, paintings by local artists, and photographs taken by the owner. The restaurant is housed in an 18th-century structure originally built for members of the Valenciana silver family. Calle Truco, a short street south of the *basílica*, runs between the Plaza de la Unión and the Plaza de la Paz. You can also reach it from the wide end of the Plaza de la Unión walking toward the Plaza de la Paz.

MEALS FOR LESS THAN $10

✪ **Café El Retiro.** Sopeña 14. ☎ **473/2-0622.** Breakfast $1.50–$3; main courses $2–$6; comida corrida $3. Daily 8am–11pm (comida corrida served 1–4:30pm). MEXICAN.

Sooner or later everyone—local, student, or visitor—winds up at El Retiro, which recently expanded into the building next door. One of the best and least expensive comida corridas in town is served here and consists of soup, rice with cheese, two or three choices of meat dish, dessert, and coffee. From the à la carte menu, you can choose from a variety of antojitos such as tacos and enchiladas or a quarter chicken. The service is quick and informally friendly. El Retiro is half a block south of the Jardín de la Unión, catercorner to the Teatro Juárez.

Tasca de los Santos. Plaza de la Paz 28. ☎ **473/2-2320.** Breakfast $1.25–$3.75; main courses $4–$9. Daily 8am–midnight. MEXICAN REGIONAL.

This is one of Guanajuato's snazzier restaurants with a completely à la carte menu. The food, service, and heavy Spanish decor are particularly pleasing. Paella is a house specialty. The restaurant also serves chicken in white-wine sauce and beef à la andaluza. You can order wine by the bottle or glass.

GUANAJUATO AFTER DARK

If long ago city planners had known the **Plaza de la Unión** was going to be so popular, they might have made it larger. This tiny plaza, shaded by Indian laurel trees, is the true heart and best hangout in the city day and night. No other spot in town rivals its benches and sidewalk restaurants. The quality of the food is less important than the viewing perch, but all the restaurants serve a variety of coffees over which you can linger. Among the best places on the plaza are the living room–type bar and inside/outside restaurant of the **Hotel Santa Fe** and the bar/restaurant of the **Hotel San Diego** overlooking the plaza. Other nearby gathering spots include the ever-popular **Café El Retiro,** half a block off the Plaza de la Union, and the cozy **Truco 7** restaurant, at that address a block from the plaza.

If you don't happen to be in Guanajuato during the Festival Cervantino, you can still catch some worthwhile theater—free—in Plazuela de San Roque at 8pm on any Sunday when the university is in session. These *entremeses* (literally "intermissions") presented by students, are short sketches written to be delivered between performances during the Cervantino Festival. In Guanajuato, they are a very special entertainment during which you can enjoy an evening under the stars in a medieval-style courtyard with about 90 minutes of acting and action by students and faculty of the University of Guanajuato. The show takes place in a real courtyard with galloping horses, water thrown from windows, church bells ringing, gusts of wind blowing out the candles, and people in authentic period costumes looking not too out of place in 20th-century Guanajuato. Don't miss it!

ALONG THE WAY FROM GUANAJUATO TO SAN MIGUEL

Although the fastest route from Guanajuato to Mexico City is to go south on Highway 45 and connect with Highway 45D to the capital (the entire route is a four-lane roadway), a far more scenic route to Mexico City is to take Highway 110 north to Dolores Hidalgo, then follow Highway 51 south through San Miguel de Allende.

Dolores Hidalgo (pop. 80,000) is famous as the site where local priest Miguel Hidalgo first made his proclamation of the independence of Mexico—the *grito,* or "Cry of Dolores"—on the night of September 15, 1810. The church on the main plaza was the site of the proclamation, and **Hidalgo's house,** at Morelos 1 (one block from the bus station), is now a museum filled with flags, photos, and documents. Besides this historic claim to fame, Dolores Hidalgo is also famous for its exotic flavors of ice cream and for its hundreds of workshops making furniture and ceramics. For details on shopping in Dolores Hidalgo, see "Side Trips from San Miguel de Allende," below. Since the drive from Guanajuato to San Miguel takes only about two hours, an overnight stop in Dolores isn't really necessary, however, there are several perfectly adequate and inexpensive hotels on or near the main plaza. If you want refreshments, check out the several restaurants on the plaza.

3 San Miguel de Allende

180 miles NW of Mexico City, 75 miles E of Guanajuato

San Miguel de Allende, founded in 1542, is one of the prettiest towns in Mexico and, like Taxco, has been declared a national monument. Virtually all the buildings you see date from the colonial era, and newer buildings must conform to existing architecture. Because so much of the city remains as it did during the days of silver mining in the region, many of the hotels, restaurants, and shops are housed in beautiful mansions dating from those years. Its cobbled streets are reminiscent of those in

Cornwall or Nantucket, and the best-known view of the town, where the highway enters it from the south, has been featured in innumerable movies and postcards.

You'll awaken early in San Miguel with the bells of a score of churches clanging like a score of hammers on a score of different-shaped anvils, and soon the booming of the *parroquia* (parish church) will superimpose itself as the others begin to fade away.

You'll find the cast that makes up San Miguel's streetlife perched on the iron benches of El Jardín. Mornings, the plaza is occupied by resident Americans on their way to and from the post office. By midmorning, tourists passing through for San Miguel's great shopping arrive, filling the plaza and fanning out through the maze of adjoining streets. (This is one of Mexico's best dining towns, too.) Language students come with their tutors, and artists sit sketching a slice of San Miguel life. And the locals are here as well, settled on benches, or passing through on their way to the striking Parroquia church across the street or to the market several blocks in the other direction. Some sell baskets and balloons, and others, painted pottery. At night, bands of mariachis tune up and wait under surrounding portals to be hired.

A sizable colony of American students and pensioners has established itself here, although the major portion of this group tends to turn over about twice a year. Apart from the affluent, which includes those who have retired here to live relatively well, the town's American colony is always composed of teachers, writers, painters, and others who have saved up enough to buy themselves six months in the sun.

If you can, try to get a look around at least one of the houses in which resident Americans are living (see "More Attractions," below). Shabby and almost universally drab from the outside, they open inside onto pretty, cool, flower-filled patios with French doors, and breathtaking views.

ESSENTIALS

GETTING THERE & DEPARTING **By Plane** The nearest international airport is two hours away in León. (For complete plane and ground transportation information, see "Getting There & Departing," above, in Guanajuato.) Querétaro, one hour away, has a small national airport served by **AeroLitoral,** which flies from San Antonio, Texas.

By Bus **To/From Guanajuato: Flecha Amarilla** has nine buses a day to San Miguel, some of which run via Dolores. If you miss the last one, buses run every 20 minutes to Dolores Hidalgo, and buses from there run every 15 minutes to San Miguel. Flecha Amarilla operates buses between San Miguel and Celaya about every 20 minutes from 5:20am to 9pm.

To/From Mexico City: It's a three- to five-hour trip to San Miguel from Mexico City's Terminal Norte (ticket area 6), depending on whether you take a nonstop directo (with one stop in Querétaro) or a local bus with many stops. **Primera Plus** runs four direct deluxe buses a day; **Satelite** has similar service as do **Elite, Tres Estrellas,** and **Omnibus de Mexico. Flecha Amarilla** has service every half hour (check to see which is directo) between 5:30am and 7pm. **Herradura de Plata** buses leave every half hour (several of them operate directo). **AeroPlus** runs luxury buses direct from the Mexico City airport to Querétaro, and from thence it's an easy jump to San Miguel; see the sidebar in chapter 12 for more information.

To/From Querétaro and Dolores Hidalgo: Satelite buses run to Querétaro and Dolores Hidalgo every half hour; **Flecha Amarilla** serves Dolores Hidalgo every 15 minutes.

To/From Nuevo Laredo: Transportes de la Frontera/Estrella Blanca deluxe buses (☎ in Nuevo Laredo **87/14-0829**), with 26 seats, leave Nuevo Laredo at

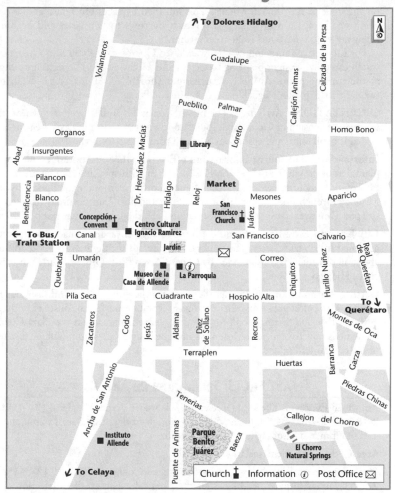

To Dolores Hidalgo

Volanteros

Guadalupe

Calzada de la Presa

Callejón Animas

Pueblito   Palmar

Organos

Homo Bono

Abad

Insurgentes

Dr. Hernández Macías

Loreto

■ Library

Pilancon

Beneficencia

Blanco

Hidalgo

Reloj

Market

Mesones

Aparicio

Concepción✝
Convent

Centro Cultural
Ignacio Ramírez ■

San
Francisco✝
Church

Juárez

← To Bus/
Train Station

Canal

San Francisco

Calvario

Quebrada

Jardín

✉

Correo

Chiquitos

Hurillo Nuñez

Real de Querétaro

Umarán

Museo de la
Casa de Allende ■

■ ⓘ
La Parroquia

Pila Seca

Cuadrante

Hospicio Alta

To ↓
Querétaro

Zacateros

Codo

Jesús

Aldama

Diez
de Soliano

Recreo

Montes de Oca

Garza

Terraplen

Huertas

Barranca

Piedras Chinas

Ancha de San Antonio

Tenerias

Callejon del Chorro

Instituto
Allende ■

Puente de Animas

Parque
Benito
Juárez

Baeza

El Chorro
Natural Springs

↙ To Celaya

| Church ✝ | Information ⓘ | Post Office ✉ |

6:30pm, arrive in Monterrey at 9pm, in San Luis Potosí at 4am, and in San Miguel de Allende between 7 and 8am the next morning. The return bus leaves San Miguel at 7pm, arrives in Monterrey at 5am, and in Nuevo Laredo between 7 and 8am the next morning. Make reservations several days in advance.

By Car   From Guanajuato: The quick route is going south from the city a short distance on Highway 110, then east on a secondary, though paved, road passing near the village of Joconoxtle. The long-but-**scenic route** is northeast on Highway 110 through Dolores Hidalgo, then south on Highway 51. If you drive the scenic route, take a break and experience a slice of rural Mexican life, especially near the small community of Santa Rosa, where small restaurants serve the local brew, **mezcal de la sierra,** and Mexican specialties such as chorizo, dried meat, and barbacoa (Mexican-style barbeque).

From Mexico City: You have a choice of two routes for the three-hour trip—via a Querétaro bypass or via Celaya. The former is shorter—take Highway 57 north, a four-lane freeway toward Querétaro. Past the Tequisquiapan turnoff, there is an exit on the right marked to San Miguel. This toll road bypasses Querétaro and crosses Highway 57 again north of town. Here it narrows to two lanes and becomes Highway 111. San Miguel is 20 miles farther.

For the Celaya route, follow Highway 57 to Querétaro. As you near Querétaro, watch carefully for signs pointing to Celaya and Highway 45. The signs are almost at the turning point. At Celaya, turn right (north) on Highway 51, a narrow two-lane road, to San Miguel.

ORIENTATION Arriving The bus station is 1¹/₂ miles west of town on the westward extension of Calle Canal. Buses to town stop in front. Taxis are generally available at all hours and cost about $2 to $3 for the trip to town.

Information The **tourist information office** is on the southeastern corner of the plaza, left of the church (☎ 415/2-1747). The English-speaking staff has maps and information about attractions in San Miguel and the surrounding region. It's open Monday through Friday from 10am to 2:45pm and 5 to 7pm, Saturday from 10am to 1pm. Don't get transportation information here, though, as it may not be current.

City Layout San Miguel's beautiful central square, **El Jardín** is shaded by perfectly groomed Indian laurel trees. The center of city life, it's the point of reference for just about all directions and is bounded by Calles Correo (Post Office Street), San Francisco, Hidalgo, and Reloj.

Getting Around In San Miguel there are regular inner-city **minibuses** but no minivans, or colectivos, as in other narrow-street cities in Mexico. Buses to outlying villages (Taboada thermal pool, for example) leave from around the Plaza Cívica. Some **taxis** now have meters. Most of San Miguel's sights are within walking distance of the central Jardín.

FAST FACTS: San Miguel de Allende

American Express The local representative is Viajes Vertiz, Hidalgo 1 (☎ 415/2-1856; fax 415/2-0499), open Monday through Friday from 9am to 2pm and 4 to 6:30pm and Saturday from 10am to 2pm.

Area Code The telephone area code is 415.

Bookstores An English-language bookstore, El Colibrí, Sollano 30 (☎ 415/2-0751), near Hospicio two blocks off the plaza, offers an excellent selection of current literature, classics, magazines, and books on Mexico, as well as an ample selection of art supplies. It's open Monday through Saturday from 10am to 2pm and 4 to 7pm.

Climate San Miguel can be warm in summer and cold enough for wool clothing at night and early morning in winter. Hotels aren't heated, and in winter long johns and warm socks are a comfort for sleeping.

Communication Services San Miguel has two unofficial message centers: La Conexión and Pack 'N Mail. For a small monthly charge, residents and visitors can rent post boxes, send and receive faxes, make local or long-distance calls, and have access to both UPS and private messenger and courier services. La Conexión is located at Aldama 1 (☎ and fax **415/2-1599** or 415/2-1687), where it shares space with a photo store and a small restaurant. Pack 'N Mail has sizable space at Jesús 2-A (☎ and fax **415/2-3191**). Both have Laredo addresses and will pack, mail, and transport your gifts. Their hours are generally weekdays from 8am to 5pm and Saturday from 8am to 3pm.

Currency Exchange   Two convenient places near the Jardín change money. Centro Cabiaro, Correo 13, is open Monday through Friday from 8am to 6pm, Saturday from 9am to 5pm, and Sunday from 9am to 2pm. Lloyds, at San Francisco 33, is open Monday through Friday from 9am to 3pm.

Drugstore   For medicine needs try the Farmacia Agundis (☎ **415/1-1198**), Canal 26 at Macías. It's open daily from 10am to midnight.

Elevation   6,143 feet.

Library   The Biblioteca Pública (Public Library), Insurgentes 25 (☎ **415/ 2-0293**), is the gathering point for the American community. It has a good selection of books in Spanish and English. There is a courtyard with tables at which you can relax and read a book or magazine. It's open Monday through Saturday from 10am to 2pm and 4 to 7pm.

Newspaper   *Atención,* the English-language paper, has local news as well as a full list of what to see and do. If you want to keep up with what's going on in San Miguel even after you leave, buy a subscription, which costs $53. Write *Atención,* Biblioteca Pública de San Miguel, Insurgentes 25 (Apdo. Postal 119), San Miguel de Allende, Gto. 37700, México (☎ and fax **415/2-3770**).

Parking   San Miguel is congested, and street parking is scarce. White poles and/ or signs at the ends of streets mark the stopping point for parking (so that other cars can make a turn). Police are vigilant about parking order and ticket with glee.

Population   60,000.

Post Office   The post office and telegraph office are at Calle Correo 16, open Monday through Friday from 8am to 7pm and Saturday from 9am to 1pm.

Seasons   Because of the fast freeway access from Mexico City, San Miguel is becoming popular with weekending citizens from the capital. Arrive early on Friday or make a reservation ahead of time if you're there for a weekend. There's also a squeeze on rooms around the Christmas and Easter holidays and around San Miguel's patron saint festival on September 29. October and November are slack months, as are January and February.

EXPLORING SAN MIGUEL

It's difficult to be bored in San Miguel. The shopping is excellent, and you'll run out of time before you can try all the good restaurants. San Miguel is ideally situated for side trips to Dolores Hidalgo, Querétaro, Guanajuato, and San Luis Potosí. This is also one of Mexico's most popular towns for Spanish and arts classes, just in case you find a lull during your vacation.

FESTIVALS

Holy Week, a movable date in the spring, is special in San Miguel, with numerous processions almost daily beginning the Saturday a week before Easter Sunday. On June 13, **Saint Anthony's Day,** children bring decorated animals for a blessing at the Parroquia church—it's quite an event. San Miguel's main festivity, however, is the **Fiesta de San Miguel** on September 29, honoring the town's patron saint. Events center on El Jardín and begin the week prior to the 29th and continue for at least three days. For at least two days prior to the 29th, there are almost nonstop parades of colorful regional dancers from all over the country and elaborate nightly fireworks, all of which continue until at least the 30th. It's an absolutely incredible cultural extravaganza, and everything is free.

Learning at the Source: Going to School in San Miguel

San Miguel is known for its Spanish-language and art schools. These institutions cater to Americans and often provide a list of apartments from which to choose for long-term stays. Rates for language classes are usually by the hour and get lower the more hours you take. If you want a chance to practice, it's best to look for small classes.

Instituto Allende, Calle Ancha de San António 20, San Miguel de Allende, Gto. 37700 (☎ **415/2-0190;** fax 415/2-4538), put San Miguel on the map back in the 1930s. It was opened by Enrique Fernández Martínez, the former governor of the state of Guanajuato, and Stirling Dickinson, an American. Today it thrives in the 18th-century home of the former counts of Canal, a beautiful place with big grounds, elegant patios and gardens, art exhibits, and murals. You can wander past classrooms where weavers, sculptors, painters, ceramicists, photographers, and struggling language students are at work. The notice board in the entrance lobby carries interesting offers ("Ride offered to L.A." or "Paperbacks for sale, Shayne to Schopenhauer"), and the office maintains a list of local families who rent rooms for stays of a month or more. The institute offers an MFA degree, and the school's credits are transferable to at least 300 colleges and universities in the United States and Canada; noncredit students are also welcome.

Academia Hispano Americana has a reputation for being a comparatively tougher language school with an emphasis on grammar as well as conversation. Classes are limited to 12 people. The work is intensive, and the school is particularly interested in students who plan to use Spanish in their future careers and in people who sincerely feel the need to communicate and understand the other Americas. The school has a continuous program of study of 12 four-week sessions for 35 hours a week. Private lessons cost $10 per hour. It's a member of the International Association of Language Centers. A brochure is available from the Registrar, Academia Hispano Americana, Mesones 4 (Apdo. Postal 150), San Miguel de Allende, Gto. 37700 (☎ **415/2-0349;** fax 415/2-2333). Office hours are Monday through Friday from 8am to 1pm and 3:30 to 6:30pm.

Inter/Idiomas is another school that readers have written to praise. Information is available from Inter/Idiomas School of Languages, 20 de Enero Sur #42, Col. San Antonio, 37750 San Miguel de Allende, Gto. ☎ **411/7-8646.** Fax 415/2-0135.

Also see the **Centro Cultural Ignacio Ramírez,** in "The Top Attractions," below.

THE TOP ATTRACTIONS

La Parroquia. South side of El Jardín. No phone. Free admission. Daily 6am–9pm.

La Parroquia, the parish church, is an imposing Gothic structure of local sandstone built in the late-19th century by a self-made architect, Ceferino Gutiérrez. The story goes that he had never seen such a church and used a picture to fashion his creation. Neoclassical stone altars have replaced the original ones made of gilded wood, but the bell is original. Step inside on any day, and you're likely to find parishioners from surrounding villages carrying on an ancient rite that has both Catholic and pre-Hispanic overtones.

Museo de la Casa de Allende. Southwest corner of El Jardín. No phone. Free admission. Tues–Sun 10am–4:30pm.

Impressions

[The traveler] is bound to spend long evenings in the company of compatriots who have gone virtually native, listening as they remove cover after cover from the surface of Mexico until he stares dizzily into a bottomless pit of mysteries, atavisms, sorceries and primitive profundities.

—Stuart Chase, Mexico: *A Study of Two Americas*, 1931

The birthplace of the famous independence leader Ignacio Allende has been converted into a museum housing colonial-era furnishings and historical documents. Inside you'll see fossils, pre-Hispanic pottery, and a biography of Allende. Exhibits also detail the fight for independence, which began in nearby Dolores Hidalgo. In 1810, Allende plotted with Padre Miguel Hidalgo of Dolores and Josefa Domínguez of neighboring Querétaro, among others, to organize for independence from Spain. Both Allende and Hidalgo were executed in Chihuahua a year later.

Centro Cultural Ignacio Ramírez (Bellas Artes/El Nigro-Mante). Hernández Macías 75. ☎ **415/2-0289.** Free admission. Mon–Fri 9am–9pm, Sat 10am–7pm, Sun 10am–2pm.

Housed in the former Convento de la Concepción (1755), between Canal and Insurgentes two blocks west of El Jardín, the center is a branch of the Palacio Bellas Artes of Mexico City. Built on two levels surrounding an enormous courtyard of lush trees, it consists of numerous rooms housing art exhibits and classrooms for drawing, painting, sculpture, lithography, textiles, ceramics, dramatic arts, ballet, regional dance, piano, and guitar. The grand mural by David Alfaro Siqueiros and memorabilia of the artist are worth seeing. A bulletin board lists concerts and lectures given at this institute and elsewhere in the city. The pleasant restaurant, Las Musas, serves Mexican and Italian food daily between 10am and 8pm. Before you leave, notice the magnificent dome behind the convent. It belongs to the Iglesia de la Concepción and was designed by the same unschooled architect who designed the Parroquia (see above).

MORE ATTRACTIONS

The **Centro de Crecimiento,** Zamora Ríos 6, a donation-supported school for handicapped children, conducts regular Saturday tours (usually at 10am) to interesting places in the country around San Miguel. Donations are $15 per person; tickets are available at Casa Maxwell.

The **House and Garden Tour,** sponsored by the Biblioteca Pública, is a regular attraction in San Miguel. The tour opens the doors of some of the city's most interesting colonial and contemporary homes. Tours leave Sunday at 11:30am from the library at Insurgentes 25 (☎ 415/2-0293) and last about two hours. A $10 donation goes to support various library projects benefiting the youth of San Miguel.

The **Travel Institute of San Miguel,** Cuna de Allende 11 (☎ 415/2-1630 or 415/2-0078, ext. 4; fax 415/2-0121), holds walking tours, field trips to colonial and archaeological sites, adventure and nature tours, visits to artisans at work, and workshops in marketing, among other things. The office is open Monday through Saturday from 9am to 2pm and 4 to 7pm.

A couple of the most enjoyable walks in town are to the lookout point **El Mirador,** especially at sunset, which colors the whole town and the lake beyond, and to **Parque Juárez,** a lovely, spacious, and shady park.

The town's **movie theater,** the Aldama, is on San Francisco, in the block between El Jardín and the San Francisco Church. There's another movie theater in the Gigante Shopping Center on the road to Querétaro.

One great way to see the mountains around San Miguel is by **Hire-a-Horse.** For $35 per person, it will provide a horse, a guide, refreshments, and a two- to four-hour outing. Inquire at the Casa Mexas restaurant, Canal 15 Centro, or call **415/2-3620** for information or reservations.

The **Taboada hot springs** are located just 5 miles outside San Miguel, about 15 minutes away by car. The Hotel Balneario Taboada is out of budget range, but next door to it is the most popular hot springs/swimming pool in the area, which you can use for about $7. Buses to Taboada leave from Calle San Francisco by the market, supposedly at 9 and 11am and 1 and 3pm. If you should have trouble getting a bus, you can always take a taxi out to any of the three hot springs; it will cost about $7 to $12—not a bad deal if you have several people to split the cost. You can ask the taxi driver to return and pick you up at the end of the day.

NEARBY ATTRACTIONS

One of the most interesting side trips you can make from San Miguel is to **Atotonilco el Grande.** Though the town itself is depressingly poor and nearly deserted, a wonderful 16th-century *oratorio* (the church of an Augustinian monastery) makes it worth a visit. The imaginative and animated frescoes depicting biblical scenes were used to teach Indians. The trip itself provides a pleasant introduction to picturesque Mexican country life. By the market, hop an "El Santuario" bus on Calle Humaran and Colegio, which passes every hour on the hour; past Taboada, the route goes left at signs reading *Manantiales de la Gruta* and *La Flor del Cortijo.* The road passes two large mansions that are now spas (see "More Attractions," above) then an aqueduct and a little narrow bridge. In no time you're in the empty town square of Atotonilco with the oratorio in front of you.

Querétaro, Guanajuato, and **Dolores Hidalgo** are easy day-trips from San Miguel. See "Getting There & Departing," above, for transportation information and "Side Trips," below.

Two companies use San Miguel as a base for trips to see the **monarch butterflies** in the state of Michoacán west of Mexico City. The **Travel Institute of San Miguel** (see "More Attractions," above) offers this trip between November and March. Another company, **Columbus Travel,** also originates the trip from either San Miguel or Mexico City. Contact them in Texas at ☎ **210/885-2000,** or 800/843-1060 in the U.S. and Canada.

SHOPPING

In general, stores in San Miguel open at 9am, close between 2 and 4pm, and reopen from 4 to 7pm. Most are closed Sunday. The town is known for its **metalwork— brass, bronze, and tin**—and for its **textiles** and **pottery,** especially Talaveraware (which is made in Dolores Hidalgo). For metalwork try **Calle Zacateros,** a street of shops selling pewter-, tin-, and ironwork. Shopping, however, is by no means limited to those items. Also, ask to see the charming **children's art** for sale at the public library; the proceeds help support the children's program.

A **Mercado de Artesanías** is located along the walkway near the entrance to Quinta Loreto; here you can bargain with vendors during most daylight hours. On the eastern edge of town along the road to Querétaro is a **shopping center** with food concessions, a grocery store, and shops. Gigante, is a supermarket with everything from folk art to Barbie dolls to barbacoa; it accepts credit cards.

Art

Galería San Miguel. Plaza Principal 14. ☎ **415/2-1046.**

This is the best local art gallery. It is run by a charming, stylish Mexican-American woman, fluent in English, who is a well-known art dealer. She exhibits the work in all price ranges of local residents as well as artists from all over Mexico. The gallery is open Monday through Friday from 10am to 2pm and 4 to 7pm, Saturday from 10am to 2pm and 4 to 8pm, and Sunday from 10am to 2pm.

Crafts

Casa Anguiano. Corner of Canal and Macías. ☎ **415/2-0107.**

You will want to return here again and again just to see what's new. The inventory of colorful Michoacán foot-loomed fabric by the bolt is extensive, as is the inventory of blown glass, copper, brass, and Nativity scenes. It's open Monday through Saturday from 9:30am to 8:30pm and Sunday from 9:30am to 6:30pm.

Casa Cohen. Reloj 12. ☎ **415/2-1434.**

Located half a block north of the square, this is the place to find brass and bronze bowls, plates, house numbers, doorknobs, knockers, and drawer pulls, as well as other utilitarian objects made of iron, aluminum, and carved stone. There's also hand-carved wood furniture. It's open the usual San Miguel hours (see the introduction to "Shopping," above).

Casa Maxwell. Canal 14. ☎ **415/2-0247.**

This is a beautiful house and garden with every imaginable craft displayed, some high-priced, others fairly reasonable. It's well worth a look around. Hours are Monday through Saturday from 9am to 2pm and 4 to 7pm.

Izcuinapán. Canal 42 at Umaran. ☎ **415/2-0594.**

Don't worry about pronouncing the name, but do go here for a very fine display of folk art, particularly Huichol masks and textiles, and an expanding line of furniture. This place offers something for everyone—from those with a limited budget to serious collectors. Look especially for the carved animals with hidden compartments from Michoacán. The store, between Zacateros and Quebrada, is open Monday through Saturday from 10am to 2pm and 4 to 7:30pm.

Mesón de San José. Mesones 38. ☎ **415/2-1367.**

This lovely old mansion, across from the market between Juárez and Nuñez, houses a dozen shops and a restaurant. One of the shops, Ono, specializes in children's toys, as well as a smattering of folk art from around Mexico. Another, Talisman, has an outstanding selection of gifts in every price range. All are open daily from 10am to 6pm.

Veryka. Zacateros 6A. ☎ **415/2-9114.**

A popular place, this small shop has a very complete collection of folk art from Mexico and the rest of Latin America, as well as fabrics, wallhangings, clothing, and jewelry. The staff is very knowledgeable, and most speak some English. It's open the standard hours (see the introduction to "Shopping," above), plus Sunday from 11am to 3pm.

Furniture

Casa María Luisa. Canal 40, at Zacateros. ☎ **415/2-0130.**

If your interests are architectural or decorative, you may enjoy browsing here. Among the crowded aisles, you'll find the store's own line of furniture, which might appeal to those who like southwestern decor. Stacked and displayed here and there are decorative ironwork, lamps, masks, pottery, and more. The staff will pack and ship your treasures. Hours are Monday through Saturday from 9am to 2pm and 4 to 7pm and Sunday from 11am to 5pm.

Masks

Tonatiu Metztli. Umarán 24, near Zacateros. ☎ **415/2-0869.**

This shop is a must for the mask collector. In addition to the masks hanging all over the shop walls, owner Jorge Guzman has a private collection he shows by appointment. He recently added some fine Huichol art, including figures decorated with exquisite beadwork. It is open the usual San Miguel hours (see the introduction to "Shopping," above), plus Sunday from 9am to 2pm.

WHERE TO STAY

There are plenty of accommodations for visitors in San Miguel; for a long stay in San Miguel (more than a month), check at the instituto or the academia (see "Learning at the Source," above) for their lists of apartments or rooms to rent. Most apartments are equipped with kitchens and bedding; some come with maid service. San Miguel is becoming popular as a weekend getaway for residents from the capital, and at least one hotel I checked raised rates on weekends, but it doesn't seem to have started a trend. Secured parking is at a premium in San Miguel; if it's not provided by your hotel, you'll pay around $12 to $15 daily in a guarded lot.

DOUBLES FOR LESS THAN $20

⑤ Casa de Huespedes. Mesones 27, 37700 San Miguel de Allende, Gto. ☎ and fax **415/2-1378.** 7 rms (all with bath). $10 single; $14 double.

A welcome addition to the budget category, this second-floor hostelry is reached by a stairway from a busy street. Owner Amelia Coglan is usually on hand. The rooms are attractive for this price category, and there is a lovely patio. There are kitchenettes in five units. The staff is friendly, and longer stays are encouraged with a discount. To get there from the Jardín, go north one block on Reloj, then right on Mesones. The casa will be on your left.

Parador San Sebastián. Mesones 7, 37700 San Miguel de Allende, Gto. ☎ **415/2-0707.** 13 rms (all with bath). $15 single; $17 double. Parking $3 daily.

The San Sebastián is a colonial-era convent-turned-inn with spacious rooms that face a lovely courtyard and garden. The rooms are simple and comfortable, and the rooftop is great for enjoying morning coffee, sunning, or taking in the city views. They don't take reservations here, so you have to try your luck. From the Jardín, walk east on Correo one block to the post office, then left two blocks to Mesones. Turn right on Mesones, go past the Mercado, and walk another half a block. The hotel is on the north (left) side of the street, across from the academia.

DOUBLES FOR LESS THAN $35

Hotel Mansion Virreyes. Canal 19, 37700 San Miguel de Allende, Gto. ☎ **415/2-3355** or 2-0851. Fax 415/2-3865. 26 rms (all with bath). TV TEL. Weekend $28 single; $38 double; weekday $23 single; $30 double. Free parking.

Previously called the Hotel Central, the Mansion Virreyes has lost none of its old charm, and some judicious remodeling has improved the comfort of the 350-year-old building. It was once a private home and became the first hotel in San Miguel following the Mexican Revolution. Located half a block west of the Jardín, it is nestled among shops and restaurants. The rooms are simple but very comfortable, and the pleasant restaurant (open daily from 8am to 9pm) serves good, moderately priced meals; the excellent comida corrida costs around $5. There is a TV bar behind the restaurant.

Quinta Loreto. Calle Loreto 15, 37700 San Miguel de Allende, Gto. ☎ **415/2-0042.** 38 rms (all with bath). $20–$25 single; $24–$28 double. Weekly and monthly discounts available. Free parking.

This motel is tucked away amid cobblestone lanes and manicured gardens. It has a large pool, a tennis court, a lovely garden, an excellent restaurant, a friendly atmosphere, and simple but pleasant rooms. Meals here are a bargain. Make reservations—the Loreto is very popular and is often booked up months in advance. Outsiders can come for breakfast (which costs $2–$3) and for lunch (which costs around $4). To get here from the Jardín, walk one block east on Correo. Turn left onto Juárez at the post office, go two blocks to Mesones, then continue for three long blocks (the street curves); the motel is on a small street off Calle Loreto.

DOUBLES FOR LESS THAN $50

Posada Carmina. Allende 7, 37700 San Miguel de Allende, Gto. ☎ **415/2-0458.** Fax 415/2-0135. 12 rms (all with bath). $33 single; $42 double.

Located on the south side of the plaza next to the Parroquia is this charming and friendly over-200-year-old colonial-era mansion. Rooms are nicely furnished and built around a central courtyard full of orange trees and flowering vines. Around the upstairs terrace are two comfortable living rooms, chairs, and chaise lounges. A restaurant serving good food, and comida corrida for around $5, is open in the courtyard daily from 8am to 9:30pm.

WORTH A SPLURGE

Mi Casa B&B. Canal 58 (Apdo. Postal 496), 37700 San Miguel de Allende, Gto. ☎ **415/2-2492.** 1 rm, 1 junior suite (both with bath). $65 single or double; $85 suite (all include breakfast). Discounts for stays of a week or more.

This charming colonial home is professionally decorated, very comfortable, and in a convenient location. The hostess, Carmen McDaniel, is a gracious expatriate and an excellent source of information on San Miguel and the surroundings. Both rooms have a garden-style bath, and the junior suite has a sitting area and fireplace. The flower-filled rooftop patio is a wonderful place for cocktails (honor bar) or morning coffee. This B&B is about three blocks west of the Jardín on Calle Canal, across from Posada de las Monjas.

۞ Pensión Casa Carmen B&B. Correo 31 (Apdo. Postal 152), 37700 San Miguel de Allende, Gto. ☎ and fax **415/2-0844.** 11 rms (all with bath). $40 single; $75 double (including breakfast); monthly rate $35 daily single; $55 daily double (including breakfast).

This small, quiet pension operated by Natalia Mooring offers a friendly, relaxed atmosphere and is often booked months in advance. The rooms, all of which have gas heaters, face a lovely colonial courtyard with plants and a fountain; meals are served in a European-style common dining room. You can reserve rooms by the day, week, or month (monthly rates are discounted). You can get here from the Jardín by walking east on Correo past the Parroquia and post office for 2¹/₂ blocks; it's near the corner of Recreo.

Villa Mirasol B&B. Pila Seca 35, 37700 San Miguel de Allende, Gto. ☎ **415/2-1564.** 6 rms (all with bath). $63–$75 single or double (including breakfast and high tea).

This delightful bed-and-breakfast, previously known as Casa de Lujo, has individually decorated Mexican-style rooms with bright colors, private entrances, and a patio area. Short-term membership is available at a local country club for swimming, golf, and tennis. To get here, go south from the Jardín one block, then right (west) on Pila Seca for 4^1/$_2$ blocks. It's between Quebrada and Ladrillera.

WHERE TO EAT

Because of its large expatriate colony and its popularity with Mexican tourists, San Miguel has the best quality and assortment of restaurants of any small city in Mexico. New places open all the time, and eateries only a few years old close down overnight. As in every Mexican town, the **mercado** offers the least expensive food in town. It contains rows of fruits and vegetables, and stands with cooked food offer basic meals like chiles rellenos, frijoles, and rice with broth.

MEALS FOR LESS THAN $5

Apolo XI. Mesones 43. ☎ **415/2-1260.** Main course (roast pork, beans, and tortillas) $2.25–$3.25. Fri–Wed 9am–7pm. MEXICAN.

Carnivores will delight in this hole-in-the-wall place that serves up slabs of *chicharrones* and *manteca* (lard) by the kilo in the front and delicious *carnitas de puerco* (roast pork) to hungry diners at the few tables in the back. An order of roast pork will more than satisfy two hearty appetites since it comes with tortillas and beans.

⑤ Café Colón. San Francisco 21 at Corregidora. ☎ **415/2-0989.** Breakfast $1.25–$3; main courses $2.50–$5. Daily 8am–10pm. MEXICAN.

Run by the friendly Espinosa family, this clean restaurant has excellent, quick service. Cloth-covered wood tables are nicely spaced for a view of the Plaza San Francisco through open doors. Traditional Mexican food is the specialty here—carne Tampiqueña, chilaquiles, and the like. I especially like this place for a quick breakfast. It's one block east of the Jardín, opposite the Plaza San Francisco and the statue of Cristóbal Colón.

✪ El Correo. Correo 23. ☎ **415/2-1051.** Breakfast $1.50–$3; main courses $2–$5. Thurs–Tues 9am–9:30pm. AMERICAN.

Housed in a colonial-era building opposite the post office half a block east of the Jardín, this place is ideally suited for watching the morning mail ritual among resident Americans. You'll see them lingering over coffee and conversation here—and for that reason, the nine tables are often full, especially around breakfast. Persevere—it's worth it! Walls are stenciled to resemble pale turn-of-the-century wallpaper. For breakfast, the *migas natural* comes with onions, tomatoes, and chile or ranchero sauce, or you can tank up on apple fritters, orange juice, or fruit with yogurt and granola. For homesick stomachs, at lunch there's fried chicken, stuffed baked potatoes, and soup.

✪ El Pegaso Café and Deli. Corregidora 6 at Correo. No phone. Breakfast $2–$4; soups, salads, sandwiches $2–$5. Mon–Sat 8:30am–10pm. DELICATESSEN/INTERNATIONAL.

You'll notice the full tables at this trendy corner restaurant one block east of the Jardín. Inside, it's cute and cozy with walls of paintings for sale. Meals are light, with soup and salad or sandwich, nachos, sopes, and other deli combinations. Regulars swear they have the best eggs Benedict in town.

Villa de Ayala. Ancha de San Antonio 1. ☎ **415/2-3883.** Breakfast $1.75–$3.50; main courses $2.50–$5; comida corrida $3. Daily 8:30am–10pm (comida corrida served 1–5pm). MEXICAN.

This restaurant is a favorite with families and students from the Instituto de Allende. Reached by a staircase, the place consists of one large room with the kitchen to one side and a video nook in a corner. Piñatas and balloons help dress up the plain tables and brick walls. A specialty of the house, *memelas*, consists of large thick tortillas with beans, salsa, cheese, and a choice of meat on top. Recorded music during the day is lively but not loud; there is occasional live music on weekends. The restaurant is across the street and a few doors toward town from the instituto; it's a long walk or short taxi ride from the Jardín.

MEALS FOR LESS THAN $10

✪ **Fonda Mesón de San José.** Mesones 38. ☎ **415/2-3848.** Breakfast $1.75–$3; soup $2.50; main courses $5–$8; margarita $2. Daily 8am–9pm. MEXICAN/AMERICAN.

Located in the midst of several interesting shops, this open-courtyard restaurant is considered by many locals to be the best restaurant in town. It's an excellent place to have an entire meal or just relax over the excellent coffee or a giant margarita. The intriguing menu is so tempting it may be hard to decide between the vegetarian plate with Yucatecan tacos and vegetarian pasta or a main course of chicken curry. Everything is fresh and attractively presented. In the evenings from 7 to 9:30pm you can enjoy the soft music of a quartet of musicians playing Mexican classics.

Olé Olé. Loreto 66. ☎ **415/2-0896.** Main courses $2.75–$8.50. Daily 1–8pm. MEXICAN.

Festive and friendly, this small restaurant is a riot of red and yellow banners, colorful streamers, and bullfight memorabilia. The small menu features delicious beef, chicken, or shrimp fajitas, shrimp brochettes, and quesadillas. The place is wildly busy at lunch. To find this restaurant from the San Francisco Plaza, walk north on Juárez and cross Mesonas; jog left then right where the street becomes Loreto and continue for three or four blocks—it's on the left with a small sign.

MEALS FOR LESS THAN $15

✪ **Casa Mexas.** Canal 15 Centro. ☎ **415/2-0044.** Main courses $2.50–$10.50; children's plate $2–$3. Daily noon–11pm. MEXICAN.

A riot of baskets and colorful piñatas hang from the ceiling of this place above white tables and chairs and white napkins stuffed into whimsical papier-mâché napkin rings. As the name suggests, it serves a blend of Mexican food and Tex-Mex, but the fare is much better than standard Tex-Mex. Prices are moderate for the large portions of well-seasoned food. This is a place kids will like, and it offers plate meals with children in mind. It's across from the Casa Maxwell, half a block west of the Jardín on Canal.

✪ **Mama Mía.** Umarán 8. ☎ **415/2-2063.** Breakfast $1.25–$3; pastas $6.25–$11; main courses $4–$11; coffees $1–$4.50. Daily 9am–11:30pm (bar til 2am Thurs–Sat). ITALIAN.

Perennially the "in" spot, this casual and hip spot offers good-quality Italian food and entertainment in a tree-shaded brick courtyard. You can dine al fresco and enjoy live folkloric South American and flamenco music nightly. In addition to the Italian specialties, Mexican and American specials dot the menu along with a large breakfast section. Coffee-based drinks with Kahlúa or brandy can top off a meal. At night it's one of the most popular spots in town, with dancing and live jazz. The restaurant is two blocks southwest of El Jardín on Umarán between Jesús and Macías.

✪ **Restaurant/Bar Bugambilia.** Hidalgo 42. ☎ **415/2-0127.** Antojitos $3–$5; main courses $5–$10. Daily noon–11pm. MEXICAN TRADITIONAL.

Both the food and the atmosphere make this place well worth a long meal. It's delightful, with its tree-filled patio, soft music, good service, and such specialties as *pollo en pulque* (pulque-marinated chicken) and *chiles en nogada* (pepper stuffed with meat, raisins, cream, and topped with pomegranate seeds). To find it from the Jardín, walk 2¹/₂ blocks north on Hidalgo.

SAN MIGUEL AFTER DARK

Clubs and discos here tend to spring up and die quickly. If you want to have dinner and drinks with live music (including piano, guitar, South American folkloric, and flamenco), see "Where to Eat," above; I've mentioned all the places where there's live music. San Miguel has many such enjoyable restaurants. Be sure also to check San Miguel's English-language paper, *Atención,* for other happenings around town.

La Fragua. Cuna de Allende 3. ☎ **415/2-1144.**

San Miguel's artists and writers drift in and out all afternoon and evening at this popular long-standing gathering spot. Housed in an old colonial home, the restaurant has tables around the courtyard where Mexican musicians perform every evening from 8 to 10:30pm. Several other dining rooms and a comfy bar resembling a living room are off the courtyard. The emphasis here is on standard Mexican fare. Bar hours are daily from noon to 2am, and the restaurant serves from 1pm to midnight.

La Princesa. Calle Recreo 5. ☎ **415/2-1403.**

This restaurant/bar has a guitar soloist or trio nightly from 8 to 2am. La Princesa is open daily from 1pm to 2am.

Pancho y Lefty's. Mesones 99. No phone. Cover $5 in high season, free in low season.

Entertainment runs the spectrum here from reggae to rock and country to blues and jazz. It's open from 7pm to 3am Wednesday, Friday, and Saturday. Wednesday night happy hour lasts the whole evening with two drinks for the price of one.

El Ring. Hidalgo 25–27. ☎ **415/2-1998.** Free Sun and Tues–Thurs, $8–$10 Fri–Sat.

Located in a lovely old building on the right side of the street as you come from the main plaza, this disco has an elaborate layout, including strobe lights and other visual hallucinogens. Every Wednesday is two-for-one tequila night. El Ring is open Tuesday through Sunday from 10pm to 4 or 5am.

Tío Lucas. Mesones 103 at Macias. ☎ **415/2-4996.** No cover.

Though this is a full-blown restaurant, it's most popular in the evenings when live music—blues, jazz, and bossanova—is on tap between 8:30pm and midnight. The restaurant opens at 1pm, and there are several cozy, dark dining rooms and a small bar with seating. Happy hour is from 6 to 8pm.

SIDE TRIPS FROM SAN MIGUEL DE ALLENDE
DOLORES HIDALGO: FINE POTTERY—AND SHRIMP ICE CREAM?

Dolores Hidalgo was made famous when Fr. Miguel Hidalgo de Costilla began the War of Independence on the steps of the parish church. Today, it is famous for its ice cream and pottery. Parlors on the four corners of the main square sell exotic ice cream flavors—tequila, shrimp, and alfalfa are just a few shocking examples, as well as mango, guanabana, and other more familiar scoops.

Only 30 miles from San Miguel, you'll see the pottery factories and store outlets beginning on the outskirts of town and continuing into town almost everywhere you look. Pottery made here is distinct from the Talaveraware of Tlaxcala and Puebla, although just as colorful and inspired. In fact, the fame of Dolores Hidalgo's ceramics is overtaking that of Tlaxcala's and Puebla's products, primarily because the items produced here are less expensive and produced in greater quantity. Some of Mexico's best hotels turn Dolores ginger jars into lamps and decorate bathrooms with Dolores-made soap dishes and towel and tissue holders. Tiles from Dolores have been popular for years. Prices here are considerably lower than in San Miguel. It could be daunting to tackle this town without a few recommendations, so I've listed a few factories and shops below. You'll discover even more as you walk the streets. Of course, it's best to go in a car if you plan to purchase much. If you arrive by bus, a box and luggage cart are handy to haul your loot around from store to store.

The stores below are listed in the order you will find them on the road from San Miguel.

Talavera San Gabriel. 14 miles from San Miguel on the outskirts of Dolores. ☎ and fax **418/2-0139.**

Here you'll find a large selection of ceramic-framed mirrors and drawer knobs, tiles, sinks, candelabras, casseroles, bowls, platters, anthropomorphic jars and candlestick holders, ginger jars, and tissue holders. If you have the bus let you off here, you'll need a taxi to continue into town. Open Monday through Saturday from 8am to 5pm and Sunday from 8am to 2pm.

Talavera Amora. Farther along the road to Dolores and past the Talavera San Gabriel. ☎ **418/2-0336;** fax 2-22029.

This is another factory outlet; you will see this signature pottery in many San Miguel stores. Items include dinnerware with a blue and yellow fish motif, chicken and frog planters, and much more. Open daily from 9am to 6pm.

Talavera Cortes. Districto Federal 8, at Tabasco. From the highway, turn left on Veracruz, go three blocks, then go left one block; it's on the corner.

Homeowners in San Miguel patronize this store for sinks, tiles and knobs, towel racks, and paper holders. You can watch craftspeople at work upstairs and browse the large showroom/warehouse downstairs. Open Monday through Friday from 7am to 4:30pm and Saturday from 7am to 1pm

Azulejos Talavera Vazquez. Puebla at Tamaluipas.

Like the other places I've listed, this is a cornucopia of ceramics, from giant ginger jars to ashtrays and sinks. This store has good prices on colorful picture frames in many sizes. The store is about two blocks south of the church with the gold and green tile dome. Open Monday through Friday from 7am to 4:30pm and Saturday from 7am to 1pm.

QUERÉTARO

Querétaro (elevation 5,873 feet), just 63 miles from San Miguel and 138 miles north of Mexico City, is the capital of the state of Querétaro and a prosperous city of 455,000 with a fascinating history. It was here that Mexico's fight for independence was instigated by Hidalgo in 1810, and it was here that the peace of the Mexican War was sealed with the Treaty of Guadalupe Hidalgo. Emperor Maximilian was executed here in 1866, and finally, the present Mexican constitution was drafted here in 1916.

The **Dirección de Turismo** has a small tourism information office next to the Mesón Santa Rosa on Pasteur at the southwest corner of the Plaza Independencia; it's open Monday through Friday from 9am to 8pm and Saturday and Sunday from 9am to 3pm. From here, the Dirección de Turismo offers a very good **guided walking tour** of the city, for around $3 daily at 10:30am.

Arriving by bus from San Miguel, you'll be at the new bus station, south of town. Catch a bus marked "Centro" or take a taxi for around $5.

A Road Trip from Querétaro: The Fray Junípero Serra Missions

If you're driving, this is a road trip worth taking. Five little-known missions established by Fray Junípero Serra before his journey to California lie in the Sierra Gorda mountain region east of Querétaro. The beautiful buildings have been restored, and the state operates the following three hotels along the route: **Mesón Concá,** near Misión Concá ($40 for a double in the old section of a hacienda); **Mesón de San Joaquín,** at San Joaquín ($15 for a double); and **Mesón de Fray Junípero Serra,** at Jalpan ($25 for a double). Each has a small restaurant. My favorite is the hacienda section of Mesón Concá. The master suite opens to a porch, yard, and steamy thermal water stream. The largest town is **Jalpan,** where an excellent small museum has just opened; the other towns are only small farming villages.

From Querétaro the drive (which begins at the Cadereyta turnoff south of Querétaro) is a winding, mountainous one that takes at least five hours. En route are two **archaeological sites—Las Ranas,** easily accessible, and **Toluquilla,** reached via a rutted road after which you must climb a mountain to get to the site. Another, less winding route begins far north of Querétaro at the San Luis Potosí turnoff east to Río Verde. From there, go south to Concá and Jalpan.

Whichever route you choose, plan to spend a minimum of two nights in the mission zone. The drive is tiring, and although the missions can be seen in one day, you'd be pushing it to drive out the second afternoon, not to mention rushing through the experience.

AeroPlus runs luxury buses direct from the Mexico City airport to Querétaro; see the sidebar in chapter 12 for more information.

Exploring Querétaro
A STROLL AROUND THE HISTORIC CENTER   Launch your visit to the city from the pedestrians-only **Plaza de la Independencia** (also called Plaza de Armas), on 5 de Mayo. It's the historic heart of the city, and the most beautiful plaza, graced by manicured umbrella-shaped trees, a beautiful fountain, and colonial-era stone mansions now housing government offices.

Of all the colonial-era buildings surrounding Plaza de la Independencia, the **Casa de la Corregidora/Palacio Municipal** is the most famous. It's a magnificent building, and tourists are welcome to step inside the interior courtyard. The building has taken its name from association with a genuine martyr of Mexican independence, Doña Josefa Ortíz de Domínguez, wife of the mayor (*corregidor*) of Querétaro. On the second floor is her room—where, while under lock and key, she managed to send a warning to Father Hidalgo that their conspiracy to declare Mexico's independence from Spain had been discovered. Hidalgo got the message and hurried to publicly shout "independence" in Dolores Hidalgo. The rest is history. Ask the guard if you can see the room and take your camera—the view of the square from here is good.

La Corregidora, as she is known, was imprisoned several times between 1810 and 1817 for her support of Mexican independence. She died impoverished and forgotten, but today she is much revered. She was the first woman to appear on a Mexican coin, the five-centavo piece, minted from 1942 to 1946.

Across the plaza opposite La Corregidora's house is the **Instituto de las Artesanías,** Pasteur 16, at the corner of Libertad (☎ **42/12-9100,** ext. 215), a state crafts shop housed in another colonial gem. Walk through the rooms with nicely displayed

Querétaro Orientation

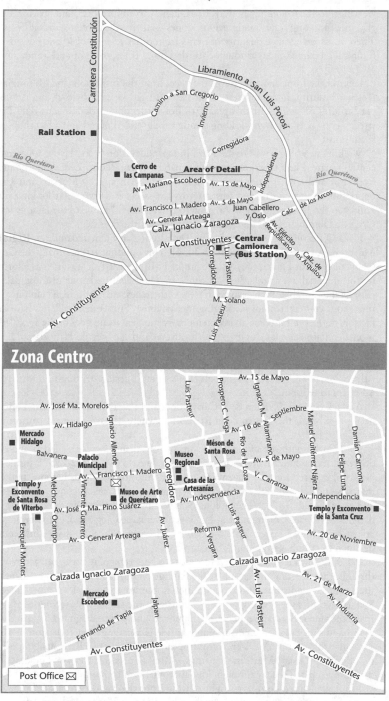

Zona Centro

Post Office ✉

weavings, regional clothing, pottery, onyx, hand-carved furniture, and opals and jewelry incorporating other semiprecious stones—all from Querétaro and all for sale. There is, as well, a nice quantity of items from other regions of Mexico on its two floors. It's open Monday through Saturday from 10am to 8pm and Sunday from 10am to 5pm.

Left out the front door and across the street from the Instituto is the **Mesón Santa Rosa,** a beautiful hotel and restaurant (see "Where to Eat," below) in a colonial-era building. Leading off this plaza are flower-decorated pedestrians-only brick streets, known as *andadores*, leading to other well-tended plazas and a few shops and restaurants.

Walking two blocks west of the Plaza Independencia on 5 de Mayo is Querétaro's central square, **Plaza Obregón** (recently renamed **Plaza Benito Zenea**). It's bounded by Juárez and Corregidora running north and south and by Madero and 16 de Septiembre running east and west. Across the street is a triangular-looking plaza known as the **Jardín Corregidora,** centered on a graceful statue of the famous Josefa Ortíz de Domínguez and lined with restaurants on the far side.

Plaza Obregón is also flanked by the Templo de San Francisco and the **Regional Museum,** at Corregidor 3 (☎ **42/12-2036**). This building was originally the Grand Convent of Saint Francis of Assisi, begun in 1540. In 1861, it was used as a fortress by the Imperialists, who backed Maximilian. The structure is one of those palatial edifices the "humble" friars favored, replete with arches and Corinthian columns. The first room you enter holds fascinating memorabilia. Subsequent galleries have artifacts from the pre-Hispanic and contemporary indigenous peoples of the area. Other rooms contain colonial paintings and furniture, and the Sala de Historia holds numerous items of perhaps morbid interest, including Maximilian's coffin and countless period photographs. The museum bookshop sells mostly Spanish-language books. Admission is $3.50; free on Tuesday. It's open Tuesday through Sunday from 10:30am to 6:30pm.

A block beyond the Plaza de la Corregidora and Plaza Obregón, at Juárez and 16 de Septiembre, is the **Teatro de la República,** where Mexico's present constitution was signed in 1917.

Two blocks southwest of the Plaza Obregón, on Allende between Madera and Pino Suárez, is the architecturally fascinating **Museo de Arte** (☎ **42/12-2537**). Inside this beautiful restored former convent is a fine museum in a fabulous baroque building that was originally an 18th-century Augustinian convent. Construction began in 1731 and was finished in 1745. The building was occupied by soldiers in the 1860s. It was designated a historic monument in 1935, yet it remained neglected, even housing the jail at one time. I saw it years ago when it housed the post office and seemed destined to crumble away chunk by chunk.

What a rebirth it's had! Now visitors are torn between going on an obligatory walk through the museum and gazing at the fabulous interior stonework. The names of the architects and stonemasons are unknown, but an excellent 15-minute video in Spanish unlocks the mystery of the symbolism in the stone. In case your Spanish is rusty, the video tells that elephants, ducks, horses, and pelicans signify Christ and that each hand sign has a different meaning. Inside is a magnificent collection of 16th-through 18th-century Mexican and European paintings, as well as changing exhibits of contemporary Mexican paintings. Admission is $2; free on Tuesday. The museum is open Tuesday through Sunday from 11am to 7pm.

From the Museo de Arte go right out the front door and right again at the first street, Pino Suárez, and continue for three blocks to E. Montes and turn left. Ahead one block on the left corner at Arteaga is the **Convent of Santa Rosa de Viterbo.**

It was built in the 18th century by Mexico's greatest religious architect, Eduardo Tresguerras. It's known for the unusual inverted flying buttresses on the outside and the magnificent baroque retablos on the inside. It's closed more often than it's open, but try around 4 or 5pm.

Backtracking to the Plaza de la Independencia, take a break in the Mesón Santa Rosa. Then continue straight ahead on 5 de Mayo eight blocks to M. Najera and turn right two blocks to V. Carranza, where you turn left one block to the **Templo y Ex-Convento de la Cruz,** on Avenida Independencia near Carmona. Building began in 1654, with major additions continuing for the next century. A tour through this massive complex will give you some feel for the life of an 18th-century cleric. From these cloisters Fr. Junípero Serra departed for California, and Fr. António de San Buenaventura stopped on his way to found the mission that was to become San Antonio, Texas. Hours are a bit irregular, but ask at the small bookstore about fascinating tours guided by one of the brothers. Nearby is a spectacular view of the aqueduct that supplied the convent and city at that time.

You'll want to take a taxi to the final touring highlight, the **Cerro de las Campanas (Hill of Bells),** Avenida Hidalgo, between Técnológico and Highway 57 to San Luis Potosí. One of the most historic places in Mexico, it can be easily spotted from Highway 57 as a giant hill topped by a titanic statue of Juárez. Just below the statue is the site of the execution of Maximilian, ruler of the short-lived Empire of Mexico. In 1901, the Austrian government built an Expiatory Chapel on the side of the hill. The caretaker (who is rarely around to let you in) takes pleasure in showing you the three small columns in front of the altar, the stones that mark the exact spot where Maximilian and his generals, Miramón and Mejia, stood before the firing squad. Maximilian was in the middle but gave that place of honor to Miramón; then he gave each member of the firing squad a gold coin so they would aim at his chest instead of his head (they complied). It's open daily from dawn to dusk.

One final place of interest is the **Lapidaria de Querétaro,** at 15 de Mayo and Peralta (☎ **42/12-0030**). Since the region is known for its opal mines, it would be a shame not to see the best in stones and mountings at this trustworthy store. Many of the stones you see here come from the family opal mine, La Catalina, 25 miles from Querétaro. But they also sell agate, turquoise, topaz, and lapis lazuli in stones, or gold or silver mountings. Besides seeing artisans working the raw stones in the store's adjacent workshop, visitors are invited to tour the mines as well. The only charge is for gasoline. The trip starts at 9am and returns to Querétaro by around 1pm. Arrange the mine trip a day or so in advance of your intended visit. If you're eating at the Mariposa Restaurant, the store is only a block and a half away.

Where to Eat

Restaurant Santa Rosa. Pasteur 17, Querétaro, Qro. 76000. ☎ **42/14-5681;** fax 42/ 12-5522. Main courses $5–$11. Daily 7am–1am. MEXICAN/INTERNATIONAL.

The state-owned Mesón Santa Rosa is the most elegant and refreshing place to eat in the historic center and also the loveliest hotel in Querétaro. Once an 18th-century stable, then quarters for Juárez's troops, and later a tenement house, it became a hotel and restaurant in the late 1980s. Iron-studded doors open to sienna-colored walls, and there are two large patios dripping with fuchsia bougainvillea and white-iron tables and chairs. The patio is usually filled with patrons sipping cappuccino and eyeing the dessert cart. Inside the elegant dining room to the right, the color scheme is rose and white, and the deep-rose walls are stenciled to resemble white doilies. Tables are covered in white linen, and waiters wear black jackets and bow ties. Often there's a pianist or violinist in the adjacent bar. The international menu emphasizes Mexican cuisine. (The enchiladas verdes were featured in Patricia Quint-ana's *The Taste of Mexico*.)

If you're up for a splurge and want to stay overnight in this historic city, this is the place. Junior suites cost $72–$80 single or double, and master suites run $90–$95.

Cafetería La Mariposa. Angela Peralta 7. ☎ **42/12-1166.** Main courses $2–$4. Daily 8am–9:30pm. MEXICAN.

Look for the wrought-iron butterfly sign when you turn left on Peralta (two blocks north of Plaza Obregón [Zenea]) to find one of the city's most popular restaurants. This is a good place for light lunches—enchiladas, a fruit salad, or a club sandwich—or pastries, ice cream, and coffee. Next door is a wickedly tempting sweet shop featuring such irresistibles as candied figs, peaches, bananas, and papaya. You can also order these delicacies in the restaurant, as the two enterprises are under the same management.

Guadalajara 10

Guadalajara (gwa-da-la-HA-ra), Mexico's second largest city, is also considered by many to be the most authentically Mexican. Much of Mexican tradition developed here or nearby. The *jarabe tapatío* (the Mexican hat dance) was developed here, and Guadalajara is considered the center for *charrarería* (Mexican-style rodeo). Mariachi music, the most robust in the country, was born nearby, and tequila, the fiery liquor that's the foundation of the margarita, is produced a few miles south of the city.

In the city's charter, Emperor Charles V called Guadalajara a *muy leal y muy noble ciudad* ("most loyal and noble city"). As a result of its isolated position southwest of Mexico City, Guadalajara developed into a sophisticated city largely on its own, without a great deal of interference from Spain. Today, it is capital of the state of Jalisco, and 5 million people live here.

As though to emphasize the great things expected from it, Guadalajara's Spanish builders gave the city not one, but four, beautiful plazas in its center. Today the city's leaders have given it a fifth, the enormous Plaza Tapatía, an ambitious stretch of redevelopment extending for about a mile through the urban landscape. Scattered with trees and monuments and sprinkled with fountains, the superplaza links the city's major colonial buildings and joins the past with the great new buildings of the present.

By the way, *tapatío* (or *tapatía*) is a word you'll come across often in this city. In the early days of the city, people from this area were known to trade in threes (three of this for three of that) called tapatíos. Gradually the people were called tapatíos too, and the word has come to mean "Guadalajaran" in reference to a thing, a person, and even an idea. The way a *charro* (Mexican cowboy) gives his all, or the way a mariachi sings his heart out—that's tapatío!

1 Orientation

ARRIVING & DEPARTING

BY PLANE   Guadalajara's international airport is a 25- to 45-minute ride from the city. Taxi and colectivo (shared ride) tickets to Guadalajara or Chapala are sold outside in front of the airport. Tickets are sold by zone. A shared taxi ride to the heart of Guadalajara costs around $10, and a private taxi costs $14. A taxi to Chapala costs around $30.

On departure from Guadalajara, you'll be required to check in at least 1 1/2 hours before takeoff for international flights, and at least 1 hour before takeoff for domestic flights. Local taxis are the only transport from town to the airport.

Major Airlines   See chapter 2, "Planning a Trip to Mexico," for a list of international airlines serving Mexico. Local numbers for airlines currently flying from Guadalajara to points abroad are **Alaska Airlines** (☎ **91/800-426-0333** in Mexico) **American Airlines** (☎ **3/616-4090**) **Continental Airlines** (☎ **3/647-6672** or 3/647-4605) **Delta** (☎ **3/630-3530**) and **United** (☎ **91-800/0-0307** in Mexico).

Aero California (☎ **3/826-1901** or 3/826-8850) serves Guadalajara from Tijuana, Mexico City, Los Mochis, La Paz, and Puebla; **Aeroméxico** (☎ **3/669-0202;** 3/689-0028 at the airport) flies from numerous points in the United States and Monterrey, Puerto Vallarta, Manzanillo, Mazatlán, Chihuahua, Acapulco, and Tijuana in Mexico; **Mexicana** (☎ **3/647-2222;** at the airport 3/689-0119) connects with a number of U.S. cities and Cancún, León, Los Cabos, Nuevo Laredo, Zihuatanejo, Puerto Vallarta, and Tijuana in Mexico. **Saro** (**3/614-7571;** at the airport 3/688-5876) flies to Mexico City, Monterrey, and Tijuana. **Taesa** (☎ **3/679-0900**) flies from Mexico City, Tijuana, Morelia, some U.S. cities, and seasonally to Puerto Vallarta.

BY TRAIN   **Major Trains**   Guadalajara is the country's second-largest train hub, but not all trains are worth taking. The **National Railways of Mexico** (☎ **3/650-0826** or 3/650-1082) runs *El Tapatío,* which goes from Mexico City to Guadalajara, leaving Mexico City at 8:30pm and arriving in Guadalajara at 8:30am. It offers seats as well as sleeping compartments. It takes 12 1/2 hours and costs between $15 and $80 one way. Considering that a bus takes five hours and costs $10 to $14, taking the train is the less attractive option. Other trains go to Mazatlán and Mexicali at the U.S. border, but they also take forever.

The Train Station   The station, on Calzada Independencia, is within walking distance (with light luggage) of at least one of the hotels I recommend. Buses marked "Centro" go downtown, and those marked "Estación" go to the station from downtown. Otherwise, you're at the mercy of taxis that charge $4 to go the short distance anywhere between the station and the city center.

BY BUS   Two bus stations serve Guadalajara—the old one near downtown, and the new one 6 miles out on the way to Tonala. A convenient place to get bus information is **Servicios Coordinados,** Calzada Independencia 254, a kind of "bus travel agency" located under Plaza Tapatía. There, travelers can make reservations, buy tickets, and receive information on the six main bus lines to all points in Mexico. The **ETN** bus line (☎ **3/614-8875** or 3/614-2479) has an office in the Hotel Carlton downtown.

To get from either station to your hotel, look for the **city buses** and white minivans marked "Centro," which pick up passengers in front of each terminal building. These are convenient only if you have a very small suitcase. **Linea Turquesa** (TUR) buses are air-conditioned and offer the most comfortable service since they accept only the number of passengers for whom there are seats. From the bus station, some go to Tonala, and others follow a route along Calzada Tlaquepaque to Tlaquepaque, Revolución, and 16 de Septiembre/Alcalde to the Centro Histórico. Some of these skip Tonala; look for the sign on the front of each bus.

You can also take a **taxi.** Taxi tickets, sold inside each terminal building, are priced by zone. A taxi from the Central Camionera to the downtown Plaza Tapatía area (a 30-minute ride) costs about $7.

The Old Bus Station   For bus trips within a 60-mile radius of Guadalajara, including to **Lake Chapala, Ajijic, Jocotepec, Mazamitla,** and **San Juan Cosola,** go to the old bus terminal on Niños Héroes off Calzada Independencia Sur and look for **Transportes Guadalajara-Chapala** (☎ **3/619-5675**), which has frequent bus and combi service beginning at 6am to Chapala (see "Side Trips from Guadalajara," below).

The New Bus Station   The **Central Camionera,** about 6 miles and a 35-minute ride east of downtown toward Tonala, provides bus service to and from virtually any point in Mexico. None of the buses from here is of the school bus variety—while the price difference between first and second class is small, the difference in speed, comfort, and convenience is often great. The new terminal resembles an international airport—seven separate buildings are connected by a covered walkway in a U shape, with one-way traffic entering on the right. Each building houses several first- and second-class bus lines. That's the only drawback—you must go to each one to find the line or service that suits you best.

Here is a breakdown of the various parts of the new station, beginning with the first building on the right: **Building 1** holds Primera Plus with deluxe service to Puerto Vallarta (5 hours), Lagos de Moreno, Colima, Manzanillo (4¹/₂ hours), and Melaque (5 hours). This building also has the ETN deluxe line to Mexico City (7 hours) and to Aguascalientes (but ETN buses leave from building 2); **Building 2** has many buses to Aguascalientes and Zacatecas. Autotransportes Mazamitla goes to Tuxcueca, La Manzanilla, and Mazamitla hourly between 6am and 6:30pm; these buses don't go through Chapala and Ajijic; instead they pass at the crossroads at Jocotopec. **Building 3** has Primera Plus and Autocamiones Cihuatlan with service to Manzanillo six times daily as well as to Talpa and Macota; **Building 5** has Estrella Blanca with hourly service until 6pm to Puerto Vallarta. Linea Azul Oriente has six buses to San Jan del Lago, and Turistar's deluxe buses go to Aguascalientes and Lagos de Moreno; **Building 6** has Omnibus de Mexico buses going to Mexico City and many to Zacatecas and Colima, as well as ETN buses with service to Colima, Manzanillo, Puerto Vallarta, Mexico City, Morelia, and Aguascalientes; **Building 7** has the Expreso Futura line with many buses to Mexico City, the Rojos al Altos line with hourly service to Zacatecas, and Turistar Primera with frequent service to Lagos de Moreno, León, and Puerto Vallarta.

This station is one of the nicest in Mexico, with amenities like shuttle buses, restaurants, gift shops, luggage storage (*guarda equipaje*), book and magazine shops, liquor stores, Ladatel long-distance telephones, and hotel information. There's also a large new budget hotel next door (see "Where to Stay," below). To get there by bus, take any bus marked **"Central"** on Avenida 16 de Septiembre/Alcalde opposite the Rotonda de los Ilustres in downtown Guadalajara.

BY CAR   Directions   From Nogales on the **California border,** follow Highway 15 south. You can also take a toll road between Guadalajara and Tepic, a six-hour drive. From **Barra de Navidad** or southeast on the coast, take Highway 80 northeast. A new toll road, running from **Puerto Vallarta** on the Pacific nearly to Tequila (30 miles west of Guadalajara), is scheduled for completion by June 1995. The trip will take four hours. From **Mexico City,** take the free Highway 90 (six to eight hours) or the new toll road, which takes 4¹/₂ hours. Coming from **Colima,** there's another toll road which takes about four hours.

VISITOR INFORMATION

The **State of Jalisco Tourist Information Office** is at Calle Morelos 102 (☎ **3/ 658-2222** or 3/658-0305; fax 3/613-0335) in the Plaza Tapatía at the crossroads of

Paseo Degollado and Paraje del Rincón del Diablo. It's open Monday through Friday from 9am to 8pm and Saturday, Sunday, and festival days from 9am to 1pm. This is one of the most efficient and informative tourism offices in the country. They have a supply of maps as well as a monthly calendar of cultural happenings in the city.

CITY LAYOUT

Guadalajara is not a difficult city to negotiate, but it certainly is big. Although most of the main attractions are within walking distance of the historic downtown area, others—such as Tonala and Tlaquepaque (which are both nearby) and Lake Chapala and Ajijic (which are both farther away)—are accessible by bus. Street names downtown change at the cathedral.

NEIGHBORHOODS IN BRIEF

Centro Histórico   The heart of the city takes in the Plaza de Armas, Plaza de los Laureles, Plaza de los Hombres Ilustres, Plaza Liberación, and Plaza Tapatía. It's the tourist center and contains major museums, theaters, restaurants, hotels, and the largest covered market in Latin America, all linked by wide boulevards and pedestrians-only streets. It's bounded east and west by Avenidas 16 de Septiembre/Alcalde and Prosperidad (across Calzada Independencia) and north and south by Avenida Hidalgo and Calle Morelos.

Parque Agua Azul   An enormous city park 20 blocks south of the Centro Histórico, it has a children's area and rubber-wheeled train. Nearby are the state crafts shop, performing-arts theaters, and the anthropology museum.

Chapultepec   A fashionable neighborhood with shops and restaurants 25 blocks west of the Centro Histórico, it is reached by Avenida Vallarta. Chapultepec is the main artery through the neighborhood.

Minerva Circle   Almost 40 blocks west of the Centro Histórico, Minerva Circle is at the confluence of Avenidas Vallarta and López Mateos and Circunvalación Washington. It's a fashionable neighborhood with several good restaurants and the Hotel Fiesta Americana, all reached by the Par Vial.

Plaza del Sol   The largest shopping center in the city, it lies south of Minerva Circle and southwest of the Centro Histórico near the intersection of Avenidas López Mateos and Mariano Otero.

Zapopan   Once a separate village founded in 1542, now it's a full-fledged suburb 20 minutes northwest of the Plaza Tapatía via Avenida Ávila Camacho. It's noted for its 18th-century basilica and the revered 16th-century image of the Virgin of Zapopan, made of corn paste and honored every October 12. The city's fashionable country club is just south of Zapopan.

Tlaquepaque   Seven miles southeast of the Centro Histórico, it's a village of former mansions turned into shops that front pedestrians-only streets and plazas.

Tonala   Four miles from Tlaquepaque, it's a village of more than 400 artists working in metal, clay, and paper. A huge street market is held on Thursday and Sunday.

GETTING AROUND

BY BUS & TREN LIJERO   The city has six kinds of city buses, and a rapid transit system called the **Tren Lijero.** Many of the buses run the same routes but offer different kinds of service. **Gray buses with maroon stripes** are better city buses and cost 35¢. **School bus–style buses** cost 25¢. Both of these buses carry seated passengers as well as passengers packed into the aisles. Privately operated **minivans** cost about

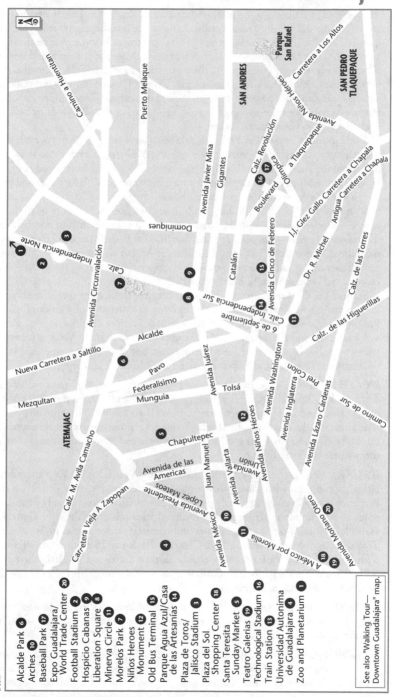

Greater Guadalajara

SAN ANDRES

Parque San Rafael

SAN PEDRO TLAQUEPAQUE

Carretera a Los Altos

Avenida Niños Héroes

J.J. Glez Gallo Carretera a Chapala

Antigua Carretera a Chapala

Calz. de las Torres

Calz. de las Higuerillas

Dr. R. Michel

Camino de Sur

Prel Colón

Avenida Washington

Avenida Inglaterra

Avenida Lázaro Cárdenas

Avenida Morelano Otero

A México por Morelia

Avenida Niños Héroes

Avenida Unión

Avenida Vallarta

Juan Manuel

Avenida México

Chapultepec

Avenida de las Americas

Avenida Presidente López Mateos

Calz. M. Avila Camacho

ATEMAJAC

Carretera Vieja A Zapopan

Mezqultan

Nueva Carretera a Saltillo

Federalisimo

Munguia

Pavo

Alcalde

Avenida Juárez

Tolsá

Calz. Independencia Sur

6 de Septiembre

Avenida Cinco de Febrero

Calz. Independencia Norte

Calz. Circunvalación

Avenida Circunvalación

Camino a Huentitan

Puerto Melaque

Avenida Javier Mina

Gigantes

Dominiques

Catalán

Calz. Revolución

Olímpica

Boulevard a Tlaquepaque

① ② ③ ④ ⑤ ⑥ ⑦ ⑧ ⑨ ⑩ ⑪ ⑫ ⑬ ⑭ ⑮ ⑯ ⑰ ⑱ ⑲ ⑳

2-0017

See also "Walking Tour— Downtown Guadalajara" map.

the same as city buses. Some are numbered, and others have their destination written on the windshield. **Linea Turquesa** (turquoise line) buses, colored a pale turquoise, have the distinguishing letters "TUR" on the side and run several routes around the city. These cost $1, are air-conditioned, have padded seats, and best of all, carry only as many passengers as there are seats. Frequent TUR buses also run between the Centro Histórico, Tlaquepaque, Central Camionera (new bus station), Tonala, and Zapopan. Some of these go to Tonala and not Zapopan, or Zapopan but not Tonala. For information on getting to Tlaquepaque and Tonala by bus, see "Side Trips from Guadalajara," below.

Two bus routes of the **"Par Vial"** (electric buses) will satisfy 90% of your intracity transportation needs. Buses bearing the sign "Par Vial" run a rectangular route going east along Independencia/Hidalgo, passing the Mercado Libertad and going as far west as the Minerva Circle, where they turn back east on Vallarta/Juárez and pass by the Plaza de Armas on their run east.

Many buses run north-south along the Calzada Independencia (not to be confused with Calle Independencia), but the **"San Juan de Dios–Estación"** bus goes between the points you want—San Juan de Dios church, next to the Mercado Libertad, and the railroad station ("estación") past Parque Agua Azul. This bus is best because most other buses on Calzada Independencia have longer routes (out to the suburbs, for instance) and thus tend to be heavily crowded at all times.

Section 1 of the **Tren Lijero** (rapid transit system), serves a few tourist needs since it runs north-south along Federalismo, curving the distance of Camino de Sur/ Prelongación Colón. More helpful for visitors, Section 2 runs east-west along Vallarta/Juárez and Avenida Javier Mina, the eastern extension of Vallarta/Juárez. It takes passengers between the Mercado Liberación and the Parque Revolución (near the restaurants Suehiro and Copenhagen and the Museo de las Artes).

BY COLECTIVO   Colectivos are minivans that run throughout the city day and night, picking up and discharging passengers at fixed and unfixed points. They are often a faster and more convenient way to travel than the bus. There are no printed schedules, and the routes and fixed pick-up points change frequently. However, locals know the routes by heart and can tell you where and how to use them if you tell them where you want to go.

BY CAR   Keep in mind several main arteries. The **Periférico** is a loop around the city that connects with most other highways entering the city. Traffic on the Periférico is slow because it's heavily potholed, filled with trucks, and only a two-lane road. Several important freeway-style thoroughfares crisscross the city. **Gonzalez Gallo** leads south from the town center and connects with the road to Tonala and Tlaquepaque or leads straight to Lake Chapala. **Highway 15** from Tepic intersects with both **Avenida Vallarta** and **Calzada Lázaro Cárdenas.** Vallarta then goes straight to the Plaza Tapatía area. **Cárdenas** crosses the whole city and intersects the road to Chapala and to Tlaquepaque and Tonala.

BY TAXI   Taxis are an expensive way to get around town. A short 10- to 15-minute ride—for example, from the Plaza de Armas to the Zoo and Planetarium—costs an exorbitant $6 or $7, while a bus there costs only 25¢.

BY HORSE-DRAWN CARRIAGE   Take one of the elegant horse-drawn carriages for a spin around town. The cost is about $15, depending on route and length of ride—usually about 45 minutes. Drivers congregate in front of the Museo Regional, near the Mercado Libertad, and also behind the Plaza/Rotonda de los Hombres Ilustres and other spots around town.

FAST FACTS: Guadalajara

American Express   The local office is at Av. Vallarta 2440, Plaza Los Arcos (☎ 3/615-8910); it's open Monday through Friday from 9am to 6pm and Saturday from 9am to noon.

Area Code   The telephone area code is 3.

Bookstores   Gonvil, a popular chain of bookstores, has a branch across from Plaza de los Hombres Ilustres on Avenida Hidalgo and another a few blocks south at Avenida 16 de Septiembre 118 (Alcalde becomes 16 de Septiembre south of the cathedral). Sanborn's, at the corner of Juárez and 16 de Septiembre, always has a tremendous selection of English-language magazines, newspapers, and books.

Climate & Dress   Guadalajara has a mild, pleasant, and dry climate year-round. Bring a sweater for evenings during November through March. The warmest months—April and May—are hot and dry. From June through September, it's rainy and a bit cooler. Guadalajara is as sophisticated and at least as formal as Mexico City. Dress is conservative; resortwear (short shorts, halters, and the like) is out of place here, but knee-length shorts, skirts, slacks, and blouses for women or slacks, bermudas, and a shirt for men are fine for all but the few formal restaurants or events.

Consulates   The world's largest American consular offices are here at Progreso 175 (☎ 3/625-2998 or 3/625-2700). The offices are open Monday through Friday from 8am to 4:30pm.

Currency Exchange   Banks will change money and traveler's checks Monday through Friday from 9am to noon.

Drugstores   Ask at your hotel about the location of the closest pharmacy. For late-night service, try Farmacías Guadalajara, a chain throughout the city with a branch near downtown on Avenida López Cotilla (☎ 3/614-2810) open daily from 8am to 10pm.

Emergencies   Dial 02 for help in most emergencies. For the state police (☎ 3/617-5838); for the highway police (☎ 3/612-7194). During the day, call the tourist office (☎ 3/614-0606, ext. 114).

Holidays   See "Festivals," below. February and October are the big festival months. At Christmas and Easter, many establishments are closed or have revised hours.

Hospitals   For a medical emergency, there's the Hospital México-Americano, Colomos 2110 (☎ 3/614-0089).

Language Study   Foreigners can study Spanish at the Foreign Student Study Center, University of Guadalajara, Calle Guanajuato 1047 (Apdo. Postal 12130), Guadalajara, Jal. 44100 (☎ 3/653-2150; fax 3/653-0040).

Luggage Storage/Lockers   Luggage storage is available in the main bus station, the Central Camionera, and at the Guadalajara airport.

Newspapers/Magazines   The Hotel Fenix, on the corner of Corona and López Cotilla, has English-language newspapers, magazines, and maps. It's also a good place to buy Guadalajara's English newspaper, *The Colony Reporter*, published every Saturday, if you don't spot it on the newsstand. Sanborn's, at the corner of Juárez and 16 de Septiembre, has a wide selection of U.S. and Mexican newspapers and magazines.

Post Office   The main post office (correo) is at the corner of Carranza and Calle Independencia, about four blocks northeast of the cathedral. Standing in the plaza behind the cathedral and facing the Degollada Theater, walk to the left and turn left on Carranza; walk past the Hotel Mendoza, cross Calle Independencia, and look for the post office on the left side.

Safety   As in any large city, don't be careless with your belongings. There are people on the streets at all hours, but to be safe, avoid walking around alone late at night on unlit streets. As in the rest of Mexico, pedestrians don't have the right of way, so be sure to look left, right, and behind you when crossing any street, even if you cross with the light.

2 Where to Stay

DOWNTOWN
DOUBLES FOR LESS THAN $15

Hotel Las Américas. Hidalgo 76, 45120 Guadalajara, Jal. ☎ **3/613-9622** or 3/614-1604. 49 rms (all with bath). TV TEL. $10 single; $14 double.

This four-story budget hotel with a very friendly proprietor, Señor Valcarcel, is a surprisingly quiet retreat from a very noisy street. New carpeting lines the marble-edged halls and rooms, and there's plenty of purified water available. The clean, carpeted rooms, each with one or two double beds, have windows facing either the street or ample airshafts (rooms off the street, of course, are quieter). The higher prices in each category are for rooms with a color TV and ceiling fan. To find Las Américas from the cathedral, walk seven blocks east on Hidalgo and look for the hotel on the left.

⑤ Posada Tapatía. López Cotilla 619, 44100 Guadalajara, Jal. ☎ **3/614-9146.** 10 rms (all with bath). $9 single; $12.50 double.

Under the care of Alberto Guzman, the hospitable and friendly new owner, this faded beauty of a mansion (formerly the Posada de la Plata) has been infused with new life. New mattresses, bedframes, colorful bedspreads, shower curtains, and new bathroom fixtures make this a great budget choice. Beautiful old tile floors and plants enliven the once-dreary interior courtyard. Rooms are large, with high ceilings and tall etched-glass double doors. The rooms are basically furnished with bedside lamps and usually a table and chairs and armoire. Guests can use the washing machine and hang clothes on the rooftop to dry. To find the hotel from the Plaza de Armas, walk south down 16 de Septiembre/Alcalde and turn right on Cotilla; it's about 6 1/2 blocks farther on the left, between Barcelona and 8 de Julio.

DOUBLES FOR LESS THAN $25

Hotel Continental. Corona 450, 44100 Guadalajara, Jal. ☎ **3/614-1117.** 129 rms (all with bath). TV TEL. $15 single; $21 double. Free parking.

The Continental, on the corner of Libertad, is well worn despite its modern exterior appearance. The receptionists can be rather uncommunicative. All rooms are carpeted, and some have large windows. The cheerful restaurant downstairs is open from 8am to 9pm. To get here, walk eight blocks from the cathedral on Avenida 16 de Septiembre, turn left onto Libertad, and walk one block to Avenida Corona.

✪ Hotel San Francisco Plaza. Degollado 267, 44100 Guadalajara, Jal. ☎ **3/613-8954** or 3/613-8971. Fax 3/613/3257. 76 rms (all with bath). A/C TV TEL. $22 single; $24–$27 double. Free parking.

For a touch of class, try this highly recommended hotel facing a tiny square near Priciliano Sánchez. You get a lot for your money. Stone arches, brick-tile floors, bronze sculptures, and potted plants decorate the four spacious central courtyards. All rooms are large and attractive, and each includes either a double bed, a king-size bed, or two double beds. The English-speaking staff is friendly and helpful. A very good, inexpensive restaurant off the lobby is open daily from 8am to 10pm. To get here from the Plaza de Armas, walk five blocks south on 16 de Septiembre, turn left onto Sánchez, and walk two blocks to Degollado and the hotel.

⑤ Posada Regis. Corona 171, 44100 Guadalajara, Jal. ☎ **3/613-3026** or 3/614/8633. 19 rms (all with bath). TV TEL. $15 single; $19 double. Discounts for stays of a week or more.

Opposite the Hotel Fenix, the Posada Regis occupies the second floor of a restored old mansion. The large, carpeted rooms are simply furnished and arranged around a tranquil, covered courtyard, a small restaurant, and potted plants. Rooms with balconies facing the street are quite noisy. Windowless interior rooms are stuffy, so ask for a fan. The mattresses have plastic covers and "nonbreathing" nylon-type sheets. Baths have open ceilings and no doors. I've stayed here and find it particularly serves my budget and my needs for safety and proximity to downtown. Video movies are shown every evening on the lobby TV. The restaurant serves a very good and inexpensive breakfast ($1.75–$2.25) between 8am and 11am and lunch ($2.75) from 2 to 4pm. I especially enjoy the good lunch here. Nonguests take meals too. It's best to call ahead and tell them you're coming, but you can also try dropping in. There's personal laundry service. To find the hotel from the Plaza de Armas, walk 2½ blocks on Corona. It's on the left almost at the corner of Madero opposite the Hotel Fenix. Enter through a small doorway and go up a flight of stairs to the second-floor hotel and lobby.

WORTH A SPLURGE

✪ Calinda Roma. Juárez 170, 44100 Guadalajara, Jal. ☎ **3/614-8650,** or 800/228-5151 in the U.S., 91-800/9-000 in Mexico. Fax 3/613-0557. 172 rms (all with bath). A/C MINIBAR TV TEL. $44 single; $44–$52 double. Parking $1 daily.

Perfectly situated, this hotel is within walking distance of all downtown sights and restaurants. It is one of the best hotels in the city center. For its 100th birthday in 1993, rooms were renovated. Bathrooms will be updated next. Some rooms have exercise bicycles. Higher priced rooms are larger. It's not outrageously expensive considering its location and quality; it's also quiet and very comfortable. There's an excellent restaurant and bar in the lobby. The rooftop garden, with a grass putting green and a pool, is a great place to unwind. To find the hotel from the Plaza de Armas, walk two blocks south on Corona. Turn left on Juárez; the hotel is two blocks ahead at the corner of Degollado.

3 Where to Eat

Some travelers find it comforting to know that such U.S. franchise restaurants as Kentucky Fried Chicken, McDonald's, and Dunkin' Donuts are beginning to proliferate in Guadalajara. But as long as you're in Guadalajara or anywhere in the state of Jalisco for that matter, I urge you to try a local dish called *birria*—a hearty soup of lamb, pork, or goat meat in a tasty chicken-and-tomato broth, lightly thickened with *masa* (corn meal) and cooked with oregano, garlic, onions, cumin, chilies, allspice, and cilantro. Restaurants around El Parian in Tlaquepaque have birria on the menu daily. Another local delicacy is the *lonche,* a sandwich made from a scooped-out *bolillo* (a large roll) filled with a variety of meats and topped with sour cream, avocado, onions, and chiles. If you're traveling in the countryside, on weekends you'll

Impressions

In all Latin-American cities a certain group of older men seem to spend their evenings about the plaza or in the City Club nearby. Perhaps as their wives grow older and the children grow up they lose interest at home.

　　　　　　　—Leonidas W. Ramsey, *Time Out for Adventure: Let's Go to Mexico,* 1934

often see signs for *borrego* (wood-roasted lamb), which is absolutely delicious and usually served with beans and tortillas.

For those on a very strict budget, the second floor of the **Mercado Libertad** will look like heaven. You can get a full comida corrida here for between $1.75 and $3 at any of the seemingly hundreds of little restaurant stands. There's a vegetarian section, and there are lots of places for tacos, tamales with atole, and enchiladas. However, be wary of cleanliness—some people say you should not eat here. Nonetheless, hundreds of people do eat here every day and seem to be surviving just fine—I've even done it myself. Check it out—it's a fascinating slice of Mexican life. The best time to go is early in the morning, while the food is the freshest. When I'm in town I take as many meals as possible at the **Posada Regis,** which serves a very economical and filling home-style breakfast and lunch (see "Where to Stay," above.)

MEALS FOR LESS THAN $5

Acuarius. Prisciliano Sánchez 416. ☎ **3/613-6277.** Breakfast $1.75–$3; main courses $2.50–$4.50; soup $1.50–$2; comida corrida $4. Daily 9:30am–8pm (comida corrida served 1–4pm). VEGETARIAN.

This immaculate, airy little lunch room has soft music playing and shelves of soy sauce and vitamins. The restaurant offers breakfast, an à la carte menu, and comida corrida. For the comida corrida, there's a choice of two main dishes, which you can sample first if you can't make up your mind. When I was here, the choice was zucchini sautéed with mushrooms in tangy tomato sauce or mixed-vegetable stew. Whole-grain bread and whole-grain tortillas come with the meal in addition to soup, fruit, and yogurt or a salad, a tall glass of fruit juice, and dessert. If that's too much food, consider ordering from the menu that offers a daily choice of three main courses made from soy and two of vegetables. From the Plaza de Armas, walk four blocks south on 16 de Septiembre, turn right onto P. Sánchez, and walk 3 ¹/₂ blocks; the restaurant is on the right between D. Guerro and Ocampo.

⑤ Café Madrid. Juárez 264. ☎ **3/614-9504.** Breakfast $1.50–$3; main courses $1.75–$4; Daily 7am–11pm. MEXICAN.

The coffee aroma wafts outside the café in the morning—americano, espresso, cappuccino, and cafe con leche are all excellent eye-openers. Conveniently located, this popular café serves the best coffee in Guadalajara. Tourists take tables beside the men whose morning ritual is solving the nation's problems while lingering over coffee. Signs above the counter advertise *chilaquiles* and "ricos hot cakes," which are indeed rich and are served with warm syrup. The extra-hearty *platillo tapatío* includes fried chicken, a taco, an enchilada, and potatoes. From the Plaza de Armas, walk one block on Corona to Juárez and turn right; the café is on the right.

La Chata Restaurant. Corona 129. ☎ **3/613-0588.** Breakfast $2–$3.25; main courses $1.75–$4. Daily 9am–11pm. REGIONAL.

This place doesn't look like much from the street, but people are drawn in by the colorful tables, the bandannaed women stirring and frying, and the wonderful food smells. Locals frequent La Chata for Tapatian fare from *pozole* and *torta ahogadas* (a spicy pork sandwich) to the steaming hot atole, which some people drink over ice. To find La Chata from the Plaza de Armas, walk 1 1/2 blocks south on Corona; it's on the right between Juárez and López Cotilla.

✪ **Los Itacates Restaurant.** Chapultepec Nte. 110. ☎ **3/825-1106.** Breakfast $1.75–$3.50; tacos 60¢; main courses $2–$5. Mon–Sat 8am–11pm, Sun 8am–7pm. MEXICAN.

Locals can't say enough about the authenticity and quality of the Mexican food here. The atmosphere is festive with colorfully painted chairs and table coverings. You can choose the sidewalk dining in front or the three interior rooms. Among the specialties are *pozole, sopa medula* (bone marrow soup), *lomo adobado* (baked pork), and *chiles rellenos*. The chicken Itacates comes with a quarter of a chicken, two cheese enchiladas, potatoes, and rice. To find the restaurant, take the Par Vial west on Independence/Hidalgo. Get off at Chapultepec and walk to the right (north) on Chapultepec about three blocks. It's on the right.

Lonchería La Playita. Av. Juárez 242. ☎ **3/614-5747.** Hamburgers $1.75–$2.25; tostadas and sandwiches $1.75–$2.50; chicken dinner $1.75–$3. Daily 9am–2am. SANDWICHES/MEXICAN.

This branch of La Playita is one of several in the city. Invitingly clean with white tile and hot-pink accents, it's also one of the best *loncherías* (sandwich shops) in town. The small but good menu features *lonches*, quesadillas, tostadas, hamburgers, hot dogs, and beer, soda, or coffee. To find this place from the Plaza de Armas, walk one block on Corona to Avenida Juárez and turn left; it's on the left.

MEALS FOR LESS THAN $10

Sanborn's. Juárez at 16 de Septiembre. ☎ **3/613-6264.** Breakfast $2–$4; main courses $2–$6. Daily 7:30am–1am. INTERNATIONAL.

Opened in 1992, Sanborn's is filled with patrons at almost any time of day. Like other branches of this Mexican chain, this restaurant features waitresses wearing festive dresses and serving clients swiftly and politely. The varied menu features everything from tacos and hotcakes to steaks and sandwiches. When you're finished eating, the section filled with drug items, English-language books and magazines, and gifts is *the* place to get back in touch with the world; Sanborn's is always well stocked. To find it from the Plaza de Armas, walk one block south on 16 de Septiembre to Juárez; it's on the left corner.

✪ **La Trattoría Pomodoro Ristorante.** Niños Héroes 3051. ☎ **3/122-1977.** Pasta $3–$5; chicken, beef, and seafood $5–$9. Mon–Sat 1pm–midnight, Sun 1pm–8pm. ITALIAN.

Sooner or later, visitors learn about the good food at this popular restaurant. Service is friendly and swift, and the newly decorated restaurant is refreshingly appealing with natural wood chairs, cushioned seats, and linen-clad tables. A large span of windows looks out onto Nios Héroes. There's separate seating for smokers and nonsmokers. For starters, you might want to sample the antipasto bar or the shrimp in white wine cream sauce with chiles. As a main course, the fettucine Alfredo is excellent. The superb salad bar and garlic bread are included in the price of main courses. To find this place, take the Par Vial going west on Independencia/Hidalgo. Get off when the bus turns back at the Minerva Circle. Walk one block farther to Avenida Mexico, cross the street, and get a bus going south to Niños Héroes (about 14 blocks). Cross Avenida Mexico to Niños Héroes and walk about half a block; the restaurant is on the right behind a church.

4 Exploring Guadalajara

FESTIVALS

During September, Mexicans celebrate their **independence** from Spain in a month-long celebration, but Guadalajara really goes all out. Look for poster-size calendars listing attractions that include many performances in theaters all over the city. On September 15, the Governor's Palace fills with well-dressed invited guests as they and the massive crowd in the park below await his reenactment of the traditional *grito* (shout for independence) at 11pm. The grito commemorates Fr. Miguel Hidalgo de Costilla's pronouncement that began the Mexican War of Independence in 1810. The celebration features live music on a temporary street stage, spontaneous dancing, much shouting of "*Viva México!*" and fireworks. On September 16, there's a parade that lasts an hour or so. For the next couple of days the park in front of the Degollado Theater resembles a country fair and Mexican market. There are games of chance with stuffed-animal prizes and a variety of food, including cotton candy and candied apples. Live entertainment goes on in the park day and night.

October is another month-long celebration called **Fiestas de Octubre** that originally began with the procession of Our Lady of Zapopan. Now the month is a celebration of everything that is notable about Guadalajara and Jalisco. The celebration kicks off with an enormous parade, usually on the Sunday (or possibly the Saturday) nearest the first of the month. The parade includes people from San Antonio, Texas, Guadalajara's sister city. Festivities continue all month long with performing arts, rodeos (*charreadas*), bullfights, art exhibits, regional dancing, a food fair, and a Day of Nations involving all the consulates of Guadalajara. Much of the ongoing displays and events takes place in the Benito Juárez Auditorium.

On October 12 around dawn, the small, dark figure of **Our Lady of Zapopan** begins her 5-hour ride from the Cathedral of Guadalajara to the Cathedral of Zapopan in a suburb. The original figure dates from the mid-1500s, and the tradition of the procession began 200 years later. Crowds spend the night all along the route and vie for position as the Virgin passes by in a new car donated to her for the occasion. During the months prior to October 12, the figure is carried to churches all over the city. During that time, you may see neighborhoods decorated with paper streamers and banners honoring the passing of the figure to the next church.

The last two weeks in February are marked by a series of **cultural events** before the beginning of Lent.

WALKING TOUR

DOWNTOWN GUADALAJARA

Start: Plaza de Armas.
Finish: Mercado Libertad.
Time: Approximately 3 hours, not including museum and shopping stops.
Best Times: After 10am, when museums are open.
Worst Times: Mondays or holidays, when the museums are closed.

This walk through downtown Guadalajara will acquaint you with the major historical, cultural, and architectural treasures of the city. Begin the tour in the plaza beside the main cathedral on Avenida Alcalde between Avenida Hidalgo and Calle Morelos in the charming:

1. **Plaza de Armas.** This pleasant plaza has wrought-iron benches and walkways that lead like spokes to the ornate French-made iron central bandstand (where the Jalisco State Band puts on **free concerts** Tuesdays, Thursdays, and Sundays from 7pm on; arrive early if you want a seat in the park). The bandstand is directly in front of the:

2. **Palacio del Gobierno.** This eye-catching arched structure dominating the plaza was built in 1774 and combines the Spanish and Moorish influences prevalent at the time. Be sure to go inside to view the spectacular mural of Hidalgo by Clemente Orozco over the beautiful wooden-railed staircase to the right. The panel to the right is called *The Contemporary Circus,* and the one on the left, *The Ghost of Religion in Alliance with Militarism.* The highly esteemed Orozco was a native of Guadalajara.

   Going back out the front entrance, turn right and walk to the:

3. **Cathedral.** Begun in 1561, the unusual multispired facade combines several 17th-century Renaissance styles, including a touch of Gothic. An 1818 earthquake destroyed the original large towers; the present ones were designed by architect Manuel Gómez Ibarra. Inside, look over the sacristy to see the painting believed to be the work of renowned 17th-century artist Bartolomé Murillo (1617–1682).

   Leave the cathedral and turn right out the front doors and walk along Avenida Alcalde to the:

4. **Rotonda de los Hombres Ilustres.** Sixteen gleaming-white columns without bases or capitals stand as monuments to Guadalajara's—and the state of Jalisco's—distinguished sons. To learn who they are, visitors need only to stroll around the flower-filled green park and read the names on the 11 nearly life-size statues of the state's heros. There are 98 burial vaults in the park, only 4 of which are occupied.

   East of the plaza, cross Liceo to the:

5. **Regional Museum of Guadalajara.** This building (☎ 3/614-9957), built in 1701 in the churrigueresque style, exhibits some of the region's archaeological finds, fossils, historic objects, and art. Among the highlights is a gigantic reconstructed skeleton of a mammoth and a meteorite weighing 1,715 pounds found in 1792 in Zacatecas. In addition, on the first floor there's a fascinating exhibit of pre-Hispanic pottery featuring unusual pieces that have been in the collection and some exquisite recent pottery and clay figures found near Tequila during the construction of the toll road. On the second floor is a small, interesting ethnography section showing the contemporary dress of the state's indigenous cultures, including the Coras, Huichols, Mexicaneros, Nahuas, and Tepehuanes. It's open Tuesday through Sunday from 9am to 3:45pm. Admission is $4.50 for adults; children enter free.

   Outside the museum and to the right is the:

6. **Palacio de Justicia.** Built in 1588 as the first convent in Guadalajara, Santa María de Gracia later became a teachers' college and girls' school. In 1952 it was officially designated as the Palace of Justice. Inside, above the stairway, is a huge mural honoring the law profession in Guadalajara; it depicts historic events, including Benito Juárez with the 1857 constitution and laws of reform.

   Outside the palacio and directly to the right, continuing east on Avenida Hidalgo is the:

7. **Church of Santa María de Gracia,** one of Guadalajara's oldest churches, which was built along with the convent next door.

   Opposite the church is the:

8. **Teatro Degollado** (Deh-goh-yah-doh), a beautiful neoclassic 19th-century opera house named for Santos Degollado, a local patriot who fought with Juárez against

the French and Maximilian. Notice the seven muses in the theater's triangular façade above the columns. The theater hosts various performances during the year, including the excellent Ballet Folklórico on Sunday at 10am. Plaza Libertad links the cathedral and the Degollado Theater. It's open Monday through Friday from 10am to 2pm.

To the right of the theater, on the opposite side of the plaza from the Santa María de Gracia church, is the:

9. **University of Guadalajara School of Music and the San Agustín Church.** There are continuous services in the church, and sometimes the music school is open to the public. Continuing east on the plaza, you should be sure to notice the spectacular fountain behind the Degollado Theater; it depicts Mexican history in low relief. You'll next pass the charming children's fountain followed by the unusual sculpture of a tree with lions and nearby slabs of text by Charles V proclaiming Guadalajara's right to be recognized as a city.

The plaza opens up into a huge pedestrian expanse called Plaza Tapatía, framed by department stores and offices and dominated by the:

10. **Quetzalcoatl Fountain.** This towering, abstract sculpture/fountain represents the mythical plumed serpent Quetzalcoatl, which figures so prominently in Mexican legend and ancient culture and religion. The smaller pieces represent the serpent and birds; the centerpiece is the serpent's fire.

☕ **TAKE A BREAK** Take a short break at one of the small ice-cream shops or fast-food restaurants along the plaza or wait to go to the small cafeteria inside the Hospicio, which serves hot dogs, sandwiches, cake, soft drinks, coffee, and snacks.

Looking down at the far end of the plaza, you'll spot the:

11. **Hospicio Cabañas.** Formerly called the Cabañas Orphanage and known today as the **Instituto Cultural Cabañas** (☎ 3/617-4322), this impressive structure was designed by the famous Mexican architect Manuel Tolsá. It housed homeless children from 1829 until 1980. Today it's a thriving cultural center offering art shows and classes. The main building has a fine dome, and the walls and ceiling are covered by murals painted in 1929 by José Clemente Orozco (1883–1949). Orozco's powerful painting in the dome, *Man of Fire*, is said to represent the spirit of humanity projecting itself toward the infinite. Several other rooms hold more of Orozco's work, and there are also excellent temporary exhibits. A contemporary art exhibit in the south wing features fascinating and unusual paintings by Javier Arevalo. The institute's own Ballet Folklórico performs here every Wednesday at 8:30pm. To the left of the entrance is a bookstore.

For a real change of pace, turn left out the front entrance of the Cabañas and look for a stairway that leads down to the:

12. **Mercado Libertad,** Guadalajara's gigantic covered central market, said to be the largest in Latin America. The site has been used for a market plaza since the 1500s, and the present buildings were constructed in the early 1950s. This is a great place to buy leather goods, pottery, baskets, rugs, kitchen utensils, and just about anything else. (See "Shopping," below.)

MORE ATTRACTIONS

Museo de las Artes de la Universidad de Guadalajara. Juárez 975. ☎ 3/625-7553. Admission $2. Tues–Sat 10am–8pm, Sun and holidays noon–8pm.

Walking Tour—Downtown Guadalajara

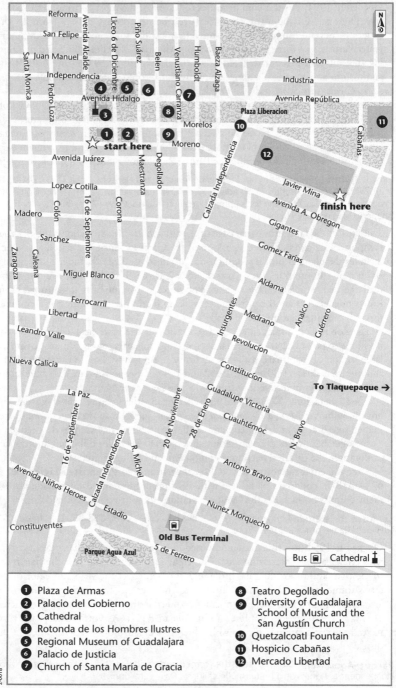

1. Plaza de Armas
2. Palacio del Gobierno
3. Cathedral
4. Rotonda de los Hombres Ilustres
5. Regional Museum of Guadalajara
6. Palacio de Justicia
7. Church of Santa María de Gracia
8. Teatro Degollado
9. University of Guadalajara School of Music and the San Agustín Church
10. Quetzalcoatl Fountain
11. Hospicio Cabañas
12. Mercado Libertad

Opened in 1994, this museum promises to be one of the most exciting in the country. The excellent opening show featured contemporary artists from all the Americas. Several rooms house the university's collection, mostly of Mexican and Jaliscan artists, and there is always a traveling exhibition. The beautiful building housing the museum was constructed as a primary school in 1914. One wall of the auditorium and the cupola above show two of Orozco's vigorous murals entitled *Man, Creator and Rebel* and *The People and Their False Leaders.*

To reach the museum, take the Par Vial west on Independencia/Hidalgo. Get off after it makes the right turn onto Vallarta/Juárez. From the bus stop on Juárez, walk back (east) two or three blocks; it's on the right opposite the University of Guadalajara. It's also about an 11-block walk from Alcalde/16 de Septiembre, straight west on Juárez; it's four blocks beyond the Parque Revolución, which will be on your left.

Parque Natural Huentitán. Calz. Independencia Nte. and Flores Magón. ☎ **3/674-0318** or 3/674-0266. Zoo admission $1.50 Adults, $1 children; planetarium $2 (movie additional $1); Pasaporte Mágico $2. Zoo daily 9am–6pm; planetarium Mon–Sat 9am–7pm, Sun 9am–6:30pm; Pasaporte Mágico daily 10am–5pm.

This area, at the far northeastern edge of the city, holds three attractions: the city zoo, Pasaporte Mágico (a children's park), and the Centro Ciencia y Tecnología, which includes the planetarium. By local bus no. 60 north on Calzada Independencia, it's about a 30-minute ride; a taxi costs $6 to $7. Those going by bus should look for the large, yellow pillars on the right side of the street coming from downtown. From Independencia, it's another 15-minute walk up Flores Magón to the zoo's entrance through the huge parking lot on the left.

The **Zoo** is set in a manicured, shaded, spread-out area with meandering walkways; it's home to polar bears, gorillas, jaguars, ocelots, tecuanes, monkeys, exotic birds, a large section of mammals, sea lions, and others. An aviary show is presented in the auditorium daily at 11:30am and 12:30 and 1:30pm. Sergio Bustamante's blue sculptures of monkeys in different positions dot the steps as you enter.

The **Planetarium** (☎ 3/674-4106) is like many others you've probably seen. The hour-long movie *Mundo Desconocido (Unknown World)* is shown daily on a dome-shaped screen at 10 and 11:30am and 2:30, 4, and 5pm. The Centro de Ciencias y Tecnología that houses the planetarium also offers rather dull exhibitions about space exploration, the galaxies, telephone equipment, and military aircraft.

After you enter the zoo area, you'll see the entrance to **Pasaporte Mágico** (☎ **3/ 674-0318**), a children's park filled with all kinds of mechanical rides made just for them. Admission includes the "Mundo Marino" show at noon, 2, 4, and 6pm.

✪ Museo de la Ciudad. Independencia 684 at M. Barcena. ☎ **3/658-2531.** Admission $1. Tues–Sat 10am–5pm, Sun 10am–3pm.

Opened in 1992, this fine museum housed in a wonderful old stone convent chronicles Guadalajara's interesting past. The eight *salas,* beginning with the first room to the right and proceeding in chronological order, cover the years just prior to the city's founding by 63 Spanish families to the present. Interesting and unusual artifacts, including rare Spanish armaments and equestrian paraphernalia, give a sense of what day-to-day life was like in Guadalajara's past. As you browse, take time to read the explanations (in Spanish), which give details not otherwise noted in the displays.

Parque Agua Azul. Located near the former bus station at the south end of Calzada Independencia. Admission $1 adults; 50¢ children. Daily 7am–6pm.

This park is a perfect refuge from the bustling city. It contains plants, trees, shrubbery, statues, and fountains. Many people come here to exercise early in the morning. For children, there's a **Museo Infantil** (Children's Museum) with displays of traditional toys as well as shows. *El Chuku, Chuku,* a rubber-tired minitrain, circulates through the grounds daily in the summer (on Saturday and Sunday the rest of the year) from 11am to 6pm. A ride costs 75¢. The museum is open daily from 10am to 6pm.

Across Independencia, catercorner from the flower market in a small one-story rock building, is the **Museo Arqueología del Occidente de Mexico.** It houses a fine collection of pre-Hispanic pottery from the states of Jalisco, Nayarit, and Colima and is well worth your time. The museum is open Tuesday through Sunday from 10am to 2pm and 4 to 7pm. There's a small admission charge.

Also across the Independencia (opposite Parque Agua Azul) is the **Casa de la Cultura,** between Avenida 16 de Septiembre and Calzada Independencia (☎ 3/619-3611). It offers a variety of classes in local culture by day, as well as a packed evening schedule to which the public is invited. The Nahuatl language is taught on Thursday from 7 to 8:30pm. The state-run **Casa de las Artesanías** (☎ 3/619-4664) is just past the park entrance at the crossroads of Calzada Independencia and Gallo (for details, see "Shopping," below).

Plaza de los Mariachis.

Half a block from the Mercado libertad on Calzada Independencia and Calle Javier Mina beside the San Juan de Dios Church is the Plaza de los Mariachis, actually a short street lined with restaurants and cafés. During the day, small bands of mariachis loaf around or sip drinks, but at night the place is packed with them (see "Guadalajara After Dark," below).

Plaza and Ex-Convento del Carmen. Avenida Juarez. No phone. Tues–Sun 9am–10pm.

The **Ex-Convento del Carmen,** on Avenida Juárez four blocks west of the Centro Histórico, offers a full range of theater, films, and musical events almost nightly. It's open tickets are usually sold here just a short while before the performance. Across the street, the **Plaza del Carmen,** with a bubbling fountain, roses, and shade trees, is a nice place to relax. Lovers' embraces may lead to a wedding at the small **Templo del Carmen,** an old church on the plaza. There's usually a mass, wedding, or christening in progress.

The Tequila Plant. Avenida Vallarta 3273. ☎ **3/615-6990** or 3/630-0707. Free admission. Tours Mon–Fri 10am.

You might want to take a tour of the Tequila Sauza bottling plant, on the left on the way out of town. After the tour there's a "happy hour" during which you can enjoy a variety of tequila drinks prepared by masters of the art. You can skip the tour and come just to drink from 10am to 1pm. Both the tours and the drinks are free.

By the way, this is just a bottling plant. The distillery is in the town of **Tequila,** off Highway 15 about 25 miles east of Guadalajara. You'll see the spiny blue agave plant, from which tequila is made, growing everywhere around the little town. It takes a good hour or two to get to Tequila due to traffic and potholes.

ORGANIZED TOURS

Several times daily, **Panoramex** (☎ **3/610-5005** or 3/610-5109) offers bilingual tours of Guadalajara, Lake Chapala, Tequila, and Zapopan; tours range from $10 to $20. Those without a car might want to consider a tour, especially to the outlying regions. Inquire at the Panoramex office (open Monday through Friday from 9am to 7pm) or at your hotel.

SPECTATOR SPORTS

BULLFIGHTS   Many say that Guadalajara and Mexico City host the best bull-fights in the country. Every Sunday at 4:30pm (4pm in summer), there's a bullfight at the Plaza de Toros "Nuevo Progreso," across from the football stadium on Calzada Independencia Norte north of town. Tickets range from $4 for seats in the sun to $40 for the best seats in the shade. Buy tickets downtown in the reception area of the Hotel Francés on Thursday from 10am to 2pm or 4 to 7pm or at the Plaza de Toros.

CHARREADA   To the east of Agua Azul is the **Aceves Galindo Lienzo,** or rodeo ring, at the corner of Dr. R. Michel and Calzada de las Palmas (☎ 3/19-3232). There's a Mexican rodeo (*charreada*) on Sunday at noon. Mexican rodeos are a special extrava-ganza with elegant costumes and grand shows of prowess in riding, roping, rope tricks, and a traditional grand promenade. Sometimes there are evening shows.

5 Shopping

The mammoth **Mercado Libertad** (see "Walking Tour: Downtown Guadalajara," above) features fresh and cooked food, crafts (including baskets, puppets, wood carv-ings, pottery, dance costumes), clothing, a great selection of inexpensive watches on the second floor, household wares, and a spectacular glimpse of daily life. Although it opens at 7am, it isn't in full swing until around 10am.

In addition, Guadalajara houses the largest modern shopping center in Latin America. The **Plaza del Sol** megacomplex sprawls over 120,000 square yards in an area at the junction of Avenidas López Mateos and Mariano Otero, outside the center of town. Here you can buy anything from a taco to a Volkswagen; you can also cash a check, make a plane reservation, or buy a lottery ticket. Hotels and restaurants of-fer respite for weary shoppers. Take any bus marked "Plaza del Sol" from Calzada Independencia near the Mercado libertad or on Alcalde in front of the Rotonda de los Ilustres.

One block past the entrance of Agua Azul Park in the direction of the city center (on your right at the crossroads of Calzada Independencia and Gallo) is the **Casa de las Artesanías,** Gallo 20 (☎ 3/619-4664). It's an enormous two-story state-run crafts store that sells pottery, silver jewelry, dance masks, and regional clothing from around the state and the country. There's often a great selection of colorful nativity scenes (*natividades*). However, if you're going to the villages, such as Tonala and Tlaquepaque, you may want to postpone buying such items. On the right as you enter are museum displays showing crafts and regional costumes from the state of Jalisco. The craft store is open Monday through Friday from 10am to 6pm, Satur-day from 10am to 5pm, and Sunday from 11am to 3pm.

Some of Mexico's best pottery and crafts are made in the suburbs of **Tlaquepaque** and **Tonala.** These two villages are a must, especially on Thursday or Sunday when Tonala spreads out a huge street market. (See "Tlaquepaque & Tonala" under "Side Trips from Guadalajara," below.)

6 Guadalajara After Dark

JALISCAN PERFORMING ARTS

Ballet Folklórico de la Universidad de Guadalajara. ☎ **3/626-9280** or 3/614-4773, ext. 144 or 143. Tickets $3–$12.

This wonderful dance company, acclaimed as the best *folklórico* company in all of Mexico, provides light, color, movement, and music that are pure Jalisco. For more than a decade it has been performing at the Degollado Theater. Performances are on Sunday at 10am.

Ballet Folklórico Nacional del Instituto Cultural Cabañas. ☎ **3/618-6003.** Tickets $4–$6.

Performances are every Wednesday at 8:30pm at the theater of the Instituto Cultural Cabañas.

Casa de la Cultura. Between Av. 16 de Septiembre and Calzada Independencia. ☎ **3/ 619-3611.**

A variety of performances is offered. The Association of Composers of Jalisco offers new works on Tuesday evenings at 8pm. The state chorus group, the Coral del Estado, also performs here. On Thursday there are literary readings at 8pm, and there are experimental dance performances and Aztec music. Call for information.

Ex-Convento del Carmen. Av. Juárez 638. ☎ **3/614-7184.** Admission varies; call for information.

A former convent just a few blocks from the central plaza, this venue hosts many inexpensive concerts. Performances are usually on Monday and Tuesday at 8 or 8:30pm, and tickets are usually sold shortly before the performance.

HANGIN' WITH THE MARIACHIS

For rousing music and local ambience, go to the **Plaza de los Mariachis,** down by the San Juan de Dios Church and the Mercado Libertad, at the junction of Calzada Independencia and Avenida Juárez/Calle Javier Mina. Every evening the colorfully dressed mariachis, in various states of inebriation, play for money (if they can get it) or for free. Enjoy a meal, a snack, or a soft drink here or just stand around spending nothing but time. It's fun and free; spend at least one evening here. Pickpockets are ever-present, so be careful. It costs nothing to listen as the mariachis belt away around other diners' tables, but if you request a song, ask the price first.

Few places in Guadalajara are more enjoyable to me than **El Parian** in Tlaquepaque, where mariachis serenade diners under the portals (see "Side Trips from Guadalajara," below).

CABARET & JAZZ CLUBS

Hotel Fiesta Americana. Glorieta Minerva. ☎ **3/625-3434** or 3/625-4848. Cover varies.

Songs and imitations are presented in the **Caballo Negro Bar** from 11pm until 1am. There is also a continually changing show in the **lobby bar** daily from 7pm until 1am. In another salon, **Estelaris,** there are occasional performances by nationally known artists.

Restaurant/Bar Copenhagen 77. Marcos Castellanos 140-Z. ☎ **3/625-2803.** No cover: Mon–Sat 8:30am–12:30am.

This dark, cozy jazz club is by the little Parque de la Revolución, on your left as you walk down López Cotilla/Federalismo. There are linen cloths and a red rose on every table. You can come just for a drink or for the restaurant's specialty—the delicious paella Copenhagen al vino. The paella takes a while to prepare, but it's an enjoyable wait as you sip a drink and listen to the jazz.

DANCE CLUBS/DISCOS

Lobby Bar, Hotel Francés. Maestranza 35. ☎ **3/613-1190.**

Though too noisy to recommend as a place to sleep, the stately Hotel Francés is a popular downtown meeting place. Check out the lobby bar, open from 8am to

10:30pm. There's a happy hour from noon to 8pm with two national (not imported) drinks for the price of one. There's often live piano music in the late afternoon and evening.

Maxim's Disco Club. In the Hotel Francés, Maestranza 35. ☎ **3/613-1190.** No cover Mon–Thurs; $4 Fri–Sun. Daily 8pm–midnight.

Despite its name, Maxim's is not a disco but a dance hall with a singer or a live band. There are tables around the dance floor and in the lower bar section.

7 Side Trips from Guadalajara

There are a number of interesting places to visit near Guadalajara. Tlaquepaque and Tonala are distant suburbs, and Lake Chapala is a popular vacation spot, especially with foreign visitors.

TLAQUEPAQUE & TONALA
7 & 11 miles S of Guadalajara

ESSENTIALS
GETTING THERE & DEPARTING   By Bus   Two types of buses go to Tlaquepaque and Tonala (a 25-minute ride). Both leave from the corner of Alcalde and Independencia in front of the Cathedral. **Linea Turquesa** buses (numbered 275 A or B) pass every 10 minutes, carry only seated passengers, and cost 75¢. Linea Turquesa buses pass within a block of Tlaquepaque's main square (it won't be obvious, so tell the driver you want off in Tlaquepaque) and stop several times on the main street going to Tonala (where you'll see the shops and street stalls). Other public buses (also numbered 275 A or B) cover the route, cost 25¢, and are often packed with both standing and seated passengers. On the public buses you'll have to watch for the welcoming arch on the left at Tlaquepaque then get off two stops later and ask for directions to El Parian, Tlaquepaque's central building on the main square. The last stop for this bus is Tonala (another 15 minutes), where it turns around for the return to Guadalajara.

ORIENTATION   Information   The **Tlaquepaque Tourism Office** is in the Presidencia Municipal (opposite El Parian), Calle Guillermo Prieto 80 (☎ **3/ 635-1503** or 3/635-0596); it's open Monday through Friday from 9am to 3pm and Saturday from 9am to 1pm.

The **Tonala Tourism Office** (☎ **3/683-1740;** fax 3/683-0590) is in the Artesanos building set back a bit from the road at Atonaltecas 140 Sur (the main street leading into Tonala) at Matamoros. Free **walking tours** are held Monday, Tuesday, Wednesday, and Friday at 9am and 2pm and Saturday at 9am and 1pm. They include visits to artisans' workshops (exhibiting ceramic, stoneware, blown-glass, papier-mâché, and the like). Tours last between 3 and 4 hours and require a minimum of five people. Hours are Monday through Friday from 9am to 3pm and Saturday from 9am to 1pm. Also in Tonala, catercorner from the church, you'll see a small **tourism information kiosk** that's staffed on market days and provides maps and useful information.

Tlaquepaque and Tonala are special treats for shoppers. **Market days** are Sunday and Thursday in Tonala, but on Sunday many of Tlaquepaque's stores are open only from 10:30am to 2:30pm. Thursday is the best day to combine a trip to both villages, about 4 miles apart. Monday through Saturday, stores in Tlaquepaque usually close between 2:30 and 4pm. A nice day consists of wearing yourself out in Tonala

Impressions

Not so many years ago the stagecoach between [Zapotlán] and Guadalajara used to be held up regularly, sometimes at several places in one trip. The highwaymen who came last would take from the passengers even their underwear, though with inborn chivalry they allowed the ladies to keep their crinolines. The unfortunate travelers would arrive at Zapotlán gowned in newspapers and the curtains of the coach. Whenever the curtains were seen not to be in their proper places it was at once understood in the town what had happened.

—Carl Lumholtz, *Unknown Mexico,* 1902

then relaxing at one of Tlaquepaque's pleasant outdoor restaurants for a sunset meal and waiting for the mariachis to warm up at El Parian.

TLAQUEPAQUE

This suburban village is famous for its **fashionable stores** in handsome old stone mansions fronting pedestrians-only streets and for its pottery and glass factories. The village is also known for **El Parian,** a circular building dating from the 1800s in the town center, where innumerable mariachis serenade diners in sidewalk cafés. The mariachis are especially plentiful, loud, and entertaining on weekend evenings (Sunday is best), but you'll hear them serenading there just about any time of day. The stores, especially on Calle Independencia, offer the pottery and glass for which the village is famous, plus the best of Mexico's crafts, such as *equipales* furniture, fine wood sculptures, and papier-mâché.

Exploring Tlaquepaque

Tlaquepaque's **Regional Ceramics Museum,** Independencia 237 (☎ **3/35-5404**), is a good place to see what traditional Jalisco pottery is all about. There are high-quality examples dating back several generations. Note the cross-hatch design known as *petatillo* on some of the pieces; it's one of the region's oldest traditional motifs. One impressive section of the museum has a wonderful old kitchen and dining room, complete with pots, utensils, and dishes. The museum is open Tuesday through Saturday from 10am to 4pm and Sunday from 10am to 1pm. There is also the National Museum of Ceramics in Tonala (see below).

Across the street from the museum is **La Rosa Fábrica de Vidrio Soplado,** a glass-blowing factory. From 9:30am to 2:30pm Monday through Friday, the public is invited to go to the rear patio and watch as a dozen scurrying men and boys heat glass bottles and jars on the end of hollow steel poles. Then, blowing furiously, they chase across the room, narrowly missing spectators and fellow workers as they swing the red-hot glass within an inch of a man who sits placidly rolling an elaborate jug out of another chunk of cooling glass. Nonchalantly, the old man will interrupt his own task long enough to clip off the end of the approaching vase at the exact moment at which it comes within reach of his hand. Then he drops the clippers and returns once more to his own task as the blower charges back across the room to reheat the vase in the furnace.

Where to Eat

Read the fine print on menus. The 10% value-added tax may not be included in Tlaquepaque; ask before ordering.

Birrería El Sope. D. Guerra 142. ☎ **3/35-6338.** Birria $3–$5. Mon–Sat 8am–8pm, Sun 8am–10pm. BIRRIA.

This is where locals go for that wonderful Jalisco specialty—birria. Cheery and clean, the restaurant is a long, narrow room in a quiet neighborhood. The decor of cushioned French provincial chairs pulled up to covered tables topped with artificial carnations doesn't quite go along with the country menu, but the food is tasty. The somewhat indifferent waitresses have little patience for questions posed by the uninitiated, so here's the lowdown: Choose your birria by the meat—goat (*cabra* or *cabrito*), lamb (*borrego*), or pork (*puerco*)—and by the cut—leg (*pechuga*), ribs (*costilla*), and so on. The leg portion has the most meat. An order comes with fresh salsa, chips, and tortillas and beans. Side orders of quesadillas or queso fundido are extra. To find this restaurant from Tlaquepaque's main plaza, walk north on Madero two blocks and turn left on Guerra; it's half a block down on the right.

✪ **Mariscos Progreso.** Progreso 80. ☎ **3/657-4995.** main courses $5–$9. Daily 8am–6pm. SEAFOOD/MEXICAN.

On a cozy tree-shaped patio filled with leather-covered tables and chairs, this restaurant makes an inviting place to take a break from shopping. Charcoal-grilled seafood, Mexican style, is the specialty here. To get here, walk two blocks south on Madero, cross Juárez (one of the streets that borders El Parian), and look for this corner restaurant on the right.

Restaurant with No Name (Sin Nombre). Madero 80. ☎ **3/635-4520** or 3/635-9677. Breakfast $4.75–$10; main courses $8–$13. Sun–Thurs 8:30am–9pm, Fri–Sat 8:30am–midnight. HAUTE MEXICAN.

One of my all-time favorites, this place offers excellent Mexican cuisine with a flair. It's set in a spectacular garden shaded by banana, peach, palm, and other tropical trees and guarded by strutting peacocks. A trio plays music in midafternoon. The menu is spoken by the bilingual waiter, not written, so ask for prices as you order. The excellent "no name chicken" is cooked in onions, green peppers, and a buttery sauce and spread around a mound of rice. The quesadillas are outstanding. To get here from the main plaza, face the plaza (with the church to your right) and walk on Madero to the right for 1$^{1}/_{2}$ blocks; the restaurant is on the right, between Independencia and Constitución.

TONALA

Tonala is a pleasant, unpretentious village about 4 miles from Tlaquepaque that you may find more authentic and easier on the wallet than Tlaquepaque. The streets were paved only recently, but there aren't any pedestrians-only thoroughfares yet. The village has been a center for potterymaking since pre-Hispanic times; half of the more than 400 artists who reside here produce high- and low-temperature pottery in different colors of clay with a dozen different finishes. Other local artists also work with forged iron, cantera stone, brass and copper, marble, miniatures, papier-mâché, textiles, blown glass, and gesso.

Exploring Tonala

On Thursday and Sunday **market days,** vendors and temporary street stalls under flapping shade cloths fill the streets; "herb-men" sell multicolored dried medicinal herbs from wheelbarrows; magicians entertain crowds with sleight-of-hand tricks; and craftspeople spread their colorful wares on the plaza's sidewalks. Those who love the handblown Mexican glass and folksy ceramics will wish they had a truck to haul the gorgeous and inexpensive handmade items back home. There is certainly greater variety here than in Tlaquepaque—tacky and chic are often side by side.

Tonala is the home of the **National Museum of Ceramics,** Constitución 104, between Hidalgo and Morelos (☎ **3/683-0494**). The museum occupies a huge two-story mansion and displays work from Jalisco as well as pottery from all over the country. There's a large shop in the front on the right as you enter. The museum is open Tuesday through Friday from 10am to 5pm and Saturday and Sunday from 10am to 2pm. A fee of $5 per camera is charged for use of any cameras.

Where to Eat

Los Geranios. Hidalgo 71. ☎ **3/683-0010;** fax 3/683-0700. Main courses $3–$6. Daily 11am–5pm. MEXICAN/INTERNATIONAL.

This narrow, inviting restaurant next to El Bazar de Sermel offers a cool respite from the blazing sun. Diners can relax in the clean and comfortable white canvas chairs at white-clothed tables or in the small booths. The menu includes Mexican specialties. Try the fish with almonds and mushrooms or the pork baked in orange sauce with baked potato and vegetables or something quick like nachos. To get here, face the church on the plaza, walk to the right turn on that street (Hidalgo) for about half a block; look on the left for a pretty stained-glass sign with red flowers.

LAKE CHAPALA: PICTURE-PERFECT LAKESIDE TOWNS

26 miles SE of Guadalajara

Mexico's largest lake and the area surrounding it have long been popular with foreign vacationers because of the near-perfect climate, gorgeous scenery, and several charming little lakeshore towns—Chapala, Ajijic, and Jocotepec among them—each with its own distinct ambience. There's a large permanent expatriate community of around 4,000 people living in settlements along the shoreline and in the villages stretching all the way from Chapala to Jocotepec.

From the mid-1970s until 1991, pollution of the Lerma River, one of the lake's water sources, caused serious concern. During that period, the lake's depth and perimeter diminished dramatically due to its heavy use as a water source by both Mexico City and Guadalajara. Recently Guadalajara developed another source of water, and the government intervened to stop pollution of the Lerma. Heavy rains in recent years have raised the lake level so much that it laps the original shore almost as it did in the past, and when you first see it, you'll think it looks like an ocean. It's a stunning sight, ringed by high, forested mountains and fishing villages.

Note: The year-round climate is so agreeable that few hotels offer air-conditioning, and only a few have fans; neither is necessary.

ESSENTIALS

GETTING THERE & DEPARTING   By Bus   Buses to Chapala go from Guadalajara's old Central Camionera. **Transportes Guadalajara-Chapala** (☎ 376/ 619-5675 in Guadalajara) serves the route. Buses and minibuses run every half hour to Chapala and every hour to Jocotepec.

In Chapala, the bus station (☎ 376/5-2212) is about seven blocks north of the lake pier. To get to Ajijic and San Juan Cosalá from Chapala, walk toward the lake (left out of the front of the station) and look for the local buses lined up on the opposite side of the street. These buses travel between Chapala and San Juan Cosalá. At San Juan Cosalá change buses to get to Jocotepec or take one of the buses that goes directly to Jocotepec from the Chapala bus station every half hour until 8pm. The last bus back to Guadalajara from Chapala is at 9pm.

By Car   Those driving will be able to enjoy the lake and the surrounding towns more fully. From Guadalajara, drive to Lake Chapala via the new four-lane Highway 15/80. Leave Guadalajara via Avenida Gonzalez Gallo, which intersects with Calzada Independencia just before Playa Azul Park. Going south on Independencia, turn left onto Gallo and follow it all the way out of town past the airport, where it becomes Highway 15/80 (which may also have signs calling it Highway 44), the main road to Chapala. The first view of the lake isn't until just outside the town of Chapala.

The highway from Guadalajara leads directly into Chapala and becomes Madero, which leads straight to Chapala's pier, malecón (waterfront walkway and street), and small shopping and restaurant area. The one traffic light in town (a block before the pier) is the turning point (right) to Ajijic, San Antonio, San Juan Cosalá, and Jocotopec. Chapala's **main plaza** is three blocks north of the pier, and the central food **market** flanks the park's back side.

ORIENTATION   Information   The **Jalisco State Information Office** is in Chapala at Aquiles Serdan 26 (☎ 376/5-3141). Serdan is a narrow side street going toward the lake, one block before the Correo (post office). The office is open Monday through Friday from 9am to 6pm and Saturday and Sunday from 10am to 6pm. The staff is willing to help but doesn't have a lot of information. You may be able to get a map of the area here.

FAST FACTS: LAKE CHAPALA

The **Area Code** for the whole northern lakeshore (Chapala, Ajijic, San Juan Cosalá, and Jocotopec) is 376. **Currency exchange** can be handled at the local Banamex, located on the right side of Madero just before the light, in Chapala. It's open Monday through Friday from 9am to 5pm; U.S. dollars can be changed all day, and Canadian dollars can be changed between 9am and 1:30pm. There's a Banamex automated teller machine (ATM) for Visa cards to the right of the bank's front door. Just down from Banamex (walking away from the lake), opposite the food market and main plaza, is **Lloyds Money Exchange,** by Lloyds's front door. It's open Monday through Friday from 9am to 4pm. To the left of the Hotel Nido, **Agencias de Cambios** is another money exchange office. It's open Monday through Saturday from 9am to 7pm and Sunday from 9am to 2pm.

Several outlets offer **communications services,** including fax, telephone, mail, and messages. Centro de Mensajes Mexicano-Americano is the local affiliate for UPS. They also have 24-hour telephone message and fax receiving service, court-approved translation ability, and secretarial service. It's at Hidalgo 236 (Apdo. Postal 872), Chapala, Jal. 45900 (☎ and fax **376/5-2102**), and it's open Monday through Friday from 10am to 6pm and Saturday from 10am to 2pm. Almost next door, Aero Flash, Hidalgo 236 (☎ **376/5-3696;** fax 376/5-3063), has a 24-hour fax service and specializes in package mailing. It's the local Federal Express office. The **post office** is on Hidalgo two blocks from the intersection of Madero. Enter down the hill and in back. It's open Monday through Friday from 9am to 1pm and 3 to 6pm and Saturday from 9am to 1pm.

Probably the most convenient **groceries store** is Supergrisa, at the corner of Hidalgo and Madero opposite the Restaurant Superior. It's open daily from 8am, closing most days at 8pm (at 3pm on Thursday and 6pm on Sunday). A good local **bookstore** is Libros y Revistas, at Madero 230 (☎ **376/5-2021**), near the Chamber of Commerce and Lloyds and opposite the plaza; it carries a wide assortment of English-language newspapers, magazines, and books—from the latest paperback novels to *Mirabella, Family Circle, Texas Monthly,* and *Scientific American.* It's open daily from 9am to 4pm.

CHAPALA

Chapala, Jalisco, founded in 1538, is the district's business and administrative center as well as the oldest resort town on Lake Chapala. Much of the town's prosperity comes from the retirees, primarily American and Canadian, who live on the outskirts and come into Chapala to change money, buy groceries, and check the stock ticker. Except on weekends, when throngs of visitors fill the area around the pier and lake's edge, the town of 36,000 can be a pretty sleepy place. There are a couple of hotels in Chapala, but Ajijic is the preferable place to stay in the area.

Where to Eat

Lake Chapala's regional specialties include caviar de Chapala, caldo michi, charales, and tortas ahogados. *Viuda de Sánchez Sangrita* (a tequila chaser) is made locally, as is Cholula brand hot sauce.

Mariscos Guicho. Corona 20. ☎ **376/5-3232.** Main courses $4–$6. Wed–Mon 11am–8pm. SEAFOOD.

This brightly colored restaurant, with its lime-green walls and pink-and-purple table cloths, is one of the most popular restaurants on the lake. The menu includes fish served many ways, large juicy garlic shrimp, frog legs, and caviar tacos. Most main courses come with rice and bread. To find this place from Chapala's main pier, walk to the left and head for the restaurants lining the lake. It's one long block ahead on the right.

Restaurant Cozumel. Corona 22 A. ☎ **376/5-4606.** Seafood and steaks $5–$8. Wednesday dinner special $7. Tues–Sun 10am–9pm. SEAFOOD/STEAKS.

A place that's secured a loyal clientele, this restaurant offers a bit more mood than others here, with its brick archways, hot-pink walls, ceiling-full of hanging plants, and low lighting in the evening. It snares extra business by offering a free margarita and wine with the evening meal. The menu holds some popular choices such as seafood brochettes, shrimp, and fish. Local favorites include breaded *charales* and caviar tacos. To find it from Chapala's main pier, walk left heading for the restaurants lining the lake. It's one long block ahead on the right, two doors down from Mariscos Guicho (see above).

AJIJIC

Ajijic, another lakeside village, is a quiet place inhabited by fishermen, artists, and retirees. As you reach Ajijic, the highway becomes a wide tree-lined boulevard through **La Floresta,** a wealthy residential district. The La Floresta sign signals you've entered Ajijic, but the central village is about a mile farther on the left. To reach Ajijic's main street, Colón (which changes to Morelos), turn left when you see the six (corner grocery) sign on the left. Colón/Morelos leads straight past the main plaza and ends at the lake and the popular Restaurant La Posada Ajijic. The cobblestone streets and arts-and-crafts stores give the town a quaint atmosphere. (See "Lake Chapala," above, for bus information to Ajijic.)

The **Clínica Ajijic** (☎ 376/6-0662; in an emergency 376/6-0875 or 376/6-0500), on the main highway at the corner of Javier and Mina, has a two-bed emergency section with oxygen and electrocardiogram, ambulance, and five doctors with different specialties. Their 16-bed hospital opened in 1993. The pharmacy there is available after hours for an emergency.

Linea Professional (☎ 376/6-0187; fax 376/6-0066) is a locally owned car rental agency in Ajijic. Make reservations as soon as you can—the cars are often all booked.

Exploring Ajijic

In La Floresta, immediately after the modernistic sculpture on the left, you'll see a cluster of buildings, one of which is marked **artesanías.** The state-owned shop

Ajijic

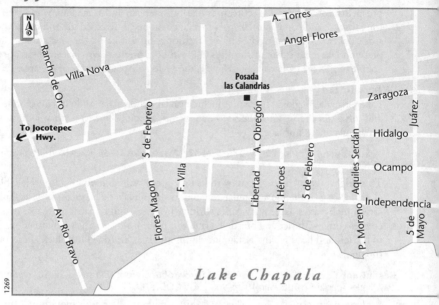

(☎ **376/6-0548**) has a good selection of pottery from all over Mexico as well as locally made crafts such as pottery, glassware, rugs, and wall tapestries. The shop is open Monday through Saturday from 10am to 6pm and Sunday from 10am to 2pm.

Ajijic has long been a center for weavers, but there seem to be fewer now than in the past. Still, it offers moderately good shopping; the best streets are Colón and those leading immediately off of it for a block or so. You'll find designer clothing and decorative accessories such as handloomed fabrics made into pillows and bedspreads, furniture, and pottery—but no one item in great abundance.

As for performing arts in the region, productions of **The Lakeside Little Theater** are usually announced in the local paper or the bulletin board at the Nueva Posada Ajijic.

Meeting the local foreign residents is easy; just go to the popular hangouts—the Restaurant Posada Ajijic, La Nueva Posada Ajijic, the Rose Café, and Los Veleros Restaurant and Sports Bar.

Where to Stay

La Laguna Bed and Brunch. Zaragoza 29, 45900 Ajijic, Jal. ☎ **376/6-1174** or 376/6-1186. Fax 376/6-1188. 4 rms (all with bath). $20 single or double (including brunch).

The rooms in this small inn are handsomely furnished with king-size beds covered in bright loomed bedspreads, thick tile floors, and fireplaces. Breakfast/brunch is served Monday through Friday from 8:30am to noon, Sunday 9am to noon. As you dine in a lovely glassed-in dining room facing the back patio, your meal begins with fruit and apple-bran muffins, which are followed by a choice of eggs as you like them. Nonguests can also partake of brunch for $3 to $4.50. To find La Laguna from the main highway, turn left on Colón and left again on the first street. It's 1 1/2 blocks down on the left behind the Laguna Ajijic Real Estate Office (which faces the main highway).

✪ **Los Artistas.** Constitución 105, 45900 Ajijic, Jal. ☎ **376/6-1027.** Fax 376/6-0066. 6 rms (all with bath). $35 to $40 single; $35–$45 double (including breakfast).

One of Ajijic's lovely walled-in homes, this inn is tucked ino a beautiful garden setting with a swimming pool, cordially served daily breakfast, and one of the best and most relaxing lodging values in Mexico. All rooms except one have private entry, and all are colorfully decorated but completely different in size and arrangement. The lowest price is for the smallest room. Guests have use of the pool and run of the downstairs, which includes the dining room and a comfortable living room with stereo. Breakfast is served inside or out by the pool and patio. To find Los Artistas from the intersection of Colón/Morelos and Constitución, turn left on Constitución and walk $5^1/_2$ blocks. It's on the left between Aldama and J. Alvarez with its name is on a small tile plaque on the brick wall beside the iron gate.

⑤ Suites Plaza Ajijic. Colón 33, 45920 Ajijic, Jal. No phone. 10 rms (all with bath). $15 per night single or double; $80 per week; $200 per month for 3-month stay.

Located on the right side of Colón opposite Ajijic's central square, this simple but pleasant and clean hotel reopened in 1992. The lobby, which faces the street, doubles as a real-estate office. Rooms, located behind the lobby, line two sides of a fairly narrow patio. All rooms are one-bedroom apartmentlike quarters; the bedrooms are separated from the kitchen areas with dining tables. A refrigerator and stove are available on request. A pleasant room in the back of the patio serves as the common living room with a game table, a TV, a stereo, and a paperback library that operates on the honor system.

Where to Eat

✪ Manix Restaurant. Ocampo 57. ☎ **376/6-0061.** Comida corrida $5–$6. Mon–Sat 1–9pm. INTERNATIONAL.

This is one of my favorite restaurants in Mexico because I can always count on a delicious meal that's politely served in an extremely pleasant setting. Rainbow-colored napkins brighten the dark carved-wood furniture in this serene atmosphere. There are usually two different international comidas daily. Seafood, beef, and sometimes chicken Cordon Bleu, ossu bucco, or chicken Parmesan are served. Servings are generous, and each comida comes with soup and dessert. To get here from the plaza, turn your back to the church, walk straight ahead on Colón for two blocks, and turn right on Ocampo; the restaurant is down the street on the right, but the sign is obscured by the lone tree on the street.

Restaurant La Posada Ajijic. Morelos and Independencia. ☎ **376/6-0744.** Sandwiches $2–$4; main courses $3.50–$7; Sunday brunch $4–$5. Mon–Thurs and Sun noon–10pm, Fri–Sat 10am–11pm, Sun brunch 9am–1pm. MEXICAN/INTERNATIONAL.

Formerly under the management of the owners of La Nueva Posada Ajijic, this restaurant facing the lake has reopened with graceful Mexican-inspired decor and good service. The menu covers traditional fare, including soups, salads, sandwiches, and more filling Mexican specialties, as well as imaginatively prepared beef, chicken, and seafood main courses. Sunday brunch is served on the patio facing the gardens. The bar, opposite the restaurant, is a favorite Ajijic hangout. The restaurant is at the end of Colón/Morelos; you enter through the back by the lake, where there's parking.

✪ **Rose Café.** Carretera Poniente 26. ☎ **376/6-1599.** Breakfast $2–$3; lunch special $3–$4. Tues–Sun 9am–4:30. VEGETARIAN.

Everyone enjoys the Rose Café, both for its food and for its casual and friendly atmosphere. Tables are set outside under the pink awning and inside back a bit from the highway. Among the best breakfast selections are fresh banana and chocolate muffins, delicious hot cakes, waffles with apple-raisin sauce, fruit salad, yogurt, and a variety of omelets and fritatas. The daily lunch special might include calzones, salad, and a grapefruit drink. The café is beside the Second Hand Rose thrift shop on the outskirts of town on the highway going west.

✪ **La Rusa.** Donato Guerra no. 9. ☎ **376/6-1444.** Reservations recommended Dec–Apr. Breakfast $2.50–$4; lunch $4–$7; dinner main courses $5–$9; Sun brunch $4.50–$6; garden grill $5–$7. Mon–Sat 8am–9pm, Sun 9am–8pm (Sun brunch served 9am–1pm; grill in the garden Mon–Fri 5–10pm). INTERNATIONAL.

Once you step inside the dining/drinking area of the La Nueva Posada Ajijic, you'll find just the right spot, whether you choose the equipales-furnished bar, the elegant dining room with garden and lake view, or the garden. La Rusa continues to be a popular dining spot with locals and *tapatíos*. The lunch menu is simple—crêpes, sandwiches, and salads. The dinner menu, printed on a large poster, has a dozen meat, seafood, and chicken main courses, plus soup, salad, and dessert. The Sunday brunch offers an entirely different selection and might include scrambled eggs in a potato nest with sausage; broccoli rarebit; or shrimp-asparagus crêpes Newburg. The higher-priced brunch includes wine. There's live music on Fridays and Saturdays. To reach the restaurant from the Ajijic plaza, walk toward the lake on Colón, turn left on Independencia/16 de Septiembre, and look for Donato Guerra. Turn right; La Rusa is on the right by the lake.

✪ **Los Telares.** Morelos 6. ☎ **376/6-0428.** Pasta $6–$7; main courses $7–$12. Wed–Thurs and Sun noon–9pm, Fri–Sat noon–10pm. ITALIAN/INTERNATIONAL.

Sophisticated but casual, this fashionable eatery opened in 1994. Dining tables set with handwoven cloths and napkins are arranged around an open courtyard. The pottery was made exclusively for the restaurant by Ken Edwards of Tlaquepaque, and works of well-known international artists decorate the walls. Vegetables and herbs are organically grown in the restaurant's garden, and breads are made fresh daily. Main courses include filet of sea bass in a smooth tamarindo sauce and Pacific prawns in key lime sauce. Try the outrageously rich and unforgettably fresh fettuccine Alfredo. Each evening live musicians—a guitarist, pianist, or trio of singers—provide romantic background music for diners. Los Telares is almost at the end of Colón/Morelos near the corner of Independencia/16 de Septiembre.

Ajijic After Dark

There's almost always a group or a crowd at the **Posada Ajijic Cantina,** Calle 16 de Septiembre no. 2, where a band (of sorts) plays music for dancing on Saturday and Sunday evenings. There's a happy hour Monday through Friday from noon to 1:30pm and 5 to 6pm with complimentary snacks. On Friday and Saturday evenings, between 5 and 10pm, there's a cover charge of $5. The **Nueva Posada Ajijic,** Donato Guerra 9, is a place to socialize almost anytime; happy hour, with complimentary snacks, runs from noon to 1:30pm and 5 to 6pm. For catching the latest in sports on a wide-screen TV or for just hanging out, **Patty's Los Veleros Restaurant and Sports Bar,** on Colón near the highway, is another popular place. It's open Sunday through Friday from 10am to 10pm and Saturday from 10am to midnight. More sophisticated than the rest is **Los Telares** (see "Where to Eat," above) where a trio, pianist, or guitarist plays softly while guests dine from Wednesday through Monday between 6 and 9pm.

JOCOTOPEC

West of Ajijic, this small colonial village is becoming a weaving center. Beginning on Hidalgo at the plaza, you'll find several weavers' shops with locally loomed rugs and wallhangings. Thursday, the market is open at the corner where the main street curves and becomes Hidalgo.

Important note for motorists: The main highway from Ajijic once went straight through Jocotopec, but your progress into town will now be a bit stilted and complicated—the highway becomes one way in the opposite direction as it approaches the town center. At the point where this occurs and you have to exit, you'll see a large sign over the highway advising drivers to veer left to Guadalajara and Morelia and right to Guadalajara and Centro (Jocotopec town center). You'll also see another sign, an arrow and line through it indicating that further travel straight ahead is illegal. If you want to reach the town plaza, turn right, then turn left at the next street, then watch for the plaza on your left. You can park here; Hidalgo's shopping is a block away. You can also turn left off the highway and follow the Guadalajara/Morelia signs until you reach Hidalgo; turn right onto Hidalgo, where you can park. You'll then be facing back in the direction of Ajijic when it's time to leave. There are several restaurants on Hidalgo near the main plaza.

11 Mexico City

An imposing, memorable place of monuments, palaces, parks, broad boulevards, handsome centuries-old buildings, and skyscrapers, Mexico City churns with the vitality of a major world capital. But it smarts under a burden of too many people—23,000,000 at last estimate—too many cars, and on many days, especially during the winter months, a dense pall of pollution.

On the one hand its world-class museums, historic center, and fine restaurants beckon world travelers to stay, explore, and linger in search of more—and they do. On the other hand its clogged sidewalks, traffic-laden streets, increasing number of begging poor, and recent upsurge in crime can repel even a New Yorker. Yet, with all its faults, it's one of the most fascinating cities in the world. I adore this city, and covet my days here.

Mexicans always refer to this city as "Mexico" rather than "Mexico City." One finds here a microcosm of all that is happening in the rest of the country—it's the fountainhead of government and in every way the center of Mexican life. Mexico's history continues to be played out in the streets of the capital, and in turn, these fascinating events have made the city what it is today. Deservedly or not, it's viewed as the city of hope throughout the country—for masses of rural migrants, going to the capital to live is synonymous with "making it."

Despite the setback caused by the late 1994 peso devaluation, Mexico is becoming more and more a part of the modern global economy, and the capital is the stage on which this exciting new chapter in the country's history is being played out. Foreign business travelers seem undeterred by gloomy news of the shelving of Mexican and foreign partnerships because of the devaluation and still fill the best hotels in the city; foreign and Mexican business connections *are* being made.

In fact, the capital city's hotels and restaurants are often packed with visitors. Though immense, Mexico City is easily walkable and terrifically enjoyable on foot. And though large, it is not an impersonal place. It's easy to make eye contact and exchange pleasantries with perfect strangers. *Capitalinos*, as residents call themselves, usually take time to be helpful to tourists—they will go out of their way to help you with directions or tell you when your bus stop is approaching.

1   Orientation

The thought of tackling one of the world's largest cities is enough to make the most experienced traveler pause, but fortunately Mexico City is quite well organized for the arriving traveler. Almost all touristically important sites are grouped in several areas that are easily walkable and easy to reach.

ARRIVING
BY PLANE

Mexico City's **Benito Juárez International Airport** is something of a small city, where you can grab a bite or buy a wardrobe, books, gifts, and insurance, as well as arrange a hotel room or take a bus directly to Puebla or Cuernavaca. There are also numerous money exchange counters and several ATM machines.

Near Gate A (*Sala* A in Spanish) is a guarded **baggage-storage area** (another is near Gate F). The key-locked metal storage lockers measure about 2 feet by 2 feet by 18 inches and cost $2.75 daily. Larger items are stored in a warehouse; cost for each 24 hours is $3.50 to $8.50, depending on the size; they'll hold your items up to a month.

The airport's **bookstores** include one near Gate A (Local #11) operated by the Instituto Nacional de Antropología (INAH) that has a large selection of historic, artistic, and scholarly books. A privately owned bookstore located near Gate D (Local #79) has a larger, more eclectic selection that includes novels and Mexican cookbooks. A **map store**, operated by the Instituto Nacional Estadistica, Geografia e Información (INEGI) occupies a tiny location near Gate C (Local #61). Another INEGI office at the exit of the Insurgentes metro station has a much greater inventory, including topographic maps.

The Mexico City Hotel and Motel Association offers a **hotel-reservation service** at their member hotels. Look for their booth just before you leave the baggage-claim area near Gate A on the concourse. They'll make the call according to your specifications for location and price. If they book the hotel, they require one night's advance payment and will give you a voucher showing payment, which you present at the hotel. Ask about hotels with specials, which can substantially reduce the rate. Special low-cost **long-distance telephones** (Ladatel) are strategically placed all along the public concourse (for instructions on how to use them, see the Appendix). For individual airline telephone numbers, see "Moving On—Travel Services," below.

GETTING INTO TOWN   The **authorized airport taxis** provide good, fast, reliable service but are relatively expensive. Here's how to use them: Either in the baggage claim area, or after exiting it onto the the public concourse, you'll see yellow booths marked "Taxi." These authorized taxi booths are staffed by personnel wearing bright-yellow jackets or bibs emblazoned with "Taxi Autorizado" (authorized taxi). Tell the ticket-seller your hotel or destination, as the price is based on a zone system. Expect to pay around $7 for a ticket to the Alameda. Count your change! A yellow-shirted escort will then show you to an available taxi in front of the airport, or to the end of a line if there is one. Present your ticket to the driver. Avoid turning your luggage over to an unauthorized taxi "assistant" who does nothing but lift your luggage into the waiting taxi—naturally he will want a tip. Putting your luggage in the taxi is the driver's job, and these "assistants" seem to whiz in and out of nowhere to do the job.

Important: Ignore those who approach you offering taxis in the arrivals hall; they are unlicensed and unauthorized. Take only an authorized cab with all the familiar markings: yellow car, white taxi light on the roof, and TRANSPORTACIÓN TERRESTRE painted on the doors.

The authorized cabbies maintain a monopoly of the airport business. You can try to beat the system by first seeing what authorized taxis charge, then walking to the Terminal Area Metro station (see below), at the intersection of the busy Bulevar Aeropuerto and the airport entrance, and look for a **regular city taxi.** When you see a yellow or green VW Beetle or little Datsun cab, flag it down. You may save as much as 25%. To get a proper, trustworthy cab, be sure to read the information on taxis in "Getting Around," below.

Colectivo van transportation from the airport was about to be reinstated after several years of no such service. Before selecting a colectivo, consider the cost savings versus the time; you could go around the city in snarling traffic letting others off long before arriving at your destination. If they are organized by destination—Zócalo area, Zona Rosa etc., then your chance of speedy arrival to your hotel is increased.

The **Metro,** Mexico City's modern subway system, is cheaper and faster than a taxi. As you come from your plane into the arrivals hall, turn left toward Gate A and walk all the way through the long terminal, out the doors, and along a covered sidewalk. Soon you'll see the distinctive Metro logo that identifies the Terminal Area station, down a flight of stairs. The station is on Metro Line 5. Follow the signs for trains to Pantitlán. At Pantitlán, change for Line 1 ("Observatorio"), which will take you to stations that are just a few blocks south of the Zócalo and the Alameda Central: Pino Suárez, Isabel la Católica, Salto del Agua, Balderas. The fare is astoundingly low—7¢—but you may not be able to go by Metro if you have luggage. Read carefully the Metro information in "Getting Around." If you decide to go by Metro with luggage, don't plan to take a Metro route that requires you to change trains at La Raza station (Lines 3 and 5 pass intersect here). The walk between lines is 10 to 15 minutes, and you'll be carrying your luggage.

BY TRAIN

If you must come or go by train, the Buenavista railroad station (☎ 5/547-1097 or 5/547-1084) is located three blocks north of the Revolución Metro station along Insurgentes. Though it is officially called the **Terminal de Ferrocarriles Nacionales de México,** you can get away with "Estación Buenavista." If you're arriving, walk out the right-hand set of front doors of the terminal and get your bearings on the front steps. You're facing south. The big boulevard on the right is Insurgentes, the city's main north-south axis. To the left of where you are standing, the spire of the Latin American Tower juts skyward from the intersection of Juárez and Lázaro Cárdenas. Taxis are always waiting at the train terminal.

BY BUS

Mexico City has a bus terminal for each of the four points of the compass: north, east, south, and west. You can't necessarily tell which terminal serves which area of the country by looking at a map, however. All stations have restaurants, book and magazine stands, money-exchange booths or banks, post offices, and long-distance telephone booths.

Note: Each station has a taxi system based on fixed-price tickets to various zones within the city, operated from a booth or kiosk in or near the entry foyer of the terminal. Locate your destination on a zone map or tell the seller where you want to go, buy a *boleto* (ticket), and most important, count your change—*more travelers are*

Greater Mexico City

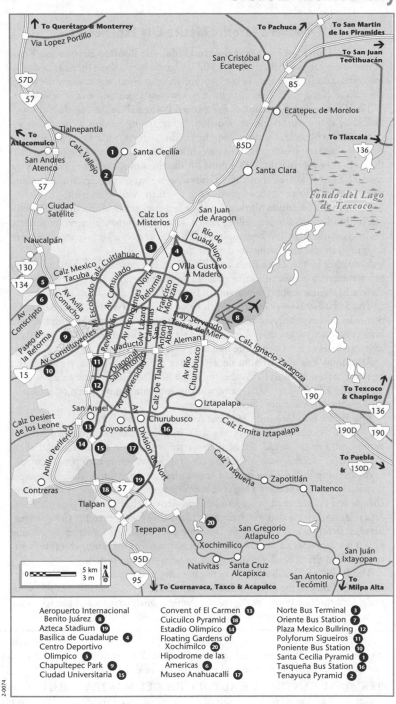

To Querétaro & Monterrey
Via Lopez Portillo

To Pachuca

To San Martin de las Piramides

To San Juan Teotihuacán

57D
57

To Atlacomulco

Tlalnepantla

Calz Vallejo

San Cristóbal Ecatepec

85

San Andres Atenco

① Santa Cecilía

②

Ecatepec de Morelos

To Tlaxcala
136

57

85D

Santa Clara

Ciudad Satélite

Calz Los Misterios

San Juan de Aragon

Fondo del Lago de Texcoco

Naucalpán

130

134

Calz Mexico Tacuba

③

Río de Guadalupe

④

⑤ Centro Deportivo

Av Avila Comacho

Villa Gustavo A Madero

⑥

Av Conscripto

Calz Cuitlahuac

Av Consulado

Av Insurgentes Norte

Francisco Monzán

⑦

Fray Servando Teresa de Mier

⑧

Paseo de la Reforma

⑨

Revolucion

Viaducto

Av Lazaro Cardenas

San Antonio Abad

Aleman

Calz Ignacio Zaragoza

Av Constituyentes

⑪

Diagonal San Antonio

Av Universidad

Av Rio Churubusco

To Texcoco & Chapingo

15

⑩

⑫

136

San Angel

Calz De Tlalpan

Iztapalapa

190

Calz Desiert de los Leone

⑬ Coyoacán

Churubusco

⑯

Calz Ermíta Iztapalapa

190D 190

Anillo Periferico

⑭

⑮

⑰

Av Division de Nort

To Puebla & 150D

Contreras

⑲

⑱ 57

Zapotitlán

Tlaltenco

Tlalpan

Calz Tasqueña

Tepepan

⑳

San Gregorio Atlapulco

San Juán Ixtayopan

95D

Xochimilco

Nativitas Santa Cruz Alcapixca

San Antonio Tecómitl

To Milpa Alta

0   5 km
     3 m

95

To Cuernavaca, Taxco & Acapulco

Aeropuerto Internacional Benito Juárez ⑧
Azteca Stadium ⑲
Basilica de Guadalupe ④
Centro Deportivo Olimpico ⑤
Chapultepec Park ⑨
Ciudad Universitaria ⑮

Convent of El Carmen ⑬
Cuicuilco Pyramid ⑱
Estadio Olimpico ⑭
Floating Gardens of Xochimilco ⑳
Hipodrome de las Americas ⑥
Museo Anahuacalli ⑰

Norte Bus Terminal ③
Oriente Bus Station ⑦
Plaza Mexico Bullring ⑫
Polyforum Sigueiros ⑪
Poniente Bus Station ⑩
Santa Cecilia Pyramid ①
Tasqueña Bus Station ⑯
Tenayuca Pyramid ②

2-0074

Frommer's Favorite Mexico City Experiences

Breakfast, Lunch, or Dinner at the Hotel Majestic Rooftop Restaurant. Enjoy at least one meal under one of the colorful umbrellas overlooking the historic downtown and Zócalo. If you arrive by 5:45pm, you can watch the military file out of the Palacio Nacional and perform the flag-lowering ceremony on the Zócalo.

The Ethnography Section of the Museo Nacional de Antropología. Overlooked by many visitors, the second-floor Ethnography Section is the perfect introduction to Mexican life away from the beaches, resorts, and cities. Fine, unusual weavings, pottery, handcrafts, furniture, huts, plows, and canoes are presented in the context of everyday life. It's a must for those about to visit the interior of the country, those who are curious about the villagers seen on the capital's streets, and those who expect their Mexico journeys to be off the well-worn path.

The Sunday Lagunilla Market. The best flea market in Mexico, this one spreads out for blocks with vendors selling santos, jewelry, antiques, pottery, miniatures, brass, glass, old locks and keys, a piece of Spanish armor, a 16th-century religious sculpture, an elkhorn earring, and much more.

Shopping in the Zona Rosa and Polanco. The dozens of fashionable shops lining the streets of these attractive areas sell designer clothing, jewelry, and antiques; there are lots of tempting restaurants in between.

The Saturday Bazaar in San Angel. Only on Saturdays (thus Bazar Sábado) is this colonial-era suburb of mansions near Parque San Jacinto invigorated with hundreds of artists, antiques dealers, street vendors, and sellers of popular art; the area restaurants consequently are mobbed.

Afternoon Tea at the Salón de Thé Duca d'Este. In Mexico, tea and coffee breaks are taken seriously. This cheerful Zona Rosa restaurant/pastry shop is great for sipping a frothy cappuccino and whiling away some time watching passersby through the huge windows facing the street.

The Ballet Folklórico de México. Among the best folkloric ballet groups in Mexico are those that perform in Mexico City either at the Teatro Bellas Artes or at the Teatro de la Ciudad. At the Bellas Artes you'll get to see the famed Tiffany glass curtain, which is usually (but not always) shown before each performance.

An Evening in the Zona Rosa. The popular Zona Rosa sidewalk cafés and pedestrian streets are ideal for a night of hopping from place to place, without cover charges and taxis, and all to see and be seen. Arrive before dusk to get a good seat for a relaxing drink and to watch the zone come alive for the evening. Copenhague, between Reforma and Hamburgo, is among the best streets for an entire evening or just for drinks. It's a narrow artery with awning-covered dining, bustling waiters, and food that's usually good enough to keep the places packed.

The Ruins of Teotihuacán. There's nothing to compare with walking down the wide Avenue of the Dead, with the Pyramid of the Moon at one end and pyramidal structures on both sides, imagining what it must have looked like when the walls were embellished with murals on brilliantly colored stucco.

shortchanged at this moment than at any other point! Present your ticket to the driver out front. For bus rider's terms and translations, see the Appendix.

TERMINAL CENTRAL DE AUTOBUSES DEL NORTE   Called by shorter names as "Camiones Norte," "Terminal Norte," "Central del Norte," or even just "C.N.," this is Mexico's largest bus station, on Avenida de los 100 ("Cien") Metros.

It handles most buses coming from the United States–Mexico border. All buses to/from the Pacific coast as far south as Puerto Vallarta and Manzanillo, and Acapulco (but most Acapulco buses use TAPO); several to and from Oaxaca (but most Oaxaca buses use the TAPO station); to/from the Gulf Coast as far south as Tampico and Veracruz; and to/from such cities as Guadalajara, San Luis Potosí, Durango, Zacatecas, Morelia, and Colima arrive and depart from here. There's also frequent first class service to Puebla. You can also get to the pyramids of San Juan Teotihuacán and Tula from here.

The Central del Norte is a mammoth place where you can change money (during normal banking hours), have a meal or a drink, take out insurance, or rent a car. You'll even find a post office and a long-distance phone installation.

To get downtown from the Terminal Norte, you have a choice: The Metro has a station (Estación Terminal de Autobuses del Norte, or T.A.N.) right here, so it's easy to hop a train and connect for all points. Walk to the center of the terminal, go out the front door, straight ahead, down the steps, and to the Metro station. This is Línea 5. Follow the signs that say DIRECCIÓN PANTITLÁN. For downtown, you can change trains at either La Raza or Consulado (see the Mexico City Metro map). Be aware that if you change at La Raza, you'll have to walk for 10 to 15 minutes and will encounter stairs. The walk is through a marble-lined underground corridor, but it's a long way with heavy luggage.

Another way to get downtown is by trolley bus. The stop is on Avenida de los Cien Metros, in front of the terminal. The trolley bus runs right down Avenida Lázaro Cárdenas, the "Eje Central" (Central Artery). Or try the Central Camionera del Norte–Villa Olímpica buses, which go down Avenida Insurgentes, past the university.

TERMINAL DE AUTOBUSES DE PASAJEROS DE ORIENTE (TAPO) The terminal is known by all as **TAPO.** Buses from the east (Puebla, Cholula, Amecameca, the Yucatán Peninsula, Veracruz, San Cristóbal de las Casas, and others) arrive here. Most buses originating in Oaxaca arrive here as well, since they pass through Puebla, which is east of Mexico City (see also Central de Autobuses del Norte above). Underneath the station's broad green dome are ticket counters, toilets, a post office, a cafeteria, bookstalls, and snack shops. Taxi tickets to anywhere in the city are sold inside on the main concourse near the exit doors; they are priced by zone. *Count your change!*

TERMINAL CENTRAL DE AUTOBUSES DEL SUR Mexico City's southern bus terminal is at Avenida Taxqueña 1320, right next to the Taxqueña Metro stop, the last stop on that line. The Central del Sur handles buses to/from Cuernavaca, Taxco, Acapulco, Zihuatanejo, and intermediate points. The easiest way to get to or from the Central del Sur is on the Metro. The station for the terminal is Taxqueña (or Tasqueña, as it's also spelled). Watch for the signs that say DIRECCIÓN PANTITLÁN to get downtown. Or take a trolley bus on Avenida Lázaro Cárdenas.

TERMINAL PONIENTE DE AUTOBUSES The western bus terminal is conveniently located right next to the Observatorio Metro station at Sur 122 and Río Tacubaya. This is the station you'll arrive at if you're coming from Acapulco, Cuernavaca, Ixtapa, Taxco, Zihuatanejo, Morelia, and Toluca.

BY CAR

If you are brave enough to drive in Mexico City here are a few tips. First, check whether your license tag number is permitted to drive in the city that day (see **Prohibited Driving Days** later in this chapter). Plan to arrive and depart before dawn,

Downtown Mexico City

Colegio Militar —

José Antonio Atzate

0 ——— 400 m / 437 y

N

Av Insurgentes Norte

Mosqueta

Normal

Av Ribera de San Cosme

San Cosme

Puente de Alvarado

Av Jesús

Zaragoza

COLONIA ANAHUAC

Av Marina Nacional

Bahía Ascensión

(Circuito Interior)

Manuel María Contreras

COLONIA SAN RAFAEL

Revolución

P Arriaga

COLONIA TABACALERA

A. Caso

Av Parque Vía

Serapio Rendón

Av Insurgentes Centro

J Sullivan

I Ramírez

Reforma Circle

Donato Guerr

Av Morelos

Villalongin

COLONIA CUAUHTEMOC

Calz Melchor Ocampo

Río Sena
Río Rhin
Río Amazonas
Río Neva
Río Marne
Río Tamesis
Río Tigris
Río Danubio
Río Po
Río Tiber
Río Boro
Río Guadalquivir
Río Niágara
Río Nilo
Río Lerma

Atenas
Gral Prim
Bucareli

Cuauhtémoc Circle

Lucerna

Versalles

Paseo de la Reforma

Cénova
Niza
Havre
Nápoles

Roma
Bruselas
Berlin
Dinamarca

Mississippi

COLONIA JUAREZ

ZONA ROSA

Cutzmala Fountain

Praga

Hamburgo

Florencia

Amberes

Av Chapultepec

Cuauhtémoc

Niños Heroes

Sevilla

Londres

Varsovia

Liverpool

Fonda El Refugio

Insurgentes

Durango

Niños Heroes

Salamanca

Monterrey

Av Insurgentes Sur

Córdoba

Av Sonora

Durango

Veracruz

COLONIA ROMA NORTE

Hospital General

Dr. Erazo

Alameda	10	Fonda Don Chon	28
Artes Populares	11	Hotel Fiesta Americana Reforma	4
Buenavista Railway Station	6	Hotel María Isabel Sheraton	1
Carretones Glass Factory	31	Lagunilla Market	20
Casa de Azulejos	14	Merced Convent	29
Catedral Metropolitana	23	Merced Market	30
Ciudadela Market	9	Museo Charrería	27
Fonart	8	Museo de la Ciudad	26

2-0020

when there is very little traffic. This way you can arrive at your destination without the added distraction of a zillion cars all coming at you from as many directions. Then park the car in a guarded lot and don't drive it again until you are ready to leave—at dawn. Driving in this city is best left to those who know it.

VISITOR INFORMATION

The most convenient **Infotur** office is in the Zona Rosa at Amberes 54, at the corner of Londres (☎ 5/525-9380; fax 5/525-9387). But it offers minimal information. Others are at the TAPO bus terminal and at the airport. They're open daily from 9am to 9pm.

The **Mexico City Chamber of Commerce** (☎ 5/592-2665) maintains an information office with a very friendly, helpful staff. And for 75¢ you can buy a detailed map of the city (or country). It's conveniently located at Reforma 42—look for the Cámara Nacional de Comercio de la Ciudad de México, open Monday through Thursday from 9am to 2pm and 3 to 6pm and Friday from 9am to 2pm and 3 to 5:30pm.

CITY LAYOUT

FINDING AN ADDRESS Despite its size, Mexico City is not outrageously hard to understand. The city is divided into 350 *colonias* (koh-lohn-ee ahs), or neighborhoods. If you are venturing out of the Colonia Centro (city center), you'll need to know colonia names. Besides Colonia Centro, a few to know are Colonia Juárez (better known as the Zona Rosa), and Colonia Polanco, a fashionable neighborhood immediately north of Chapultepec Park, and all the Lomas—Lomas de Chapultepec, Lomas Tecamachalco, etc.—which are very exclusive neighborhoods west of Chapultepec Park, the "in" addresses so to speak. The names of colonias are included in our Downtown Mexico City map. In addresses the word is abbreviated *Col.*; the full colonia name is vital in addressing correspondence and in directing taxi drivers.

Taxi drivers are notoriously ignorant of the city, including the major tourist sights and popular restaurants. Before getting in the taxi always give them, in addition to a street address and colonia, cross streets as a reference and locate your destination on a map that you carry with you.

A LANDMARK Probably the most frequently used and noticed landmark in Mexico City is the Monumento a la Independencia, often referred to as the Angel of Independence Monument, at the intersection of Reforma, Florencia, and Río Tiber. Set upon a tall marble shaft, the golden angel is an important and easily discerned guidepost for travelers. A creation of Antonio Rivas Mercado, the 22-foot-high gold-plated bronze angel—cast in Florence, Italy was completed in 1906 at a cost of $2.5 million. With its base of marble and Italian granite, the monument's total height is 150 feet.

STREET MAPS Should you want more detailed maps of Mexico City than the ones included in this guide, you can obtain them easily. A few bookstores carry a local map-guide entitled *Mexico City Trillas Tourist Guide,* a soft bound book of block-by-block pictorial maps covering most areas of the city that are of interest to visitors. The English text includes interesting facts and statistics on Mexico City and its sights.

More readily available are maps published by **Guía Roji** in both sheet and soft bound book form. Quite detailed, they are valuable if you plan to venture much out of the Centro Histórico or the Zona Rosa.

The **American Automobile Association** publishes a motorist's map of Mexico, which includes a map of downtown Mexico City. The map is available free to AAA members at any AAA office in the United States; it's not available in Mexico.

Neighborhoods in Brief

Centro Histórico   Centro Histórico refers to the heart of Mexico City, its business, banking, and historic center, including the areas in and around the Parque Alameda and Zócalo.

Chapultepec   A huge area west of the city center, it mainly includes Chapultepec Park—with its numerous museums—and its immediate environs.

Coyoacán   Thirteen miles from the city center, south of San Angel and east of the Ciudad Universitaria, Coyoacán is another colonial-era suburb noted for its beautiful town square, cobblestone streets lined with fine old mansions, and several of the city's most interesting museums.

Polanco   A district immediately north of Chapultepec Park, Polanco is the city's trendiest neighborhood. It's dotted with glitzy boutiques, luxury hotels, interesting antique shops, and some of the city's best restaurants. President Masaryk is the main artery running through it.

San Angel   Nine miles south of the city center, San Angel was once a distinct village but is now surrounded by the city. Yet the neighborhood remains a beautiful suburb of cobbled streets and beautiful colonial-era homes.

Xochimilco   Fifteen miles south of the town center, Xochimilco is noted for its famed canals and "floating gardens," which date from pre-Hispanic times.

Zona Rosa   West of the Centro Histórico, the "Pink Zone" is a trendy area noted for its pedestrian-only streets, shops, restaurants, and hotels.

2 Getting Around

Luckily for budget travelers, Mexico City has a highly developed and remarkably cheap public transportation system. The Metro, first- and second-class buses, and minibuses (colectivos will take you anywhere you want to go for very little money). The yellow or green VW taxis are also reasonable—providing traffic isn't heavy. When the roads are gridlocked, though, taxis merely inch along while the meter continues to run.

BY METRO   The subway system in Mexico City offers a smooth ride for one of the lowest fares anywhere in the world—7¢. Ten lines spider-web the sprawling city. Each train usually has nine cars, each seating 39 people. Another 50 or more can be accommodated standing.

As you enter the station, buy a ticket (*boleto*) at the glass ticket booth (*taquilla*). Insert your ticket into the slot at the turnstile and pass through; inside you'll see two large signs showing the line's destination (for example, for Line 1, it's "Observatorio" and "Pantitlán"). Follow the signs for the destination you want and *know where you're going*, since there is usually only one map of the routes, at the entrance to the station. There are, however, two signs you'll see everywhere: *salida*, which means "exit," and *andenes*, which means "platforms." Once inside the train, you'll see several linear maps of the station stops for that line, with symbols and names.

Transfer of lines is indicated by correspondencias. The ride is smooth, fast, and efficient (although hot and crowded during rush hours). The stations are clean and beautifully designed and have the added attraction of several archaeological ruins unearthed during construction. There is also a subterranean passage that goes between the Pino Suárez and Zócalo stations so you can avoid the crowds and the rain along Pino Suárez. The Zócalo station features dioramas and large photographs of the different periods in the history of the Valley of Mexico, and at Pino Suárez you'll see the foundation of an Aztec pyramid.

Important Notes: The Metro system runs workdays from 5am to 12:30am, Saturday from 6am to 1:30am and Sunday and holidays from 7am to 1:30am. Large baggage is not allowed into the system. In practice this means that bulky suitcases or backpacks sometimes make you *persona non grata* (but a large shoulder bag such as I use is not classed as luggage, nor is an attaché case or even a case that's slightly bigger). The reason is that on an average day Mexico City's Metro handles over 5 million riders and that leaves precious little room for bags. But, in effect, if no one stops you as you enter, you're in.

Metro travel is crowded during daylight hours on weekdays and consequently pretty hot and muggy in summer. In fact, you may find that between 4 and 7pm on weekdays the Metro is virtually unusable downtown because of sardine-can conditions. At some stations there are even separate lanes roped off for women and children because the press of the crowd is so great someone might get molested. Buses, colectivos, and taxis are all heavily used during these hours. You can possibly beat the mob scene by choosing one of the fore or aft cars—they seem to be less crowded. Or wait a few minutes for the next train.

Note on pickpockets: Metro pickpockets prey on the unwary (especially foreigners), so watch your belongings and carry valuables inside your clothing.

BY BUS   Moving millions of people through this sprawling urban mass is a gargantuan task, but the city officials do a pretty good job of it, though they tend to change bus numbers and routes frequently. Maps of the entire system are impossible to find.

The large buses that ran on the major tourist routes (Reforma and Insurgentes) tended to become suffocatingly overpacked and have been phased out in favor of small buses, and more of them. Thus, crowding is uncommon except perhaps during peak hours. The cost in pesos is usually the U.S. equivalent of around 7¢ to 20¢. Although the driver usually has change, try to have the exact fare when you board. Bus stops on the major tourist streets usually have a map with the full route description.

One of the most important bus routes is the one that runs between the Zócalo and the Auditorio (National Auditorium in Chapultepec Park) or the Observatorio Metro station. The route is via Avenida Madero or Cinco (5) de Mayo, Avenida Juárez, Paseo de la Reforma. Buses marked **"Zócalo"** run this route.

Another important route is **"Indios Verdes-Tlalpan,"** which runs along Avenida Insurgentes connecting the northern bus terminal (Terminal Norte), Buenavista railroad station, Reforma, the Zona Rosa, and—far to the south—San Angel and University City.

BY TAXI   Mexico City is pretty easy to negotiate by Metro and bus, and these methods bring you few hassles. Taxis are another matter, but there are times when nothing else will do. Cabs operate under several distinct sets of rules, established in early 1991, that *may* make using one less of a combat zone situation than in the past. Don't use a car that is not an official taxi. All official taxis, except the expensive "Turismo" cabs, are painted yellow or green, have white plastic roof signs bearing the word TAXI have TAXI or SITIO painted on the doors, and have meters. Look for all of these indications, not just one or two of them.

Metered Taxis Yellow or green Volkswagen Beetles (with white tops) and "sitio" (radio-operated) Datsun cabs are your best bet for good low-cost service. Though you will often encounter a gouging driver ("Ah, the meter just broke yesterday; I'll have it fixed tomorrow!"), or one who advances the meter (yes, I've seen it), or drives farther than necessary to run up the tab, most of the service will be quick and adequate. As of early 1991, these taxis began operating strictly by the meter. The meter should start at three pesos and advance by centavos, not by leaps of pesos. If the driver says his meter isn't working, find another taxi.

Important note: Don't get in a taxi that doesn't have the driver's taxi permit, with picture ID that looks like the driver, prominently displayed. It's a laminated license, about 5" x 7", and it's often above the rearview mirror or attached to a string near the glove box. It's illegal for a taxi to operate without the license in view. A taxi operating without it usually means the person driving the taxi is not a registered driver. These drivers are most often the ones who will try to cheat the passenger and you have no recourse if something goes wrong with the service. *There have also been reports of unauthorized drivers using authorized taxis to rob passengers.* So it's important to be aware of the driver's credentials before accepting a ride. This caution applies to street taxis, not the authorized ones that service airports and bus stations—these *should be* safe to use.

"Turismo" Taxis These cabs are unmarked, have special license plates, have bags covering their meters, are usually well-kept big cars, and are assigned to specific hotels. The drivers negotiate rates with individual passengers for sightseeing, but rates to and from the airport are established, although higher than the Datsun or VW taxis. Ask the bell captain what the airport rate should be and establish the rate before taking off. These drivers are often licensed English-speaking guides and can provide exceptional service.

There is no need to tip any taxi driver in Mexico, unless the driver has performed a special service, such as carrying your luggage inside a hotel.

BY COLECTIVO Also called *peseros,* these are sedans or minibuses, usually green and gray, that run along major arteries. They pick up and discharge passengers along the route, charge established fares, and provide more comfort and speed than the bus. Routes are displayed on cards in the windshield; often a Metro station will be the destination. One of the most useful routes for tourists runs from the **Zócalo** along **Avenida Juárez,** along **Reforma** to **Chapultepec,** and back again. Get a colectivo with a sign saying ZÓCALO, not VILLA. A "Villa" bus or pesero goes to the Basílica de Guadalupe.

Note that some of the minibuses on this route have automatic sliding doors—you don't have to shut them, a motor does.

As the driver approaches a stop, he may put his hand out the window and hold up one or more fingers. This is the number of passengers he's willing to take on (vacant seats are difficult to see if you're outside the car).

RENTAL CARS The least expensive rental car is the manual-shift Volkswagen Beetle, which is manufactured in Mexico. The price jump is considerable after the VW Beetle, and you pay more for automatic transmission and air-conditioning in any car. Hertz, Budget, National, and Avis car rentals, among others, are represented at the airport, and each has several city offices as well. Daily rates and deductibles vary considerably. (See also "Getting Around By Rental Car" in chapter 2.)

Pollution Control To control pollution in the capital, regulations for car use according to day of the week, tag number, and color are in force as shown here:

Prohibited Driving Days

	Mon.	Tues.	Wed.	Thurs.	Fri.
Tag color	Yellow	Pink	Red	Green	Blue
Tag ends in	5 or 6	7 or 8	3 or 4	1 or 2	9 or 0

This means that if your car tag is yellow and ends in a 5 or 6, you are prohibited from driving in Mexico City on Monday, but you can drive any other day of the week. Note that this applies to rental cars and to tourist cars (for foreign license plates, it's the last digit that counts), but it is not in effect on Saturday or Sunday. There's a stiff fine for violating this regulation.

FAST FACTS: Mexico City

In "Fast Facts: Mexico" in chapter 2 you'll find the answers to all sorts of questions about daily life in Mexico City. But here are a few essentials for getting along in this charming, enormous metropolis:

American Express   The Mexico City office is at Reforma 234 (☎ **5/207-7282** or 5/514-0629) in the Zona Rosa. It's open for banking, the pickup of American Express clients' mail, and travel advice Monday through Friday from 9am to 6pm and Saturday from 9am to 1pm.

Area Code   The telephone area code for Mexico City is 5.

Banks   Banks are usually open Monday through Friday from 9am to 5pm. Banamex is open Monday through Friday from 9am to 5:50pm. Bank branches at the airport are open whenever the airport is busy, including weekends. They usually offer ATM machines and very good rates of exchange.

Bookstores   In Mexico City, Sanborn's always has books in English, as well as magazines and newspapers. So does the American Bookstore, Madero 25 off Bolívar (☎ **5/512-7284**); it's open Monday through Saturday from 9:30am to 7pm.

French and English books and magazines, especially those dealing with Mexico and its history, archaeology, and people, are the specialty of Librería de Porrua Hermanos y Cia. One of its branches is located across from the Palacio de Bellas Artes at Juárez 16.

One of the most convenient foreign- and Spanish-language bookstore, in Mexico City, with a good selection of guidebooks and texts on Mexico, is Librería Gandhi (formerly Librería Mizrachi), Juárez 4, near Avenida Lázaro Cárdenas (☎ **5/ 510-4231**), right across from the Bellas Artes. Inside the Bellas Artes is an excellent bookstore with a wide assortment of titles in English and Spanish. Another nearby shop, the Librería Británica, Madero (☎ **5/521-0180**), also has a small coffee bar.

Currency Exchange   The alternative to a bank is a currency-exchange booth, or *casa de cambio*. These are often open Monday through Friday from 8:30am to 5:30pm, and some are open Saturday from 8:30am to 2:30pm as well; many stay open until 6pm. The exchange rates offered by casas de cambio are sometimes better—and sometimes worse—than those offered by banks. Usually, their rates are much better than the rates offered by most hotels.

Currency-exchange booths are found in parts of the city where foreigners circulate.

Drugstores   The drug departments at Sanborn's stay open late. Check the phone directory for the location nearest you. After hours, check with your hotel staff, who can usually contact the drugstore *de turno* (on call).

Elevation   Remember you are now at an elevation of 7,240 feet—almost a mile and a half in the sky—where there's a lot less oxygen in the air than you're used to. If you run for a bus and feel dizzy when you sit down, it's the elevation; if you think you're in shape but huff and puff getting up Chapultepec Hill, again it's the elevation. It takes about 10 days or so to adjust to the scarcity of oxygen. Go easy on food and alcohol the first few days in the city.

Emergencies   A government-operated service, **Locatel** (☎ 5/658-1111) is most often associated with finding missing persons anywhere in the country. With a good description of a car and its occupants, they'll search for motorists who have an emergency back home. **SECTUR** (Secretaria de Turismo) staffs telephones 24 hours daily (☎ 5/250-0123 or 5/250-0493) to help tourists in difficulty. Dialing 06 is similiar to dialing 911 in the United States, but the emergency number is only valid to subscribing users. Thus if the phone you are using isn't a subscriber, 06 gets you nowhere.

Hospitals   Catering to foreigners, the American-British Cowdray (A.B.C.) Hospital is located at Calle Sur. 132 no. 136, at the corner of Avenida Observatorio, Colonia Las Américas (Sur 132 is the name of the street) (☎ 5/272-8500, or for emergencies 5/515-8359 or 5/516-8077).

Hotlines   If you think you've been ripped off in a purchase, try calling the consumer protection office, the Procuraduría Nacional del Consumidor (☎ 5/761-3811 or 5/761-3801); phones may not be staffed. Perhaps a more helpful number is the 24-hour tourist assistance line (☎ 5/250-0123 or 5/20-0493).

Legal Assistance   If you need legal help, call SECTUR at ☎ 5/525-9380, 5/525-9381, or 5/525-9382.

Libraries   Mexico City has several libraries of English-language books connected with its diplomatic missions. Check out the Benjamin Franklin (American) Library, at Londres 16, just east of the George Washington statue (☎ 5/211-0042, ext. 3482 or 3483).

Luggage Storage/Lockers   There are *guarda equipaje* rooms at the airport and bus stations. Most hotels have a key-locked storage area for guests who want to leave possessions for a few days.

Newspapers/Magazines   *The Mexico City News* and *The Mexico City Times* are the country's only English-language daily newspapers. See also "Bookstores," above.

Pollution   September and October seem to be light months for pollution, while mid- to late November, as well as December and January, are months noted for heavy pollution. During January, schools are often closed because of it, and restrictions on driving usually imposed only on weekdays may be imposed on weekends during heavy pollution; be sure to check before driving into or around the city. (See "By Car" under "Getting Around" earlier in this chapter.) Be careful if you have respiratory problems; being at an elevation of 7,240 feet will make your problems even worse. Just before your planned visit, call the Mexican Government Tourist Office nearest you (see "Visitor Information, Entry Requirements & Money" in chapter 2 for the address) and ask for the latest information on pollution in the capital. Minimize your exposure to the fumes by refraining from walking busy streets during rush hour. Make Sunday, when many factories are closed and many cars escape the city, your prime sightseeing day.

Post Office The city's main post office, the Correos Mayor, is a block north of the Palacio de Bellas Artes on Avenida Lázaro Cárdenas, at the corner of Tacuba.

Although I don't recommend mailing a package in Mexico, since it may never get to its intended destination, if you must mail one in Mexico City, here's what to do: Take it to the post office called Correos Internacional no. 2, Calle Dr. Andrade and Río de la Loza (Metro: Balderas or Salto del Agua), open Monday through Friday from 8am to noon. Don't wrap up your package securely until an inspector examines it. (For a glossary of mail terms, see the Appendix.)

Alternatively, packages may be sent via the familiar UPS, Federal Express, MexPost, or DHL.

Safety Read the "Safety" section in chapter 2. Don't wear expensive jewelry or watches. Watch for pickpockets. Crowded subway cars and buses provide the perfect workplace for petty thieves, as do major museums (inside and out), thronged outdoor markets and bullfights, and indoor theaters. The "touch" can range from light-fingered wallet lifting or purse opening to a fairly rough shoving by two or three knife-wielding thieves. Sometimes the ploy is this: Someone drops a coin, and while everyone is looking, pushing, and shoving, your wallet disappears. Watch out for any place tourists go in numbers: on the Metro, in buses, in crowded hotel elevators, at the Ballet Folklórico, and at museums. Until the peso crisis, muggings were pretty infrequent in Mexico City. But people of all walks of life have become desperate, and some have resorted to theft. Robberies now happen in broad daylight on crowded streets in "good" parts of town. If you find yourself up against a handful of these guys, the best thing to do is give up the demanded possession, flee, and then notify the police. (You'll need the police report to file an insurance claim.) If you're in a crowded place, you could try raising a fuss—no matter whether you do it in Spanish or in English. Just a few shouts of "¡Ladrón!" ("Thief!") might put them off. But that could also be risky. Overall, it's wise to leave valuables in the hotel safe and to take only the cash you'll need for the day. Conceal a camera in a shoulder bag draped across your body and hanging in front of you—not on the side.

Taxes Mexico's 15% sales tax may be included in posted prices, or it may be added to a posted price. It's wise to ask "Más IVA?" (plus tax?) or "Con IVA?" (with tax?). There are also airport taxes for domestic and international flights. (See "Getting Around" in chapter 2.)

Telephones Generally speaking, Mexico City's telephone system is in terrible shape. A number you reached five seconds ago may not be reachable again for days. As elsewhere in the country, the telephone company changes numbers without informing the telephone owners or the information operators. Telephone numbers are registered in the name of the corporation, which may be different from the name of a hotel or restaurant owned by the corporation. A telephone number is accessed by the operator under the corporate name unless the corporation pays for separate listing. Changes of telephone numbers are ongoing in the capital—numbers that were correct at the time this edition was updated may have changed by the time you visit. So you never know if the number you have is an operating one or not. The local number for information is 04, and you are allowed to request three numbers with each information call. However, reaching the information operator can be difficult, so make every call count.

Capable of holding up to $70 in coins, coin-operated phones are prone to vandalism and are being replaced by card-only Ladatel phones. Ladatel cards are usually available for purchase at pharmacies and newsstands near public phones. They come in denominations of 10, 30, 50, and 100 New Pesos. If you expect to do much calling, buy at least a 30-peso card—the 10-peso card goes fast. Long-distance calls within Mexico and to foreign points are astoundingly expensive. Consult "Telephones & Mail" in the Appendix for how to use phones. Hotels are beginning to charge for local calls, but budget-priced hotels are less likely to do this because they lack the equipment to track calls from individual rooms.

Weather/Clothing   Mexico City's high elevation means you'll need a warm jacket and sweater in winter. The southern parts of the city, such as the university area and Xochimilco, are much colder than the central part of the city. In summer, it gets warm during the day and cool, but not cold, at night. The rainy season runs between May and October (this is common all over Mexico)—take a raincoat or rain poncho. The showers may last all day or for only an hour or two.

For dining in better restaurants or an unexpected invitation to a private home, men may want to bring along something of the jacket-and-tie class, and women might pack a nice dress or suit; Mexico City is rather formal.

3 Moving On—Travel Services

BY PLANE   For local information on flights, times, and prices, contact the airlines directly. Although airline numbers seem to change every year, the following numbers may be useful: **Aero California** (☎ **5/207-1392** for reservations or flight information), **Aeroméxico** (☎ **5/228-9910** for reservations, or 5/762-4000 for flight information), **American** (☎ **5/237-1400** for reservations, or 5/571-3219 at the airport), **Aviacsa** (☎ **5/559-1955** for reservations, or 5/369-0810 at the airport), **Continental** (☎ **5/280-3434** for reservations, or 5/571-3661 for flight information), **Delta** (☎ **5/207-3411** for reservations, or 5/785-1700 at the airport), **Mexicana** (☎ **5/325-0990** for reservations or flight information), **Saro** (☎ **5/273-1766** for reservations, or 5/726-0156 at the airport), **Taesa** (☎ **5/227-0700** for reservations or flight information), and **United** (☎ **5/208-8816** for reservations, or 5/784-4814 at the airport).

For information on reconfirmation of flights, see chapter 2. *Note:* Telephoning an airline in Mexico City can be frustrating because the city's telephone system is old, and in certain sections of the city it's downright nonfunctional. Besides, the airlines often don't have enough telephone lines to handle calls—keep trying. Also check the latest telephone directories for new or additional numbers.

Be sure to allow at least 45 minutes' travel time from either the Zona Rosa or the Zócalo area to the airport. Check in at least 90 minutes before international flights and 60 minutes before domestic flights.

BY TRAIN   From Mexico City's **Buenavista Station,** it's possible to journey by rail to just about any region in the country. It's the hub of a number of trains heading for the far corners of the country. (For details on these trains, how to make reservations, and where to get information and timetables, see chapter 2.) Train travel in Mexico, however, is very slow, and passenger service has deteriorated severely in the past several years. Buses are faster and more comfortable. To get a timetable, go to the administrative offices of the train station—not the information desk. The following is a glimpse of regions covered by rail from Mexico City:

• The *Constitucionalista* links Mexico City with popular colonial cities a short distance north of the capital including Querétaro and Guanajuato.
• The *Regiomontaño* runs between Mexico City, San Luis Potosí, Saltillo, and Monterrey.
• *El Oaxaqueño* goes to Puebla, Tehuacán, and Oaxaca.

- *El Jarocho* goes to Veracruz, Fortín de las Flores, Orizaba, and Córdoba.
- *El Purépecha* goes to Morelia, Pátzcuaro, and Uruapan.

Guadalajara is another hub—see chapter 10 for details on train travel along the west coast. If you plan to get on and off the train en route, you must tell the agent your exact on/off schedule at the time of your ticket purchase. Make your reservation early.

BY BUS   Getting from Juárez International Airport to Cuernavaca, Toluca, Puebla, and Querétaro/Celaya/Guanajuato   If your destination is **Cuernavaca**, **Suburban** (☎ **73/22-0445** or 73/22-0456 in Cuernavaca; **5/549-3506** in Mexico City) will take up to seven passengers in a (guess what) Suburban. They leave about every two hours between 6:15am and 9:15pm daily; the cost is $13 per person. It's affiliated with the Pullman de Morelos busline. The Suburban ticket kiosk is near Gate A. These supposedly take you directly to your hotel in Cuernavaca—but verify that. You can make reservations, but if the Mexico City number doesn't work, calling Cuernavaca is your only other choice. **Pullman de Morelos** also runs almost hourly buses from the airport to Cuernavaca between 9am and 10pm for $3.25. Pay aboard.

Estrella Roja buses depart for **Puebla** from the airport hourly beginning at 6 or 7:30am. Some of these go to a bus stop on the western edge of the Puebla at 4 Poniente and 21 Norte, and others go directly to Puebla's main bus terminal CAPU. **Estrella Roja/Flecha Amarillo** buses also go to **Toluca** and **Querétaro;** their schedule is similar to buses bound for Puebla. Buses for all these lines are found in front of the covered concourse outside the terminal between exit doors for Gates C and D. If you have trouble locating any of these, ask for help at one of the **information desks** on the airport's main concourse. Most important, since this airport bus transportation service is new and could change and/or if precise scheduling is essential to your trip, you could verify information by calling the **Airport Information Office** (☎ **5/728-4811** or 5/571-3600) to verify names of buses, the place to find them, and the current schedule.

Terminal Central de Autobuses del Norte   This is the city's largest terminal and covers the most destinations. It's the one to use if you're going to nearby Pachuca; the ruins of Teotihuacán; or north to San Miguel de Allende, Querétaro, Morelia, and Guanajuato.

Terminal de Autobuses de Pasajeros de Oriente (TAPO)   This is the place to go if you are looking for a bus to Oaxaca, Puebla, Tlaxcala, Pachuca, Amecameca, Jalapa, Yucatán, or Guatemala. You'll find ticket counters, restrooms, a post office, a cafeteria, bookstalls, and snack shops within. Companies that sell tickets here include Autobuses Unidos (AU), Autobuses de Oriente, ADO, ADO GL, Lilnea Uno, Pullman Plus, Estrella Roja, ATAH, and Cristóbal Colón. AU and ATAH buses have the most frequent departures for Huamantla, Tlaxcala, Tehuacán, Veracruz, Cuetzálan, and Jalapa. Deluxe Pullman Plus buses are the most comfortable for a trip to Puebla and Tlaxcala with departures every 15 minutes or so. ADO has "GL" (luxury) service to Oaxaca (six times daily), Jalapa, Puebla, and Veracruz. You can reserve a seat on GL buses from anywhere in the country using the toll free number (☎ **91-800/ 7-0362**) and your credit card. Linea Uno offers luxury service to Oaxaca (five times daily) Jalapa (four times daily), and Veracruz (six times daily). To get to TAPO, take a "Hipodromo-Pantitlán" bus east along Alvarado, Hidalgo, or Donceles; if you take the Metro, get off at the San Lázaro station on the eastern portion of Line 1 (between Candelaria and Moctezuma stations). See also "Arriving by Plane" for information on buses to Puebla directly from the airport.

Terminal de Autobuses del Sur   This terminal is fairly easy to figure out. If you're going to Cuernavaca, head straight for the ticket counters of Autobuses Pullman de Morelos, as its buses depart every 10 or 15 minutes throughout the day for that destination; there's hardly ever a problem getting a seat. If, however, you're headed for Acapulco or Zihuatanejo, go to the first-class line named Estrella de Oro; at its ticket counter, you can choose your bus seat on a computer screen. The best service to Taxco is on Estrella Blanca/Flecha Roja. Second-class lines will save you a minuscule sum of money over first-class lines, so I recommend going first class. See also "Arriving by Plane" for information on buses to Cuernavaca directly from the airport.

Terminal Poniente de Autobuses   The smallest of the terminals is the Terminal Poniente (also known as the Observatorio station), and its main reason for being is to serve the route between Mexico City and Toluca. But other cities to the west and northwest are served also, including Ixtapan de la Sal, Valle de Bravo, Morelia, Uruapan, and Guadalajara. In general, if your chosen destination is also served from the Terminal Norte, you'd be better off going there. The Terminal Norte simply has more buses and better bus lines. Metro Observatorio is next to the bus station.

BY CAR   Insurgentes Sur becomes Highway 95 to Taxco and Cuernavaca. Insurgentes Norte leads to Teotihuacán and Pachuca. Highway 57, the Periférico (loop around the city), is called Camacho as it goes north and leads out of the city north to Tula and Querétaro. Constituyentes leads west out of the city past Chapultepec Park and connects with Highway 15 to Toluca, Morelia, and Pátzcuaro. Zaragoza leads east to Highway 150 to Puebla and Veracruz.

4 Where to Stay

It costs less to stay in Mexico City than it does in most European capitals or almost any U.S. city of any size. The city is a bargain when you consider that for $15 to $33 you can find a double room in a fairly central hotel complete with a bath and often such extras as air-conditioning and TV. Many hotels have their own garages where guests can park free. Most new construction in the last decade has been luxurious hotels with central air-conditioning, elevators, restaurants, and the like; these are usually at the top of our budget and beyond. Cheaper hotels tend to be the older ones, well kept and with a restaurant, but without all the extras that inflate prices.

My recommendations for lodging and dining in Mexico City are grouped around the city's major landmarks, places that are easily found and explored by first-time visitors.

The **Zona Rosa** was once Mexico City's status address. Though that honor has recently been usurped by Polanco, it's still a popular tourist hub. Many chic boutiques, fancy restaurants and cafés, and expensive hotels are here. My hotel choices, in and near the Zona Rosa, are thus at the top of our daily budget. **Sullivan Park** (Jardín del Arte) is a wedge-shaped park extending west from the intersection of Paseo de la Reforma and Avenida Insurgentes. It has a good range of hotels, old and new, colonial and modern, flashy and humble. Many are on quiet streets, some have views of the park, and all are close to the Zona Rosa and to transportation.

The **Monumento a la Revolución** is in the large Plaza de la República, at the very western end of Avenida Juárez. Here you're centrally located, about equidistant from the Zona Rosa and the Zócalo, close to the Alameda and major transportation routes, but most of the hotel streets are quiet. The **Alameda Central,** next to the Palacio de Bellas Artes, is closer to the downtown shopping district, a bit farther from the Zona Rosa. Transportation is still good. Most of the hotels are well-used structures (although many have been remodeled) on streets to the south of the Alameda. The **Zócalo** is the heart of the historic Mexico City, surrounded by colonial buildings and Aztec ruins. It's also the heart of the downtown shopping district, with interesting small stores to the west and the gigantic Mercado Merced to the east. Excellent, reasonably priced hotels and restaurants are found here.

AROUND THE ZONA ROSA

Casa González. Río Sena 69, 06500 Mexico, D.F. ☎ **5/514-3302.** 21 rms, 1 suite (all with bath). $20–$22 single; $23–$27 double; $40 suite for four. Metro: Insurgentes (four blocks away).

Casa González is a two-story hostelry made up of two mansions that have been converted to guest rooms, each heated for those chilly mornings. With little grassy patios out back and a huge shade tree, the houses make a pleasant and quiet oasis in the middle of the city. Meals (optional) are taken in a dining room bright with stained glass and international conversation. Casa González is especially good for women traveling alone, although there are only three single rooms. There's limited parking in the driveway. The hotel is between Río Lerma and Río Panuco.

Hotel María Cristina. Río Lerma 31, 06500 Mexico, D.F. ☎ **5/566-9688.** Fax 5/566-9194. 150 rms (all with bath). TV TEL. $34 single; $37.75 double. Free parking.

The colonial-style María Cristina, in a quiet residential section, is within three blocks of Sullivan Park and five blocks from the heart of the Zona Rosa. It's popular with out-of-towners because of its price (although a bit high for what you get) and location. Unfortunately the reception desk staff's attitude still fluctuates between surly and indifferent. The lobby shows rich use of blue-and-white tiles, red velvet, dark wood, and wrought iron. A lounge off the lobby has a big fireplace; beside the hotel is a shady lawn. The hotel is at Río Guadiana between Río Amazonas and Río Neva.

NEAR SULLIVAN PARK

Ⓢ **Hotel Astor.** Antonio Caso 83, 06470 Mexico, D.F. ☎ **5/546-2611** or 5/546-2645. Fax 5/535-7420. 200 rms (all with bath). TV TEL. $23 single or double; $41 with jacuzzi. Free parking. Metro: San Cosme (five blocks away).

The Astor still has the smell of newness, and at a very good price. Carpeted and well-lit halls lead to ample rooms containing king-size beds. Bathrooms are large with marble basins and floors, plus bath mats and absorbent towels. Five rooms have whirlpool baths. A dining room is across from the lobby. The hotel is on the north side of Antonio Caso at the corner of Serapio Rendón, one block from the Sullivan Park.

Hotel Compostela. Sullivan 35, 06470 Mexico, D. F. ☎ and fax **5/566-0733.** 79 rms. TV TEL. $17 single; $19 double.

Tucked in a quiet corner opposite Sullivan Park, this older five-story (with elevator) hotel, is a little off the main tourist track, but worth considering. Each clean and freshly painted room is furnished with Formica furniture, matching bedspreads and drapes, and good overbed lights. Halls are brightly lighted. Rooms facing inside (with an airshaft window) may be quieter but more stuffy than those with windows on Sullivan or Rendón. While its shiny marble lobby and the rest of the hotel are well maintained, it's not in the heart of the tourist zone—so it's worth it to ask for a discount. It's at the corner of Sullivan and Rendón.

Ⓢ **Hotel Mallorca.** Serapio Rendón 119, 06470 Mexico, D.F. ☎ **5/566-4833.** Fax 5/566-1789. 140 rms. TV TEL. $17.50 single; $19.75–$21 double. Free parking.

Almost catercorner from the Hotel Compostela (above) and opposite the eastern end of the Jardín del Arte, the five-story (with elevator) Mallorca is an excellent budget choice. Rooms are freshly painted, and bedspreads coordinate with the drapes. Single rooms with a twin or double bed are small, however. Going from the Jardín, the hotel is between Sullivan and A. Caso, on the left side of the street.

Hotel Sevilla. Serapio Rendón 126, 06470 Mexico, D.F. ☎ **and fax 5/566-1866.** 225 rms (all with bath). TV TEL. $20 single; $25.50 double. Free parking. Metro: San Cosme or Insurgentes.

The nine-story (with elevator) Hotel Sevilla has clean, carpeted rooms, each with a tiled bath, radio, desk and chairs, and purified water. The hotel's restaurant/bar provides room service. The hotel is at the corner of Rendón and Sullivan, across from the Hotel Compostela.

NEAR THE MONUMENTO A LA REVOLUCIÓN
DOUBLES FOR LESS THAN $20

Ⓢ **Gran Hotel Texas.** Ignacio Mariscal 129, 06030 Mexico, D.F. ☎ **and fax 5/705-5782** or 5/705-6496. 52 rms (all with bath). TV TEL. $14.75 single; $16.50–$18 double. Free parking. Metro: Revolución (1 block away).

At the low end of the price scale, this modest five-story hotel gets high marks for effort. It's consistently clean, friendly, and low priced. Don't look for anything fancy here; rather, notice the smiles that greet you and the tidiness of the premises. Free local calls are a plus. The street is relatively quiet, and the location quite convenient. The hotel is between Arriaga and Iglesias.

Ⓢ **Hotel Edison.** Edison 106, 06030 Mexico, D.F. ☎ **5/566-0933.** 45 rms (all with bath). TV TEL. $14.75 single; $16.50–$19.75 double. Free parking. Metro: Revolución (two blocks away).

The Hotel Edison, a block north of the Monumento a la Revolución, is a real find. Its odd three-story construction around a narrow court with grass and trees gives a sense of sanctuary from the city's noise and bustle. Some rooms are built in tiers overlooking the court, and even larger ones are hidden away down hallways. These latter rooms tend to be dark but big and comfortable with king-size beds. Blond wood and light colors, piped-in music, and sunlight make this a cheerful place. All rooms include baths with separate washbasin areas, and some have bidets, plus tub/shower combinations. The hotel is at the corner of Iglesias.

Hotel New York. Edison 45, 06030 Mexico, D.F. ☎ **and fax 5/566-9700.** 45 rms (all with bath). TV TEL. $14.75 single; $16.50–$21.50 double. Free parking. Metro: Revolución (five blocks away).

The New York, two short blocks from the jai alai fronton, is a large four-story building (with elevator) that's a cubist's dream of mosaic tile, grass-green paneling, and glass. The carpeted rooms have Formica-topped furniture, wood paneling on one wall, and hanging glass lamps. The hotel's small restaurant is open daily from 7am to 10pm. The hotel is on the north side of the street between Emparan and Baranda.

DOUBLES FOR LESS THAN $30

Hotel Mayaland. Antonio Caso 23, 06030 Mexico, D.F. ☎ **5/566-6066.** Fax 5/535-1273. 91 rms (all with bath). TV TEL. $22.25 single; $24.75–$26.25 double. Metro: Juárez (5¹/₂ blocks away).

This conveniently located six-story hotel features coordinated drapes and spreads in its pleasant rooms. Baths have an additional faucet for purified water. You can't miss the Maya mural on one lobby wall, and another stained-glass wall separates the lobby from the hotel's small restaurant. The hotel is between Ramírez and Vallarta, a block and a half west of Reforma.

Hotel Palace. Ignacio Ramírez 7, 06030 Mexico, D.F. ☎ **5/566-2400.** Fax 5/535-7520. 200 rms (all with bath). TV TEL. $22.75–$24.75 single; $26.50–$34 double. Free parking. Metro: Revolución (five blocks away).

One of Mexico's outstanding luxury hotels a few decades ago, today the nine-story Palace retains its comfort, experienced staff, and well-kept rooms. The bustle of a large hotel surrounds you here, with a tobacco kiosk and travel desk in the lobby, bag-bearing bellboys scurrying here and there, and the occasional busload of tourists. The hotel is 1½ blocks south of Plaza de la República.

☼ Hotel Regente. Paris 9, 06030 Mexico, D.F. ☎ **5/566-8933.** Fax 5/592-5794. 138 rms (all with bath). TV TEL. $28.50–$35.75 single or double. Free parking. Metro: Revolución (six blocks away).

This remodeled hotel is within walking distance of Sullivan Park, the Alameda, and the Zona Rosa. Once a frumpy hotel with mismatched furnishings and a horrible phone system, today it's state-of-the-art. Rooms have matching bedspreads and drapes; carpeted floors themed around pastel green, orange, and blue; overbed reading lights; full-length mirrors; and new tile baths. The hotel's excellent Restaurant Corinto, open daily from 7am to 11pm, is off the small lobby. The hotel is between Madrid and Insurgentes Centro, four blocks southwest of the Monumento a la Revolución.

NEAR THE ALAMEDA CENTRAL

Hotel Capitol. Uruguay 12, 06000 Mexico D.F. ☎ **5/518-1750.** Fax 5/521-1149. 75 rms, 3 suites (all with bath). TV TEL. $19.75 single; $24.75 double; $29.50 suite. Metro: Bellas Artes or Salto de Agua (five blocks away).

The four-story Capitol opened in late 1989. Rooms open to the lobby atrium, and there's a restaurant in back. You'll find such extras as carpeting and reading lights. Each double room is furnished with either a king-size bed or two doubles. Rooms and baths are large, except for the three "suites," which are tiny but have enormous whirlpool tubs big enough for two. Unfortunately, towels are flimsy. Rooms along the front have small balconies opening to Uruguay, while others have interior windows opening to the lobby atrium. It's within walking distance of the Alameda, Bellas Artes, and historic Zócalo. The hotel is between Cárdenas and Bolívar.

⑤ Hotel El Salvador. República del Salvador 16, 06080 Mexico, D.F. ☎ **and fax 5/521-1008** or 5/521-2160. 94 rms (all with bath). TV TEL. $19.75 single; $24.75 double. Free parking. Metro: Salto de Agua (six blocks away).

The five-story El Salvador, half a block east of Lázaro Cárdenas, completed a total remodeling in 1994. The impressive new lobby, aswirl in beige marble, is up a wide staircase from the sidewalk. Rooms have natural-colored pine furniture, fresh stucco and paint, carpeting, over-bed reading lights, and coordinated pastel drapes and spreads. Baths are small, but there's plenty of room for luggage storage, either in the closets or on built-in benches. Halls are narrow and dark, with only a few lights visible during the day. A small restaurant is adjacent. It's a very nice, quiet, and convenient place to stay at budget prices. The hotel is between Cárdenas and Bolívar on the north side of the street.

☼ Hotel Fleming. Revillagigedo 35, 06050 Mexico, D.F. ☎ **5/510-4530.** 75 rms (all with bath). TV TEL. $22.75 single; $28.50 double; $37.75 room with whirlpool tub. Free parking. Metro: Juárez.

In 1992, the mismatched ancient furnishings gave way to soft cool colors, coordinated carpeting and textiles, mirrored closet doors, and updated baths with lots of towels—even some with whirlpool tubs. Each room comes with either one king-size bed, two doubles, or two twin-size beds. The hotel's clean, dependable restaurant is off the lobby. It's excellently located near the Alameda and within walking distance of the Zócalo. The hotel is between Articulo 123 and Victoria.

✪ **Hotel Metropol.** Luís Moya 39, 06050 Mexico, D.F. ☎ **5/521-4901** or 5/510-8660. Fax 5/512-1273. 165 rms (all with bath). TV TEL. $34 single; $37.75 double. Free parking. Metro: Juárez (two blocks away).

After a total facelift, each room at the Metropol is beautifully furnished and carpeted, with a safety deposit box, a color TV receiving U.S. channels, and purified water from a special tap. If the essence of luxury is what you want at relatively low prices, this is the place. A small restaurant and video bar enhance the feeling. The location is choice—within walking distance of both the Zócalo and the Alameda. The hotel is between Articulo 123 and Independencia.

NEAR THE ZÓCALO

⑤ **Hotel Canada.** Av. 5 de Mayo No. 47, 06000 Mexico, D.F. ☎ **5/518-2106.** Fax 5/512-9310. 85 rms, (all with bath). TV TEL. $18 single; $23 double. Metro: Zócalo (1½ blocks away).

The Hotel Canada, opened in 1984, has an up-to-date decor, Formica furnishings, double or king beds, and showers. It's comfortable and so different from many of the downtown hotels, which tend to be older and somewhat worn. Hallways are brightly lit, and each room has a safe-box. The hotel is on the south side of the street between Isabel la Católica and Palma.

Hotel Catedral. Calle Donceles 95, 06020 Mexico, D.F. ☎ **5/518-5232.** Fax 5/512-4344. 116 rms (all with bath). TV TEL. $23 single; $28 double. Free parking. Metro: Zócalo.

One block north of Tacuba is Calle Donceles, a street noted for its bookstores, stationery stores, and gunsmith shops. Here, set back from the street by a shopping arcade, is the eight-story (with elevator) Hotel Catedral, half a block from the Templo Mayor and very popular with Mexico's middle class. In front of the big, cool lobby is the restaurant/bar, bustling with white-jacketed waiters. Rooms are well kept, and some have tub/shower combinations. Ice is available on each floor. Bonuses are a bar, good housekeeping standards, and rooms on the upper floors with views of Mexico City's mammoth cathedral. The hotel is between Brasil and Argentina.

✪ **Hotel Gillow.** Isabel la Católica 17, 06000. Mexico, D.F. ☎ **5/518-1440.** Fax 5/512-2078. 110 rms (all with bath). TV TEL. $21.50 single; $24 double. Metro: Zócalo.

Personal friends and many readers give this hotel high praise, as do I. The dignified looking, seven-story Gillow is a modern hotel with six stories of rooms grouped around a long glass-canopied rectangular courtyard with a colonial fountain. Were it in the Zona Rosa, the Gillow would easily cost three times the price. Clean, well-kept, newly carpeted rooms with comfortable beds, a tub/shower combination, excellent lighting, and remote control TV are among the best features in each room. Some rooms are small, with one double bed and enough room for one person's luggage. Others are quite spacious with a long carpeted bench for suitcases. Interior windows open to an airshaft. Ice machines are on several floors. An excellent restaurant on the first floor offers long hours, good food, friendly service, and an excellent comida corrida. The hotel is on the west side of the street between 5 de Mayo and Madero. It's hard to beat the location.

Hotel Isabel. Isabel La Católica 63, 06000 Mexico, D.F. ☎ **5/518-1213.** 72 rms, (64 with bath). TV TEL. $12.50 single; $14.75 double. Metro: Isabel la Católica (five blocks away).

The five-story Isabel (with elevator) is an older place with a mix of Mexican and foreign clientele. In the lobby, a somber painting of Queen Isabel gazes out over the vast lobby. The rooms are old-fashioned and spacious, with dark wood or painted furniture and carpeting. Larger rooms have tubs as well as showers, little tiled entrance halls, and frosted-glass doors opening onto wrought-iron balconies. There's a good restaurant and bar. You can wangle yourself a reduction if the place is not full.

The hotel is between Uruguay and República del Salvador on the west side of the street.

Hotel Montecarlo. Uruguay 69, 06000. Mexico, D.F. ☎ **5/518-1418** or 5/521-2559. Fax 5/510-0081. 60 rms (45 with bath). TEL. $10–$13 single; $13–$16.50 double. Free parking. Metro: Zócalo or Isabel la Católica.

This building, erected about 1772 as an Augustinian monastery, later became the residence of D.H. Lawrence for a time. The large assortment of rooms at the Montecarlo come in various sizes, some with modern baths, others with baths lacking toilet seats. Rooms in the original monastery section, plus the added third story, tend to carry lobby and hallway noise; rooms in the newer section in back are quieter. Note that some rooms have windows looking onto hallways and courtyards, not the outside. Lower-priced rooms don't have private bathrooms. The Montecarlo is often full, so it's best to call ahead to see about availability. One caveat: I've had the same problem readers have also complained about: They take a reservation, but lose it or rent the room they promised before you get there—even as you travel across town! Parking for six or seven cars is reached by driving through the lobby. The hotel is between 5 de Febrero and Isabel la Católica, next to the Biblioteca Nacional.

NEAR THE AIRPORT

Hotel Aeropuerto. Bulevar Aeropuerto 380, 15530 Mexico, D.F. ☎ **5/785-6928.** Fax 5/784-1329. 52 rms (all with bath). A/C TV TEL. $24.75 single; $29.50 double. Free parking; guarded. Metro: Terminal.

Don't let the glassed-in front desk intimidate you: The Hotel Aeropuerto is actually an excellent choice just across from the airport, next to the more visible and much more expensive JM Hotel Aeropuerto. The brown-on-brown decor, with nice natural pine accents, is comfortable if not particularly cheerful. Rooms are clean, with new mattresses, large baths, and powerful showers. However, you'll have to make peace with the sound of jets roaring overhead. The reasonably priced coffee shop serves very good coffee. Taxis are easy to flag down in front of the hotel. It's possible to walk to the terminal, though you must climb the steep stairway to the overpass over the main road into the airport—a difficult feat with luggage.

Hotel Riazor. Viaducto Miguel Alemán 297, 08310 Mexico, D.F. ☎ **5/726-9998.** Fax 5/654-3840. 175 rms (all with bath). TV TEL. $28 single; $34.50 double. Transportation: Take a taxi from the airport.

The six-story Riazor is only a short cab ride from the airport. You can take shelter in any one of the modern, comfy rooms, each complete with king-size bed, shower, and perhaps even a view of the city. There are a pool, restaurant, and bar. The hotel fills up by nightfall, but if you arrive early there's a good chance to get a room.

5 Where to Eat

Everybody eats out in Mexico City—from the wealthy executive to the peasant. Consequently, you can find restaurants of every type, size, and price range scattered across the city. In this section I have tried to give you a list of some of the tried-and-true establishments. I have sifted through myriad restaurants and listed those that give the best food for the best price in budget, medium-price, splurge, and specialty categories.

If you get one of those unfortunate cravings for home perhaps McDonald's, Sub-way, Burger King, Pizza Hut, VIP's, Denny's, or Lyni's can satisfy—you'll see them all over town. The latter three—which have branches all over the city—have familiar fare at reasonable prices.

In the more expensive restaurants, particularly in the Zona Rosa, you'll be able to pay with a major credit card.

IN & AROUND THE ZONA ROSA
MEALS FOR LESS THAN $5

Kobá-ich. Londres 136-A. ☎ **5/208-5791.** Breakfast $1.25–$2.50; main course $2–$4.50; daily special $2.75–$3.25. Mon–Sat 8am–10pm. Metro: Insurgentes. YUCATECAN.

Two narrow steps lead down into this small Yucatecan experience. With your first taste of chamorro (pork in a heavenly sauce), you feel yourself beamed directly to Mérida or Valladolid. Other specialties include sopa (seca) de arroz con platano (rice with banana), poc-chuc, and papadzules. A menu card with color photos of unfamiliar dishes can help you decide on your order. All this is yours between Reforma and Hamburgo.

Restaurante Vegetariano Yug. Varsovia 3 Reforma. ☎ **5/533-3296.** Breakfast 50¢–75¢; main courses $1.75–$4; buffet lunch or dinner $4.25. Mon–Fri 7am–11:30pm, Sat 8:30am–8pm, Sun 1–8:30pm (buffet served Sun–Fri 1–5pm). Metro: Sevilla (six blocks away). VEGETARIAN.

This upbeat modern place offers several fixed-price breakfasts, a dozen fantastic salads (the "Africa" features spinach and nuts), plus crêpes, spinach lasagna, and soya "meat" Mexican style. Portions are huge, and prices are low. It's on the west side of the street between Reforma and Hamburgo.

Ⓢ Restaurant Marianne. Río Rhin 63. ☎ **5/207-8831.** Breakfast $1.25–$3; comida corrida $2–$3.75; pastries $1.75; cappuccino $1.25. Mon–Fri 8am–7pm. Metro: Insurgentes. CONTINENTAL.

Tucked away one block from the British Embassy is the little Restaurant Marianne, where the atmosphere is that of a European coffeehouse, and the specialties are pastries and cappuccino and an excellent three-course lunch. No children under 12 are accepted. The restaurant is two blocks north of Reforma between Río Lerma and Río Panuco.

Ⓢ Restaurant Taquería Beatriz. Londres 179, Florencia. ☎ **5/525-5857.** Tacos 75¢; soup $1–$2. Mon–Thurs 9:30am–6:30pm, Sat–Sun 10:30am–6:30pm. Metro: Sevilla. MEXICAN.

You don't have to wander long to find the Beatriz—just follow your nose. Tortillas will be on the grill as you enter a narrow room embellished with brick arches, and tables covered in blue-and-white-checked cloths. It's all sparkling clean. Grab a table and choose from the 24 fillings for tacos or the many soups. The tacos de barbacoa or puerco come packed with shredded beef or tender pork and topped with guacamole sauce and shredded white cheese. Orders are per taco, with additional guacamole and onions separate. This gem is between Florencia and Varsovia.

MEALS FOR LESS THAN $10

✪ Café Konditori. Genova 61. ☎ **5/208-1846.** Main courses $4–6.25; coffee and dessert $2.75–$4. Daily 8am–midnight. Metro: Insurgentes; it's between Hamburgo and Londres. DANISH.

Located in the Zona Rosa, the Café Konditori advertises itself as a Danish restaurant, bar, and coffee shop. It's not what you'd call aggressively Danish (a specialty is Bavarian sausage with sauerkraut and mashed potatoes), but it does have a very pleasant sidewalk-café section. You can sit out in the open air and watch traffic along the pedestrian-way in good weather (which is nearly always) or by a window in the restaurant proper anytime. Choose from 11 different coffees. The cappuccino is the perfect accompaniment for one of the Konditori's luscious cakes or tarts. Be sure to inspect the dessert display before you sit. The café is open for breakfast, lunch, and dinner.

✪ **Chalet Suizo.** Niza 37. ☎ **5/511-7529.** Main courses $4.25–$10. Daily 12:30pm–midnight. Metro: Insurgentes. INTERNATIONAL.

Founded in 1950 and still one of the most dependable and cozy restaurants around, Chalet Suizo features Swiss decor, of course: checkered tablecloths, pine walls, beamed ceilings, and alpine landscapes. The menu features hearty French onion soup and a wide range of interesting main dishes, some of which are changed daily. Among these are veal with morel mushrooms, smoked pork chops, German-style pot roast, chicken tarragon, veal goulash, sauerbraten, and excellent fondue. The food is delicious, the portions are large, and the service is friendly and quick. One caveat: The bread and butter placed on your table are not included in the price of the meal and cost extra. It's on the west side of the street between Hamburgo and Londres.

✪ **Fonda El Refugio.** Liverpool 166. ☎ **5/207-2732** or 5/525-8128. Main courses $6–$8.50. Mon–Sat 1pm–midnight. Metro: Insurgentes. MEXICAN.

Fonda El Refugio, with service, food, and an atmosphere shaped by more than 40 years of tradition, is a very special place to dine à la mexicana. Although small, it's unusually congenial, with a large fireplace decorated with gleaming copper pots and pans; rows and rows of culinary awards and citations hang behind the desk. The restaurant manages the almost impossible task of being both elegant and informal. The menu runs the gamut of Mexican cuisine—*arroz con platanos* (rice with fried bananas) to enchiladas con mole poblano, topped with the rich, thick, spicy chocolate sauce of Puebla. There's a daily specialty; for example, on Tuesday it's *manchamanteles* (tablecloth stainer), and on Saturday it's *albondigas en chile chipotle* (meatballs in chipotle sauce). Fonda El Refugio is very popular, especially on Saturday night, so get there early. Valet parking is provided. It's between Florencia and Amberes.

WORTH A SPLURGE

Restaurant Passy. Amberes 10. ☎ **5/208-2084.** Reservations recommended. Main courses $16.50. Mon–Sat 1–11pm. Metro: Insurgentes. INTERNATIONAL.

The Restaurant Passy is an elegant old favorite of locals and tourists alike. The attractive, classic, and restrained decor features low lights, antiques, linen, and candles. The service is polished and polite, and the menu is traditional French: Oysters Rockefeller, onion or oyster soup, chicken Cordon Bleu, canard (duck) à l'orange, and coq au vin are among the continental favorites. There's also a good selection of fish. It's between Reforma and Hamburgo.

NEAR THE MONUMENTO A LA REVOLUCIÓN

Ⓢ **Los Arcos.** José Maria Iglesias 26. ☎ **5/535-0816.** Breakfast $1.50; soup 75¢–$1.75; main courses $1.25–$4; comida corrida $1.25. Daily 7am–10pm. Metro: Revolución. TACOS.

This small restaurant with red brick arches and orange formica tables and booths offers fast, economical meals. To the left as you enter is the juice bar, beyond which you can watch the cooks grill your choice of meats. Straight ahead, beyond some booths, is the soup kitchen where four enormous soup pots simmer. The comida corrida is a four course affair: soup, rice, a meat dish (perhaps beef in mole sauce or pork pibil), and a dessert. You truly get value for your peso here at the corner of

Iglesias and Mariscal, three blocks north of the Plaza a la Revolución and a block from the Gran Hotel Texas.

⑤ El Caminero. Ramirez 17. ☎ **5/566-3981.** Tacos (3) $2.25; soft drinks 50¢. Mon–Fri 10am–midnight, Sat 1pm–1am, Sun 1–11pm. TACOS.

Take a stool at one of the tall tables and gaze at the wall menu for your desired taco combination—steak, pork, or sausage with or without cheese, onions, bacon, and so on. Some orders come with three tacos, others have six or eight. Side orders to taste include grilled onions, beans, and quesadillas. Draft beer is available, and the café de olla is superior. This branch is between the Monumento a la Revolución and the Colón Monument, which is on Reforma.

NEAR THE ALAMEDA

Fonda Santa Anita. Calle Humboldt 48. ☎ **5/518-4609.** Main courses $2.50–$5.25; fixed–price meal $3.75. Mon–Fri noon–10pm, Sat–Sun 1:30–9pm. Metro: Juárez. MEXICAN.

Situated in the block south of Avenida Juárez near the Hotel Ambassador, the Fonda Santa Anita has moderate prices and speedy service. It's plain on the outside, but inside it's festooned with colorful banners, *papel picado* (artfully cut paper), and gaily painted walls. The large menu includes cheese-stuffed peppers, black-bean soup with tortilla strips and epazote, pork loin in red sauce, or breakfast at any hour. It's between Juárez and Donato Guerra.

❂ Restaurant Danúbio. Uruguay 3. ☎ **5/512-0912.** Main courses $4.25–$9; comida corrida $7.50 (Sunday $8.25). Daily 1pm–midnight (comida corrida served 1–4pm). Metro: Bellas Artes or Salto de Agua. INTERNATIONAL.

Elbow your way past the crowds for a gigantic fixed-price comida corrida that's practically an institution—it's plenty for two. A typical lunch consists of a shrimp or oyster cocktail, maybe Valencia soup or tomato consommé, boiled lentils, a choice of hot or cold fish dish, a choice of three main courses, custard or fruit, and coffee or tea. The à la carte menu is extensive, but you get better service during the busy time if you stick to the fixed-price meal. An upstairs room accommodates the lunchtime overflow. The house specialty, *langostinos* (baby crayfish), are well worth the splurge! The restaurant is south of the Alameda near the corner of Lázaro Cárdenas.

Sanborn's Casa de Azulejos. Madero 4. ☎ **5/518-6676.** Main courses $3.25–$6.50; dessert and coffee $2–$2.50. Daily 7:00am–1am. Metro: Bellas Artes. MEXICAN/AMERICAN.

Known today as Sanborn's House of Tiles (for the tiles covering the outside walls), this gorgeous antique building was once the palace of the counts of the Valley of Orizaba. For many years now it has housed a branch of the Sanborn's restaurant and variety-store chain. Dining tables are set in an elaborate courtyard complete with carved pillars, tiles, and peacock frescoes. Closed for nearly a year following a disastrous fire, it reopened in March 1995 with the conversion of much of the second floor into lovely secluded dining areas and a handsome bar. It's directly across Madero from the San Francisco church and diagonally across from the Latin American Tower.

AROUND THE ZÓCALO

Café Cinco de Mayo. 5 de Mayo No. 57. ☎ **5/510-1995.** Breakfast $1–$2.75; main courses $2.50–$6.50; comida corrida $2.50–$4. Daily 7am–11pm. Metro: Zócalo. MEXICAN.

An old-fashioned standby and a real money-saver near the Zócalo, the Café Cinco de Mayo is the very picture of a Mexican lunchroom. Less than a block west of the cathedral on the south side of the street, it's bright with fluorescent lights and often loud with conversation. Waiters scurry here and there bearing enormous glasses of fresh orange juice, cups of hot coffee, baskets of pan dulce, sandwiches, pork chops, soup—well, you name it. The Sunday special of barbacoa en salsa borracha is worth a try. Draft beer is available. If you order café con leche, a waiter will approach with a big metal coffeepot, pour an inch of thick, bitter coffee into the bottom of your glass, then fill it up with hot milk. The restaurant is between the Zócalo and Palma.

✪ **Café de Tacuba.** Tacuba 28. ☎ **5/512-8482.** Breakfast $4–$8.25; main courses $5.25–$9.50; comida corrida $9–$13. Daily 8am–11:30pm. Metro: Allende. MEXICAN.

One of the city's best-established and popular restaurants, the Café de Tacuba has a handsome colonial-era look but dates from 1912. A stately atmosphere welcomes guests to the two long dining rooms, with brass lamps, dark and brooding oil paintings, and a large mural of several nuns working in a kitchen. The customary fixed-price comida corrida offers a selection of daily lunch plates served with soup. In the front window and pastry case is a tempting selection of homemade cakes and pies and candied fruit. On Thursday through Sunday from 6pm until closing a wonderful group of medieval-costumed singers entertains; their sound is like the melodious estudiantina groups of Guanajuato accompanied by mandolins and guitars. Other musicians may be entertaining on other evenings. The café is between República de Chile and Bolívar.

⑤ **Café El Popular.** 5 de Mayo No. 52. ☎ **5/518-6081.** Breakfast $1–$1.75; main courses $1.75–$3.75; comida corrida $2.50; Oaxaca tamal $1. Daily 24 hours (comida corrida served 1–5pm). Metro: Zócalo. MEXICAN.

Café El Popular is not only popular for its prices but it looks like a cozy French café with inviting streetside windows filled with pastries. Go on in—it only looks expensive. You'll find one of the best-priced menus downtown. If the lower level is full, take the narrow stairs up to the loft level. Either way, expect your waitress to greet you with a heaping basket of pastries (they charge you for what you eat). Breakfast or *merienda* (tea time) specials include Oaxaca tamal, beans, *atole* (a sweet, thick corn drink), or coffee. Soups are rather greasy. You'll find the restaurant between Isabel la Católica and Palma.

Hostería de Santo Domingo. Domínguez 72. ☎ **5/510-1434.** Breakfast $3–$4.50; main courses $4–$10; specialties of the day $9. Daily 9am–11pm. Metro: Allende. MEXICAN.

Established in 1860, the Hostería de Santo Domingo is said to be the oldest restaurant in the city still in operation. A mural at one end of the main dining room shows the Plaza Domingo during colonial times. The player piano will fool you into thinking a pianist is playing nonstop. The food is excellent, with large portions. At lunchtime the place is generally packed, so come early. Try the stuffed peppers with cheese, the pork loin, or the unusual bread soup. But beware of the cecina, which is very salty. *Note:* The bread placed on your table costs extra. The restaurant is north of the Zócalo, between República de Brazil and República de Chile, near Palma.

Restaurante Vegetariano y Dietético. Madero 56. ☎ **5/521-6880.** Breakfast $2.25–$2.75; main courses and comida corrida $2.75–$3.25; soups and salads $1.25–$2.50. Mon–Sat 9am–6pm. Metro: Zócalo. VEGETARIAN.

There's only a small brass plaque with the restaurant's name next to the doorway, so look for a stairway with the menu posted outside on the entrance; walk one flight up (past a tailor shop) to enter the restaurant. The decor is nothing special—the restaurant was founded in 1942 and probably never redecorated—but the food is darn good. A typical meal starts with a huge salad, followed by superb soup, a choice of two main courses, and a delicious cake made of whole wheat and honey, served with coffee or tea. The restaurant is upstairs, between Isabel la Católica and Palma.

TEA HOUSES

Auseba. Hamburgo 159b. ☎ **5/511-3769.** Breakfast 50¢–75¢; coffee or tea 25¢–50¢; pastries 25¢–50¢; light meals 50¢–75¢. Mon–Sat 9am–10pm, Sun 11am–1pm. Metro: Insurgentes. CONTINENTAL.

One of the finest places for afternoon coffee (excellent) or tea is Auseba, which serves pastries, light meals, and all kinds of coffee concoctions along with tea. The glass cases display delicious-looking cookies, meringues, bonbons, cakes, pies, and puddings— all prepared daily in the restaurant's own bakery. Service can be very slow, though, and some of their pastries dry out when heated in the microwave. The restaurant is between Florencia and Estocolmo.

✪ **Salón de Thé Duca d'Este.** Hamburgo 164b. ☎ **5/525-6374.** Breakfast $2–$3.75; ice cream or pastry $1.25–$2; salads $2.75–$3.25; soups $1.75. Sun–Thurs 8am–11pm, Fri–Sat 8am–midnight. Metro: Insurgentes. CONTINENTAL.

This is another favorite of mine, opposite the above-mentioned Auseba. Small tea tables draped in apricot cloths look out onto the bustle of pedestrian traffic. But many of the customers are absorbed in gazing at the Duca d'Este's refrigerated display cases, which shelter many kinds of pastries, fresh and candied fruits, ice creams, and other fare. There's a good selection of coffees, teas, and hot chocolates. You can have a light lunch or supper by ordering soup, salad, or salmon. It's at the corner of Florencia and Hamburgo.

CANTINAS

La Opera Bar. 5 De Mayo 10. ☎ **5/512-8959.** Reservations recommended at lunch. Main courses $3.75–$7.50; mixed drinks $2.50–$5. Mon–Sat 1pm–midnight. Metro: Bellas Artes. INTERNATIONAL.

La Opera Bar, three blocks east of the Alameda, is the most opulent of the city's cantinas. Below gilded baroque ceilings, slide into one of the darkwood booths with patches of beveled mirror and exquisite small oil paintings of pastoral scenes or grab a linen-covered table with a basket of fresh bread. La Opera is the Mexican equivalent of a London club, although it has become so popular for dining that fewer and fewer men play dominoes. In fact, you see more and more people enjoying romantic interludes in one of the cavernous booths, but tables of any kind are hard to find. Service is best if you arrive for lunch when it opens or go after 5pm when the throngs have diminished. The menu is sophisticated and extensive. While you wait for one of the jacketed waiters to bring your meal, look on the ceiling for the bullet hole that legend says Pancho Villa left when he galloped in on a horse. It's half a block toward the zócalo from Sanborn's House of Tiles.

Salón Victoria. López 43. ☎ **5/512-4340.** Reservations recommended before 3pm and for lunch. Main courses $3.50–$9. Mon–Sat 10am–11pm. Metro: Bellas Artes. MEXICAN.

The Salón Victoria looks a bit like a classy English pub. With brass chandeliers and lamps and colorfully framed prints, this is not quite the Salón Victoria of nearly 50 years ago—maybe it's better. Specialties here include paella valenciana, *mole roja* (a turkey dish with almost 20 ingredients), and goat-head tacos. The last are an acquired taste; if you want to try them, you must reserve an order in advance—the supply is limited, and the Victoria hoards them for its best customers. It's at the corner of Victoria.

6　Exploring Mexico City

You'll find that in Mexico City such a routine activity as walking in the park can bring delightful surprises, and even an ordinary stroll in the city's markets presents the opportunity to admire exotic items unavailable at home.

Mexico City was built on the ruins of the ancient city of Tenochtitlán. A downtown portion of the city comprising almost 700 acres and 1,500 buildings has been designated a **Historical Zone (Centro Histórico).** The area is being reclaimed from years of neglect and restored to its former colonial charm.

In summer, always be prepared for rain, which comes daily. In winter, carry a jacket or sweater—stone museums are cold inside, and when the sun goes down, the outside air gets chilly. There are often surprise rainstorms in winter as well.

THE TOP ATTRACTIONS

✪ **Museo Nacional de Antropología.** Chapultepec Park. ☎ **5/553-6638**1. Admission $2.25; free Sun. $1.50 fee for still cameras; personal video cameras $3.50; no tripods permitted. Tues–Sat 9am–7pm, Sun 10am–6pm. Metro: Auditorio.

Occupying 44,000 square feet, Mexico City's anthropology museum is regarded as one of the top museums in the world. First-floor rooms are devoted to the pre-Hispanic cultures of Mexico. Second-floor rooms cover contemporary rural cultures through their crafts and everyday life. This museum offers the single best introduction to Mexico. (See the walking tour, below, for detailed guidance.)

✪ **Museo del Templo Mayor (Great Temple).** Off the Zócalo. ☎ **5/542-0606;** Fax 5/542-1717. Admission $2.25 (valid for both ruins and museum); free Sun. $1.50 fee for still cameras; personal video camera $3.50. Tues–Sun 9am–6pm (last ticket sold 5pm). Metro: Zócalo.

Opened in 1987 at the site of the newly excavated Aztec Templo Mayor, this quickly became one of the city's top museums. At the time of the 1521 Conquest the site was the center of religious life for the city of 300,000. No other museum shows the variety and splendor of the Aztec Empire the way this one does. All 6,000 pieces came from the relatively small plot of excavated ruins just in front of the museum. (See "Walking Tour 1—The Zócalo" later in this chapter.)

✪ **The Historic District.** Metro: Zócalo or Bellas Artes.

At least 1,500 buildings and an area of almost 700 acres of historic downtown Mexico City around the Alameda and Zócalo have been earmarked for preservation. A good portion of the history of Mexico from the 16th to the 20th century is reflected in the grand palaces and buildings in these two areas. (See the walking tours of the Zócalo and the Alameda later in this chapter.)

Diego Rivera Murals. Diego Rivera, one of Mexico's top muralists, left an indelible stamp on Mexico City's walls and, through his painted political themes, affected the way millions view Mexican history. See his stunning and provocative interpretations at the Palacio Nacional, the Bellas Artes, the National Preparatory School (his first ones), the Department of Public Education, the National School of Agriculture at Chapingo, the National Institute of Cardiology, and the Museo Mural Diego Rivera (housing the mural formerly in the Hotel Del Prado). (See the walking tours of the Alameda and the Zócalo later in this chapter.)

✪ **Museo Franz Mayer.** Hidalgo 45, facing the Alameda. ☎ **5/518-2265.** Admission $1.25; free Sun. Tues–Sun 10am–5pm. Metro: Hidalgo or Bellas Artes.

German immigrant Franz Mayer spent a lifetime collecting rare furniture and other utilitarian decorative pieces dating from the 16th to the 19th century. When he died in 1975, he bequeathed them to the Mexican people with a trust fund for their care and display. (See "Walking Tour 2—Near the Alameda" later in this chapter.)

MORE ATTRACTIONS
NEAR THE ALAMEDA

North, west, and south of the Alameda proper are other attractions worthy of note. For the major highlights, see "Walking Tour 2—Near the Alameda" later in this chapter.

Plaza and Cemetery of San Fernando. Puente de Alvarado and Vicente Guerrero. Free. Daily dawn–dusk.

At one end of the plaza is the 18th-century San Fernando Church and behind it, $2^1/2$ blocks west of the Alameda, is a small cemetery by the same name where a few of Mexico's elite families are buried. It's the only cemetery remaining in the city from the 19th century, and President Benito Juárez was the last person buried here, on July 23, 1872. His tomb is like a Greek temple with a sculpture representing the motherland cradling a beloved son. (Many of Mexico's more infamous are buried in the cemetery behind the original Basilica of Guadalupe.)

Museo de San Carlos. Puente de Alvarado 50. ☎ **5/592-3721** or 5/566-8522. Admission $1; free Sun. Wed–Mon 10am–6pm. Walk $5^1/2$ blocks west of the Alameda ($2^1/2$ blocks west of San Fernando Plaza); it's at the corner of Arizpe.

The San Carlos Museum shows works from students of the Academy of San Carlos. Most of the country's great painters—Diego Rivera among them—count it as their alma mater. The beautiful converted mansion that houses the museum was built in the early 1800s by architect Manuel Tolsá and was later the home of the Marqués de Buenavista.

In the mansion's elliptical court are displays of the 19th-century Mexican statuary and busts by Manuel Vilar and his pupils, and off to one side is a pretty garden court shaded by rubber trees.

The various rooms on the first and second floors hold some of Mexico's best paintings, by both Mexican and European artists. In Sala I, for instance, you can view *Christ in Limbo* by Mostaert (ca. 1534–1598) and also two paintings by Lucas Cranach the Elder: *Adam and Eve* and *Federico de Sajonia*. Other treats include *La Coquea y el Jovenzuelo* by Fragonard and a portrait of Sir William Stanhope attributed to Sir Joshua Reynolds. There is also a gallery with prints and engravings.

✪ Monumento a la Revolución & Museo Nacional de la Revolución. Av. Juárez and La Fragua. ☎ **5/546-2115** or 5/566-1902. Free admission. Tues–Sat 9am–5pm, Sun 9am–3pm. From the Colón Monument on Reforma, walk two blocks north on I. Ramírez; the monument will loom ahead.

The stocky art deco Monument to the Revolution, set in the large **Plaza de la República,** has a curious and ironic history. The government of Porfirio Díaz, perennially "reelected" as president of Mexico, began construction of what was intended to be a new legislative chamber. However, only the dome was raised by the time the Mexican Revolution (1910) put an end to his plans—not to mention his dictatorship. In the 1930s, after the turmoil of the revolution diminished, the dome was finished as a monument: The mortal remains of two revolutionary presidents, Francisco Madero and Venustiano Carranza, were entombed in two of its pillars, and it was dedicated to the revolution. Later, the bodies of Presidents Plutarco Elías Calles and Lázaro Cárdenas were buried there.

Beneath the Monument to the Revolution is the Museo Nacional de la Revolución (the entrance is directly across from the Frontón). The tumultuous years from 1867 through the revolution (which started in 1911) to 1917, when the present constitution was signed, are chronicled in excellent exhibits of documents, newspaper stories, photographs, drawings, clothing, costumes, uniforms, weapons, and furnishings. The museum is well worth a visit if you're at all interested in the period or the revolution.

Plaza de las Tres Culturas. At the corner of Lázaro Cárdenas and Flores Magón. Free admission. Daily dawn–dusk. Directions: It's about 2 miles north of the Alameda at Flores Magón, just off Reforma, in Colonia Tlatelolco. To walk there from the Alameda, go north on Lázaro Cárdenas straight for six long blocks to Reforma and the traffic circle with the Cuitláhuac Monument. Cross Reforma and go ¹/₄ of the way around the circle, then left on Flores Magón for two blocks. Turn right across Magón, and there you are. Metro: Line 3 to Tlatelolco; leave the terminal by the exit to Manuel González and turn right on this street; walk two blocks to the Avenida Lázaro Cárdenas and turn right again. The plaza is a long half block south, on the left, just past the Clínico Hospital. Either way, the walk takes less than 15 minutes.

Here three cultures converge—Aztec, Spanish, and contemporary. Surrounded by modern office and apartment buildings are large remains of the **Aztec city of Tlatelolco,** site of the last battle of the Conquest of Mexico, and off to one side is the **Cathedral of Santiago Tlatelolco.** During the Aztec Empire, Tlatelolco was on the edge of Lake Texcoco, linked to the Aztec capital by a causeway. Bernal Díaz de Castillo, in his *True Story of the Conquest of New Spain*, described the roar from the dazzling market there. Later he described the incredible scene after the last battle of the Conquest in Tlatelolco on August 13, 1521—the dead bodies were piled so deep that walking there was impossible. That night determined the fate of the country and completed the Spanish Conquest of Mexico.

View the pyramidal remains from raised walkways over the site. The cathedral, off to one side, was built in the 16th century entirely of volcanic stone. The interior has been tastefully restored, preserving little patches of fresco in stark-white plaster walls, with a few deep-blue stained-glass windows and an unadorned stone altar.

Sunday is a good day to combine a visit here with one to the Sunday Lagunilla street market (for details, see "Shopping" later in this chapter), which is within walking distance south across Reforma.

Sullivan Park/Jardín del Arte. Two blocks north of the intersection of Insurgentes and Reforma. Free admission. Daily; artists exhibit on Sun.

Though this is not strictly "near the Alameda," you might want to continue your tour on a 10-minute walk southwest along Reforma to Sullivan Park, which on Sunday becomes Jardín del Arte (Garden of Art). This pretty park begins with the Monumento a la Maternidad (Monument to Motherhood) and continues with trees, shrubs, benches, fountains, and sculpture into Sullivan Park. On Sunday, it's crowded with artists displaying their wares for sale.

IN CHAPULTEPEC PARK

One of the biggest city parks in the world (more than 1,700 acres), Chapultepec Park is more than a playground. The park is open for entry from 5am till 5pm, although one can exit later. Besides accommodating picnickers on worn-away grass under centuries-old trees, it offers a lake with canoes; vendors selling balloons, trinkets, and food; a garden for senior citizens only; a miniature train; an auditorium; and Los Pinos, home of Mexico's president. Most important for tourists, it contains a

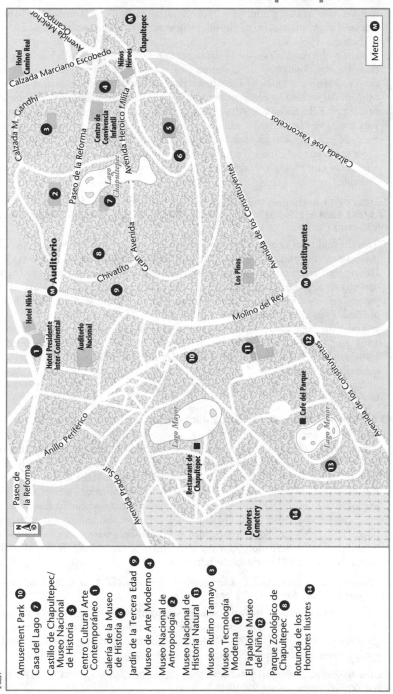

Metro **Ⓜ**

Calzada José Vasconcelos

Avenida Melchor Ocampo

Hotel Camino Real

Calzada Marciano Escobedo

Niños Héroes

Calzada M. Gandhi

Chapultepec Ⓜ

③

④

Centro de Convivencia Infantil

Paseo de la Reforma

Lago Chapultepec

⑤

⑥

Avenida Heroico Militar

②

⑦

Avenida de los Constituyentes

⑧

Gran Avenida

Chivatito

Los Pinos

Constituyentes Ⓜ

Auditorio Ⓜ

⑨

Molino del Rey

Hotel Nikko

①

Hotel Presidente Inter-Continental

Auditorio Nacional

⑩

⑪

⑫

Anillo Periférico

Avenida Prado Sur

Café del Parque ■

Lago Mayor

Restaurant de Chapultepec ■

Lago Menor

⑬

Avenida de los Constituyentes

Paseo de la Reforma

N

⑭

Dolores Cemetery

2-0021

number of interesting museums. (See the detailed Walking Tour of the Museo Nacional de Antropología later in this chapter for information on the most famous of these attractions.)

Most of the things to see are in the rather loosely defined Section 1, reached most easily by any "Auditorio" or "Reforma/Chapultepec" bus on Reforma, which will drop you within a block of the Museo Rufino Tamayo and the Museo de Arte Moderno or within two blocks of the Museo Nacional de Antropología. All these are situated off Reforma, about half a mile past the Diana Statue, near the Chapultepec Park zoo. The Metro, Line 1 will take you to the Chapultepec station, just outside the park, or Line 7 will take you to Auditorio, closer to the National Auditorium.

Section 2 has the Museo Tecnológico and Museo Nacional de Historia Natural, reached by a long walk from the Constituyentes station (Line 7). A taxi may be more desirable.

Castillo de Chapultepec/Museo Nacional de Historia. Chapultepec Park, Section 1. ☎ **5/553-6224** or 5/553-6396. Admission $2.50; free Sun. Tues–Sun 9am–5pm (tickets sold only till 4pm).

This site had been occupied by a fortress since the days of the Aztecs; the present palace wasn't built until the 1780s. The castle offers a beautiful view of Mexico City. During the French occupation of the 1860s, Carlota (who designed the lovely garden surrounding the palace) could sit up in bed and watch her husband, Maximilian, proceeding down Reforma on his way to work. Later, this became the official home of Mexico's president, until 1939.

Today the castle houses a variety of historical artifacts covering the period between 1521 and 1917. You'll see murals by Orozco, Siqueros, and others; elaborate European furnishings brought here by Maximilian and Carlota; and jewelry and colonial art objects.

Note: Hold onto your ticket the entire time you're on the hill—you may be asked to show it.

✪ **Galería de la Museo de Historia.** Chapultepec Park, Section 1. Admission $1; free Sun. Tues–Sat 9am–4:30pm; Sun 10am–3:30pm.

About 200 yards below Chapultepec Castle is this circular glass building, also known as the Museo Caracol (Snail Museum) because of its spiral shape, and as the Museo de la Lucha del Pueblo Mexicano por su Libertad (Museum of the Mexican People's Fight for Their Liberty) because of its content. It's a condensed chronological history of Mexico from 1800 to 1917, complete with portraits, reproductions of documents, and dramatic dioramas. The more recent years are also represented, with large photographic blowups. Some scenes, such as Maximilian's execution, are staged with great drama and imagination. In many ways, this museum is more riveting than the Museo Nacional de Historia on the hill above.

✪ **Museo de Arte Moderno.** Chapultepec Park, Section 1. ☎ **5/553-6233.** Admission $1.50; free Sun. Tues–Sun 10am–5:30pm.

The museum is actually in two buildings set together, but its only entrance is on Reforma. The museum features both Mexican and foreign artists, including such greats as Kahlo, Rivera, Orozco, Montenegro, Tamayo, Coronel, and Magritte. Its garden serves as a sculpture gallery.

Museo Nacional de Historia Natural. Chapultepec Park, Section 2. ☎ **5/515-2222.** Admission 50¢; free Sun. Tues–Sun 10am–5pm.

The 10 interconnecting domes that form the Museum of Natural History contain stuffed and preserved animals and birds; tableaux of different natural environments with the appropriate wildlife; and exhibits on geology, astronomy, biology, the origin of life, and more. It's a fascinating place for anyone with the slightest curiosity about nature, and it's totally absorbing for youngsters.

✪ El Papalote, Museo del Niño (Children's Museum). Avenida de los Constituyentes, Chapultepec Park, Section 2. ☎ **5/224-1260.** Admission $3 adults ($5 including IMAX show); $2.50 children ($3.50 including IMAX show). Daily 9am–1pm and 2–6pm.

This interactive children's museum opened in 1993 in three separate buildings. The Building of the Pyramids holds most of the exhibits, while in the IMAX building two films alternate for 10 shows daily. There's virtually nothing here that children can't touch; once they discover this, they'll want to stay a long time. Children must be accompanied by an adult.

Rotonda de los Hombres Ilustres. Dolores Cemetery, Section 3 of Chapultepec Park, Constituyentes and Av. Civil Dolores. Free admission. Daily 6am–6pm.

The din of traffic recedes in the serene environment where Mexico's illustrious military, political, and artistic elite are buried. It's more like an outdoor museum of monuments than a cemetery; the stone markers are grouped in a double circle around an eternal flame. A stroll here will enliven a conversation about who's who in Mexican history. Among the famous buried here are artists Diego Rivera, Alfredo Siqueiros, José Clemente Orozco, and Gerardo Murillo; presidents Sebastian Lerdo de Tejada, Valentín Gómez Farías, and Plutarco Calles; musicians Jaime Nuño (author of the Mexican national anthem), Juventino Rosas, and Agustín Lara; and outstanding citizens such as Carlos Pellicer. Stop in the entrance building and the guard will give you a map with a list of those buried here, which includes biographical information.

✪ Museo Rufino Tamayo. Chapultepec Park, Section 1. ☎ **5/286-5889** or 5/286-5939. Admission $2.25; free Sun. Tues–Sun 10am–6pm. Free guided tours Sat–Sun 10am–2pm.

Oaxaca-born painter Rufino Tamayo not only contributed a great deal to modern Mexican painting, but also collected pre-Hispanic, Mexican, and foreign works, including pieces by de Kooning, Warhol, Dalí, and Magritte. Tamayo's pre-Hispanic collection is in Oaxaca, but here you can see a number of his works and the remainder of his collection, unless they are temporarily displaced by a special exhibit. If you see one advertised (in *The News*, for instance), don't miss it.

Museo Tecnológico Moderno (Museum of Technology). Chapultepec Park, Section 2. ☎ **5/516-0964** or 5/277-5779. Free admission. Tues–Sun 9am–4:45pm.

This museum is always filled with students madly taking notes on scientific developments through the ages. Inside and outside are trains and planes (both real and models), mockup factories, displays on the experiments of Morse and Edison, and various energy exhibits. The polyhedral dome outside is the planetarium, which has six shows between 10am and 4pm daily. When you're thoroughly exhausted, head for the cafeteria near the aircraft exhibit where they serve a really fine comida corrida for $4 (9–11am and 1–3pm).

NORTH OF THE CITY CENTER

Basilica of Our Lady of Guadalupe. No phone. Free admission; Museum 50¢. Tues–Sun 10am–6pm. Metro: Line 3 to the "Basílica" station; take the exit marked SAALIDA AV. MONTIEL. Walk a block or so north of the Metro station to a major intersection (Montevideo; you'll know it by the VIP's and Denny's across the street to the left). Turn right onto Avenida Montevideo and cross the overpass; after about 15 minutes' walk, you'll see the great church looming ahead. From La Villa station, walk north on Calzada de Guadalupe.

Within the northern city limits is the famous Basilica of Guadalupe. Tour groups often combine a trip to the basilica with the Plaza of Three Cultures (see above) and the Pyramids of Teotihuacán (see chapter 12), which makes a rushed and exhausting day.

The Basilica of Our Lady of Guadalupe is on the site where, on December 9, 1531, a poor Indian named Juan Diego is reputed to have seen a vision of a beautiful lady in a blue mantle. The local bishop, Zumarraga, was reluctant to confirm that Juan had indeed seen the Virgin Mary, so he asked the peasant for some evidence. Juan saw the vision a second time, on December 12, and it became miraculously emblazoned on the peasant's cloak. The bishop immediately ordered the building of a church on the spot, and upon its completion the image was hung in the place of honor, framed in gold. Since that time millions of the devout and the curious have come to view the miraculous image that experts, it is said, are at a loss to explain. The blue-mantled Virgin of Guadalupe is the patron saint of Mexico.

So heavy was the flow of visitors—many of whom approached for hundreds of yards on their knees—that the old church, already fragile, was insufficient to handle them, and an audacious new basilica was built, designed by Pedro Ramírez Vazquez, the same architect who did the breathtaking Museo Nacional de Antropología.

For a view of the miraculous cloak, which hangs at the altar, go to the lower level of the church. The architect has designed it so you can look at the image from below while gliding past on a moving sidewalk.

To the right of the modern basilica is an old basilica, actually the second one built to house the cloak—the original is higher up on the hill. Restoration of this basilica has been ongoing for at least 10 years, and portions are open to the public. To the back of it is the entrance to the Basilica Museum, with a very good display of religious art in restored rooms. One of the side chapels, with a silver altar, is adjacent to the museum.

At the top of the hill, behind the basilica, is the Panteón del Tepeyac, a cemetery for Mexico's more infamous folk (Santa Anna among them) and also several gift shops specializing in religious objects, trinkets encased in seashells and other folk art. The steps up this hill are lined with flowers, shrubs, and waterfalls, and the climb, although tiring, is worthwhile for the view from the top.

Should you be lucky enough to visit Mexico City on December 12, you can witness the grand festival in honor of the Virgin of Guadalupe. The square in front of the basilica fills up with the pious and the party-minded as prayers, dances, and a carnival atmosphere attract thousands of the devout.

SOUTH OF THE CITY CENTER
San Angel
San Angel is a fashionable colonial-era suburb of cobblestone streets with several worthwhile museums. The nearest Metro station is M. A. Quevedo. From downtown, take a colectivo ("San Angel") or bus ("Indios Verdes–Tlalpan" or "Central Norte—Villa Olímpica") south along Insurgentes near the Zona Rosa. Ask to get off at La Paz. To the east is a pretty park, the Plaza del Carmen, and on the west side of Insurgentes is a Sanborn's store/restaurant, good for a quick, moderately priced meal.

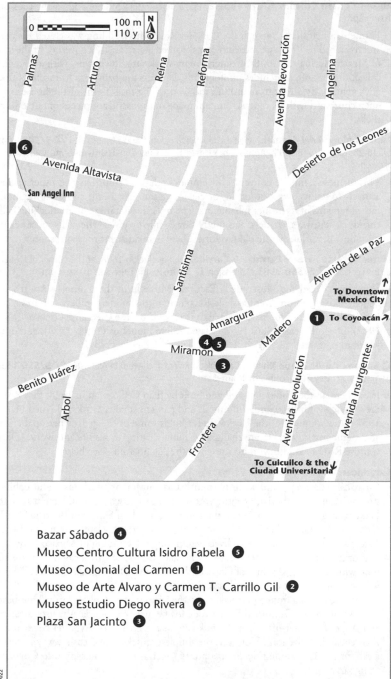

Bazar Sábado **4**

Museo Centro Cultura Isidro Fabela **5**

Museo Colonial del Carmen **1**

Museo de Arte Alvaro y Carmen T. Carrillo Gil **2**

Museo Estudio Diego Rivera **6**

Plaza San Jacinto **3**

2-0022

Museo Centro Cultura Isidro Fabela. Plaza San Angel 15. Free admission. Tues–Sun 10am–5pm.

Formerly a mansion known as the Casa del Risco, this building was closed for years and reopened in 1992 as a museum of art, named after Fabela, a governor of the state of Mexico during the 1940s. Contemporary works are downstairs, with a changing collection that often includes photographs. Upstairs are paintings from the 16th to 18th century by artists from around the world. The focal point of the house is the open courtyard with its central fountain made of thousands of pieces of pottery and shells.

Museo Colonial del Carmen. Avenida de la Revolución 4 and Monasterio. ☎ **5/548-9849,** 5/548-2838, or 5/548-5312. Admission $2; free Sun. Tues–Sun 10am–4:45pm. Cameras not allowed.

This former Carmelite convent now employs religious paintings and other ancient artifacts to tell its own history. In the cellar one can view skulls and even the mummified remains of its former inhabitants. The museum is a maze of interlocking halls, corridors, stairways, chapels, and pretty flower-filled patios. One of its most beautiful rooms is, curiously, the old lavatory. There is an adjacent museum shop.

Museo de Arte Alvar y Carmen T. Carrillo Gil. Revolución 1608, at the corner of Desierto de los Leones. ☎ **5/550-3983.** Admission $1.50; free Sun. Tues–Sun 10am–6pm.

Sometimes called the Museo de la Esquina (Museum of the Corner) since it's at a major intersection on Avenida de la Revolución, this modern gallery features a collection that includes rooms dedicated to the works of José Clemente Orozco (1883–1942), Diego Rivera (1886–1957), David Alfaro Siqueiros (1896–1974), and other Mexican painters.

✪ **Museo Estudio Diego Rivera.** Calle Diego Rivera and Avenida Altavista. ☎ **5/550-1139.** Admission $1; free Sun. Tues–Sun 10am–5pm.

It was here, in the studio designed and built by Juan O'Gorman in 1928, that Rivera drew sketches for his wonderful murals and painted smaller works. He died here in 1957. Now a museum, the Rivera studio holds some of the artist's personal effects and mementos, and there are changing exhibits relating to his life and work. (Don't confuse Rivera's studio with his museum, the Anahuacalli—see below.)

Coyoacán

Coyoacán is a pretty and wealthy suburb boasting many old houses and cobbled streets dating from the 16th century. At the center are two graceful large plazas, the Plaza Hidalgo and Jardín Centenario, and the Church of San Juan Bautista (1583). Once the capital of the Tepanec kingdom, Coyoacán was later conquered by the Aztecs and then by Cortés, who lived here during the building of Mexico City.

From downtown, the Metro Line 3 can take you to the Coyoacán or Viveros station, within walking distance of Coyoacán's museums. Or "Iztacala-Coyoacán" buses will get you from the center to this suburb.

If you're coming from San Angel, catch the "Alcantarilla–Col. Agrarista" bus heading east along the Camino al Desierto de los Leones or Avenida Altavista, near the San Angel Inn. Get off when the bus gets to the corner of Avenida Mexico and Xicoténcatl in Coyoacán. However, the simplest, quickest, and easiest way is to take a cab for the 15-minute ride. Sosa, a pretty street, is the main artery into Coyoacán from San Angel.

✪ **Museo Nacional de Culturas Populares (National Museum of Popular Cultures).** Hidalgo 289. ☎ **5/554-3800** or 5/554-8882. Donation 75¢. Tues–Sun 10am–6pm.

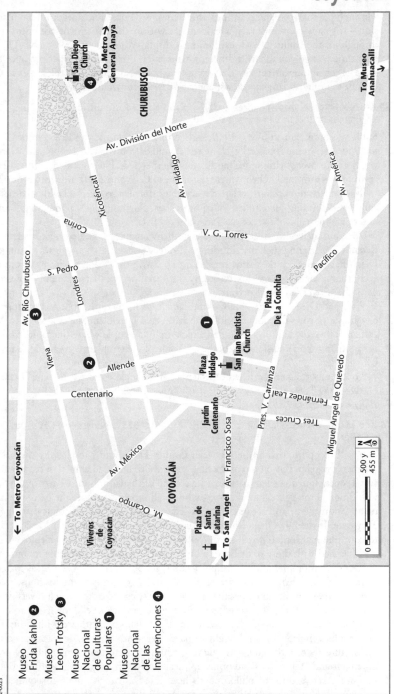

San Diego Church

To Metro →
General Anaya

CHURUBUSCO

To Museo
Anahuacalli →

Av. División del Norte

Av. Hidalgo

Xicoténcatl

Corina

Av. América

V. G. Torres

S. Pedro

Av. Río Churubusco

Pacífico

Londres

Plaza
De La Conchita

Viena

Allende

San Juan Bautista
Church

Plaza
Hidalgo

Centenario

Pres. V. Carranza

Fernández Leal

Tres Cruces

Jardín
Centenario

Miguel Ángel de Quevedo

Av. México

Av. Francisco Sosa

COYOACÁN

M. Ocampo

Viveros
de
Coyoacán

Plaza de
Santa
Catarina

To San Angel ←

← To Metro Coyoacán

N
500 y
0   455 m

2-0023

Museo
Frida Kahlo ❷

Museo
Leon Trotsky ❸

Museo
Nacional
de Culturas
Populares ❶

Museo
Nacional
de las
Intervenciones ❹

Through photographs and paintings, this museum—housed in a beautiful old mansion—displays contemporary Mexican life within the context of communities throughout the country. Each exhibition is displayed for about six months. Thus, each time you go you'll have a different experience, often finding a performance or some other significant activity that complements the display. Call the museum or consult the English-language newspaper, *The News*, for what's current.

⊙ **Museo Frida Kahlo.** Londres 247. ☎ **5/554-5999.** Admission $1.50. Tues–Sun 10am–6pm. Note that no cameras are allowed.

Kahlo was born here on July 7, 1910, and occupied the house with Rivera from 1929 to 1954. The house is basically as she left it, and as you wander through the rooms you'll get an overwhelming feeling for the life they led. Their mementos are in every room—from the kitchen, where the names Diego and Frida are written on the walls, to the studio upstairs, where a wheelchair sits next to the easel with a partially completed painting surrounded by paintbrushes, palettes, books, photographs, and other paraphernalia of the couple's art-centered lives.

The bookshelves are filled with books in many languages, nestled against a few of Rivera's files bearing such inscriptions as "Protect Rockefeller Vandalism," "Amigos Diego Personales," and "Vários Interesantes y Curiosos." Frida's paintings hang in every room, some of them dominated by the gory imagery that apparently obsessed her in her final surgery-filled years.

Frida and Diego collected pre-Columbian art, so many of the rooms contain jewelry and terra-cotta figurines from Teotihuacán and Tlatelolco. She even went to the extreme of having built in the garden a mockup of a temple where she could exhibit her numerous pots and statues. On the back side of the temple are several skulls from Chichén-Itzá.

To learn more about the lives of this remarkable couple, I can recommend Bertram D. Wolfe's *Diego Rivera: His Life and Times* and Hayden Herrara's *Frida: A Biography of Frida Kahlo.*

Museo Leon Trotsky. Río Churubusco 410. ☎ **5/658-8732.** Admission $1.50. Tues–Sun 10am–5pm.

You will recognize this house, between Gómez Farías and Morelos, by the brick riflemen's watchtowers on top of the high stone walls. During Lenin's last days, Stalin and Trotsky fought a silent battle for leadership of the Communist Party in the Soviet Union. Trotsky stuck to ideology, while Stalin took control of the party mechanism. Stalin won, and Trotsky was exiled, to continue his ideological struggle elsewhere. Invited by Diego Rivera, he settled here on the outskirts of Mexico City to continue his work and writing on political topics and communist ideology. His ideas clashed with those of Stalin in many respects, and Stalin, wanting no opposition or dissension in world Communist ranks, set out to have Trotsky assassinated. A first attempt failed, but it served to give a warning to Trotsky and his household, and from then on the house became a veritable fortress, with the watchtowers' steel doors (Trotsky's bedroom was entered only through thick steel doors), and round-the-clock guards, several of whom were Americans who sympathized with Trotsky's philosophies. Finally a man thought to have been paid, cajoled, or blackmailed by Stalin, directly or indirectly, was able to get himself admitted to the house by posing as a friend of Trotsky's and of his political views. On August 20, 1940, he put a mountaineer's ax into the philosopher's head. He was caught, but Trotsky died of his wounds shortly afterward. Because Trotsky and Rivera had previously had a falling out, both Rivera and Kahlo were suspects for a short time after the murder.

The museum is divided into two parts. In the first section you pass through displays of newspaper clippings chronicling the life of Trotsky and his wife in Mexico and the assassination. Then you enter the home, which is much more meager in its furnishings than you might expect for such a famous person.

If you saw the film *The Death of Trotsky* (with Richard Burton), you already have a good idea of what the house looks like; although the movie was not made here, the set was a very good replica of the house and gardens. You can visit Natalia's (Trotsky's wife's) study, the communal dining room, and Trotsky's study (with worksheets, newspaper clippings, books, and cylindrical wax dictating records still spread around) and fortresslike bedroom. Closets still hold their personal clothing. Some of the walls still bear the bullet holes left from the first attempt on his life. Trotsky's tomb, designed by Juan O'Gorman, is in the garden.

Museo Nacional de las Intervenciones (National Museum of Interventions). 20 de Agosto y General Anaya, Churubusco. ☎ **5/604-0699.** Admission $2; free Sun. Tues–Sun 9am–6pm.

If your country has been invaded as many times as Mexico has, and for some of the most unusual reasons, there would be a museum about it, too. Housed in a beautiful old convent, the well-done displays chronicle each intervention, including the French invasions in 1838 and 1862, the war with the United States between 1846 and 1848, and the U.S. invasions of 1914 and 1916. Visitors from France or the States, rather than being in for some American or French bashing, discover just the facts—very well displayed. The building itself was the site of a battle with Mexican General Anaya, his troops, and U.S. deserters on one side and U.S. Gen. Winfield Scott and his troops on the other.

San Pablo Tepetlapa

The Anahuacalli (Diego Rivera Museum). Calle Museo 150, Col. Tepetlapa. ☎ **5/677-2873.** Free admission. Tues–Sun 10am–2pm and 3–6pm. It's in the southern outskirts of the city in the suburb of San Pablo Tepetlapa, south of the Frida Kahlo Museum. Take the Metro (Line 2) to the Tasqueña terminal and change to Saro bus ("Tasqueña–Peña Pobre") west, which passes the museum. Another way to get there is on buses labeled "Zacatenco-Tlalpan" south along Balderas, or "El Rosario–Xochimilco" south along Avenidas Vasconcelos, Nuevo León, and Division del Norte; hop off at the Calle del Museo stop.

Not to be confused with Rivera's Studio Museum near the San Angel Inn, this is probably the most unusual museum in the city. Designed by Rivera before his death in 1957, it's devoted to his works as well as to his extensive collection of pre-Columbian art. Called the Anahuacalli ("House of Mexico") Museum and constructed of pedregal (the lava rock in which the area abounds), it resembles Maya and Aztec architecture. The name *Anahuac* was the old name for the ancient Valley of Mexico.

In front of the museum is a reproduction of a Toltec ball court, and the entrance to the museum itself is via a coffin-shaped door. Light filters in through translucent onyx slabs and is supplemented by lights inside niches and wall cases containing the exhibits. Rivera collected nearly 60,000 pre-Columbian artifacts, and the museum showcases thousands of them, in 23 rooms in chronological order, stashed on the shelves, tucked away in corners, and peeking from behind glass cases.

Upstairs, a replica of Rivera's studio has been constructed, and there you'll find the original sketches for some of his murals and two in-progress canvases. His first sketch (of a train) was done at the age of three, and there's a photo of it, plus a color photograph of him at work later in life in a pair of baggy pants and a blue denim jacket. Rivera (1886–1957) studied in Europe for 15 years and spent much of his life as a devoted Marxist. Yet he came through political scrapes and personal tragedies with no apparent diminution of creative energy, and a plaque in the museum proclaims him "A man of genius who is among the greatest painters of all time."

Xochimilco

The Canals and "Floating Gardens." Admission to the area is free; charge for boat rides is $16.50 per boat; boats can be shared by up to 8 to 10 people. Daily, morning to dusk. Metro: Take the metro to the Tasqueña stop, then the *tren ligero* (light train), which stops at the outskirts of Xochimilco. From there take a taxi to the main plaza of the town of Xochimilco. Buses run all the way across the city from north to south to end up at Xochimilco, but they take longer than the Metro. Of the buses coming from the center, the most convenient is "La Villa-Xochimilco," which you catch going south on Correo Mayor and Pino Suárez near the Zócalo; or near Chapultepec on Avenida Vasconcelos, Avenida Nuevo Leon, and Avenida Division del Norte.

The canals of Xochimilco (so-chee-MEEL-co), about 15 miles south of the historic center, are a survivor from the civilization of the Aztecs; the name means "flower cultivators." They built *chinampas* (gardens/cultivated fields) on a lake by filling them with fertile lake bottom mud and anchoring them in a shallow part of the lake, first with poles and then by tall, vertical ahuehuete trees around the edges. The lake eventually filled in with chinampas and, contrary to popular thought, they don't float. They are narrow, rectangular-shaped islands flanked on all sides by canals. In fact there are at least 50 miles of canals in Xochimilco.

If you've not been to Xochimilco in a while, you'll see a big difference. The long-announced revival and cleanup of Xochimilco has finally happened.

There are two main parts to Xochimilco, the **tourism-oriented area** in the historic center of town, where colorful boats take loads of tourists (some of them picnicking along the way) through a portion of the canals. Lively music is a staple, some of it provided by mariachi and trio musicians for hire who board the boats. The area is flanked by historic buildings, restaurants, souvenir stands, curio sellers, and boat vendors who pester you to take one boat over another. The other section, north of the center of town, is the **ecology-oriented area—Parque Natural Xochimilco.** Colorful boats also take tourists through the latter canals to see farming of the chinampas, and abundant bird life. Food and drink, however, are not allowed on boats in this section, though there are food, drink, and curio vendors where you board the boats. The chinampas have been used agriculturally for more than 500 years, and after almost 30 years of neglect are being reclaimed and put to use again as farmland. Descendants of the families that worked them in the past can be seen planting the fertile rectangular-shaped fields with flowers, as well as broccoli, corn, cabbage, squash, and other vegetables. Among the more than 170 species of birds is the rare Martín pescador. A water treatment plant cleans the water in the canals, and a lake has been created to funnel fresh water into them and is stocked with carp for fishing. Fronting the lake is a huge **modern visitors center** with a restaurant, book and gift shop, boat rentals (for the lake), and picnicking area. Beside it a **botanical garden** grows species of plants native to different areas around the city—Tlalpan, Texcoco, the Pedregal, Mixquic, and Xochimilco. The ecologically oriented section is calmly pastoral compared to the lively atmosphere of the more tourist-oriented area. Though the two are connected by canal, boats from one aren't allowed to go to the other.

On Sunday, Xochimilco (especially the tourist-oriented section) is jammed with foreign tourists and Mexican families with babies and picnic hampers; on weekdays, it's nearly deserted.

Xochimilco

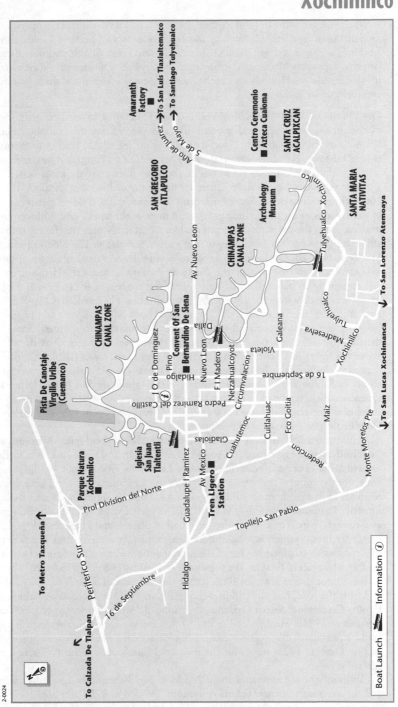

2-0024

When you get to the town of Xochimilco, you'll find a busy market in operation, specializing in rugs, ethnic clothing, and brightly decorated pottery. As you enter Xochimilco proper you will see many places to board boats. Should you miss them, however, turn along Madero and follow signs that say "Los Embarcaderos" (the piers). If you can resist the blandishment of the inevitable curio salesmen and shills, you will eventually arrive at the docks.

The Village of Xochimilco. Xochimilco (pop. 300,000), a colonial-era gem, with its bricked streets and light traffic, seems like a small town despite it's sizable population. Leave the hubbub of the colorful canals behind and take an hour or so to stroll around the town. Restaurants are at the edge of the canal and shopping area, and historically significant churches are within easy walking distance of the main square.

Among these, facing the main square (at the corner of Pino and Hidalgo), is the **16th-century Convent of San Bernardino de Siena,** with its flower petals carved in stone—a signature of the Indians who did most of the work—and 16th-century retables, one of the country's three such retables miraculously preserved for more than 400 years. (Another is at Huejotzingo, near Puebla; see chapter 12, "Side Trips from Mexico City.") The last Indian governor of Xochimilco, Apoxquiyohuatzin, is buried here. Inside and to the right, the skull over the font is from a pre-Hispanic skull rack signifying an Indian/Christian mixture of the concept of life and death. Eight lateral retablos date from the 16th to the 18th centuries. The fabulous gold gilt main altar, also from the 16th century, is like an open book with sculpture and religious paintings. A profusion of cherubic angels decorates columns and borders. Some of the altar paintings are attributed to Baltasar Echave Orio the Elder. Over the altar, above the figure of Christ, is San Bernardino with the *caciques* (local authorities) dressed in clothing with Indian elements and without shoes. Five blocks away at the corner of Sabino and J. O. de Dominguez is the **Iglesia de San Juan Tlaltentli.** Quetzalcoatl is symbolized by a snail and Aztec face on walls. The enormous ahuehuete tree across the street is hundreds of years old. From February through October the tree is loaded with nesting cranes.

A mile and a half south of the central plaza is the **Archeological Museum of Xochimilco,** at the crossroads of Avenida Tenochtitlán and Calle La Planta in the town of Santa Cruz Acalpixcan. The building dates from 1904 when it was the pump house for the springs. It houses artifacts from the area, many of them found when residents built their homes—10,000-year-old mammoth bones and figures dating from the Teotihuacán period—figures of Tlaloc (god of water and life) Ehecatl (god of the wind), Xipe Totec (god of renewal and of plants), and Huehueteotl (god of fire), polychrome pottery, carved abalone, and tombs showing funerary practices of 23 Teotihuacán inhabitants. One of the most unique pieces is a clay figure of a child holding a bouquet of flowers. The museum (☎ **5/675-0168** or 5/675-0426) is open Tuesday through Sunday from 10am to 5pm and admission is free.

Across the road, but not within walking distance, is the **archaeological zone/ Centro Ceremonial Azteca Cualama,** consisting of a series of petroglyphs meandering up a rocky hill. Steps go up the incline. On top is a large clearing which is still used for ceremonial dancing on March 21, for Fiesta de la Primavera Tlacaxipeualiztli, and on October 12, at noon, for the Fiesta del Pueblo Altepeilhuitl. There's no admission.

Continuing on the same road about 2 miles is the village of Santiago Tulyehualco and the **amaranth factory/Tehutl-Amaranto** (☎ **5/842-0752** and 5/842-2778). Amaranth was the sacred crop of the Aztecs, a plant yielding tiny whitish lysine-loaded round seeds that can be toasted or ground, and nutritious leaves that look like spinach. (Lysine is an essential amino acid that's sometimes absent in plant protein.) Because the Aztecs used amaranth in their rituals, the Spaniards forbid its cultivation, but as we see they weren't entirely successful. As you enter the front door, amaranth plants are on the left. Ask permission to see the process in back, of separating, grading, toasting, and packaging of products. To the right of the entrance is a store selling amaranth products, which include amaranth mixed with powdered chocolate for a hot drink, flour, cereal, pasta for soup, cookies, and granola. During the Days of the Dead amaranth skulls are sold at street markets countrywide. Amaranth is grown commercially in Puebla and Morelos states and locally on family plots. Green and black olives and olive oil are also sold, made from trees grown in the area. Each February the village hosts an **Olive and Amaranth fair.** The factory is open daily from 8am to 4pm; telephone ahead to arrange a tour.

Xochimilco celebrates with at least **422 festivals** annually, the most famous of which is for the **Niñopa,** a figure of the Christ child that since 1875 has been believed to possess miraculous powers. The figure is venerated on **January 6** (Three Kings Day), **February 2** (changing of the Niñopa's custodian), **December 16 through 24** (posadas for the Niñopa), and **April 30** (Day of the Child). Caring for the Niñopa is a coveted privilege that lasts a year, and the schedule of approved caretakers is filled through the year 2031.

Other significant festivals and commemorative occasions include the Olive and Alegria Fair **January 30–February 14** in Santaigo Tulyehualco (but the dates vary somewhat from this). During Days of the Dead, **November 1 through 2,** families decorate graves and perform cemetery vigils. **December 12,** Day of Guadalupe, is especially celebrated in the barrio (neighborhood) of La Guadalupita Xochitenco. **March 28 through April 4** (it varies slightly) is the *Feria de la Flor Más Bella del Ejido,* a flower fair when the most beautiful girl with Indian features and costume is selected. For more information and exact dates, contact the Xochimilco Tourist Office (Subdireccion de Turismo), Pino No 36, (☎ 5/676-5844; fax 5/676-0978) two blocks from the main square. It's open Monday through Saturday from 8am–3pm and 6–9pm.

Museo Dolores Olmedo Patiño. Avenida México 5843, Col. La Noria, Xochimilco. ☎ **5/555-1016.** Admission $1.50. Tues–Sun 10am–6pm.

Art collector and philanthropist Olmedo left her former home, the grand Hacienda La Noria, as a museum featuring the works of her friend and lover Diego Rivera. At least 137 of his works are displayed here, including his portrait of Olmeda, 25 paintings of Frida Kahlo, and 37 portraits of Angelina Beloff (Rivera's first wife), many of them drawings and engravings. Besides the paintings there are fine pre-Hispanic pieces on display, colonial furniture and other hacienda artifacts, and a collection of folk art. An excellent gift shop and a cafeteria are on the premises. The building and gardens alone are beautiful enough to justify a visit, and as you stroll the grounds you may see turkeys and hairless dogs. *Note:* It's a long walk to the museum from the main entrance, and the main building has many levels.

WALKING TOUR 1
The Zócalo

Start: The Palacio Nacional, on the east side of the Zócalo (Metro: Zócalo).
Finish: Burial vault of Hernán Cortés at the Hospital de Jesús Nazareño.
Time: Spread across 1 or 2 days, depending on the length of time you spend at each stop.

Best Times: Sunday, when the streets are relatively uncrowded, or the week before or after September 15 (Mexican Independence Day), when the Zócalo and surrounding streets are festooned in ribbons and lights.

Worst Times: Monday, when the museums are closed.

1. The Zócalo. Every Spanish colonial city in North America was laid out according to a textbook plan, with a plaza at the center surrounded by a church, government buildings, and military headquarters. Since Mexico City was the capital of New Spain, its Zócalo is one of the grandest and is graced on all sides by stately 17th-century buildings.

Zócalo actually means "pedestal" or "plinth." A grand monument to Mexico's independence was planned and the pedestal built, but the project was never completed. Nevertheless, the pedestal became a landmark for visitors, and soon everyone was calling the square after the pedestal, even though the pedestal was later removed. Its official name is Plaza de la Constitución. It covers almost 10 acres and is bounded on the north by 5 de Mayo, on the east by Pino Suárez, on the south by 16 de Septiembre, and on the west by Monte de Piedad. The downtown district, especially to the north of the Templo Mayor site, one of the oldest in the city, has suffered long neglect, but a restoration project is slowly renewing much of its colonial charm. Occupying the entire east side of the Zócalo is the majestic, red tezontle stone.

2. Palacio Nacional, begun in 1692 on the site of Moctezuma's "new" palace, which became the site of Hernán Cortés's home and the residence of colonial viceroys. It has changed much in 300 years, taking on its present form in the late 1920s when the top floor was added. The complex of countless rooms, wide stone stairways, and numerous courtyards adorned with carved brass balconies is also where the president of Mexico works. But to most visitors it's better known for the fabulous second-floor Diego Rivera murals depicting the history of Mexico. Just 30 minutes here with an English-speaking guide will provide a good background for your understanding of Mexico's history. The cost of a guide is negotiable, $8.25 or less, depending on your negotiating ability.

Enter by the central door, over which hangs the bell from Dolores Hidalgo rung by Padre Miguel Hidalgo when he proclaimed Mexico's independence from Spain in 1810. Each September 15, Mexican Independence Day, the president of Mexico stands on the balcony above the door to echo Hidalgo's cry to thousands of spectators filling the Zócalo. Take the stairs to the Rivera murals, which were painted during a 25-year period. If you know something of the history of Mexico their content is easy to understand. The Legend of Quetzalcoatl depicts the famous legend of the flying serpent bringing a blond-bearded white man to the country. When Cortés arrived, many of the Aztecs remembered this legend and believed him to be Quetzalcoatl. Another mural tells of the American Intervention when American invaders marched into Mexico City during the War of 1847. It was on this occasion that the military cadets of Chapultepec Castle (then a military school) fought bravely to the last man. The most notable of Rivera's murals is the Great City of Tenochtitlán, a pictorial study of the original settlement in the Valley of Mexico. The city takes up only a small part of the mural, and the remainder is filled with what appear to be four million extras left over from a Hollywood epic. In fact, no matter what their themes, most of the murals incorporate a piece of ancient Mexican history, usually featuring Cortés and a cast of thousands. It's open daily from 9am to 5:30pm. Admission is free but, visitor tags are required; be prepared to leave some form of identification in exchange.

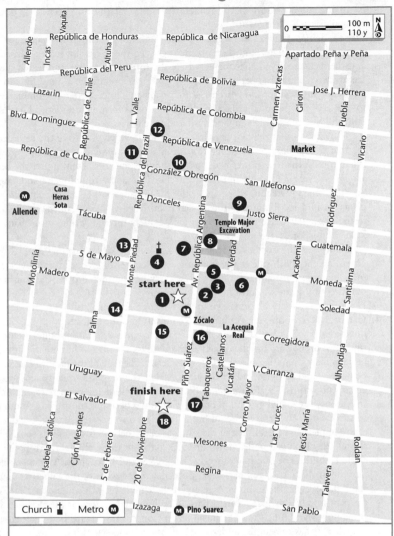

República de Honduras
República de Nicaragua
Vaquita
Allende
Incas
Altuha
Apartado Peña y Peña
República del Peru
República de Bolivia
Jose J. Herrera
Lazarin
República de Chile
República de Colombia
Carmen Aztecas
Giron
Puebla
Blvd. Dominguez
L. Valle
Vicario
12
República de Venezuela
Market
11
República de Cuba
República del Brazil
González Obregón
10
San Ildefonso
Rodriguez
Casa Heras Sota
Donceles
Av. República Argentina
Allende
Tácuba
9
Justo Sierra
Motolinía
5 de Mayo
13
Monte Piedad
Templo Major Excavation
8
7
Guatemala
Academia
Madero
4
5
Verdad
M
Moneda
Santisima
start here
3
6
Soledad
1
2
M
14
Zócalo
La Acequia Real
Corregidora
Palma
15
16
Alhondiga
Uruguay
Piño Suárez
Castellanos
Yucatán
V.Carranza
Correo Mayor
El Salvador
finish here
17
Isabela Católica
Cjón Mesones
5 de Febrero
20 de Noviembre
18
Mesones
Las Cruces
Jesús María
Roldan
Talavera
Regina
Church ✝ Metro Ⓜ
Izazaga
Ⓜ Pino Suarez
San Pablo

1. The Zócalo
2. Palacio Nacional
3. Museo Benito Juárez
4. Catedral Metropolitana
5. Calle de la Moneda
6. Museo de las Culturas
7. The Model of the Lake Region
8. Museo del Templo Mayor
9. Escuela Nacional Preparatoria
10. Secretaria de Educación Pública
11. Plaza de Santo Domingo
12. Palacio de la Inquisición
13. Monte de Piedad Nacional
14. Gran Hotel Ciudad de Mexico
15. Old and New Federal District Building
16. Suprema Corte de Justicia
17. Museo de la Ciudad de México
18. Iglesia y Hospital de Jesús Nazareño

Inside the corridors of the Palacio Nacional, at the northern end, is the comparatively little known:

3. **Museo Benito Juárez** (☎ 5/522-5646). Walk north inside the palace, to the statue of Benito Juárez and then up the stairs. To the left is the Juárez Museum and the well-preserved apartments where the former president of Mexico died. Handwritten letters and papers are kept in glass cases around the room. Other cases hold tablecloths, silverware, medals, shirts, watches, a briefcase, and symbolic keys to the city—all personal effects of the much-loved former president. There's a beautiful library in which anyone may study the books.

The last room at the rear is Juárez's bedroom, which gives one the eerie feeling that the former president might walk in at any moment—his dressing gown is laid out on the four-poster bed, and a chamber pot peeks from under the bed. *Important Note:* This Museum has been closed for some time for "remodeling," but spokesmen predict its reopening soon. Meanwhile most of the contents are on display at Hidalgo 79, next to the Museo Franz Mayer by the Alameda. If the one in the National Palace is open, hours are Monday through Friday from 9am to 7pm. Admission is free.

Before heading north, you may want to take a look at La Acequia Real (Royal Canal) on the south side of the building at the corner of Corregidora. It was the most important canal in colonial times, carrying commerce from the southern outskirts of the city. A portion of it was recently restored.

From the Palacio Nacional, go to the northern edge of the Zócalo and the:

4. **Catedral Metropolitana**. An impressive, towering cathedral, begun in 1573 and finished in 1667, it blends Greek and Mexican *churrigueresque* (baroque) architecture. In your look around the cathedral and the Sagrario next to it, note the sinkage of the building into the soft lake bottom beneath. The base of the facade is far from being level and straight, and when one considers the weight of the immense towers, it's no surprise. Scaffolding is in place because stabilizing repairs are ongoing. In Mexico, the sacred ground of one religion often becomes the sacred ground of its successor. Cortés and his Spanish missionaries converted the Aztecs, tore down their temples, and used much of the stone to construct a church on this spot. The church they built was pulled down in 1573 so the present Catedral Metropolitana could be built. The building of today has 5 naves and 14 chapels. As you wander past the small chapels, you may hear guides describing some of the cathedral's outstanding features: the tomb of Agustín Iturbide perhaps, placed here in 1838, or the paintings by the Spanish artist Bartolomé Esteban Murillo, or the fact that the stone holy-water fonts ring like metal when tapped with a coin. Like many huge churches, it has catacombs underneath. The much older looking church next to the cathedral is the chapel known as El Sagrario, another tour de force of Mexican baroque architecture built in the mid-1700s.

As you walk around the cathedral you will notice a scene reminiscent of medieval times: The west side of the cathedral is the gathering place of tradesmen—carpenters, plasterers, plumbers, painters, and electricians—who have no shops. Each craftsperson displays the tools of his trade, sometimes along with pictures of his work. Go out the front door of the cathedral and turn left toward the Palacio Nacional. Continue straight ahead across Seminario to the pedestrians-only street on the north side of the Palacio Nacional:

5. **Calle de la Moneda (Street of the Treasury or Mint)**. The street is lined with aged buildings constructed of tezontle, the local volcanic rock. On the left, at the corner of Calle Verdad, is the Edificio Arzobispal, the former archbishop's palace. True to Spanish tradition, the chief ecclesiastical official's power base was built

smack on top of the Aztec Temple of Tezcatlipoca, the multifaceted god who gave life and governed a host of lesser gods. It was on this site that the child Juan Diego revealed the cloak with the figure of the Virgin of Guadalupe for the first time to the archbishop. The building from which the street takes its name is at no. 13, on the right about halfway down, and it houses the:

6. Musco de las Culturas (☎ 5/512-7452). Formerly La Casa de Moneda (the mint), built as a part of the Palacio Nacional in the 1500s, this building was home for a time to the national anthropology museum before the new one opened in 1964 in Chapultepec Park. It remains a museum, and holds a fascinating assortment of exhibits relating to world cultures, with especially good pieces from Asia and Africa. It's open Tuesday through Friday from 9:30am to 6pm and Saturday and Sunday from 9:30am to 5:45pm. Admission is free.

☕ **TAKE A BREAK** If you are ready for a break, backtrack across the Zócalo to **Los Metates,** next to the entrance of the Hotel Majestic. It's small, but the service is fast.

Return across the Zócalo to the plaza on the east side of the cathedral. At ground level you'll see:

7. The Model of the Lake Region. The model shows the area in what today is the Zócalo and surrounding region as it was when Cortés first entered the city. The two cities of Tenochtitlán (the area where you're standing) and Tlatelolco (roughly the area around the Plaza of Three Cultures) were surrounded by the waters of Lake Texcoco and linked by raised causeways and canals. The model's fountain fills the canal-like "streets" with water just as they did in the heyday of the Aztec capital.

Continue on Seminario. Straight ahead and on the right are remnants of pre-Conquest Mexico at the:

8. Templo Mayor Archaeological Site and Museum (☎ 5/542-0606; fax 5/542-1717). A small corner of the site has been exposed for years, but it was never excavated. In 1978, a workman digging on the east side of the Catedral Metropolitana, next to what is now the Palacio Nacional, unearthed an exquisite Aztec stone of the moon goddess Coyolxauhqui. Mexican archaeologists followed up the discovery with major excavations, and what they uncovered were interior remains of the Pyramid of Huitzilopochtli, also called the Templo Mayor (Great Temple), the most important religious structure in the Aztec capital. What you see are actually remains of pyramids that were covered by the great pyramid the Spaniards saw on their arrival in the 16th century.

Strolling along the walkways built over the site, you pass a water-collection conduit constructed during the presidency of Porfirio Díaz (1877–1911), as well as far-earlier constructions. Building dates are on explanatory plaques (in Spanish). Shelters cover the ruins to protect traces of original paintwork and carving. Note especially the Tzompantli, or Altar of Skulls, a common Aztec and Maya design.

To enter the Museo del Templo Mayor (Museum of the Great Temple), take the walkway to the large building in the back portion of the site, which contains the fabulous artifacts from on-site excavations.

Inside the door, a model of Tenochtitlán will give you a good idea of the scale of the vast city of the Aztecs, which flourished in the century before Cortés arrived. The rooms and exhibits are organized by subject on many levels around a central open space. You'll see some marvelous displays of masks, figurines, tools, jewelry, and other artifacts, including the huge stone wheel of the moon goddess

Coyolxauhqui, "she with bells painted upon her face," on the second floor. The goddess ruled the night, so the Aztecs believed, but died at the dawning of every day, slain and dismembered by her brother Xiuhcoatl, the Serpent of Fire.

Look also for the striking jade-and-obsidian mask and the full-size terra-cotta figures of the *guerreros aguilas,* or "eagle warriors." A cutaway model of the Templo Mayor shows the layers and methods of construction.

Here's a quick guide to the exhibit rooms: Sala 1, "Antecedentes," contains exhibits about the early days of Tenochtitlán. Sala 2, "Guerra y Sacrificio," goes into the details of the Aztec religious duties of war and human sacrifice. Sala 3, "Tributo y Comercio," deals with Aztec government and its alliances and commerce with tributary states. Sala 4, "Huitzilopochtli," treats this most important of Aztec gods, a triumphant warrior, the son of Coatlicue, who bore him without losing her virginity. Huitzilopochtli, the "hummingbird god," was the one who demanded that human sacrifices be made to sustain him. In Sala 5, "Tlaloc," are exhibits explaining the role of the Aztec rain god in daily and religious life. Sala 6, "Faunas," deals with the wild and domesticated animals common in the Aztec Empire at the time when the capital flourished. Sala 7, "Religion," explains Aztec religious beliefs, which are amazingly complex and sometimes confusing because they are so different from the familiar religions of Europe and the Middle East. Sala 8, "Caida de Tenochtitlán," recounts the fall of the great city and its last emperors, Moctezuma and Cuauhtémoc, to Hernán Cortés and his conquistadores. The museum is open Tuesday through Sunday from 9am to 6pm (tickets sold only till 5pm). The entry fee is $2.25; free for all on Sunday. Use of your still camera is an additional $1.50; video camera $3.50. The admission is for both the ruins and the museum.

When you're finished at the museum, exit and come back around to the entrance on Seminario opposite the cathedral. The street changes to República de Argentina in front of the archaeological site. Continue north half a block, to the corner of Argentina and Donceles, and then turn right; half a block ahead on the left is the:

9. **Escuela Nacional Preparatoria,** constructed in 1740 by the Jesuits as the Colegio de San Ildefonso, houses murals by three Mexican greats: Rivera, Orozco, and Siqueiros. Today the building is a school, but the murals may be viewed Tuesday through Sunday from 11am until 5:30pm (till 8:30pm on Wednesday). Admission is $1.50.

Continue north on Argentina, cross and turn left on Calle González Obregón; on the right will be the entrance to the:

10. **Secretaría de Educación Pública,** built in 1922 and decorated with a great series of more than 200 Diego Rivera murals dating from 1923 and 1924. Other artists did a panel here and there, but it's the Rivera murals that are superb. The building is open Monday through Friday from 9:30am to 5:30pm.

As you exit the front door of the Secretaría, turn right (west) and walk half a block to the corner of República de Brasil; across the street on the right is the:

11. **Plaza de Santo Domingo,** featuring a wonderful slice of Mexican life. A fascinating plaza with arcades on one side, a Dominican church on the other, it's dominated by a statue of the Corregidora of Querétaro, Josefa Ortiz de Domínguez. The plaza is best known for the scribes who compose and type letters for clients unable to do so for themselves. Years ago, it was full of professional public writers clacking away on ancient typewriters, and a few still ply their trade on ancient electric typewriters among a proliferation of small print shops and presses. Emperor Cuauhtémoc's palace once occupied this land, then Dominicans built their monastery here.

Catercorner across the street, at the corner of Venezuela and Brasil, is the:

12. Palacio de la Inquisición (Inquisition Palace), built in 1732. For more than 200 years (1571–1820), accused Mexican heretics and other religious "criminals" were strangled and/or burned at the stake; for almost 100 years this was the building in which they were held prisoner and their fates decided. The last accused heretic to be executed was José María Morelos, hero of the Mexican Independence. Today the palace houses several rooms devoted to the very interesting Museum of the History of Mexican Medicine, with displays of modern and pre-Hispanic medicine. Informational signs are in Spanish only. To the left of the palace as you enter is a small bookstore/historical library of art, medicine, and culture. Outside the bookstore is a small restaurant serving light refreshments. The building and museum are open daily from 9am to 6:30pm.

☕ **TAKE A BREAK**   From the front door of the palacio, cross Brazil and go one block on Domínguez; on the right, ¹/₂ block past Palma, is the **Hostería de Santo Domingo,** Domínguez 72 (☎ **5/510-1434**), established in 1860 and reputed to be the oldest restaurant in Mexico City. Meals and drinks are a little expensive, but it's lively at midday, and the service and atmosphere are delightful. It's open daily from 9am to 11pm.

From the Hostería de Santo Domingo, return to the corner of Domínguez and Brasil and turn right on Brazil (toward the Zócalo), walking 3¹/₂ blocks. On the right is the:

13. Monte de Piedad Nacional, or National Pawn Shop (☎ **5/597-3455**), at the corner of Monte de Piedad and 5 de Mayo. Whoever heard of touring a pawn shop? In Mexico City it's done all the time in what could be described as the world's largest and most elegant Goodwill/Morgan Memorial thrift store. Electric power tools, jewelry, antique furniture, heavy machine tools, sofa beds, and a bewildering array of other things from trash to treasure are all on display. Buying is not required, but taking a look is recommended. Be sure to see the "Sala de Arte y Regalos" (art and gift shop); it's a hodgepodge of items ranging from the ridiculous to the exquisite. The building is on the site of Moctezuma's old Axayácatl palace" where the captive Emperor was killed. Cortés used the site to build a viceregal palace. The present building was given by Pedro Romero de Terreros, the Count of Regla, an 18th-century silver magnate from Pachuca, so that Mexican people might obtain low-interest loans. It's open Monday through Friday from 8:30am to 6pm and Saturday from 8:30am to 3pm.

☕ **TAKE A BREAK**   For a pause in your walking tour, continue south half a block and cross 5 de Mayo and Madero; here on the corner is one of the city's most popular hotels and rooftop restaurants, the **Hotel Majestic.** From the seventh-floor indoor/outdoor rooftop restaurant is a wonderful view of the Zócalo. For the best seat in town for the impressive flag-lowering ceremonies, get there by 5:45pm. On a clear day you can even see the Ixta and Popo volcanoes. It's great to begin your Zócalo tour here, to stop at midday, or to pay a late visit to the bar adjoining the restaurant, where there's a live singer nightly. It's open daily from 7:30am to 10:30pm.

With the Majestic Hotel on your right and the Zócalo on your left, go to the next corner, 16 de Septiembre; turn right a few steps to the:

14. Gran Hotel Ciudad de México. Originally a department store and later converted to a hotel, it is now operated by the Howard Johnson chain. It boasts one of the most splendid interiors of any downtown building. Step inside to see the lavish lobby, topped with its breathtaking Tiffany stained-glass canopy, and gilded open elevators on both sides.

Backtrack on 16 de Septiembre toward the Zócalo. Catercorner to your right are the:

15. **Arcades of the 16th-century Old Federal District Building and the New Federal District Building,** which dates from 1935 but looks like the older building. Both are on the south side of the Zócalo.

Continue east two blocks, crossing Pino Suárez; with the Palacio Nacional on the left, to your right is the:

16. **Suprema Corte de Justicia** (Supreme Court of Justice), built in the mid-1930s. Inside, on the main staircase and its landings are José Clemente Orozco murals, following a theme of justice that he was given the liberty to interpret.

Only 2¹/₂ blocks farther south on Pino Suárez, on the left at the corner of República del Salvador, is the:

17. **Museo de la Ciudad de México,** Pino Suárez 30 (☎ 5/542-8356 or 5/ 542-0487). Before you enter, go to the corner of República del Salvador and look at the enormous stone serpent head, a corner support at the building's base. The stone was once part of an Aztec pyramid. At the entrance, a stone doorway opens to the courtyard of this mansion built in 1528 as the House of the Counts of Santiago de Calimaya. This classic old building was converted into the Museum of the City of Mexico in 1964 and should be visited by anyone interested in the country's past. Dealing solely with the Mexico Valley, where the first people arrived around 8000 B.C., the museum contains some fine maps and pictographic presentations of the initial settlements and outlines of the social organization as it developed as well as models of several famous buildings of the city. Since its opening, the Museo Templo Mayor has somewhat overshadowed this one.

Much of the space upstairs has become either offices or meeting rooms. However, there are some beautiful religious paintings and the sun-drenched studio of Mexican impressionist Joaquin Clausell (1866–1935).

The museum is open Tuesday through Sunday from 10am to 6pm; admission is free.

Catercorner from the museum, at the corner of Suárez and Salvador, is the:

18. **Iglesia y Hospital de Jesús Nazareño,** founded by Hernán Cortés soon after the Conquest. A stone marker on Pino Suárez marks it as the spot where Cortés and Moctezuma reportedly met for the first time. Cortés died in Spain in 1547, but his remains are in a vault inside the chapel (entered by a side door on República del Salvador). Vaults on the opposite wall store the remains of Cortés's relatives. Notice the Orozco mural The Apocalypse on the choir ceiling. The chapel is open Monday through Saturday from 7am to 8pm and Sunday from 7am to 1pm and 5 to 8pm.

At the end of your tour here, the nearest Metro station is Pino Suárez or Zócalo (equal distance).

WALKING TOUR 2
Near the Alameda

Start: The Alameda Central (Metro: Bellas Artes).
Finish: Museo de Artes e Industrías Populares.
Time: Spread across 1 or 2 days, depending on the time spent at each location.

Walking Tour—Near the Alameda

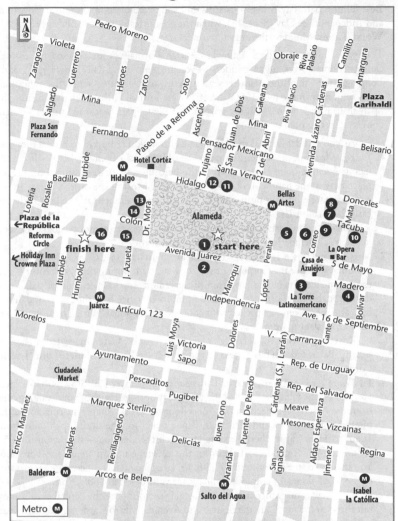

Metro **M**

1. Juárez Monument
2. Museo de Artes e Industrías Populares
3. La Torre Latinoamericano
4. Palacio de Iturbide
5. Palacio de Bellas Artes
6. Correos
7. Plaza Tolsá and El Caballito
8. Museo Nacional de Arte
9. Palacio Minería
10. Museo del Ejército y F.A.M.
11. Museo de la Estampa
12. Museo Franz Mayer
13. Pinacoteca Virreinal de San Diego
14. Museo Mural Diego Rivera
15. Jardín de la Solidaridad
16. Exposición Nacional de Arte Popular

Best Times: Saturday, when museums and shops are open, and around Christmas and Independence Day (Sept. 15), when the area is festooned in holiday color.
Worst Times: Monday; the museums are closed.

Today, the lovely tree-filled Alameda Central is a magnet for pedestrians, cotton-candy vendors, lovers, organ grinders—everyone enjoying a daily repast in the park. Long ago, the site of the Alameda was an Aztec marketplace. When the conquistadores took over in the mid-1500s, heretics were burned at the stake there under the Spanish Inquisition. In 1592, the governor of New Spain, Viceroy Luís de Velasco, converted it to a public park.

As you wander around the Alameda Central, you're bound to notice the:

1. Juárez Monument, sometimes called the **Hemiciclo** (hemicycle or half-circle), facing Avenida Juárez. Enthroned as the hero he was, Juárez assumes his proper place here in the pantheon of Mexican patriots. Most of the other statuary in the park was done by European sculptors (particularly French) in the late 19th and early 20th centuries.

   Folk-art enthusiasts will delight in the excellent government-operated craft shop just across Avenida Juárez from the monument, the:

2. Museo de Artes e Industrias Populares, at Juárez 44 (☎ 5/521-6679). The building was once the Corpus Christi Convent, built during the 17th century. You can see the upstairs museum portion (if the remodeling has been completed) Tuesday through Friday between 9am and 6pm; its entrance is in the rear of the building. The showrooms are packed with good-quality regional crafts. The store is open daily from 9am to 6pm.

   Leaving the Museo, turn right for three blocks. Catercorner from the imposing Palacio de Bellas Artes, at the corner of Juárez (Madero) and Lázaro Cárdenas, is:

3. La Torre Latino Americana, or Latin American Tower (☎ 5/521-0844). Here you can see the fabulous views of the whole city and the route of your walking tour from the observation deck on the 42nd floor of this skyscraper soaring above the intersection of Juárez and Cárdenas. Buy a ticket for the deck (open daily from 10am to 11pm) at the booth as you approach the elevators—admission is $2.50 for adults, $2 for children. Tokens for the telescope up top are on sale here, too. You then take an elevator to the 37th floor, cross the hall, and take another elevator to the 42nd floor. An employee will ask for your ticket as you get off.

   The view is magnificent, with mountains surrounding the capital on all sides, but those to the north are the nearest and Avenida Lázaro Cárdenas seems to head straight for them. To the north just below is the white-marble Bellas Artes, and west of it is the green patch of the Alameda. Due west is the Monument to the Revolution, just beyond the intersection of Juárez and Reforma. You can't see Reforma too well because it's hidden by the buildings that line it, but the green swath of Chapultepec Park and its palace on the hilltop are easy to spot. To the east is the Zócalo, dominated by the cathedral. To the south is an area densely packed with homes, factories, and tall apartment buildings.

   From the front door of the tower, turn right to the corner, then right again on Madero (the street name has changed from Juárez). Go 1 1/2 blocks (past the Church of San Francisco) to the magnificent:

4. Palacio de Iturbide, at Madero 17. This ornate stone palace with huge hand-carved wooden doors and a wildly baroque 40-foot-high carved-stone archway was built in 1780 for the Conde de San Mateo Valparaíso as a gift for his daughter. It was later the residence of Don Agustín de Iturbide, and briefly, in 1847, it served

as a prison where Americans captured during the U.S. invasion of Mexico were held.

The building now takes its name from Don Agustín de Iturbide, who later became the self-proclaimed Agustín I, Emperor of Mexico (1822–1823). His reign lasted only a matter of months, for although he was a partisan of Mexican independence, his political outlook was basically royalist and conservative. The future of Mexico lay in the liberal social reforms advocated by the great revolutionaries Hidalgo and Morelos. Iturbide was exiled and, later, on his unauthorized return, was executed in Padilla, Tamaulipas, and buried there. Years later his contribution to Mexican independence was recognized, and his body was reburied in the Catedral Metropolitana (see "Walking Tour 1—The Zócalo"), where it remains today.

Banamex, the present owner of the building, restored the palace in 1972, and the result is beautiful. Enter a courtyard with three tiers of balconies: The ground floor is a banking office and has a temporary art-exhibition area; the upper floors have executive offices. Period paintings and statues grace walls and corners, and the second-floor chapel has been beautifully restored. Banamex has a brief (but free) printed guide to the building; ask the guard for one and come in and have a look at any time daily from 10am to 7pm.

While you're here you may want to stop in a few doors down at the American Book Store or take a look at the exterior of the Casa Borda that belonged to the silver baron from Taxco, on the same side of the street at the corner of Madero and Allende.

Now cross the street to the north side of Madero and double back toward the Alameda.

☕ **TAKE A BREAK**   On the way back from the Iturbide Palace toward the Alameda, whether or not it's time for a break, you must stop in, however briefly, at a downtown institution: The **Casa de Azulejos** (House of Tiles), Madero 4 (☎ **5/518-6676**). You can't miss it, all decked out in gorgeous blue-and-white tiles. One of Mexico City's most precious colonial gems and popular meeting places, the building dates from the end of the 1500s, when it was built for the Count of the Valley of Orizaba. The most popular story goes that during the count's defiant youth, his father proclaimed: "You will never build a house of tiles," a tiled house being a sign of success at the time—the father was sure his son would amount to nothing. So when success came, the young count covered his house in tiles, which are a fine example of Puebla craftspeople's work. Today the tile-covered house is a branch of Sanborn's restaurant/newsstand/giftshop/drugstore chain. You can stroll through to admire the interior and have a refreshing drink or a full meal. Pause to see the Orozco mural *Omniscience*, on the landing leading to the second floor (where the bathrooms are). It's open daily from 7:30am to 11pm.

Continuing back toward the Alameda on Madero, turn right at the next corner, the busy Avenida Lázaro Cárdenas, and cross it to the beautiful white marble:

5. **Palacio de Bellas Artes** (*bay*-yahs *arr*-tehs), at the east end of the Alameda (☎ **5/512-2592**, ext. 152). The building is a supreme achievement of art deco lyricism. In addition to being the concert hall, it houses permanent and traveling art shows.

The theater is very turn-of-the-century, built during the Porfiriato and covered in Italian Carrara marble on the outside; however, it's completely 1930s art deco inside. It has sunk into the soft belly of Lake Texcoco some 12 feet since construction was begun in 1900 (it was opened in 1934). The palacio is the work of several masters: Italian architect Adamo Boari, who made the original plans; António Muñoz and Frederico Mariscal, who modified Boari's plans considerably; and Mexican painter Gerardo Murillo ("Doctor Atl"), who designed the fabulous art nouveau glass curtain that was constructed by Louis Comfort Tiffany in the Tiffany Studios of New York. Made from nearly a million iridescent pieces of colored glass, the curtain portrays the Valley of Mexico with its two great volcanoes. You can see the curtain before important performances at the theater and on Sunday mornings.

On the third level are the famous murals by Rivera, Orozco, and Siqueiros. The controversial Rivera mural *Man in Control of His Universe* was commissioned in 1933 for Rockefeller Center in New York City. He completed the work there just as you see it: A giant vacuum sucks up the riches of the earth to feed the factories of callous, card-playing, hard-drinking white capitalist bullies, while the noble workers of the earth, of all races, rally behind the red flag of socialism and its standard-bearer, Lenin. Needless to say, the Rockefellers didn't enjoy their new purchase. Much to their discredit, however, they had it painted over—destroyed. Rivera duplicated the mural here as *Man at the Crossing of the Ways* to preserve it.

There's a restaurant and good bookstore on the first floor to the left of the entrance. You can look around in the building Tuesday through Saturday from 11am until 7pm and on Sunday from 9am until 7pm. For information on tickets to performances of the Ballet Folklórico, see "Evening Entertainment" later in this chapter.

Go back across Cárdenas. The huge building at the corner of Cárdenas and Tacuba is the:

6. **Correos** (post office). The beautiful white stone building, built between 1902 and 1907, was designed by Italian architect Adamo Boari, who also contributed to the Bellas Artes. On the ground level you transact postal business, while the second level houses an interesting exhibit of postal related items from the past, such as old post-boxes and a carriage that once carried mail between Mexico City and Veracruz.

From the Correos and the corner of Tacuba, with your back to Cárdenas, walk a block. Here on the left is the:

7. **Plaza Tolsá and El Caballito,** a huge equestrian statue in front of the Museo Nacional de Arte. The gallant statue of King Carlos IV of Spain (1788–1808) atop a high-stepping horse was crafted by Mexican sculptor Manuel Tolsá. Mexicans call the statue El Caballito ("The Little Horse"), and the name reveals a lot: They prefer not to mention Carlos, who was king shortly before Mexico's Independence movement from Spain began in 1810. The statue is actually one of the largest and most finely crafted equestrian statues in the world. Erected first in the Zócalo, it was later moved (1852) to a traffic circle in the Paseo de la Reforma. A few years ago El Caballito was moved to this more dignified and appropriate position in front of the museum opposite the handsome Palacio de Minería (see below), also designed by Tolsá and one of the capital's most handsome buildings.

Just behind the statue is the entrance to one of the city's best, but least-visited, museums, the:

8. **Museo Nacional de Arte** (☎ **5/512-3224** or 5/521-7320). The palacelike building, designed by Italian architect Silvio Contri and completed in 1911, another legacy of the years of Europe-loving Porfirio Díaz, was built to house the government's offices of Communications and Public Works. The National

Museum of Art took over the building in 1982. Wander through the immense rooms with polished wooden floors as you view the wealth of paintings showing Mexico's art development, primarily covering the period from 1810 to 1950. It's open Tuesday through Sunday from 10am to 5:30pm. Admission is $1.50; free on Sunday.

The beautiful building across from the Museo Nacional de Arte is the:

9. **Palacio de Minería,** built in the 1800s, one of architect Manuel Tolsá's finest works. Formerly the school of mining, it's used today for concerts and cultural events (see "Evening Entertainment" later in this chapter). If it's open, step inside for a look at the several patios and fabulous stone work.

Just past the Minería at the next corner (Mata), turn right a few steps and on your left will be the:

10. **Museo del Ejército y F.A.M.,** Calle de Tacuba and Filomeno Mata 6 (☎ 5/512-3215; fax 5/512-7586), a rather new museum. Ejército means "army," and delicately and artistically displayed inside these high-ceilinged, serene rooms are select instruments used in warfare—from coats of armor and swords to modern weapons. Blood and suffering seem like they could never have been a part of anything so tastefully designed and presented. It's open daily from 10am to 6pm.

Return to Tacuba and turn left back to Cárdenas. Cross Cárdenas and continue 1¹/₂ blocks west. Opposite the north side of the Alameda, near the corner of Hidalgo and Trujano, is the:

11. **Museo Nacional de la Estampa,** Hidalgo 39 (☎ 5/521-2244), next door to the Museo Franz Mayer (see below). Estampa means "engraving" or "printing," and the museum is devoted to understanding and preserving the graphic arts. Housed in a beautifully restored 16th-century building, the museum has both permanent and changing exhibits. Displays include those from pre-Hispanic times when clay seals were used for designs on fabrics, ceramics, and other surfaces. But the most famous works here are probably those of José Guadalupe Posada, Mexico's famous printmaker, who poked fun at death and politicians through his skeleton figure drawings. If your interest in this subject is deep, ask to see the video programs on graphic techniques—woodcuts, lithography, etching, and the like. It's open Tuesday through Sunday from 10am to 6pm. Admission is $1.25; free on Sunday.

From here, go right a few steps to the entrance of the:

12. **Museo Franz Mayer,** Hidalgo 45 (☎ 5/518-2265), one of the capital's foremost museums, which opened in 1986 in a beautifully restored 16th-century building on Plaza de la Santa Veracruz. It's also on the north side of the Alameda. The extraordinary 10,000-piece collection of antiques, mostly from Mexico's 16th through 19th centuries, was amassed by one man, Franz Mayer. A German immigrant, he adopted Mexico as his home in 1905 and grew rich there. Before his death in 1975, Mayer bequeathed the collection to the country and arranged for its permanent display through a trust with the Banco Nacional. The pieces, all utilitarian objects (as opposed to pure art objects), include inlaid and richly carved furniture; an enormous collection of Talavera pottery; gold and silver religious pieces; sculptures; tapestries; rare watches and clocks (the oldest is a 1680 lantern clock); wrought iron; old master paintings from Europe and Mexico; and 770 Don Quixote volumes, many of which are rare editions or typographically unique. There's so much to see that it may take two visits to absorb it. The museum is open Tuesday through Sunday from 10am to 5pm. Admission is $1.25; free on Sunday. There are guided tours Monday through Saturday at 10:30 and 11:30am and 12:30pm.

(Next to the Museo Franz Mayer, is the **temporary Museo Benito Juárez,** Hidalgo 79, (☎ 5/228-3887). While the Juárez rooms at the Palacio Nacional are being remodeled, the contents are on display here and include the personal effects of Juárez and his family, his personal letters, a library that's open to the public, and 180 paintings of Mexico's historic elite.

☕ **TAKE A BREAK** If a break is in order at this point, try a light snack at the Cafeteria of the **Museo Franz Mayer,** at its marble-top tables in a pleasant courtyard. It's open the same days and hours as the museum. Or take in another ancient religious structure. Continue one block farther west of the Franz Mayer on Hidalgo to the corner of Reforma, where you'll find the Hotel de Cortés. It was constructed in the 18th-century as a hospice for Augustinian monks. After their suppression in 1821, it served, among other things, as an insane asylum and more lately as a lovely hotel. Step inside the red tezontle stone edifice to the open courtyard dripping with pink bougainvillea and outfitted in umbrella-shaded tables. The restaurant serves rather high-priced Mexican and international dishes. Drinks, however, are relatively inexpensive. It's open daily from 7:30am to 10pm.

From the Hotel de Cortés, cross Hidalgo toward the park. Just at the corner on your right, opposite the Alameda and past the Centro Cultural José Martí, is the:

13. **Pinacoteca Virreinal de San Diego,** Dr. Mora 7 (☎ **5/510-2793** or 5/512-2079). This former church is now a gallery of paintings, most from the 16th and 17th centuries and ecclesiastical in theme. Highlights are apparent immediately as you walk around: In the wing to the right of where the altar would have been is a room featuring a gorgeous blue-and-gilt ceiling with gleaming rosettes and a striking mural by Frederico Canto (1959), one of the few modern works. Upstairs in a cloister are many small paintings by Hipolito de Rioja (who worked in the second half of the 17th century), Baltazar de Echave Ibia (1610–1640), and others. By the way, the tremendous painting on the cloister wall, *Glorificación de la Inmaculada* by Francisco Antonio Vallejo (1756–1783), should be viewed from upstairs—the lighting is better. The Pinacoteca is open Tuesday through Sunday from 10am to 5pm; admission is $1.25; free on Sunday.

Turn right out the front door and right again on Colón, a short street facing the Plaza de la Solidaridad; walk to the entrance, on the right, of the:

14. **Museo Mural Diego Rivera** (☎ **5/510-2329**), housing Diego Rivera's famous mural *Dream of a Sunday Afternoon in Alameda Park*, which was painted on a wall of the Hotel Prado in 1947. The hotel was demolished after the 1985 earthquake, but the precious mural, perhaps the best known of Rivera's works, was saved and transferred to its new location in 1986. The huge picture, 50 feet long and 13 feet high, chronicles the history of the park from the time of Cortés onward. Among the historical figures who have made their mark in Mexican history are these, portrayed more or less from left to right (but not in chronological order): Cortés; a heretic suffering under the Spanish Inquisition; Sor Juana Inés de la Cruz, a brilliant and progressive woman who became a nun in order to continue her scholarly pursuits; Benito Juárez, putting forth the laws of Mexico's great Reforma; the conservative Gen. Antonio López de Santa Anna, handing the keys to Mexico to the invading American Gen. Winfield Scott; Emperor Maximilian and Empress Carlota; José Martí, the Cuban revolutionary; Death, with the plumed serpent (Quetzalcoatl) entwined about his neck; Gen. Porfirio Díaz, great with age and medals, asleep; a police officer keeping the Alameda free of "riffraff" by ordering a poor family out of the elitists' park; and Francisco Madero, the martyred democratic president who caused the downfall of Díaz, whose betrayal and alleged

murder by Gen. Victoriano Huerta (pictured on the right) resulted in years of civil turmoil in Mexico. The museum is open Tuesday through Sunday from 10am to 7pm; admission is $1.25; free on Sunday.

Facing the Museo Mural, on the west side of the Alameda, is the:

15. Jardín de la Solidaridad, or Solidarity Garden, built in 1986 in remembrance of those who died during the 1985 earthquake.

From the Avenida Juárez side of the Jardín de la Solidaridad, go west on Juárez one block, crossing Zarco. Here on the corner on the right is the:

16. Exposición Nacional de Arte Popular, Juárez 89 (☎ **5/518-3058**), described in more detail under "Shopping" later in this chapter. The ground floor of the 18th-century mansion is loaded with crafts from all over Mexico. It's open daily from 10am to 6pm.

WINDING DOWN   As you leave the Exposición, turn right on Juárez to the next corner, Humboldt. Turn left, crossing Juárez, and go a long block. Here on the left is the **Fonda Santa Anita,** Humboldt 48 (☎ **5/518-4609**), a good place to finish a stroll around the Alameda. The Fonda provides traditional Mexican food and margaritas served in quaint ceramic jugs. It's a great for kicking back and reviewing the day amid colorful banners and painted chairs. And it's only a block from the Juárez metro station. Hours are Monday through Friday from noon to 10pm and Saturday and Sunday from 1:30 to 9pm.

WALKING TOUR 3
The Museo Nacional de Antropología

Start: Sala (Room) 1.
Finish: Sala (Room) 22.
Time: At least two or three hours, even if you're a dedicated museum-rusher.
Best Times: Early any weekday, or Sunday, when it's free.
Worst Times: Monday, when the museum is closed, or a national holiday, when it's crowded.

The Museo Nacional de Antropología (☎ **5/553-6381**) is breathtaking in its splendor, with a tall fountain designed by José Chávez Morado. It's open Tuesday through Saturday from 9am to 7pm and Sunday from 10am until 6pm. Admission costs $2.25 (free on Sunday). Free tours are available on request (for a minimum of five people) in English, French, or Spanish Tuesday through Saturday from 10am to 5pm. See "In Chapultepec Park" earlier in this chapter for details on how to get to the museum.

There are three sections. First is the entrance hall to the museum proper, with a checkroom on the right and the museum bookstore on the left. The bookstore has a superior collection of guides to cultural, culinary, and archaeological attractions in Mexico.

Inside the museum proper is an open courtyard (containing the Chávez Morado fountain) with beautifully designed spacious rooms running around three sides on two levels. The ground-floor rooms are theoretically the most significant, and they are the most popular among studious visitors, devoted as they are to history and pre-historic days all the way up to the most recently explored archaeological sites. These rooms include dioramas of the way Mexico City looked when the Spaniards first arrived and reproductions of part of a pyramid at Teotihuacán. The Aztec calendar stone "wheel" takes a proud place here.

Save some of your time and energy, though, for the **ethnographic rooms** upstairs. This portion is a "living museum," devoted to the way people throughout Mexico live today, complete with straw-covered huts, tape recordings of songs and dances, crafts, clothing, and lifelike models of village activities. To me, both floors are equally interesting, one dealing with the past and the other dealing with the living past so to speak, because so much Mexican village life today retains vestiges of pre-Hispanic customs.

There is a lovely restaurant in the museum with moderate prices, air-conditioning, and cheerful patio tables.

Note: Most of the museum is wheelchair accessible; however, assistance will be needed in places. Signs are in Spanish only. A systematic room-at-a-time renovation and reorganization started in 1995, so a room or portion of one may be closed during your visit.

Pass the ticket taker and enter the courtyard. Here are the museum's highlights, room (sala) by room, beginning on your right:

1. **"Introducción a la Antropología"**: The entrance mural by Z. González Camarena depicts women of various nations. Exhibits deal with the various races of humanity throughout the world, their progress and development, and how these aspects are studied by anthropologists.

2. **"Mesoamerica"**: Here you see the cultural interrelation of the Mesoamerican people even though they are dispersed over a large landscape, demonstrated by a large color map showing locations of the great cultures. A timeline puts them in perspective. A mural by Raul Anguiano shows the Maya cosmogony: Thirteen heavens are held up by a giant ceiba tree; nine hells are beneath. The mural is directly above an exhibit of burial customs. You'll see other fascinating displays of pottery, jewelry, skeletal remains, painting, sculpture, and architecture.

The next sign you'll see, SALAS DE ETNOGRAFÍA, EN LA PLANTA ALTA, means "Ethnographic Rooms on the Upper Floor." There's a stairway here so you can reach those rooms. But, for now, continue around the right side of the courtyard on the main level to:

3. **"Origenes"**: This "Room of Origins" traces the history of the earliest men and women in the Americas, with specific emphasis on their remains in Mexico. Don't miss the *mamut 2* (mammoth 2) of Santa Isabel Iztapan discovered in 1954 northwest of Mexico City. Of considerable interest is the miniature display of the diverse architectural styles evidenced in Mexico's pyramids.

4. **"Preclásica y Teotihuacána"**: Exhibits here are of Preclassic times (2000 B.C.–A.D. 300), just before the Mesoamerican cultures reached their zenith. Religion, agriculture, hieroglyphic writing, numbering, and art were in place. One display shows a reconstructed archaeological site found in place during digs at Tlatilco (1300–800 B.C.), including pottery, figures, and skeletal remains. The people of Tlatilco were known for their appliqué technique using clay pieces for figure decoration, and many of their pieces were formed in the shape of animals, birds, frogs, and squash. Among the most interesting displays are clay figures that effectively show the appearance of people in those times, including pottery pieces attributed to the Olmecs.

5. **"Teotihuacán"**: First view the model of this important site that flourished just outside Mexico City between 100 B.C. and A.D. 700. Outside on the back patio is another mockup view of the site at eye level. This sala will prepare you for seeing the ruins in person—something you must do. Chronologically displayed pottery gives a clear picture of the development of this utilitarian art at Teotihuacán. Other exhibits show tools for building, sculpture, fresco painting, jewelry making,

Walking Tour —
The Museo Nacional de Antropología

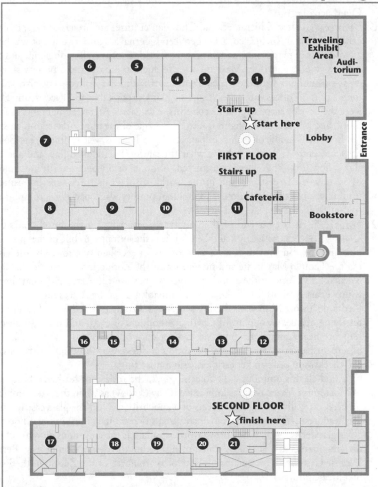

FIRST FLOOR:
1. "Introducción a la Antropología"
2. "Mesoamerica"
3. "Origenes"
4. "Preclásica y Teotihuacana"
5. "Teotihuacán"
6. "Tolteca"
7. "Mexica"
8. "Oaxaca"
9. "Golfo de Mexico"
10. "Maya"
11. "Norte y Occidente"

SECOND FLOOR:
12. "Introductoría"
13. "Los Coras y Huicholes"
14. "Purepecha"
15. "Otomianos"
16. "Sierra Norte de Puebla"
17. "Oaxaca"
18. "Costa Golfo"
19. "Maya"
20. "Noroeste de México"
21. "Las Nahuas"

and weaving. There's a reproduction of the mural *Paradise of the God Tlaloc*, and visitors are dwarfed beside the life-size replica of a portion of the Temple of Quetzalcoatl.

6. **"Tolteca":** Toltec, Chichimec, and Cholulan cultures are preserved here, but the exhibit begins at Xochicalco, a site between Cuernavaca and Taxco that was both a crossroads of many cultures and perhaps a bridge between Teotihuacán, and the Toltecs at Tula, north of Mexico City. Xochicalco building and pottery show a cross-cultural mix with the Maya, Teotihuacán, and the Toltecs. The artistic elements of the Toltecs influenced those of many groups that followed them: They were the developers of serpentine columns, *chac mools*, Atlantean figures, the eagle motif, and pilasters of war figures. Also here is one of the huge Atlantean-men statues from the Temple of Tlahuizcalpantecutli, at Tula, as well as other great monoliths and pottery. A model shows what the site of Tula looked like, and another shows how it may have been constructed. A model of the pyramid site at Cholula, by volume the largest pyramid in the world, displays its three superimpositions (buildings one on top of another). Cholulan pottery was especially accomplished, so don't miss the displays of it here.

7. **"Mexica":** At the far end of the courtyard, lettering on the lintel reads CEM ANAHUAC TENOCHCA TLALPAN, and beneath it is the entrance to one of the most important rooms in the museum. This room is an excellent one to see before visiting the Templo Mayor site and museum near the Zócalo in the historical zone of Mexico City. Among the amazing carved stones are the Aztec Calendar Stone, which bears symbols for all the ages of humankind (as the Aztecs saw them); the Piedra de Tizoc; Xiuhcoatl, the fire serpent; a Tzompantli, or wall of skulls; the terrifying headless monolith of Coatlicue, goddess of earth and death, with two serpents' heads coming from her neck, a necklace of hands and hearts, and a skirt of serpents; and the stone head of the moon goddess, Coyolxauhqui, with bells on her cheeks, sun disks in her earlobes, and a nose ring.

Amid all this ominous dark volcanic rock, the iridescent feathered headdress of Moctezuma blazes away, as impressive today (a copy) as when the Aztec emperor proceeded regally through the streets of Tenochtitlán. Near the glass case holding the headdress is a large model of Moctezuma's rich capital city; a mural echoes the city's grandeur as well. One of my favorite displays is the enormous diorama of the thriving market at Tlatelolco, which brings to life the description of it by Bernal Díaz de Castillo. (The remains of Tlatelolco are north of the Zócalo in the Plaza of Three Cultures.)

8. **"Oaxaca":** After the Mexico room comes that of Oaxaca, with its Zapotec and Mixtec cultures, Olmec influences, and priceless artifacts from the Monte Albán excavations. The huge display of pottery is arranged chronologically to show its evolution, and a deerskin Mixtec codice exemplifies picture writing. The Mixtecs were accomplished metalworkers, gemsmiths, and woodcarvers; and you'll see fine examples of their work. Take time to admire the reproduction of Tomb 105 from Monte Albán. Go down the stairs to a reproduction of Tomb 104, complete with wall frescoes and burial figures surrounded by offerings. A huge mural shows how the mountaintop ruins of Monte Albán looked at their apogee.

9. **"Golfo de Mexico":** Divided into four sections, this hall covers the rich cultures of the Huastecas from the northern part of Veracruz and Tamaulipas; the Remojadas and Totonacs, who occupied the middle portion of the region; and the Olmecs, who occupied southern Veracruz and northern Tabasco but whose influence was felt far away. Certainly the most visible highlight here is an enormous multiton, basaltic rock head, though one of the finest is the graceful and beautifully sculpted "wrestler," both by Olmec master stone carvers. The Huastecas were known for their exquisite polychrome pottery with anthropomorphic and zoomorphic forms, and the pottery display does justice to the culture. But the tall, slender stone-carved figure of the "Huasteca Adolescent," with a baby on its back, is one of Mesoamerica's most graceful. There are models of the archaeological sites at El Tajín, near Papantla, and Zempoala, near Veracruz.

10. "Maya": Don't miss this room! Not only are the exhibits wonderful, but also Maya art and culture have tremendous intrinsic interest. Displays here include a fine collection of well-preserved beautiful Maya carvings, not just from Mexican territory but from other parts of Mesoamerica (Central America) as well.

Models of ancient cities include Copan (Honduras), Yaxchilán (Chiapas), Tulum (Quintana Roo), and Uaxactun (Guatemala). Downstairs is a model of the fabulous tomb discovered in the Temple of the Inscriptions at Palenque, complete with a rich jade mask for the deceased monarch. Outside the exhibit room is a full-scale replica of a temple at Hochob (Campeche) and another of the Temple of Paintings at Bonampak, plus replicas of stele from Quirigua (Guatemala). In all these examples, notice especially the fineness of the carving. In the Tablero de la Cruz Enramada, from Palenque, note the fine work in the glyphs.

11. "Norte y Occidente": These rooms deal with the "culture of the desert" from northern and western Mexico. If you're familiar with the culture of the Indians of the southwestern United States, you'll notice numerous similarities here. Many of the artifacts are from the Casas Grandes pueblo in the state of Chihuahua, where the people lived in adobe pueblos and crafted pottery very much like that of New Mexico and Arizona.

The occidental (western) exhibits hold echoes of the great civilization of the Valley of Mexico, mostly from such sites as Tzintzuntzán (Michoacán), Ixtlan (Nayarit), Ixtepete (Jalisco), and Chupicuaro (Guanajuato), but they also include objects from San Miguel de Allende and San Luis Potosí. The *chac-mool* from Ihuatzio, for instance, looks like a bad copy or a stylized rendering of the great chac-mools of Tula and Chichén-Itzá. There's also a model of a *yácata*, a vast stepped ceremonial platform, as found in the western zone.

☕ **TAKE A BREAK**   After touring the Maya room, descend a wide staircase to reach the reasonably priced **Cafetería Museo.** Beer and mixed or soft drinks are served, as well as breakfast, soups, salads, sandwiches, and more substantial main courses. It's open Tuesday through Saturday from 9am to 7pm and Sunday from 9am to 6pm.

From here, cross to the end of the patio next to the Sala de Origenes and take the stairs up to the splendid displays of daily life in the Ethnographic Section. Begin in the first room on the right:

12. "Introductoría": Murals, maps, photographs, textiles, jewelry, and other objects give perspective on Mexico's daily life from pre-Hispanic times to the present.

13. "Cora y Huichol": Devoted to inhabitants of the west-coast states of Nayarit and Jalisco, this room displays lifelike figures, clad in traditionally embroidered clothing and seated on equipale stools before an authentic indigenous hut. Particularly note the pottery and *morales* (woven bags), all of which are in use in villages today.

14. "Purépecha": The Purépecha, more generally known as Tarascans, live in the state of Michoacán and carry on crafts learned centuries ago under the influence of the first Bishop of Pátzcuaro, Vasco de Quiroga. The main calling card of this display is the enormously long dugout canoe at the entrance. You'll see examples of guitars from Paracho, copper objects from Santa Clara del Cobre, and samples of fine dinnerware from potters around Lake Pátzcuaro. Occasionally on display is the exquisite reversible black-and-white serape trimmed with stylized quetzal bird designs that is produced by weavers from Angahuan, a village near the Paricutín volcano.

15. **"Otomianos":** Otomi Indians, who speak several languages within the Otomangue language group, live in the states of Hidalgo, México (which almost surrounds Mexico City), San Luis Potosí, and Querétaro. This group of Indians includes the Nahua, Azteca, Mazahua, and Matlatzinca, all of which are believed to be descendants of the Toltec. Here you see figures weaving *ixtle* fibers of the maguey plant. There are also cases of products made for everyday use and trade, such as baskets, belts, jars, blouses, and serapes.

16. **"Sierra Norte de Puebla":** The northern part of the state of Puebla is one of the country's most interesting areas, yet it's little visited by tourists. Note the villagers of San Pablito pounding bark into paper, the unfinished pink and black *quechquemitl* on an unusual loom that rounds corners, and the finely embroidered blouses with flower and animal designs.

17. **"Oaxaca":** The southern state of Oaxaca is one of the most interesting in the country, due in part to the numerous varieties of colorful *huipiles* (loose garments) worn by women from different indigenous groups. A full-size hut is complete with furnishings, weaving looms, and pottery, plus an oxcart outside. Another section shows the different styles of huts used along the coast of Oaxaca, and men and boys weaving palm.

18. **"Costa Golfo":** This region is composed of indigenous groups of Huastecas, Totonacas, and Nahuas. The Huasteca Indians speak a language related to Maya. Inside the hut, women wearing embroidered blouses and ribbons twisted through their braided hair are surrounded by pottery and frozen in the motion of decorating and forming clay by hand.

19. **"Maya":** The land of the Maya comprises the states of Tabasco, Chiapas, Yucatán, Campeche, and Quintana Roo; of these, the most colorful is Chiapas. Besides the cases of costumes and pottery, there are examples of musical instruments and furnished huts showing life today. A market scene from the Chiapas highlands shows men and women in regional attire—heavy wool tunics and colorful, richly brocaded loomed *huipiles*. In another scene, a woman from the Yucatán weaves henequen fiber on a stick loom.

20. **"Noroeste de México":** Seri, Tarahumara, and Yaqui Indians live in northwestern Mexico in the states of Sonora, Chihuahua, and Sinaloa, as well as in Baja California. Among the unusual items you'll see are beautiful basketry that's quite similar to some made in the southwestern United States. A painting shows how the Seri women decorate their faces.

21. **"Las Nahuas":** The last room is devoted to this Indian group in modern Mexico who live in central Veracruz, Hidalgo, Guerrero, Morelia, Durango, Tlaxcala, Jalisco, and the state of México. It portrays them in various acts of their daily life, which is based on the corn culture. A written narrative states that this group is in a precarious situation due to poor health care, unemployment, illiteracy, injustice, and oppression.

ORGANIZED TOURS

I've already mentioned that Mexico City is a great place for looking around on your own, and in general this is the cheapest way to see whatever you like. However, if your time is limited, you may wish to acclimate yourself quickly by taking a tour or two.

Among the noncommercial offerings are **free guided tours** sponsored by the **Mexico City Historical Center** (☎ 5/510-2541 or 5/510-4737, ext. 1499), which is housed in the 18th-century home of Don Manuel de Heras y Soto, at Donceles and República de Chile. Groups meet each Sunday at 10:45am at a central gathering place for that day's tour, which varies from week to week. These tours might explore a historic downtown street, cafés and theaters, cemeteries, or the colonial churches of Xochimilco. Most tours, which last about two hours, are in Spanish, and as many as 300 people may be divided among 10 guides; however, visitors with other language requirements can ask a day in advance for a guide who speaks their language. Since the center's phone is almost always busy, you'll have to visit the office in the far back of the building, on the right and up a spiral staircase, to obtain a list of upcoming tours and gathering locations. Office hours are Monday through Friday from 9am to 3pm and 6 to 9pm. Don Manuel, by the way, was one of the notables who signed Mexico's Act of National Independence in 1821.

A one-hour **trolley-bus tour** of the Centro Histórico is sponsored by the Chamber of Commerce Tourism Services (☎ 5/512-1012) Tuesday through Sunday. Buses load across Pino Suarez from the Museo de La Ciudad and leave every 30 minutes between 10am and 4pm. Cost is $3.

Many commercial tours are offered, such as a four-hour city tour including such sites as the **National Cathedral,** the **Palacio Nacional,** and **Chapultepec Park** and **Castle;** a longer tour to the **Shrine of Guadalupe** and nearby pyramids in the **Teotihuacán archaeological zone;** and the Sunday tour that begins with the **Ballet Folklórico,** moves on to the floating **gardens of Xochimilco,** and may or may not include lunch and the afternoon bullfights. Almost as popular are the one-day and overnight tours to Puebla, Cuernavaca, Taxco, and Acapulco. There are also several nightclub tours.

I feel that I must give some caveats: Many readers have written to say they were unhappy with the sightseeing tours of this or that company. The reasons are myriad: The tour was too rushed; the guide knew nothing and made up stories about the sights; or the tour spent most of its time in a handcrafts shop (chosen by the tour company) rather than seeing the sights. Do tour companies get a kickback from souvenir shops? You bet they do! If you meet someone who has recently taken a guided tour and liked it, go with the same company. Otherwise, you might do well to see the sights on your own, following the detailed guidance in this book.

Or I can highly recommend the services of my friend for many years, **Guillermo Arias** (☎ and fax **5/397-2838**), a licensed English-speaking guide who can take you anywhere inside or outside the city. Write him at Acacias 82, Viveros de la Loma, 54080 Estado de México. That address is just north of the city center, but he can meet you anywhere.

SPECTATOR SPORTS

JAI ALAI Fronton de México, Plaza de la República (☎ **5/546-5369,** 5/546-1479, or 5/546-3240). Jai alai (hi-lie) must be the fastest game in the world and is exciting to watch even without prior knowledge of the sport. It doesn't much matter when you arrive, as there are several games on each night's schedule. As you walk into the fronton, the ticket office is to your left: There you pay and pick up a program, then take a seat.

Jai alai players wear on their right arms small baskets with which they catch and sling a fantastically resilient ball against the wall to the right of where you're sitting. In the best game, four players, two with blue armbands and two with red ones, compete against each other in a fashion similar to squash. The member of one team throws the ball against the wall, and the other team has to return it. The whole thing is done at an incredible speed—how they manage to see, much less catch, a ball traveling at about 80 miles per hour is marvelous.

The most fun is in the betting; it's amazing how much more exciting a game can be when you have money riding on the result. Wait until the program announces a game of 30 points (*partido a treinta tantos*) and watch the bookies. These colorful gentlemen, wearing burgundy vests, carry little pads of betting slips edged in red (*rojo*) or blue (*azul*), and when the game begins they'll be offering only a slight edge on one team or another. Bets are placed inside of slashed tennis balls and thrown to bookies during the game. When the scoring starts, however, the odds will change. If you're as good a mathematician as most jai alai aficionados, you'll be able to bet with impunity on both sides at different points of the game—and still finish ahead.

Note: This has become a game for elite spectators, meaning that for men coats and ties are required. Women must be similarly nicely dressed.

Admission is $14.25. The box office opens at 6:30pm, and games are held on Tuesday through Sunday at 5pm year-round. To get there, head for the northeast corner of Plaza de la República (at the corner of Calle Ramos Arizpe, six blocks along Juárez west of Reforma). Any bus going west along Juárez will take you to the Juárez-Reforma intersection, and it's a short walk from there. Or you can take the Metro to the Revolución station and walk three blocks down Arriaga (south) to the plaza.

BULLFIGHTS   The capital's **Plaza de Toros Monumental México** is among the largest bullrings in the world. It seats 64,000 people, and on Sunday during the professional season (usually December through April, but no fixed dates) most seats are taken. On other Sundays through the year the arena is given over to the beginners (*nouvilleros*), most of whom are as bad as the beginners in any other sport. Six fights make up a corrida, which begins precisely at 4pm and is one of the few things in Mexico that's always on time.

There are several ways to reach Plaza de Toros, which is situated 2 or 3 miles south along Insurgentes. Any big hotel or tour agency will be happy to book you onto a tour with transportation. In about 25 minutes, the bus will pass the bullring on the right. Most of the people on the bus will alight here, so you'll know you're at the bullring, which is just around the corner ahead.

Dozens of men and women sell nuts, hats, and all kinds of whatnots. Look for a woman, or *muchacha*, selling chewing gum and waving small "programs." If you buy the chewing gum, she'll give you (free) the one-page sheet that lists the names of the day's *toreros*.

Unless you want to pay more, take your place in the line at one of the windows marked *sol general.* It will be in the sun, and it will be high up; but the sun isn't too strong (it sets soon, anyway), and you won't see many other tourists that way. (Try to avoid the seats numbered 1 to 100; for some reason, the roughnecks prefer to gather in this section.) Seats in *la sombra* (shade) are more expensive, of course. Tickets cost between $2.50 and $24.75. Fights start at 4pm, but get there well in advance for a good seat.

Usually, there are six separate bulls to be fought (two by each matador) in a corrida, but I'd suggest you leave just before the last bull—to avoid the crowds. Outside, around two sides of the bullring is a scene of frantic activity. Hundreds of tiny stalls have masses of food frying, cold beer stacked high, and radios blaring with a commentary on the action inside the ring.

To get there, take the Metro (to the San Antonio station on Line 7) or a colectivo; the number of colectivos that normally roam Insurgentes is supplemented by Sunday-afternoon taxis headed for the plaza, and they'll often pick up extra passengers going their way. Or you can catch one of the buses marked "Plaza México" that travels down Insurgentes on Sunday afternoon.

7 Shopping

Mexico City is a marvelous place to buy crafts of all types. You'll come across numerous places displaying fascinating native products, and you're certain to find something you want as a souvenir. Here's the rundown on the best places to shop, from small, selective crafts shops to vast general markets.

Today it often costs only a little more money to buy these things in the capital than at the source, if one knows a good shop. Several government-run shops and a few excellent privately run shops have exceptionally good collections of Mexico's arts and crafts. As fascinating as a fine-art gallery, these shops deserve a visit whether or not you intend to buy.

Two districts are particularly good for browsing. The first is the area on and off Avenida Juárez (facing the Alameda), Avenida Madero, and the streets parallel them. Within the Zona Rosa (for jewelry, Calle Amberes is the place, for instance), there are also many great places to browse. A few unique shops deserve particular mention.

SHOPPING A TO Z

Crafts

Artesanías de México. Londres 117. ☎ **5/514-2025** or 5/514-7455.

This shop, in the Zona Rosa, brings crafts from the state of Michoacán. It isn't large, but it's a good place to see a wide selection of that state's pottery, textiles, and copper. Open Monday through Saturday from 10am to 7pm.

Exposición Nacional de Arte Popular (FONART). Juárez 89. ☎ **5/521-6681.** Metro: Hidalgo or Juárez.

This government-operated store is usually loaded with crafts: papier-mâché figurines, textiles, earthenware, colorfully painted candelabras, hand-carved wooden masks, straw goods, beads, bangles, and glass. It is operated by the Fonda Nacional para el Fomento de las Artes (FONART), a government organization that helps village craftspeople. It's open daily from 10am to 6pm.

FONART. Londres 136A. ☎ **5/525-2026.** Metro: Hidalgo or Juárez.

Another branch of the government-operated store (see above) is in the heart of the Zona Rosa. Though in a small, narrow upstairs quarters, it is absolutely packed with folk art, much of it not duplicated at the larger store on Juárez. Open Monday through Saturday from 10am to 7pm.

Museo Nacional de Artes e Industrias Populares. Juárez 44. ☎ **5/521-6679.** Metro: Hidalgo or Juárez.

The museum store here, located across from the Benito Juárez statue in Alameda Park, has an enormous selection of high-quality Mexican crafts for sale. Because the prices are fixed, you can get an idea of quality versus cost for later use in market bargaining. (Upstairs with the entrance in back is the museum, which was recently closed for renovation.) Open daily from 10am to 6pm; the museum is normally open Monday through Saturday from 10am to 6pm.

Glass

Avalos Brothers. Carretones 5. ☎ **5/522-5311;** fax 5/522-6420.

For more than 100 years, blown glass has been issuing forth from this run-down location in the old section of town. You can watch men and women scurry around with red-hot glass in various stages of shaping until it cools. A sales showroom to the left of the entrance holds shelves full of glass objects—pitchers, vases, plates, glasses, flowers, cream and sugar containers, and the like in various colors. Few tourists seem to find their way here, but among locals this is the store of choice for selection and price. It is near the La Merced market where Carretones dead-ends into Tapacio, a short block south of San Pablo. It's open Monday through Friday from 10am to 5pm and Saturday from 10am to 2pm.

Markets

Bazar Sábado. San Angel.

The Bazar Sábado is held every Saturday, as its name indicates, in an expensive colonial-era suburb of cobbled streets, mansions, and parks a few miles south of the city. This is the only day the actual bazaar building (a fine two-story mansion built around a courtyard) is open. It showcases dozens of permanent stalls offering high-quality decorative art. On adjacent plazas, hundreds of easel artists display their paintings, and members of indigenous groups from Puebla and elsewhere bring their folk art—baskets, masks, pottery, textiles, and so on. Restaurants (some in mansions) lining the streets play host to leisurely diners seated at umbrella-shaded tables. Plan to spend all Saturday touring the attractions on the southern outskirts of the city. (See also "San Angel" earlier in this chapter.)

Centro Artesanal (Mercado de Curiosidades). At the corner of Ayuntamiento and Dolores. Metro: Salto del Agua.

This rather modern building set back off a plaza is composed of a number of stalls on two levels, selling everything from leather to tiles. They have some lovely silver jewelry and, as in most non-fixed-price stores, the asking price is high, but the bargained result is often very reasonable.

Lagunilla Market. Three blocks east of Plaza de Garibaldi. Metro: Allende.

This is another market well worth visiting. The best day is Sunday, when the Lagunilla becomes a colorful outdoor market filling the streets for blocks. Vendors sell everything from axes to antiques. Be careful about pickpockets. The two enclosed sections are open all week and are separated by a short street, Calle Juan Alvarez. They have different specialties: The one to the north is noted for clothes, rebozos, and blankets; the one to the south for tools, pottery, and household goods, such as attractive hanging copper lamps. This is also the area to find old and rare books, many at a ridiculously low cost, if you're willing to hunt and bargain.

Mercado de Artesanías "La Ciudadela." Plaza de la Ciudadela. Metro: Juárez.

An interesting market that's large and clean, the Mercado de Artensanías rambles on forever just off Balderas and Ayuntamiento in the Plaza de la Ciudadela. The merchandise is of good quality and well displayed, and bartering may help.

Mercado Insurgentes. On Londres between Florencia and Amberes.

Mercado Insurgentes is a full-fledged crafts market tucked in the Zona Rosa. Because of its address you might expect exorbitant prices, but vendors in the maze of stalls are eager to bargain, and good buys aren't hard to come by.

Merced Market. This is the biggest market in the city, and it's among the most fascinating in the country, with an intense activity and energy level akin to the Abastos market in Oaxaca and the Friday Ocotlán market south of there. Several years ago the city tried to move this market because of the traffic congestion around the market and because it's semipermanent street-vendor sprawl had almost reached the steps of the Palacio Nacional. The effort was fruitless because the Merced has been functioning successfully here for centuries, although there's a limit to street vendors now. Officially it consists of several modern buildings, but shops line tidy-but-people-filled streets all the way to the Zócalo. Near the market, street vendors hawk their wares as well. The first building is mainly for fruits and vegetables; the others contain just about everything you would find if a department store joined forces with a discount warehouse—a good place to shop especially for housewares. The main market is east of the Zócalo on Circunvalación between General Anaya and Adolfo Gurrión. To get here from the Zócalo take Corregidor, the street to the right of the Palacio Nacional, and follow it five blocks to Circunvalación and turn right. Walk for two long blocks and you'll see the entrance to the market on the left. It's also interesting to meander past all the shops on other streets zigzagging your way to the market. Or take the Metro from the Zócalo to the Merced stop right outside the market. To return to the Zócalo or anywhere else within the city, take the Metro (Line 1) from the Merced station, which is just outside the enclosed market. You can change at Pino Suárez (first stop) to take you to the Zócalo.

8 Mexico City After Dark

If you have any energy left after sightseeing at this high elevation, the capital of Mexico offers up quite a variety of nighttime entertainment from mariachi and reggae to the opera, regional folkloric dancing to classic ballet, and dinner shows to drinking establishments; the choice is enormous. In addition, you can enjoy them in Mexico City at a price that is lower than comparable entertainment in other major cities of the world. On the other hand, if you're willing to let *la vida Mexicana* put on its own fascinating show for you, the bill will be much less. People-watching, café-sitting, music, even a dozen mariachi bands all playing at once, can be yours for next to nothing.

THE ENTERTAINMENT SCENE

For current information on cultural offerings at all of the establishments listed below, the best source is the Sunday edition of *The News* or *The Times,* both of which have a full listing of cultural events. A limited number of events are printed other days. *Donde,* a magazine found in hotels, is another good source for locating the newest places, but it doesn't list changing entertainment or current exhibits. For performances of major attractions tickets can usually be obtained through **TicketMaster** (☎ 5/325-9000).

Lobby bars tend to have live entertainment of the low-key type in the late afternoon and on into the evening. Disco dancing is alive and well in Mexico with flashy light shows and megadecibel music. Discos and dinner dance establishments tend to get going around 9 or 10:30pm and last until at least 3am. Most discos operate only Thursday through Saturday. Fiesta nights give visitors a chance to dine on typical Mexican food and see Mexico's wonderful regional dancing, which seems always to be a treat no matter how many times you've seen them.

Much of the city's nightlife takes place around the **Zona Rosa,** a traditional place to stroll, sip, and eat at several places if you want—appetizers one place, dinner another, and dessert somewhere else, winding up at a nearby disco or dancing establishment, hotel lobby bar, or cozy coffeehouse. Outdoor cafés on **Copenhague street** are among the liveliest for being in the thick of the Zona Rosa scene, but with one or two exceptions, they have become more expensive than they are good. Another tradition is Garibaldi Square, where mariachis tune up and wait to be hired.

Restaurants and drinking establishments there feature them in a typical Mexican atmosphere. It's a slice of Mexican life that every traveler must experience at least once.

For cultural events the **National Auditorium** in Chapultepec Park (☎ 5/520-3502) is usually the biggest bargain in town. Symphonies, international ballet, opera, and theater companies play here. Prices vary depending on the performance.

FOLKLORIC BALLET

Palacio de Bellas Artes. Lázaro Cárdenas, on the east side of the Alameda. ☎ **5/512-2592,** ext. 152. Tickets $19.75–$29.50. Metro: Bellas Artes.

Besides hosting traveling ballet and opera companies from around the world, performances of Mexico's famed Ballet Folklórico de Mexico are held here several times weekly. (See also "Walking Tour 2—Near the Alameda.")

The Ballet Folklórico is a celebration of pre- and post-Hispanic dancing in Mexico. A typical program will include Aztec ritual dances, agricultural dances from Jalisco, a fiesta in Veracruz, a Christmas celebration—all welded together with mariachis, marimba players, singers, and dancers.

Since many other events are held in the Bellas Artes—visits by foreign opera companies, for instance—there are times when the Ballet Folklórico is moved. Usually, it reappears in the National Auditorium in Chapultepec Park. Check at the Bellas Artes box office. There are two companies—three, if you count the one usually on tour. The show is popular and tickets are bought up rapidly (especially by a tour agency at twice the cost). The box office is on the ground floor of the Bellas Artes, main entrance. *Note:* The theater tends to be very cold so you may want to bring a sweater. The box office is open Monday through Saturday 11am to 7pm, Sunday 8:30am to 7pm; Ballet Folklórico performances, Sunday 9:30am; Wednesday 8:30pm.

Teatro de la Ciudad. Donceles 36. ☎ **5/521-2355.** Tickets $6.50–$16.50 to the Ballet Folklórico; call about other performances. Shows Sun 9:30am; Tues 8:30pm. Metro: Bellas Artes.

An alternative to the Ballet Folklórico de Mexico is the Ballet Folklórico Nacional Aztlán, in the beautiful turn-of-the-century Teatro de La Ciudad, a block northeast of the Bellas Artes between Xicoténcatl and Allende. Performances here are as good as the better-known ones in the Bellas Artes, but tickets are a lot cheaper and much easier to obtain. Other major performances of ballet, concerts, and the like also appear here.

MARIACHIS

At some time or other, everybody—Mexicans and turistas alike—goes to see and hear the mariachi players. The mariachis are strolling musicians who wear distinctive costumes, which make them look like Mexican cowboys dressed up for a special occasion. Their costume—tight spangled trousers, fancy jackets, and big floppy bow ties—dates back to the French occupation of Mexico in the mid-19th century, as indeed, does their name. *Mariachi* is believed to be the Mexican mispronunciation of the French word for marriage, which is where they were often on call for music.

In Mexico City, the mariachis make their headquarters around the **Plaza de Garibaldi,** five blocks north of the Palacio de Bellas Artes up Avenida Lázaro Cárdenas, at Avenida República de Honduras. You will pass dozens of stores and a couple of burlesque houses. The Plaza itself was torn up for most of 1995, due to construction of an underground parking garage, but have patience, the plaza is taking on charm with new paving and ornamental street lamps.

In the Plaza de Garibaldi, especially in the evenings, mariachi players are everywhere. At every corner, guitars are stacked together like rifles in an army training camp. Young musicians strut proudly in their flashy outfits, on the lookout for señoritas to impress. They play when they feel like it, when there's a good chance to gather in some tips, or when someone orders a song—the going rate seems to be around $1.50 to $3.25 per song.

In any of the eating and drinking establishments around the plaza you can enjoy the mariachi music that swirls through the air. **Tlaquepaque,** across the square, is a well-known tourist-oriented restaurant where you can dine to strolling mariachis. But remember—if you give a bandleader the sign, you're the one who pays for the song, just like outside in the square.

Pulquería Hermana Hortensia, Amargura 4 (☎ **5/529-7828**), is perhaps the most adventurous spot for newcomers to Mexico City. It's on the Plaza Garibaldi near the northeast corner at Amargura and República de Honduras. It's open Monday through Saturday from 5pm until 2am and on Sunday from noon until 3am. Unlike most pulque bars, La Hermana Hortensia is a *pulquería familiar* (a "family" bar, that is, you can bring your wife—but not your kids). *Pulque* (*pool*-keh) is a thick and flavorsome drink made by fermenting the juice of a maguey (century) plant. Invented by the ancient Toltecs and shared with the Aztecs, pulque was a sacred drink forbidden to the common people for centuries. One of the effects of the Spanish Conquest was to liberate pulque for the masses. Was this good or bad? Ask your neighbor in La Hermana Hortensia as you quaff the thick brew (sold by the glass or liter). Pulque packs a wallop, although it's not nearly so strong as those other maguey-based drinks, tequila and mezcal. By the way, pulque here can be ordered with nuts blended in.

Don't get the idea that you'll see only your countryfolk in the Plaza Garibaldi, for it is indeed a Mexican phenomenon. As evening falls, lots of people from the neighborhood come to stroll or sit. (See also Jorongo Bar, below.) *A note of caution:* Crime focused on tourists has increased around Garibaldi Square, both day and night. For now, until police are more evident in the area, don't take excess money, and go with a crowd of friends or take one of the Garibaldi tours.

TRIO MUSIC, JAZZ & FIESTAS

El Chato la Posta. Londres 25. Col. Juárez. ☎ **5/546-1199** or 5/705-1457. Cover $25.

This popular bar features great trio music and botanas (snacks) with the drinks. Several different groups entertain. Open Thursday through Saturday 10:30 to 3am.

Jorongo Bar. Hotel María Isabel–Sheraton, Reforma 325. ☎ **5/207-3933.**

For wonderful Mexican trio music in plush surroundings, make your way to Jorongo Bar at the María Isabel—Sheraton Hotel, facing the Angel Monument. The reputation for this bar's good trio/mariachi music has been good for decades—it's an institution. From 7pm to 2am, you can enjoy the smooth and joyous sounds for the price of a drink ($2.50 to $5) and a cover charge of about $8.25.

Maquiavelo. Hotel Krystal, Liverpool 155. ☎ **5/211-0092** or 5/211-3460. Cover $8.25 or more, depending on performers.

This little-known nightclub, in the heart of the Zona Rosa, changes from an informal bar during the day to a jazz center in the evenings. Open 9pm to 3am.

El Patio. Atenas 9, Col. Juárez. ☎ **5/566-1743.** Call for current charge.

Some of Mexico's most famous singers and entertainers perform in a lengthy after-dinner show. It's at the far eastern edge of the Zona Rosa. Open Tuesday through Saturday from 10pm to 3am.

Hotel María Isabel—Sheraton. Reforma 325, at Río Tiber, ☎ **5/507-3933.** Cover $21–$30.

The elaborate Fiesta Mexicana dinner and show here has also been a staple of capital entertainment for years, featuring good dinner and a lively show of Mexican regional dancers in colorful attire. Open Monday through Friday from 7 to 10pm.

NIGHTCLUBS & DISCOS

Dynasty Disco. Hotel Nikko, Campos Elíseos 204, Polanco. ☎ **5/280-1111.** Cover Mon–Thurs $8 and Fri–Sat $15.

This upscale disco is in one of the capital's top hotels. Besides the disco there are two nightly live shows of mariachi or trio music, which last about 45 minutes each, all for the price of admission. Drinks, of course, are extra. Open Monday through Thursday 9pm to 1:30am and Friday and Saturday from 9pm to 3am.

Hotel Majestic. Av. Madero 73, Mexico, D.F. 06000. ☎ **5/521-8600.** No cover.

The popular rooftop bar of this hotel overlooks the Zócalo and the Catedral Metropolitana. A variety of good singers (usually) entertains, although there could be a trio crooning romantic Mexican favorites. Open daily noon to 1am; entertainment 7pm to 1am.

LOBBY BARS

Hotel Camino Real. Mariano Escobedo 700, Col. Nueva Anzures. ☎ **5/203-2121.** No cover.

You'll be surrounded by people enjoying the piano music at this very popular lobby bar. Order a drink and kick back for a relaxing respite. Open daily noon to 1am.

Hotel Galería Plaza. Hamburgo 195, at Varsovia. ☎ **5/211-0014.** No cover.

Ever since this luxury hotel opened in the early 1980s it's been known for its inviting Lobby Bar entertainment. The type of music varies, but often includes jazz. Open 11am to 1am; live music 7pm to 1am.

Caviar Bar. Hotel Marquís Reforma, Reforma 465, Col. Cuauhtémoc. ☎ **5/211-3600.**

While guests enjoy light meals and drinks in the lobby Caviar Bar of this stylish hotel, a string quartet plays in the evening hours. It's totally elegant and wonderfully soothing, and is open from 1pm until 1am.

Side Trips from Mexico City

Just as Paris has its Versailles and Rome its Villa d'Este, so Mexico City is surrounded by suburban areas that are every bit as fascinating as the city itself—and all can be reached by a bus ride that is ridiculously cheap and relatively easy. The places described in this chapter are suitable for one-day trips that can be followed by an evening back in town (for Taxco, and perhaps Tlaxcala and Puebla, you may want to make an exception and stay overnight).

The first and most exciting stop is at the breathtaking ancient pyramids of Teotihuacán, then the volcanoes and Puebla, the "City of Tiles," then Tlaxcala. Later I take you farther afield, southwest over the mountains to Toluca and Cuernavaca, and then to the silver city of Taxco, on the road to Acapulco.

1 The Pyramids of Teotihuacán

30 miles NE of Mexico City

The ruins of Teotihuacán are among the most remarkable in Mexico, and you shouldn't miss them. The name means "place where gods were born." Occupation of the area of Teotihuacán began around 500 B.C., but it wasn't until 100 B.C. that construction of the enormous Pyramid of the Sun at Teotihuacán was begun. Teotihuacán's rise corresponds to the time when the Classical Greeks were building their great monuments on the other side of the world, and to the beginning of cultures in Mexico's Yucatán Peninsula, Oaxaca, and Puebla. Teotihuacán was the dominant city in Mesoamerica during the Classical Period, covering 8 square miles with its magnificent pyramids and palaces. At its zenith around A.D. 500 there were at least 200,000 inhabitants—more than Rome had at that time. Through trade and other contact, its influence was known in other parts of Mexico and as far south as Mexico's Yucatán peninsula and Guatemala. But little is known about the city's inhabitants, what they looked like, what language they spoke, where they came from, or why they abandoned the place in A.D. 700. It is known that at the beginning of the first century A.D. the Xitle volcano erupted near Cuicuilco (south of Mexico City) and decimated that city, which was the most dominant city of the time. Those inhabitants probably migrated to Teotihuacán. Scholars believe that Teotihuacán's decline was gradual, and perhaps occurred over

Side Trips from Mexico City

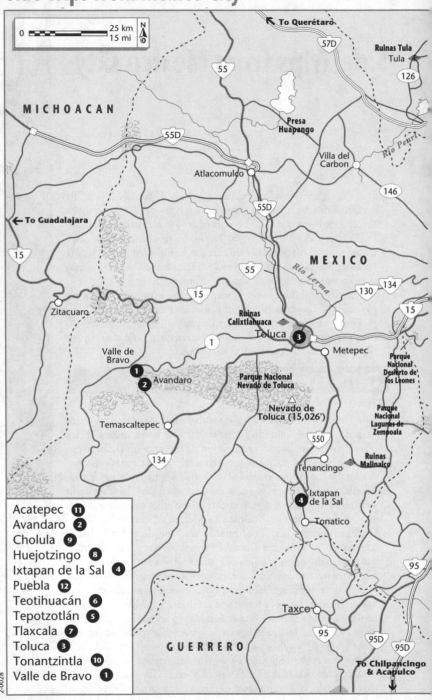

0 ━━━━━━ 25 km
0 ━━━━━━ 15 mi
N

← To Querétaro

57D

Ruinas Tula
Tula

126

55

MICHOACAN

55D

Presa
Huapango

Villa del
Carbon

Atlacomulco

55D

146

← To Guadalajara

15

MEXICO

55

Río Lerma

130 134

15

Zitacuaro

15

Ruinas
Calixtlahuaca

Toluca 3

Metepec

Parque
Nacional
Desierto de
los Leones

1

Valle de
Bravo

1

2 Avandaro

Parque Nacional
Nevado de Toluca

Parque
Nacional
Lagunas de
Zempoala

Temascaltepec

Nevado de
Toluca (15,026')

550

Ruinas
Malinalco

134

Tenancingo

Ixtapan
de la Sal

4

95

Tonatico

Acatepec 11
Avandaro 2
Cholula 9
Huejotzingo 8
Ixtapan de la Sal 4
Puebla 12
Teotihuacán 6
Tepotzotlán 5
Tlaxcala 7
Toluca 3
Tonantzintla 10
Valle de Bravo 1

Taxco

95

95

95D 95D

GUERRERO

To Chilpancingo
& Acapulco

2-0028

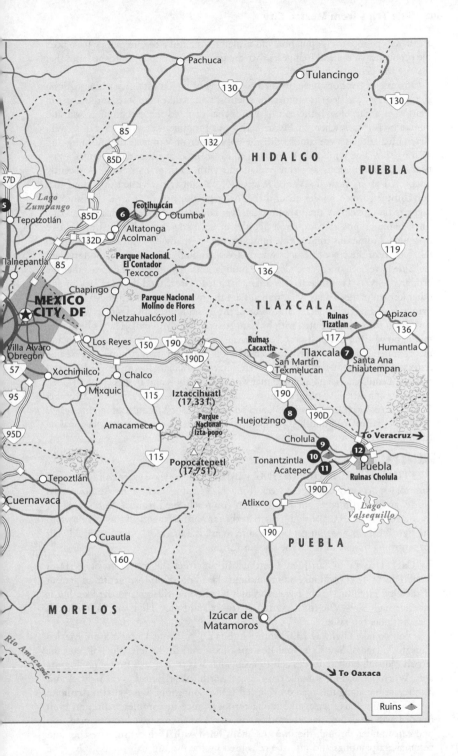

a 250-year period; overpopulation and depletion of natural resources may have been the problems. In the end it appears that the people were poorly nourished and that the city was deliberately burned.

Ongoing excavations have revealed something of the culture. According to John B. Carlson, an archaeoastronomer (or scientist who studies the stars and planets in relation to archaeology), the cult of Venus that dictated the execution of war and human sacrifice elsewhere in Mesoamerica was prominent at Teotihuacán as well. Ceremonial rituals were timed with the appearance of Venus as the morning and evening star. The symbol of Venus at Teotihuacán (as at Cacaxtla, 50 miles away, near Tlaxcala), appears as a star or half star with a full or half circle. A recently discovered room in the La Ventilla secton of Teotihuacán revealed this motif in a polychromed fresco border around the lower portions of the room. Carlson also suggests the possibility that Teotihuacán was conquered by people from Cacaxtla, since name glyphs of conquered peoples at Cacaxtla showed Teotihuacán-like pyramids. Numerous tombs with human remains (many of them either sacrificial inhabitants of the city or perhaps war captives), and objects of jewelry, pottery, and daily life have been uncovered along the foundations of buildings. It appears that the primary deity at Teotihuacán was a female called "Great Goddess" for lack of any other known name. Today what remains are the rough stone structures of the three pyramids and sacrificial altars, and some of the grand houses, all of which were once covered in stucco and painted with brilliant frescos (mainly in red). The Toltecs, who rose in power after the decline of Teotihuacán, were fascinated with Teotihuacán and incorporated many of the Teotihuacán symbols into their own cultural motifs. The Aztecs, who came after the Toltecs, were likewise fascinated with the Toltecs and ruins of Teotihuacán, and adopted many of *their* symbols and motifs.

Fascinating articles about Teotihuacán appear in *National Geographic* (December 1995), *Archeology* (December 1993), and on the murals of Teotihuacán in *Arqueología* (Vol. III—Num 16) published in Spanish in Mexico by the Instituto Nacional de Antropología e Historia.

ESSENTIALS

GETTING THERE & DEPARTING   By Bus   Buses leave every half hour (from 5am to 10pm) every day of the week from the Terminal Central de Autobuses del Norte, and the trip takes one hour. When you reach the Terminal Norte, look for the AUTOBUSES SAHAGUN sign located at the far northwest end all the way down to the sign 8 ESPERA. As you get off, be sure to ask the driver where you should wait for returning buses and when the last bus leaves.

By Car   Driving to San Juan Teotihuacán on either the toll Highway 85D or free Highway 132D will take about an hour. Head north on Insurgentes to get out of the city. Highway 132D passes through picturesque villages and the like, but is excruciatingly slow, due to the surfeit of trucks and buses; Highway 85D, the toll road, is duller but faster.

If you do take Highway 132D through the villages, about 15 miles from Mexico City the village of **San Cristóbal Ecatepec** looms off to the left. Note also on the left an old wall built centuries ago to keep what was then a lake from flooding the area. When the road forks a mile or so farther north, take the road to the right. About 3 miles farther along this road on your left is the Convent of **San Agustín Acolman** (1539–1560). This fortresslike monastery was once in complete ruin and even flooded with mud. Now, however, the monastery and church have been restored, and you can wander through the immense halls lined with 16th-century frescoes and colonial-era paintings and into the cells used by the Augustinian monks. Over the

SAN MARTIN

Tepantitla ①
La Cueva
Villas Archeologicas
Entrance
Parking
Parking
⑩
⑪
Pyramid ⑥
⑧
⑨
⑦
Avenue of the Dead
Avenue of the Dead
⑫
Parking
Parking
Entrance
⑤
Roadside Cookshops
Entrance
⑬ Parking ℗
Pyramid Charlie's
⑯
⑰ ⑮
⑭
To San Juan Teotihuacán ↓ Terraced Road
To Mexico City ↓
Parking ℗

Atetelco ⑭
The Citadel ⑪
El Corso ⑤
The High Priest's Home ⑦
New Museum Location ⑧
Old Museum Building ⑫
Palace of Quetzalpapálotl ③
Palace of the Jaguars ④
Pyramid of the Moon ②

Pyramid of the Sun ⑥
The Temple of Quetzalcoatl ⑩
Tepantitla ①
Tetitla ⑮
La Ventilla ⑬
The Viking Group ⑨
Yayahuala ⑰
Zacuala ⑯

2-0029

arched entry are a sculpted lion, angel heads, and horses whose hind portions become leaves and flowers. There's a charge to see the small museum showcasing a small collection of religious art. Museum Admission is $1.50, and the monastery is open daily from 10am to 1pm and 3 to 6pm.

ORIENTATION The museum and cultural center are in a new location, and parking lots and souvenir stands are on the outer edges of the site. A small train to take visitors from entry booths to various stops within the site is planned.

Do keep in mind these important points: You will be doing a great deal of walking, and perhaps some climbing, at an altitude of more than 7,000 feet. Take it slowly; bring sunblock and a hat; be prepared for the summer rainy season, when it rains almost every afternoon—but rain is possible any time.

A good place to start is at the **new museum.** Opened in 1995, this excellent museum is state-of-the-art, with interactive exhibits, and in one part, a glass floor on which visitors walk above mockups of the pyramids which are below. Findings during recent digs are on display including several tombs with skeletons wearing necklaces of human and simulated jawbones, and newly discovered sculpture.

The ruins of Teotihuacán are open daily from 8am to 5pm. Admission Monday through Saturday is $2.25; free on Sunday; there is a $4.25 fee for use of a video camera.

The Layout The grand buildings of Teotihuacán were laid out in accordance with celestial movements. The front wall of the **Pyramid of the Sun** is exactly square to (facing) the point on the horizon where the sun sets twice annually—if a line were drawn from the pyramid to the sun at noon on the day when the sun reaches its highest point, the line would in theory be perfectly vertical. The rest of the ceremonial buildings were laid out at right angles to the Pyramid of the Sun.

The main thoroughfare, called by archaeologists the **Avenue of the Dead,** runs roughly north–south. The **Pyramid of the Moon** is at the northern end, and the **Ciudadela** is on the southern part of the thoroughfare. Actually, the great street was several miles long in its heyday, but only a mile or so has been uncovered and restored.

EXPLORING THE TEOTIHUACÁN ARCHAEOLOGICAL SITE

THE CIUDADELA   The Ciudadela, or Citadel, was named by the Spaniards. Actually, this immense sunken square was not a fortress at all, although the impressive walls make it look like one. It was the grand setting for the Feathered Serpent Pyramid and the Temple of Quetzalcoatl. Scholars aren't certain that the Teotihuacán culture embraced the Quetzalcoatl deity so well known in the Toltec, Aztec, and Maya cultures. The feathered serpent is featured in the Ciudadela, but whether it was worshipped as Quetzalcoatl or a similar god isn't yet known. Once you've admired the great scale of the Ciudadela, go down the steps into the massive court and head for the ruined temple, in the middle.

The Temple of Quetzalcoatl was covered over by an even larger structure, a pyramid. As you walk toward the center of the Ciudadela's court, you'll be approaching the pyramid. The Feathered Serpent Pyramid will be on your left. Walk around to the right of it, and soon you'll see the reconstructed temple close behind the pyramid. There's a narrow passage between the two structures, and foot traffic is supposed to be one way—which is why I directed you to the right.

Early temples were often covered over by later ones in Mexico and Central America. The Pyramid of the Sun may have been built up in this way. Archaeologists have tunneled deep inside the Feathered Serpent Pyramid and found numerous ceremonially buried human remains, interred with precise detail and position, but as yet no person of royalty. Drawings of how the building once looked show that every level was covered with faces of a feathered serpent. As for the Temple of Quetzalcoatl, you'll notice at once the big carved serpents' heads jutting out from collars of feathers carved in the stone walls. Other feathered serpents are carved in relief lower on the walls. You can get a good idea of the glory of Mexico's ancient cities from this temple.

AVENUE OF THE DEAD   The Avenue of the Dead got its strange and forbidding name from the Aztecs, who mistook the little temples that line both sides of the avenue for tombs of kings or priests.

As you stroll north along the Avenue of the Dead toward the Pyramid of the Moon, look on the right for a bit of wall sheltered by a modern corrugated roof. Beneath the shelter, the wall still bears a painting of a jaguar. From this fragment, you might be able to build a picture of the breathtaking spectacle that must have met the eye when all the paintings along the avenue were intact.

PYRAMID OF THE SUN   The Pyramid of the Sun is located on the east side of the Avenue of the Dead. As pyramids go, this is the third largest in the world. The Great Pyramid of Cholula, near Puebla, is the largest structure ever built. Second largest is the Pyramid of Cheops on the outskirts of Cairo, Egypt. Teotihuacán's Pyramid of the Sun is, at the base, 730 feet per side—almost as large as Cheops. But at 210 feet high, the Sun pyramid is only about half as high as its Egyptian rival.

No matter. It's still the biggest restored pyramid in the Western Hemisphere, and an awesome sight. Although the Pyramid of the Sun was not built as a great king's tomb, it does have secret tunnels and chambers beneath it, but they aren't open to the public.

The first structure of the pyramid was probably built a century before Christ, and the temple that used to crown the pyramid was finished about 400 years later (A.D. 300). By the time the pyramid was discovered and restoration was begun (early in our century), the temple had completely disappeared, and the pyramid was just a mass of rubble covered with bushes and trees.

If you're game, trudge up the 248 steps to the top. The view is marvelous, if the smog's not too thick.

PYRAMID OF THE MOON   The Pyramid of the Moon faces an interesting plaza at the northern end of the avenue. The plaza is surrounded by little temples, and by the Palace of Quetzal-Mariposa (or Quetzal-Butterfly), on the left (west) side. You get about the same range of view from the top of the Pyramid of the Moon as you do from its larger neighbor, because the moon pyramid is built on higher ground. The perspective straight down the Avenue of the Dead is magnificent.

PALACE OF QUETZAL-MARIPOSA   The Palace of Quetzal-Mariposa lay in ruins until the 1960s, when restoration work began. Today it echoes wonderfully with its former glory, as figures of Quetzal-Mariposa (a mythical exotic bird-butterfly) appear painted on walls or carved in the pillars of the inner court.

Behind the Palace of Quetzal-Mariposa is the Palace of the Jaguars, complete with murals showing a lively jaguar musical combo and some frescoes.

WHERE TO DINE

You may want to pack a **box lunch** to take to the ruins—doing so will save you a long walk to any of the restaurants. Almost any hotel or restaurant in the city can prepare it for you. At press time, the **restaurant** over the old museum was still operating; if it's still running when you visit you'll find it the most convenient place for a meal or a drink at the ruins. Vendors at the ruins also sell drinks and snacks.

La Gruta. ☎ 595/6-0127; 595/6-0104. Main courses $3.50–$8.50. Daily 11am–7pm. A bit northwest of Gate 5 on the Peripheral Highway. MEXICAN.

La Gruta is a huge, delightfully cool natural grotto filled with natty waiters and the sound of clinking glasses. Soft drinks and beer are served until the full bar opens. You have the option of ordering a five-course set-price lunch, or choosing your own combination—perhaps a hamburger and a soft drink.

2 Ixta-Popo National Park

50 miles SE of Mexico City

Amecameca, a town of 37,000 situated at a height of 7,500 feet, is blessed with a big square, a 200-year-old parish church constructed in the 16th century for priests of the Dominican order, and fresh, clear air. But the reason you're here is to see or perhaps to hike or climb in Ixta-Popo National Park, whose raison d'être is the volcanoes Popocatépetl and Ixtaccíhuatl. Popocatépetl last erupted in December 1994, rumbled throughout most of 1995 (causing periodic closing of the park), and remains very active at press time—**no hiking up the slope is allowed at the moment.** Still, Popo's enormous snow-capped peak is a magnificent beauty to see from the lodge, and worth the drive if you're in the vicinity.

ESSENTIALS

GETTING THERE & DEPARTING **By Bus** Take Metro Line 1 east (toward Pantitlán) to the San Lázaro stop. As you come to the surface, you'll see the green-domed **TAPO** (Terminal de Autobuses de Pasajeros de Oriente), Mexico City's eastern bus terminal. Walk along Tunnel 1, the corridor to the central domed area, and look for **Líneas Unidas–Cristóbal Colón** buses to Amecameca and Popo Park. Buses leave every half hour every day. The bus will let you off a block and a half from the central square in Amecameca.

To get to Ixta-Popo National Park and the mountain lodge, about 8 miles from Amecameca, you'll have to hire a taxi for about $22 one way. Check at the Hotel San Carlos, on the square, for other passengers and perhaps you'll be able to split the cost. Make a deal with the taxi driver to pick you up later since there's no telephone at the lodge; or you can take a chance and try to thumb a ride down the mountains, which is often easily done. Hitchhiking from Amecameca to the lodge isn't recommended because there's little traffic.

By Car Take the Puebla road (Route 190) out of Mexico City, turning off to the right on Route 115 to the village of Chalco. A few miles farther on is Amecameca. From there, ask directions for the road to the park, 8 miles farther up the mountain on a good paved road that twists through alpine beauty.

HIKING & CLIMBING IN THE PARK

Outside the Albergue lodge (see below) is the snow-covered summit of **Popocatépetl,** 18,177 feet high at the rim. In the morning the clouds may drift away for an hour, yielding an incomparable closeup view. Across the valley, Popo's sister volcano, **Ixtaccíhuatl,** may be exposed as well. When you see them gleaming in the morning sun, surrounded by the chilly morning air, you'll remember the moment for a lifetime.

THE TRAILS Popocatépetl is no mountain for rookie climbers or for any expert climber who's not in top shape. At the lodge trailhead the air is so thin that even walking makes a normal, healthy person dizzy—and the air's considerably thinner at 17,887 feet! Besides, it's cold up here, even in the sweltering heat of summer. But if you're an expert climber, check in at the lodge reception or the rescue hut next to the lodge. You may be asked to pass an equipment check and sign your name in the hiker's register before you set out. *A safety note:* Despite the name "rescue hut" on one of the buildings, there is no staff rescue team on hand. *You climb at your own risk,* and rescue—if any—will come from those on hand who pitch in to help.

Maps of the various trails to the summit, showing the several huts and shelters, are on view in the lodge hut. The trek to the summit takes two days or longer, depending on what shape you're in and which trail you choose. You camp below the summit.

When you return to the lodge, if all the bunks are taken, no one will mind if you pitch a tent in the pine grove just below the lodge.

WHERE TO STAY & EAT

Albergue Vicente Guerrero. Río Elba 20 10th Floor, Col. Cuauhtémoc, 06500 México, D.F. ☎ **5/553-5896.** Fax 5/553-9073. $1.75 bunk with sheet, pillow case, and blanket.

The Albergue Vicente Guerrero at Tlamacas (elev. 12,800 ft.), in the Parque Nacional Ixta-Popo, was opened in 1978. It's beautiful—a modern mountain lodge done in native stone and natural wood, complete with bunkrooms, showers, a cafeteria, and a restaurant. If you want to stay the night, especially on a weekend, it's best to call or drop by the Mexico City office of the lodge for a reservation at the above address. There are several bunkrooms with six sections of four bunk beds each, which you share with others of mixed gender.

3 Puebla, City of Tiles

80 miles SE of Mexico City

Puebla, Mexico's fourth-largest city, has such a wealth of preserved architectural beauty dating from colonial times that it's been named a UNESCO World Heritage Site. The city's church domes and building facades are embellished with richly colored tiles—a style so attractive that generations of tourists and collectors have come here in search of pottery and tiles to accent their own homes. And Puebla is considered the cradle of Mexican cuisine, for here were created some of the country's classic dishes.

Puebla was founded sometime around 1531 as a safe haven on the route between the capital and the coast; its colonial mansions were built to serve as comfortable way stations for wealthy travelers. The city's wonderful pottery and tile tradition was born when Talavera artisans from Toledo, Spain, arrived and mixed their work with that of Puebla's Native artisans, who'd been known for pottery-making before the Conquest.

Certainly seeing the colorful tiles in use on building facades and church domes whets the shopper's appetite for bringing a little of it home. In fact, exploring Puebla's Talavera pottery workshops in search of a set or piece of fine, handpainted tiles or dinnerware is the main reason many travelers visit Puebla. You certainly have ample opportunity to see it in use both architecturally and decoratively.

Catholicism was pervasive in New Spain, and it flourished throughout the country until 1857, when an anti-Catholic movement closed (but did not destroy) many churches and convents. Of these at, least 99 churches survive in Puebla (most with tile domes), along with many grand monasteries, convents, and a magnificent Bishop's Palace next to the cathedral. The church chose Puebla as a major center, along with San Luis Potosí and Oaxaca.

Today Puebla (elev. 7,049 ft.; pop 1,750,000) is growing at an amazing rate. Off the historic zócalo, streets are jammed with street markets, cars, and the ever-present buses, which trumpet, roar, and spew fumes.

ESSENTIALS

GETTING THERE & DEPARTING   By Bus   The bus trip from Mexico City to Puebla takes about two hours. Buses usually follow the new highway, but be sure to ask; otherwise you'll be in for a lot of tedious stops. From Mexico City's TAPO bus station, **Pullman Plus** runs deluxe service to Puebla every half hour. **ADO** has departures every 15 minutes, and **Autobuses Unidos** provides service every 10 minutes.

If you are arriving by plane in Mexico City and wish to go directly to Puebla, **Estrella Roja** buses depart from the airport hourly (beginning at 6 and 7:30am) for

Impressions

I make solemn affidavit that not even in Russia have I seen such an abnormal proportion of bankrupt plumbing systems, [and] ill-advised electric wiring.
—Stuart Chase, Mexico: *A Study of Two Americas*, 1931

Puebla. Some of these go to a bus stop on the western edge of Puebla at 4 Poniente and 21 Norte, and others go directly to Puebla's main bus terminal, CAPU. These buses depart from the front of the airport, at the Gate D exit.

If you're going on from Puebla to Tlaxcala or to Pachuca from Puebla, **Flecha Azul** has direct service. **ERCO** goes to Izúcar de Matamoros every 10 minutes, and the trip takes about 90 minutes. **Autobuses Surianos** goes directly to Huamantla every 20 minutes, as does **ATAH.**

By Car   There are two roads to Puebla from the capital: Highway 190, an old, winding one that you'll drive with great frustration, following strings of lumbering trucks with little chance to pass; and Highway 150D, a new toll road that's faster.

ORIENTATION   **Arriving**   Buses arrive at a modern **bus terminal,** known by its acronym CAPU; it's located on the outskirts of the city. To get to downtown Puebla, look for one of several booths marked "Taxi Autorizado." As in Mexico City, you pay by the zone (to the city center costs $1.75 to $2.25). A city bus marked "CAPU Central Camionera-Centro" will also get you downtown.

Information   The **State Tourist Office** (☎ 22/46-1285 or fax 22/46-2044, ask for tone) is at Av. 5 Oriente no. 3, across from the side of the cathedral and next to the Biblioteca Palafoxiana; the office is open Monday through Saturday from 9am to 8:30pm, and Sunday from 9am to 2pm. The friendly staff can sell you a good map of the city, as well as other literature about the city and state. The **City Tourist Office** faces the main plaza at Portal Hidalgo 14 (☎ 22/32-0357; fax 22/32-1399), and its staff is eager to please. On the same side of the plaza as the Royalty Hotel, it's open daily from 10am to 8:30pm.

City Layout   For visitors, the heart of town will be the shady zócalo, known as the **Plaza de la Constitución,** a beautiful place with a central fountain and tile-covered benches. On one side are the cathedral and Avenida 3 Oriente, and the other sides are flanked by the *portales* (arcades) of colonial-era buildings that today house restaurants, hotels, and shops. These are on Calle 16 de Septiembre, Calle 2 Sur, and Avenida de la Reforma where it meets Avenida Camacho. Most of the museums, shops, and hotels mentioned here are within walking distance of the zócalo.

Most streets running east and west are avenidas, and those running north and south are calles. **Avenida de la Reforma**, which becomes **Avenida General Maximino Avila Camacho** on the east, divides the city north and south, with even-numbered avenues to the north and odd-numbered avenues to the south. **Calle 16 de Septiembre,** which becomes **Calle 5 de Mayo** north of Reforma, is the east–west dividing line, with even-numbered streets to the east. City streets are further divided by direction: North "Norte" (Nte.), South "Sur," West "Poniente" (Pte.), and East "Oriente" (Ote.). In practice, the "Avenida" and "Calle" are often dropped.

FAST FACTS: PUEBLA

American Express   The American Express office is on Calle 5 de Mayo, at Plaza Dorada 2 (☎ 22/37-5551).

Area Code   The telephone area code is 22.

Cooking School   Since Puebla is the distinguished cradle of Mexican cuisine, it's only fitting that cooking lessons be available to the uninitiated. At the Restaurant/ Bar Las Chinas de Puebla you can learn all about chiles and their use in sauces, how a good mole poblano and mixiotes should taste and how to fix them, and much more in even a short class of around three hours. Classes are simple but extremely beneficial with the excellent restaurant cook Trinidad Becerra. For details see "Where to Dine" below.

Puebla

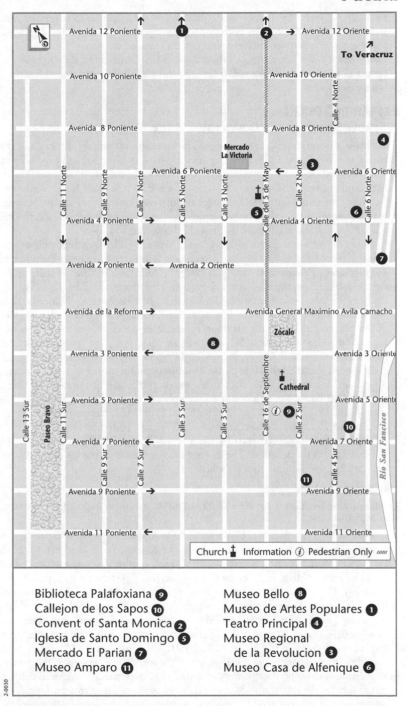

Church ✝ Information ⓘ Pedestrian Only /////

2-0030

413

Parking   If you're driving, be aware that downtown Puebla is so congested with traffic that it's almost impossible to find a parking spot. It's best to find a guarded parking garage on arrival and leave your car until you depart.

Post Office   The *correos* (post office) is in the Archbishop's Palace next to the cathedral, at the corner of Avenida 5 Oriente and Calle 16 de Septiembre, but there is no sign.

EXPLORING PUEBLA
A STROLL THROUGH THE DOWNTOWN AREA

Puebla is a fascinating place to explore. The immense **cathedral**, just south of the zócalo and fronting on Calle 16 de Septiembre was commissioned by King Philip of Spain in 1562, and it was completed in 1649. The cathedral towers are the tallest in Mexico. Bells hang in the tower closer to the zócalo (the other tower is empty). According to legend, additional bells were not installed because the Pueblans believed their weight would make the cathedral sink into an underground sea. The cathedral is open daily to tourists from 10:30am to 12:30pm and 4 to 6pm.

Beside the cathedral, on Avenida 5 Oriente between Calle 16 de Septiembre Calle 2 Sur, is the old Archbishop's Palace, which now houses the **Casa de la Cultura** and the **Biblioteca Palafoxiana.** After you enter the courtyard, the marble stairs to the right will take you to the Biblioteca Palafoxiana. This library, the oldest in the Americas (also the most beautiful), was built in 1646 by Juan de Palafox y Mendoza, then archbishop and founder of the College of Saints Peter and Paul. It bespeaks the glory of this period with its elegant tile floor, hand-carved wood walls and ceiling, inlaid tables, and gilded wooden statues. Bookcases are filled with 17th-century books and manuscripts in Spanish, Créole, French, and English.

Be sure to visit the **Iglesia de Santo Domingo,** on the corner of 5 de Mayo and 4 Poniente. Finished in 1611, the church was originally part of a monastery. Don't miss the **Capilla del Rosario,** a fantastic symphony of gilt and beautiful stone dedicated to the Virgin of the Rosary and built in 1690. Puebla has many other beautiful churches and convents that date from the 17th and 18th centuries.

Near the **Barrio del Artísta/El Parián** is the **Teatro Principal,** said to be the oldest theater in the Americas. The interior has been restored, but it's open only for concerts (ask the tourism office for schedules).

MUSEUMS

✪ **Museo Amparo.** Calle 2 Sur 708. ☎ **22/46-4200.** Admission $1.50 adults; free Mon. Wed–Mon 10am–6pm.

Opened in 1991 and dedicated by her husband to Amparo Rugarcia de Espinoza, this is among the top archaeological museums in the country. It's housed in a colonial-era building that was first a hospital in 1534, then a college for women founded by Juan de Palafox y Mendoza, later the Colegio San José de Gracia for married women, and lastly the Colegio Esparza before its adaptation as a museum. You can rent audio phones to guide you through or simply pass on your own. *Sala* (room) "Arte Rupestre" contains examples of cave paintings throughout the world, and in the Sala "Codice del Tiempo" a wonderful wall-size timeline marks important world cultures and events from 2500 B.C. to A.D. 1500. Viewing benches in front of it provide a place to ponder the development of the world's civilizations. Other rooms include information on the discovery of corn and its importance to Mexican culture, techniques for the production of art, and the function of art in society. Upstairs is a fabulous collection of pre-Hispanic art covering the pre- to post-Classic periods. Some of the clay figures from Nayarit and Colima are especially amazing. Signs are in Spanish and English. One final room contains furniture from various periods. No cameras are permitted. The museum is located three blocks south of the zócalo near the corner of Avenida 9 Pte.

⭕ **Museo Bello y Gonzaléz.** Av. 3 Pte. No. 302. ☎ **22/32-9475.** Admission 75¢; free Tues. Tues–Sun 10am–4:30pm.

Located near the corner of Calle 3 Sur and Avenida 3 Poniente, a block and a half west of the zócalo, this museum is definitely worth a visit. The collection includes fine 17-, 18th-, and 19th-century art. Señor Bello made his fortune in tobacco and began to collect art from all over the world. He never traveled, but he hired art dealers who did. Later, Señor Bello, who was a fine artist and an accomplished organist, founded a museum, which he left to the state when he died. His taste is evident throughout the house: velvet curtains, French porcelain, beautiful hand-carved furniture, several very fine organs, and numerous paintings. The mandatory guided tour (in English or Spanish) is included in the price of admission.

⭕ **Museo Casa de Alfeñique/State Regional Museum.** Avenida 4 Ote. 416. ☎ **22/32-4296.** Admission 75¢; free Tues. Tues–Sun 10am–4:30pm.

One of the most interesting parts of this museum is the building itself, called the Casa de Alfeñique. The 18th-century house resembles an elaborate wedding cake; in fact, the name means "sugar-cake house." Inside, it's architecturally embellished with an elaborate plaster doorway and brick-and-beam ceilings. The exhibits include a good collection of pre-Hispanic artifacts and pottery, displays of regional crafts, colonial-era furniture, and a sizable collection of china poblana costumes. The museum is four blocks northeast of the zócalo, between Calles 4 and 6 Norte.

⭕ **Exconvento de Santa Mónica.** Av. 18 Pte. no. 103. ☎ **22/32-0178.** Admission $1; free Sun. Tues–Sun 10am–4:30pm.

When the convents of Puebla were closed in 1857, this one and two others operated secretly, using entrances through private homes, which hid the convent from public view. Very few people knew this convent existed before it was rediscovered in 1935 by a tax collector. Today it's a museum, kept as it was found. It's some 10 blocks north of the zócalo near the corner of Avenida 18 Poniente and 5 de Mayo, at Callejón de la Av. 18 Pte.

⭕ **Museo de Artes Populares and the Cocina de Santa Rosa.** Calle 3 Nte. at 12 Pte. ☎ **22/46-4526.** Admission 75¢. Tues–Sun 10am–4:30pm.

The largest convent in Puebla, Santa Rosa belonged to the Dominican order. It has been beautifully restored and is worth a visit just to see the cavernous, beautifully tiled kitchen (*cocina*) where many native Mexican dishes were created. The museum has two floors of elaborate Mexican arts and crafts, including a 6-foot earthenware candelabra, regional costumes, minute scenes made of straw and clay, and hand-tooled leather. A small shop sells local crafts, but they aren't as good as those at the government shops in other cities. Twenty-minute tours of the museum and kitchen are offered, the last starting at 4:30pm. The museum is eight blocks northwest of the zócalo, between Avenida 12 and Avenida 14 Poniente. The front door, which is closed and locked, is on Calle 3 Nte. Go around the corner to a public parking lot at Av. 14 Pte. 305; the entry is through there.

Museo Regional de la Revolución (Casa de Aquiles Serdán). Av. 6 Ote. no. 206. ☎ **22/42-1076.** Admission 75¢; free Tues. Tues–Sun 10am–4:30pm.

This war museum is 3½ blocks north of the zócalo, between Calle 2 and Calle 4 Norte, in the Casa de Aquiles Serdán, an 18th-century structure complete with bullet holes in the front facade of the house. The collection includes arms and photos of the great turmoil of the mid-19th century: the battle between the *Juaristas* (liberals) and those who followed the imperialists (conservatives). Since Puebla lies between the main seaport of Veracruz and the capital, it was often under bombardment by besieging armies.

SHOPPING

If you're in the market for a set of **Talavera dinnerware,** this is the city. Numerous workshops produce this famous, expensive pottery. **Uriarte Talavera,** Calle 4 Pte. 911 (☎ **22/32-1598**), is one of the most established (since 1824) potters in Puebla. Behind an unprepossesing doorway, the factory produces exquisite pieces, many examples of which are displayed in its sophisticated showrooms. Some are for sale there; others are samples from which to order. Tours of the factory are given Monday through Friday at 11am, noon, and 1pm. It's open Monday through Saturday from 9am to 6:30pm, and Sunday from 11am to 6pm. The **Centro Talavera Poblana,** Calle 6 Ote. 11 (☎ **22/42-0848**), offers a wide range of Talaveraware from producers in Puebla as well as Tlaxcala. The huge showroom has full sets with between 6 and 12 place settings ready for you to take home. Prices are fixed. Between Calle 2 Norte and Calle 5 de Mayo, it's open daily from 9:30am to 8pm. The **Mercado de Artisanías,** or **El Parián** as it's also called, is a pedestrians-only open-air shopping area just east of Calle 6 Norte between Avenidas 2 and 6 Oriente. You'll see rows of neat brick shops selling crafts and souvenirs. Don't judge all Talavera pottery by what you see here, though. Artists seem to have gone overboard with design. The shops are open daily from 10am to 8pm. Bargain to get a good price. While you're in this area, you can take a look at the Teatro Principal.

A good selection of the better-quality Talaveraware, along with other fine crafts such as textiles, can be found under the portales at **Tienda DIF,** Portal Hidalgo 14, (☎ **22/32-10-17**), a government-owned shop. The proceeds benefit local families. It's open daily from 10am to 8pm.

For some good **antique browsing,** go to **Callejón de los Sapos** (Alley of the Frogs), about three blocks southeast of the zócalo near Calle 4 Sur and Avenida 7 Oriente. Wander in and out, for there's good stuff both large and small. Shops are generally open daily from 10am to 2pm and 4 to 6pm. Bargain to get a good price.

WHERE TO STAY

Puebla hotels are still overpriced, though the peso devaluation has brought several downtown hotels into the reasonable range.

Hotel Colonial. Calle 4 Sur no. 105, 72000 Puebla, Pue. ☎ **22/46-4199.** Fax 22/46-0818. 70 rms (all with bath). TEL. $21.50 single; $28 double.

The four-story hotel (with elevator) is charming in an old way, with arches and lots of tiles on the interior public areas. The rooms, too, have tile floors and are neatly furnished. It's comfortable and close to all the sights, and the restaurant is popular with locals. Expensive garage parking is around the corner. The Colonial is one block east of the zócalo, on a pedestrian-way between Camacho and Avenida 3 Oriente.

Hotel Palace. Av. 2 Ote. no. 13, 72000 Puebla, Pue. ☎ **22/32-2430** or 22/42-4030. Fax 22/42-5599. 60 rms (all with bath) TV TEL. $22.75 single; $24.75–$30 double.

Opened in 1993, this is a modern five-story hotel convenient to everything in the downtown area. The shocking-orange halls are carpeted, as are the small rooms. Each room comes with one or two beds, a desk, an overstuffed chair, and overbed reading lights. The restaurant/bar off the lobby is open daily from 8am to 11pm. The hotel is between Calle 2 Norte and Calle 5 de Mayo.

✪ **Hotel Posada San Pedro.** Av. 2 Ote. no. 202, 72000 Puebla, Pue. ☎ **22/46-5077.** Fax 22/46-5376. 76 rms (all with bath). AC TV TEL. $34 single; $47 double. Free parking.

Behind its rather uninspiring front, the San Pedro is a choice little five-story hostelry. Only slightly out of the budget range, it is much less expensive and of much higher quality than some other downtown "luxury" hotels. The rooms have high ceilings, heavily textured walls, and modern furnishings. Bathrooms are large and equipped with bath mats, large towels, and all the toiletry amenities. A swimming pool in the atrium is a welcome attraction after padding Puebla's streets. An intimate bar is discreetly located on the mezzanine floor. This is a family hotel, with afternoon videos for the kids and child care by prior arrangement. It's conveniently located between Calles 2 and 4 Nte., only two blocks from the zócalo.

✪ **Hotel San Angel.** Av. 4 Pte. no. 504, 72000 Puebla, Pue. ☎ and fax **22/32-3845.** 37 rms (all with bath). TV TEL. $21.50 single or double. All rates include breakfast.

This cheery little hotel, renovated in 1993, occupies a large three-story 19th-century townhouse (with an elevator) centered on a covered interior patio. The hotel's welcoming little restaurant occupies the central patio, where guests take the complimentary breakfast or other meals. The carpeted rooms are exceedingly cheerful, with matching bedspreads and drapes and overbed reading lights. The baths are small, but the sinks are conveniently outside the toilet/shower area. It's near the corner of Calle 5 Norte.

Hotel San Miguel. Av. 3 Pte. no. 721, 72000 Puebla, Pue. ☎ **22/42-4860.** Fax 22/42-4863. 65 rms (all with bath). TV TEL. $13.25 single; $16.50 double.

The tile hallways here gleam; the rooms are large and clean; and they've put money into good towels. I recommend a quiet interior room. The only drawback is the limited supply of hot water: It's available from 6 to 11am and 5 to 11pm only. The San Miguel is 3¹/₂ long blocks west of the cathedral, between Calles 7 and 9 Sur.

WHERE TO EAT

Puebla is known throughout Mexico for the famous *mole poblano,* a sauce with more than 20 ingredients, as well as *mixiotes,* a dish of beef, pork, or lamb in a spicy red sauce baked in maguey paper. Should you want to try your hand at making the delicious mixiotes, mague-paper wrappers are sold in the market. *Tinga,* a delicious beef stew, is another state specialty. And if you're looking for a gift, *Rompope,* an eggnog-like drink spiked with rum, is sold in liquor and grocery stores. *Dulces* (sweets) shops are scattered along Avenida 6 Oriente, with display windows brim-full of marzipan crafted into various shapes and designs, candied figs, guava paste, and *camotes,* which are little cylinders of a fruity sweet-potato paste wrapped in waxed paper.

There are more small, inexpensive Puebla-style eateries on **Calle 6 Norte,** all doing their part to uphold the reputation Puebla bears as a culinary fount. Great pots of boiling mole and other mysteriously delectable regional sauces bubble temptingly. Find something you like by peeking into the kitchens right in front. Most restaurants are open daily, but several are closed on Wednesday.

✪ **Las Chinas de Puebla.** Av 5 Oriente 3, in the Tourism Office. ☎ **22/46-1569.** Appetizers 50¢–$3; main courses $2–$3.50. Daily 9am–9pm. PUEBLA CUISINE.

After eating one meal here and having a cooking lesson with super-chef Trini Becerra, I decided I could pay more to eat the same regional specialties elsewhere but I wouldn't dine better anywhere—so I returned again and again.

The idea of this new restaurant was to replicate the look of an authentic 19th-century Puebla pulquería, like those painted by the famous Pueblan costumbrista artist Augustine Arrieta (1803–1874); reproductions of his works decorate the walls. Furthermore, it was to be an example of what the best Puebla cuisine is all about. So here you can try *cemitas* (the local name for a sandwich made with a special delicious bread), *chanclas,* a sandwich covered in a delicious red-pepper sauce, extraordinarily good mixiotes and mole poblano, plus a full range of meal-size appetizers such as *molotes,* which in Puebla are deep-fried flour wrappers stuffed with cheese, potatoes, or meat, epazote, and jalapeño pepper—it's not *picante*. All the sauces are made fresh daily. On Sundays manchamanteles are the off-the-menu special. Cooking lessons can be arranged evenings except on Tuesday. Speak with manager María Esther Rodríguez a day or so in advance of your desired lesson time, or write to arrange it before you arrive. Costs hadn't been determined when I checked, but lessons should be inexpensive. To find it, facing the cathedral, it's to the right on Avenida 5 Oriente in the State Tourism Office.

✪ **El Cortijo.** Calle 16 de Septiembre no. 506. ☎ **22/42-0503.** Main courses $5–$7.50; comida corrida $5.75. Daily 1pm–6pm (comida corrida served 1–3pm). MEXICAN.

This enclosed patio restaurant has a comfortable atmosphere and tasty food. Dishes range from pork chops to delicious jumbo shrimp or paella. The *cubierto* (or comida corrida) starts with a fruit cocktail; followed by a choice of two soups; a midcourse of perhaps paella or spaghetti; then the main course, which might include a choice of pork leg, mole, fish, or chicken. This is a good place for that large afternoon meal and a bottle of wine. The restaurant is $2^{1}/_{2}$ blocks south of the zócalo, between Avenidas 5 and 7 Ote.

Fonda de San Agustín. Av. 3 Pte. 531. ☎ **22/32-5089.** Breakfast $3.25; comida corrida $2. daily 8am–6pm. MEXICAN.

Just to the right of the entrance to the Hotel San Agustín you'll see this little eatery. A short row of booths plus three tables hold diners who converge here daily for the good lunch deal. The set-price meal includes soup, a main course, and a dessert. It's between Calles 5 and 7 Sur.

✪ **Fonda de Santa Clara.** Av. 3 Pte. no. 307. ☎ **22/42-2659.** Lunch $3.75–$8.25; dinner $1.75–$3.25. Tues–Sat noon–10pm, Sun 11am–10pm. REGIONAL.

This is one of the city's most popular and traditional restaurants, serving regional food. It's busy but cozy and slightly formal. The menu includes such local dishes as pollo mole poblano, mixiotes, and tinga. There are seasonal specialties as well, like fried grasshoppers in October and November, maguey worms in April and May, chiles en nogada from July through September, and huitlacoche in June. The light dinner menu features such specials as *tacos de sesos* (brain tacos), tamales, *pozole, mole de panza* (mole over stomach meat), and atole. The restaurant is $1^{1}/_{2}$ blocks west of the zócalo, opposite the Bello Museum.

Mac's Tavern and Bar. Avenida Camacho and Portal Morelos. ☎ **22/46-0211.** Breakfast $2–$4.25; sandwiches $2.25–$4; main courses $2.30–$4.50; weekday buffet $3.50; Sat–Sun special poblano buffet $5.75. Daily 7am to midnight (buffet served 1–5pm). MEXICAN.

Here on the northeast corner of the zócalo is one of Puebla's most popular places for lunch. Hungry Poblanos don't come here for the modern setting but for the buffet, which will last you the rest of the day.

Sanborn's. Av. 2 Ote. 6. ☎ **22/42-3986.** Breakfast $1.25–$3.25; main courses $4.75–$6.50. Daily 7am–11pm. MEXICAN.

The dining room, in a fine colonial courtyard, has tables set around a stone fountain. The menu, as at others at this reliable chain, covers the culinary spectrum from chicken, fajitas, and fish, to enchiladas, chilaquiles, and sandwiches. Apart from the restaurant a large section of the store is devoted to the sale of books, magazines, cameras, jewelry, gifts, luggage, and the like. It's 1 ¹/₂ blocks north of the zócalo, between Calle 2 Nte. and 5 de Mayo.

Vittorio's Pizzería. Portal Morelos 106. ☎ **22/32-7900.** Pastas and salads $1.75–$3.50; pizza $4–$16.50; main courses $3.25–$5. Daily 12pm–12am. ITALIAN.

This pleasantly cozy restaurant on the east side of the zócalo serves cheese-smothered pizzas, pastas, and regional poblano cuisine. You can dine inside or outside on the plaza. Pizzas come in three sizes: small (for one or two), medium (for two or three), and large (for four to six). There are cappuccino and espresso, plus there's an extensive wine and liquor list. It's closed on major holidays.

PUEBLA AFTER DARK

Mariachis play daily, beginning at 6pm, on **Plaza de Santa Inés,** at Avenida 11 Poniente and Calle 3 Sur. They stroll through the crowds that gather at the sidewalk cafés. Another square that attracts mariachis is **Plaza de los Sapos,** Avenida 7 Oriente near Calle 6 Sur. To get there, walk two blocks from the zócalo and take a left onto Avenida 7 Oriente, toward the river. The plaza will be on your left spreading out between Avenida 7 and Avenida 5 Oriente just passed Calle 4 Sur. If you use Avenida 5 Oriente from the cathedral to reach the Plaza de los Sapos you'll pass several local hangouts where students, artists, and others gather for conversation, coffee, drinks, and snacks. But for the best evening entertainment in town try the **Mesón Sacristía de la Compañía** at Calle 6 Sur 304 (Calle 6 Sur is also called Callejon de los Sapos and is known for its numerous antique shops—see "Shopping" above). Leonardo Espinosa turned his antique shop into the trendiest patio restaurant in Puebla and transformed the 200-year-old building into a small hotel. All the furniture in the nine hotel rooms is for sale as is just about everything else you see in the dining areas as well. During the late afternoon a pianist plays soft music. At 9pm a singer/guitarist entertains with popular ballads until midnight. The rooms are out of our price range ($75 and up) but the restaurant, which fills the inner patio and adjacent rooms, is moderately priced, so you can dine or drink and enjoy the free entertainment without breaking the bank.

Teorema, Reforma 540 near Calle 7 Norte (22/42-1014), is a wonderful coffee shop/bookstore that features guitarists and folksingers every evening. This is a good place to meet young local residents. It's open daily from 9:30am to 2:30pm and 4:30pm to midnight.

SIDE TRIPS FROM PUEBLA
CHOLULA: CITY OF CHURCHES

Six miles northwest of Puebla along Highway 190 (not the toll road, 190D), the colonial town of Cholula (pop. 45,000) is one of the holiest places in Mexico. Legend says that Quetzalcoatl, the famed feathered serpent, lived here in exile after he was forced to leave his city of Tula, capital of the Toltecs, in A.D. 900. During pre-Hispanic days pilgrims came here to pay their respects to the legendary leader. Today it's very easy to get to Cholula from Puebla by taking one of the small white vans marked "Cholula," at the corner of Avenida 10 Poniente and Calle 11 Norte.

The Cholulans strongly resisted Cortés and his men. When the Spaniards discovered the residents of this town were plotting to overthrow them, at least 3,000 Cholulans were killed.

Cholula boasts so many churches it's often said there's one for every day of the year. It's also the home of the **University of the Americas**—popular with American students. From Cholula's main plaza, you can see a large yellow church. Behind it, atop what looks like an enormous hill, you'll see the white **Los Remedios Church** etched against the sky. The "hill," however, is the **Great Tepanapa Pyramid,** only a five-minute walk away. To get there from the plaza, walk on Morelos and across the railroad tracks. On the right, about a football field's length from the tracks, is the entrance. The pyramid is actually several pyramids built one on top of the other. Around the perimeter reconstructed portions show what parts of the pyramid once looked like, and other areas show excavations. The famous frescoes deep inside date back to the Classic Period, but they've been closed to the public for some time.

The lighted interior tunnels were dug by archaeologists and are easy to follow by yourself, but a hired guide can provide interesting details and show where one pyramid stops and another begins. Prices for guides are about $8.25 for a tour inside and out and $4.25 for a tour inside only.

The ruins are open daily from 10am to 5pm. Admission is $2.25; free on Sunday and holidays; $4.25 for use of your video camera.

If you take the stone walkway up the hill (to the top of the pyramid), you'll reach the lovely chapel of the Virgen de los Remedios. The gilded interior of this little gem is as pretty as its exterior. While regaining your breath, you'll enjoy the spectacular view of the town's steeples and plaza.

HUEJOTZINGO'S MARKET & MONASTERY

On Saturday fine woolen goods, especially serapes and blankets, are sold at the open-air market in Huejotzingo, Puebla (elev. 7,550 ft.; pop. 30,000), a pleasant town with a large main square 9 miles northwest of Cholula. Even if you don't come for market day, you can stop and enjoy a glass or two of the sparkling (alcoholic) cider, a local specialty.

While in town, be sure to visit the **Franciscan monastery,** right across the main road from the town plaza. It was built between 1529 and 1570 and is one of the oldest in Mexico. As you walk up the stairs from the main road and enter the monastery compound, stop to admire the little square chapels (posas) topped by pyramidal roofs at each corner of the enclosure. The cross mounted on a pedestal in the courtyard dates from the 1500s as well.

The church, very austere on the outside, has a wonderfully lacy Gothic vault inside, plus a dazzling altar in the plateresque style. The monastery building next door, entered through the double-arch doorway, has a few excellent friezes in black and white painted by Fray António de Roldan in 1558. There is a lovely chapel, a cloister for the monks, kitchens, and a dining room. The monastery is open Tuesday through Sunday from 10am to 4:30pm; admission is $1.

From Puebla, buses leave every 15 minutes or so. From Cholula, take a taxi from the central plaza for around $5.

A FESTIVAL   The colorful story of bandit Agustín Lorenzo's kidnapping of a beautiful young girl is reenacted in Huejotzingo the Tuesday before Ash Wednesday with a colorful firecracker-filled **Carnaval** featuring a cast of thousands wearing brilliantly colored costumes. The story goes that during the colonial era in Huejotzingo, Lorenzo kidnapped the daughter of a rich landowner and spirited her away into the mountains in order to wed her. During the wedding celebration local

Two Churrigueresque Churches

If you go to Cholula, try to visit the churches of **Santa María Tonanzintla** and **San Francisco Acatepec,** 3 miles southeast of Cholula. Called Indian baroque because the Indians used pre-Hispanic ideas to present Christian concepts, the churches are elaborately decorated with beautifully colored Puebla tiles and wood carved by local artisans. Saints are swaddled in stylized quetzal bird feathers, once used to depict the god Quetzalcoatl, and faces protrude from a headdress of corn leaves, in the same way they did in pre-Christian times. The interior of the Tonanzintla church is covered floor to ceiling in fabulous gilded and polychrome faces, cherubs, and foliage—an unforgettable sight. The facade of the Acatepec church is a fantasy of tile, though it has a less elaborate interior than the Tonanzintla church.

The churches are only 8 miles outside Cholula and are easy to reach from there: Take one of the buses marked "chipito," which go by the entrance to the ruins. Hours are unpredictable, but the caretaker is usually not far away; ask around for him, and chances are he'll appear.

soldiers came to her rescue. It's one of the most colorful Carnaval celebrations in Mexico; the carnaval market is at least 10 blocks square.

TLAXCALA & THE NEARBY CACAXTLA/XOCHITÉCATL RUINS

Located 25 miles north of Puebla and 75 miles east of Mexico City, Tlaxcala is the capital of Mexico's smallest state (same name) and is a pretty colonial-era city with several unique claims to fame. Tlaxcalan warriors, for one thing, allied themselves with Hernán Cortés against the Aztecs and were essential to the conquistador's victory. As a reward for their help in the Conquest, the Tlaxcalans were allowed to govern themselves and were exempted from paying taxes to Spain; and they were the first permitted to own guns and horses supplied by the Spaniards. Tlaxcalan chiefs were also the first to be baptized by the Spaniards; the baptismal font used for them is found in the **Templo de San Francisco** (located two blocks from the main plaza and just above the bullring). The Templo is noted for its elaborately inlaid Moorish ceiling below the choir loft. A painting inside the Chapel of the Third Order shows the baptism of the chiefs.

To the right of the Templo is the **Exconvento museum,** containing early paintings and artifacts from nearby archaeological sites. The **Government Palace,** on the handsome tree-shaped central zócalo, is painted inside with vivid murals showing Tlaxcala history by a local artist, Desiderio Hernández Xochitiotzin. The expanded **Museo de Artesanías** on Sanchez Piedras between Lardizabal and 1 de Mayo, showcases the state's wide-ranging crafts and customs. Here local artisans give visitors demonstrations in such crafts as embroidery, weaving, and pulque making. The museum is open Tuesday through Sunday, 10am–6pm; admission is $1.

A bit more than $^{1}/_{2}$ mile from the town center is the famed **Ocotlán Sanctuary,** constructed after Juan Diego Bernardino claimed to have seen an apparition of the Virgin Mary on that site in 1541. Baroque inside and out, the elaborate interior decorations of carved figures and curling gilded wood date from the 1700s. These carvings are attributed to Francisco Miguel Tlayotehuanitzin, an Indian sculptor who labored for more than 20 years to create them. **Santa Ana,** a wool-weaving village, is only 1$^{1}/_{2}$ miles east of Tlaxcala. Shops selling large rugs, serapes, and sweaters woven locally line the main street. **Huamantla,** 30 miles southeast of Tlaxcala, is a small village noted for its commemoration of the Assumption of the Virgin on August 12 (see below). Tlaxcala's main attractions, however, are **Cacaxtla** (kah-*kahsh*-tlah) and the recently opened **Xochitécatl** (soh-she-*teh*-kettle), both unique pre-Hispanic hilltop sites 12 miles southwest of the city of Tlaxcala.

In general, this wonderfully pleasant city hosts few tourists and because of that retains its small-town atmosphere and generally low prices. It's worthy of a day— perhaps several days—of your journey.

The excellent **Oficina del Turismo del Estado** (State Tourism Office) is located a block north of the zócalo at the corner of Juárez and Lardizábal (☎ **246/2-5037;** fax 246/2-5306). **City Tours** are offered on weekends by the State Tourism Office. On Saturday there's tour of the city and on Sunday a tour of the Cacaxtla/Xochitécatl sites. Tours leave from the front of the Posada San Francisco Villas Arqueologícas at 10am both mornings. Board the bus; the guide will collect the $1.75 fee as you go.

Exploring the Cacaxtla/Xochitécatl Archaeological Site

Scholars were startled by the 1975 discovery at Cacaxtla of vivid murals in red, blue, black, yellow, and white, showing Maya warriors (from the Mexican Yucatán Peninsula 500 miles south). Since then more murals, more history, and at least eight construction phases have been uncovered.

Presently, scholars attribute the influence of the site to a little-known tri-ethnic group (Náhua, Mixtec, and Chocho-popoloca) known as Olmec-Xicalanca from Mexico's Gulf Coast. Among the translations of the people's name, "merchant's trade pack" seems most revealing. Like Casas Grandes north of Chihuahua City, or Xochicalco (also with distinctive Maya influence) between Cuernavaca and Taxco, Cacaxtla apparently was an important crossroads for merchants, astronomers, and others in the Mesoamerican world. Its apogee, between A.D. 650 and 900, corresponds with the abandonment of Teotihuacán (near Mexico City), the beginning of Casas Grandes culture, and in the final phase, the decline of the Maya in Yucatán, the emergence of the Toltec culture at Tula (also near Mexico City), and the spread of Toltec influence to Yucatán. How, or even if, those events affected Cacaxtla isn't known yet. Apparently the mural is a victory scene with warrior figures clothed magnificently in jaguar skins and seemingly victorious over figures dressed in feathers who were to be sacrificial victims. Some of the victims are even depicted lying on the floor, where they will undergo the ultimate humiliation of being walked on by the victors. Numerous symbols of Venus (a half star with five points) found painted at the site have led archaeoastronomy scholar John Carlson to link historical events such as wars, captive-taking, and ritual sacrifice with the appearance of Venus; all of this was likely undertaken in hopes of assuring the continued fertility of crops. These symbols of blood, along with toads and turtles (all water symbols), sacrifice, and Venus, together with others of corn stalks and cacao trees (symbolizing fertility), were to appease the gods to assure a productive cycle of rains, crops, and trade. The latest mural discoveries show a wall of corn and cacao trees leading to a merchant whose trade pack is laden with these symbolic crops. The murals flank a grand acropolis with unusual architectural motifs. For a lavishly illustrated account of the site, read "Mural Masterpieces of Ancient Cacaxtla" (*National Geographic*, September 1992). The grand plaza and murals are now protected by a giant steel roof.

Xochitécatl is a small ceremonial center located on a hilltop overlooking Cacaxtla, 2¹/₂ miles to the east. A curious circular pyramid stands atop this hill, 600 feet above the surrounding countryside. Besides this are two other pyramids (one of which is the fourth largest in Mexico), and three massive boulders (one about 10 feet in

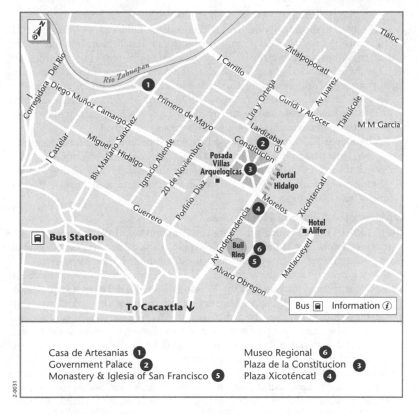

Casa de Artesanias **1**
Government Palace **2**
Monastery & Iglesia of San Francisco **5**

Museo Regional **6**
Plaza de la Constitucion **3**
Plaza Xicoténcatl **4**

diameter), which were hollowed out for some obscure reason. Hollowed boulders appear to have been restricted to the Puebla-Tlaxcala valley. Excavation of the Edificio de la Espiral (circular pyramid), dated between 1000–800 B.C. (middle formative period), encountered no stairways, hence access is thought to have been via its spiral walkway. Rounded boulders from the nearby Zahuapan and Atoyac rivers were used in its construction. Rounded pyramids, in this part of Mexico, are thought to have been dedicated to Ehécatl, god of the wind. The base diameter exceeds 180 feet, and it rises to a height of 50 feet.

The stepped and terraced Pyramid of the Flowers, made of rounded boulders, was begun during the middle formative period, though modifications continued into colonial times as exemplified by faced-stone and stucco-covered adobe. Of the 30 bodies found during excavations, all but one were children. Little is known yet about the people who built Xochitécatl, but at least part of the time they were contemporaneous with neighboring Cacaxtla. Evidence suggests that the area was dedicated to Xochitl, goddess of flowers and fertility. There is a small site museum building containing pottery and small sculpture, and a garden with display of larger sculpture.

To get to Cacaxtla from Tlaxcala, take a *combi* (collective minivan) or city bus to the village of San Miguel Milagro or Nativitas (nearest the Cacaxtla ruins). From there, walk the paved mile or so or take a taxi to the entrance. From the parking lot it is a fairly stiff 100 yard climb to the archaeological site. Be careful of the slippery and crudely made wooden steps and use the handrails.

To arrive at Xochitécatl, stay on the bus until you get to Xochitécatitla, then walk or take a cab to the ruins, which are another couple of miles on a blacktop road. If you're driving from Tlaxcala, take the road south to Tetlatlahuaca and turn (right) there to Xochitécatitla or Nativitas. There are signs to the ruins in both towns.

From Puebla, take Highway 119 north to the crossroads near Zacualpan and turn left passing Tetlatlahuaca; turn right when you see signs to Nativitas and Cacaxtla. From Mexico City, take Highway 190 to San Martin Texmelucan, where you should ask directions for the road leading directly to the ruins, which are about 6 miles ahead. (This is the southern road you can use without going to Tlaxcala.)

Admission is $2.75 (one ticket is good for both sites), plus $4.25 for a video camera; free Sundays and holidays. At Cacaxtla, since neither a flash nor a tripod is allowed, the site is difficult to photograph from the inside because of dust and low light caused by shading from the giant roof. Both sites are open Tuesday through Sunday from 10am to 5pm.

Exploring the Village of Huamantla

On August 11, the evening preceding the **Assumption of the Virgin** event, the streets are decorated in murals made of flower petals and colored sawdust, all of which are destroyed when a figure of the virgin is carried through downtown streets. The following weekend a running of the bulls takes place through the downtown streets. Just as colorful and fascinating is the **Museo Nacional del Titere Rosete Aranda** (Rosete Aranda National Puppet Museum), a rare collection of handmade puppets from the Aranda family, who lived in Huamantla. As early as 1835 the family toured the state and went to the capital with their puppet plays—poking fun at politics and history, and performing dances, parades, cockfights, bullfights, and circus acts, complete with marching bands playing instruments—all with puppets. The idea for the character of Cantinflas (a Mexican comedian played by Mario Moreno), came from an Aranda puppet called Vale Coyote. The museum also houses puppets from around the world and from several centuries. (More puppets by this family are in the Rafael Coronel Museum in Zacatecas). The museum is near the main plaza; ask for directions to it from there. Admission is $2.50, and the museum is open Tuesday through Sunday from 10am to 4pm.

Where to Stay & Eat in Tlaxcala

Tlaxcala has several good restaurants beneath the portal on the east side of the zócalo, and budget hotels are nearby and along the road to Apizaco.

Hotel Alifer. Morelos 11. Tlaxcala, 90000 Tlax. ☎ **246/2-5678.** 18 rms (all with bath). TV TEL. $14.75 single; $19.75 double. Free parking.

The Alifer's clean rooms—with a black-and-red Spanish colonial decor—are carpeted and come with tile-and-marble baths with showers. To get there from the Plaza Constitución, with your back to the Posada San Francisco walk to the right two blocks; the second block is a steep one guaranteed to get your blood running by the time you reach the hotel entrance, just before the street turns to the right. The parking lot is next to the lobby entrance.

4 Toluca

45 miles W of Mexico City

The capital of the state of México, Toluca is, at 8,760 feet, the highest city in Mexico. The hour-long trip here from Mexico City offers spectacular scenic views: Pine trees and icy-looking blue lakes dot the landscape, and only an occasional cactus plant or brightly colored painting, drying in the sun, will remind you that you're in Mexico.

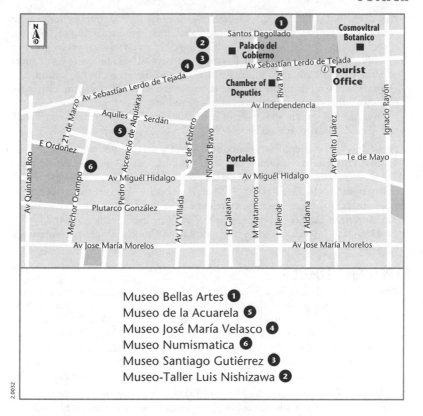

Museo Bellas Artes ❶
Museo de la Acuarela ❺
Museo José María Velasco ❹
Museo Numismatica ❻
Museo Santiago Gutiérrez ❸
Museo-Taller Luis Nishizawa ❷

Toluca's Friday market was once so popular that a parade of buses loaded up tourists every hour from Chapultepec Park in Mexico City. Toluca declined in popular tourism in the 1970s after its famous Friday market moved from its downtown location to its present one, nearer the outskirts of town by the bus station. Though tourism dropped, business boomed, and the market is still enormous and churning with activity. Today Toluca is a thriving industrial center; you'll see the plants lining the highway as you drive into town. With healthy business growth came city beautification, as well as new museums and restaurants. In short, with city sights and excellent shopping in Toluca, and easily reached nearby villages, there's good reason to put Toluca back on the tourist itinerary.

ESSENTIALS

GETTING THERE & DEPARTING   By Bus   It's easy to get to Toluca and the market by bus from Mexico City. Take the Metro to the Observatorio station, which is also called the **Terminal Poniente** bus station. Reserved-seat buses ("Toluca-Directo") of various companies depart every 5 or 10 minutes for the hour-long trip. **ETN,** at the far end of the concourse, offers deluxe service to Toluca and is well worth the little extra in cost over that for standard buses.

By Car   From Mexico City, follow Paseo de la Reforma west until it merges with Carretera a Toluca (Highway 15).

ORIENTATION   Arriving   From Mexico City you'll enter town on the broad **Paseo Tollocán,** a four-lane highway lined with industrial plants like Chrysler and

Pfizer. The bus will discharge passengers at the central bus station in front of the famed Friday market. Both are on **Isidro Fabela** near the intersection of Tollocán. If you're going directly to the market, it's behind the bus station. If you're going to a hotel first and have luggage, you'll want to get a taxi. They line up on a side street opposite the bus station's front exits. Slash the quoted price by half or a third, and you may strike a reasonable bargain. If you're traveling light, use the city buses ("Centro") that go to the city center and are also lined up in front.

From the bus station, the center of town is northwest between Lerdo de Tejada and Avenida Hidalgo. It's too far to walk.

Fast Facts   The **telephone area code** is 72. The well-staffed and helpful **State Tourist Office** is in the central city at Lerdo Poniente 101 in the Edificio Plaza Toluca, second floor (☎ **72/14-1342;** fax 72/13-3142). Hours are Monday through Friday from 9am to 3pm and 4 to 9:30pm. It stocks a wide variety of booklets with maps outlining the state's regions, as well as Toluca maps and museum information. The **American Express** representative is Viajes Corona, Villada no. 445 (☎ **72/ 12-4189;** fax 72/14-2655), at the corner of Ramón Corona. Toluca's **population** is 490,000.

EXPLORING TOLUCA

Plan your Toluca foray for a Friday, just so you can say you saw the **market,** even if you don't stay long. The crowds and hubbub are taxing, and an hour or two should do it, even for a die-hard market lover. Follow that by a trip to ✪ **CASART,** the state crafts store a long block from the market. Then catch a bus ("Centro") for downtown. The first two should take the better part of the morning. After lunch, you'll have time to see some of the city's terrific museums and walk around the historic town center. A trip to nearby archaeological sites and the craft villages takes another day.

THE MARKET   The gigantic **Mercado Juárez,** at the edge of town on the highway to Mexico City, has both market buildings and open-air grounds. Shops in the buildings are open all week, but it's on Friday that the people from surrounding villages come and crowd the plaza. The bus from Mexico City pulls into a terminal right across the street from the Mercado Júarez. You'll recognize the market by the pair of slender concrete slabs that tower above it to serve as a landmark.

Because of the natives' bargaining powers, a peaceful walk around the market is not easy. Every time you pause to admire such unfamiliar sights as a boxful of chattering chickens, a 2-foot-high pile of assorted shoelaces, or an array of framed saints' pictures, some man or boy will accost you with cries of "Serapes, rebozos, very cheap." Some sights will make you pause—a marimba band banging away cheerfully between the stalls or a little open-fronted bakery where chains of tortillas can be seen pouring off a conveyor belt into a basket. But sooner or later the heat and crowdedness of the market will begin to get you down; the man with the pig under his arm or the woman with a turkey sticking its head out from the back of her shawl probably won't even cause you to bat an eye.

THE HISTORIC CENTER   This area in the heart of Toluca is bounded by Avenidas Hidalgo, Juárez, and Sebastián Lerdo de Tejada. Here you'll see the housing for the heart of state government in stately buildings framing the square—the Palace of Justice, Chamber of Deputies, Government Palace, Municipal Palace, Cosmovitral Botánico, and the cathedral, which was established by the Franciscans in the mid-1800s.

The famous *portales* (arcades) of Toluca, begun in 1832, are one block east of the main plaza. They are a popular meeting, shopping, and dining place. From the Days of the Dead (November 1 and 2) through Christmas, they're filled with temporary vendors selling the candy for which the state is famous.

Located at the corner of Juárez and Lerdo off Plaza de los Martires and between the Chamber of Deputies and the Government Palace, the **Cosmovitral Botánico**, or Botanical Garden (☎ 72/14-6785), is an indoor garden inside the walls of a 19th-century art nouveau building and is one of the city's greatest creations. It was the site of the famed Toluca market until 1975. In 1980, it reopened to house the botanical gardens. The upper half of the building is emblazoned with 54 bold stained-glass panels telling the story of humanity in relation to the cosmos. All the elements of a good tale are there—good and evil, happiness and sadness, freedom and imprisonment. From design to completion, it took local artists three years. The stained glass, however, is only the frame for the gardens showing plants native to the state of México and other countries. The gardens are open Tuesday through Sunday from 9am to 5pm; admission is $1.50.

Velasco was one of the state's favorite sons, so it's only fitting the man known as Mexico's foremost 19th-century landscape painter should have a museum here in his honor. The **Museo José María Velasco,** Lerdo de Tejada 400, at the corner of N. Bravo (☎ 72/13-2814) is a showcase for Velasco's vast landscapes that feature enormous Mexican valleys, usually with a volcano in the background. Viewers of his work may feel as though they are standing on the same mountaintop as the painter himself. Some of these works are on display, and it's well worth the short time it takes to see them. The museum is opposite the main plaza, across from the Palacio del Gobierno and a block from the Cosmovitral Botánico. It's open Tuesday through Sunday from 10am to 6pm; admission is free.

In a grand mansion connected and next door to the Velasco Museum, the **Museo Santiago Gutiérrez,** at Nicolas Bravo Nte. 303 (☎ 72/13-2647) pays homage to another of the state's famous painters. Gutiérrez and Velasco were friends, and both studied at the San Carlos Museum. Gutiérrez was the country's foremost 19th-century portrait, figure, and *costumbrista* artist. (Costumbrista paintings used Mexican themes with figures clad in Mexican attire.) He traveled and studied widely, eventually founding the Academia de Artes de Bogotá, Colombia, during his years there. The Museo Gutiérrez in Toluca houses the largest collection of his work, one of which was included in the spectacular "Thirty Centuries of Mexican Art" exhibit that toured the United States in 1990. The Museum is open Tuesday through Sunday from 10am to 6pm; admission is free.

You may never have heard of this master painter, but you won't forget him once you see his work housed on two floors here in the ✪ **Museo-Taller Luis Nishizawa** at Nicolas Bravo Nte. 305 (☎ 72/135-7468). His oil portraits and skilled use of color are unforgettable. Born to a Japanese father and a Mexican mother, he moved with his parents from Toluca to Mexico City in 1925. At 24 he entered the San Carlos Academy and within three years was given the title "Master of Plastic Arts." In his long career he has won hundreds of awards. Now in his 70s, he divides his time between residing in Mexico City and teaching at the museum between 10am and 2pm each Saturday. The stained-glass ceiling over the patio is a Nishizawa creation. The beautifully restored house dates from 1781 and has a colorful history, including tales of ghosts that are said to appear even today. The Instituto Mexiquense de Cultura published in 1993 an illustrated history of the house, *La Vieja Casona de Nicolas Bravo Norte 305.* The museum is located farther up the street from the Museo Santiago Gutiérrez (see above); it's one block north of the main plaza between Lerdo de Tejada and Santo Degollado. This is a top museum you should not miss. It's open Tuesday through Sunday from 10am to 6pm, and admission is free.

Impressions

*In the Maison de la Providencia, at Toluca, yesterday, a hungry guest shot Margarito
López, a waiter of the establishment, through the hand, because the waiter did not
answer his call promptly.*

—W. E. Carson, *Mexico: The Wonderland of the South*, 1909

Housed in a part of the former Convento de la Purisma Concepción, the **Museo
de Bellas Artes,** at Santos Degollado Pte. 102 (☎ 72/15-5329), displays furniture,
sculpture, and paintings from the 16th to the 18th century. Paintings here include
those by Indian artists Miguel Cabrera (1728–1768), Agnolo de Broznino (1503–
1563), José Juárez (1615–1660), and Cristóbal de Villalpando (1651–1714). The
rarest piece, however, is a four-tiered funerary painting (*tumelo*) possibly dating from
the early 18th century. Only one other is known in Mexico, at the Museo Virreynal
de Taxco (between Cuernavaca and Acapulco). It isn't known for whom the one in
Toluca was intended, but besides the painted scenes, it has several poems and Latin
phrases. To find the museum from the main plaza, walk up Bravo to the corner of
Santos Degollado and turn right; the museum is half a block farther on the left.
If you're at the Nishizawa museum, go out the front door, turn left, walk to the
corner, and turn right; it's ahead on the left. The museum is open Tuesday through
Sunday from 10am to 6pm; admission costs 75¢.

The ✪ **Museo de la Acuarela,** Pedro Ascencio at Nigromante (☎ 72/14-7304),
housed in a mansion built early this century and restored recently, is devoted entirely
to watercolor paintings. Featured here are either the works of state-born artists or
paintings about the state by artists from around the world. Since the state of México
is so large and almost surrounds the Federal District, the subject matter—from
archaeological sites to landscapes and village streets—is vast. The work, too, is
wonderful, and you may find yourself lingering to admire it or to identify recognizable places artists have captured in watercolor. The museum is only 1 1/2 blocks west
of the central square. To find it from the northwest corner of the main plaza (where
Bravo meets Independencia), turn left onto Independencia (which becomes Serdán)
and walk straight one block, then turn left on Pedro Ascencio de Alquisiras; the
museum is on the right about half a block. It's open Tuesday through Sunday from
10am to 6pm; admission is free.

The **Museo de Numismatica,** Av. Hidalgo Pte. 506 (☎ 72/13-1927), is housed
in a grand turn-of-the-century stone mansion. It features Mexican currency from
pre-Hispanic times to the present. Among the most interesting are the pre-Hispanic
beads and *cacao* (chocolate beans), once used as currency among various tribes.
Regional money printed during the tumultuous years of the Mexican Revolution is
another fascinating exhibit. The museum is billed as tops in the country and Latin
America—you be the judge. To find it from the southwest corner of the main plaza,
walk west on Hidalgo, crossing 5 de Febrero and Pedro Ascencio de Alquisiras; it's
in the middle of the next block on the right. If you're coming from the Museo de
la Acuarela (see above), turn right out the front door and walk two blocks to Hidalgo.
Turn right; it's on the right. The museum is open Tuesday through Saturday from
10am to 6pm and Sunday from 10am to 4pm; admission is free.

✪ **CENTRO CULTURAL MEXIQUENSE**   Seeing this cultural center is reason
enough to stay on in Toluca. In 1987, the Centro Cultural Mexiquense (☎ 72/
12-4738) opened on the sprawling grounds of the former Hacienda de la Pila, in a
southeastern suburb of the city. The ambitious and beautiful museum incorporates
four cultural entities and a library that were once scattered throughout Toluca. The

various buildings form a one-story U shape around an enormous central yard where orchestras and dancers sometimes entertain.

English-speaking guides are often available for the asking at the library, on your left as you approach the cluster of buildings. Or you are free to wander at your leisure, but all signs are in Spanish.

The center and all its museums are open Tuesday through Sunday from 9am to 5pm; the restaurant is closed on Sunday. The $3.25 admission price includes all the buildings and museums at the Centro. Admission is paid at the kiosk in the parking lot—not in the museums. It's free for all on Sunday.

Don't miss the **Popular Arts Museum,** on the right, in the original hacienda building, if you plan to visit any of the state's crafts villages. You'll get not only a great overview of what the state has to offer and where but also an idea of quality. As you enter, you can't miss the spectacular, building-size polychrome-clay "trees of life" from the artisans of Metepec. They would have been too huge to bring into the building, so the artists made and fired them inside before the museum opened. As you walk through the salons you'll find exhibits of regional costumes, Persian-like tapestries from Temoaya, leather-covered chests from San Mateo Atenco, and embroidery from Ameyalco among the thousands of objects. In the **Charro Museum** you'll see lariats and swords, a great sombrero display, spurs, bits, and saddles. There's even a 16th-century stirrup and a charro wedding suit. A cozy restaurant (inexpensive), bookstore, and sales shop are in this building.

Opposite the Popular Arts Museum and next to the **library** is the **Museum of Modern Art** in a building originally intended as an observatory. Here you can study paintings by Rufino Tamayo, Juan O'Gorman, José Chávez Morado, Orozco, and Diego Rivera, all of whom were better known for their murals. The works are quite good, and you'll likely discover other lesser-known artists whose efforts rival their better-known contemporaries.

In the middle, straight ahead from the entrance, between the Popular Arts and Modern Art museums, is the **Museum of Anthropology.** The massive number of artifacts are well displayed in a broad and spacious building. Objects from the state's 10 most important archaeological sites include beautiful pottery and mural fragments from Teotihuacán and the famous wood drum from Malinalco, showing carved jaguars and eagles. Other excellent displays show the forests and animals by region, insects, butterflies, and a considerable collection of stuffed animals. Memorabilia from colonial days to the present include a bust of Emperor Maximilian, a fan and lace gloves that belonged to Empress Carlota, French dresses from the time of Porfirio Díaz, photographs, and the first soft-drink machine in the state of México.

SHOPPING   Besides the famous Mercado Juárez mentioned above, Toluca and environs offer several good options for shopping, especially for regionally made crafts. The Centro Cultural Mexequense and the Toluca Market give you two insights into regional crafts; **CASART,** Paseo Tollocán and Urawa (☎ **72/17-5144** or 72/17-5108), gives another. You can't miss the showy building on the main road by the central market and bus station. Inside is an enormous showroom and sales outlet for a majority of the state's crafts—blown glass; dinnerware; textiles; wood carving; Persian-style rugs from nearby Temoaya; hand-woven sweaters, rugs, and serapes from Gualapita; baskets of all kinds; silver jewelry from San Felipe el Progreso; and pottery from Metepec. A few crafts from other regions in Mexico are for sale as well, such as lacquer chests from Olinalá, Guerrero. Local women sell and demonstrate textile and basket weaving as well. Upstairs are more crafts and excellent photographs of artisans at work, with labels describing the regions and crafts. CASART is open daily from 10am to 7pm.

WHERE TO STAY & EAT

If you should decide to spend the night, good choices near the portales and main plaza include the inexpensive but very nice **Hotel Colonial,** 50000 Hidalgo Oriente 103, Toluca, Edo. de México (☎ **72/72/15-9700** or 72/14-7066); the even less expensive **Hotel San Carlos,** Portal Madero 210, 50000 Toluca, Edo. de México (☎ **72/14-9422;** fax 72/14-9704); or the best hotel downtown, the moderately priced **Hotel San Francisco,** Rayon Sur 104, 50000 Toluca, Edo. de México (☎ **72/13-3114;** fax 72/13-2482). Restaurants are by the Toluca market, downtown along Hidalgo, and inside the portales just off the main square.

SIDE TRIPS FROM TOLUCA

THE POTTERY OF METEPEC   Known for its pottery and polychrome "trees of life," **Metepec,** approximately 5 miles from the edge of Toluca, is probably the most famous of the area crafts villages. A trip here is worth the little time it takes: Frequent buses leave the central bus station in Toluca, and the trip takes less than 30 minutes. Avoid arriving between 2 and 4pm when shops are closed. Pottery shops line the main street into town. Potters generally have their workshops away from the city center, so if you want to see them at work, ask around for directions.

ARCHAEOLOGICAL SITES   There are two nearby archaeological sites—**Teotenango** and **Calixtlahuaca.** The latter is the easier to reach by local bus from Toluca's bus station.

Frequent buses make the 20-minute trip to the town of Calixlahuaca. From there it's a short hike up the hill. The zone is small and dates back more than 3,000 years. The most notable edifice is the circular one devoted to Ehecatl, god of the wind. If your visit coincides with lunch, bring it along and eat while sitting there listening to the sounds of the village drift up. You can see for miles. Locals may try to sell you artifacts they've found, but it's illegal to buy them. There's a small museum at the site.

About 15 miles south of Toluca is the huge, ancient fortified city of Teotenango. It was occupied between A.D. 900 and 1200.

The archaeological sites are open Tuesday through Sunday from 9am to 5pm. Admission is $1 for each site.

5 Cuernavaca

64 miles SW of Mexico City, 50 miles NE of Taxco

Cuernavaca, capital of the state of Morelos, has been popular as a resort for people from Mexico City ever since the time of Moctezuma. Emperor Maximilian built a retreat here over a century ago. Mexicans say the town has a climate of "eternal spring," and on weekends the city is crowded with day-trippers from surrounding cities, especially the capital. On weekends the roads between Mexico City and Cuernavaca are jammed, and restaurants and hotels may be full as well. Cuernavaca has a large American colony, plus students attending one of the myriad language and cultural institutes that crowd the city.

The Indian name for this town was Cuauhnahuac, which means "at the edge of the forest." The city's symbol today is an Indian pictogram of a tree speaking. People have lived here, next to whispering trees, since about A.D. 1200, but in the early 1400s it came under the sway of the Aztecs, who established huge hunting parks—beginning a tradition of Cuauhnahuac as a resort for the wealthy and powerful. The conquistadores, when they arrived, heard "Cuauhnahuac" but said "Cuernavaca," so the forest's edge became a cow's horn.

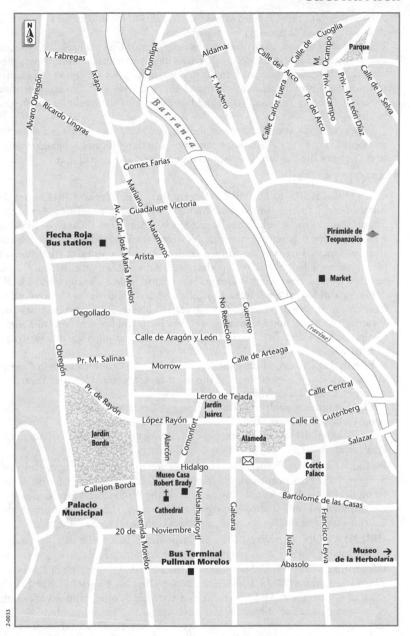

2-0033

Emperor Charles V gave Cuernavaca to Cortés as a fief, and the conquistador built a palace here in 1532 (now the Museo Cuauhnahuac) and lived there on and off for half a dozen years before returning to Spain. Cortés introduced sugarcane cultivation to the area, and Caribbean slaves were brought in to work in the cane fields. His sugar hacienda at the edge of town is now the luxurious Hotel de Cortés. The economics of large sugarcane growers failed to serve the interests of the indigenous farmers and there were numerous uprisings in colonial times.

After independence, mighty landowners from Mexico City gradually dispossessed the remaining small landholders, converting them to virtual serfdom. It was this condition that led to the rise of Emiliano Zapata, the great champion of agrarian reform, who battled the forces of wealth and power, defending the small farmer with the cry of "Tierra y Libertad!" (Land and Liberty!) during the revolution that began in 1911.

In this century, Cuernavaca has seen the influx of wealthy foreigners and of industrial capital. The giant CIVAC industrial complex on the outskirts has brought wealth to the city but also the curse of increased traffic, noise, and air pollution.

ESSENTIALS

GETTING THERE & DEPARTING   By Bus   The Mexico City **Central de Autobuses del Sur** follows the route Mexico City–Cuernavaca–Taxco–Acapulco–Zihuatanejo, so you'll have little trouble getting a bus. **Autobuses Pullman de Morelos** is the line with the most frequent departures (every 10 minutes). Pullman has two stations in Cuernavaca; the downtown station is at the corner of Abasolo and Netzahualcoyotl, four blocks south of the center of town. Their other station, Casino de la Selva, is less conveniently located near the railroad station. The trip takes an hour.

Lineas Unidas del Sur/Flecha Roja offers 33 buses daily from Mexico City to Cuernavaca. Its new terminal in Cuernavaca at Morelos 505, between Arista and Victoria, is six blocks north of town center. Here you'll find frequent buses to Toluca, Chalma, Ixtapan de la Sal, Taxco, Acapulco, the Cacahuamilpa Caves, Querétaro, and Nuevo Laredo.

Estrella Roja, a second-class station at Galeana and Cuauhtemotzin in Cuernavaca, about eight blocks south of the town center, serves Cuautla, Yautepec, Oaxtepec, and Izúcar de Matamoros.

The **Autobuses Estrella de Oro** terminal in Cuernavaca is at Morelos Sur 900, at the corner of Tabasco, about 15 blocks south of the center of town. This is the terminal with buses to Taxco (three per day); Zihuatanejo (two per day); Acapulco, Iguala, and Chilpancingo (five per day); and Mexico City (six per day).

By Car   From Mexico City, take Paseo de la Reforma to Chapultepec Park and merge with the Periférico, which will take you to Highway 95D, the toll road on the far south of town that goes to Cuernavaca. From the Periférico, take the Insurgentes exit and continue until you come to signs for Cuernavaca/Tlalpan. Choose either the Cuernavaca Cuota (toll) or the old Cuernavaca Libre (free) road on the right.

ORIENTATION   Arriving   Most bus stations are close to the town center and within walking distance of several of my hotel recommendations.

Information   Cuernavaca's **State Tourist Office** is at Av. Morelos Sur 802, between Jalisco and Tabasco (☎ **73/14-3860** or 72/14-3920; fax 72/14-3881), half a block north of the Estrella de Oro bus station and about a 15- to 20-minute walk south of the cathedral. It's open Monday through Friday from 9am to 8pm and Saturday and Sunday from 9am to 5pm. A better bet is the City Tourism kiosk stuck in the wall of the cathedral grounds on Hidalgo close to Morelos. It's open Monday through Friday 9am to 4pm and Saturday from 9am to 2pm.

City Layout   In the center of the city are two contiguous plazas. The small and more formal of the two, across from the post office, has a Victorian gazebo (designed by Gustave Eiffel of Eiffel Tower fame) at its center. This is the **Alameda.** The larger, rectangular plaza planted with trees, shrubs, and benches is the **Plaza de Armas.**

These two plazas are known collectively as the **zócalo** and are the hub for strolling vendors selling balloons, baskets, bracelets, and other crafts from surrounding villages. It's all easy-going, and one of the pleasures is grabbing a park bench or table in a nearby restaurant just to watch. On Sunday afternoons orchestras play from the gazebo. At the eastern end of the Alameda is the **Cortés Palace,** the conquistador's residence that now serves as the Museo de Cuauhnahuac.

You should be aware that this city's street-numbering systems are extremely confusing. It appears that the city fathers, during the past century or so, became dissatisfied with the street numbers every 10 or 20 years and imposed a new numbering system each time. Thus you may find an address given as "no. 5" only to find that the building itself bears the number "506," or perhaps "Antes no. 5." One grand gateway I know bears no fewer than five different street numbers, ranging from 2 to 567! In my descriptions of hotels, restaurants, and sights, I'll note the nearest cross street so you can find your way to your chosen destination with a minimum of fuss.

Getting Around   Frequent **buses** go from downtown to all the outlying centers. Just tell a local where you want to go, and most will go out of their way to help you. **Taxis** are relatively inexpensive in Cuernavaca; $2.50 should get you from downtown to the outlying herb museum, for example. Determine the fare before taking off.

FAST FACTS: CUERNAVACA

American Express   The local representative is Viajes Marin, Edificio Las Plazas, Loc. 13 (☎ **73/14-2266;** fax 73/12-9297).

Area Code   The telephone area code is 73.

Banks   Money can be changed from 9:30am to 1pm only. There are several banks in town, but the handiest to the zócalo is Bancomer at the corner of Matamoros and Lerdo de Tejada, catercorner to Jardín Juárez.

Elevation   The city sits at 5,058 feet.

Population   Cuernavaca has 450,000 residents.

Post Office   The post office (☎ **73/12-4379**) is on the Alameda, next door to the Café Los Arcos.

Spanish Lessons   As much as for its springlike weather, Cuernavaca is known for its Spanish-language schools, aimed at the foreigner. Generally the schools will help students find lodging with a family or provide a list of potential places to stay. Rather than make a long-term commitment in a family living situation, try it for a week, then decide. Below are the names and addresses of some of the schools. The whole experience—from classes to lodging—can be quite expensive, and the school may accept credit cards for the class portion. Contact the Center for Bilingual Multicultural Studies, San Jeronimo 304 (Apdo. Postal 1520), 62000 Cuernavaca, Mor. 62000 (☎ **73/17-0696**); or in the United States contact them at 3133 Lake Hollywood Drive, P. O. Box 1860, Los Angeles, CA 90078 (☎ and fax **213/851-3403** or 800/426-4660); or Universal Centro de Lengua y Comunicación Social A.C. (Universal Language School), H. Preciado 332 (Apdo. Postal 1-1826), 62000 Cuernavaca, Mor.(☎ **73/18-2904** or 72/12-4902).

EXPLORING CUERNAVACA

If you plan to visit Cuernavaca on a day-trip from Mexico City, the best days to do so are Tuesday, Wednesday, or Thursday (and perhaps Friday). On weekends the roads, the city, and its hotels and restaurants are filled with people from Mexico City, and prices jump dramatically. On Monday, the museum—which you definitely must see—is closed. So make it Tuesday through Friday.

Take a Luxury Bus Direct to Your
Destination from the Mexico City Airport

This new airport-to-destination service takes the hassle out of travel to a number of the most alluring cities in central Mexico. Buses serving these routes are deluxe, air-conditioned, and have video movies and a restroom. In most cases there's complimentary soft-drink service; you either help yourself or are served by a hostess.

If your destination is **Cuernavaca,** Suburban (☎ **73/22-0445** or 72/22-0456 in Cuernavaca, or 72/549-3506 in Mexico City) takes up to seven passengers in a—you guessed it—Chevrolet Suburban, leaving the airport about every two hours between 6:15am and 9:15pm daily at a cost of $13 per person. It's affiliated with the Pullman de Morelos bus line. The Suburban ticket kiosk is near Sala (gate) A. These supposedly take you directly to your hotel in Cuernavaca—but verify that. You can make reservations, but if the Mexico City number doesn't work, calling Cuernavaca is your only other choice. Pullman de Morelos also runs almost hourly buses from the airport to Cuernavaca (the first leaves at 8am, the last at 10pm) for $6.45.

If you're going to **Puebla,** Estrella Roja and Pullman Plus buses depart from the airport hourly (beginning at 6 or 7:30am), from in front of the airport, at the Sala D exit, and tickets cost $6.45 one way. Some of these go to a bus stop on the western edge of the Puebla at 4 Poniente and 21 Norte, and others go directly to Puebla's main bus terminal, CAPU.

TMT Caminante buses (☎ **72/277-2746** or 72/271-1433 in Mexico City) go to **Toluca** approximately every two hours beginning at 7:30am at a cost of $4.50.

To **Querétaro** and **Celaya,** AeroPlus buses run the route at 8 and 10am, noon, and 2, 5, 6:30, and 10:15pm for a cost of $9.50. This is the bus to take if your destination is **San Miguel de Allende**; from Querétaro you take one of the frequent buses to San Miguel.

To **Pachuca,** Aguila buses run three times at 9am and 5 and 8pm.

There's no sign, but buses for all these lines, and attendants for them, are found in front of the covered concourse outside the terminal between exit doors for Gates C and D. If you have trouble locating any of these, ask for help at one of the information desks on the airport's main concourse, or ask any porter. Most important, since this airport bus transportation service is new and could change, and/or if precise scheduling is essential to your trip, you could try calling the airport information office (☎ **72/728-4811** or 72/571-3600) to verify names of buses, where they depart from, and the current schedule.

You can spend one to two days sightseeing in Cuernavaca pleasantly enough. If you've come on a day trip from Mexico City, you may not have time to rove afield to all the outskirts-of-town sights mentioned below, but you'll have enough time to see the sights in town.

✪ **Museo de Cuauhnahuac.** In the Cortés Palace, Levya 100. No phone. Admission $2; free Sun. Tues–Sun 10am–5pm.

The museum is housed in the Cortés Palace, the former home of the greatest of the conquistadores, Hernán Cortés. Begun by Cortés in 1530, it was finished by the conquistador's son, Martín, and later served as the legislative headquarters for the state of Morelos. It's in the town center at the eastern end of the Jardín de los Héroes.

Once you're inside the main door, go to the right and pass through exhibits of humanity's early times, followed by a little court with ruins of a Tlahuica temple. In keeping with conquistador policy, Cortés had his mansion built right on top of an older structure.

The northern wing of the palace, on the ground floor, houses exhibits and relics from the colonial era. Upstairs in the northern wings are costumes, domestic furnishings, carriages, and farm implements from the Mexico of the 1800s, mostly from *haciendas azucareras* (sugar plantations). There are also mementos of the great revolutionaries Francisco Madero and Emiliano Zapata.

Through the door on the right are more colonial exhibits including several fascinating pages from "painted books," or Indian codices, which survived the book burnings of the Spaniards. There's also a clock mechanism (*reloj*) from Cuernavaca's cathedral, thought to be the first public clock on the American continent.

When you get to the east portico on the upper floor, you're in for a treat. A large Diego Rivera mural commissioned by Dwight Morrow, U.S. ambassador to Mexico in the 1920s, depicts the history of Cuernavaca from the coming of the Spaniards to the rise of Zapata (1910). It's fascinating to examine the mural in detail. Above the north door, the Spaniards and their Indian allies, armed with firearms, crossbows, and cannons, battle the Aztecs, who have clubs, spears, slings, and bows and arrows. Above the door is a scene of Aztec human sacrifice.

Moving southward along the wall, men struggle with a huge tree, perhaps symbolizing the Aztec "universe." Next, the inhabitants of Mexico are enslaved, branded, and made to yield their gold. The figure in a white headscarf is José María Morelos, one of the leaders in Mexico's fight for independence from Spain.

Moving along, malevolent priests, backed by lancers, subjugate the Indians spiritually; dressed in white, they stand peaceably and respectfully at the orders of the priests. The Spaniards build a new society using the Indians as slave labor.

The scenes on the sugar plantations are from the time after independence when the wealthy and powerful dispossessed the native population of their land in order to create the huge sugar haciendas. While the Indians slave away, the blancos recline in hammocks. Nearby, priests and friars direct the building of churches and monasteries by native labor; the churchmen accept gold from the Indians; and only one poor friar sits with the women and children, teaching them the doctrines of the church.

Above the south door is an *auto-da-fé*, or burning of heretics, from the Spanish Inquisition. The scene is chronologically out of place, but Rivera obviously meant to contrast it to the Aztec sacrifice over the north door, opposite. He's saying, "Aztecs or Catholics, the more it changes, the more it stays the same." Rivera firmly believed communism would break the cycle of man's inhumanity to man—the Stalinist purges of the 1930s were yet in the future when Rivera painted this superb mural. It's ironic that his "religion" (communist ideology) led to the same excesses of ideological fanaticism as did Aztec cosmology and the Catholic Inquisition.

In the upper-left corner of the southern door, Indian revolutionaries are hanged by slave drivers. In the lower left, Zapata leads a group of revolutionary campesinos brandishing their farming tools as weapons. The frieze beneath the mural is interesting as well, done in a chunky 1930s style that is very art deco but also very Rivera. It looks to me as though he was inspired in the many Aztec friezes.

Catedral de la Asunción. At the corner of Hidalgo and Morelos. Free admission. Daily 8am–2pm and 4–10pm. Walk three blocks southwest of the Plaza de Armas.

As you enter the church precincts and pass down the walk, try to imagine what life in Mexico was like in the old days. Construction on the church was begun in 1533, a mere 12 years after Cortés conquered Tenochtitlán (Mexico City) from the Aztecs. The churchmen could hardly trust their safety to the tenuous allegiance of their new converts, so they built a fortress as a church. The skull-and-crossbones above the main door is not a comment on their feelings about the future, however, but a symbol for the Franciscan order, which had its monastery here in the church precincts.

Inside, the church is stark, even severe, having been refurbished in the 1960s. The most curious aspect of the interior is the mystery of the frescoes painted in Japanese style. Discovered during the refurbishing, they depict the persecution and martyrdom of St. Felipe de Jesús and his companions in Japan. No one is certain who painted them.

Museo Casa Robert Brady. Calle Netzahualcoyotl 4. ☎ **72/18-8554.** Admission $2. Tues–Sun 10am–6pm.

This museum, in what was the private home of Robert Brady, contains more than 1,200 works of art. Brady, an avid art collector, came to Mexico in 1960. He bought a portion of a 16th-century Franciscan monastery in 1962 and turned it into his home cum gallery, where he lived and entertained until his death in 1986. In this collection are pre-Hispanic and colonial pieces; oil paintings by Frida Kahlo and Rufino Tamayo; and handcrafts from America, Africa, Asia, and India. Admission includes a guide in Spanish; English and French guides are available if requested at the time of your reservation.

Palacio Municipal. At the corner of Av. Morelos and Callejón Borda. No phone. Free admission Mon–Fri 9am–3pm (hours are erratic).

To the right of the door on Cuernavaca's Palacio Municipal (Town Hall) there's a ceramic tile plaque that reads HONORABLE AYUNTAMIENTO DE CUERNAVACA (town council); to the left is a plaque that says CUAUHNAHUAC, with the city's tree symbol. Walk into the brick, stone, and stucco courtyard any time the building is open. Besides the unusual and attractive building, you should tour the large old paintings hung in the arcades on the first and second floors. On the north wall, on the ground floor, paintings explain the making of "feathered mosaics." In the north arcade, on the upper floor, are scenes from Cuernavaca's pre-Hispanic culture: Tlahuicans making pottery, storing corn (maize), being shaken down by an Aztec tax collector, and harvesting cotton. On the east wall, the scenes continue: The Indians gather maguey leaves, pound them to release the fibers, and weave cloth; a priest offers a chicken to the god Tepuztecatl. The Aztec goldsmiths' craft is explained in a canvas with 17 smaller panels. In the southeastern corner are two murals, done by R. Cueva in 1962, with scenes from the Revolution.

Jardín Borda. Morelos 103, at Hidalgo. ☎ **72/18-5101** or 72/14-1529. Admission 75¢. Tues–Sun 10am–5pm.

Half a block west of the cathedral is the Jardín Borda (Borda Gardens). One of the many wealthy builders to choose Cuernavaca was José de la Borda, the Taxco silver magnate, who ordered a sumptuous vacation house built here in the late 1700s. The large enclosed garden next to the house was actually a huge private park, laid out in Andalusian style with little kiosks and an artificial pond. Maximilian found it worthy of an emperor and took it over as his private preserve in the mid-1800s. But after Maximilian, the Borda Gardens fell on hard times. Decades of neglect followed.

The paintings of the French Intervention prepare you for a stroll through the gardens. Here are the scenes you'll see: Emperor Maximilian and Empress Carlota arrive in Cuernavaca for the first time; then, Maximilian, while out for a ride, gets his first glimpse of La India Bonita, who was to become his lover. The next scene is of court festivities in the Borda Gardens, with courtiers taking turns rowing little boats. Finally, Maximilian's niece pleads with President Benito Juárez, after the siege of Querétaro, to spare the emperor's life. (At that time, Carlota was off in Europe, trying to round up support for her husband's cause, without result.) Juárez refused her request, and Maximilian, along with two of his generals, was executed by firing squad on the Hill of Bells in Querétaro a few days thereafter.

On your stroll through the gardens you'll see the same little artificial lake on which Austrian, French, and Mexican nobility rowed in little boats beneath the moonlight. Ducks have taken the place of dukes, however, and there are rowboats for rent. The lake is now artfully adapted as an outdoor theater, with seats for the audience on one side and the stage on the other.

The Borda Gardens have been completely restored and were reopened in October 1987 as the Jardín Borda Instituto Cultural de Morelos. In the gateway buildings are several galleries for changing exhibits, a café for refreshments and light meals, and several large paintings showing scenes from the life of Maximilian and from the history of the Borda Gardens.

Museo de la Herbolaría. Matamoros 200, Acapantzingo. ☎ **72/12-5956.** Admission $2. Daily 10am–5pm.

This museum of traditional herbal medicine, in the southern Cuernavaca suburb of Acapantzingo, has been set up in a former resort residence built by Maximilian, the Casa del Olindo, or Casa del Olvido. It was here, during his brief reign, that the Austrian-born emperor would come for trysts with La India Bonita, his Cuernavacan lover. Restored in 1960, the house and gardens now preserve the local wisdom in folk medicine. The shady gardens are lovely to wander through, and you shouldn't miss the 200 orchids growing near the rear of the property. However, the lovers' actual house, the little dark-pink building in the back, is closed. Catch combi no. 6 at the mercado on Degollado. Ask to be dropped off at Matamoros near the museum. Turn right on Matamoros and walk 1 1/2 blocks; the museum will be on your right.

Pirámide de Teopanzolco. Northeast of the center of town. Admission $1.50. Daily 10am–5pm.

You'll need a taxi or bus to reach the curious Teopanzolco pyramid. Now set in a park, the pyramid was excavated beginning in 1921. As with most Mesoamerican cultures, the local Tlahuicans reconstructed their principal religious monuments at the end of a major calendar cycle by building a new, larger structure right on top of the older one. Here you can clearly see the two different older and newer structures. Catch combi no. 10 (Barona) on Galeana catercorner to Jardín Juárez.

WHERE TO STAY

Because so many capitalinos come down from Mexico City for the day or for the weekend, the hotel trade here may be heavy on weekends and holidays, light at other times. A few local hoteliers adapt their policies and prices to these shifts.

✪ **Hotel Cadiz.** Alvaro Obregón 329, 62000 Cuernavaca, Mor. ☎ **73/18-9204.** 17 rms (all with bath). FAN. $14.75 single; $19.75 double.

Every now and then I discover a hotel with the kind of homey charm that makes me want to return. Such is the Hotel Cadiz, run by the gracious Aguilar family. You may have known it as the Hotel María Cristina. Each of the fresh, simple rooms is furnished uniquely, and there's a lot of nostalgic tile and big old (but well-kept) freestanding sinks. The grounds, set back from the street, make a pleasant respite, plus there are a pool and a small inexpensive restaurant open from 9am to 4pm. To find it from Morelos, turn left on Ricardo Linares and go past Las Mañanitas. The first street is Obregón. Turn left, and the hotel is a block ahead on the right.

Hotel Colonial. Agustín y León 104, 62000 Cuernavaca, Mor. ☎ 73/18-6414. 14 rms (all with bath). $10–$11.50 single or double, one bed; $14.75 double, two beds.

The simple little rooms at the Colonial, 4½ blocks north of Jardín Juárez between Matamoros and Morelos, are the best buys on a street full of budget hotels; get there early before they fill up. The rooms are arranged around a cheery courtyard.

Hotel Las Hortensias. Hidalgo 22, 62000 Cuernavaca, Mor. ☎ 73/18-5265. 23 rms (all with bath). $12.50 single; $17 double.

The Las Hortensias, two blocks south of Jardín Juárez, is a convenient downtown hotel converted from an old house on an odd hillside site. Rooms are small, simple, and modernish with colonial accents. Look at your prospective room first—some are dark, and some have only windows that look onto the walkways. The nice, quiet little garden with a fountain and green grass provides an oasis in the midst of the city.

WORTH A SPLURGE

✪ **Las Mañanitas.** Ricardo Linares 107, 62000 Cuernavaca, Mor. ☎ 73/14-1466 or 72/12-4646. Fax 73/18-3672. 22 rms (all with bath). TEL. $85.75 double; $114–$210 suite double. Buses going north on Morelos stop within half a block of the hotel. Valet parking.

Among Cuernavaca's best-known luxury lodgings is Las Mañanitas, 5½ long blocks north of the Jardín Borda. It's one of the best run hotels in Mexico. Rooms are outfitted with exquisitely kept antique furniture and large baths; brass and wood everywhere are polished to a sheen. Many have verdant, vine-encumbered balconies big enough for sitting and sipping while overlooking the emerald lawns where peacocks and other exotic birds strut and preen and fountains tinkle musically. Thirteen rooms have fireplaces, and the hotel also has a heated pool. After a few hours, most of the personnel address you by name.

Although suites are available, it's the standard rooms that interest us. These simple but charming accommodations allow you to splurge and live the good life when others, staying in the terrace suites, patio suites, and luxurious garden suites, are paying a great deal more. Formerly this luxury hotel did not accept credit cards, but now American Express cards are accepted.

WHERE TO EAT

✪ **Flash Tacos.** Blv. Juarez #2. ☎ 72/12-13-37. Tacos 50¢–$2; main courses $3.75–$5.25. Daily 1pm–1am. MEXICAN.

This restaurant/video bar provides a great view of the Palacio de Cortés, especially from its upper deck. Or, if you prefer, the latest rock videos can be seen from any of its 49 small monitors. And in spite of its name, the food is very good. There is a full menu of appetizers, a great selection of tacos, and complete meals of grilled chicken and beef dishes, including fajitas. Full bar service is also provided. You can't miss it; look for the colorful umbrellas that shield its outside tables at the corner of Hidalgo facing the Cortés Palace.

La Parroquia. Guerrero 102. ☎ 72/18-5820. Breakfast $1.75–$2.30; main courses $2.30–$4.25; comida corrida $3.25. Daily 7:30am–12am. MEXICAN/PASTRIES.

This place does a teeming business, partly because of its great location (half a block north of the Alameda, opposite the Parque Juárez), partly because of its Arab specialties, and partly because it has fairly reasonable prices for Cuernavaca. It's open to the street with a few outdoor café tables, perfect for watching the changing parade of street vendors and park life.

◐ **Restaurant Las Mañanitas.** Ricardo Linares 107. ☎ **72/14-1466** or 72/12-4646. Reservations recommended. Main courses $8.50–$23.50. Daily noon–5pm and 7–11pm. Buses going north on Morelos stop within half a block of the restaurant. MEXICAN/INTERNATIONAL.

Las Mañanitas, 5½ long blocks north of the Jardín Borda, sets the standard for lush and sumptuous in Cuernavaca. Dining tables are set out on an airy, shaded terrace with a view of the gardens. The decor and ambience are lightly colonial, and the service is extremely friendly and attentive. When you arrive, you can enjoy cocktails in the cozy *sala* (living room); and when you're ready to dine, a waiter will present a large blackboard menu of at least half a dozen daily specials. The specialty is Mexican with an international flare, including whatever fruits and vegetables are in season and offering a full selection of fresh seafood, beef, pork, veal, and fowl.

◐ **Restaurant Los Arcos.** Jardín de Los Héroes 4. ☎ **72/12-4486.** Breakfast $1.50–$2.50; main course $2.30–$5.75; fixed-price lunch $2.75; sandwiches $1–$1.75. Daily 7am–12am. MEXICAN.

Cuernavaca's best-located sidewalk café is Los Arcos, next to the post office on the Alameda. Wrought-iron tables and chairs, shaded by umbrellas, are set out within view of the Cortés Palace, and all three meals are served. The menu runs the gamut from sandwiches and enchiladas to chicken and steaks. The fixed-price lunch is called the *menu del día.*

Restaurant Vienés. Lerdo de Tejada 4. ☎ **72/18-4044** or 72/14-3404. Breakfast $1.50–$3.25; main courses $6–$8. Daily 8am–10pm. VIENNESE.

An indication of Cuernavaca's Viennese immigrant heritage is the Restaurant Vienes, a tidy and somewhat Viennese-looking place a block from the Jardín Juárez between Lerdo de Tejada and Comonfort. The menu also has echoes of the Old World, such as grilled trout with vegetables and German potato salad, with Apfelstrudel for dessert, followed by Viennese coffee. The restaurant has a pastry/coffee shop next door called Los Pasteles de Vienes. Although the menu is identical, the coffee shop's atmosphere is much more leisurely, and there the pastries are on full, tempting display in glass cases.

SIDE TRIPS FROM CUERNAVACA

If you have enough time, you should try to make some side trips around Cuernavaca. To the north you'll find pine trees and an alpine setting; to the east, lush hills and valleys. On the road north to Mexico City you will climb several thousand feet within half an hour into some gorgeous mountain air.

TEPOZTLÁN'S STREET MARKET & MONASTERY This Tlahuica village predates the Conquest and still holds the ruins of a temple, plus a **Dominican monastery** (1580) and the thatched huts of the residents. It was also the subject of a study in cultural anthropology by Oscar Lewis. There's generally a very good street market around the central square on weekends and holidays, especially during Carnaval (three days before Ash Wednesday, a movable date usually in February). To get to Tepoztlán, take one of the frequent buses or minivans by the market on Degollado. Tourists don't use these much, and other passengers generally go out of their way to be helpful and will let you know when to get off.

XOCHICALCO RUINS About 16 miles south of Cuernavaca along Highway 95 (the "Libre"—no-toll-road to Taxco) is the town of Alpuyeca, and 9½ miles northwest of Alpuyeca are the ruins of Xochicalco, the "House of Flowers." High on a mountaintop, Xochicalco boasts a magnificent situation and an interesting complex of buildings dating from about A.D. 600 through 900. Most interesting is the **Temple**

of the Feathered Serpents, with beautiful bas-reliefs showing distinctively Maya figures. There are also a ball court, some underground passages, and other temples. Archaeologists believe the Teotihuacán, Toltec, Zapotec, and Maya cultures may have met and interacted here. You can visit the ruins from 8am to 5pm daily. Catch a bus to the *crucero* (crossing) from the Pullman de Morelos station. Buses run frequently. From the crucero take a combi to the ruins for about $1.75. Admission is $2; additional $4.25 for use of a personal video camera.

SPELUNKING IN THE CACAHUAMILPA CAVES The Grutas (Caves) de Cacahuamilpa lie 46 miles southwest of Cuernavaca, 5 miles north of the Taxco road, Highway 95. You can join the group tour (every hour on the hour) of these mammoth caverns, said to stretch some 43 miles within the earth (don't worry—you don't get to see the entire 43 miles!). If you have a car and are driving to Taxco, this makes a nice detour. To travel by bus, go to the Líneas Unidas/Flecha Roja bus station and take one of the crowded buses that leaves each hour for $1.50. The last bus is at 6pm.

The caves are truly awesome, worth a visit even if you're not generally a cave fancier. Judging by the graffiti in the caves, everyone important—from Empress Carlota to Mexican presidents—has come to admire them. The caves are open daily from 10am to 3pm; admission costs $4.25. Tours are in Spanish only, but you'll pick up the salient points, and the geologic grandeur and beauty speak for themselves.

IXTAPAN DE LA SAL: SPA TOWN The road to Cacahuamilpa, Highway 55, is also the road to Toluca, which is 79 miles north from Highway 95. On the way, 28 miles from Highway 95, is the pretty spa town of Ixtapan de la Sal, with at least a dozen inexpensive hotels specializing in the cure: bathing in the natural mineral waters of the area.

6 Taxco: Picturesque Silver City

111 miles SW of Mexico City, 50 miles SW of Cuernavaca, 185 miles NE of Acapulco

Taxco (*tahs*-ko), famous for its silverwork, sits at nearly 6,000 feet on a hill among hills, and almost everywhere you walk in the city there are fantastic views.

Taxco's renowned silver mines, first worked in the time of Cortés, four centuries ago, were revived, for all practical purposes, by an American, William Spratling, in the 1930s. Today its fame rests more on the over 200 silver shops, most little one-man factories, that line the cobbled streets all the way up into the hills. Whether you'll find bargains depends on how much you know about the quality and price of silver. But there is no doubt that nowhere else in the country will you find the quantity and variety of silver. The artistry and imagination of the local silversmiths are evident in each piece.

You can get the idea of what Taxco's like by spending an afternoon, but there's much more to this picturesque town of 87,000 than just the Plaza Borda and the shops surrounding it. You'll have to stay overnight if you want more time to climb up and down its steep cobblestone streets, discovering little plazas and fine churches. The main part of town stretches up the hillside from the highway, and although it's a steep walk, it's not a particularly long one. But you don't have to walk: Vehicles make the circuit through and around town picking up and dropping off passengers along the route. There are *burritos*, the local name for white VW minibuses that run the route from about 7am until 9pm. Taxis in town are around 75¢ to $1.25.

Warning: Self-appointed guides will undoubtedly approach you in the zócalo (Plaza Borda) and offer their services—they get a cut (up to 25%) of all you buy in the shops

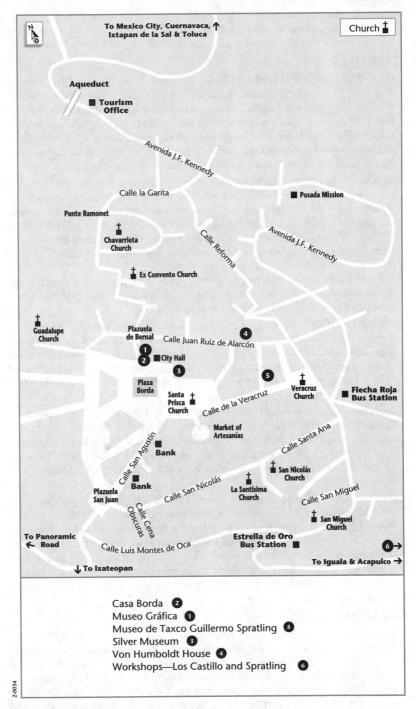

Taxco

To Mexico City, Cuernavaca, Ixtapan de la Sal & Toluca

Church

Aqueduct

■ Tourism Office

Avenida J.F. Kennedy

Calle la Garita

■ Posada Mission

Punte Ramonet

✝ Chavarrieta Church

Calle Reforma

Avenida J.F. Kennedy

✝ Ex Convento Church

✝ Guadalupe Church

Plazuela de Bernal

Calle Juan Ruiz de Alarcón

❹

❶
❷ ■ City Hall
❸

❺

✝ Veracruz Church

■ Flecha Roja Bus Station

Plaza Borda

Santa Prisca ✝ Church

Calle de la Veracruz

Market of Artesanías

Calle San Agustín

■ Bank

Calle Santa Ana

✝ San Nicolás Church

Calle San Nicolás

Plazuela San Juan

■ Bank

Calle Cena Obscuras

✝ La Santisima Church

Calle San Miguel

✝ San Miguel Church

To Panoramic ← Road

Calle Luis Montes de Oca

Estrella de Oro Bus Station ■

❻ →

↓ To Ixateopan

To Iguala & Acapulco →

Casa Borda ❷
Museo Gráfica ❶
Museo de Taxco Guillermo Spratling ❺
Silver Museum ❸
Von Humboldt House ❹
Workshops—Los Castillo and Spratling ❻

2-0034

441

they take you to. Before hiring a **guide,** ask to see his Departamento de Turismo credentials. The Department of Tourism office on the highway at the north end of town can recommend a licensed walking guide for about $4.25 to $5.75 per hour.

ESSENTIALS

GETTING THERE & DEPARTING By Bus From Mexico City, buses to Taxco depart from the Central de Autobuses del Sur station (Metro: Tasqueña) and take two to three hours. **Estrella Blanca** and its **Líneas Unidas del Sur/Flecha Roja** lines have service to Taxco every hour or so with a variety of bus types. Your best bet is their "Plus" service for $7. These buses have air-conditioning, a TV, soft drinks, and bathrooms. **Estrella de Oro** has five (three direct) no-frills buses a day to Taxco for $5.50. **From Cuernavaca,** see details in "Side Trips from Cuernavaca," above.

By Car From Mexico City, take Paseo de la Reforma to Chapultepec Park and merge with the Periférico, which will take you to Highway 95D on the south end of town. From the Periférico, take the Insurgentes exit and merge until you come to the sign to Cuernavaca/Tlalpan. Choose either CUERNAVACA CUOTA (toll) or CUERNAVACA LIBRE (free). Continue south around Cuernavaca to the Amacuzac interchange and proceed straight ahead for Taxco. The drive from Mexico City takes about 3$^1/_2$ hours. Fill up with gas at Cuernavaca.

From Acapulco you have two options: Highway 95D, the new toll road through Iguala to Taxco is open. Or you can take the old two-lane road (95) that winds through villages and is slower, but it's in good condition.

ORIENTATION Arriving Taxco has two **bus** stations. **Estrella de Oro** buses arrive at their own station on the southern edge of town. **Flecha Roja** buses arrive at the station on the eastern edge of town on Avenida Kennedy. Both stations present a hard walk to town. If you have only a small suitcase, take a white minivan marked "Santa Prisca" or "Zócalo" from the front of either station to get to the town center. Taxis cost around 75¢ to the zócalo.

Information The State of Guerrero Dirección de Turismo (☎ 762/2-6616; fax 762/2-2274) has offices at the arches on the main highway at the north end of town, useful if you're driving into town. The office is open daily from 9am to 3pm and 6 to 9pm. To get there from Plaza Borda, take a combi ("Zócalo Arcos") and get off at the arch over the highway. As you face the arches, the tourism office is on your right.

City Layout The center of town is the tiny Plaza Borda, shaded by perfectly manicured Indian laurel trees. On one side is the imposing twin-towered, pink-stone **Santa Prisca Church,** and the other sides are lined with whitewashed red-tile buildings housing the famous **silver shops** and a restaurant or two. Beside the church, deep in a crevice of the mountain is the **city market.** Brick-paved streets fill out from here in a helter-skelter fashion up and down the hillsides. Besides the silver-filled shops, the plaza swirls with vendors of everything from hammocks to cotton candy and bark paintings to balloons.

FAST FACTS: TAXCO

Area Code The telephone area code is 762.

Bookstores The Casa Domínguez, Calle Arco 7 (☎ 762/2-0133), stocks a small assortment of English-language magazines, newspapers, and books. It's on the narrow street on the right side of the Santa Prisca Church (as you face it) and is open Monday through Saturday from 10am to 2pm and 4 to 8pm, and on Sunday from 10am to 2pm. Another bookstore, Agencia de Publicaciones is next door and open daily from 9am to 2pm and 5 to 8pm.

Climate   Generally Taxco is warm during the day, usually in the 80s, but cool enough for a sweater in the mornings and after sunset. There can be torrential rains in summer.

Long-Distance Phone   Farmacia Oscarin, Av. Kennedy 47 (☎ 762/2-1847), opposite the Flecha Roja bus station, used to serve as the community long-distance telephone center. However, many small businesses now provide long-distance service, including the bus station itself. Look for the sign LARGA DISTANCIA.

Post Office   The post office is on the outskirts of Taxco on the highway heading toward Acapulco. It's in a row of shops with a black-and-white sign reading CORREO.

Scam   Some taxi drivers at the bus station and tour guides who greet you on arrival in town receive a payoff to take you to certain hotels in Taxco. They'll even go so far as to tell you the hotel at which you have reservations is closed or in horrible disrepair in order to take you to a hotel for which they get a kickback. Proceed with your own plans and leave these guys to their dirty tricks.

Shoes   Because Taxco's stone-paved streets are steep and slick, wear only sturdy, rubber-soled shoes.

Spanish/Art Classes   In 1993, the Universidad Nacional Autónoma de Mexico (UNAM) opened its doors in the buildings and grounds of the Hacienda del Chorillo, formerly part of the Cortés land grant. Here students can study silversmithing, Spanish, drawing, composition, and history under the supervision of UNAM instructors. Classes contain between 10 and 15 students, and courses are generally for three months at a time. The school will provide a list of prospective town accommodations that consist primarily of hotels. As an alternative, I suggest you select an inexpensive hotel for the first several nights, then search for something more reasonable for a lengthy stay. At locations all over town are notices of furnished apartments or rooms for rent at reasonable prices. For information about the school, contact either the Dirección de Turismo (tourist office) in Taxco (see under "Information," above) or write the school directly: UNAM, Hacienda del Chorillo, Taxco, Gro. 40200 (☎ 762/2-3690).

EXPLORING TAXCO

Since Taxco boasts more than 200 shops selling silver, shopping for the brilliant metal is the major pastime—and the main reason most tourists come. But Taxco's cultural show is on an upward move. You have, besides the opulent, world-renowned **Santa Prisca y San Sebastián Church,** the **Spratling Archaeology Museum,** the **Silver Museum,** and the **von Humboldt House/Museo Virreynal de Taxco.** In Taxco, museums seem to have "official" hours and "real" hours, so you may find some are closed when they should be open.

You also might consider taking a look at Juan O'Gorman's mural beside the pool at the Hotel Posada de la Misión (on the highway; go via minibus).

FESTIVALS & EVENTS

Taxco's **Silver Fair** starts the last Saturday in November and continues for one week. It includes a competition for silver sculptures from among the top silversmiths. **Holy Week** in Taxco is one of the most compelling in the country, beginning the Friday a week before Easter with nightly processions and several during the day. The most riveting procession, on Thursday evening, lasts almost four hours and includes villagers from the surrounding area carrying saints, followed by hooded members of a society of self-flagellating penitents chained at the ankles and carrying huge wooden crosses and bundles of penetrating thorny branches. On the Saturday morning before Easter, the Plaza Borda fills for the procession of three falls, reenacting the three times Christ stumbled and fell while carrying his cross. The **Jornadas Alarconianas,** featuring plays and literary events in honor of Juan Ruíz de Alarcón (1572–1639), a world-famous dramatist who was born in Taxco, were traditionally in the spring, but switched to the fall in recent years.

SIGHTS IN TOWN

✪ **Santa Prisca y San Sebastian Church.** Plaza Borda. No phone. Free admission. Daily 8am–11pm.

This is Taxco's centerpiece parish church, around which village life takes place. Facing the pleasant Plaza Borda, it was built with funds provided by José de la Borda, a French miner who struck it rich in Taxco's silver mines. Completed in 1758 after eight years of labor, it's one of Mexico's most impressive baroque churches. Outside, the ultracarved facade is flanked by two elaborately embellished steeples and a colorful tile dome. Inside, the intricacy of the gold-leafed saints and cherubic angels is positively breathtaking. The paintings by Miguel Cabrera, one of Mexico's most famous colonial-era artists, are the pride of Taxco. The room behind the altar is now open and contains even more Cabrera paintings.

Guides, both boys and adults, will approach you outside the church offering to give a tour, and it's worth the small price to get a full rendition of what you're seeing. Make sure the guide's English is good, however, and establish whether the price is per person or per tour. Give him 75¢.

✪ **Silver Museum.** Plaza Borda. ☎ **762/2-0558.** Admission 50¢. Daily 10am–4pm.

The Silver Museum is operated by a local silversmith. After entering the building next to Santa Prisca (upstairs is Sr. Costilla's restaurant), look for a sign on the left; the museum is downstairs. It's not a traditional public-sponsored museum. Nevertheless, it does a much-needed job of describing the history of silver in Mexico and Taxco, as well as displaying some historic and contemporary award-winning pieces. Time spent here seeing quality silverwork will make you a more discerning shopper in Taxco's dazzling silver shops.

✪ **Museo de Taxco Guillermo Spratling.** Porfirio A. Delgado 1. ☎ **762/2-1660.** Admission $1.50; free Sun. Tues–Sun 10am–5pm.

A plaque (in Spanish) explains that most of the collection of pre-Columbian art displayed here, as well as the funds for the museum, came from William Spratling, an American born in 1900 who studied architecture in the United States, later settled in Taxco, and organized the first workshops to turn out high-quality silver jewelry. From this first effort in 1931 the town's reputation as a center of artistic silverwork grew to what it is today. In a real sense, Spratling "put Taxco on the map." He died in 1967 in a car accident. You'd expect this to be a silver museum, but it's not—to see Spratling silver, go to the Spratling Ranch Workshop (see "Nearby Attractions," below). The entrance floor of this museum and the one above display a good collection of pre-Columbian statues and implements in clay, stone, and jade. The lower floor has changing exhibits.

To find the museum, turn right out of the Santa Prisca Church and right again at the corner; continue down the street. Jog right, then immediately left. There it is, facing you.

✪ **Von Humboldt House/Museo Virreyenal de Taxco.** Calle Juan Ruíz de Alarcón 6. ☎ **762/2-5501.** Admission $1.50. Tues–Sun 10am–5pm.

Stroll along Ruíz de Alarcón (the street behind the Casa Borda and just downhill from the Posada de Los Castillo), and look for the richly decorated facade of the von

Humboldt House, where the renowned German scientist/explorer Baron Alexander von Humboldt (1769–1859) visited Taxco and stayed one night in 1803. The new museum houses 18th-century memorabilia pertinent to Taxco, most of which came from a secret room discovered during the recent restoration of the Santa Prisca y San Sebastian Church. It's a fascinating museum, especially if you take a guided tour; however, signs with detailed information are in both Spanish and English. The von Humboldt House has known many uses, including 40 years as a guesthouse run until the mid-1970s by the von Wuthenau family. To the right as you enter are two huge and very rare *tumelos* (three-tiered funerary paintings). The bottom two were painted in honor of the death of Carlos III of Spain; the top one, with a carved phoenix on top, was supposedly painted for the funeral of José de la Borda.(The only other known tumelo in Mexico is at the Museo Bellas Artes in Toluca.)

The three stories of the museum are divided by eras and persons famous in Taxco's history. In the *sala* (room) dedicated to José de la Borda is a copy of a painting (which hangs in the church) showing him dressed in the finery of his times, with samples of such garments in other cases. In a room of photographs are pictures of Taxco's 10 principal churches. Another room shows paintings of what workshops must have been like during the construction of Santa Prisca y San Sebastian. Another section is devoted to historical information about Don Miguel Cabrera, Mexico's foremost 18th-century artist. Fine examples of clerical garments decorated with gold and silver thread hang in glass cases. More excellently restored Cabrera paintings are hung throughout the museum; some were found in the frames you see, others were haphazardly rolled up. And, of course, a small room devoted to von Humboldt shows what this young explorer looked like and gives a short history of his sojourns through South America and Mexico.

✪ **Casa de la Cultura Casa Borda.** Plaza Borda. ☎ and fax **762/2-6617.**

Catercorner from the Santa Prisca Church and facing Plaza Borda, this was the home José de la Borda built for his son around 1759. It is now the Guerrero State Cultural Center, housing classrooms and exhibit halls where period clothing, engravings, paintings, and crafts are displayed, as well as traveling exhibits, such as a recent display of codices.

Mercado Central. Plaza Borda. Daily 7am–6pm.

To the right of the Santa Prisca Church, behind and below Berta's, Taxco's central market meanders deep inside the mountain. Take the stairs off the street. Among the curio stores you'll find the food stalls and cookshops, always the best place for a cheap meal.

NEARBY ATTRACTIONS

For a spectacular view of Taxco, ride the **cable cars** (gondola) to the Hotel Monte Taxco. Catch them across the street from the state tourism office, left of the arches, near the college campus. Take a combi marked "Los Arcos" and exit just before the arches, turn left, and follow the signs to the cable cars. Daily hours are 7am to 7pm. A round-trip ride is $3.25.

Spratling Ranch Workshop. 6 miles south of town on the Acapulco Hwy. No phone. Free admission. Mon–Sat 9am–5pm.

Spratling's hacienda-style home/workshop on the outskirts of Taxco once again hums with busy hands reproducing his unique designs. A trip here will show you what distinctive Spratling work was all about, for the designs crafted today show the same fine work—even Spratling's workshop foreman is employed again overseeing the development of a new generation of silversmiths. Prices are high, but the designs are unusual and considered collectible. There's no store in Taxco, and unfortunately, most of the display cases hold only samples. With the exception of a few jewelry pieces, most items are by order only. Ask about their U.S. outlets.

Los Castillo. 5 miles south of town on the Acapulco Hwy., and in Taxco on Plaza Bernal. ☎ **762/2-1016** (workshop) or 762/2-3471 (store). Free admission. Workshop, Mon–Fri 9am– 5pm; store, Mon–Fri 9am–6:30pm, Sat 9am–1pm, Sun 10am–3pm.

Don Antonio Castillo was one of hundreds of young men to whom William Spratling taught the silversmithing trade in the 1930s. He was also one of the first to branch out with his own shops and line of designs, which over the years have earned him a fine name. Now his daughter Emilia creates her own noteworthy designs, among which are decorative pieces with silver fused onto porcelain. You can visit Don Antonio's workshop, 5 miles south of town, Monday through Friday between 9am and 5pm . Emilia's work is for sale at Los Castillo, on the ground floor of the Posada de Los Castillo, just below the Plazuela Bernal. Another store, featuring the designs of Don Antonio and another daughter, Kitty, is in Mexico City's Zona Rosa, at Amberes 41.

WHERE TO STAY

Compared to Cuernavaca, Taxco is an overnight-stop visitor's dream: charming and picturesque, with a respectable selection of well-kept and delightful hotels. Since the devaluation, prices are so affordable that Taxco is once again the budget traveler's haven. But prices tend to "bulge" at holiday times (especially Easter week).

Hotel Casa Grande. Plazuela de San Juan 7, 40200 Taxco, Gro. ☎ and fax **762/2-1108.** 12 rms (all with bath). $9 single; $11.50 double; $13.25 triple.

One of Taxco's most basic hotels is housed in one of its oldest buildings, ideally located on Plazuela San Juan. Rooms are dark and small but nicely kept, with tile baths but no toilet seats. Some rooms have one or two double beds; others have twin beds; all have overbed lights. Mattresses are soft, so test yours before signing in. There's a small restaurant/bar, La Concha Nostra, in the front that overlooks the plazuela and is open daily from 8:30am to 12am.

Hotel Los Arcos. Juan Ruíz de Alarcón 12, 40200 Taxco, Gro. ☎ **762/2-1836.** Fax 762/ 2-3211. 21 rms (all with bath). $14 single; $19 double.

Los Arcos occupies a converted 1620 monastery. The handsome inner patio is bedecked with Puebla pottery and a gaily dressed restaurant area to the left, all around a central fountain. The rooms are nicely but sparsely furnished, with natural tile floors and colonial-style furniture. You'll be immersed in colonial charm and blissful quiet. To find it from the Plaza Borda, follow the hill down past the Casa Borda. Make an immediate right at the Plazuela Bernal; the hotel is a block down on the left, opposite the Posada de los Castillo (see below).

✪ **Hotel Rancho Taxco Victoria.** Apdo. Postal 83, 40200 Taxco, Gro. ☎ and fax **762/ 2-0010.** 64 rms (all with bath). $24.75 standard; $33 deluxe; $41 junior suite.

The Rancho Taxco Victoria clings to the hillside above town, with breathtaking views from its flower-covered verandas. It's a personal favorite partly for the views and partly because it exudes all the charm of old-fashioned Mexico. The furnishings, beautifully kept as if purchased yesterday, whisper comfortably of the hotel's heyday in the 1940s. In the guest rooms—nestled into nooks and crannies of the rambling hillside buildings—are vanities constructed of handmade tiles; local tin-craft reading lamps; old prints of Mexico and Taxco; beamed ceilings; craftwork bedspreads and throw rugs; a plant or two; baths with tubs; and in many cases, small private terraces. Each standard room comes with a bedroom and in front of each is a table and chairs set out on the tiled common walkway. Each deluxe room has a bedroom and private terrace; each junior suite has a bedroom, a nicely furnished large living room, and a spacious private terrace overlooking the city. There's a lovely pool, plus an overpriced restaurant—both with a great view of Taxco. Even if you don't stay here, come for a drink in the comfortable bar/living room, then stroll on the terrace to take in the fabulous view. From Plazuela de San Juan, go up a narrow, winding cobbled street named Carlos J. Nibbi to no. 57 on the hilltop.

Hotel Santa Prisca. Plazuela de San Juan 1, 40200 Taxco, Gro. ☎ **762/2-0080** or 762/2-0980. Fax 762/2-2938. 34 rms (all with bath). $22 double standard room; $24.75 double suite; $41 single or double suites nos. 25 and 26.

The Santa Prisca, one block from Plaza Borda on Plazuela de San Juan, is one of the older and nicer hotels in town. Rooms are small but comfortable, with older baths (showers only), tile floors, wood beams, and a colonial atmosphere. If your stay is long, ask for a room in the adjacent "new addition," where the rooms are sunnier, more spacious, and quieter. There is a reading area in an upstairs salon overlooking Taxco, a lush patio with fountains, and a lovely dining room done in mustard and blue.

☯ Posada de los Castillo. Juan Ruíz de Alarcón 3, 40200 Taxco, Gro. ☎ **762/2-1396.** Fax 762/2-3471. 14 rms (all with bath). $14 single; $18 double.

Each room in this delightful small hotel is simply but beautifully furnished with handsome carved doors and furniture; baths have either tubs or showers. Just off the lobby is a branch of the Los Castillo silver store. (The Castillo family also owns the hotel.) The helpful manager, Don Teodoro Contreras, is a fountain of information about Taxco. To get here from the Plaza Borda, go down hill a short block to the Plazuela Bernal; make an immediate right, and the hotel is a block farther on the right, opposite the Hotel Los Arcos (see above).

WHERE TO EAT

Taxco gets a lot of people from the capital for the day or passing through on their way to Acapulco; there are not enough restaurants to fill the demand, so prices are high for what you get. If you have a big breakfast and pack a lunch, you'll save money.

A special note: One of my old favorites, La Taberna Restaurant, was in transition at press time. When it reopens after renovation, it will be called Sotavento, serve a slightly revamped menu, and also serve double duty as a gallery. See if it's open when you travel; it's on the same side of the street as the post office, but just beyond it as you turn left around the bend.

Cielito Lindo. Plaza Borda 14. ☎ **762/2-0603.** Breakfast $2.75–$6.25; main courses $4.50–$6.50. Daily 10am–11pm. MEXICAN/INTERNATIONAL.

Cielito Lindo is probably the most popular place on the plaza for lunch, perhaps more for its visibility and colorful decor than for its food—which is okay, not great. The tables, covered in white and blue and laid with blue and white local crockery, are usually packed, and plates of food disappear as fast as the waiters can bring them. You can get anything from soup to roast chicken, enchiladas, tacos, steak, and dessert, as well as frosty margaritas.

La Hamburguesa. Plazuela de San Juan 5. ☎ **762/2-0941.** Breakfast $1.50–$2.50; hamburgers and tacos $1–$2.30; main courses $1–$2.50; comida corrida $2.50. Daily 8am–midnight (comida corrida served 1–5pm). MEXICAN.

The tables are always full at this small restaurant just steps off Plazuela San Juan. A few cloth-covered tables are set outside on the porch and others inside, but both have a view of the busy plaza. The menu offers soup, yogurt and fruit, Mexican plate meals, burgers and fries, and tacos—all filling, tasty, and cheap.

✪ **Restaurante Ethel.** Plazuela de San Juan 14. ☎ **762/2-0788.** Soup $1.50; main courses $3.75–$5; comida corrida $3.75. Daily 9am–10pm (comida corrida served 1–5pm). MEXICAN.

A family-run place opposite the Hotel Santa Prisca on Plazuela de San Juan, one block from Plaza Borda, Restaurante Ethel is kept clean and tidy, with white table-cloths and colorful crumb cloths on the tables and a homey atmosphere. The hearty daily comida corrida consists of soup or pasta, meat (perhaps a small steak), dessert, and good coffee.

Sr. Costilla's ("Mr. Ribs"). Plaza Borda 1. ☎ **762/2-3215.** Main courses $4.25–$11.50. Daily 1pm–midnight. INTERNATIONAL.

The offbeat decor of this member of the Carlos Anderson chain includes a ceiling festooned with the usual assortment of cultural flotsam and jetsam. Several tiny balconies hold a few minuscule tables that afford a view of the plaza and church (it's next to the Santa Prisca Church, above Patio de las Artesanías), and these fill up long before the large dining room does. The menu, with a large selection of everything from soup through steaks, sandwiches, and pork ribs to desserts and coffee is certainly varied. But the quality and taste are slipping, so until you know better, confine this to a good spot for margaritas and snacks while gazing over the plaza, and leave the big meal for another place.

TAXCO AFTER DARK

Taxco's nighttime action is centered in the luxury hotels. **Paco's** is just about the most popular place overlooking the square for sipping, nibbling, people-watching, and people-meeting, all of which continues until midnight daily. And there's Taxco's dazzling disco, **Windows,** high up the mountain in the Hotel Monte Taxco. The whole city is on view from there, and music runs the gamut from the hit parade to hard rock. For a cover of $5 you can boogie Saturday nights from 9pm to 3am.

Completely different in tone is **Berta's,** next to Santa Prisca Church. Opened in 1930 by a lady named Berta, who made her fame on a drink of the same name (tequila, soda, lime, and honey), Berta's is traditionally the gathering place of the local gentry. Spurs and old swords decorate the walls, and a saddle is casually slung over the banister of the stairs leading to the second-floor room where tin masks leer from the walls. A Berta costs about $2; rum, the same. Open daily from 11am to around 10pm.

Tarascan Country

Perennially off the beaten tourist track, Tarascan Country offers a distinctive, unusual taste of Mexico without the bad aftertaste of high prices. The area is situated northwest of Mexico City, in Michoacán (Meech-oh-ah-kahn), Mexico's sixth-largest state. Its best-known towns are Morelia, Pátzcuaro, and Uruapan. All of them are old colonial towns with their own unique charms, and they're all within range of Michoacán's seemingly timeless fascinations: trips through the countryside to see volcanoes or millions of monarch butterflies, to wander through Purépecha ruins, or to visit the area's many small, colorful villages—where centuries-old craft traditions are alive today.

The land of the Tarascans has maintained a special place in the country's history since before the Spanish conquest of Mexico. Unconquered by the Aztecs, the proud and courageous Tarascan people held themselves and their land apart in majestic forested mountains dotted with misty lakes. Their language and influence were known as far north as the present-day states of Querétaro, Guerrero, Colima, Jalisco, and Guanajuato. Even the name Guanajuato is a Spanish corruption of the Tarascan word *guanaxuato*, meaning "hill of the frogs." Their pyramids, connecting half circles and rectangles, were called *yacatas*, the most visible of which are at Tzintzuntzán, near Pátzcuaro. Good examples of their pottery, stonework, and metalwork are displayed at the Museo del Estado in Morelia, at La Huatapera in Uruapan, and at the Museo de Arte Regional y Popular in Pátzcuaro.

The true name of the indigenous people here, and their language, is not Tarascan but Purépecha (sometimes spelled Purápecha), a word heard often in the region. When Spaniards married into Indian families, the Indians called them *tarasco*, which means "son-in-law" in Purépecha. The Spaniards heard the name so often they named the people Tarascans—and it stuck. The Purépecha language is still spoken by more than 200,000 people; according to the Cultural Atlas of Mexico, it's remotely linked to the Mixe and Zoque languages in Mexico and to the Quecha language of Peru. But even from village to village, there are differences in pronunciation within the language.

Two very different leaders stand out in the colonial history of Pátzcuaro. Conquistador Nuño de Guzman is remembered for his infamous greed and brutality; he terrorized the Tarascan population

Michoacán State

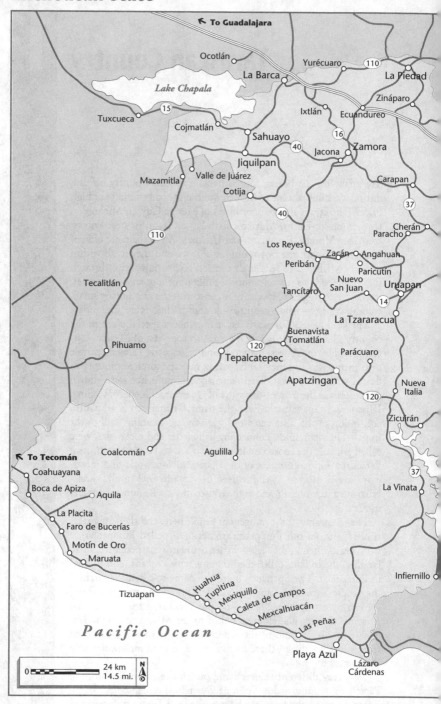

To Guadalajara

Ocotlán

Yurécuaro
110
La Piedad

La Barca

Lake Chapala

Zináparo

Ixtlán
Ecuandureo

Tuxcueca

Cojmatlán
Sahuayo
16
Zamora

40
Jacona

Jiquilpan

Mazamitla
Valle de Juárez

Carapan

Cotija
40
37

Cherán
Paracho

Los Reyes
Zacán
Angahuan

Peribán
Paricutín

110
Nuevo
San Juan
Uruapan

Tecalitlán
Tancítaro
14

La Tzararacua

Buenavista
Tomatlán
Parácuaro

Pihuamo
120
Tepalcatepec

Apatzingan

Nueva
Italia
120

Zicuirán

Coalcomán
Agulilla

To Tecomán

37

La Vinata

Coahuayana

Boca de Apiza
Aquila

La Placita

Faro de Bucerías

Motín de Oro

Maruata

Infiernillo

Huahua
Tupitina

Tizuapan
Mexiquillo

Caleta de Campos

Mexcalhuacán

Las Peñas

Pacific Ocean

Playa Azul
Lázaro
Cárdenas

0   24 km
          14.5 mi.   N

450

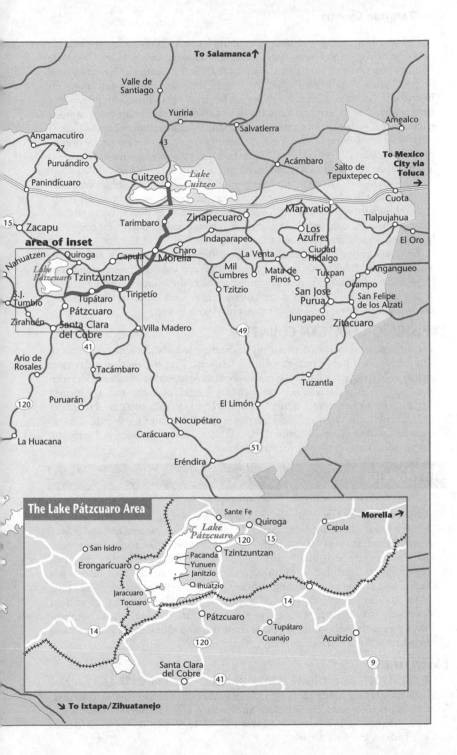

To Salamanca↑

Valle de Santiago

Yuriria

Salvatierra

Amealco

Angamacutiro

27

Puruándiro

43

Acámbaro

To Mexico City via Toluca →

Salto de Tepuxtepec

Panindícuaro

Cuitzeo

Lake Cuitzeo

Cuota

15

Zacapu

area of inset

Tarimbaro

Zinapecuaro

Maravatio

Tlalpujahua

El Oro

Nahuatzen

Quiroga

Capula

Charo

Morelia

Indaparapeo

La Venta

Los Azufres

Ciudad Hidalgo

Angangueo

Lake Pátzcuaro

Tzintzuntzan

Mil Cumbres

Mata de Pinos

Tuxpan

Ocampo

San Felipe de los Alzati

S.J. Tumbio

Tupátaro

Tiripetío

Tzitzio

San Jose Purua

Jungapeo

Zitácuaro

Zirahuén

Pátzcuaro

Santa Clara del Cobre

Villa Madero

49

41

Ario de Rosales

Tacámbaro

Tuzantla

120

Puruarán

El Limón

Nocupétaro

Carácuaro

51

La Huacana

Eréndira

The Lake Pátzcuaro Area

Sante Fe

Quiroga

Capula

Morella →

Lake Pátzcuaro

120

15

San Isidro

Pacanda

Tzintzuntzan

Erongarícuaro

Yunuen

Janitzio

Jaracuaro

Tocuaro

Ihuatzio

14

Pátzcuaro

Tupátaro

Cuanajo

Acuitzio

14

120

9

Santa Clara del Cobre

41

↘ To Ixtapa/Zihuatanejo

451

and burned their chief alive because he wouldn't—or couldn't—disclose the location of gold deposits. After Guzman was arrested, a humane bishop named Vasco de Quiroga was sent to reconstruct the area. De Quiroga taught the Indians several trades, a different one in each village. As a result, today the region is well known for its crafts, including handsome hand-loomed fabrics made in Pátzcuaro; pottery and straw weavings in Tzintzuntzán and Ihuatzio; and hand-carved furniture and wood sculptures in Quiroga, Tzintzuntzán, Cuanaja, and Pátzcuaro. Santa Clara del Cobre's shops shimmer with copper, and both Pátzcuaro and Uruapan are known for distinctive lacquerware. The bishop became so revered that he is still honored today. Streets and hotels are named after him, and his statue stands in the main plaza of Pátzcuaro.

Although most Tarascans have given up truly distinctive regional dress, women still wear their hair braided and interlaced with satin ribbons in the traditional manner, don embroidered blouses and hand-loomed skirts, and wrap themselves in rebozos. In remote villages, older men (more often than young men or boys) wear traditional homespun white cotton pants and shirts.

While the region is completely integrated into the commerce of mainstream Mexico—through agriculture (avocados and coffee) and industry (furniture and lumber)—it is still culturally set apart, primarily because of the beautiful but mountainous terrain. Architecturally, it's almost unchanged from colonial times. Its unique culture makes it one of the most enjoyable regions in Mexico to visit.

EXPLORING TARASCAN COUNTRY

The time required to travel between any of the three major cities is no more than an hour or two, and public transportation is frequent. Plan no less than a day (two nights) in Morelia and a minimum of two days (three nights) in Pátzcuaro. Uruapan is an easy day-trip, but you may want to stay longer for a visit to the Paricutín volcano. During Easter week or the Day of the Dead (actually two days, November 1–2), the plazas in Pátzcuaro and Uruapan are loaded with regional crafts. Processions and other traditional customs make Easter week exceptional in Pátzcuaro. Reserve rooms well in advance for these holidays.

1 Morelia

195 miles W of Mexico City, 228 miles SE of Guadalajara

Morelia, the capital of the wildly beautiful state of Michoacán, is a lovely colonial city. Over the years, it has earned a reputation as one of Mexico's intellectual and artistic centers. As with much of Mexico, there is layer upon layer of fascinating history here. The area was inhabited first by the indigenous peoples, notably the Tarascans. Founded by the Spanish in 1541, the city was originally named Valladolid and was changed later to honor the revolutionary hero José María Morelos, who once lived here.

Morelia's many original colonial buildings add a special touch of ancient Mexican/Spanish elegance. To preserve the architectural harmony, the city government long ago decreed that all new major construction continue in the same style and be built no taller than the existing structures.

ESSENTIALS

GETTING THERE & DEPARTING   By Plane   Aerolitoral (☎ 43/3-6202, or 91-800/9-0999 toll free in Mexico), an Aeroméxico affiliate, flies from Guadalajara, Mexico City, León, and Tijuana. **Aero SudPacífico** (☎ 43/15-8952) flies daily to Lázaro Cárdenas, and Zihuatanejo. **Taesa** (☎ 43/15-7463) has flights to Mexico City, Tijuana, and Guadalajara.

Morelia

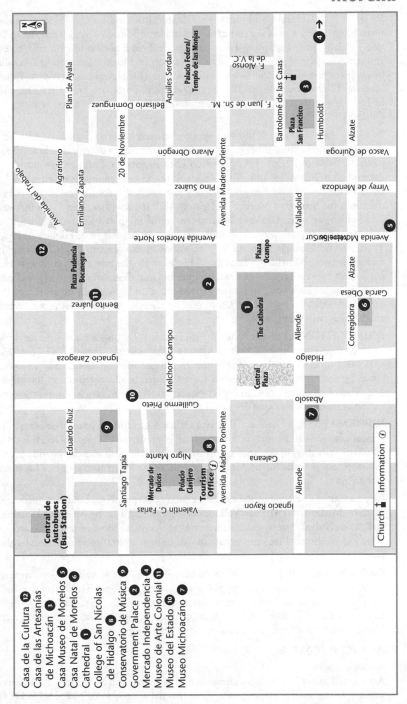

Casa de la Cultura **12**
Casa de las Artesanías
de Michoacán **3**
Casa Museo de Morelos **5**
Casa Natal de Morelos **6**
Cathedral **1**
College of San Nicolas
de Hidalgo **8**
Conservatorio de Música **9**
Government Palace **2**
Mercado Independencia **4**
Museo de Arte Colonial **11**
Museo del Estado **10**
Museo Michoacáno **7**

By Bus   The **Central Camionera** is at Eduardo Ruíz and Valentín Gómez Farías, seven blocks northwest of the cathedral. To and from Mexico City, **Flecha Amarilla** runs 42 daily buses (including 14 deluxe), while **Tres Estrellas** has 10 daily buses, and the deluxe line **ETN** also has frequent service. In Mexico City, Flecha Amarilla buses leave from both the Norte and Poniente (Observatorio) stations. From Morelia, Flecha buses also go hourly to Querétaro, Pátzcuaro, and Uruapan, and to León (four-hour trip) every 20 minutes. ETN also runs nine daily buses to Guadalajara.

By Car   With the new toll highway running between Mexico City and Guadalajara, the trip to Morelia from either city now takes only 2 1/2 to 3 hours (formerly a tedious four- to five-hour trip). From Mexico City it goes to Toluca then north to Atlacomulco, Marvatio, and Zinapecuaro. From Guadalajara it goes direct to La Barca (northeast of Lake Chapala), passing just south of Lake Cuitzeo. From either direction, the turnoff to Morelia is Highway 43. The new, free, four-lane Highway 120 (which, on a map, looks like an extension of Highway 43) links Morelia to Pátzcuaro; the trip takes about 40 minutes. (The left turnoff from Highway 120 to Tupátaro and Guanajo, covered in "Excursions from Pátzcuaro," below, is about midway between Morelia and Pátzcuaro.) Highway 15 (the long route) runs west and north from Mexico City and east and south from Guadalajara. Both sections of Highway 15 are mountainous and have hairpin curves. Highway 43 north is a fairly direct and noncurvy route from San Miguel de Allende through Celaya (two hours) and Guanajuato (four hours).

ORIENTATION   Arriving   Aeropuerto Francisco J. Mugica is a 45-minute drive from the city center on the Carretera Morelia-Cinepecuaro, 27km (☎ **43/13-6074,** 43/13-6177, or 43/13-6178). Taxis meet each flight and cost around $17 to town; return by taxi costs the same. The bus station is seven blocks northwest of the cathedral. Taxis line up out front to collect passengers. A ride to hotels around the central plaza should cost around $3.

INFORMATION   The **State Tourism Office** is in a former Jesuit monastery, the Palacio Clavijero, at the corner of Madero and Nigromante (☎ **43/13-2654;** fax 43/ 12-9816). Members of the helpful staff usually speak English and can provide excellent maps and information on Morelia and Michoacán. The office is open daily from 9am to 9pm.

City Layout   The heart of the city is the pretty **central plaza,** bounded north and south by **Madero** and **Allende/Valladolid** and east and west by **Abasolo, Hidalgo,** and the **cathedral.** Streets change directions at the plaza. Most of the major attractions and the hotels I recommend are in this historic central zone anchored by the plaza.

Getting Around   Taxis are a fairly good bargain here. Although there are no meters, cab drivers are supposed to charge 50¢ per kilometer, or about $1.80 between various points downtown. Here, as anywhere in Mexico, settle the fare before you enter the cab. **Combis,** at 35¢ per ticket, are cheaper than taxis. These customized vans hold up to 15 passengers and are color-coded according to route.

FAST FACTS: MORELIA

Altitude   6,368 ft.

American Express   The local representative is Lopsa Travel Agency, in the Servi Center, Avenida del Campestre and Artilleros del 47 no. 1520 (☎ **43/15-3211;** fax 43/14-7716).

Area Code   The telephone area code is 43.

Climate   At an altitude of more than 6,000 feet, Morelia can be a bit chilly mornings and evenings, especially from November through February.

Newspapers   The local paper, *La Voz de Michoacán,* has a "What's New in Morelia This Week" page that appears every Monday and lists all kinds of interesting cultural events around Morelia.

Population   484,000.

Post Office/Telegraph Office   Both are in the Palacio Federal, on the corner of Madero and Serapio Rendón, five blocks east of the cathedral.

EXPLORING MORELIA

FESTIVALS & EVENTS   In March, the **International Guitar Festival** attracts musicians from all over the world. The **International Organ Festival** is held in May at the cathedral. In June, there is the **Fiesta de Corpus,** with a special cathedral-lighting ceremony, and the **International Festival of Music.** In September, for the **birthday of Revolutionary hero Don José María Morelos,** there are independence celebrations.

A STROLL THROUGH THE COLONIAL CENTER   Morelia is a beautiful city that's perfect for walking, since most of the museums, restaurants, and shops are all within strolling distance of downtown hotels and restaurants.

The walk outlined below begins at the cathedral and winds up at the Casa de la Cultura. Set aside a whole day to do it, or spread it out over two days. The museums open at 9am; you'll find a lot of places are closed on Mondays and holidays and on other days between 2 and 4pm.

In the heart of Morelia, on Madero between Ignacio Zaragoza and Avenida Morelos Norte, past the plaza, is the **cathedral,** which took 104 years to build (1640–1744) and has two impressive spires over 220 feet high that can be climbed (the doors are locked, but the man with the key is usually hanging around at midday). The interior of the church is awesome, particularly if you're fortunate enough to be there when the organist is playing. The organ, with its 4,600 pipes, is one of the best in Latin America. Great organists perform here during the International Organ Festival in May.

Across the street (Madero) from the cathedral, is the **Government Palace,** built in 1732 as a seminary. It now contains grand, colorful murals depicting the history of the state of Michoacán and of Mexico. Some of them were done by a well-known local artist named Alfredo Zalce. Notice the building's lovely arches.

If you wish to visit one of the best regional museums of art and showrooms of crafts, walk two blocks east on Madero (turn left out the door of the Government Palace), then turn south (right) onto Vasco de Quiroga for one block to the **Casa de Artesanías,** across Plaza de San Francisco in the colonial building attached to the church of the same name. Outside, rows of crafts vendors have set up semipermanent stalls. Inside, high quality traditional-style crafts of all sorts are displayed in both a museum and a large sales outlet upstairs and downstairs. (See "Shopping," below.) It's open daily from 9am to 8pm; admission is free.

Leaving the Artesanías, turn left to the first street (Humboldt), turn left again to Calle Vicente Santa María (it runs north-south behind the Artesanías), then turn right (south) for five blocks to the huge **Mercado Independencia,** which is open daily. Browse and enjoy the wonders of the Mexican street market—everything from clothing to cookware to flowers is sold here.

From the market, walk three blocks west to Avenida Morelos Sur and two blocks north to visit the **Casa Museo de Morelos,** Morelos Sur 323 (☎ **43/13-2651**), where the city's namesake José María Morelos lived as an adult. It's a pleasant house with an authentically preserved kitchen, in addition to furniture and personal effects of the hero. It's open daily from 9am to 7pm; admission costs $3.50. For those who still want to learn more about Morelos, walk another block west to García Obesa, turn right, and on the corner of Corregidora is the **Casa Natal de Morelos (Birthplace of Morelos)**, at Corregidora and Obeso (☎ 43/12-2793). There's more memorabilia, including historical documents, old posters, and modern murals depicting the Revolution. A terrific bookstore selling local and national historic and ethnographic literature is on the right as you enter. Open daily from 9am to 7pm.

From here, turn left out the front door and go half a block to Hidalgo and turn right, then turn left again for another block to Allende and the **Museo Michoacano,** Allende and Abasolo (☎ 43/12-0407). This is a good introduction to the history of the state from prehistoric times to Mexico's Cardenist period of the 1930s. The building, finished in 1775, was originally owned by Isidor Huarte, father of Ana Huarte (Emperor Iturbide's wife).

To the right as you enter, a great bookstore features literature on Mexico's archaeology as well as pottery reproductions from the Museum of Anthropology in Mexico City. The museum is open Tuesday through Saturday from 9am to 7pm and Sunday from 9am to 2pm. Admission is $4.

Head north across the park to Madero for a rest stop. Back on Madero in front of the cathedral is a choice of cafés, beginning with El Paraíso, across from the cathedral on the corner of Benito Juárez, and running down past the Café Catedral and Hotel Casino to Prieto.

Continue west on Madero one block to the corner of Nigromante, where, on the right corner, you'll find the **College of San Nicolas de Hidalgo,** a beautiful colonial-era university that claims to be the "oldest in the western hemisphere." Founded in Pátzcuaro in 1540, it was moved to Valladolid (present-day Morelia) in 1580 and incorporated into the University of Michoacán in 1917. Turn north (right) on Nigromante and walk three short blocks to Santiago Tapia and turn right; on the left side is the **Conservatorio de Música,** in the former Convento de Las Rosas, established as a convent for Dominican nuns in 1500. In 1785, it became a school for boys with musical skill, and it is now the home of the internationally acclaimed Morelia Boys' Choir. Don't miss them if there's a practice or performance while you're in town; you can listen and observe quietly.

Catercorner across the street is the **Museo del Estado,** at the corner of Tapia and Guillermo Prieto (☎ 43/13-0629), a delightfully well done free museum with information about Michoacán from cavemen and fossils, to an on-site, intact 19th-century apothecary shop, to contemporary art on the second floor. This was the childhood home of Ana Huerta, first empress of Mexico and wife of Emperor Agustín de Iturbide. The museum is open Monday through Friday from 10am to 2pm and 4 to 8pm and Saturday, Sunday, and holidays from 10am to 7pm.

For another interesting museum, continue east on Santiago Tapia two blocks to Benito Juárez and turn north (left) to the **Museo de Arte Colonial,** Av. Benito Juárez 240 (☎ 43/13-9260). It's filled with religious art from the 16th to the 18th century, housed in another old town house with a central courtyard. It's open Tuesday through Sunday from 10am to 2pm and 5 to 8pm.

To find out about local cultural events, cross the small street to the north (around the corner to the right from the museum) and turn left onto the next street (Avenida Morelos Norte). Follow the high wrought-iron fence enclosing whimsical, contemporary sculpture made from machine parts to reach the entrance of the **Casa de la Cultura.** This cultural complex (☎ 43/13-1320) includes a mask museum, an open-air café, and several art galleries. It's open daily from 10am to 8pm, and there's no

Into the Mountains to See Michoacán's Monarch Butterflies

Visiting the winter nesting grounds of the monarch butterfly in the mountains of Michoacán—a very long day-trip from Morelia—is an awesome experience. The monarchs wing down from Canada for the winter, so the best time to see them is from November through February. In the tiny, unpaved village of El Rosario, the brilliant butterflies welcome visitors with a blizzard of orange and black. At the nearby El Rosario Sanctuary (admission $3; open daily from 10am to 5 or 6pm), a guide (who should be tipped a few dollars) accompanies each group of visitors along the loop trail (about an hour's steep walk at high altitude). It's worth the time, effort, and expense to get here to be surrounded by the magic of millions of monarchs. Be quiet and you'll hear almost a billion wings—this is one of the few places in the world where one can hear the soft sound of butterflies flying.

At the high point of the trail, the branches of the tall pine trees bow under their burden of butterflies. For folks unable to tackle the walk, monarchs are visible around the car park. There's also a comprehensive video show at the nearby information center, as well as snacks, soft drinks, and toilets.

Take one of the tours offered by a number of travel agents in Morelia or rough it by taking a bus on your own. Having done the latter, I recommend the former, since in the long run the tour involves less time, money, and effort.

Organized Tours   Tour companies in Morelia offer this trip frequently during peak months for about $30 to $45. The tour takes about 10 to 12 hours by van. The Wagon-Lits travel agent (☎ **43/12-7766;** fax 43/12-7660), in the lobby of the Hotel Alemeda on the corner of Madero and G. Prieto (just west of the cathedral), handles this and other tours through Auto Turismo de Michoacán (☎ **43/2-4987** or 43/2-6810). You might also try Viajes Flamingo, Zaragoza 93 (☎ **43/12-0059** or 43/12-4833; fax 43/12-4833). Monarch tours generally leave at 10am and return at 7:30pm; tours require a minimum of five people.

Tours from Elsewhere   Travel agencies from San Miguel de Allende often have monarch tours. See the section on San Miguel in chapter 9 for details. Columbus Travel (☎ **800/843-1060** in the U.S. and Canada) has frequent trips to the butterflies via Mexico City.

On Your Own   An alternative is to stay overnight in Zitácuaro and get an early start in your own car or by public bus to Ocampo. In Ocampo, hired transportation is readily available for the last stretch on the rough dirt road to the sanctuary. To drive your own car, just follow the main roads to the towns described above. Zitácuaro is on Highway 15 between Toluca and Morelia. A Volkswagen Beetle carried me up the final dirt road from Ocampo to El Rosario.

admission charge. Posters in the entryway announce events taking place here and at other locations in town.

SHOPPING

✪ **Casa de Artesanías.** Plaza de San Francisco. ☎ **43/12-1248.**

This is one of the best crafts shops in the country. In the showroom, to the right as you enter on the first floor, you'll find fantastic carved wooden furniture; people-size ceramic pots; beautiful handwoven clothing; embroidered scenes of daily life; wooden masks; lacquerware from Pátzcuaro and Uruapan; cross-stitch embroidery from Taracuato; waist-loomed table runners (they use them for mufflers), and carved pine furniture from Cuanajo; woodwork and guitars from Paracho; and close-woven hats from the Isla de Jaracuaro. Straight ahead in the fabulous interior courtyard of this monumental structure are showcases laden with the best regional crafts. Upstairs individual villages have sales outlets for fabric, wood carving, weaving, copper, and the like. Everything on display is for sale at reasonable prices. Also upstairs is a living crafts museum where workers create and display their art. The shop is open daily from 9am to 8pm; admission is free.

Mercado de Dulces. Beside the Palacio Clavijero, along Valentín Gómez Farías.

This delightful jumble of shops, west on Madero from the cathedral and north on Nigromante, sells *cubitos de áte* (candied fruit wedges), jelly candies, honey, goat's milk, strawberry jam, and *chongos* (a combination of milk, sugar, cinnamon, and honey). Upstairs is a shop with all kinds of regional artesanías and hundreds of picture postcards from all over Michoacán. The mercado is open daily from 7am to 10pm.

WHERE TO STAY

Hotel Casino. Portal Hidalgo 229, 58000 Morelia, Mich. ☎ **43/13-1003.** Fax 43/12-1252. 50 rms (all with bath). TV TEL. $35 single; $40 double.

This fine old hotel features several nice touches—beams, chandeliers, and columns—along with an excellent location practically across the street from the cathedral. The immaculate rooms have wall-to-wall carpeting. The restaurant, located in the covered courtyard on the first floor and outside under the portals, is one of the best in town.

Hotel Concordia. Valentín Gómez Farías 328, 58000 Morelia, Mich. ☎ **43/12-3052.** 51 rms (all with bath). TV TEL. $15 single; $20 double.

Many of my readers have recommended this quiet four-story hotel, conveniently located near the bus station and a few blocks from the town center. The rooms are large and modern; the elevator is functional; and the staff is friendly. Ask for one of the rooms facing the street—they have the most light, with almost a full wall of windows. To find the hotel from the bus station, walk to the left out the front door and to the corner (Gómez Farías), then left again; it's half a block on the right.

✪ Posada de la Soledad. Ignacio Zaragoza 90, 58000 Morelia, Mich. ☎ **45/12-1888.** 58 rms, 9 suites (all with bath). TV TEL. $40–$45 single; $45–$50 double. Free parking.

A tranquil, beautiful hacienda-style manor, the hotel was built in 1719 as the home and carriage house of a rich Spaniard. Old carriages are handsomely placed around the first floor. Some of the rooms have a fireplace, a tub as well as a shower, and a small balcony. Standard rooms are small, and most are plainly furnished with one or two double beds and colonial-style furniture. The hotel restaurant/bar, one of the most inviting in Mexico, is open daily from 7:30am to 10:30pm, with tables set under the portals. To reach the hotel from the cathedral, walk one block west on Madero to Zaragoza; turn right and you'll find the hotel on the right, near Ocampo.

WHERE TO EAT

Across from the main plaza and cathedral, on the same side of the street as the Hotel Casino and the Restaurant El Paraíso, is an entire block replete with sidewalk cafés. This is local life on parade—people linger for hours sipping coffee in its many varieties or downing whole meals. All the restaurants here are popular, so pick one that's appealing.

La Cueva de Chucho. Eduardo Ruíz 620. ☎ **43/12-3885.** Breakfast $2–$3; main courses $3–$5; comida corrida $4. Daily 7am–11pm (comida corrida served noon–3:30 or 4pm). MEXICAN.

With its beige-and-yellow decor, plastic chairs, and tile floors, this place has the atmosphere of a bowling alley, but it's spotlessly clean; the waitresses are neatly dressed in clean uniforms; and the food is great and inexpensive. Try the tortitas de carne—delectable, melt-in-your-mouth, lean meat in a spicy tomatillo sauce with a side order of beans. On Sunday the special is paella for $5. From the bus terminal, turn right and cross the first street; the restaurant is on the right.

✪ **Las Mercedes Restaurant.** León Guzman 47. ☎ **43/2-6113.** Main courses $5–$9. Mon–Sat 1:30–11:30pm. MEXICAN/INTERNATIONAL.

If you eat only one meal in Morelia take it here, in a stone-arched inner courtyard filled with palms, flowers, and succulents in tubs and pots. One wall is lined with colorful birds in cages and others with exotic murals. At night, small spotlights illuminate each table's colorful, fresh bouquet. Pastel-clothed tables are set with hand-painted ceramic plates bearing charming scenes, and wine is presented in a translucent, handblown fluted green glass. A plate of small tacos is automatically brought while diners make their choices. Homemade bread also arrives with a small tub of herb-flavored butter. The menu includes pasta; crêpes with piñons and pistachios; beef brochette; and various seafood and meat offerings. To get here from the cathedral, walk six short blocks west on Madero. Turn right on León Guzman and look for a small sign on the left over the door.

✪ **Las Viandas de San José.** Alvaro Obregón 263 at Emiliano Zapata. ☎ **43/2-3728.** Breakfast $2–$2.50; main courses $4–$7; comida corrida $5.50. Daily 8am–11pm. REGIONAL/INTERNATIONAL.

Dining is a pleasure under the arcades or adjacent rooms of this mansion, built around an open interior patio. Service is gracious, and the menu offers intriguing regional specialties such as uchepos; corrundas; bone-marrow soup; rabbit in wine sauce; chicken placero with enchiladas; and 11 different fish dishes, including Pátzcuaro whitefish. Beef and chicken prepared home-style round out the menu. You can't go wrong with the huge comida corrida. Las Viandas is a sibling of Los Comensales at Zaragoza 148, a block and a half from the main plaza. The menus are almost the same, but Las Viandas has superior service. To find Las Viandas from the cathedral, walk three blocks east on Madero Oriente and turn left on Alvaro Obregón. Walk straight for three blocks; it's on the corner opposite the Iglesia San José.

MORELIA AFTER DARK

Morelia's cafés (see "Where to Dine," above) become its nightspots after dark. Hot coffee and cold beer are served to a lively college crowd. Another nice cafe and nightspot is Colibri, Galeana 36, a block behind Hotel Virrey de Mendoza (go two blocks west of the cathedral then turn left on Galeana; Colibri is on the right side). Softly strumming his guitar, a singer entertains patrons with a variety of lovely ballads, mostly Mexican and Latin American. On winter evenings around Christmas, the owner personally serves complimentary cups of the traditional hot fruit punch.

2 Pátzcuaro

231 Miles W of Mexico City, 178 miles SE of Guadalajara, 43 miles SW of Morelia

Pátzcuaro is a well-preserved colonial town with low overhanging red-tile roofs, white-washed buildings, two plazas, and no traffic lights. Coming from Morelia, you'll immediately notice the difference between that city's regal colonial architecture and Pátzcuaro's rural colonial-era structures. No new buildings interfere with the timeworn harmony of Pátzcuaro's colonial roofline.

Except for its paved streets, little has changed about Pátzcuaro's appearance since colonial times. Here, as in San Miguel de Allende, you have the feeling of traveling centuries back in time. More than San Miguel or even Morelia, Pátzcuaro has Indian roots that still run deep. Though distinct regional costumes are seldom seen, Indian women still braid their hair with ribbons and wear bright blue rebozos, and women from several villages wear a distinctive cross-point stitched apron—a new kind of costume. The ancient Tarascan language is heard frequently, especially in the central market. The town is known for its lake, one of the world's highest at 7,250 feet, where fishermen catch delicious whitefish with nets of such delicate texture and wide-winged shape that they've been compared to butterflies. If there is any drawback to Pátzcuaro, it is that its lovely stone park benches are dirty and the unkempt appearance of both plazas obscures their beauty.

ESSENTIALS

GETTING THERE & DEPARTING   By Bus   The bus station is on the outskirts of Pátzcuaro, about a 20-minute bus ride to town or 10 minutes by taxi. **From Mexico City:** Service is more frequent to Morelia than directly to Pátzcuaro. It may therefore be more efficient to take a bus first to Morelia and then one of the frequent buses running from there to Pátzcuaro. **Flecha Amarilla and Autobuses de Occidente** have two buses from Mexico City to Pátzcuaro that cost about $12. **From Morelia: Autotransportes Galeana** runs between Pátzcuaro and Morelia every 15 minutes; the 40-minute to one-hour trip costs $1.50 to $2. The same line has buses to and from Uruapan every 20 minutes, and the one-hour trip costs $1.50 to $2. ETN has 10 daily buses to Morelia. **Parhikuni** buses run every few minutes between Pátzcuaro and Morelia. **To Tocuaro and Erongaricaro:** Occidente buses make the 30- to 40-minute trip every 20 minutes. **To Tupátaro and Cuanajo:** Buses of the Herradura de Plata line run hourly between 7am and 9pm. **To Tzintzuntzán:** Frequent buses of the Galeana and Occidente lines labeled "Quiroga" go frequently to Tzintzuntzán (40 minutes). **To Santa Clara del Cobre:** Frequent buses labeled "Ario de Rosales" pass first through Santa Clara del Cobre (the so-called "Copper Capital" of Mexico), a 30-minute drive from Pátzcuaro. Occidente or Galeana buses are among the several buses that go there. **To Ihuatzio:** Frequent minivans and buses pass by the Plaza Chica in Pátzcuaro en route to Ihuatzio. **To San Miguel de Allende:** Flecha Amarilla has four daily buses making the four- to five-hour trip.

By Car   See "Getting There & Departing: By Car" in Morelia, above, for information from Mexico City, Guadalajara, San Miguel de Allende, and Morelia. From Morelia there are two routes to Pátzcuaro: The fastest route is the new four-lane Highway 120, which passes near Tiripetío and Tupátaro/Cuanajo (see "Excursions from Pátzcuaro," below). The longer route via Highway 15 takes about an hour and passes near the pottery-making village of Capula and then through Quiroga, where you follow signs to Pátzcuaro and Tzintzuntzán (see "Excursions from Pátzcuaro," below).

ORIENTATION   Arriving   The bus station, on Libramiento Ignacio Zaragoza Highway, is on the outskirts of town—too far to walk from the center. City buses and minivans (15¢ to 25¢) arrive in the lot adjacent to the bus station or out on the highway (half a block away). Those marked "Centro" go either to the Plaza Grande or the Plaza Chica; ask which one if you have a specific destination in mind. Small bags can be accommodated. A taxi will cost about $2.50.

Information   The **State Tourism Office,** catercorner from the northwest corner of the Plaza Grande at Ibarra 3 (☎ **343/2-1214**), is open daily from 9am to 2pm and

Pátzcuaro

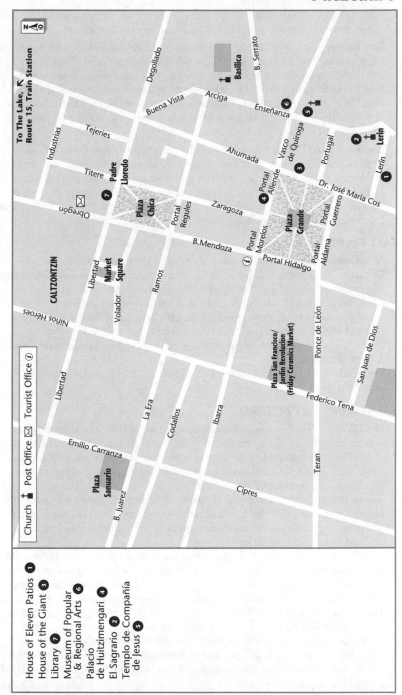

Church ✝ | Post Office ⊠ | Tourist Office ⓘ

To The Lake, ↖
Route 15, Train Station

Basílica

B. Serrato

Degollado

Arciga

Buena Vista

Enseñanza

Tejerías

Industrias

Ahumada

Vasco de Quiroga

Portugal

Lerín

Padre Lloredo

Titere

Obregón

Plaza Chica

Portal Regules

Zaragoza

Portal Allende

Dr. José Maria Cos

Plaza Grande

Portal Morelos

Portal Guerrero

B. Mendoza

Portal Hidalgo

Portal Aldama

CALITZONTZIN

Libertad

Market Square

Volador

Ramos

Niños Héroes

Ponce de León

San Juan de Dios

Libertad

La Era

Codallos

Ibarra

Plaza San Francisco / Jardín Revolución (Friday Ceramics Market)

Federico Tena

Teran

Emilio Carranza

B. Juárez

Plaza Sanuario

Cipres

House of Eleven Patios ❶
House of the Giant ❸
Library ❼
Museum of Popular & Regional Arts ❻
Palacio de Huitzimengari ❷
El Sagrario ❹
Templo de Compañía de Jesus ❺

4 to 7:30pm. Although you might not find someone who speaks English, the staff will try to be helpful, and you can pick up useful maps and brochures.

City Layout   In a way, Pátzcuaro has two town centers, both of them plazas a block apart from each other. Plaza Grande, also called Plaza Principal or Plaza Don Vasco de Quiroga, is a picturesque tranquil plaza centered on a fountain and a statue of Vasco de Quiroga. It is flanked by hotels, shops, and restaurants in colonial-era buildings. Plaza Chica, also known as Plaza de San Agustín or Plaza Gertrudis Bocanegra, flows into the market, and around it swirls the commercial life of Pátzcuaro. Plaza Chica is north of Plaza Grande.

Getting Around   With the exception of Lake Pátzcuaro, the lookout, and hotels on Lázaro Cárdenas, everything is within easy walking distance from almost any hotel in Pátzcuaro. Although the lake is over a mile from town, buses make the run every 15 minutes from both the Plaza Grande and the Plaza Chica, going all the way to the pier (the embarcadero or muelle), passing by the train station and all the places I name on Avenida Lázaro Cárdenas (formerly Avenida de las Américas).

FAST FACTS: PÁTZCUARO

Area Code   The telephone area code changed in 1994 from 454 to 434.

Climate   The climate is delightful most of the year, but occasional blustery days bring swirls of dust and a chill of air across the lake, causing everyone to shutter themselves inside. From October through April, it's cold enough for a heavy sweater, especially in the morning and evening. Thick walls in many of the hotels retain a chill so that it may be several degrees cooler inside than outside. Since few hotels have fireplaces or any source of heat in the rooms, long johns and socks may make sleeping more comfortable.

Post Office   The Correo is located half a block north of Plaza Chica, on the right side of the street.

EXPLORING PÁTZCUARO

FESTIVALS   The island of Janitzio has achieved world fame for the candlelight vigil local residents hold at the cemetery during the nights of November 1 and 2, the Day of the Dead. Tzintzuntzán also hosts very popular festivities, including folkloric dances in the main plaza and in the nearby yácatas (pre-Hispanic ruins), concerts in the church, and decorations in the cemetery. If you wish to avoid crowds, however, skip Janitzio and Tzintzuntzán and go to one of the smaller lakeside villages or other islands on the lake that also have extraordinary rituals. The Tourism Office (see "Information," above) has a schedule of events for the entire area and publishes an explanatory booklet "Día de los Muertos."

Easter week, beginning the Friday before Palm Sunday, is special here, too. Most activity centers around the basílica. There are processions involving the surrounding villages almost nightly, and in Tzintzuntzán there's a reenactment of the betrayal of Christ and a ceremonial washing of the feet. Although written in 1947, Frances Toor's description of Holy Week in Pátzcuaro, in *A Treasury of Mexican Folkways* (Crown), is still accurate and a good preparation for a visit.

During both events, the Plaza Grande is loaded with regional crafts.

Important note: Make hotel reservations months in advance for either event. Most hotels require a three-night minimum stay during Holy Week and Day of the Dead.

A STROLL AROUND TOWN   Pátzcuaro is a beautiful town, worthy of leisurely strolls through its ancient, unchanged streets and plazas. **The Plaza Chica,** crisscrossed by walkways, has a statue of Gertrudis Bocanegra, heroine of Mexican independence, in the middle. Immediately west of and across the street from the Plaza Chica, the **market** and large market plaza has myriad stalls where vendors sell pottery, copper, rebozos, serapes, and food. North of the market across the street, facing the Plaza Chica, is the **public library,** also named for Doña Bocanegra. Occupying the former monastery of San Agustín, the library contains a huge mural painted by Juan O'Gorman (the artist's first mural), depicting the history of the area from the Tarascan legends up to the Revolution. The former living quarters of the monks, next door, were converted into the Teatro Emperador Caltzontzin.

Just one long block south is the splendid **Plaza Grande,** surrounded by colonial-era buildings. It's a vast tree-shaded expanse of roughly kept lawns; in the center is an elaborate stone fountain with a large figure of beloved Vasco de Quiroga, "Tata Vasco," in a benevolent posture. On the north side of the plaza is the **Palacio de Huitzimengari,** built by the Spaniards for the Tarascan emperor—one of the few instances in colonial Mexico of respect and equitable treatment for the indigenous people. Local Indian artisans now occupy the slowly deteriorating building.

One of the oldest buildings in Pátzcuaro is the **House of the Giant,** on the east side of Plaza Grande at Portal de Matamoros 40. It was named after the 12-foot-high painted statue that supports one of the arches around the patio. This residence was built in 1663 by a Spanish count and represents the colonial taste of that period—carved stone panels, thick columns, and open courtyards.

The **basílica,** east of the small plaza on top of a small hill, was built in the 16th century at the prompting of Bishop Don Vasco and designated a basílica by papal decree in 1907. It opened in 1554, but Don Vasco died before it was completed. Now reconstructed, it has been through many catastrophes from earthquakes to the civil war of the mid-19th century. Be sure to go to the main altar to see the Virgin, which is made of "corn-stalk pulp and a mucilage obtained from a prized orchid of the region." She is a very sacred figure to the Indians of this area, and on the eighth day of each month they come from the villages to pay homage to her, particularly for her miraculous healing power.

Two blocks to the south of the basílica is the **Museum of Popular and Regional Arts** (☎ 434/2-1029). It's yet another beautiful colonial building (1540), originally Don Vasco's College of San Nicolás. The rooms, filled with fine examples of regional crafts and costumes, are located off the central courtyard. The museum is open Tuesday through Saturday from 9am to 7pm and Sunday from 9am to 3pm. Admission is $4; free on Sunday.

Of the many old churches in Pátzcuaro, one of the most interesting is the **Temple of the Compañía de Jesús,** just south of the museum. This church was Don Vasco's cathedral before the basílica and afterward was given to the Jesuits. The buildings across the street from the church were once part of the complex, containing the hospital, soup kitchen, and living quarters for religious scholars.

The **House of the Eleven Patios,** located between José María Cos and Enseñanza, is one of the most outstanding architectural achievements of the colonial period. Formerly a convent of the Catherine nuns, today it houses the Casa de las Artesanías de Michoacán, with every type of local artistry for sale. (See "Shopping," below.)

SHOPPING

Pátzcuaro is one of Mexico's best shopping towns because of the textiles, copper, wood carving, lacquer work, and straw weavings made in the region. Most shops are on the Plaza Grande and the streets leading from it to the Plaza Chica, the place of choice for copper vendors. There are also a couple of shops on the street facing the basílica. In addition to the shops in Pátzcuaro, nearby Tzintzuntzán, Ihuatzio,

Cuanaja, Tupátaro, and Santa Clara del Cobre are must-stops for shoppers (see "Side Trips from Pátzcuaro," below).

✪ Casa de las Artesanías de Michoacán/House of the Eleven Patios. Calle Lerin between José Cos and Enseñanza. No phone.

Housed in a former convent (see "A Stroll Around Town," above), this is the best one-stop shopping in the village. Much of what's produced in the region is for sale here—textile arts, pottery and ceramic dishes, lacquerwork, paintings, wood carvings, jewelry, copperwork, and musical instruments, including the famous Paracho guitars. Most of the shops are open daily from 9am to 2pm and 4 to 7pm.

✪ Comunidad de Santa Cruz. José María Cos 3. No phone.

Berta Servin Barriga is the helpful powerhouse behind this cooperative. Women of the farming community of nearby Santa Cruz, where she lives, send their embroidery work to be sold here. Scenes of village life are embroidered on colorful cloth panels ranging from 3 by 5 inches to 20 by 40 inches, plus tablecloths and clothing. Ask Berta or her daughter Esther to explain the events in each festive scene. The delightful panels are fabulous framed or as pillows. There's no sign, but it's next to Mantas Típicas (see below), near the corner of Lerin. The shop is open Monday through Friday from 10am to 8pm and Saturday and Sunday from 10am to 5pm.

Diseño Artesania. José Cos 1. No phone.

Owner Esperanza Sepulveda designs one-of-a-kind clothing using locally made fabrics. It's on the west side of the Plaza Grande and open daily from 10am to 3pm and 4:30 to 8pm.

✪ Friday Pottery Market. Plaza San Francisco, Ponce de León at Federico Tena. No phone.

Early each Friday morning this plaza, one block west of the Plaza Grande, fills with sellers of various styles of regionally made pottery, most of it not for sale in Pátzcuaro on other days. This is a market for the locals, and few tourists seem to know about it. Prices are incredibly cheap.

Galería del Arcangel. Corner of Enseñaza and Vasco de Quiroga. ☎ and fax **434/2-0172.**

Catercorner from the basílica and a block east of the Plaza Grande, this store offers a fine collection of quality regional pottery and hand-carved furniture, plus some of the best crafts from other parts of Mexico. It's open daily from 10am to 7pm.

✪ Galería de Arte Iturbe. Portal Morelos 59. ☎ **434/2-0368.**

If you are an art afficionado, this powerful collection of works by Michoacán artists will impress you. There's also a small selection of folk art from Ocumichu and Michoacán and books on Mexican art. Enter either through the Hotel Iturbe (go all the way to the back) or on Ahumada off the Plaza Grande. The gallery is open daily from 10am to 8pm.

Herrajes Artísticos. José Cos 36. ☎ **434/2-0674.**

Beautiful "drawn-work" (fabric threads pulled apart to make elaborate designs) is a diminishing art in the region. This store still carries some of the best-made drawn-work, including elegant jackets and tableware. The shop is on the west side of the Plaza Grande and is open Monday through Saturday from 10am to 8pm and Sunday from 10am to 6pm.

Mantas Típicas. José Cos 5. ☎ **434/2-1324.** Fax 434/2-0522.

A factory outlet for the company's textile mill, this is one of several textile outlets on the Plaza Grande. Shelves are laden with colorful foot-loomed tablecloths, napkins, bedspreads, and bolts of fabric. It's at the corner of Lerin. Open daily from 9am to 7pm.

Market Plaza. West of Plaza Chica.

The House of the Eleven Patios (above) should be your first stop, and this should be your second. The entire plaza fronting the food market is filled with covered stalls selling crafts, clothing, rugs, rebozos, and more. Locally knitted sweaters are a good buy. Streets surrounding the plaza churn with exuberant sellers of fresh vegetables and caged birds.

WHERE TO STAY
DOUBLES FOR LESS THAN $20

Hotel Valmen. Av. Lloreda 34, 61600 Pátzcuaro, Mich. ☎ **434/2-1161.** 16 rms (all with bath). $6 single; $12 double.

You'll find an attractively tiled entryway and small courtyard in this old-fashioned three-story hotel. On the second floor is a sunny, glassed-in patio, and the entire building is decorated with pretty brown, turquoise, and gold tile. Accommodations are basic but comfortable; the clean rooms are arranged around a lovely glass-roofed courtyard. It's an excellent budget choice, though the lime-green and yellow walls could use cleaning or painting, it may be a bit noisy on the busy corner, and the front doors are locked tight at 10pm. To get here from Plaza Grande, walk two blocks north on Ahumada; the hotel is on the left, on the corner of Libertad.

✪ **Posada de la Salud.** Serrato 9, 61600 Pátzcuaro, Mich. ☎ **434/2-0058.** 15 rms (all with bath). $10 single; $15 double. Street parking available.

This posada offers two tiers of exceptionally quiet rooms built around an attractive courtyard. All rooms have beautiful beds with carved wooden headboards and matching desks. Two rooms have fireplaces. To get here from the Plaza Grande, walk one block east on P. Allende/V. De Quiroga and turn left on Arciga; walk a block and turn right onto Serrato (not marked, but on the right side of the basílica). The hotel is a long half-block up on the right.

DOUBLES FOR LESS THAN $30

Hotel Los Escudos. Portal Hidalgo 73, 61600 Pátzcuaro, Mich. ☎ **434/2-0138** or 434/2-1290. Fax 434/2-0207. 30 rms (all with bath). TV. $23 single; $29 double. Parking $2.

The rooms in this handsome colonial-style hotel on the west side of Plaza Grande are decorated with lush red or blue carpeting, red drapes, lace curtains, and scenes of an earlier Pátzcuaro painted on the walls. Some of the rooms have fireplaces, while others have private balconies overlooking the plaza. There's an excellent restaurant off the lobby.

✪ **Hotel Fiesta Plaza.** Plaza Bocanegra 24, 61600 Pátzcuaro, Mich. ☎ **434/2-2515** or 2-2516. Fax 434/2-2515. 60 rms (all with bath). TV TEL. $24 single; $27 double. Free parking.

When you enter the Fiesta Plaza's inviting courtyard, you're surrounded by three tiers of rooms (no elevator) with richly lustrous pine columns and wrought-iron banisters. The comfortable rooms have pine furniture, small tile baths, and carpets. Each has windows opening onto covered walkways, which are furnished with tables and chairs. A restaurant/bar is on the open patio as you enter. It faces the north side of the Plaza Chica/Bocanegra at the corner of Libertad/Pade Lloreda.

✪ **Hotel Posada de la Basílica.** Arciga 6, 61600 Pátzcuaro, Mich. ☎ **434/2-1108.** 11 rms (all with bath). TV. $17 single; $20 double. Children under 12 stay free in parents' room. Free enclosed parking.

A mansion-turned-hotel, this appealing colonial-style inn across from the basílica is built around a lovely patio. The sunny rooms have wonderful views, red curtains, heavy Spanish-style furniture, and little brick fireplaces. The hotel's restaurant, whose tables are decorated with regional pottery, is open for breakfast and lunch. Service is slow, but there's a fabulous view of the village while you wait. The hotel is opposite the basílica, at the corner of Arciga and La Paz.

Posada San Rafael. Plaza Grande, 61600 Pátzcuaro, Mich. ☎ **434/2-0770** or 434/2-0779. 103 rms (all with bath). $20–$25 single; $23–$30 double. Free parking in courtyard.

This comfortable, colonial-style inn on the south side of Plaza Grande has rooms that open onto a sunny central courtyard filled with lush potted plants and a fountain. Rooms are small and traditionally furnished; some are carpeted. The higher price in each category is for remodeled rooms, but the difference in room quality is not worth the extra price. Note that the rooms can be quite cold in winter, and desk clerks have been known to be stingy with blankets. The second-story restaurant is open daily from 8am to 9pm.

DOUBLES FOR LESS THAN $45

✪ **Hotel Mansión Iturbe Bed and Breakfast.** Portal Morelos 59, 61600 Pátzcuaro, Mich. ☎ **434/2-0368**. 15 rms (all with bath). $30 single; $40 double; $52 suite. All rates include breakfast. Free parking.

Located on the north side of the Plaza Grande, this 17th-century building was formerly a combination home (upstairs), commercial outlet (first floor), and stable (in back) for muleteers traversing Mexico's mountains with trade goods. Today the ground floor (where the shops once were) holds Doña Paca, the hotel's excellent restaurant (see "Where to Eat," below), and the Viejo Gaucho (see "Pátzcuaro After Dark," below), the local venue for evening music, is located in the stable area. The hotel also houses the fine Galería de Arte Iturbe, featuring Michoacán artists. Music from Viejo Gaucho can't be heard in the front guestrooms. Rooms are on the second floor and have original plank flooring; heavy, dark Spanish-style wooden furniture; deep-red drapes; and plaid bedspreads.

Bathrooms are large, and hot water is slow to come but plenty hot when it finally arrives. Though there are bedside lights, lighting in general in this hotel is on the dim side. Rates include a welcome drink, full breakfast with delicious cappuccino or coffee, two hours' use of a bicycle, and a free daily paper; in addition, the fourth night is free. Instant coffee and hot water are in the lobby early in the morning before the restaurant opens. This deal is hard to beat in Pátzcuaro.

WHERE TO EAT

Restaurants open late and close early in Pátzcuaro, so don't plan on hot coffee if you're up to catch the early-morning train and plan ahead for late-evening hunger pangs. For inexpensive food, try the tamal and atole vendors in front of the basílica. Even more prolific are the pushcart taco stands that line up near Plaza Chica and the market in the mornings to sell tacos containing meat from different parts of the cow (don't ask which parts; they simply taste good); there are also steamy cups of atole, hot *corrundas* (little triangular-shaped tamales with hot sauce and cream), and huge tamales sold by housewives. Breakfast will cost $1 or less here.

In the afternoons, different vendors show up to sell other parts of the cow. In the evenings, Plaza Chica is filled with small sidewalk restaurants selling another specialty—Pátzcuaro chicken with enchiladas (tortillas with sauce) and heaps of fried potatoes and carrots. Buñelos come dripping with honey. Café Botafumeiro, a

coffee shop on the southwest corner of Plaza Grande, dispenses a variety of excellent Uruapan coffees by the cup or kilo and chocolate steaming hot in cups or cakes of it packaged by the kilo.

🟢 **El Patio.** Plaza Grande 19. ☎ **434/2-0484**. Breakfast $2.50–$5; main courses $4.50–$8; comida corrida $4.50–$5. Daily 8am–8pm (comida corrida served 1:30–4pm). MEXICAN.

Wood-beamed ceilings, charming chandeliers woven in basketry, and paintings of local scenes make this a very pleasant restaurant. Be sure to notice the unusual bar made of bottles and a gun embedded in the stucco. El Patio, on the south side of Plaza Grande, offers delicious, inexpensive meals. Hot bread and butter are served with dishes like carne asada. The three-course comida corrida is delicious and plentiful.

🟢 **Restaurant Doña Paca.** Hotel Iturbe, Portal Morelos 59. ☎ **434/2-0366**. Main courses $3–$6. Daily 8am–9pm. MEXICAN REGIONAL.

This is one of the best places for regional Michoacán cuisine. Warmly inviting, with leather equipale chairs, beamed ceilings, French doors facing the portales and Plaza Grande, and photos of old Pátzcuaro decorating the walls, it's a good place to linger. Try the corrundas or the trout served al gusto (as you like it) with a choice of cilantro (marvelous), garlic, or other herbs. This is one of the few places featuring churipo, a regional beef and vegetable stew served with corrundas. For a tasty encore try a buñelo topped with delicious coconut yogurt. Margarita Arriaga, the English-speaking owner, prides herself on the coffee she serves—and with good reason. The cappuccino is the best in Mexico. The wonderful hot chocolate comes in a big cup frothed to a puffy frenzy. The food is spectacular, but the service is slow—don't expect to dine in a hurry.

NEARBY DINING

The traditional place to dine on whitefish is at one of the many restaurants lining the road to the lake. For an economical meal, wander down to the little open-air restaurants on the wharf (embarcadero), where señoras fry up the delicious fish while you watch. Fish, garnishes, and a soft drink cost $7 to $10. The restaurants are open daily from 8am to 6pm. Morelia.

🟢 **Camino Real.** Carretera Patz-Tzurumutaro. No phone. Main courses $4–$9; comida corrida $4. Daily 7am–midnight. MEXICAN.

Locals claim that this hard-to-find restaurant serves the best food in town. Its eggs with chilaquiles or potatoes will keep you going for hours. The chicken and fish dishes are also delicious, and the comida corrida is a three-course feast. Service is good even when the restaurant is full. Camino Real is about a mile outside of town on the road to Morelia (Highway 14), shortly before the turnoff to Tzintzuntzán-Quiroga and beside the Pemex station.

Restaurant las Redes. Av. Lázaro Cárdenas 6. ☎ **434/2-1275**. Main courses $3–$7; comida corrida $4.50–$5. Daily 9am–8pm (comida corrida served 1–8pm). Bus: On the road to the wharf. MEXICAN.

Local residents gather at this rustic restaurant on the road to the wharf for the comida corrida, which comes with soup, rice, fish or meat, frijoles, and coffee. The restaurant is famous for its pescado blanco (whitefish).

PÁTZCUARO AFTER DARK

Generally speaking, Pátzcuaro closes down before 10pm, so bring a good book or plan to rest up for the remainder of your travels.

The Dance of the Little Old Men

The **Danza de los Viejitos** is an ancient mask dance created by the Tarascans to ridicule the Spaniards during the Conquest. Dancers in traditional regional costume, including comical pink masks with hooked noses and big red smiles, perform a skillful dance. Clacking on the floor with wooden sandals, they are bent over all the while like old men hobbling on wooden canes—but, oh, do their feet fly! The dance is still performed each Saturday night at 8pm at the reasonably priced Restaurant Los Escudos in the patio of the Hotel Los Escudos on the Plaza Grande (see "Where to Stay," above).

The dance is also performed every Wednesday and Saturday at 9pm in the restaurant of the Hotel Posada de Don Vasco, on Avenida de Lázaro Cárdenas going toward the lake. A full dinner costs around $12, but you can dine for much less. After the dancers, an eight-piece mariachi group performs. You can reserve a table if you wish on the day of the performance. There's no admission charge for people dining during the performance in either place.

Late-night music lovers flock to the Viejo Gaucho for performances that include Mexican trios, Peruvian music, and jazz. The small restaurant serves empanadas, steaks, hamburgers, beer, and mixed drinks. It's in the Hotel Iturbe, Portal Morelos 59 (☎ **434/2-0366**), but the entry is on Ahumada. It's open Thursday through Sunday from 6pm to 2am. Music starts between 8:30 and 9pm. After the music starts there's a cover charge of $2.50–$5.

SIDE TRIPS FROM PÁTZCUARO
BY BOAT TO THE ISLAND VILLAGE OF JANITZIO

No visit to Pátzcuaro is complete without a trip on the lake, preferably across to the isolated island village of Janitzio, dominated by a hilltop statue of José María Morelos. The village church is famous for the annual ceremony on the Day of the Dead, held at midnight on November 1, when villagers climb to the churchyard carrying lighted candles in memory of their dead relatives and then spend the night in graveside vigil. The celebration begins October 30 and lasts through November 2.

The most economical way to get to Janitzio is by colectivo launch, which makes the trip when enough people have gathered to go—about every 20 to 30 minutes from about 7:30am to 6pm. Round-trip fare is $2 for those five years and older; a private boat costs $33 round trip; a trip to three islands costs $35. The ticket office (☎ **434/2-0681**) is open daily from 7am to 5pm.

At the ticket office on the pier (*embarcadero*), a map of the lake posted on the wall shows all the boat trips possible around the lake to various islands and lakeshore towns. Launches will take you wherever you want to go. Though prices are high (see above), up to 20 people can split the cost.

EL ESTRIBO: A SCENIC OVERLOOK

For a good view of the town and the lake, head for the **lookout** at El Estribo, 2 miles from town on the hill to the west. Driving from the main square on Calle Ponce de León, following the signs, will take you 10 to 15 minutes. Walking will take you about 45 minutes since it's up a continuously steep hill. Once you reach the gazebo, you can climb the more than 400 steps to the very summit of the hill for a bird's-eye view. The gazebo area is great for a picnic; there are barbecue pits and sometimes a couple selling soft drinks and beer.

TZINTZUNTZÁN: TARASCAN RUINS, STRAW HANDCRAFTS, CERAMICS & WOVEN GOODS

Tzintzuntzán is an ancient village 10 miles from Pátzcuaro on the road to Quiroga (see "Getting There & Departing: By Bus," above). In earlier centuries, Tzintzuntzán was the capital of a Tarascan empire that controlled over a hundred other towns and villages. On a hill on the right before you enter town, pyramids upon pyramids still remind visitors of the glorious (and bloody) past. Today the village is known for its straw handcrafts—mobiles, baskets, and figures (skeletons, airplanes, reindeer, turkeys, and the like)—as well as for its pottery and woven goods. The old market is now housed in a neocolonial building. Across from the **basket market** are several open-air wood-carving workshops full of photogenic life-size wooden saints and other figures. There is a footpath along the shore of Lake Pátzcuaro.

During the week of February 1, the whole village honors **Nuestro Señor del Rescate** (Our Lord of the Rescue) with religious processions. The village also takes part in Holy Week celebrations.

SANTA CLARA DEL COBRE: COPPER CRAFTS

Although the copper mines that existed here during pre-Conquest times have been lost forever, local artisans still make copper vessels using the age-old method by which each piece is pounded out by hand. The streets are lined with shops, and little boys pounce on every visitor to direct them to stores (where they get a commission). The **Museo del Cobre** (Copper Museum), half a block from the main plaza, at Morelos and Pino Suárez, is a fine introduction to the quality and styles of local work. A sales showroom to the left as you enter features the work of 77 local craftsmen. There's no admission; the museum is open daily from 10am to 3pm and 5 to 7pm.

The **National Copper Fair** is held here each August, which coincides on August 12 with the **Festival of Our Lady of Santa Clara de Asis,** and on August 15 with the **Festival of the Virgin of the Sacred Patroness,** with folk dancing and parades.

To get here from Pátzcuaro, take a bus from the Cental Camionera (see "Getting There & Departing: By Bus," above). Buses back to Pátzcuaro run approximately every few minutes (or more) from the plaza. Cabs crammed full of people head back to Pátzcuaro for the same price as the bus.

During Easter Week and Day of the Dead, when Pátzcuaro's hotels fill up, it may be useful to know of two inexpensive hotels that face Santa Clara's main plaza: The **Hotel Oasis,** Portal Allende 144 (☎ 434/3-0040), the better of the two; and **Hotel Real del Cobre,** Portal Hidalgo 19 (☎ 343/3-0205), which has a restaurant.

TOCUARO & ERONGARICARO: MASKS & ONE-OF-A-KIND FURNITURE

Tocuaro, a village of mask carvers, and Erongaricaro, noted for its colonial center and furniture factory, are both easy jaunts from Pátzcuaro. Both are on the same road skirting the lake.

To find Tocuaro, walk the equivalent of three or four blocks from the highway where the bus lets you off. As you stroll the streets, villagers will ask you if you're interested in masks and invite you to their homes. When you want to return, go back to the highway and flag down a bus.

A few miles farther is Erongaricaro, formerly known for its textiles. Today its most famous factory, **Muebles Finos Artesanales Erongarícaro** [MFA/ERONGA] (☎ and fax **434/4-0017**), is the creator of whimsical folk-art-style furniture, some of which is copied by regional furniture makers. There's nothing quite like the fine furniture here, decorated with the likeness of Frida Kahlo, plump Botero-inspired figures, and forms that recall Gauguin or Picasso, among others. Their fine furniture designs are featured in the luxury Casa Que Canta hotel in the Pacific Coast village of Zihuatanejo, among other upscale places in Mexico and the States. Each piece is unique and expensive. This is a working factory and there's no showroom, so the owners, Maureen and Steve Rosenthal, kindly ask that only serious buyers arrive for a look around. The factory is open Monday through Friday from 9am to 2pm and 4 to 6pm. Their wholesale warehouse in Tucson, Arizona (☎ **602/798-1086**) has a catalog.

TUPÁTARO & CUANAJO: A HISTORIC CHURCH & HAND-CARVED FURNITURE

The turnoff into these two colonial-era villages is about 20 miles northwest of Pátzcuaro off Highway 120 going to Morelia (see "Getting There & Departing," above).

The narrow paved road passes first through tiny Tupátaro (pop. 600), which in Tarascan means "place of tule" (tule is a reed of Chuspata). Just opposite the small main plaza is the Templo del Señor Santiago Tupátaro, unique in Mexico for its 18th-century painted ceiling. Restored in 1994 under a civilian program, it's still a parish church but is overseen by the Institute of Anthropology and History. The church was built in 1775 after the miraculous discovery of a crucifix formed in a pine tree. Indian artists, whose names are unknown today, brilliantly painted the entire wood-plank ceiling with scenes of the life and death of Christ and Mary. The magnificent gilt retablo, still intact, behind the altar features Solomonic columns and paintings. In the center of the retablo is Santiago (St. James), above which appears the face of the Eternal Father; above all is the sign of the dove.

When visitors arrive at the church, electric lights are turned on to illuminate the fabulous colors. There's no admission charge and no photos are permitted. The church is open daily from 8am to 8pm. Days of religious significance here include the Tuesday of Carnaval week and July 25, which honors Santiago (St. James). Across the plaza a small café serves soft drinks and snacks and sells regional crafts.

Five miles farther is Cuanajo (pop. 8,000), a village devoted to hand-carved pine furniture and weaving. On the road as you enter and around the pleasant, tree-shaded main plaza, you'll see storefronts with colorful furniture inside and on the street. Parrots, plants, the sun, moon, and faces are among the myriad subjects carved into furniture, which is then painted with a fabulous combination of colors. Furniture is also sold at a cooperative on the main plaza. Here too you'll find softspoken women who weave exquisite tapestries and thin belts on waist looms. Motifs in their handsome tapestries include birds, people, and plants. Everything is for sale. It's open daily from 9am to 6pm.

Festival days in Cuanajo include March 8 and September 8, both of which honor the patron saint Virgin María de la Natividad. These are solemn occasions when neighboring villages make processions carrying figures of the holy virgin.

IHUATZIO: TULE FIGURES & PRE-HISPANIC ARCHITECTURE

This little lakeside village is noted for its weavers of tule figures—fanciful animals such as elephants, pigs, and bulls made from a reed that grows on the edge of the lake— and for a rather spread-out group of pre-Hispanic buildings. The turnoff to Ihuatzio is on a paved road a short distance from the outskirts of Pátzcuaro on the road to Tzintzuntzán (see "Getting There & Departing: By Bus," above).

ZIRAHUÉN: A PRISTINE LAKE

To see one of the few lakes in Mexico that remains more or less in its natural state, visit Zirahuén, about 7½ miles west of Pátzcuaro on the road to Uruapan. Since there are no regular buses, it's difficult to get to Zirahuén without a car. A taxi costs about $12 one way. Lakeside restaurants serve fish (inspect fish carefully for cleanliness by look and by smell).

URUAPAN: CRAFTS, A VISIT TO A VOLCANO & OTHER SIDE TRIPS

Uruapan, Michoacán, 38 miles west of Pátzcuaro and an hour away, has long been known for its lacquered boxes and trays. Although this city of 217,000 people has few tourist attractions of its own, it makes a good base for several interesting side trips, the most famous of which is to the Paricutín volcano and the lava-covered church and village near Angahuán. If you leave Pátzcuaro early and change buses in Uruapan for Angahuán, you can see Uruapan and Angahuán in a day. Otherwise you may wish to spend the night in Uruapan and start for Angahuán early the next day.

ESSENTIALS   The tourist office (☎ 542/3-6172), is in the shopping area below the Hotel Plaza, just off the main plaza. It's open Monday through Saturday from 9am to 2pm and 4 to 7pm.

The main plaza, **Jardín Morelos,** is actually a very long rectangle running east to west, with the churches and La Huatapera Museum on the north side and the Hotel Victoria on the south. Everything you need is within a block or two of the square, including the market, which is behind the churches.

Uruapan's main square is 20 blocks from the bus station. Minivans labeled "Centro" and "Central" (central bus station) circulate from the street in front of the bus station to the south side of the main plaza all day.

Be prepared for cold mornings and evenings from October through April; bring a heavy sweater and gloves. Few hotels have heat.

WHERE TO STAY & EAT   If you want to spend the night in Uruapan, consider the inexpensive but neat **Hotel Villa de Flores,** Emiliano Carranza 15 (☎ 452/4-2800), and the slightly more expensive **Nuevo Hotel Alameda,** Av. 5 de Febrero 11 (**452/3-3635**), both of which are by the main plaza. The best hotel in downtown and also by the plaza is the **Hotel Plaza Uruapan,** Ocampo 64 (☎ 452/3-3980). All three have restaurants, and there are numerous good restaurants on or near the plaza.

EXPLORING URUAPAN   Uruapan's main plaza fills with craftspeople from around the state during the week before and after the **Day of the Dead** (November 1 and 2) and before and during **Easter week.** It's an unbelievable array of wares, all neatly displayed.

The **antojitos market,** opposite the monument in the middle of the main square, has copper, crosspoint blouses and tablecloths, hats, huaraches, caged birds, fresh vegetables, and lots of cookshops.

La Huatapera, attached to the cathedral on the main square, is a fabulous museum of regional crafts. It is housed in a former hospital built in 1533 by Fray Juan de San Miguel, a Franciscan. It's open Tuesday through Sunday from 9:30am to 1:30pm and 3:30 to 6pm. Admission is free.

For the finest in foot-loomed tablecloths, napkins, and other beautifully made textiles, take a taxi to **Tellares Uruapan** (☎ 452/4-0677 or 452/4-6135), in the Antigua Fabrica de San Pedro. Call in advance, and the English-speaking owners may give you a tour of the factory, which contains fascinating turn-of-the-century machinery.

When you enter the **Parque Nacional Eduardo Ruíz,** a botanical garden eight blocks west of the main plaza, you'll feel like you're deep in the tropics. This multi-acre semitropical paradise includes jungle paths, deep ravines, rushing water, and clear

Uruapan

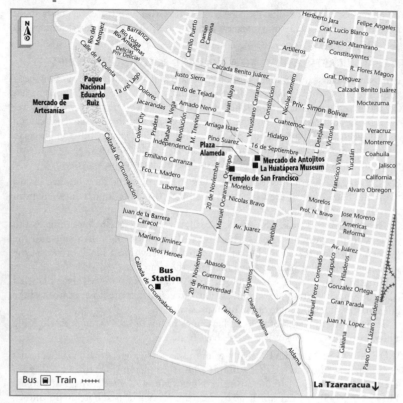

N

Barranca
Río Volga
Río Amazonas
Delicias
Priv Delicias

Heriberto Jara   Felipe Angeles
Gral. Lucio Blanco
Gral. Ignacio Altamirano
Artilleros   Constituyentes

Río del Marquez
Calle de la Quinta

Carrillo Puerto
Damian Carmona

Calzada Benito Juárez

R. Flores Magon
Gral. Dieguez

Calzada Benito Juárez

Moctezuma

Paque Nacional Eduardo Ruiz

Mercado de Artesanías

1a del Lago
Dolores
Jacarandas
Colver City
Pradera
Rafael M. Vega
Revolución
Independencia
Emiliano Carranza
Fco. I. Madero
Libertad

Justo Sierra
Lerdo de Tejada
Amado Nervo

Juan Aldya

Venustiano Carranza

Nicolas Romero

Constitución

Priv. Simon Bolivar

Veracruz
Monterrey
Coahuila
Jalisco
California
Alvaro Obregon

Calzada de Circunvalación

Arriaga Isaac
Pino Suarez
M. Trevino

Plaza Alameda

Cuauhtemoc
Hidalgo

16 de Septiembre

■ Mercado de Antojitos
■ La Huatápera Museum

L Detejada
Victoria

Francisco Villa
Yucatán

■ Templo de San Francisco
Morelos
Nicolas Bravo

Morelos

Prol. N. Bravo
Jose Moreno
Americas
Reforma

20 de Noviembre
Manuel Ocaranza Ocampo

Av. Juarez

Pueblita

Av. Juárez
Acapulco
Hiladeros

Juan de la Barrera
Caracol
Mariano Jiminez
Niños Heroes

Calzada de Circunvalación

■ Bus Station

20 de Noviembre

Abasolo
Guerrero
Primoverdad

Triguetos

Diagonal Aldama

Tamucua

Aldama

Manuel Perez Coronado

Gonzalez Ortega
Gran Parada
Juan N. Lopez

Galeana

Paseo Gra. Lázaro Cárdenas

Bus 🚌 Train ├──┤

La Tzararacua ↓

waterfalls. Children pester visitors, offering to be their guides, but you'll enjoy touring more with only a map (25¢). The garden is open daily from 8am to 6pm, and there is a small admission fee. Buses marked "Parque" leave from in front of the telegraph office on the main square and stop at the park.

OUTSIDE URUAPAN   A Waterfall   A bus marked "Tzaráracua" goes to the impressive **Waterfall at Tzaráracua,** 6 miles from the main plaza. The Río Cupatitzio originates as a bubbling spring in the national park and then forms a cascade on its way to the Pacific. A trip to Tzaráracua and to the national park can be made in a day, even in an afternoon. The falls are reached down a steep pathway.

Handmade Guitars   Often called Mexico's "Guitar Capital" for its fine handmade guitars, **Paracho** is a 30-minute bus ride from Uruapan's Central Camionera. Take the Flecha Amarilla or Servicios Coordinados lines.

Angahuán & Paricutín Volcano   Twenty-one miles away from Uruapan, Angahuán is the village from which to launch trips to **Paricutín Volcano,** which began an extended eruption in 1943 that would eventually cover portions of this village under lava. Autotransportes Galeana buses leave every 30 minutes from Uruapan's Central Camionera for the hour-long trip.

If you don't know the story of how Paricutín appeared, stop by the plaza in Angahuán and take a look at the carved wooden door of a nearby house that faces the church, around the stone fence to the right, two doors down. The story of the volcano, carved in pictures and words, shows how a local man was plowing his cornfield in the valley on February 20, 1943, when at 3pm, the ground began to boil. At first he tried to stop it up; when that proved impossible, he decided to run. By that evening, rocks, smoke, and fire were flying up out of the ground. Some villagers fled that same night; others days later. The volcano was active for nine years, growing larger and larger, until finally it breathed its last breath on March 6, 1952, stopping as suddenly as it had begun.

On arrival in Angahuán, tourists are besieged by guides ready to take them on horseback to see the half-buried **Church of San Juan Parangaricutiro,** looming silently up out of the lava, and to the crater of the volcano. Though a horse is not necessary, a guide is advisable.

The road to the volcano—not at all obvious (or marked) in the village—is a few blocks to the left of the plaza, with the church to the right. About half a mile down the road from Angahuán toward old San Juan and the lava flow is a state-run lodge/restaurant with bathrooms (the only ones in the area) and a stone patio with a good view of the church and volcanic cone. Unless there's an abundance of hikers or riders headed for the church, orient yourself here; once you're down in the woods, the church is not visible and there is a maze of unmarked trails in every direction. The walk to the church takes about an hour or so. There you can climb over the lava to the bell tower and see the mighty gray volcano in the distance.

Those who want to climb the volcano should allow at least eight hours from Angahuán. The round-trip is about 14 miles. Take plenty of food and water because there's none along the way. The hike is mostly flat, with some steeper rises toward the end. Climbing the steep crater itself takes only about 40 minutes for those who exercise regularly, but count on more time to walk around the crater's rim on top ($1^1/_4$ to 2 miles) to enjoy the spectacular view.

By horse, the trip to the church and volcano takes about six or seven hours and costs $20 to $30, plus tip. The asking price for a horse to the volcano is $15 to $20 per horse—and you must also pay that amount for the guide's horse. It's possible to bargain the price down to a total of $25 (for two horses and a guide). However, don't be surprised when, a few kilometers into the ride, the guide asks for a tip to be paid at the end of the trip. My guide climbed to the top of the crater with me; pointed out various interesting features, including steaming fumeroles; and provided riding instructions and a good history of the area. Acting as a guide to the volcano is one of the few opportunities to earn money for the obviously poor Angahuán villagers. Just don't pay until the ride is over and the services were delivered as promised.

Plan to spend an entire day for the trip from Uruapan, the ride to the foot of the volcano, the short climb, the return to Angahuán, and the trip back to Uruapan.

14 The Southernmost States: Oaxaca, Chiapas & Tabasco

These three neighboring Mexican states span the distance from the Gulf of Mexico to the Pacific Ocean. **Oaxaca** is one of the country's poorest states but is richly endowed with tradition and culture. Its handsome colonial-era capital city (likewise called Oaxaca) and the vast archaeological sites, vibrant Indian cultures, and market villages that surround it have drawn increasing numbers of tourists over the last 10 or so years. (Oaxaca's two laid-back beach towns, Puerto Escondido and Puerto Angel, are a day's drive from the capital; see chapter 7 for information.) **Tabasco** and its burgeoning Gulf Coast oil cities are for most tourists little more than a way station near Palenque and between the main body of Mexico and the Yucatán Peninsula. In the Maya ruins of Palenque, the old city of San Cristóbal de las Casas, and the fascinating patchwork of living Maya villages around San Cristóbal, **Chiapas** offers some of the richest and strongest cultural flavor in all Mexico. (And Chiapan coffee is among Mexico's best, too.)

All three states have a strong indigenous character, evident even now in the everyday clothing, customs, festivals, and holiday costume of their peoples. The famous Olmec site, La Venta, is in Tabasco state; museums in Villahermosa, the capital, hold Olmec sculpture and artifacts. Numerous Indian groups in the state still speak Maya-related languages. In Chiapas, each of the indigenous villages around San Cristóbal de las Casas has unique language, cultural, and craft traditions. And Oaxaca city is sandwiched between Mitla and Monte Albán, two important archaeological sites; several lesser but still fascinating sites are nearby.

EXPLORING OAXACA, CHIAPAS & TABASCO

Many people who travel to this southernmost part of Mexico want to hit the highlights of all three states in one visit. Improved airline and bus service makes doing so easier than ever before. Some people arrive by bus or air in Villahermosa and continue inland by bus to Palenque and San Cristóbal, then on to Tuxtla Gutiérrez, flying from Tuxtla to Oaxaca. Others take the opposite approach, beginning at Oaxaca, flying to Tuxtla Gutiérrez, and from there traveling by bus to San Cristóbal, Palenque, and Villahermosa. This works well if you'll be moving on to the Yucatán Peninsula.

Oaxaca city can be so engrossing that five days won't be nearly enough, particularly if you go during Christmas or the Days of the

Dead. Try to plan on no less than four days there, allowing at least two days for seeing the ruins, at least a day in the city itself, and a day at craft villages and markets.

Palenque and San Cristóbal de las Casas are the two stellar attractions in the Tabasco-Chiapas area. You might budget your time in the following manner: Spend one day in Villahermosa and no less than a day (two nights) at Palenque. You'll want at least two days amid San Cristóbal's captivating culture and another two days to visit the outlying villages—try to spend at least four days there.

1 Oaxaca City

325 miles SE of Mexico City, 144 miles SE of Tehuacán, 168 miles NE of Puerto Escondido

Set in a 5,070-foot-high valley amid rugged mountains, Oaxaca has become the destination of choice for travelers seeking colonial surroundings, archaeological sites, and very creative indigenous crafts (particularly wood carvings, handwoven textiles, and pottery). It's a beautiful city, with many fine homes and shops; the purple blooms of jacaranda trees are everywhere, a contrast against the cobalt sky. The museums display gold and jade antiquities; the galleries exhibit the fine work of local artists; and the mountains and valleys of the surrounding countryside are a photographer's dream. American and European expatriates have fostered something of a bohemian subculture, and Zapotecs and Mixtecs live much as their ancestors did long ago.

Most visitors to Oaxaca (Wah-HAH-kah) leave still unaware that the city is a booming commercial and industrial center. Prosperity has given the city a cosmopolitan touch, and the outskirts of town have a definite industrial air; but Oaxaca's 800,000 residents, who call themselves Oaxaqueños (Wah-HAH-kehn-yos), have carefully preserved the colonial beauty of the central city.

The Zapotecs came to this high valley around 800 B.C. and over the centuries built a beautiful city and a flourishing culture at Monte Albán, 6 miles from modern-day Oaxaca city. They weren't the first people to live here: Evidence from White Cave, near Mitla, indicates the presence of primitive inhabitants in the valley as early as 10,000 B.C. Some authorities consider that Olmec influence reached the Oaxaca valley around 1200 B.C. However, it was the Zapotecs who created the city and a high-level culture, building monuments visible at the site today.

After this flowering of Zapotec culture (ca. A.D. 300–700), another tribe, the Mixtecs, built a rival center at Mitla, 36 miles away on the other side of what is today Oaxaca, and the two tribes struggled for control of the valley until they united against a powerful common enemy from the north, the Aztecs. Even together the two tribes were outmatched: In the late 1400s and the early 1500s Aztec influence predominated in the valley.

The local tribes didn't have to worry about the Aztecs for long, however—an even more formidable enemy appeared in 1521. After the Spanish subdued the valley, they set up a military post called Antequera here; six years later the town of Oaxaca was founded. Hernán Cortés was later given the title of Marqués del Valle de Oaxaca by the Hapsburg emperor Charles V, and with the title came grants of land, some of which were controlled by Cortés's descendants until the Mexican Revolution in 1910.

Two of Mexico's presidents, Porfirio Díaz and Benito Juárez, were born near Oaxaca. Nobody does much to remember Díaz these days, but monuments to Juárez are everywhere: statues, murals, streets named for him, even a Benito Juárez University. In fact, the city's official name is Oaxaca de Juárez.

A Zapotec, Juárez was born in the nearby village of Guelatao and "adopted" by a wealthy Oaxacan family who clothed, educated, and taught him Spanish in return for his services as a houseboy. He fell in love with the daughter of the household and promised he would become rich and famous and return to marry her. He managed all three, and Oaxaca adores him for it. Juárez attended law school, was the governor of the state of Oaxaca (1847–1852), and later became a resistance leader and president of the republic. He is a national hero.

ESSENTIALS

GETTING THERE & DEPARTING   By Plane   Mexicana (☎ **951/6-7352,** 951/6-8414, or 951/1-5337 at the airport) has several daily flights to Oaxaca from Mexico City. **Aeroméxico** (☎ **951/6-1066** or 951/1-5055 at the airport) has daily flights to Mexico City. **AeroCaribe** (affiliated with Mexicana, ☎ **951/6-0229,** or 951/6-0266 or 951/1-5247 at the airport) flies once a day to Tuxtla Gutiérrez, Villahermosa, Mérida and Cancún. **Aviacsa** (☎ **951/3-1801**) flies once a day to Tuxtla Gutiérrez. **Aeromorelos** (☎ **951/6-0974,** 951/6-0975, or 951/1-5100 and fax 951/6-1002 at the airport) flies a turboprop between Oaxaca and the Pacific coast resorts of Puerto Escondido and Bahías de Huatulco, at least once daily and more during Christmas, Easter, Days of the Dead, and the Guelaguetza. Aeromorelos flights within the state of Oaxaca can be booked in the United States through Zapotec Tours (☎ **800/444-OAXACA**). **AeroVega** (☎ **951/6-6294** or 951/6-2777) flies a five-passenger twin-engine Aero-Commander from Puerto Escondido and Bahías de Huatulco once daily (twice if there are enough passengers). Arrangements for AeroVega are made at the Monte Alban Hotel facing the Alameda (next to the Zócalo).

Inexpensive transportation from hotels in town to the airport can be arranged by **Transportes Aeropuerto Oaxaca** (☎ **951/4-4350**), located a few doors from the Hotel Monte Albán on the Alameda. They don't accept phone reservations, so drop by Monday through Saturday from 9am to 2pm or 5pm to 8pm to buy your ticket. And since the office is closed on Sunday, buy tickets on Saturday if you plan to leave on Monday. The cost is $2 from downtown hotels and around $4 from outlying hotels. The staff also charges more if you have more than two suitcases and one small carry-on.

By Bus   On long trips to and from Oaxaca, be sure to ask if your potential bus is *con escalas* (with stops), *directo* (with fewer stops), or *sin escalas* (no stops). And if you are traveling between Mexico City and Oaxaca, ask if the bus goes by way of the *autopista* (a six-hour trip) or the federal highway (nine hours). You'll thank yourself if you've packed some water and food for longer trips (especially nonstop trips).

The first-class line **ADO** (☎ **951/5-1703** or 951/5-0903) handles most traffic north and west.

Cristóbal Colón (☎ **951/5-1214**) serves the region south and east of Oaxaca—including Tuxtla Gutiérrez (five a day), San Cristóbal de las Casas (two overnight buses), and Huatulco, Pochutla, and Puerto Escondido on the coast (two a day, stopping at all three towns). The Cristóbal Colón bus takes nine hours to reach Puerto Escondido because it goes by way of Huatulco; for a faster trip see below. Colón also serves the areas north and east of Oaxaca; at least 50 buses a day run to Mexico City's TAPO (East) and Central del Norte (North) stations. Another 10 go to Puebla, and four to Tehuacán; other destinations are Tapachula (one bus a day), Veracruz (three a day), and Villahermosa (two a day).

The deluxe **Linea UNO** (☎ **951/3-3350**) has six nonstop departures daily for Mexico City using the *autopista*; the trip costs $21 one-way. Also deluxe, **ADO GL** buses have five nonstop departures for Mexico City with four going to the TAPO station and one to the Norte station. A seat costs $18. The latter two feature movies, help-yourself free soft drinks, decent leg room, reclining seats, and bathroom.

Oaxaca Area

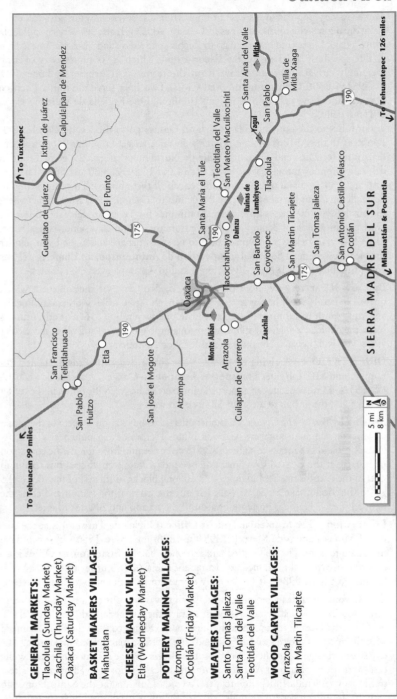

GENERAL MARKETS:
Tlacolula (Sunday Market)
Zaachila (Thursday Market)
Oaxaca (Saturday Market)

BASKET MAKERS VILLAGE:
Miahuatlan

CHEESE MAKING VILLAGE:
Etla (Wednesday Market)

POTTERY MAKING VILLAGES:
Atzompa
Ocotlán (Friday Market)

WEAVERS VILLAGES:
Santo Tomas Jalieza
Santa Ana del Valle
Teotitlán del Valle

WOOD CARVER VILLAGES:
Arrazola
San Martin Tilcajete

These are very popular so it's wise to book your seat several days in advance, especially during heavily touristed times in Oaxaca. ADO GL also has service to Puebla (three a day). Linea Uno buses also go to Puebla (one a day) and Veracruz (one a day).

The speediest buses to **Puerto Escondido**—which is six hours away over an extremely curvaceous road—leave from the terminal at Armenta y López 721 (☎ **951/4-0806**) across from the Red Cross. Two lines serve the route. **Pacifico Oaxaca** buses leave daily at 8:30am and 10:30pm. One **Estrella de Valle** bus leaves at 11pm daily.

For buses to the outlying villages around Oaxaca go to the second-class bus station next to the Abastos Market. **Fletes y Pasajes**, at gate number 9, has frequent departures for Mitla and Tlacolula. **Valle de Norte** buses, at gate 29, go to Teotitlán del Valle Monday through Saturday at 11am, and 12:30, 2, 3:30 and 5pm. They return at 12:30, 2, 5 and 6pm (but double check all these hours). To get to Teotitlán del Valle on a Sunday take a Fletes y Pasaje bus to Tlacolula, and from there (where the bus lets you off) buses leave every 20 minutes for Teotitlán del Valle. Buses for Guelatao (birthplace of Benito Juárez) leave from the second-class station several times daily. Buy your tickets a day in advance to be sure of space and a good seat. Under the breathless name of **Sociedad Cooperativo de Autotransportes Choferes del Sur** you'll find buses to Etla every 40 minutes, and to Atzompa every 30 minutes.

By Car It's an easy five-hour drive from Mexico City, via the toll road, which opened in late 1994. It begins at Cuacnoapalan, about 50 miles southeast of Puebla, and runs south to terminate in Oaxaca; the one-way toll is $16. For adventurous souls, the old federal highway still winds through the mountains and offers spectacular views; you will, however, be on the road for 9 or 10 hours.

ORIENTATION   Arriving by Plane   The airport is south of town, about a 20-minute (and $10) cab ride. **Transportes Aeropuerto Oaxaca,** Alameda de León 1A (☎ **951/4-4350**), operates an airport minibus service between the hotels in the center of town and the airport at a cost of $2–$4 each way.

Arriving by Bus   The Central Camionera first-class bus station is north of the center of town on the main highway (Calzada Niños Héroes de Chapultepec). Taxis between here and the zócalo cost about $2. If you're coming from the Pacific coast, you may arrive at the Central Camionera de Segunda Clase (second-class bus terminal) next to the Abastos market buildings. It's 10 long blocks southwest of the zócalo. To get to the zócalo, take a taxi, or walk left out the front of the station and cross the railroad tracks. Traffic is horrendous around the station and Abastos Market.

Information   The **Municipal Tourist Office** (Oficina de Turismo) is at the corner of Morelos and 5 de Mayo (☎ **951/6-4828;** fax 951/6-1550); it's open daily from 8am to 8pm. The well-staffed and extremely helpful **State Tourist Office** is located across from the Alameda at Independencia 607, (corner of García Vigil; ☎ and fax **951/6-0984**). It's open daily from 9am to 3pm and 6 to 8pm.

City Layout   Oaxaca's central historic section was laid out on a north–south and east–west grid. The cathedral faces west toward the Alameda Park, and the Palacio del Gobierno faces north overlooking the zócalo. Do not confuse the Plaza Alameda with the zócalo. Oaxaca's **zócalo** is one of the prettiest main plazas in Mexico. The city streets change names here. North–south streets change at Independencia, while east–west streets change at Alcalá/Bustamante. Alcalá is closed to all but cross-street traffic from Avenida Independencia to Avenida Gurrión (at the Santo Domingo church), forming a pedestrian mall. Most of the more expensive hotels, restaurants, and galleries are located north of the zócalo; the market and inexpensive hotels are south.

North, near the first-class bus station, is **Parque Paseo Juárez,** also known as El Llano. This is where families, children, teens, and lovers congregate both by day and by night: groups practicing dance steps, children learning to skate, joggers running or stretching, they are all here. Here you see the life of the city.

GETTING AROUND   By Bus   Buses to the outlying villages of Guelatao, Teotitlán del Valle, Tlacolula, and Mitla leave from the second-class station just north of the Abastos Market (see "Getting There & Departing," above, for details). City buses run along Juárez and Pino Suárez, Tinoco y Palacios and Porfirio Díaz, and others.

By Taxi   Colectivo taxis depart to the villages from Calle Mercadores, on the south side of the Abastos Market. You can negotiate rides to the ruins based on the number of people in your group. The average cost is around $10 per hour, which can be shared with up to five people. A regular taxi stand is along Independencia at the north side of the Alameda, while another is on Calle Murguía just south of the Hotel Camino Real. An honest, careful, and dependable English-speaking driver, **Tomás Ramírez,** can be found here, or reached at his home (☎ **951/1-5061**).

FAST FACTS: OAXACA CITY

American Express   The office, in Viajes Misca, is at Valdivieso and Hidalgo (northeast corner of the zócalo; ☎ **951/6-2700;** fax 951/6-7475). American Express office hours are Monday through Friday from 9am to 2pm and 4 to 6pm and on Saturday from 9am to 1pm. However, the travel agency is open Monday through Friday from 9am to 8pm and Saturday from 9am to 6pm. Here you will find both their travel agency and financial services office.

Area Code   The telephone area code is 951.

Bookstores   There's a good Spanish-English bookstore, Librería Universitaria, off the southeast corner of the zócalo at Guerrero 104. Most are new books, but there are a few used-book racks. Used books are even cheaper at the Biblioteca Circulante (Oaxaca Lending Library), located at Alcalá 305. For an extensive collection of books about Oaxaca, visit the Librería y Papelería Proveedora Escolar. This two-story bookstore is at Independencia 1001, at the corner of Reforma.

Consulates   Several consulates can be contacted through Grupo Consular, upstairs at Hidalgo 817 #4 (☎ **951/4-2744**). The U.S. Consular Agency is at Alcalá 201 (☎ and fax **951/6-4272** or 951/4-3054). Hours are Monday through Friday from 9am to 1pm.

Currency Exchange   Banks change dollars only from Monday through Friday, from 9am to 12:30pm. Look for a window displaying COMPRA Y VENTA DE DIVISAS. Most banks charge a commission for cashing travelers checks, and Banpaís charges a small fee for changing dollars. There are several *casas de cambio* (money-changing storefronts) around the plaza, most of which offer a slightly lesser exchange rate than the banks. Most require a Tourist Card or passport as identification.

One such storefront is Interdisa (☎ **951/6-3399** or 951/4-3098) near the corner of Valdivieso and the zócalo, just around the corner (to the right) from the Hotel Marqués del Valle. It's open Monday through Saturday from 8am to 8pm and Sunday from 9am to 5pm.

Canadian visitors can exchange money at the above-mentioned casa de cambio and at Banamex, Bancomer, Comermex, and others.

Newspapers/Magazines   The English-language newspaper *The News,* published in Mexico City, is sold at newsstands. There is a supply of English-language magazines at the Biblioteca Circulante. The monthly give-away *Oaxaca Times,* published in English, is available at the tourist offices and many hotels. Another monthly, *OAXACA*, is tri-lingual (English, Spanish, and French) and is widely available.

Post Office   The *correos* (main post office) is at the corner of Independencia and the Alameda Park. It is open Monday to Friday from 9am to 7pm and Saturday 9am to 1pm.

Safety   Petty crime is increasing in Oaxaca. Take normal precautions and you should have no trouble: Park your car in a lot overnight; don't leave anything in the car within view; watch your property at all times when you're waiting in the bus station; and be especially careful of very professional pickpockets in the markets and buses—they can take your wallet out of your back or front pocket, handbag, or knapsack, and you won't know it until the time comes to pay for dinner. Luckily, violent crime (including mugging) is still very rare here. In most cases, the police are of little help.

Shipping   Oaxaca is a shopper's delight, and it's hard to keep from accumulating huge quantities of pottery, rugs, and other heavy goods that must be sent home. Many of the better shops can arrange shipping, but if your goods have come from the markets and villages you'll need to ship them yourself. The first rule of shipping is this: You must have a receipt. That means carrying a notebook and asking merchants to write out a receipt for you when you shop. All shipped items must be stamped HECHO EN MÉXICO (Made in Mexico). Mexicana airlines has a cargo office at Libres 617 (☎ **951/5-3711**), open Monday through Saturday from 9am to 8pm, and it can ship your goods to any gateway cities in the United States that have U.S. customs offices. Mexicana requires eight copies of your receipts and charges a minimum of $120 for 1 to 20 kilos (2 to 44 lbs.) to send a package to, for example, Los Angeles. To avoid shipping, however, remember you're allowed two suitcases on a flight.

EXPLORING OAXACA

There are several very good museums, convents, and colonial buildings in Oaxaca, as well as a wonderful zócalo where the community band plays every other night, and sidewalk cafés around the zócalo provide the perfect place for travelers and locals to watch the action. There are also many interesting short road trips through the surrounding countryside—to nearby ruins at Monte Albán and Mitla, or to the outlying villages for pottery, wood carving, and textiles. You'll want to visit Oaxaca's market and the various popular art shops around town; the craft work of this state is some of the finest in Mexico. Remember that most shops and museums will be closed from 2 to 4pm.

The life of the city centers around the zócalo, bordered by Avenidas Hidalgo, Trujano, Magón, and Valdivieso. Calle Magón becomes García Vigil to the north and Cabrera to the south, while Valdivieso becomes Alcalá to the north and Bustamante to the south. The white wrought-iron gazebo in the center and several fountains along the pathways make it a delightful place to walk or sit. This is the place from which to orient yourself.

To get a feel for this lovely city, I recommend walking around town to see the churches and monuments, and then (mañana) a visit to the Regional Museum and the Rufino Tamayo Museum of pre-Hispanic art.

FESTIVALS

Oaxaca is famous for its colorful, exuberant, and tradition-filled festivals. The most important ones are during Holy Week at Easter, the Guelaguetza in July, Días de los Muertos in November, and the Night of the Radishes and Christmas in December.

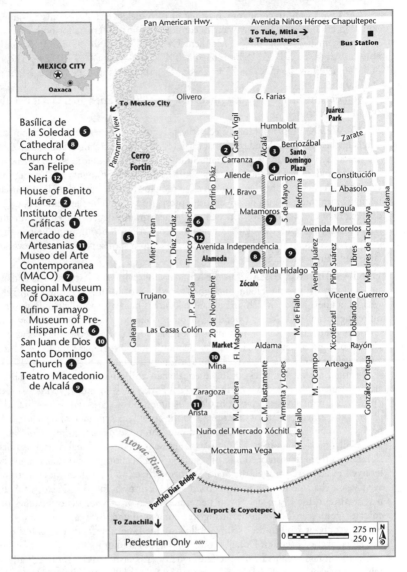

MEXICO CITY
★
Oaxaca

Basílica de
la Soledad **5**
Cathedral **8**
Church of
San Felipe
Neri **12**
House of Benito
Juárez **2**
Instituto de Artes
Gráficas **1**
Mercado de
Artesanias **11**
Museo del Arte
Contemporanea
(MACO) **7**
Regional Museum
of Oaxaca **3**
Rufino Tamayo
Museum of Pre-
Hispanic Art **6**
San Juan de Dios **10**
Santo Domingo
Church **4**
Teatro Macedonio
de Alcalá **9**

Pan American Hwy.
Avenida Niños Héroes Chapultepec
To Tule, Mitla →
& Tehuantepec
Bus Station

To Mexico City
Panoramic View
Cerro Fortin

Olivero
G. Farias
Juárez Park

García Vigil
Humboldt
Zarate
Alcalá
Berriozábal
Santo Domingo Plaza
Carranza
Constitución
Porfirio Díaz
Allende
Gurrion
L. Abasolo
M. Bravo
5 de Mayo
Reforma
Murguía
Matamoros
Aldama
Mier y Teran
G. Díaz Ordaz
Tinoco y Palacios
Avenida Morelos
Avenida Independencia
Alameda
Avenida Juárez
Piño Suárez
Libres
Martires de Tacubaya
Avenida Hidalgo
Zócalo
Trujano
J.P. García
M. de Fiallo
Vicente Guerrero
Xicoténcatl
Doblando
Las Casas Colón
20 de Noviembre
González Ortega
Galeana
Market
Fl. Magon
Aldama
Rayón
Mina
Arteaga
M. Ocampo
Zaragoza
Arista
M. Cabrera
C.M. Bustamente
Armenta y Lopes
M. de Fiallo
Nuño del Mercado Xóchitl
Moctezuma Vega
Atoyac River
Porfirio Díaz Bridge
To Zaachila ↓
To Airport & Coyotepec →

0   275 m
      250 y
N

Pedestrian Only

Make hotel reservations at least two months in advance if you plan to visit during these times.

At festival time in Oaxaca, sidewalk stands are set up in the market areas and near the cathedral to sell buñuelos, the Mexican equivalent of a papadum (the crunchy, spiced wafers that often begin an Indian meal), only sweet. You'll be served your buñuelo in a cracked or otherwise flawed dish or bowl, and after you're finished you smash the crockery on the sidewalk for good luck. Don't be timid! After a while, you may find yourself buying more and more buñuelos—which cost about 75¢ each— just for the fun of smashing plates. Besides buñuelos, hot punch (*ponche*), loaded with fruit, and atole are served and cost about 60¢ each.

Note: If you want to come for Christmas or the Guelaguetza but rooms and transportation are booked, you may want to consider **Sanborn's Tours** for both festivals. Contact them at 2015 S. 10th St., McAllen, TX 78502 (☎ **800/395-8482**). **Remarkable Journeys,** P.O. Box 31855, Houston, TX 77231-1855 (☎ **713/721-2517,** or 800/856-1993 in the U.S.; fax 713/728-8334), also arrives in time for the Night of the Radishes.

For more activities see "Oaxaca After Dark" and "Road Trips from Oaxaca" at the end of this section.

HOLY WEEK   During Holy Week (the principal activities of which begin the Thursday before Easter Sunday), figurines made of palm leaves are made and sold on the streets by village families. On Palm Sunday (the Sunday before Easter) there are colorful parades, and on the following Thursday, Oaxaca residents follow the Procession of the Seven Churches. Hundreds of the pious move from church to church, taking communion in each one to ensure a prosperous year. The next day, Good Friday, many of the barrios have "Encuentros," where groups depart separately from the church, carrying relics through the neighborhoods, then "encountering" each other back at the church. Throughout the week each church sponsors concerts, fireworks, fairs, and other entertainment.

FIESTA GUELAGUETZA   On the Mondays following the last two weekends in July you can witness the Fiesta Guelaguetza, or Feast of Monday of the Hill. In the villages, a guelaguetza (which literally means gift) is held by a family needing to acquire the means of holding a wedding or other obligatory community celebration. Gifts are catalogued and will be repaid in kind at other guelaguetzas. In Oaxaca the custom of a guelaguetza, which includes elaborately staged regional dancing, has been a civic celebration since 1974, when the stadium was built.

During these last two weeks in July there are fairs and exhibits, and regional dances are performed in the stadium on the Cerro del Fortin each Monday (about 10am to 1pm). It's a marvelous spectacle of color, costumes, music, and dance in which the dancers toss small candies or other treats to the crowds as symbolic of a guelaguetza or a gift. Some 350 different huipils and dresses can be seen during the performance as the villages of the seven regions of Oaxaca present their traditional dances. Admission ranges from free (in Section C) to $50–$75 (in Section A), and tickets must be reserved in advance through the State Tourism office (no later than May). A travel agency may be able to help you. I recommend Sections 5 and 6 in Palco A for the best seating in the Cerro del Fortin stadium. The color of your ticket matches the color of your seat. You will be sitting in strong sunlight, so wear a hat and long sleeves. At about 7:30 in the evening, following the Guelaguetza dances, a free performance of the Legend of Donaji is presented in the stadium.

On the Sunday nights before the Guelaguetza, university students present an excellent program in the Plaza de la Danza at the Soledad church. The production is called the *Bani Stui Gulal,* and is an abbreviated history of the Oaxaca valley. The program begins at 9pm, but since the event is free and seating is limited, you should get there quite early.

DÍAS DE LOS MUERTOS   The Days of the Dead (November 1 and 2), blend Indian and Hispanic customs and trail only Easter in importance to local people. Markets brim with marigolds and offerings for altars built to honor the dead. Be sure to take one of the night cemetery tours offered around this time. An excellent one is offered out of Casa Arnel (☎ **951/5-2856;** fax 951/3-6285). They leave for Xoxo (pronounced "ho-ho") around 10pm on October 31, taking flowers and candles to be placed on tombs that have no visitors, and return about 1:30am. Cost is $15.50. They also visit other villages on the nights of November 1 and 2.

Xoxo is the most traditional on October 31, but other villages have different kinds of festivities on the next two nights, some of them quite carnival-like with masked street dancers and no cemetery vigil.

DECEMBER FESTIVALS   The December Festivals begin on the 12th, with the festival of the Virgen de Guadalupe, and continue on the 16th with a *calenda,* or procession, to many of the older churches in the barrios, all accompanied by dancing and costumes. Festivities continue on the 18th with the Fiesta de la Soledad in honor of the Virgen de la Soledad, patroness of Oaxaca state. On that night there is a cascade of fire from a "castle" erected for the occasion in Plaza de la Soledad. December 23 is **the Night of the Radishes,** when the Oaxaqueños build fantastic sculptures out of enormous radishes (the most prized vegetable cultivated during the colonial period), as well as flowers and corn husks. Displays on three sides of the zocalo are set up from 3pm on. By 6pm, when the show officially opens, lines to see the amazing figures are four blocks long. It's well organized and overseen by a heavy police presence. On December 24, around 8:30pm, each Oaxacan church organizes a procession with music, floats, enormous papier-mâché dancing figures (*caros allegoricos*), and crowds bearing candles, all of which culminate on the zócalo.

NEW YEAR'S EVE   The New Year is rung in with the Petition of the Cross, where villagers from all over come to a forlorn chapel on the hill beyond Tlacolula (about 22 miles southeast of Oaxaca, near Mitla) to light candles and express their wishes for the coming new year. Mock bargaining, with sticks and stones to represent livestock and produce, is part of the traditional way of expressing hope for the new year. Tiny symbolic farms and fields are built, proxies for dreams of real prosperity.

MUSEUMS

Regional Museum of Oaxaca. Gurrión at Alcalá. ☎ **951/6-2991.** Admission $2; free Sun and holidays. Tues–Fri 10am–6pm. Sat, Sun & holidays 10am–5pm.

This former convent next to the Santo Domingo Church six blocks north of the zócalo has had a colorful history, including having been used as an army barracks during the War of Independence. All the rooms open onto the lovely arched interior courtyard, where the only sound is that of the fountain. There are remnants of elaborate frescoes along the walls and ceilings. The building is still magnificent, and you can feel the pervasive peacefulness of the place.

The contents of Monte Albán's Tomb 7 are probably the most popular exhibit here. Discovered in 1932, they're housed in the room immediately to the left after you enter the museum; seeing these incredible treasures first may make the rest of the rooms on the first floor more meaningful. The tomb contained the remains of 12 to 14 individuals. Some scholars believe the Zapotecs built the tomb about A.D. 500, but—though there's still debate—the tomb's contents are generally thought to be Mixtec, dating to about A.D. 1250. All agree, however, that the jewelry—made of gold (almost 8 pounds), turquoise, conch shell, amber, and obsidian—and the bowls of onyx and rock crystal are very beautiful. Some 500 pieces of jewelry and art were found, and the display is breathtaking.

A few hints on interpreting recurring visual motifs you'll see as you move through the rest of the museum (there's no guidebook to the museum, and all the plaques are in Spanish): The Zapotecs had a number system of bars and dots, similar to that of the Olmecs and the Maya, and a collection of glyphs that, perhaps, represent a calendar. Another thing to note is that most of the ceramic sculpture here has the characteristic Zapotec touches of prominent teeth, elaborate headgear (often as an eagle or jaguar mask), and large ear plugs. Many of the figures have mouths similar to the ones found in Olmec sculpture—it's thought that the Olmecs influenced the early development of Monte Albán.

Next stop should be the room that's straight ahead on the first floor as you enter the museum, which displays objects and artifacts that will lead you through some 8,000 years of human history in the Oaxaca valley. The next rooms are dedicated to exquisite finds from the nearby ruins of Monte Albán, the Zapotec city that flourished from 600 B.C. until beginning to decline around A.D. 800. The Mixtecs moved in and remained until the 15th century.

On the upper floor are rooms devoted to an ethnographic exhibit of regional crafts and costumes; mannequins dressed in authentic regional dress portray facets of religious, social, and cultural life. These rooms, and an exhibit devoted to the Dominican presence in Oaxaca, are not always open.

Until 1994 a portion of the convent was occupied by the military. That area has been returned to the state which has begun restoration. It will be a part of the museum.

Rufino Tamayo Museum of Pre-Hispanic Art. Av. Morelos 503. ☎ **951/6-4750.** Admission $1.50 Mon and Wed–Sat 10am–2pm and 4–7pm, Sun 10am–3pm. Closed Tuesday and holidays. Open all day December 17–30.

The artifacts displayed in this unique museum were chosen "solely for the aesthetic rank of the works, their beauty, power, and originality." The result is one of the most important collections of pre-Hispanic art in Mexico. The collection was amassed over a 20-year period by artist Rufino Tamayo, born in Oaxaca. The artifacts range from the Pre-Classical Period up to the Aztecs: terra-cotta figurines, scenes of daily life, lots of female fertility figures, Olmecan and Totonac sculpture from the Gulf Coast, and Zapotec long-nosed god figures. Plaques in Spanish give the period, culture, and location of each find, but you'll find yourself ignoring this information and just admiring the works and displays. Missing, however, is information on the sites where most of the figures were found, although most are noted to be from a particular area of the country. To get to the museum, walk two blocks north of the zócalo on Alcalá to Morelos, then left two and a half blocks. It's between Tinoco y Palacios and Porfirio Díaz.

Oaxaca Museum of Contemporary Art. Alcalá 202, between Matamoros and Morelos. ☎ **951/6-8499.** Free admission (donation requested). Daily 9am–9pm.

Also known as the House of Cortés (and formerly the Museum of the City of Oaxaca), this museum is 2¹/₂ blocks north of the zócalo. It exhibits the work of contemporary artists, primarily from Oaxaca state. The museum also hosts international exhibits. If there's an opening night, join the crowd; concerts and other cultural events are also held in the main patio. A second patio has a café and cine club. A fine small bookstore is to your right as you enter. The beautifully restored 16th-century building housing the museum was supposedly built on the order of conqueror Hernán Cortés after receiving the title of Marqués of the Valley of Oaxaca (he died in Spain without seeing it).

Institute of Graphic Arts. Alcalá 507. ☎ **951/6-6980.** Free admission (donation requested). Wed–Mon 10:30am–8pm. Closed Tues.

Also known simply as IAGO, the Institute features an outstanding national and international graphic arts collection, which contains the works of Goya, Posada, Tamayo, Toledo, and others. Prints, drawings, and posters make up the collection and there is a fine library of over 6,000 volumes (including videos) spread over several rooms. The front gallery features traveling exhibits, and there is a small bookstore. Housed in the former residence of the Toledo family, the Institute is located across (catercorner to the right) from the front of the Santo Domingo church. A small coffee and pastry shop in the back courtyard is open daily from 8am to 8pm.

CHURCHES

Cathedral of Oaxaca. Fronting the Parque Alameda. No phone. Free admission. Daily 7am–9pm.

Anchoring the east end of the Alameda is the cathedral, originally built in 1553 and reconstructed in 1773. It has an elaborate 18th-century baroque facade and a glittering interior with three naves and many side chapels. It contains a bronze sculpture above the altar, a huge pipe organ, stained-glass windows, and fine etched-glass doors.

Basílica de la Soledad. Independencia at Galeana. No phone. Museum 25¢. Museum, Mon–Sat 10am–2pm and 4–6pm, Sun 11am–2pm; basílica, daily 7am–2pm and 4–9pm.

The basílica, the most important religious center in Oaxaca, is seven blocks west of the zócalo. A sculpted black-stone representation of the Virgen de la Soledad, patron saint of the state, rests high on the west wall (around to the left as you face the church). A huge celebration on and around December 18th honors this patron saint, attracting penitents from all over the state. The basílica is actually a huge complex of buildings, including a garden, convent, and museum. A small outdoor patio/theater (Plaza de la Danza), with stone and concrete step/seats, lies just in front of the church grounds; here spectators can witness the famous *Bani Stui Gulal* (see "Guelaguetza" under "Festivals," above). The original church, begun in 1582, was much damaged by the many earthquakes that occurred during the early years of the Conquest and was rebuilt between 1682 and 1690. The basílica has four levels on the outside, each decorated with carvings of saints. The interior is an overpowering array of chandeliers, angels, gilt ceiling, paintings, and statues. A figure of La Virgen de la Soledad is above the altar in the basílica. A copy is in the museum at the back of the church, to your right as you exit. Both statues are draped in black velvet, and the copy resides in a chapel filled with white wedding regalia made of glass, pearl, and plastic. Other items of interest include a 3-foot-square case containing innumerable miniature glass figurines (birds, angels, animals, and flowers) surrounding the Christ Child, many 18th-century *retablos* (altarpieces) expressing thanks for favors granted, and a four-panel stained-glass representation of the legend of the finding of the Virgen's carved head and hands. The garden outside the museum has a life-size metal sculpture of the legendary mule train in which the mysterious chest was found.

Santo Domingo Church. Corner of Gurrión and Alcalá. No phone. Free admission. Daily 7am–2pm and 4–11pm.

There are 27 churches in Oaxaca, but you should make a special effort to see this one, next to the Regional Museum of Oaxaca, six blocks north of the zócalo. Don't judge a church by its facade. Started in the 1550s by Dominican friars and finished a century later, it contains the work of all the best artists of that period. The walls and ceiling are covered with ornate plaster statues and flowers, most of them gilded. The sun shines through the yellow stained-glass window, casting a golden glow over the whole interior. There is a large gilded rosary chapel to the right as you enter. If you are there around 11am Monday through Saturday, you are likely to hear the lovely sound of the gift shop operator singing her devotions in the Rosario chapel. It is worth timing your visit for this.

Church of San Felipe. Tinoco y Palacios at Independencia. No phone. Free admission. Daily 8am–11pm.

This church 2¹/₂ blocks northeast of the zócalo was built in 1636 and displays all the architectural opulence of that period: The altar and nave are covered with ornately carved and gilded wood, and the walls are frescoed—ornate but not overpowering. In the west transept/chapel is a small figure of St. Martha and the dragon; the faithful have bedecked her with ribbons, praying that she assist them in vanquishing their woes (often a spouse).

San Juan de Dios. 20 de Noviembre s/n, corner Aldama and Arteaga. No phone. Free admission. Daily 6am–11pm.

This is the earliest church in Oaxaca, built in 1521 or 1522 of adobe and thatch. The present structure was begun during the mid-1600s and included a convent and hospital (where the 20 de Noviembre market is now). The exterior is nothing special, but the interior has an ornate altar and paintings on the ceiling by Urbano Olivera. A glass shrine to the Virgin near the entrance and one to Christ (off to the right) are especially revered by Oaxaqueños. Because it's by the market, one block west and two blocks south of the zócalo, many of the people who visit the church are villagers who've come in to buy and sell. There's an interesting guitar mass on Sunday at 1pm.

SPANISH & ART CLASSES

The **Instituto Cultural Oaxaca A.C.,** Av. Juárez 909 (Apdo. Postal 340), Oaxaca, Oax. 68000, Mexico (☎ 951/5-3404; fax 951/5-3728), offers Spanish classes for foreigners, as well as workshops with Mexican artisans such as weavers, potters, and cooks. There are also lectures emphasizing Oaxaca's history, archaeology, anthropology, and botany. Although the normal course length is four weeks, arrangements can be made for as short a period as a week, and the Institute will arrange inexpensive housing with local families. The Institute itself is housed in a lovely old hacienda next to the Pan American Highway. Even a short time at the Institute will give you a better understanding of both the language and Oaxaca.

The **Instituto de Comunicación y Cultura,** Alcalá 307-12, Oaxaca, Oax. 68000 (☎/fax. **951/6-3443**), provides group or private Spanish instruction to many satisfied students. They can also arrange for home-stays with a Mexican family.

OTHER ATTRACTIONS

Teatro Macedonio de Alcalá. Independencia at Armenta y López. No phone. Open only for events.

This beautiful 1903 belle époque theater, two blocks east of the zócalo, holds 1,300 people and is still used for concerts and performances in the evening. Peek through the doors to see the marble stairway and Louis XV vestibule. A list of events is sometimes posted on the doors.

Cerro del Fortín. Díaz Ordaz at Calle Delmonte. No phone.

To take all this sightseeing in at a glance, those with cars can drive to this hill at the west of town for a panoramic view of the city, especially good just before sunset. Recognize the hill by a statue of—who else?—Benito Juárez and a stadium built to hold 15,000 spectators? The annual Fiesta Guelaguetza is held here.

You can walk to the hill as well. Head up Díaz Ordaz/Crespo and look for the Escaleras del Fortín (Stairway to the Fortress) shortly after you cross Calle Delmonte; the 180 plus steps (interrupted by risers) are a challenge, but the view is worth it.

SHOPPING

It's a toss-up as to what tourists do first in Oaxaca: see the nearby ruins or shop. Oaxaca and the surrounding villages have some of the country's best buys in locally hand-crafted pottery, wood carvings, and textiles. It's easy to buy more than you ever imagined, so come prepared with extra suitcases.

For market days in outlying villages and directions to the wood-carvers and other crafts villages of importance, see "Road Trips from Oaxaca," below.

Note: Before you load down with tons of pottery, wood carvings, and weavings, however, keep in mind that your luggage is weighed at flight check-in. You'll be charged a fee for bags over 25 kilos (slightly over 55 lbs.). The transport bus to the airport also charges extra for passengers with overly bulky or excess baggage. See also "Shipping" under "Fast Facts" above for more information.

Arts & Crafts

Several of the stores mentioned below are on the pedestrians-only Alcalá (but watch out for motorbikes), which has been closed to traffic from Independencia to Gurrión, making it a most pleasant place to browse. The Benito Juárez Market (see "City Markets," below) mainly features meat, produce, and household needs. The 20 de Noviembre Market, a block farther south, has a huge crafts section. Both markets can be accessed from either Cabrera or 20 de Noviembre streets, both of which are open to traffic.

Artesanías y Industrias Populares del Estado de Oaxaca (ARIPO). García Vigil 809. ☎ **951/4-4030.**

The State of Oaxaca runs ARIPO, which includes a workshop and store. It is located two blocks farther up the hill beyond the Benito Juárez house. You can hear looms working in the back as you browse through the handicrafts expertly displayed in the many rooms. ARIPO has possibly the widest selection of black pottery in the city. There's also a good supply of masks, clothing, and cutlery. Open Monday through Saturday from 9am to 7pm, at the corner of Vigil and Cosijopi.

Arte y Tradición. García Vigil 406. ☎ **951/6-3552.**

Four blocks north of the zócalo and just around the corner from the FONART store, a brightly painted doorway leads one into this attractive arcade of shops with an open patio in the center. Each shop functions as a cooperative, with articles on consignment from the various villages, such as Teotitlán del Valle and Arrazola. Individuals from these villages are on hand to explain the crafts (weaving, wood carving, and the like) as practiced by their townspeople. You'll also find an excellent restaurant serving authentic Oaxacan cuisine, the Belaguetza Travel Agency, and a small bookstore. The English-speaking manager, Judith Reyes, is a real dynamo and has tremendous pride in her Mixtec heritage. The store is open daily 9am to 8pm, although the individual shop hours may vary.

FONART. M. Bravo 116. ☎ **951/6-5764.**

Oaxaca's branch of this government-supported chain is on M. Bravo at García Vigil. The name stands for Fondo Nacional para el Fomento de las Artesanías. Prices are fixed. Featuring a wide selection of native crafts from all over Mexico, the store is open Monday through Saturday from 9am to 2pm and 4 to 7pm. During Christmas it's open daily from 9am to 5pm.

Galería Arte de Oaxaca. Murguía 105. ☎ and fax **951/4-0910** or 951/4-1532.

Owner Nancy Mayagoitia has made this the city's best showcase for the state's leading contemporary artists. There's always something artistically exciting happening here.

Open Monday through Friday from 11am to 3pm and 5 to 9pm; Saturday 11am to 3pm. You'll find it two blocks north and one block east of the zócalo.

La Mano Mágica. Alcalá 203. ☎ **951/6-4275.**

This gallery of contemporary and popular art is across from the city museum. The name means "magic hand," and it's a true celebration of Oaxacan artistic creativity. Fine exhibits of paintings by local artists occupy the front room. The back rooms are full of regional folk art by the area's best artisans, folk who carry on an inherited artistic tradition in their village homes. Pieces are personally selected by owners Mary Jane and Arnulfo Mendoza (don't miss his weavings). They can help you ship purchases anywhere in the world via DHL courier service. Located between Morelos and Matamoros opposite the Museum of Contemporary Art/MACO (House of Cortés), it's open Monday through Saturday from 10am to 1:30pm and 4 to 7:30pm.

Mercado de Artesanías. J. P. García at Zaragoza.

If the crafts section of the Benito Juárez market mentioned under "City Markets," below, leaves you wanting, this is a good place to get an overview of Oaxaca's folk arts, particularly textiles. Women and men weave rugs, belts, *huipils*, serapes, and bags on looms and display their finest work. Ask the artisans where they're from, and you'll get an idea of which villages you'd like to visit. Located one block south and one block west of the 20 de Noviembre Market and four blocks south and two blocks west of the zócalo, it's open daily from 10am to 4pm.

Victor's. Porfirio Díaz 111. ☎ **951/6-1174.**

This art shop in a 17th-century monastery is managed by Sr. Ramón Fosado, who goes to the villages himself in search of the best native art. He speaks English and is very pleasant. If you're shopping for serapes and blankets, be sure to stop at Victor's to do a little research. The quality of these goods varies, but the friendly staff here is willing to tell you about the differences in materials (wool versus synthetic), dyes (natural and chemical), and designs. You should also scout around and compare the various products in the open markets. Open Monday through Saturday from 9am to 2pm and 4 to 8pm.

Yalalag de Oaxaca. Alcalá 104. ☎ **951/6-2108.**

This old mansion near the corner of Alcalá and Morelos displays a multifarious but affordable collection of art. Black pottery, Talavera ceramics, terra-cotta figurines, tin sculpture, table linens, apparel, papier-mâché sculpture, and other quality crafts from all over Mexico can be found here. Open Monday through Saturday from 9:30am to 1:30pm and 4:30 to 8pm.

Chocolate & Mole

Although Oaxaca produces some chocolate, most that is processed here comes from Tabasco and Chiapas. The state is better known for its 20 (more or less) varieties of mole (moh-lay), of which chocolate is often an ingredient; it comes in colors of red, yellow, black, brown, and green. Mole is used to make a sauce usually served over turkey or chicken but also as a flavoring in regional tamales. In the market area, strolling vendors sell chocolate in thick half-dollar–size cakes, usually six or eight to the package. However, you'll have more choices (and more fun deciding) if you buy it in a store specializing in chocolate. Establishments that sell fresh chocolate often also grind and mix the ingredients for mole and sell it in a paste. Mole can be found in heaps in both the Abastos and Benito Juárez markets (see "City Markets," below), at grinders on Mina, or at the Chocolate Mayordomo mentioned below. Mole keeps for a year if stored in a refrigerator.

Chocolate Mayordomo. 20 de Noviembre at Mina. ☎ **951/6-1619** or 951/6-0246.

This corner store is actually a huge operation with another outlet across the street on Mina and several others throughout the city. All sell chocolate and mole, their mix or ground to your specifications. Here you'll find shelves of boxed chocolate either *amargo* (unsweetened) or *semidulce* (semisweet), with or without almonds and/or cinnamon, in small, hard cakes or in a soft paste. Either is used in cooking or for making hot chocolate. A half-kilo of chocolate costs around $1.50; gift boxes of plastic-wrapped fresh black or red mole are also found here for $2.50 per kilo. They make excellent gifts for friends back home. Ask General Manager Salvador Flores about chocolate—you'll learn a lot! The store is open daily from 8am to 8:30pm.

City Markets

Abastos Market. Across the railroad tracks and just south of the second-class bus station.

The Abastos Market is open daily but is most active on Saturday, when Indians from the villages come to town to sell and shop. You'll see huge mounds of dried chilies, herbs, vegetables, crafts, bread, and even burros for sale at this bustling market.

Benito Juárez Market. Bordered by Las Casas, Cabrera, Aldama, and 20 de Noviembre.

One block south of the zócalo, this covered market is big and busy every day, but especially on Saturday. The area around it is then an open street market, teeming with vendors of chilies, string, parrots, talismans, food, spices, cloth, dresses, blankets— one of the most exciting markets in Mexico, because the people who come to sell their wares are so colorful. The bulk of the produce trade has been relocated to the Abastos Market (see above), where the local color is even more profound.

20 de Noviembre Market. Bordered by Las Casas, Cabrera, Mina, and 20 de Noviembre.

Anchored on the northwest corner by the San Juan de Dios church and immediately south of, and truly a continuation of, the Juárez Market, this one has its own separate name. It occupies the area where once stood the convent and hospital of the San Juan de Dios church. In addition to many food products, there are innumerable cookshops offering juices and complete meals.

WHERE TO STAY

Oaxaca is in the midst of a tourism boom—and a shortage of hotel rooms. You can generally arrive and find a room easily enough, but in the high tourist periods of Easter, July, November, and December, it's best to make reservations at least two to three months in advance.

The SEDETUR Tourist Office in Oaxaca (across from the Alameda; ☎ **951/ 6-0123** or 951/6-4828; fax 951/6-0984) has a hand in maintaining small **one-bedroom houses** for tourists in nine Zapotec villages in the Oaxaca valley. They are called "Tourist Yu'u" (*yu'u* means house in Zapotec); are equipped with bare kitchen necessities, sheets, towels, and bathrooms; and rent for $5 per person. The idea was to give tourists and locals opportunity to know each other, but most of these houses are so far from the villages that mingling is difficult without a car. Villages with Yu'u huts are Abasolo, Teotitlán del Valle, Papalutla, Benito Juárez, Tlacolula, Quialana, Tlapozola, and Santa Ana del Valle. Contact SEDETUR for reservations or more information.

DOUBLES FOR LESS THAN $15

Hotel Reforma. Reforma 102, 68000 Oaxaca, Oax. ☎ **951/6-0939.** 16 rms (all with bath). $8.50 single; $10 double.

If you're on a tight budget, try this hotel, centrally located two blocks northeast of the plaza. Remodeled, repainted, and refurnished in 1992, the clean rooms feature brightly painted walls in pastel pink and green, tile floors, and chenille or cotton bedspreads. Some rooms are so crowded with furniture it creates a tight squeeze to the bath or requires creative luggage placement. In general, baths are small, and although the commodes are new, most don't have toilet seats; also look out for the curtainless showers, which may spray the whole bathroom. The Reforma is between Independencia and Morelos.

Hotel Santa Clara. Morelos 1004, 68000 Oaxaca, Oax. ☎ **951/6-1138.** 14 rms. $11 single; $13 double.

Opened in 1993 by the owners of the Hotel Reforma, this simple two-story hotel has a lot of charm for the few bucks you pay. Beyond the lobby is a nice paved inner courtyard with white iron tables and chairs. Rooms are back of this, and two of them face the courtyard with big windows that let in the light. The carpeted rooms have armoires for clothing, matching furniture, and tile baths. Rooms behind the patio may be a bit dark, so check first. The hotel is near the corner of Reforma.

Hotel Virreyes. Morelos 1001,68000 Oaxaca, Oax. ☎ **951/6-5141.** 30 rms (all with bath). $8.50 single; $11 double.

The courtyard at the Virreyes is covered with painted glass that lets in such a mellow light the air seems to be colored beige. The hotel is a converted mansion that's looking a bit run-down. Rooms are large, with tile floors and high ceilings, but some are very dark and have no windows. Be sure to look at your room before signing in. This is not a hotel for the light sleeper because of the street noise and the echo-chamber effect created by the enclosed courtyard. The hotel is a few steps between Juárez and Reforma.

DOUBLES FOR LESS THAN $25

✪ **Las Golondrinas.** Tinoco y Palacios 411, 68000 Oaxaca, Oax. ☎ **951/6-8726.** Fax 951/ 4-2126. 24 rms (all with bath). $21.25 double.

Owned and personally managed by Guillermina and Jorge Velasco, Las Golondrinas ("The Swallows") has been growing more popular every year. This charming one-story hotel is situated amid rambling patios with roses, fuchsia, bougainvillea, and mature banana trees. The 24 simply furnished rooms, with windows and doors opening onto courtyards, are individually accented with Mexican crafts; all have tile floors and a small desk and chairs. Breakfast (nonguests welcome) is served between 8 and 10am in a small tile-covered café in a garden setting. It's 6$^{1/2}$ blocks northwest of the zócalo, between Allende and Bravo.

Hotel Antonio's. Independencia 601, Oaxaca, Oax. 68000 ☎ **951/6-7227.** Fax 951/6-3672. 15 rms (all with bath). TV. $20 single; $23.50 double.

Opened in 1991, this comfortable and conveniently located hotel was converted from an old two-story town home, with an interior patio surrounded by an arcaded walkway. There is a small restaurant on the patio. Each room has a tile floor, colonial-style pine furniture, some with two double beds, and a small tile bath. Wall hooks solve the storage problem in rooms without closets. It's located a block and a half west of the cathedral, at the corner of Porfirio Díaz and Independencia.

❸ **Hotel Casa Arnel.** Aldama 404, Col. Jalatlaco, 68000 Oaxaca, Oax ☎ **951/5-2856.** Fax 951/3-6285. 30 rms (22 with bath). $12.25 double without bath; $16.75 double with bath. Furnished apartment $300 monthly. Parking $1.25 daily.

This favorite and excellent budget choice is slightly removed from the city center but still within walking distance of most sights. It's a U-shaped two-story building built around a cool tropical garden behind the home of the Cruz family, owners of the Casa Arnel. Sooner or later you'll meet a member of this large extended family; you'll also be on a first-name basis with several resident parrots and a dozing cat or two. The dining tables and chairs in the cool garden are the gathering spot where guests (who are an international lot, by the way) write postcards or read something from the hotel's enormous lending library.

The rooms are plain but clean and comfortable and have tile floors and tile baths; some share a bath among four rooms. If you crave a firm mattress, this is the place— some of them are almost brick-hard. Across the street in the new wing (Hostal Miriam) are three additional rooms with double beds and private baths, plus four furnished apartments with fully equipped kitchens. In the apartments, stays of 15 days are allowed at half the monthly rate. Breakfast and dinner are served on the family patio.

For a number of years the Hotel Casa Arnel has held Posadas—reenactments of Joseph and Mary's search for an inn before Jesus was born—for its guests during the nine days prior to Christmas. On Christmas Eve a procession wends its way to the zócalo, after which everyone returns for an 11:30pm Christmas Eve dinner. Take advantage of this—it is seldom that a tourist has the opportunity to be included in a Mexican family celebration.

Arnel Cruz and his wife Lilia also operate a **travel agency** here and can obtain bus and airline tickets and arrange tours of the area. They have special nightly tours for the Days of the Dead (Oct 31–Nov 2). Just snag one of them to make the arrangements.

To get to the hotel from the first-class bus station, turn right out the front door of the station, go two blocks, and turn right onto Aldama. The casa is seven blocks ahead on your left across from the Iglesia San Matias Jalatlaco.

Hotel Francia. Calle 20 de Noviembre no. 212, 68000 Oaxaca, Oax.☎ **951/6-4811.** Fax 951/6-4251. 46 rms (all with bath). FAN TEL. $17.25 single; $20 double.

Built in 1834, the Francia was one of the city's first hotels, but it's still functional, pleasant, and nicely kept. Arranged around a central patio, the clean, high-ceilinged rooms have French doors and are filled with somewhat ancient furniture, firm beds with blanket spreads, table and chairs, and small but adequate baths. Consider street noise when selecting a room and be aware that it can be cold and drafty here in winter. It's at the corner of Trujano one block west of the zócalo.

Hotel Monte Albán. Alameda de León, 68000 Oaxaca, Oax. ☎ **951/6-2777.** Fax 951/6-3265. 20 rms (all with bath). TEL. $11.50–$15.25 single; $14.25–$19 double.

Impressions

In Mexico there is always a brooding sense of the past. Turn off the highway, and the rutted road leads you over humpbacked bridges, past the gates of old haciendas, through the villages where the church stands on the plaza as it always has. The high mesa blossoms pink with cosmos in late August, and far away on the edge of the hills shine the tile domes. Farther up the hills are markets where not everyone speaks Spanish, where women are still wearing garments which they weave for themselves.

—Elizabeth Wilder Weismann, *Art and Time in Mexico,* 1985

The location is one good reason to stay at this hotel, which fronts the Alameda and is a half block west of the zócalo, opposite the cathedral. But don't expect a friendly welcome. The large, airy rooms in the front are the most colonial, but the smaller interior rooms are also fine and may be a bit lower in price. All rooms have tile showers and colonial furnishings. The courtyard restaurant is topped by a glass skylight canopy.

The hotel hosts a delightful show of folk dances in the courtyard every night from 8:30 to 10pm. Guests who go to bed early might not find the show so delightful night after night.

Hotel Principal. 5 de Mayo no. 208, 68000 Oaxaca, Oax. ☎ and Fax **951/6-2535.** 16 rms (all with bath). $19 single; $23 double.

The Principal, 1 block east and 2¹/₂ blocks north of zócalo, is a longtime favorite of budget travelers, for good reason. The location, near shops, museums, and restaurants, is great, and rooms are clean and filled with sunlight. Six upstairs rooms have balconies. Make reservations in advance, since the hotel is often full.

Hotel Las Rosas. Trujano 112, 68000 Oaxaca, Oax. ☎ **951/4-2217.** 19 rms (all with bath). FAN. $17 single; $20 double.

Las Rosas, formerly the Plaza Hotel, has been renovated and painted bright white. A narrow flight of stairs leads up from the street to the second-story lobby and colonial courtyard. Rooms open onto the courtyard, and some have windows; those without windows are claustrophobic. Rooms are cheerily decorated with a few regional crafts and colorful tile work; in some you'll find a turquoise wall and coordinated bedspreads. Some rooms have floor fans. The hotel is situated one-half block west of the zócalo, between Magón and 20 de Noviembre.

DOUBLES FOR LESS THAN $40

Hotel Casona del Llano. Av. Juárez 701, 68000 Oaxaca, Oax. ☎ **951/4-7719** or 47703. Fax 951/6-2219. 28 rms (all with bath). FAN TV TEL. $24 single; $31 double. Free parking.

In an elegant mansion with a beautiful stone verandah, this hotel definitely has curb appeal. The grand-looking but reasonably priced restaurant is on the left as you enter; there are two stories of rooms in this building as well as a new section in back that fronts a handsome inner lawn. There's no elevator. Guestquarters are tastefully decorated in pastel and earth tones, with tile floors, large windows, and rattan furniture. The restaurant is open daily from 7am to 11pm. The hotel's across the street from El Llano, a park popular with Oaxacan families and children, but for all the activity there, it is quiet. Located on the west side of Parque Paseo Juárez (known locally as El Llano), this hotel is a short (15-minute) walk or shorter bus ride from the zócalo. To find it from the zócalo, walk three blocks east on Hidalgo to Juárez and turn left (north) for seven blocks; it's at the corner of Humbolt.

✪ **Hotel Gala.** Bustamante 103, 68000 Oaxaca, Oax. ☎ **915/4-1308.** Fax 915/6-3660. 36 rms (all with bath). FAN TV TEL. $31 single; $36 double.

This hotel's lobby and sweeping staircase are so impressive and its rooms are so nicely kept that you'd expect it to charge much more. Opened in 1992, occupying the old Hotel Ruiz, the three stories of rooms (no elevator) are carpeted and have coordinated furnishings and firm mattresses. Some rooms have windows overlooking Bustamante, and others have windows on the hall. Some rooms have minuscule bathrooms, and in most cases there's not a lot of room for luggage, but it's otherwise a very comfortable and excellently located hotel. The hotel restaurant is to the right of the front door. The Gala is ¹/₂ block south of the zócalo near the corner of Bustamante and Guerrero.

✪ **Marqués del Valle.** Portal Clavería s/n, 68000 Oaxaca, Oax. ☎ **951/6-3677** or 951/6-6294. Fax 951/6-9961. 95 rms (all with bath). TV TEL. $38 double.

One of the most charming traditional hotels in Oaxaca, the five-story (with elevator) Marqués del Valle has large rooms built around an inner courtyard. It's across from the zócalo and next to the cathedral, yet this side of the plaza isn't very noisy (except for Sunday afternoon band concerts). Rooms with French doors facing the plaza have a grand view. Be sure to try one of the coffees in the cafe under the colonnade in front of the hotel. Service is slow, but the coffee is the best in town. Walk-in customers get lower hotel rates than those who reserve ahead.

DOUBLES FOR LESS THAN $50

Calesa Real. García Vigil 306, 68000 Oaxaca, Oax. ☎ **951/6-5544.** Fax 951/6-7232. 77 rms. FAN TV TEL. $45 double. Free parking.

The Calesa Real, in a colonial building 3 1/2 blocks north of the zócalo, is a traditional favorite that hosts a lot of tour groups. One of the nicest features here is the small pool, set in a cool courtyard. Eight of the rooms on the first floor have French doors opening to the pool area; others on the second and third floors have small balconies. There is a second-story terrace and restaurant overlooking the pool. The large rooms have blue-tile baths and double beds. The hotel is between Bravo and Matamoros.

WORTH A SPLURGE

✪ **Hostal de la Noria.** Av. Hidalgo 918, 68000 Oaxaca, Oax. ☎ **951/4-7844,** or 800/528-1234 in the U.S. Fax 951/6-3992. 43 rms. TV TEL. High season $57 single; $66 double. Low season $50 single; $57 double.

Behind this gracious colonial-era facade is one the city's newest hotels, complete with handsome courtyard restaurant, elegant bar, and three stories (no elevator) of large rooms. Pastel yellow walls with lavender accent trim around the wooden doors lead to rooms overlooking both the interior courtyard or exterior streets. Rooms are large, with high ceilings, carpeting, handsome armoires for clothing, and remote control TV. Some baths have a tub/shower combination. The hotel, which is affiliated with Best Western, is two blocks east of the zócalo at the corner of Fiallo/Reforma.

WHERE TO EAT

Oaxaca's regional foods are among the best in Mexico. The state is known for its varieties of mole, cheese, tamales, peppers, tortillas, bread, and chocolate. Tasajo, a thin cut of beef, and cecina, a thin cut of pork, are two other regional specialties. To see a magnificent array of these foods, walk through the Abastos Market on Saturday; the quantity and variety are unforgettable. When you hear women shouting "*tlayuda, tlayuda,*" take a look at the 12-inch tortillas they're selling. Oaxaca is also known for pozole Mixteco, a delightfully different version of the hearty soup—it includes chicken and red mole sauce. Restaurants in the city often feature mole, tamales, and Oaxaca cheese. Fortunately, and at last, good restaurants are becoming easier to find in Oaxaca, and the prices here are better than in almost any other city in Mexico.

For a snack or light breakfast, pick up your fill of pastries, cookies, sweet rolls, and breads from the large **Panificadora Bamby,** at the corner of Morelos and García Vigil, two blocks north of the zócalo. It's open daily from 7am to 9pm.

MEALS FOR LESS THAN $5

Cafetería Bamby. García Vigil 205. ☎ **951/6-3285.** Breakfast $1.50–$3; soups/salads $1.75–$5; main courses $3.50–$5; comida corrida $3.50. Mon–Sat 8am–10pm. MEXICAN.

When you're feeling a bit homesick for homestyle food, this is the place to come. Only 2 1/2 blocks north of the zócalo, this bright, clean U.S.–type café offers prompt, courteous service, and a nice selection of dishes that attracts both local and tourist clientele. And the bathrooms are way above average!

○ **Doña Elpidia.** Miguel Cabrera 413. ☎ **951/6-4292.** Fixed-price lunch $4.15. Daily 8:30–10am, 1–5pm. REGIONAL.

This restaurant is a Oaxaca institution; Doña Elpidia and now her son have been catering to a refined, selective local clientele for decades. Inside the deceptively shabby-looking door is a beautiful and heavily shaded courtyard filled with birds and plants. Five tables are set out in the shaded arcade, and there are a dozen more in the indoor dining rooms. The five-course comida corrida includes a basket of bread, an appetizer, vegetable or pasta soup, a meat or enchilada course, a dessert, and Mexican coffee. There's usually a different mole daily. The place is a bit hard to find since the sign says only RESTAURANT, but it's 5¹/₂ blocks south of the zócalo, between Arista and Nuño del Mercado.

○ **Gecko Coffee Shop.** 5 de Mayo 412. ☎ **951/4-8024.** Sandwiches $1.25; desserts $75¢–$1.25; coffee 75¢; chocolate $1. Mon–Sat 7am–8pm. SANDWICHES/CHOCOLATE/COFFEE.

Less than half a block south of the Santo Domingo church is this little habit-forming gem. A variety of delicious sandwiches and pastries are served along with hot chocolate and coffee either in a small dining room or in the more ample patio. Here you have peace and quiet to sip, snack, and read or write the ever-necessary postcards. And when you finally tear yourself away, a gallery, small bookstore, and the wonderful Instituto Welte (of Oaxaca studies) are just off the patio.

Ⓢ **Restaurant El Decano.** 5 de Mayo 210. ☎ **951/4-4153.** Appetizers $2–$5; main courses $3.25–$5.50; comida corrida $2–$2.50. Mon–Sat 9am–9pm. MEXICAN/REGIONAL.

People in the know find their way to this simple lunchroom, known primarily for its filling comida corrida. The midday repast includes a choice of two soups, then choose between entreés such as two kinds of mole, fish, stuffed squash, a small steak, or the plato Oaxaca. These are accompanied by beans, rolls, or tortillas and followed by an ample dessert. The restaurant is four blocks north of the zócalo near the corner of Murgía.

Ⓢ **Restaurant El Mesón.** Av. Hidalgo 805 at Valdivieso. ☎ **951/6-2729.** Breakfast and lunch buffet $3; comida corrida $1.80; tacos $1.60–$2.80; Mexican specialties $1.35–$6. Daily 8am–1am (breakfast buffet 8am–noon; lunch buffet noon–6pm and comida corrida noon–4.30pm). MEXICAN/REGIONAL.

As you enter El Mesón you see señoritas patting out fresh tortillas, and if you sit at the counter you can watch all the kitchen preparations. The menu and prices are printed on a sheet the waitress gives you; just check off what you want and present the waitress with your selection. The food is good and reasonably priced, and it's a great place to try regional specialties. What's more, the excellent all-you-can-eat buffets include fresh fruit, and at lunch fresh salads are added, plus a variety of main courses. The comida corrida is a shortened version of the lunch buffet—soup and a main course of your choice. Taco prices are per order (usually two tacos). Besides the large range of tacos, they serve some "especialidades" such as tamal Oaxaqueño, pozole, and puntas de filete albañil (bricklayers' beef tips). There's the regular assortment of beer and soft drinks, but this is a good place to try chocolate with water or milk (so hot and good on a chilly morning) or the equally delicious atole. The location is excellent and it's a popular meeting place for fellow travelers and locals alike.

○ **Restaurant Las Quince Letras.** Abasolo 300. ☎ **951/4-3769.** Breakfast $1.75–$5.25; appetizers $1.50–$4.25; main courses $3.65–$5.25; comida corrida $3. Daily 8am–9pm. MEXICAN/REGIONAL.

Though it has only one small dining room, and it's a bit off the well-worn path, the restaurant has a loyal following of foreigners who know value and good taste. If you come with at least one companion, complementary *memelitas* are served while you decide what to order. This regional masa creation is similar to a sope. The fresh salads are huge and unadorned with dressing. The tasajo, prepared several ways, is cooked in a wonderful marinade. If you order the filling botana Oaxaqueña, the dozen different enticements leave barely enough room for a light dessert. To find it from the zócalo, walk north on Alcalá four blocks to Abasolo, then right 3¹/₄ blocks. It's on the right, just past the corner of Juárez; look for a bright blue entryway with the restaurant's name painted vertically in white on it.

Restaurant T.L.C. J. P. García at Aldama. ☎ **951/6-4331.** Breakfast $1.65–$2.50; main courses $1.35–$3.50; comida corrida $2. Mon–Sat 7am–midnight. MEXICAN.

Should you find yourself on Mina in the chocolate part of town at lunch time, walk to the corner of J.P. García and Aldama for a treat. As a rather crowded streetcorner lunchroom, it isn't particularly inviting, but the food is good. T.L.C. stands for tacos, liquados, comida but there's much more than that. The tostadas are a two fisted affair; the alambre especial features three kinds of meat and fresh vegetables; plus there are quesadillas, seafood, burgers, and tlayudas that are loaded or semi-loaded. It is a block west of the markets on Aldama and four blocks southwest of the zócalo.

MEALS FOR LESS THAN $10

✪ Restaurant/Bar Catedral. García Vigil 105. ☎ **951/6-3285.** Breakfast $1.75–$2.75; main courses $5–$10. Daily 8am–2am. MEXICAN/REGIONAL/STEAKS.

Casually elegant, with both open patio and interior dining, the Catedral is also a serene place to enjoy a leisurely meal. The restaurant is known for its excellent cuts of beef. Among its international selections is veal cordon bleu, and the regional choices include poblano soup, and delicious chicken estofado. (The latter is one of the 20 moles of Oaxaca.) It's two blocks north of the zócalo, at the corner of Morelos.

OAXACA AFTER DARK

Among the best entertainments in Oaxaca are the **band concerts** in the zócalo—and they're free, too! The State band plays on Tuesday, Thursday, and Sunday, while Monday, Wednesday, Friday, and Saturday the marimbas take over. Oaxaca has the jolliest and most active zócalo in all of Mexico, enjoyed by everyone in town, young and old, rich and poor, citizen or tourist.

A smaller version of the **Guelaguetza,** the famous regional dance of Oaxaca, is performed at the Hotel Camino Real on Friday from 7 to 10pm by a group of highly professional dancers. The cost of $28 per person includes a buffet and elaborate show. The Hotel Monte Albán presents more reasonably priced **folk dances** daily from 8:30 to 10pm for $5 for the show alone. Dinner and drinks are extra. Buy your ticket the day before; then when you enter, you'll find your name card placed at your reserved seat.

Concerts and dance programs are offered all year long at the **Teatro Macedonio de Alcalá,** at Independencia and Armenta y López. Schedules are often posted by the front doors of the theater. The **Casa de la Cultura** (ex-convent of the Seven Princes), at the corner of Colón and G. Ortega, offers exhibits, lectures, films, and various art and music classes, as does the **Centro Cultural Ricardo Flores Magón** (Alcalá 302).

One of Oaxaca's hottest **discos** is in the **Hotel Victoria,** on the Cerro del Fortín, northwest of the center of town (☎ **951/5-2633**). It's active from 10pm till 2am on Friday and Saturday. You'll need a taxi to get there, or at least to get home. At the **Hotel Mision de los Angeles,** Calz. P. Diaz 102 (☎ **951/5-1500**), north of the

Parque Juárez, the **Disco Tequila Rock** is open Wednesday through Saturday from 9pm to 3am. The **Disco Eclipse** (Calle Porfirio Díaz 219, between Matamoros and Morelos, ☎ **951/6-4236**) kicks it from Thursday through Sunday (10pm until the crowd decides to leave).

For night owls who are not up to the disco scene, there's **live music** at **El Sagrario** (Valdivieso 120, behind the cathedral; ☎ **951/4-0303**); the club provides food and beverages while (from 8pm on) you listen to salsa, guitar, and Andean pan pipes. The **Terranova,** facing the zócalo at Portal Benito Juárez 116 (☎ **951/4-0533**), is a popular restaurant with live music between 8pm and 11pm. And near Santo Domingo Church is **La Candela,** Allende 211, a block and a half west of Santo Domingo (☎ **951/6-7933**). It's a good enough restaurant in its own right, but it's a popular night spot with live salsa, reggae, etc., and dancing from about 9:30pm till 1:30am Tuesday through Saturday. **El Sol y La Luna,** Bravo 109 between Alcala and Vigil, ☎ **951/4-8105,** is another good restaurant, serving crêpes, pasta, pizza, etc., and attracting a loyal following of diners and live-music lovers. It's open Monday through Saturday from 5pm to midnight.

ROAD TRIPS FROM OAXACA

Monte Albán and Mitla are the two most important archaeological sites near Oaxaca, but there are several smaller ruins that are also interesting. In addition, I've mentioned a few day-trips to the more interesting villages outside Oaxaca. (For Puerto Escondido, Huatulco, and San Angel, see chapter 6, "Acapulco & the Southern Pacific Coast.") The tourist office will give you a map showing the nearby villages where beautiful handicrafts are made. It's a fun excursion by car or bus.

Monte Albán: Fabled Mountaintop Ceremonial Center

For some 1,500 years prior to 500 B.C., the Oaxaca valleys were inhabited by more or less settled village-dwelling peoples, whose origins are mysterious. Then, between 800 and 500 B.C., a new ceramic style appeared, presumably produced by an influx of new peoples, now called Zapotec. Around 500 B.C. these peoples began to level the top of a mountain upon which to build the magnificent city we know as Monte Albán (*mon*-teh al-*ban*).

Very little of the original structures remain—they've been either obscured beneath newer structures or recycled, their stones reused. However, the Danzantes friezes (see below) are of this period.

Monte Albán was an elite center of Zapotec culture, although affected by contemporary cultures outside the valley of Mexico. You can see Olmec influence in the early sculptures; more recent masks and sculptures reflect contact with the Maya. When Monte Albán was at its zenith in A.D. 300, architectural ideas were borrowed from Teotihuacán. By around A.D. 800, the significance of Monte Albán in Zapotec cosmology began to decline. Although probably never totally abandoned, it became a mere shell of its former grandeur. Then, around the beginning of the 13th century, the remnants of this star of the valley were appropriated by the Mixtecs. The Mixtecs, who had long coexisted in the area with the Zapotecs, now imposed their own, by now more highly developed, culture. At Monte Albán, they did very little building of their own but are renowned for the treasure they left in Tomb 7.

Monte Albán covers about 15 square miles and is centered on the Great Plaza, a large grassy area that was once a mountain top. From this plaza, aligned north–south, you can overlook the lush Oaxacan valley, a gorgeous setting for any civilization. The excavations at Monte Albán have revealed more than 170 tombs, numerous ceremonial altars, stelae, pyramids, and palaces.

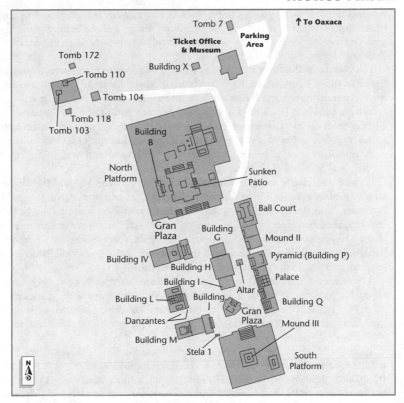

Begin your tour of the ruins on the eastern side of the Great Plaza at the **I-shaped ball court.** This ball court differs slightly from Maya and Toltec ball courts in that there are no goal rings and the sides of the court are sloped. Also on the east side of the plaza are several altars and pyramids that were once covered with stucco. Note the sloping walls, wide stairs, and ramps, which are typical of Zapotec architecture and resemble the architecture of Teotihuacán. The building slightly out of line with the plaza (not on the north–south axis) is thought by some to have been an observatory and was probably aligned with the heavenly bodies rather than with the points of the compass.

The south side of the plaza has a large platform that bore several stelae, most of which are now in the National Museum of Anthropology in Mexico City. There's a good view of the surrounding area from the top of this platform.

The west side has more ceremonial platforms and pyramids. On top of the pyramid substructure are four columns that probably held the roof of the temple at one time.

The famous **building of the Dancers (Danzantes)** is on the west side of the plaza and is the earliest known structure at Monte Albán. This building is covered with large stone slabs carved into distorted naked figures (these are copies; the originals are protected in the site museum). There is speculation as to who carved these figures and what they represent. There is certainly a distinct resemblance to the Olmec "baby faces" seen at La Venta, in Tabasco state. The distorted bodies and pained expressions of the faces perhaps imply disease. There are clear examples of figures representing childbirth, dwarfism, and infantilism. Because of the fluidity of the figures, they became known as the Danzantes, but this is only a modern label for these ancient and mysterious carvings.

The **Northern Platform** is a maze of temples and palaces interwoven with subterranean tunnels and sanctuaries. Wander around here, for there are numerous reliefs, glyphs, paintings, and friezes along the lintels and jambs as well as the walls.

Leaving the Great Plaza, head north to the cemetery and tombs. Of the tombs so far excavated, the most famous is Tomb 7, to the east of the cemetery. Inside were found some 500 pieces of jewelry made of gold, amber, and turquoise, as well as art objects made of silver, alabaster, and bone. This amazing collection is on display at the Regional Museum of Oaxaca.

If you have a day to spend at Monte Albán, be sure to visit some of the tombs, for they contain some really magnificent glyphs, paintings, and stone carvings of gods, goddesses, birds, and serpents. Two tombs that are especially absorbing, Tombs 104 and 105, are guarded and can be entered via ladders; the guards are usually helpful about pointing out areas of special interest. Ignore the vendors hawking "original" artifacts, supposedly found at the site—if they were real, these guys would hardly need to wander around in the midday sun trying to sell them!

As you enter the site you'll see an on-site museum, a shop selling guidebooks to the ruins, a café, and a craft shop. I recommend you purchase one of the guidebooks. Admission to the ruins is $3.50; free on Sunday and holidays. The site is open daily from 8am to 5pm. Licensed guides charge $13.50 per person for a walking tour. Video camera permits cost $5.50.

To get to Monte Albán, take a bus from the Hotel Mesón del Angel, Mina 518, at Mier y Terán. Autobuses Turísticos makes seven runs daily, leaving at 8:30, 9:30, 10:30, and 11:30am and 12:30, 1:30, and 3:30pm. Return service leaves the ruins at 11am, noon, and 1, 2, 3, 4, and 5:30pm. The round-trip fare is $1.75. The ride takes half an hour, and your scheduled return time is two hours after your arrival. It's possible to take a later return for an additional $1; inform the driver of your intent (but you won't be guaranteed a seat). During high season there are usually additional buses.

THE ROAD TO MITLA: RUINS & RUG WEAVERS

East of Oaxaca, the Pan American Highway to Mitla rolls past several important archaeological sites, markets, and craft villages. En route you can visit the famous El Tule tree; the church at Tlacochahuaya; the ruins at Dainzú, Lambityeco, and Yagul; the weaver's village of Teotitlán del Valle; and the Saturday market village of Tlacolula.

Without a car, it's impossible to cover all these destinations in a day, and by car the route takes a very long day. On a Sunday you could combine the Tlacolula market with all the archaeological sites, which have free admission on Sunday. Save the weaving village of Teotitlán del Valle and the church of Tlacochahuaya for another day.

The **Fletes y Pasajes** bus line (☎ **951/6-2270**) runs buses every 20 minutes from 6am to 8pm to Mitla from the second-class terminal. The terminal is eight long blocks west of the zócalo on Trujano. The trip takes an hour and 15 minutes and costs $1 each way. The driver will stop at any point along the way; let him know in advance.

SANTA MARÍA DEL TULE'S 2,000-YEAR-OLD TREE Santa María del Tule is a small town (8 miles outside Oaxaca) that's filled with turkeys, children, and rug vendors. The town is famous for the immense **El Tule Tree,** an *ahuehuete* tree (Montezuma cypress) in a churchyard just off the main road. It was 2,001 years old in 1995. The enormous ancient tree is still growing today, as is evidenced by the foliage, but pollution and a sinking groundwater level are posing a serious threat. This whole region around Santa María del Tule was once very marshy; in fact, the word *tule* means "reed." A private foundation has been established in an effort to provide protection for this survivor. Beyond El Tule is agricultural country, and at siesta time you'll see whole families resting in the shade of giant cacti. You can see the tree from outside the churchyard fence, or pay $1.50 to go inside, close to the tree.

The **Church of San Jerónimo Tlacochahuaya** is a fine example of how the Spanish borrowed from Zapotec architectural design. Inside you'll see how the church leaders artistically melded the two cultures. Note the elaborately carved altar and the crucified Christ fashioned from ground dried corn cobs. Also, don't miss the still-functional organ (dated 1620) in the choir loft. The church is open from 10am to 2pm and 4 to 6pm. It's on the right side of the road, past El Tule Tree, and 14 miles from Oaxaca.

The Mitla bus will drop you off at the road leading into town. You can either hitch a ride with locals or walk the distance.

DAINZÚ: ZAPOTEC RUINS Sixteen miles from Oaxaca, this site (first excavated in the 1960s) dates to sometime between 700 and 600 B.C. Increasingly sophisticated building continued until about A.D. 300. One of the major buildings was constructed against a west-facing hill; incorporated into the lower portion of this building were found some 35 carvings resembling Monte Albán's Danzantes. These carvings are now housed in a protective shed, which a caretaker will unlock for interested parties. There is a partially reconstructed ball court. The site provides an outstanding view of the valley. Admission is $1.50.

Dainzú (dine-*zoo*), beautiful in the afternoon sun, lies less than a mile south of Highway 190, at the end of a mostly paved road. Look for a sign 16 miles from Oaxaca.

LAMBITYECO: ANOTHER ARCHAEOLOGICAL SITE On the south side of Highway 190, a few miles east of the turnoff to Dainzú, is the small site of Lambityeco. Part of a much larger site containing over 200 mounds, it is thought to have been inhabited from about 600 B.C., although the fully studied part belongs to the period following the decline of Monte Albán. Of particular interest are the two beautifully executed and preserved stucco masks of the rain god Cocijo. A product of Lambityeco was salt, distilled from saline groundwaters nearby. Admission is $1.50; $5.50 for use of your video camera.

TEOTITLÁN DEL VALLE: BEAUTIFUL RUGS This town is famous for weaving; its products can be found in the shops in Oaxaca, but if you're serious about rug shopping there's a lot of pleasure in buying them at the source and meeting the weavers in the process. Most weavers sell out of their homes and give demonstrations. The prices are considerably lower than in Oaxaca, and here you have the opportunity to visit weavers in their homes.

The church in town is well worth a visit, as is the community museum opposite the artisan's market and adjacent to the church. The museum has an interesting exhibit of the natural dye making using herbs, plants, and cochineal.

For a place to eat consider the **Restaurant Tlaminalli,** Av. Juárez 39 (☎ **952/ 4-4157**), run by six lovely Zapotec sisters who serve authentic Oaxacan cuisine. Its reputation as the shrine of Oaxacan cooking brings in lots of foreigners, but my last meal there was just average. It could have been an off day. Prices on the à la carte

Shopping at the Source: Oaxaca's Splendid Market Villages

You could spend a full week in Oaxaca just visiting the various markets held in nearby villages. Each has its specialty—cheese, produce, livestock, weaving, and pottery—and its unique character. Market days in the villages are as follows:

Wednesday	Etla, known for its cheese; $9^1/2$ miles north.
Thursday	Zaachila, ruins and agriculture; 11 miles southwest.
	Ejutla, agriculture; 40 miles south.
Friday	Ocotlán, pottery, textiles, and food; $18^1/2$ miles south.
Saturday	Oaxaca, Abastos Market.
Sunday	Tlacolula, agriculture and crafts (visit the chapel as well); $19^1/2$ miles southeast.

You can get to any of these craft villages by taking a bus from the second-class bus station, eight blocks west of the zócalo on Trujano. On market days these buses are crammed with passengers. If you get off a bus between destinations—say, at Dainzú on the way to Mitla or at Cuilapan on the way to Zaachila—but want to continue to the next place, return to the highway and hail a passing bus.

It's also possible to take a colectivo taxi to the villages that don't have bus service. To find a colectivo, head to the south end of the Abastos Market. On Calle Mercaderos you'll see dozens of parked maroon-and-white colectivo taxis. The town each one serves is written on the door, trunk, or windshield. There are also posted metal signs for destinations. They fill up relatively fast and are an economical way to reach the villages. Be sure to go early; by afternoon the colectivos don't fill up as fast and you'll have to wait.

Tours to all the markets as well as the craft villages and ruins can easily be arranged through **Tours Arnel,** at Hotel Casa Arnel, Aldama 404 (☎ 951/5-2856), or **Belaguetza,** at Arte y Tradición, García Vigil 406, (☎ 951/6-3552). There are, of course, many tour agencies in Oaxaca, but these both offer friendly, personal, English-speaking guide service at competitive prices. Three- to four-hour tours to Monte Albán or Mitla will cost about $9 per person (plus site entry). Other villages can be included at minimal cost.

Many of these historical and/or craft villages have, in the past several years, developed some truly fine small municipal museums. **San José El Mogote,** site of one of the very earliest pre-Hispanic village-dweller groups, has a display of carvings and statues found in and around the town and a display model of an old hacienda and details of its produce and social organization. **Teotitlán del Valle** is another with such a municipal museum; it features displays on the weaving process. Ask at the State Tourism Office (north side of the Alameda on Independencia) for more information on these and others.

menu seem a bit steep at $2 for soup and $5 for a smallish main course. It's on the main street as you approach the main part of town, in a red brick building on the right with black wrought iron window covers. It's open Monday through Friday from 1 to 4pm. A bit farther on, there's another nice restaurant on the left where the main street intersects with the town center.

Direct buses make the run between Oaxaca and Teotitlán from the second-class bus station. If you're coming from or going to Mitla, you'll have to hitch or walk from the highway crossroads.

TLACOLULA: A FINE MARKET & UNIQUE CHAPEL   Located about 19 miles from Oaxaca, southeast on the road to Mitla, Tlacolula is famous for its market and **Dominican chapel,** which is considered by many to be the most beautiful of the Dominican churches in the Americas. The wrought iron gates, the choir loft, and the wrought iron pulpit, considered to be unique in Mexico, are worth a look, as are the frescoes and paintings in relief. A few years ago a secret passage was found, leading to a room that contained valuable silver religious pieces. The silver was hidden during the Revolution of 1916 when there was a tide of antireligious sentiment; the articles are now back in the church.

Sunday is market day in Tlacolula, with rows of textiles fluttering in the breeze, and aisle after aisle of pottery and baskets.

YAGUL: RUINS OF A ZAPOTEC FORTRESS   This was a fortress city on a hill overlooking the valley. It's 20 miles southeast of Oaxaca, about half a mile off the road to Mitla. There's a small sign indicating the turnoff to the left; go up the paved road to the site. The setting is absolutely gorgeous, and because the ruins are not as fully reconstructed as those at Monte Albán, you're likely to have the place to yourself. It's a good place for a picnic lunch.

The city was divided into two sections: the fortress at the top of a hill and the area of palaces lower down. The center of the palace complex is the plaza, surrounded by four temples. In the center is a ceremonial platform, under which is the Triple Tomb. The door of the tomb is a large stone slab decorated on both sides with beautiful hieroglyphs. The tomb may or may not be open for viewing.

Look for the beautifully restored ball court, typical of Zapotec ball courts (which are without goal rings). North of the plaza is the incredible palace structure built for the chiefs of the city. It's a maze of huge rooms with six patios, decorated with painted stucco and stone mosaics. Here and there you can see ceremonial mounds and tombs decorated in the same geometric patterns that are found in Mitla. This is one of the most interesting palaces in the area. The panoramic view of the valley from the fortress is worth the rather exhausting climb.

Admission is $1.25; free on Sunday and holidays. Still cameras are free, but use of a video camera will cost you $4.15. Save your receipt—it will serve for any other sites visited the same day. The site is open daily from 8am to 5:30pm, but be prepared to blow 11¢ for parking.

It's just a few miles farther southeast to Mitla. The turnoff comes at a very obvious fork in the road.

MITLA: LARGE ZAPOTEC & MIXTEC SITE   Mitla is 2³/₄ miles from the highway, and the turnoff terminates at the ruins by the church. If you've come here by bus, it's about half a mile up the road from the dusty town square to the ruins; if you want to hire a cab, there are some available in the square.

Mitla was settled by the Zapotecs around 600 B.C., but became a Mixtec bastion in the late 10th century. This city of the Mixtecs was still flourishing at the time of the Spanish Conquest, and many of the buildings were used through the 16th century.

The town of Mitla (pop. 10,000) is often bypassed by the tour groups but is worth a visit. The University of the Americas maintains the **Museum of Zapotec Art** (previously known as the Frissell collection) in town. It contains some outstanding Zapotec and Mixtec relics. Admission is $1.50. Be sure to look at the Leigh collection, which contains some real treasures. The museum is housed in a beautiful old hacienda. In a back patio is the excellent **Restaurant La Sorpresa,** Av. Juárez #2 (☎ 952/8-0194), that's a pleasant place to relax. You can dine on the patio daily between 9am and 5pm. Breakfast costs from $3.50; the daily lunch special costs $5.50

Shopping for Handwoven Zapotec Rugs

For centuries the Zapotecs have been among the most skilled of Mexican weavers, and now collectors worldwide are discovering their work. So it's no secret that sleuthing for the perfect rug in the weaving village of Teotitlán del Valle is a primary quest for many foreigners. The high quality rugs are reversible and are made by families who've passed the craft on for generations.

Rug vendors and weavers with little shops begin the minute you turn left off the highway from Oaxaca to Teotitlán, and almost all of these along the stretch going into town are worth a stop. There's an artisans' rug market in town, but as you'll discover in a stroll through the dirt streets of this prosperous town, a weaver resides inside almost every house. You're welcome to knock and enter. Piles of rugs are neatly folded on tables and chairs, and they will patiently unfold them and spread them upon the floor for as long as you are willing to look.

Designs, colors, and quality vary. A few people are selling uninspired, mass produced-looking rugs made of cheap cotton or acrylic, but on the whole, craftsmanship is excellent here, with wool being the yarn of choice. The natural wool colors of white, dark brown, and black are incorporated into the rugs, and some wools are dyed using natural plants. However, most colors of blue, red, yellow, orange, and green are achieved through artificial dying.

Buying a colorfast wool rug with colorfast dyes is usually a given, but I've noticed that many shop owners will stretch the truth regarding the dyes. Perhaps because past visitors have asked for naturally dyed rugs (thinking that they're always more desirable), some storeowners (not necessarily the weavers) proclaim untruthfully that the rugs are made with naturally dyed yarn. They may also proclaim that a rug with a Navajo design is instead thoroughly Zapotec. Some weavers, but more often store owners, present a bowl of dried cochineal bugs (harvesting these insects from maguey cactus is being revived in the area), as proof that the colors appearing in their rugs are natural as opposed to commercially produced. Cochineal dye was a dynamic business in pre-Hispanic times and was coveted by Europeans after the Conquest of Mexico. But the tiny insect is difficult to cultivate even now (it attracts a host of natural predators), so the dried insects are expensive to buy. Thus any rug incorporating cochineal-dyed yarn is very expensive. And in truth adeptness in using this elusive insect as a dye (or any other natural dye for that matter), is limited to only a few dye specialists in Teotitlán. Depending on the natural or man-made chemical the insect is mixed with to achieve color variation, the color can range from pale lavender to yellow and deep orange/red. Natural indigo blue, made from leaves of a plant *(indigofera anil)*, is another widely touted color, but use of it too is exaggerated, even though it's grown in Oaxaca. In either case, a rug incorporating these natural dyes would lack uniformity of color, so any rug with perfectly matching blue or orange/red throughout probably isn't made with either

and includes soup, salad, a main course, and dessert. The lunch special is truly delicious and worth the bucks.

You can easily see the most important buildings in an hour. Mixtec architecture is based on a quadrangle surrounded on three or four sides by patios and chambers, usually rectangular in shape. The chambers have a low roof, which is excellent for defense but which makes the rooms dark and close. The stone buildings are inlaid with small cut stones to form geometric patterns.

There are five groups of buildings divided by the Mitla River. The most important buildings are on the east side of the ravine. The Group of the Columns consists of these natural colors. Knowledgeable collectors often prefer the irregularity of the same color in a rug, which is often found when natural colors are used; however, it's also true that skilled weavers may show variations of one color in an portion or rug without using naturally died yarn. Varying the same color with a different hue is an artistic weaving technique—not a ploy to fool buyers.

Traditional Zapotec rugs in pastel earthtones and with designs (usually a Greek-like fret motif) from area pyramids continue to be made; however, within the last decade a strong Navajo rug influence swept through town, radically changing local designs while deepening the colors into rich blue-greens, pale to medium yellows, strong orange-reds, handsome dark green, and dark navy to aquamarine and pale blue. These master Zapotec weavers adopted the Navajo designs readily, failing only in conquering the pleasing color combinations of the Navajos—though some weavers are excellent color designers. Purists disdain outside influence on traditional styles, but realists acknowledge the prosperity this new work brings the village. Versatile Zapotec weavers offer to weave anything to specification—show them a picture of your desired rug, and the finished work demonstrates mastery of their craft. But be prepared to present rug, specifications in meters, not inches or feet.

If you're a serious shopper, plan to spend the day going from house to shop to house, narrowing your choices as you go. In the warren of streets it's wise to collect names and addresses too, so you can retrace your steps if necessary. Prices start high, and you're expected to bargain (that's why it can take a wearying, but very interesting, day to accomplish purchases). Cut the starting price in half and see where bargaining leads. As an example, a small bathmat size rug costing $25 to $35 in Oaxaca, may cost $10 to $15 in Teotitlán. But there are large rugs too, some big enough to show handsomely under a dining room table or to become the center-piece on a large wall. Price is also affected by the complication of design and variation and number of colors. The weavers are uniformly pleasant about show-ing you many rugs without making you feel uncomfortable if you don't buy immediately—but don't ponder endlessly—time spent with you is time away from weaving. Besides rugs, the woven goods appear as pillow covers and are fashioned into purses with leather trim. These you'll find in shops on the main street rather than in homes.

Getting carried away while rug hunting here isn't unusual, so what a relief it is to discover that credit cards are accepted at most of the better storefront shops. But it's cash only in weaver's homes. Most people will accept dollars, but the exchange rate will be lower than you'd get at an exchange house or bank. Whatever currency you use, bring plenty—the rugs are so appealing that you'll probably buy more than you planned.

of two quadrangles, connected at the corners with palaces. The building to the north has a long chamber with six columns and many rooms decorated with geometric designs. The most common motif is the zigzag pattern, the same one seen repeatedly on the Mitla blankets. Human or animal images are rare in Mixtec art. In fact, only one frieze has been found (in the Group of the Church, in the north patio). Here you'll see a series of figures painted with their name glyphs.

Admission to the site is $1.50; free on Sunday and holidays. Use of a video cam-era costs $4.25. Entrance to the museum is included in the price. It's open daily from 8am to 5pm.

Outside the ruins you'll be bombarded by vendors. The moment you step out of a car or taxi, every able-bodied woman and child for 10 miles around will come charging over with shrill cries and a basket full of bargains—heavily embroidered belts, small pieces of pottery, fake archaeological relics, cheap earrings. Offer to pay half the price the vendors ask. There's a modern handicrafts market near the ruins, but prices are lower in town.

In Mitla and on the highway going south, you'll find **mezcal outlets** *(expendios de mezcal)*, which are factory outlets for little distilleries that produce the fiery cactus *aguardiente*. To be authentic, a bottle of mezcal must have a worm floating in it. The liquor is surprisingly cheap; the bottle labels are surprisingly colorful; and the taste is quite different. It is not unlike tequila—mix a shot of mezcal with a glass of grapefruit or pomegranate juice, and you've got a cocktail that will make you forget the heat, even in Mitla. Watch out for the worm!

SOUTH OF MONTE ALBÁN: ARRAZOLA, CUILAPAN & ZAACHILA

ARRAZOLA: WOOD-CARVING CAPITAL   Arrazola (ar-a-ZO-la) is in the foothills of Monte Albán, about 15 miles southwest of Oaxaca. The tiny town's most famous resident is **Manuel Jimenez,** the septuagenarian grandfather of the resurgence in wood carving as a folk art. Jimenez's polar bears, anteaters, and rabbits carved from copal wood are shown in galleries throughout the world; his home is a mecca of sorts for folk-art collectors. Now the town is full of other carvers, all making fanciful creatures painted in bright, festive colors. Among those who should be sought out are Antonio and Ramiro Aragon; their delicate and imaginative work should rank them with Jimenez. Little boys will greet you at the outskirts of town offering to guide you to individual homes for a small tip. Following them is a good way to know the town, and after a bit you can dismiss them.

If you're driving to Arrazola, take the road out of Oaxaca city that goes to Monte Albán, then take the left fork after crossing the Atoyac River and follow the signs for Zaachila. Turn right after the town of Xoxo and you will soon be there. There are no road signs, but other travelers along the way will direct you. The bus from the second-class station in Oaxaca will let you off at the side of the road to Arrazola where it meets the highway. From there it's a pleasant 3 1/2-mile walk to the town, past a few homes, the occupants of which are wood carvers who will invite you in for a look at their work. To return, colectivo taxis make the run to Zaachila and Oaxaca for around $2, which can be shared—it's worth it.

CUILAPAN: A DOMINICAN MONASTERY   Cuilapan (kwi-LAP-an) is located about 10 miles southwest of Oaxaca. The Dominican friars began their second monastery here in 1550. However, parts of the convent and church were never completed due to political machinations of the late 16th century. The roof of the monastery has fallen, but the cloister and the church remain. The church is being restored and is still used today. There are three naves with lofty arches, large stone columns, and many frescoes. It is open daily from 10am till 6pm; entry is $5.50, plus $8.50 for a video camera. The monastery is visible on the right a short distance from the main road to Zaachila, and there's a sign as well. The bus from the second-class station stops within a few hundred feet of the church.

ZAACHILA: MARKET TOWN WITH MIXTEC TOMBS   Farther on from Cuilapan, 15 miles southwest of Oaxaca, Zaachila (Za-CHEE-la) has a Thursday market; baskets and pottery are sold for local household use, and the produce market is always full. Also take note of the interesting livestock section and a *mercado de madera* (wood market) just as you enter town.

Near and behind the church is the entrance to a small archaeological site containing several mounds and platforms and two quite interesting tombs. Artifacts found there now reside in the National Museum of Anthropology in Mexico City, but Tomb 1 contains carvings worth seeing.

At the time of the Spanish Conquest, Zaachila was the last surviving city of the Zapotec rulers. When Cortés marched on the city, the Zapotecs did not resist and instead formed an alliance with him, which outraged the Mixtecs, who invaded Zaachila shortly afterward. The site and the tombs are open daily from 9am till 4pm, and the entrance fee is $1.50.

To return to Oaxaca, you have a choice of walking several blocks back to the second-class bus station near the animal market or lining up with the locals for one of the colectivo taxis on the main street across from the market. I prefer the taxi.

South Along Highway 175

SAN BARTOLO COYOTEPEC: BLACK POTTERY San Bartolo is the home of the black pottery you've seen in all the stores in Oaxaca. It's also one of several little villages named Coyotepec in the area. Buses frequently operate between Oaxaca and this village, 23 miles south on Highway 175. In 1953, a native woman named Doña Rosa invented the technique of smoking the pottery during firing to make it black and rubbing the fired pieces with a piece of quartz to produce a sheen. Doña Rosa died in 1979, but her son, Valente Nieto Real, carries on the tradition. It is an almost spiritual experience to watch Valente change a lump of coarse clay into a work of living art with only two crude plates used as a potter's wheel. The family's home/factory is a few blocks off the main road; you'll see the sign as you enter town. It's open daily from 9am to 5:30pm.

Black pottery is sold at many shops on the little plaza or in the artists' homes. Villagers who make pottery often place a piece of their work near their front door, by the gate, or on the street. It's their way of inviting prospective buyers to come in.

SAN MARTÍN TILCAJETE: ANOTHER WOOD-CARVING CENTER San Martín Tilcajete is a recent addition to the tour of folk-art towns. Located about 10 miles south of San Bartolo Coyotepec, San Martín is noted, as is Arrazola, for its wood-carvers and their fantastical, brightly painted animals and dragons. The Sosa and Hernández families are especially prolific, and you can easily spend half a day wandering from house to house to see the amazing collections of hot-pink rabbits, 4-foot-long bright blue twisting snakes, and two-headed Dalmatians.

OCOTLÁN: MARKET TOWN & THE AGUILAR POTTERS One of the best markets in the area is held on Friday in Ocotlán de Morelos, 35 miles south of Oaxaca on Highway 175. The variety of goods includes modern dishware and cutlery, hand-molded earthenware jugs, polyester dresses, finely woven cotton or wool rebozos (scarves), hand-dyed and tooled leather, and electronics, as well as produce. You won't find a more varied selection except in Oaxaca. On other than market day, you can always visit Ocotlán's most famous potters, the noted Aguilar family—Josephina, Guillermina, and Irena. On the right, just at the outskirts of Ocotlán, their row of home-workshops is distinguished by pottery pieces stuck up on the fence and the roof. Their work, often figures of daily life, is colorful, sometimes humorous, and highly prized by collectors. Visitors are welcome daily.

North of Oaxaca

GUELATAO: BIRTHPLACE OF BENITO JUÁREZ Set high in the mountains north of Oaxaca, this town has become a living monument to its favorite son, Benito

Juárez. Although usually peaceful, this lovely town comes to life on Juárez's birthday (March 21). The museum, statues, and plaza all attest to the town's obvious devotion to the patriot.

To get here, a second-class bus departs from Oaxaca's first-class station six times daily. There are also several departures from the second-class station. The trip will take at least two hours, through gorgeous mountain scenery. Buses return to Oaxaca every two hours until 8pm.

2 Tuxtla Gutiérrez

51 miles W of San Cristóbal, 173 miles S of Villahermosa, 151 miles NW of Ciudad Cuauhtémoc on the Guatemalan border

Tuxtla Gutiérrez (alt. 1,838 ft.; pop. 300,000) is the boom town capital of the wild, mountainous state of Chiapas. Long Mexico's coffee-growing center, the city has recently become an oil prospector's mecca. While Tuxtla is not exactly an unpleasant town, it hasn't been able to manage growth with any aesthetic considerations. To tourists, who are more of a footnote than a feature of town, Tuxtla Gutiérrez is a necessary crossroads for getting to San Cristóbal. If you have some time to spare, visit the Tuxtla zoo and Sumidero Canyon.

ESSENTIALS

GETTING THERE & DEPARTING   By Plane   Aviación de Chiapas (also known as Aviacsa, ☎ **961/2-6880** or 961/2-8081; fax 961/3-5029; at the airport 961/5-1011) connects Tuxtla to Cancún, Chetumal, Mérida, Mexico City, Guatemala City, Villahermosa, and Oaxaca. **Mexicana** (☎ **961/2-0020** or 961/2-5402; at the airport 961/3-4921) has daily flights from Mexico City, Cancún, Mérida, Oaxaca, and Villahermosa. Check with the local offices of Mexicana about van departures to the airport. They leave from the downtown office or will pick you up at your hotel if you reserve in advance. When the office is closed, the van departs from the plaza in front of the Gran Hotel Humberto. Vans leave about two hours before each scheduled departure from the Llano San Juan airport. **Aerocaribe** (☎ **961/1-1490;** fax 961/2-2053; at the airport 961/5-1530), a Mexicana affiliate, flies between Tuxtla and Oaxaca from Tuxtla's small Aeropuerto Terán and to Cancún from the larger Llano San Juan airport. Aerocaribe and other commuter flights arrive at Tuxtla's downtown airport, a short taxi ride from the town center. Aviacsa seems to have more passengers on its flights from Tuxtla and seems to keep more to its schedule than Aerocaribe.

Tuxtla's large airport, Llano San Juan, about 40 minutes from town, is subject to closures and delays because of rain, high winds, and fog. If the weather looks bad, double-check your flight departure. It's possible the smaller Aeropuerto Terán, which is closer to town, will be expanded to accommodate larger planes.

Important note: If you're flying on Aerocaribe and Aviacsa, be sure to clarify from which airport you'll be departing. Your ticket *may not* indicate the right airport or the right name of the airline, so check with the airline directly or a travel agent in Tuxtla.

By Bus   First-class **Omnibus Cristóbal Colón** (☎ 961/2-2624) goes every half hour to San Cristóbal (from 5am to 9:15pm) and runs seven daily buses to Tuxtla from Villahermosa, three to Oaxaca, and fourteen to Comitán and Ciudad Cuauhtémoc on the Guatemalan border. There are four "deluxe plus" buses to Palenque between

7am and midnight. The first-class San Cristóbal buses are generally easy to book, unless it's a holiday; at such times, you may face a wait. **Transportes Rudolfo Figueroa** also provides deluxe service daily to and from Palenque.

By Car   From Oaxaca or Veracruz, you enter Tuxtla by Highway 190. From Villahermosa or San Cristóbal, you'll enter at the opposite end of town. Eventually, you will end up at the big main square, Plaza Cívica.

From Tuxtla to Villahermosa, take Highway 199 then cut north on Highway 195 to Villahermosa. To San Cristóbal, take Highway 199 all the way. Because the road from Tuxtla to San Cristóbal and Villahermosa is mountainous and curvy, don't be in a hurry. It's in good repair to San Cristóbal, but there are many bad spots between San Cristóbal and Palenque. The trip from Tuxtla to Villahermosa takes eight hours by car, and the scenery is beautiful.

By Taxi   Taxi drivers solicit riders to San Cristóbal outside the bus station and airports. The going rate of $27 to $33 per car can be shared by up to four passengers. You'll have to wait for them to assemble, however, unless fewer than four agree to split the fare. I've used this service several times, and it's worked well.

ORIENTATION   Arriving   From the international airport off Highway 190, it's a 40-minute ride to the center of town. The colectivo into town costs $7.50, more if there are only a few passengers. Don't tarry at the airport—the vans fill up and leave immediately, and taxis charge about five times the price of a colectivo for the same trip downtown.

The Cristóbal Colón bus terminal, 2a Avenida Norte and 2a Calle Poniente, is two blocks west of Calle Central.

For information about getting to San Cristóbal directly from the airport, see "Arriving & Departing: By Taxi," above.

Information   The **tourist office** (☎ 961/2-5509 or 961/2-4535) is in the Secretaría de Fomento Económico building (previously called the Plaza de las Instituciones) on Avenida Central/Bulevar Domínguez, near the Hotel Bonampak Tuxtla. It's on the first floor of the plaza and is open Monday through Friday from 8am to 9pm. Most questions can be answered at the information booth in front of the office. There are also information booths at the international airport (staffed when flights are due) and at the zoo (open Tuesday through Sunday from 9am to 3pm and 6 to 9pm). Another kiosk (open the same hours as the one at the zoo) is located on Highway 190 about three miles west of town.

City Layout   The city is divided by two "Central" streets: **Calle Central,** running north to south, and **Avenida Central** (also called Avenida 14 de Septiembre), running east to west. The main highway is Avenida Central (also named Bulevar Domínguez west of downtown). Streets are numbered from these central arteries, with the suffix *norte, sur, oriente,* or *poniente* designating the direction of progress from the central arteries.

Getting Around   **Buses** to all parts of the city converge upon the Plaza Cívica along Calle Central. **Taxi** fares are higher here than in other regions; for example, a taxi across town from the bus station to the tourist office is $4.50.

Fast Facts   The local **American Express** representative is Viajes Marabasco, Plaza Bonampak, Loc. 4, Col. Moctezuma, near the tourist office (☎ **961/2-6998;** fax 961/2-4053). The **telephone area code** is 961.

TUXTLA'S MUSEUM & ZOO

The majority of travelers simply pass through Tuxtla on their way to San Cristóbal or Oaxaca. The excellent zoo and the Sumidero Canyon are the best places to spend time you have to spare.

Calzada de los Hombres Illustres. 1A Oriente Nte. at 5A Oriente Nte. Park and botanical garden, free; museum, $3.50; free on Sunday. Open: Museum, Tues–Sun 9am–4pm; botanical garden, daily 8:30am–5pm; children's area, Tues–Sun 8am–8pm. The park is 11 blocks northwest of the main plaza; catch a colectivo along Avenida Central or walk about 15 minutes west along Calle 5a Oriente Norte.

Tuxtla's cultural highlights are clustered in this area, once referred to as the Parque Madero. The park is one part of the area, which also includes the **Regional Museum of Anthropology,** a botanical garden, a children's area, and the city theater. The museum features exhibits on the lifestyles of the people of Chiapas and some artifacts from the state's archaeological sites. In one short stop you can learn about Chiapas's past civilizations, its flora, and its present-day accomplishments. It also has a FONART (government crafts) shop and cafeteria.

Miguel Alvarez del Toro Zoo (ZOOMAT). Bulevar Samuel León Brinois, southeast of downtown. Free admission; donations solicited. Tues–Sun 9am–5:30pm. The zoo is about 5 miles southeast of downtown; buses for the zoo can be found along Avenida Central and at the Calzada.

Located in the forest called El Zapotal, ZOOMAT is one of the best zoos in Mexico, and it's one of my personal favorites. The collection of animals and birds indigenous to this area gives the visitor a tangible sense of what the wilds of Chiapas are like. Jaguars, howler monkeys, owls, and many more exotic animals are kept in roomy cages that replicate their home terrain, and the whole zoo is so deeply buried in vegetation that you can almost pretend you're in a natural habitat. Unlike at other zoos I've visited, the animals are almost always on view; many will come to the fence if you make a kissing noise.

SHOPPING

The government-operated **Casa de las Artesanías,** Bulevar Domínguez 2035 (☎ **961/3-3478**), is both a shop and gallery. The two stories of rooms feature a fine, extensive collection of crafts grouped by region and type from throughout the state of Chiapas. It's open Monday through Saturday from 9am to 2pm and 5 to 8pm and Sunday from 9am to 1pm.

WHERE TO STAY

As Tuxtla booms, the center of the hotel industry has moved out of town, west to Highway 190. As you come in from the airport, you'll notice the new motel-style hotels such as the Hotel Flamboyant, Palace Inn, Hotel Laganja, La Hacienda, and the older Hotel Bonampak Tuxtla. All these are more expensive than those listed below, which are in the heart of town.

Gran Hotel Humberto. Av. Central 180, Tuxtla Gutiérrez, Chi. 29000. ☎ **961/2-2080.** Fax 961/2-9771. 112 rms (all with bath). TV TEL. $27 single; $37 double.

This older 10-story inner-city hotel is your best budget bet in booming Tuxtla. It's clean and comfortable enough, with well-kept furnishings dating from the 1950s. However, it isn't always an oasis of peace and quiet, especially on weekends when church bells compete with the ninth-floor nightclub. The location is ideal—it's in the center of town half a block from Plaza Cívica restaurants and the Mexicana airline office and 1¹/₂ blocks from the Cristóbal Colón bus station.

Hotel Esponda. 1a Calle Poniente Nte. 142, Tuxtla Gutiérrez, Chi. 29030. ☎ **961/2-0080** or 961/2-9771. 50 rms (all with bath). FAN TV TEL. $14 single; $18 double. Free parking.

In a city where inexpensive rooms are hard to come by, the Esponda is an excellent choice. Its rooms are in a nondescript five-story building with an elevator. The brown, green, and yellow decor is a bit unsettling, but the rooms are perfectly satisfactory— each has one, two, or three double beds; showers (without doors or curtains); big closets; and powerful ceiling fans. The hotel is conveniently located one block from the Plaza Cívica, near the Cristóbal Colón bus station.

WHERE TO EAT

Tuxtla's main plaza, the **Plaza Cívica** (Avenida Central at 1 Poniente), is actually two plazas separated by Avenida Central. Rimming the edges are numerous restaurants, many of which serve customers outdoors under umbrella-shaded tables. The restaurants change names with frequency, so I won't recommend one over another. Just stroll the area and pick one that looks interesting, clean, and reasonably priced.

♦ **Las Pichanchas.** Av. Central Ote. 837. ☎ **961/2-5351.** Tamales $1.50–$1.75 each; main courses $4–$8. Daily 8am–11:30 (live marimba music 2:30–5:30pm and 8:30–11:30pm; patio dinner show Tues–Sun at 9pm). Closed New Year's Day and the two days following Easter. MEXICAN.

No trip to Tuxtla Gutiérrez is complete without a meal at this colorfully decorated restaurant devoted to the regional food and drink of Chiapas. Inverted *pichanchas* (pots full of holes used to make *nixtamal* masa dough) are hung on posts as lanterns. For a sampler plate, try the *platón de carnes frías* (cold meat platter, which includes different local sausages, ham, cheese, and tortillas) or the *platón de botana regional* (a variety of hot tidbits). The cold meat platter and the especially tasty *butifarra* both feed two or three people nicely. Since Chiapan tamales are tastier and larger than those you may have eaten elsewhere, you must try at least one. From the Hotel Humberto in the center of town, walk six to eight blocks south; you'll find the restaurant on the left.

ROAD TRIPS FROM TUXTLA GUTIÉRREZ

CHIAPA DE CORZO: HOME OF A LACQUER-PAINTING MUSEUM   The small town of Chiapa de Corzo is a 30-minute, 8-mile ride by bus from the main square (buses leave every 15 minutes in the morning, every 30 minutes in the afternoon), or a 10- to 15-minute ride by taxi. Those going on to San Cristóbal or over the mountains to the Yucatán (see chapter 15) will pass through this town on their way.

Chiapa de Corzo has a small **museum** on the main square dedicated to the city's lacquer industry; an interesting church; a colonial fountain; and a small **pyramid,** somewhat restored and visible from the road. In the museum, you can often see women learning the regional craft of lacquer painting, and sometimes mask makers give carving demonstrations and lessons.

EL SUMIDERO: AN AWESOME, SHEER-WALLED CANYON   Another, more spectacular trip is to the canyon of El Sumidero, 10 miles northeast of the center of town along a country road. You can hire a taxi for a road tour of the canyon's rim and five lookout points for about $15 per hour. Boat rides through the canyon can be arranged through some travel agencies and hotels in Tuxtla and through the Tuxtla office of **Transportes al Cañon** (☎ 961/3-3584). You can tour the canyon on your own by taking a bus or taxi to Chiapa de Corzo and negotiating a ride along the riverbed; the cost should be around $40 for five persons for a two-hour ride. You can also go by bus to Cahuare from the main square and arrange for a boat under the Grijalva River Bridge; the rate may be somewhat lower here.

3 San Cristóbal de las Casas

143 miles SW of Palenque, 50 miles E of Tuxtla Gutiérrez, 46 miles NW of Comitán, 104 miles NW of Cuauhtémoc, 282 miles E of Oaxaca

San Cristóbal is a colonial town set in a lovely valley—itself nearly 7,000 feet high—where the centuries-old Maya civilization continues to flourish. Part of the town's name is derived from the 16th-century bishop Fray Bartolome de las Casas, who sought to protect native peoples from exploitation. Nearly all the Indians in the immediate area speak languages such as Tzotzil or Tzeltal, which are derived from the ancient Maya. The town of 90,000 is the major market center for Maya Indians of various groups who trek down from the surrounding mountains, but some groups, such as the Lacandóns (who number only about 450) don't come into town at all; they live so far off in the forests of eastern Chiapas that it takes six days on horseback to get to their territory.

Probably the most visible among the local indigenous groups are the Chamula. The men wear baggy thigh-length trousers and white or black serapes, while the women wear blue rebozos, gathered white blouses with embroidered trim, and black wool wraparound skirts.

Another local Indian group is the Zinacantecan, whose male population dresses in light-pink overshirts with colorful trim and tassels and sometimes short pants. Hat ribbons (now a rare sight) are tied on married men, while ribbons dangle loosely from the hats of bachelors and community leaders. The Zinacantecan women wear beautiful, brightly colored woven shawls along with black wool skirts. You may also see Tenejapa men clad in knee-length black tunics and flat straw hats and Tenejapa women dressed in beautiful reddish and rust-colored *huipils*. Women of all groups are barefooted, while men wear handmade sandals or cowboy boots.

There are several Indian villages within access of San Cristóbal by road—Chamula, with its weavers and non-Christian church; Zinacantán, whose residents practice a unique religion and wear brilliantly colored clothing; Tenejapa, San Andrés, and Magdalena, known for brocaded textiles; Amatenango del Valle, a town of potters; and Aguacatenango, known for embroidery. Most of these "villages" consist of little more than a church and the municipal government building, with homes scattered for miles around and a general gathering only for church and market days (usually Sunday).

You'll hear the word *ladino* here—it refers to non-Indian Mexicans or people who have taken up modern ways, changed their dress, dropped their Indian traditions and language, and decided to live in town. It may be used derogatorily or descriptively, depending on who is using the term and how it's used.

Other local lingo you should know about includes *Jovel*, San Cristóbal's original name, used often by businesses, and *coleto*, meaning someone or something from San Cristóbal. You'll see signs for tamales coletos, coleto bread, and coleto breakfast.

In recent years, San Cristóbal has become more popular with Mexicans, not to mention North Americans and Europeans in search of a charming, "unspoiled" traditional town to visit. Evangelical Protestant missionaries recently have converted large numbers of indigenous peoples, and in some villages new converts find themselves expelled from their homelands—in Chamula, for example, as many as 30,000 people have been expelled. Many of these people, called *expulsados* (expelled ones), have taken up residence in new villages on the outskirts of San Cristóbal de las Casas.

They still wear their traditional dress. Other villages, such as Tenejapa, allow the Protestant church to exist, and villagers to attend it without prejudice.

Although the influx of tourists is increasing and the influence of outsiders (including Mexicans) is inevitably chipping away at the culture, the Indians aren't really interested in being or looking like the foreigners in their midst. They may steal glances at tourists or even stare curiously, but mainly they pay little attention to outsiders. Just in case we think they are envious of our clothing, possessions, or culture, I'll repeat an interesting comment made one night during dinner at Na-Bolom with a Maya specialist living in San Cristóbal: "They think we are the remains of a leftover civilization and that we eat our babies."

Important note: In January 1994, Indians from this area led a revolt against the *ladino*-led towns and Mexican government over health care, education, land distribution, and representative government. Finally, after two years of on-again-off-again negotiations between the Indians and the government, both sides have agreed to resolve a portion of the disagreement. Discussions about remaining issues are ongoing and tension still exists in the area. However, the conflict seems not to have deterred travelers from Europe from visiting, and hotels are often filled with them. The only tourists missing are those from the United States. Polite armed military personnel are still stopping traffic at several roadblocks on all highways leading to San Cristóbal. At these stops, travelers may be required to present personal travel documents such as tourist permits, passports, or other identification and to state the purpose of their travel. Some vehicles are searched.

ESSENTIALS

GETTING THERE & DEPARTING   By Plane   For the status of services at a proposed new airport near San Cristóbal, check with the Municipal Tourism Office (see "Information," below). Until the new airport is open, there are no commercial flights to San Cristóbal—only charter flights to Comitán. Tour agencies in Palenque and San Cristóbal can arrange charter flights between the two cities for a minimum of four people, but the flights are costly.

Charter-flight arrangements or flight changes on any airline in another city can be made through ATC Tours and Travel, across from El Fogón de Jovel Restaurant in San Cristóbal (☎ 967/8-2550; fax 967/8-3145).

By Bus   To/From Palenque: From both Tuxtla Gutiérrez and Palenque, **Transportes Rudolfo Figueroa, Mundo Maya,** and **Autotransportes Cristóbal Colón** all have deluxe service several times a day. Three first-class Cristóbal Colón buses go to Palenque daily at 9:30am and 4:45 and 5:15pm. In either city, buy your ticket the day before your planned departure to ensure a seat.

To/From Tuxtla Gutiérrez: The best way to get to San Cristóbal from Tuxtla Gutiérrez is to hop on one of the 12 direct buses from the first-class Cristóbal Colón bus station for the 1¹/₂-hour trip or to take one of the deluxe Autotransportes Cristóbal Colón or Transportes Rudolfo Figueroa buses. The road between Tuxtla and San Cristóbal is curvy and the buses cover it rapidly, so motion sickness is a consideration. The highway climbs to almost 7,000 feet in a matter of 50 miles, and the scenery is spectacular. To Tuxtla, **Cristóbal Colón** (☎ 967/8-0291) has hourly first-class buses (called locales) from 6:30am to 9:30pm originating in San Cristóbal; nine others pass through (de paso). There are deluxe "plus" Cristóbal Colón buses departing for Tuxtla daily at 4 and 5:30pm.

To/From Villahermosa: One daily Cristóbal Colón bus leaves for Villahermosa at 10am and takes seven to eight hours.

San Cristóbal de las Casas

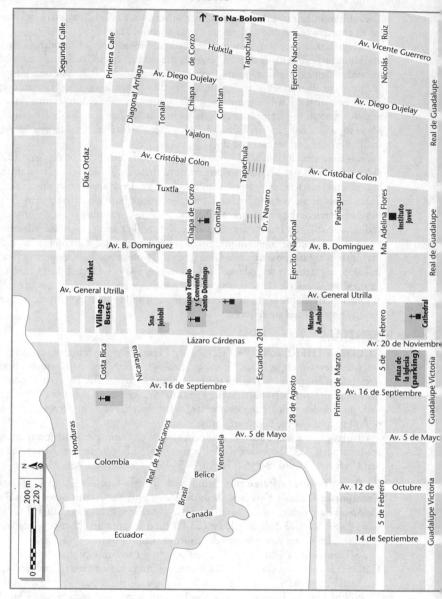

To/From Oaxaca: There's daily service on Cristóbal Colón to Oaxaca at 10am and 5:15pm; be prepared for a 12-hour trip.

To/From Mérida: Deluxe "plus" Cristóbal Colón buses leave for Mérida at 9am and 8pm (a 14-hour trip). Purchase your ticket a day or two in advance.

By Taxi Taxis from Tuxtla Gutiérrez to San Cristóbal leave from both the airport and the Cristóbal Colón bus station. See "Getting There & Departing" in Tuxtla Gutiérrez for details.

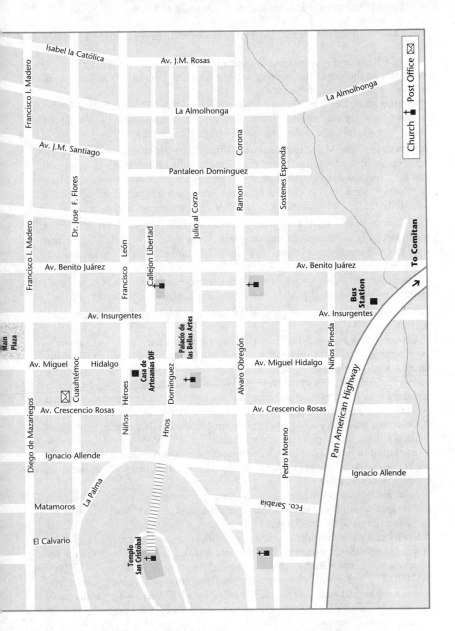

By Car From Tuxtla, a 1½-hour trip, the road winds through beautiful mountain country. The road between Palenque and San Cristóbal de las Casas is adventurous and provides jungle scenery, but portions of it may be heavily potholed, washed out, or have dangerous dips. The trip takes about five hours.

ORIENTATION Arriving The **first-class Cristóbal Colón bus station** is on Highway 190, which runs on the southern outskirts of San Cristóbal. The street that intersects the highway in front of the bus station is Avenida de los Insurgentes. From the station, the main plaza is nine blocks north along Insurgentes (a 10- or 15-minute walk).

Deluxe **Rudolfo Figueroa** buses traveling between Palenque and Tuxtla drop off passengers on the side of the highway near the first-class bus station. To catch a cab or minibus, walk over to the station.

Urbano minibuses (see "Getting Around," below) pass by the station on Utrilla headed toward the central plaza. Use these if you have only a small bag; if you have heftier luggage, take one of the taxis from in front of the station.

Information   The **Municipal Tourism Office** (☎ 967/8-0660, ext. 126), on the main square in the town hall, across the street from the cathedral, is well organized and has a friendly, helpful staff. The office keeps especially convenient hours: Monday through Saturday from 9am to 8pm and Sunday from 9am to 2pm. Check the bulletin board here for apartments, shared rides, cultural events, and local tours.

City Layout   The cathedral marks the main plaza, where Avenida de los Insurgentes becomes Utrilla. All streets crossing the plaza change their names here. The market is nine blocks north along Utrilla, while the bus station is south. From the market, minibuses (colectivos) trundle to outlying villages.

Take note that this town has at least three streets named "Domínguez." There's Hermanos Domínguez, Belisário Domínguez, and Pantaleón Domínguez.

Getting Around   Most of the sights and shopping in San Cristóbal are within walking distance of the plaza.

Urbano buses are minibuses that take residents to and from town and the outlying neighborhoods. All buses pass by the market and central plaza on their way through town. Utrilla and Avenida 16 de Septiembre are the two main arteries; all buses use the market area as the last stop. Utrilla is one-way going toward the market, and any bus on that street will take you to the market. "María Auxiliadora" buses pass by all the bus stations on the way to the distant barrio of the same name.

Colectivo buses to outlying villages depart from the public market at Avenida General Utrilla. Buses late in the day are usually very crowded. Always check to see when the last or next-to-last bus returns from wherever you're going, then take the one before that—those last buses sometimes don't materialize, and you'll be stranded. I speak from experience!

As traffic increases in the city, it often seems quicker to walk to your destination than to grab a taxi. Rides from the plaza to most parts of the city are less than $2. There is a taxi stand on the east side of the plaza.

Rental cars come in handy for trips to the outlying villages and may be worth the expense when shared by a group, but keep in mind that insurance is invalid on unpaved roads. There's a **Budget** rental-car office here at Av. Mazariegos 36 (☎ **961/ 8-3100**). You'll save money by arranging the rental from your home country; otherwise, a day's rental with insurance will cost $62 for a VW Beetle with manual transmission, the cheapest car for rent. Office hours are from 8am to 1pm and 5 to 8pm Monday through Sunday.

Rental bicycles are another option for getting around the city; a day's rental is about $10. Bikes are available at **Rent a Bike,** Av. Insurgentes 57 (☎ 961/8-4157), and at some hotels.

FAST FACTS: San Cristóbal de las Casas

Area Code   The telephone area code is 967.

Books   *Living Maya* (Abrams) by Walter Morris, with photography by Jeffrey Fox, is the best book to read to understand the culture around San Cristóbal de las Casas.

The People of the Bat: Mayan Tales and Dreams from Zinacantán (Smithsonian) by Robert M. Laughlin is a priceless collection of beliefs from that village near San Cristóbal. Another good book with a completely different overview of today's Maya is *The Heart of the Sky* by Peter Canby chronicling his recent travels among the Maya and their struggles.

Bookstore For a good selection of books about local Indians and crafts, go to Librería Soluna, Real de Guadalupe 13B and Insurgentes 27. Another good bookstore is La Pared de Las Casas, located in the Centro Cultural El Puente (Real de Guadalupe #55). Here you'll find a selection of both new and used books, as well as a collection of travel guides and postcards.

Climate San Cristóbal can be very cold day or night year-round, especially during the winter. Most hotels are not heated, although some have fireplaces. Come prepared to bundle up in layers that can be peeled off. I always bring heavy socks, gloves, long johns, and a wool jacket, except in June, July, and August, when I take only heavy socks and a medium-weight jacket or sweater. Some sort of rain gear is handy year-round as well, especially in summer, when rains can be torrential.

Currency Exchange Banamex is on the main plaza opposite the municipal palace; it's open Monday through Friday from 9:30am to 1pm. However, the most convenient place to exchange money is the Lacantún Money Exchange on Real de Guadalupe 12A, half a block from the plaza and next to the Real del Valle Hotel. It's open Monday through Saturday from 9am to 2pm and 4 to 8pm and Sunday from 9am to 1pm.

Parking If your hotel does not have parking, use the underground public lot (*estacionamiento*) located in front of the cathedral, just off the main square on 16 de Septiembre. Entry is from Calle 5 de Febrero. They charge $1.50 for 12 hours, $3 for 24 hours.

Photography Warning Photographers should be very cautious about when, where, and at whom or what they point their cameras. In San Cristóbal, taking a photograph of even a chile pepper can be a risky undertaking, partly because of the native belief that a photograph endangers the soul and partly because the native people are tired of being photographed. Especially in the San Cristóbal market, people who think they or their possessions are being photographed may angrily pelt photographers with whatever object is at hand. Be respectful and ask first. You might even try offering a small amount of money in exchange for taking a picture. Young handcraft vendors will sometimes offer to be photographed for money.

Important note: In villages outside San Cristóbal, there are strict rules about photography. To ensure proper respect by outsiders, villages around San Cristóbal, especially Chamula and Zinacantán, require visitors to go to the municipal building upon arrival and sign an agreement (written in Spanish) not to take photographs. The penalty for disobeying these regulations is stiff—confiscation of your camera and perhaps even a lengthy stay in jail. They mean it!

Post Office The post office (Correo) is at Crecencio Rosas and Cuauhtémoc, half a block south of the main square. It's open Monday through Friday from 8am to 7pm for purchasing stamps and mailing letters, 9am to 1pm and 4 to 5pm for mailing packages, and Saturday and holidays from 9am to 1pm.

Spanish Classes The **Centro Bilingue,** at the Centro Cultural El Puente, Real de Guadalupe 55, San Cristóbal de las Casas, Chi. 29250 (☎ and fax **967/8-3723,** or 800-303-4983 in the U.S.), offers classes in Spanish. The Director, Roberto Rivas, customizes instruction, be it one-on-one or in a small group, and strongly recommends that students expand their study by lodging with a local family. The

Instituto Jovel, María Adelina Flores 21 (Apdo. Postal 62), San Cristóbal de las Casas, Chi. 29250 (☎ and fax **967/8-4069**) is another well-regarded center for learning Spanish. Living with a local family is also part of the learning experience.

EXPLORING SAN CRISTÓBAL

Although San Cristóbal, a mountain town, is hard to get to, it continues to draw more and more visitors who come to enjoy the scenery, air, and hikes in the mountains. The town's biggest attraction is its colorful, centuries-old indigenous culture. The Chiapan Maya, attired in their beautifully crafted native garb, surround tourists in San Cristóbal, but most travelers take at least one trip to the outlying villages for a truer vision of Maya life.

FESTIVALS

In nearby Chamula, **Carnaval,** the big annual festival that takes place days before Lent, is a fascinating mingling of the Christian pre-Lenten ceremonies and the ancient Maya celebration of the five "lost days" at the end of the 360-day Maya agricultural cycle. Around noon on Shrove Tuesday, groups of village elders run across patches of burning grass as a purification rite, and then macho residents run through the streets with a bull. During Carnaval, roads are closed in town, and buses drop off visitors at the outskirts.

Warning: No photography of any kind is allowed during the Chamula Carnaval celebrations.

Nearby villages (except Zinacantán) also have celebrations during this time, although they're perhaps not as dramatic. Visiting these villages, especially on the Sunday before Lent, will round out your impression of Carnaval in all its regional varieties. In Tenejapa, the celebrants are still active during the Thursday market after Ash Wednesday.

San Cristóbal explodes with lights, excitement, and hordes of visitors during the week after Easter, when the annual **Feria de Primavera** (Spring Festival) is held. Activities, which fill an entire week, include carnival rides, food stalls, handcraft shops, parades, and band concerts. Hotel rooms are scarce, and room prices rise accordingly.

Another spectacle is staged July 22–25, the dates of the annual **Fiesta of San Cristóbal,** the town's patron saint. The steps up to San Cristóbal church are lit with torches at night. Pilgrimages to the church begin several days earlier, and on the night of the 24th, there's an all-night vigil.

ATTRACTIONS IN TOWN

✪ **Na-Bolom.** Av. Vicente Guerrero 3, San Cristóbal de las Casas, Chi. 29200. ☎ and fax **967/8-5586** for the cultural center; ☎ and fax 967/8-1418 for hotel reservations. Admission $2 individual tours; $3 group tour and film *La Reina de la Selva*—an excellent 50-minute film on the Bloms, the Lacandóns, and Na-Bolom. Individual tours (in Spanish) are available daily 11:30am–1:30pm. The group tour and film *La Reina de la Selva* (in English) is offered Tues–Sun 4:30–7:30pm. Leave the square on Real de Guadalupe, walk 4 blocks to Avenida Vicente Guerrero, and turn left; Na-Bolom is 5¹/₂ blocks up Guerrero, just past the intersection with Comitán.

If you're interested in the anthropology of this region, you'll want to visit this house-cum-museum and stay here if you can. The house, built as a seminary in 1891, became the headquarters of anthropologists Frans and Trudy Blom in 1951 and the gathering place of outsiders interested in studying the region. Frans Blom led many early archaeological studies in Mexico, and Trudy was noted for her photographs of the Lacandón Indians and her efforts to save them and their forest homeland. A room at Na-Bolom contains a selection of her Lacandón photographs, and postcards of the photographs are on sale. A tour of the home includes the displays of pre-Hispanic artifacts collected by Frans Blom, the cozy library with its numerous volumes about the region and the Maya, and the gardens Trudy Blom started for the ongoing reforestation of the Lacandón jungle. Trudy Blom died in 1993, but Na-Bolom continues to operate as a nonprofit public trust.

The 13 guest rooms, named for surrounding villages, are decorated with local objects and textiles. All rooms have fireplaces. Guests are allowed to use the extensive library devoted to Maya literature. Prices for rooms (including breakfast) are $28 single and $30 double.

Even if you're not a guest here you can come for a meal, usually a delicious assortment of vegetarian dishes. Just be sure to make a reservation and be on time. The colorful dining room has one large table; it's a gathering place for scholars, anthropologists, archaeologists, and the like, and the eclectic mix can make for interesting conversation. After dinner, if there's interest, a host will light a fire in the library, and guests can gather there for coffee and conversation amidst more of the Bloms' pre-Hispanic artifacts. Breakfast costs $3.25, lunch and dinner $4.25 each. Following breakfast at 9am, tours to San Juan Chamula and Zinacantán are offered. (See "The Nearby Maya Villages & Countryside" below.)

Museo Templo y Convento Santo Domingo. Av. 20 de Noviembre. ☎ **967/8-1600.** Church, free. Museum, Tues–Sat $3; Sun and holidays free. Museum, Tues–Sun 10am–5pm.

Inside the front door of the carved-stone plateresque facade, there's a beautiful gilded wooden altarpiece built in 1560, walls with saints, and gilt-framed paintings. Attached to the church is the former Convent of Santo Domingo, which houses a small museum about San Cristóbal and Chiapas. The museum, housed on three floors, has changing exhibits and often shows cultural films. It's five blocks north of the zócalo.

The Cathedral. 20 de Noviembre at Guadalupe Victoria. No phone. Free admission. Daily 7am–6pm.

San Cristóbal's main cathedral was built in the 1500s and boasts fine timberwork and a very fancy pulpit.

Palacio de las Bellas Artes. Av. Hidalgo, four blocks south of the plaza. No phone.

Be sure to check out this building if you are interested in the arts. It periodically hosts dance events, art shows, and other performances. The schedule of events is usually posted on the door if the Bellas Artes is not open. There's a public library next door.

Templo de San Cristóbal. Leave the zócalo on Avenida Hidalgo and turn right onto the third street (Hermanos Domínguez); at the end of the street are the steps you've got to climb.

For the best view of San Cristóbal, climb the seemingly endless steps to this church and *mirador* (lookout point). A visit here requires stamina. By the way, there are 22 more churches in town, some of which also require a strenuous climb.

Museo de Ambar. Plaza Sivan, Utrilla 10. ☎ **967/8-3507.** Free admission. Daily 9:30am–7pm. From the plaza, walk 2¹/₂ blocks north on Utrilla (going toward the market); the museum will be on your left.

Seen from the street, this place looks like just another store selling Guatemalan clothing, but pass through the small shop area and you'll find the long, narrow museum—a fascinating place to browse. It's the only museum in Mexico devoted to amber, a vegetable-fossil resin thousands of years old mined in Chiapas near Simojovel. Owner José Luís Coria Torres has assembled more than 250 sculpted amber pieces as well as a rare collection of amber with insects trapped inside and amber fused with fossils. Amber jewelry and other objects are also for sale.

HORSEBACK RIDING

The **Casa de Huespedes Margarita** and **Hotel Real del Valle** (see "Where to Stay," below) can arrange horseback rides for around $15 for a day, including a guide. Reserve your steed at least a day in advance. A horse-riding excursion might go to San Juan Chamula, to nearby caves, or just up into the hills.

THE NEARBY MAYA VILLAGES & COUNTRYSIDE

Na Bolom (see "Attractions in Town," above) offers daily trips to San Juan Chamula and Zinacantán at 10am. Minivan transporation, and a knowledgeable guide are included in the $7.50 per person price. The tour returns to San Cristóbal between 2 and 3pm.

Another tour is led by a very opinionated mestiza woman, **Mercedes Hernández Gómez.** Mercedes, a largely self-trained ethnographer, is extremely well informed about the history and folkways of the villages. She explains (in English) the religious significance of what you see in the churches, where shamans try to cure Indian patients of various maladies. She also facilitates tourists' firsthand contact with Indians. Her group goes by minivan to the village or villages she has selected; normally the return to the plaza is at about 2:30pm. You can meet her near the kiosk in the main plaza at 9am (she will be carrying an umbrella). The tour costs $10 per person.

Important note: Do not take photographs in the villages around San Cristóbal (see the "Photography Warning" in "Fast Facts," above). During Carnaval in 1990, I met a French photographer who took one picture from a hill above Chamula, after which villagers hiding in the bushes wrestled him to the ground and seized his Nikon.

For trips farther afield, see "Road Trips from San Cristóbal" at the end of this section.

CHAMULA & ZINACANTÁN   A side trip to the village of San Juan Chamula will really get you into the spirit of life around San Cristóbal. Sunday, when the market is in full swing, is the best day to go shopping, but other days, when you'll be unimpeded by anxious children selling their crafts, are better for seeing the village and church. Colectivos (minibuses) to San Juan Chamula leave the municipal market in San Cristóbal about every half hour and charge 75¢. Don't expect anyone in these vans to speak English or Spanish.

The village, five miles northeast of San Cristóbal, is the Chamula cultural and ceremonial center. Activity centers on the huge church, the plaza, and the municipal building. Each year, a new group of citizens is chosen to live in the municipal center as caretakers of the saints, settlers of disputes, and enforcers of village rules. As in other nearby villages, on Sunday local leaders wear their leadership costumes with beautifully woven straw hats loaded with colorful ribbons befitting their high position. They solemnly sit together in a long line somewhere around the central square. Chamula is typical of other villages in that men are often away working in the "hot lands" harvesting coffee or cacao, while women stay home to tend the sheep, the children, the cornfields, and the fires. It's almost always the women's and children's work to gather sticks for fires, and you see them along roadsides bent against the weight.

I don't want to spoil your experience of the interior of the Chamula church for the first time by describing it too much. Just don't leave Chamula without seeing it. As you step from bright sunlight into the candlelit interior, it will take a few minutes for your eyes to adjust. The tile floor is covered in pine needles scattered amid a meandering sea of lighted candles. Saints line the walls, and before them people are often kneeling and praying aloud while passing around bottles of soft drinks. Shamans are often on hand, passing eggs over sick people or using live or dead chickens in a curing ritual. The statues of saints are similar to those you might see in any Mexican Catholic church, but they take on another meaning to the Chamulas that has no similarity to the traditional Catholic saints other than in name. Visitors can walk carefully through the church to see the saints or stand quietly in the background and observe.

Carnaval, which takes place just before Lent, is the big annual festival. The Chamulas are not a very wealthy people as their economy is based on agriculture, but the women are the region's best wool weavers, producing finished pieces for themselves and for other villages.

In Zinacantán, a wealthier village than Chamula, you must sign a rigid form promising not to take any photographs before you are allowed to see the two side-by-side sanctuaries. Once permission is granted and you have paid a small fee, an escort will usually show you the church, or you may be allowed to see it on your own. Floors may be covered in pine needles here, too, and the rooms are brightly sunlit. The experience is an altogether different one from that of Chamula.

AMATENANGO DEL VALLE About an hour's ride south of San Cristóbal is Amatenango, a town known mostly for its women potters. You'll see their work in San Cristóbal—small animals, jars, and large water jugs—but in the village, you can visit the potters in their homes. All you have to do is arrive and walk down the dirt streets. Villagers will lean over the walls of family compounds and invite you in to select from their inventory. You may even see them firing the pieces under piles of wood in the open courtyard or painting them with color derived from rusty iron water. The women wear beautiful red-and-yellow *huipils*, but if you want to take a photograph, you'll have to pay.

To get here, take a colectivo from the market in San Cristóbal, but before it lets you off, be sure to ask about the return-trip schedule.

AGUACATENANGO Located 10 miles south of Amatenango, this village is known for its embroidery. If you've been in San Cristóbal shops before arriving here, you'll recognize the white-on-white or black-on-black floral patterns on dresses and blouses for sale. The locals' own regional blouses, however, are quite different.

TENEJAPA The weavers of Tenejapa make some of the most beautiful and expensive work you'll see in the region. The best time to visit is on market day (Sunday and Thursday, though Sunday is best). The weavers of Tenejapa taught the weavers of San Andrés and Magdalena, which accounts for the similarity in their designs and colors. To get to Tenejapa, try to find a colectivo in the very last row of colectivos by the market or hire a taxi for around $30. On Tenejapa's main street, several stores sell locally woven regional clothing, and you can bargain for the price.

THE HUITEPEC CLOUD FOREST **Pronatura,** a private nonprofit ecological organization, offers environmentally sensitive tours of the cloud forest. The forest is a haven for migratory birds, and over 100 bird species and 600 plant species have been discovered here. In the past, tours have been offered Tuesday, Thursday, and Saturday at 9:30am at a cost of $6 per person; these tours have been temporarily suspended because Pronatura has moved its office. Inquire for its address and phone number at the Municipal Tourism Office in San Cristóbal (see "Information," above). To reach the reserve on your own, drive on the road to Chamula; the turnoff is at 3.5km. The reserve is open Tuesday through Saturday from 9am to 5pm.

SHOPPING

Many Indian villages near San Cristóbal are noted for their weaving, embroidery, brocade work, leather, and pottery, making the area one of the best in the country for shopping. The craftspeople make and sell beautiful serapes, colorful native shirts, and magnificently woven *huipils* (women's long overblouses), all of which often come in vivid geometric patterns. In leather they are artisans of the highest rating, making sandals and men's handbags. There's a proliferation of tie-dyed jaspe from Guatemala, which comes in bolts and is made into clothing, as well as other textiles from that country. There are numerous shops up and down the streets leading to the market. Calle Real de Guadalupe houses more shops than any other street.

Crafts

La Albarrada, Centro Desarrollo Comunitario DIF. Barrio María Auxiliadora. No phone.

At this government-sponsored school, young men and women from surrounding villages come to learn how to hook Persian-style rugs, weave fabric on foot looms, sew, make furniture, construct a house, cook, make leather shoes and bags, forge iron, and grow vegetables and trees for reforestation. Probably the most interesting crafts for the general tourist are the rugmaking and weaving. Artisans from Temoaya in Mexico State learned rugmaking from Persians, who came to teach this skill in the 1970s. The Temoaya artisans in turn traveled to San Cristóbal to teach the craft to area students, who have since taught others. The beautiful rug designs are taken from brocaded and woven designs used to decorate regional costumes. Visitors should stop at the entrance and ask for an escort. You can visit all the various areas and see students at work or simply go straight to the weavers. There's a small sales outlet at the entrance selling newly loomed fabric by the meter, leather bags, rugs, and baskets made at another school in the highlands. The rug selection is best here, but the Casa de Artesanías DIF in the town center (see "Textile Shops," below) features these crafts and more from around Mexico. La Albarrada is in a far southern suburb of the city off the highway to Comitán, to the right. To get here take the "María Auxiliadora" urbano bus from the market. Ask the driver to let you off at La Albarrada. The same bus makes the return trip, passing through town center and ending its route at the market.

Central Market. Av. Utrilla. No phone.

The market buildings and the streets surrounding them offer just about anything you need. The market in San Cristóbal is open every morning except Sunday (when each village has its own local market), and you'll probably enjoy observing the sellers as much as the things they sell. See the "Photography Warning" in "Fast Facts," above, regarding photography here. The mercado is north of the Santo Domingo church, about nine blocks from the zócalo.

El Encuentro. Calle Real de Guadalupe 63-A. ☎ **967/8-3698.**

This place is tended by a pair of *dueñas muy simpáticas*, and you'll find some of your best bargains here—or at least you'll think the price is fair. The shop carries many regional ritual items, such as new and used men's ceremonial hats, false saints, and iron rooftop adornments, plus many *huipils* and other textiles. It's open Monday through Saturday from 9am to 8pm. It's between Dujelay and Guerrero.

La Galería. Hidalgo 3. ☎ **967/8-1547.**

This lovely shop beneath a great café has a wonderful selection of paintings and greeting cards by Kiki, a German artist who has found her niche in San Cristóbal. There is also an extensive selection of Oaxacan rugs and pottery, plus unusual silver jewelry. Open daily from 10am to 9pm.

Textile Shops

Casa de Artesanías DIF. Niños Héroes at Hidalgo. ☎ **967/8-1180.**

Crafts made under the sponsorship of DIF (a governmental agency that assists families) are sold in a fine showroom in one of the city's old houses. Here you'll find such

Impressions

No other race that I can call to mind allowed so wide a disparity between the simple bread with which they feed their bodies and the arts by which they nourished their souls. . . . Even today, Mexican Indians have only a rudimentary development of the so-called instinct of acquisition, and a very sophisticated development of artistic appreciation as reflected in their craftsmanship.

—Stuart Chase, Mexico: *A Study of Two Americas,* 1931

quality products as lined wool vests and jackets, bolts of foot-loomed fabrics, Persian-style rugs made at La Albarrada (see "Crafts," above), pillow covers, amber jewelry, and more. In back is a museum showing costumes worn by villagers who live near San Cristóbal. Open Monday through Saturday from 9am to 2pm and 5 to 8pm.

Plaza de Santo Domingo. Av. Utrilla.

The plazas around this church and the nearby Templo de Caridad are filled with women in native garb selling their wares. Here you'll find women from Chamula weaving belts or embroidering, surrounded by piles of loomed woolen textiles from their village. More and more Guatemalan shawls, belts, and bags are included in their inventory. There are also some excellent buys in Chiapan-made wool vests, jackets, rugs, and shawls similar to those in Sna Jolobil (see below), if you take the time to look and bargain. Vendors arrive between 9 and 10am and begin to leave around 3pm.

Sna Jolobil. Av. 20 de Noviembre. No phone.

Meaning "weaver's house" in the Maya language, this place is located in the former convent (monastery) of Santo Domingo, next to the Templo de Santo Domingo between Navarro and Nicaragua. This cooperative store is operated by groups of Tzotzil and Tzeltal craftspeople and has about 3,000 members who contribute products, help in running the store, and share in the moderate profits. Their works are simply beautiful; prices are set and high—as is the quality. Be sure to take a look. Open Monday through Saturday from 9am to 2pm and 4 to 6pm; credit cards are accepted.

Tzontehuitz. Real de Guadalupe 74. ☎ and fax **967/8-3158.**

About 3½ blocks from the plaza, this shop is one of the best on Calle Real de Guadalupe, near the corner of Diego Dujelay. Owner Janet Giacobone specializes in her own textile designs and weavings. Some of her work is loomed in Guatemala, but you can also watch weavers using foot looms in the courtyard. Hours are Monday through Saturday from 9am to 2pm and 4 to 7pm.

Unión Regional de Artesanías de los Altos. Av. Utrilla 43. ☎ **967/8-2848.**

Another cooperative of weavers, this one is smaller than Sna Jolobil (see above) but not necessarily any cheaper and not as sophisticated in its approach to potential shoppers. Also known as J'pas Joloviletic, it's worth looking around, and credit cards are accepted (though they weren't in the past). Open Monday through Saturday from 9am to 2pm and 4 to 7pm and Sunday from 9am to 1pm.

WHERE TO STAY

Keep in mind that among the most interesting places to stay in San Cristóbal is an anthropologist's dream—the house/museum of **Na-Bolom.** See "Attractions in Town," above, for details.

For really low-cost accommodations, there are basic but acceptable hospedajes and posadas, which charge about $6 for a single and $8–$12 for a double. Usually these places are unadvertised; if you're interested in a very cheap hospedaje, ask around in a restaurant or café, and you're sure to find one, or go to the tourist office, which often displays notices of new hospedajes on the metal flip rack in the office.

Some of the best economical offerings are on Calle Real de Guadalupe, east of the main square.

Important note about hotel prices: The prices quoted below are the highest rates hotels charge and usually apply only during July, August, Easter week, and Christmas. In the past, *rates were 20% lower at all other times*, but with the peso devaluation, this could change.

DOUBLES FOR LESS THAN $20

Casa de Huespedes Lupita. Juárez 12, San Cristóbal de las Casas, Chi. 29200. ☎ **967/ 8-1421.** 15 rms (none with bath). $3.35 single; $6.70 double.

Forget luxury, privacy, and amenities and concentrate on your budget at this basic hostelry. Guests share a simple bath without shower curtains or doors. Each room has a good mattress, a wooden chair, and a bedside table. Guests can use the locked kitchen, keep perishables in the refrigerator, and wash their clothes in the laundry tubs. The proprietress does her best to beautify the surroundings, painting every wall lavender and distributing plants about the hallways. To find this place, walk one block south and one block east of the plaza.

Casa de Huespedes Margarita. Real de Guadalupe 34, San Cristóbal de las Casas, Chi. 29200. ☎ and fax **967/8-0957.** 26 rms (none with bath). $3.80 dorm bed; $5.30 single; $8.50 double; $11.50 triple.

Part hotel and part youth hostel, this establishment offers rooms arranged around a courtyard where the young backpackers congregate. The rooms have sagging mattresses and flimsy locks; the shared baths are only fair. The hotel's popular restaurant is filled with youths in the evening, and there is live music at 8pm. Margarita's also has horse rentals and offers tours to the nearby ruins and to the Sumidero Canyon near Tuxtla Gutiérrez. You'll find this lodging 1¹/₂ blocks east of the plaza between Avenida B. Domínguez and Colón.

⑤ Hotel Don Quijote. Colón 7, San Cristóbal de las Casas, Chi. 29230. ☎ and fax **967/ 8-0346.** 22 rms (all with bath). TV. $11 single; $13.50 double; $15 triple. Free secure parking.

Upon entering this three-story hotel in a former residence built around a small patio, you'll see walls decorated with costumes from area villages. Throughout the hotel there are photos of old San Cristóbal and murals depicting Don Quixote. The small rooms are crowded with furniture and closets are small, but the rooms are carpeted and coordinated with warm, beautiful textiles foot-loomed in the family factory. All have two double beds with lamps over them, private tiled baths, and plenty of hot water. To find the hotel from the plaza, walk two blocks east on Real de Guadalupe then left on Colón; the hotel is on the right.

⑤ Hotel Real de Valle. Real de Guadalupe 14, San Cristóbal de las Casas, Chi. 29200. ☎ **967/8-0680.** Fax 967/8-3955. 36 rms (all with bath). $10 single; $15 double.

The helpful staff at the Real de Valle is quick to assist guests in any way possible. The 24 new rooms in the back three-story section have new baths, big closets, and a brown-and-cream decor. In addition to a rooftop solarium with chaise lounges, you'll find a small cafeteria and an upstairs dining room with a big double fireplace. Services include a travel agency offering personally guided tours, horse rental, laundry,

Spanish-language study, and use of a fax and photocopy machine. To find the hotel from the plaza, walk a half block east of the central plaza on Real de Guadalupe.

⊗ **Posada Jovel.** Flavio Paniagua 28, San Cristóbal de las Casas, Chi. 29200. ☎ **967/8-1734.** 18 rms (9 with bath). $7.50 single, $10.50 double without bath; $6.75 single, $7.50 double without bath; $8.50 single, $10 double with bath.

If you're low on funds and want to stay a while in cheery surroundings, then you may find this modest two-story inn to your liking. The bright, freshly painted rooms have tile floors and colorful blanket/bedspreads and *ixtle* (basket) lamps. Shelves and hooks hold belongings, and beds are firm. This place belongs to an association of posadas, so they'll recommend another budget lodging if they're full. The posada is between the market and main plaza, 2$^1/_2$ very long blocks east of Utrilla.

DOUBLES FOR LESS THAN $25

✪ **Hotel Palacio de Moctezuma.** Juárez 16, San Cristóbal de las Casas, Chi. 29200. ☎ **967/ 8-0352** or 967/8-1142. Fax 967/8-1536. 42 rms (all with bath). TV TEL. $17 single; $22 double. Free limited parking.

An excellent choice near the plaza, this three-story hotel is delightfully filled with bougainvillea and geraniums. Fresh-cut flowers tucked around tile fountains are a hallmark of this hotel. The rooms have lace curtains on French windows, handsome coordinated drapes and bedspreads, red carpeting, and modern tiled showers. Two suites have a TV and refrigerator. Overstuffed couches face a large fireplace in the lobby bar, and the cozy restaurant looks out on the interior courtyard. On the third floor is a solarium with comfortable tables and chairs and great city views. To find the hotel from the plaza, walk two blocks south on Insurgentes and turn left on León; the hotel is on the next corner on the left.

Hotel Plaza Santo Domingo. Utrilla 35, San Cristóbal de las Casas, Chi. 29200. ☎ and fax **967/8-1927.** 29 rms (all with bath). TV TEL. $16 single; $17 double. Limited parking.

New in 1992, this hotel is ideally situated close to the Santo Domingo Church, near the bustling market area. Behind the lobby and plant-filled entry courtyard are the nicely furnished, carpeted rooms. Each comes with a small closet and small desk below the TV, which is set high on the wall. Baths are trimmed in blue-and-white tile, and the sink area is conveniently placed outside the shower area. A large pleasant indoor dining room is off the lobby, along with a smaller patio dining area and a large bar. This is one of the few places near Santo Domingo and the market where you can get a good meal and use clean restrooms.

Hotel Posada de los Angeles. Calle Francisco Madero 17, San Cristóbal de las Casas, Chi. 29200. ☎ **967/8-1173** or 967/8-4371. Fax 967/8-2581. 20 rms (all with bath). TV TEL. $17 single; $21 double.

With beautiful etched-glass doors opening to the street, this inn, which opened in 1991, deserves your attention. The vaulted ceilings and skylights make the three-story hotel seem much larger and brighter than many others in the city. Rooms have either two single or two double beds, and the baths are large, modern, and immaculately clean; windows open onto a pretty courtyard with a fountain. The rooftop sundeck is a great siesta spot. The hotel is a half block east of the plaza between Insurgentes and Juárez.

DOUBLES FOR LESS THAN $40

✪ **Hotel Casavieja.** Ma. Adelina Flores 27, San Cristóbal de las Casas, Chi. 29200. ☎ and fax **967/8-5223** and 967/8-0385. 40 rms (all with bath). TV TEL. $32 single; $37 double. Free parking.

The Casavieja is undoubtedly one of the choice hotels in Mexico. Originally built in 1740, restoration and new construction have faithfully replicated the original design and detail. The size and beautiful furnishings of the rooms make you want to stay in them rather than going out sightseeing. The hotel's restaurant, Doña Rita, offers delicious authentic Mexican dishes at reasonable prices.

✪ **Hotel Rincón del Arco.** Ejército Nacional 66, San Cristóbal de las Casas, Chi. 29200. ☎ **967/8-1313.** Fax 967/8-1568. 36 rms (all with bath). TV TEL. $20 single; $25 double. Free parking.

The original section of this former colonial-era home is built around a small interior patio and dates from 1650. Rooms in this part, with tall ceilings and carpet over hardwood floors, exude charm. Those in the adjacent new section face a large grassy inner yard and are clean, sizable, and each is distinct. Some are furnished in antiques, others in colonial style. Some have small balconies; all have fireplaces. Throughout the hotel there are coordinated drapes and bedspreads loomed in the family factory. Owner José António Hernánz is eager to make your stay a good one. There's an excellent restaurant just behind the lobby. The hotel offers special discounted prices to students, but make arrangements in advance and be able to show university identification. To find the hotel from the plaza, walk three blocks north on Utrilla to Ejército Nacional, then turn right and walk five blocks; the hotel is on the corner of Avenida V. Guerrero.

WORTH A SPLURGE

✪ **Hotel Casa Mexicana.** 28 de Agosto No. 1, San Cristóbal de las Casas, Chi. 29200. ☎ **967/8-1348.** Fax 967/8-2627. 31 rms (all with bath). TV TEL. $40 single; $45 double. Free secure parking.

This lovely new hotel is a luxurious addition to the San Cristóbal scene. Tastefully designed, decorated, and furnished, the hotel has a colonial feel enhanced by two courtyards. Rooms have electric heaters for those chilly mornings and either one or two double beds. There's a reasonably priced restaurant as well. To find the hotel from the Museo de Ambar, walk a half block north on Utrilla and turn left on Agosto/Eje Nacional; the hotel is on the right.

WHERE TO EAT

San Cristóbal is one of the country's best dining-out towns because of the sheer quality of its food—not for luxury establishments. In addition to the restaurants mentioned below, most hotels have their own restaurants and serve good meals. Be sure to look for regional Chiapan food like large tamales, *butifarra* (a delicious sausage), and *pox* (pronounced posh, a local firewater similar to *aguardiente*). For baked goods, try the **Panadería Mercantil** at Mazariego 17 (☎ **967/8-0307**). It's open Monday through Saturday from 8am to 9:30pm and Sunday from 9am to 9pm. Remember that you're about a mile and a half high here, and therefore you digest your food more slowly.

MEALS FOR LESS THAN $5

⑤ **Café el Puente.** Real de Guadalupe 55. ☎ **967/8-2250.** Breakfast $1.50–$2; soups and salads $2–$2.50; pastries 50¢–$2. Mon–Sat 8am–10:30pm. MEXICAN.

Ex-Californian Bill English has turned a huge old mansion into a café/cultural center where tourists and locals can converse. The café takes up the main part of the building; and there are a weaver's shop and travel agency to the side. The Centro Bilingue language school is headquartered here as well, and movies, plays, and lectures are presented nightly in an interior patio and meeting room. It's the kind of place you return to often, for fresh waffles and coffee in the morning, for an inexpensive lunch or dinner of brown rice and veggies, or for good conversation at any time of day. Guests are welcome to post notices, messages, and advertisements on the long bulletin board, which is well worth checking out if you're looking for a ride, a place to stay, or information on out-of-the-way destinations. It's 2¹/₂ blocks east of the plaza.

⑤ Normita's II. Av. Juárez at F. Flores. No phone. Breakfast $1.25–$2.25; comida corrida $2,75; pozole $2; tacos $1. Daily 8am–10pm (comida corrida served 1:30–3pm). MEXICAN.

This is the place for cheap, dependable, short-order Mexican mainstays. Everything is homemade—from the wood tables and checked tablecloths to the tacos and pozole. It's a very humble restaurant; the open kitchen takes up one corner of the room and tables are scattered in front of a large paper mural of a fall forest scene from some faraway place. To find it from the plaza, walk one block south on Insurgentes, then turn left on J. Flores and walk one block; it's on the right at the corner of Flores and Juárez.

MEALS FOR LESS THAN $10

✪ El Fogón de Jovel. 16 de Septiembre no. 11. ☎ **967/8-1153.** Corn soup $2; Chiapan tamales $3.25 for 5; main courses $3,75–$5.50. Daily 1–5pm and 7–11pm. CHIAPAN.

If word-of-mouth doesn't lead you here, the lively sounds of marimba music will. Chiapan food is served at this handsome old town house, with dining under the portals and rooms built around a central courtyard. The waiters wear local costumes. Walls are hung with Guatemalan and Chiapan prints and folk art. Each dish and regional drink such as *pox* (a distilled sugar-and-corn drink) is explained on the menu, which is available in English. I highly recommend the Chiapan tamales, the corn soup, and the beef-stuffed chiles rellenos. A basket of steaming warm tortillas with six condiments arrives before the meal. The restaurant is only a block northwest of the plaza at the corner of Guadalupe Victoria/Real de Guadalupe.

✪ Madre Tierra. Insurgentes 19. ☎ **967/8-4297.** Main courses $2–$5.50; comida corrida $6. Restaurant, daily 8am–9:45pm (comida corrida served 1–5pm); bakery, Mon–Sat 9am–8pm, Sun 9am–noon. MEXICAN/VEGETARIAN.

This restaurant satisfies the cravings of meat lovers and vegetarians alike. The bakery specializes in whole-wheat breads, pastries, pizza by the slice, quiche, grains, granola, and dried fruit. The restaurant serves the bakery's goods and other delicious fare in an old mansion with wood-plank floors, long windows looking onto the street, and tables covered in colorful Guatemalan *jaspe*. Classical music plays softly in the background. It's a good place for a cappuccino and pastry or an entire meal; the comida corrida is very filling, and I also recommend the chicken curry, lasagna, and fresh salads. Madre Tierra is on Insurgentes, 3¹/₂ blocks south of the plaza.

✪ Paris-Mexico Restaurant. Madero 20. ☎ **967/8-0695.** Crêpes $1.75–$4; pizzas $4.25–$6; comida corrida $3.50–$4.50. Daily 7am–11pm. MEXICAN/FRENCH/ITALIAN.

Decorated with plain, nicely finished wood tables and chairs, the Paris-Mexico resembles a cozy neighborhood café. The food is wonderfully prepared. The comida corrida might consist of salad, grilled chicken breast, potatoes or rice, fruit salad, and coffee or tea. You can also choose from an endless list of crêpes for breakfast, lunch, dinner, or dessert; pizza served 10 ways; five variations on spaghetti; or a small selection of beef and chicken dishes. The Paris-Mexico is on Madero half a block east of the plaza.

✪ Restaurant Tuluc. Insurgentes 5. ☎ **967/8-2090.** Breakfast $1.75–$3.50; main course $2.75–$3.50; comida corrida $3.50. Daily 7am–10pm (comida corrida served 1–5pm). MEXICAN.

This warm and inviting restaurant has lustrous wooden booths and tables with Guatemalan fabric. It's a cozy place for a cup of hot chocolate or espresso, but above all, the comida corrida is an exceptional value here. The evening menu is equally popular. The house specialty is the *filete Tuluc*, a beef filet wrapped around spinach and cheese served with fried potatoes and green beans. The Chiapaneco breakfast is a filling quartet of juice, toast, two Chiapan tamales, and your choice of tea, coffee, cappuccino, or hot chocolate. The owner speaks seven languages. Tuluc is 1 1/2 blocks south of the plaza between Cuauhtémoc and F. León.

COFFEEHOUSES

Since Chiapan-grown coffee is highly regarded, it's natural to find a proliferation of coffeehouses here. Most are concealed in the nooks and crannies of San Cristóbal's side streets.

Café Altura and Casa Naturista. Primero de Marzo #6C. ☎ **967/8-4038.** Soy burgers $2; salads $2; coffee 75¢–$1.25. Daily 7am–9pm. VEGETARIAN.

Café Altura specializes in organic vegetarian meals. Breakfasts include granola, yogurt, fruit, and whole-wheat breads, and a variety of coffees is available all day. Grains, granola, teas, and coffee beans are sold in bulk. The café is three blocks north of the plaza near the corner of Primero de Marzo and 16 de Noviembre.

Café San Cristóbal. Cuauhtémoc 1. ☎ **967/8-3861.** Coffee 50¢–$1; cake $1.25–$2.50. Mon–Sat 9am–10pm, Sun 10am–2pm and 5–10pm. COFFEE/CAKE.

Not only is this a café, but it also sells coffee beans by the kilogram (2.2 lb.) for $4. Chess is the game of choice at the few tables and booths; men hunker over their chessboards for hours, drinking coffee and visiting with friends. A cup of coffee here provides a respite from the rush outside. The restaurant is one block south of the plaza near the corner of Cuauhtémoc and Insurgentes.

SAN CRISTÓBAL AFTER DARK

The cafés and restaurants of San Cristóbal are also home to the area's nightlife. The coffeehouses, with their international clientele, invite the pastime of conversation; you'll also see notices posted around town advertising live music, particularly in the cafés.

ROAD TRIPS FROM SAN CRISTÓBAL

Several travel agencies in town offer trips to nearby villages (see "San Cristóbal's History & Culture," above) and those farther away. Strangely, except where noted otherwise, the cost of the trip includes a driver but does not necessarily include either a bilingual guide or guided information of any kind. You pay extra for those services, so if you want to be informed while taking a tour, be sure to ask if the tour is merely transportation or if it includes a knowledgeable guide as well.

RUINS OF TONINÁ The Maya ruins of Toniná (which means "house of rocks") are two hours from San Cristóbal and 8 1/2 miles east of Ocosingo. Dating from the Classic Period, the terraced site covers an area of at least 9 square miles. Extensive excavations are under way here during the dry season.

As early as A.D. 350, Toniná emerged as a separate dynastic center from the Maya and has the distinction of having the last recorded date of the long count yet found (A.D. 909) on a small stone monument. Another stone, dated A.D. 711, discovered here depicts the captured King Kan-Xul of Palenque (the younger brother of Chan-Bahlum and the son of King Pacal); the portrait shows him with his arm tied by a rope but still wearing his royal headdress. Recently a huge stucco panel was unearthed

picturing the Lord of Death holding Kan-Xul's head, confirming long-held suspicions that the king died at Toniná.

At the moment there are no signs to guide visitors through the site, so you're on your own. The caretaker can also show you around (in Spanish), after which a tip is appreciated. Ask at the Casa Margarita in San Cristóbal (see "Where to Stay," above) about guided trips to Toniná for $18 per person, with a four-person minimum. The trip includes the services of a bilingual driver, a tour of the site, lunch, and a swim in the river. From November through February you'll see thousands of swallows swarming near the ruins.

You can go on your own by bus to Ocosingo and from there take a taxi to the ruins, but have the taxi wait for your return. The ruins are open daily from 8am to 5pm; admission is $3.

PALENQUE, BONAMPAK & YAXCHILÁN   Many visitors to San Cristóbal want to visit the ruins of Palenque near Villahermosa and the Bonampak and Yaxchilán ruins on Mexico's border with Guatemala. A trip to Palenque can be accomplished in a long day-trip from San Cristóbal, but I don't recommend it because Palenque should be savored. Bonampak and Yaxchilán are easier to see from Palenque.

For arranging these trips from San Cristóbal, I highly recommend **ATC Tours and Travel,** located across from El Fogón restaurant, Calle 5 de Febrero no. 15 at the corner of 16 de Septiembre (☎ **967/8-2550;** fax 967/8-3145). The agency has bilingual guides and good vehicles. There's also a branch in Palenque. See the Palenque section, below, for details on Bonampak and camping overnight at Yaxchilán; see "Outdoor Sports, Adventure Travel & Wilderness Trips" in chapter 2 for other ATC regional tours focusing on birds and orchids, textiles, hiking, and camping.

If you're considering a day-trip to the archaeological site of Palenque using ATC (mentioned above) or a similar travel agency, here's how your tour will be arranged. You start at 7 or 8am and within three hours reach the Agua Azul waterfalls, where there's a 1 1/2-hour stop to swim. From there it's another 1 1/2-hour drive to Palenque. You'll have about two hours to see the site. If your group agrees, you can skip the swim and have more time at Palenque. It'll be a minimum 16-hour day and costs about $80 per person with a minimum of four people traveling.

CHINCULTIC RUINS, COMITÁN & MONTEBELLO NATIONAL PARK
Almost 100 miles southeast of San Cristóbal, near the border of Guatemala, is the Chincultic archaeological site and Montebello National Park, with 16 multicolored lakes and exuberant pine-forest vegetation. Forty-six miles from San Cristóbal is Comitán, a pretty hillside town of 40,000 inhabitants known for its flower cultivation and a sugarcane-based firewater called *comitecho*. It's also the last big town along the Pan American Highway before the Guatemalan border, and it's the location of the nearest airport to San Cristóbal.

The Chincultic ruins, a Late-Classic site, have barely been excavated, but the main acropolis, set high up against a cliff, is magnificent to see from below and worth the walk up for the vista. After passing through the gate, you'll see the trail ahead; it passes ruins on both sides. Steep stairs leading up the mountain to the acropolis are flanked by more unexcavated tree-covered ruins. From there, you can gaze upon distant Montebello Lakes and miles of cornfields and forest. The paved road to the lakes passes six lakes, all different colors and sizes, ringed by cool pine forests; most have car parks and lookouts. The paved road ends at a small restaurant. The lakes are best seen on a sunny day, when their famous brilliant colors are optimal.

Most travel agencies in San Cristóbal offer a day-long trip that includes the lakes, the ruins, lunch in Comitán, and a stop in the pottery-making village of Amatenango del Valle. If you're driving, follow Highway 190 south from San Cristóbal through the pretty village of Teopisca and then through Comitán; turn left at La Trintaria, where there's a sign to the lakes. After the Trintaria turnoff and before you reach the lakes, there's a sign pointing left down a narrow dirt road to the Chincultic ruins.

4 Palenque

89 miles SE of Villahermosa, 143 miles NE of San Cristóbal

The ruins of Palenque are one of the most spectacular of the Maya archaeological sites, with roof-combed temples ensconced in lush vegetation high above the savannas. The ruins, located on the edge of the jungle in the state of Chiapas, are part of a reserve known as the Parque Nacional Palenque. The flora of the surrounding countryside continues to encroach on the park, and it takes a team of machete wielders to hold the jungle back.

Were it not for the local ruins, the town of Palenque (pop. 16,000) would hardly exist. This slow-paced, somnolent village is accustomed to visitors passing through, but it pays them little heed.

ESSENTIALS

GETTING THERE & DEPARTING   By Plane   A new airport at San Cristóbal de las Casas should be open by the time you travel to handle smaller private and charter aircraft. Check with travel agencies in Villahermosa, Tuxtla Gutiérrez, and San

Cristóbal de las Casas for information. Until the new airport was slated to open in San Cristóbal, the airport at Comitán (about 50 miles southeast of San Cristóbal de las Casas) served all Palenque charter flights; however, it was closed when I checked.

By Bus Four bus stations serve Palenque, and all are within three blocks of the hospital on Avenida Juárez. Of these, the Transportes Cristóbal Colón and Transportes Rudolfo Figueroa (which share a building) should be the first choice when looking for transportation. ADO and Autotransportes Tuxtla Gutiérrez offer limited service.

From Tuxtla Gutiérrez, with stops in San Cristóbal, both **Omnibus Cristóbal Colón** (☎ 934/5-0140) and **Transportes Rudolfo Figueroa** (☎ 934/5-0369) run several deluxe buses to Palenque. The trip from Palenque to San Cristóbal takes around six hours. When TRF buses reach San Cristóbal, passengers are only dropped off on the highway near the bus station and cannot board for a return to ride to Palenque or Tuxtla. TRF buses are the most deluxe buses traveling this route, with movies, curtained windows, air-conditioning, and heat. The bathroom is never unlocked. If you tend toward claustrophobia or nausea, however, be forewarned that the windows do not open. From Mérida, the trip to Palenque takes around nine hours. Twice daily, deluxe Cristóbal Colón buses make the trip with onboard bathroom, movies, snacks, and soft drinks.

From Villahermosa's first-class **ADO** station (☎ 934/5-0400), there are eight buses to Palenque daily; the trip takes 1 1/2 to 3 hours. From San Cristóbal there are three buses, which leave at 9am, and 7 and 8pm for the three-hour run. Three buses run to Mérida at 8am and 8 and 9:30pm, eight to Villahermosa, one to Chetumal at 10:30pm, and three to Escárcega at 8am and 8 and 8:30pm.

Almost directly across the street from the Pemex station is the **Terminal de Transportes Dag Dug** (no phone). It's known locally as the **Mérida station,** although only one bus daily goes to Mérida. There are so few buses operating from here that this should be a choice only when all other lines are full.

By Car The 143-mile trip from San Cristóbal to Palenque takes five to six hours and passes through lush jungle and mountain scenery. Take it easy since potholes and other hindrances occur. Highway 186 from Villahermosa is in good condition, and the trip from there and on the Palenque turnoff should take about 1 1/2 hours.

ORIENTATION Arriving Most travelers reach Palenque on buses, which arrive four or five blocks from the zócalo. Taxis from the bus stations to most hotels cost less than $1.50; only those hotels surrounding the zócalo are within walking distance if you're carrying heavy luggage.

Information The **State Tourism Office** (☎ 934/5-0760 or 934/5-0828) is located a block west of the zócalo on Juárez at the corner of Abasolo (north side of the street). The office is open Monday through Saturday from 8am to 9pm.

City Layout The **ruins** are about 5 miles southwest of town. The road from Villahermosa forks just west of town at the impossible-to-miss Maya statue; the ruins are southwest of the statue, and the town lies to the east.

Palenque has three separate areas where tourists tend to congregate. The most central area is around the **main plaza,** bordered by Avenidas Hidalgo, 20 de Noviembre, Independencia, and Jiménez. **La Cañada** is a pleasant area located five very long blocks west of the main plaza on Merle Green, a partially paved road that runs through a tropical forest. Here, you'll find a few small hotels and restaurants and stands of artists who carve and paint. Aside from the main plaza area, this is the best location for travelers without cars, since the town is within a few blocks and the buses that run to the ruins pass by La Cañada. The third tourist zone is along the **road to**

the ruins, where small hotels, RV parks, and campgrounds are tucked into the surrounding jungle. This is an ideal location for those with cars.

Getting Around   The cheapest way to get back and forth from the ruins is on the Chambalu colectivo buses, which depart from the terminal at Avenidas Juárez and Allende every 10 minutes from 6am to 6pm; the fare is 50¢. Chambalu also runs buses five times daily to Misol Ha and Agua Azul; the fare is $6. The buses pass La Cañada and hotels along the road to the ruins, but they may not stop if they're full.

   Taxis from town to the ruins cost $3 to $4.50; drivers may charge more from the ruins back to town.

Fast Facts   The **telephone area code** is 934. As for the **climate,** Palenque's constant humidity is downright oppressive in the summer, especially after rain showers. During the winter, the damp air can be chilly, especially in the evenings, so a jacket is a good idea. Rain gear is important any time of year.

EXPLORING PALENQUE

The real reason for being here is the ruins, which can be toured in a morning; but many people like to savor Palenque. Despite the fame of the ruins, the village of Palenque remains rather uncommercialized, though more shops are opening and new hotel construction has started on the road into town. There are no must-see sights in the town; if you have time to spare, sit on the main plaza and observe the goings-on. The La Cañada area west of town (see "City Layout," above) is a pleasant spot for a leisurely lunch and for browsing through Maya reproductions made by local artists.

PARQUE NACIONAL PALENQUE   The archaeological site of Palenque underwent several changes in 1994, which culminated in the opening of a new museum/visitors' center on the highway to the ruins. The complex includes a large parking lot, a refreshment stand serving snacks and drinks, and two shops with an impressive display of quality folk art from throughout Chiapas. The **museum,** although not large, is worth an additional entrance fee and the time it takes to see it. Inside are well-chosen and artistically displayed exhibits. Explanatory texts, in both Spanish and English, explain the life and times of the magnificent city of Palenque. New pieces are constantly being added as they are uncovered in ongoing excavations. The **main entrance,** about a mile beyond the museum, is at the top of a hill at the end of the paved highway. There, you'll find a large parking lot, a refreshment stand, a ticket booth, and two shops displaying folk art. Among the vendors selling souvenirs by the parking lot are Lacandón Indians wearing white tunics and hawking bows and arrows.

   Admission to the ruins is $2.50; free on Sunday. There's a $4.50 charge for each video camera used. Parking at the main entrance and at the visitors' center is free. The site and visitors' center shops are open daily from 8am to 5pm; the crypt is open daily from 10am to 4pm. Admission to the museum is an additional $3.75; it's open Tuesday through Sunday from 10am to 5pm.

Touring the Ruins   Pottery found during the excavations shows that people lived in this area as early as 300 B.C. During the Classic Period (A.D. 300–900), the ancient Maya city of Palenque was a ceremonial center for the high priests; the civilization peaked at around 600 to 700.

   When John Stephens visited the site in the 1840s, the cleared ruins you see today were buried under centuries of accumulated earth and a thick canopy of jungle. The dense jungle surrounding the cleared portion still covers yet unexplored temples, which are easily discernible even to the untrained eye. Of all the ruins in Mexico open to the public, this is the most haunting because of its majesty and sense of the past.

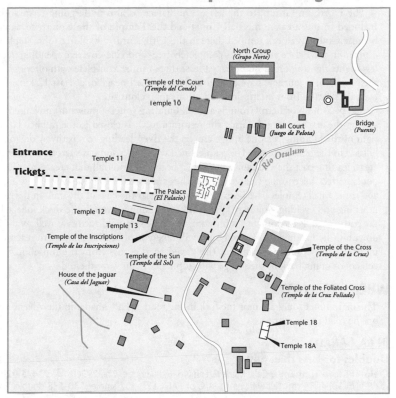

Scholars have unearthed names of the rulers and their family histories, putting visitors on a first-name basis with these ancient people etched in stone.

As you enter the ruins from the entrance, the building on your right is the **Temple of the Inscriptions,** named for the great stone hieroglyphic panels found inside.

Just to your right as you face the Temple of the Inscriptions is **Temple XIII,** which is receiving considerable attention from archaeologists. Recently, the burial of another important male personage was discovered here. He was richly adorned and was accompanied in death by an adult female and an adolescent. These remains are still being studied.

When you're back on the main pathway, the building directly in front of you will be the **Palace,** with its unique watchtower. A new pathway between the Palace and the Temple of the Inscriptions leads to the **Temple of the Sun,** the **Temple of the Foliated Cross,** the **Temple of the Cross,** and **Temple XIV.** This group of temples—now cleared and in various stages of reconstruction—was built by Pacal's son, Chan-Bahlum, who is usually shown on inscriptions as having six toes. Chan-Bahlum's plaster mask was found in Temple XIV next to the Temple of the Sun. Archaeologists have recently begun probing the depths of the Temple of the Sun in search of Chan-Bahlum's tomb. Little remains of this temple's exterior carving. Inside, however, behind a fence, a carving of Chan-Bahlum shows him ascending the throne in A.D. 690. The panels, which are still in place, depict Chan-Bahlum's version of his historic link to the throne.

The Northern Group, to the left of the Palace, is also undergoing restoration. Included in this area are the **Ball Court** and the **Temple of the Count,** so named because Count Waldeck camped there in the 19th century. Explorer John Stephens camped in the Palace when it was completely tree- and vine-covered, spending sleepless nights fighting off mosquitoes. At least three tombs, complete with offerings for the underworld journey, have been found here. The lineage of at least 12 kings has been deciphered from inscriptions left at this marvelous site.

Just past the Northern Group is a small building (once a museum) now used for storing the artifacts found during the restorations. It is closed to the public. To the right of the building, a stone bridge crosses the river, leading to a pathway down the hillside to the new museum. The path is lined with rocks and has steps in the steepest areas, leading past the **Cascada Motiepa,** a beautiful waterfall that creates a series of pools perfect for cooling weary feet. Benches are placed along the way as rest areas, and some small temples have been reconstructed near the base of the trail. In the early morning and evening, you may hear monkeys crashing through the thick foliage by the path; if you keep noise to a minimum, you may spot wild parrots as well. Walking downhill (by far the best way to go), it will take you about 20 minutes to reach the main highway. The path ends at the paved road across from the museum. The colectivos going back to the village will stop here if you wave them down.

WHERE TO STAY

The main hotel zones are near the fork in the road at La Cañada; in the village; and on the road to the ruins.

In La Cañada
Doubles for Less than $40

✪ **Hotel Maya Tulipanes.** Calle Merle Green No. 6, Palenque, Chi. 29960. ☎ **934/5-0201.** Fax 934/5-1004. 34 rms (all with bath). A/C or FAN. $27–$32 single; $30–$38 double. Free parking.

Maya statues, carvings, and paintings fill the hallways and public areas in this rambling, overgrown, but comfortable two-story hotel. Some of the windows are even shaped like the Maya corbeled arch. You definitely feel as if you're in the jungle here, and the dark shade is a cool respite from the sun's glare. Higher prices are for rooms in the new section. The hotel is one long block north of the Maya statue in La Cañada.

La Posada. Calle Inominada La Cañada, Palenque, Chi. 29960. ☎ **934/5-0437.** Fax 934/5-0193. 8 rms (all with bath). FAN. $12 single; $15 double.

Owner Lourdes Chávez de Grajales took over this hotel in 1993 and continues its tradition of budget-priced rooms in pleasant surroundings. The original rooms are basic; each has one cement-platform double bed, a portable fan, and a large tiled bath with hot showers. Room numbers are painted in Maya symbols. A second story has been added with eight new rooms, each with two beds, fans, and tiled baths. The rooms face a wide lawn where tables and chairs are set out for guests, and the owner reports that she has spotted howler monkeys in the nearby trees. Cold sodas, water, beer, and snacks are sold from a refrigerator in the lobby, near the Ping-Pong table. La Posado is off Merle Green on a dirt road just past the Hotel Maya Tulipanes.

In Town
Doubles for Less than $30

Hotel Casa de Pakal. Av. Juárez 10, Palenque, Chi. 29960. ☎ **934/5-0393.** 15 rms (all with bath). A/C. $15 single; $18 double.

This bright, relatively new four-story hotel far surpasses most others on Juárez. Air-conditioning is a big plus here. The rooms are small but far brighter and cleaner than those at nearby establishments, and they come with either one double or one single bed covered with chenille spreads. A good restaurant is on premises. The hotel is a half block east of the main plaza.

Hotel Kashlan. 5 de Mayo no. 105, Palenque, Chi. 29960. ☎ **934/5-0297.** Fax 934/5-0309. 58 rms (all with bath). FAN (30) A/C (28). $15 $25 single, $17–$25 double.

You'll be well located if you lodge in the Kashlan. The clean rooms have interior windows opening onto the hall, marble-square floors, nice bedspreads, tile baths, small vanities, and luggage racks. Your *Frommer's* book may get you a discount. Higher prices are for rooms with air-conditioning. To find this hotel from the ADO station, walk to the corner on your right, which is 5 de Mayo, and turn right; it's half a block ahead.

WHERE TO EAT

Avenida Juárez is lined with many small eateries, none of which is exceptional. Good options are the many markets and *panaderías* (bakeries) along Juárez. **Panificadora La Tehuanita,** near the bus stations, has fresh cookies firm enough to withstand hours in the bottom of a purse, and **La Bodeguita** has a beautiful display of fresh fruit—just stick with those you can peel.

MEALS FOR LESS THAN $5

La Cañada. Calle Merle Green s/n. ☎ **934/5-0102.** Main courses $2.25–$7; beer $1.25. Daily 7am–10pm. MEXICAN.

This palapa-topped restaurant tucked into the jungle is said to be one of the best in town, though it never seems crowded. Though the dining room has a dirt floor, the place is spotless, the service attentive, and the food good—if not exceptional. Try one of the local specialties such as pollo mexicano or bean soup. Near the restaurant lies the two-story thatched disco La Nuit, the most popular dance spot in town. This restaurant is in La Cañada in the Hotel La Cañada on the left, about midway down the road.

Chan-Kah Centro. Av. Independencia s/n. ☎ **934/5-0318.** Breakfast buffet (7–11am) $3; comida corrida $3; quesadillas $2. Daily 7am–11pm. MEXICAN.

This attractive hotel restaurant, on the east side of the main plaza at the corner of Independencia, is the most peaceful place to eat. The waiters are extremely attentive, and the food is fairly well prepared (avoid the tough beef though). The second-story bar overlooks the main plaza and has live music on some weekend nights.

Girasoles. Av. Juárez 189. ☎ **934/5-0383.** Comida del día $3; main courses $2–$3.75. Daily 7am–11pm. MEXICAN.

There's always a smattering of locals and foreigners here taking advantage of the good prices. The simple decor boasts cloth-covered tables, wicker lampshades on ceiling lights, and fans. It's a good place for resting your feet and watching the action, in addition to getting a good deal on the food. The menu covers the basics and has fish, poultry, and Mexican specialties, including decent tacos that are more like flautas. The freshly brewed coffee comes from Chiapas, and you can buy it ground by the kilo. Girasoles is on 5 de Mayo across from the ADO bus station.

✪ Restaurant Maya. Av. Independencia s/n. No phone. Breakfast $2–$3; main courses $3–$5. Daily 7am–10pm. MEXICAN.

The most popular place in town among tourists and locals, Restaurant Maya is opposite the northeast corner of the main plaza near the post office. Breezy and open, it's managed by a solicitous family. At breakfast, there are free refills of very good coffee. Try the tamales.

MEALS FOR LESS THAN $10

✪ **La Chiapaneca.** Carretera Palenque. ☎ **934/5-0363.** Main courses $6.50–$8. Daily 11am–10pm. MEXICAN.

Palenque's traditional "best" restaurant continues to serve top-notch regional cuisine in a pleasant tropical setting. Though it has a thatched roof, the dining room is large and refined. The *pollo Palenque* (chicken with potatoes in a tomato-and-onion sauce) is a soothing choice; save room for the flan. Mexican wines are served by the bottle. La Chiapaneca is about a 20-minute walk from the Maya statue toward the ruins.

ROAD TRIPS FROM PALENQUE

AGUA AZUL & CASCADA DE MISOL HA: SPECTACULAR WATER FALLS
The most popular excursion from Palenque is a day-trip to the Agua Azul cascades. Trips can be arranged through Shivalva Tours and ATC Tours and Travel (see "Bonampak & Yaxchilán," below). Minivans from the Chambalu Colectivo Service make the trip to Agua Azul and the Cascada de Misol Ha every day with two round-trips beginning at 10am; the last van departs Agua Azul for Palenque at 6:30pm. They may wait until six or eight people want to go, so check a day or two in advance of your proposed trip. Several new travel agencies have popped up in town, most offering the same tours and services. Prices have become a bit more competitive, so it's worth checking out a few of the agencies along Avenida Juárez. Be sure to ask if private or public transportation is used for the tours.

BONAMPAK & YAXCHILÁN: RUINS & RUGGED ADVENTURE
Intrepid travelers might consider the two-day excursion to the Maya ruins of Bonampak and Yaxchilán. The ruins of Bonampak, southeast of Palenque on the Guatemalan border, were discovered in 1946. The mural discovered on the interior walls of one of the buildings is the greatest battle painting of pre-Hispanic Mexico. Reproductions of the vivid murals found here are on view in the Regional Archeology Museum in Villahermosa.

You can fly or drive to Bonampak. Several tour companies offer a two-day (minimum) tour by four-wheel-drive vehicle to within 4 1/2 miles of Bonampak. You must walk the rest of the way to the ruins. After camping overnight, you continue by river to the extensive ruins of the great Maya city, Yaxchilán, famous for its highly ornamented buildings. Bring rain gear, boots, a flashlight, and bug repellent. All tours include meals but vary in price ($80 to $120 per person); some take far too many people for comfort (the seven-hour road trip can be unbearable).

Among the most reputable tour operators is **Viajes Shivalva,** Calle Merle Green 1 (Apdo. Postal 237), Palenque, Chi. 29960 (☎ **934/5-0411;** fax 934/5-0392). Office hours are Monday through Friday from 7am to 3pm. A branch office is now open a block from the zócalo at the corner of Juárez and Abasolo (across the hall from the State Tourism Office). Their phone is 934/5-0822, and they are open Monday through Saturday from 9am to 9pm.

Information about **ATC Tours and Travel** (☎ and fax **934/5-0297**) can be obtained at the Hotel Kashlan, 5 de Mayo and Allende (see "Where to Stay," above, in Palenque). This agency has a large number of clients (and thus the best chance of making a group) and offers a large number of tours. Among its offerings is a one-day trip to the ruins of Tikal in Guatemala for five people; another tour takes in Yaxchilán, Bonampak, and Tikal with a minimum of four people. Though rustic, they have the only permanent overnight accommodations at Yaxchilán at their Posada del Río Usumacinta. Their headquarters are in San Cristóbal (see "San Cristóbal de las Casas," above), so you can make arrangements there as well.

An alternative way to reach Bonampak and Yaxchilán is via tours run by the **Chambalu Colectivo Service** at Juárez and Allende. A minimum of five people is needed to make the trip. The Palenque-Bonampak portion takes five hours by road and another 2¹/₂ hours to hike, and then there's an overnight stay in rustic huts with wood-slat beds and no meals or mosquito netting, another two-hour bus ride, a river trip to Yaxchilán, and the long ride back to Palenque. It's a strenuous, no-frills trip that can be absolutely wonderful if you don't expect great service and if you bring plenty of food and drink, a hammock and net, and a great deal of patience. The two-day trip costs about $75 to $85 per person.

When negotiating the deal, be sure to ask how many will be in the bus, or you may not have a place to sit for hours on bumpy dirt roads. Recent road improvements should shorten the trip and may alter tour arrangements considerably.

5 Villahermosa

89 miles NW of Palenque, 293 miles SW of Campeche, 100 miles N of San Cristóbal de las Casas

Villahermosa (pop. 265,000), the capital of the state of Tabasco, is right at the center of Mexico's oil boom, but it's off-center from just about everything else. Were it not for oil and the city's proximity to the ruins of Palenque, visitors would have little reason to come here. Nevertheless, oil wealth has helped transform this dowdy provincial town into a more attractive and obviously prosperous modern city, making it a comfortable crossroads in your Mexican journeys.

Prosperity has recently brought the city a number of developments, including a beautiful park surrounding the Parque-Museo La Venta; a high-class business, residence, and hotel development called Tabasco 2000 (containing gleaming office buildings, a convention center, golf course, and exclusive residences); the CICOM development, with theaters and the Museo Regional de Antropología Carlos Pellicer Camara; and the pedestrians-only shopping area along Avenida Benito Juárez. You really shouldn't miss the Parque Museo La Venta, which contains the Olmec remains found at La Venta west of Villahermosa.

ESSENTIALS

GETTING THERE & DEPARTING   By Plane   Mexicana (☎ **93/16-3785** or 93/16-3132; at the airport 93/12-1164) flies to Villahermosa from Mexico City, Tuxtla Gutiérrez, and Guadalajara. **Aeroméxico** (☎ **93/12-1528**, at the airport 93/14-1675) flies from Mexico City, Guadalajara, Mérida, Acapulco, and U.S. gateways. **Aviación de Chiapas (Aviacsa)** (☎ **93/14-5770** or 93/14-5780; at the airport 93/14-4755) flies to and from Mérida, Mexico City, Tuxtla Gutiérrez, and Oaxaca. **AeroLitoral,** another regional airline and a subsidiary of Aeroméxico, is at the airport (☎ **93/12-6991**) and serves the route to and from Veracruz, Tampico, Minatitlán, Ciudad del Carmen, and Monterrey. **Aerocaribe** (☎ **93/16-5046;** fax 93/16-5047), a Mexicana affiliate, serves Cancún, Cozumel, Tuxtla Gutiérrez, Oaxaca, and Mérida.

By Bus   The two bus stations in Villahermosa are about five blocks apart. The first-class **ADO** station (☎ **93/12-4446**) is at Mina and Merino, three blocks off Highway 180. This nice bus station has a clean waiting area, luggage storage at 50¢ per bag, souvenir shops, and snack bars. Buses for most destinations leave from here, and the station houses many lines. Most ticket booths offer computerized ticketing, and you can look at the computer screen and select your seat. Eight first-class **ADO**

buses leave for Palenque (three hours) between 6am and 7:45pm. Deluxe service to Palenque (two hours) leaves at 8am and 1:30pm. Additional first-class buses go to most major Gulf Coast cities, Jalapa, and Mexico City. **Autotransportes Cristóbal Colón** (☎ 93/12-7692) has seven daily buses to Tuxtla Gutiérrez (passing through Palenque and San Cristóbal de las Casas), Tapachula, Oaxaca, and Mexico City. **UNO** (☎ 93/14-5818) runs luxury buses with 25 seats, smoking and no-smoking sections, self-service refreshments, video movies, and air-conditioning. They go to Mexico City (five daily), Veracruz (three daily), Puebla, and Mérida. You can reserve seats up to two days in advance.

The **Central Camionera de Segunda Clase** (second-class bus station) is on Highway 180/186, about five blocks from the ADO station. From the second-class bus station you can ride **Sureste del Caribe** to Tuxtla and Campeche at 6 and 11am and 3 and 7pm; and to Mérida four times daily. **Servicio Somellera** (☎ 93/12-3973) goes to Comalcalco every 30 minutes. **Autobuses Unidos de Tabasco** travels to Veracruz and Mexico City. Be forewarned that this bus station is horrid and the buses are even worse.

By Car   Paved Highway 195 connects the Tabascan capital of Villahermosa with Tuxtla Gutiérrez, the capital of the state of Chiapas. Between these cities lie Palenque and San Cristóbal de las Casas. The road to Palenque is a good one, and the drive should take about two hours. Between Villahermosa and San Cristóbal de las Casas, the road, although paved, sometimes has stretches with many potholes. Often a portion of the roadway caves in and traffic slows to one lane to avoid it; these conditions occur more frequently during the rainy season between May and October. The trip to San Cristóbal takes a minimum of five hours from Villahermosa. The paved, mountainous (and very curvy) road between San Cristóbal and Tuxtla is in good condition, and the trip takes about 1 1/2 hours.

The drive between Villahermosa and Chetumal (about 350 miles) can seem interminable if the road is in poor condition. It had recently been repaired when I checked. One possible stopover between the two would be at Xpujil, 62 miles west of Chetumal. Another potential stopover is Francisco Escárcega, but only in an emergency. Once here, you're not too far from wherever you're going.

ORIENTATION   Arriving   Coming in from Villahermosa's airport, which is 6 1/2 miles east of town, you'll cross a bridge over the Río Grijalva; turn left to reach downtown. The airport minibuses charge $7.50; taxis begin at $15. Don't linger in the terminal and expect a minibus to still be at the curb when you're ready; the ticket seller is in cahoots with the taxi drivers and would rather you take a taxi than a van.

From the bus station, local buses marked "Mercado—C. Camionera" or simply "Centro" leave frequently for the center of town. A taxi from either bus station to downtown hotels will cost about $1.25 to $1.50.

Parking downtown can be difficult, but there are several parking lots near the hotels I recommend below. Use one that's guarded around the clock.

Information   The best source of information is at the **State Tourism Office** in the Tabasco 2000 complex, Paseo Tabasco 1504, SEFICOT Building, Centro Administrativo del Gobierno (☎ **93/16-3633** or 93/16-2890). Inconveniently located opposite the Liverpool department store and an enclosed shopping center on the second floor of the building, it's open Monday through Friday from 8am to 4pm. There are two other branches—the **airport office** is staffed daily from 10am to 5pm, and **La Venta Park** has an office open Tuesday through Sunday from

10am to 5pm. The staff can supply rates and telephone numbers for the hotels, as well as useful telephone numbers for bus companies and airlines.

City Layout The hotels and restaurants I recommend are located off the main streets: **Madero, Pino Suárez,** the **Malecón,** and **Grijalva/Ruíz Cortinez.** Highway 180 skirts the city, so a turn onto Madero or Pino Suárez will take you into the center of town.

Your point of reference in town can be **Plaza Juárez,** or the main square, bounded by the streets Zaragoza, Madero, Sánchez, and Carranza. The plaza is just off the center of the downtown district, at the north end of the pedestrian zone, with the Río Grijalva to its east and Highway 186 to its north. Within this area is the **pedestrian zone,** with roads closed to traffic for five blocks. This zone is often called **Centro,** or **Zona Luz.** At the south end of the pedestrian zone is the **Plaza de Armas** bounded by 27 de Febrero, Guerrero, Maquiliz, and Independencia, and with the Palacio de Gobierno at its north end. Villahermosa's main thoroughfare is Avenida Madero, running south from Highway 186 past the Plaza Juárez to the river, where it intersects with the riverside avenue, the **Malecón.** I have used the Plaza Juárez, Plaza de Armas, and the popular Restaurant Galerías Madan as points of reference.

Getting Around All the **city buses** converge on Avenida Pino Suárez at the market and are clearly labeled for Tabasco 2000, Parque La Venta, and Centro; most rides cost about 30¢.

A **taxi** from the center of town to the Parque La Venta is about $1.25. If you're getting around **by car,** you'll be glad to know that Villahermosa's streets are well marked, with arrows clearly designating the direction of traffic.

Fast Facts   American Express is represented by Turismo Nieves, Bulevar Simón Sarlat 202 (☎ **93/14-1888;** fax 93/12-5130). The telephone **area code** is 93.

EXPLORING VILLAHERMOSA

Major sights in Villahermosa include the **Parque-Museo La Venta,** the **Pellicer Anthropology Museum,** the **History of Tabasco Museum,** and the **Museum of Popular Culture** (see below). You can hit the high points in a day.

If you need to shop for any necessities or luxuries, head for the indoor shopping mall at **Tabasco 2000** or the shops lining **Avenida Madero.**

The most popular side trip from Villahermosa is to the **archaeological site of Palenque,** covered earlier in this chapter.

✪ **Parque Museo La Venta.** Av. Ruíz Cortinez. ☎ **93/12-8910.** Museum $1; still camera free (no flash); no video. Archaeological Park $1; no video. Daily 9am–5pm. Take Paseo Tabasco northeast to Highway 180 and turn right; it's less than a mile down on your right next to the Exposition Park.

This park incorporates not only the fascinating outdoor La Venta Museum, but also the regional zoo and the Museo Olmeca de La Venta (Olmec Museum of La Venta), an exceptionally well-done explanation of the Olmec civilization.

La Venta was one of three major Olmec cities during the Pre-Classic Period (2000 B.C.–A.D. 300). The mammoth heads you see in the park were found when the ruins of La Venta were discovered in 1938. Today all that remains of the once-impressive city are some grass-covered mounds—once earthen pyramids—84 miles west of Villahermosa. All the gigantic heads and other important sculptures have been moved from the site to this interesting museum/park. Allow at least an hour to wander through the junglelike sanctuary and to look at the 3,000-year-old sculpture and listen to the birds that inhabit the grounds. *Important note:* Mosquitoes can be thick certain times of the year, so bring insect repellent.

On a walk through the park, you'll see Olmec relics, sculptures, mosaics, a mockup of the original La Venta, and, of course, three colossal Olmec heads. Carved around 1000 B.C., these heads are 6¹/₂ feet high and weigh around 40 tons. The faces seem to be half-adult, half-infantile, with the fleshy undulating lips characteristic of Olmecan art. The basalt rock was transported from the nearest source, over 70 miles from La Venta, which is all the more impressive when you realize the sculptors had no wheels to move it. The multiton rock was brought by raft from the quarry to the site. At least 16 heads have been found: four at La Venta, nine at San Lorenzo, and three at Tres Zapotes—all Olmec cities on Mexico's east coast.

On your stroll through the park, notice the other fine stone sculptures and artistic achievements of the Olmecs, who established the first art style in Mesoamerica with their monumental works (chiseled without the use of metal). Their exquisite figurines in jade and serpentine, which can be seen in the Museo Regional de Antropología (see below), far excelled any other craft of this period.

✪ **Museo Regional de Antropología Carlos Pellicer Camara.** Av. Carlos Pellicer 511. ☎ **93/12-1803.** Admission $1.50. Tues–Sun 10am–4pm; gift shop, Tues–Sat 9am–4pm.

This museum, on the west bank of the river a mile south of the town center, is architecturally bold and attractive and very well organized. The pre-Hispanic artifacts on display include not only Tabascan finds (Totonac, Zapotec, and Olmec) but also those of other Mexican and Central American cultures.

The first floor contains the auditorium, bookstore, and gift shop; most of what interests visitors is on the upper floors, reached by an elevator or the stairs. The second floor is devoted to the Olmecs, while the third floor features artifacts relating to central Mexico, including the Tlatilco and Teotihuacán cultures; the Huasteca culture of Veracruz, San Luis Potosí, and Tampico states; and the west-coast cultures of Nayarit state. Photographs and diagrams provide vivid images, but the explanatory signs are mostly in Spanish. Look especially for the figurines that were found in this area and for the colorful *Codex* (an early book of pictographs).

Museo de Historia de Tabasco (Casa de los Azulejos). At the corner of 27 de Febrero and Av. Juárez. No phone. Admission 75¢. Daily 10am–4pm.

Take half an hour and head to the pedestrians-only zone to see this museum, which presents the history of Tabasco from pre-Columbian times to the present through documents, artifacts, and pictures. Every room is decorated with tiles in the Spanish and Italian baroque style, and the building's blue-and-white-tiled exterior, with wrought iron balconies, is worth a snapshot. Only some explanations are in English. There's a nice gift shop off the lobby featuring books and products of the state of Tabasco.

✪ **Museo de Cultura Popular.** Calle Zaragoza 810, at Juárez. ☎ **93/12-1117.** Free admission. Daily 10am–4pm; gift shop, daily 10am–4pm.

This museum is 3 blocks north and 4¹/₂ blocks west of the Museo de Historia (see above). As you enter, on the right there's a small gift shop with baskets, carved gourds, embroidered regional clothing, and chocolate from Tabasco. Displays in the next room show the state's regional clothing and dance costumes. In the back is a Chontal hut, complete with typical furnishings and a recorded conversation of two female villagers talking about the high cost of living. Student guides are often on hand for a free explanation. Another room shows ceremonial pottery and household utensils.

WHERE TO STAY

The area around the intersections of Avenidas Juárez and Lerdo, sometimes referred to as the "Zona Luz," is now one of the best places to stay; the streets are pedestrian malls closed to traffic. One drawback to this plan is parking, though there are guarded lots on the outskirts of the mall.

Room rates in Villahermosa are distressingly high, especially considering what you get. The price headings used below are for doubles during high season.

DOUBLES FOR LESS THAN $25

Hotel Palomino Palace. Av. Mina 222, Villahermosa, Tab. 86000. ☎ **93/12-8431.** 45 rms (all with bath). FAN. $17 single or double. Free parking on the street.

Directly across from the first-class bus station, the Palomino is surprisingly clean and quiet. The rooms are small, with a couple of shelves for clothes, no closets, and blue-tiled baths with hot showers. Those overlooking Avenida Mina are the noisiest; there are a few rooms away from the street that should be your first choice. The restaurant off the lobby is open daily from 6am to midnight.

DOUBLES FOR LESS THAN $50

⑤ Hotel Madan. Pino Suárez 105, Villahermosa, Tab. 86000. ☎ **93/12-1650.** Fax 93/14-3192. 20 rms (all with bath). A/C TV TEL. $18 single; $19 double. Free parking; secured.

The two-story Madan is another convenient downtown hotel within walking distance of the pedestrians-only zone and central-city museums. The pleasant rooms are clean and carpeted. On the second floor, you'll find a comfortable sitting room and cold water dispenser. It's between Reforma and Lerdo, on the street behind the popular Restaurant Galerías Madan.

✪ Hotel Plaza Independencia. Independencia 123, Villahermosa, Tab. 86000. ☎ **93/12-7541,** 93/12-1299. Fax 93/14-4724. 90 rms (all with bath). A/C TV TEL. $35 single or double. Free parking.

Of the many hotels in this price range, the Plaza Independencia is one of the best. The rooms, which are on six floors served by an elevator, contain avocado drapes and rugs and nice bamboo furnishings, including small desks. Some rooms have balconies and from the top floor you can see the river. It's the only budget hotel with a pool and enclosed parking. There's an off-lobby restaurant, open for all meals, plus a bar that's open Monday through Saturday. Try to reserve your room in advance. To find the hotel from the Plaza de Armas, face in the direction of the Malecón and walk to the right on Guerrero a half block to the corner of Macuiliz. Turn right and walk a block to Independencia and turn left; the hotel is a half block ahead on the right.

WHERE TO EAT

As other Mexican cities, Villahermosa is beginning to receive U.S.-franchise eateries such as Dunkin' Donuts, which is opposite the Museo de la Historia.

⑤ Galerías Madan. Madero 408. ☎ **93/12-1650.** Breakfast $1.50–$3.50; comida corrida $3.50; hamburgers $2.25–$3. Daily 7am–11:30pm (comida corrida served 1–4pm). MEXICAN.

Situated in a lobby of shops, this calm, soft pink, air-conditioned restaurant serves a comida corrida of soup, rice, a main course, vegetables, coffee, and dessert. The *empanadas de carne* (meat pies) are superior, and the tamales are just plain good. Large windows look onto the street, and the room has the feel of a hotel coffee shop where downtown shoppers and business types gather. It's between Lerdo de Tejada and Reforma.

⑤ **Ric's Coffee Shop.** Inside Las Galas, Av. Mina. ☎ **93/14-0717.** Breakfast $2–$3.25; soup $1.75–$2.50; main dishes $3–$5. Daily 8am–10pm. MEXICAN.

A clean, brightly lit coffee shop, Ric's is a blessing to those stranded at the nearby ADO bus station. Breakfasts are the best deal here, with a pot of coffee included in the price of the meal; special meals served throughout the day include drinks. The air-conditioning is powerful; the waiters and waitresses are friendly; and the restrooms are large and clean. To find this restaurant, turn left on Mina as you exit the bus station and walk about half a block to the entrance of the Las Galas center; Ric's is inside. The center also contains several bakeries and juice stands.

✪ **Los Tulipanes.** CICOM Center, Periférico Carlos Pellicer Camara 511. ☎ **93/12-9209** or 93/12-9217. Seafood courses $7–$11; beef courses $8–$11.50. Daily 1–9pm. SEAFOOD/STEAKS.

Supremely popular with the local upper class, Los Tulipanes offers pricey but good food and excellent service. The staff seems to serve a full house with ease, and on busy days, a trio strolls and serenades. Since the restaurant is located by the Río Grijalva and the Pellicer Museum of Anthropology, you can combine a visit to the museum with lunch here. They may bring you a plate of *tostones de plátano*—a monster-size tortilla made of banana instead of corn. In addition to seafood and steaks, there are such Mexican specialties as chiles rellenos, tacos, and *rejelagarto* empanadas.

Ask these folks about their Barco Restaurant Capitan Buelo. For a romantic interlude, dine on board the riverboat as it cruises the majestic Río Grijalva. They offer two afternoon seatings and one in the evening from November through August.

Mérida & the Maya Cities

Mérida and its environs in Campeche, and Yucatán state in the western Yucatán, are abundantly endowed with the qualities that can make a Mexican vacation something to remember. The area is rich in living pre-Hispanic traditions—you'll find clothing, crafts, and village life that hearken back to Maya ways of 10 centuries ago. And there are plenty of the more traditional reminders of the past—the ruins of spectacular Maya cities such as Chichén-Itzá, Uxmal, and others, along with walled Spanish colonial cities like Campeche. The western half of the Yucatán also offers the budget-minded traveler a wide choice of economical lodgings, and you'll enjoy the relaxed pace of Yucatecan life and warm, friendly people.

Maya village women wear cool embroidered cotton shirts and go about village life oblivious to the peninsula's fame as a premier resort destination. Their day-to-day cultural and belief system holds many elements that can be traced to pre-Hispanic times.

Though shy, the Maya are immensely courteous and helpful, and they eagerly chat with strangers even when there's a language barrier. More than 350,000 Maya living in the Yucatán peninsula's three states speak a Maya dialect, and many, particularly men, speak Spanish, too. Many, especially those serving tourists, slip easily between Maya, Spanish, and English. You'll get along even if English is your only language.

EXPLORING THE YUCATÁN'S MAYA HEARTLAND

The cultural center of the Yucatán, beautiful Mérida is a natural launching pad for trips to the Yucatán's major archaeological sites, to the Gulf Coast, and to the Yucatán's northern coast. This part of the Yucatán Peninsula is among the best places in Mexico to take a driving tour—there are no mountains; roads are fairly well maintained; traffic is light; and stopovers in the many rock-walled villages are delightful.

Celestún National Wildlife Refuge: A Wetlands Reserve This flamingo sanctuary and offbeat sand-street fishing village on the Gulf Coast is a one-hour drive from Mérida. Plan a long day—with a very early start—for the 7am flamingo trip. However, some people might find this a welcome respite for a week.

Dzibilchaltún: Maya Ruins This Maya site, now a national park, is located 9 miles north of Mérida along the Progreso road. Here

The Yucatán Peninsula

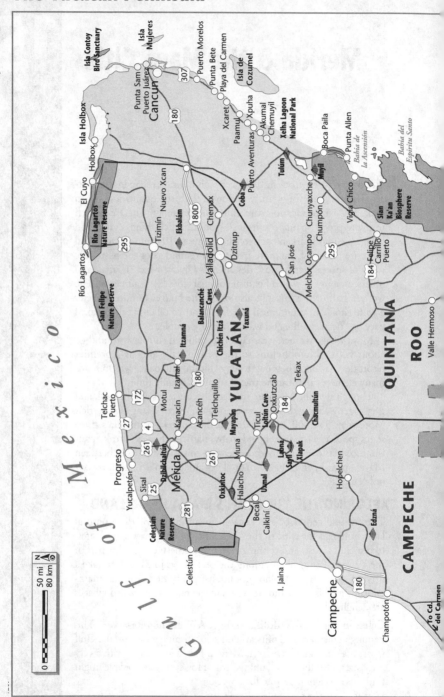

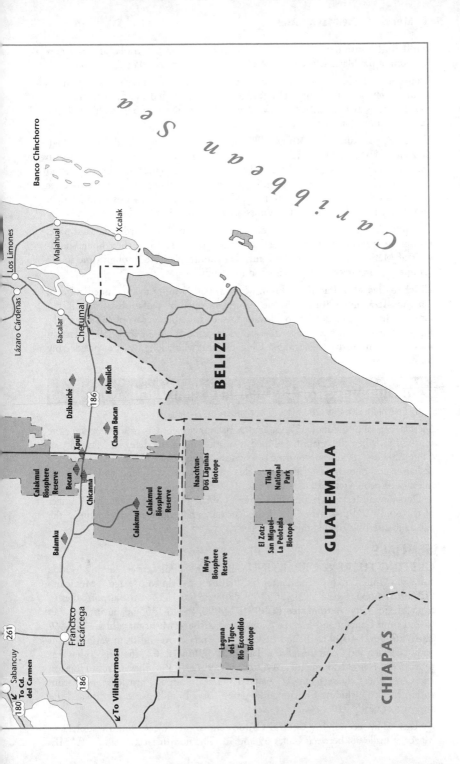

Banco Chinchorro

Caribbean Sea

Xcalak

Majahual

Los Limones

Lázaro Cárdenas

Bacalar

Chetumal

BELIZE

Dzibanché

Kohunlich

186

Chacan Bacan

Xpujil

Calakmul
Biosphere
Reserve

Becan

Naachtun-
Dós Lagunas
Biotope

Chicanná

Balamku

Calakmul

Calakmul
Biosphere
Reserve

Tikal
National
Park

El Zotz-
San Miguel-
La Palotada
Biotope

Maya
Biosphere
Reserve

GUATEMALA

Francisco
Escárcega

261

180 ↙ Sabancuy
To Cd.
del Carmen

186

↙To Villahermosa

Laguna
del Tigre-
Río Escondido
Biotope

CHIAPAS

543

you'll find a number of pre-Hispanic structures, nature trails, and the new Museum of the Maya. Make this one a half-day trip in the cool of the morning.

Progreso: Gulf Coast City   A modern city and Gulf Coast beach escape 21 miles north of Mérida, Progreso has a beautiful oceanfront drive and a vast beach lined with coconut palms that's popular on the weekends. Plan a full day-trip if you like beaches, but there's not a lot else to do.

Uxmal: Spectacular Maya Ruins   The best way to visit the splendid archaeological zone of Uxmal ("Oosh-mahl"; it's about 50 miles to the south of Mérida) is to rent a car, stay two nights in a hotel at Uxmal or a less expensive hotel in Ticul, and allow for two full days of sightseeing. It's also possible—though a bit rushed—to see Uxmal and the quartet of ruins south of there on a day-trip by bus from Mérida. Sunday is a good day to go, since admission is free to the archaeological sites.

Campeche: Walled Colonial City   A pretty colonial city with a relaxed pace, Campeche is also somewhat off the main tourist path. It's about three hours southwest of Mérida. Two nights and a full day should give you enough time to see Campeche's architectural highlights and museums.

Chichén-Itzá & Valladolid   From Mérida, it's 75 miles to the famed ruins of **Chichén-Itzá,** and 100 miles to the somnolent town of **Valladolid.** The ruins at Chichén-Itzá are so vast that you'll want to spend the better part of two days, taking your time in the heat, to see this site. The colonial city of Valladolid offers an inexpensive alternative to staying at Chichén-Itzá, where lodgings are considerably more expensive.

1 Mérida: Gateway to the Maya Heartland

900 miles NE of Mexico City, 200 miles W of Cancún

Mérida, capital of the state of Yucatán, has been the major city in the area since the mid-1500s, when the Spanish founded it on the site of the defeated Maya city of Tihó. Although it's a major touristic crossroads—within range of both the peninsula's archaeological ruins and its glitzy coasts—this modern city is easygoing, and the friendliness of its people remains its trademark.

Downtown Mérida is full of fine examples of colonial-style architecture. Vestiges of the opulent 19th-century era of the Yucatán's henequen boom remain in the ornate mansions sprinkled throughout the city.

ESSENTIALS

GETTING THERE & DEPARTING   By Plane   For carriers serving Mérida from the United States, see chapter 3, "Planning a Trip to Mexico." **Mexicana** (☎ **99/24-6633,** 99/24-7421, or 99/23-0508; 99/46-1332 at the airport) flies in from Mexico City. **Aeroméxico** (☎ **99/27-9000;** 99/46-1305 at the airport) flies to and from Cancún and Mexico City. **AeroCaribe**, a Mexicana affiliate (☎ **99/ 28-6786;** 99/28-6790 at the airport), provides service to and from various cities within Mexico and Central America. **Taesa** (☎ **99/46-1826** at the airport) has seasonal flights from Mexican cities. **Aviateca** (☎ **99/24-4354**) flies in from Houston and Guatemala City. **Aviacsa** (☎ **99/46-1344** at the airport) provides service from within Mexico including Cancún and Mexico City. Taxis between the city and the airport cost nearly $10.

By Bus   The second-class **Central Camionera** is seven blocks southwest of Plaza Mayor at Calle 68, between Calles 69 and 71. The new first-class station, **CAME,**

is directly behind it on Calle 70, between Calles 69 and 71. A separate station for travelers to **Progresso** is at Calle 62 no. 524, between Calles 65 and 67.

To/From Uxmal: Autotransportes del Sur (☎ 99/24-9374) buses depart at 6 and 9am, noon, and 2:30pm; return trips are at 2:30, 3:30, and 7:30pm. The same company also offers one bus daily on the Mérida–Uxmal–Kabah–Sayil–Labná–Xlapak route. The trip costs $11; it departs Mérida at 8am and returns at 4pm. The driver allows passengers to spend around two hours at Uxmal and 30 minutes at each of the other archaeological sites before returning. There is no evening departure for the sound-and-light show at Uxmal.

To/From Chichén-Itzá: There are first-class **ADO** (☎ 99/24-8391) buses at 7:30am and 3:30pm, leaving from the CAME. If you're planning a day-trip (something I don't recommend because you'll want more time to see the impressive ruins), take the 7:30am bus and reserve a seat on the 3:30pm return bus.

To/From Pisté: Autotransportes de Oriente (☎ 99/22-2387) runs second-class buses every hour from 5am till midnight, and a luxury bus at 11am.

To/From Valladolid and Cancún: Expresso de Oriente (☎ 99/22-2387) offers deluxe service—video, restroom, and refreshments—to Cancún (a four- to five-hour trip) 19 times daily between 6am and 11:15pm. The line also has eight deluxe buses daily to Valladolid between 6am and 11:45pm. **Caribe Express** (☎ 99/24-4275) runs nine deluxe buses daily to Cancún between 7:15am and 10pm. **Autotransportes del Caribe** goes to Cancún at 6:30am and 5:30 and 11:45pm, and **ADO** runs three buses to Valladolid.

To/From Playa del Carmen, Tulum, and Chetumal: Three deluxe **ADO** buses go to Valladolid and on to Playa del Carmen between 7:30am and midnight. ADO also has deluxe buses to Chetumal at 10:10am and 5:30pm. **Caribe Express** buses to Playa del Carmen and Tulum depart at 6:15am and 11pm; Caribe Express buses to Chetumal depart at 7:30 and 10:30am and 1, 10, and 11pm. **Autotransportes Peninsulares** (☎ 99/24-1844) offers Servicio Plus deluxe service to Chetumal at 8:30am and 6pm.

To/From Campeche: Autotransportes Peninsulares offers deluxe service to Campeche at 8am and 3pm. **ADO** has first-class service to Campeche every half hour between 6am and 10pm; **Autotransportes del Sur** (☎ 99/24-9374) buses leave every 45 minutes from 6am to 11:30pm.

To/From Palenque and San Cristóbal de las Casas: ADO has first-class service to Palenque at 8am and 10pm. **Autotransportes del Sureste** offers second-class service to Palenque and San Cristóbal de las Casas at 6pm.

To/From Progreso, Dzibilchaltún, and Celestún: Buses depart from the Progreso Station at Calle 62 no. 524, between Calles 65 and 67.

By Car Highway 180 from Cancún, Chichén-Itzá, or Valladolid leads into Calle 65 past the market and within one block of the Plaza Mayor. Highway 281 from Uxmal (via Muna and Uman) becomes Avenida Itzáes (if you arrive by that route, turn right on Calle 63 to reach the Plaza Mayor). From Uxmal (via Ticul and the ruins of Mayapán) the road passes through Kanasín before joining Highway 180 from Valladolid into Mérida.

A traffic loop encircles Mérida, making it possible to skirt the city and head for a nearby city or site. Directional signs are generally good into the city, but going around the city on the loop requires constant vigilance.

The eight-lane toll highway (autopista) between Mérida and Cancún was completed in 1993 and cuts the driving between the two cities by about one hour. The highway begins about 35 miles east of Mérida at Kantunil, intersecting with

Highway 180. It ends at Nuevo Xcan, which is about 50 miles before Cancún. One-way tolls cost about $15.

See "En Route to Uxmal," below, at the end of the Mérida section for suggested routes from Mérida.

ORIENTATION Arriving by Plane Mérida's airport is 8 miles from the city center on the southwestern outskirts of town where Highway 180 enters the city. The airport has desks for renting a car, reserving a hotel room, and getting tourist information. *A Note of Caution:* Customs inspectors at the Mérida airport have been known to hassle tourists by confiscating and refusing to return the legal, legitimate, and allowable contents of their luggage. Upon arrival at all airports in Mexico passengers receive a customs statement with all allowable items listed. If you are within your rights according to that list, tell the officials that you are reporting them to SEDOCAM ("say-doh-kahm"), which is the Comptroller and Adminstrative Development Secretariat (☎ **91-800/0-0148** toll free in Mexico). Of course their idea is to relieve you of your possessions, but threatening to go over their heads to their superiors *may* save you further discussion. The allowable items per person include a portable computer, a video camera, two still cameras, personal clothing, used fishing equipment for one person, etc.

Taxi tickets to town are sold outside the airport doors under the covered walkway. A colectivo ticket costs $6 per person, but you have to wait for a group of five to assemble. Private taxis cost $10.

City bus no. 79 ("Aviación") operates between the town center and the airport (40¢), but the buses do not have frequent service. Other city buses run along Avenida Itzáes, just out of the airport precincts, heading for downtown.

Arriving by Bus From Mérida's main bus station you're only six blocks from the Plaza Mayor and within walking distance of several hotels. Buses to town stop on the corner to the left of the bus station's front door.

Information The most convenient source of information is the downtown branch of the **State of Yucatán Tourist Information Office,** in the hulking edifice known as the Teatro Peón Contreras, on Calle 60 between Calles 57 and 59 (☎ **99/24-9290** or 99/24-9389). It's open Monday through Sunday from 8am to 8pm, as are the information booths at the **airport** (☎ **99/24-6764**), the bus station, and on Calle 62 next to the Palacio Municipal. **Yucatán Information Office,** P. O. Box 140681, Coral Gales, FL 33114-0681, is a nonprofit service of the Mesoamerica Foundation. They offer helpful information about the Yucatán, such as the current cost of admission to archaeological sites, new museums, and customs scams.

City Layout As in many colonial Mexican cities, Mérida's streets were originally laid out in a grid: **Even-numbered streets** run north–south; **odd-numbered streets** run east–west. In the last few decades the city has expanded well beyond the grid, and several grand boulevards have been added on the outskirts to ease traffic flow.

When looking for an address, you'll notice that street numbers progress very slowly because of the many unnumbered dwellings and the addition of letters (A, B, C, etc.) to numbered dwellings. For example, the distance from 504 to 615D on Calle 59 is 12 blocks.

The center of town is the very pretty **Plaza Mayor** (sometimes called the **Plaza Principal**), with its shady trees, benches, vendors, and a social life all its own. Around the Plaza Mayor are the massive cathedral, the Palacio de Gobierno (state government headquarters), the Palacio Municipal, and the Casa de Montejo. Within a few blocks are several smaller plazas, the University of Yucatán, and the sprawling market district.

Mérida's most fashionable address is the broad tree-lined boulevard called **Paseo de Montejo** and the surrounding neighborhood. The Paseo de Montejo begins seven blocks northwest of the Plaza Mayor and is home to Yucatán's anthropological museum, several upscale hotels, and the U.S. consulate. New high-rise deluxe hotels are opening just off the Paseo on **Avenida Colón,** another shaded boulevard containing some of the city's finest old mansions. Within the next few years, this neighborhood will become Mérida's more exclusive tourism zone, with fine restaurants and boutiques catering to the travelers drawn to the new hotels.

GETTING AROUND   By Bus   A ride on a city bus costs only 35¢. You can take a bus to the large, shady **Parque Centenario** on the western outskirts of town. Look for a bus of the same name ("Centenario") on Calle 64. Most buses on Calle 59 go to the zoo or to the **Museum of Natural History.** "Central" buses stop at the bus station, and any bus marked "Mercado" or "Correo" (post office) will take you to the **market district.**

By Taxi   Taxi drivers are beginning to overcharge tourists in Mérida the way they do in Mexico City. Taxi meters start at $2.50.

By Car   A car is handy for your explorations of Mayapán, Uxmal, and Kabah, but you don't need one to get around Mérida or to reach Chichén-Itzá or Cancún. Rental cars are expensive, averaging $45 to $75 per day for a VW Beetle. As you scour the city for a rental-car deal, be sure the price quoted includes tax, insurance, and unlimited mileage, and get deductible information before settling the deal. For tips on saving money on car rentals by renting in advance from your home country see "Getting Around" in chapter 2.

By Horse-Drawn Carriage   Look for a line of *coches de caleta* near the cathedral and in front of the Hotel Casa del Balam. Haggle for a good price; a one-hour tour of the city costs around $8.

On Foot   Most tourist attractions are within walking distance of the Plaza Mayor.

FAST FACTS: Mérida

Area Code   The telephone area code is 99.

Bookstore   The Librería Dante, Calle 60 at Calle 57 (☎ **99/24-9522**), has a selection of English-language cultural-history books on Mexico. It's open Monday through Friday from 8am to 9:30pm, Saturday from 8am to 2pm and 5 to 9pm, and Sunday from 10am to 2pm and 4 to 8pm.

Climate   From November through February the weather can be chilly, windy, and rainy. You'll need a light jacket or sweater for occasional cool winter weather and thin, light clothes for summer days. Light rain gear is suggested for the brief showers in late May, June, and July, but there's a chance of rain year-round in the Yucatán.

Complaints   Tourists experiencing difficulties with public officials such as police officers can call ☎ **91-800/0-0148** toll free in Mexico to report incidents.

Consulates   The U.S. Consulate is at Paseo de Montejo 453, at the corner of Avenida Colón (☎ **99/25-5011**), near the Holiday Inn. It's open Monday through Friday from 7:30am to 4pm. Visa matters are dealt with only on Monday, Tuesday, Wednesday, and Friday from 7:30 to 11am; other kinds of problems are considered the same days from noon to 3:30pm and Thursday until 4pm. The telephone number of a duty officer is posted at the entrance. The British Vice-Consulate is at

Calle 58 no. 498 (☎ 99/28-6152). Though in theory it's open Monday through Friday from 9:30am to 1pm, you may find no one there. The vice-consul fields questions about travel to Belize as well as British matters.

Currency Exchange   Banamex, in the Palacio Montejo on the Plaza Mayor, usually provides a better rate of exchange than other banks, but the lines are often maddeningly long. Exchange hours are Monday through Friday from 9:30am to 1:30pm. Another option is the money-exchange office just as you enter the bank gates, and more banks are located on and off Calle 65 between Calles 62 and 60.

Hospitals   Hospital O'Horan is on Avenida Itzáes at Calle 59A (☎ 99/24-8711), north of the Parque Centenario.

Post Office   Mérida's main post office ("correo") is located in the midst of the market at the corner of Calles 65 and 56. A branch office is located at the airport. Both are open Monday through Friday from 8am to 5pm and Saturday from 8am to 2pm.

Seasons   There are two high seasons—one in July and August when the weather is very hot and humid and when Mexicans most commonly take their vacations, and one between November 15 and Easter Sunday when the northerners flock to the Yucatán to escape winter weather and when weather in the Yucatán is cooler.

Spanish Classes   Maya scholars, Spanish teachers, and archaeologists from the United States are among the students at the **Centro Idiomas del Sureste,** Calle 14 no. 106 at Calle 25, Colonia México, Mérida, Yucatán, 97000 (☎ 99/26-1155; fax 99/26-9020). The school has two locations: in the Colonia México, a northern residential district, and on Calle 66 at Calle 57 in the downtown area. Students live with local families or in hotels; sessions running two weeks or longer are available for all levels of proficiency and areas of interest. For brochures and applications, contact Chloe Conaway de Pacheco, directora.

Telephone   There are long-distance *casetas* at the airport and the bus station. Look also for the blue-and-silver Ladatel phones appearing in public places all over Mexico. Also see "Telephones" in chapter 1. *Important note:* Telephone numbers are being changed throughout the city, so if you have difficulty reaching a number, ask the telephone operator for assistance.

EXPLORING MÉRIDA

Most of the city's attractions are within walking distance of each other in the downtown area.

FESTIVALS & EVENTS

On the evening of the **first Friday** of each month, Dennis LaFoy of the Yucatán Trails Travel Agency (☎ 99/28-2582) invites the English-speaking community to a casual get-together. They usually gather at the Hotel Mérida Misión Park Plaza on Calle 60, across from the Hotel Casa del Balam, but call Dennis to confirm the location.

Many Mexican cities offer weekend concerts in the park, but Mérida surpasses them with almost-daily high-quality public events, most of which are free.

Sunday   Each Sunday from 9am to 9pm there's a fair called **Domingo en Mérida** (Sunday in Mérida). The downtown area, blocked off from traffic for the day, bustles with activity; there are children's art classes, antique vendors, and food stands, as well as concerts of all kinds. At 11am in front of the Palacio del Gobierno, musicians play everything from jazz to classical and folk music. Also at 11am the police orchestra performs Yucatecan tunes at the Santa Lucía park. At 11:30am, marimba music brightens the Parque Cepeda Peraza (Parque Hidalgo) on Calle 60 at Calle 59. At 1pm in front of the Palacio Municipal on the Plaza Mayor, folk ballet dancers reenact a typical Yucatecan wedding. All events are free.

Monday The **City Hall Folklore Ballet** and the **Police Jaranera Band** perform at 8pm in front of the Palacio Municipal. The music and dancing celebrate the Vaquerías feast, which occurs after the branding of cattle on Yucatecan haciendas. Among the featured performers are dancers with trays of bottles or filled glasses on their heads—a sight to see. Admission is free.

Tuesday The theme for the Tuesday entertainment, held at 9pm in Parque Santiago, on Calle 59 at Calle 72, is **Musical Memories**. Tunes range from South American and Mexican to North American. Admission is free. Also at 9pm in the Teatro Peón Contreras on Calle 60 at Calle 57 the **University of Yucatán Folklore Ballet** presents "Yucatán and Its Roots." Admission is $5.

Wednesday The **University of Yucatán Folklore Ballet,** along with guitarists and poets, performs at 8pm at the Maya Culture House on Calle 63, between Calles 64 and 66. Admission is free.

Thursday Typical Yucatecan music and dance are presented at the **Serenata** in Parque Santa Lucía at 9pm; admission is free.

Friday At 9pm in the patio of the University of Yucatán, Calle 60 at Calle 57, the **University of Yucatán Folklore Ballet** often performs typical regional dances from the Yucatán. Admission is free.

WALKING TOUR
Mérida

Start: Plaza Mayor.
Finish: Palacio Cantón.
Time: Allow approximately two hours, not counting time for browsing or refreshment.
Best Times: Tuesday through Sunday before noon.
Worst Times: Monday, when the Anthropology Museum is closed.

Downtown Mérida is a visitor's visual delight, with several tree-shaded parks and most of the finest examples of both colonial and late-19th-century architecture the city has to offer. The downtown is within an easy stroll of the:

1. Plaza Mayor. Flanked east and west by Calles 61 and 63 and north and south by Calles 60 and 62, the plaza began its history as the Plaza de Armas—a training field for Montejo's troops. It was renamed Plaza de la Constitución in 1812 and then Plaza de la Independencia in 1821 before assuming its current name. Other common names for it include Plaza Grande, Plaza Principal, and the zócalo. Today this beautiful town square, shaded by topiary laurel trees, is decked out in manicured shrubs and lawns with iron benches. Numerous entertainment events open to the public take place here throughout the year. On the east side of the plaza stands the:

2. Cathedral. Built between 1561 and 1598, it looks like a fortress, as do many other early churches in the Yucatán. (For several centuries, defense was actually one of the functions of such churches, as the Maya did not take kindly to European domination.) Much of the stone in the cathedral's walls came from the ruined buildings of Tihó, the former Maya city. Inside, decoration is sparse, with altars draped in fabric colorfully embroidered like a Maya woman's shift. The most notable feature is a picture over the right side door of Ah Kukum Tutul Xiú visiting the Montejo camp.

To the left of the main altar is a smaller shrine with a curious charred cross recovered from the church in the town of Ichmul, which burned down. The figure was carved by a local artist in the 1500s from a miraculous tree that burned but did not char. The figure, along with the church, broke out in blisters as the flames enveloped it. The local people named it Cristo de las Ampollas (Christ of the Blisters). Also take a look in the side chapel (open from 8 to 11am and 4:30 to 7pm), which contains a life-size diorama of the Last Supper. The Mexican Jesus is covered with prayer crosses brought by supplicants asking for intercession.

To the right (south) of the cathedral is a:

3. Seminary and the former site of the archbishop's palace. The palace was torn down during the Mexican Revolution in 1915; part of the seminary remains but now contains shops. On the south side of the Plaza Mayor is the:

4. Palacio Montejo, also called the Casa de Montejo. Started in 1542 by Francisco Montejo *el mozo* (the Younger, i.e., the first Montejo's natural son) it was occupied by Montejo descendants until the 1970s. It now houses a Banamex bank branch, which means you can get a look at parts of the palace just by wandering in during banking hours: Monday through Friday from 9am to 1:30pm. Note the arms of the Spanish kings and of the Montejo family on the plateresque facade, along with figures of the conquistadores standing on the heads of "barbarians." Look closely and you'll find the bust of Francisco Montejo the Elder, his wife, and his daughter.

Facing the cathedral across the Plaza Mayor (on the west side) is the:

5. Palacio Municipal (City Hall) with its familiar clock tower. It started out as the *cabildo*—the colonial town hall and lockup—in 1542. It had to be rebuilt in the 1730s and again in the 1850s, when it took on its present romantic aspect. On the north side of the Plaza Mayor is the:

6. Palacio de Gobierno, dating from 1892. Large murals painted by the Meridiano artist Fernando Pacheco Castro between 1971 and 1973 decorate the interior walls. Scenes from Maya and Mexican history abound, and the painting over the stairway depicts the Maya spirit with ears of sacred corn, the "sunbeams of the gods." Nearby is a painting of the mustached benevolent dictator Lázaro Cárdenas, who in 1938 expropriated 17 foreign oil companies and was hailed as a Mexican liberator. The palace is open Monday through Saturday from 8am to 8pm and Sunday from 9am to 5pm.

☕ **TAKE A BREAK** Revive your motor with a cup of coffee and some pan dulce or a bolillo from the **Pan Montejo** on the southwest side of the plaza on the corner of Calles 63 and 62. Add a glass of fresh orange or papaya juice from **Jugos California** next door, take a seat at the plaza, and enjoy the morning sun.

Exploring Calle 60 Continuing north from the Plaza Mayor up Calle 60, you'll see many of Mérida's old churches and little parks. Several stores catering to tourists along Calle 60 sell gold-filigree jewelry, pottery, and folk art. A stroll along this street leads to the Parque Santa Ana and continues to the fashionable boulevard Paseo de Montejo and its Museo Regional de Antropología. On your left as you leave the northeast corner of the Plaza Mayor, the:

7. Teatro Daniel Ayala offers a continuous schedule of performing artists from around the world. A few steps beyond and across the street is the:

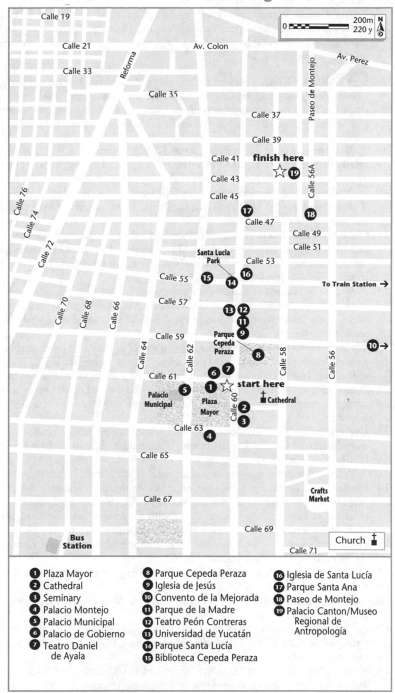

Calle 19
Calle 21
Av. Colon
Calle 33
Reforma
Av. Perez
Paseo de Montejo
Calle 35
Calle 37
Calle 39
Calle 41
finish here
Calle 43
☆ ⑲
Calle 56A
Calle 45
⑰
Calle 47
⑱
Calle 76
Calle 74
Calle 72
Calle 49
Calle 51
Santa Lucia Park
Calle 53
Calle 55
⑮ ⑭ ⑯
To Train Station →
Calle 57
⑬ ⑫
Calle 70
Calle 68
Calle 66
⑪
Calle 59
⑨
Parque Cepeda Peraza
Calle 64
Calle 62
⑧
Calle 58
Calle 56
⑩ →
Calle 61
⑥ ⑦
Palacio Municipal
⑤ ①
☆ **start here**
Plaza Mayor
Calle 60
† **Cathedral**
②
Calle 63
③
④
Calle 65
Calle 67
Crafts Market
Calle 69
Church †
Bus Station
Calle 71

① Plaza Mayor
② Cathedral
③ Seminary
④ Palacio Montejo
⑤ Palacio Municipal
⑥ Palacio de Gobierno
⑦ Teatro Daniel de Ayala
⑧ Parque Cepeda Peraza
⑨ Iglesia de Jesús
⑩ Convento de la Mejorada
⑪ Parque de la Madre
⑫ Teatro Peón Contreras
⑬ Universidad de Yucatán
⑭ Parque Santa Lucía
⑮ Biblioteca Cepeda Peraza
⑯ Iglesia de Santa Lucía
⑰ Parque Santa Ana
⑱ Paseo de Montejo
⑲ Palacio Canton/Museo Regional de Antropología

8. Parque Cepeda Peraza (also called the Parque Hidalgo), named for the 19th-century general Manuel Cepeda Peraza, was part of Montejo's original city plan. Small outdoor restaurants front hotels on the *parque*, making it a popular stopping-off place at any time of day.

☕ **TAKE A BREAK**   Any of the several outdoor restaurants on the Parque Cepeda Peraza makes an inviting respite. My favorite is **Giorgio,** where you can claim a table and write postcards while bartering for hammocks, amber jewelry, and baskets displayed by wandering artisans. It's in front of the Gran Hotel.

Bordering Parque Cepeda Peraza across Calle 59 is the:

9. Iglesia de Jesús, or El Tercer Ordén (the Third Order), built by the Jesuit order in 1618. The entire city block on which the church stands was part of the Jesuit establishment, and the early schools developed into the Universidad de Yucatán. Walk east on Calle 59, five blocks past the Parque Cepeda Peraza and the church, and you'll see the former:

10. Convento de la Mejorada, a late-1600s work by the Franciscans. While here, go half a block farther on Calle 59 to the **Museo Regional de Artes Populares** (see "More Attractions," below). Backtrack to Calle 60 and turn north. Just beyond the church (Iglesia de Jesús) is the:

11. Parque de la Madre (also called the Parque Morelos), which contains a modern statue of the Madonna and Child. The statue is a copy of the work by Renoir that stands in the Luxembourg Gardens in Paris. Beyond the Parque de la Madre and across the pedestrian way is:

12. Teatro Peón Contreras, an enormous beige edifice designed by Italian architect Enrico Deserti in the early years of this century. In one corner you'll see a branch of the State Tourist Information Office facing the Parque de la Madre. The main theater entrance, with its Carrara marble staircase and frescoed dome, is a few steps farther. Domestic and international performers appear here frequently. On the west side of Calle 60, at the corner of Calle 57, is the:

13. Universidad de Yucatán, founded in the 19th century by Felipe Carrillo Puerto with the help of General Cepeda Peraza. The founding is illustrated by a fresco (1961) by Manuel Lizama.

A block farther on your left, past the Hotel Mérida Misión Park Inn, is the:

14. Parque Santa Lucía. Surrounded by an arcade on the north and west sides, the *parque* was once where visitors first alighted in Mérida after arriving in their stage-coaches. On Sunday, Parque Santa Lucía holds a used-book sale and small swap meet, and several evenings a week it hosts popular entertainment. On Thursday nights performers present Yucatecan songs and poems. A block west from the *parque* on Calle 55 at the corner of Calle 62 is:

15. Biblioteca Cepeda Peraza, a library founded by the general in 1867. Back to the Parque Santa Lucia and facing it is the ancient:

16. Iglesia de Santa Lucía (1575). To reach Paseo de Montejo, continue walking north on Calle 60 to the:

17. Parque Santa Ana, four blocks up Calle 60 from the Parque Santa Lucía. Turn right here on Calle 47 for 1 1/2 blocks; then turn left onto the broad, busy boulevard known as the:

18. Paseo de Montejo, a broad tree-lined thoroughfare with imposing banks, hotels, and several 19th-century mansions erected by henequen barons, generals, and other Yucatecan potentates. It's Mexico's humble version of the Champs-Elysées.

☕ **WINDING DOWN**   Before or after tackling the Palacio Cantón (see below), stop for a break at the **Dulcería y Sorbetería Colón,** on Paseo de Montejo one block north of the Palacio between Calles 39 and 41. Far grander than its sister cafe at the Plaza Mayor, this bakery/ice-cream shop/candy shop has a long glass counter displaying sweet treats. Unfortunately, coffee and tea are not available.

At the corner of Calle 43 is the:

19. Palacio Cantón (entrance on Calle 43), which houses the **Museo Regional de Antropología** (Anthropology Museum; ☎ **23-0557**). Designed and built by Enrico Deserti, the architect who designed the Teatro Peón Contreras, this is the most impressive mansion on Paseo de Montejo and the only one open to the public. It was constructed between 1909 and 1911 during the last years of the Porfiriato as the home of General Francisco Cantón Rosado. The general enjoyed his palace for only six years before he died in 1917. The house was converted into a school and later became the official residence of the governor of the Yucatán.

This is an interregional museum covering not only the state but also the rest of the peninsula and Mexico. Its exhibits include cosmology, pre-Hispanic time computation and comparative timeline, musical instruments, weaving examples and designs, and stone carving from all over the country.

On the right as you enter is a room used for changing exhibits, usually featuring "the piece of the month." After that are the permanent exhibits with captions mostly in Spanish. Starting with fossil mastodon teeth, the exhibits take you through the Yucatán's history, paying special attention to the daily life of its inhabitants. You'll see how the Maya tied boards to babies' skulls to create the slanting forehead that was then a mark of great beauty, and how they filed teeth to sharpen them or drilled teeth to implant jewels. Enlarged photos show the archaeological sites, and drawings illustrate the various styles of Maya houses and how they were constructed. The one of Mayapán, for instance, clearly shows the city's ancient walls. Even if you know only a little Spanish, the museum provides a good background for explorations of Maya sites. The museum is open Tuesday through Saturday from 8am to 8pm and Sunday from 8am to 2pm. Admission is $4.50; free on Sunday. There's a museum bookstore on the left as you enter.

MORE ATTRACTIONS

The **Museo de la Ciudad** is on Calle 61 at Calle 58, in recently renovated quarters. The museum collection relates the city's past in the form of photographs, drawings, and dioramas. It's open Tuesday through Saturday from 9am to 8pm and Sunday 9am to 1pm. Admission is $2.

The **Museo de Arte Contemporáneo Ateneo de Yucatán** (MACAY) opened in April 1994 in a rambling 15-room building from colonial days. Now refurbished, it has on permanent exhibit the works of Fernando García Ponce, Gabriel Ramirez Asnar, and others, and it hosts traveling exhibits every three months or so. It is located on Paseo de la Revolución (Calle 61-A), just south across the street from the cathedral; it's open Wednesday through Monday from 9am to 5pm. Admission is $3.50.

ECO-TOURS & ADVENTURE TRIPS

Companies that organize nature and adventure tours of the Yucatán Peninsula are just beginning to establish themselves. **Ecoturismo Yucatán,** Calle 3 no. 235, Col. Pensiones, Mérida, Yuc. 97219 (☎ **99/25-2187;** fax 99/25-9047), is run by Alfonso and Roberta Escobedo. Alfonso has been guiding adventure tours for more than a dozen years, and Roberta runs the office with professional efficiency. The various tours emphasize remote ruin sites and culture in the Yucatán, Campeche, Chiapas, Tabasco, Oaxaca, Belize, and Guatemala. Customized tours are available.

Another specialty tour agency is **Yucatán Trails,** Calle 62 no. 482 (☎ 99/28-2582). Canadian Dennis LaFoy, well known and active in the English-speaking community, is a font of information and can arrange a variety of individualized tours.

Roger Lynn at **Casa Mexilio Guest House** (☎ 99/28-2505), mentioned in "Where to Stay," below, arranges a variety of specialized trips. Concentrating on nature, Yucatán train trips, and haciendas, these are among the most unique trips in the area. Roger is operations manager for the Turquoise Reef Group, so you can request information through them at P.O. Box 2664, Evergreen, CO 80439 (☎ 800/538-6802).

SHOPPING

Mérida is known for hammocks, *guayaberas* (short-sleeve, lightweight men's shirts that are worn untucked), and Panama hats. There are also good buys in baskets made in the Yucatán, and pottery and crafts from all over Mexico, especially at the central market. The Mérida market is also the place to pick up prepared *achiote*—a mixture of ground achiote, oregano, garlic, masa, and other spices used in Yucatecan cuisine.

Mérida's bustling **market district,** bounded by Calles 63 to 69 and Calles 62 to 54, is a few blocks southeast of the Plaza Mayor. The streets surrounding the market can be as interesting and crowded as the market itself. Heaps of prepared achiote are sold in a pastelike substance in the food section. You mix it with vinegar to a soupy consistency for a marinade for grilled chicken and fish. It's also the sauce that makes baked chicken and cochinta pibil. On occasion, achiote is also found bottled and already mixed with juice of the sour orange. I don't leave the Yucatán without achiote, and it makes a great gift when given along with the recipe for using it. At home it keeps well for years in the freezer, so you can cut off the amount you need and save the remainder for another feast.

Crafts

Casa del las Artesanías. Calle 63 no. 513, between Calles 64 and 66. ☎ 99/23-5392.

ThisMérida beautiful restored monastery houses an impressive selection of crafts from throughout Mexico. Stop by here before going to the various crafts markets to see what high-quality work looks like. The monastery's back courtyard is used as a gallery, with rotating exhibits on folk and fine arts. It's open Monday through Saturday from 8am to 8pm.

Crafts Market. In a separate building of the main market, Calle 67 at Calle 56.

Look for a large pale-green building behind the post office. Climb the steps and wade into the clamor and activity while browsing for leather goods, hammocks, Panama hats, Maya embroidered dresses, men's formal guayabera shirts, and craft items of all kinds.

Museo Regional de Artes Populares. Calle 59 no. 441, between Calles 50 and 48. No phone.

A branch of the Museo Nacional de Artes y Industrías Populares in Mexico City, this museum displays regional costumes and crafts in the front rooms. Upstairs is a large room full of crafts from all over Mexico, including filigree jewelry from Mérida, folk pottery, baskets, and wood carving from the Yucatán. Open Tuesday through Saturday from 8am to 8pm and Sunday from 9am to 2pm. Admission is free.

Guayaberas

T-shirts, polo shirts, dress shirts, and the like can be horrendously hot and uncomfortable in Mérida's soaking humidity. For this reason, businessmen, politicians, bankers, and bus drivers alike don the guayabera—a loose-fitting button-down shirt worn outside pants. Mérida could well be called the hotbed of guayaberas, which can be purchased for under $10 at the market or for over $50 custom-made by a tailor. A guayabera made of Japanese linen can set you back about $65. The most comfortable shirts are made of light, breathable cotton, though polyester is surprisingly common, despite its tendency to seal in perspiration against the skin. Several guayabera shops are located along Calle 59; most display ready-to-wear shirts in several price ranges.

Jack Guayaberas. Calle 59 no. 507A. ☎ **99/28-6002.**

The tailors at Jack's, known for their craftsmanship since the mid-1950s, can make you the guayabera of your dreams in three hours. Connoisseurs have very definite opinions on color, the type of tucks that will run down the front, and the embroidery that will swirl around the buttons. Check out the shirts on the racks for your first guayabera or perhaps a blouse or dress. The shop is open daily from 9am to 1pm and 4 to 8pm.

Hammocks

The comfortable Yucatecan fine-mesh hammocks (*hamacas*) are made of string woven from silk, nylon, or cotton. Silk is extremely expensive and only for truly serious hammock sleepers. Nylon is long-lasting. Cotton is attractive, fairly strong, and inexpensive, but it wears out sooner than nylon. Here's how to select a hammock: Hold the hammock loosely and make sure the space between the weave is no larger than the size of your little finger. Grasp the hammock at the point where the wide part and the end strings meet and hold your hand level with the top of your head. The body should more than touch the floor; if not, the hammock is too short.

Hammocks are sold as *sencillo* (single, about $15); *doble* (double, $20); and *matrimonial* (larger than double, about $25). The biggest hammock of all is called *matrimonial especial.* Buy the biggest hammock you can afford—the bigger ones take up no more room than smaller ones and are more comfortable, even for just one person.

Street vendors selling hammocks will approach you at every turn, *"¿Hamacas, señor, señorita?"* Their prices will be low, but so is the quality of their merchandise. If you buy from these vendors, be sure to examine the hammock carefully. Booths in the market have a larger selection and offer hammocks at only slightly higher prices.

La Poblana. S.A., Calle 65 no. 492, between Calles 60 and 58. No phone.

La Poblana has been well recommended for years. Prices are marked, so don't try to bargain. Upstairs there's a room hung wall-to-wall with hammocks where you can give your prospective purchase a test-drive. La Poblana sells ropes and mosquito nets for hammocks, as well as Maya women's dresses and men's guayaberas. The store is open Monday through Saturday from 8am to 7pm.

Panama Hats

Another very popular item are these soft, pliable hats made from the palm fibers of the jipijapa in several towns along Highway 180, especially Becal, in the neighboring state of Campeche. There's no need to journey all the way to Campeche, however, as Mérida sells the hats in abundance. Just the thing to shade you from the fierce Yucatecan sun, the hats can be rolled up and carried in a suitcase for the trip home. They retain their shape quite well.

Jipi hats come in three grades determined by the quality (pliability and fineness) of the fibers and closeness of the weave. Hats with the coarser, more open weave of fairly large fibers cost a few dollars (street vendors in Cancún and Cozumel charge up to $10). The middle grade—a fairly fine, close weave of good fibers—should cost about $15 in a respectable shop. The finest weave, truly a beautiful Panama-style hat, can cost more than $50.

WHERE TO STAY

Mérida is easier on the budget than other Yucatán cities. Most hotels offer at least a few air-conditioned rooms, and a few of the places also have pools. You may find every room taken in July and August, when Mexicans vacation in Mérida.

DOUBLES FOR LESS THAN $20

Casa Becil. Calle 67 no. 550C, Mérida, Yuc. 97000. ☎ **99/24-6764.** 14 rms (all with bath). FAN. $10 single; $14 double. Parking on the street; unguarded.

A pleasant family runs this homey *casa de huéspedes* between Calles 66 and 68. Most of the plain but serviceable rooms are around a tiny, shady, quiet court in back. Toilets may not have seats and the windows are not well screened, but the tap water is purified and there's a small sun deck on the second floor. There's laundry service, and the English-speaking owner can arrange airline tickets and tours. You can rent TVs for a small daily charge. To find the hotel from the bus station, turn right out the front door to Calle 68, then left one block to Calle 67, then right; the hotel is a half block down on the right. Parking is scarce on the street and not very secure. Parking lots in the area charge $3 to $5 per day.

Hotel Monjas. Calle 66-A no. 509, 97000 Mérida, Yuc. ☎ **99/28-6632.** 30 rms (all with bath). A/C (2) or FAN. $9 single or double with one bed; $11 double with two beds. Parking on the street; limited.

The lobby here is a bit small and dark, but the basically furnished rooms are clean. The proprietor and his wife speak English. Rooms come with either one or two double beds or a double and a twin. The location, slightly away from traffic and city hubbub, is excellent. A small snack bar in the lobby functions on weekends; breakfast pastries and soft drinks are sold at any time. They also have posted phone numbers of consulates and doctors, as well as bus schedules. From the southwest corner of the Plaza Mayor, walk three blocks west on Calle 63 to Calle 66-A; the hotel is two doors down.

Ⓢ Hotel Mucuy. Calle 57 no. 481, 97000 Mérida, Yuc. ☎ **99/28-5193.** Fax 99/23-7801. 22 rooms (all with bath). FAN. $10 single; $12 double.

One of the most hospitable budget hotels in the country, the Mucuy is named for a small dove said to bring good luck to places where it alights. You'll see doves fluttering about the flower-filled interior courtyard. Owners Alfredo and Ofelia Comin strive to make guests feel welcome with conveniences such as a communal refrigerator in the lobby and laundry and clothesline facilities for guest use. Outside there are comfortable tables and chairs. Inside, two floors of freshly painted rooms with window screens, showers, and ceiling fans face the courtyard. Señora Comin speaks English. To find the hotel from the Plaza Mayor walk two blocks north on Calle 60, then turn right on Calle 57 and go a block and a half; it's between Calles 56 and 58.

DOUBLES FOR LESS THAN $30

Ⓢ Hotel Dolores Alba. Calle 63 no. 464, 97000 Mérida, Yuc. ☎ **99/28-5650.** Fax 99/ 28-3163. 40 rms (all with bath). A/C or FAN. $19 single; $21 double. Limited free parking; guarded.

The Sánchez family converted the family home into this comfortable hotel, which boasts a large open court and a smaller courtyard with a nice clean pool. The rooms, half of which have air-conditioning, are decorated with local crafts and all have showers. The highest prices are for rooms with air-conditioning. A small dining room opens for breakfast between 7 and 9am. The Sánchez family also operates the Hotel Janeiro (see above) and the Hotel Dolores Alba outside Chichén-Itzá, so you can make reservations at one hotel for another. To find this hotel from the Plaza Mayor, walk east on Calle 63 for 3¹/₂ blocks; it's between Calles 52 and 54.

Hotel Santa Lucía. Calle 55 no. 508, 97000 Mérida, Yuc. ☎ **99/24-6233.** Fax 99/28-2662. 51 rms (all with bath). A/C or FAN TV TEL. $17–$23 single; $19–$21 double. Free parking nearby; guarded.

This small hotel opened in 1990. The rooms are in a three-story building with windows facing the inner hallways or the courtyard, which contains a long, inviting pool. The highest rates are for rooms with air-conditioning. The management is very helpful, providing information on tours, restaurants, and sights. They also run the Hotel San Clemente in Valladolid. To find the hotel from the Santa Lucía Park, walk west on Calle 55; the hotel is on the left less than half a block down, between Calles 60 and 62.

Hotel Trinidad Galería. Calle 60 no. 456, 97000 Mérida, Yuc. ☎ **99/23-2463.** Fax 99/24-2319. 31 rms, 1 suite (all with bath). A/C or FAN. $14 single; $15 double; $18–$20 suite with A/C and TV. Limited free parking.

Once an enormous home, this rambling hotel offers its guests a small shaded pool, a communal refrigerator, a shared dining room, oodles of original art and antiques, and lots of relaxing nooks with comfortable furniture. Upstairs, a covered porch decorated with antiques and plants runs the length of the hotel, providing yet another place to read or converse. Rooms are rather dark and simply furnished, and most don't have windows, but the overall ambience of the hotel is comparable to that of more expensive inns. To find the hotel from the Plaza Mayor, walk five blocks north on Calle 60; it's at the corner of Calle 51, two blocks north of the Santa Lucía Park.

DOUBLES FOR LESS THAN $40

✪ **Casa Mexilio Guest House.** Calle 68 no. 495, 97000 Mérida, Yuc. ☎ and fax **99/28-2505,** or 800/538-6802 in the U.S. 7 rms, 1 suite (all with bath). High season, $55–$75 single or double. Low season, $35–$55 single or double (including breakfast). Parking on street.

Roger Lynn, part owner and host, has created the atmosphere of a private home rather than that of a hotel in this 19th-century town house. Guests have the run of this three-story home built around indoor and outdoor patios. Each room is unique, and throughout the house pleasant decorative use is made of Mexican crafts. On the back patio are a small pool and whirlpool. The hotel is connected with the Turquoise Reef Group, which runs inns on Mexico's Caribbean coast between Cancún and Chetumal. You can make reservations here for those inns and sign up for a variety of trips in the Yucatán (see "Eco-Tours & Adventure Trips," above).

To find the hotel from the Plaza Mayor, walk one block north on Calle 62. Turn left on Calle 59 and walk for three blocks. Turn right on Calle 68; the hotel is half a block down on the left.

✪ **Hotel Caribe.** Calle 59 no. 500, 97000 Mérida, Yuc. ☎ **99/24-9022,** or 800/826-6842 in the U.S. Fax 99/24-8733. 18 rms, 38 suites (all with bath). A/C (2) or FAN (16) TV TEL. $28–$32 single; $30–$37 double; $45 suite for two with A/C. Free parking; guarded.

Step inside the entry of this small two-story central hotel and discover a well-located, comfortable jewel. Well-coordinated colonial-style furnishings accent new pastel tile floors. Comfortable sitting areas along the three stories of covered open-air walkways are like extended living rooms offering a cozy respite at any time of day. From the top floor, where there's a small pool and sun deck, are great views of the cathedral and town. Rooms with air-conditioning are the most expensive. The interior restaurant is arranged around a quiet central courtyard, while the hotel's sidewalk café, El Mesón, is set out in front in the shady Parque Cepada Peraza. *A Reservation Note:* If you reserve a room through the 800 number, all the nights of your reservation will be charged on your credit card, which may arrive befor you leave home; the rate will be higher than if you paid and reserved directly with the hotel. To get to the hotel from the Plaza Mayor, walk a half block to the Parque Cepeda Peraza. The hotel is in the back right corner of the park.

Posada Toledo. Calle 58 no. 487, 97000 Mérida, Yuc. ☎ **99/23-1690.** Fax 99/23-2256. 21 rms, 2 suites (all with bath). A/C (16) or FAN (5) TEL. $19–$21 single; $21–$23 double. Free parking next door.

This colonial inn was once a private mansion. It's now a cross between a garden dripping with vines and a fading museum with beautifully kept antique furnishings. Two of the grandest rooms have been remodeled into a suite with ornate cornices and woodwork. Most rooms have no windows, but high ceilings and appropriately creaky hardwood floors are standard. The highest rates are for air-conditioned rooms. The rooftop lounge area is excellent for viewing the city. Five rooms have TVs. To find the inn from the Plaza Mayor, walk two blocks north on Calle 60, then right one block on Calle 57 to Calle 58; it's on the left.

WHERE TO EAT

Calle 62 between the Plaza Mayor and Calle 57 contains a short string of small budget food shops. To make your own breakfast, try the **Panificadora Montejo,** at the corner of Calles 62 and 63 on the southwest corner of the Plaza Mayor, and choose from a number of delectable treats. For those who can't start a day without fresh orange juice, **juice bars** have sprouted up all over Mérida, and several are on or near the Plaza Mayor.

MEALS FOR LESS THAN $5

Café Alameda. Calle 58 no. 474. ☎ **99/28-3635.** Breakfast $2.25–$2.50; main courses $3–$6. Mon–Sat 8am–10pm. YUCATECAN/MIDDLE EASTERN.

At about 10am on weekdays, the Alameda is filled with businesspeople all eating the same late breakfast—a shish kebab of marinated beef, a basket of warm pita bread, and coffee. If eggs are more your style, order them with beans; otherwise, you'll get a small plate with a little pile of eggs. Vegetarians can choose from tabbouleh, hummus, cauliflower, eggplant or spinach casseroles, and veggie tamales. The umbrella-shaded tables on the back patio are pleasant places to eat. To find the café from the Plaza Mayor, walk east on Calle 61 for one block, then turn left on Calle 58 and walk three blocks north, near the corner of Calle 55.

Café Amaro. Calle 59 no. 507. ☎ **99/28-2451.** Breakfast $2–$2.50; main courses $3–$3.75. Mon–Sat 8am–11pm. REGIONAL/VEGETARIAN.

This pleasant, small restaurant serves guests in an open courtyard to the accompaniment of soft background music. Their *crema de calabacitas* soup is delicious, as is the apple salad. The avocado pizza is terrific. There is also a limited menu of meat and chicken dishes. To find it from the Plaza Mayor, walk one block north on Calle 60 and turn left on Calle 59.

El Louvre. Calle 62 no. 499. ☎ **99/24-5073.** Main courses $2–$4; comida corrida $3. Daily 24 hours (comida corrida served 1–5pm). MEXICAN.

This big, open restaurant feeds everybody from farm workers to townspeople. There's also an English menu. The comida corrida might include beans with pork on Monday, pork stew on Tuesday, and so on, plus there are sandwiches, soups, and other full meals. From the Palacio Municipal, cross Calle 61 and walk north on Calle 62 a few steps; it's near the corner of Calle 61.

⑤ Restaurante Los Amigos. Calle 62 no. 497. ☎ **99/23-1957.** Comida corrida $1.75. Fri–Wed 1pm–midnight. MEXICAN.

This place serves a comida corrida of Yucatecan specialties, which includes soup, main course, and dessert. It's not classy, but the price is right. To find it from the Palacio Municipal (which faces the Plaza Mayor), walk north on Calle 62 half a block; it's on the left between Calles 61 and 59.

✪ Vito Corleone. Calle 59 at Calle 60. ☎ **99/28-5777.** Pizza $2–$6; spaghetti $2; beer $1. Daily 9:30am–11:30pm. PIZZA/SPAGHETTI.

Aside from the food, the most impressive aspect of this tiny pizza parlor is the interesting use of ollas (clay pots) embedded in the wall above the hand-painted tile oven. The oven's golden yellow tiles are as handsome as those that decorate church domes. The tables by the sidewalk are the only bearable places to sit when it's warm, since the oven casts incredible heat. Another section upstairs in the back is also tolerable. The thin-crusted pizzas taste smoky and savory, and on Thursdays there's a pizza special of two pizzas for the price of one. To find it from the Plaza Mayor, walk north on Calle 60 one block and turn left on Calle 59; it's half a block ahead.

MEALS FOR LESS THAN $10

✪ Los Almendros. Calle 50A no. 493. ☎ **99/28-5459.** Main courses $3–$7; daily special $4–$8. Daily 9am–11pm. YUCATECAN.

The original Los Almendros is located in Ticul, deep in the Maya hinterland, but the branch in Mérida has become a favorite spot to sample local delicacies. The colorful chairs and tables will put you in a festive mood. Ask to see the menu with color photographs of the offerings accompanied by descriptions in English. Their famous poc chuc—a marinated and grilled pork dish created at the original restaurant in Ticul some years ago—is a must. To arrive at the restaurant from the Parque Cepeda Peraza, walk east on Calle 59 for five blocks, then left on Calle 50A; it's half a block on the left facing the Parque de Mejorada.

✪ La Casona. Calle 60 no. 434. ☎ **99/23-8348.** Reservations recommended. Pasta courses $4–$7; meat courses $5–$8. Daily 1pm–midnight. CONTINENTAL/ITALIAN.

A gracious old Mérida house and its lush interior garden make a charming and romantic restaurant. The cuisine is Yucatecan and continental, especially Italian, so you can choose among such dishes as *pollo pibil,* filet mignon with brandy and cream, linguine with mushrooms, and lasagne. It's also a fine place to wind up the day sipping espresso or cappuccino. To find it from the Plaza Mayor, walk north on Calle 60 six blocks and it's at the corner of Calle 47.

El Patio de Las Fajitas. Calle 60 no. 467. ☎ **99/28-3782.** Main courses $5–$8; comida corrida $4–$6. Mon–Sat 1–11pm. MEXICAN.

Fajitas are the specialty at this mansion-turned-restaurant where you dine around a central courtyard decorated with plants and colorful tablecloths. The fajitas, grilled before you on the patio, come with guacamole, tortillas, and fresh Mexican salsa cruda. The portions are not large, so you may want to order a baked potato on the side. The menu also offers an economical fixed-price afternoon meal, which can include soup, poc chuc or *pollo mole*, rice, beans, and tortillas. To find the restaurant, walk north on Calle 60 for four blocks; it's at the corner of Calle 53.

✪ **Restaurante Portico del Peregrino.** Calle 57 no. 501. ☎ **99/28-6163.** Reservations recommended. Main courses $5–$8. Daily noon–11pm. MEXICAN/INTERNATIONAL.

This romantic restaurant captures the spirit of 19th-century Mexico with its patio dining on the side of the street and outdoor patio dining in back. Inside is an air-conditioned dining room decorated with antique mirrors and elegant sideboards. The extensive menu offers soup, fish filet, grilled gulf shrimp, spaghetti, *pollo pibil,* baked eggplant with chicken and cheese, and coconut ice cream topped with Kahlúa. To find it from the Plaza Mayor, walk 2^1/$_2$ blocks north on Calle 60, turn left on Calle 57, and it's half a block down on the right before Calle 62.

MÉRIDA AFTER DARK

For a full range of free or low-cost evening entertainment, as well as daily public events in Mérida, see "Special Events," above.

Teatro Peón Contreras, at Calles 60 and 57, and the **Teatro Ayala,** on Calle 60 at Calle 61, both feature a wide range of performing artists from around the world. Stop in and see what's showing.

The scene at the hotel bars, lounges, and discos depends on the crowd of customers presently staying at each hotel. Most of Mérida's downtown hotels, however, are filled with tour groups whose members prefer to rest after an exhausting day.

SIDE TRIPS FROM MÉRIDA
CELESTÚN NATIONAL WILDLIFE REFUGE: FLAMINGOS & OTHER WATERFOWL

This flamingo sanctuary and offbeat sand-street fishing village on the Gulf Coast is a 1^1/$_2$-hour drive from Mérida. To get here, take Highway 281 (a two-lane road) past numerous old henequen haciendas. Around 10 **Autobuses de Occidente** buses leave Mérida for Celestún from the terminal at Calles 50 and 67 daily between 6am and 6:30pm.

One **telephone** at the Hotel Gutiérrez (☎ **99/28-0419**) serves as the public phone for the entire village. You'll find a bank, two gas stations (but no unleaded gas), and a grocery store. Bus tickets are purchased at the end of the row of market stalls on the left side of the church. Celestún hotels don't furnish drinking water, so bring your own or buy it in town.

December 8 is the Feast Day of the Virgen de Concepción, the patron saint of the village. On the Sunday that falls nearest to **July 15,** a colorful procession carries Celestún's venerated figure of the Virgen de Concepción to meet the sacred figure of the Virgen de Asunción on the highway leading to Celestún. Returning to Celestún, they float away on decorated boats and later return to be ensconced at the church during a mass and celebration.

Seeing the Waterfowl

The town is on a narrow strip of land separated from the mainland by a lagoon. Crossing over the lagoon bridge, you'll find the 14,611-acre **wildlife refuge** spreading out on both sides without visible boundaries. You'll notice the small boats moored on both sides waiting to take visitors to see the flamingos. In addition to flamingos, you may see frigate birds, pelicans, cranes, egrets, sandpipers, and other waterfowl feeding on shallow sandbars at any time of year. Of the 175 bird species that come here, some 99 are permanent residents. At least 15 duck species have also been counted. Flamingos are found here all year; some nonbreeding flamingos remain year-round even though the larger group takes off around April to nest on the upper Yucatán Peninsula east of Río Lagartos.

A 1¹/₂- to 2-hour **flamingo-sighting trip** costs around $25 for four persons or twice that much if you stay half a day. The best time to go is around 7am, and the worst is midafternoon, when sudden storms come up. Be sure not to allow the boatmen to get close enough to frighten the birds; they've been known to do it for photographers, but it will eventually cause the birds to permanently abandon the habitat. Your tour will take you a short distance into the massive mangroves that line the lagoon to a sulfur pool, where the boatman kills the motor and poles in so you can experience the stillness and density of the jungle, feel the sultry air, and see other birds.

Where to Stay

To find restaurants and hotels, follow the bridge road a few blocks to the end. On the last street, Calle 12, paralleling the oceanfront, you'll find restaurants and hotels, all of which have decent rooms but marginal housekeeping standards. Always try to bargain for lower rates, which can go down by as much as 30% in the off-season.

Hotel María del Carmen. Calle 12 no. 111, Celestún, Yuc. 97367. ☎ **99/28-0152.** 9 rms (all with bath). FAN. $10 single; $12 double.

New in 1992, this three-story hotel on the beach is a welcome addition to Celestún's modest accommodations lineup. Spare but clean and large, each room has terrazzo floors, two double beds with sheets but no bedspread, screened windows (check screens for holes), and a small balcony or patio facing the ocean. Best of all, there's hot water in the baths (not necessarily a hallmark of other Celestún hotels) but not always toilet seats. Lorenzo Saul Rodríguez and María del Carmen Gutiérrez own the hotel and are actively involved in local conservation efforts, particularly in protecting the sea turtles that nest on the beach in early summer. Look for the sign for Villa del Mar, the hotel's restaurant; the rooms are behind it across the parking area.

Where to Eat

Calle 12 is home to several rustic seafood restaurants aside from the place listed below. All have irregular hours of operation.

✪ **Restaurant Celestún.** Calle 12, on the waterfront. No phone. Main courses $3–$7. Daily 10am–6pm (sometimes). SEAFOOD/MEXICAN.

I highly recommend this ocean-view restaurant, owned by Elda Cauich and Wenseslao Ojeda; the service is friendly and swift. Tables and chairs fill a long room that stretches from Calle 12 to the beach. The house specialty is a super-delicious shrimp, crab, and squid omelet (called a *torta*). But if you're a fan of stone crabs (*manitas de cangrejo* on the menu), this is definitely the place to chow down. Trapped in the gulf by Celestún fishermen, they come freshly cooked and seasoned with lime juice. Also popular during the fall season is *pulpo* (octopus). Other local specialties include *liza* (mullet) and caviar de Celestún (mullet eggs). To find the restaurant, follow the bridge road to the waterfront (Calle 12); turn left and the restaurant is immediately on the right.

DZIBILCHALTÚN: MAYA RUINS

This Maya site, now a national park located 9 miles north of Mérida along the Progreso road and 4¹/₂ miles east off the highway, is worth a stop. Though it was founded about 500 B.C. and flourished around A.D. 750, Dzibilchaltún was in decline long before the coming of the conquistadores but may have been occupied until A.D. 1600—almost a hundred years after the arrival of the Spaniards. Since its discovery in 1941, more than 8,000 buildings have been mapped. The site, which was probably a center of commerce and religion, covers an area of almost 10 square miles with a central core of almost 65 acres. At least 12 *sacbeob* (causeways), the longest of which is 4,200 feet, have been unearthed. Dzibilchaltún means "place of the stone writing," and at least 25 stelae have been found, many of them reused in buildings constructed after the original ones were covered or destroyed.

Today, the most interesting buildings are grouped around the **Cenote Xlacah,** the sacred well, and include a complex of buildings around Structure 38; the **Central Group** of temples; the raised **causeways;** and the **Seven Dolls Group,** centered on the **Temple of the Seven Dolls.** It was beneath the floor of the temple that seven weird little dolls (now in the museum) showing a variety of diseases and birth defects were discovered. The Yucatán State Department of Ecology has added nature trails and published a booklet (in Spanish) of birds and plants seen at various points along the mapped trail. The booklet tells where in the park you are likely to see specific plants and birds.

The federal government has spent over a million pesos for the **Museum of the Maya** on the grounds of Dzibilchaltún; the museum should open in 1995. The museum will be a replica of a Maya village of houses, called *nas,* staffed by Maya demonstrating traditional cooking, gardening, and folk-art techniques.

To get to Dzibilchaltún by bus from Mérida, go to the Progreso bus station at Calle 62 no. 524, between Calles 65 and 67. There are five buses per day on Monday through Saturday at 7:10 and 9am and 1, 2, and 3:20pm to the pueblo of Chanculob; it's a 1-km walk to the ruins from there. On Sunday there are only three buses to Chanculob—at 5:40 and 9am and 2pm. The return bus schedule is posted at the ticket window by the ruins. The last bus is at 4:15pm.

The site and nature trails are open daily from 8am to 5pm. Admission is $2.75; free on Sunday; video camera use costs $4. Parking costs $1, and a guided tour costs about $15 for a small group.

PROGRESO: GULF COAST CITY

For another beach escape, go to Progreso, a modern city facing the gulf less than an hour from Mérida. Here, the Malecón, a beautiful oceanfront drive, borders a vast beach lined with coconut palms that's popular on the weekends. A long pier, or *muelle* (pronounced "mu-wey-yeh"), extends 5 miles out into the bay to reach water deep enough for oceangoing ships. Progreso is part-time home to many Americans and Canadians who come to escape northern winters and also to many Meridianos who want to escape Mérida.

Along or near the Malecón are several of the more desirable restaurants and hotels.

From Mérida, buses to Progreso leave the special bus station at Calle 62 no. 524, between Calles 65 and 67, every 15 minutes during the day, starting at 5am. The trip takes 45 minutes.

In Progreso, the bus station is about four blocks south of Calle 19, or Malecón, which runs along the beach.

EN ROUTE TO UXMAL

There are three routes to Uxmal, about 50 miles south of Mérida. The most direct is Highway 261 via Uman and Muna. A second possibility is to follow Highway 180 through Uman and the ruins of Oxkintok near Maxcanú and Calcehtok, turn east onto Highway 184, then at Muna rejoin Highway 261 South to Uxmal. And your third choice is a scenic but meandering trip down State Highway 18. Additional details on this last route are provided in "The Ruins of Mayapán & Village of Ticul," below.

HIGHWAY 261: YAXCOPOIL & MUNA   Ten miles beyond Uman along Highway 261 is Yaxcopoil (yash-koh-poe-EEL), the tongue-twisting Maya name of a fascinating 19th-century hacienda on the right side of the road between Mérida and Uxmal. It's difficult to reach by bus.

This hacienda, dating from 1864, was originally a cattle ranch comprising over 23,000 acres. Around 1900, it was converted to growing henequen (for the manufacture of rope). Take half an hour to tour the house (which boasts 18-foot ceilings and original furniture), factory, outbuildings, and museum. You'll see that such haciendas were the administrative, commercial, and social centers of vast private domains; they were almost little principalities carved out of the Yucatecan jungle. It's open Monday through Saturday from 8am to 6pm and Sunday from 9am to 1pm.

From Mérida via Uman, it's 20 miles to the Hacienda Yaxcopoil and 40 miles to Muna on Highway 261. Uxmal is 10 miles from Muna.

HIGHWAY 180: OXKINTOK & GRUTAS CALCEHTOK   Only 35 miles south of Mérida and 28 miles northwest of Uxmal is a Maya site that dates from pre-Classic times, perhaps as early as 300 B.C., and covers 3 square miles. Before recent excavations it suffered extensive looting, but new discoveries still thrill archaeologists. Although the architecture is predominantly Puuc, as in other nearby sites, scholars believe it was an important crossroads because there is great evidence of influence from as far away as Guatemala. Building and habitation continued until at least the Late Classic Period, around A.D. 1000.

Archaeologists have mapped more than 200 buildings, including at least 12 pyramids. Deep inside several pyramids, numerous tombs containing jade masks have been uncovered. Today several restored structures are visible, including the Tzat Tun Tzat, the Ch'ich Palace, and the Devil's Palace. The most interesting of these is probably the Tzat Tun Tzat. Its depths revealed a labyrinth of tunnels, passageways, stairs, and rooms, one of which was a tomb. Based on the placement of its windows, it was probably an observatory. The 10-room Ch'ich Palace still has two of the four anthropomorphic columns that once decorated the portico. The Devil's Palace contains an anthropomorphic column with holes in its head supporting the northern portico. Visually, the site doesn't rival Uxmal or Chichén-Itzá, but it's interesting if you're following a ruins itinerary. The site is open more or less daily from 8am to 5pm. Admission is $2.50; free on Sunday; use of a personal video camera costs $8.

The undeveloped **Grutas (caves) Calcehtok,** with almost 3 miles of underground passageways in which to get lost, are about 2 miles from Oxkintok. To explore them, contact Roger Cuy, a guide in Calcehtok.

To get to Oxkintok, follow Highway 180 south through Uman to an intersection 2 miles short of Maxcanú. Turn east here (an overhead sign points to Manu) for about 5 miles. This takes you to the village of Calcehtok. A sign points south (right) to the Grutas Calcehtok and Oxkintok. After about a mile, another sign points to the Grutas (straight ahead) or to Oxkintok (right). Follow this road (which gives new meaning to the word *narrow*) for a mile and a half (the last half mile is dirt) to a locked gate. A caretaker *may* show up to let you in and accept admission.

HIGHWAY 18: KANASIN, ACANCEH, MAYAPÁN & TICUL   Taking Calle 67 east, head out of Mérida toward Kanasin (kahn-AH-seen) and Acanceh (ah-KAHN-keh), for about 12 miles. When Calle 67 ends, bear right, then go left at the next big intersection. Follow the wide divided highway with speed bumps. At Mérida's periférico (the road that circles the city), you'll see signs to Cancún. You can either cross the periférico and go straight into Kanasin or turn and follow the Cancún signs for a short distance and then follow the signs into Kanasin. In **Kanasin,** watch for signs that say CIRCULACIÓN or DESVIACIÓN. As in many Yucatán towns, you're being redirected to follow a one-way street through the urban area. Go past the market, church, and the main square on your left and continue straight out of town. The next village you come to, at km 10, is **San António Tehuit,** an old henequen hacienda. At km 13 is **Tepich,** another hacienda-centered village, with those funny little henequen-cart tracks criss-crossing the main road. After Tepich comes **Petectunich** and finally Acanceh.

Across the street from and overlooking **Acanceh's** church is a partially restored pyramid. From Acanceh's main square, turn right (around the statue of a smiling deer) and head for **Tecoh** with its huge crumbling church (5¹/₂ miles farther along Highway 18) and **Telchaquillo** (7 miles farther). This route takes you past several old Yucatecan haciendas, each with a big house, chapel, factory with smokestack, and workers' houses.

Shortly after the village of Telchaquillo, a sign on the right side of the road will point to the entrance of the ruins of Mayapán.

2 The Ruins of Mayapán & Village of Ticul

THE RUINS OF MAYAPÁN

30 miles S of Mérida; 25 miles NE of Ticul; 37 miles NE of Uxmal

Founded, according to Maya lore, by the man-god Quetzalcoatl (Kukulkán in Maya) in about A.D. 1007, Mayapán ranked in importance with Chichén-Itzá and Uxmal and covered at least 2¹/₂ square miles. For more than two centuries, it was the capital of a Maya confederation of city-states that included Chichén and Uxmal. But before the year 1200 the rulers of Mayapán ended the confederation by attacking and conquering Chichén and by forcing the rulers of Uxmal to live as vassals in Mayapán. Eventually a successful revolt by the captive Maya rulers brought down Mayapán, which was abandoned during the mid-1400s.

Though ruined, the main pyramid is still impressive. Next to it is a large cenote (a natural limestone cavern used as a well), now full of trees, bushes, and banana plants. Beside it is a small temple with columns and a fine high-relief mask of Chaac, the hook-nosed rain god. Jungle paths lead to other small temples, including El Caracol, with its circular tower. These piles of stones do not reflect the grandeur of the walled city of Mayapán in its heyday. Supplied with water from 20 cenotes, it had over 3,000 buildings in its enclosed boundaries of several square miles. Today, all is covered in dense jungle.

The site is open daily from 8am to 5pm. Admission is $1.25; free on Sunday; use of a personal video camera is $4.

FROM MAYAPÁN TO TICUL   The road is a good one, but directional signs through the villages are almost nonexistent. Stop and ask directions frequently. From Mayapán, continue along Highway 18 to **Tekit** (5 miles), turn right and go to **Mama** on a road as thrilling as a roller-coaster ride (4 miles), then turn right again for **Chapab** (8 miles).

If you're ready for a break, take time out to visit the **tortilla factory** in Chapab. Turn left when you see a building named Centro Educativo Comunitario Chapab, and the factory will be a couple of blocks farther on the left. As you came into town, you probably noticed young Maya girls, masa dough up to their elbows, carrying large pans and buckets of it atop their heads. They're returning from the daily ritual of corn grinding, and they'll use the masa to make their own tortillas at home. Other youngsters are carrying large stacks of finished tortillas hot off the press. The Matos Sabino family owns the factory, and they don't mind if you stop in and watch the action, which goes on daily from 8am to around 3pm. Better yet, buy some tortillas; fill them with avocados, tomatoes, and cheese; and have a picnic on the lawn across the street. After Chapab you reach **Ticul** (6¼ miles), the largest town in the region.

TICUL

12 miles E of Uxmal, 53 miles SE of Mérida

Many of the 27,000 inhabitants of this sprawling town make their living embroidering *huipiles* (the Maya women's shiftlike dress), weaving straw hats, making shoes and gold-filigree jewelry, and shaping pottery. Workshops and stores featuring most of these items are easy to find, especially in the market area.

ESSENTIALS

GETTING THERE & DEPARTING   There are frequent buses from Mérida. The Ticul bus station is near the town center on Calle 24 between Calles 25 and 25A. Buses return to Mérida daily at 7 and 10am and 5:30 and 7pm. Also check with the drivers of the minivans that line up across from the bus station. Buses run twice hourly to Muna, where you can change for a bus to Uxmal. For car information, see "En Route to Uxmal," above.

ORIENTATION   The market, most hotels, and Los Almendros, Ticul's best-known restaurant, are on the main street, **Calle 23,** also called Calle Principal. The **telephone area code** is 997. Since cars, buses, trucks, bicycles, and tricycles all compete for space on the narrow potholed streets, **parking and driving** have become difficult. Consider parking several streets away from the center of town and walking around from there. Directional signs that allow drivers to bypass the most congested part of town are beginning to appear.

EXPLORING TICUL

Ticul's **annual festival,** complete with bullfights, dancing, and carnival games, is held during the first few days of April.

SHOPPING

Ticul is best known for the cottage industry of huipil embroidery and for the manufacture of ladies' dress shoes. It's also a center for large-size commercially produced pottery. Most of the widely sold sienna-colored pottery painted with Maya designs comes from Ticul. If it's a cloudy, humid day, the potters may not be working since part of the process requires sun drying, but they still welcome visitors to purchase finished pieces.

Arte Maya. Calle 23 No. 301, Carretera Ticul Muna. ☎ **997/2-1095.** Fax 997/2-0334.

Owned and operated by Luis Echeverria and Lourdes Castillo, this shop and gallery produces museum-quality art in alabaster, stone, jade, and ceramics. Much of the work is done as it was in Maya times; soft stone or ceramic is smoothed with the leaf of the siricote tree, and colors are derived from plant sources. If you buy from them, hang onto the written description of your purchase—their work looks so authentic that U.S. customs have delayed entry of people carrying their wares.

Ticul

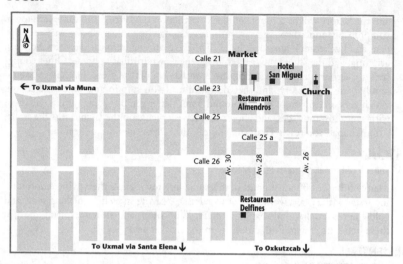

WHERE TO STAY

Only 12 miles northeast of Uxmal, Ticul is an ideal spot from which to launch regional sightseeing trips and to avoid the high cost of hotels in Uxmal.

Hotel Bougambillias Familiar. Calle 23 no. 291A,97860 Ticul, Yuc. ☎ **997/2-0761.** 20 rms (all with bath). FAN. $9 single or double, one bed; $12 double, two beds. Free parking.

Ticul's nicest inn is more like a motel, with parking outside the rooms. The half-circle drive into the arched entrance is lined with plants and pottery from the owner's local factory. Ceiling-height windows don't let in much light; the rooms have saggy beds; and bathrooms come without shower curtains and toilet seats. But the cool tile floors and ready hot water are attractions. In back is the hotel's pretty restaurant, Xux-Cab, which has erratic hours. To find the hotel, follow Calle 23 through Ticul on the road to Muna. It's on the right before you leave town, past the Santa Elena turnoff.

WHERE TO EAT

Good restaurants are few in Ticul, but in addition to checking out those listed here, don't overlook the busy **market** on Calle 23, where you can pick up fresh fruit and grab a bite at one of the little eateries.

✪ **Los Almendros.** Calle 23 no. 207. ☎ **993/2-0021.** Main courses $4–$7. Daily 9am–7pm. YUCATECAN.

Set in a big old Andalusian-style house with interior-courtyard parking, this is the first of a chain that now has branches in Mérida and Cancún. The Maya specialties include *papadzules* (sauce-covered, egg-filled tortillas), poc chuc (which originated here), and the spicy *pollo ticuleño*; as in Mérida, the quality of the food can vary. Ask for the illustrated menu in English (also Spanish and French) that explains the dishes in detail. To find it, walk 1½ blocks west of the plaza/church on Calle 23; it's on the left.

Restaurant Los Delfines. Calle 27, no. 216. No phone. Main courses $4–$5. Daily 8am–6pm. MEXICAN.

A favorite, although I've often found it closed, the Restaurant Los Delfines is in a beautiful garden setting near the center of town. The menu offers chiles rellenos stuffed with shrimp, *carne raja asada* with *achiote,* pork, garlic-flavored fish, and other seafood. The filling complimentary *botanas* (appetizers) are a refreshing treat. You can park off the street in the courtyard. If the restaurant appears to be closed, just bang on the large metal doors and someone will open. To find the restaurant from the corner of Calles 23 and 26 (by the church), go two blocks west on Calle 23 to Calle 28; turn left (south) for three blocks to Calle 27, then right half a block. It's on the left.

SPELUNKING IN THE YAXNIC CAVES

Just outside the village of Yotolín (also spelled Yohtolín), between Ticul and Oxkutzcab (along Highway 184), are some impressive caves called **Yaxnic** (yash-NEEK), on the grounds of the old, private Hacienda Yotolín. Virtually undeveloped and full of colored stalactites and stalagmites, the caves are visited by means of a perilous descent in a basket let down on a rope.

Arranging this spelunking challenge takes time, but the thrill may be worth it. Here's the procedure: Several days (or even weeks or months) before your intended cave descent, go to Yotolín and ask for the house of the *comisario,* a village elder. He will make the proper introductions to the hacienda owners, who in turn will tell you how to prepare for the experience.

FROM TICUL TO UXMAL

From Ticul to Uxmal, follow the main street (Calle 23) west through town. Turn left at the sign to **Santa Elena.** It's 10 miles to Santa Elena; then, at Highway 261, cut back right for about 2 miles to Uxmal. The easiest route to follow is via Muna, but this route is also longer and less picturesque than driving straight through Ticul, 14 miles to Muna. At Muna, turn left and head south on Highway 261 to Uxmal, 12 miles away.

3 The Ruins of Uxmal

50 miles SW of Mérida, 12 miles W of Ticul, 12 miles S of Muna

One of the highlights of a vacation in the Yucatán, the ruins of Uxmal, noted for their rich geometric stone facades, are the most beautiful on the peninsula. Remains of an agricultural society indicate that the area was occupied possibly as early as 800 B.C. However, the great building period took place a thousand years later, between A.D. 700 and 1000, during which time the population probably reached 25,000. Then Uxmal fell under the sway of the Xiú princes (who may have come from the Valley of Mexico) after the year 1000. In the 1440s, the Xiú conquered Mayapán, and not long afterward the glories of the Maya ended when the Spanish conquistadores arrived.

Close to Uxmal, four other sites—Sayil, Kabah, Xlapak, and Labná—are worth visiting. With Uxmal, these ruins are collectively known as the Puuc route, for the Puuc Hills of this part of the Yucatán. See the "Excursions" section below if you want to explore these sites.

ESSENTIALS

GETTING THERE & DEPARTING By Bus See "Getting There & Departing" in Mérida, above, for information about bus service between Mérida and Uxmal. To return, wait for the bus on the highway at the entrance to the ruins. There is no evening departure from Mérida for the sound-and-light show at Uxmal.

By Car   Three routes to Uxmal from Mérida—via Highway 261, via Highways 180 and 184, or via State Highway 18—are described in "En Route to Uxmal," at the end of the Mérida section, above. *Note:* There's no gasoline at Uxmal, so top off the tank in Mérida, Muna, or Ticul before continuing.

ORIENTATION   Uxmal consists of the archaeological site and its visitor center, four hotels, and a highway restaurant. The visitor center—open daily from 8am to 9pm—has a restaurant (with good coffee); toilets; a first-aid station; and shops selling soft drinks, ice cream, film, batteries, and books. There are no phones except at the hotels. Restaurants at hotels near Uxmal and at the visitor center are expensive, so if you're coming for the day, bring a lunch. Most public buses pick up and let off passengers on the highway at the entrance to the ruins. The site itself is open daily from 8am to 5pm. Admission to the archaeological site of Uxmal is $3.75, but a Sunday visit will save money since admission is free to Uxmal and other recommended sites nearby. There's a $4 charge for each video camera you bring in (save your receipt; it's good for other area sites on the same day). Parking costs $1.

Guides at the entrance of Uxmal give tours in a variety of languages and charge $20 for one person or a group. The guides frown on an unrelated individual joining a group (presumably a group is people traveling together). They'd rather you pay as a single entity, but you can hang around the entrance and ask other English speakers if they would like to join you in a tour and split the cost. As at other sites, the guides' information is not up-to-date, but you'll see areas and architectural details you might otherwise miss.

A 45-minute **sound-and-light show** is staged each evening in Spanish for $2 at 7pm and in English for $3 at 9pm. The bus from Mérida is scheduled to leave near the end of the Spanish show; confirm the exact time with the driver. If you stay for the English show, the only return to Mérida is via an expensive taxi. After the impressive show, the chant *"Chaaac, Chaaac"* will echo in your mind for weeks.

A TOUR OF THE RUINS

The Pyramid of the Magician   As you enter the ruins, note the chultún (cistern) inside the entrance to the right. Besides the natural underground cisterns (such as cenotes) formed in the porous limestone, chultúnes were the principal source of water for the Maya.

Just beyond the chultún, Uxmal's dominant building, the Pyramid of the Magician (also called the Soothsayer's Temple) with its unique rounded sides, looms majestically on the right as you enter. The name comes from a legend about a mystical dwarf who reached adulthood rapidly after being hatched from an egg and who built this pyramid in one night. Beneath it are five temples, since it was common practice for the Maya to build new structures atop old ones as part of a prescribed ritual.

The pyramid is unique because of its oval shape, height, steepness, and odd doorway on the opposite (west) side near the top. The doorway's heavy ornamentation, a characteristic of the Chenes style, features 12 stylized masks of the rain god Chaac, and the doorway itself is a huge open-mouthed Chaac mask.

The tiring and even dangerous climb to the top is worth it for the view. From on top you can see Uxmal's entire layout. Next to the Pyramid of the Magician, to the west, is the Nunnery Quadrangle, and left of it is a conserved ball court, south of which are several large complexes. The biggest building among them is the Governor's Palace, and behind it lies the partially restored Great Pyramid. In the distance is the Dovecote, a palace with a lacy roofcomb (false front) that looks like the perfect apartment complex for pigeons. From this vantage point, note how Uxmal is special

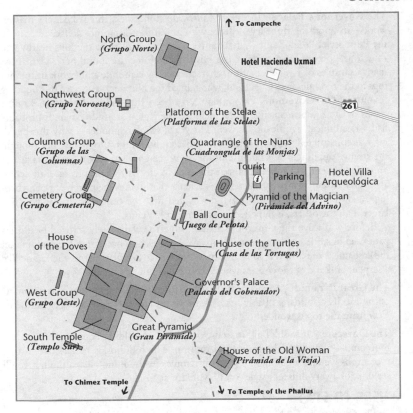

among Maya sites for its use of broad terraces or platforms constructed to support the buildings; look closely and you'll see that the Governor's Palace is not on a natural hill or rise but on a huge square terrace, as is the Nunnery Quadrangle.

The Nunnery   The 16th-century Spanish historian Fray Diego López de Cogullado gave the building its name because it resembled a Spanish monastery. Possibly it was a military academy or a training school for princes, who may have lived in the 70-odd rooms. The buildings were constructed at different times: The northern one was first, then the southern, then the eastern, then the western. The western building has the most richly decorated facade, composed of intertwined stone snakes and numerous masks of the hook-nosed rain god Chaac.

The corbeled archway on the south was once the main entrance to the Nunnery complex; as you head toward it out of the quadrangle to the south, look above each doorway in that section for the motif of a Maya cottage, or *na*, looking just like any number of cottages you'd see throughout the Yucatán today. All this wonderful decoration has been restored, of course—it didn't look this good when the archaeologists discovered it.

The Ball Court   The unimpressive ball court is conserved to prevent further decay, but keep it in mind to compare with the magnificent restored court at Chichén-Itzá.

The Turtle House   Up on the terrace south of the ball court is a little temple decorated with colonnade motif on the facade and a border of turtles. Though it's small and simple, its harmony is one of the gems of Uxmal.

The Governor's Palace   In size and intricate stonework, this is Uxmal's master-work—an imposing three-level edifice with a 320-foot-long mosaic facade done in the Puuc style. Puuc means "hilly country," the name given to the hills nearby and thus to the predominant style of pre-Hispanic architecture found here. Uxmal has many examples of Puuc decoration, characterized by elaborate stonework from door tops to the roofline. Fray Cogullado, who named the Nunnery, also gave this building its name. The Governor's Palace may have been just that—the administrative center of the Xiú principality, which included the region around Uxmal. It probably had astronomical significance as well. For years, scholars pondered why this building was constructed slightly turned from adjacent buildings. Originally they thought the strange alignment was because of the *sacbe* (ceremonial road) that starts at this building and ends 11 miles distant at the ancient city of Kabah. But recently scholars of archaeoastronomy (a relatively new science that studies the placement of archeological sites in relation to the stars), discovered that the central doorway, which is larger than the others, is in perfect alignment with Venus.

Before you leave the Governor's Palace, note the elaborately stylized headdress patterned in stone over the central doorway. As you stand back from the building on the east side, note how the 103 stone masks of Chaac undulate across the facade like a serpent and end at the corners where there are columns of masks.

The Great Pyramid   A massive, partially restored nine-level structure, it has interesting motifs of birds, probably macaws, on its facade, as well as a huge mask. The view from the top is wonderful.

The Dovecote   It wasn't built to house doves, but it could well do the job in its lacy roofcomb—a kind of false front on a rooftop. The building is remarkable in that roofcombs weren't a common feature of temples in the Puuc hills, although you'll see one (of a very different style) on El Mirador at Sayil.

WHERE TO STAY

Unlike Chichén-Itzá, which has several classes of hotels from which to choose, Uxmal has, with a single exception, only one type—comfortable but expensive. This might just be the place to blow your budget. If you've already done that by renting a car, more affordable rooms can be found at nearby Ticul.

Hotel Hacienda Uxmal. Km 80 Carretera Mérida-Uxmal, 97840 Uxmal, Yuc. ☎ & fax **99/ 49-4754** (for reservations contact Mayaland Resorts, Hotel Casa del Balam, Calle 60 at Calle 57 [Apdo. Postal 407], Av. Mérida, Yuc. 97000; ☎ **99/23-685,** or 800/235-4079 in the U.S.; fax 24-6290). 75 rms (all with bath). A/C (21) or FAN (54). $45–$65 single; $50–$80 double. Free parking; guarded.

One of my favorites, this is also the oldest hotel in Uxmal. Located on the highway across from the ruins, it was built as the headquarters for the archaeological staff years ago. Rooms are large and airy, exuding an impression of a well-kept yesteryear, with patterned tile floors, heavy furniture, and well-screened windows. All rooms have ceiling fans, and TVs are being added. Guest rooms surround a handsome central garden courtyard with towering royal palms, a bar, and a pool. Other facilities include a dining room and gift shop. Meals are expensive here: breakfast costs $4 to $6; lunch $7 to $11; dinner, $9 to $15. A guitar trio usually plays on the open patio in the evenings. Checkout time is 1pm, so you can spend the morning at the ruins and take a swim before you hit the road again. It's on the highway opposite the road entrance to the ruins.

Mayaland Resorts, owners of the hotel, offers tour packages that include free car rental for the nights you spend in its hotels. Car rental is free, but there's a daily insurance charge, which for a manual-shift Volkswagen Beetle is $18 per day. They also have Ford Escorts at a higher price. Mayaland also has a transfer service between the hotel and Mérida for about $30 one way.

Rancho Uxmal. Km 70 Carretera Mérida-Uxmal, 97840 Uxmal, Yuc. No local phone. (For reservations contact Sr. Macario Cach Cabrera, Calle 26 #156, Ticul, Yuc, 97860; ☎ **997/2-0277** or 99/23-1576). 20 rms (all with bath.) A/C or FAN. $18–$24 single or double; $4 per person campsite. Free parking; guarded.

This modest little hotel is an exception to the high-priced places near Uxmal, and it gets better every year. Air-conditioning has been added to 10 of the rooms, all of which have good screens, hot-water showers, and 24-hour electricity. The restaurant is good; a full meal of poc chuc, rice, beans, and tortillas costs about $5, and breakfast is $2.25 to $3. It's a long hike to the ruins from here, but the manager may help you flag down a passing bus or combi or even drive you himself if he has time. A primitive campground out back offers electrical hookups and use of a shower. The hotel is 2¹/₄ miles north of the ruins on Highway 261.

WHERE TO EAT

Besides the hotel restaurants mentioned above, there are few other choices.

Café-Bar Nicte-Ha. In the Hotel Hacienda Uxmal, across the highway from the turnoff to the ruins. ☎ **993/24-7142.** Soups and salads $2–$4; pizzas and enchiladas $5; main courses $5–$8; fixed-price lunch $9. Daily 1–8pm. MEXICAN.

This small restaurant attached to the Hotel Hacienda Uxmal is visible from the crossroads entrance to the ruins. The food is decent, though the prices tend to be high. If you eat here, take full advantage of the experience and spend a few hours by the pool near the café—use is free to customers. This is a favorite spot for bus tours, so come early.

Las Palapas. Hwy. 261. No phone. Breakfast $3; comida corrida $3.75; soft drinks $1. Daily 9am–6pm (comida corrida served 1–4pm). MEXICAN/YUCATECAN.

Three miles north of the ruins on the road to Mérida you'll find this pleasant restaurant with open-air walls and large thatched palapa roof. The amiable owner, María Cristina Choy, has the most reasonable dining prices around. Individual diners can sometimes become lost in the crowd if a busload of tourists arrives, but otherwise the service is fine and the food quite good. There's also a small gift shop with regional crafts and a few books.

THE PUUC MAYA ROUTE & VILLAGE OF OXKUTZCAB

South and east of Uxmal are several other Maya ruins worth exploring. Though smaller in scale than either Uxmal or Chichén-Itzá, each has gems of Maya architecture. The facade of masks on the Palace of Masks at **Kabah,** the enormous palace at **Sayil,** and the fantastic caverns of **Loltún** may be among the high points of your trip. Also along the way are the **Xlapak** and **Labná** ruins and the pretty village of **Oxkutzcab.**

Note: All these sites are currently undergoing excavation and reconstruction, and some buildings may be roped off when you visit. And for photographers: You'll find afternoon light the best. The sites are open daily from 8am to 5pm. Admission is $1.75 each for Sayil, Kabah, and Labná, and for Xlapak $1.25, and Loltún $2.75. All except the caves of Loltún are free on Sunday. Use of a video camera at any time costs $4, but if you're visiting Uxmal in the same day, you pay only once for video permission and present your receipt as proof at each ruin.

Kabah is 17 miles southeast of Uxmal. From there it's only a few miles to Sayil. Xlapak is almost walking distance (through the jungle) from Sayil, and Labná is just a bit farther east. A short drive beyond Labná brings you to the caves of Loltún. And Oxkutzcab is at the road's intersection with Highway 184, which can be followed west to Ticul or east all the way to Felipe Carillo Puerto.

If you are driving, between Labná and Loltún you'll find a road and a sign pointing north to Tabi. A few feet west of this road is a narrow dry-weather track leading into the seemingly impenetrable jungle. A bit over a mile up this track, the jungle opens to remains of the fabulous old henequen-producing **Hacienda Tabí.** The hewn-rock, two-story main house extends almost the length of a city block, with the living quarters above and storage and space for carriages below. In places it looks ready to collapse. Besides the house, you'll see the ruined chapel, remnants of tall chimneys, and broken machinery. Though not a formal public site, the caretaker will ask you to sign a guestbook and allow you to wander around the hulking ruins—without climbing to the second story.

If you aren't driving, a daily bus from Mérida goes to all these archaeological sites, with the exception of Loltún. (See "By Bus" under "Getting There and Departing," in Mérida, above, for more details).

KABAH   If you're off to Kabah, head southwest on Highway 261 to Santa Elena (8 miles), then south to Kabah ($8^1/2$ miles). The ancient city of Kabah is on both sides along the highway. Make a right turn into the parking lot.

The most outstanding building at Kabah is the huge **Palace of Masks,** or *Codz Poop* (rolled-up mat), named for a motif in its decoration. You'll notice it first on the right, up on a terrace. Its outstanding feature is the Chenes-style facade, completely covered in a repeated pattern of 250 masks of the rain god Chaac, each one with curling remnants of Chaac's elephant-trunk-like nose. There's nothing like this facade in all of Maya architecture. For years stone-carved parts of this building lay lined up in the weeds like pieces of a puzzle awaiting the master puzzlemaker to put them into place. Now workers are positioning the parts, including the broken roofcomb, in place. Sculptures from this building are in the museums of anthropology in Mérida and Mexico City.

Once you've seen the Palace of Masks, you've seen the best of Kabah. But you should take a look at the other buildings. Just behind and to the left of the Codz Poop is the **Palace Group** (also called the East Group), with a fine Puuc-style colonnaded facade. Originally it had 32 rooms. On the front you see seven doors, two divided by columns, a common feature of Puuc architecture. Recent restoration has added a beautiful L-shaped colonnaded extension to the left front. Further restoration is underway at Kabah, so there may be more to see when you arrive.

Across the highway, a large, conical dirt-and-rubble mound (on your right) was once the **Great Temple,** or Teocalli. Past it is a **great arch,** which was much wider at one time and may have been a monumental gate into the city. A sacbe linked this arch to a point at Uxmal. Compare this corbeled arch to the one at Labná (below), which is in much better shape.

SAYIL   Just about 3 miles south of Kabah is the turnoff (left, which is east) to Sayil, Xlapak, Labná, Loltún, and Oxkutzcab. And $2^1/2$ miles along this road are the ruins of Sayil (which means "place of the ants").

Sayil is famous for **El Palacio,** the tremendous 100-plus-room palace that's a masterpiece of Maya architecture. Impressive for its simplistic grandeur, the building's facade stretching three terraced levels is breathtaking. Its rows of columns and colonnettes give it a Minoan appearance. On the second level, notice the upside-down stone figure of the diving god of bees and honey over the doorway; the same motif was used at Tulum several centuries later. From the top of El Palacio there is a great view of the Puuc hills. Sometimes it's difficult to tell which are hills and which are unrestored pyramids, since little temples peep out at unlikely places from the jungle. The large circular basin on the ground below the palace is an artificial catch basin for a chultún (cistern) because this region has no natural cenotes (wells) to catch rainwater.

In the jungle past El Palacio is **El Mirador,** a small temple with an oddly slotted roofcomb. Beyond El Mirador, a crude **stele** has a phallic idol carved on it in greatly exaggerated proportions.

XLAPAK   Xlapak (pronounced "Shla-pahk") is a small site with one building; it's 3¹/₂ miles down the road from Sayil. The **Palace at Xlapak** bears the masks of the rain god Chaac.

LABNÁ   Labná, which dates to between A.D. 600 and 900, is 18 miles from Uxmal and only 1³/₄ miles past Xlapak. Like other archaeological sites in the Yucatán, it's also undergoing significant restoration and conservation. Descriptive placards fronting the main buildings are in Spanish, English, and German.

The first thing you see on the left as you enter is **El Palacio,** a magnificent Puuc-style building much like the one at Sayil but in poorer condition. There is an enormous mask of Chaac over a doorway with big banded eyes, a huge snout nose, and jagged teeth around a small mouth that seems on the verge of speaking. Jutting out on one corner is a highly stylized serpent's mouth out of which pops a human head with a completely calm expression. From the front you can gaze out to the enormous grassy interior grounds flanked by vestiges of unrestored buildings and jungle.

From El Palacio you can walk across the interior grounds on a newly reconstructed sacbe leading to Labná's **corbeled arch,** famed for its ornamental beauty and for its representation of what many such arches must have looked like at other sites. This one has been extensively restored, although only remnants of the roofcomb can be seen, and it was part of a more elaborate structure which is completely gone. Chaac's face is on the corners of one facade, and stylized Maya huts are fashioned in stone above the doorways.

You pass through the arch to **El Mirador,** or **El Castillo,** as the rubble-formed, pyramid-shaped structure is called. Towering on the top is a single room crowned with a roofcomb etched against the sky.

There's a refreshment/gift stand with restrooms at the entrance.

LOLTÚN   The caverns of Loltún are 18¹/₂ miles past Labná on the way to Oxkutzcab, on the left side of the road. The fascinating caves, home of ancient Maya, were also used as a refuge and fortress during the War of the Castes (1847–1901). Inside, examine statuary, wall carvings and paintings, chultúnes (cisterns), and other signs of Maya habitation, but the grandeur and beauty of the caverns alone are impressive. In front of the entrance is an enormous stone phallus. The cult of the phallic symbol originated south of Veracruz and appeared in the Yucatán between A.D. 200 and 500.

The 1¹/₂-hour tours in Spanish are given daily at 9:30 and 11am and 12:30, 2, and 3pm and are included in the price. Before going on a tour, confirm these times at the information desk at Uxmal.

To return to Mérida from Loltún, drive the 4¹/₂ miles to Oxkutzcab and from there go northwest on Highway 184. It's 12 miles to Ticul, and (turning north onto Highway 261 at Muna) 65 miles to Mérida.

OXKUTZCAB

Oxkutzcab (ohsh-kootz-KAHB), 7 miles from Loltún, is the heartland of the Yucatán's fruit-growing region, particularly oranges. The tidy village of 21,000, centered on a beautiful 16th-century church and the market, is worth a stop if for no other reason than to eat at Su Cabaña Suiza (see below) before heading back to Mérida, Uxmal, or Ticul.

During the last week in October and first week in November is the **Orange Festival,** when the village celebrates with a carnival and orange displays in and around the central plaza.

Where to Eat

✪ **Su Cabaña Suiza.** Calle 54 no. 101. ☎ **997/5-0457.** Main dishes $3; soft drinks or orange juice 75¢. Daily 7:30am–6:30pm. CHARCOAL-GRILLED MEAT/MEXICAN.

It's worth a trip from Loltún, Ticul, or Uxmal just to taste the delicious charcoal-grilled meat at this unpretentious eatery dripping with colorful plants. Park in the gravel courtyard, then take a seat at one of the metal tables either under the palapa roof or outdoors where caged birds sing. Señora María Antónia Puerto de Pacho runs the spotless place with an iron hand, and family members provide swift, friendly service. The primary menu items include filling portions of charcoal-grilled beef, pork, or chicken served with salad, rice, tortillas, and a bowl of delicious bean soup. But you can also find a few Yucatecan specialties, such as *costillos entomatados, escabeche, queso relleno,* and *pollo pibil.* The restaurant is between Calles 49 and 51 in a quiet neighborhood three blocks south of the main square.

EN ROUTE TO CAMPECHE

From Oxkutzcab, head back 27 miles to Sayil, then drive south on Highway 261 to Campeche (78 miles). Along the way are several ruins and caves worth visiting.

XTACUMBILXUNA CAVES   Highway 261 heads south for several miles, passing through a lofty arch marking the boundary between the states of Yucatán and Campeche. Continue on through Bolonchén de Rejón (Bolonchén means "nine wells").

About 1³/₄ miles south of Bolonchén a sign points west to the Grutas de Xtacumbilxuna, though the sign spells it "Xtacumbinxunan." Another sign reads: IT'S WORTH IT TO MAKE A TRIP FROM NEW YORK TO BOLONCHÉN JUST TO SEE XTACUMBILXUNA CAVES (JOHN STEPHENS—EXPLORER). The caves are open whenever the guide is around, which is most of the time. Follow him down for the 30- or 45-minute tour in Spanish, after which a $1 to $3 tip is customary.

Legend has it that a Maya girl escaped an unhappy love affair by hiding in these vast limestone caverns, which wouldn't be hard to do, as you'll see. Unlike the fascinating caves at Loltún, which are filled with traces of Maya occupation, these have only the standard bestiary of limestone shapes: a dog, an eagle, a penguin, a Madonna and child, a snake, and so on—figments of the guide's imagination.

CHENES RUINS   On your route south, you can also take a detour to see several unexcavated, unspoiled ruined cities in the Chenes style. You have to be adventurous for these; pack some food and water. When you get to Hopelchén, take the turn-off for Dzibalchén. When you get back to Dzibalchén (25 ¹/₂ miles from Hopelchén), ask for directions to Hochob, San Pedro, Dzehkabtún, El Tabasqueño, and Dzibilnocac.

EDZNÁ   From Hopelchén, Highway 261 heads west, and after 26 miles you'll find yourself at the turnoff for the ruined city of Edzná, 12 miles farther along to the south.

Founded probably between 600 and 300 B.C. as a small agricultural settlement, it developed into a major ceremonial center during the next 1,500 years. Archaeologists estimate that to build and maintain such a complex center must have required a population in the tens of thousands. Once a network of Maya canals crisscrossed this entire area, making intensive cultivation possible.

The **Great Acropolis** is a unique five-level pyramid with a temple complete with roofcomb on top. Edzná means "House of Wry Faces," which undoubtedly there were at one time. Though the buildings at Edzná were mostly in the heavily baroque Chenes, or "well country" style, no vestige of these distinctive decorative facades remains at Edzná. Several other buildings surround an open central yard. Farther back, new excavations have revealed the **Temple of the Stone Mask,** a structure with several fine stucco masks similar to those of Kohunlich in the Río Bec region near Chetumal. The site takes only 30 minutes or less to see and is perhaps not worth the price of entry, especially if you've seen many other sites in the Yucatán. (*Note:* The afternoon light is better for photographing the temple.)

It's open daily from 8am to 5pm. Admission costs $2.50, plus $4 to use your video camera.

Back on Highway 261, it's 12 miles to the intersection with Highway 180, then another 26 miles to the very center of Campeche.

4 Campeche

157 miles SW of Mérida, 235 miles NE of Villahermosa

Campeche, capital of the state bearing the same name, is a pleasant, beautifully kept coastal city (pop. 172,000) with a leisurely pace. You'll be able to enjoy this charming city without the crowds because many tourists bypass Campeche on their way to Mérida in favor of the road via Kabah and Uxmal.

Founded by Francisco de Córdoba in 1517 and claimed for the Spanish crown by the soldier Francisco de Montejo the Elder in 1531, Campeche was later abandoned and refounded by Montejo the Younger in 1540. To protect it against pirates who pillaged the gulf coastal towns, the townspeople built a wall around the city in the late 1600s. Remnants of this wall, called *baluartes* (bulwarks), are among the city's proudest links with the past.

ESSENTIALS

GETTING THERE & DEPARTING   By Plane   Aeroméxico (at the airport ☎ 981/6-6656) flies once daily to and from Mexico City.

By Bus   The **Camioneros de Campeche** line (☎ 981/6-2332) runs second-class buses to Mérida every half hour for the two- to three-hour trip. There are direct buses to Mérida at 7am and 1:30 and 5:30pm, daily buses to Uxmal at 7 and 11am and 5pm, and buses to Edzná at 8am and 2:30pm (this bus drops you off and picks you up 1 km from the ruins). These tickets are sold on the Calle Chile side of the bus station at the Camioneros de Campeche ticket booth. **ADO** (☎ 981/6-0002), in the front of the station, offers a first-class de paso bus to Palenque at 11pm and buses to Mérida every hour or less from 5:30am to midnight. **Caribe Express** (☎ 981/1-3972) has direct deluxe service to and from Mérida and Cancún. Their office and bus yard is on the north side of the Centro Comercial Ah Kin Pech, Local 304.

By Car   Highway 180 goes south from Mérida, passing near the basket-making village of Halacho and near Becal, known for Panama-hat weavers. At Tenabo, take the shortcut (right) to Campeche rather than going farther to the crossroads near Chencoyí. The longer way from Mérida is along Highway 261 past Uxmal. From

Uxmal, Highway 261 passes near some interesting ruins and the Xtacumbilxuna caves (see "En Route to Campeche," above).

When driving the other direction, toward Celestún and Mérida, use the Vía Corta (short route) by going north on Avenida Ruíz Cortínez, bearing left to follow the water (this becomes Avenida Pedro Sainz de Baranda, but there's no sign). Follow the road as it turns inland to Highway 180, where you turn left (there's a gas station at the intersection). The route takes you through Becal and Halacho. Stores in both villages close between 2 and 4pm.

If you're leaving Campeche for Edzná and Uxmal, go north on either Cortínez or Gobernadores and turn right on Madero, which becomes Highway 281. To Villahermosa, take Cortínez south; it becomes Highway 180.

ORIENTATION   Arriving   The **airport** is several miles northeast of the town center, and you'll have to take a taxi ($5) into town. The **ADO bus station,** on Av. Gobernadores, is nine long blocks from the Plaza Principal. Turn left out the front door and walk one block. Turn right (Calle 49) and go straight for five blocks to Calle 8. Turn left here, and the Plaza Principal is three blocks ahead. Taxis cost around $5 to the plaza.

Information   The **State of Campeche Office of Tourism** (☎ **981/6-6767** or ☎ and fax 981/6-6068) is in the Baluarte Santa Rosa on the south side of town on Circuito Baluartes, between Calles 12 and 14. It's open Monday through Friday from 9am to 9pm, Saturday and Sunday from 9am to 1pm.

City Layout   Most of your time in Campeche will be spent within the confines of the old city walls. The administrative center of town is the modernistic **Plaza Moch-Couoh** on Avenida 16 de Septiembre near the waterfront. Next door to the plaza rises the modern office tower called the Edificio Poderes or Palacio de Gobierno, headquarters for the state of Campeche. Beside it is the futuristic Cámara de Diputados or Casa de Congreso (state legislature chamber), which looks like an enormous square clam. Just behind it, the **Parque Principal** (central park) on Calle 8 will most likely be your reference point for touring.

Campeche's systematic street-numbering plan can be both clear-cut and confusing. Streets are all called "Calle" regardless of which way they run—that's the confusing part. The easy part is that those running roughly north to south have even numbers, and those running east to west have odd numbers. In addition, the streets are numbered so that numbers ascend toward the south and west. After walking around for five minutes you'll have the system down pat.

Getting Around   Most of the recommended sights, restaurants, and hotels are within walking distance of the Parque Principal. Campeche isn't easy to negotiate by bus, so I recommend taxis for the more distant areas.

FAST FACTS: CAMPECHE

American Express   Local offices are at Calle 59 no. 4–5 (☎ **981/1-1010**), in the Edificio Belmar, a half block toward town from the Ramada Hotel. They're open Monday through Friday from 9am to 2pm and 5 to 7pm and Saturday from 9am to 1:30pm. They do not cash traveler's checks.

Area Code   The telephone area code is 981.

Post Office   The post office (Correo) is in the Edificio Federal at the corner of Avenida 16 de Septiembre and Calle 53 (☎ **981/6-2134**), near the Baluarte de Santiago; it's open Monday through Saturday from 7:30am to 8pm. The telegraph office is here as well.

Campeche

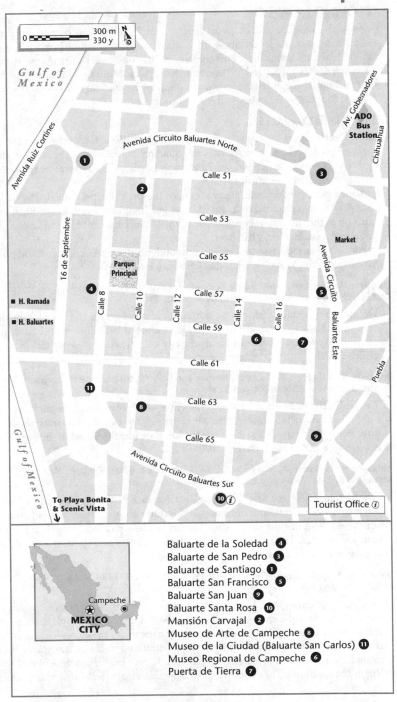

Gulf of Mexico

Avenida Ruiz Cortines

Av. Gobernadores

ADO Bus Station

Chihuahua

Avenida Circuito Baluartes Norte

Calle 51

Market

Calle 53

16 de Septiembre

Calle 55

Parque Principal

Avenida Circuito Baluartes Este

Calle 8

Calle 10

Calle 12

Calle 57

Calle 14

Calle 16

Puebla

■ H. Ramada
■ H. Baluartes

Calle 59

Calle 61

Calle 63

Calle 65

Gulf of Mexico

Avenida Circuito Baluartes Sur

To Playa Bonita & Scenic Vista

Tourist Office ⓘ

Campeche

MEXICO CITY

Baluarte de la Soledad ❹
Baluarte de San Pedro ❸
Baluarte de Santiago ❶
Baluarte San Francisco ❺
Baluarte San Juan ❾
Baluarte Santa Rosa ❿
Mansión Carvajal ❷
Museo de Arte de Campeche ❽
Museo de la Ciudad (Baluarte San Carlos) ⓫
Museo Regional de Campeche ❻
Puerta de Tierra ❼

EXPLORING CAMPECHE

With its city walls, clean brick-paved streets, friendly people, easy pace, and orderly traffic, Campeche is a lovely city worthy of at least a day in your itinerary. Besides taking in the museums built into the city walls, you'll want to stroll the streets (especially Calles 55, 57, and 59) and enjoy the typical Mexican colonial-style architecture. Look through large doorways to glimpse the colonial past—high-beamed ceilings, Moorish stone arches, and interior courtyards.

INSIDE THE CITY WALLS

As the busiest port in the region during the 1600s and 1700s, Campeche was a choice target for pirates. The Campechanos began building impressive defenses in 1668, and by 1704, the walls, gates, and bulwarks were in place. Today three of the seven remaining baluartes are worth visiting.

A good place to begin is the pretty zócalo, or **Parque Principal,** bounded by Calles 55 and 57 running east and west and Calles 8 and 10 running north and south. Construction of the church on the north side of the square began in 1650 and was finally completed a century and a half later.

For a good introduction to the city, turn south from the park on Calle 8 and walk five blocks to the Museo de la Ciudad (city museum).

Baluarte de San Carlos/Museo de la Ciudad. Circuito Baluartes and Av. Justo Sierra. No phone. Free admission. Tues–Sat 8am–8pm, Sun 8am–2pm.

This museum features a permanent exhibition of photographs and plans about the city and its history. The model of the city shows how it looked in its glory days and gives a good overview for touring within the city walls. There are several excellent ship models as well.

Baluarte de Santiago. Av. 16 de Septiembre and Calle 49. No phone. Free admission. Tues–Fri 8am–3pm and 6–8:30pm, Sat–Sun 9am–1pm.

The **Jardín Botánico Xmuch'haltun** grows in a jumble of exotic and common plants within the stone walls of this baluarte. More than 250 species of plants and trees share what seems like a terribly small courtyard. Some are identified, and, if the projector is working, a film explains the garden.

Baluarte de la Soledad. Calle 57 and Calle 8, opposite the Plaza Principal. No phone. Free admission. Tues–Sat 8am–8pm, Sun 8am–1pm.

This bastion houses the Sala de Estelas, or **Chamber of Stelae,** a display of Maya votive stones brought from various sites in this ruin-rich state. Many are badly worn, but the excellent line drawings beside the stones allow you to admire their former beauty. Three additional rooms also have interesting artifacts; each room is dedicated to a different Maya scholar.

Museo de Arte de Campeche. Calles 10 and 63. ☎ **981/6-1424.** Admission 50¢. Tues–Fri 9am–1pm and 4–8pm.

To glimpse colonial glitter and a touch of modern art, visit this museum, which is actually the restored Templo de San José (1640). The museum displays traveling exhibits of Mexican art. The temple also holds the library for the university next door, and students' paintings and photographs are displayed in the gallery space. Peer around corners and behind shelves at the walls. Don't miss the large mural of the Virgin of Guadalupe. The temple is one block inland from the Museo de la Ciudad (see above).

Museo Regional de Campeche. Calle 59 no. 36, between Calles 14 and 16. ☎ **981/6-9111.** Admission $3. Tues–Sat 8am–8pm, Sun 8am–1pm.

Just 2¹/₂ blocks farther inland from the Museo de Arte de Campeche (see above) is the city's best museum. Housed in the former mansion of the Teniente de Rey (royal governor), it features original Maya artifacts, pictures, drawings, and models of Campeche's history. The exhibit on the skull-flattening of babies practiced by the Maya includes actual deformed skulls. Another highlight is the Late Classic (A.D. 600–900) Maya stele carved in a metamorphic rock that does not exist in the Yucatán but was brought from a quarry hundreds of miles away. Many clay figures show scarified faces and tools, such as manta-ray bones, obsidian, and jade, used for cutting the face.

Other unusual pre-Hispanic artifacts include clay figures with movable arms and legs, as well as jade masks and jewelry from the tomb of Calakmul—a site in southern Campeche that is undergoing study and excavation. Among the other Calakmul artifacts found in Structure VII are the remains of a human between 30 and 40 years old; the remains show the burial custom of partially burning the body then wrapping it in a woven straw mat and cloth. Beans, copal, and feathers—all items deemed necessary to take the person through the underworld after death—were discovered in pottery vessels.

A model of the archaeological site at Becán shows Maya society in daily life. Other displays demonstrate Maya architecture; techniques of water conservation; and aspects of their religion, commerce, art, and considerable scientific knowledge. There's a bookstore on the left as you enter.

Puerta de Tierra (Land Gate). Calle 59 at Circuito Baluartes/Av. Gobernadores. No phone. Museum, free; show, $3. Tues–Sun 8am–2pm and 4–8pm.

At the Land Gate there's a small museum displaying portraits of pirates and the city founders. The 1732 French 5-ton cannon in the entryway was found in 1990. On Tuesday and Friday at 8pm there's a light-and-sound show.

Mansión Carvajal. Calle 10 no. 584. No phone. Free admission. Mon–Sat 9am–2pm and 4–8pm.

Restoration was completed in 1992 on this early 20th-century mansion, originally the home of the Carvajal family, owners of a henequen plantation. In its latest transformation, the blue-and-white Moorish home contains government agencies. Join the crowd purposefully striding along the gleaming black-and-white tile and up the curving marble staircase. No signs mark the entrance to the building—look for fresh blue-and-white paint inside the entrance on the west side of Calle 10 between Calles 53 and 51.

MORE ATTRACTIONS

If you're looking for a **beach,** the Playa Bonita is 4 miles south of town; it's often dirty.

A Scenic Vista

For a dramatic view of the city and gulf, go south from the tourism office on Avenida Ruíz Cortínez and turn left on Ruta Escénica, winding up to the **Fuerte San Miguel.** Built in 1771, this fort was the most important of the city's defenses. Santa Anna later used it when he attacked the city in 1842. It is currently being used as a museum with a recent exhibit of pirate-related items.

Shopping

Artesanías DIF. Calle 55 #25 (between Calles 12 and 14). ☎ **981/6-9088.**

This newly opened store in a restored mansion features quality textiles, clothing, and locally made furniture. DIF is the family-assistance arm of the government, and proceeds support government programs. It's open Monday through Friday from 9am to 1:30pm and 5 to 8pm, Saturday from 9am to 1:30pm.

WHERE TO STAY

Campeche's tourist trade is small and there are relatively few good places to stay. If you're driving, there are a few motels on the waterfront road, but you don't get a lot for the money.

DOUBLES FOR LESS THAN $35

Hotel América. Calle 10 no. 252, 24000 Campeche, Camp. ☎ **981/6-4588.** 52 rms (all with bath). FAN TV. $14 single; $19 double. Free parking three blocks away; guarded.

This centrally located hotel is a choice only if La Posada del Angel is full. It is old and worn, semiclean, and gets no high marks for maintenance. The three stories of rooms (no elevator) have one, two, or three double beds and come with tile floors. Corner rooms are quieter than those with windows on the street. To find the hotel from the Parque Principal, walk south on Calle 10 for 2½ blocks; it's on the right between Calles 61 and 63.

La Posada del Angel. Calle 10 no. 307, 24000 Campeche, Camp. ☎ **981/6-7718.** 14 rms (all with bath). FAN or A/C. $12–$14 single; $14–$16 double.

Rooms, with windows opening onto the dim narrow hall, are a little dark in this three-story hotel, but they are clean and freshly painted, and each comes with either two double beds or a single and a double. Carpeted halls in the upper two stories cut down on noise. To find the hotel from the Parque Principal, walk north on Calle 10 (with the cathedral on your left); the hotel is opposite the cathedral's right wall, a half block north of the Plaza Principal.

WHERE TO EAT

For regional food, try *colados,* which are delicious regional tamales, *tacos de salchicha* (an unusual pastry), *cazón de Campeche* (a tasty shark stew), and *pan de cazón* (another shark dish for those with more adventurous palates).

MEALS FOR LESS THAN $5

Panificadora Nueva España. Calle 10 no. 256. ☎ **981/6-2887.** All items 50¢–$2. Mon–Sat 6:30am–9:30pm. BAKERY.

A block and a half south of the Parque Principal is Campeche's best downtown bakery. Besides the usual assorted breads and pastries, you can stock up on food for the road—mayonnaise, catsup, cheese, butter, yogurt, and fruit drinks. This is the place to try the unusual *tacos de salchicha,* also called *feite.* Fresh breads come out of the oven at 5pm. A second location is on Calle 12 between Calles 57 and 59.

La Parroquia. Calle 55 no. 9. ☎ **981/6-8086.** Breakfast $1–$3; main courses $2–$5; comida corrida $3. Daily 24 hours (comida corrida served 1–4pm). MEXICAN.

La Parroquia, a popular local hangout, has friendly waiters and offers excellent inexpensive fare. Here, you can enjoy great breakfasts and colados, the delicious regional tamal. Selections on the comida corrida might include pot roast, meatballs, pork or fish, rice or squash, beans, tortillas, and fresh-fruit-flavored water.

La Perla. Calle 10 no. 345. ☎ **981/6-4092.** Breakfast $1:75; main courses $2–$4; sodas 75¢. Mon–Sat 7am–10pm. MEXICAN.

A popular student lounge (the Instituto Campechano is down the street near the Templo San José), La Perla has a youthful clientele with prices to match student budgets. The *arroz con camarones,* a filling meal of rice and shrimp, is a great bargain, and the *licuados* made with purified water and fresh pineapple or cantaloupe are refreshing. The coffee is instant, not brewed! At times, La Perla is noisy, but sometimes just a few customers are scattered about, seriously reading textbooks. To find the lounge from the Art Museum (at Calle 63 and Calle 10), walk one block north.

MEALS FOR LESS THAN $10

Restaurant Miramar. Calle 8 no. 293 (corner of Calle 61). ☎ **981/6-2883.** Main courses $3.25–$6; sandwiches $2–$3. Mon–Fri 8am–midnight, Sat 8am–1am, Sun 11am–7pm. SEAFOOD/MEXICAN.

One of the best choices in Campeche, this restaurant has airy and pleasant decor with light-colored stone arches, dark wood, and ironwork. The menu offers typical Campeche seafood dishes, including lightly fried breaded shrimp (ask for *camarones empanizados*); *arroz con mariscos* (shellfish and rice); and *pargo poc chuc*. For dessert there's *queso napolitana*, a very rich, thick flan. Ask about the changing daily specials. To find the restaurant from the Plaza Principal, walk two blocks south on Calle 8; it's near the corner of Calle 61.

♦ **La Pigua.** Av. Miguel Alemán no. 197A. ☎ **981/1-3365.** Main courses $4–$6. Daily noon–6pm. SEAFOOD/MEXICAN.

You can easily pass the entire afternoon in this jungle-like dining room with glass walls between the diners and the trees. The most filling meal on the menu (in a sharkskin folder) is the plateful of rice with octopus and shrimp; the most unusual is chiles rellenos stuffed with shark. The *cangrejo* (stone crab) is a house specialty. To reach La Pigua from the Plaza Principal, walk north on Calle 8 for three blocks. Cross the Avenida Circuito by the botanical garden, where Calle 8 becomes Miguel Alemán. The restaurant is 1½ blocks north, on the east side of the street.

5 The Ruins of Chichén-Itzá & Village of Pisté

112 miles SW of Cancún, 75 miles SE of Mérida

The fabled pyramids and temples of Chichén-Itzá are the Yucatán's best-known ancient monuments. You must go, since you can't say you've *really* seen the Yucatán until you've gazed at the towering El Castillo, seen the sun from the Maya observatory called El Caracol, or shivered on the brink of the gaping cenote that may have served as the sacrificial well.

This Maya city was established by Itzáes perhaps sometime during the ninth century A.D. Linda Schele and David Friedel, in *A Forest of Kings* (Morrow, 1990), have cast doubt on the legend that Kukulkán (called Quetzalcoatl by the Toltecs—a name also associated with a legendary god) came here from the Toltec capital of Tula, and, along with Putún Maya coastal traders, built a magnificent metropolis that combined the Maya Puuc style with Toltec motifs (the feathered serpent, warriors, eagles, and jaguars). According to Schele and Friedel, readings of Chichén's bas-reliefs and hieroglyphs fail to support that legend and instead show that Chichén-Itzá was a continuous Maya site that was influenced by association with the Toltecs but not by an invasion. So, Kukulkán's role in the Yucatán is once again in question. (See also "History" in chapter 16.)

Though it's possible to make a round-trip from Mérida to Chichén-Itzá in one day, it will be a long, tiring, and very rushed day. Try to spend at least one night at Chichén-Itzá (you'll actually stay in the nearby village of Pisté) or two if you can and take your time seeing the ruins in the cool of the morning or the afternoon after 3pm; take a siesta during the midday heat. The next morning, get to the ruins early; when the heat of the day approaches, catch a bus to your next destination. This may involve paying the admission fee more than once (unless you're there on a Sunday, when it's free), but the experience is worth it. Day-trip groups generally arrive when it's beginning to get hot, rushing through this marvelous ancient city in order to catch another bus or have lunch.

ESSENTIALS

GETTING THERE & DEPARTING   By Plane   Day-trips on charter flights from Cancún and Cozumel can be arranged by travel agents in the U.S. or in Cancún.

By Bus   From Mérida, first-class **ADO buses** leave at 7:30am and 3:30pm. If you go round-trip in a day (a two-hour trip one way), take the 8:45am bus and reserve a seat on the return bus. There are direct buses to Cancún at 11:15am and 6pm and to Mérida at 3pm. De paso buses to Mérida leave hourly day and night, as do those to Valladolid and Cancún.

By Car   Chichén-Itzá is on the main Highway 180 between Mérida and Cancún.

ORIENTATION   Arriving   You'll arrive in the village of Pisté, at the bus station next to the Pirámide Inn. From Pisté there's a sidewalk to the archaeological zone, which is a mile or so east of the bus station.

City Layout   The small town of **Pisté,** where most hotels and restaurants are located, is about a mile and a half from the ruins of Chichén-Itzá. Public buses from Mérida, Cancún, Valladolid, and elsewhere discharge passengers here. A few hotels are at the edge of the ruins, and one, the **Hotel Dolores Alba** (see "Where to Stay," below), is out of town about 1¹/₂ miles from the ruins on the road to Valladolid.

Fast Facts   The telephone area code is 985.

EXPLORING THE RUINS

The site occupies 4 square miles, and it takes a strenuous full day (from 8am to noon and 2 to 5pm) to see all the ruins, which are open daily from 8am to 5pm. Service areas are open from 8am to 10pm. Admission is $3.50; free for children under 12, and free for all on Sunday and holidays. A permit to use your own video camera costs an additional $4. Parking costs $1. *You can use your ticket to reenter on the same day, but you'll have to pay again for another day.*

The huge visitor center, at the main entrance where you pay the admission charge, is beside the parking lot and consists of a museum, an auditorium, a restaurant, a bookstore, and restrooms. You can see the site on your own or with a licensed guide who speaks either English or Spanish. These guides are usually waiting at the entrance and charge around $20 for one to six people. Although the guides frown on it, there's nothing wrong with your approaching a group of people who speak the same language and asking if they would like to share a guide with you. (The guide, of course,

Impressions

The architects of pre-Columbian America were more fortunate than most of those of Europe. Their masterpieces were never condemned to invisibility, but stood magnificently isolated, displaying their three dimensions to all beholders. European cathedrals were built within the walls of cities; the temples of the aboriginal American seem, in most cases, to have stood outside.

—Aldous Huxley, *Beyond the Mexique Bay,* 1934

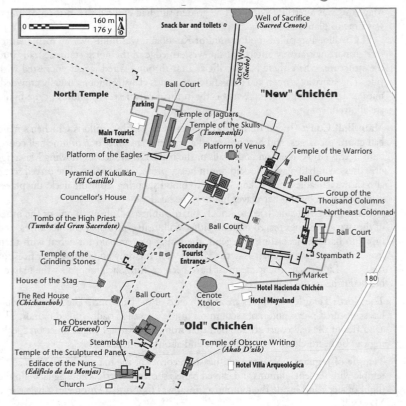

would like to get $20 from you alone and $20 each from other individuals who don't know one another.) Don't believe all the history they spout—some of it is just plain out-of-date, but the architectural details they point out are enlightening.

Chichén-Itzá's light-and-sound show was completely revamped in 1993 and is well worth seeing. The Spanish version is shown nightly at 7pm and costs $2.50; the English version is at 9pm and costs $3. The show may be offered in French and German as well. Ask at your hotel.

There are actually two parts of Chichén-Itzá (which dates from around A.D. 600 to 900). There's the northern (new) zone, which shows distinct Toltec influence, and the southern (old) zone, which is mostly Puuc architecture.

El Castillo As you enter from the tourist center, the beautiful 75-foot El Castillo pyramid will be straight ahead across a large open area. It was built with the Maya calendar in mind. There are 364 stairs plus a platform to equal 365 (days of the year), 52 panels on each side (which represent the 52-year cycle of the Maya calendar), and nine terraces on each side of the stairways (for a total of 18 terraces, which represents the 18-month Maya solar calendar). If this isn't proof enough of the mathematical precision of this temple, come for the spring or fall equinox (March 21 or September 21 between 3 and 5pm). On those days, the seven stairs of the northern stairway and the serpent-head carving at the base are touched with sunlight and become a "serpent" formed by the play of light and shadow. It appears to descend into the earth as the sun hits each stair from the top, ending with the serpent head. To the

Maya this was a fertility symbol: The golden sun had entered the earth, meaning it was time to plant the corn.

El Castillo, also called the Pyramid of Kukulkán, was built over an earlier structure. A narrow stairway entered at the western edge of the north staircase leads into the structure, where there is a sacrificial altar-throne—a red jaguar encrusted with jade. The stairway is open at 11am and 3pm and is claustrophobic, usually crowded, humid, and uncomfortable. A visit early in the day is best. No photos of the figure are allowed.

Main Ball Court (Juego de Pelota)   Northwest of El Castillo is Chichén's main ball court, the largest and best preserved anywhere, and only one of nine ball courts built in this city. Carved on both walls of the ball court are scenes showing Maya figures dressed as ball players decked out in heavy protective padding. The carved scene also shows a headless player kneeling with blood shooting from the neck; the player is looked upon by another player holding the head.

Players on two teams tried to knock a hard rubber ball through one or the other of the two stone rings placed high on either wall, using only their elbows, knees, and hips (no hands). According to legend, the losing players paid for defeat with their lives. However, some experts say the victors were the only appropriate sacrifices for the gods. Either way, the game must have been exciting, heightened by the marvelous acoustics of the ball court.

The North Temple   Temples are at both ends of the ball court. The North Temple has sculptured pillars and more sculptures inside, as well as badly ruined murals. The acoustics of the ball court are so good that from the North Temple a person speaking can be heard clearly at the opposite end about 450 feet away.

Temple of Jaguars   Near the southeastern corner of the main ball court is a small temple with serpent columns and carved panels showing warriors and jaguars. Up the flight of steps and inside the temple, a mural was found that chronicles a battle in a Maya village.

Temple of the Skulls (Tzompantli)   To the right of the ball court is the Temple of the Skulls with rows of skulls carved into the stone platform. When a sacrificial victim's head was cut off, it was stuck on a pole and displayed in a tidy row with others. As a symbol of the building's purpose, the architects provided these rows of skulls. Also carved into the stone are pictures of eagles tearing hearts from human victims. The word *Tzompantli* is not Maya but came from central Mexico. Reconstruction using scattered fragments may add a level to this platform and change the look of this structure by the time you visit.

Platform of the Eagles   Next to the Tzompantli, this small platform has reliefs showing eagles and jaguars clutching human hearts in their talons and claws, as well as a head coming out of the mouth of a serpent.

Platform of Venus   East of the Tzompantli and north of El Castillo near the road to the Sacred Cenote is the Platform of Venus. In Maya-Toltec lore, Venus was represented by a feathered monster or a feathered serpent with a human head in its mouth. It's also called the tomb of Chaac-Mool because a Chaac-Mool figure was discovered "buried" within the structure.

Sacred Cenote   Follow the dirt road (actually an ancient sacbe) that heads north from the Platform of Venus, and after five minutes you'll come to the great natural well that may have given Chichén-Itzá (the Well of the Itzáes) its name. This well was used for ceremonial purposes, not for drinking water, and according to legend, sacrificial victims were drowned in this pool to honor the rain god Chaac. Anatomical research done early this century by Ernest A. Hooten showed that bones of both children and adults were found in the well. Judging from Hooten's evidence, they may have been outcasts, diseased, or feeble-minded.

Edward Thompson, American consul in Mérida and a Harvard professor, bought the ruins of Chichén early this century, explored the cenote with dredges and divers, and exposed a fortune in gold and jade. Most of the riches wound up in Harvard's Peabody Museum of Archeology and Ethnology. Later excavations in the 1960s brought up more treasure, and studies of the recovered objects show offerings from throughout the Yucatán and even farther away.

Temple of the Warriors (Templo de los Guerreros)   Due east of El Castillo is one of the most impressive structures at Chichén—the Temple of the Warriors—named for the carvings of warriors marching along its walls. It's also called the **Group of the Thousand Columns** for the many columns flanking it. During the recent restoration, hundreds more of the columns were rescued from the rubble and put in place, setting off the temple more magnificently than ever. Climb up the steep stairs at the front to reach a figure of Chaac-Mool and several impressive columns carved in relief to look like enormous feathered serpents. South of the temple was a square building that archaeologists called the market (mercado). Its central court is surrounded by a colonnade. In the jungle beyond the temple and the market are mounds of rubble, parts of which are being reconstructed.

The main Mérida–Cancún highway used to run straight through the ruins of Chichén, and though it has now been diverted, you can still see the great swath it cut. South and west of the old highway's path are more impressive ruined buildings.

Tomb of the High Priest (Tumba del Gran Sacerdote)   Past the refreshment stand to the right of the path is the Tomb of the High Priest, which stood atop a natural limestone cave in which skeletons and offerings were found, giving the temple its name.

This building is being reconstructed, and workers are unearthing other smaller temples in the area. As the work progresses, some buildings may be roped off and others will open to the public for the first time. It's fascinating to watch the archaeologists at work, meticulously numbering each stone as they take apart what appears to be a mound of rocks and then reassembling the stones into a recognizable structure.

House of Metates (Casa de los Metates)   This building, the next one on your right, is named after the concave corn-grinding stones used by the Maya.

Temple of the Deer (Templo del Venado)   Past the House of Metates is this fairly tall though ruined building. The relief of a stag that gave the temple its name is long gone.

Little Holes (Chichan-chob)   This next temple has a roofcomb with little holes, three masks of the rain god Chaac, three rooms, and a good view of the surrounding structures. It's one of the older buildings at Chichén, built in the Puuc style during the Late Classic Period.

Observatory (El Caracol)   Construction of the Observatory, a complex building with a circular tower, was carried out over a long period of time. Without a doubt, the additions and modifications reflected the Maya's increasing knowledge of celestial movements and their need for increasingly exact measurements. Through slits in the tower's walls, Maya astronomers could observe the cardinal directions and the approach of the all-important spring and autumn equinoxes, as well as the summer solstice. The temple's name, which means "snail," comes from a spiral staircase, now closed off, within the structure.

On the east side of El Caracol, a path leads north into the bush to the **Cenote Xtoloc,** a natural limestone well that provided the city's daily water supply. If you see any lizards sunning there, they may well be *xtoloc*, the lizard for which the cenote is named.

Temple of Panels (Templo de los Tableros)   Just to the south of El Caracol are the ruins of a **steambath** (*temazcalli*) and the Temple of Panels, named for the carved panels on top. This temple was once covered by a much larger structure, only traces of which remain.

Edifice of the Nuns (Edificio de las Monjas)   If you've visited the Puuc sites of Kabah, Sayil, Labná, or Xlapak, the enormous nunnery here will remind you at once of the "palaces" at the other sites. Built in the Late Classic Period, the new edifice was constructed over an older one. Suspecting that this was so, Le Plongeon, an archaeologist working earlier in this century, put dynamite in between the two and blew part of the newer building to smithereens, thereby revealing part of the old. You can still see the results of Le Plongeon's indelicate exploratory methods.

On the eastern side of the Edifice of the Nuns is an annex (Anexo Este) constructed in highly ornate Chenes style with Chaac masks and serpents.

The Church (La Iglesia)   Next to the annex is one of the oldest buildings at Chichén, ridiculously named The Church. Masks of Chaac decorate two upper stories. Look closely, and you'll see among the crowd of Chaacs an armadillo, crab, snail, and tortoise. These represent the Maya gods called *bacah*, whose job it was to hold up the sky.

Temple of Obscure Writing (Akab Dzib)   This temple is along a path east of the Edifice of the Nuns. Above a door in one of the rooms are some Maya glyphs, which gave the temple its name, since the writings have yet to be deciphered. In other rooms, traces of red handprints are still visible. Reconstructed and expanded over the centuries, this building has parts that are very old; it may well be the oldest building at Chichén.

Old Chichén (Chichén Viejo)   For a look at more of Chichén's oldest buildings, constructed well before the time of Toltec influence, follow signs from the Edifice of the Nuns southwest into the bush to Old Chichén, about half a mile away. Be prepared for this trek with long trousers, insect repellent, and a local guide. The attractions here are the **Temple of the First Inscriptions** (*Templo de los Inscripciones Iniciales*), with the oldest inscriptions discovered at Chichén, and the restored **Temple of the Lintels** (*Templo de los Dinteles*), a fine Puuc building.

WHERE TO STAY

It's difficult to reach Chichén and Pisté by phone; however, many hotels have reservation services in Mérida or in Mexico City.

DOUBLES FOR LESS THAN $15

Posada Chac Mool. Carretera Mérida-Valladolid, 97751 Pisté, Yuc. No phone. 8 rms (all with bath). FAN. $10 single; $12 double. Free limited parking; unguarded.

Clean and plain, this no-frills single-story motel opened in 1990. The basically furnished rooms have new mattresses, red-tile floors, and well-screened windows. Little tables and chairs outside each room on the covered walkway make an inviting place to enjoy a self-made meal. The motel is located at Calle 15, next to the Restaurant Las Mestizas, and almost opposite Hotel Misión.

Posada El Paso. Calle 15 no. 48F, Carretera Mérida-Valladolid, 97751 Pisté, Yuc. No phone. 13 rms (all with bath). FAN. $5–$7 single; $7–$9 double. Parking on the street in front of the hotel.

If you can handle the traffic noise, this small new hotel may be perfect for you. The buses and trucks roar past on Pisté's main drag, but the rooms are set back a bit from the road. Shower curtains are nonexistent, but the bathrooms are clean and the mattresses adequate.

Posada Novelo. Carretera Mérida-Valladolid, 97751 Pisté, Yuc. ☎ and fax **985/1-0122.** 11 rms (all with bath) FAN. $10 single or double. Free parking in front.

Operated by the Stardust Inn next door, this very basic hotel may serve well if your budget is more important than a status address. Rooms, attached in a row and linked by a covered walkway, all have one or two beds and are sparsely furnished but clean. Hot water is a rarity.

DOUBLES FOR LESS THAN $40

Stardust Inn. Calle 15A no. 34A, Carretera Mérida-Valladolid, 97751 Pisté, Yuc. ☎ and fax **985/1-0122** (For reservations contact Calle 81A no. 513, 97000 Mérida, Yuc.; ☎ **99/ 84-0072.**) 53 rms (all with bath). AC TV. $35 single or double. Free parking; guarded.

The two-story Stardust Inn is built around a pool and a shaded courtyard. Each of the comfortable rooms has a tile floor, a shower, nice towels, and one or two double beds or three single beds; check the condition of your mattress before selecting a room. During high season there's a video bar/disco on the first floor; it's open during other times of the year if there are groups. If tranquility is one of your priorities, ask if the disco is functioning before you rent a room. The very nice air-conditioned restaurant adjacent to the lobby and facing the highway serves all three meals and is open from 7:30am to 9:30pm.

WHERE TO EAT

Food is available near the ruins in the expensive hotels. In Pisté there's little difference in prices or fare at the various restaurants. Most of the better restaurants cater to large groups that converge after 1pm for lunch.

MEALS FOR LESS THAN $10

Cafetería Ruinas. In the Chichén-Itzá visitors' center. No phone. Breakfast $4; sandwiches $4; main courses $5–$6. Daily 9am–5pm. MEXICAN/ITALIAN.

Though it has the monopoly on food at the ruins, this cafeteria actually does a good job with such basic meals as enchiladas, spaghetti, and baked chicken. Eggs are cooked to order, as are burgers, and their coffee is very good. Sit outside at the tables farthest from the crowd and relax.

La Fiesta. Carretera Mérida-Valladolid, Pisté. No phone. Main courses $4–$5; comida corrida $6. Daily 7am–9pm (comida corrida served 12:30–5pm). REGIONAL/MEXICAN.

With Maya motifs on the wall and colorful decorations, this is one of Pisté's long-established restaurants catering especially to tour groups. Though expensive, the food is very good. You'll be quite satisfied unless you arrive when a tour group is being served, in which case service to individual diners may suffer. Going toward the ruins, La Fiesta is on the west end of town.

Restaurant Bar "Poxil." Calle 15 s/n, Carretera Mérida-Valladolid, Pisté. ☎ **985/1-0123.** Breakfast $3; main courses $3.50. Daily 7am–8pm. MEXICAN/REGIONAL.

A *poxil* is a Mayan fruit somewhat akin to a guanabana. Although this place doesn't serve them, what is on the menu is good, though not gourmet, and the price is right.

You will find the Poxil near the west entrance to town on the south side of the street.

MEALS FOR LESS THAN $12

Puebla Maya. Carretera Mérida-Valladolid, Pisté. No phone. Fixed-price lunch buffet $7. Daily 1–5pm. MEXICAN.

Opposite the Pirámide Inn, the Puebla Maya looks just like its name, a Maya town with small white huts flanking a large open-walled palapa-topped center. Inside, however, you cross an artificial lagoon, planters drip with greenery, and live musicians play to the hundreds of tourists filling the tables. Service through the huge buffet is quick, so if you've been huffing around the ruins all morning, you have time to eat and relax before boarding the bus to wherever you're going. You can even swim in a lovely landscaped pool.

AN EXCURSION TO THE GRUTAS (CAVES) DE BALANKANCHE

The Grutas de Balankanche are $3^{1}/_{2}$ miles from Chichén-Itzá on the road to Cancún and Puerto Juárez. Expect the taxi to cost about $6. (Taxis are usually on hand when the tours let out.) The entire excursion takes about half an hour, and the walk inside is hot and humid. The natural caves became wartime hideaways. You can still see traces of carving and incense burning, as well as an underground stream that served as the sanctuary's water supply. Outside, take time to meander through the botanical gardens, where most of the plants and trees are labeled with their common and scientific names.

The caves are open daily. Admission is $2.50; free on Sunday. Use of your video camera will cost an additional $4. Children under six aren't admitted. Guided tours in English are at 11am and 1 and 3pm, and in Spanish, at 9am, noon, and 2 and 4pm. Tours go only if there are a minimum of six people and take up to 30 people at a time. Double-check these hours at the main entrance to the Chichén ruins.

6 Valladolid

25 miles E of Chichén-Itzá & Pisté, 100 miles SW of Cancún

The somewhat sleepy town of Valladolid (BYE-yah-doh-LEET), 25 miles east of Pisté/Chichén-Itzá, is an inexpensive alternative to staying in Pisté near the ruins of Chichén. You can get an early bus from Mérida, spend the day at the ruins, then travel another hour to Valladolid to overnight.

ESSENTIALS

GETTING THERE & DEPARTING   By Bus   Buses leave almost hourly from Mérida, passing through Pisté and Chichén-Itzá on the way to Valladolid and Cancún. There are also regular buses from Cancún and at least six daily buses from Playa del Carmen. Because of the frequency of buses to Mérida and Cancún, advance purchase of tickets isn't usually necessary.

Autotransportes Oriente (☎ 985/6-3449) offers de paso buses to Pisté (the town nearest the Chichén-Itzá ruins) every hour from 2am to midnight; these same buses go on to Mérida. De paso buses on this same line go to Cobá at 4:30am and 1pm. Buses to Tizimín leave every hour from 5am to 10pm. **Expresso de Oriente** buses (☎ 985/6-3630) go to Mérida six times daily, to Playa del Carmen six times daily, and to Cancún five times daily. **Autobuses del Centro del Estado** offers five daily buses to Tinum and several other small towns on the way to Mérida.

By Car   From Valladolid, there are frequent signs directing you via the toll road (*cuota*) to Mérida and Chichén-Itzá ($6) or Cancún ($11). No signs point you to the free (*libre*) road, but don't despair. To take the free road to Pisté/Chichén-Itzá and Mérida, take Calle 39, a one-way street going west on the north side of the Parque Cantón (the main plaza); this becomes the free Highway 180. Calle 41, a one-way east-bound street on the south side of the zócalo, becomes the free highway to Cancún.

Highway 180 links Valladolid with both Cancún and Mérida. It's a good, well-marked road and goes right past the main square in town. If you come from the toll road, the exit road leads to the Parque Cantón (the main plaza).

ORIENTATION   Information   There is a small tourism office in the Palacio Municipal, which will furnish you with some good information and maps. Señora Tete Mendoza B. is extremely helpful and knows her city and its history.

City Layout   All hotels and restaurants are within walking distance of Valladolid's pretty **main square,** the **Parque Francisco Cantón Rosado.** The Valladolid **bus station** is at the corner of Calles 37 and 57, ten very long blocks from the parque and too far to haul heavy luggage. Taxis are usually in front of the station.

Fast Facts   The **telephone area code** is 985.

EXPLORING VALLADOLID

Valladolid was founded in 1543 on the shore of a lagoon near the coast. As it lacked good agricultural land, two years later it was moved to its present location on the site of a Maya religious center called Zací (meaning White Hawk). The Franciscans built an impressive monastery here, the **Convento de San Bernardino de Siena** (1552); the town boasts another half-dozen colonial churches, including the Templo de Santa Ana built in the 1500s, originally for the exclusive use of the Maya. Two cenotes, one only two blocks east of the Parque Cantón, supplied water during colonial times. A small park, with a restaurant, a small bowl for the performing arts, and three Maya-style stick-and-thatched-roof houses, have been created around the cenote Zací. These houses are meant to depict a typical Maya settlement, and inside are some old photographs of Valladolid and a few arts and crafts for sale. **El Parroquia de San Servasio** (1545), the parish church, is on the south side of the main square, and the **Palacio Municipal** (Town Hall) is on the east.

SHOPPING   Embroidered Maya dresses can be purchased at the Mercado de Artesanías de Valladolid at the corner of Calles 39 and 44 and from women around the main square. The latter also sell—of all things—Barbie-doll-size Maya dresses! Just ask "¿Vestidos para Barbie?" and out they come.

The **food market** is on Calle 32 between Calles 35 and 37. Though it's open other days, the main market time is Sunday morning, when it's most active and colorful.

WHERE TO STAY

Hotel El Mesón del Marqués. Calle 39 no. 203, 97780 Valladolid, Yuc. ☎ **985/6-3042** or 985/6-2073. Fax 985/6-2280. 38 rms (all with bath). A/C and FAN TV TEL. $31 single or double; $39 double, suite. Free interior parking; secure.

This comfortable colonial-era mansion-turned-hotel on the north side of the Parque Cantón opposite the church offers rooms in both the original 200-year-old mansion and a new addition built around a pool in back. There is always hot water, and most of the rooms are sheltered from city noise. On the first floor there's a travel agency, gift shop, and restaurant (see "Where to Eat," below).

Hotel María de la Luz. Calle 42 no. 195, 97780 Valladolid, Yuc. ☎ and fax **985/6-2071.** 33 rms (all with bath). A/C and FAN TV. $18 single or double. Free parking; secure.

The two stories at the María de la Luz are built around an inner pool. The freshly painted rooms have been refurbished with new tile floors and baths and new mattresses. A couple of rooms have balconies overlooking the square. The wide interior covered walkway to the rooms is a nice place to relax in comfortable chairs. The hotel is on the west side of the Parque Francisco Cantón Rosado (the main square) between Calles 39 and 41.

WHERE TO EAT

The lowest restaurant prices are in the **Bazar Municipal,** a little arcade of shops beside Hotel El Mesón del Marqués (see "Where to Stay," above) right on the Parque Cantón. The cookshops open at mealtimes, when tables and chairs are set in the courtyard. You won't find many printed menus, let alone one in English, but a quick look around will tell you what's cooking, and you can order with a discreetly pointed finger. Ask the price beforehand so you won't be overcharged.

✪ Casa de los Arcos Restaurant. Calle 39 no. 200A. ☎ **985/6-2467.** Breakfast $3; antojitos $3–$4.50; main courses $3–$6; comida corrida $4. Daily 7am–10pm (comida corrida served 1–4pm). MEXICAN/YUCATECAN.

A lovely, breezy courtyard with a black-and-white tiled floor makes this restaurant especially appealing. Waiters are efficient, the menu is in English and Spanish. The hearty comida corrida might feature a choice of meat and include red beans, tortillas, and coffee. There's also a full menu of beef, chicken, seafood, and a few Mexican specialties, one of which is the delicious *longaniza a la Valladolid.* To reach the restaurant from the main square (with the Hotel El Mesón del Marqués on your left), take Calle 39 two blocks; the restaurant is on the right across from the Hotel Don Luís.

Hostería del Marqués. Calle 39 no. 203. ☎ **985/6-2073.** Breakfast $2–$4; Mexican plates $2–$3; main courses $4–$7; sandwiches $2–$3. Daily 7am–11:30pm. MEXICAN/YUCATECAN.

This place is part of the Hotel El Mesón del Marqués facing the main square. Its patrons often spill out of the air-conditioned dining room onto the hotel's open *portales* on the interior courtyard, where tables have fresh flowers and are festively decorated in hot pink and turquoise. It's definitely a popular place, often crowded at lunch. The guacamole is great.

Hotel María de la Luz. Calle 2 no. 195. ☎ **985/6-2070.** Breakfast buffet $3; main courses $4–$6; tamales and sandwiches $2–$3; comida corrida $3. Daily 7am–10pm (breakfast buffet served 7–11am). MEXICAN/YUCATECAN.

This restaurant has some fine touches such as rattan chairs drawn up to cloth-covered tables. Open to the street on the west side of the main square, this hotel-lobby restaurant is well known for its breezy and inexpensive meals served in large portions. If you eat here and at the Mesón del Marqués, you'll have the town's "in" gathering spots covered.

SIDE TRIPS FROM VALLADOLID

CENOTE DZITNUP   The Cenote Dzitnup (also known as Cenote Xkeken), 2¹/₂ miles west of Valladolid off Highway 180, is worth a visit, especially if you have time for a dip. Descend a short flight of rather perilous stone steps, and at the bottom, inside a beautiful cavern, is a natural pool of water so clear and blue it's like something from a dream. If you decide to take a swim, be sure you don't have creams or other chemicals on your skin, as they damage the habitat for the small fish and other organisms living there. Also, no alcohol, food, or smoking is allowed after you enter the cavern.

Admission is $1. The cenote is open daily from 8am to 5pm.

EKBALAM: NEWLY EXCAVATED MAYA RUINS About 21 miles northeast of Valladolid is Ekbalam (which in Maya means "star jaguar"), a newly opened archaeological site. Excavations of these ruins, which date from 100 B.C. to A.D. 1200, are ongoing.

To get here from Valladolid, go north on Highway 259 for 11 miles. Watch for the sign pointing right to the village of **Hunuku** and turn right there, following the road for 8¹/₂ miles. When you reach Hunuku, a small village, ask someone to point to the dirt road that leads about 1 mile to the ruins. Caretaker Felipe Tuz Cohuo or willing young children can point out the highlights (the children have absorbed a lot of information during the years the ruins have been excavated). A tip to the caretaker is greatly appreciated. Pencils or ballpoint pens are good gifts for the children.

To really get a lot out of this site, you should be prepared to climb up the mountainlike pyramids with sides made of loose dirt and even looser rocks. Some of the important parts can also be seen from the pathway, but climbing is much more rewarding.

You can park at the entry sign and walk from there. Located on 2,500 wooded acres, the buildings are grouped closely around a large central area; along 350 feet of the perimeter are the remains of two low walls. The largest building, called **Structure 1** or **The Tower,** is impressive for its dimensions—it's 100 feet high, 517 feet long, and 200 feet wide. From the top you can see the tallest building of Cobá, 30 miles southeast as the crow flies. Scholars believe that Ekbalam was the center of a vast agricultural region. From this lofty vantage point, all around you can see fertile land that still produces corn, cotton, and honey.

Structure 3, also called **The Palace of the Nuns,** has a row of corbel-arched rooms. Though greatly destroyed, this architecture resembles the Puuc style of other Yucatecan sites. A few badly weathered stelae fragments are on display under flimsy thatched coverings. Structures show partial walls, some made of irregular rocks and others of carefully fitted and cut rock. Sacbeob (causeways) fan out in several directions, but so far none is thought to go farther than a mile or so. If you do any climbing at all, seeing the area will take a minimum of two hours.

The site is open daily from 8am to 5pm. Admission is $1.25, free on Sunday. A video-camera permit costs $4.

RÍO LAGARTOS WILDLIFE REFUGE: NESTING FLAMINGOS North of Valladolid, about 50 miles and 25 miles north of Tizimin on Highway 295, is Río Lagartos, a 118,000-acre refuge established in 1979 to protect the largest nesting population of flamingos in North America. Found in the park's dunes, mangrove swamps, and tropical forests are jaguars, ocelots, sea turtles, and at least 212 bird species (141 of which are permanent residents).

You can make the trip in one long day from Valladolid, but you'll have to leave by at least 5am to get to Río Lagartos by 7am, in time to arrange a trip to see the flamingos with one of the local boatmen. There's one down-and-out hotel in Río Lagartos, which I can't recommend. If you prefer to overnight closer to the refuge, then a good choice is **Tizimin** (pop. 50,000), 35 miles north of Valladolid. This pleasant city is the agricultural hub of the region, and hotels and restaurants are on or near the main square. From Tizimin to Río Lagartos is about a 30-minute drive.

Seeing the Río Lagartos Refuge Río Lagartos is a small fishing village of around 3,000 people who make their living from the sea and from the occasional tourist who shows up to see the flamingos. Colorfully painted homes face the Malecón (the ocean-front street), and brightly painted boats dock along the same half-moon-shaped port. While Río Lagartos is interesting, if you have time for only one flamingo foray, make it in Celestún (west of Mérida). I've seen more flamingos and other kinds of birds at Celestún.

Plan to arrive in Río Lagartos around 7am and go straight to the dock area. There, boatmen will offer to take you on an hour-long trip to the flamingo lagoons for around $30 for up to six people in a motor-powered wooden boat. Ask around for Filiberto Pat Zem, a reliable boatman who takes the time to give a good tour.

Although thousands of flamingos nest near here from April to August, it is pro-hibited by law to visit their nesting grounds. Flamingos need mud with particular ingredients (including a high salt content) in order to multiply, and this area's mud does the trick. On your boat tour you'll probably see flamingos wading in the waters next to Mexico's second-largest salt-producing plant—the muddy bottom is plenty salty here. Flamingos use their special bills to suck up the mud, and they have the ability to screen the special contents they need from it. What you see on the boat trip is a mixture of flamingos, frigates, pelicans, herons in several colors, and ducks. Don't allow the boatman to frighten the birds into flight for your photographs; it causes the birds to eventually leave the habitat permanently.

Cancún 16

Say the word "Cancún" to most people, and they'll think of fine sandy beaches, limpid, incredibly blue Caribbean waters—and expensive luxury resorts. It's all that and then some.

Cancún actually is two places with one name. **Isla Cancún** (the island) is lined with upscale resorts, flashy shopping centers, restaurants, and nightclubs. **Ciudad Cancún,** on the mainland opposite the island, grew up with hotels more for the budget-minded traveler and a downtown area chockablock with restaurants, small hotels, and T-shirt and curio shops.

In 1994 Cancún celebrated its 20th anniversary, having risen up on an uninhabited island miles from any civilization. These days Cancún is the magic word in Mexican vacations.

Cancún *is* a perfect resort site: with lush Yucatecan jungle and the long island's powdery limestone sand beaches; and air and water temperatures that are just right. Cancún can be a starting point for exploration of other Yucatecan lures. The older, less expensive island resorts of Isla Mujeres and Cozumel are close at hand. The Maya ruins at Tulum, Chichén-Itzá, and Cobá are within driving distance, as are the snorkeling reserves of Xcaret and Xel-Ha. And along the coast south of Cancún, in places such as Playa del Carmen, new hotels and resorts in all price ranges are popping up in incredible numbers.

Cancún today is a city of 450,000 people and boasts more than 18,000 hotel rooms between the mainland city and the resort-filled island. The 14-mile-long island's resorts together make for quite a variegated display of modern architectural style; they seem to get grander and more lavish each year.

Lovers of Cancún see its similarity to U.S. resort life as a plus—a foreign vacation with diluted foreign overtones. If you've never been to Mexico, Cancún is a good place to ease into the culture—though it's not at all like the rest of the country. But especially if you like beaches, Cancún and the coast south of it have the best beaches in Mexico.

If you're beginning your Yucatecan foray in Cancún, you should read up on the history of the Yucatán in Chapter 15.

Downtown Cancún

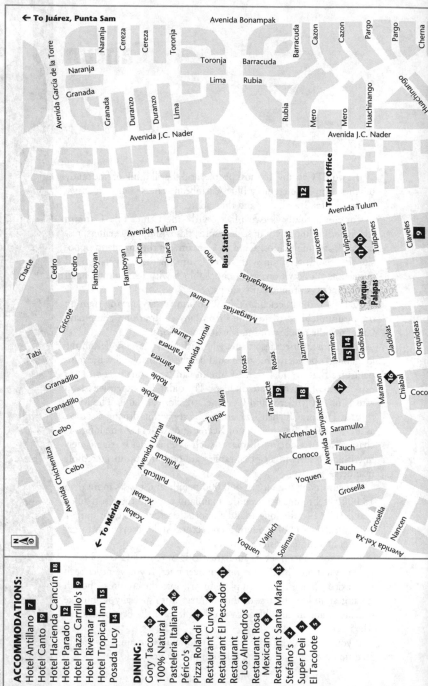

← To Juárez, Punta Sam

Avenida Bonampak

Avenida García de la Torre

Naranja
Cereza
Cereza
Toronja
Barracuda
Cazon
Cazon
Pargo
Pargo
Cherna

Naranja
Toronja
Barracuda

Granada
Lima
Rubia

Duranzo
Duranzo
Lima
Rubia
Mero
Mero
Huachinango

Huachinango

Avenida J.C. Nader
Avenida J.C. Nader

Tourist Office

12

Avenida Tulum

Avenida Tulum

Chacte

Cedro
Cedro
Cedro

Flamboyan

Flamboyan
Chaca
Chaca

Pino

Bus Station

Azucenas
Azucenas
Tulipanes

11 **10**

Tulipanes
Claveles

9

Margaritas

Laurel
Laurel

Margaritas

13

Parque
Palapas

Tabi

Ciricote

Laurel

Palmera
Laurel

Avenida Uxmal

Rosas
Rosas

Jazmines
Jazmines

15 **14**

Gladiolas
Gladiolas
Orquideas

Granadillo
Granadillo

Robie
Palmera

Tanchacte

19
18

17

Marañon

16

Chiabal
Coco

Ceibo

Avenida Uxmal
Allen

Tupac
Allen

Nicchehabi
Saramullo

Avenida Chichenitza

Ceibo

Pulticub
Pulticub

Conoco
Tauch

Avenida Sunyaxchen
Tauch

Yoquen

Grosella

Xcabal
Xcabal

← To Mérida

Grosella
Nancen

Yoquen
Valpich
Soliman

Avenida Xel-xa

N

2-0053

ACCOMMODATIONS:

Hotel Antillano **7**
Hotel Canto **19**
Hotel Hacienda Cancún **18**
Hotel Parador **12**
Hotel Plaza Carrillo's **9**
Hotel Rivemar **6**
Hotel Tropical Inn **15**
Posada Lucy **14**

DINING:

Gory Tacos **10**
100% Natural **17**
Pasteleria Italiana **16**
Périco's **6**
Pizza Rolandi **4**
Restaurant Curva **19**
Restaurant El Pescador **11**
Restaurant Los Almendros **1**
Restaurant Rosa Mexicano **8**
Restaurant Santa María **13**
Stefano's **2**
Super Deli **3**
El Tacolote **5**

594

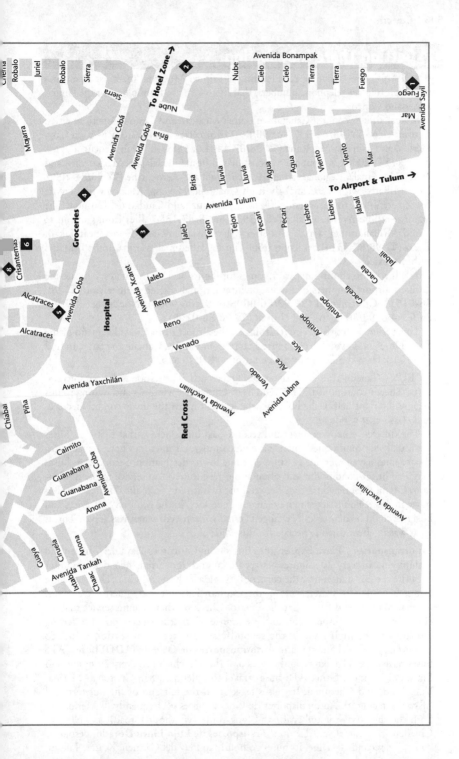

1 Getting There & Departing

BY PLANE   See Chapter 2, "Planning a Trip to Mexico," for a list of airlines (and their toll-free telephone numbers) that fly to Cancún from points in the United States and Canada.

Several airlines connect Cancún with other Mexican and Central American cities. **Aeroméxico** (☎ **98/84-3571** or 98/84-1186) offers service from Mexico City, Mérida, and Tijuana. **Mexicana** (☎ **98/87-4444** or 98/87-2769 in Cancún and toll free 800/5-0220 for 24-hour reservations) flies in from Guadalajara, Mexico City, and Flores, Guatemala. Regional carriers **Aerocozumel** and **Aerocaribe** (☎ **98/84-2000,** both affiliated with Mexicana) fly from Cozumel, Havana, Mexico City, Tuxtla Gutiérrez, Villahermosa, Mérida, Oaxaca, Veracruz, and Ciudad del Carmen. The regional airline **Aviateca** (☎ **98/84-3938** or 98/87-1386) flies from Cancún to Mérida, Villahermosa, Tuxtla Gutiérrez, Guatemala City, and Flores (near Tikal). **Taesa** (☎ **98/87-4314**) has flights from Tijuana, Chetumal, Mérida, and other cities within Mexico.

You'll want to confirm departure times for flights back to the States; here are the Cancún airport numbers of the major international carriers: **American** (☎ **98/ 86-0151**), **Continental** (☎ **98/86-0005** or 98/86-0006), **Northwest** (☎ **98/ 86-0044** or 98/86-0046), and **United** (☎ **98/86-0158**).

There is no colectivo service returning to the airport from Ciudad Cancún or the Zona Hotelera, so you'll have to hire a taxi. From Ciudad Cancún the fare's around $9 to $10; from the Zona Hotelera it's around $10 to $15.

BY BUS   Cancún's bus terminal has been renovated. The station is divided into two parts: The air conditioned ADO and Green Line ticket windows and waiting rooms occupy the right half of the building; the left half holds the unair-conditioned second class ticket windows.

The difference between first- and second-class buses here is that first-class buses are usually air conditioned, often have video movies, sometimes have a snack area aboard, and have fewer, if any, stops en route to the destination. Second-class buses may also be air-conditioned and often also offer limited stop service to the destination. Often, the price difference between the two is not great. *Bus Travel Note:* Bus travel in this region changes more than any I check on in the country. So services and buslines could be dramatically changed (usually improved) when you travel. This is what was in effect when I checked for this edition.

Autotransportes   Playa Express runs buses from Cancún to Playa del Carmen and Tulum almost every 20 minutes between 6am and 9pm from their ticket counter opposite the bus station near the corner of Avenida Tulum and Pino. They also have frequent service to Xcaret, Tulum, the Capitan Lafitte resort, Puerto Aventuras, Xpuha, Akumal, and Felipe Carrillo Puerto. Check on their Tulum service that includes entry and transportation to the entrance to the ruins (as opposed to letting you off on the highway). In the second-class bus terminal section are: **ATS** (Autotransportes del Sureste) **and Autotransportes de Oriente (ADO) buses.** ATS buses have large ATS letters on the sides of its buses, which run every 20 minutes to Playa del Carmen. Other ATS buses travel to Palenque, San Cristóbal, Mérida, Valladolid, and Chetumal. Its buses leave from the left end of the bus terminal (if you're facing it). Autotransportes de Oriente buses go frequently to Mérida, on both the short (via the toll road) and long route (via the free road), as well as to Chichén-Itzá, Izamal, and Tizimin. **Transportes de Lujo Linea Dorado,** despite its name, is a second-class line. Its buses go hourly to Play del Carmen, Xcaret, Tulum,

Lago Bacalar, Oxkutzcab, and Ticul. In the first-class part of the station are **Greenline Paquete** and **ADO** buses with their separate air-conditioned waiting room on the far right. **ADO** buses go to Mérida and Valladolid almost twice hourly until 11:30pm; the company also has daily service to Mexico City, Veracruz, and Villermosa. They have three classes of service: GL buses have air conditioning, a small snack area, bathroom, spacious seating, and video. UNO buses are similarly equipped but some have 25 super reclining seats, and some have 40 seats. **Greenline Paquetes** offer packages (paquetes) to popular nearby destinations. To Chichén-Itzá the bus leaves at 9am, and the round-trip ticket includes the round-trip air-conditioned bus ride, with video, for the 3-hour trip to Chichén-Itzá, entry to the ruins, two hours at the ruins, lunch, a brief stop for shopping, visit to a cenote, and return to Cancún by 5pm. The trip to Xcaret (which is much cheaper than the same trip offered at the Xcaret terminal office), includes round-trip transportation and entry to the park. Departures are at 9 and 10 am daily with return at 5pm. To Cozumel, the departures leave at 8, 9, and 10am with return at 5pm, and include a bus and ferry escort, round-trip, air-conditioned transportation to Playa del Carmen, and the ferry ticket to and from Cozumel. This takes the mystery out of getting to Cozumel, but you can do this simple trip on your own, by bus from this terminal, for half the price.

BY FERRY   For ferry service to Cozumel or to Isla Mujeres, see Chapter 17.

2 Orientation

ARRIVING   Special vans run from Cancún's international airport into town for $5 per person. Rates for a cab are double or triple the colectivo fare depending on your destination. From the airport there's no minibus transportation to the Puerto Juárez passenger ferry to Isla Mujeres. The least expensive way to get there is to take the minibus to the bus station in downtown Cancún and from there bargain for a taxi, which should cost around $5. Most major rental-car firms have outlets at the airport, so if you're renting a car, consider picking it up and dropping it off at the airport to save on airport-transportation prices.

The bus station is in downtown Ciudad Cancún at the intersection of Avenidas Tulum and Uxmal, within walking distance of several of my hotel suggestions. All out-of-town buses arrive there.

INFORMATION   The **State Tourism Office** (☎ 98/84-8073) is centrally located downtown on the east side of Avenida Tulum immediately left of the Ayuntamiento Benito Juárez building between Avenidas Cobá and Uxmal. It's open daily from 9am to 9pm. A second tourist information office (☎ 84-3238 or 84-3438) is located on Avenida Cobá at Avenida Tulum, next to Pizza Rolandi, and is open Monday through Friday from 9am to 9pm. Hotels and their rates are listed at each office, as well as ferry schedules.

A Warning: The friendliest people in town are often representatives of time-share real estate businesses who snag your attention by offering "information." However, their real mission is to get you to attend a spiel about the wonders of a Cancún time-sharing or condo purchase. They'll go so far as to shout at you across a busy street, just to get your attention. You represent dollars, and they are paid a bounty for convincing you to attend one of their sales talks. If you get suckered in by these sales professionals you will spend no less than half a day of your vacation listening to them; you probably won't, however, receive the gift they'll promise.

Pick up free copies of the monthly *Cancún Tips* booklet and a seasonal tabloid of the same name. Both are useful and have fine maps. The publications are owned by the same people who own the Captain's Cove restaurants, a couple of sightseeing boats, and time-share hotels, so the information (though good) is not completely unbiased. Don't be surprised if, during your stay, one of their army of employees touts the joys of time-sharing, though more subtly than the others.

CITY LAYOUT   There are two Cancúns: **Isla Cancún** (Cancún Island) and **Ciudad Cancún** (Cancún City). The latter, on the mainland, has restaurants, shops, and less expensive hotels, as well as all the other establishments that make life function—pharmacies, dentists, automotive shops, banks, travel and airline agencies, car-rental firms—all within an area about nine blocks square. The city's main thoroughfare is **Avenida Tulum.** Heading south, Avenida Tulum becomes the highway to the airport, as well as to Tulum and Chetumal; heading north, it intersects the highway to Mérida and the road to Puerto Juárez and the Isla Mujeres ferries.

The famed **Zona Hotelera** (alternately called the **Zona Turística**) stretches out along Isla Cancún, a sandy strip 14 miles long, shaped like a "7." It's now joined by bridges to the mainland at the north and south ends. **Avenida Cobá** from Cancún city becomes **Paseo Kukulkán,** the island's main traffic artery. Cancún's international airport is just inland from the south end of the island.

Finding an Address   The street-numbering system is left over from Cancún's early days. Addresses are still given by the number of the building lot and by the *manzana* (block) or *super-manzana* (group of city blocks). So, it's a little difficult to find a place in Ciudad Cancún just by street number. However, the city is still relatively small, and the downtown section can easily be covered on foot.

On the island, addresses are given by kilometer number on Paseo Kukulkán or by reference to some well-known location.

3 Getting Around

BY BUS   In town, almost everything is within walking distance. **Ruta 1** and **Ruta 2** ("Hoteles") city buses travel frequently from the mainland to the beaches along Avenida Tulum (the main street) and all the way to Punta Nizuc at the far end of the Zona Hotelera on Isla Cancún. **Ruta 8** buses go to Puerto Juárez/Punta Sam for ferries to Isla Mujeres. They stop on the east side of Avenida Tulum. Both these city buses operate between 6am and midnight daily. The public buses have the fare amount painted on the front.

BY TAXI   Settle on a price in advance. The trip from Ciudad Cancún to the Hotel Camino Real, for example, should cost $4; from Ciudad Cancún to the airport, $9 to $10; within Cancún proper, $3 to $5.

BY RENTAL CAR   There's really no need to have a car in Cancún, since bus service is good, taxis on the mainland are relatively inexpensive, and most things in Ciudad Cancún are within walking distance. But if you do rent, the cheapest way is to arrange for the rental before you leave your home country. If you rent on the spot after arrival, the daily cost of a rental car will be around $65–$75 for a VW Beetle. For more details on renting the least expensive way, see "Getting Around" in Chapter 2.

Important Note: Speed limits are posted on Paseo Kukulkán in the Zona Hotelera, slowing cars to around 60 kilometers per hour (40 m.p.h.) in most of the zone. Traffic lights have also been installed, and raised concrete pedestrian walkways across Avenida Tulum make motorists slow down while people cross. Police give tickets to speeders!

FAST FACTS: Cancún

American Express   The local office is at Av. Tulum 208 and Agua (☎ **98/ 84-1999,** 98/84-4243, or 98/87-0831), open Monday through Friday from 9am to 2pm and 4 to 6pm and Saturday from 9am to 1pm. It's one block past the Plaza México.

Area Code   The telephone area code is 98.

Climate   Hot! The rainy season is May through October. August through October is the hurricane season, which brings erratic weather. November through February can be cloudy, windy, rainy, and cool; a sweater and rain gear are handy.

Consulates   The U.S. Consular Agent is in the Maruelos Building at Av. Nader 40 (☎ **98/84-2411**). The agent is available Monday through Friday from 9am to 2pm and 3 to 5pm; the office is open Monday through Friday from 9am to 2pm and 3 to 6pm. In an emergency, call the U.S. Consulate in Mérida (☎ **99/47-2285**).

Crime   Car break-ins are just about the only crime, and they happen frequently, especially around the shopping centers in the Zona Hotelera. VW Beetles and Golfs are frequent targets. Don't leave valuables in plain sight.

Currency Exchange   Most banks are downtown along Avenida Tulum and are usually open Monday through Friday from 9:30am to 1:30pm. In the hotel zone you'll find banks in the Plaza Kukulkán and next to the Convention Center. There are also many *casas de cambio* (exchange houses). Avoid changing money at the airport as you arrive, especially at the first exchange you see—its rates are less favorable than any in town or others farther inside the airport concourse.

Doctors   Ask at your hotel or call one of the hospitals under "Emergencies," below.

Drugstores   Next to the Hotel Caribe Internacional, Farmacia Canto, at Avenida Yaxchilán 36, at Sunyaxchen (☎ **98/84-4083** or 98/84-9330), is open 24 hours.

Emergencies   To report an emergency dial 06, similar to 911 in the United States. For first aid, Cruz Roja (Red Cross; ☎ **98/84-1616**) is open 24 hours on Avenida Yaxchilán between Avenidas Xcaret and Labná, next to the Telemex building. Total Assist, a small nine-room emergency hospital with English-speaking doctors at Claveles 5, SM22, at Avenida Tulum (☎ **98/84-1058** or 98/84-1092), is open 24 hours. Desk staff may have limited English. Clínica Quirurgica del Caribe, at SM63, Mz Q, Calle 3 inte. no. 36 (☎ **98/84-2516**), is open 24 hours.

Luggage Storage/Lockers   Hotels will generally tag and store excess luggage while you travel elsewhere.

Newspapers/Magazines   For English-language newspapers and books, go to Fama on Avenida Tulum between Tulipanes and Claveles (☎ **98/84-6586**), open daily from 8am to 10pm.

Photographic Needs   For batteries and film, try Omega on Avenida Tulum at Tulipanes (☎ **98/84-3860**).

Police To reach the police (Seguridad Pública), dial **98/84-1913** or 98/84-2342.

Post Office   The main post office is at the intersection of Avenidas Sunyaxchen and Xel-Ha (☎ **98/84-1418**). It's open Monday through Friday from 8am to 7pm and Saturday from 9am to 1pm.

Restrooms   There are few public restrooms. Use those in restaurants, hotels, and other public establishments.

Safety There is very little crime in Cancún. People in general are safe late at night in touristed areas; just use ordinary common sense. As at any other beach resort, don't take money or valuables to the beach. See "Crime," above.

Swimming on the Caribbean side presents real dangers from undertow. See "Beaches" in "What to See & Do," below, for flag warnings.

Seasons Technically, high season is December 15 through Easter, when prices are higher; low season is May through November, when prices are reduced 10% to 30%. Some hotels are starting to charge high-season rates between July and September during school-holidays and European vacation time.

Telephones The phone system for Cancún changed in 1992. The area code, which once was 988, is now 98. All local numbers now have six digits instead of five; all numbers begin with 8. If a number is written 988/4-1234, when in Cancún you must dial 84-1234.

4 Where to Stay

Cancún hoteliers, even in budget and moderately priced hotels are beginning to quote rates in dollars instead of pesos, to buffer themselves against the falling value of the peso. You're usually better off insisting on a quote in pesos. Ciudad Cancún has many good budget and moderately priced hotels. During off-season (from April to November), prices go down, and it doesn't hurt to bargain for further reductions. Ask for the *tarifa promocional* (promotional rate), which hotels often have. The hotels below are categorized by high-season, double-room prices.

If the recommendations below are full, the **Posada Lucy,** Gladiolas 8, ☎ and fax **98/84-4165,** is one of Cancún's budget standbys, good for a long-term stay. And the cheapest beds in town can be found at **Albergue de la Juventud,** Paseo Kukulkán km 3.2, ☎ **98/83-1337.** This youth hostel is located at the beginning of the Zona Hotelera, and a bed costs a mere $5.

DOUBLES FOR LESS THAN $25

Hotel Canto. Yaxchilán at Tanchate, 77500 Cancún, Q. Roo. ☎ and fax **98/84-1267.** 23 rms (all with bath). A/C TV TEL. $13 single, $16 double.

Rooms in this three-story hotel (no elevator) are tidy and freshly painted, though maintenance could be better. Each room has a window but no views, plus small TVs broadcasting U.S. channels. The hotel will be on your right by the Hotel Caribe Internacional, at the intersection with Tanchate, as you head south on Yaxchilán. Street parking is scarce.

ⓢ Hotel Rivemar. Tulum 49–51, 77500 Cancún, Q. Roo. ☎ **98/84-1199.** 36 rms (all with bath). A/C or FAN TV TEL. $21–$26 single or double.

Right in the heart of downtown Cancún, this hotel is perfectly located. Rooms are clean, each with tile floors, two double beds, and small baths. Most rooms have air conditioning with only seven having fan only. All rooms have windows, some with street views and some with hall view. The hotel is at the corner of Crisantemas, 1¹/₂ blocks north of the corner of Avenidas Cobá and Uxmal.

DOUBLES FOR LESS THAN $35

Hotel Hacienda Cancún. Sunyaxchen 39–40, 77500 Cancún, Q. Roo. ☎ **98/84-3672.** Fax 98/84-1208. 40 rms (all with bath). A/C TV. High season, $23 single or double. Low season, $17 single or double.

Isla Cancún (Zona Hotelera)

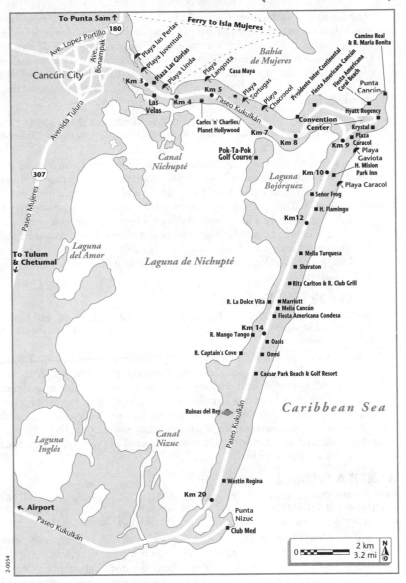

This is an extremely pleasing little hotel with rooms that are clean and plainly furnished but very comfortable. All have two double beds and windows (but no views). There's a nice small pool and café under a shaded palapa in the back. The hotel is also a member of the Imperial Las Perlas beach club in the Zona Hotelera. To find it from Avenida Yaxchilán turn west on Sunyaxchen; it's on your right next to the Hotel Caribe International, opposite 100% Natural. Parking is on the street.

Hotel Parador. Tulum 26, 77500 Cancún, Q. Roo. ☎ **98/84-1922.** Fax 98/84-9712. 66 rms (all with bath). A/C TV TEL. High season, $37 single or double. Low season, $28 single or double. Ask about promotional rates.

One of the most popular downtown hotels, the three-story Parador is conveniently located. Guest rooms are arranged around two long, narrow garden courtyards leading back to a pool (with separate children's pool) and grassy sunning area. The rooms are modern, each with two double beds, a shower, and cable TV. Help yourself to bottled drinking water in the hall. There's a restaurant/bar, plus it's next to Pop's restaurant almost at the corner of Uxmal. Rates are almost always discounted from those quoted here. Street parking is limited.

Hotel Plaza Carrillo's. Claveles 5, 77500 Cancún, Q. Roo. ☎ **98/84-1227.** Fax 98/84-2371. 43 rms (all with bath). A/C TV TEL. High season, $30 single, $33 double. Low season, $25 single, $27 double.

Rooms at this three story hotel (no elevator) are excellently located, comfortable, and well kept, if totally nondescript.You're paying more for location than anything especially when comparing this hotel to the Hotel Hacienda, for example. Some rooms are small and dark; others large and bright. Some beds are on concrete platforms that occasionally are a little low to the floor. The nice second-story patio facing the street is a good place to relax with a breeze and a book. The scarcely used pool is in the center behind the streetside restaurant. From Avenida Tulum, the hotel is a half block west on Claveles. Parking spaces are available around the Parque Palapas, a half block farther.

DOUBLES FOR LESS THAN $55

✪ Hotel Antillano. Claveles 37, 77500 Cancún, Q. Roo. ☎ **98/84-1532.** Fax 98/84-1878. 46 rms, 2 suites (all with bath). A/C TV TEL. High season, $38 single, $50 double. Low season, $31 single, $35 double.

This is an excellent choice and one of the nicer downtown establishments. For the quality, you'd expect to pay a good deal more. Rooms overlook Avenida Tulum, the side streets and the interior pool, with the latter being the most desirable since they are quieter. Each room has nicely coordinated furnishings, one or two double beds, a sink area separate from the bath, red-tile floors, and a small TV. There's a small bar to one side of the reception area and a travel agency in the lobby. To find it from Tulum, walk west on Claveles a half block; it's opposite the Restaurant Rosa Mexicana. Parking is on the street.

WORTH A SPLURGE

Hotel Aristos. Paseo Kukulkán km 12 (Apdo. Postal 450), 77500 Cancún, Q. Roo. ☎ **98/ 83-0011,** or 800/527-4786 in the U.S. 244 rms (all with bath). A/C TV TEL. High season, $87 single or double. Low season, $71 single or double. Free parking; unguarded.

One of the island's first hotels, rooms are neat and cool, with red-tile floors, small balconies, and yellow Formica furniture. All rooms face either the Caribbean or the paseo and lagoon; rooms with the best views (and no noise from the paseo) are on the Caribbean side. Here you'll find one restaurant and several bars, plus room and laundry service, a travel agency, and baby-sitting service. The central pool overlooks the ocean with a wide stretch of beach one level below the pool and lobby. You'll also find a marina with water-sports equipment and two lighted tennis courts. Beware of spring break here; the hotel caters to the crowd with loud music poolside all day.

Hotel Tropical Inn. Yaxchilán 31. SM 22. Cancún, Q. Roo. ☎ **98/84-3078.** Fax 84/34-7881. 81 rms. A/C TV TEL. High season, $50–$70 single; $64–$84 double. Low season, $46–$52 single; $56–$60 double.

The former Hotel Plaza del Sol has been incorporated into a shopping mall and has new owners. The three stories of rooms (with elevator) front a lovely palm-shaded pool area with comfortable tables and chairs and restaurant. Standard rooms have two double beds framed with wrought iron headboards, tile floors, large tile baths with sink separate, desks, and overbed reading lights. Single rooms, with one double bed, are spacious with plenty of room for luggage. It's a nice hotel, but the prices are high for the location. Ask about a discount. The hotel is between Jazmines and Gladiolas catercorner from Perico's.

5 Where to Eat

Restaurants change names with amazing rapidity in Cancún, so those I've chosen are a mix of those with dependable quality and staying power and those that were new or newly thriving when I checked them for this edition. Restaurants that survive tend to be more expensive. And many of the survivors feature menus and ambience aimed at the package-tour traveler who comes into Ciudad Cancún for "an authentic Mexican dining experience."

On the other hand, Cancún has been invaded by U.S. franchise restaurants, which you will see in more than one location. Among them are **Wendy's, Subway, McDonald's, Pizza Hut, Tony Roma's, Ruth's Chris Steak House, Kentucky Fried Chicken,** and **Burger King.** Among the most economical chains are **VIP's** and **Denny's,** which also have several locations.

CIUDAD CANCÚN
MEALS FOR LESS THAN $5

Ⓢ **Gory Tacos.** Tulipanes 26. No phone. Breakfast $1.50–$2.50; sandwiches $2–$3; tacos $2.25–$3.25; grilled specialties $5–$6; daily special $6.50; soft drinks 65¢; beer 80¢. Daily 9am–11pm. MEXICAN.

The clean decor here, with 10 pine benches and pink-tile tables, welcomes you to sit and sample the excellent food. The hamburgers are close to stateside fixings, and the french fries are thick. Sandwiches come on big fresh rolls; the quesadillas are packed with cheese and enveloped in fresh flour tortillas. Besides fast food, you can order grilled fish, beef, and chicken—all of which come with french fries, beans, salad, and tortillas. The daily special is a real tanker-upper with two choices of meat or seafood, rice, salad, baked potato, and bread. It's a half block from Tulum on the first Tulipanes and next to the Restaurant El Pescador.

Ⓢ **Restaurant Curva.** Av. Yaxchilán at Sunyaxchen. No phone. Breakfast $1.75–$2.50; comida corrida $2.50–$3. Mon–Sat 9am–5pm. MEXICAN.

It's worth a wait for a seat at one of the six tables in this tiny, and spotless, storefront café. You'll join young office workers and students for an inexpensive lunch. The daily comida includes soup, rice, beans, and meat. There's usually a choice of main courses, such as beef tips, pozole, pollo adobado, and pollo frito. Lingering is not appreciated during lunchtime. The restaurant is at the bend where Avenida Yaxchilán meets Avenida Sunyaxchen.

MEALS FOR LESS THAN $10

Ⓢ **El Tacolote.** Av. Coba 19 at Alatraces. ☎ **98/87-3045.** Delivery 98/87-3045. Appetizers $1.50–$2.50; main courses $5.50–$8; grilled dinner for two $16. Daily noon–2am. MEXICAN/GRILLED MEAT.

The ranch theme of red brick, wagon wheels, glossy dark-wood tables and chairs, and an open grill is fitting for a place specializing in grilled meats. Steaks are the specialty, and northern Mexico-style charro beans are a staple. Tacos come many ways and are made with several meats—pork, chicken, beef, and al pastor—with a wide variety of garnishes—cheese, onions, bacon, mushrooms, tomatoes, and cilantro. The same meats are featured as dinner specials. There's a nice size drink list. If you'd rather order in, they'll deliver. It's at the corner of Av. Cobá and Alcatrases.

⭕ **100% Natural.** Av. Sunyaxchen 6. ☎ **98/84-3617.** Breakfast $1.50–$2.50; spaghetti $5; fruit or vegetable shakes $2; sandwiches and Mexican plates $3–$5; coffee $1.50. Daily 7am–11pm. SEMI-VEGETARIAN.

Of all the 100% naturals around Mexico, this has one of the most appealing settings with white rattan tables on white tile floor and large dining areas on the street or interior patio. For great mixed-fruit shakes and salads, this is the place. Coffee is expensive but comes with several refills. Full meals include large portions of chicken or fish, spaghetti, or soup and sandwiches. Dine on the pretty patio in back to avoid the roar of Sunyaxchen. The restaurant is near the corner of Avenidas Yaxchilán and Sunyaxchen opposite the Hotel Caribe Internacional. Two other locations with higher prices are in the Zona Hotelera at Plaza Terramar ☎ 83-1180; open 24 hours) and Plaza Kukulkán ☎ 85-2904; open 7am to 11pm).

Pizza Rolandi. Cobá 12. ☎ **98/84-4047.** Appetizers $2.50–$7; pasta $5–$7; pizza and main courses $4.50–$9. Mon–Sat 1pm–midnight, Sun 1pm–11pm. ITALIAN.

At this shaded outdoor patio restaurant you can choose from almost two dozen different wood-oven pizzas and a full selection of spaghetti, calzones, and Italian-style chicken and beef and desserts. There's a full bar list as well. To find it from the corner of Tulum and Cobá, walk east (toward the island) a few steps; Rolandi's is on the left.

⭕ **Restaurant Los Almendros.** Av. Bonampak and Sayil. ☎ **98/87-1332.** Appetizers $1.50–$6; main courses $4–$6. Daily 10:30am–11pm. YUCATECAN.

To steep yourself in Yucatecan cuisine head directly to this large, colorful, and air-conditioned restaurant. Many readers have written to say they ate nearly every meal here, since the food and service are good, and the illustrated menu, with color pictures of dishes, makes ordering easy. Some of the regional specialties include lime soup, *poc-chuc*, chicken or pork pibil, and such appetizers as *panuchos yucatecos*. The combinado Yucateco is a sampler of four typically Yucatecan main courses—pollo, poc-chuc, sausage, and *escabeche*. A second location opened in 1994 on Paseo Kulkulkán across from the convention center. To find the downtown location, go to the corner of Tulum and Cobá, walk toward Cancún island (east) two long blocks, and turn right on Avenida Bonampak; it's opposite the bullring seven short blocks ahead.

Restaurante Santa María. Azucenas at Parque Palapas. No phone. Appetizers $1.75–$4; tacos 75¢–$5; main courses $3.50–$9. Daily 5pm–10pm. MEXICAN.

The open-air Santa María restaurant is a clean, gaily decked out place to sample authentic Mexican food. It's cool and breezy with patio dining that's open on two sides and furnished in leather tables and chairs covered in multicolored cloths. A bowl of frijoles de olla and an order of beefsteak tacos will fill you up for a low price. You may want to try tortilla soup or enchiladas, or go for one of the grilled U.S. cut steaks, or an order of fajitas, ribs, or grilled seafood, all of which arrive with a baked potato. The restaurant is opposite the north end of the Parque Palapas 2¹/₂ blocks west of Tulum.

Stefano's. Bonampak 177. ☎ **98/84-1715.** Appetizers $3–$5; main courses $4.75–$6.25; pizza $4.75–$6.75. Wed–Mon 2pm–midnight. ITALIAN/PIZZA/PASTA.

Tourists are beginning to find Stefano's, with its Italian decor and food with a few Mexican accents. For example there's a huitlacoche and shrimp pizza, rigatoni in tequila sauce, and seafood with chile peppers, nestled proudly with the Stefano special pizza made with fresh tomato, cheese, and pesto and calzones stuffed with spinach, mozzarella, and tomato sauce. For dessert the ricotta strudel is something out of the ordinary, plus tiramisú and lots of different coffees and mixed drinks. Stefano's is on Bonampak just around the corner from Cobá, on the west side of the street opposite the Pemex station.

A Fun Theme Restaurant

Périco's. Av. Yaxchilán 61. ☎ **98/84-3152.** Appetizers $3.50–$8; main courses $6–$17. Daily 1pm–1am. MEXICAN/SEAFOOD/STEAK.

With colorful murals of Mexico's culture and illustrious persons that almost dance off the walls, a ceiling full of baskets over the bar area, saddles for bar stools, colorfully bedecked leather tables and chairs, and witty waiters, Périco's is always booming and festive. The extensive menu offers well-prepared steak, seafood, and traditional Mexican dishes for moderate rates (except lobster). This is a place not only to eat and drink but to let loose and join in the fun, so don't be surprised if everybody drops their forks and dons huge Mexican sombreros to bob and snake in a conga dance around the dining room. It's fun whether or not you join in. There's marimba music from 7:30 to 10:30pm, and mariachis from 10:30pm to midnight. To find it, go west of Avenida Tulum to the Parque Palapas. Cross the middle of the park and continue west one block on Gladiolas to Yaxchilán. Périco's is across Yaxchilán at the corner of Chiabal.

Worth a Splurge

✪ **Restaurant El Pescador.** Tulipanes 28, off Av. Tulum. ☎ **98/84-2673.** Appetizers $5–$10; Seafood $7–$25; Mexican plates $5–$9; beef and chicken $7–$12. Daily 11am–10:30pm. SEAFOOD.

There's often a line at this restaurant, which opened in 1980 serving well-prepared fresh seafood in its streetside patio and upstairs venue overlooking Tulipanes. Feast on cocktails of shrimp, plus conch, fish, octopus, Créole-style shrimp (*camarones à la criolla*), charcoal-broiled lobster, and stone crabs. Zarzuela is a combination seafood plate cooked in white wine and garlic. There's a Mexican-specialty menu as well. Another branch, La Mesa del Pescador, is in the Plaza Kukulkán and is open the same hours, but is more expensive. The downtown restaurant is a half block east of Avenida Tulum.

Restaurant Rosa Mexicano. Claveles 4. ☎ **98/84-6313.** Reservations recommended for parties of six or more. Main courses $6.75–$11; lobster $20. Daily 5–11pm. MEXICAN HAUTE.

This beautiful little place has candlelit tables and a plant-filled patio in back, and it's almost always packed. Colorful paper banners and piñatas hang from the ceiling, efficient waiters wear bow ties and cummerbunds color-themed to the Mexican flag, and a trio plays romantic Mexican music nightly. The menu features "refined" Mexican specialties. Try the *pollo almendro*, which is chicken covered in a cream sauce sprinkled with ground almonds, plus rice and vegetables, or the pork baked in a banana leaf with a sauce of oranges, lime, chile ancho, and garlic. The steak tampiqueño is a huge platter that comes with guacamole salad, quesadillas, beans, salad, and rice. The restaurant is a half block east of Avenida Tulum.

Coffee and Pastries

Pastelería Italiana. Av. Yaxchilán 67, SM 25, near Sunyaxchen. ☎ **98/84-0796.** Pastries $1.75–$2.25; ice cream $2; coffee $1–$2. Mon–Sat 9am–10pm, Sun 2–9pm. COFFEE/PASTRIES/ICE CREAM.

More like a casual neighborhood coffeehouse than a place aimed at tourists, this shady little respite has been doing business here since 1977. You'll spot it by the white awning that covers the small outdoor, plant filled table area. Inside are refrigerated cases of tarts, and scrumptious looking cakes, ready to be carried away in their entirety or by the piece. The coffeehouse is in the same block as Perico's, between Marañon and Chiabal.

A DELICATESSEN

Super Deli. Tulum at Xcaret/Cobá. ☎ **98/84-1412.** Breakfast $2–$7.50; sandwiches $5–$7.50; pizzas $5.75–$8. Daily 24 hours. DELICATESSEN.

You can't miss the trendy awning and outdoor restaurant here. It's very popular for light or substantial meals any time, and inside is a well-stocked, medium-size grocery store with an excellent delicatessen. Dining choices include pizza, pasta, steaks, burgers, baguette sandwiches, a variety of coffees, wine, and beer. There's another branch on the island in the Plaza Nautilus. This Cancún City location is on the west side of Tulum just past the intersection of Tulum and Xcaret, almost next to the Hotel Handall.

ON CANCÚN ISLAND

Finding something decent to eat in the Zona Hotelera is never a problem—you'll choose from spare-no-expense luxury restaurants, barnlike tourist traps, and familiar fast-food chains nearly everywhere. But finding a truly memorable meal isn't all that easy—and chances are that you'll pay handsomely for top-flight dining. Besides this highly recommended restaurant below, scout out the restaurants in the open-air plaza of the **Mayfair Shopping Center,** which flows into the **Costa Brava** and **La Mansión** Centers. (They're so close it's impossible to tell where one ends and the other begins, but there are lots of restaurants.) Below is one place that's definitely worth the expense.

✪ **La Dolce Vita.** Av. Kulkulkán, Km 14.6. ☎ **98/84-1384.** Reservations required for dinner. Main courses $10–$19. Mon–Fri 1pm–midnight; Sat–Sun 5pm–midnight. ITALIAN.

Prepare to dine on some the best Italian food in Mexico. Now at its new location on the lagoon, and opposite the Marriot Hotel, the casually elegant La Dolce Vita is even more pleasant and popular. Appetizers include pâté of quail liver and carpaccio in vinaigrette or watercress salad. You can order such pastas as green tagliolini with lobster medallions, linguine with clams or seafood, or rigatoni Mexican style (with chorizo, mushrooms, and chives), as an appetizer for half price or as a main course for full price. Other main courses include veal with morels, fresh salmon with cream sauce, scampi, and various fish.

6 Beaches, Water Sports & Other Things to Do

Although most people come to Cancún to kick back and relax on the beach, options for exploring beyond your selected beach chair are numerous. If you need a travel agent, I highly recommend **Mayaland Tours,** Avenida Tulum at Cóba in the Hotel América (☎ **98/87-2450;** fax 98/87-2438). The company pioneered tourism in the Yucatán and has a better handle on it than most others. I've seen their double-decker buses running the route south to Tulum and Xel-Ha and elsewhere, and now they're a full-service travel agency handling not only tours all over the Yucatán Peninsula, but also plane reservations. They own hotels in Mérida, Uxmal, and Chichén Itzá and can arrange a free rental car with reservations at their hotels.

The first thing to do is explore the Zona Hotelera on Isla Cancún, just to see the fabulous resort itself and to get your bearings. Frequent **Ruta 1** or **Ruta 2 buses** marked "Hoteles" run from the mainland city along the full 12 miles to the end of the island and cost around 50¢ per ride. You can get on and off anywhere to visit hotels, shopping centers, and beaches (but you pay to ride again). The best stretches of beach are dominated by the big hotels.

THE BEACHES All of Mexico's beaches are public property, however you may be stopped if you try to enter one through a hotel where you are not a guest. Be especially careful on beaches fronting the open Caribbean, where the undertow can be deadly. Swim where there's a lifeguard. By contrast, the waters of Mujeres Bay (Bahía Mujeres) at the north end of the island are usually calm. Get to know Cancún's water-safety pennant system, and make sure to check the flag at any beach or hotel before entering the water. Here's how it goes:

- White—Excellent
- Green—Normal conditions (safe)
- Yellow—Changeable, uncertain (use caution)
- Black or Red—Unsafe—use the swimming pool instead!

Here in the Caribbean, storms can arrive and conditions can change from safe to unsafe in a matter of minutes, so be alert: If you see dark clouds heading your way, make your way to shore and wait until the storm passes and the green flag is displayed again.

Playa Tortuga (Turtle Beach) is the public beach. Besides swimming, you can rent a sailboard and take lessons there. Shuttle boats to Isla Mujeres also depart from here along with some tour boats. There's a small but beautiful portion of public beach on **Playa Caracol,** by the Xcaret Terminal. Both of these face the calm waters of Bahía Mujeres and for that reason are much better than those facing the Caribbean.

WATER SPORTS Many beachside hotels offer water-sports concessions that include rental of rubber rafts, kayaks, and snorkeling equipment. On the calm Nichupte Lagoon are outlets for renting sailboats, water jets, and water skis. Prices vary and are often negotiable, so check around.

Besides **snorkeling** at Garrafón National Park (see "Boating Excursions," below), travel agencies offer an all-day excursion to the natural wildlife habitat of Isla Contoy, which usually includes time for snorkeling. It costs much more than doing it on your own from Isla Mujeres (see Chapter 17 for details).

You can arrange a day of **deep-sea fishing** at one of the numerous piers or travel agencies for around $150 to $250 for four hours for up to four people.

Scuba trips run around $60 and include two tanks. **Scuba Cancún,** Paseo Kukulkán, km 5, on the lagoon side (☎ **83-1011,** fax 84-2336, open 8:30am to 6pm, phone reservations also available in the evenings from 7:30 to 10:30pm using the fax line), offers a four-hour resort course for $70. Full certification takes four to five days and costs around $350. Scuba Cancún also offers diving trips to 12 nearby reefs, including Cuevones at 30 feet and the open ocean at 50 to 60 feet (offered in good weather only). The average dive is around 35 feet. The farthest reef is about 40 minutes away. Drift diving is the norm here, and the big attractions are the coral reefs where there are hundreds of fish. One-tank dives cost $45, and two-tank dives cost $56. Dives usually start around 10am and return by 2:15pm. **Snorkeling** trips cost $24 and leave every afternoon after 2pm going to shallow reefs about a 20-minute boat ride away.

For windsurfing, go to the Playa Tortuga public beach, where there's a **Windsurfing School** (☎ **84-2023**) with equipment for rent.

BOATING EXCURSIONS   The island of Isla Mujeres, just 10 miles offshore, is one of the most pleasant day-trips from Cancún. At one end is **El Garrafón National Underwater Park,** which is excellent for snorkeling. And at the other end is the delightful village with small shops, restaurants, and hotels, and Playa Norte, the island's best beach. (See Chapter 17 for more on Isla Mujeres.)

There are four ways to get there: by frequent public ferry from Puerto Juárez, which takes between 20 and 45 minutes; by a shuttle boat from Playa Linda or Playa Tortuga (a one-hour ride) but with irregular service; by the Watertaxi (also with limited service), next to the Xcaret Terminal; and by one of the day-long pleasure boats, most of which leave from the Playa Linda pier.

It's easy to go on your own. The Puerto Juárez **public ferries** are just a few miles from downtown Cancún. From Cancún city, take the Ruta 8 bus on Avenida Tulum to Puerto Juárez; the ferry docks in downtown Isla Mujeres by all the shops, restaurants, hotels, and Norte beach. You'll need a taxi to go to Garrafón Park at the other end of the island. You can stay as long as you like (even overnight) and return by ferry, but be sure to ask about the time of the last returning ferry—don't depend on the posted hours. Taxi fare from downtown Cancún to the pier will cost around $6. The ferry costs $1.50 to $3 one way. (For more details and a ferry schedule, see Chapter 17.) The Isla Mujeres Shuttle departs from Playa Linda and Playa Tortuga in the Zona Hotelera. The round-trip fare is $13.50, and the trip takes about one hour. The Watertaxi costs around $12. (For more details and shuttle schedule see Chapter 17.)

Pleasure boat cruises to Isla Mujeres are a favorite pastime here. Modern motor yachts, catamarans, trimarans, and even old-time sloops take swimmers, sunners, snorkelers, and shoppers out into the limpid waters. Some tours include a snorkeling stop at Garrafón, lunch on the beach, and a short time for shopping in downtown Isla Mujeres. Most leave at 9:30 or 10am; last about five or six hours; and include continental breakfast, lunch, and rental of snorkel gear. Others, particularly the sunset and night cruises, go to beaches away from town for pseudo-pirate shows and include a lobster dinner or Mexican buffet. If you want to actually see Isla Mujeres, go on a morning cruise, or go on your own and return on the public ferry.

Tour companies are also beginning to offer cruises that emphasize Cancún's natural attributes. The **lagoons** along the Zona Hotelera are ideal for spotting herons, egrets, and crabs in the mangroves. Often billed as **jungle cruises,** they don't go to a jungle, but they usually include time for lagoon snorkeling. Other excursions go to the **reefs** in glass-bottom boats, so you can have a near-scuba-diving experience and see many colorful fish. However, the reefs are a distance from shore and impossible to reach on windy days with choppy seas. They've also suffered through overuse, and their condition is far from pristine. The **Nautibus** (☎ **83-3552** or 83-2119), one of those offering glass-bottom boat trips to the reefs, has been around for years. The trip in a glass-bottom boat from the Playa Linda pier to the Chitale coral reef to see colorful fish, takes about one hour and 20 minutes. Around 50 minutes is consumed going to and from the reef. Cokes are included in the price of the trip, which costs $24 per person. Still other boat excursions visit Isla Contoy, a **national bird sanctuary** that's well worth the time. However, if you are planning to spend time in Isla Mujeres, the Contoy trip is easier and more pleasurable to take from there.

The operators and names of boats offering excursions change often. To find out what's available when you're there, check with a local travel agent or hotel tour desk, for they should have a wide range of options. You can also go to the Playa Linda Pier either a day ahead or the day of your intended outing and buy your own ticket. If you go on the day of your trip, arrive at the pier around 8:45am since most boats leave around 9 or 9:30am.

RUINAS EL REY   Cancún has its own Maya ruins. It's a small site and not impressive compared to ruins at Tulum, Cobá, or Chichén-Itzá. The Maya fishermen built this small ceremonial center and settlement very early in the history of Maya culture. It was then abandoned, to be resettled later near the end of the post-Classic Period, not long before the arrival of the conquistadores. The platforms of numerous small temples are visible amid the banana plants, papayas, and wildflowers. A new golf course has been built around the ruins, but there is a separate entrance for sightseers. You'll find the ruins about 13 miles from town, at the southern reaches of the Zona Hotelera, almost to Punta Nizuc. Look for the Caesar's Palace hotel on the left (east), then the ruins on the right (west). Admission is $4.50 (free on Sundays and holidays); the hours are daily from 8am to 5pm.

A MUSEUM   To the right side of the entrance to the Cancún Convention Center is the **Museo Arqueológico de Cancún,** a small but interesting museum with relics from archaeological sites around the state. Admission is $1.75 (free on Sundays and holidays); the hours are Tuesday to Saturday from 9am to 7pm, Sunday from 10am to 5pm.

BULLFIGHTS   Cancún has a small bullring (☎ **98/84-8372**) near the northern (town) end of Paseo Kukulkán opposite the Restaurant Los Almendros. Bullfights are held every Wednesday at 3:30pm during the winter tourist season. There are usually four bulls. Travel agencies in Cancún sell tickets: $45 for adults and $25 for children.

7 Shopping

Although shops in Cancún are more expensive than their equivalents in any other Mexican city, most visitors spend a portion of their time browsing.

There are several open-air **crafts markets** easily visible on Avenida Tulum in Cancún city and near the convention center in the hotel zone.

Cancún's **"people market,"** selling food, spices, housewares, piñatas, party supplies, and the like is behind the post office at Sunyaxchen and Xel-Ha. It's open Monday through Saturday from 9am to 1pm and 4 to 9pm and Sunday from 9am to 2pm. There you can also find **Disco Tinhorot II** (☎ **84-3728**), with a large selection of Mexican tapes and CDs. It's open the same hours as the market.

Malls on Cancún Island are air-conditioned, sleek, and sophisticated. Most of these are located one after another on Paseo Kukulkán between 7 and 12km —Plaza Lagunas, Costa Brava, La Mansión, Mayfair, Plaza Terramar, Plaza Caracol, Plaza Flamingo, and Plaza Kulkulán. These malls offer shops selling anything from fine crystal and silver to designer clothing and decorative objects. Numerous restaurants are interspersed among the shops, many with prices higher than their branches on the mainland. Stores are generally open daily from 10am to 8 or 10pm. Stores in malls near the convention center generally stay open all day, but some, and especially in malls farther out, close between 2 and 4pm. Here's a brief rundown on the malls and some of the shops each contain.

Inside the **Plaza Kukulkán** you'll find a branch of Banco Serfin; the OK Maguey Cantina Grill; a movie theater with U.S. movies; Tikal, a shop with Guatemalan textile clothing; several crafts stores; a liquor store; a bathing suit specialty store; a record and tape outlet; all leather goods including shoes and sandals; and another specializing in silver from Taxco. In the food court are a number of U.S. franchise restaurants plus one featuring specialty coffee.

Planet Hollywood anchors the **Plaza Flamingo,** but inside you'll also pass a branch of the Bancrecer, Denny's, Subway sandwiches, and La Casa del Habana for Cuban Cigars.

The long meandering **Plaza Caracol** holds outlets for Cartier jewelry, Aca Joe, Guess, Señor Frog clothing, Waterford crystal, Samsonite luggage, Thomas Moore Travel, Gucci, Fuji film, Mr. Papa's, and La Fisheria restaurant.

Mayfair Plaza is the oldest, with an open bricked center that's lively with people sitting in open-air restaurants and bars such as Tequila Sunrise, Fat Tuesday, El Mexicano, Hard Rock Cafe, Pizza Hut, and several stores selling silver, leather, and crafts.

8 Cancún After Dark

One of Cancún's draws is its active nightlife. Sometimes there's entertainment enough just strolling along thriving **Avenida Tulum,** where restaurant employees show off enticing sample plates to lure in passersby. But there are also snazzy discos and a variety of lobby entertainment at island hotels. But the **Centro Comercio Mayfair** (shopping center) is just about the liveliest place for spending an evening hanging out, going from restaurant to drinking establishment to restaurant. It's one of the first shopping centers on the island, and the only one with a large open-air center that's ideal for sitting outside to eat and drink and meet other vacationers having a good time.

CONVENTION CENTER The convention center glistens with slick (and I mean slick) marble floors, arcades of fashionable shops and restaurants, entertainment, meeting rooms, and an auditorium.

THE PERFORMING ARTS Nightly performances of the **Ballet Folklórico de Cancún** (☎ 98/83-0199, ext. 193 and 194), are held at the Cancún Convention Center. Tickets are sold between 8am and 9pm at a booth just as you enter the convention center. You can go for dinner and the show, or just the show. Dinner/show guests pay around $35, and arrive at 6:30pm for drinks, which is followed by dinner at 7pm, and the show at 8pm. The price includes an open bar, dinner, show, tax, and tip. Guests preferring only the show arrive at 7:30pm and pay $22. Several hotels host **Mexican fiesta nights,** including a buffet dinner and a folkloric dance show; admission, including dinner, ranges from $35 to $50. A Ballet Folklórico appears Monday through Saturday nights in a one hour and 15 minute show at the **Continental Villas Plaza** (☎ 85-1444, ext. 5690). The **Hyatt Regency Cancún** (☎ 83-1234) has a dinner, folkloric, and mariachi fiesta, Tuesday through Sunday nights during the high season, as does the Camino Real (☎ 83-1200). **El Mexicano** restaurant (☎ 84-4207) in the Costa Blanca shopping center hosts a tropical dinner show every night as well as live music for dancing. The entertainment alternates each night with mariachis entertaining intermittently from 7:30 to 11pm and a folkloric show from 8 to 9:30pm.

Mango Tango, Paseo Kukulkán km 14 (☎ 98/85-0303). Get in a party mood at this lagoon side restaurant/dinner show establishment. Diners can choose from two levels, one nearer the music and the other overlooking it all. Music is loud and varied. The one hour and 20 minute dinner show begins at 8pm nightly and costs $25 to $35. At 9:30pm live reggae music begins and there's no cover. If you want to enjoy the show without a meal, just order a drink and be seated at an upper level table. It's opposite the Jack Tar Village.

On Fridays at 7:30pm the downtown **Parque de las Palapas** hosts Noches Caribeños with tropical music and dancing.

THE CLUB & MUSIC SCENE Clubbing in Cancún, still called discoing here, is a raucous affair. Many of the big hotels have nightclubs, usually a disco or at least live music, and a lobby bar. However, they're expensive: Expect to pay a cover charge of $8 to $20 per person in the discos or show bars and $4 to $7 for a drink. Numerous restaurants, such as **Carlos 'n Charlie's, Planet Hollywood, Hard Rock Cafe, Señor Frog, TGI Friday,** and **Périco's** (for the last see "Where to Eat," above), double as late-night party spots; the first four attract hordes of spring breakers and offer wildish fun at a fraction of the prices of more costly evening entertainment.

Carlos O'Brien's, Tulum 29, SM 22 (☎ **98/84-1659**). With taped music, this is one of the tamer of the Carlos Anderson restaurants/night spots in town (Señor Frog and Carlos 'n Charlie's are two others), but it has its lively moments, depending on the crowd. It's open daily from 11am to 12:30am.

Christine's, at the Hotel Krystal on the island (☎ **98/83-1793**), is one of the most popular discos. The dress code is no shorts or jeans. It's open at 9:30pm nightly.

Dady'O, Paseo Kukulkán, 9.5 km, is the current heavyweight champion, with lines long enough to make you think you're in New York or L.A. It opens at 9:30pm nightly.

La Boom, Bulevar Kukulkán, km 3.5 (☎ **98/83-1152**), has two sections: On one side is a video bar, and on the other is a bilevel disco with the required cranium-cracking music. There's blessed air-conditioning in both places. Each night there may be a special client-getting attraction like no cover, free bar, ladies' night, or bikini night. It's open nightly from 8pm to 6am. A sound-and-light show begins at 11:30pm in the disco.

Azucar Bar Caribeño, adjacent to the Hotel Camino Real (☎ **98/83-0441**), offers spicy tropical dancing of the salsa, merengue, and bolero kind, with bands from Cuba, Jamaica, and the Dominican Republic; it's open Monday to Saturday from 9:30pm to 4am.

Tequila Sunrise Grill Bar & Fiesta, in the Mayfair Shopping Center above the Pizza Hut, is a restaurant, but it's also a lively dancing spot with tempting music drifting down to the plaza below; there's no cover, and it's open daily from 7pm to 4am.

Hard Rock Cafe, also in the Mayfair Shopping Center (☎ **98/83-2024**) entertains with a live band at 10:30pm every night except Wednesday. Other hours you'll get your share of lively recorded music, to munch by—the menu combines the most popular foods from American and Mexican cultures. It's open daily from 10am to 2am.

Planet Hollywood, Flamingo Shopping Center, Paseo Kukulkán km 11 (☎ **98/ 85-3022**), is the trendy brainchild of Sylvester Stallone, Bruce Willis, and Arnold Schwarzenegger. It's both a restaurant and nighttime music/dance spot with mega-decibel live music. It's open daily from 11am to 2am.

Carlos 'n Charlie's, Paseo Kukulkán, km 4.5 (☎ **98/83-0846**), is a reliable place to find both good food and frat-house-level entertainment in the evenings. There's a dance floor to go along with the live music that starts nightly around 9pm. A cover charge is implemented if you're not planning to eat. It's open daily from noon to 2am.

SPORTS WAGERING This form of entertainment seems to be sweeping Mexico's resorts. TV screens mounted around the room at **LF Caliente** (☎ **98/83-3704**), at the Fiesta Americana Hotel, show all the action in racetrack, football, soccer, and so on in a bar/lounge setting.

9 Road Trips from Cancún

Outside of Cancún are all the many wonders of the Yucatán Peninsula; you'll find the details in chapters 15 and 17. Cancún can be a perfect base for day- or overnight trips or the starting point for a longer exploration. The Maya ruins to the south at

Tulum or **Cobá** should be your first goal, then perhaps the *caleta* (cove) of **Xel-Ha** or the new lagoon day-trip to **Xcaret.** And if you're going south, consider staying a night or two on the island of **Cozumel** or at one of the budget resorts on the **Tulum coast** or **Punta Allen,** south of the Tulum ruins. **Isla Mujeres** is an easy day-trip off mainland Cancún (see chapter 17).

About 80 miles south of Cancún begins the **Sian Ka'an Biosphere Reserve,** a 1.3-million-acre area set aside in 1986 to preserve a region of tropical forests, savannas, mangroves, canals, lagoons, bays, cenotes, and coral reefs, all of which are home to hundreds of birds and land and marine animals (see chapter 17 for details). The Friends of Sian Ka'an, a nonprofit group based in Cancún, offers biologist-escorted day-trips from the Cabañas Ana y José on the Punta Allen Peninsula *south of Tulum,* Monday, Tuesday, Friday, and Saturday (weather permitting) at $50 per person in their vehicle, or $40 per person if you drive yourself. The price includes chips and soft drinks, round-trip van transportation to the reserve from the Cabañas Ana y José, a guided boat/birding trip through one of the reserve's lagoons, and use of binoculars. Tours can accommodate up to 18 people. Trips start from the hotel at 9:30am and return there around 2:30pm. For reservations, contact Amigos de Sian Ka'an, Plaza America (☎ 98/84-9583; fax 98/87-3080). Their office is on Avenida Cobá 5, 3rd floor, Plaza America. Office hours are 9am to 3pm and 6 to 8pm.

Although I don't recommend it, by driving fast or catching the right buses, you can go inland to **Chichén-Itzá,** explore the ruins, and return in a day, but it's much better to spend at least two days seeing Chichén-Itzá, Mérida, and Uxmal. See chapter 15 for transportation details and further information on these destinations.

Isla Mujeres, Cozumel & the Caribbean Coast

Once obscured by Cancún's glitter, Mexico's other Caribbean vacation spots have shouldered their way into the tourist spotlight. **Isla Mujeres,** just a short ferry ride from Cancún, offers low-priced and low-key Caribbean relaxation. The island of **Cozumel,** somewhere on the spectrum between Isla Mujeres' slow pace and Cancún's fast-lane bustle, has scuba and snorkeling possibilities that compare with any in the world. And the Quintana Roo coast, dubbed the **Costa Turquesa** (Turquoise Coast), stretches south from Cancún all the way to Chetumal—230 miles of powdery white-sand beaches, lush jungle, crystal-clear lagoons full of coral and colorful fish, flashy new resorts, and inexpensive hideaways.

Chapter 15 supplies full information on points west of Cancún, such as Chichén-Itzá and Mérida. In this chapter we look at the islands off the peninsula and the mainland coast south of Cancún.

EXPLORING MEXICO'S CARIBBEAN

Isla Mujeres   Many Cancún vacationers see Isla Mujeres via a brief day-trip on a party boat, which is fine if you don't have much time. However, most of those trips provide little time in the village, and you get no sense of what island life is like or how enjoyable a longer stay could be. Besides loafing, fishing, and snorkeling, diving is one of its main attractions. I recommend at least two nights here, but watch it—the pace is so relaxing here your two-day plan might stretch into weeks before you know it.

Local passenger ferries go to Isla Mujeres from Puerto Juárez near Cancún, and car ferries to Isla Mujeres leave from Punta Sam, also near Cancún. More expensive passenger ferries, with less frequent departures, also go to Isla Mujeres from Playa Linda on Cancún island.

Cozumel   This truly laid-back island getaway is a perfect place to relax for a week or more. The best diving in Mexico is here, plus there's good fishing, and excursions to villages and ruins are only a ferry-ride away on the mainland. If you're considering a package (usually offered for three or four nights) remember that you'll spend a day coming and going. Buy a longer package if you can. But remember too that there are many inexpensive places to stay that won't be part of a package deal, and you can still do all the diving and sightseeing you want. Passenger ferries also run between Playa del Carmen and Cozumel—another, less expensive, way to go if you aren't flying direct from your home base. A car/passenger ferry runs between Puerto Morelos (south of Cancún) and Cozumel.

The Costa Turquesa   Signs pointing to brand-new, and expensive, resort developments are sprouting up all along Highway 307 from Cancún south to Tulum, a stretch known as the "Tulum Corridor." Some are actually under construction, and others may never progress farther than a big sign and a pipe dream. This frenzy of construction is changing the character of the Corridor, but there are still plenty of small, inexpensive beachfront hideaways, just a short distance from the highway. And south of Tulum, almost 100 miles of this coast has been saved from developers and set aside as the **Sian Ka'an Biosphere Reserve.** A trip down the coast is a great way to spend a day of a vacation centered in Cancún. The most popular agency-led tour out of Cancún is to the ruins of Tulum, followed by a stop at **Xel-Ha** for swimming and/or snorkeling in the beautiful clear lagoon. Once a placid and little-known spot, **Xcaret Lagoon** opened in 1991 as a full-blown tourist attraction widely touted in Cancún for people who plan to spend the day.

Though **Chetumal** is the capital of Quintana Roo state, it has little to recommend it. It's best to think of it as a gateway to Guatemala, Belize, the several ruins near the city, and the excellent diving and fishing to be had off the Xcalak Peninsula. The reexcavation of many of the ruins near Chetumal may be a reason for a detour there, but Lago Bacalar is the preferred place to stay near Chetumal.

Between Lago Bacalar and Escarcega is the **Río Bec** ruin route where several "new" sites are open to the public, and others are available with special permission.

The Costa Turquesa is best experienced in a car. (See Chapters 2 and 16 for information on rentals.) It's not impossible to get around by bus, but doing so requires careful planning, more time, and lots of patience. Besides Cancún, Playa del Carmen has the best selection of bus services. There are frequent buses between Cancún and Chetumal that stop at the more populous towns—Playa del Carmen, Tulum, and Felipe Carrillo Puerto. These buses will also let you off if you want to go to Xel-Ha, Xcaret, Paamul, or other spots, but in many cases you'll have to walk the mile or so from the highway to your destination. However, a few buslines now take passengers directly into these popular day-trip destinations. (See "Arriving & Departing By Bus" in Chapter 16 for details.) To return on buses not offering door-to-door service, you'll have to walk back and wait on a sweltering highway to flag a passing bus—and be prepared to watch buses pass you by if they're full. Hitching a ride with other travelers is another possibility, though I don't recommend hitchhiking on the highway.

Highway 307 south of Cancún is flanked by jungle on both sides, except where there are beaches and beach settlements. Traffic, which was once scarce, is dangerously dense now. (See the "Traveler's Advisory" box.)

Here are some drive-times from Cancún: Puerto Morelos (port for the car-ferry to Cozumel), 45 minutes; Playa del Carmen (a laid-back beachside village), one hour; Xcaret lagoon and Paamul, one hour; Akumal, one hour; Xel-Ha and Tulum, around two hours; and Chetumal, about five hours.

1 Isla Mujeres

10 miles N of Cancún

For total, laid-back, inexpensive Caribbean relaxation, it's hard to beat Isla Mujeres. Often called the "poor man's Cancún," Isla Mujeres is a bargain compared to Cancún—and I much prefer it. The sand streets have been bricked, and some of the original Caribbean-style clapboard houses remain to add a colorful and authentic reminder of the island's past. Suntanned visitors hang out in open-air cafés and

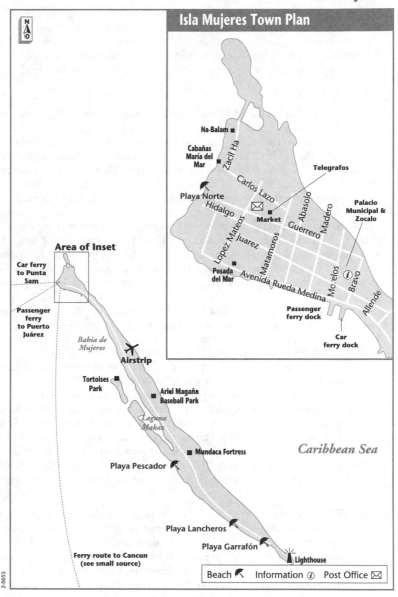

Isla Mujeres Town Plan

N

Area of Inset

Car ferry to Punta Sam

Passenger ferry to Puerto Juárez

Bahia de Mujeres

Airstrip

Tortoises Park

Ariel Magaña Baseball Park

Laguna Makax

Mundaca Fortress

Playa Pescador

Playa Lancheros

Playa Garrafón

Lighthouse

Ferry route to Cancun (see small source)

Caribbean Sea

Na-Balam

Cabañas María del Mar

Zacil Ha

Carlos Lazo

Telegrafos

Playa Norte

Hidalgo

Lopez Mateos

Juarez

Market

Abasolo

Guerrero

Madero

Palacio Municipal & Zocalo

Posada del Mar

Matamoros

Avenida Rueda Medina

Mo elos

Bravo

Allende

Passenger ferry dock

Car ferry dock

Beach   Information ⓘ   Post Office ✉

2-0055

stroll streets lined with frantic souvenir vendors who beckon them like carnival barkers.

As packed as days can be, with trips to the Isla Contoy bird sanctuary and excellent diving, fishing, and snorkeling, in the evenings most people find the slow, relaxing pace one of the island's biggest draws. At night it's bathed in a cool breeze that's perfect for casual open-air dining and drinking in small streetside eateries. Most people pack it in as early as 9 or 10pm, when most of the businesses close. Restless night owls, however, will find kindred souls at a few bars on Playa Norte that stay open until the wee hours.

There are two versions of how Isla Mujeres ("Island of Women") got its name. The more popular story claims that pirates parked their women here for safekeeping while they were marauding the Spanish Main. The other account attributes the name to conquistador Francisco Hernández de Córdoba, who was reportedly impressed by the large number of female terra-cotta figurines he found in temples on the island.

ESSENTIALS

GETTING THERE & DEPARTING   Puerto Juárez, just north of Cancún, is the dock for the passenger ferries to Isla Mujeres. The *Caribbean Queen* makes the trip many times daily; it takes 45 minutes, and the fare is $1.50. The newer *Caribbean Express* makes the trip in 20 minutes; the cost is $3. Ferries run frequently between 6am and 8pm. Pay at the ticket office, or if the ferry is about to leave, you can pay aboard. Taxi fares are now posted at the lot where the taxis park. The fare to the Cancún airport is $10; to downtown Cancún, $4; and to the Hotel Zone, $6 to $8.50.

Isla Mujeres is so small that a vehicle isn't necessary, but if you're taking a vehicle to Isla Mujeres, you'll use the Punta Sam port a little farther past Puerto Juárez. The ferry runs the 40-minute trip five or six times daily all year except in bad weather (check with the tourist office in Cancún for a current schedule). Cars should arrive an hour in advance of the ferry departure to register for a place in line and pay the posted fee.

There are also boats from the Playa Linda pier in Cancún, but they're less frequent and much more expensive—$13 one way—than those from Puerto Juárez. The Playa Linda ferries simply don't run if there isn't a crowd. When I checked, a new **Watertaxi** (☎ **86-4270** or 86-4847) to Isla Mujeres was operating from Playa Caracol, between the Fiesta Americana Coral Beach Hotel and the Xcaret terminal on the island, at a cost of $12. Their scheduled departures were 9 and 11am and 1 and 3pm with returns from Isla Mujeres at 10am, noon, and 2 and 5pm.

To get to either Puerto Juárez or Punta Sam from Cancún, take any Ruta 8 city bus from Avenida Tulum. If you're coming from Mérida, you can either fly to Cancún and then proceed by bus to Puerto Juárez, or you can take a first- or second-class bus directly from the Mérida bus station to Puerto Juárez; they leave several times a day. From Cozumel, you can either fly to Cancún (there are daily flights) or take a ferry to Playa del Carmen (see the Cozumel section below for details), where you can catch a bus to Puerto Juárez.

ORIENTATION   Arriving   Ferries arrive at the dock in the center of town. Unless you're loaded with luggage, you don't need transportation (most hotels are close by), but taxis are always lined up in front of the dock, and they ask around $1 to $2 to take you to almost any hotel. The price gets lower if you wait until all passengers have left the area. Negotiate directly with the driver, not a representative who recruits passengers by quoting half the price the driver actually charges. Rates are posted at the taxi co-op to the right of the pier as you leave the ferry. Tricycle taxis are the least expensive.

Visitor Information   The **City Tourist Office** (☎ and fax **987/7-0316**) has moved again with its latest location on the second floor of the Plaza Isla Mujeres. You'll find it at the northern end of Juárez, between López Mateos and Matamoros. It's open Monday through Friday 9am to 2:30pm and 7 to 9pm. Also look for "Islander" a free publication with history, local information, advertisements, and list of events (if any).

Island Layout   Isla Mujeres is about 5 miles long and 2¹/₂ miles wide. The **ferry docks** are right at the center of town, within walking distance of most hotels. The street running along the waterfront is **Rueda Medina,** commonly called the **Malecón.** The **market** (Mercado Municipal) is by the post office on **Calle Guerrero,** an inland street at the north edge of town, which, like most streets in the town, is un-marked.

Getting Around   A popular form of transportation on Isla Mujeres is the electric golf cart, available for rent at many hotels for $10 per hour or $50 per day. They don't go more than 20 miles per hour, so don't expect to speed around the island, but they're fun. Anyway on Isla Mujeres you aren't there to hurry. Many people enjoy touring the island by moto, the local sobriquet for motorized bikes and scooters. If you don't want to fool with shifting gears, rent a fully automatic one for around $30 per day or $6 per hour. They come with seats for one person, but some are large enough for two. Whatever you rent, take time to get familiar with how the vehicles work, and be careful on the road as you approach blind corners and hills where vis-ibility is poor. There's only one main road with a couple of offshoots, so you won't get lost. Be aware that the rental price does not include insurance, and any injury to yourself or the vehicle will come out of your pocket. Bicycles are also available for rent at some hotels for $5 per day.

FAST FACTS: ISLA MUJERES

Area Code   The area code of Isla Mujeres is 987. The first digit for all telephone numbers on the island has been changed from 2 to 7.

Hospital   The Hospital de la Armada (☎ **987/7-0001**), is on Medina at Ojon P. Blanco.

Post Office/Telegraph Office   The correo is on Calle Guerrero, by the market.

Telephone   There's a long-distance telephone office in the lobby of the Hotel María José, Avenida Madero at Medina, open Monday through Saturday from 9am to 1pm and 4 to 8pm. There are Ladatel phones accepting coins and pre-paid phone cards at the plaza.

Tourist Seasons   Isla Mujeres' tourist season (when hotel rates are higher) is a bit different from that of other places in Mexico. High season runs December through May, a month longer than in Cancún; some hotels raise their rates in August and some hotels raise their rates beginning in mid-November. Low season is June through mid-November.

BEACHES, WATER SPORTS & OTHER ATTRACTIONS

THE BEACHES   The sand on Isla's beaches is the same beautiful white powdery stuff seen in Cancún and the rest of the coast. The most popular beach in town used to be called Playa Cocoteros (Coco for short). Then, in 1988, Hurricane Gilbert de-stroyed the coconut palms on the beach. Gradually, the name has been changed to **Playa Norte,** referring to the long stretch of beach that extends around the north-ern tip of the island, to your left as you get off the boat. New palms are beginning to sprout all over Playa Norte and it won't be long until it will be deserving of its previous name. The beach is easily reached on foot from the ferry and from all down-town hotels. Water-sports equipment, beach umbrellas, and lounge chairs are avail-able for rent. The latter go for $1.75 to $2.25 per day. Those in front of restaurants usually cost nothing if you use the restaurant as your headquarters for drinks and food.

   Garrafón National Park is best known as a snorkeling area, but there is a nice stretch of beach on either side of the park. **Playa Lancheros** is on the Caribbean side of Laguna Makax. Local buses go to Lancheros, then turn inland and return downtown. The beach at Playa Lancheros is nice, but the few restaurants there are high-priced.

WATER SPORTS   Swimming   Wide Playa Norte is the best swimming beach, with Playa Lancheros second. There are no lifeguards on duty on Isla Mujeres, and the system of water-safety flags used in Cancún and Cozumel isn't used here. Be very careful!

Snorkeling   By far the most popular place to snorkel is **Garrafón National Park,** at the southern end of the island, where you'll see numerous schools of colorful fish. The well-equipped park has beach chairs, changing rooms, lockers, showers, and a snack bar. Taxis from the central village cost around $3.50 one way. Admission is $2; lockers rent for $1.50. Also good for snorkeling is the **Manchones reef,** which is just offshore and reached by boat, where a bronze cross was installed in 1994.

Another excellent location is around the lighthouse in the **Bahía de Mujeres** (bay) opposite downtown, where the water is about 6 feet deep. Boatmen will take you for around $10 per person if you have your own snorkeling equipment or $15 more if you use theirs.

Diving   Several dive shops have opened on the island, most offering the same trips. The traditional dive center is **Buzos de México,** on Rueda Medina at Morelos (☎ **987/7-0500**), next to the boat cooperative. Dive instructor Carlos Gutiérrez speaks English, French and Italian and offers certification (five–six days for $300), and resort courses ($80 with three dives), and makes sure all dives are led by certified dive masters. **Bahia Dive Shop,** on Rueda Medina 166 across from the car-ferry dock (☎ and fax **987/7-0340**), is a full-service shop with dive equipment for sale and rent and resort and certification classes. The most popular reefs are Manchones, Banderas, and Cuevones. All 30- to 40-foot dives cost $40 to $70 for a two-tank trip; equipment rental costs $15. Cuevas de los Tiburones (Caves of the Sleeping Sharks) is Isla's most famous dive site and costs $60 to $80 for a two-tank dive at a depth of 70 feet. There are actually two places to see the sleeping sharks at the Cuevas de Tiberones and La Punta. During a storm the arch collapsed that was featured in Jacques Cousteau film showing the sleeping sharks, but the caves are still there. However, your chance of actually seeing sleeping sharks, by the way, is 25 percent to 30 percent, with fewer sharks being present than in the past. The best time to see them is January through March. Other dive sites include a sunken ship 9 kilometers offshore, Banderas between Isla Mujeres and Cancún where there's always a strong current, Tabos reef on the eastern shore, and Manchones 1 kilometer off the southeastern tip of the island where the water is 15 to 35 feet deep. The best season for diving is from June through August, when the water is calm.

Fishing   To arrange a day of fishing, ask at the **Sociedad Cooperativa Turística** (boatmen's cooperative; ☎ **987/7-8500**) or the travel agency mentioned below, under Isla Contoy. The cost can be shared with four to six others and includes lunch and drinks. All year you'll find bonito, mackerel, kingfish, and amberjack. Sailfish and sharks (hammerhead, bull, nurse, lemon, and tiger) are in good supply in April and May. In winter, larger grouper and jewfish are prevalent. Four hours of fishing close to shore costs around $100, with eight hours farther out for $240. The cooperative is open Monday through Saturday from 8am to 1pm and 5 to 8pm and Sunday from 7:30 to 10am and 6 to 8pm.

OTHER ATTRACTIONS   A Turtle Sanctuary   Easily the most interesting outing on the island is to this reserve dedicated to preservation of Caribbean sea turtles and to educating the public about them. It's on the west side of the island—the best way to get there is by taxi.

As few as 20 years ago fishermen converged on the island nightly from May through September waiting for these monster size turtles to lumber ashore to deposit their flimsy ping-pong-ball-sized eggs. Totally vulnerable once the turtles begin laying their eggs and exhausted when they finish, the turtles were easily captured and slaughtered for their highly prized meat, shell, and eggs. Then a concerned fisherman, Gonzalez Cahle Maldonado, began convincing fishermen to spare at least the eggs, which he protected. It was a start. Following his lead, the Fishing Secretariat founded this **Centro de Investigaciones** 10 years ago; it's funded by both the government and private donations. Since then at least 28,000 turtles have been released, and every year local school children participate in the event, thus planting the notion of protecting the turtles within a new generation of islanders.

Six different species of sea turtle nest on Isla Mujeres. An adult green turtle, the most abundant species, measures 4 to 5 feet in length and can weigh as much as 450 pounds when grown. At the center, visitors walk through the indoor and outdoor turtle pool areas, watching the creatures paddling around. The turtles are separated by age, from newly hatched up to one year. Besides protecting the turtles that nest on Isla Mujeres of their own accord, the program also calls for capturing the turtles at sea and bringing them to enclosed compounds to mate and later to be freed to nest on Isla Mujeres. They are tagged and then released. While in the care of the center these guests receive a high protein diet and reportedly grow faster than in the wild. People who come here usually end up staying at least an hour, especially if they opt for the guided tour, which enhances a visit. The permanent shelter has large wall paintings of all the sea turtles of the area. Admission is $1; the shelter is open daily from 9am to 5pm.

A Maya Ruin   Just beyond the lighthouse, at the southern end of the island, is a pile of stones that formed a small Maya pyramid before Hurricane Gilbert struck. Believed to have been an observatory built to the moon goddess Ixchel, now it's reduced to a rocky heap. However, the location, on a lofty bluff overlooking the sea, is still worth seeing. If you're at Garrafón National Park and want to walk, it's not too far. Turn right from Garrafón. When you see the lighthouse, turn toward it down the rocky path.

A Pirate's Fortress   The Fortress of Mundaca is about 2 miles in the same direction as Garrafón, about half a mile to the left. The fortress was built by the pirate Mundaca Marecheaga, who in the early 19th century arrived at Isla Mujeres and proceeded to set up a blissful paradise in a pretty, shady spot while making money from selling slaves to Cuba and Belize.

A Visit To Isla Contoy   If at all possible, plan to visit this pristine uninhabited island, 19 miles by boat from Isla Mujeres, that was set aside as a national wildlife reserve in 1981. The oddly shaped 3.8-mile-long island is covered in lush vegetation and harbors 70 species of birds as well as a host of marine and animal life. Bird species that nest on the island include pelicans, brown boobies, frigates, egrets, terns, and cormorants. Flocks of flamingos arrive in April. June, July, and August are good months to spot turtles that bury their eggs in the sand at night. Most excursions troll for fish (which will be your lunch), anchor en route for a snorkeling expedition, and skirt the island at a leisurely pace for close viewing of the birds without disturbing the habitat, then pull ashore. While the captain prepares lunch visitors can swim, sun, follow the nature trails, and visit the fine nature museum. For a while the island was closed to visitors, but it's reopened now. The trip from Isla Mujeres takes a minimum of $1^1/2$ hours one way, more if the waves are choppy. Because of the tight-knit boatmen's cooperative, prices for this excursion are the same everywhere—$50. You can buy a ticket at the **Sociedad Cooperativa Turística** (☎ 987/7-0274) on Avenida Rueda Medina, next to Mexico Divers and Las Brisas restaurant, or at one of several travel agencies, such as **La Isleña,** on Morelos between Medina and Juárez (☎ 987/7-0578). La Isleña is open daily from 7am to 9pm and is a good source for tourist information. Contoy trips leave at 8:30am and return around 4pm.

Three types of boats go to Contoy. Small boats have one motor and seat eight or nine people. Medium-size boats have two motors and hold 10. Large boats have a toilet and hold 16. Most boats have a sun cover. The first two types are being phased out in favor of the larger, better boats. Boat captains should respect the cooperative's regulations regarding capacity and should have enough life jackets to go around. Snorkeling equipment is usually included in the price, but double-check that before heading out. I highly recommend the services of English-speaking boat owner **Ricardo Gaitan** (☎ 987/7-0434) who has two boats—the *Afroditi,* a 30-foot speedboat holding up to 15 people, and the 37-foot trimaran *Pelicano,* good for overnight excursions. It sleeps up to six people or carries 15 passengers for day-trips. Call him, or write to him directly at: P.O. Box 42, 77400 Isla Mujeres, Q. Roo.

SHOPPING   Shopping is a casual activity here. The few glittery, sleek shops mostly sell fine jewelry. Otherwise you are bombarded by shop owners (especially on Hidalgo) selling Saltillo rugs, onyx, silver, Guatemalan clothing, blown glassware, masks, folk art, beach paraphernalia, and T-shirts in abundance. Prices are also lower than in Cancún or Cozumel, but with the eager sellers bargaining is necessary to achieve a satisfactory price. One store stands out from the rest: **La Loma,** Guerrero 6 (☎ 987/7-0223), stocks a great variety of good folk art, including Huichol yarn "paintings," masks, silver chains and coins, a good selection of textiles, Oaxacan wood carvings, Olinalá lacquer objects, and colorful clay candelabras from Izúcar de Matamoros. You'll see it opposite the left side of the church beside La Peña restaurant, and almost next to the Hotel Perla del Caribe II. It's open Monday through Saturday from 10am to 3pm and 5 to 8pm.

WHERE TO STAY

There are plenty of hotels in all price ranges on Isla Mujeres. Rates are at their peak during high season, which is the most expensive and most crowded time to go. Elizabeth Wenger of Four Seasons Travel in Montello, WI (☎ 800/552-4550) specializes in Mexico travel and especially books a lot of hotels in Isla Mujeres. Her service is invaluable in high season when hotel occupancy is high.

DOUBLES FOR LESS THAN $15

Autel Carmelena. Guerrero 4, 77400 Isla Mujeres, Q. Roo. ☎ 987/7-0005. 18rms. FAN. $7–$10 single; $10–$13.50 double.

With so few cars in Isla, it's odd to see a motel but not odd that no cars are parked here since so few tourists bring a vehicle. Nevertheless there's plenty of room to park in front of the two tiers of coral- and white-colored rooms all facing the lot. Rooms, which have windows facing the common walkway and parking lot, are plain but clean, with tile floors, striped cotton bedspreads, desks, and small bathrooms. Only two rooms have air conditioning, and the highest prices are for these. Bike rentals can be arranged at the reception desk; you can also order roast chicken between 11am and 3:30pm (another of the owner's interests). It's between Madero and Abasolo.

Hotel Caribe Maya. Av. Madero 9, 77400 Isla Mujeres, Q. Roo. ☎ **986/1-0523.** 26 rms (all with bath). A/C or FAN. $11–$18 single or double.

The rooms in this basic three-story hotel have green-tile floors, nylon ruffled bedspreads, reading lights over the beds, showers, and furniture that may have seen service in some older and long-gone establishment. Upstairs rooms are brighter, and higher prices are for the seven rooms with air conditioning. To get here from the main pier, turn left one block, then go right for 1 1/2 blocks; it's between Guerrero and Hidalgo.

Hotel María José. Avs. Madero and Rueda Medina, 77400 Isla Mujeres, Q. Roo. ☎ **987/ 7-0244** or 987/7-0245. 15 rms (all with bath). FAN. High season, $10 single or double.

Near the ferry dock, this three-story hotel is a good budget deal. Rooms are bright, cheery, clean, and comfortable. Only triple rooms have balconies overlooking the street. Incredibly (considering the already low price), they offer a discount for stays of three or more days. The busy long-distance telephone office is in the lobby. To find it from the main pier, turn left on the Malecón, walk one block to a hot-pink arch, and turn right; the hotel is on your left.

Hotel Vistamar. Av. Rueda Medina, 77400 Isla Mujeres, Q. Roo. ☎ **987/7-0209.** 36 rooms (all with bath). A/C or FAN. High season, $9–$15 single; $12–$15 double. Low season, $7–$10 single; $9–$13.50 double.

The name means "sea view," which is indeed what you get if you select a room facing the Malecón. Other rooms have interior windows without views. All units have green-tile floors and ruffled bedspreads and are extremely simple but well kept. Of course, rooms with air-conditioning command the highest prices. The hotel is across from a nice stretch of beach and shoreline, and Playa Norte is almost around the corner. The hotel is on the Malecón, between Abasolo and Matamoros, 1 1/2 blocks to the left of the ferry pier.

Poc-Na. Calle Matamoros 15, 77400 Isla Mujeres, Q. Roo. ☎ **987/7-0090.** Fax 987/7-0059. 4 bunk rms, 3 hammock rms, 3 private rms (none with bath). FAN. Rates: $4 bunk; $3 hammock; private room $7–$10; Towels 35¢ extra; breakfast $1.50–$2.50; lunch 75¢–$1.75; dinner or pizza $1.75–$4.50.

The Poc-Na claims to be "a basic clean place to stay at the lowest price possible"— and it is. Deposits of your passport or ID are necessary for all rentals. The communal sleeping rooms are arranged around a central palapa-shaded dining area with picnic tables. Meals are served cafeteria-style from a small kitchen. Conveniently located, the hotel is only a short walk from Playa Norte. It's at the end of Calle Matamoros, near the market.

Posada San Jorge. Av. Juárez 29A, 77400 Isla Mujeres, Q. Roo. ☎ **987/7-0155.** 16 rms. FAN. High season $11.50 single; $14.75 double. Low season $11.50 single or double (including continental breakfast).

The two-story (no elevator) San Jorge got a facelift in 1995 that puts it back into the acceptable category again. New paint, mattresses, and bath fixtures have revitalized the hotel, which had deteriorated grimly from lack of care. Most rooms have two double beds, and all have green tile floors, overbed reading lights, and windows opening to the hall. A refrigerator in the lobby is filled with soft drinks for sale to guests, and there's a breezy balcony on the second floor overlooking Juárez. The ambitious plans for the future call for a TV and small refrigerator in each room, a bar in a room off the lobby, and continuation of the small restaurant across the street. Prices will be higher for rooms with TV and air conditioning. The hotel is located between Matamoros and López Mateos.

DOUBLES FOR LESS THAN $40

Hotel Belmar. Av. Hidalgo 110, 74000 Isla Mujeres, Q. Roo. ☎ **987/7-0430.** Fax 987/7-0429. 11 rms (all with bath). A/C FAN TV TEL. High season, $30 single; $35 double. Low season, $23 single; $27 double.

Situated above Pizza Rolandi (consider the restaurant noise), this hotel is run by the same people who serve up those wood-oven pizzas. Each of the simple but stylish rooms comes with two twin or double beds and handsome tile accents. Prices are high for no views, but the rooms are very pleasant, and a satellite dish brings in U.S. channels. The hotel is between Madero and Abasolo, 3¹/₂ blocks from the passenger ferry pier.

✪ **Hotel D'Gomar.** Rueda Medina 50, 77400 Isla Mujeres, Q. Roo. ☎ **987/7-0540.** 16 rms A/C or FAN. High season, $23–$27 single or double. Low season, $14–$17 single or double.

You can hardly beat this hotel for comfort at reasonable prices. Rooms, in rattan furniture, all have two double beds, pink walls and drapes, and a wall of windows with great breezes and picture views. The higher prices are for air conditioning, which is hardly needed with fantastic breezes and ceiling fans. The manager Manuel Serano says "We make friends of all our clients," and indeed I think he does. The only drawback is that there are five stories of rooms and no elevator. But it's conveniently located catercorner (look right) from the ferry pier, and the rooftop views can't be beat anywhere on the island. The name of the hotel is the most visible sign on the "skyline."

✪ **Hotel Francis Arlene.** Guerrero 7, 77400 Isla Mujeres, Q. Roo. ☎ and fax **987/7-0310,** in Cancún 98/84-3302. 17 rms (all with bath). A/C or FAN. High season, $15–$27 single; $20–$27 double. Low season, $12–$15 single; $18–$20 double.

The Magaña family operates this neat little two-story inn behind the family home, which is built around a small shady courtyard. You'll notice the tidy cream-and-white facade of the building from the street. Rooms are clean and comfortable, with tile floors and all-tile baths, and soap and towels laid out on your bed. Each downstairs room has a refrigerator and stove; each upstairs room comes with a refrigerator and toaster. All have either a balcony or a patio. Rates were substantially better if quoted in pesos when I checked and are reflected above. In dollars they are 15% to 20% higher. It's 5¹/₂ blocks inland from the ferry pier, between Abasolo and Matamoros.

WORTH A SPLURGE

✪ **Hotel Na Balam.** Zacil Ha 118, 77400 Isla Mujeres, Q. Roo. ☎ **987/7-0279.** Fax 987/7-0446. 31 suites (all with bath). A/C FAN. High season, $100–$125 suite for one or two. Low season, $80–$115 suite for one or two. Free parking; unguarded.

This two-story hotel near the end of Norte Beach is my favorite of the island's lodgings, with its comfortable rooms on a quiet, ideally located portion of the beach. It seems to get better each year. Suites are in three sections, with some facing the beach, and others across the street in a garden setting where there's a swimming pool. All rooms have either a patio or balcony. Each nicely furnished and spacious suite contains two double beds, a seating area, and folk-art decorations. Though other rooms are newer, my preference is the older section with a bottom floor patio facing the peaceful palm-filled sandy inner yard and Norte beach. Tuesday through Thursday yoga lessons are offered; ask about the time and price. The restaurant, Zacil-Ha, is one of the island's most popular (see "Where To Eat," below). To find it from the pier, walk five blocks to López Mateos; turn right and walk four blocks to Lazo (the last street). Turn left and walk to the sandy road parallel to the beach and turn right. The hotel is half a block farther.

✪ **Hotel Posada del Mar.** Av. Rueda Medina 15, 77400 Isla Mujeres, Q. Roo. ☎ **987/ 7-0300,** or 800-221-6509 in the U.S. Fax 987/7-0266. 40 rms (all with bath). A/C TEL. $40–$55 single; $45–$65 double. (Ask about specials.)

Attractively furnished, quiet, and comfortable, this long-established hotel faces the water and a wide beach three blocks north of the ferry pier. The very spacious rooms, all with a fresh coat of white paint, are in a large garden palm grove in either a three-story building or in one-story bungalow units. For the spacious quality of the rooms and the location, this is among the best buys on the island. A wide, seldom-used but appealing stretch of Playa Norte is across the street. An extremely appealing casual palapa-style bar and a lovely pool are set on the back lawn, and the popular restaurant Pinguino (see "Where To Eat," below) is by the sidewalk at the front of the property. Ask about specials—four nights for the price of three and seven nights for the price of five. From the pier, go left for four blocks; the hotel is on the right.

WHERE TO EAT

The **Municipal Market,** next door to the telegraph office and post office on Avenida Guerrero, has several little cookshops operated by obliging and hard-working señoras and enjoyed by numbers of tourists. On Sunday, Nacho Beh, El Rey del Taco (The King of the Taco), prepares sublime cochinita pibil tacos. Get there early.

At the **Panadería La Reyna,** at Madero and Juárez, you can pick up inexpensive sweet bread, muffins, cookies, and yogurt. It's open Monday through Saturday from 7am to 9:30pm.

As in the rest of Mexico a **cocina economica** restaurant literally means "economic kitchen." Usually aimed at the local population, these are almost universally great places to find good food at rock bottom prices. That's especially so on Isla Mujeres, where you'll find several.

MEALS FOR LESS THAN $5

✪ **Chen Huaye.** Bravo 6. No phone. Breakfast $1.25–$2; appetizers $1–$1.50; main courses $1.25–$4.25. Thurs–Tues 9am–11pm. MEXICAN/HOME COOKING.

The Juanito Tago Trego family owns this large lunchroom where tourists and locals find a variety of pleasing dishes at equally pleasing prices. Light meals include empanadas, Yucatecan salubites, panucos, and quesadillas. The tamal costado, a tamal stuffed with hunks of chicken and baked in a banana leaf, is a daily special. Main courses might include breaded pork chops, or chicken in adobado or fried. The name, by the way, is Maya for "only here." It's between Guerrero and Juárez; you'll spot it by the wagon wheel in front.

⑤ **Cocina Economica Carmelita.** Calle Juárez 14. ☎ **987/7-0136.** Meal of the day $3. Daily 12:30–5pm. MEXICAN/HOME COOKING.

Few tourists find their way to this tiny restaurant, open only for lunch. But locals know they can get a filling, inexpensive home-cooked meal prepared by Carmelita in the back kitchen and served by her husband at the three cloth-covered tables in the front room of their home. Two or three comida corridas are available each day and are served until they run out. They begin with black bean soup and include a fruit water drink. If offered, try the *Brazo de la Reyna*, which is a large, sliced, very flavorful, and filling Maya tamal stuffed with hard-boiled eggs and spices. If it's not on the menu, make a request and see if it can be prepared during your stay. Other selections include paella or *cochinita pibil*, and Sunday is *pozole* day. It's two blocks from the passenger ferry pier, between Bravo and Allende.

La Lomita II. Juarez s/n. No phone. Breakfast $1.50–$1.75; main courses $2.50–$5; comida corrida $2.25. Mon–Sat 9:30am–11pm. MEXICAN.

Narrow and plain, this is a tiny branch of the larger mother restaurant, La Lomita I, on Juárez (the larger restaurant was closed each time I checked, but it's near Cocina Economica Carmelita). This one offers the same menu as the original. The comida corrida starts with soup, then beans or rice, then the main course with a vegetable. Drinks are extra. It's between Madero and Morelos.

☉ Cocina Economica. Juárez 5. ☎ **987/7-0298.** Comida corrida $2.50. Mon–Sat 11am–6pm. HOME COOKING.

Step into another living room just off the street, and enter the homey world of Daniel Canol and his wife Susana Martinez, who is master of the cocina. It's in one of the island's original wood-frame houses with Cuban-style mosaic tile on the floor. It's a very informal place with a few plastic-draped tables and walls with religious memorabilia. The daily menu comes with rice and beans or soup, and a main course that might be pollo adobado, fried fish, milanesa, or a Yucatecan flavored pork chop seasoned with achiote. There's no sign, but you'll see a handwritten paper menu tacked to the door, and it's next to La Lomita II, between Madero and Morelos.

MEALS FOR LESS THAN $10

☉ Cafecito. Calle Juárez. ☎ **987/7-0438.** Coffee drinks $1–$3; crêpes $1.25–$3.25; breakfast $2–$3; main courses $4.25–$6.25. Mon–Wed and Fri–Sat 8am–noon, and 6–10pm; Thurs and Sun 8am–noon. CRÊPES/ICE CREAM/COFFEES/FRUIT DRINKS.

Sabina and Luis Rivera own this cute, Caribbean-blue corner restaurant, where you can begin the day with flavorful coffee and a croissant and cream cheese or end it with a hot fudge sundae. Terrific crêpes are served with yogurt, ice cream, fresh fruit, or chocolate sauces, as well as ham and cheese. The two-page ice cream menu satisfies most any craving—even one for waffles with ice cream and fruit. The three-course fixed-price dinner starts with soup, then a main course such as fish or curried shrimp with rice and salad, followed by dessert. It's four blocks from the pier at the corner of Juárez and Matamoros.

Las Palapas Chimbo's. Norte Beach. No phone. Breakfast $1.85–$3; sandwiches and fruit $2–$3.50; seafood $3.80–$5.50. Daily 8am–6pm. SEAFOOD.

If you're looking for a beachside palapa-covered restaurant where you can wiggle your toes in the sand while scarfing down fresh seafood, this is the best of them. Locals recommend it as their favorite on Norte Beach. Try the delicious fried fish (a whole one), which comes with rice, beans, and tortillas. You'll notice the bandstand and dance floor that's been added to the middle of the restaurant, and especially the sex-hunk posters all over the ceiling—that is when you aren't gazing at the beach and Caribbean (see "Isla Mujeres After Dark" below for details). To find it from the pier, walk left to the end of the Malecón, then right onto the Playa Norte beach; it's about half a block on the right.

☉ Pinguino. In the Hotel Posada del Mar, Av. Rueda Medina 15. ☎ **987/7-0300.** Breakfast $1.75–$3; main dishes $3.50–$5.75; daily special $5.75. Daily 7am–9pm; bar open to midnight. MEXICAN/SEAFOOD.

The best seats on the waterfront are on the deck of this restaurant/bar, especially in late evening when islanders and tourists arrive to dance and party. This is the place to splurge on lobster—though you'll pay dearly, you'll get a beautifully presented, large, sublimely fresh lobster tail with a choice of butter, garlic, and secret sauces. Breakfasts include fresh fruit, yogurt, and granola or sizable platters of eggs, served with homemade wheat bread. At night it's one of "the" places to be. Pinguino is in front of the hotel, three blocks west of the ferry pier.

Pizza Rolandi. Av. Hidalgo. ☎ **987/7-0429.** Main courses $5.25–$9; pizza $4.75–$8.25. Daily 1–11pm. ITALIAN.

Pizza Rolandi, the chain that saves the day with dependably good, reasonably priced food in otherwise expensive resorts, comes through in Isla Mujeres as well. The casual dining room, in an open courtyard of the Hotel Belmar, is the scene for consumption of plate-size pizzas, pastas, and calzones cooked in a wood oven. There's also a more expensive "cuisine" menu with fish, beef, and chicken dishes. Guitarists often perform in the evenings. It's 3¹/₂ blocks inland from the pier, between Madero and Abasolo.

✪ **Zacil-Ha.** At the Hotel Na Balam, Norte Beach. ☎ **987/7-0279.** Breakfast $3.50–$4.50; main courses $6–$9. Daily 7:30am–10:30am, 12:30–3:30pm, and 7–10pm. INTERNATIONAL.

At this restaurant you can enjoy some of the island's best food while sitting among the palms and gardens at tables on the sand. The serene environment is enhanced by the food—terrific pasta with garlic, shrimp in tequila sauce, fajitas, seafood pasta, and delicious mole enchiladas. Main courses come with vegetable and rice. Between the set hours for meals you can have all sorts of enticing food such as blender vegetable and fruit drinks, tacos, sandwiches, ceviche, and terrific nachos. It's likely you'll stake this place out for several meals before you leave. It's at the end of Playa Norte and almost at the end of Calle Zacil-Ha.

ISLA MUJERES AFTER DARK

Those in a party mood by day's end might want to start out at the beach bar of the **Hotel Na Balam** on Playa Norte, which hosts a crowd until around midnight. On Saturday and Sunday there's live music here between 4 and 7pm. **Las Palapas Chimbo's** restaurant on the beach becomes a jivin' dance joint with a live band from 9pm until . . . Farther along the same stretch of beach, **Buho's,** the restaurant/beach bar of the Posada María del Mar, was a popular, low-key hangout when I was there. **Pinguino's** in the Hotel Posada del Mar has two places to be—the restaurant/bar, where the manager, Miguel, whips up some potent concoctions at the bar and the band plays nightly during high season from 9pm to midnight, and the more tranquil but totally delightful poolside bar with its swings at the bar under a giant palapa.

2 Cozumel

44 miles S of Cancún

Cozumel, 12 miles east of Playa del Carmen, comes from the Maya word *Cuzamil,* meaning "land of the swallows." It's Mexico's largest Caribbean island, 28 miles long and 11 miles wide, but it's only 3% developed, leaving vast stretches of jungle and uninhabited shoreline. The only town is San Miguel de Cozumel, usually called just San Miguel.

Today Cozumel is one of the Yucatán's top resort destinations as well as the country's scuba-diving capital. It's also home to two species of birds that are found nowhere else—the Cozumel vireo and the Cozumel thrasher. If Cancún is the jet-set's port of call and Isla Mujeres is the poor man's Cancún, Cozumel is a little bit of both. More remote than the other two, this island (pop. 60,000) is a place where people come to get away from the day-tripping atmosphere of Isla Mujeres or the megadevelopment of Cancún.

All the necessaries for a good vacation are here: excellent snorkeling and scuba places, sailing and water sports, expensive resorts and modest hotels, elegant restaurants and taco shops, even a Maya ruin or two. If, after a while, you do get restless, the ancient Maya city of Tulum, the lagoons of Xel-Ha and Xcaret, or the nearby village of Playa del Carmen provide convenient and interesting excursions.

During pre-Hispanic times the island was one of three important ceremonial centers (Izamal and Chichén-Itzá were the other two). Salt and honey, trade products produced on the island, further linked Cuzamil with the mainland; they were brought ashore at the ruins we know today as Tulum. The site was occupied when Hernán Cortés landed here in 1519. Before his own boat docked, Cortés's men sacked the town and took the chief's wife and children captive. According to Bernal Díaz del Castillo's account, everything was returned. Diego de Landa's account says Cortés converted the Indians and replaced their sacred Maya figures with a cross and a statue of Mary in the main temple at Cozumel. After the Spanish Conquest, the island was an important port; however, diseases brought by the foreigners decimated the population, and by 1570 it was almost uninhabited.

The inhabitants returned later, but the War of the Castes in the 1800s severely curtailed Cozumel's trade. Cozumel continued on its economic roller coaster, and after the Caste War it again took its place as a commercial seaport. Merchants exported henequen, coconuts, sugarcane, bananas, chicle, pineapple, honey, and wood products, though in 1955 Hurricane Janet all but demolished the coconut palm plantations. In the mid-1950s Cozumel's fame as a diving destination began to grow, and real development of the island as the site for a vacation resort evolved along with Cancún beginning in the mid-1970s.

ESSENTIALS

GETTING THERE & DEPARTING   By Plane   Aero Cozumel, a Mexicana affiliate, has numerous flights to and from Cancún and Mérida. **Mexicana** flies from Mexico City, and Continental arrives from Houston. **Taesa** flies from Cancún, Chetumal, and Mérida.

Here are some telephone numbers for confirming departures to and from Cozumel: Aero Cozumel (☎ **998/2-3456** or 988/4-2002 in Cancún; fax 987/2-0877 in Cozumel); Continental (☎ **987/2-0847** in Cozumel); Mexicana (☎ **987/2-0157** or 987/2-2945 at the airport; fax 987/2-2945); and Taesa (☎ **987/2-4420**).

You can't get a colectivo van from town to the airport, but taxis go to the airport for $5 to $7.

By Ferry   Passenger ferries to Cozumel depart from Playa del Carmen on the mainland; there is also a car ferry from Puerto Morelos. You can catch a bus to Playa del Carmen from Cancún.

The Car Ferry from Puerto Morelos: The first thing to know is that you're better off without a car in Cozumel; parking is difficult. A solution is to drive to Playa del Carmen, find a reliable place to leave your car, and take the passenger ferry. If you do want to take your car over, the terminus in Puerto Morelos (☎ **987/1-0008**), the largest establishment in town, is very easy to find. The car-ferry schedule is complicated and may change, so double-check it before arriving in Puerto Morelos. On Monday, the ferry leaves at 7pm; on Tuesday at 11am; on Wednesday through Sunday at 6am. The crossing takes approximately three hours.

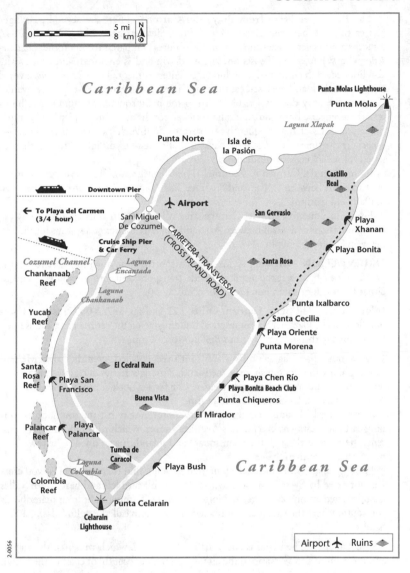

Cargo takes precedence over cars. Officials suggest that camper drivers stay overnight in the parking lot to be first in line for tickets. In any case, *always arrive at least three hours in advance of the ferry's departure to purchase a ticket and to get in line.*

Since passenger-boat service between Playa del Carmen and Cozumel is quite frequent now, I don't recommend that foot passengers bother with this boat.

When returning to Puerto Morelos from Cozumel, the ferry departs from the international cruise-ship pier daily. Get in line about three hours before departure, and double-check the schedule by calling **987/2-0950.** The fare is $35 for a car and $6 per passenger.

The Passenger Ferry from Playa del Carmen: There are several passenger ferries running between Cozumel and Playa del Carmen. The WJ *México III*, a modern water jet, makes the trip in 45 minutes compared to 60 on the *Cozumeleño*. The WJ *México III* costs $8.25 round-trip and is enclosed, and usually air-conditioned, with cushioned seats and video entertainment. The *Cozumeleño*, a vessel with a roof deck and enclosed cabin, runs the route for $5 round-trip. In Playa del Carmen, the ferry dock is 1½ blocks from the main square and from where buses let off passengers. Both companies have ticket booths at the main pier in Cozumel. Since schedules change frequently, be sure to double-check them at the docks—especially the time of the last ferry back, if that's the one you intend to use. Be prepared for seasickness on windy days.

From Playa del Carmen to Cozumel, The WJ *Mexico III* runs every hour or every two hours between 5:30am and 8:45pm. The *Cozumeleño* runs five times between 9:30am and 6:30pm.

From Cozumel to Playa del Carmen, the WJ *Mexico III* runs approximately every hour or hour and a half between 4am and 8pm. The *Cozumeleño* runs four times, between 8am and 5:30pm.

ORIENTATION **Arriving** Cozumel's airport is near downtown. Aero Transportes colectivo vans at the airport provide transportation into town for $3 and to either the north or south hotel zone for $5 to $7.50.

Information The **State Tourism Office** (☎ and fax **987/2-0972**) is on the second floor of the Plaza del Sol commercial building facing the central plaza and is open from Monday through Friday from 8:30am to 2:30pm.

City Layout San Miguel's main waterfront street is called **Avenida Rafael Melgar,** running along the western shore of the island. Passenger ferries dock right in the center, opposite the main plaza and Melgar. Car-ferries dock south of town near the hotels Sol Caribe, La Ceiba, and Fiesta Inn.

The town is laid out on a grid, with avenidas running north and south, calles running east and west. The exception is **Avenida Juárez,** which runs right from the passenger-ferry dock through the main square and inland. Juárez divides the town into northern and southern halves.

Heading inland from the dock along Juárez, you'll find that the avenidas you cross are numbered by fives: 5a av., 10a av., 15a av. If you turn left and head north, calles are numbered evenly: 2a Norte, 4a Norte, 6a Norte. Turning right from Juárez heads you south, where the streets are numbered: 1a Sur (also called Adolfo Salas), 3a Sur, 5a Sur.

Island Layout The island is cut in half by one road, which runs past the airport and the ruins of San Gervasio to the almost uninhabited southern coast of the island. The northern part of the island has no paved roads. It's scattered with small badly ruined Maya sites, from the age when "Cuzamil" was a land sacred to the moon goddess Ixchel. San Gervasio is accessible by motor scooter and car.

Most inexpensive hotels are in the town of San Miguel. Moderate to expensive accommodations are north and south of town. Many cater to divers. Beyond the hotels to the south is **Chankanaab National Park,** centered on the beautiful lagoon of the same name. Beyond Chankanaab are **Playa Palancar** and, offshore, the **Palancar Reef** (arrecife). At the southern tip of the island are **Punta Celarain** and the lighthouse.

The eastern, seaward shore of the island is mostly surf beach, beautiful for walking but dangerous for swimming.

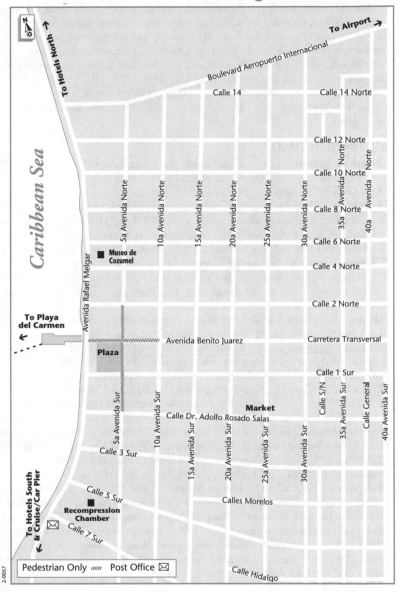

Getting Around You can walk to most destinations in town. The trip from town to the Chankanaab Lagoon by taxi costs around $4. For a day at the beach, finding some like-minded fellow travelers and sharing the cost of a cab is the most economical way to go. Taxis should charge no more than $5 from the town center to the farthest hotels.

Car rentals are as expensive here as in other parts of Mexico. Open-top jeeps are popular for rental, but they roll over easily and many tourists have been injured or killed using them. See "By Car" under "Getting Around" in Chapter 2 for specifics.

Moped rentals are all over the village and cost about $25 for 24 hours, but terms and prices vary. Carefully inspect the actual moped you'll be renting to see that all the gizmos are in good shape: horn, light, starter, seat, mirror. And be sure to note all damage to the moped on the rental agreement. Most important, read the fine print on the back of the rental agreement, which states that you are not insured, are responsible for paying any damage to the bike (or for all of it if it's stolen or demolished), and must stay on paved roads. It's illegal to ride a moped without a helmet. *Important Note:* North/south streets have the right of way, and these drivers don't slow down.

FAST FACTS: COZUMEL

American Express   The local representative is Fiesta Cozumel, Calle 11 no. 598 (☎ **987/2-0725** or 987/2-0433; fax 987/2-1044).

Area Code   The telephone area code is 987.

Bookstore   The Agencia de Publicaciones Gracia, next to the Farmacia Joaquin, is a small store facing the zócalo at Avenida 5 (☎ **987/2-0031**), with a good selection of English-language novels and magazines. It's open Monday through Saturday from 8am to 10pm and Sunday from 10am to 2pm and 6 to 10pm.

Climate   From October through December there can be strong winds all over the Yucatán, as well as some rain. In Cozumel, wind conditions in November and December can make diving dangerous. May through September is the rainy season.

Diving   If you intend to dive, remember to bring proof of your diver's certification. Underwater currents can be very strong here, so be cautious.

Parking   Since many of the downtown hotels are on streets closed to traffic, parking space and parking lots are scarce. There is a public lot, Estacionamiento Cozumel, behind the church on Avenida 10 Sur. Parking is 50¢ per hour or $5 overnight.

Post Office   The post office (correo) is on Avenida Rafael Melgar at Calle 7 Sur, at the southern edge of town; it's open Monday through Friday from 9am to 6pm and Saturday from 9am to noon.

Recompression Chamber   The recompression chamber (*cámara de recompreción*) is on Calle 5 Sur one block off Melgar between Melgar and Avenida 5 Sur (☎ **987/ 2-2387;** fax 987/2-1430). Normal hours are 8am to 1pm and 4 to 8pm.

Seasons   High season is Christmas through Easter, and in August.

Telephone   The **Calling Station** on Melgar at Calle 3 Sur is a full-service phone center with air-conditioned booths, no surcharges, fax service, and a bulletin board where you can leave messages for friends. It's open Monday through Saturday from 8am to 11pm and Sunday from 9am to 10pm. You can also make collect calls from the Sports Page restaurant. Besides these, long-distance telephones are on Salas between Avenidas 5 Sur and 10 Sur on the exterior of the telephone building. Use a credit card to get an American operator; or make it collect; or have a pile of coins ready to feed the phone.

DIVING, EXPLORING THE ISLAND & OTHER THINGS TO DO

For **diving** and **snorkeling** it's best to go directly to the recommended shops below. For **island tours, ruins tours** on and off the island, **glass-bottom boat tours, fiesta nights, fishing,** and other activities I can recommend the travel agency **InterMar Cozumel Viajes,** Calle 4 Norte 101-B (☎ **987/2-1098;** fax 987/2-0895). The office is close to the main plaza between Ave 5 and 10 Norte. But many of these you can do on your own without purchasing a tour.

A FESTIVAL   Carnaval/Mardi Gras is Cozumel's most colorful fiesta. It begins the Thursday before Ash Wednesday with daytime street dancing and nighttime parades on Thursday, Saturday, and Monday (the best).

FUN ON & UNDER THE WATER   Snorkeling   Anyone who can swim can go snorkeling. Rental of the snorkel (breathing pipe), goggles, and flippers should cost only about $4 for half a day; a two-hour snorkeling trip costs $15. The brilliantly colored tropical fish provide a dazzling show. Chankanaab Park is one of the best places to go on your own for an abundant fish show.

Agency arranged **snorkeling excursions** cost around $40 for a 10am to 3pm trip that includes snorkeling at three different reefs, lunch, beer, and soft drinks. Two-hour snorkeling trips through the dive shops recommended below cost $15 and usually leave around 2:30pm.

Scuba Diving   Cozumel is Mexico's dive capital. Various establishments on the island rent scuba gear—tanks, regulator with pressure gauge, buoyancy compensator, weight belts, mask, snorkel, and fins. Many will also arrange a half-day expedition in a boat, complete with lunch, for a set price—usually around $40. Sign up the day before if you're interested. A two-tank morning dive costs around $50; some shops are now offering an additional afternoon one-tank dive for $9 for those who took the morning dives, or $25 for a one-tank dive. However, if you're a dedicated diver, you'll save many dollars by buying a diving package that includes air transportation, hotel, and usually two dives a day. There's a recompression chamber on the island (see "Fast Facts," above).

The underwater wonders of the famous **Palancar Reef** are offshore from the beach of the same name. From the car-ferry south to Punta Celarain are more than 20 miles of offshore reefs. In the famous blue depths, divers find caves and canyons, small and large colorful fish, and an enormous variety of sea coral. The **Santa Rosa Reef** is famous for its depth, sea life, coral, and sponges. **San Francisco Reef,** off the beach by the same name south of town, has a drop-off wall, but it's still fairly shallow and the sea life is fascinating. The **Chankanaab Reef,** where divers are joined by schools of tropical fish, is close to the shore by the national park of the same name. It's shallow and good for novice divers, as is **Paradise Reef** by the La Ceiba hotel. Next after Chankanaab going south on the eastern road, **Yucab Reef** has beautiful coral.

Numerous vessels on the island operate daily diving and snorkeling tours, so if you aren't traveling on a prearranged dive package, the best plan is to shop around and sign up for one of those. Of Cozumel's many dive shops, two are among the top: **Aqua Safari,** in front of the Aqua Safari Inn and next to the Vista del Mar Hotel on Melgar at Avenida 5 (☎ **987/2-0101,** fax 987/2-0661) and in the Hotel Plaza Las Glorias (☎ **987/2-3362** or 987/2-2422), is a PADI five-star instructor center, has full equipment and parts, a good selection of books, and its own pier just across the street. **Dive House,** on the main plaza (☎ **987/2-1953** and fax 987/2-0368), offers PADI, NAUI SSI instruction. Both shops offer morning and night dives, and afternoon snorkeling trips.

You can save money by renting your gear at a beach shop, such as the two mentioned above, and diving from shore. The shops at the Plaza Las Glorias and La Ceiba hotels are good for shore diving—you'll find plenty to see as soon as you enter the water. It costs about $6 to rent one tank and weights.

A new twist in underwater Yucatán is **cenote diving and snorkeling.** The peninsula's underground cenotes (say-*noh*-tehs), or sink holes—which were sacred to the Maya—lead to a vast system of underground caverns, where the gently flowing water is so clear divers appear to be floating on air through caves that look just like those on dry land, complete with stalactites and stalagmites, plus tropical fish, eels, and turtles. The caverns were formed millions of years ago during the last two glacial eras, but only in recent years has this other world been opened to certified divers. The experienced cave diver/owners of **Yucatec Expeditions** (☎ and fax **987/2-4618** or 987/4-7835), offer this unique experience five times weekly from Playa del Carmen (you take the ferry with your gear and they meet you with vans there). Cenotes are 30 to 45 minutes from Playa and a dive in each cenote lasts around 45 minutes. Snorkelers paddle around the cenotes, while divers explore the depths. Dives are within the daylight zone, about 130 feet into the caverns and no more than 60 feet deep. There's plenty of natural light. Company owners Sheila Gracey, German Yañez Mendoza, and Jorge Gonzalez inspect diving credentials carefully and have a list of requirements divers must meet before cave diving is permitted. They also offer the equivalent of a resort course in cave diving and a full cave diving course. A cenote snorkeling trip to two cenotes runs around $65, while a two-cenote dive costs around $120, and a two-cavern dive runs $150.

Windsurfing   One of Mexico's top windsurfing champions, Raul de Lille, offers windsurfing classes and equipment rentals at the beach in front of Sol Cabãas del Caribe, on the north side. For information call **987/2-0017;** fax 987/2-1942.

Boat Trips   Boat trips are another popular pastime at Cozumel. Some excursions include snorkeling and scuba diving or a stop at a beach with lunch. Various types of tours are offered, including rides in **glass-bottom boats** for around $30. These usually start at 9am and end at 1pm and include beer and soft drinks.

Fishing   The best months for fishing are April through September, when the catch will be blue and white marlin, sailfish, tarpon, swordfish, dorado, wahoo, tuna, and red snapper. Fishing costs $450 for six people all day or $76 per person for a half day for four people.

TOURING THE ISLAND   Travel agencies can book you on a group tour of the island for around $35, depending on whether the tour includes lunch and a stop for snorkeling. A taxi driver charges $60 for a four-hour tour. A four-hour horseback riding tour of the island's interior to the ruins and jungle costs around $40; call the InterMar travel agency mentioned above for information.

You can easily rent a motorbike or car for half a day to take you around the southern part of the island (42 miles). North of town, along Avenida Rafael Melgar (which becomes Carretera Pilar), you'll pass a yacht marina and a string of Cozumel's first hotels as well as some new condominiums. A few of the hotels have nice beaches, which you are welcome to use (on Cozumel this public ownership is more important than ever, since beaches are relatively few—most of the island is surrounded by coral reefs). This road ends just past the hotels; you can backtrack to the transversal road that cuts across the island from west (the town side) to east and link up with the eastern highway that brings you back to town.

The more interesting route begins by going south of town on Melgar (which becomes Costera Sur or Carretera a Chankanaab) past the Hotel Barracuda and **Sol Caribe.** After about 3 miles you'll see a sign pointing left down an unpaved road a short distance to the **Rancho San Manuel,** where you can rent horses. There are only seven horses here, but a guide and soft drink are included in the price. Rides cost $20 per hour. It's open daily from 8am to 4pm.

About 5 miles south of town you'll come to the big **Sol Caribe** (which is closed) and La Ceiba hotels and also the car-ferry dock for ferries to Puerto Morelos. Go snorkeling out in the water by the Hotel La Ceiba and you might spot a sunken airplane, put there for an underwater movie. Offshore, from here to the tip of the island at Punta Celarain, 20 miles away, is **Underwater National Park,** so designated to protect the reef from damage by visitors. Dive masters warn not to touch or destroy the underwater growth.

Chankanaab National Park   This lagoon and botanical garden is a mile past the big hotels and 5¹/₂ miles south of town. It has long been famous for the color and variety of its sea life. The intrusion of sightseers began to ruin the marine habitat, so now visitors must swim and snorkel in the open sea, not in the lagoon. The beach is wide and beautiful, with plenty of shady thatched umbrellas to sit under, and the snorkeling is good—lots of colorful fish. Arrive early to stake out a chair and palapa before the cruise-ship visitors arrive. There are restrooms, lockers, a gift shop, several snack huts, a restaurant, and a snorkeling-gear-rental palapa.

Surrounding the lagoon, the botanical garden, with shady paths, has 352 species of tropical and subtropical plants from 22 countries and 451 species from Cozumel. Several Maya structures have been re-created within the gardens to give visitors an idea of Maya life in a jungle setting. There's a small natural-history museum as well. Admission to the park costs $3; it's open daily from 8am to 5pm.

Beaches   After another 10 miles, you'll come to **Playa San Francisco** and, south of it, **Playa Palancar.** Besides the beach at Chankanaab Lagoon, they're the best on Cozumel. Food (usually overpriced) and equipment rentals are available.

The **Playa Bonita Beach Club** near Playa Chiqueros has water-sports and windsurfing equipment rentals. The restaurant is open daily from 10am to 5pm.

Punta Celarain   After Playa San Francisco, you plow through the jungle on a straight road for miles until you're 17¹/₂ miles from town. Finally, though, you emerge near the southern reaches of the island on the east coast. The **lighthouse** you see in the distance is at Punta Celarain, the island's southernmost tip. The sand track is unsuitable for motorbikes, but in a car you can drive to the lighthouse in about 25 minutes.

The Eastern Shore   The road along the east coast of the island is wonderful. There are views of the sea, the rocky shore, and the pounding surf. On the land side are little farms and forests. Exotic birds take flight as you approach, and monstrous (but harmless) iguanas skitter off into the undergrowth.

Most of the east coast is unsafe for swimming because the surf can create a deadly undertow that will pull you far out to sea in a matter of minutes. There are always cars pulled off along the road here, with the occupants spending the day on the beach, but not in the churning waters. Three restaurants catering to tourists are along this part of the coast, complete with sombrero-clad iguanas for a picture companion.

Halfway up the east coast, the paved eastern road meets the paved transversal road (which passes the ruins of San Gervasio) back to town, 9¹/₂ miles away. The east-coast road ends when it turns into the transversal, petering out to a narrow track of sandy road by a nice restaurant in front of the Chen Río beach; vehicles, even motorbikes, will get stuck on the sand road. If you're a birdwatcher, leave your vehicle on the highway here and walk straight down the sandy road. Go slowly and quietly, and at the least you'll spot many herons and egrets in the lagoon on the left that parallels the path. Much farther on are Maya ruins.

Maya Ruins   One of the most popular island excursions is to **San Gervasio** (100 B.C. to A.D. 1600). A road leads there from the airport, or you can continue on the eastern part of the island following the paved transversal road. The worn sign to the ruins is easy to miss, but the turnoff (left) is about halfway between town and the eastern coast. Stop at the entry gate and pay the $1 road-use fee. Go straight ahead over the potholed road to the ruins about 2 miles farther and pay the $3.50 to enter; camera permits cost $4 for each still or video camera you want to bring in. A small tourist center at the entrance has cold drinks and snacks for sale.

When it comes to Cozumel's Maya remains, getting there is most of the fun, and you should do it for the trip, not for the ruins. The buildings, though preserved, are crudely made and would not be much of a tourist attraction if they were not the island's only cleared and accessible ruins. More significant than beautiful, the site was once an important ceremonial center where the Maya gathered, coming from as far away as the mainland. The important deity here was Ixchel, known as the goddess of weaving, women, childbirth, pilgrims, the moon, and medicine. Although you won't see any representations of her at San Gervasio today, Bruce Hunter, in his *Guide to Ancient Maya Ruins*, writes that priests hid behind a large pottery statue of her and became the voice of the goddess speaking to pilgrims and answering their petitions. She was the wife of Itzamná, preeminent among Maya gods.

Tour guides charge $10 for a tour for one to six people, but it's not worth it. Find a copy of the green booklet "San Gervasio," sold at local checkout counters or bookstores, and tour the site on your own. Seeing it takes 30 minutes. Taxi drivers offer a tour to the ruins for about $25; the driver will wait for you outside the ruins.

Parque Arqueológica This park contains reproductions of many of Mexico's important archaeological treasures, including the 4-foot-high Olmec head and the Chaac-Mool seen in Chichén-Itzá. A Maya couple demonstrate the lifestyle of the Maya in a *na,* or thatch-roofed oval home. The park is a nice addition to the island's cultural attractions and is well worth visiting—but slather on the bug repellent before you begin exploring. The park is open daily from 8am to 6pm; admission is $1.50. To get there, turn left on the unmarked road across from the International Pier, off Costera Sur just south of the La Ceiba hotel, then left on Avenida 65 Sur and follow the signs.

A HISTORY MUSEUM The **Museo de la Isla de Cozumel,** on Avenida Melgar between Calles 4 and 6 Norte, is more than just a nice place to spend a rainy hour. On the first floor an excellent exhibit showcases endangered species, the origin of the island, and its present-day topography and plant and animal life, including an explanation of coral formation. Upstairs, showrooms feature the history of the town; artifacts from the island's pre-Hispanic sites; and colonial-era cannons, swords, and ship paraphernalia. It's open daily from 10am to 6pm. Admission is $1.75; guided tours in English are free. There's a rooftop restaurant open long hours.

TRIPS TO THE MAINLAND **Playa del Carmen, Xcaret & Xcalacoco** Going on your own to the nearby seaside village of **Playa del Carmen** and **Xcaret** is as easy as a quick ferry ride from Cozumel. (For ferry information, see "Getting There & Departing," above.) All are covered in detail later in this chapter. Cozumel travel agencies offer an Xcaret tour that includes the ferry fee, transportation to the park, and admission for $45 (only about $6 more than it costs to do the trip on your own).

CHICHÉN-ITZÁ, TULUM & COBÁ Travel agencies can arrange day-trips to the fascinating ruins of **Chichén-Itzá** either by air for around $120, or by bus for $85, Departure times vary depending on which transportation you choose. For an excursion to the ruins of **Tulum,** overlooking the Caribbean, and **Cobá,** in a dense jungle setting, you'll shell out $85, but these ruins are closer, and are a complete architectural contrast to Chichén-Itzá. Such a trip begins at 9am and returns around 6pm.

SHOPPING Shopping has improved beyond the ubiquitous T-shirt shops into expensive resortwear, silver, and better decorative and folk art. Most of the stores are on Avenida Melgar; the best shops for high-quality Mexican folk art are **Los Cinco Soles, Talavera,** and **Playa del Angel.** Prices for serapes, T-shirts, and the like are normally less expensive on the side streets off Melgar.

If you want to pick up some Mexican tapes and CDs, head to **Discoteca Hollywood,** at Juárez 421 (☎ **987/2-4090**); it's open Monday through Saturday from 9am to 10pm. Self-billed as the "Paradise of the Cassette," this store stocks a large selection.

WHERE TO STAY

Cozumel's hotels are in three separate locations: The oldest resorts, most of which are expensive, line beaches and coral and limestone outcroppings north of town; the more budget-oriented inns are in the central village; and other relatively expensive hotels lie both immediately north and south of town. Since tourism to Cozumel has been down, many hoteliers have not raised their prices as dramatically as in the past. Generally speaking, they've been so cautious and fickle that prices may be even lower than the ones quoted here by the time you travel. As an alternative to a hotel **Casa Cozumel Vacation Villas and Condos,** Av. 10 Sur no. 124, 77600 Cozumel, Q. Roo (☎ **987/2-2259;** fax 987/2-2348, or 800/558-5145 in the U.S.), offers a wide range of accommodations and prices that may appeal to people traveling together.

DOUBLES FOR LESS THAN $20

Hotel Flores. Adolfo Rosado Salas 72, 77600 Cozumel, Q. Roo. ☎ **987/2-1429.** Fax 987/2-2475. 30 rms (all with bath). A/C or FAN. $10–$12.25 single; $12.25–$15 double.

Some rooms with fresh paint and new mattresses make the three-story Flores (no elevator) a good downtown choice. The rooms with windows facing interior halls and stairs are rather dreary; ask to see a few rooms before choosing one. Corner rooms have two windows to the outside and are brighter, though it's hard to make this older, dark hotel look good. To find the Flores walk inland one block from the plaza on Melgar and turn left on Salas; it's on your right a few doors from the Hotel Suites Elizabeth.

Posada Edem. Calle 2 Nte. no. 12, Cozumel, 77600 Q. Roo. ☎ **987/2-1166.** 15 rms (all with bath). FAN. $12 single; $14 double.

This small, modest hotel is near the Sports Page restaurant. The rooms are plain but functional, each with tile floors, sheets (but no bedspreads), and a single light hanging from the ceiling. The showers in some bathrooms drip constantly—check it out before you unpack. Four rooms have air conditioning. To get there from the Sports Page turn left and walk 1¹/₂ blocks on Calle 2; it's on your right.

DOUBLES FOR LESS THAN $30

Ⓢ **Hotel Flamingo.** Calle 6 Nte. no. 81, 77600 Cozumel, Q. Roo. ☎ **987/2-1264.** 22 rms (all with bath). FAN. High season, $25 single; $29 double. Low season, $17 single; $21 double.

Built in 1986, the Flamingo offers three floors of quiet rooms, a grassy inner courtyard, and very helpful management. Second- and third-story rooms are spacious. All have white tile floors. Rooms on the front have balconies overlooking the street. Some doubles have one bed; others have two. Soft drinks and bottled water are available from the refrigerator in the lobby. Trade paperbacks are by the reception desk and a TV in the lobby is for guests. You get a lot for your money here. To find it, walk five blocks north on Melgar from the plaza and turn right on Calle 6; the hotel is on the left between Melgar and Avenida 5. Street parking is available.

Ⓢ **Hotel Pepita.** Av. 15 Sur (Apdo. Postal 120), 77600 Cozumel, Q. Roo. ☎ **987/2-0098.** Fax 987/2-0201. 30 rms (all with bath). A/C or FAN. $25 single or double.

Quiet and laid-back, this small two-story inn is an economical hideaway in a peaceful residential neighborhood. The rooms are simple and clean, with good screens on the windows, tiled baths, and mismatched toilet seats. The narrow courtyard is filled with tables and chairs and large bird cages with green parrots. Mornings, between 5 and 10am, complimentary coffee and cookies are available in the lobby. The price seems a bit high, so ask for a discount. To get there from the pier, walk two blocks south on Melgar to Salas, go left three blocks to Avenida 15 Sur, then turn left. The hotel is on your left.

DOUBLES FOR LESS THAN $40

Hotel Aguilar. Calle 3 Sur no. 95, 77600 Cozumel, Q. Roo. ☎ **987/2-0307.** Fax 987/2-0769. 32 rms (all with bath). A/C and FAN. High season, $35 single or double. Low season, $29 single or double.

Behind its white stucco walls you'll find a clean, quiet little respite focused on a large pool and a plant-filled courtyard within walking distance of downtown action. The spotless rooms come with fresh paint, lights over the beds, tile floors, two double beds (firm) covered with ruffled spreads, and glass windows with good screens. You can rent a car (expensive), boat, or motor scooter in the lobby. To find the hotel, turn right at the ferry pier on Melgar, then turn left on Calle 3 Sur.

Hotel El Marqués. Av. 5 Sur no. 180, 77600 Cozumel, Q. Roo. ☎ **987/2-0677.** Fax 987/2-0537. 40 rms (all with bath). A/C. High season, $32 single or double. Low season, $22 single or double (discounts for two or more nights).

Each of the sunny rooms here has gold trim and Formica-marble countertops, French provincial overtones, gray-and-white tile floors, and two double beds. The junior suites have refrigerators; full suites have refrigerators, stoves, and sitting areas. Third-floor rooms have good views. The staff is friendly and attentive. To find it from the plaza, turn right (south) on Av. 5 Sur; the hotel near the corner of Salas, on the right up the stairs next to Coco's restaurant.

Hotel Mary-Carmen. Av. 5 Sur no. 4 (Apdo. Postal 14), 77600 Cozumel, Q. Roo. ☎ **987/2-0581.** 30 rms (all with bath). A/C or FAN. High season, $32 single or double. Low season, $27 single or double.

Watched over by eagle-eyed señoras, the two stories of rooms at the Mary-Carmen surround an interior courtyard shaded by a large mamey tree. Rooms are clean and carpeted, with well-screened windows facing the courtyard. Most have two double beds. Upstairs rooms have fan only, while first floor rooms have both fan and air conditioning. It's half a block south of the zócalo on the right.

Hotel Maya Cozumel. Calle 5 Sur (Apdo. Postal 23), 77600 Cozumel, Q. Roo. ☎ **987/2-0011.** Fax 987/2-0781. 38 rms (all with bath). A/C TEL. $34 single; $40 double.

Maya touches decorate the lobby and rooms in this pretty, apricot-and-white hotel. A long green lawn and small, clean pool are framed by two three-story buildings and flowering shrubs. Paintings of Maya deities decorate the blue, green, and white walls in the large rooms; some have leather lounge chairs, and TVs with cable connection are available in 15 rooms. The rates stay the same year-round. Street parking is limited. From the ferry pier turn right (south) and walk three blocks on Melgar, then turn left on Calle 5. The hotel is on the left between Melgar and 5 Avenida Sur.

DOUBLES FOR LESS THAN $50

✪ **Hotel Safari Inn.** Av. Melgar at Calle 5 Sur (Apdo. Postal 41), 77600 Cozumel, Q. Roo. ☎ **987/2-0101.** Fax 987/2-0661. 12 rms (all with bath). A/C. High season, $42 single; $45 double. Low season, $31 single; $35 double.

The nicest budget hotel in town is above and behind the Aqua Dive Shop. Natural colors and stucco pervade the interior of this three-story establishment. The huge rooms come with firm beds, built-in sofas, and tiled floors. The hotel caters to divers and offers some good dive packages. To find it from the pier turn right (south) and walk 3½ blocks on Melgar; the hotel is on your left facing the Caribbean at the corner of Calle 5 Sur.

DOUBLES FOR LESS THAN $70

B & B Caribo. 799 Avenida Juárez, 77600 Cozumel, Q. Roo. ☎ and fax **987/2-3195**. 800/830-5558 in the U.S. 10 rms (8 with bath). FAN. $350 per week single or double; $700 per month single; $850 per month double. Rates include continental breakfast.

The blue and white residence behind a short white iron fence looks like one of the finer residences in this neighborhood. The 10 rooms continue the crisp blue and white decor and come with cool tile floors, white furniture, blue bedspreads, and big bottles of purified drinking water. Eight of the rooms have air conditioning and private baths. Two rooms have a shared bath in the middle, and these have fans but no air conditioning. A bakery with breads and pastries is located in the front of the house. To find the Caribo from the plaza, walk 6½ blocks inland on Juárez, and it's on the left.

Hotel Barracuda. Av. Rafael Melgar 628 (Apdo. Postal 163), 77600 Cozumel, Q. Roo. ☎ **987/2-0002** or 987/2-1243. Fax 987/2-0884 or 987/2-3633. 50 rms (all with bath). A/C FAN. High season, $60 single; $65 double. Low season, $42 single; $48 double.

You won't think much of this plain tan colored building a short walk south of town, but the view from within is outstanding. Rustic carved-wood furnishings decorate the cozy rooms, all with balconies looking out to sea. There's a refrigerator in each room as well. An inner hallway leading to the rooms blocks out the noise from the road. There's no pool, but lounge chairs are lined up on an elevated strip of sand, and stairs lead down to a good snorkeling area. There is a small oceanfront café serving breakfast and snacks, plus a good dive shop. The hotel is on Costera Sur, a 10-minute walk from town; from the pier walk right; the hotel is on your right. Street parking is readily available.

Hotel Suites Bazar Colonial. Av. 5 Sur no. 9 (Apdo. Postal 286), 77600 Cozumel, Q. Roo. ☎ **987/2-0506**. Fax 987/2-1387. 28 rms (all with bath). A/C TV TEL. High season, $55 single; $60 double. Low season, $40 single; $50 double.

Across the street from the El Marqués is a collection of shops and this nice four-story hotel—with an elevator. It's a good deal for the money. The lobby is far back past the shops. You get a quiet, spacious, furnished studio or a one-bedroom apartment with red-tile floors on the first floor; second- and third-floor rooms have kitchenettes. The street is closed to traffic. From the plaza, walk half a block south on Avenida 5 Sur; the hotel is on the left.

WORTH A SPLURGE

As with hotels south of town, most of the hostelries along the northern part of the island are far out of our budget range. However, the place below is within splurge range, especially if you can get a discount or package deal.

Hotel Fontan. Carretera Santa Pilar km 2.5, 77600 Cozumel, Q. Roo. ☎ **987/2-0300** or 987/2-0194, or 800/221-6509 in the U.S. Fax 987/2-0105. 48 rms. A/C TV TEL. High season, $106 single; $118 double. Low season, $88 single; $100 double. Free parking; unguarded.

Rooms on all four floors of this tan-colored hotel are well maintained and have private balconies; most have ocean views. Baths all have showers. There's a nice pool by the beach (held up by a retaining wall) that's surrounded by lounge chairs. There's a restaurant/bar, plus a dock for water sports. Though somewhat outdated, it's an excellent value for your money.

WHERE TO EAT

There are inexpensive ways to eat well in Cozumel. On Calle 2 Norte, half a block in from the waterfront, is the **Panificadora Cozumel,** excellent for a do-it-yourself breakfast or for picnic supplies. It's open daily from 6am to 9pm. **Zermatt,** at Avenida 5 Norte and Calle 4 Norte is an excellent place to stock up on baked goodies. It's open daily from 7am to 9pm. Cookshops in the **market** always have something brewing—just look for what's hot and freshly cooked. Most of the island's hotels have good restaurants; however, most of the popular restaurants are located in the downtown area. Fast-food franchises are slowly making their way onto the island, and you'll find branches of Dairy Queen, Pizza Hut, Kentucky Fried Chicken, and Subway.

MEALS FOR LESS THAN $5

✪ **Café Caribe.** Av. 10 Sur 215. ☎ **987/2-3621.** Coffee and pastries $1–$3. Mon–Sat 8am–1pm and 6–9:30pm. PASTRIES & COFFEE.

This cute little eatery behind a facade of fuchsia and dark green may become your favorite place to start or finish the day or for something in between. You'll find ice cream, milkshakes, freshly made cheesecake and carrot cake, waffles, bagels, croissants, and biscuits filled with cheese and cream or ham and cheese or butter and marmalade. Nine different coffees are served, including Cuban, cappuccino, espresso, and Irish. To get there from the plaza turn right (south) on Av. 5 Sur, walk one block and turn left on Calle Salas, then right on Av. 10; it's on your left.

❸ **Casa de Denis.** Calle 1 Sur. ☎ **987/2-0067.** Breakfast $1.25–$3; main courses $4–$12. Mon–Sat 7am–11pm. REGIONAL/INTERNATIONAL.

This yellow wooden house holds a great home-style Mexican restaurant. Small tables are scattered outside on the pedestrians-only street and in two rooms separated by a foyer filled with family photos. More tables are set in the back on the shady patio. You can make a light meal from empanadas filled with potatoes, cheese, or fish or go for the full comida of fried grouper, rice, and beans; or better yet try one of the regional specialties such as pollo pibil or pork brochette seasoned with the subtle flavor of achiote. Groups of four or more can request a special meal in advance. To get there from the plaza walk a half block inland up Calle 1 Sur; it's on your right.

❸ **Cocina Económica Mi Chabelita.** Av. 10 Sur. ☎ **987/2-0896.** Breakfast $2.25–$5.75; main courses $3–$7. Mon–Sat 7am–9pm. MEXICAN.

Few tourists have discovered this cheery and informal eatery that caters to locals. It seems to get better every year. Breakfast features omelets and traditional Yucatecan eggs motuleño style or more filling fare such as enchiladas verdes or mole, and quesadillas. At lunch and dinner the menu offers tacos, liver and onions, steak and potatoes, fried fish, soup, and homemade mole. To get there from the plaza walk one block south on Calle 1 Sur and turn right on Av. 10 Sur; it's on your left near the corner of Salas.

✪ **Coco's.** Av. 5 Sur no. 180, at the corner of Calle Salas. ☎ **987/2-0241.** Breakfast $2.50–$5. Tues–Sun 7am–noon. Closed the last two weeks of September and the first week of October. MEXICAN/AMERICAN.

Once discovered, Coco's becomes a favorite. Tended by owners Terri and Daniel Ocejo, it's clean and welcoming to the tourist, right down to the free coffee refills and the ready purified ice water. Plan to indulge in stateside favorites like hash browns, cornflakes and bananas, and gigantic blueberry muffins, cinnamon rolls, and cream stuffed rolls, plus something unique like a bagelwich or a sandwich on an English muffin. Mexican specialties include huevos rancheros, huevos mexicana, and eggs scrambled with chilies and covered with melted cheese. And you can order them with Egg Beater eggs, if you wish. The really famished should inquire about the inexpensive but outrageously filling "Loco" breakfast. A gift section at the front includes gourmet coffee, local honey, bottles of hot pepper, chocolate, *rompope*, and vanilla. Plus there's a paperback-book exchange. To get there from the plaza turn right (south) on Av. 5 Sur. It's on your right beside the Hotel El Marqués.

Comida Casera Toñita. Calle Salas 265, between Calles 10 and 15 Norte. ☎ **987/2-0401.** Breakfast $1.50–$2; main courses $3.75–$5; daily specials $2.50; fruit drinks $1. Mon–Sat 8am–6pm. HOME-STYLE YUCATECAN.

The owners have taken the living room of their home and made it into a comfortable dining room, complete with filled bookshelves and classical music playing in the background. Whole fried fish, fish filet, fried chicken, and beefsteak prepared as you wish are on the regular menu. Daily specials give you a chance to taste authentic regional food, including a pollo a la naranja, chicken mole, pollo en escabeche, and pork chops with *achiote* seasoning. To reach Toñita's, walk south from the plaza on Avenida 5 Sur for one block, then turn left on Salas and walk east 1¹/₂ blocks; the restaurant is on your left.

✪ **Frutas Selecta.** Calle Rosado Salas 352. ☎ **987/2-5560.** Breakfast $1.35–$2.75; salads $1.35–$3; sandwiches $1.35–$2; fruit and vegetable juices 75¢–$1.35; coffee 75¢. Mon–Sat 7am–2pm and 5–9pm. FRUIT/PASTRIES.

The sweet smell of fruit will greet you as you enter Frutas Selecta. Downstairs is a grocery store specializing in fresh fruit, and upstairs is the sleek and cheery restaurant with windows on two sides. The yellow and green sign reads only NATURAL. Juices, licuados, "the best coffee in town," yogurt, veggie sandwiches, a salad bar, fruit shakes, baked potatoes with a variety of toppings, and pastries are served. From the plaza, turn right and walk one block south on Avenida 5 Sur, then turn left on Salas and walk three blocks east. It's on your right between 15th and 20th Norte.

MEALS FOR LESS THAN $10

✪ **D'Pub.** Calle 4 Norte. ☎ **987/2-4132.** Reservations recommended in high season. Main courses $5–$14. Mon–Sat 11pm–midnight; Sun 5pm–midnight; Pub/Botanera Mon–Sat 11am–5pm. SEAFOOD/INTERNATIONAL.

Nothing here is quite what you expect. It's in a new building that's architecturally like the old island frame houses with cutout wood trim. Then it's a handsome English-style pub with mahogany bar glimmering with shiny glass and brass while coupling the best of Mexican cantina (the equivalent of a Mexican pub) tradition offering delicious snacks free with inexpensive drinks—but that's only between 11am and 5pm. After 5pm it's transformed from casual to elegant, becoming a stylish restaurant with cloth covered tables where good service brings terrific crispy fresh salads, curried chicken, large seafood platters, fish and chips, barbecue chicken, dip roast-beef sandwiches, fajitas, stir-fried vegetables, steaks, and an enormous Mexican combo including roasted chicken, rice, beans, guacamole, an enchilada, and a quesadilla. You can dine inside or on the veranda or patio in back overlooking the shaded garden. In the main room as you enter, casual couches and conversational areas are conducive to leisurely drinking; chatting; playing cards or backgammon; or watching ESPAN, CNN, WGNC Chicago, or sporting events. The latter two are played at low volume. The gracious owners Anibal and Mercedes de Iturbide are almost always on hand. To get there from the plaza turn left (north) on Av. 5 Norte, walk two blocks and turn right on Calle 4 Norte; it's behind Zermatt bakery, on your right midway up the block.

El Moro. 75 bis Norte 124. ☎ **987/2-3029**. Main courses $3–$10; margarita $3.30; beer $1.15. Fri–Wed 1–11pm. Closed Thurs. REGIONAL.

Crowds flock to El Moro for its wonderfully prepared food and service, but not the decor, which is orange, orange, orange, and Formica. And it's away from everything—a taxi is a must—costing around $1.30 one way. But you won't care as soon as you taste anything, and especially if you sip even a little of their giant, whallop-packing margaritas. The pollo Ticuleño (a specialty from the town of Ticul), is a rib-sticking, delicious, layered plate of smooth tomato sauce, mashed potatoes, crispy baked corn tortilla, batter-fried chicken breast, all topped with shredded cheese and green peas. Besides the regional food, other specialties of Mexico bolt from the kitchen piping hot, such as enchiladas and seafood many ways, plus grilled steaks, sandwiches, and, of course, nachos to go with that humdinger margarita. El Moro is inland from Melgar 12½ blocks and between Calles 2 and 4 Norte.

Pizza Rolandi. Av. Melgar, between Calles 6 and 8 Norte. ☎ **987/2-0946**. Appetizers $3.80–$8.25; main courses $8.50–$13; pizza $9–$11; daily specials $4.25–$13. Mon–Sat 11am–11pm, Sun 5–11pm. ITALIAN.

Deck chairs and glossy wood tables make the inviting interior garden a restful place in daytime, and it becomes romantic with candlelight at night. The specialty here (as in their branches in Isla Mujeres and Cancún) is wood-oven-baked pizzas. But for a change, look for pasta prepared five ways and the weekly specials, which may be a special appetizer of sea bass carpaccio, pizza, pasta, or fish with an Italian twist. To get there from the pier turn left (north) on Melgar and walk four blocks; it's on your right.

✪ Prima. Calle Salas 109. ☎ **987/2-4242**. Appetizers $3.30–$9; pizzas $5–$12; pastas $5–$15; calzone $3–$5.25; early bird special $5. Daily 3–11pm. ITALIAN.

One of the few good Italian restaurants in Mexico, Prima gets better every year. Everything is fresh—the pastas, calzones, and sourdough pizza. Owner Albert Domínguez grows most of the vegetables in his hydroponic garden on the island. The menu changes daily and might include shrimp scampi, fettucine with pesto, and lobster and crab ravioli with cream sauce. The fettucine Alfredo is wonderful, as are the puff-pastry garlic "bread" and crispy house salad. Dining is upstairs on the breezy terrace. Next door is **Prima Deli** serving great sandwiches on fresh baked bread and aromatic coffee from 9am to 7pm. To get to either place from the pier turn right (south) on Melgar and walk two blocks to Calle 5 Sur and turn left. Prima is visible on your left between Calles 5 and 10 Sur. Hotel delivery is available.

✪ The Waffle House. Av. Melgar. ☎ **987/2-0545** or 987/2-3065. Waffles $2.80–$4.50; breakfast $2.80–$4; main courses $5–$9. Daily 6am–1pm and 6–10pm. BREAKFAST/DESSERTS/MEXICAN.

Tables are often full since the Waffle house has far more business than it has space to handle. The name is a bit misleading since you can order way more than waffles, and you can also have breakfast any time. Jeanie De Lille, the island's premier pastry chef, bakes crisp, light waffles and serves them in many ways, including the waffle ranchero with eggs and salsa, the waffle Benedict with eggs and hollandaise sauce, and waffles with whipped cream and chocolate. Hash browns, homemade breads, and great coffee are other reasons to drop in for breakfast mornings and evenings. The menu has been expanded to include fried fish, tamales, *carne asada tampiqueña*, and several pasta dishes; and there is a full bar. To get there from the pier turn right (south) on Melgar and walk four blocks; it's on your left between the Aqua Safari and the Hotel Vista del Mar.

Meals for Less Than $15

✪ **La Choza.** Salas 198 at Av. 10 Sur. ☎ **987/2-0958.** Breakfast $2.50; appetizers $2.50–$3.50; main courses $7–$12; Daily 7:30am–11pm. YUCATECAN.

The filled tables looking out the big open-air windows on the corner of Salas and 10th Sur announce that this is a favorite of both tourists and locals. It looks like a big Maya house with white stucco walls and thatched roof. Platters of chiles stuffed with shrimp, *pollo en relleño negro* (chicken in a blackened pepper sauce), *puerco entometado* (pork stew), and beef steak in a poblano pepper sauce are among the truly authentic specialties.

La Mission. Av. Juárez 23. ☎ **987/2-1641.** Seafood dishes $8–$18; meat dishes $8–$10; Mexican specialties $7–$9. Daily 3pm–midnight. GRILLED MEAT/MEXICAN.

You can tell by the crowds that this is a popular restaurant, where foreign visitors leave saying "We'll see you next year." The first thing you'll notice is the colorfully tiled open kitchen on the right where cooks prepare the dependably good flame-broiled food for which La Mission is known. The tender fajita platter comes with guacamole, beans, rice, and fresh flour tortillas. The seafood platter includes shrimp and lobster, and the garlic bread is great. The owner says, "If you don't like it, don't pay." From the plaza turn right (east) on Juárez and walk one block; it's on your right between Avenidas 10 and 15 Sur.

Worth a Splurge

✪ **Café del Puerto.** Av. Melgar 3. ☎ **987/2-0316.** Reservations recommended. Main courses $11–$35. Daily 5–11pm. INTERNATIONAL.

For a romantic dinner with a sunset view, try this restaurant. After being greeted at the door, climb the spiral staircase to the main dining room or continue to a higher loft, overlooking the rest of the dining room. Soft piano music entertains in the background. The service is polished and polite, and the menu is sophisticated, with dishes like mustard steak flambé, shrimp brochette with bacon and pineapple, and prime rib. From the pier cross the street and turn left on Melgar; it's almost immediately on your right.

COZUMEL AFTER DARK

Cozumel is a town frequented by sports-minded visitors who play hard all day and wind down early at night. People sit in outdoor cafés around the zócalo enjoying the cool night breezes until the restaurants close. **Carlos 'n Charlie's** and the **Hard Rock,** both on Melgar left of the pier are two of the liveliest places in town. **Karen's Grill and Pizza** on Avenida 5 between Juárez and Calle 2 Norte features live entertainment in the evenings.

Scaramouche, a popular disco, on Melgar at Salas, is open nightly from 10pm to 3am. The cover charge varies.

3 Puerto Morelos

21 miles S of Cancún

Most people come here to take the car-ferry to Cozumel, several hours away. Puerto Morelos has begun to resume the building boom that was beginning when Hurricane Gilbert came through.

ESSENTIALS

GETTING THERE   By Bus   Buses from Cancún's bus station going to Tulum and Playa del Carmen usually stop here, but be sure to ask in Cancún if your bus makes the Puerto Morelos stop.

By Car   Drive south from Cancún along Highway 307 to the km 31 marker. There are a couple of worthwhile stops along Highway 307 on the way to Puerto Morelos. **Croco Cun,** a zoological park where crocodiles are raised, is one of the most interesting attractions in the area—don't be put off by the comical name. Though far from grand, the park has exhibits of crocodiles in all stages of development, as well as animals of nearly all the species that once roamed the Yucatán Peninsula. The snake exhibit is fascinating, though it may make you think twice about roaming in the jungle. The rattlesnakes and boa constrictors are particularly intimidating, and the tarantulas are downright enormous. Children enjoy the guides' enthusiastic tours and are entranced by the spider monkeys and wild pigs. Wear plenty of bug repellent and allow an hour or two for the tour, followed by a cool drink in the restaurant. Croco Cun is open daily from 8:30am to 5:30pm. Admission is $5, and free for children under 6. The park is at km 31 on Highway 307.

About half a mile before Puerto Morelos is a 150-acre **Jardín Botánico,** opened in 1990 and named after Dr. Alfredo Barrera, a biologist who studied the selva (a common geographical term meaning "tropical evergreen broadleaf forest"). A natural, protected showcase for native plants and animals, it's open Tuesday through Sunday from 9am to 4pm. Admission is $3; it's worth the money—and every minute of the hour or more it will take to see it. Slather on the mosquito repellent, though.

The park is divided into six parts: an epiphyte area (plants that grow on others); Maya ruins; an ethnographic area, with a furnished hut and typical garden; a chiclero camp, about the once-thriving chicle (chewing gum) industry; a nature park, where wild vegetation is preserved; and mangroves. Wandering along the marked paths, you'll see that the dense jungle of plants and trees is named and labeled in English and Spanish. Each sign has the plant's scientific and common names, use of the plant, and the geographic areas where it is found in the wild. It's rich in bird and animal life, too, but to catch a glimpse of something you'll have to move quietly and listen carefully.

By the Puerto Morelos–Cozumel Car-Ferry   The dock (☎ **987/1-0008**), the largest establishment in town, is very easy to find. Look to the Cozumel section above for details on the car-ferry schedule, but several points bear repeating here: The car-ferry schedule is complicated and may change, so double-check it before arriving. And always arrive at least three hours in advance of the ferry's departure to purchase a ticket and to get in line.

ORIENTATION   There's one public telephone in Puerto Morelos (☎ **987/ 2-0070**; fax 987/1-0081), at the Caseta de Larga Distancia, next to the Zenaida Restaurant a block south of the main entry street leading to the highway. You can make calls there, and supposedly they'll take messages and pass along hotel-reservation requests. It's open Monday through Saturday from 8am to 1pm and 4 to 7pm. On the highway, near the Puerto Morelos junction, you'll see a gas station with public phones (including Ladatel phones that accept pre-paid phone cards) and a supermarket on the right.

EXPLORING AROUND PUERTO MORELOS

Puerto Morelos is attracting more of its own clientele—people seeking seaside relaxation without the crowds and high prices. You make your own fun here. But for

The Yucatán's Upper Caribbean Coast

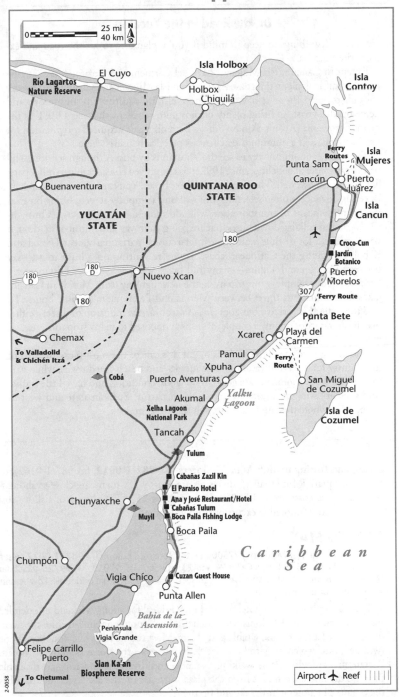

0 | 25 mi
| 40 km
N

Río Lagartos Nature Reserve

El Cuyo

Isla Holbox

Holbox
Chiquilá

Isla Contoy

Ferry Routes

Punta Sam

Cancún

Isla Mujeres

Puerto Juárez

Isla Cancun

Buenaventura

QUINTANA ROO STATE

YUCATÁN STATE

180

Croco-Cun

Jardín Botanico

Puerto Morelos

180 D

180 D

180 D

180

Nuevo Xcan

307

Ferry Route

Punta Bete

Chemax

To Valladolid & Chichén Itzá

Cobá

Xcaret

Playa del Carmen

Pamul

Xpuha

Ferry Route

Puerto Aventuras

San Miguel de Cozumel

Akumal

Yalku Lagoon

Xelha Lagoon National Park

Tancah

Isla de Cozumel

Tulum

Cabañas Zazil Kin
El Paraiso Hotel
Ana y José Restaurant/Hotel
Cabañas Tulum
Boca Paila Fishing Lodge

Chunyaxche

Muyil

Boca Paila

Chumpón

Caribbean Sea

Vigia Chíco

Cuzan Guest House

Punta Allen

Bahía de la Ascensión

Felipe Carrillo Puerto

Peninsula Vigia Grande

Sian Ka'an Biosphere Reserve

To Chetumal

Airport ✈ Reef ||||||

2-0058

On the Road in the Yucatán

Here are a few things to keep in mind if you're planning to hit the road and explore the Yucatán.

Except in Cancún, Isla Mujeres, Playa del Carmen, and Cozumel, exchanging money is difficult along this coast. And though Isla Mujeres and Cozumel are breezy enough to keep them at bay, everywhere else mosquitoes are numerous and fierce on this coast, so bring plenty of mosquito repellent that has DEET as the main ingredient. (Avon's Skin So Soft, a bath oil that's acquired a reputation for its effectiveness as a mosquito repellent, is practically useless here.)

The most economical way to see the Yucatán is by bus. Although service is still best between the major cities, since 1992 it has improved considerably to other parts of the peninsula as well. There are more deluxe buses. You can sometimes purchase tickets in advance—often selecting your seat on a computer screen. Using buses as the primary means of transportation will add more days to your trip. On highways, you can still flag down buses that are going your way and hop aboard, though you'll spend a lot of time waiting at intersections, particularly near Uxmal and Kabah and along the Caribbean coast. If you're waiting on a busy route—say between Cancún and Tulum—many full buses will pass you by. Distances are deceiving. For example, a bus trip using the new highway from Mérida to Cancún takes four hours; bus travel between Mérida and Palenque takes nine hours. To find the fastest bus, ask if a bus goes *sin escalas* or *directo* (nonstop or direct); either may mean no stops or only a couple of stops as opposed to many stops on a regular bus.

The best way to see the Yucatán is by car. It's one of the most pleasant parts of the country for a driving vacation. The jungle- and beach-lined roads, while narrow and without shoulders, are generally in good condition and have little traffic. And they are straight, except in the southern part of Yucatán state and west to Campeche, where they undulate through the Yucatán Alps.

diving and fishing try **Sub Aqua Explorers** (☎ 987/1-0012; fax 987/1-0162), on the main square. More than 15 dive sites are nearby . . . many are close to shore. A two-tank dive costs around $60 and night dives $55. Two hours of fishing cost around $80 and snorkeling excursions run around $5.

WHERE TO STAY

Ojo de Agua. Calle Ejer Mexicano, 77500 Puerto Morelos, Q. Roo. ☎ **987/1-0027** (reservations: Calle 12 no. 96, between Calles 21 and 23, Mérida, Yuc. 97050. ☎ **99/25-0292**; fax 99/28-3405). 16 rms (all with bath). FAN. High season, $45–$55 single or double. Low season, $40–$50 single or double.

This family-style two-story hotel on the beach is ideal for a long weekend or extended stay, especially in the 12 rooms with kitchens. Each room contains a white-tile floor, natural-tone furniture, and a table and chairs. Most rooms have one double and one twin bed, but two come with king-size beds. There's a free-form pool by the ocean. Restaurants are within easy walking distance, and dive gear and trips are available through the hotel. To find it from the plaza, turn left on the last street that parallels the ocean. The hotel is at the far end on the left.

The four-lane toll road between Cancún and Mérida is complete but actually ends short of either city. Costing around $15 one-way, it cuts the trip from five to around four hours. The old two-lane free road is still in fine shape and passes through numerous villages with many speed-control bumps (*topes*)—this route is much more interesting. New directional signs seem to lead motorists to the toll road (*cuota*) and don't mention the free road (*libre*), so if you want to use it, ask locals for directions.

A new four-lane stretch of road is finished going out of Cancún south for several miles. Originally it was to extend to Chetumal, but the local rumor is that a new toll road instead will parallel the existing two-lane Highway 307 and connect Cancún and Chetumal; construction hasn't yet begun. Meanwhile, traffic is quite heavy from Cancún to Tulum, and drivers go too fast. A stalled or stopped car is hard to see, and there are no shoulders for pulling off the roadway. Follow these precautions for a safe journey: Never turn left while on the highway (it's against Mexican law anyway). Always go to the next road on the right and turn around and come back to the turnoff you want. Occasionally, a specially constructed right-hand turnoff, such as at Xcaret, allows motorists to pull off to the right in order to cross the road when traffic has passed. Don't speed and don't follow the next car too closely. There have been many accidents and fatalities on this road lately, and these precautions could save your life. After Tulum, traffic is much lighter, but follow these precautions anyway.

Be aware of the long distances in the Yucatán. Mérida, for instance, is 400 miles from Villahermosa, 125 miles from Campeche, and 200 miles from Cancún. Leaded gas (*Nova*) is readily available in the Yucatán; unleaded gas (*Magna Sin*) is available at most stations. *Note:* Gas stations are found in all major towns, but they're only open from around 8am to around 7pm. If you're planning to rent a car to travel the area, see Chapter 2, "Getting Around by Rental Car."

Posada Amor. Apdo. Postal 806, 77580 Cancún, Q. Roo. ☎ **987/1-0033.** 20 rms (8 with bath). $16.50 single without bath; $20 double without bath; $22 single with bath; $25 double with bath; $29 for a room with four beds and bath.

The simple, cheery little rooms at the Posada Amor, with screens and mosquito netting, are plain but adequate and overpriced. They're clustered around a patio in back of the restaurant. The posada's restaurant is rustic and quaint like an English cottage—with whitewashed walls, small shuttered windows, and open rafters—and decorated with primitive paintings and flowers on each table. The food is tasty, with many regional specialites, sandwiches, a comida corrida for $3.50, and a Sunday buffet for $5. It's open daily from 7:30am to 11pm. To get here, when you enter town, turn right; with the town square on the left, follow the main street leading to the ferry; the hotel is about a block down on the right.

WHERE TO EAT

Besides the above-mentioned Posada Amor, Los Pelicanos is worth trying.

Los Pelicanos. On the oceanside behind and right of the zócalo. ☎ **987/1-0014.** Main courses $4–$13; lobster $25. Daily 10am–10pm. SEAFOOD.

Sea Turtles of the Yucatán

At least four of Mexico's nine species of marine turtles nest on the beaches of Quintana Roo—the loggerhead, green, hawksbill, and leatherback varieties. Of these, the leatherback is almost nonexistent, and the loggerhead is the most abundant—but all are endangered.

Most turtles lay eggs on the same beach year after year, and as often as three times in a season. Strolling along the beach late at night in search of giant turtles (prime egg-laying hours are between 10pm and 3am) is a special experience that will make you feel closer to the Yucatán's environment. It may take you a while to get used to the darkness, but don't use your flashlight—lights of any kind repel the turtles. Laying the eggs is tough work—a female will dig nonstop with back flippers for more than an hour; the exercise leaves its head and legs flushed. Depositing the 100 or more eggs takes only minutes, then she makes the nest invisible by laboriously covering it with sand and disappears into the sea. Each soft-shelled egg looks like a Ping-Pong ball.

Hatchlings scurry to the sea 45 days later, but successful incubation depends on the temperature and depth of the nest. When conditions are right, the hatch rates of fertile eggs are high; however, only 5% of those that do make it to the sea escape predators long enough to return.

Despite recent efforts to protect Mexico's turtles, the eggs are still considered an aphrodisiac, and there's a market for them; turtles are killed for their shells and meat as well. Since turtle life expectancy is more than 50 years, killing one turtle kills thousands more. Costly protection programs include tagging the female and catching the eggs as they are deposited and removing them to a protected area and nest of identical size and temperature.

Since this village has few restaurants, Los Pelicanos holds almost a captive audience for beachside dining. You'll notice the inviting restaurant down a block to the right of the plaza on the street paralleling the ocean. Select a table inside under the palapa or outside on the terrace (wear mosquito repellent in the evenings). From the terrace you have an easy view of pelicans swooping around the dock. The seafood menu has all the usual offerings, from ceviche to conch made three ways to shrimp, lobster, and fish. There are grilled chicken and steak for those who don't want seafood.

EN ROUTE TO PLAYA DEL CARMEN

Heading south on Highway 307 from Puerto Morelos, you'll find the village of Muchi to be the next landmark. It's only 20 miles from Puerto Morelos to Playa del Carmen, so you'll be there in half an hour or less. However, you'll pass several small beach resorts en route. Less than 3 miles before Playa del Carmen, you'll see a sign pointing left to **Punta Bete,** which is the name of a fine beach—not a town. For an out-of-the-way place on a private beach, turn left here for the Cabañas Bahia Xcalacoco, and Cabañas Xcalacoco, for which you'll see a faded sign on the highway. Though close to Playa del Carmen, you might as well be a thousand miles from civilization for the secluded feeling you get. The narrow, overgrown road you follow isn't much, and you may even wonder if it's the right one. Have faith and keep bearing right. Soon you'll see a sign pointing to the right to the Cabañas Bahia Xcalacoco, or go straight ahead to the Cabañas Xcalacoco both facing the ocean. (There's another cabaña just to the left of the Cabañas Xcalacoco, with nearly the same name, but upkeep and service are undependable, and I don't recommend it.) Even if you don't stay here, you can use the restaurants as a base and come for the day from Playa del Carmen. The beach is beautiful and almost uninhabited.

WHERE TO STAY & EAT

Cabañas Bahia Xcalacoco. Apdo. Postal 176, 77710 Playa del Carmen, Q. Roo. 2 rms (all with bath).

Ricardo and Rosa Novelo opened their own small inn in 1996, with two small white-washed rooms in a shady thicket by the beach. Rosa, the powerhouse cook and general manager, keeps things running smoothly while Ricardo takes guests fishing and snorkeling. The rooms are small and plain, but comfortable—however, there's no electricity so you learn to work the kerosene lamp. Rosa serves guests in the small restaurant—expect sizeable portions at very reasonable prices. The fish dinner is large and excellent. Ask about jungle trails to Maya ruins near the cabañas.

Cabañas Xcalacoco. Carretera Cancún-Tulum km 52 (Apdo. Postal 176), 77710 Playa del Carmen, Q. Roo. No phone. 7 cabañas (all with bath). $25 with one bed, $35 with two beds; RVs and campers $4 per person. Discounts available in low season. Free parking.

Next door to the Cabañas Bahia is this long-established set of cabañas, which are tidy whitewashed buildings with small porches, all right on the beach. All have baths; five have king-size beds, and the others have two double beds each. Since there's no electricity, kerosene lamps light rooms in the evenings. Camping facilities are available for those in recreational vehicles and others wishing to hang a hammock under a thatched-roof covering. For these folks there's a shower and bathroom but no electricity. A small restaurant serves guests, but it's always a good idea to bring along packaged and canned snacks, water, and soft drinks.

4 Playa del Carmen

20 miles SW of Puerto Morelos, 44 miles SW of Cancún

This rapidly expanding Caribbean village grew up around the mainland terminus of the passenger-boat service to Cozumel. Travelers soon discovered that Playa del Carmen's long stretches of white beach were far better than those on Cozumel, and it has developed quite a tourist trade of its own. The tide of progress is rolling on with the appearance of the all-inclusive Diamond Resort and the Hotel Continental Plaza Playacar, both new resorts south of the center of town, as well as new sewage and water lines, telephone service, and more brick-paved streets. Playa del Carmen severed its political apron strings from Cozumel and now has its own mayor and is contained in its own separate *municipio* (like a county). The town doubled in size in 1993 and is preparing for 50,000 inhabitants by the year 2000.

Time-share hawkers ply their same fake friendly ways in Playa, but not in the numbers present in Puerto Vallarta or Cancún. Topless sunbathing, though against the law in Mexico, seems condoned here—including leisurely topless strolling anywhere there's a beach. It's so casually topless, in fact, that there was a sign in the post office to the effect of no topless in here.

Avenida Juárez (also known as Avenida Principal) leads into town and has always been considered "main street," but the four-lane Avenida 30, five blocks from the beach, has been paved and is positioned as another "main street."

Playa del Carmen is something of a fork in the road for southbound travelers—you can go by ferry east to Cozumel or continue south to Akumal, Tulum, Cobá, Punta Allen, and Chetumal on Highway 307.

Though Playa has lost its innocence, it's still a peaceful place where you can hang out on the beach for hours without feeling the need to explore. However, get there quickly—it's changing fast.

ESSENTIALS

GETTING THERE & DEPARTING   By Bus   There are three bus stations in Playa del Carmen, all on Avenida Principal (the main street): **Transportes de Oriente, Playa Express,** and **ATS,** are a half block north of the main square and Avenida 5 on Avenida Principal; **Expreso Oriente** is on the corner of Avenida 5 and Avenida Principal; and the **ADO** station is four blocks north of the ferry dock and two blocks north of the plaza.

ATS offers service to and from Cancún every 15 minutes. ATS buses also go to Xcaret (five times) and to Tulum (11 times), as well as to Cobá, Chetumal, and Palenque. Second-class Oriente buses travel the route to and from Tulum, Cobá, and Bacalar. Several de paso ADO buses pass through Playa del Carmen on the way to Cancún. And several ADO buses go to Valladolid, Chichén-Itzá, and Mérida.

Expreso Oriente goes to Villahermosa, Mérida, Tulum, Cancún, Felipe Carrillo Puerto, and Chetumal.

By Car   The turnoff to Playa del Carmen from Highway 307 is plainly marked, and you'll arrive on the divided Avenida Principal, also known as Avenida Benito Juárez (not that there's a street sign to that effect).

By the Playa del Carmen–Cozumel Passenger Ferry   See the Cozumel section above for the details on the passenger ferry service between Playa del Carmen and Cozumel.

By Taxi   Taxi fares to the Cancún airport are prohibitively high, but there is a service offering shared taxi rides for $10 per person. Ask about it at your hotel.

ORIENTATION   Arriving   The ferry dock in Playa del Carmen is one block from the main square and within walking distance of hotels. Buses are along Avenida Principal, a short distance from hotels, restaurants, and the ferry pier. Tricycle taxis are the only vehicular traffic allowed between the bus stations and the ferry. A number of these efficient taxis meet each bus and ferry and can transport you and your luggage between the two or to any hotel in town.

City Layout   Villagers know and use street names, but few street signs exist. The main street, **Avenida Principal,** also known as **Avenida Benito Juárez,** leads into town from Highway 307, crossing Avenida 5 one block before it ends at the beach next to the main plaza or zócalo. Traffic is diverted from Avenida Principal at Calle 10. The other main artery (closed to traffic from Avenida Principal to Calle 8), **Avenida 5,** leads to the ferry dock, two blocks from the zócalo; most restaurants and hotels are either on Avenida 5, or a block or two off it. The village's beautiful beach parallels Avenida 5 and is only a block from it.

FAST FACTS: PLAYA DEL CARMEN

Area Code   The telephone area code is 987.

Money Exchange   There are two branches of the Cicsa Money exchange, one at the foot of the pier and the other at the Rincón del Sol plaza on Av. 5 at Calle 8. Both are open from Monday through Friday from 7:30am to 7:30pm and Saturday from 7:30am to 1pm and 3:30 to 6:30pm. Exchange rates are less favorable in Playa than in either Cancún or Cozumel.

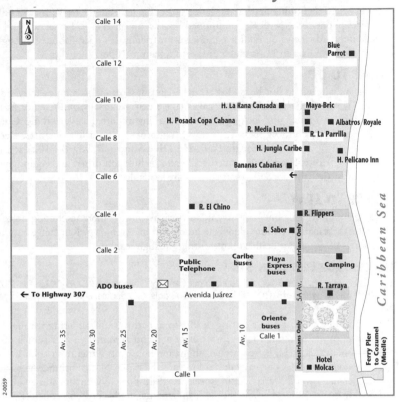

Messages Mom's Hotel acts as an unofficial message center, with a bulletin board posting messages for traveling friends, people needing rides, house or room rental, or items for sale.

Parking Because of the pedestrians-only blocks and the increasing population and popularity of Playa, parking close to hotels has become somewhat difficult. There was talk of prohibiting vehicular traffic inside the village by corralling all vehicles into a pay lot, which would be serviced by special taxis. For now, the most accessible parking lot is the Estacionamiento Mexico at the corner of Avenida Principal and Avenida 10, open daily 24 hours.

Post Office The post office is on Avenida Principal three blocks north of the plaza, on the right past the Hotel Playa del Carmen and the launderette.

Seasons High season is December through Easter and August. Low season is all other months, but November is becoming very popular, and some hoteliers raise rates then.

Spanish Lessons The Centro Bilingue de Playa del Carmen (☎ and fax **987/3-0558**) offers informal classes in conversational Spanish as well as Spanish geared toward government and business. For a reasonable fee they'll arrange transport to the Cancún airport and confirm airline tickets. The school is on Avenida 5 between Calles 4 and 6 above the Panadería Caribe.

Telephones Many hotels have phones and faxes now; often both are on the same phone line. So, to send a fax, call and ask for the fax tone: "Por favor, dar me el tono por el fax." The **Calling Station** on the street leading up from the ferry pier, is a full-services phone center with air-conditioned booths, no surcharges, fax service, and a bulletin board where you can leave messages for friends. It's open Monday through Saturday from 8am to 11pm and Sunday from 9am to 10pm.

WHAT TO DO

Playa is for relaxing. But beyond that, the island of Cozumel is a quick ferry ride away; Tulum, Xel-Ha, Xcaret, and Xcalacoco are easy excursions; and Avenida 5a is lined with two dozen nice-looking small shops selling imported batik clothing, Guatemalan fabric clothing, masks, pottery, hammocks, and a few T-shirts. Reef diving can be arranged through **Tank-Ha Dive Shop** (☎ 987/3-0302) at the Hotel Maya-Bric. Snorkeling trips cost $25 and include soft drinks and equipment. Two-tank dive trips are $60; resort courses are available.

WHERE TO STAY

There are motel-style hotels on Avenida Principal, but the more interesting hostelries are the cabaña-style inns along the beach and on Avenida 5. Rate ranges in the headings below are for double rooms during the high season.

DOUBLES FOR LESS THAN $40

Cabañas Tuxatah. Calle 5 Sur, 77710 Playa del Carmen, Q. Roo . ☎ 987/3-0025. Fax 987/3-0148. 9 rms (all with bath). FAN. High season, $18 single; $25 double. Low season, $15 single; $20 double.

In a Robinson Crusoe–like setting, with stone pathways meandering through a ravine of overgrown jungle foliage, this place will appeal to many for its casual, offbeat rusticity. Caged birds are scattered about and house cats skitter from sight, while family dogs join in lockstep as you head toward the rooms hidden behind the bush. The German owner, María Weltin, speaks English, French, German, and Spanish. The tidy quarters in a two-story building all have one double bed on a concrete platform, speckled tile floors, screened and louvered windows, and nice baths. To find Tuxatah, walk inland from the pier on Avenida Principal two blocks. Turn left on Calle 5 at the Continental Plaza Playacar sign and walk 1 1/2 blocks. The hotel is on your right; the entrance is down a pathway behind the sign for Villas y Condominios Playacar. There is ample parking in front of the entrance.

✪ **Hotel Maya-Bric.** Av. 5 Norte, 77710 Playa del Carmen, Q. Roo. ☎ and fax **987/3-0011.** 29 rms (all with bath). A/C or FAN. High season, $35 single or double. Low season, $25 single or double. Free parking; guarded.

The colorful exterior and flowers draw your eye to this two-story beachfront inn. The well-kept rooms have two double beds with fairly firm mattresses; some have ocean views. The buildings frame a small pool where guests gather for card games and conversation. The Maya-Bric is one of the quietest hotels in town; it's well-supervised by the Briseño family owners and is frequented by loyal guests who return annually. The gates are locked at night, and only guests are allowed to enter. A small restaurant by the office sometimes serves breakfast and snacks during the high season. Air conditioning is being added to all rooms. The on-site dive shop, Tank-Ha (see "What to Do," above), rents diving and snorkeling gear and arranges trips to the reefs.

⬡ **Mom's Hotel.** Av. 30 at Calle 4. 77710 Playa del Carmen, Q. Roo. ☎ and fax **987/3-0315.** 12 rms (all with bath). FAN. High season, $25 single; $35 double. Low season (May, June, Sept-Nov), $20 single; $25 double. Discounts for lengthy stays.

Though away from the beach, this is a good choice if all the beachside inns are full or if your stay is long. Rooms, all facing the interior courtyard, are fairly large and sunny; each comes with tile floors, one or two double beds, and bedside reading lights. Three rooms have air conditioning. There's a small pool in the sunny court-yard, and a bulletin board for messages to other travelers. A bar and restaurant were in the planning stage when I checked. To find it from the corner of Avenida 5 and Calle 4, walk five blocks inland, and it's at the corner of Calle 4 and Avenida 30.

Posada Copa Cabaña. Av. 5 (Apdo. Postal 103), 77710 Playa del Carmen, Q. Roo. ☎ **987/ 3-0218.** 8 rms, 2 cabañas (all with bath). FAN. High season, $30 single; $35 double. Low sea-son, $20 single; $30 double.

Hammocks are stretched in front of each room and on the porch of each cabaña at this pleasant palm-shaded inn, and the patio Restarant Soluna fills up the courtyard to the right. Each of the clean, simply furnished rooms has one or two double beds on concrete platforms and pink-and-gray tile floors. Vanities and sinks are conve-niently placed outside the baths. There's good cross ventilation through well-screened windows. To get here from the plaza turn right on Avenida 5 and walk three blocks; it's on your right between Calles 6 and 8. There is no parking on Avenida 5, but there's limited parking nearby.

WORTH A SPLURGE

✪ **Albatros Royale.** Calle 8 (Apdo. Postal 31), 77710 Playa del Carmen, Q. Roo. ☎ **987/ 3-0001,** or 800/538-6802 in the U.S. and Canada. 31 rms (all with bath). FAN. High season, $60–$80 single or double. Low season, $50–$60 single or double. Rates include breakfast.

This "deluxe" sister hotel to the neighboring Cabañas Albatros (see below) rises up on a narrow bit of land facing the beach. The two stories of rooms all have tile floors, tile baths with marble vanities and showers, and balconies or porches; most have ocean views. Most have two double beds, but seven have queen-size beds. Breakfast is taken almost next door at the Pelicano Inn. To get here from the corner of Avenida 5 and Calle 8 (where you'll see the Rincón del Sol center) turn toward the water on Calle 8; it's midway down the block on your left. Street parking is scarce.

Pelicano Inn. On the beach between Calles 6 and 8 (Apdo. Postal 31), 77710 Playa del Carmen, Q. Roo. ☎ **987/3-0997,** or 800/538-6802 in the U.S. Fax 987/3-0998. 38 rms. FAN or A/C. High season, $75 single or double garden view; $85 single or double sea view. Low season, $55 single; $60 double. Rates include breakfast.

Larry Beard demolished his old seaside hotel Albatros and in its place created a beau-tiful white-stucco pueblo-style hotel bearing no resemblance to its predecessor. The spacious rooms, in one-, two- and three-level tiers, have tile floors and baths, overbed reading lights, and balconies or patios outfitted with hammocks. Most rooms have two double beds, but several have only one. Once you see it, you'd expect to pay a good deal more. The restaurant, open from 7:30am to 6pm, is one of the best in Playa (see "Where to Eat" below), and guests partake of the all-you-can-eat break-fast buffet. From the Avenida Principal, walk four blocks north on Avenida 5, then turn right a half a block on Calle 8, where a path on the right between two lots leads into the hotel. (You don't have to trudge across the beach as in the past.)

Treetops. Calle 8 s/n, 77710 Playa del Carmen, Q. Roo. ☎ and fax **987/3-0351.** 15 rms (all with bath). FAN. High season, $30–$50 single or double. Low season, $25–$45 single or double.

Owners Sandy and Bill Dillon changed the name from Cuevo Pargo and added more rooms during their stem to stern cleaning and revamp. Set in a small patch of un-disturbed jungle, with bungalows linked by stone pathways, this place is cooler than any in town and comes complete with its own cenote. The older bungalows (each a separate unit) are rustic but comfortable and come with small charms like thatched roofs and rock walls and unusual architecture—no two are alike. Two bungalows have kitchens. One room has a loft bed overlooking a living area. The new rooms, in a two-story fourplex have a choice of air conditioning or fan (you pay extra to turn on the A/C), refrigerators, and nice balconies or patios. The hotel's restaurant serves free coffee to guests each morning, a limited menu of charcoal-broiled hot dogs and hamburgers (with U.S. beef), homemade potato salad, Tex-Mex chili, tacos, and pizza. The Safari bar, to the left after you enter, is a good place to come for an evening drink and meet fellow travelers. The bar is open daily from 3pm to midnight. Happy hour is from 5 to 7pm. There's a TV broadcasting U.S. channels in the "lobby." A new restaurant, to be built over a new swimming pool was in the planning stages. From the Avenida Principal, walk four blocks north on Avenida 5, then turn right for half a block on Calle 8; the hotel is on the left, half a block from the beach.

Hotel Alejari. Calle 6 (Apdo. Postal 166), 77710 Playa del Carmen, Q. Roo. ☎ **987/3-0374.** Fax 987/3-0005. 23 rms (all with bath). A/C FAN. High season, $50 single or double; $60 single or double with kitchenette; $55 single or double two-story unit with kitchen. Low season, $45 single or double; $55 single or double two-story unit with kitchen. Rates include breakfast. Free parking; guarded.

Built around a fastidiously kept flower-filled inner yard, this small hotel is just off Avenida 5 and half a block from the beach. Though somewhat overpriced, rooms are clean, each with white walls, ruffled nylon bedspreads, and a small vanity with mirror in the bedroom. Ground-level rooms have two double beds. Rooms with kitchens have a kitchen and living room downstairs, and the bedroom, with a king-size bed, is up a narrow stairway. The restaurant is open daily from 8am to 4pm, and breakfast is served between 8 and 11am.

La Rana Cansada. Calle 10, 77710 Playa del Carmen, Q. Roo. ☎ and fax **987/3-0389.** 12 rms (all with bath). High season, $50 single or double. Low season, $20 single or double.

The "Tired Frog" is one of the most simply pleasant inns in the village, though a bit overpriced in high season. Behind an elegant hacienda-style wall and handsome iron gate, the plainly furnished, but neat and clean rooms face an inner courtyard with a small snack bar under a large thatched palapa. Hammocks are strung on the covered porch outside the row of rooms. Some have concrete ceilings, and others a thatched roof; all have well-screened doors and windows. New rooms were on the drawing board as well as a small pool and breakfast service. Trade paperbacks are available at the front desk, and manager John Swartz is very accommodating with tips on seeing the area. It's a block and a half inland from the beach. To find it, from the main plaza, walk five blocks north on Avenida 5 and turn left on Calle 10; the hotel is on the left.

A YOUTH HOSTEL

From the bus station, walk toward the highway and follow the signs. A bed in an 18-bunk room with cold and hot water costs $5, including sheets, pillowcase, and a locker. You can also rent a cabaña with shared bath for $15. The hostel is a 10- to 15-minute walk from the bus station.

CAMPING

Playa del Carmen has many little camping areas down along the water. Turn to the left at the beach and head for **Campamiento, Cabañas Las Ruinas** (☎ 987/ 3-0405), right on the beach and across the street from a tiny Maya ruin. Everyone pays a refundable entry deposit of $8, and cabin renters deposit $20. Hammocks rent for $2, and sheets, towels, and blankets (no pillows) rent for 75¢. Lockers cost $1.50; safety boxes cost $5 for money, passports, and so forth. Hammock space in a covered palapa comes with a locker and costs $5. Small cabins cost $10 to $35 (with bath in high season); tent, trailer, and camper spaces run $4 to $8; and auto space is $4. The property is very run-down and casually operated; I strongly recommend you get a locker or safety deposit box for your valuables. A shady palapa serves as a restaurant and general gathering area.

Coming in from the highway, turn left (north) on Avenida Principal, left on Avenida 10, and right on Calle 6; go straight for one block and cross Avenida 5, and it's a half block down on the left near the beach.

WHERE TO EAT
MEALS FOR LESS THAN $5

Daily Doughnuts. Av. 5, between Calles 8 and 10. ☎ **987/3-0396.** Doughnuts 75¢; doughnut centers 30¢; sandwiches $2–$3; molletes $1; coffee 75¢. Mon–Sat 7am–9pm. DOUGHNUTS/CROISSANTS/SANDWICHES.

Paulino and Federico Suárez, a pair of enterprising Mexico City youths, opened this delicious doughnut shop in 1993. The variety is mouthwatering—50 kinds in all, with terrific toppings of glaze, chocolate, or nuts or combined flavorings of coffee, almonds, cream, blueberries, strawberries, peanut butter, and more. The Chiapan blend they use makes the best cup of coffee in town.

Sabor. Av. 5 between Calles 2 and 4. No phone. Yogurt and granola $1–$1.75; sandwiches $1.50–$2; vegetarian plates $1.50–$2.50; pastries 50¢–$1. Daily 8am–11pm. BAKERY/HEALTH FOOD.

Melinda Burns offers her popular bakery products to a patio full of patrons—it's always full. The list of hot and cold drinks has expanded to include espresso and cappuccino, café frappe, hot chocolate, tea, and fruit and vegetable drinks; and Sabor now has Blue Bell ice cream and light vegetarian meals. Try a cup of something with a slice of pie and watch village life stroll by.

MEALS FOR LESS THAN $10

✪ **El Chino.** Calle 4 at Av. 15. ☎ **987/3-0015.** Breakfast $1.50–$2.50; main courses $3–$7.50. Daily 8am–11pm YUCATÁN/MEXICAN.

Despite its name there's nary a Chinese dish on El Chino's menu. But locals highly recommend this place, as do I. Though slightly off the popular Avenida 5 row of restaurants, it has its own clean, cool ambience with tile floors and plastic-covered polished wood tables set below a huge palapa roof with whirring ceiling fans. A side patio is open air with uncovered tables that are good for evening meals. The standard breakfast menu applies, plus you can order fresh blended fruit drinks. Main courses include such regional favorites as poc-chuc, chicken pibil, and Ticul-style fish, plus shrimp-stuffed fish, beef, chicken, and shrimp borcettes. Other selections are lobster and shrimp crêpes, fajitas, and ceviche.

El Tacolote. Av. Juárez. ☎ **987/3-0066.** Main courses $2–$11. Daily 11am–3am. (Shortened hours in low season.) GRILLED MEATS/SEAFOOD.

There's a good selection of tacos, hamburgers, and mixed brochettes offered here. The "vegetarian plate" is grilled shrimp with peppers; the "gringas plate" comes with flour tortillas, grilled pork, and cheese. The restaurant faces the main plaza and has expanded to fill up half the block. Marimbas and mariachis play on weekend nights in high season. There's another branch of this restaurant in Cancún; if you've tried and enjoyed that one, you'll likely enjoy this one, too, especially with its cool patio in back.

✪ **Media Luna.** Av 5 corner of Calle 8. No phone. Breakfast $2.50–$4; main courses $3–$7. Tues–Sun 7:30am–3pm and 6:30–11:30pm. INTERNATIONAL.

Open only a short while when I passed by, I couldn't resist adding it to my list. Few restaurants have such mouthwatering aromas coming from the kitchen. When you read the menu you'll know why. The spinach and mushroom breakfast crêpes arrive with fabulous herb, onion, and garlic flavored potatoes. Other crêpes are filled with fresh fruit. For dinner there are savory Greek salads, black bean quesadillas, grilled shrimp salads, fresh grilled fish, and pastas with fresh herbs and sauces, plus other entres featuring Indian, Italian, Mexican, and Chinese specialties. It's a casual, inviting place, with soft taped guitar music in the background and decorated in textiles from Guatemala, with a few unfinished pine tables for dining outside on the street or a larger area inside.

✪ **Pelicano Inn.** On the beach, at Calle 6. ☎ **987/3-0997.** Buffet breakfast $6; main courses $2–$30. Buffet breakfast daily 7–11am; lunch daily 11:30–6pm (happy hour noon–1pm and 4–6pm). MEXICAN/AMERICAN.

Located on the beach, this is a good place to meet Americans who live here and while away some hours munching and people-watching. The food is dependably good. The cost of a breakfast buffet is for all you can eat. Apart from breakfast you have a choice of peel-your-own-cajun shrimp with U. S. style tarter and shrimp sauce, hamburgers, hot dogs, quesadillas, pastries, ice cream, beer, wine, and coffee. From Avenida Principal, walk four blocks north on Avenida 5, turn right ¹/₂ block on Calle 8 to a marked Pelican Inn pathway, and turn right, or go to the beach and turn right; the hotel/restaurant is on the beach.

✪ **Tarraya Restaurant/Bar.** Calle 2 Norte at the beach. No phone. Appetizers $1.50–$3.50; main courses $3–$6; whole fish $5. Daily noon–9pm. SEAFOOD.

"The restaurant that was born with the town" proclaims the sign. This is also the restaurant locals recommend as the best for seafood. Since it's right on the beach, with the water practically lapping the foundations, and since the owners are fishermen, the fish is so fresh it's practically still wiggling. The wood hut doesn't look like much, but you can have fish fixed almost any way imaginable. If you haven't tried the Yucatecan specialty Tikin xic fish—this would be a good place. It's on the beach opposite the basketball court.

PLAYA DEL CARMEN AFTER DARK

It seems like everyone in town is out on Avenida 5 or Juárez across from the square until 10 or 11pm; there's pleasant strolling, meals and drinks at streetside cafes, buskers to watch and listen to, and shops to duck into. Later in the evening your choices diminish: there's a **Señor Frog's** down by the ferry dock, dishing out its patented mix of thumping dance music, Jello shots, and frat-house antics; **Karen's Pizza** on Avenida 5, with live entertainment nightly; and then there's the beachside bar at the **Blue Parrot,** which seems to draw most of the European and American expatriate community, has swings for barstools, and stays open late (somewhere around 2 to 3am). This last is the coolest. *A Caution:* Ladies—stay clear of Playa's unusual number of would-be gigolos; they're slick. And lately there have been a few reports of drug involvment in tourist robberies—don't do drugs in Mexico, and don't flash money.

5 Highway 307 from Xcaret to Xel-Ha

This section of the mainland coast—between Playa del Carmen and Tulum—is right on the front lines of the Caribbean coast's transformation from idyllic backwater to developing tourist destination. South of Playa del Carmen along Highway 307 are a succession of brand-new planned resorts and nature parks, commercially developed beaches, and—for now, anyway—a few rustic beach hideaways and unspoiled coves. From north to south, this section will cover Xcaret, Paamul, Xpuha, Puerto Aventuras, Akumal, Chemuyil, Xcacel, and Xel-Ha.

Of the fledgling resorts south of Playa del Carmen, **Akumal** is one of the most developed, with moderately priced hotels and bungalows scattered among the graceful palms that line the beautiful, soft beach and gorgeous bay. **Puerto Aventuras** is a privately developed, growing resort city aimed at the well-heeled traveler. **Paamul** and **Xpuha** offer inexpensive inns on gorgeous beaches 2¹/₂ miles apart. If the offbeat beach life is what you're after, grab it now before it disappears. (Other little-known and inexpensive getaways can be found on the Punta Allen Peninsula south of Tulum; see the next section for details.) You'll also enjoy a swim in the nearby lagoon of **Xel-Ha,** one of the coast's prettiest spots. And the new parklike development of **Xcaret** will appeal to some for an all-day excursion.

EN ROUTE SOUTH FROM PLAYA DEL CARMEN   Bus transportation from Playa del Carmen south is no longer as chancy as it used to be, but it's still not great. There are several bus companies in Playa; buses depart fairly frequently for Chetumal, stopping at every point of interest along the way. There's even bus service to and from Cobá. Though buses originate in Playa, you may be told you can't buy tickets ahead of time. If you choose to hire a car and driver, be sure to find a driver you like; remember, you'll be with him all day.

XCARET: A DEVELOPED NATURE PARK

Three miles south of Playa del Carmen is the turnoff to Xcaret (ISH-car-et), a heavily commercialized, specially built tourist destination that promotes itself as a 150-acre ecological park. Meant as a place to spend the day, it's open daily from 9am to 5:30pm.

Xcaret may celebrate mother nature, but its builders rearranged quite a bit of her handiwork in completing it. If you're looking for a place to escape the commercialism of Cancún, this may not be it; it's expensive and contrived and may even be very crowded, thus diminishing the advertised "natural" experience. Children, however, seem to love the park. Without exaggeration, everywhere you look in Cancún are signs advertising Xcaret, or someone handing you a leaflet about it. They even have their own bus terminal to take tourists from Cancún at regular intervals, and they've added an evening extravaganza. Once past the entry booths (built to resemble small Maya temples) you'll find pathways that meander around bathing coves, the snorkeling lagoon, and the remains of a group of Maya temples. You'll have access to swimming beaches with canoes and pedal boats; limestone tunnels to snorkel through; marked palm-lined pathways; and a visitors' center with lockers, first aid, and gifts. There's also a museum, a "farm," and a botanical garden. Visitors aren't allowed to bring in food or drinks, so you're at the mercy of the high-priced restaurants. Personal radios are a no-no, as is use of suntan lotion if you swim in the lagoon; chemicals in lotion will poison the lagoon habitat.

The price of $30 per person entitles you to all the facilities—boats, life jacket, snorkeling equipment for the underwater tunnel and lagoon, lounge chairs, and other facilities. However, there are often more visitors than equipment (such as beach chairs), so bring a beach towel and your own snorkeling gear. Travel agencies in Cancún offer Xcaret as a day-trip that includes transportation and admission. You can also buy a ticket to the park at the Xcaret Terminal (☎ **987/8-30654** or 987/8-30743) next to the Hotel Fiesta Americana Coral Beach on Cancún island. Xcaret's colorfully painted buses haul people to and from Cancún. From Cancún the price including transportation and admission is $45 for adults and $33 for children.

"Xcaret Night," costs $80 for adults and $70 for children and includes round-trip transporation from Cancún, a charreada festival, lighted pathways to a Maya Village, dinner, and folkloric show.

PAAMUL: A BEACH HIDEAWAY

About 10 miles south of Xcaret, 60 miles southwest of Cancún, and half a mile east of the highway is Paamul (also spelled *Pamul*), which in Maya means "a destroyed ruin." Turn when you see the Minisuper (a spot for reasonably priced snacks and drinks), which is also owned by the Cabañas Paamul (see below). Here you can enjoy a beautiful beach and a safe cove for swimming; it's a delightful place to leave the world behind. Thirty years ago the Martin family gave up coconut harvesting, gained title to the land, and established this comfortable out-of-the-way respite. Plans are to soon begin building more rooms on the unoccupied portion of the bay.

Mark and Lester Willis established their PADI- and SSI-certified fully equipped dive shop here a few years ago and opened **Scuba Max** (☎ 987/3-0667 and fax 987/ 4-1729), next to the cabañas. Using three 38-foot boats, they takes guests on dives 5 miles in either direction. If it's too choppy, the reefs in front of the hotel are also excellent. The cost per dive is $25–$45 if you have your own equipment or $35–$65 if you rent. The snorkeling is excellent in this protected bay and the one next to it. They were establishing an office at the Hotel La Jungla Caribe in Playa del Carmen when I checked.

WHERE TO STAY & EAT

✪ **Cabañas Paamul.** Carretera Cancún-Tulum, km 85 (Apdo. Postal 83), Playa del Carmen, Q. Roo 77710. ☎ **99/25-9422.** Fax 99/25-6913 in Mérida. 12 bungalows (all with bath); 80 trailer spaces (all with full hookups). FAN. Dec–Feb $40 single or double. March–June $30 single or double. July–Aug $40 single or double. Sept–Nov $30 single or double. RV space with hookups $13 per day, $300 per month.

When you reach this isolated, relaxing hotel you'll see an extremely tidy lineup of mobile homes and beyond them a row of coral-and-white beachfront bungalows, with covered porches, steps away from the Caribbean. Despite the number of mobile homes (which are occupied more in winter than any other time) there's seldom a soul on the beautiful little beach. I eagerly anticipate reaching Paamul, for the bit of peace it gives me during hectic days of updating. Each cabaña contains two double beds, tile floors, rattan furniture, ceiling fans, hot water, and 24-hour electricity. A new large breezy palapa restaurant serves delicious food at more than reasonable prices. Try the pescado Paamul or shrimp Paamul; both are wonderful baked medleys devised by the gracious owner Eloiza Zapata. For stays longer than a week, ask for a discount, which can sometimes be as much as 10% to 20%. The trailer park is among the nicest I've seen; some trailers have decks or patios and thatched palapa shade covers. Trailer guests have six showers and separate baths for men and women. Laundry service is available. Turtles nest here June through September. The Paamul turnoff is clearly marked on the highway; then it's almost a mile on a straight, narrow, paved but rutted road to the cabañas. Visitors not staying here are welcome to use the beach, though the owners request that they not bring in drinks and food and use the restaurant instead.

PUERTO AVENTURAS: A RESORT COMMUNITY

About 2¹/₂ miles south of Paamul (65 miles south of Cancún), you'll come to the new city-size development of Puerto Aventuras on Chakalal Bay. Though it's on 900 oceanfront acres, you don't see the ocean unless you walk through one of the three hotels. A complete resort, it includes a state-of-the-art marina, hotels, several restaurants, and multitudes of fashionable condominiums winding about the grounds and around the marina. The golf course has nine holes open for play.

The hotels are far beyond our budget, but even if you don't stay here, the **Museo CEDAM** on the grounds is worth a stop. CEDAM means Center for the Study of Aquatic Sports in Mexico, and the museum houses displays on the history of diving on this coast from pre-Hispanic times to the present. Besides dive-related memorabilia, there are displays of pre-Hispanic pottery, figures, and copper bells found in the cenote of Chichén-Itzá; shell fossils; and sunken ship contents. It's supposed to be open daily from 10am to 1pm and 2 to 6pm. Donations are requested.

XPUHA: ANOTHER BEACH HIDEAWAY

Almost 3 miles beyond Pamul, east of the highway, is an area known as Xpuha (*ish*-poo-hah) consisting of an incredibly beautiful wide bay and fine stretch of sand. Before October 1995's Hurricane Roxanne, tall palms leaned over the beach, but unfortunately the storm destroyed the trees and toppled the encroaching jungle, revealing the seamier side of Xpuha. Some of this heavenly beach is junked with trashy looking abodes and tacky restaurants, with the all-inclusive Robinson Club at the far southern end (though it was closed when I was there). The two hotels listed below are on a nicely kept part of beach (comparatively speaking). Finding Xpuha can be confusing since several crude signs mark entry; crude, narrow rutted roads cut through the jungle to the beach. To get to the best portion of beach take the one marked Villas Xpuha.

Though they call these inns "villas," that word implies much more than the reality of these simply furnished, painted cinder-block buildings. The **restaurant** of the Villas Xpuha offers home-style cooking with a simple-but-varied menu and several fish entrées to choose from. It's open daily from 7am to 8pm. It's ideal for day-trippers who want to spend the day on the beach and have restaurant facilities, too; they request that visitors not bring food. As long as you use the restaurant of the Villas Xpuha, there's no charge for the two public baths and showers. Besides the beach, a huge lagoon is within walking distance, and the reef is not far offshore.

WHERE TO STAY & EAT

Villas del Caribe Xpuha. Carretera Cancún-Tulum, km 88, Playa del Carmen, Q. Roo 77710. No phone. 9 rms (all with bath). High season, $30 single or double. Low season, $22 single or double.

Not quite as nice as its neighbor (see Villas Xpuha below), this inn is still a good choice. The two stories of rooms face the beach, with communal porches for lounging. Rooms have blue-tile floors and matching blue walls, and each comes with one or two double beds, an all-tile bath, and windows facing the beach; one room has a kitchen. There's 24-hour electricity and hot water here, too. The management has radio communication with the Hotel Flores in Cozumel (☎ **987/2-1429**), so if you're there, you can reserve a room ahead (or vice versa).

✪ **Villas Xpuha and Restaurant.** Carretera Cancún-Tulum, 88km (Apdo. Postal 115), Playa del Carmen, Q. Roo 77710. No phone. 5 rms (all with bath). FAN. High season, $40 single or double. Low season, $32 single or double.

The five rooms here line up in a row of blue buildings; four have a porch area on the beach and ocean, and one is an island-style wooden structure. The rooms are plain but clean, each with nice tile floors, two windows, two single beds, two plastic chairs, hammock hooks, and a place for a suitcase—but no closet. A single bare bulb in the center of each ceiling provides light. Count on 24-hour electricity and hot water. The hotel has a dive shop offering diving and snorkeling trips and kayak rentals.

AKUMAL: RESORT ON A LAGOON

Continuing south on Highway 307 a short distance, you'll come to Akumal, a resort development built around and named after a beautiful lagoon. Signs point the way in from the highway, and the white arched Akumal gateway is less than half a mile toward the sea. The resort complex here consists of five distinct establishments sharing the same wonderful, smooth palm-lined beach and the adjacent Half Moon Bay and Yalku Lagoon. The hotel's signs and white entry arches are clearly visible from Highway 307.

The hotels are all far beyond our budget, so I don't recommend staying here, but you don't have to be a guest to enjoy the **beach,** swim in the beautiful clear bay, and eat at the restaurants. It's an excellent place to spend the day while on a trip down the coast. This is one of the best and easiest places to snorkel along the whole coast—the water's calm; it's rarely crowded; and the reef is both within an easy swim and teeming with all variety of sea creatures. It's easy to spot lots of live coral, sea urchins, countless species of colorful fish, barracuda, and manta ray. Besides swimming and snorkeling, ask at the reception desk about **horseback rides** on the beach ($30) and a tour of the Sian Ka'an Biosphere Reserve that starts at the Hotel Ana y José on the Punta Allen Peninsula south of the ruins of Tulum. For **scuba diving,** two completely equipped dive shops with PADI-certified instructors serve the hotels and bungalows in this area. Both are located between the two hotels. There are almost 30 dive sites in the region (from 30 to 80 feet), and two-tank dives cost around $55. Both shops offer resort courses as well as complete certification. **Fishing trips** can also be arranged through the dive shops. You're only 15 minutes from good fishing. Two hours (the minimum period) costs $80, and each additional hour is $25 for up to four people with two fishing lines.

CHEMUYIL & XCACEL: DEVELOPED BEACHES

Three miles south of Akumal (70 miles southwest of Cancún) is the pay beach, camping, and trailer park at **Chemuyil.** Though the sign says the most beautiful beach in the world, it's no longer a pretty place and really not worth a stop.

More idyllic, **Xcacel** is 1 1/2 miles south of Chemuyil and a quarter mile east of the highway. It's a nice place where you can spend the day for $2 or pitch your tent or park your van for $5 per person per night, including use of changing rooms, toilets, and showers. There's a nice restaurant here as well, but you can cook out in a portable grill (yours) as long as you bring your own charcoal and don't cook on the beach.

When I was last here, a state-supervised volunteer group had established a "save the turtle" program on the beach, left of the restaurant. It's unfunded, so there's a contribution box at the entrance to the turtle area. Visitors can see turtles in shaded water flats before they are released. Loggerheads are so rare that this may be your only chance to ever see one. Between May and September, at least half of the coast's loggerhead turtles nest between here and Cancún—or they will until driven away by development. In 1991, the volunteers protected 550 loggerhead and green turtle nests, and more than 2,500 of these endangered species have been hatched, tagged, and released.

A CAVERN TOUR/SCUBA DIVING OPERATOR

On the right side of the road (if coming from Cancún) about 11 1/2 miles south of Xcacel (and about 9 miles north of Tulum), is **Divers of the Hidden Worlds** (☎ 98/74-4081; it's a cellular phone in Cancún). Experienced divers lead certified divers, snorkelers, and hikers on a variety of unusual trips. Some require hiking in the jungle to dry caves, others to caves where divers penetrate the underground world of watery caves with glass-clear water. Snorkelers investigate the *cenotes* (sink holes leading to underground caves). Some dives are for more advanced divers, and some trips last all day while others consume a half a day. They also offer reef dives and resort courses and cave diving certification. They'll provide transportation from Cancún.

XEL-HA: SNORKELING & SWIMMING

The Caribbean coast of the Yucatán is carved by the sea into hundreds of small *caletas* (coves) that form the perfect habitat for tropical marine life, both flora and fauna. Many caletas remain undiscovered and pristine along the coast, but Xel-Ha, 8 miles south of Akumal and 1 1/2 miles from Xcacel, is enjoyed daily by snorkelers and scuba divers who come to luxuriate in its warm waters and swim among its brilliant fish. Xel-Ha (s*hell*-hah) is a swimmer's paradise, with no threat of undertow or pollution.

The entrance to Xel-Ha is half a mile in from the highway. You'll be asked to pay a "contribution" to the upkeep and preservation of the site of $10 per adult and $7 for children from ages 5 to 12. It's open daily from 8am to 4:30pm.

Once in the park, you can rent snorkeling equipment and an underwater camera—but it's much cheaper to bring your own. You can also buy an outrageously priced drink or meal, change clothes, and take showers. When you swim, be careful to observe the SWIM HERE and NO SWIMMING signs. (The greatest variety of fish can be seen right near the ropes marking off the "no swimming" areas and near any groups of rocks.) Xel-Ha is an exceptionally beautiful place.

Just south of the Xel-Ha turnoff on the west side of the highway, don't miss the **Maya ruins** of ancient Xel-Ha. You'll likely be the only one there as you walk over limestone rocks and through the tangle of trees, vines, and palms. There is a huge, deep, and dark cenote to one side and a temple palace with tumbled-down columns, a jaguar group, and a conserved temple group. A covered palapa on one pyramid guards a partially preserved mural. Admission is $2.50.

Xel-Ha is close to the ruins at Tulum—it's a good place for a dip when you've finished clambering around the Maya castles. You can make the short 8-mile hop north from Tulum to Xel-Ha by bus. When you get off at the junction for Tulum, ask the restaurant owner when the next buses come by—otherwise you may have to wait as much as two hours on the highway. Most tour companies in Cancún and Cozumel include a trip to Tulum and a swim at Xel-Ha in the same journey.

6 Tulum, Punta Allen & Sian Ka'an

Tulum (80 miles southwest of Cancún) and the Punta Allen Peninsula (110 miles southwest of Cancún at its tip) are the southernmost points many travelers reach in their wanderings down the Caribbean coast (although there is more to discover farther on). The walled Maya city of Tulum—a large post-Classic Maya site that dramatically overlooks the Caribbean—is a natural beacon to visitors to Quintana Roo, and from Cancún it's within a two-hour drive. Tour companies and public buses make the trip regularly from Cancún and Playa del Carmen. And for those who want to leave the modern world a long, long way behind, Punta Allen (which can take between 1 1/2 to 3 hours to reach from Tulum, depending on how miserable the road's condition is) may be the ultimate. It's a place without the crowds, frenetic pace, or the creature comforts of the resorts to the north—down here, the generator shuts down at 10pm (if there is one). What you will find is great fishing and snorkeling, the natural and archaeological riches of the Sian Ka'an Biosphere Reserve, and a chance to rest up at what truly feels like the end of the road. A few beach cabañas now offer reliable power, telephones, and hot showers.

ESSENTIALS

ORIENTATION   When traveling south of Highway 307, get your bearings on Tulum by thinking of it as several distinct areas: First, on your left will be the junction of Highway 307 and the old access road to the Tulum ruins (it no longer provides access); here you'll find two small hotels, two restaurants, and a Pemex gas station. Next, a few feet south of the old road on Highway 307, also on the left, is the new Tulum ruins access road, leading to a large parking lot. And a few feet farther along 307 is the left turn onto the road leading to the hotels and campgrounds south of the ruins.

This is the road south along the narrow **Punta Allen Peninsula** to **Boca Paila,** a portion of the **Sian Ka'an Biosphere Reserve,** and **Punta Allen,** a lobstering/fishing village at the tip's end. Though most of this 30-mile-long peninsular stretch of sandy, potholed road is uninhabited, there are several rustic inns along a fabulous beach south of the ruins.

(Across the highway from the turnoff to the Punta Allen Peninsula on Highway 307 is the road to Cobá, another fascinating Maya city 40 miles inland. See "Cobá," below, for details.)

Finally, south of the Punta Allen road on Highway 307 is the **village of Tulum.** The highway here is lined with businesses, including the bus stations, auto repair shops, markets, and pharmacies. The village of Tulum, by the way, has the look of an up-and-coming place, with sidewalks and restaurants it's never sported before.

EXPLORING THE TULUM ARCHAEOLOGICAL SITE

Located 8 miles south of Xel-Ha, Tulum is a Maya fortress overlooking the Caribbean. At the end of the Classic Period, in A.D. 900, Maya civilization began to decline, and most of the large ceremonial centers were deserted. During the post-Classic Period (A.D. 900 to the Spanish Conquest), small rival states developed with a few imported traditions from north central Mexico. Tulum is one such walled city-state; built in the 10th century, it functioned as a seaport. Aside from the spectacular setting, Tulum is not an impressive city when compared to Chichén-Itzá or Uxmal. There are no magnificent pyramidal structures as are found in the Classic Maya ruins. The stone carving is crude, and the site looks as though it was put together in a hurry or by novice apprentices rather than skilled masters. The primary god here was the diving god, depicted on several buildings as an upside-down figure above doorways. Seen at the Palace at Sayil and Cobá, this curious, almost comical figure is also known as the bee god.

The most imposing building in Tulum is the large stone structure on the cliff called the **Castillo** (castle), actually a temple as well as a fortress, once covered with stucco and painted. In front of the Castillo are several unrestored palacelike buildings partially covered with stucco. And on the beach below, where the Maya once came ashore, tourists frolic, combining a visit to the ruins with a dip in the Caribbean.

The **Temple of the Frescoes,** directly in front of the Castillo, contains interesting 13th-century wall paintings inside the temple, but entrance is no longer permitted. Distinctly Maya, they represent the rain god Chaac and Ixchel, the goddess of weaving, women, the moon, and medicine. On the cornice of this temple is a relief of the head of the rain god. If you get a slight distance from the building you'll see

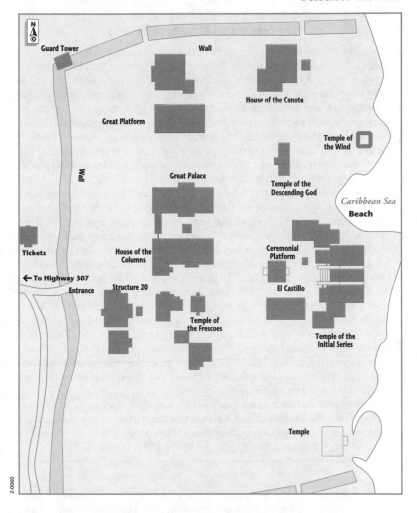

the eyes, nose, mouth, and chin. Notice the remains of the red-painted stucco on this building—at one time all the buildings at Tulum were painted a bright red.

Much of what we know of Tulum at the time of the Spanish Conquest comes from the writings of Diego de Landa, third bishop of the Yucatán. He wrote that Tulum was a small city inhabited by about 600 people, who lived in dwellings situated on platforms along a street and who supervised the trade traffic from Honduras to the Yucatán. Though it was a walled city, most of the inhabitants probably lived outside the walls, leaving the interior for priestly hierarchy and religious ceremonies. Tulum survived about 70 years after the Conquest, when it was finally abandoned.

Because of the excessive amount of visitors this site receives, it is no longer possible to climb the ruins. Visitors are asked to remain behind roped-off areas to view them.

In late 1994 a new entrance to the ruins was constructed about a 10-minute walk from the archaeological site. Cars and buses enter a large parking lot; some of the

The Sian Ka'an Biosphere Reserve

Down the peninsula a few miles south of the Tulum ruins, you'll pass the guard house of the Sian Ka'an Biosphere Reserve, 1.3 million acres set aside in 1986 to preserve tropical forests, savannas, mangroves, coastal and marine habitats, and 70 miles of coastal reefs. The area is home to jaguars; pumas; ocelots; margays; jaguarundis; spider and howler monkeys; tapirs; white-lipped and collared peccaries; manatees; brocket and white-tailed deer; crocodiles; and green, loggerhead, hawksbill, and leatherback sea turtles. It also protects 366 species of birds—you might catch a glimpse of an ocellated turkey; a great curassow; a brilliantly colored parrot; a toucan or trogon; a white ibis; a roseate spoon-bill; a jabiru or wood stork; a flamingo; or one of 15 species of herons, egrets, and bitterns.

The park is separated into three parts: a "core zone," restricted to research; a "buffer zone," where visitors and families already living there have restricted use; and a "cooperation zone," outside the reserve but vital to its preservation. If you drive on Highway 307 from Tulum to an imaginary line just below the Bahía (bay) of Espíritu Santo, all you see on the Caribbean side is the reserve; but except at the ruins of Muyil/Chunyaxche, there's no access. At least 22 archaeological sites have been charted within Sian Ka'an. The best place to sample the reserve is the Punta Allen Peninsula, part of the "buffer zone." The inns were already in place when the reserve was created. Of these, only the Cuzan Guest House (see "Where To Stay & Eat," below) offers trips for birding. But bring your own binoculars and birding books and have at it—the birdlife anywhere here is rich. At the Boca Paila bridge you can often find fishermen who'll take you into the lagoon on the landward side, where you can fish and see plenty of birdlife; but it's unlikely the boatman will know bird names in English or Spanish. Birding is best just after dawn, especially during the April through July nesting season.

Day-trips to the Sian Ka'an are led from Cozumel (see "Cozumel," above) by a biologist from the **Friends of Sian Ka'an** in Cancún. For more information about the reserve or trip reservations, contact them at Plaza América, Av. Cobá 5, 3a Piso, Suite 48–50, Cancún, Q. Roo 77500 (☎ **98/84-9583;** fax 98/87-3080).

public buses from Playa del Carmen go directly to the visitors center. There are artisans' stands, a bookstore, museum, restaurant, several large restrooms, and a ticket booth for Inter-Playa buses, which depart for Playa del Carmen and Cancún frequently between 7:40am and 4:40pm. After walking through the center, visitors pay the admission fee to the ruins, and another fee ($1.50 round trip) to ride an open-air shuttle to the ruins. You can easily walk, however. Admission is $5; free on Sunday. There's an additional charge of $4 for a permit to use a video camera at the site. Parking costs $1.50. Licensed guides have a stand by the path to the ruins and charge $20 for a 45-minute tour in English, French, or Spanish for up to four persons. They will point out many architectural details you might otherwise miss, but their history information may not be up-to-date.

WHERE TO STAY & EAT

Motel El Crucero. Carretera Cancún-Tulum (Hwy. 307), Tulum Junction (Apdo. Postal 4), Tulum, Q. Roo. ☎ **987/3-0230** or 987/3-0232. 16 rms (all with bath). FAN. $12 single; $15 double. Free parking; unguarded.

This motel, opposite the more expensive Hotel Acuario, has a very good and festive restaurant with the best food in the area; main courses cost $4 to $6. The pollo pibil is excellent. The guest rooms, however, are quite basic and may or may not have hot water. There's also a tiny "convenience store."

EN ROUTE TO FELIPE CARRILLO PUERTO

If you continue along the main Highway 307 past the Cobá turnoff, it heads south-west through Tulum village. About 14 miles south of Tulum village are the ruins of **Muyil** (ca. A.D. 1–1540) at the settlement of **Chunyaxche,** on the left side. Although archaeologists have done extensive mapping and studies of the ruins, only a few of the more than 100 or so buildings, caves, and subterranean temples have been excavated; new excavations take place off and on, so keep checking the progress. One of the objects of this research is to find evidence of an inland port, since canals link the site to the Caribbean 9 miles east of the Boca Paila cut.

The Friends of Sian Ka'an in Cancún (see "Sian Ka'an Biosphere Reserve," above) organizes trips through the canals from Boca Paila. The Cuzan Guest House in Punta Allen and the Cabañas Ana y José south of the Tulum ruins (see listings below) also guide visitors here through the lagoons and canals. *Note:* The mosquito and dive-bombing fly population is fierce, but this is one of the best places along the coast for birding—go early in the morning.

Admission is $1.75; free for children under 12, and free for everyone on Sunday and festival days. It's open daily from 8am to 5pm.

After Muyil and Chunyaxche, Highway 307 cuts through 45 miles of jungle to Felipe Carrillo Puerto (see below).

THE PUNTA ALLEN PENINSULA

About 3 miles south of the Tulum ruins on the Punta Allen Road, the pavement ends, and the road becomes narrow and sandy, with many potholes during the rainy season. Beyond this point is a 30-mile-long peninsula called Punta Allen, split in two at a cut called Boca Paila, where a bridge connects the two parts of the peninsula, and the Caribbean enters a large lagoon on the right. It's part of the far eastern edge of the 1.3-million-acre **Sian Ka'an Biosphere Reserve** (see below). Along this road you'll find several cabaña-type inns, all on beautiful beaches facing the Caribbean. Taxis from the ruins can take you to most of these; then you can find a ride back to the junction at the end of your stay. *A Note About Hurricane Roxanne:* Tulum and the Punta Allen Peninsula were among the hardest hit when Hurricane Roxanne raged through in October 1995. However, within a month hotels sported new paint, windows, roofs, and furnishings. The path of the storm was evident by the acres of broken trees, but the businesses seemed to have survived.

EXPLORING THE PUNTA ALLEN PENINSULA

The natural environment is the peninsula's marquee attraction, whether your tastes run to relaxing on the beaches or going on bird-watching expeditions (these are available between June and August, with July being best). Sea turtles nest on the beaches along here from May to October. The turtles lumber ashore at night, usually between 10pm and 3am. *A Note About Provisions:* Since the Punta Allen Peninsula is remote and there are no stores, handy provisions to bring along are a flashlight, mosquito repellent, mosquito coils, and water. Most hotels along here charge for bottled water in your room and for meals. From October through December winds may be accompanied by nippy nights, so come prepared—the hotels don't have blankets.

WHERE TO STAY & EAT

Lodgings here vary in quality—some are simple but quite comfortable, while others are a lot like camping out. One or two have electricity for a few hours in the evening—but shut it off around 10pm—and there are no electrical outlets; most don't have hot water. The first one is half a mile south of the ruins, and the farthest is 30 miles down the peninsula.

The following hotels are listed in the order you'll find them as you drive south on the Punta Allen road (from Tulum). To reach the first one you'll need to take the Punta Allen exit from Highway 307, then turn left when it intersects the coastal road. The rest of the hotels are to the right.

Cabañas Zazil Kin Don Armando. Apdo. Postal 44, 77780 Tulum, Q. Roo. ☎ **987/4-3856.** 30 bungalows (none with bath). $10 bed with hammock; $13 double with two beds. $10 deposit for bedding, key, and flashlight. Free parking; unguarded.

Casual accommodations on a big beautiful beach, these stick-walled bungalows are spread over the large stretch of sand, mingled with clotheslines flapping with guests' laundry and a restaurant that's notably good. Each of these basic bungalows has a bed on a concrete slab, sheets, a blanket, and occasional mosquito netting, but there's electricity only in the restaurant. (Bring your own soap, towel, and mosquito netting.) Some of the bungalows have no windows or ventilation, except through the cracks, unless the door is open. There are separate shared bath facilities for men and women. The friendly English-speaking owners also run the restaurant. An average meal of chicken, beans, and rice costs $3 to $5. At night Don Armando's restaurant is *the* place to be while you're in the area, offering the best food and service and conviviality among guests.

From here you can arrange taxi service to and from the Tulum ruins and to the Cancún airport. It's half a mile south of the Tulum ruins; the sign on the right as you drive toward the ruins says ZAZIL KIN.

Restaurant y Cabañas Ana y José. Punta Allen Peninsula, Carretera Tulum, 7km (Apdo. Postal 15), 77780 Tulum, Q. Roo. ☎ **98/80-6022** in Cancún. Fax 98/80-6021 in Cancún.16 rms (all with bath). High season, $50–$60 single or double. Low season, $40–$50 single or double. Free parking; unguarded.

This place started as a restaurant and blossomed into a comfortable inn on the beach, although it's somewhat overpriced. All rooms have tiled floors, one or two double beds, baths with cold-water shower, patios or balconies, and electricity between 6 and 10pm. However, 24-hour electricity is said to be on its way, so expect prices to skyrocket. The rock-walled cabañas in front are a little larger than the other rooms, and some face the beautiful wide beach just a few yards off; but these are also the most expensive rooms. New rooms have been added on a second level in back. The only drawback is the lack of cross ventilation in some of the lower rooms in the back section, which can be uncomfortable at night without electricity to power fans. The inn also offers bicycle and kayak rentals, snorkeling, and dive trips. Biologist-led boat excursions to the Sian Ka'an Biosphere Reserve begin here at 9:30am Monday, Tuesday, Friday, and Saturday (weather permitting) for $50 per person. The price includes chips and soft drinks and round-trip van transportation to the reserve from the cabañas.

The excellent, screened-in restaurant, with sand floors under the palapa, offers modest prices and is open daily from 8am to 9pm. It's 4 miles south of the Tulum ruins. Reservations are a must in high season, or arrive very early in the day before it fills up.

Cabañas Tulum. Punta Allen Peninsula, Carretera Tulum, 7km (Apdo. Postal 63), 77780 Tulum, Q. Roo. No phone. 18 rms (all with bath). FAN. High season, $34 single or double. Low season, $23 single or double.

Next door to Ana y José's (above) is a row of bungalows facing a heavenly stretch of ocean and beach. Each bungalow includes a cold-water shower, two double beds, screens on the windows, a table, one electric light, nice-size tiled baths, and a verandah where you can hang a hammock. Mattresses, which rest on a cement platform, are too thin to cushion against the hard surface. Flat top sheets, which are also used as bottom sheets, immediately work off the mattress leaving guests either wrestling with them all night or giving up to settle in on the bare mattress. The electricity is on from 5:30 to 10pm only, so bring candles or a flashlight. A small restaurant serves beer, soft drinks, and all three meals for reasonable prices—just don't expect a gourmet meal. The cabañas are often full between December 15 and Easter and July and August, so arrive early or make reservations. It's 4 miles south of the ruins.

✪ **Cuzan Guest House.** Punta Allen (reservations: Contact Apdo. Postal 24, 77720 Felipe Carrillo Puerto, Q. Roo; ☎ **983/4-0358** and fax 983/4-0383 in Felipe Carrillo Puerto). 8 rms (six with bath). $40–$60 single or double. All-inclusive seven-day fly-fishing package $1,499.

About 30 miles south of the Tulum ruins is the end of the peninsula and Punta Allen, the Yucatán's best-known lobstering and fishing village planted on a palm-studded beach. Isolated and rustic, it's part Indiana Jones, part Robinson Crusoe, and certainly the most laid-back end of the line you'll find for a while. The small town has a lobster cooperative, a few streets with modest homes, and a lighthouse at the end of a narrow sand road dense with coconut palms and jungle on both sides. So it's a welcome sight to see the beachside Cuzan Guest House and its sign in English that reads STOP HERE FOR TOURIST INFORMATION. A stay here could well be the highlight of your trip, provided you're a flexible traveler.

Two rooms are plainly furnished Maya-style oval stucco buildings with concrete floors, shared bath, and a double bed with mosquito netting. Three comfortable spacious huts with thatched roofs and private bathrooms are at the water's edge, with three more similar accommodations set back from the water, but with an ocean view. A room in the owner's house with a front verandah is sometimes available. A house in the village is often rented as well, but readers have reported that the neighborhood is extremely noisy at night. Unfortunately Cuzan's delightful thatched teepees disappeared during Hurricane Roxanne. Everything is solar powered. The real charmer here is the sand-floored restaurant run by co-owner Sonja Lilvik, a Californian who makes you feel right at home. If it's lobster season you may have lobster at every meal, always prepared with a deliciously different recipe. But you might also be treated to a pile of heavenly stone crabs or some other gift from the sea.

Sonja arranges fly-fishing trips for bone, permit, snook, and tarpon to the nearby saltwater flats and lagoons of Ascension Bay. The $25 per-person boat tour of the coastline that she offers is a fascinating three hours of snorkeling, slipping in and out of mangrove-filled canals for birdwatching, and skirting the edge of an island rookery loaded with frigate birds. November through March is frigate-mating season, and the male frigate shows off his big billowy red breast pouch to impress potential mates. The all-day Robinson Crusoe Tour costs $100 per person and includes a boat excursion to remote islands, beaches, reefs, ruins (Muyil/Chunyaxche), jungles, lagoons, and birdwatching areas. Or you can simply relax in a hammock on the beach or in your room or go kayaking along the coast.

7 Cobá

105 miles SW of Cancún

The impressive Maya ruins at Cobá, deep in the jungle, are a worthy detour from your route south. You don't need to stay overnight to see the ruins, but there are a few hotels. The village is small and poor, gaining little from the visitors who pass through to see the ruins. **Used clothing** (especially for children) is a welcome gift.

ESSENTIALS

GETTING THERE & DEPARTING   By Bus   From Playa del Carmen there are several buses to Cobá. Two buses leave Valladolid for Cobá, but they may fill early, so buy tickets as soon as possible.

Several buses a day leave Cobá: At 6:30am and 3pm a bus goes to Tulum and Playa del Carmen, and at noon and 7pm there's a bus to Valladolid.

By Car   The road to Cobá begins in Tulum, across Highway 307 from the turn-off to the Punta Allen Peninsula. Turn right when you see the signs to Cobá and continue on that road for 40 miles. When you reach the village, proceed straight until you see the lake; when the road curves right, turn left. The entrance to the ruins is at the end of that road past some small restaurants. Cobá is also about a three-hour drive south from Cancún.

ORIENTATION   The highway into Cobá becomes one main paved street through town, which passes El Bocadito restaurant and hotel on the right (see "Where to Stay & Eat," below) and goes a block to the lake. If you turn right at the lake you reach the Villas Arqueológicas a block farther. Turning left will lead past a couple of informal/primitive restaurants on the left facing the lake, and to the ruins, straight ahead, the equivalent of a block.

EXPLORING THE COBÁ RUINS

The Maya built many breathtaking cities in the Yucatán, but few were grander in scope than Cobá. Much of the 42-square-mile site, on the shores of two lakes, is unexcavated. A 60-mile-long sacbe (a pre-Hispanic raised road or causeway) through the jungle linked Cobá to Yaxuná, once a Maya center 30 miles south of Chichén-Itzá. It's the Maya's longest-known sacbe, and there are at least 50 or more shorter ones from here. An important city-state, Cobá, which means "water stirred by the wind," flourished between A.D. 632 (the oldest carved date found here) until after the founding of Chichén-Itzá, around 800. Then Cobá slowly faded in importance and population until it was finally abandoned. Scholars believe Cobá was an important trade link between the Yucatán Caribbean coast and inland cities.

Once in the site, keep your bearings—it's very easy to get lost on the maze of dirt roads in the jungle. Bring your bird and butterfly books; this is one of the best places to see both. Branching off from every labeled path you'll notice unofficial narrow paths into the jungle, used by locals as shortcuts through the ruins. These are good for scouting for birds, but be careful to remember the way back.

The **Grupo Cobá** boasts a large, impressive pyramid, the **Temple of the Church** (La Iglesia), which you'll find if you take the path bearing right after the entry gate. Walking to it, notice the unexcavated mounds on the left. Though the urge to climb the temple is great, the view is better from El Castillo in the Nohoc Mul group farther back at the site.

From here, return back to the main path and turn right. You'll pass a sign pointing right to the ruined *juego de pelota* (ball court), but the path is obscure.

Continuing straight ahead on this path for 5 to 10 minutes, you'll come to a fork in the road. To the left and right you'll notice jungle-covered, unexcavated pyramids, and at one point you'll cross a raised portion crossing the pathway—this is the visible remains of the sacbe to Yaxuná. Throughout the area, intricately carved stelae stand by pathways, or lie forlornly in the jungle underbrush. Though protected by crude thatched roofs, most are so weatherworn as to be indiscernible.

The left fork leads to the **Nohoc Mul Group,** which contains El Castillo, the tallest pyramid in the Yucatán (rising even higher than the great El Castillo at Chichén-Itzá and the Pyramid of the Magician at Uxmal). So far, visitors are still permitted to climb to the top. From the magnificent lofty position you can see unexcavated jungle-covered pyramidal structures poking up through the forest all around. The right fork (more or less straight on) goes to the **Conjunto Las Pinturas.** Here, the main attraction is the **Pyramid of the Painted Lintel,** a small structure with traces of the original bright colors above the door. You can climb up to get a close look. Though maps of Cobá show ruins around two lakes, there are really only two excavated buildings to see after you enter the site.

Note: Because of the heat, visit Cobá in the morning or after the heat of the day has passed. Mosquito repellent, drinking water, and comfortable shoes are imperative.

Admission is $3.50; children under 12 enter free daily, and Sunday and holidays it's free to everyone. Camera permits are $4 for each video. The site is open daily from 8am to 5pm.

WHERE TO STAY & EAT

✪ **El Bocadito.** Calle Principal, Cobá, Q. Roo. No phone. (reservations: Apdo. Postal 56, 97780 Valladolid, Yuc.). 8 rms (all with bath). FAN. $12–$15 single or double. Free parking; unguarded.

El Bocadito, on the right as you enter town, could take advantage of being the only game in town besides the much more expensive Villas Arqueológicas—but it doesn't. Next to the hotel's restaurant of the same name, the rooms are arranged in two rows facing an open patio. They're simple, each with tile floors, two double beds, no bedspreads, a ceiling fan, and a washbasin separate from the toilet and cold-water shower cubicle. It's agreeable enough and always full by nightfall, so to secure a room, arrive no later than 3pm.

The clean open-air restaurant offers good meals at reasonable prices, served by a friendly, efficient staff. Busloads of tour groups stop here at lunch (always a sign of approval). I enjoy the casual atmosphere of El Bocadito, and there's a good bookstore and gift shop adjacent to the restaurant.

Villas Arqueológicas Cobá. Cobá, Q. Roo. ☎ **5/203-3086** in Mexico City or 800/258-2633 in the U.S. 44 rms (all with bath). A/C. $70 single; $80 double (including all charges and taxes). Free parking; guarded.

Operated by Club Med but nothing like a Club Med village, this lovely lakeside hotel is a 10-minute walk from the ruins. The hotel has a French polish, and the restaurant is top-notch, though expensive. Breakfast costs $10; lunch and dinner cost $20. A room rate including meals is available. The rooms, built around a plant-filled courtyard and beautiful pool, are stylish and soothingly comfortable. The hotel also has a library on Mesoamerican archaeology (with books in French, English, and Spanish). Make reservations—this hotel fills with touring groups.

To find it, drive through town and turn right at the lake; the hotel is straight ahead on the right.

8 Felipe Carrillo Puerto

134 miles SW of Cancún

Felipe Carrillo Puerto (pop. 47,000) is a busy crossroads in the jungle along the road to Ciudad Chetumal. It has gas stations, a market, small ice plant, bus terminal, and a few modest hotels and restaurants.

Since the main road intersects the road back to Mérida, Carrillo Puerto is the turning point for those making a "short circuit" of the Yucatán Peninsula. Highway 184 heads west from here to Ticul, Uxmal, Campeche, and Mérida.

As you pass through, consider its strange history: This was where the rebels in the War of the Castes took their stand, guided by the "Talking Crosses." Some remnants of that town (named Chan Santa Cruz) are still extant. Look for signs in town pointing the way.

ESSENTIALS

GETTING THERE   By Bus   There's frequent bus service south from Cancún and Playa del Carmen.

By Car   Coastal Highway 307 from Cancún leads directly here.

ORIENTATION   The highway goes right through the town, becoming **Avenida Benito Juárez** in town. Driving in from the north, you'll pass a traffic circle with a bust of the great Juárez. The town **market** is here. Small, inexpensive hotels are on the left, and the **Pemex station** is on the right.

The directions given above assume you'll be driving. If you arrive by bus, the **bus station** is right on the plaza. From there it's a 10-minute walk east down Calle 67, past the cathedral and banks, to Avenida Juárez. Turn left onto Juárez to find the recommended restaurants and hotels and the traffic circle I use as a reference point.

Fast Facts   The telephone **area code** is 983. **Banks** here don't exchange foreign currency. The only gas station between Tulum and Chetumal is here.

9 Lago Bacalar

65 miles SW of Felipe Carrillo Puerto, 23 miles NW of Chetumal

If you can arrange it, staying in Bacalar sure beats staying in Chetumal or Carrillo Puerto. The crystal-clear spring-fed waters of Lake Bacalar, which is Mexico's second largest lake at slightly over 65 miles long, empty into the Caribbean. Known as the Lake of Seven Colors, mismanagement of the natural mixture of spring and seawater in recent years changed the characteristic varied deep blue colors. It's still beautiful to gaze upon, and the colors range from crystal clear to deep bluegreen to Caribbean turquoise. Spaniards fleeing coastal pirates used Maya pyramid stones to build a fort in Bacalar, which is now a modest museum. The area is very quiet—the perfect place to swim and relax. At least 130 species of birds have been counted in the area. If you're in a car, take a detour through the village of Bacalar and down along the lakeshore drive. To find the lakeshore drive, go all the way past town on Highway 307, where you'll see a sign pointing left to the lake. When you turn left, that road is the lakeshore drive. You can double back along the drive from there to return to the highway. The Hotel Laguna is on the lakeshore drive. From here it's a 30-minute drive to Chetumal and to the Corozol Airport in Belize. Besides its location on Lago Bacalar, this area is also perfect for launching excursions into the Río Bec ruin route, described below.

ESSENTIALS

GETTING THERE   By Bus   Buses going south from Cancún and Playa del Carmen stop here.

By Car   Signs into Bacalar are plainly visible from Highway 307.

WHERE TO STAY

Hotel Laguna. Costera de Bacalar 143, 77010 Lago Bacalar, Q. Roo . ☎ **983/2-3517** in Chetumal. 30 rms, 4 bungalows (all with bath). FAN. $23 single or double. $50 bungalow for five persons.

The Laguna is off the beaten path, so there are almost always rooms available—except in winter, when it's full of Canadians. Rooms overlook the pool and have a lovely view of the lake. The water along the shore is very shallow, but you can dive from the hotel's dock into 30-foot water. The hotel's restaurant offers main courses costing about $4 to $8. It's open daily from 8am to 8pm. To find it, go through town toward Chetumal. Just at the edge of town you'll see a sign pointing left to the hotel and lakeshore drive.

⊙ **Rancho Encantado.** Carretera Felipe Carrillo Puerto-Chetumal (Apdo. Postal 233), 77000 Chetumal, Q. Roo. ☎ and fax **983/8-0427.** (reservations: Contact P.O. Box 1256, Taos, NM 87571. ☎ 800/505 MAYA in the U.S.; fax 505/776-5878). 12 casitas. FAN. Including continental breakfast and dinner, Nov–April, $120 single or double; May–Oct, $96 single or double ($17.50 per person less without food).

What an Edenic, serene place to unwind. Rancho Encantado's immaculate white stucco individual casitas are spread out on a shady manicured lawn beside the smooth Lago Bacalar. Each spacious, sublimely comfortable, and beautifully kept room has mahogany-louvered windows, a shiny red-tile floor, mahogany dining table and chairs, a living room or sitting area, a porch with chairs, and hammocks strung between trees. Some have a handsome blue-tile kitchenette and others have a coffee area; coffeemakers and coffee are provided in each room. Some rooms have cedar ceilings and red-tiled roofs and others have handsome thatched roofs. All are decorated with folk art, footloomed pastel colored bedspreads, and Zapotec rugs from Oaxaca. The newest rooms are the four waterfront casitas (rooms 9 through 12) with white stucco walls, thatched roofs, and fabulous hand-painted murals inspired by those at Bonampak. Two of these have murals plus a striking large rust-colored plaster face resembling those Olmec-like faces at nearby Kohunlich. These rooms prime you for a trip to nearby archaeological sites. Casita 8 sleeps five, and casita 1 sleeps four.

The large palapa-topped restaurant overlooks the lake and serves all three meals. There's no beef on the menu, but plenty of chicken, fish, vegetables, and fresh fruit. The honey here is from Rancho hives. You can swim from the hotel's dock, and kayaks and canoes are available for guest use. Orange, lime, mango, sapote, ceiba, and banana trees; palms; oaks; wild orchids, and bromeliads on the expansive grounds make great bird shelter attracting flocks of chattering parrots, turquoise browed motmots, toucans, and at least a hundred more species, many of which are easy to spot outside your room. Ask the manager, Luis Tellez, for a copy of the extensive birding list.

Tellez also keeps abreast of developments at the nearby archaeological sites and is the only source of current information before you reach the ruins. He's developed a lot of knowledge about the sites and leads several trips himself. Almost a dozen excursions are available through the hotel. Among them are day-trips to the Río Bec ruin route, an extended visit to Calakmul, a ruins visit and lunch with a local family (a guest favorite), outings to the Majahual Peninsula, and a riverboat trip to the

Maya ruins of Lamanai deep in a forest in Belize. This is the only hotel offering guided trips to the Río Bec ruins, many of which are available only by special permit, which Tellez can obtain. Several ruins are easily reachable from the road and others are so deep in the jungle that a guide is necessary to find them, and a four-wheel drive vehicle is a must. With advance notice, the hotel can arrange guides and transportation. They also work with Río Bec specialist Serge Ríou (see Chetumal "What to See and Do," below). Excursions range in price from $55 to $115 per person depending on the length and difficulty of the trip, and several have a three-person minimum. Groups interested in birding, yoga, archaeology, and the like are invited to bring a leader and use Rancho Encantado as a base. Special packages and excursions can be arranged in advance from the hotel's U.S. office. To find it, look for the hotel's sign on the left about 1 mile before Bacalar.

WHERE TO EAT

Besides the lakeside restaurant of Rancho Encantado you may enjoy the **Restaurant Cenote Azul,** a comfortable open-air thatched-roof restaurant on the edge of the beautiful Cenote Azul. In both places, main courses cost from $5 to $10. To get there, follow the highway to the south edge of town and turn left at the restaurant's sign; follow that road around to the restaurant. At Rancho Encantado you can swim in Lago Bacalar, and at the Restaurant Cenote you can take a dip in placid Cenote Azul—but without skin lotion of any kind because it poisons the cenote.

EXCURSIONS FROM BACALAR: THE RÍO BEC RUIN ROUTE

A few miles west of Bacalar begins the Yucatán's southern ruin route, generally called the Río Bec region, although other architectural styles are present. Until recently the region enjoyed little attention. However, all that is rapidly changing. Within the last several years, the Mexican government has spent millions of pesos to build a new highway, conserve previously excavated sites, and uncover heretofore unexcavated ruins. This is an especially ruin-rich but little-explored part of the peninsula. With the opening in late 1994 of **Dzibanché,** an extensive "new" site; paved road access to **Calakmul** in 1994; and the **Museo de la Cultura Maya** also in 1995 in Chetumal; together with other "new sites" and discoveries at existing ruins, the region is poised to become the peninsula's "newest" tourist destination. With responsible guides, other jungle-surrounded but difficult-to-reach sites may also be available soon. A new, four-lane highway leads from close to Bacalar for several miles before it becomes two-lane again; construction crews are continuing to work widening the road even farther. Touristic services (restaurants, hotels) are slowly being added along the route; informed guides must be arranged before you arrive, and there are no visitors' centers. Rancho Encantado trucks in water to the bathrooms at the ruins of Kohunlich, making them the only public restrooms on the route. Part of what makes this area so special is the feeling of pioneering into unmarked land—and with that comes a bit of inconvenience. However, this area is definitely worth watching and visiting now. And finally I must mention the richness of the bird and animal life in the whole route. Toucans flying across the highway and orioles are extremely common. Grey fox, wild turkey, tesquintle (a bushy-tailed, plant-eating rodent), the raccoon relative coatimundi with its long tapered snout and tail, and armadillos will surely cross your path. At Calakmul a family of howler monkey's resides in the trees overlooking the parking area. To make the most of your visit, preparatory reading would include *A Forest of Kings: The Untold Story of the Ancient Maya* by Linda Schele and David Friedel (William Morrow, 1990), *The Blood of Kings: Dynasty and Ritual in Maya Art,* By Linda Schele and Mary Ellen Miller (George Braziller, Inc., 1968), and the *Maya Cosmos* by David Freidel and Linda Schele (William Morrow, 1993). *Arqueológica Mexicana* magazine, which is written in Spanish, devoted its July-August 1995 issue to the Quintana Roo portion of the Río Bec ruin route. And finally, though it lacks historic and cultural information, and many sites have expanded since it was written, Joyce Kelly's *An Archeological Guide to Mexico's Yucatán Peninsula* (University of Oklahoma, 1993), is the best companion book to have. To learn the most in a short time, focus your learning on the meaning of the jaguar, Xibalba (the underworld), and the earth monster.

The route starts just 9 miles from the edge of Bacalar where there's the turnoff from Highway 307 to Highway 186, which leads to the Río Bec ruin route as well as to Escarcega, Villahermosa, and Palenque. You can divide your sightseeing into several day-trips. If you get an early start, many of the ruins mentioned below can be easily visited in a day from Bacalar. These sites will be changing, though, since swarms of laborers are still busy with further exploration. Evidence shows that these ruins, especially Becán, were part of the trade route linking the Caribbean coast at Cobá to Edzná and the Gulf Coast and with Lamanai in Belize and beyond. Once this region was dense with Maya cities, cultivated fields, lakes, and an elaborate system of rivers that connected the region with Belize and Central America. Today many of these ancient cities hide under a dense cover of jungle, which has overtaken the land from horizon to horizon. There are no visitor facilities or refreshments at these sites, so bring your own water and food. However, in the village of Xpujil (just before the ruins of Xpujil), the **Restaurant Posada Calakmul** (☎ 983/2-3304), under the watchful eye of Doña María Cabrera, serves excellent home-style food and caters to ruins enthusiasts—note the photos and descriptions of little-known sites by Serge Ríou. The new **hotel rooms** behind the restaurant cost $16 single or double and are clean and comfortable, with tile floors, private bathrooms with hot water, good beds, and a small porch. Near the entrance to Chicanná, on the north side of the road, is the new **Ramada Inn Eco Village,** Km. 144 Carretera Excarcega (☎ 983/2-8863). Though the name suggests an ecological bent, approximately 20 acres of jungle were completely leveled to build an as yet unpaved parking lot for all the buses and cars that will one day come, a swimming pool, restaurant, and 28 nicely furnished rooms in sets of two stories. One room is single level and built like a Maya house. Manicured lawns with flower beds and pathways link the rooms, which have a Polynesian architecture. There are no ecologically oriented tours. For the moment, the hotel attracts primarily bus tours and individual travelers. Electricity is generated between 6pm and 10am. Restaurant prices are high and don't include the 15 percent tax. A 15 percent service charge might also be added. Single rooms go for $90 single and $100 double including breakfast.

Luis Tellez at Rancho Encantado, at Bacalar (see "Where to Stay," above), is the best source of information about the status of these sites and any new ones. Entry to each site is $1.75 to $3, and all are free on Sunday. Informational signs at each building within the sites are in Maya, Spanish, and English. Wear loads of mosquito repellent. The following list of sites is in order if you're driving from Bacalar or Chetumal.

DZIBANCHÉ Dzibanché (or Tzibanché) means "place where they write on wood." Exploration began here in 1993, and it opened to the public in late 1994. Scattered over 26 square miles (though only a small portion is excavated), it's both a pre- and a post-Classic site (A.D. 300-900) that was occupied for around 700 years. Two enormous and adjoining plazas have been cleared. The site shows influence from Río Bec, Petén, and Teotihuacán. The Temple of the Owl, on the Plaza de Xibalbá, has a miniature version of Teotihuacán-style *talud tablero* (slant and straight facade) architecture flanking the sides of the main stairway leading to the top with its lentil and entrance to an underground tomb. (Teotihuacán ruins are near Mexico City, but their influence was strong as far as Guatemala.) Despite centuries of an unforgiving wet climate, a wood lintel, in good condition and with a date carving, still supports a partially preserved corbeled arch on top of this building. Inside the temple, a tomb was discovered, making this the second-known temple in Mexico built specifically as a tomb (the first discovered is the Temple of Inscriptions at Palenque). However, the tomb at Dzibanché predates Pacal's at Palenque by about 350 years. A diagram of this temple shows interior steps leading from the top, then down inside the pyramid to ground level, just as at Palenque. The stairway is first reached by a deep, well-like drop that held remains of a sacrificial victim and which was sacked during pre-Hispanic times. Uncovered at different levels of the stairwell were a number of beautiful polychromed lidded vessals one of which has an owl painted on the top handle, with its wings spreading onto the lid. White owls were messengers of the gods of the underworld in the Maya religion. This interior stairway isn't open to the public, but you can clearly see the lintel just behind the entrance to the tomb. Further exploration of the tomb awaits stabilization of interior walls. Opposite the Temple of the Owl is the Temple of the Cormorant, so named after a polychromed drinking vessal found there picturing a cormorant. Here too archaeologists have found evidence of an interior tomb similar to the one in the Temple of the Owl, but excavation of it has not begun. Other magnificently preserved pottery pieces found during excavations include an incense burner with an almost three-dimensional figure of the diving god attached to the outside, and another incense burner with an elaborately dressed figure of the god Itzamná attached. The site also incorporates another section of ruins called Kinichná (keen *eech* nah), about 1¹/₂ miles north, and which is reachable only by a rutted road that's impassable in the rainy season. There, an Olmec-style jade figure was found. A formal road to these ruins had not yet been built, but there's a sign pointing to the right turn to Morocoy approximately 18 miles from the Highway 307 turnoff. You follow that paved road, which becomes unpaved and pass the small settlement (not really a town) of Morocoy, to another rough dirt road to the right (there's a sign to the ruins there), and follow it for about a mile to the ruin entrance. Ask at Rancho Encantado, near Bacalar (see "Where To Stay," above), about the condition of the unpaved portion of road.

KOHUNLICH Kohunlich (koh-*hoon*-leek), 26 miles from the intersection of Highways 186 and 307, dates from around A.D. 100 to 900. Turn left off the road, and the entrance is 5¹/₂ miles ahead. From the parking area you enter the grand park-like site, crossing a large and shady ceremonial area flanked by four large conserved pyramidal edifices. Continue walking and just beyond this grouping you'll come to Kohunlich's famous **Pyramid of the Masks** under a thatched covering. The masks, actually enormous plaster faces, date from around A.D. 500 and are on the facade of the building. Besides characteristic Olmec undulating lips, the masks show vestiges of blue and red paint. Note the carving on the pupils, which show a cosmic connection possibly with the night sun that illuminated the underworld. It's speculated that masks covered much of the facade of this building, which is built in the Río Bec style with rounded corners, false stairway, and false temple on the top. At least one theory is that the masks are a composite of several rulers at Kohunlich. During recent excavations of buildings immediately to the left after you enter, two intact pre-Hispanic skeletons and five decapitated heads were uncovered that were once probably used in a ceremonial rite. To the right after you enter (follow a shady path through the jungle) is another recently excavated plaza. It's thought to have housed elite citizens due to the high quality of pottery found there and the fine architecture of the rooms. Scholars believe that Kohunlich became overpopulated, leading to its decline. The bathrooms here are the only ones at any site on the route.

CHACAN BACAN Chacan Bacan (chah-*kahn* bah-*kahn*), which dates from around 200 B.C., was first discovered in 1980 with excavation begining in 1995. It's scheduled to open sometime in 1997, with 30 to 40 buildings uncovered. Only one imposing 107 feet high pyramid was being excavated when I was there. However, the discovery of huge Olmec-style heads on the facade of it can only lend excitement to future digs. The heads, showing from the middle of the skull forward, have helmetlike caps similar in style to the full multiton Olmec heads unearthed in Veracruz and Tabasco on Mexico's Gulf Coast, where the Olmecs originated. These heads are thought to be older than the figures at both Kohunlich and Balamkú. The exact size of the site hasn't been determined, but it's huge. In a densely forested setting, with thousands of tropical hardwood trees, plants, birds, and wild animals, it's been earmarked as an ecological/touristic center. Though not open to the public when I was there, it's about 50 miles and a 1 1/2-hour drive from Bacalar. The turnoff (left) to it is at Caoba where you follow a paved road for about 1 1/2 miles, then turn left on an unmarked path. From the paved portion you can look left and see the uncovered pyramid protruding over the surrounding jungle. Ask at Rancho Bacalar about the accessibility of this site.

XPUJIL Xpujil (also spelled Xpuhil) means either "cat tail" or "forest of kapok trees" and flourished between A.D. 400 and 900. Ahead on the left after you enter, you'll see a rectangular ceremonial platform 6 1/2 feet high and 173 feet long holding three once-ornate buildings. These almost-conical edifices resemble the towering ruins of Tikal in Guatemala and rest on a lower building with 12 rooms. Unfortunately, they are so ruined you can only ponder how it might have been. To the right after you enter are two newly uncovered structures, one of which is a large acropolis. From the highway, a small sign on the right points to the site that is just a few yards off the highway and 49 miles from Kohunlich.

BECÁN Becán, once surrounded by a moat, means "canyon filled by water" and dates from Early Classic to Late Classic—600 B.C. to A.D. 1200. It is surrounded by a moat that once had seven bridges leading to the seven cities that were pledged to Becán. Extensive excavations will continue through 1997. Following jungle paths beyond the first visible group of ruins, you'll find at least two recently excavated acropolises. Though the site was abandoned by 850, ceramic remains indicate there may have been a population resurgence between A.D. 900 and 1000, and it was still used as a ceremonial site as late as A.D. 1200. Becán was a governmental and ceremonial center with political sway over at least seven other cities in the area including Chicanná, Hormiguerro, and Payan. To really understand this site, you need a good guide. But for starters, the first plaza group you see after you enter was the center of grand ceremonies. From the highway you see the backside of a pyramid (Temple 1) with two temples on top. From the highway you can see between the two pyramid-top temples to Temple 4, which is opposite Temple 1. When the high priest appeared through the mouth of the earth monster in the center of Temple 4 (which he reached via a hidden side stairway that's now partly exposed), he was visible from what is now the highway. It's thought that commoners had to watch ceremonies from outside the ceremonial plaza, thus the site was positioned for good viewing purposes. The backside of Temple 4 is believed to have been a civic plaza where rulers sat on stone benches while pronouncing judgements. The recently uncovered second plaza group dates from around A.D. 850 and has perfect twin towers on top where there's a big platform. Under the platform are 10 rooms that are thought to be related to Xibalba (shee-*bahl*-bah), the underworld. Earth monster faces probably covered this building (and they appeared on other buildings as well). Remains of at least one ball court have been unearthed. Becán is about 4¹/₂ miles beyond Xpujil and is visible on the right side of the highway, about half a mile down a rutted road.

CHICANNÁ Slightly over a mile beyond Becán, on the left side of the highway, is Chicanná, which means "house of the mouth of snakes." Trees loaded with bromeliads shade the central square surrounded by five buildings. The most outstanding edifice features a monster-mouth doorway and an ornate stone facade with more superimposed masks. As you enter the mouth of the earth monster, note that you are walking on a platform that functions as the open jaw of the monster with stone teeth on both sides.

CALAKMUL This area is both a massive Maya archaeological zone with at least 60 sites and a 178,699-acre rain forest designated in 1989 as the Calakmul Biosphere Reserve, which includes territory in both Mexico and Guatemala.

The Archaeological Zone Since 1982, archaeologists have been excavating the ruins of Calakmul, which dates from 100 B.C. to A.D. 900. It's the largest of the area's 60 known sites. Nearly 7,000 buildings have been discovered and mapped. At its zenith at least 60,000 people may have lived around the site, but by the time of the Spanish conquest of Mexico in 1519, there were fewer than 1,000 inhabitants. Discoveries include more stelae than any other site. One of them by building 13 is a stelae of a woman dating from A.D. 652. Of the buildings, Temple 3 is the best preserved. In it were found offerings of shells, beads, and polychromed tripod pottery. The tallest, at 178 feet, is Temple 2. From the top of it you can see the outline of the ruins of El Mirador 30 miles across the forest in Guatemala. Temple 4 charts the line of the sun from June 21 when it falls on the left (north) corner, to Sept. 21 and March 21 when it lines up in the east behind the middle temple on the top of the building, to December 21 when it falls on the right (south) corner. Numerous jade pieces including spectacular jade masks were uncovered here, most of which are on display in the Museo Regional in Campeche. Temple 7 is largely unexcavated except for the top where in 1984 the most outstanding jade mask was found. In *A Forest of Kings,* Linda Schele and David Freidel tell of wars between Calakmul, Tikal, and Naranjo (the latter two in Guatemala) and how Ah-Cacaw, king of Tikal (75 miles south of Calakmul) captured King Jaguar-Paw in A.D. 695 and later Lord Ox-Ha-Te Ixil Ahau, both of Calakmul. From January to May the site is open Tuesday through Sunday from 7am to 7pm. The site will be so wet during the rainy season from June through October that it's best not to go.

Calakmul Biosphere Reserve Set aside in 1989, this is the peninsula's only high forest selva, a rain forest that annually records as much as 16 feet of rain. Among the plants are cactus, epiphytes, and orchids. Endangered animals include the white-lipped peccary, jaguar, and puma. So far more than 250 species of birds have been recorded. At the moment there are no guided tours in the reserve, and no overnight stays or camping are permitted. But a hint of the region can be seen around the ruins. Howler monkeys are often peering down on visitors as they park their cars near the entrance to the ruins.

The turnoff on the left for Calakmul is located approximately 145 miles from the intersection of Highways 186 and 307, just before the village of Conhuas. There's a guard station there where you pay to enter the road/site. From the turnoff it's an 1¹/₂ hour drive on a newly paved, but very narrow, and somewhat rutted road that may be difficult during the rainy season from May through October. *A driving caution:* Numerous curves in the road make seeing oncoming traffic (what little there is) difficult, and there have been head-on collisions. (I nearly had one.)

BALAMKÚ   Balamkú (bah-*lahm*-koo) was literally snatched from the incredibly destructive hands of looters by INAH archaeologist Florentino García Cruz in October 1990. Amateur archaelogist and guide Serge Rìou was close behind him to photograph the site before looters hit one last time destroying the head of one of the figures. An uncharted site at the time it was saved by García, who had been alerted by locals that looters were working there, today it's open to the public and though small, it's worth the time to see it since the facade of one building is among the most unusual on this route. When you reach the clearing, about 2 miles from the highway via a narrow dirt path through the jungle, are two buildings, one on the right and one on the left. The right building is really three continuous, tall, but narrow, pyramids dating from around A.D. 700. The left building, which dates from around A.D. 400, holds the most interest because of the cross legged figures resembling those found at Copan, in Honduras. Originally there were four of these regal figures (probably representing kings), seated on crocodiles or frogs above the entrance to the underworld, but looters destroyed two on each end and further disfigured the others. Still, enough remains to see the beauty; the whole concept of this building, with its molded stucco facade, is of life and death. On the head of each almost three dimensional figure are the eyes, nose, and mouth of a jaguar figure; followed by the full face of the human figure; then a neck formed by the eyes and nose of another jaguar; and an Olmec-like face on the stomach, its neck decorated by a necklace; then the crossed legs of the figure seated upon a frog or crocodile. The earth monster is represented by a half-snake, half-crocodile animal, all symbols of death, water, and life. The May 1992 issue of *Mexico Desconocido* features the discovery of Balamkú written by Florentino García Cruz.

10 Chetumal

85 miles S of Felipe Carrillo Puerto, 23 miles S of Lago Bacalar

Quintana Roo became a state in 1974, and Chetumal (pop. 170,000) is its capital. While Quintana Roo was still a territory, it was a free-trade zone to encourage trade and immigration between neighboring Guatemala and Belize. The old part of town, down by the river (Río Hondo), has a Caribbean atmosphere and wooden buildings, but the newer parts are modern Mexican. There is lots of noise and heat, so your best plan would be not to stay—it's not a particularly interesting or friendly town. It is, however, worth a detour to see the wonderful **Museo de la Cultural Maya,** especially if your trip involves seeing the Río Bec ruin route described above.

ESSENTIALS

GETTING THERE & DEPARTING   By Plane   Aerocaribe (Mexicana) has daily flights to and from Cancún and flights several times weekly between Chetumal and the ruins of Tikal in Guatemala. **Taesa** flies from Cancún and Cozumel.

By Bus   The bus station of **Autotransportes del Caribe** (☎ 983/2-0740) is 20 blocks from the town center on Insurgentes at Niños Héroes. Buses go to Cancún, Tulum, Playa del Carmen, Puerto Morelos, Mérida, Campeche, Villahermosa, and Mexico City. **Caribe Express** (☎ 983/2-7889 or 983/2-8001) has deluxe buses to Mérida and Cancún. This service features a 28-seat bus with video movies, steward service, and refreshments. Sixteen second-class buses run to and from Bacalar daily.

   To Belize: Two companies make the run from Chetumal (through Corozal and Orange Walk) to Belize City. **Batty's Bus Service** runs 10 buses per day, and

Venus Bus Lines (☎ 04/2-2132 in Corozal) has seven daily buses, the first at 11am; the 2pm bus is express with fewer stops. Seven buses go to Belize City (☎ 02/7-3354 in Belize); the first leaves at 4am and the last at 10am. Though it's a short distance from Chetumal to Corozal, it may take as much as 1 1/2 hours, depending on how long it takes the bus to pass through Customs and Immigration.

By Car It's a 2 1/2-hour ride from Felipe Carrillo Puerto. If you're heading to Belize you'll need a passport and special auto insurance, which you can buy at the border. You can't take a rental car over the border, however.

To get to the ruins of Tikal in Guatemala you must first go through Belize to the border crossing at Ciudad Melchor de Mencos. For more details on crossing into Guatemala and Belize, see *Frommer's Costa Rica, Guatemala & Belize*.

ORIENTATION The **telephone area code** is 983. Chetumal has many "no left turn" streets, with hawk-eyed traffic policemen at each one. Be alert—they love to nail visitors and may even motion you into making a traffic or pedestrian violation, then issue a ticket, or take a bribe instead.

You'll arrive following Obregón into town. Niños Héroes is the other main cross street. When you reach it, turn left to find the hotels mentioned below.

WHERE TO STAY & EAT

Hotel Nachacan. Calz. Veracruz 379, 77000 Chetumal, Q. Roo. ☎ **983/2-3232**. 20 rms. A/C TV. $15 single; $19 double.

Opposite the new market, this nice hotel offers rooms that are plain, but clean and comfortable. A restaurant is off the lobby. It's relatively convenient to the bus station, but not close enough to walk if you arrive by bus; and it's within walking distance of the Museo de la Cultura Maya. To find it from Avenida Obregón, turn left on Calzada Veracruz and follow it for at least 10 blocks; the hotel will be on the right.

Hotel Continental Caribe. Niños Héroes 171, Chetumal, Q. Roo 77000. ☎ **983/2-1100**. 800/465-4329 in the U. S. Fax 983/2-1676. 75 rms (all with bath). A/C TV TEL. $50–$75 single or double. Free parking.

This modern hotel (formerly the Continental), located across from the central market, was remodeled in 1995 and became a Holiday Inn. The hotel has a good-sized pool (a blessing in muggy Chetumal) and a good restaurant. If you stay here it's only two blocks farther to the Museo de la Cultura Maya. You can contact Río Bec specialist Serge Rìou (see below) through the travel agency here. To find it as you enter town on Obregón, turn left on Niños Heroes, go six blocks, and look for the hotel on the right, opposite the market.

EXPLORING CHETUMAL

Chetumal is really the gateway to Belize or to the Río Bec ruins and is not in itself an interesting city to visit. But it's worth a detour to Chetumal to see the Museo de la Cultura Maya. If you can arrange it, see the museum before you tour the Río Bec ruins, since it will all make more sense after getting it in perspective here.

If you're coming to this part of the Yucatán specifically to see the Río Bec ruins, the services of Serge Rìou, "Maya Lowland Specialist," will probably be indispensable to you. Several years ago young Mr. Rìou visited the Río Bec ruin route on a vacation from France. He fell so in love with the culture, romance, and history of the ruins, that he returned to live and learn all that was possible about these little-known ruins. Living in Xpujil, he hiked the forests daily in search of ruins, worked with archaeologists on the trail of new sites, photographed the ruins, attended conferences of Maya specialists, and read everything he could find on Mexican archaeology.

Today his encyclopedic knowledge of the nearby ruins makes him the most informed guide. He speaks excellent English and Spanish and charges around $60 to $100 per person a day to guide up to three people to a variety of sites. The higher price is for Calakmul, the farthest site from Chetumal. He can arrange necessary permits to un-opened sites. You can contact him directly (Apartado Postal 238, 77000 Chetumal, Q. Roo; ☎ **983/2-9819** or 983/2-1251); or arrange for his services through Rancho Encantado at Lago Bacalar (see "Bacalar," above), which has all the necessary types of vehicles, or contact him through the Holiday Inn in Chetumal.

⊙ **Museo de la Cultura Maya.** Av. Heroes s/n. ☎ **983/2-6838.** Admission $1; children 50¢. Tues–Thurs 9am–7pm, Fri–Sat 9am–8pm, Sun 9am–2pm. Between Colón and Primo de Verdad, eight blocks from Avenida Obregón, on the left past the Holiday Inn.

Sophisticated, impressive, and informative, this new museum provides the keys to understanding the complex world of the Maya. Push a button, and an illustrated description appears explaining the medicinal and domestic uses of plants with their Maya and scientific names; another describes the five social classes of the Maya by the way they dress; and yet another shows how the beauty signs of cranial deforma-tion, crossed eyes, and facial scarification were achieved. An enormous screen flashes moving pictures taken from an airplane flying over more than a dozen Maya sites from Mexico to Honduras. Another large television shows the architectural variety of Maya pyramids and how they were probably built. Then a walk on a glass floor takes you over representative ruins in the Maya world so that you can see the variety of shapes and particular sites. And finally one of the most impressive sections is the three-story sacred ceiba tree, which the Maya believed represented the under-world (Xibalba) on the bottom (the bottom floor of the museum), earth (the middle floor of the museum), and the 13 heavens (the third floor of the museum). From this you'll have a better idea of the significance of symbolism on the pyramids in the Maya world. Plan no less than two hours here. Even then, especially if your interest is high, you may want to take a break and return with renewed vigor—there's a lot to see and learn. What a museum!

ONWARD FROM CHETUMAL

From Chetumal you have several choices. You can go south to Belize and Guatemala (though not in a rental car), and after Bacalar you can cut diagonally across the pen-insula to Mérida or retrace your steps to Cancún. You can take Highway 186 west to Escarcega, Villahermosa, and Palenque, but I don't recommend it. It's a long, hot, and lonely trip on a highway that is often riddled with potholes after you cross into Campeche state. Permanent ZONA DE DESLAVE signs warn motorists that parts of the roadbed are missing entirely or so badly dipped they might cause an accident. It improves from time to time, but annual rains cause constant problems. At the Campeche state line there's a military guard post with drug-sniffing dogs; every vehicle is searched. A military guard post at the Reforma intersection just before Bacalar requires motorists to present identification you used to enter Mexico (birth certificate or passport), plus your Tourist Permit. Other photo identification may be required, as well as information on where you are staying or where you are headed. The whole procedure should take only minutes.

Appendix

A Telephones & Mail

USING THE TELEPHONES

Area codes and city exchanges are being changed all over the country. If you have difficulty reaching a number, ask an operator for assistance. Mexico does not have helpful recordings to inform you of changes or new numbers.

Most **public pay phones** in the country have been converted to Ladatel phones, many of which are both coin- and card-operated. Instructions on the phones tell you how to use them. When your time limit for local calls is about to end (about three minutes), you'll hear three odd sounding beeps, and then you'll be cut off unless you deposit more coins. Ladatel cards come in denominations of 10, 20, and 30 New Pesos. If you're planning to make many calls, purchase the 30 New Peso card; it takes no time at all to use up a 10 peso card (about $1.65). They're sold at pharmacies, bookstores, and grocery stores near Ladatel phones. You insert the card, dial your number, and start talking, all the while watching a digital counter tick away your money.

Next is the *caseta de larga distancia* (long-distance telephone office) found all over Mexico. Most bus stations and airports now have specially staffed rooms exclusively for making long-distance calls and sending faxes. Often they are efficient and inexpensive, providing the client with a computer printout of the time and charges. In other places, often pharmacies, the clerk will place the call for you; then you step into a private booth to take the call. Whether it's a special long-distance office or a pharmacy, there's usually a service charge of around $3.50 to make the call, which you pay in addition to any call costs if you didn't call collect.

For **long-distance calls** you can access an English-speaking AT&T operator by pushing the star button twice then 09. If that fails, try dialing 09 for an international operator. To call the United States or Canada tell the operator that you want a collect call (*una llamada por cobrar*) or station-to-station (*teléfono a teléfono*), or person-to-person (*persona a persona*). Collect calls are the least expensive of all, but sometimes caseta offices won't make them, so you'll have to pay on the spot.

To make a long-distance call from Mexico to another country, first dial 95 for the United States and Canada, or 98 for anywhere else in the world. Then, dial the area code and the number you are calling.

To call long distance (abbreviated "lada") within Mexico, dial 91, the area code, then the number. Mexico's area codes (claves) may be one, two, or three numbers and are usually listed in the front of telephone directories. In this book the area code is listed under "Fast Facts" for each town. (Area codes, however, are changing throughout the country.)

To place a phone call to Mexico from your home country, dial the international service (011), Mexico's country code (52), then the Mexican area code (for Cancún, for example, that would be 98), then the local number. Keep in mind that calls to Mexico are quite expensive, even if dialed direct from your home phone.

Better hotels, which have more sophisticated tracking equipment, may charge for each local call made from your room. Budget or moderately priced hotels often don't charge, since they can't keep track. To avoid check-out shock, it's best to ask in advance if you'll be charged for local calls. These cost between 50¢ and $1 per call. In addition, if you make a long-distance call from your hotel room, there is usually a hefty service charge added to the cost of the call.

POSTAL GLOSSARY

Airmail   Correo Aereo
Customs   Aduana
General Delivery   Lista de Correos
Insurance (insured mail)   Seguros
Mailbox   Buzón
Money Order   Giro Postale
Parcel   Paquete
Post Office   Oficina de Correos
Post Office Box (abbreviation)   Apdo. Postal
Postal Service   Correos
Registered Mail   Registrado
Rubber Stamp   Sello
Special Delivery   Express Entrega Inmediata
Stamp   Estampilla or Timbre

B Basic Vocabulary

Most Mexicans are very patient with foreigners who try to speak their language; it helps a lot to know a few basic phrases.

I've included a list of certain simple phrases for expressing basic needs, followed by some common menu items.

ENGLISH-SPANISH PHRASES

English	Spanish	Pronunciation
Good day	**Buenos días**	*bway*-nohss-*dee*-ahss
How are you?	**¿Cómo esta usted?**	*koh*-moh *ess*-tah oo-sted
Very well	**Muy bien**	mwee byen
Thank you	**Gracias**	*grah*-see-ahss
You're welcome	**De nada**	day *nah*-dah
Good-bye	**Adios**	ah-dyohss
Please	**Por favor**	pohr fah-*bohr*

Yes	Sí	see
No	No	noh
Excuse me	Perdóneme	pehr-*doh*-ney-may
Give me	Déme	*day*-may
Where is . . . ?	¿Dónde esta . . . ?	*dohn*-day *ess*-tah
the station	la estación	la ess-tah-see-*own*
a hotel	un hotel	oon oh-*tel*
a gas station	una gasolinera	oon-nuh gah-so-lee-nay-rah
a restaurant	un restaurante	oon res-tow-*rahn*-tay
the toilet	el baño	el *bahn*-yoh
a good doctor	un buen médico	oon bwayn *may*-dee-co
the road to	el camino a . . .	el cah-*mee*-noh ah
To the right	A la derecha	ah lah day-*ray*-chuh
To the left	A la izquierda	ah lah ees-ky-*ehr*-dah
Straight ahead	Derecho	day-*ray*-cho
I would like	Quisiera	keyh-see-*air*-ah
I want	Quiero	*kyehr*-oh
to eat	comer	*ko*-mayr
a room	una habitación	oon-nuh ha-bee tah-see-*own*
Do you have?	¿Tiene usted?	tyah-nay oos-*ted*
a book	un libro	oon *lee*-bro
a dictionary	un diccionario	oon deek-see-own-ar-eo
How much is it?	¿Cuanto cuesta?	*kwahn*-to *kwess*-tah
When?	¿Cuando?	*kwahn*-doh
What?	¿Que?	kay
There is (Is there?)	¿Hay . . .	eye
Yesterday	Ayer	ah-*yer*
Today	Hoy	oy
Tomorrow	Mañana	mahn-*yawn*-ah
Good	Bueno	*bway*-no
Bad	Malo	*mah*-lo
Better (best)	(Lo) Mejor	(loh) meh-*hor*
More	Más	mahs
Less	Menos	may-noss
No Smoking	Se prohibe fumar	seh pro-*hee*-beh foo-mahr
Postcard	Tarjeta postal	tahr-*hay*-ta pohs-tahl
Insect repellent	Rapellante contra insectos	rah-pey-*yahn*-te *cohn*-trah een-sehk-tos

MORE USEFUL PHRASES

Do you speak English?	¿Habla usted inglés?
Is there anyone here who speaks English?	¿Hay alguien aquí qué hable inglés?

I speak a little Spanish.	Hablo un poco de español.
I don't understand Spanish very well.	No lo entiendo muy bien el español.
The meal is good.	Me gusta la comida.
What time is it?	¿Qué hora es?
May I see your menu?	¿Puedo ver su menu?
The check please.	La cuenta por favor.
What do I owe you?	¿Cuanto lo debo?
What did you say?	¿Mande? (colloquial expression for American "Eh?")
I want (to see) a room	Quiero (ver) un cuarto (una habitación) . . .
for two persons	para dos personas
with (without) bath.	con (sin) baño.
We are staying here only	Nos quedaremos aqui solamente . . .
one night.	una noche
one week.	una semana.
We are leaving tomorrow.	Partimos mañana.
Do you accept traveler's checks?	¿Acepta usted cheques de viajero?
Is there a laundromat near here?	¿Hay una lavandería cerca de aquí?
Please send these clothes to the laundry.	Hágame el favor de mandar esta ropa a la lavandería.

NUMBERS

1	**uno** (*ooh*-noh)	18	**dieciocho** (dee-*ess*-ee-*oh*-choh)
2	**dos** (dohs)		
3	**tres** (trayss)	19	**diecinueve** (dee-*ess*-ee-*nway*-bay)
4	**cuatro** (*kwah*-troh)		
5	**cinco** (*seen*-koh)	20	**veinte** (*bayn*-tay)
6	**seis** (sayss)	30	**treinta** (*trayn*-tah)
7	**siete** (*syeh*-tay)	40	**cuarenta** (kwah-*ren*-tah)
8	**ocho** (*oh*-choh)	50	**cincuenta** (seen-*kwen*-tah)
9	**nueve** (*nway*-bay)	60	**sesenta** (say-*sen*-tah)
10	**diez** (dee-ess)	70	**setenta** (say-*ten*-tah)
11	**once** (*ohn*-say)	80	**ochenta** (oh-*chen*-tah)
12	**doce** (*doh*-say)	90	**noventa** (noh-*ben*-tah)
13	**trece** (*tray*-say)	100	**cien** (see-en)
14	**catorce** (kah-*tor*-say)	200	**doscientos** (*dos*-se-en-tos)
15	**quince** (*keen*-say)	500	**quinientos** (*keen*-ee-ehn-tos)
16	**dieciseis** (de-*ess*-ee-sayss)		
17	**diecisiete** (de-*ess*-ee-*syeh*-tay)	1,000	**mil** (meal)

BUS TERMS

Bus	Autobus
Bus or truck	Camion
Lane	Carril
Nonstop	Directo
Baggage (claim area)	Equipajes

Intercity	Foraneo
Luggage storage area	Guarda equipaje
Gates	Llegadas
Originates at this station	Local
Originates elsewhere; stops if seats available	De paso
First class	Primera
Second class	Segunda
Nonstop	Sin escala
Baggage claim area	Recibo de equipajes
Waiting room	Sala de espera
Toilets	Sanitarios
Ticket window	Taquilla

C Menu Glossary

Achiote   Small red seed of the annatto tree.

Achiote preparada   A prepared paste found in Yucatán markets made of ground achiote, wheat and corn flour, cumin, cinnamon, salt, onion, garlic, and oregano. Mixed with juice of a sour orange or vinegar and put on broiled or charcoaled fish (tikin chick) and chicken.

Agua fresca   Fruit-flavored water, usually watermelon, canteloupe, chia seed with lemon, hibiscus flour, or ground melon seed mixture.

Antojito   A Mexican snack, usually masa-based with a variety of toppings such as sausage, cheese, beans, onions; also refers to tostadas, sopes, and garnachas.

Atole   A thick, lightly sweet, warm drink made with finely ground rice or corn and usually flavored with vanilla.

Birria   Lamb or goat meat cooked in a tomato broth, spiced with garlic, chiles, cumin, ginger, oregano, cloves, cinnamon, and thyme and garnished with onions, cilantro, and fresh lime juice to taste; a specialty of Jalisco state.

Botana   A light snack—an antojito.

Buñuelos   Round, thin, deep-fried crispy fritters dipped in sugar.

Cabrito   Grilled kid; a northern Mexican delicacy.

Carnitas   Pork that's been deep-cooked (not fried) in lard, then steamed and served with corn tortillas for tacos.

Ceviche   Fresh raw seafood marinated in fresh lime juice and garnished with chopped tomatoes, onions, chiles, and sometimes cilantro and served with crispy, fried whole corn tortillas.

Chiles rellenos   Poblano peppers usually stuffed with cheese, rolled in a batter and baked; other stuffings include ground beef spiced with raisins.

Chayote   Vegetable pear or merleton, a type of spiny squash boiled and served as an accompaniment to meat dishes.

Churro   Tube-shaped, bread-like fritter, dipped in sugar and sometimes filled with cajeta or chocolate.

Cochinita pibil   Pig wrapped in banana leaves, flavored with pibil sauce and pit-baked; common in Yucatán.

Corunda   A triangular tamal wrapped in a corn leaf, a Michoacán specialty.

Enchilada   Tortilla dipped in a sauce and usually filled with chicken or white cheese and sometimes topped with tomato sauce and sour cream (enchiladas Suizas—Swiss enchiladas), or covered in a green sauce (enchiladas verdes), or topped with onions, sour cream, and guacamole (enchiladas Potosiños).

Epazote   Leaf of the wormseed plant, used in black beans and with cheese in quesadillas.

Escabeche   A lightly pickled sauce used in Yucatecan chicken stew.

Frijoles charros   Beans flavored with beer; a northern Mexican specialty.

Frijoles refritos   Pinto beans mashed and cooked with lard.

Garnachas   A thickish small circle of fried masa with pinched sides, topped with pork or chicken, onions, and avocado or sometimes chopped potatoes and tomatoes; typical as a botana in Veracruz and Yucatán.

Gorditas   Thickish fried-corn tortillas, slit and stuffed with choice of cheese, beans, beef, and chicken, with or without lettuce, tomato, and onion garnish.

Gusanos de maguey   Maguey worms, considered a delicacy, and delicious when charbroiled to a crisp and served with corn tortillas for tacos.

Horchata   Refreshing drink made of ground rice or melon seeds, ground almonds, and lightly sweetened.

Huevos Mexicanos   Eggs with onions, hot peppers, tomatoes.

Huevos Motulenos   Eggs atop a tortilla, garnished with beans, peas, ham, sausage, and grated cheese; a Yucatecan specialty.

Huevos rancheros   Fried egg on top of a fried corn tortilla covered in a tomato sauce.

Huitlacoche   Sometimes spelled "cuitlacoche," a mushroom-flavored black fungus that appears on corn in the rainy season; considered a delicacy.

Machaca   Shredded dried beef scrambled with eggs or as salad topping; a specialty of Northern Mexico.

Manchamantel   Translated means "tablecloth stainer"; a stew of chicken or pork with chiles, tomatoes, pineapple, bananas, and jícama.

Masa   Ground corn soaked in lime used as basis for tamales, corn tortillas, and soups.

Mixiote   Lamb baked in a chile sauce, or chicken with carrots and potatoes both baked in parchment paper made from the maguey leaf.

Mole   Pronounced "*moh*-lay," a sauce made with 20 ingredients including chocolate, peppers, ground tortillas, sesame seeds, cinnamon, tomatoes, onion, garlic, peanuts, pumpkin seeds, cloves, and tomatillos; developed by colonial nuns in Puebla, usually served over chicken or turkey; especially served in Puebla, State of Mexico, and Oaxaca with sauces varying from red, to black and brown.

Molletes   A bolillo cut in half and topped with refried beans and cheese, then broiled; popular at breakfast.

Pan de Muerto   Sweet or plain bread made around the Days of the Dead (Nov.1–2), in the form of mummies, dolls, or round with bone designs.

Pan dulce   Lightly sweetened bread in many configurations usually served at breakfast or bought at any bakery.

Papadzules   Tortillas stuffed with hard-boiled eggs and seeds (cucumber or sunflower) in a tomato sauce.

Pavo   Relleno negro stuffed turkey Yucatán-style, filled with chopped pork and beef, cooked in a rich, dark sauce.

Pibil   Pit-baked pork or chicken in a sauce of tomato, onion, mild red pepper, cilantro, and vinegar.

Pipian Sauce   Made with ground pumpkin seeds, nuts, and mild peppers.

Poc-chuc   Slices of pork with onion marinated in a tangy sour orange sauce and charcoal broiled; a Yucatecan specialty.

Pollo   Calpulalpan Chicken cooked in pulque; a specialty of Tlaxcala.

Pozole A soup made with hominy and pork or chicken, in either a tomato-based broth Jalisco-style, or a white broth Nayarit-style, or green chile sauce Guerrero-style, and topped with choice of chopped white onion, lettuce or cabbage, radishes, oregano, red pepper, and cilantro.

Pulque Drink made of fermented sap of the maguey plant; best in state of Hidalgo and around Mexico City.

Quesadilla Four tortillas stuffed with melted white cheese and lightly fried.

Queso relleno "Stuffed cheese" is a mild yellow cheese stuffed with minced meat and spices; a Yucatecan specialty.

Rompope Delicious Mexican eggnog, invented in Puebla, made with eggs, vanilla, sugar, and rum.

Salsa verde A cooked sauce using the green tomatillo and puréed with mildly hot peppers, onions, garlic, and cilantro; on tables countrywide.

Sopa de calabaza Soup made of chopped squash or pumpkin blossoms.

Sopa de lima A tangy soup made with chicken broth and accented with fresh lime; popular in Yucatán.

Sopa Tlalpeña A hearty soup made with chunks of chicken, chopped carrots, zucchini, corn, onions, garlic, and cilantro.

Sopa Tlaxcalteca A hearty tomato-based soup filled with cooked nopal cactus, cheese, cream, and avocado with crispy tortilla strips floating on top.

Sopa Tortilla A traditional chicken broth-based soup, seasoned with chiles, tomatoes, onion, and garlic, bobbing with crisp fried strips of corn tortillas.

Sopa Tarascan A rib-sticking pinto-bean based soup, flavored with onions, garlic, tomatoes, chiles, and chicken broth and garnished with sour cream, white cheese, avocado chunks, and fried tortilla strips; a specialty of Michoacán state.

Sopa Seca Not a soup at all, but a seasoned rice, which translated means "dry soup."

Sope (*Soh*-pay) A botana similar to a garnacha, except spread with refried beans and topped with crumbled cheese and onions.

Tacos al pastor Thin slices of flavored pork roasted on a revolving cylinder dripping with onion slices and juice of fresh pineapple slices.

Tamal Incorrectly called tamale (tamal singular, tamales plural), meat or sweet filling rolled with fresh masa, then wrapped in a corn husk or banana leaf and steamed; many varieties and sizes throughout the country.

Tepache Drink made of fermented pineapple peelings and brown sugar.

Tikin Xic Also seen on menus as "tikin chick," char-broiled fish brushed with achiote sauce.

Tinga A stew made with pork tenderloin, sausage, onions, garlic, tomatoes, chiles, and potatoes; popular on menus in Puebla and Hidalgo states.

Torta A sandwich, usually on bolillo bread, usually with sliced avocado, onions, tomatoes, and a choice of meat and often cheese.

Torta Ahogado A specialty of Lake Chapala is made with scooped out roll, filled with beans and beef strips and seasoned with a tomato or chile sauce.

Tostadas Crispy fried corn tortillas topped with meat, onions, lettuce, tomatoes, cheese, avocados, and sometimes sour cream.

Venado Venison (deer) served perhaps as pipian de venado, steamed in banana leaves and served with a sauce of ground squash seeds.

Xtabentun (Shtah-ben-*toon*) A Yucatán liquor made of fermented honey and flavored with anise. It comes *seco* (dry) or *crema* (sweet).

Zacahuil Pork leg tamal, packed in thick masa, wrapped in banana leaves, and pit baked; sometimes pot-made with tomato and masa; specialty of mid-to-upper Veracruz.

Index

NOTES

NOTES

FOR RESERVATIONS CALL:

▣ Sleep	1-800-62-SLEEP
▣ Comfort	1-800-228-5150
▣ Quality	1-800-228-5151
▣ Clarion	1-800-CLARION
Econo Lodge	1-800-55-ECONO
RODEWAY	1-800-228-2000

Advance reservations are required through 1-800-4-CHOICE. Discounts are based on availability at participating hotels and cannot be used in conjunction with other discounts or promotions.

MEXICANA 🦅

ARC reporting procedure
1. Treat as Type A - Discount certificate.
2. No REN is required.
3. Enter the discount certificate number or 8132 4630 000 001 1
   on the ticket in the Endorsements/Restrictions area.
4. Place discount certificate on top of the auditor's coupon for a
   cash sale or on top of the charge form for a credit sale.
5. Refer to Industry Agents' Handbook, Section 6.0 for details.
6. Fare basis code is the code used plus the letters "FB".
   Example: MXR is used to calculate fare, then on discount
   ticket fare code would be "MXRFB".

Mexicana ticket office procedure:
1. For details refer to rule #1345.
2. Attach coupon to auditor's coupon in sales report.
3. Fare basis code is the code used plus the letters "FB".
   Example: MXR is to calculate fare, then on discount ticket
   fare code would be "MXRFB".

Posada del Mar
BEACH HOTEL
Isla Mujeres, Q.Roo, Mexico

SPECIAL PROMOTION
May 20 - December 15, 1997

STAY 4 NIGHTS AND PAY FOR 3 NIGHTS
OR
STAY 7 NIGHTS AND PAY FOR 5 NIGHTS

For reservations call
Ph. (987) 700 44/ 703 00/Fax 70266
Av. Rueda Medina No. 15 - A Isla Mujeres, Q.Roo Mexico 77400

Las Golodrinas Hotel
Tinoco y Palacios #411
Oaxaca, Oax. C.P. 68000

Provincial Atmosphere • Friendly • Clean

One Complimentary Breakfast Per Person
in our Cafeteria Includes: 1 Juice, 1 Coffee, 1 Yogurt,
Eggs Las Golondrinas or Similar Style.

Offer available to guests of Las Golodrinas Hotel. Valid if paid in advance for one week
stay or more. Original coupon must be used for acceptance. No other discounts apply.

Expires December 31, 1997

ARISTOS INTERNATIONAL, INC.

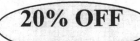

20% OFF

Aristos Hotels in Cancun, Ixtapa, Mexico City,
Puebla, Zacatecas and San Miguel Allende.

For Reservations
Call 1 (800) 5 ARISTO in the US or (210) 631-2000

Valid May 1st through December 15th 1997 and 1998
EXCEPT HOLIDAYS

10% OFF   10% OFF

Now you can save even more at any of more than 1,700 Days Inns throughout the United States and internationally. Just present this coupon upon check-in and Days Inn will take 10% off our regular room rate for your entire length of stay! Advance reservations recommended, so call now!

1-800-DAYS INN
see details on back.

Valuable discount coupon good for 15% OFF your first order from

AMERICA'S LEADING SOURCE OF TRAVEL SUPPLIES

*If it makes travel more comfortable,
safe and rewarding, we have it!*

Phone 1-800-962-4943
for a FREE CATALOG

Mention code "afbg" when you place
your first order and receive 15% OFF.

Offer expires December 31, 1998

PO Box 5485-AF, Santa Barbara, CA 93150

Follow the Sun

- Available at participating properties.
- This coupon cannot be combined with any other special discount offer.
- Limit one coupon per room, per stay.
- Not valid during blackout periods or special events.
- Void where prohibited.
- No reproductions accepted.
- Expires December 31, 1997.

1-800-DAYS INN

Discover Oaxaca

HOTEL CHOICE:
- Camino Real
- Victoria
- Misión de Los Angeles

TOUR CHOICE:
  (Four tours included)
- Archeological Site of Monte Albán
- Archeological Site of Mitla and Tule tree
- Monastery of Cuilapan and Village of Zaachila
- Craft Villages of Coyotepec, Jalieza and Ocotlan
- Weaving Village of Teotitlan del Valle
- City and Museum Tour

ALSO AVAILABLE:
- Private car and driver
- Cooking classes
- Spanish classes

Place
Stamp
Here

The Kemwel Group, Inc.
106 Calvert Street
Harrison, NY 10528-3199

FROMMER'S COMPLETE TRAVEL GUIDES

*(Comprehensive guides to destinations around the world, with
selections in all price ranges—from deluxe to budget)*

Acapulco/Ixtapa/Zihuatenjo
Alaska
Amsterdam
Arizona
Atlanta
Australia
Austria
Bahamas
Bangkok
Barcelona, Madrid &
    Seville
Belgium, Holland &
    Luxembourg
Berlin
Bermuda
Boston
Budapest & the Best of
    Hungary
California
Canada
Cancún, Cozumel & the
    Yucatán
Caribbean
Caribbean Cruises & Ports
    of Call
Caribbean Ports of Call
Carolinas & Georgia
Chicago
Colorado
Costa Rica
Denver, Boulder &
    Colorado Springs
Dublin
England

Florida
France
Germany
Greece
Hawaii
Hong Kong
Honolulu/Waikiki/Oahu
Ireland
Italy
Jamaica & Barbados
Japan
Las Vegas
London
Los Angeles
Maryland & Delaware
Maui
Mexico
Mexico City
Miami & the Keys
Montana & Wyoming
Montréal & Québec
    City
Munich & the Bavarian
    Alps
Nashville & Memphis
Nepal
New England
New Mexico
New Orleans
New York City
Northern New England
Nova Scotia, New
    Brunswick & Prince
    Edward Island

Paris
Philadelphia & the Amish
    Country
Portugal
Prague & the Best of the
    Czech Republic
Puerto Rico
Puerto Vallarta, Manzanillo
    & Guadalajara
Rome
San Antonio & Austin
San Diego
San Francisco
Santa Fe, Taos &
    Albuquerque
Scandinavia
Scotland
Seattle & Portland
South Pacific
Spain
Switzerland
Thailand
Tokyo
Toronto
U.S.A.
Utah
Vancouver & Victoria
Vienna
Virgin Islands
Virginia
Walt Disney World &
    Orlando
Washington, D.C.
Washington & Oregon

FROMMER'S FRUGAL TRAVELER'S GUIDES

*(The grown-up guides to budget travel, offering dream vacations
at down-to-earth prices)*

Australia from $45 a Day
Berlin from $50 a Day
California from $60 a Day
Caribbean from $60 a Day
Costa Rica & Belize from
    $35 a Day
Eastern Europe from
    $30 a Day

England from $50 a Day
Europe from $50 a Day
Florida from $50 a Day
Greece from $45 a Day
Hawaii from $60 a Day
India from $40 a Day
Ireland from $45 a Day
Italy from $50 a Day

Israel from $45 a Day
London from $60 a Day
Mexico from $35 a Day
New York from $70 a Day
New Zealand from $45 a Day
Paris from $60 a Day
Washington, D.C. from
    $50 a Day

FROMMER'S PORTABLE GUIDES

(Pocket-size guides for travelers who want everything in a nutshell)

Charleston & Savannah　　Las Vegas　　Washington, D.C.　　New Orleans　　San Francisco

FROMMER'S FAMILY GUIDES

(The complete guides for successful family vacations)

California with Kids	New England with Kids	San Francisco with Kids
Los Angeles with Kids	New York City with Kids	Washington, D.C. with Kids

FROMMER'S AMERICA ON WHEELS

(Everything you need for a successful road trip, including full-color road maps and ratings for every hotel)

California & Nevada	Midwest & the Great	Northwest & the	Southwest
Florida	Lake States	Great Plains States	Texas & the South-
Mid-Atlantic	New York & the New	Southeast	Central States
	England States		

FROMMER'S WALKING TOURS

(Memorable neighborhood strolls through the world's great cities)

Berlin	Montréal & Québec City	Spain's Favorite Cities
Chicago	New York	Tokyo
England's Favorite Cities	Paris	Venice
London	San Francisco	Washington, D.C.

SPECIAL-INTEREST TITLES

Arthur Frommer's Branson!
Arthur Frommer's New World of Travel
The Civil War Trust's Official Guide to the
　Civil War Discovery Trail
Frommer's America's 100 Best-Loved State
　Parks
Frommer's Caribbean Hideaways
Frommer's Complete Hostel Vacation Guide to
　England, Scotland & Wales
Frommer's Food Lover's Companion to France
Frommer's Food Lover's Companion to Italy
Frommer's Great European Driving Tours

Frommer's National Park Guide
Outside Magazine's Adventure Guide to New
　England
Outside Magazine's Adventure Guide to
　Northern California
Places Rated Almanac
Retirement Places Rated
USA Sports Traveler's and TV Viewer's
　Golf Tournament Guide
USA Sports Minor League Baseball Book
USA Today Golf Atlas
Wonderful Weekends from NYC

FROMMER'S IRREVERENT GUIDES

(Wickedly honest guides for sophisticated travelers)

Amsterdam	Manhattan	Paris	U.S. Virgin Islands
Chicago	Miami	San Francisco	Walt Disney World
London	New Orleans	Santa Fe	Washington, D.C.

UNOFFICIAL GUIDES

(Get the unbiased truth from these candid, value-conscious guides)

Atlanta	Euro Disneyland	Mini-Mickey
Branson, Missouri	The Great Smoky & Blue	Skiing in the West
Chicago	Ridge Mountains	Walt Disney World
Cruises	Las Vegas	Walt Disney World Companion
Disneyland	Miami & the Keys	Washington, D.C.

BAEDEKER

(With four-color photographs and a free pull-out map)

Amsterdam	Florence	London	Scotland
Athens	Florida	Mexico	Singapore
Austria	Germany	New York	South Africa
Bali	Great Britain	Paris	Spain
Belgium	Greece	Portugal	Switzerland
Budapest	Greek Islands	Prague	Thailand
California	Hawaii	Provence	Tokyo
Canada	Hong Kong	Rome	Turkish Coast
Caribbean	Ireland	San Francisco	Tuscany
China	Israel	St. Petersburg	Venice
Copenhagen	Italy	Scandinavia	Vienna
Crete	Lisbon		

FROMMER'S BY NIGHT GUIDES

(The series for those who know that life begins after dark)

Amsterdam	London	Miami	Paris
Chicago	Los Angeles	New Orleans	San Francisco
Las Vegas	Manhattan		

FROMMER'S BEST BEACH VACATIONS

(The top places to sun, stroll, shop, stay, play, party, and swim, with ratings for each beach)

California	Hawaii	New England
Carolinas & Georgia	Mid-Atlantic (from New	
Florida	York to Washington, D.C.)	

FROMMER'S BED & BREAKFAST GUIDES

(Selective guides with four-color photos and full descriptions of the best inns in each region)

California	Great American Cities	New England	The Rockies
Caribbean	Hawaii	Pacific Northwest	Southwest

FROMMER'S DRIVING TOURS

(Four-color photos and detailed maps outlining spectacular scenic driving routes)

Australia	France	Italy	Spain
Austria	Germany	Scandinavia	Switzerland
Britain	Ireland	Scotland	U.S.A.
Florida			

FROMMER'S BORN TO SHOP

(The ultimate guides for travelers who love to shop)

France	Hong Kong	Mexico
Great Britain	London	New York

TRAVEL & LEISURE GUIDES

(Sophisticated pocket-size guides for discriminating travelers)

Amsterdam	Hong Kong	New York	San Francisco
Boston	London	Paris	Washington, D.C.